THE
BOOK OF MORMON
Another Testament of Jesus Christ

THE
BOOK OF MORMON

AN ACCOUNT WRITTEN BY

THE HAND OF MORMON

UPON PLATES

TAKEN FROM THE PLATES OF NEPHI

Wherefore, it is an abridgment of the record of the people of Nephi, and also of the Lamanites—Written to the Lamanites, who are a remnant of the house of Israel; and also to Jew and Gentile—Written by way of commandment, and also by the spirit of prophecy and of revelation—Written and sealed up, and hid up unto the Lord, that they might not be destroyed—To come forth by the gift and power of God unto the interpretation thereof—Sealed by the hand of Moroni, and hid up unto the Lord, to come forth in due time by way of the Gentile—The interpretation thereof by the gift of God.

An abridgment taken from the Book of Ether also, which is a record of the people of Jared, who were scattered at the time the Lord confounded the language of the people, when they were building a tower to get to heaven—Which is to show unto the remnant of the House of Israel what great things the Lord hath done for their fathers; and that they may know the covenants of the Lord, that they are not cast off forever—And also to the convincing of the Jew and Gentile that JESUS is the CHRIST, the ETERNAL GOD, manifesting himself unto all nations—And now, if there are faults they are the mistakes of men; wherefore, condemn not the things of God, that ye may be found spotless at the judgment-seat of Christ.

TRANSLATED BY JOSEPH SMITH, JUN.

Published by
The Church of Jesus Christ
of Latter-day Saints
Salt Lake City, Utah, U.S.A.

First English edition published in 1830

Printed in the United States of America 05/2010

ISBN 978-1-59297-500-6 (Hardcover blue 30922)
ISBN 978-1-59297-501-3 (Paperback blue 30923)

INTRODUCTION

The Book of Mormon is a volume of holy scripture comparable to the Bible. It is a record of God's dealings with the ancient inhabitants of the Americas and contains, as does the Bible, the fulness of the everlasting gospel.

The book was written by many ancient prophets by the spirit of prophecy and revelation. Their words, written on gold plates, were quoted and abridged by a prophet-historian named Mormon. The record gives an account of two great civilizations. One came from Jerusalem in 600 B.C., and afterward separated into two nations, known as the Nephites and the Lamanites. The other came much earlier when the Lord confounded the tongues at the Tower of Babel. This group is known as the Jaredites. After thousands of years, all were destroyed except the Lamanites, and they are the principal ancestors of the American Indians.

The crowning event recorded in the Book of Mormon is the personal ministry of the Lord Jesus Christ among the Nephites soon after his resurrection. It puts forth the doctrines of the gospel, outlines the plan of salvation, and tells men what they must do to gain peace in this life and eternal salvation in the life to come.

After Mormon completed his writings, he delivered the account to his son Moroni, who added a few words of his own and hid up the plates in the hill Cumorah. On September 21, 1823, the same Moroni, then a glorified, resurrected being, appeared to the Prophet Joseph Smith and instructed him relative to the ancient record and its destined translation into the English language.

In due course the plates were delivered to Joseph Smith, who translated them by the gift and power of God. The record is now published in many languages as a new and additional witness that Jesus Christ is the Son of the living God and that all who will come unto him and obey the laws and ordinances of his gospel may be saved.

Concerning this record the Prophet Joseph Smith said: "I told the brethren that the Book of Mormon was the most correct of any book on earth, and the keystone of our religion, and a man would get nearer to God by abiding by its precepts, than by any other book."

In addition to Joseph Smith, the Lord provided for eleven others to see the gold plates for themselves and to be special witnesses of the truth and divinity of the Book of Mormon. Their written testimonies are included herewith as "The Testimony of Three Witnesses" and "The Testimony of Eight Witnesses."

We invite all men everywhere to read the Book of Mormon, to ponder in their hearts the message it contains, and then to ask God, the Eternal Father, in the name of Christ if the book is true. Those who pursue this course and ask in faith will gain a testimony of its truth and divinity by the power of the Holy Ghost. (See Moroni 10: 3–5.)

Those who gain this divine witness from the Holy Spirit will also come to know by the same power that Jesus Christ is the Savior of the world, that Joseph Smith is his revelator and prophet in these last days, and that The Church of Jesus Christ of Latter-day Saints is the Lord's kingdom once again established on the earth, preparatory to the second coming of the Messiah.

THE TESTIMONY OF THREE WITNESSES

BE IT KNOWN unto all nations, kindreds, tongues, and people, unto whom this work shall come: That we, through the grace of God the Father, and our Lord Jesus Christ, have seen the plates which contain this record, which is a record of the people of Nephi, and also of the Lamanites, their brethren, and also of the people of Jared, who came from the tower of which hath been spoken. And we also know that they have been translated by the gift and power of God, for his voice hath declared it unto us; wherefore we know of a surety that the work is true. And we also testify that we have seen the engravings which are upon the plates; and they have been shown unto us by the power of God, and not of man. And we declare with words of soberness, that an angel of God came down from heaven, and he brought and laid before our eyes, that we beheld and saw the plates, and the engravings thereon; and we know that it is by the grace of God the Father, and our Lord Jesus Christ, that we beheld and bear record that these things are true. And it is marvelous in our eyes. Nevertheless, the voice of the Lord commanded us that we should bear record of it; wherefore, to be obedient unto the commandments of God, we bear testimony of these things. And we know that if we are faithful in Christ, we shall rid our garments of the blood of all men, and be found spotless before the judgment-seat of Christ, and shall dwell with him eternally in the heavens. And the honor be to the Father, and to the Son, and to the Holy Ghost, which is one God. Amen.

OLIVER COWDERY
DAVID WHITMER
MARTIN HARRIS

THE TESTIMONY OF EIGHT WITNESSES

BE IT KNOWN unto all nations, kindreds, tongues, and people, unto whom this work shall come: That Joseph Smith, Jun., the translator of this work, has shown unto us the plates of which hath been spoken, which have the appearance of gold; and as many of the leaves as the said Smith has translated we did handle with our hands; and we also saw the engravings thereon, all of which has the appearance of ancient work, and of curious workmanship. And this we bear record with words of soberness, that the said Smith has shown unto us, for we have seen and hefted, and know of a surety that the said Smith has got the plates of which we have spoken. And we give our names unto the world, to witness unto the world that which we have seen. And we lie not, God bearing witness of it.

CHRISTIAN WHITMER
JACOB WHITMER
PETER WHITMER, JUN.
JOHN WHITMER
HIRAM PAGE
JOSEPH SMITH, SEN.
HYRUM SMITH
SAMUEL H. SMITH

TESTIMONY OF THE PROPHET JOSEPH SMITH

The Prophet Joseph Smith's own words about the coming forth of the Book of Mormon are:

"On the evening of the... twenty-first of September [1823]... I betook myself to prayer and supplication to Almighty God....

"While I was thus in the act of calling upon God, I discovered a light appearing in my room, which continued to increase until the room was lighter than at noonday, when immediately a personage appeared at my bedside, standing in the air, for his feet did not touch the floor.

"He had on a loose robe of most exquisite whiteness. It was a whiteness beyond anything earthly I had ever seen; nor do I believe that any earthly thing could be made to appear so exceedingly white and brilliant. His hands were naked, and his arms also, a little above the wrists; so, also, were his feet naked, as were his legs, a little above the ankles. His head and neck were also bare. I could discover that he had no other clothing on but this robe, as it was open, so that I could see into his bosom.

"Not only was his robe exceedingly white, but his whole person was glorious beyond description, and his countenance truly like lightning. The room was exceedingly light, but not so very bright as immediately around his person. When I first looked upon him, I was afraid; but the fear soon left me.

"He called me by name, and said unto me that he was a messenger sent from the presence of God to me, and that his name was Moroni; that God had a work for me to do; and that my name should be had for good and evil among all nations, kindreds, and tongues, or that it should be both good and evil spoken of among all people.

"He said there was a book deposited, written upon gold plates, giving an account of the former inhabitants of this continent, and the source from whence they sprang. He also said that the fulness of the everlasting Gospel was contained in it, as delivered by the Savior to the ancient inhabitants;

"Also, that there were two stones in silver bows—and these stones, fastened to a breastplate, constituted what is called the Urim and Thummim—deposited with the plates; and the possession and use of these stones were what constituted *Seers* in ancient or former times; and that God had prepared them for the purpose of translating the book.

* * * * * * *

"Again, he told me, that when I got those plates of which he had spoken—for the time that they should be obtained was not yet fulfilled—I should not show them to any person; neither the breastplate with the Urim and Thummim; only to those to whom I should be commanded to show them; if I did I should be destroyed. While he was conversing with me about the plates, the vision was opened to my mind that I could see the place where the plates were deposited, and that so clearly and distinctly that I knew the place again when I visited it.

"After this communication, I saw the light in the room begin to gather immediately around the person of him who had been speaking to me, and it continued to do so, until the room was again left dark, except just around him, when instantly I saw, as it were, a conduit open right up into heaven, and he ascended until he entirely disappeared, and the room was left as it had been before this heavenly light had made its appearance.

"I lay musing on the singularity of the scene, and marveling greatly at what had been told to me by this extraordinary messenger; when, in the midst of my meditation, I suddenly discovered that my room was again beginning to get lighted, and in an instant, as it were, the same heavenly messenger was again by my bedside.

"He commenced, and again related the very same things which he had done at his first visit, without the least variation; which having done, he informed me of great judgments which were coming upon the earth, with great desolations by famine, sword, and pestilence; and that these grievous judgments would come on the earth in this generation. Having related these things, he again ascended as he had done before.

"By this time, so deep were the impressions made on my mind, that sleep had fled from my eyes, and I lay overwhelmed in astonishment at what I had both seen and heard. But what was my surprise when again I beheld the same messenger at my bedside, and heard him rehearse or repeat over again to me the same things as before; and added a caution to me, telling me that Satan would try to tempt me (in consequence of the indigent circumstances of my father's family), to get the plates for the purpose of getting rich. This he forbade me, saying that I must have no other object in view in getting the plates but to glorify God, and must not be influenced by any other motive than that of building His kingdom; otherwise I could not get them.

"After this third visit, he again ascended into heaven as before, and I was again left to ponder on the strangeness of what I had just experienced; when almost immediately after the heavenly messenger had ascended from me the third time, the cock crowed, and I found that day was approaching, so that our interviews must have occupied the whole of that night.

"I shortly after arose from my bed, and, as usual, went to the necessary labors of the day; but, in attempting to work as at other times, I found my strength so exhausted as to render me entirely unable. My father, who was laboring along with me, discovered something to be wrong with me, and told me to go home. I started with the intention of going to the house; but, in attempting to cross the fence out of the field where we were, my strength entirely failed me, and I fell helpless on the ground, and for a time was quite unconscious of anything.

"The first thing that I can recollect was a voice speaking unto me, calling me by name. I looked up, and beheld the same messenger standing over my head, surrounded by light as before. He then again related unto me all that he had related to me the previous night, and commanded me to go to my father and tell him of the vision and commandments which I had received.

"I obeyed; I returned to my father in the field, and rehearsed the whole matter to him. He replied to me that it was of God, and told me to go and do as commanded by the messenger. I left the field, and went to the place where the messenger had told me the plates were deposited; and owing to the distinctness of the vision which I had had concerning it, I knew the place the instant that I arrived there.

"Convenient to the village of Manchester, Ontario county, New York, stands a hill of considerable size, and the most elevated of any in the neighborhood. On the west side of this hill, not far from the top, under a stone of considerable size, lay the plates, deposited in a stone box. This stone was thick and rounding in the middle on the upper side, and thinner towards the edges, so that the middle part of it was visible above the ground, but the edge all around was covered with earth.

"Having removed the earth, I obtained a lever, which I got fixed under the edge of the stone, and with a little exertion raised it up. I looked in, and there indeed did I behold the plates, the Urim and Thummim, and the breastplate, as stated by the messenger. The box in which they lay was formed by laying stones together in some kind of cement. In the bottom of the box were laid two stones crossways of the box, and on these stones lay the plates and the other things with them.

"I made an attempt to take them out, but was forbidden by the messenger, and was again informed that the time for bringing them forth had not yet arrived, neither would it, until four years from that time; but he told me that I should come to that place precisely in one year from that time, and that he would there meet with me, and that I should continue to do so until the time should come for obtaining the plates.

"Accordingly, as I had been commanded, I went at the end of each year, and at each time I found the same messenger there, and received instruction and intelligence from him at each of our interviews, respecting what the Lord was going to do, and how and in what manner His kingdom was to be conducted in the last days.

* * * * * * *

"At length the time arrived for obtaining the plates, the Urim and Thummim, and the breastplate. On the twenty-second day of September, one thousand eight hundred and twenty-seven, having gone as usual at the end of another year to the place where they were deposited, the same heavenly messenger delivered them up to me with this charge: That I should be responsible for them; that if I should let them go carelessly, or through any neglect of mine, I should be cut off; but that if I would use all my endeavors to preserve them, until he, the messenger, should call for them, they should be protected.

"I soon found out the reason why I had received such strict charges to keep them safe, and why it was that the messenger had said that when I had done what was required at my hand, he would call for them. For no sooner was it known that I had them, than the most strenuous exertions were used to get them from me. Every stratagem that could be invented was resorted to for that purpose. The persecution became more bitter and severe than before, and multitudes were on the alert continually to get them from me if possible. But by the wisdom of God, they remained safe in my hands, until I had accomplished by them what was required at my hand. When, according to arrangements, the messenger called for them, I delivered them up to him; and he has them in his charge until this day, being the second day of May, one thousand eight hundred and thirty-eight."

For the complete record, see Joseph Smith—History, in the Pearl of Great Price, and *History of The Church of Jesus Christ of Latter-day Saints*, volume 1, chapters 1 through 6.

The ancient record thus brought forth from the earth as the voice of a people speaking from the dust, and translated into modern speech by the gift and power of God as attested by Divine affirmation, was first published to the world in the year 1830 as THE BOOK OF MORMON.

A BRIEF EXPLANATION ABOUT

THE BOOK OF MORMON

The Book of Mormon is a sacred record of peoples in ancient America, and was engraved upon sheets of metal. Four kinds of metal record plates are spoken of in the book itself:

1. *The Plates of Nephi*, which were of two kinds: the Small Plates and the Large Plates. The former were more particularly devoted to the spiritual matters and the ministry and teachings of the prophets, while the latter were occupied mostly by a secular history of the peoples concerned (1 Nephi 9: 2–4). From the time of Mosiah, however, the large plates also included items of major spiritual importance.
2. *The Plates of Mormon*, which consist of an abridgment by Mormon from the Large Plates of Nephi, with many commentaries. These plates also contained a continuation of the history by Mormon and additions by his son Moroni.
3. *The Plates of Ether*, which present a history of the Jaredites. This record was abridged by Moroni, who inserted comments of his own and incorporated the record with the general history under the title "Book of Ether."
4. *The Plates of Brass* brought by the people of Lehi from Jerusalem in 600 B.C. These contained "the five books of Moses, . . . And also a record of the Jews from the beginning, . . . down to the commencement of the reign of Zedekiah, king of Judah; And also the prophecies of the holy prophets" (1 Nephi 5: 11–13). Many quotations from these plates, citing Isaiah and other biblical and nonbiblical prophets, appear in the Book of Mormon.

The Book of Mormon comprises fifteen main parts or divisions, known, with one exception, as books, each designated by the name of its principal author. The first portion (the first six books, ending with Omni) is a translation from the Small Plates of Nephi. Between the books of Omni and Mosiah is an insert called The Words of Mormon. This insert connects the record engraved on the Small Plates with Mormon's abridgment of the Large Plates.

The longest portion, from Mosiah to Mormon, chapter 7, inclusive, is a translation of Mormon's abridgment of the Large Plates of Nephi. The concluding portion, from Mormon, chapter 8, to the end of the volume, was engraved by Mormon's son Moroni, who, after finishing the record of his father's life, made an abridgment of the Jaredite record (as the Book of Ether) and later added the parts known as the Book of Moroni.

In or about the year A.D. 421, Moroni, the last of the Nephite prophet-historians, sealed the sacred record and hid it up unto the Lord, to be brought forth in the latter days, as predicted by the voice of God through his ancient prophets. In A.D. 1823, this same Moroni, then a resurrected personage, visited the Prophet Joseph Smith and subsequently delivered the engraved plates to him.

About this edition: Some minor errors in the text have been perpetuated in past editions of the Book of Mormon. This edition contains corrections that seem appropriate to bring the material into conformity with prepublication manuscripts and early editions edited by the Prophet Joseph Smith.

ILLUSTRATIONS

1. *The Lord Jesus Christ*
   Painting by Heinrich Hofmann

2. *The Prophet Joseph Smith*
   Painting by Alven Gittins
   See the "Testimony of the Prophet Joseph Smith," Introduction

3. *Lehi discovers the Liahona*
   Painting by Arnold Friberg
   See 1 Nephi 16, pages 33–36

4. *Lehi and his people arrive in the promised land*
   Painting by Arnold Friberg
   See 1 Nephi 18, pages 41–43

5. *Alma baptizes in the Waters of Mormon*
   Painting by Arnold Friberg
   See Mosiah 18, pages 180–183

6. *Samuel the Lamanite prophesies*
   Painting by Arnold Friberg
   See Helaman 16, pages 404–406

7. *Jesus Christ visits the Americas*
   Painting by John Scott
   See 3 Nephi 11, pages 427–430

8. *Moroni buries the Nephite record*
   Painting by Tom Lovell
   See Mormon 8, pages 481–484

A. FRIBERG

TOM
LOVELL

NAMES AND ORDER OF BOOKS IN

THE BOOK OF MORMON

Name	*Page*
First Book of Nephi	1
Second Book of Nephi	53
Book of Jacob	117
Book of Enos	136
Book of Jarom	138
Book of Omni	140
The Words of Mormon	143
Book of Mosiah	145
Book of Alma	207
Book of Helaman	368
Third Nephi	406
Fourth Nephi	465
Book of Mormon	469
Book of Ether	487
Book of Moroni	518

ABBREVIATIONS AND DESIGNATIONS IN FOOTNOTES AND INDEX

Old Testament

Gen.	Genesis
Ex.	Exodus
Lev.	Leviticus
Num.	Numbers
Deut.	Deuteronomy
Josh.	Joshua
Judg.	Judges
Ruth	Ruth
1 Sam.	1 Samuel
2 Sam.	2 Samuel
1 Kgs.	1 Kings
2 Kgs.	2 Kings
1 Chr.	1 Chronicles
2 Chr.	2 Chronicles
Ezra	Ezra
Neh.	Nehemiah
Esth.	Esther
Job	Job
Ps.	Psalms
Prov.	Proverbs
Eccl.	Ecclesiastes
Song.	Song of Solomon
Isa.	Isaiah
Jer.	Jeremiah
Lam.	Lamentations
Ezek.	Ezekiel
Dan.	Daniel
Hosea	Hosea
Joel	Joel
Amos	Amos
Obad.	Obadiah
Jonah	Jonah
Micah	Micah
Nahum	Nahum
Hab.	Habakkuk
Zeph.	Zephaniah
Hag.	Haggai
Zech.	Zechariah
Mal.	Malachi

New Testament

Matt.	Matthew
Mark	Mark
Luke	Luke
John	John
Acts	Acts
Rom.	Romans
1 Cor.	1 Corinthians
2 Cor.	2 Corinthians
Gal.	Galatians
Eph.	Ephesians
Philip.	Philippians
Col.	Colossians
1 Thes.	1 Thessalonians
2 Thes.	2 Thessalonians
1 Tim.	1 Timothy
2 Tim.	2 Timothy
Titus	Titus
Philem.	Philemon
Heb.	Hebrews
James	James
1 Pet.	1 Peter
2 Pet.	2 Peter
1 Jn.	1 John
2 Jn.	2 John
3 Jn.	3 John
Jude	Jude
Rev.	Revelation

BD	Bible Dictionary
HC	History of the Church
JST	Joseph Smith Translation
TG	Topical Guide

Book of Mormon

1 Ne.	1 Nephi
2 Ne.	2 Nephi
Jacob	Jacob
Enos	Enos
Jarom	Jarom
Omni	Omni
W of M	Words of Mormon
Mosiah	Mosiah
Alma	Alma
Hel.	Helaman
3 Ne.	3 Nephi
4 Ne.	4 Nephi
Morm.	Mormon
Ether	Ether
Moro.	Moroni

Doctrine and Covenants

D&C	Doctrine and Covenants
OD	Official Declaration

Pearl of Great Price

Moses	Moses
Abr.	Abraham
JS-M	Joseph Smith—Matthew
JS-H	Joseph Smith—History
A of F	Articles of Faith

THE FIRST BOOK OF NEPHI

HIS REIGN AND MINISTRY

An account of Lehi and his wife Sariah, and his four sons, being called, (beginning at the eldest) Laman, Lemuel, Sam, and Nephi. The Lord warns Lehi to depart out of the land of Jerusalem, because he prophesieth unto the people concerning their iniquity and they seek to destroy his life. He taketh three days' journey into the wilderness with his family. Nephi taketh his brethren and returneth to the land of Jerusalem after the record of the Jews. The account of their sufferings. They take the daughters of Ishmael to wife. They take their families and depart into the wilderness. Their sufferings and afflictions in the wilderness. The course of their travels. They come to the large waters. Nephi's brethren rebel against him. He confoundeth them, and buildeth a ship. They call the name of the place Bountiful. They cross the large waters into the promised land, and so forth. This is according to the account of Nephi; or in other words, I, Nephi, wrote this record.

CHAPTER 1

Nephi begins the record of his people—Lehi sees in vision a pillar of fire and reads from a book of prophecy—He praises God, foretells the coming of the Messiah, and prophesies the destruction of Jerusalem—He is persecuted by the Jews.

I, NEPHI, having been [a]born
of [b]goodly [c]parents, therefore I
was [d]taught somewhat in all the
learning of my father; and having
seen many [e]afflictions in the course
of my days, nevertheless, having
been highly favored of the Lord in all
my days; yea, having had a great
knowledge of the goodness and the
mysteries of God, therefore I make
a [f]record of my proceedings in my
days.
2 Yea, I make a record in the
[a]language of my father, which consists of the learning of the Jews and
the language of the Egyptians.
3 And I know that the record
which I make is [a]true; and I make it
with mine own hand; and I make it
according to my knowledge.
4 For it came to pass in the commencement of the [a]first year of the
reign of [b]Zedekiah, king of Judah,
(my father, Lehi, having dwelt at
[c]Jerusalem in all his days); and in
that same year there came many
[d]prophets, prophesying unto the
people that they must [e]repent, or
the great city [f]Jerusalem must be
destroyed.
5 Wherefore it came to pass that
my father, Lehi, as he went forth
prayed unto the Lord, yea, even

---

1 1*a* TG Birthright.
b Prov. 22: 1.
c Mosiah 1: 2 (2–3); D&C 68: 25 (25, 28). TG Honoring Father and Mother.
d Enos 1: 1. TG Education; Family, Children, Responsibilities toward; Family, Love within.
e TG Affliction; Blessing; God, Gifts of.
f TG Record Keeping; Scriptures, Writing of.
2*a* Mosiah 1: 4; Morm. 9: 32 (32–33).
3*a* 1 Ne. 14: 30; 2 Ne. 25: 20; Mosiah 1: 6; Alma 3: 12; Ether 5: 3 (1–3).
4*a* 1 Ne. 2: 4; Mosiah 6: 4.
b 2 Kgs. 24: 18; 2 Chr. 36: 10; Jer. 37: 1; 44: 30; 49: 34; 52: 3 (3–5); Omni 1: 15.
c 1 Chr. 9: 3; 2 Chr. 15: 9; Alma 7: 10.
d 2 Kgs. 17: 13 (13–15); 2 Chr. 36: 15 (15–16); Jer. 7: 25; 26: 20. TG Prophets, Mission of.
e TG Repentance.
f Jer. 26: 18 (17–19); 2 Ne. 1: 4; Hel. 8: 20. TG Israel, Bondage of, in Other Lands; Jerusalem.

[About 600 B.C.]

with all his [a]heart, in behalf of his
people.
6 And it came to pass as he prayed
unto the Lord, there came a [a]pillar
of fire and dwelt upon a rock before
him; and he saw and heard much;
and because of the things which he
saw and heard he did [b]quake and
tremble exceedingly.
7 And it came to pass that he returned to his own house at Jerusalem; and he cast himself upon
his bed, being [a]overcome with the
Spirit and the things which he had
seen.
8 And being thus overcome with
the Spirit, he was carried away in a
[a]vision, even that he saw the
[b]heavens open, and he thought he
[c]saw God sitting upon his throne,
surrounded with numberless concourses of angels in the attitude of
singing and praising their God.
9 And it came to pass that he saw
One descending out of the midst
of heaven, and he beheld that his
[a]luster was above that of the sun at
noon-day.
10 And he also saw [a]twelve others
following him, and their brightness
did exceed that of the stars in the
firmament.
11 And they came down and went
forth upon the face of the earth;
and the first came and [a]stood before
my father, and gave unto him a
[b]book, and bade him that he should
read.
12 And it came to pass that as he
read, he was filled with the [a]Spirit
of the Lord.
13 And he read, saying: Wo, wo,
unto Jerusalem, for I have seen
thine [a]abominations! Yea, and
many things did my father read
concerning [b]Jerusalem—that it
should be destroyed, and the inhabitants thereof; many should
perish by the sword, and many
should be [c]carried away captive into
Babylon.
14 And it came to pass that when
my father had read and seen many
great and marvelous things, he did
exclaim many things unto the Lord;
such as: Great and marvelous are
thy works, O Lord God Almighty!
Thy throne is high in the heavens,
and thy [a]power, and goodness, and
mercy are over all the inhabitants
of the earth; and, because thou art
merciful, thou wilt not suffer those
who [b]come unto thee that they shall
perish!
15 And after this manner was the
language of my father in the praising
of his God; for his soul did rejoice,
and his whole heart was filled, because of the things which he had
seen, yea, which the Lord had
shown unto him.
16 And now I, Nephi, do not make
a full account of the things which
my father hath written, for he hath
written many things which he saw
in [a]visions and in [b]dreams; and he
also hath written many things
which he [c]prophesied and spake

5*a* Jer. 29: 13; James 5: 16; 2 Ne. 4: 24 (23–25).
6*a* Ex. 14: 24; Hel. 5: 24 (24, 43); D&C 29: 12; JS-H 1: 16, 30.
b Isa. 6: 5 (1–5).
7*a* Dan. 8: 27 (26–27); 10: 8 (8–12); 1 Ne. 17: 47; Alma 27: 17; Moses 1: 10 (9–10).
8*a* 1 Ne. 3: 18 (17–18); 5: 4. TG Vision.
b Ezek. 1: 1; Acts 7: 56 (55–56); 1 Ne. 11: 14; Alma 36: 22; Hel. 5: 48 (45–49); D&C 137: 1.
c TG God, Manifestations of; God, Privilege of Seeing.
9*a* JS-H 1: 17 (16–17), 30 (30–32).
10*a* TG Apostles.
11*a* 1 Sam. 3: 10; D&C 110: 2 (2–3).
b Ezek. 2: 9 (9–10); Rev. 10: 9 (2–11).
12*a* Gen. 41: 38; Mosiah 27: 24; Alma 18: 16.
13*a* 2 Kgs. 24: 19; 2 Chr. 36: 14; Jer. 13: 27.
b 2 Kgs. 23: 27; 24: 2; Jer. 13: 14; Ezek. 15: 6 (6–8); 1 Ne. 2: 13; 3: 17.
c 2 Kgs. 20: 17 (17–18); Jer. 52: 15 (3–15); 2 Ne. 25: 10; Omni 1: 15. TG Babylon.
14*a* TG God, Power of.
b 2 Ne. 26: 25 (24–28); Alma 5: 34 (33–36); 3 Ne. 9: 14 (13–14).
16*a* Ezek. 1: 1; JS-H 1: 24 (21–25).
b 1 Ne. 8: 2 (2–38); Jacob 2: 34.
c 1 Ne. 7: 1.

[About 600 B.C.]

unto his children, of which I shall
not make a full account.
17 But I shall make an account of
my proceedings in my days. Behold,
I make an [a]abridgment of the record
of my [b]father, upon [c]plates which I
have made with mine own hands;
wherefore, after I have abridged the
record of my [d]father then will I make
an account of mine own life.
18 Therefore, I would that ye
should know, that after the Lord
had shown so many marvelous
things unto my father, Lehi, yea,
concerning the [a]destruction of Jerusalem, behold he went forth among
the people, and began to [b]prophesy
and to declare unto them concerning
the things which he had both seen
and heard.
19 And it came to pass that the
[a]Jews did [b]mock him because of the
things which he testified of them;
for he truly testified of their [c]wicked-
ness and their abominations; and
he testified that the things which he
saw and heard, and also the things
which he read in the book, manifested plainly of the coming of a
[d]Messiah, and also the redemption of
the world.
20 And when the Jews heard these
things they were angry with him;
yea, even as with the prophets of
old, whom they had [a]cast out, and
stoned, and slain; and they also
[b]sought his life, that they might take
it away. But behold, I, Nephi, will
show unto you that the tender
[c]mercies of the Lord are over all
those whom he hath chosen, because of their faith, to make them
mighty even unto the power of
[d]deliverance.

CHAPTER 2

Lehi takes his family into the wilderness by the Red Sea—They leave their property—Lehi offers a sacrifice to the Lord and teaches his sons to keep the commandments—Laman and Lemuel murmur against their father—Nephi is obedient and prays in faith; the Lord speaks to him, and he is chosen to rule over his brethren.

FOR behold, it came to pass that
the Lord spake unto my father, yea,
even in a dream, and said unto him:
Blessed art thou Lehi, because of the
things which thou hast done; and
because thou hast been faithful and
declared unto this people the things
which I commanded thee, behold,
they seek to [a]take away thy [b]life.
2 And it came to pass that the Lord
[a]commanded my father, even in a
[b]dream, that he should [c]take his
family and depart into the wilderness.
3 And it came to pass that he was
[a]obedient unto the word of the Lord,
wherefore he did as the Lord commanded him.
4 And it came to pass that [a]he
*departed into the wilderness. And
he left his house, and the land of
his inheritance, and his gold, and
his silver, and his precious things,
and took nothing with him, save it

17*a* 1 Ne. 9: 2 (2–5); Enos 1: 13 (13, 15–18). TG Scriptures, Writing of.
b 1 Ne. 6: 1 (1–3); 8: 29 (29–30); 19: 1 (1–6).
c 1 Ne. 10: 15.
d 2 Ne. 4: 14; 5: 33 (29–33); D&C 10: 42.
18*a* 2 Ne. 25: 9; D&C 5: 20.
b TG Prophets, Mission of; Prophets, Rejection of.
19*a* TG Apostasy of Israel.
b 2 Chr. 36: 16; Jer. 25: 4 (1–4); Ezek. 5: 6; 1 Ne. 2: 13; 7: 14.
c 1 Ne. 17: 22.
d TG Jesus Christ, Prophecies about.
20*a* Jer. 13: 11; Hel. 13: 24 (24–28).
b Jer. 11: 19; 1 Ne. 2: 2 (1–4); 2 Ne. 10: 20. TG Prophets, Rejection of.
c Gen. 32: 10; Alma 34: 38; D&C 46: 15.
d TG Deliverance.

2 1*a* TG Persecution.
b 1 Ne. 7: 14.
2*a* 1 Ne. 3: 16; 4: 34; 5: 8; 17: 44; Mosiah 7: 20; Alma 9: 9. TG Called of God.
b TG Dream.
c Gen. 12: 1; 19: 12; 1 Ne. 1: 20 (18–20); 2 Ne. 10: 20; Ether 1: 42; Abr. 2: 3. TG Protection, Divine.
3*a* TG Commitment.
4*a* 1 Ne. 10: 4; 19: 8.

[*600 B.C.]

were his family, and provisions, and
tents, and departed into the wilderness.
5 And he came down by the
borders near the shore of the [a]Red
Sea; and he traveled in the wilderness in the borders which are nearer
the Red Sea; and he did travel in
the wilderness with his family,
which consisted of my mother,
Sariah, and my elder brothers, who
were Laman, Lemuel, and Sam.
6 And it came to pass that when he
had traveled three days in the wilderness, he pitched his tent in a [a]valley
by the side of a [b]river of water.
7 And it came to pass that he built
an [a]altar of [b]stones, and made an
[c]offering unto the Lord, and gave
[d]thanks unto the Lord our God.
8 And it came to pass that he called
the name of the river, Laman, and it
emptied into the Red Sea; and the
valley was in the borders near the
mouth thereof.
9 And when my father saw that the
waters of the river emptied into the
[a]fountain of the Red Sea, he spake
unto Laman, saying: O that thou
mightest be like unto this river,
continually running into the fountain of all righteousness!
10 And he also spake unto Lemuel:
O that thou mightest be like unto
this valley, [a]firm and [b]steadfast, and
immovable in keeping the commandments of the Lord!
11 Now this he spake because of
the [a]stiffneckedness of Laman and
Lemuel; for behold they did [b]mur-
mur in many things against their
[c]father, because he was a [d]visionary
man, and had led them out of the
land of Jerusalem, to leave the land
of their inheritance, and their gold,
and their silver, and their precious
things, to perish in the wilderness.
And this they said he had done
because of the foolish imaginations
of his heart.
12 And thus Laman and Lemuel,
being the eldest, did murmur against
their [a]father. And they did [b]murmur
because they [c]knew not the dealings of that God who had [d]created
them.
13 Neither did they [a]believe that
Jerusalem, that great city, could be
[b]destroyed according to the words
of the prophets. And they were like
unto the Jews who were at Jerusalem, who sought to take away the
life of my father.
14 And it came to pass that my
father did speak unto them in the
[a]valley of Lemuel, with [b]power,
being filled with the Spirit, until
their frames did [c]shake before him.
And he did confound them, that
they durst not utter against him;
wherefore, they did as he commanded them.
15 And my father dwelt in a [a]tent.
16 And it came to pass that I,
Nephi, being exceedingly young,
nevertheless being large in stature,
and also having great desires to
know of the [a]mysteries of God,

5*a* 1 Ne. 16: 14; D&C 17: 1.
6*a* 1 Ne. 9: 1.
b Joel 1: 20.
7*a* Gen. 12: 7 (7–8); 26: 25; Ex. 24: 4; Abr. 2: 17.
b Ex. 20: 25; Deut. 27: 5 (5–6); Josh. 8: 31 (30–31).
c TG Sacrifice.
d TG Thanksgiving.
9*a* IE fount, or source, like the Gulf of Akaba, which empties into the Red Sea.
10*a* IE like Ezion-geber, the Hebrew roots of which denote firmness and strength, or might of a man.
b TG Dependability.
11*a* TG Stiffneckedness.
b 1 Ne. 7: 7. TG Murmuring.
c Prov. 20: 20.
d 1 Ne. 5: 4 (2–4); 17: 20.
12*a* Lam. 4: 16 (16–17).
b 1 Sam. 3: 13; Mosiah 27: 8 (7–37); Moses 5: 16.
c Moses 4: 6.
d Deut. 32: 6; D&C 43: 23. TG Man, Physical Creation of.
13*a* Ezek. 5: 6; 1 Ne. 1: 19 (18–20).
b Jer. 13: 14; 1 Ne. 1: 13 (4–13).
14*a* 1 Ne. 9: 1; 16: 6 (6, 12).
b TG Priesthood, Power of.
c 1 Ne. 17: 45.
15*a* Gen. 12: 8; 26: 17 (17, 25); 31: 25 (25, 33); 1 Ne. 4: 38; 10: 16.
16*a* TG Mysteries of Godliness.

[About 600 B.C.]

wherefore, I did cry unto the Lord; and behold he did [b]visit me, and did [c]soften my heart that I did [d]believe all the words which had been spoken by my [e]father; wherefore, I did not [f]rebel against him like unto my brothers.

17 And I spake unto Sam, making known unto him the things which the Lord had manifested unto me by his Holy Spirit. And it came to pass that he believed in my words.

18 But, behold, Laman and Lemuel would not hearken unto my words; and being [a]grieved because of the hardness of their hearts I cried unto the Lord for them.

19 And it came to pass that the Lord spake unto me, saying: Blessed art thou, Nephi, because of thy [a]faith, for thou hast sought me diligently, with lowliness of heart.

20 And inasmuch as ye shall keep my commandments, ye shall [a]prosper, and shall be led to a [b]land of promise; yea, even a land which I have prepared for you; yea, a land which is choice above all other lands.

21 And inasmuch as thy brethren shall rebel against thee, they shall be [a]cut off from the presence of the Lord.

22 And inasmuch as thou shalt keep my commandments, thou shalt be made a [a]ruler and a teacher over thy brethren.

23 For behold, in that day that they shall [a]rebel against me, I will [b]curse them even with a sore curse, and they shall have no power over thy seed except they shall [c]rebel against me also.

24 And if it so be that they rebel against me, they shall be a [a]scourge unto thy seed, to [b]stir them up in the ways of remembrance.

CHAPTER 3

Lehi's sons return to Jerusalem to obtain the plates of brass—Laban refuses to give them up—Nephi exhorts and encourages his brethren—Laban steals their property and attempts to slay them—Laman and Lemuel smite Nephi and are reproved by an angel.

AND it came to pass that I, Nephi, returned from [a]speaking with the Lord, to the tent of my father.

2 And it came to pass that he spake unto me, saying: Behold I have dreamed a [a]dream, in the which the Lord hath commanded me that thou and thy brethren shall [b]return to Jerusalem.

3 For behold, Laban hath the record of the Jews and also a [a]genealogy of my forefathers, and they are [b]engraven upon plates of brass.

4 Wherefore, the Lord hath commanded me that thou and thy brothers should go unto the house of Laban, and seek the records, and bring them down hither into the wilderness.

5 And now, behold thy brothers murmur, saying it is a hard thing which I have required of them; but behold I have not required it of

---

16*b* Ps. 8: 4; 1 Ne. 3: 1; 19: 11; Alma 17: 10; D&C 5: 16. TG Guidance, Divine.
c 1 Kgs. 18: 37; Alma 5: 7.
d 1 Ne. 11: 5.
e TG Honoring Father and Mother.
f TG Family, Love within.
18*a* Alma 31: 24; 3 Ne. 7: 16.
19*a* 1 Ne. 7: 12 (9–13); 15: 11.
20*a* Josh. 1: 7; 1 Ne. 4: 14; Mosiah 1: 7.
b Deut. 33: 13 (13–16); 1 Chr. 28: 8 (7–8); 1 Ne. 5: 5 (5, 22); 7: 13; Moses 7: 17 (17–18). TG Promised Lands.
21*a* Josh. 23: 13; 2 Ne. 5: 20 (20–24); Alma 9: 14 (13–15); 38: 1.
22*a* Gen. 37: 8 (8–11); 1 Ne. 3: 29. TG Authority.
23*a* Job 24: 13.
b Deut. 11: 28; 1 Ne. 12: 22 (22–23); D&C 41: 1. TG Curse.
c Josh. 22: 16; Mosiah 15: 26.
24*a* Josh. 23: 13; Judg. 2: 22 (22–23).
b 2 Ne. 5: 25.
3 1*a* 1 Ne. 2: 16.
2*a* TG Dream.
b 1 Ne. 2: 4 (1–5); 7: 3.
3*a* 1 Ne. 3: 12; 5: 14.
b Jer. 17: 1; 1 Ne. 3: 24 (12, 19–24).

[Between 600 and 592 B.C.]

them, but it is a commandment of the Lord.

6 Therefore go, my son, and thou shalt be favored of the Lord, because thou hast [a]not [b]murmured.

7 And it came to pass that I, Nephi, said unto my father: I [a]will go and do the things which the Lord hath commanded, for I know that the Lord giveth no [b]commandments unto the children of men, save he shall [c]prepare a way for them that they may accomplish the thing which he commandeth them.

8 And it came to pass that when my father had heard these words he was exceedingly glad, for he knew that I had been blessed of the Lord.

9 And I, Nephi, and my brethren took our journey in the wilderness, with our tents, to go up to the land of Jerusalem.

10 And it came to pass that when we had gone up to the land of Jerusalem, I and my brethren did consult one with another.

11 And we [a]cast lots—who of us should go in unto the house of Laban. And it came to pass that the lot fell upon Laman; and Laman went in unto the house of Laban, and he talked with him as he sat in his house.

12 And he desired of Laban the records which were engraven upon the plates of brass, which contained the [a]genealogy of my father.

13 And behold, it came to pass that Laban was angry, and thrust him out from his presence; and he would not that he should have the records. Wherefore, he said unto him: Behold thou art a robber, and I will slay thee.

14 But Laman fled out of his presence, and told the things which Laban had done, unto us. And we began to be exceedingly sorrowful, and my brethren were about to return unto my father in the wilderness.

15 But behold I said unto them that: [a]As the Lord liveth, and as we live, we will not go down unto our father in the wilderness until we have [b]accomplished the thing which the Lord hath commanded us.

16 Wherefore, let us be faithful in keeping the commandments of the Lord; therefore let us go down to the land of our father's [a]inheritance, for behold he left gold and silver, and all manner of riches. And all this he hath done because of the [b]commandments of the Lord.

17 For he knew that Jerusalem must be [a]destroyed, because of the wickedness of the people.

18 For behold, they have [a]rejected the words of the prophets. Wherefore, if my father should dwell in the land after he hath been [b]commanded to flee out of the land, behold, he would also perish. Wherefore, it must needs be that he flee out of the land.

19 And behold, it is wisdom in God that we should obtain these [a]records, that we may preserve unto our children the language of our fathers;

20 And also that we may [a]preserve unto them the words which have been spoken by the mouth of all the holy [b]prophets, which have been delivered unto them by the Spirit and power of God, since the world began, even down unto this present time.

6*a* TG Sustaining Church Leaders.
b TG Murmuring.
7*a* 1 Sam. 17: 32; 1 Kgs. 17: 15 (11–15). TG Faith; Loyalty; Obedience.
b TG Commandments of God.
c Gen. 18: 14; Philip. 4: 13; 1 Ne. 17: 3, 50; D&C 5: 34.
11*a* Neh. 10: 34; Acts 1: 26.
12*a* 1 Ne. 3: 3; 5: 14; Jarom 1: 1.
15*a* TG Oath; Promise.
b TG Commitment; Dedication.
16*a* 1 Ne. 2: 4.
b 1 Ne. 2: 2; 4: 34.
17*a* 2 Chr. 36: 20 (16–20); Jer. 39: 9 (1–9); 1 Ne. 1: 13.
18*a* Jer. 26: 23 (21–24). TG Prophets, Rejection of.
b 1 Ne. 5: 21; 7: 2; 16: 8.
19*a* Omni 1: 17; Mosiah 1: 3 (2–6). TG Record Keeping.
20*a* TG Scriptures, Preservation of.
b Zech. 7: 12; Matt. 11: 13; Mosiah 15: 13.

[Between 600 and 592 B.C.]

21 And it came to pass that after this manner of language did I [a]persuade my brethren, that they might be faithful in keeping the commandments of God.

22 And it came to pass that we went down to the land of our inheritance, and we did gather together our [a]gold, and our silver, and our precious things.

23 And after we had gathered these things together, we went up again unto the house of Laban.

24 And it came to pass that we went in unto Laban, and desired him that he would give unto us the records which were engraven upon the [a]plates of brass, for which we would give unto him our gold, and our silver, and all our precious things.

25 And it came to pass that when Laban saw our property, and that it was exceedingly great, he did [a]lust after it, insomuch that he thrust us out, and sent his servants to slay us, that he might obtain our property.

26 And [a]it came to pass that we did flee before the servants of Laban, and we were obliged to leave behind our property, and it fell into the hands of Laban.

27 And it came to pass that we fled into the wilderness, and the servants of Laban did not overtake us, and we [a]hid ourselves in the cavity of a rock.

28 And it came to pass that Laman was angry with me, and also with my father; and also was Lemuel, for he hearkened unto the words of Laman. Wherefore Laman and Lemuel did speak many [a]hard words unto us, their younger brothers, and they did smite us even with a rod.

29 And it came to pass as they smote us with a rod, behold, an [a]angel of the Lord came and stood before them, and he spake unto them, saying: Why do ye smite your younger brother with a rod? Know ye not that the Lord hath chosen him to be a [b]ruler over you, and this because of your iniquities? Behold ye shall go up to Jerusalem again, and the Lord will [c]deliver Laban into your hands.

30 And after the [a]angel had spoken unto us, he departed.

31 And after the angel had departed, Laman and Lemuel again began to [a]murmur, saying: How is it possible that the Lord will deliver Laban into our hands? Behold, he is a mighty man, and he can command fifty, yea, even he can slay fifty; then why not us?

CHAPTER 4

Nephi slays Laban at the Lord's command and then secures the plates of brass by stratagem—Zoram chooses to join Lehi's family in the wilderness.

AND it came to pass that I spake unto my brethren, saying: Let us go up again unto Jerusalem, and let us be [a]faithful in keeping the commandments of the Lord; for behold he is mightier than all the earth, then why not [b]mightier than Laban and his fifty, yea, or even than his tens of thousands?

2 Therefore let us go up; let us be [a]strong like unto Moses; for he truly spake unto the waters of the Red [b]Sea and they divided hither and thither, and our fathers came through, out of captivity, on dry ground, and the armies of Pharaoh

21*a* TG Family, Love within; Persuade.
22*a* 1 Ne. 2: 4.
24*a* 1 Ne. 3: 3; 4: 24 (24, 38).
25*a* TG Covetousness.
26*a* 1 Ne. 4: 11.
27*a* Josh. 10: 16 (16–17); 1 Sam. 13: 6; Jer. 36: 26; Ether 13: 13 (13, 22).
28*a* 1 Ne. 17: 18.
29*a* 1 Ne. 4: 3; 7: 10. TG Angels.
b Gen. 41: 43 (41–43); 1 Ne. 2: 22.
c 2 Kgs. 3: 18; 3 Ne. 3: 21.
30*a* 1 Ne. 4: 3; 16: 38.
31*a* TG Murmuring.

4 1*a* TG Courage; Dependability; Faithful.
b 1 Ne. 7: 11. TG God, Power of.
2*a* Deut. 11: 8; Prov. 24: 10 (10–12).
b Ex. 14: 21 (18–30); Josh. 2: 10; 1 Ne. 17: 26; Mosiah 7: 19.

[Between 600 and 592 B.C.]

did follow and were drowned in the
waters of the Red Sea.
3 Now behold ye know that this
is true; and ye also know that an
[a]angel hath spoken unto you; wherefore can ye [b]doubt? Let us go up;
the Lord is able to [c]deliver us, even
as our fathers, and to destroy Laban,
even as the Egyptians.
4 Now when I had spoken these
words, they were yet wroth, and did
still continue to murmur; nevertheless they did follow me up until we
came without the walls of Jerusalem.
5 And it was by night; and I caused
that they should hide themselves
without the walls. And after they
had hid themselves, I, Nephi, crept
into the city and went forth towards
the house of Laban.
6 And I was [a]led by the Spirit, not
[b]knowing beforehand the things
which I should do.
7 Nevertheless I went forth, and as
I came near unto the house of Laban
I beheld a man, and he had fallen to
the earth before me, for he was
[a]drunken with wine.
8 And when I came to him I found
that it was Laban.
9 And I beheld his [a]sword, and I
drew it forth from the sheath thereof; and the hilt thereof was of pure
gold, and the workmanship thereof
was exceedingly fine, and I saw that
the blade thereof was of the most
precious steel.
10 And it came to pass that I was
[a]constrained by the Spirit that I
should kill Laban; but I said in my
heart: Never at any time have I
shed the blood of man. And I shrunk
and would that I might not slay him.
11 And the Spirit said unto me
again: Behold the [a]Lord hath
[b]delivered him into thy hands. Yea,
and I also knew that he had sought
to take away mine own life; yea,
and he would not hearken unto the
commandments of the Lord; and he
also had [c]taken away our property.
12 And it came to pass that the
Spirit said unto me again: Slay him,
for the Lord hath delivered him into
thy hands;
13 Behold the Lord [a]slayeth the
[b]wicked to bring forth his righteous
purposes. It is [c]better that one man
should perish than that a nation
should dwindle and perish in
[d]unbelief.
14 And now, when I, Nephi, had
heard these words, I remembered
the words of the Lord which he spake
unto me in the wilderness, saying
that: [a]Inasmuch as thy seed shall
keep my [b]commandments, they shall
[c]prosper in the [d]land of promise.
15 Yea, and I also thought that
they could not keep the commandments of the Lord according to the
[a]law of Moses, save they should have
the law.
16 And I also knew that the [a]law
was engraven upon the plates of
brass.
17 And again, I knew that the Lord
had delivered Laban into my hands
for this cause—that I might obtain
the records according to his commandments.
18 Therefore I did obey the voice
of the Spirit, and took Laban by the
hair of the head, and I smote off his
head with his own [a]sword.
19 And after I had smitten off his

3*a* 1 Ne. 3: 30 (29–31); 7: 10.
b TG Doubt.
c TG Deliverance.
6*a* TG Guidance, Divine; Holy Ghost, Gifts of; Inspiration.
b Heb. 11: 8.
7*a* TG Drunkenness.
9*a* 2 Ne. 5: 14; D&C 17: 1.
10*a* 1 Sam. 15: 3 (3–33).
11*a* Deut. 3: 3; 1 Sam. 17: 46 (41–49).
b 1 Ne. 7: 11.
c 1 Ne. 3: 26.
13*a* Num. 25: 17; Deut. 12: 29; Ps. 139: 19; 1 Ne. 17: 37 (33–38); D&C 98: 32 (31–32).
b TG Justice; Punishment; Wickedness.
c Alma 30: 47. TG Life, Sanctity of.
d TG Unbelief, Unbelievers.
14*a* Omni 1: 6; Mosiah 2: 22; Ether 2: 7 (7–12).
b TG Commandments of God.
c 1 Ne. 2: 20.
d 1 Ne. 17: 13 (13–14); Jacob 2: 12.
15*a* Mosiah 1: 5 (1–6).
16*a* Josh. 1: 8. TG Law of Moses.
18*a* 1 Sam. 17: 51.

[Between 600 and 592 B.C.]

head with his own sword, I took the
garments of Laban and put them
upon mine own body; yea, even
every whit; and I did gird on his
armor about my loins.
20 And after I had done this, I went
forth unto the treasury of Laban.
And as I went forth towards the
treasury of Laban, behold, I saw
the [a]servant of Laban who had the
keys of the treasury. And I commanded
him in the voice of Laban,
that he should go with me into the
treasury.
21 And he supposed me to be his
master, Laban, for he beheld the
garments and also the sword girded
about my loins.
22 And he spake unto me concerning
the [a]elders of the Jews, he knowing
that his master, Laban, had been
out by night among them.
23 And I spake unto him as if it had
been Laban.
24 And I also spake unto him that
I should carry the engravings, which
were upon the [a]plates of brass, to
my elder brethren, who were without
the walls.
25 And I also bade him that he
should follow me.
26 And he, supposing that I spake
of the [a]brethren of the [b]church, and
that I was truly that Laban whom I
had slain, wherefore he did follow
me.
27 And he spake unto me many
times concerning the elders of the
Jews, as I went forth unto my brethren,
who were without the walls.
28 And it came to pass that when
Laman saw me he was exceedingly
frightened, and also Lemuel and
Sam. And they fled from before my
presence; for they supposed it was
Laban, and that he had slain me and
had sought to take away their lives
also.
29 And it came to pass that I called
after them, and they did hear me;
wherefore they did cease to flee from
my presence.
30 And it came to pass that when
the servant of Laban beheld my
brethren he began to tremble, and
was about to flee from before me and
return to the city of Jerusalem.
31 And now I, Nephi, being a man
large in stature, and also having
received much [a]strength of the Lord,
therefore I did seize upon the servant
of Laban, and held him, that
he should not flee.
32 And it came to pass that I spake
with him, that if he would hearken
unto my words, as the Lord liveth,
and as I live, even so that if he would
hearken unto our words, we would
spare his life.
33 And I spake unto him, even with
an [a]oath, that he need not fear; that
he should be a [b]free man like unto us
if he would go down in the wilderness
with us.
34 And I also spake unto him, saying:
Surely the Lord hath [a]commanded
us to do this thing; and
shall we not be diligent in keeping
the commandments of the Lord?
Therefore, if thou wilt go down into
the wilderness to my father thou
shalt have place with us.
35 And it came to pass that [a]Zoram
did take courage at the words which
I spake. Now Zoram was the name
of the servant; and he promised that
he would go down into the wilderness
unto our father. Yea, and he
also made an oath unto us that he
would tarry with us from that time
forth.
36 Now we were desirous that he
should tarry with us for this cause,
that the Jews might not know concerning
our flight into the wilderness,
lest they should pursue us and
destroy us.
37 And it came to pass that when

20*a* 2 Ne. 1: 30.
22*a* 2 Sam. 17: 15; Ezek. 8: 1; Acts 25: 15.
24*a* 1 Ne. 3: 24 (12, 19–24); 5: 10 (10–22).
26*a* Ex. 2: 11; Num. 18: 6; 2 Sam. 19: 41.
b TG Church Organization.
31*a* TG Strength; Strengthen.
33*a* 2 Sam. 21: 7. TG Oath.
b TG Free.
34*a* 1 Ne. 2: 2; 3: 16.
35*a* 1 Ne. 16: 7; 2 Ne. 5: 6 (5–6); Jacob 1: 13; Alma 54: 23; 4 Ne. 1: 36 (36–37).

[Between 600 and 592 B.C.]

Zoram had made an [a]oath unto us,
our [b]fears did cease concerning him.
38 And it came to pass that we took
the plates of brass and the servant
of Laban, and departed into the
wilderness, and journeyed unto the
[a]tent of our father.

CHAPTER 5

Sariah complains against Lehi—Both rejoice over the return of their sons—They offer sacrifices—The plates of brass contain writings of Moses and the prophets—They identify Lehi as a descendant of Joseph—Lehi prophesies concerning his seed and the preservation of the plates.

AND it came to pass that after we
had come down into the wilderness unto our father, behold, he was
filled with joy, and also my mother,
Sariah, was exceedingly glad, for she
truly had mourned because of us.
2 For she had supposed that we
had perished in the wilderness; and
she also had [a]complained against
my father, telling him that he was a
[b]visionary man; saying: Behold thou
hast led us forth from the land of our
inheritance, and my sons are no
more, and we perish in the wilderness.
3 And after this manner of language
had my mother complained against
my father.
4 And it had come to pass that my
father spake unto her, saying: I
know that I am a [a]visionary man;
for if I had not seen the things of
God in a [b]vision I should not have
known the goodness of God, but had
tarried at Jerusalem, and had
perished with my brethren.
5 But behold, I have [a]obtained a
[b]land of promise, in the which things
I do rejoice; yea, and I [c]know that
the Lord will deliver my sons out of
the hands of Laban, and bring them
down again unto us in the wilderness.
6 And after this manner of language
did my father, Lehi, [a]comfort my
mother, Sariah, concerning us, while
we journeyed in the wilderness up to
the land of Jerusalem, to obtain the
record of the Jews.
7 And when we had returned to
the tent of my father, behold their
joy was full, and my mother was
comforted.
8 And she spake, saying: Now I
know of a surety that the Lord hath
[a]commanded my husband to [b]flee
into the wilderness; yea, and I also
know of a surety that the Lord hath
protected my sons, and delivered
them out of the hands of Laban, and
given them power whereby they
could [c]accomplish the thing which
the Lord hath commanded them.
And after this manner of language
did she speak.
9 And it came to pass that they did
rejoice exceedingly, and did offer
[a]sacrifice and burnt offerings unto
the Lord; and they gave [b]thanks unto the God of Israel.
10 And after they had given thanks
unto the God of Israel, my father,
Lehi, took the records which were
engraven upon the [a]plates of brass,
and he did search them from the
beginning.
11 And he beheld that they did
contain the five [a]books of Moses,
which gave an account of the creation of the world, and also of Adam
and Eve, who were our first parents;

37*a* Ex. 22: 11 (10–11); Josh. 9: 19 (1–21). TG Oath; Vows.
b TG Trustworthiness.
38*a* 1 Ne. 2: 15.
5 2*a* TG Murmuring.
b Gen. 37: 19 (8, 19).
4*a* 1 Ne. 2: 11; 17: 20.
b 1 Ne. 1: 8 (8–13); 3: 18 (17–18). TG Vision.
5*a* Eph. 1: 11; Heb. 6: 15 (13–15).
b 1 Ne. 2: 20; 18: 8 (8, 22–23). TG Promised Lands.
c TG Faith; Trust in God.
6*a* TG Comfort; Family, Love within.
8*a* 1 Ne. 2: 2.
b Gen. 19: 14.
c 1 Ne. 3: 7.
9*a* 1 Ne. 7: 22; Mosiah 2: 3; 3 Ne. 9: 19. TG Law of Moses.
b TG Thanksgiving.
10*a* 1 Ne. 4: 24 (24, 38); 13: 23.
11*a* Ex. 17: 14; Deut. 31: 9; Luke 16: 29; 24: 27; 1 Ne. 19: 23; Moses 1: 41 (40–41).

[Between 600 and 592 B.C.]

12 And also a [a]record of the Jews
from the beginning, even down to
the commencement of the reign of
Zedekiah, king of Judah;
13 And also the prophecies of the
holy prophets, from the beginning,
even down to the commencement of
the reign of [a]Zedekiah; and also
many prophecies which have been
spoken by the mouth of [b]Jeremiah.
14 And it came to pass that my
father, Lehi, also found upon the
[a]plates of brass a [b]genealogy of his
[c]fathers; wherefore he knew that he
was a descendant of [d]Joseph; yea,
even that Joseph who was the son
of [e]Jacob, who was [f]sold into Egypt,
and who was [g]preserved by the
hand of the Lord, that he might preserve his father, Jacob, and all his
household from perishing with
famine.
15 And they were also [a]led out of
captivity and out of the land of
Egypt, by that same God who had
preserved them.
16 And thus my father, Lehi, did
discover the genealogy of his fathers.
And Laban also was a descendant of
[a]Joseph, wherefore he and his fathers
had kept the [b]records.
17 And now when my father saw
all these things, he was filled with
the Spirit, and began to prophesy
concerning his seed—
18 That these [a]plates of brass
should go forth unto all [b]nations,
kindreds, tongues, and people who
were of his seed.
19 Wherefore, he said that these
plates of brass should [a]never perish;
neither should they be dimmed any
more by time. And he prophesied
many things concerning his seed.
20 And it came to pass that thus
far I and my father had kept the
commandments wherewith the Lord
had commanded us.
21 And we had obtained the
records which the Lord had commanded us, and searched them and
found that they were desirable; yea,
even of great [a]worth unto us, insomuch that we could [b]preserve the
commandments of the Lord unto our
children.
22 Wherefore, it was wisdom in the
Lord that we should carry them with
us, as we journeyed in the wilderness
towards the land of promise.

CHAPTER 6

Nephi writes of the things of God—His purpose is to persuade men to come unto the God of Abraham and be saved.

AND now I, Nephi, do not give the
genealogy of my fathers in [a]this part
of my record; neither at any time
shall I give it after upon these
[b]plates which I am [c]writing; for it is
given in the record which has been
kept by my [d]father; wherefore, I do
not write it in this work.
2 For it sufficeth me to say that we
are descendants of [a]Joseph.
3 And it mattereth not to me that I
am particular to give a full account
of all the things of my father, for
they cannot be written upon [a]these

12*a* 1 Chr. 9: 1.
TG Scriptures, Writing of.
13*a* 2 Kgs. 24: 18; Jer. 37: 1.
b Ezra 1: 1; Jer. 36: 32 (17–32); 1 Ne. 7: 14; Hel. 8: 20.
14*a* Mosiah 2: 34.
b 1 Ne. 3: 3, 12; Jarom 1: 1.
TG Book of Remembrance.
c TG Israel, Origins of.
d 2 Ne. 3: 4; Alma 10: 3.
TG Israel, Joseph, People of.
e Gen. 25: 26; 2 Ne. 20: 21; Alma 7: 25; D&C 27: 10.
f Gen. 37: 36 (29–36).
g TG Protection, Divine.
15*a* Gen. 15: 14 (13–14); Ex. 15: 13; Amos 3: 1 (1–2); 1 Ne. 17: 31 (23–31); 19: 10; D&C 103: 16 (16–18); 136: 22.
16*a* 2 Chr. 15: 9; 1 Ne. 6: 2.
TG Israel, Joseph, People of.
b TG Record Keeping.
18*a* Alma 22: 12.
b JS-H 1: 33.
19*a* Alma 37: 4.
21*a* TG Scriptures, Value of.
b TG Scriptures, Preservation of.
6 1*a* 2 Ne. 4: 15.
b 1 Ne. 9: 2.
c TG Scriptures, Writing of.
d 1 Ne. 1: 17 (16–17); 19: 1 (1–6).
2*a* 1 Ne. 5: 16 (14–16).
3*a* Jacob 7: 27; Jarom 1: 2 (2, 14); Omni 1: 1, 30.

[Between 600 and 592 B.C.]

plates, for I desire the room that I
may write of the things of God.
4 For the fulness of mine intent is
that I may [a]persuade men to [b]come
unto the God of Abraham, and the
God of Isaac, and the God of Jacob,
and be saved.
5 Wherefore, the things which are
[a]pleasing unto the world I do not
write, but the things which are pleasing unto God and unto those who are
not of the world.
6 Wherefore, I shall give commandment unto my seed, that they
shall not occupy these plates with
things which are not of worth unto
the children of men.

CHAPTER 7

Lehi's sons return to Jerusalem and enlist Ishmael and his household in their cause—Laman and others rebel—Nephi exhorts his brethren to have faith in the Lord—They bind him with cords and plan his destruction—He is freed by the power of faith—His brethren ask forgiveness—Lehi and his company offer sacrifice and burnt offerings.

AND now I would that ye might
know, that after my father, Lehi,
had made an end of [a]prophesying
concerning his seed, it came to pass
that the Lord spake unto him again,
saying that it was not meet for him,
Lehi, that he should take his family
into the wilderness alone; but that
his sons should take [b]daughters to
[c]wife, that they might raise up
[d]seed unto the Lord in the land of
promise.
2 And it came to pass that the
Lord [a]commanded him that I,
Nephi, and my brethren, should
again return unto the land of
Jerusalem, and bring down Ishmael
and his family into the wilderness.
3 And it came to pass that I,
Nephi, did [a]again, with my brethren,
go forth into the wilderness to go up
to Jerusalem.
4 And it came to pass that we went
up unto the house of Ishmael, and
we did gain favor in the sight of
Ishmael, insomuch that we did
speak unto him the words of the
Lord.
5 And it came to pass that the [a]Lord
did soften the heart of Ishmael, and
also his household, insomuch that
they took their journey with us
down into the wilderness to the tent
of our father.
6 And it came to pass that as we
journeyed in the wilderness, behold
Laman and Lemuel, and two of the
[a]daughters of Ishmael, and the two
[b]sons of Ishmael and their families,
did [c]rebel against us; yea, against
me, Nephi, and Sam, and their
father, Ishmael, and his wife, and
his three other daughters.
7 And it came to pass in the which
rebellion, they were desirous to
return unto the land of Jerusalem.
8 And now I, Nephi, being [a]grieved
for the hardness of their hearts,
therefore I spake unto them, saying,
yea, even unto Laman and unto
Lemuel: Behold ye are mine elder
brethren, and how is it that ye are
so hard in your hearts, and so blind
in your minds, that ye have need
that I, your [b]younger brother,
should speak unto you, yea, and set
an [c]example for you?
9 How is it that ye have not hearkened unto the word of the Lord?
10 How is it that ye have [a]forgotten
that ye have seen an angel of the
Lord?

4*a* Luke 1:4 (3–4); John 20:31 (30–31).
b 2 Ne. 9:41 (41, 45, 51).
5*a* Gal. 1:10; 1 Thes. 2:4; Heb. 13:21; W of M 1:4.
7 1*a* 1 Ne. 1:16.
b 1 Ne. 16:7.
c TG Marriage.
d Ps. 127:3.
2*a* 1 Ne. 16:8.
3*a* 1 Ne. 3:2.
5*a* TG Guidance, Divine.
6*a* 1 Ne. 16:7 (7, 17).
b 2 Ne. 4:10.
c 1 Ne. 17:18 (17–55).
8*a* Mosiah 28:3; Alma 31:2; 3 Ne. 17:14; Moses 7:41.
b 1 Chr. 29:1; D&C 1:19 (19, 23).
c TG Example.
10*a* Deut. 4:9 (9–13); 1 Ne. 4:3.

[Between 600 and 592 B.C.]

11 Yea, and how is it that ye have
forgotten what great things the
Lord hath done for us, in [a]delivering
us out of the hands of Laban, and
also that we should obtain the
record?
12 Yea, and how is it that ye have
forgotten that the Lord is able to do
all [a]things according to his will, for
the children of men, if it so be that
they exercise [b]faith in him? Wherefore, let us be faithful to him.
13 And if it so be that we are
faithful to him, we shall obtain the
[a]land of promise; and ye shall know
at some future period that the word
of the Lord shall be fulfilled concerning the [b]destruction of [c]Jeru-
salem; for all things which the Lord
hath spoken concerning the destruction of Jerusalem must be fulfilled.
14 For behold, the [a]Spirit of the
Lord [b]ceaseth soon to strive with
them; for behold, they have [c]re-
jected the prophets, and [d]Jeremiah
have they cast into prison. And they
have sought to take away the [e]life
of my father, insomuch that they
have driven him out of the land.
15 Now behold, I say unto you
that if ye will return unto Jerusalem
ye shall also perish with them. And
now, if ye have choice, go up to the
land, and remember the words which
I speak unto you, that if ye go ye
will also perish; for thus the Spirit
of the Lord constraineth me that I
should speak.
16 And it came to pass that when I,
Nephi, had spoken these words unto
my brethren, they were angry with
me. And it came to pass that they
did lay their hands upon me, for
behold, they were exceedingly
wroth, and they did [a]bind me with
cords, for they sought to take away
my life, that they might leave me
in the wilderness to be devoured by
wild beasts.
17 But it came to pass that I
prayed unto the Lord, saying: O
Lord, according to my faith which
is in thee, wilt thou deliver me from
the hands of my brethren; yea, even
give me [a]strength that I may [b]burst
these bands with which I am bound.
18 And it came to pass that when I
had said these words, behold, the
bands were loosed from off my
hands and feet, and I stood before
my brethren, and I spake unto them
again.
19 And it came to pass that they
were angry with me again, and
sought to lay hands upon me; but
behold, one of the [a]daughters of
Ishmael, yea, and also her mother,
and one of the sons of Ishmael, did
plead with my brethren, insomuch
that they did soften their hearts;
and they did cease striving to take
away my life.
20 And it came to pass that they
were sorrowful, because of their
wickedness, insomuch that they did
bow down before me, and did plead
with me that I would [a]forgive them
of the thing that they had done
against me.
21 And it came to pass that I did
frankly [a]forgive them all that they
had done, and I did exhort them
that they would pray unto the Lord
their God for [b]forgiveness. And it
came to pass that they did so. And
after they had done praying unto
the Lord we did again travel on our
journey towards the tent of our
father.
22 And it came to pass that we did

11*a* 1 Ne. 4: 1 (1–38).
12*a* Ps. 18: 32 (32–40); 1 Ne. 17: 50; Alma 26: 12.
b 1 Ne. 2: 19 (18–21); 15: 11.
13*a* 1 Ne. 2: 20. TG Promised Lands.
b 2 Kgs. 25: 4 (1–21).
c 2 Ne. 6: 8; 25: 10; Omni 1: 15; Hel. 8: 21 (20–21).
14*a* TG God, Spirit of.
b Ezek. 5: 6; 1 Ne. 1: 19 (18–20); 2: 13.
c TG Prophets, Rejection of.
d Jer. 37: 15 (15–21).
e 1 Ne. 2: 1.
16*a* 1 Ne. 18: 11 (11–15).
17*a* Judg. 14: 6.
b Jacob 4: 6; Alma 14: 28 (26–28); 3 Ne. 28: 20 (19–22).
19*a* 1 Ne. 16: 7; 18: 19 (19–20).
20*a* TG Repentance.
21*a* TG Family, Love within.
b TG Forgiveness.

[Between 600 and 592 B.C.]

come down unto the tent of our
father. And after I and my brethren
and all the house of Ishmael had
come down unto the tent of my
father, they did give [a]thanks unto the
Lord their God; and they did offer
[b]sacrifice and burnt offerings unto
him.

CHAPTER 8

Lehi sees a vision of the tree of life—He partakes of its fruit and desires his family to do likewise—He sees a rod of iron, a strait and narrow path, and the mists of darkness that enshroud men—Sariah, Nephi, and Sam partake of the fruit, but Laman and Lemuel refuse.

AND it came to pass that we had
gathered together all manner of
[a]seeds of every kind, both of grain of
every kind, and also of the seeds of
fruit of every kind.
2 And it came to pass that while
my father tarried in the wilderness
he spake unto us, saying: Behold, I
have [a]dreamed a dream; or, in other
words, I have [b]seen a [c]vision.
3 And behold, because of the thing
which I have seen, I have reason to
rejoice in the Lord because of [a]Nephi
and also of Sam; for I have reason
to suppose that they, and also many
of their seed, will be saved.
4 But behold, [a]Laman and Lemuel,
I fear exceedingly because of you;
for behold, methought I saw in my
dream, a dark and dreary wilderness.
5 And it came to pass that I saw
a [a]man, and he was dressed in a
white [b]robe; and he came and stood
before me.
6 And it came to pass that he spake
unto me, and bade me follow him.
7 And it came to pass that as I
followed him I beheld myself that I
was in a dark and dreary waste.
8 And after I had traveled for the
space of many hours in darkness, I
began to pray unto the Lord that he
would have [a]mercy on me, according to the multitude of his tender
mercies.
9 And it came to pass after I had
prayed unto the Lord I beheld a
large and spacious [a]field.
10 And it came to pass that I beheld
a [a]tree, whose [b]fruit was desirable to
make one [c]happy.
11 And it came to pass that I did
go forth and partake of the [a]fruit
thereof; and I beheld that it was
most sweet, above all that I ever
before tasted. Yea, and I beheld that
the fruit thereof was white, to exceed
all the [b]whiteness that I had ever
seen.
12 And as I partook of the fruit
thereof it filled my soul with exceedingly great [a]joy; wherefore, I began
to be [b]desirous that my family
should partake of it also; for I knew
that it was [c]desirable above all other
fruit.
13 And as I cast my eyes round
about, that perhaps I might discover
my family also, I beheld a [a]river of
water; and it ran along, and it was
near the tree of which I was partaking the fruit.
14 And I looked to behold from
whence it came; and I saw the head
thereof a little way off; and at the
head thereof I beheld your mother
Sariah, and Sam, and [a]Nephi; and
they stood as if they knew not
whither they should go.
15 And it came to pass that I

22*a* TG Thanksgiving.
b 1 Ne. 5: 9.
8 1*a* 1 Ne. 16: 11.
2*a* 1 Ne. 1: 16; 10: 2. TG Dream; Revelation; Vision.
b 1 Ne. 14: 29.
c 1 Ne. 10: 17.
3*a* 1 Ne. 8: 14 (14–18).
4*a* 1 Ne. 8: 35.
5*a* Dan. 10: 5 (2–12).
b JS-H 1: 31 (30–32).
8*a* TG God, Mercy of.
9*a* Matt. 13: 38.
10*a* Gen. 2: 9; Rev. 2: 7 (1–7); 22: 2 (1–16); 1 Ne. 11: 4, 8 (8–25).
b 1 Ne. 8: 24 (15, 20, 24); Alma 32: 42 (41–43).
c TG Happiness.
11*a* 1 Ne. 15: 36; Alma 5: 34.
b 1 Ne. 11: 8.
12*a* TG Joy.
b Enos 1: 9; Alma 36: 24. TG Family, Love within.
c Gen. 3: 6; 1 Ne. 15: 36.
13*a* 1 Ne. 12: 16 (16–18); 15: 26–27 (26–29).
14*a* 1 Ne. 8: 3 (3–4).

[Between 600 and 592 B.C.]

beckoned unto them; and I also did say unto them with a loud voice that they should come unto me, and partake of the fruit, which was desirable above all other fruit.
16 And it came to pass that they did come unto me and partake of the fruit also.
17 And it came to pass that I was desirous that Laman and Lemuel should come and partake of the fruit also; wherefore, I cast mine eyes towards the head of the river, that perhaps I might see them.
18 And it came to pass that I saw them, but they would [a]not come unto me and partake of the fruit.
19 And I beheld a [a]rod of iron, and it extended along the bank of the river, and led to the tree by which I stood.
20 And I also beheld a [a]strait and narrow path, which came along by the rod of iron, even to the tree by which I stood; and it also led by the head of the fountain, unto a large and spacious field, as if it had been a [b]world.
21 And I saw numberless concourses of people, many of whom were [a]pressing forward, that they might obtain the [b]path which led unto the tree by which I stood.
22 And it came to pass that they did come forth, and commence in the path which led to the tree.
23 And it came to pass that there arose a [a]mist of darkness; yea, even an exceedingly great mist of darkness, insomuch that they who had commenced in the path did lose their way, that they wandered off and were [b]lost.
24 And it came to pass that I beheld others pressing forward, and they came forth and caught hold of the end of the rod of iron; and they did press forward through the mist of darkness, [a]clinging to the rod of iron, even until they did come forth and partake of the [b]fruit of the tree.
25 And after they had partaken of the fruit of the tree they did cast their eyes about as if they were [a]ashamed.
26 And I also cast my eyes round about, and beheld, on the [a]other side of the river of water, a great and [b]spacious building; and it stood as it were in the [c]air, high above the earth.
27 And it was filled with people, both old and young, both male and female; and their manner of dress was exceedingly fine; and they were in the [a]attitude of [b]mocking and pointing their fingers towards those who had come at and were partaking of the fruit.
28 And after they had [a]tasted of the fruit they were [b]ashamed, because of those that were [c]scoffing at them; and they [d]fell away into forbidden paths and were lost.
29 And now I, Nephi, do not speak [a]all the words of my father.
30 But, to be short in writing, behold, he saw other multitudes pressing forward; and they came and caught hold of the end of the [a]rod of iron; and they did press their way forward, continually holding

18*a* 2 Ne. 5: 20 (20–25).
19*a* Rev. 2: 27; 12: 5; 19: 15 (also JST Rev. 19: 15); 1 Ne. 8: 30; 11: 25; 15: 23 (23–24).
20*a* Matt. 7: 14; 2 Ne. 31: 18 (17–20).
b Matt. 13: 38.
21*a* D&C 123: 12.
b TG Objectives; Path; Way.
23*a* Matt. 13: 19 (18–19); 2 Pet. 2: 17; 1 Ne. 12: 17; 15: 24 (23–24).
b TG Apostasy of Individuals.
24*a* TG Diligence; Perseverance.
b 1 Ne. 8: 10.
25*a* Rom. 1: 16; 2 Tim. 1: 8; Alma 46: 21; Morm. 8: 38.
26*a* Luke 16: 26.
b 1 Ne. 11: 35 (35–36); 12: 18.
c Eph. 2: 2 (1–3).
27*a* TG Haughtiness; Pride.
b Matt. 9: 24 (20–26). TG Mocking.
28*a* 2 Pet. 2: 20 (19–22).
b Mark 4: 17 (14–20); 8: 38; Luke 8: 13 (11–15); John 12: 43 (42–43); Rom. 3: 3. TG Fearfulness.
c TG Peer Influence.
d TG Apostasy of Individuals.
29*a* 1 Ne. 1: 17 (16–17).
30*a* 1 Ne. 8: 19; 15: 24 (23–24).

[Between 600 and 592 B.C.]

fast to the rod of iron, until they came forth and fell down and partook of the fruit of the tree.

31 And he also saw other [a]multitudes feeling their way towards that great and spacious building.

32 And it came to pass that many were drowned in the [a]depths of the [b]fountain; and many were lost from his view, wandering in strange roads.

33 And great was the multitude that did enter into that strange building. And after they did enter into that building they did point the finger of [a]scorn at me and those that were partaking of the fruit also; but we heeded them not.

34 These are the words of my father: For as many as [a]heeded them, had fallen away.

35 And [a]Laman and Lemuel partook not of the fruit, said my father.

36 And it came to pass after my father had spoken all the words of his dream or vision, which were many, he said unto us, because of these things which he saw in a vision, he exceedingly feared for Laman and Lemuel; yea, he feared lest they should be cast off from the presence of the Lord.

37 And he did [a]exhort them then with all the feeling of a tender parent, that they would hearken to his words, that perhaps the Lord would be merciful to them, and not cast them off; yea, my father did preach unto them.

38 And after he had preached unto them, and also prophesied unto them of many things, he bade them to keep the commandments of the Lord; and he did cease speaking unto them.

CHAPTER 9

Nephi makes two sets of records—Each is called the plates of Nephi—The larger plates contain a secular history; the smaller ones deal primarily with sacred things.

AND all these things did my father see, and hear, and speak, as he dwelt in a tent, in the [a]valley of Lemuel, and also a great many more things, which cannot be written upon these plates.

2 And now, as I have spoken concerning these plates, behold they are not the plates upon which I make a full account of the history of my people; for the [a]plates upon which I make a full account of my people I have given the name of Nephi; wherefore, they are called the plates of Nephi, after mine own name; and these plates also are called the plates of Nephi.

3 Nevertheless, I have received a commandment of the Lord that I should make these plates, for the special [a]purpose that there should be an account engraven of the [b]ministry of my people.

4 Upon the other plates should be engraven an account of the reign of the kings, and the wars and contentions of my people; wherefore these plates are for the more part of the ministry; and the [a]other plates are for the more part of the reign of the kings and the wars and contentions of my people.

31*a* Matt. 7: 13.
32*a* 1 Ne. 15: 29 (26–29).
b 1 Ne. 8: 14 (13–14).
33*a* Neh. 2: 19; Alma 26: 23.
TG Persecution; Scorn; Scorner.
34*a* Ex. 23: 2; Prov. 19: 27; Mosiah 2: 37 (33, 37).
35*a* 1 Ne. 8: 4 (4, 17–18); 2 Ne. 5: 20 (19–24).
37*a* TG Family, Children, Responsibilities toward.
9 1*a* 1 Ne. 2: 6 (4–6, 8, 14–15); 16: 6 (6, 12).
2*a* IE the full account is on larger plates; the special account of his ministry is on the smaller plates of Nephi. See Jacob 3: 13–14. See also 1 Ne. 1: 17 (16–17); 6: 1; 10: 1; 19: 2, 4; Omni 1: 1; W of M 1: 3 (2–11); D&C 10: 38 (38–40).
3*a* D&C 3: 19.
b 1 Ne. 6: 3.
4*a* 2 Ne. 4: 14; 5: 33 (29–33); Jacob 1: 3 (2–4); Jarom 1: 14; Omni 1: 18; W of M 1: 10.

[Between 600 and 592 B.C.]

5 Wherefore, the Lord hath commanded me to make these plates
for a [a]wise purpose in him, which
purpose I know not.
6 But the Lord [a]knoweth all things
from the beginning; wherefore, he
prepareth a way to accomplish all
his works among the children of
men; for behold, he hath all [b]power
unto the fulfilling of all his words.
And thus it is. Amen.

CHAPTER 10

Lehi predicts the Babylonian captivity—He tells of the coming among the Jews of a Messiah, a Savior, a Redeemer—He tells also of the coming of the one who should baptize the Lamb of God—Lehi tells of the death and resurrection of the Messiah—He compares the scattering and gathering of Israel to an olive tree—Nephi speaks of the Son of God, of the gift of the Holy Ghost, and of the need for righteousness.

AND now I, Nephi, proceed to give
an account upon [a]these plates of
my proceedings, and my reign and
ministry; wherefore, to proceed with
mine account, I must speak somewhat of the things of my father,
and also of my brethren.
2 For behold, it came to pass after
my father had made an end of speaking the words of his [a]dream, and
also of exhorting them to all
diligence, he spake unto them concerning the Jews—
3 That after they should be destroyed, even that great city [a]Jeru-
salem, and many be [b]carried away
captive into [c]Babylon, according to
the own due time of the Lord, they
should [d]return again, yea, even be
brought back out of captivity; and
after they should be brought back
out of captivity they should possess
again the land of their inheritance.
4 Yea, even [a]six hundred years
from the time that my father left
Jerusalem, a [b]prophet would the
Lord God raise up among the [c]Jews
—even a [d]Messiah, or, in other
words, a Savior of the world.
5 And he also spake concerning the
prophets, how great a number had
[a]testified of these things, concerning
this Messiah, of whom he had spoken, or this Redeemer of the world.
6 Wherefore, all mankind were in
a [a]lost and in a [b]fallen state, and
ever would be save they should rely
on this Redeemer.
7 And he spake also concerning a
[a]prophet who should come before
the Messiah, to prepare the way of
the Lord—
8 Yea, even he should go forth and
cry in the wilderness: [a]Prepare ye
the way of the Lord, and make his
paths straight; for there standeth
one among you whom ye know not;
and he is mightier than I, whose
shoe's latchet I am not worthy to
unloose. And much spake my father
concerning this thing.
9 And my father said he should

5*a* 1 Ne. 19: 3; W of M 1: 7; Alma 37: 14 (2, 12, 14).
6*a* Isa. 48: 3 (3–7); Moses 1: 6, 35. TG God, Foreknowledge of; God, Intelligence of; God, Omniscience of.
b Matt. 28: 18.
10 1*a* 1 Ne. 9: 2 (1–5); 19: 3 (1–6).
2*a* 1 Ne. 8: 2 (2–36).
3*a* Esth. 2: 6; 2 Ne. 6: 8; Hel. 8: 20 (20–21).
b Ezek. 36: 12 (8–15); 2 Ne. 25: 10. TG Israel, Bondage of, in Other Lands; Israel, Scattering of.
c Ezek. 24: 2; 1 Ne. 1: 13; Omni 1: 15. TG Babylon.
d Neh. 12: 1; Jer. 29: 10 (9–10); 2 Ne. 6: 9 (8–9); Abr. 2: 6.
4*a* 1 Ne. 19: 8 (8–14); 2 Ne. 25: 19; Alma 13: 25; 3 Ne. 1: 1.
b 1 Ne. 22: 21 (20–21).
c TG Israel, Judah, People of.
d Jacob 1: 6. TG Jesus Christ, Birth of; Jesus Christ, Messiah
5*a* Jacob 7: 11; Mosiah 13: 33; Hel. 8: 24 (19–24); 3 Ne. 20: 24 (23–24). TG Jesus Christ, Prophecies about.
6*a* Rom. 3: 23; 2 Ne. 2: 5 (5–8).
b TG Death, Spiritual, First.
7*a* 1 Ne. 11: 27; 2 Ne. 31: 4 (4–18). TG Foreordination.
8*a* Isa. 40: 3; Matt. 3: 3 (1–3); D&C 84: 26.

[Between 600 and 592 B.C.]

baptize in [a]Bethabara, beyond Jordan; and he also said he should [b]baptize with water; even that he should baptize the Messiah with water.

10 And after he had baptized the Messiah with water, he should behold and bear record that he had baptized the [a]Lamb of God, who should take away the sins of the world.

11 And it came to pass after my father had spoken these words he spake unto my brethren concerning the gospel which should be preached among the Jews, and also concerning the [a]dwindling of the Jews in [b]unbelief. And after they had [c]slain the Messiah, who should come, and after he had been slain he should [d]rise from the dead, and should make himself [e]manifest, by the Holy Ghost, unto the Gentiles.

12 Yea, even my father spake much concerning the Gentiles, and also concerning the house of Israel, that they should be compared like unto an [a]olive-tree, whose [b]branches should be broken off and should be [c]scattered upon all the face of the earth.

13 Wherefore, he said it must needs be that we should be led with one accord into the [a]land of promise, unto the fulfilling of the word of the Lord, that we should be scattered upon all the face of the earth.

14 And after the house of [a]Israel should be scattered they should be [b]gathered together again; or, in fine, after the [c]Gentiles had received the fulness of the [d]Gospel, the natural branches of the [e]olive-tree, or the [f]remnants of the house of [g]Israel, should be grafted in, or [h]come to the knowledge of the true Messiah, their Lord and their Redeemer.

15 And after this manner of language did my father prophesy and speak unto my brethren, and also many more things which I do not write in this book; for I have written as many of them as were expedient for me in mine [a]other book.

16 And all these things, of which I have spoken, were done as my father dwelt in a [a]tent, in the valley of Lemuel.

17 And it came to pass after I, Nephi, having heard all the [a]words of my father, concerning the things which he saw in a [b]vision, and also the things which he spake by the power of the Holy Ghost, which power he received by faith on the Son of God—and the Son of God was the [c]Messiah who should come—I, Nephi, was [d]desirous also that I might see, and hear, and know of these things, by the power of the [e]Holy Ghost, which is the [f]gift of God unto [g]all those who diligently seek him, as well in times of [h]old

9*a* John 1: 28.
b TG Jesus Christ, Baptism of.
10*a* TG Jesus Christ, Lamb of God.
11*a* Rom. 11: 1 (1–36); Jacob 4: 15 (14–18).
b Morm. 5: 14 (14–20). TG Unbelief, Unbelievers.
c TG Jesus Christ, Crucifixion of; Jesus Christ, Prophecies about.
d TG Jesus Christ, Resurrection.
e 3 Ne. 15: 23 (21–24). TG Holy Ghost, Mission of.
12*a* Gen. 49: 22 (22–26); 1 Ne. 15: 12; 2 Ne. 3: 5 (4–5); Jacob 5: 3 (3–77); 6: 1 (1–7). TG Vineyard of the Lord.
b TG Israel, Bondage of, in Other Lands.
c Deut. 32: 26; 1 Ne. 22: 3 (3–8). TG Israel, Scattering of.
13*a* 1 Ne. 2: 20. TG Promised Lands.
14*a* TG Israel, Ten Lost Tribes of.
b TG Israel, Gathering of.
c 1 Ne. 13: 42; D&C 14: 10.
d TG Gospel.
e 1 Ne. 15: 7.
f TG Israel, Remnant of.
g TG Israel, Twelve Tribes of.
h 1 Ne. 19: 15 (14–17).
15*a* 1 Ne. 1: 17 (16–18).
16*a* 1 Ne. 2: 15 (15–16).
17*a* Enos 1: 3; Alma 36: 17 (17–18).
b 1 Ne. 8: 2.
c TG Jesus Christ, Messiah.
d 2 Ne. 4: 24.
e 2 Pet. 1: 21.
f TG God, Gifts of; Holy Ghost, Gift of.
g Moro. 7: 36; 10: 7 (4–5, 7, 19).
h D&C 20: 26.

[Between 600 and 592 B.C.]

as in the time that he should manifest himself unto the children of men.
18 For he is the [a]same yesterday,
to-day, and forever; and the way is prepared for all men from the foundation of the world, if it so be that they repent and come unto him.
19 For he that diligently [a]seeketh
shall find; and the [b]mysteries of God shall be unfolded unto them, by the power of the [c]Holy Ghost, as well in these times as in times of old, and as well in times of old as in times to come; wherefore, the [d]course of the Lord is one eternal round.
20 Therefore remember, O man,
for all thy doings thou shalt be brought into [a]judgment.
21 Wherefore, if ye have sought to
do [a]wickedly in the days of your [b]probation, then ye are found [c]unclean before the judgment-seat of God; and no unclean thing can dwell with God; wherefore, ye must be cast off forever.
22 And the Holy Ghost giveth
[a]authority that I should speak these things, and deny them not.

CHAPTER 11

Nephi sees the Spirit of the Lord and is shown in vision the tree of life—He sees the mother of the Son of God and learns of the condescension of God—He sees the baptism, ministry, and crucifixion of the Lamb of God—He sees also the call and ministry of the twelve apostles of the Lamb.

FOR it came to pass after I had desired to know the things that my father had seen, and believing that the Lord was able to make them known unto me, as I sat [a]pondering in mine heart I was [b]caught away in the Spirit of the Lord, yea, into an exceedingly high [c]mountain, which I never had before seen, and upon which I never had before set my foot.
2 And the Spirit said unto me:
Behold, what [a]desirest thou?
3 And I said: I desire to behold the
things which my father [a]saw.
4 And the Spirit said unto me:
[a]Believest thou that thy father saw the [b]tree of which he hath spoken?
5 And I said: Yea, thou knowest
that I [a]believe all the words of my father.
6 And when I had spoken these
words, the Spirit cried with a loud voice, saying: Hosanna to the Lord, the most high God; for he is God over all the [a]earth, yea, even above all. And blessed art thou, Nephi, because thou [b]believest in the Son of the most high God; wherefore, thou shalt behold the things which thou hast desired.
7 And behold this thing shall be
given unto thee for a [a]sign, that after thou hast beheld the tree which bore the fruit which thy father tasted, thou shalt also behold a man descending out of heaven, and him shall ye witness; and after ye have witnessed him ye shall [b]bear record that it is the Son of God.
8 And it came to pass that the
Spirit said unto me: Look! And I

18*a* Heb. 13:8; Morm. 9:9 (9–11); D&C 20:12.
TG God, Perfection of.
19*a* TG Objectives.
b TG Mysteries of Godliness.
c TG Holy Ghost, Source of Testimony.
d Alma 7:20; 37:12; D&C 3:2; 35:1.
TG God, Eternal Nature of.
20*a* Eccl. 12:14; Ezek. 33:20. TG Judgment, The Last.
21*a* Ezek. 33:9.
b TG Probation.
c 1 Cor. 6:9 (9–10); Morm. 7:7; D&C 76:62 (50–62); 138:20, 37; Moses 6:57.
22*a* TG Holy Ghost, Mission of.
11 1*a* D&C 76:19.
TG Meditation.
b Dan. 8:2; 2 Cor. 12:2 (1–4); Rev. 21:10; 2 Ne. 4:25; Moses 1:1.
c Ex. 24:13 (12–13); Deut. 10:1; Ether 3:1.
2*a* Zech. 4:2 (1–6).
3*a* 1 Ne. 8:2.
4*a* Mosiah 5:1 (1–2).
b 1 Ne. 8:10 (10–12); 15:22 (21–22).
5*a* 1 Ne. 2:16.
6*a* Ex. 9:29; Deut. 10:14; 2 Ne. 29:7; 3 Ne. 11:14; D&C 55:1; Moses 6:44.
b TG Believe.
7*a* TG Signs.
b TG Testimony; Witnesses.

[Between 600 and 592 B.C.]

looked and beheld a tree; and it was like unto the [a]tree which my father had seen; and the [b]beauty thereof was far beyond, yea, exceeding of all beauty; and the [c]whiteness thereof did exceed the whiteness of the driven snow.

9 And it came to pass after I had seen the tree, I said unto the Spirit: I behold thou hast shown unto me the tree which is [a]precious above all.

10 And he said unto me: What desirest thou?

11 And I said unto him: To know the [a]interpretation thereof—for I spake unto him as a man speaketh; for I beheld that he was in the [b]form of a man; yet nevertheless, I knew that it was the Spirit of the Lord; and he spake unto me as a man speaketh with another.

12 And it came to pass that he said unto me: Look! And I looked as if to look upon him, and I saw him not; for he had gone from before my presence.

13 And it came to pass that I looked and beheld the great city of Jerusalem, and also other cities. And I beheld the city of Nazareth; and in the city of [a]Nazareth I beheld a [b]virgin, and she was exceedingly fair and white.

14 And it came to pass that I saw the [a]heavens open; and an angel came down and stood before me; and he said unto me: Nephi, what beholdest thou?

15 And I said unto him: A virgin, most beautiful and fair above all other virgins.

16 And he said unto me: Knowest thou the [a]condescension of God?

17 And I said unto him: I know that he loveth his children; nevertheless, I do not know the meaning of all things.

18 And he said unto me: Behold, the [a]virgin whom thou seest is the [b]mother of the Son of God, after the manner of the flesh.

19 And it came to pass that I beheld that she was carried away in the Spirit; and after she had been carried away in the [a]Spirit for the space of a time the angel spake unto me, saying: Look!

20 And I looked and beheld the virgin again, bearing a [a]child in her arms.

21 And the angel said unto me: Behold the [a]Lamb of God, yea, even the [b]Son of the Eternal [c]Father! Knowest thou the meaning of the [d]tree which thy father saw?

22 And I answered him, saying: Yea, it is the [a]love of God, which [b]sheddeth itself abroad in the hearts of the children of men; wherefore, it is the [c]most desirable above all things.

23 And he spake unto me, saying: Yea, and the most [a]joyous to the soul.

24 And after he had said these words, he said unto me: Look! And I looked, and I beheld the Son of God [a]going forth among the children of men; and I saw many fall down at his feet and worship him.

25 And it came to pass that I beheld that the [a]rod of iron, which my father had seen, was the [b]word of God, which [c]led to the fountain of [d]living waters, or to the [e]tree of life;

8a 1 Ne. 8: 10.
b TG Beauty.
c 1 Ne. 8: 11.
9a 1 Ne. 11: 22 (22–25).
11a Gen. 40: 8.
b TG Spirit Body.
13a Matt. 2: 23.
b Luke 1: 27 (26–27); Alma 7: 10.
14a Ezek. 1: 1; 1 Ne. 1: 8 (6–11).
16a 1 Ne. 11: 26. TG Jesus Christ, Condescension of.
18a Luke 1: 34 (34–35). TG Foreordination; Jesus Christ, Prophecies about.
b Matt. 1: 16; Mosiah 3: 8; Alma 19: 13. TG Jesus Christ, Birth of.
19a Matt. 1: 20.
20a Luke 2: 16.
21a TG Jesus Christ, Lamb of God.
b TG Jesus Christ, Divine Sonship.
c TG God the Father—Elohim/Eloheim.
d 1 Ne. 8: 10; Alma 5: 62.
22a TG God, Love of.
b Moro. 8: 26.
c 1 Ne. 11: 9.
23a TG Joy.
24a Luke 4: 14 (14–21).
25a See especially JST Rev. 2: 27.
b 1 Ne. 8: 19.
c TG Guidance, Divine.
d TG Living Water.
e Gen. 2: 9; Prov. 11: 30 (22–30); Moses 4: 28 (28, 31).

[Between 600 and 592 B.C.]

which waters are a representation of
the love of God; and I also beheld
that the tree of life was a representation of the love of God.
26 And the angel said unto me
again: Look and behold the [a]con-
descension of God!
27 And I looked and [a]beheld the
Redeemer of the world, of whom my
father had spoken; and I also beheld
the [b]prophet who should prepare
the way before him. And the Lamb
of God went forth and was [c]baptized
of him; and after he was baptized, I
beheld the heavens open, and the
Holy Ghost come down out of
heaven and abide upon him in the
form of a [d]dove.
28 And I beheld that he went forth
ministering unto the people, in
[a]power and great glory; and the
multitudes were gathered together
to hear him; and I beheld that they
cast him out from among them.
29 And I also beheld [a]twelve others
following him. And it came to pass
that they were [b]carried away in the
Spirit from before my face, and I
saw them not.
30 And it came to pass that the
angel spake unto me again, saying:
Look! And I looked, and I beheld
the heavens open again, and I saw
[a]angels descending upon the children
of men; and they did minister unto
them.
31 And he spake unto me again,
saying: Look! And I looked, and I
beheld the Lamb of God going forth
among the children of men. And I
beheld multitudes of people who
were [a]sick, and who were afflicted
with all manner of diseases, and with
[b]devils and [c]unclean spirits; and the
angel spake and showed all these
things unto me. And they were
[d]healed by the power of the Lamb of
God; and the devils and the unclean
spirits were cast out.
32 And it came to pass that the
angel spake unto me again, saying:
Look! And I looked and beheld the
Lamb of God, that he was [a]taken
by the people; yea, the Son of the
everlasting God was [b]judged of the
world; and I saw and bear record.
33 And I, Nephi, saw that he was
[a]lifted up upon the cross and [b]slain
for the sins of the world.
34 And after he was slain I saw the
multitudes of the earth, that they
were gathered together to [a]fight
against the apostles of the Lamb;
for thus were the twelve called by
the angel of the Lord.
35 And the multitude of the earth
was gathered together; and I beheld
that they were in a large and spacious
[a]building, like unto the building
which my father saw. And the angel
of the Lord spake unto me again,
saying: Behold the world and the
wisdom thereof; yea, behold the
house of Israel hath gathered together to [b]fight against the twelve
apostles of the Lamb.
36 And it came to pass that I saw
and bear record, that the great and
spacious building was the [a]pride of
the world; and it [b]fell, and the fall
thereof was exceedingly great. And
the angel of the Lord spake unto me

26*a* 1 Ne. 11: 16.
TG Jesus Christ, Condescension of.
27*a* 2 Ne. 25: 13.
b Mal. 3: 1; Matt. 11: 10; John 1: 6 (6–7); 1 Ne. 10: 7 (7–10); 2 Ne. 31: 4 (4–18); D&C 35: 4.
c TG Jesus Christ, Baptism of.
d TG Holy Ghost, Dove, Sign of.
28*a* D&C 138: 26.
29*a* 1 Ne. 12: 9; 13: 40 (24–26, 40).
TG Apostles.
b 1 Ne. 14: 30.
30*a* TG Angels.
31*a* TG Sickness.
b Mark 5: 15 (15–20); 7: 30; Mosiah 3: 6 (5–7); Morm. 9: 24.
c TG Spirits, Evil or Unclean.
d TG Healing.
32*a* TG Jesus Christ, Betrayal of.
b Mark 15: 19 (17–20); Luke 9: 44 (44–45).
33*a* Luke 18: 31; 2 Ne. 10: 3; Mosiah 3: 9 (9–10); 3 Ne. 27: 14.
b TG Jesus Christ, Atonement through; Jesus Christ, Death of.
34*a* Mark 13: 13; 1 Cor. 4: 9 (6–13).
35*a* 1 Ne. 8: 26; 12: 18.
b Micah 3: 5; D&C 121: 38.
36*a* TG Pride.
b TG Earth, Cleansing of; World, End of.

[Between 600 and 592 B.C.]

again, saying: Thus shall be the destruction of all nations, kindreds, tongues, and people, that shall fight against the twelve apostles of the Lamb.

CHAPTER 12

Nephi sees in vision: the land of promise; the righteousness, iniquity, and downfall of its inhabitants; the coming of the Lamb of God among them; how the twelve disciples and the twelve apostles shall judge Israel; the loathsome and filthy state of those who dwindle in unbelief.

AND it came to pass that the angel said unto me: Look, and behold thy seed, and also the seed of thy brethren. And I looked and beheld the [a]land of promise; and I beheld multitudes of people, yea, even as it were in number as many as the [b]sand of the sea.

2 And it came to pass that I beheld multitudes gathered together to battle, one against the other; and I beheld [a]wars, and rumors of wars, and great slaughters with the sword among my people.

3 And it came to pass that I beheld many generations pass away, after the manner of wars and contentions in the land; and I beheld many cities, yea, even that I did not number them.

4 And it came to pass that I saw a [a]mist of [b]darkness on the face of the land of promise; and I saw lightnings, and I heard thunderings, and earthquakes, and all manner of tumultuous noises; and I saw the earth and the rocks, that they rent; and I saw mountains tumbling into pieces; and I saw the plains of the earth, that they were [c]broken up; and I saw many cities that they were [d]sunk; and I saw many that they were burned with fire; and I saw many that did tumble to the earth, because of the quaking thereof.

5 And it came to pass after I saw these things, I saw the [a]vapor of darkness, that it passed from off the face of the earth; and behold, I saw multitudes who had not fallen because of the great and terrible judgments of the Lord.

6 And I saw the heavens open, and the [a]Lamb of God descending out of heaven; and he came down and [b]showed himself unto them.

7 And I also saw and bear record that the Holy Ghost fell upon [a]twelve others; and they were ordained of God, and chosen.

8 And the angel spake unto me, saying: Behold the twelve disciples of the Lamb, who are chosen to minister unto thy seed.

9 And he said unto me: Thou rememberest the [a]twelve apostles of the Lamb? Behold they are they who shall [b]judge the twelve tribes of Israel; wherefore, the twelve ministers of thy seed shall be judged of them; for ye are of the house of Israel.

10 And these [a]twelve ministers whom thou beholdest shall judge thy seed. And, behold, they are righteous forever; for because of their faith in the Lamb of God their [b]garments are made white in his blood.

11 And the angel said unto me: Look! And I looked, and beheld [a]three generations pass away in

---

12 1*a* TG Promised Lands.
b Gen. 22: 17 (17–18); 1 Kgs. 4: 20.
2*a* Enos 1: 24; Morm. 8: 7 (7–8). TG War.
4*a* 1 Ne. 19: 12; Hel. 14: 28 (20–28); 3 Ne. 10: 11.
b 1 Ne. 19: 10; 2 Ne. 26: 3.
c Gen. 7: 11.
d 3 Ne. 8: 14.
5*a* 3 Ne. 8: 20.
6*a* 2 Ne. 26: 1 (1, 9); 3 Ne. 11: 8 (3–17).
b 2 Ne. 32: 6; Alma 7: 8; 16: 20.
7a 3 Ne. 11: 22; 12: 1.
9*a* Matt. 10: 1; Luke 6: 13; John 6: 70; 1 Ne. 11: 29; 13: 40 (24–26, 40).
b Matt. 19: 28; D&C 29: 12. TG Judgment, The Last.
10*a* 3 Ne. 27: 27; Morm. 3: 18–19.
b Rev. 7: 14; 19: 8; Alma 5: 21 (21–27); 13: 11 (11–13); 3 Ne. 27: 19 (19–20); D&C 88: 85.
11*a* 2 Ne. 26: 9 (9–10); 3 Ne. 27: 32 (30–32).

[Between 600 and 592 B.C.]

righteousness; and their garments
were white even like unto the Lamb
of God. And the angel said unto me:
These are made white in the blood of
the Lamb, because of their faith in
him.
12 And I, Nephi, also saw many of
the [a]fourth generation who passed
away in righteousness.
13 And it came to pass that I saw
the multitudes of the earth gathered
together.
14 And the angel said unto me:
Behold thy seed, and also the seed of
thy brethren.
15 And it came to pass that I looked
and beheld the people of my seed
gathered together in multitudes
[a]against the seed of my brethren;
and they were gathered together to
battle.
16 And the angel spake unto me,
saying: Behold the fountain of
[a]filthy water which thy father saw;
yea, even the [b]river of which he
spake; and the depths thereof are
the depths of [c]hell.
17 And the [a]mists of darkness are
the temptations of the devil, which
[b]blindeth the eyes, and hardeneth
the hearts of the children of men,
and leadeth them away into [c]broad
roads, that they perish and are lost.
18 And the large and spacious
[a]building, which thy father saw, is
vain [b]imaginations and the [c]pride of
the children of men. And a great and
a terrible [d]gulf divideth them; yea,
even the word of the [e]justice of the
Eternal God, and the Messiah who
is the Lamb of God, of whom the
Holy Ghost beareth record, from the
beginning of the world until this
time, and from this time henceforth
and forever.
19 And while the angel spake these
words, I beheld and saw that the
seed of my brethren did contend
against my seed, according to the
word of the angel; and because of
the pride of my seed, and the
[a]temptations of the devil, I beheld
that the seed of my brethren did
[b]overpower the people of my seed.
20 And it came to pass that I beheld,
and saw the people of the seed
of my brethren that they had overcome
my seed; and they went forth
in multitudes upon the face of the
land.
21 And I saw them gathered
together in multitudes; and I saw
[a]wars and rumors of wars among
them; and in wars and rumors of
wars I saw [b]many generations pass
away.
22 And the angel said unto me:
Behold these shall [a]dwindle in unbelief.
23 And it came to pass that I beheld,
after they had dwindled in
unbelief they became a [a]dark, and
loathsome, and a [b]filthy people, full
of [c]idleness and all manner of
abominations.

CHAPTER 13

Nephi sees in vision: the church of the devil set up among the Gentiles; the discovery and colonizing of America; the loss of many plain and precious parts of the Bible; the resultant state of gentile apostasy; the restoration of the gospel, the coming forth of latter-day scripture, and the building up of Zion.

12*a* 2 Ne. 26: 9; Alma 45: 12 (10–12); Hel. 13: 10 (5, 9–10); 3 Ne. 27: 32; 4 Ne. 1: 14 (14–41).
15*a* Morm. 6: 7 (1–22).
16*a* TG Filthiness.
b 1 Ne. 8: 13 (13–14); 15: 27 (26–29).
c TG Hell.
17*a* 2 Pet. 2: 17; 1 Ne. 8: 23; 15: 24 (23–24).
b TG Apostasy of Individuals.
c Prov. 4: 14; Luke 13: 24.
18*a* 1 Ne. 8: 26; 11: 35 (35–36).
b Jer. 7: 24; 9: 14.
c TG Haughtiness; Pride.
d Luke 16: 26; 1 Ne. 15: 28 (28–30).
e TG God, Justice of.
19*a* TG Temptation.
b Jarom 1: 10; W of M 1: 2 (1–2).
21*a* Morm. 8: 8; Moro. 1: 2.
b 2 Ne. 1: 18.
22*a* 1 Ne. 15: 13; 2 Ne. 26: 15.
23*a* Jacob 3: 3; Alma 3: 7 (6–19).
b 2 Ne. 5: 22 (20–25). TG Filthiness.
c TG Idleness.

[Between 600 and 592 B.C.]

AND it came to pass that the angel
spake unto me, saying: Look! And I
looked and beheld many nations
and kingdoms.
2 And the angel said unto me:
What beholdest thou? And I said:
I behold many [a]nations and kingdoms.
3 And he said unto me: These are
the nations and kingdoms of the
Gentiles.
4 And it came to pass that I saw
among the nations of the [a]Gentiles
the formation of a [b]great church.
5 And the angel said unto me:
Behold the formation of a [a]church
which is most abominable above all
other churches, which [b]slayeth the
saints of God, yea, and tortureth
them and bindeth them down, and
yoketh them with a [c]yoke of iron,
and bringeth them down into captivity.
6 And it came to pass that I beheld this [a]great and [b]abominable
church; and I saw the [c]devil that he
was the founder of it.
7 And I also saw [a]gold, and silver,
and silks, and scarlets, and fine-
twined [b]linen, and all manner of
precious clothing; and I saw many
harlots.
8 And the angel spake unto me,
saying: Behold the gold, and the
silver, and the silks, and the scarlets,
and the fine-twined linen, and the
precious clothing, and the harlots,
are the [a]desires of this great and
abominable church.
9 And also for the [a]praise of the
world do they [b]destroy the saints of
God, and bring them down into
captivity.
10 And it came to pass that I looked
and beheld many waters; and they
divided the Gentiles from the seed
of my brethren.
11 And it came to pass that the
angel said unto me: Behold the
wrath of God is upon the seed of thy
brethren.
12 And I looked and beheld a man
among the Gentiles, who was
separated from the seed of my
brethren by the many waters; and I
beheld the Spirit of God, that it came
down and [a]wrought upon the man;
and he went forth upon the many
waters, even unto the seed of my
brethren, who were in the promised
land.
13 And it came to pass that I beheld
the Spirit of God, that it wrought
upon other Gentiles; and they went
forth out of captivity, upon the
many waters.
14 And it came to pass that I beheld
many [a]multitudes of the Gentiles
upon the [b]land of promise; and I
beheld the wrath of God, that it was
upon the seed of my brethren; and
they were [c]scattered before the
Gentiles and were smitten.
15 And I beheld the Spirit of the
Lord, that it was upon the Gentiles,
and they did prosper and [a]obtain
the [b]land for their inheritance; and I
beheld that they were white, and exceedingly fair and [c]beautiful, like unto my people before they were [d]slain.
16 And it came to pass that I,
Nephi, beheld that the Gentiles who
had gone forth out of captivity did
humble themselves before the Lord;
and the power of the Lord was [a]with
them.
17 And I beheld that their mother
Gentiles were gathered together

13 2*a* TG Kings, Earthly; Nations.
4*a* TG Gentiles.
b 1 Ne. 13: 26 (26, 34); 14: 10 (3, 9–17).
5*a* 2 Ne. 10: 16.
b Rev. 17: 6 (3–6); 18: 24; 1 Ne. 14: 13.
c Jer. 28: 14 (10–14). TG Bondage, Spiritual.
6*a* D&C 88: 94.
b TG Devil, Church of.
c 1 Ne. 22: 23 (22–23). TG Devil.
7*a* Morm. 8: 37 (36–38).
b Ether 10: 24.
8*a* Rev. 18: 19 (10–24); Morm. 8: 37 (36–41).
9*a* Morm. 8: 38.
b Rev. 13: 7 (4–7).
12*a* TG Guidance, Divine.
14*a* 2 Ne. 1: 11; Morm. 5: 19 (19–20).
b TG Promised Lands.
c 1 Ne. 22: 7. TG Israel, Scattering of.
15*a* Morm. 5: 19.
b 2 Ne. 10: 19.
c 2 Ne. 5: 21; 4 Ne. 1: 10; Morm. 9: 6.
d Morm. 6: 19 (17–22).
16*a* D&C 101: 80.

[Between 600 and 592 B.C.]

upon the waters, and upon the land also, to battle against them.

18 And I beheld that the power of God was with them, and also that the wrath of God was upon all those that were gathered together [a]against them to battle.

19 And I, Nephi, beheld that the Gentiles that had gone out of captivity were [a]delivered by the power of God out of the hands of all other nations.

20 And it came to pass that I, Nephi, beheld that they did prosper in the land; and I beheld a [a]book, and it was carried forth among them.

21 And the angel said unto me: Knowest thou the meaning of the book?

22 And I said unto him: I know not.

23 And he said: Behold it proceedeth out of the mouth of a Jew. And I, Nephi, beheld it; and he said unto me: The [a]book that thou beholdest is a [b]record of the [c]Jews, which contains the covenants of the Lord, which he hath made unto the house of Israel; and it also containeth many of the prophecies of the holy prophets; and it is a record like unto the engravings which are upon the [d]plates of brass, save there are not so many; nevertheless, they contain the covenants of the Lord, which he hath made unto the house of Israel; wherefore, they are of great worth unto the Gentiles.

24 And the angel of the Lord said unto me: Thou hast beheld that the [a]book proceeded forth from the mouth of a Jew; and when it proceeded forth from the mouth of a Jew it contained the fulness of the gospel of the Lord, of whom the twelve apostles bear record; and they bear record according to the truth which is in the Lamb of God.

25 Wherefore, these things go forth from the [a]Jews in purity unto the [b]Gentiles, according to the truth which is in God.

26 And after they go forth by the [a]hand of the twelve apostles of the Lamb, from the Jews [b]unto the Gentiles, thou seest the formation of that [c]great and abominable [d]church, which is most abominable above all other churches; for behold, they have [e]taken away from the gospel of the Lamb many parts which are [f]plain and most precious; and also many covenants of the Lord have they taken away.

27 And all this have they done that they might pervert the right ways of the Lord, that they might blind the eyes and harden the hearts of the children of men.

28 Wherefore, thou seest that after the book hath gone forth through the hands of the great and abominable church, that there are many plain and [a]precious things taken away from the book, which is the book of the Lamb of God.

29 And after these plain and precious things were [a]taken away it goeth forth unto all the nations of the Gentiles; and after it goeth forth unto all the nations of the Gentiles, yea, even across the many waters which thou hast seen with the Gentiles which have gone forth out of captivity, thou seest—because of the many plain and precious things which have been taken out of the

18*a* 1 Ne. 17: 35.
19*a* 2 Ne. 10: 10 (10–14); 3 Ne. 21: 4; Ether 2: 12.
20*a* 1 Ne. 13: 41 (3–41); 14: 23.
23*a* 1 Ne. 13: 38; 2 Ne. 29: 6 (4–12).
b TG Scriptures, Preservation of.
c 2 Ne. 3: 12.
d 1 Ne. 5: 10 (10–22); 19: 22.
24*a* 2 Ne. 29: 3.
25*a* 2 Ne. 29: 4 (4–6); D&C 3: 16. TG Israel, Judah, People of.
b TG Gentiles.
26*a* Luke 1: 1 (1–4); 2 Tim. 4: 13.
b Matt. 21: 43.
c 1 Ne. 13: 4 (4–6); 14: 10 (3, 9–17).
d TG Apostasy of the Early Christian Church.
e Morm. 8: 33; Moses 1: 41. TG False Doctrine; Scriptures, Lost.
f 1 Ne. 14: 21 (20–26); A of F 8.
28*a* 1 Ne. 14: 23.
29*a* 2 Pet. 3: 16.

[Between 600 and 592 B.C.]

book, which were plain unto the
understanding of the children of
men, according to the plainness
which is in the Lamb of God—
because of these things which are
taken away out of the gospel of the
Lamb, an exceedingly great many
do stumble, yea, insomuch that
Satan hath great power over them.
30 Nevertheless, thou beholdest
that the Gentiles who have gone
forth out of captivity, and have been
lifted up by the power of God above
all other nations, upon the face of
the land which is choice above all
other lands, which is the land that
the Lord God hath covenanted with
thy father that his seed should have
for the [a]land of their inheritance;
wherefore, thou seest that the Lord
God will not suffer that the Gentiles
will utterly destroy the [b]mixture of
thy [c]seed, which are among thy
brethren.
31 Neither will he suffer that the
Gentiles shall [a]destroy the seed of
thy brethren.
32 Neither will the Lord God suffer
that the Gentiles shall forever remain in that awful state of blindness, which thou beholdest they are
in, because of the plain and most
precious parts of the gospel of the
Lamb which have been kept back
by that [a]abominable church, whose
formation thou hast seen.
33 Wherefore saith the Lamb of
God: I will be [a]merciful unto the
Gentiles, unto the visiting of the
remnant of the house of Israel in
great judgment.
34 And it came to pass that the
angel of the Lord spake unto me,
saying: Behold, saith the Lamb of
God, after I have [a]visited the
[b]remnant of the house of Israel—
and this remnant of whom I speak is
the seed of thy father—wherefore,
after I have visited them in judgment, and smitten them by the hand
of the Gentiles, and after the Gentiles
do [c]stumble exceedingly, because of
the most plain and precious parts of
the [d]gospel of the Lamb which have
been kept back by that abominable church, which is the mother of
harlots, saith the Lamb—I will be
merciful unto the [e]Gentiles in that
day, insomuch that I will [f]bring
forth unto them, in mine own power,
much of my [g]gospel, which shall
be plain and precious, saith the
Lamb.
35 For, behold, saith the Lamb: I
will manifest myself unto thy seed,
that they shall write many things
which I shall minister unto them,
which shall be plain and precious;
and after thy seed shall be destroyed,
and dwindle in unbelief, and also
the seed of thy brethren, behold,
[a]these things shall be hid up, to
come forth unto the Gentiles, by
the gift and power of the Lamb.
36 And in them shall be written
my [a]gospel, saith the Lamb, and
my [b]rock and my salvation.
37 And [a]blessed are they who shall
seek to bring forth my [b]Zion at that
day, for they shall have the [c]gift and
the [d]power of the Holy Ghost; and
if they [e]endure unto the end they

30*a* TG Lands of Inheritance; Promised Lands.
b 2 Ne. 29: 12 (12–13); Alma 45: 14 (10–14); D&C 3: 17.
c 2 Ne. 3: 3.
31*a* 2 Ne. 4: 7; 10: 18 (18–19); Jacob 3: 6 (5–9); Hel. 15: 12 (10–17); 3 Ne. 16: 8 (4–13); Morm. 5: 20 (20–21).
32*a* TG Devil, Church of.
33*a* Isa. 42: 1 (1, 3–4).
34*a* D&C 124: 8; Abr. 1: 17.
b TG Israel, Joseph, People of.
c 1 Ne. 14: 1 (1–3); 2 Ne. 26: 20.
d TG Gospel.
e TG Millennium, Preparing a People for.
f TG Scriptures, Lost.
g D&C 10: 62. TG Restoration of the Gospel.
35*a* 1 Ne. 14: 7; 22: 8; 2 Ne. 27: 26 (6–26); 29: 1 (1–2). TG Book of Mormon.
36*a* 3 Ne. 27: 21.
b 3 Ne. 11: 39 (38–39). TG Rock.
37*a* Jacob 5: 75 (70–76); D&C 21: 9. TG Mission of Israel; Mission of Latter-day Saints.
b TG Zion.
c TG Holy Ghost, Gift of.
d Luke 24: 49; 1 Ne. 14: 14; D&C 38: 38 (32–38).
e 3 Ne. 27: 16. TG Endure; Perseverance; Steadfastness.

[Between 600 and 592 B.C.]

shall be [f]lifted up at the last day,
and shall be saved in the everlasting
[g]kingdom of the Lamb; and whoso
shall [h]publish peace, yea, tidings of
great joy, how beautiful upon the
mountains shall they be.
38 And it came to pass that I
beheld the remnant of the seed of
my brethren, and also the [a]book of
the Lamb of God, which had proceeded forth from the mouth of the
Jew, that it came forth from the
Gentiles [b]unto the remnant of the
seed of my brethren.
39 And after it had come forth unto
them I beheld [a]other [b]books, which
came forth by the power of the
Lamb, from the Gentiles unto them,
unto the [c]convincing of the Gentiles
and the remnant of the seed of my
brethren, and also the Jews who
were scattered upon all the face of
the earth, that the records of the
prophets and of the twelve apostles
of the Lamb are [d]true.
40 And the angel spake unto me,
saying: These [a]last records, which
thou hast seen among the Gentiles,
shall [b]establish the truth of the [c]first,
which are of the [d]twelve apostles of
the Lamb, and shall make known
the plain and precious things which
have been taken away from them;
and shall make known to all kindreds, tongues, and people, that the
Lamb of God is the Son of the
Eternal Father, and the [e]Savior of
the world; and that all men must
come unto him, or they cannot be
saved.
41 And they must come according
to the words which shall be established by the mouth of the Lamb;
and the words of the Lamb shall be
made known in the records of thy
seed, as well as in the [a]records of the
twelve apostles of the Lamb; wherefore they both shall be established in
[b]one; for there is [c]one God and one
[d]Shepherd over all the earth.
42 And the time cometh that he
shall manifest himself unto all
nations, both unto the [a]Jews and
also unto the Gentiles; and after he
has manifested himself unto the
Jews and also unto the Gentiles,
then he shall manifest himself unto
the Gentiles and also unto the Jews,
and the [b]last shall be first, and the
[c]first shall be last.

CHAPTER 14

An angel tells Nephi of the blessings and cursings to fall upon the Gentiles—There are only two churches: the Church of the Lamb of God and the church of the devil—The saints of God in all nations are persecuted by the great and abominable church—The apostle John shall write concerning the end of the world.

AND it shall come to pass, that if the
[a]Gentiles shall hearken unto the
Lamb of God in that day that he
shall manifest himself unto them in
word, and also in [b]power, in very
deed, unto the [c]taking away of their
[d]stumbling blocks—
2 And harden not their hearts

37*f* James 4: 10.
g TG Kingdom of God, in Heaven.
h Isa. 52: 7 (7–10); Mark 13: 10; 3 Ne. 20: 40.
38*a* 1 Ne. 13: 23; 2 Ne. 29: 6 (4–6).
b Morm. 5: 15; 7: 8 (8–9).
39*a* D&C 9: 2.
b TG Scriptures to Come Forth.
c Ezek. 37: 17 (15–20); 1 Ne. 14: 2 (1–5).
d 1 Ne. 14: 30.
40*a* 2 Ne. 26: 17 (16–17); 27: 6 (6–26); 29: 12. TG Book of Mormon.
b TG Scriptures, Value of.
c See the title page of the Book of Mormon. TG Bible.
d 1 Ne. 11: 29; 12: 9.
e Moses 1: 6.
41*a* 1 Ne. 13: 20 (20–28).
b Ezek. 37: 17.
c Deut. 6: 4; 2 Ne. 31: 21.
d TG Jesus Christ, Good Shepherd.
42*a* D&C 18: 6, 26; 19: 27; 21: 12; 90: 9 (8–9); 107: 33; 112: 4.
b Jacob 5: 63; Ether 13: 12.
c Luke 13: 30; 1 Ne. 10: 14; 15: 13 (13–20); D&C 14: 10.
14 1*a* 1 Ne. 22: 9 (8–9); 2 Ne. 30: 3; 3 Ne. 16: 6 (6–13). TG Gentiles.
b 1 Thes. 1: 5; 1 Ne. 14: 14; Jacob 6: 2 (2–3).
c Ether 12: 27.
d Isa. 57: 14; Ezek. 7: 19; 1 Cor. 1: 23; 1 Ne. 13: 34 (29, 34); 2 Ne. 26: 20.

[Between 600 and 592 B.C.]

against the Lamb of God, they shall
be numbered among the seed of thy
father; yea, they shall be [a]numbered
among the house of Israel; and they
shall be a [b]blessed people upon the
[c]promised land forever; they shall
be no more brought down into
captivity; and the house of Israel
shall no more be confounded.
3 And that great [a]pit, which hath
been digged for them by that great
and abominable church, which was
founded by the devil and his children, that he might lead away the
souls of men down to hell—yea,
that great pit which hath been
digged for the destruction of men
shall be filled by those who digged it,
unto their utter destruction, saith
the Lamb of God; not the destruction of the soul, save it be the casting
of it into that [b]hell which hath no
end.
4 For behold, this is according to
the [a]captivity of the devil, and also
according to the justice of God, upon
all those who will work wickedness
and abomination before him.
5 And it came to pass that the angel
spake unto me, Nephi, saying:
Thou hast beheld that if the Gentiles
repent it shall be [a]well with them;
and thou also knowest concerning
the covenants of the Lord unto the
house of Israel; and thou also hast
heard that whoso [b]repenteth not
must perish.
6 Therefore, [a]wo be unto the
Gentiles if it so be that they harden
their hearts against the Lamb of
God.
7 For the time cometh, saith the
Lamb of God, that I will work a great
and a [a]marvelous work among the
children of men; a [b]work which shall
be everlasting, either on the one
hand or on the other—either to the
convincing of them unto [c]peace and
[d]life eternal, or unto the deliverance
of them to the hardness of their
hearts and the blindness of their
minds unto their being brought
down into captivity, and also into
destruction, both temporally and
spiritually, according to the [e]cap-
tivity of the devil, of which I have
spoken.
8 And it came to pass that when the
angel had spoken these words, he
said unto me: Rememberest thou the
[a]covenants of the Father unto the
house of Israel? I said unto him, Yea.
9 And it came to pass that he said
unto me: Look, and behold that
great and abominable church, which
is the mother of abominations,
whose founder is the [a]devil.
10 And he said unto me: Behold
there are save [a]two churches only;
the one is the church of the Lamb of
God, and the [b]other is the church of
the [c]devil; wherefore, [d]whoso belongeth not to the church of the
Lamb of God belongeth to that
great church, which is the mother of
abominations; and she is the [e]whore
of all the earth.
11 And it came to pass that I

2*a* Gal. 3: 7 (7, 29); 2 Ne. 10: 18 (18–19); 3 Ne. 16: 13; 21: 6 (6, 22); Abr. 2: 10 (9–11).
b 2 Ne. 6: 12; 10: 10 (8–14); 3 Ne. 16: 6 (6–7); 20: 27; Morm. 5: 19.
c TG Israel, Deliverance of; Israel, Restoration of; Lands of Inheritance.
3*a* Ps. 57: 6; Matt. 7: 2 (1–2); 1 Ne. 22: 14 (13–14); D&C 10: 26 (25–27); 109: 25.
b Alma 19: 29. TG Damnation; Hell.
4*a* TG Bondage, Spiritual.
5*a* 1 Ne. 13: 39 (34–42); 22: 9.
b TG Repentance.
6*a* 2 Ne. 28: 32.
7*a* Isa. 29: 14; 1 Ne. 13: 35; 22: 8; 2 Ne. 27: 26; 29: 1 (1–2); D&C 4: 1. TG Restoration of the Gospel.
b TG God, Works of.
c TG Peace; Peace of God.
d Jer. 21: 8. TG Eternal Life.
e 2 Ne. 2: 29 (26–29); Alma 12: 11 (9–11).
8*a* TG Abrahamic Covenant; Israel, Mission of.
9*a* 1 Ne. 15: 35; D&C 1: 35. TG Devil, Church of.
10*a* 1 Ne. 22: 23; 2 Ne. 26: 20; Morm. 8: 28 (25–41). TG Church.
b 1 Ne. 13: 4 (4–6), 26 (26, 34).
c TG Devil, Church of; False Prophets.
d 2 Ne. 10: 16.
e Rev. 17: 15 (5, 15).

[Between 600 and 592 B.C.]

looked and beheld the whore of all the earth, and she sat upon many [a]waters; and she had dominion over [b]all the earth, among all nations, kindreds, tongues, and people.

12 And it came to pass that I beheld the church of the Lamb of God, and its numbers were [a]few, because of the wickedness and abominations of the whore who sat upon many waters; nevertheless, I beheld that the church of the Lamb, who were the saints of God, were also upon [b]all the face of the earth; and their dominions upon the face of the earth were small, because of the wickedness of the great whore whom I saw.

13 And it came to pass that I beheld that the great mother of abominations did gather together multitudes upon the face of all the earth, among all the nations of the Gentiles, to [a]fight against the Lamb of God.

14 And it came to pass that I, Nephi, beheld the power of the Lamb of God, that it descended upon the saints of the church of the Lamb, and upon the covenant people of the Lord, who were scattered upon all the face of the earth; and they were [a]armed with [b]righteousness and with the [c]power of God in great glory.

15 And it came to pass that I beheld that the wrath of God was [a]poured out upon that great and abominable church, insomuch that there were wars and rumors of wars among all the [b]nations and kindreds of the earth.

16 And as there began to be [a]wars and rumors of wars among all the nations which belonged to the mother of abominations, the angel spake unto me, saying: Behold, the wrath of God is upon the mother of harlots; and behold, thou seest all these things—

17 And when the [a]day cometh that the [b]wrath of God is poured out upon the mother of harlots, which is the great and abominable church of all the earth, whose founder is the devil, then, at that day, the [c]work of the Father shall commence, in preparing the way for the fulfilling of his [d]covenants, which he hath made to his people who are of the house of Israel.

18 And it came to pass that the angel spake unto me, saying: Look!

19 And I looked and beheld a man, and he was dressed in a white robe.

20 And the angel said unto me: Behold [a]one of the twelve apostles of the Lamb.

21 Behold, he shall [a]see and [b]write the [c]remainder of these things; yea, and also many things which have been.

22 And he shall also write concerning the end of the world.

23 Wherefore, the things which he shall write are just and true; and behold they are written in the [a]book which thou beheld proceeding out of the mouth of the Jew; and at the time they proceeded out of the mouth of the Jew, or, at the time the book proceeded out of the mouth of the Jew, the things which were written were plain and pure, and most [b]precious and easy to the understanding of all men.

11*a* Jer. 51: 13 (12–14).
b D&C 35: 11.
12*a* Matt. 7: 14; Jacob 5: 70; 3 Ne. 14: 14; D&C 138: 26.
b D&C 90: 11.
13*a* Rev. 17: 6 (1–6); 18: 24; 1 Ne. 13: 5.
14*a* TG Mission of Latter-day Saints.
b TG Deliverance; Protection, Divine.
c Luke 24: 49; 1 Ne. 13: 37; 14: 1; Jacob 6: 2 (2–3); D&C 38: 38 (32–38).
15*a* D&C 115: 6 (5–6).
b Mark 13: 8; D&C 87: 6.
16*a* 1 Ne. 22: 13 (13–14); Morm. 8: 30. TG War.
17*a* TG Last Days.
b 1 Ne. 21: 26; 22: 16 (15–16); 3 Ne. 20: 20 (19–21).
c 3 Ne. 21: 26 (7, 20–29). TG Israel, Restoration of.
d Morm. 8: 21 (21, 41). TG Abrahamic Covenant.
20*a* Rev. 1: 1 (1–3); 1 Ne. 14: 27.
21*a* Rev. 1: 1.
b 1 Ne. 13: 24 (20–40); A of F 8.
c Rev. 4: 1.
23*a* 1 Ne. 13: 20 (20–24); Morm. 8: 33; Ether 4: 16.
b 1 Ne. 13: 28 (28–32).

[Between 600 and 592 B.C.]

24 And behold, the things which this [a]apostle of the Lamb shall write are many things which thou hast seen; and behold, the remainder shalt thou see.

25 But the things which thou shalt see hereafter thou shalt not write; for the Lord God hath ordained the apostle of the Lamb of God that he should [a]write them.

26 And also others who have been, to them hath he shown all things, and they have [a]written them; and they are [b]sealed up to come forth in their purity, according to the truth which is in the Lamb, in the own due time of the Lord, unto the house of Israel.

27 And I, Nephi, heard and bear record, that the name of the apostle of the Lamb was [a]John, according to the word of the angel.

28 And behold, I, Nephi, am forbidden that I should write the remainder of the things which I saw and heard; wherefore the things which I have written sufficeth me; and I have written but a small part of the things which I saw.

29 And I bear record that I saw the things which my [a]father saw, and the angel of the Lord did make them known unto me.

30 And now I make an end of speaking concerning the things which I saw while I was [a]carried away in the spirit; and if all the things which I saw are not written, the things which I have written are [b]true. And thus it is. Amen.

CHAPTER 15

Lehi's seed are to receive the gospel from the Gentiles in the latter days—The gathering of Israel is likened unto an olive tree whose natural branches shall be grafted in again—Nephi interprets the vision of the tree of life and speaks of the justice of God in dividing the wicked from the righteous.

AND it came to pass that after I, Nephi, had been carried away in the spirit, and seen all these things, I returned to the tent of my father.

2 And it came to pass that I beheld my brethren, and they were disputing one with another concerning the things which my father had spoken unto them.

3 For he truly spake many great things unto them, which were hard to be [a]understood, save a man should inquire of the Lord; and they being hard in their hearts, therefore they did not look unto the Lord as they ought.

4 And now I, Nephi, was grieved because of the hardness of their hearts, and also, because of the things which I had seen, and knew they must unavoidably come to pass because of the great wickedness of the children of men.

5 And it came to pass that I was overcome because of my afflictions, for I considered that mine [a]afflictions were great above all, because of the [b]destruction of my people, for I had beheld their fall.

6 And it came to pass that after I had received [a]strength I spake unto my brethren, desiring to know of them the cause of their disputations.

7 And they said: Behold, we cannot understand the words which our father hath spoken concerning the natural branches of the [a]olive-tree, and also concerning the Gentiles.

8 And I said unto them: Have ye [a]inquired of the Lord?

24*a* Ether 4: 16.
25*a* John 20: 30 (30–31); 21: 25; Rev. 1: 19.
26*a* TG Scriptures, Writing of.
b Dan. 12: 9; 2 Ne. 27: 10 (6–23); 30: 17; Ether 3: 21 (21–27); 4: 5 (4–7); 12: 21; D&C 35: 18; JS-H 1: 65.
27*a* Rev. 1: 1 (1–3).
29*a* 1 Ne. 8: 2 (2–35).
30*a* 1 Kgs. 18: 12; 1 Ne. 11: 29 (19, 29).
b 1 Ne. 13: 39; 2 Ne. 25: 20.
15 3*a* 1 Cor. 2: 11 (10–12). TG Hardheartedness; Understanding.
5*a* Moses 7: 44 (41–44).
b Enos 1: 13; Morm. 6: 1.
6*a* Moses 1: 10; JS-H 1: 20, 48.
7*a* 1 Ne. 10: 14 (2–15).
8*a* 2 Ne. 1: 25 (24–27); Mosiah 10: 14. TG Problem-Solving.

[Between 600 and 592 B.C.]

9 And they said unto me: [a]We have
not; for the Lord maketh no such
thing known unto us.
10 Behold, I said unto them: How
is it that ye do not keep the commandments of the Lord? How is it
that ye will [a]perish, because of the
hardness of your hearts?
11 Do ye not remember the things
which the Lord hath said?—If ye
will not harden your hearts, and [a]ask
me in [b]faith, believing that ye shall
receive, with diligence in keeping
my commandments, surely these
things shall be made known unto
you.
12 Behold, I say unto you, that the
house of Israel was compared unto
an olive-tree, by the Spirit of the
Lord which was in our father; and
behold are we not broken off from
the house of Israel, and are we not a
[a]branch of the house of Israel?
13 And now, the thing which our
father meaneth concerning the
grafting in of the natural branches
through the fulness of the Gentiles,
is, that in the latter days, when our
seed shall have [a]dwindled in unbelief, yea, for the space of many
years, and many generations after
the [b]Messiah shall be manifested in
body unto the children of men, then
shall the fulness of the [c]gospel of the
Messiah come unto the Gentiles,
and from the [d]Gentiles unto the
remnant of our seed—
14 And at that day shall the remnant of our [a]seed [b]know that they
are of the house of Israel, and that
they are the [c]covenant people of the
Lord; and then shall they know and
[d]come to the [e]knowledge of their
forefathers, and also to the knowledge of the gospel of their Redeemer,
which was ministered unto their
fathers by him; wherefore, they
shall come to the knowledge of their
Redeemer and the very points of his
doctrine, that they may know how
to come unto him and be saved.
15 And then at that day will they
not rejoice and give praise unto their
everlasting God, their [a]rock and
their salvation? Yea, at that day,
will they not receive the strength
and nourishment from the true
[b]vine? Yea, will they not come unto
the true fold of God?
16 Behold, I say unto you, Yea;
they shall be remembered again
among the house of Israel; they shall
be [a]grafted in, being a natural
branch of the olive-tree, into the
true olive-tree.
17 And this is what our father
meaneth; and he meaneth that it
will not come to pass until after
they are scattered by the Gentiles;
and he meaneth that it shall come
by way of the Gentiles, that the
Lord may show his power unto the
Gentiles, for the very cause that he
shall be [a]rejected of the Jews, or of
the house of Israel.
18 Wherefore, our father hath not
spoken of our seed alone, but also of
all the house of Israel, pointing to
the covenant which should be fulfilled in the latter days; which
covenant the Lord made to our
father Abraham, saying: In thy
[a]seed shall all the kindreds of the
earth be [b]blessed.

9*a* D&C 58:33.
10*a* TG Apostasy of Individuals.
11*a* James 1:5 (5–6). TG Prayer.
b 1 Ne. 2:19 (18–21); 7:12 (9–13).
12*a* Gen. 49:22 (22–26); 1 Ne. 10:12 (12–14); 19:24. TG Israel, Joseph, People of.
13*a* 1 Ne. 12:22 (22–23); 2 Ne. 26:15.
b TG Jesus Christ, Messiah.
c TG Gospel; Mission of Latter-day Saints.
d 1 Ne. 13:42; 22:9 (5–10); D&C 14:10. TG Gentiles.
14*a* 2 Ne. 10:2; 3 Ne. 5:23 (21–26); 21:7 (4–29).
b 2 Ne. 3:12; 30:5; Morm. 7:9 (1, 9–10).
c TG Abrahamic Covenant.
d Jacob 3:6.
e D&C 3:18 (16–20). See also title page of the Book of Mormon.
15*a* TG Rock.
b Gen. 49:11; John 15:1.
16*a* Jacob 5:54 (1–77).
17*a* TG Jesus Christ, Betrayal of; Jesus Christ, Crucifixion of.
18*a* Gen. 12:3 (1–3); Abr. 2:11 (6–11). TG Seed of Abraham.
b TG Israel, Mission of.

[Between 600 and 592 B.C.]

19 And it came to pass that I,
Nephi, spake much unto them concerning these things; yea, I spake
unto them concerning the [a]restora-
tion of the Jews in the latter days.
20 And I did rehearse unto them
the words of [a]Isaiah, who spake
[b]concerning the [c]restoration of the
Jews, or of the house of Israel; and
after they were restored they should
no more be confounded, neither
should they be scattered again. And
it came to pass that I did speak many
words unto my brethren, that they
were pacified and did [d]humble themselves before the Lord.
21 And it came to pass that they
did speak unto me again, saying:
What meaneth this thing which our
father saw in a dream? What meaneth the [a]tree which he saw?
22 And I said unto them: It was a
representation of the [a]tree of life.
23 And they said unto me: What
meaneth the [a]rod of iron which our
father saw, that led to the tree?
24 And I said unto them that it was
the [a]word of God; and whoso would
hearken unto the word of God, and
would [b]hold fast unto it, they would
never perish; neither could the
[c]temptations and the fiery [d]darts of
the [e]adversary overpower them unto
blindness, to lead them away to
destruction.
25 Wherefore, I, Nephi, did exhort
them to give [a]heed unto the word of
the Lord; yea, I did exhort them
with all the energies of my soul, and
with all the [b]faculty which I possessed, that they would give heed
to the word of God and remember
to keep his commandments always
in all things.
26 And they said unto me: What
meaneth the [a]river of water which
our father saw?
27 And I said unto them that the
[a]water which my father saw was
[b]filthiness; and so much was his
mind swallowed up in other things
that he beheld not the filthiness of
the water.
28 And I said unto them that it was
an awful [a]gulf, which separated the
wicked from the tree of life, and also
from the saints of God.
29 And I said unto them that it was
a representation of that awful [a]hell,
which the angel said unto me was
prepared for the wicked.
30 And I said unto them that our
father also saw that the [a]justice of
God did also divide the wicked from
the righteous; and the brightness
thereof was like unto the brightness
of a flaming [b]fire, which ascendeth
up unto God forever and ever, and
hath no end.
31 And they said unto me: Doth
this thing mean the torment of the
body in the days of [a]probation, or
doth it mean the final state of the
soul after the [b]death of the temporal
body, or doth it speak of the things
which are temporal?
32 And it came to pass that I said
unto them that it was a representation of things both temporal and
spiritual; for the day should come
that they must be judged of their
[a]works, yea, even the works which
were done by the temporal body in
their days of [b]probation.

19*a* Isa. 42: 22 (22–23); 1 Ne. 19: 15. TG Israel, Gathering of; Israel, Judah, People of.
20*a* 1 Ne. 19: 23.
b Isa. 40: 9.
c TG Israel, Restoration of.
d 1 Ne. 16: 5 (5, 24, 39).
21*a* 1 Ne. 8: 10 (10–12).
22*a* 1 Ne. 11: 4; Moses 3: 9.
23*a* 1 Ne. 8: 19 (19–24).
24*a* 1 Ne. 8: 19. TG Gospel.
b Prov. 4: 13.
c 1 Ne. 8: 23. TG Temptation.
d Eph. 6: 16; D&C 3: 8; 27: 17.
e TG Devil.
25*a* D&C 11: 2; 32: 4; 84: 43 (43–44). TG Scriptures, Study of.
b W of M 1: 18.
26*a* 1 Ne. 8: 13.
27*a* 1 Ne. 12: 16 (16–18).
b TG Filthiness.
28*a* Luke 16: 26; 1 Ne. 12: 18; 2 Ne. 1: 13.
29*a* 1 Ne. 8: 32 (13–14, 32). TG Hell.
30*a* TG God, Justice of; Justice.
b Num. 11: 1 (1, 10); 2 Ne. 26: 6.
31*a* TG Probation.
b Alma 40: 11 (6–26).
32*a* TG Good Works.
b TG Probation.

[Between 600 and 592 B.C.]

33 Wherefore, if they should [a]die in their wickedness they must be [b]cast off also, as to the things which are spiritual, which are pertaining to righteousness; wherefore, they must be brought to stand before God, to be [c]judged of their [d]works; and if their works have been filthiness they must needs be [e]filthy; and if they be filthy it must needs be that they cannot [f]dwell in the kingdom of God; if so, the kingdom of God must be filthy also.

34 But behold, I say unto you, the kingdom of God is not filthy, and there cannot any unclean thing enter into the kingdom of God; wherefore there must needs be a place of [a]filthiness prepared for that which is filthy.

35 And there is a place prepared, yea, even that [a]awful [b]hell of which I have spoken, and the [c]devil is the preparator of it; wherefore the final state of the souls of men is to dwell in the kingdom of God, or to be cast out because of that [d]justice of which I have spoken.

36 Wherefore, the wicked are rejected from the righteous, and also from that [a]tree of life, whose fruit is most precious and most [b]desirable above all other fruits; yea, and it is the [c]greatest of all the [d]gifts of God. And thus I spake unto my brethren. Amen.

CHAPTER 16

The wicked take the truth to be hard—Lehi's sons marry the daughters of Ishmael—The Liahona guides their course in the wilderness—Messages from the Lord are written on the Liahona from time to time—Ishmael dies; his family murmur because of afflictions.

AND now it came to pass that after I, Nephi, had made an end of speaking to my brethren, behold they said unto me: Thou hast declared unto us hard things, more than we are able to bear.

2 And it came to pass that I said unto them that I knew that I had spoken [a]hard things against the wicked, according to the truth; and the righteous have I justified, and testified that they should be lifted up at the last day; wherefore, the [b]guilty taketh the [c]truth to be hard, for it [d]cutteth them to the very center.

3 And now my brethren, if ye were righteous and were willing to hearken to the truth, and give heed unto it, that ye might [a]walk uprightly before God, then ye would not murmur because of the truth, and say: Thou speakest hard things against us.

4 And it came to pass that I, Nephi, did exhort my brethren, with all diligence, to keep the commandments of the Lord.

5 And it came to pass that they did [a]humble themselves before the Lord; insomuch that I had joy and great hopes of them, that they would walk in the paths of righteousness.

6 Now, all these things were said

33*a* Ezek. 18: 26; Mosiah 15: 26; Moro. 10: 26.
b Alma 12: 16; 40: 26.
c TG Jesus Christ, Judge; Judgment, The Last.
d Ps. 33: 15 (13–15); 3 Ne. 27: 25 (23–27).
e 2 Ne. 9: 16; D&C 88: 35.
f Ps. 15: 1 (1–5); 24: 3 (3–4); Mosiah 15: 23; Alma 11: 37; D&C 76: 62 (50–70); Moses 6: 57 (55–59).

34*a* TG Filthiness.
35*a* 2 Ne. 9: 19; Mosiah 26: 27.
b TG Hell.
c 1 Ne. 14: 9; D&C 1: 35.
d TG Justice.
36*a* Gen. 2: 9; 1 Ne. 8: 11; 2 Ne. 2: 15.
b 1 Ne. 8: 12.
c Hel. 5: 8.
d D&C 14: 7. TG God, Gifts of.
16 2*a* Acts 7: 54; 2 Ne. 33: 5; Enos 1: 23; W of M 1: 17. TG Chastening.
b John 3: 20 (19–21); 7: 7; Hel. 13: 24 (24–27).
c Prov. 15: 10; 2 Ne. 1: 26; 9: 40.
d Acts 5: 33; Mosiah 13: 7; Moses 6: 37.
3*a* D&C 5: 21. TG Walking with God.
5*a* 1 Ne. 15: 20; 16: 24 (24, 39); 18: 4.

[Between 600 and 592 B.C.]

and done as my father dwelt in a tent in the [a]valley which he called Lemuel.

7 And it came to pass that I, Nephi, took one of the [a]daughters of Ishmael to [b]wife; and also, my brethren took of the [c]daughters of Ishmael to wife; and also [d]Zoram took the eldest daughter of Ishmael to wife.

8 And thus my father had fulfilled all the [a]commandments of the Lord which had been given unto him. And also, I, Nephi, had been blessed of the Lord exceedingly.

9 And it came to pass that the voice of the Lord spake unto my father by night, and commanded him that on the morrow he should take his [a]journey into the wilderness.

10 And it came to pass that as my father arose in the morning, and went forth to the tent door, to his great astonishment he beheld upon the ground a round [a]ball of curious workmanship; and it was of fine brass. And within the ball were two spindles; and the one [b]pointed the way whither we should go into the wilderness.

11 And it came to pass that we did gather together whatsoever things we should carry into the wilderness, and all the remainder of our provisions which the Lord had given unto us; and we did take [a]seed of every kind that we might carry into the wilderness.

12 And it came to pass that we did take our tents and depart into the wilderness, across the river Laman.

13 And it came to pass that we traveled for the space of four days, nearly a south-southeast direction, and we did pitch our tents again; and we did call the name of the place [a]Shazer.

14 And it came to pass that we did take our bows and our arrows, and go forth into the wilderness to slay food for our families; and after we had slain food for our families we did return again to our families in the wilderness, to the place of Shazer. And we did go forth again in the wilderness, following the same direction, keeping in the most fertile parts of the wilderness, which were in the borders near the [a]Red Sea.

15 And it came to pass that we did travel for the space of many days, [a]slaying food by the way, with our bows and our arrows and our stones and our slings.

16 And we did follow the [a]directions of the ball, which led us in the more fertile parts of the wilderness.

17 And after we had traveled for the space of many days, we did pitch our tents for the space of a time, that we might again rest ourselves and obtain food for our families.

18 And it came to pass that as I, Nephi, went forth to slay food, behold, I did break my bow, which was made of fine [a]steel; and after I did break my bow, behold, my brethren were angry with me because of the loss of my bow, for we did obtain no food.

19 And it came to pass that we did return without food to our families, and being much fatigued, because of their journeying, they did suffer much for the want of food.

20 And it came to pass that Laman and Lemuel and the sons of Ishmael did begin to murmur exceedingly, because of their sufferings and afflictions in the wilderness; and also my father began to murmur against the Lord his God; yea, and they were all exceedingly sorrowful,

---

6*a* 1 Ne. 2: 14 (8, 14); 9: 1.
7*a* 1 Ne. 7: 1 (1, 19); 18: 19 (19–20).
b TG Marriage.
c 1 Ne. 7: 6.
d 1 Ne. 4: 35; 2 Ne. 5: 6 (5–6).
8*a* 1 Ne. 3: 18; 5: 21; 7: 2.
9*a* Omni 1: 16.
10*a* 1 Ne. 16: 16; Alma 37: 38 (38–47).
b Ex. 13: 21.
11*a* 1 Ne. 8: 1; 18: 6; Ether 1: 41; 2: 3.
13*a* HEB twisting, intertwining.
14*a* 1 Ne. 2: 5; D&C 17: 1.
15*a* Alma 17: 7.
16*a* 1 Ne. 16: 10 (10, 16, 26); 18: 12 (12, 21); 2 Ne. 5: 12; Alma 37: 38 (38–47); D&C 17: 1.
18*a* 2 Sam. 22: 35; Ps. 18: 34.

[Between 600 and 592 B.C.]

even that they did [a]murmur against
the Lord.
21 Now it came to pass that I,
Nephi, having been afflicted with
my brethren because of the loss of
my bow, and their bows having lost
their [a]springs, it began to be exceedingly difficult, yea, insomuch that
we could obtain no food.
22 And it came to pass that I,
Nephi, did speak much unto my
brethren, because they had hardened their hearts again, even unto
[a]complaining against the Lord their
God.
23 And it came to pass that I,
Nephi, did [a]make out of wood a bow,
and out of a straight stick, an arrow;
wherefore, I did arm myself with a
bow and an arrow, with a sling and
with stones. And I said unto my
[b]father: Whither shall I go to obtain
food?
24 And it came to pass that he did
[a]inquire of the Lord, for they had
[b]humbled themselves because of my
words; for I did say many things
unto them in the energy of my soul.
25 And it came to pass that the
voice of the Lord came unto my
father; and he was truly [a]chastened
because of his murmuring against
the Lord, insomuch that he was
brought down into the depths of
sorrow.
26 And it came to pass that the
voice of the Lord said unto him:
Look upon the ball, and behold the
things which are written.
27 And it came to pass that when
my father beheld the things which
were [a]written upon the ball, he did
fear and tremble exceedingly, and
also my brethren and the sons of
Ishmael and our wives.
28 And it came to pass that I,
Nephi, beheld the pointers which
were in the ball, that they did work
according to the [a]faith and diligence
and heed which we did give unto
them.
29 And there was also written upon
them a new writing, which was plain
to be read, which did give us [a]under-
standing concerning the ways of the
Lord; and it was written and
changed from time to time, according to the faith and diligence which
we gave unto it. And thus we see
that by [b]small means the Lord can
bring about great things.
30 And it came to pass that I,
Nephi, did go forth up into the top
of the mountain, according to the
[a]directions which were given upon
the ball.
31 And it came to pass that I did
slay wild [a]beasts, insomuch that I
did obtain food for our families.
32 And it came to pass that I did
return to our tents, bearing the
beasts which I had slain; and now
when they beheld that I had obtained [a]food, how great was their
joy! And it came to pass that they
did humble themselves before the
Lord, and did give thanks unto him.
33 And it came to pass that we did
again take our journey, traveling
nearly the same course as in the
beginning; and after we had traveled
for the space of many days we did
pitch our tents again, that we might
tarry for the space of a time.
34 And it came to pass that [a]Ish-
mael died, and was buried in the
place which was called [b]Nahom.
35 And it came to pass that the
daughters of Ishmael did [a]mourn
exceedingly, because of the loss of

20*a* TG Murmuring.
21*a* Gen. 49: 24.
22*a* Ex. 16: 8; Num. 11: 1 (1–2); D&C 29: 19.
23*a* TG Initiative.
b TG Honoring Father and Mother.
24*a* TG Guidance, Divine; Prayer.
b 1 Ne. 15: 20; 16: 5.
25*a* Ether 2: 14. TG Chastening; Repentance.
27*a* TG Warnings.
28*a* Alma 37: 40. TG Faith.
29*a* TG Understanding.
b 2 Kgs. 5: 13; James 3: 4; Alma 37: 6 (6–8, 41); D&C 123: 16.
30*a* TG Guidance, Divine.
31*a* Gen. 9: 3.
32*a* 2 Ne. 1: 24. TG Food; Thanksgiving.
34*a* 1 Ne. 7: 2 (2–6, 19).
b HEB probably "consolation," from verb *naham*, "be sorry, console oneself."
35*a* TG Mourning.

[Between 600 and 592 B.C.]

their father, and because of their
[b]afflictions in the wilderness; and
they did [c]murmur against my father,
because he had brought them out of
the land of Jerusalem, saying: Our
father is dead; yea, and we have
wandered much in the wilderness,
and we have suffered much affliction, hunger, thirst, and fatigue; and
after all these sufferings we must
perish in the wilderness with hunger.
36 And thus they did murmur
against my father, and also against
me; and they were desirous to [a]re-
turn again to Jerusalem.
37 And Laman said unto Lemuel
and also unto the sons of Ishmael:
Behold, let us [a]slay our father, and
also our brother Nephi, who has
taken it upon him to be our [b]ruler
and our teacher, who are his elder
brethren.
38 Now, he says that the Lord
has talked with him, and also that
[a]angels have ministered unto him.
But behold, we know that he lies
unto us; and he tells us these things,
and he worketh many things by his
cunning arts, that he may deceive
our eyes, thinking, perhaps, that he
may lead us away into some strange
wilderness; and after he has led us
away, he has thought to make himself a king and a ruler over us, that
he may do with us according to his
will and pleasure. And after this
manner did my brother Laman [b]stir
up their hearts to [c]anger.
39 And it came to pass that the
Lord was with us, yea, even the
voice of the Lord came and did
speak many words unto them, and
did [a]chasten them exceedingly; and
after they were chastened by the
voice of the Lord they did turn
away their anger, and did repent of
their sins, insomuch that the Lord
did bless us again with food, that
we did not perish.

CHAPTER 17

Nephi is commanded to build a ship—His brethren oppose him—He exhorts them by recounting the history of God's dealings with Israel—He is filled with the power of God—His brethren are forbidden to touch him, lest they wither as a dried reed.

AND it came to pass that we did
again take our journey in the wilderness; and we did travel nearly eastward from that time forth. And we
did travel and [a]wade through much
affliction in the wilderness; and our
[b]women did bear children in the
wilderness.
2 And so great were the [a]blessings
of the Lord upon us, that while we
did live upon [b]raw [c]meat in the
wilderness, our women did give
plenty of suck for their children,
and were strong, yea, even like unto
the men; and they began to bear
their journeyings without murmurings.
3 And thus we see that the commandments of God must be fulfilled.
And if it so be that the children of
men keep the commandments of
God he doth nourish them, and
[a]strengthen them, and provide
means whereby they can accomplish
the thing which he has commanded
them; wherefore, he did [b]provide
means for us while we did sojourn
in the wilderness.
4 And we did sojourn for the space
of many years, yea, *even eight
years in the wilderness.
5 And we did come to the land
which we called [a]Bountiful, because

35*b* TG Affliction.
c TG Murmuring.
36*a* Num. 14: 4 (1–5).
37*a* 1 Ne. 17: 44; 2 Ne. 1: 24.
TG Murder.
b Gen. 37: 10 (9–11); Num. 16: 13; 1 Ne. 2: 22; 8: 10.
38*a* 1 Ne. 3: 30 (30–31); 4: 3.
b TG Provoking.
c TG Anger.
39*a* TG Chastening.
17 1*a* Ps. 69: 2 (1–2, 14).
b TG Woman.
2*a* TG Blessing.
b 1 Ne. 17: 12.
c Ex. 16: 13 (12–13); 1 Ne. 18: 6.
TG Meat.
3*a* Ex. 1: 19; Ezra 8: 22 (22–23); Isa. 45: 24; Mosiah 2: 41; Alma 26: 12.
TG Strength.
b Gen. 18: 14; 1 Ne. 3: 7.
5*a* Alma 22: 29 (29–33).

[*592 B.C.]

of its much fruit and also wild honey;
and all these things were prepared
of the Lord that we might not
perish. And we beheld the sea, which
we called Irreantum, which, being
interpreted, is many waters.
6 And it came to pass that we did
pitch our tents by the seashore;
and notwithstanding we had suffered many [a]afflictions and much
difficulty, yea, even so much that
we cannot write them all, we were
exceedingly rejoiced when we came
to the seashore; and we called the
place Bountiful, because of its much
fruit.
7 And it came to pass that after
I, Nephi, had been in the land of
Bountiful for the space of many
days, the voice of the Lord came
unto me, saying: [a]Arise, and get
thee into the mountain. And it came
to pass that I arose and went up into
the mountain, and cried unto the
Lord.
8 And it came to pass that the Lord
spake unto me, saying: Thou shalt
[a]construct a ship, after the [b]manner
which I shall show thee, that I may
carry thy people across these waters.
9 And I said: Lord, whither shall I
go that I may find ore to molten,
that I may make [a]tools to construct
the ship after the manner which
thou hast shown unto me?
10 And it came to pass that the
Lord told me whither I should go to
find ore, that I might make tools.
11 And it came to pass that I,
Nephi, did make a bellows wherewith to [a]blow the fire, of the skins
of beasts; and after I had made a
bellows, that I might have wherewith to blow the fire, I did smite two
stones together that I might make
fire.
12 For the Lord had not hitherto
suffered that we should make much
fire, as we journeyed in the wilderness; for he said: I will make thy
food become sweet, that ye [a]cook
it not;
13 And I will also be your [a]light in
the wilderness; and I will prepare
the way before you, if it so be that
ye shall keep my commandments;
wherefore, inasmuch as ye shall keep
my commandments ye shall be led
towards the [b]promised land; and ye
shall [c]know that it is by me that ye
are led.
14 Yea, and the Lord said also that:
After ye have arrived in the promised
land, ye shall [a]know that I, the Lord,
am [b]God; and that I, the Lord, did
[c]deliver you from destruction; yea,
that I did bring you out of the land
of Jerusalem.
15 Wherefore, I, Nephi, did strive
to keep the [a]commandments of
the Lord, and I did [b]exhort my
brethren to faithfulness and diligence.
16 And it came to pass that I did
[a]make tools of the ore which I did
molten out of the rock.
17 And when my brethren saw that
I was about to [a]build a ship, they
began to [b]murmur against me, saying: Our brother is a fool, for he
thinketh that he can build a ship;
yea, and he also thinketh that he
can cross these great waters.
18 And thus my brethren did
[a]complain against me, and were
desirous that they might not labor,
for they did not [b]believe that I could
build a ship; neither would they

6*a* 2 Ne. 4: 20.
7*a* Ezek. 3: 22 (22–27).
8*a* Gen. 6: 14 (14–16).
b Ex. 25: 40; 1 Chr. 28: 12 (11–12, 19); 1 Ne. 18: 2.
9*a* Deut. 8: 9; 1 Kgs. 6: 7; 1 Chr. 22: 3 (3, 14); Job 28: 2; Isa. 44: 12.
11*a* Isa. 54: 16.
12*a* 1 Ne. 17: 2.
13*a* Alma 5: 37 (37–38); D&C 88: 66.
b 1 Ne. 2: 20; 4: 14; Jacob 2: 12.
c Ex. 6: 7; 13: 21. TG Guidance, Divine.
14*a* 2 Ne. 1: 4. TG God, Knowledge about; Testimony.
b D&C 5: 2.
c TG Deliverance.
15*a* 1 Kgs. 2: 3; Prov. 7: 2.
b Acts 14: 22; Titus 2: 15; Heb. 3: 13.
16*a* TG Skill.
17*a* 1 Ne. 17: 49 (8, 49–51); 18: 1 (1–6).
b TG Murmuring.
18*a* 1 Ne. 3: 28; 7: 6 (6–19); 18: 10 (9–22).
b TG Unbelief, Unbelievers.

[About 591 B.C.]

believe that I was instructed of the
Lord.
19 And now it came to pass that
I, Nephi, was exceedingly sorrowful because of the hardness of their
hearts; and now when they saw that
I began to be sorrowful they were
glad in their hearts, insomuch that
they did [a]rejoice over me, saying:
We knew that ye could not construct
a ship, for we knew that ye were
lacking in judgment; wherefore,
thou canst not accomplish so great a
work.
20 And thou art like unto our
father, led away by the foolish
[a]imaginations of his heart; yea, he
hath led us out of the land of
Jerusalem, and we have wandered
in the wilderness for these many
years; and our women have toiled,
being big with child; and they have
borne children in the wilderness and
suffered all things, save it were
death; and it would have been better
that they had died before they came
out of Jerusalem than to have suffered these afflictions.
21 Behold, these many years we
have suffered in the wilderness,
which time we might have enjoyed
our possessions and the land of our
inheritance; yea, and we might have
been happy.
22 And we know that the people
who were in the land of Jerusalem
were a [a]righteous people; for they
kept the statutes and judgments of
the Lord, and all his commandments, according to the law of
Moses; wherefore, we know that
they are a righteous people; and our
father hath judged them, and hath
led us away because we would
hearken unto his words; yea, and
our brother is like unto him. And
after this manner of language did
my brethren murmur and complain
against us.
23 And it came to pass that I,
Nephi, spake unto them, saying:
Do ye believe that our fathers, who
were the children of Israel, would
have been led away out of the hands
of the [a]Egyptians if they had not
hearkened unto the words of the
Lord?
24 Yea, do ye suppose that they
would have been led out of bondage, if the Lord had not commanded
Moses that he should [a]lead them out
of bondage?
25 Now ye know that the children
of Israel were in [a]bondage; and ye
know that they were laden with
[b]tasks, which were grievous to be
borne; wherefore, ye know that it
must needs be a good thing for them,
that they should be [c]brought out of
bondage.
26 Now ye know that [a]Moses was
commanded of the Lord to do that
great work; and ye know that by
his [b]word the waters of the Red
Sea were divided hither and thither,
and they passed through on dry
ground.
27 But ye know that the Egyptians
were [a]drowned in the Red Sea, who
were the armies of Pharaoh.
28 And ye also know that they were
fed with [a]manna in the wilderness.
29 Yea, and ye also know that
Moses, by his word according to the
power of God which was in him,
[a]smote the rock, and there came

19*a* TG Mocking; Persecution.
20*a* 1 Ne. 2: 11; 5: 4 (2–4).
22*a* 1 Ne. 1: 19 (4, 13, 18–20).
23*a* Ex. 20: 2; Ps. 80: 8; Moses 1: 26.
24*a* Ex. 3: 10 (2–10); Hosea 12: 13 (12–14); 1 Ne. 19: 10; 2 Ne. 3: 9; 25: 20.
25*a* Gen. 15: 13 (13–14); Mosiah 11: 21; D&C 101: 79. TG Israel, Bondage of, in Egypt.
b Ex. 1: 11 (10–11); 2: 11; 1 Ne. 20: 10.
c Ex. 5: 1.
26*a* Josh. 24: 6; Jer. 2: 2; Acts 7: 27 (22–39).
b Ex. 14: 21 (19–31); Josh. 2: 10; Neh. 9: 11; 1 Ne. 4: 2; Mosiah 7: 19; Hel. 8: 11; D&C 8: 3; Moses 1: 25. TG Israel, Deliverance of.
27*a* Josh. 24: 6.
28*a* Ex. 16: 15 (4, 14–15, 35); Num. 11: 7 (7–8); Deut. 8: 3; Neh. 9: 20; Hosea 13: 6 (5–8); John 6: 49; Mosiah 7: 19.
29*a* Ex. 17: 6; Num. 20: 11; Deut. 8: 15; Neh. 9: 15; 1 Ne. 20: 21; 2 Ne. 25: 20.

[About 591 B.C.]

forth water, that the children of
Israel might quench their thirst.
30 And notwithstanding they being
led, the Lord their God, their Redeemer, going before them, [a]lead-
ing them by day and giving light
unto them by night, and doing all
things for them which were [b]ex-
pedient for man to receive, they
hardened their hearts and blinded
their minds, and [c]reviled against
Moses and against the true and
living God.
31 And it came to pass that according to his word he did [a]destroy them;
and according to his word he did
[b]lead them; and according to his
word he did do all things for them;
and there was not any thing done
save it were by his word.
32 And after they had crossed the
river Jordan he did make them
mighty unto the [a]driving out of the
children of the land, yea, unto the
scattering them to destruction.
33 And now, do ye suppose that
the children of this land, who were
in the land of promise, who were
driven out by our fathers, do ye
suppose that they were righteous?
Behold, I say unto you, Nay.
34 Do ye suppose that our fathers
would have been more choice than
they if they had been righteous?
I say unto you, Nay.
35 Behold, the Lord esteemeth all
[a]flesh in one; he that is [b]righteous is
[c]favored of God. But behold, this
[d]people had rejected every word of
God, and they were ripe in iniquity;
and the fulness of the wrath of God
was upon them; and the Lord did
curse the land against them, and
bless it unto our fathers; yea, he did
curse it against them unto their
destruction, and he did bless it unto
our fathers unto their obtaining
power over it.
36 Behold, the Lord hath created
the [a]earth that it should be [b]in-
habited; and he hath created his
children that they should possess it.
37 And he [a]raiseth up a righteous
nation, and destroyeth the nations
of the wicked.
38 And he leadeth away the
righteous into precious [a]lands, and
the wicked he [b]destroyeth, and curseth the land unto them for their
sakes.
39 He ruleth high in the heavens,
for it is his throne, and this earth
is his [a]footstool.
40 And he loveth those who will
have him to be their God. Behold,
he loved our [a]fathers, and he
[b]covenanted with them, yea, even
Abraham, [c]Isaac, and [d]Jacob; and he
remembered the covenants which he
had made; wherefore, he did bring
them out of the land of [e]Egypt.
41 And he did straiten them in the
wilderness with his rod; for they
[a]hardened their hearts, even as ye
have; and the Lord straitened them
because of their iniquity. He sent

30*a* Ex. 13: 18 (18, 20).
b D&C 18: 18; 88: 64 (64–65).
c Ex. 32: 8; Num. 14: 11 (11–12); Ezek. 20: 13 (13–16); D&C 84: 24 (23–25).
31*a* Num. 26: 65.
b Ex. 15: 13; 1 Ne. 5: 15; D&C 103: 16 (16–18).
32*a* Ex. 34: 11; Num. 33: 52 (52–53); Josh. 11: 6; 24: 8.
35*a* Acts 10: 15 (15, 34); Rom. 2: 11; 2 Ne. 26: 33 (23–33).
b Ps. 55: 22; John 15: 10; 1 Ne. 22: 17.
c 1 Sam. 2: 30; 1 Kgs. 2: 3; Ps. 97: 10; 145: 20 (1–21); Alma 13: 4; 28: 13; D&C 82: 10 (8–10).
d Gen. 15: 16; Ex. 23: 31 (28–31); Deut. 7: 10; Josh. 2: 24.
36*a* Gen. 1: 28 (26–28); Jer. 27: 5; Moses 1: 29. TG Earth, Purpose of; Man, a Spirit Child of Heavenly Father; Man, Physical Creation of.
b Isa. 45: 18.
37*a* Ps. 1: 6; Prov. 14: 34; Isa. 45: 1 (1–3); 1 Ne. 4: 13; Ether 2: 10; D&C 98: 32 (31–32); 117: 6.
38*a* TG Lands of Inheritance.
b Lev. 20: 22.
39*a* Isa. 66: 1; Lam. 2: 1; D&C 38: 17; Abr. 2: 7.
40*a* TG Israel, Origins of.
b TG Abrahamic Covenant.
c Gen. 21: 12; D&C 27: 10.
d Gen. 28: 4 (1–5).
e Deut. 4: 37 (37–38).
41*a* 2 Kgs. 17: 7 (7–23).

[About 591 B.C.]

fiery flying [b]serpents among them;
and after they were bitten he prepared a way that they might be
[c]healed; and the labor which they
had to perform was to look; and
because of the [d]simpleness of the
way, or the easiness of it, there were
many who perished.
42 And they did harden their hearts
from time to time, and they did
[a]revile against [b]Moses, and also
against God; nevertheless, ye know
that they were led forth by his
matchless power into the land of
promise.
43 And now, after all these things,
the time has come that they have become wicked, yea, nearly unto ripe-
ness; and I know not but they are
at this day about to be [a]destroyed;
for I know that the day must surely
come that they must be destroyed,
save a few only, who shall be led
away into captivity.
44 Wherefore, the Lord [a]com-
manded my father that he should
depart into the wilderness; and the
Jews also sought to take away his
life; yea, and [b]ye also have sought to
take away his life; wherefore, ye are
murderers in your hearts and ye are
like unto them.
45 Ye are [a]swift to do iniquity but
slow to remember the Lord your
God. Ye have seen an [b]angel, and he
spake unto you; yea, ye have heard
his voice from time to time; and he
hath spoken unto you in a still small
voice, but ye were [c]past feeling, that
ye could not feel his words; wherefore, he has spoken unto you like
unto the voice of thunder, which did
cause the earth to shake as if it were
to divide asunder.
46 And ye also know that by the
[a]power of his almighty word he can
cause the earth that it shall pass
away; yea, and ye know that by his
word he can cause the rough places
to be made smooth, and smooth
places shall be broken up. O, then,
why is it, that ye can be so hard in
your hearts?
47 Behold, my soul is rent with
anguish because of you, and my
heart is pained; I fear lest ye shall
be cast off forever. Behold, I am
[a]full of the Spirit of God, insomuch
that my frame has [b]no strength.
48 And now it came to pass that
when I had spoken these words they
were angry with me, and were desirous to throw me into the depths
of the sea; and as they came forth to
lay their hands upon me I spake unto
them, saying: In the name of the
Almighty God, I command you that
ye [a]touch me not, for I am filled with
the [b]power of God, even unto the
consuming of my flesh; and whoso
shall lay his hands upon me shall
[c]wither even as a dried reed; and he
shall be as naught before the power
of God, for God shall smite him.
49 And it came to pass that I,
Nephi, said unto them that they
should murmur no more against
their father; neither should they
withhold their labor from me, for
God had commanded me that I
should [a]build a ship.
50 And I said unto them: [a]If God
had commanded me to do all things
I could do them. If he should command me that I should say unto this
water, be thou earth, it should be
earth; and if I should say it, it would
be done.
51 And now, if the Lord has such
great power, and has wrought so

41*b* Num. 21: 6 (4–9); Deut. 8: 15; Alma 33: 19 (18–22).
c Hosea 11: 3; John 3: 14; 2 Ne. 25: 20.
d Alma 37: 46 (44–47); Hel. 8: 15.
42*a* Ex. 32: 23; Num. 14: 2 (1–12). TG Reviling.
b D&C 84: 23.
43*a* Hosea 7: 13. TG Israel, Scattering of.
44*a* 1 Ne. 2: 2 (1–2).
b 1 Ne. 16: 37.
45*a* Mosiah 13: 29.
b 1 Ne. 4: 3.
c Acts 17: 27; Eph. 4: 19; 1 Ne. 2: 14.
46*a* Hel. 12: 10 (6–18).
47*a* Micah 3: 8.
b Dan. 10: 8 (8, 17); 1 Ne. 1: 7; 19: 20.
48*a* Mosiah 13: 3.
b 2 Ne. 1: 27 (26–27). TG God, Power of; Priesthood, Power of.
c 1 Kgs. 13: 4 (4–7); Moses 1: 11; 6: 47.
49*a* 1 Ne. 17: 17; 18: 1 (1–6).
50*a* Philip. 4: 13; 1 Ne. 3: 7; D&C 24: 13.

[About 591 B.C.]

many miracles among the children
of men, how is it that he cannot
[a]instruct me, that I should build a
ship?
52 And it came to pass that I,
Nephi, said many things unto my
brethren, insomuch that they were
[a]confounded and could not contend
against me; neither durst they lay
their hands upon me nor touch
me with their fingers, even for the
space of many days. Now they durst
not do this lest they should wither
before me, so powerful was the
[b]Spirit of God; and thus it had
wrought upon them.
53 And it came to pass that the
Lord said unto me: Stretch forth
thine hand again unto thy brethren,
and they shall not wither before thee,
but I will [a]shock them, saith the
Lord, and this will I do, that they
may know that I am the Lord their
God.
54 And it came to pass that I
stretched forth my hand unto my
brethren, and they did not wither
before me; but the Lord did shake
them, even according to the word
which he had spoken.
55 And now, they said: We know
of a surety that the Lord is [a]with
thee, for we know that it is the power
of the Lord that has shaken us. And
they fell down before me, and were
about to [b]worship me, but I would
not suffer them, saying: I am thy
brother, yea, even thy younger
brother; wherefore, worship the
Lord thy God, and honor thy father
and thy mother, that thy [c]days may
be long in the land which the Lord
thy God shall give thee.

CHAPTER 18

The ship is finished—The births of Jacob and Joseph are mentioned—The company embarks for the promised land—The sons of Ishmael and their wives join in revelry and rebellion—Nephi is bound, and the ship is driven back by a terrible tempest—Nephi is freed, and by his prayer the storm ceases—They arrive in the promised land.

AND it came to pass that they did
[a]worship the Lord, and did go forth
with me; and we did work timbers
of curious [b]workmanship. And the
Lord did show me from time to time
after what manner I should work
the timbers of the [c]ship.
2 Now I, Nephi, did not work the
timbers after the manner which was
learned by men, neither did I build
the ship after the manner of men;
but I did build it after the manner
which the Lord had shown unto
me; wherefore, it was not after the
manner of men.
3 And I, Nephi, did go into the
mount oft, and I did [a]pray oft unto the Lord; wherefore the Lord
[b]showed unto me [c]great things.
4 And it came to pass that after I
had finished the ship, according to
the word of the Lord, my brethren
beheld that it was good, and that
the workmanship thereof was exceedingly fine; wherefore, they did
[a]humble themselves again before
the Lord.
5 And it came to pass that the voice
of the Lord came unto my father,
that we should arise and go down
into the ship.
6 And it came to pass that on the
morrow, after we had prepared all
things, much fruits and [a]meat from
the wilderness, and honey in abundance, and provisions according
to that which the Lord had commanded us, we did go down into the
ship, with all our loading and our

51*a* Gen. 6: 14 (14–16); 1 Ne. 18: 1.
52*a* IE ashamed, overawed.
b TG God, Spirit of.
53*a* IE cause to shake or tremble; see v. 54–55.
55*a* Ex. 3: 12; Alma 38: 4.
b Dan. 2: 46; Acts 14: 15 (11–15).
c Ex. 20: 12; Prov. 9: 11; Mosiah 14: 10; Hel. 7: 24; D&C 5: 33.
18 1*a* 1 Ne. 17: 55.
b TG Art.
c 1 Ne. 17: 49 (8, 17, 49–51).
3*a* Jer. 33: 3.
b TG Guidance, Divine.
c 2 Ne. 1: 24.
4*a* 1 Ne. 16: 5.
6*a* 1 Ne. 17: 2.

[About 591 B.C.]

[b]seeds, and whatsoever thing we
had brought with us, every one
according to his age; wherefore, we
did all go down into the [c]ship, with
our wives and our children.
7 And now, my father had begat
two sons in the wilderness; the elder
was called [a]Jacob and the younger
[b]Joseph.
8 And it came to pass after we had
all gone down into the ship, and had
taken with us our provisions and
things which had been commanded
us, we did put forth into the [a]sea
and were driven forth before the
wind towards the [b]promised land.
9 And after we had been [a]driven
forth before the wind for the space
of many days, behold, my brethren
and the sons of Ishmael and also
their wives began to make themselves merry, insomuch that they
began to dance, and to sing, and to
speak with much [b]rudeness, yea,
even that they did forget by what
power they had been brought
thither; yea, they were lifted up unto exceeding rudeness.
10 And I, Nephi, began to fear
exceedingly lest the Lord should
be angry with us, and smite us
because of our iniquity, that we
should be swallowed up in the depths
of the sea; wherefore, I, Nephi,
began to speak to them with much
soberness; but behold they were
[a]angry with me, saying: We will not
that our younger brother shall be a
[b]ruler over us.
11 And it came to pass that Laman
and Lemuel did take me and [a]bind
me with cords, and they did treat me
with much harshness; nevertheless,
the Lord did suffer it that he might
show forth his power, unto the fulfilling of his word which he had
[b]spoken concerning the wicked.
12 And it came to pass that after
they had bound me insomuch that
I could not move, the [a]compass,
which had been prepared of the
Lord, did cease to work.
13 Wherefore, they knew not
whither they should steer the ship,
insomuch that there arose a great
[a]storm, yea, a great and terrible
tempest, and we were [b]driven back
upon the waters for the space of
three days; and they began to be
frightened exceedingly lest they
should be drowned in the sea; nevertheless they did not loose me.
14 And on the fourth day, which
we had been driven back, the
tempest began to be exceedingly
sore.
15 And it came to pass that we
were about to be swallowed up in the
depths of the sea. And after we had
been driven back upon the waters
for the space of four days, my
brethren began to [a]see that the
judgments of God were upon them,
and that they must perish save that
they should repent of their iniquities; wherefore, they came unto me,
and loosed the bands which were
upon my wrists, and behold they
had swollen exceedingly; and also
mine ankles were much swollen, and
great was the soreness thereof.
16 Nevertheless, I did look unto
my God, and I did [a]praise him all
the day long; and I did not murmur
against the Lord because of mine
afflictions.
17 Now my father, Lehi, had said
many things unto them, and also
unto the sons of [a]Ishmael; but,
behold, they did breathe out much

6*b* 1 Ne. 8: 1; 16: 11.
c Gen. 7: 7.
7*a* 2 Ne. 2: 1.
b 2 Ne. 3: 1.
8*a* Ps. 8: 8; 2 Ne. 10: 20.
b 1 Ne. 2: 20; 5: 5 (5, 22).
TG Promised Lands.
9*a* Ether 6: 5.
b 2 Ne. 1: 2.
TG Rioting and Reveling.
10*a* 1 Ne. 17: 18 (17–55); 2 Ne. 4: 13 (13–14).
b Gen. 37: 10 (9–11); 1 Ne. 16: 37 (37–38); 2 Ne. 1: 25 (25–27).
11*a* 1 Ne. 7: 16 (16–20).
b Ex. 23: 7; Ps. 37: 9 (8–13); Alma 14: 11.
12*a* 1 Ne. 16: 16 (10, 16, 26); 2 Ne. 5: 12; Alma 37: 38 (38–47); D&C 17: 1.
13*a* Jonah 1: 4; Matt. 8: 24.
b Mosiah 1: 17.
15*a* Hel. 12: 3.
16*a* Ezra 3: 11 (11–13); 2 Ne. 9: 49; Mosiah 2: 20 (20–21); Alma 36: 28; D&C 136: 28.
17*a* 1 Ne. 7: 4 (4–20).

[About 590 B.C.]

threatenings against anyone that should speak for me; and my parents being [b]stricken in years, and having [c]suffered much grief because of their [d]children, they were brought down, yea, even upon their sick-beds.

18 Because of their grief and much sorrow, and the iniquity of my brethren, they were brought near even to be carried out of this time to meet their God; yea, their [a]grey hairs were about to be brought down to lie low in the dust; yea, even they were near to be cast with sorrow into a watery grave.

19 And Jacob and Joseph also, being young, having need of much nourishment, were grieved because of the afflictions of their mother; and also [a]my wife with her tears and prayers, and also my children, did not soften the hearts of my brethren that they would loose me.

20 And there was nothing save it were the power of God, which threatened them with destruction, could soften their [a]hearts; wherefore, when they saw that they were about to be swallowed up in the depths of the sea they repented of the thing which they had done, insomuch that they loosed me.

21 And it came to pass after they had loosed me, behold, I took the compass, and it did work whither I desired it. And it came to pass that I [a]prayed unto the Lord; and after I had prayed the winds did cease, and the storm did cease, and there was a great calm.

22 And it came to pass that I, Nephi, did guide the ship, that we sailed again towards the promised land.

23 And it came to pass that after we had sailed for the space of many days *we did arrive at the [a]promised land; and we went forth upon the land, and did pitch our tents; and we did call it the promised land.

24 And it came to pass that we did begin to till the earth, and we began to plant seeds; yea, we did put all our [a]seeds into the earth, which we had brought from the land of Jerusalem. And it came to pass that they did grow exceedingly; wherefore, we were blessed in abundance.

25 And it came to pass that we did find upon the land of promise, as we journeyed in the wilderness, that there were [a]beasts in the forests of every kind, both the cow and the ox, and the ass and the horse, and the goat and the wild goat, and all manner of wild animals, which were for the use of men. And we did find all manner of [b]ore, both of [c]gold, and of silver, and of copper.

CHAPTER 19

Nephi makes plates of ore and records the history of his people—The God of Israel will come six hundred years from the time Lehi left Jerusalem—Nephi tells of His sufferings and crucifixion—The Jews shall be despised and scattered until the latter days, when they shall return unto the Lord.

AND it came to pass that the Lord commanded me, wherefore I did make plates of ore that I might engraven upon them the [a]record of my people. And upon the plates which I made I did [b]engraven the record of my [c]father, and also our journeyings in the wilderness, and the prophecies of my father; and also many of mine own prophecies have I engraven upon them.

2 And I knew not at the time when I made them that I should be com-

17*b* Gen. 24: 1.
c TG Suffering.
d TG Family, Children, Duties of; Honoring Father and Mother.
18*a* Gen. 42: 38.
19*a* 1 Ne. 7: 19; 16: 7.
20*a* TG Hardheartedness.
21*a* Jonah 1: 6.
23*a* Mosiah 10: 13.
TG Promised Lands.
24*a* 1 Ne. 8: 1.
25*a* Enos 1: 21.
b 2 Ne. 5: 15 (14–16).
c Deut. 33: 16 (13–17).
19 1*a* TG Plate; Record Keeping.
b TG Scribe.
c 1 Ne. 1: 17 (16–17); 6: 1 (1–3); Jacob 7: 26 (26–27).

[*Probably about 589 B.C.]

manded of the Lord to make [a]these
plates; wherefore, the record of my
father, and the genealogy of his
fathers, and the more part of all our
proceedings in the wilderness are
engraven upon those first plates of
which I have spoken; wherefore,
the things which transpired before I
made [b]these plates are, of a truth,
more particularly made mention upon the first plates.
3 And after I had made these plates
by way of commandment, I, Nephi,
received a commandment that the
ministry and the prophecies, the
more plain and precious parts of
them, should be written upon [a]these
plates; and that the things which
were written should be kept for the
instruction of my people, who should
possess the land, and also for other
[b]wise purposes, which purposes are
known unto the Lord.
4 Wherefore, I, Nephi, did make a
record upon the [a]other plates, which
gives an account, or which gives a
greater account of the wars and
contentions and destructions of my
people. And this have I done, and
commanded my people what they
should do after I was gone; and that
these plates should be handed down
from one generation to another,
or from one prophet to another,
until further commandments of the
Lord.
5 And an account of my [a]making
these plates shall be given hereafter;
and then, behold, I proceed according to that which I have spoken;
and this I do that the more sacred
things may be [b]kept for the knowledge of my people.
6 Nevertheless, I do not [a]write
anything upon plates save it be that
I think it be [b]sacred. And now, if I
do err, even did they err of old; not
that I would excuse myself because
of other men, but because of the
[c]weakness which is in me, according
to the flesh, I would excuse myself.
7 For the things which some men
esteem to be of great worth, both
to the body and soul, others set at
[a]naught and trample under their
feet. Yea, even the very God of Israel
do men [b]trample under their feet; I
say, trample under their feet but I
would speak in other words—they
set him at naught, and [c]hearken not
to the voice of his counsels.
8 And behold he [a]cometh, according to the words of the angel, in [b]six
hundred years from the time my
father left Jerusalem.
9 And the world, because of their
iniquity, shall judge him to be a
thing of naught; wherefore they
scourge him, and he suffereth it;
and they smite him, and he suffereth
it. Yea, they [a]spit upon him, and he
suffereth it, because of his loving
[b]kindness and his [c]long-suffering
towards the children of men.
10 And the [a]God of our fathers,
who were [b]led out of Egypt, out of
bondage, and also were preserved
in the wilderness by him, yea, the

2*a* 2 Ne. 5: 30; Jacob 3: 14.
b 1 Ne. 9: 2 (1–5); Omni 1: 1.
3*a* 1 Ne. 10: 1; Jacob 1: 1 (1–4); 3: 13 (13–14); 4: 1 (1–4).
b 1 Ne. 9: 5 (4–5); W of M 1: 7; D&C 3: 19 (19–20); 10: 38 (1–51).
4*a* 1 Ne. 9: 4 (2–5); 2 Ne. 5: 33.
5*a* 2 Ne. 5: 30 (28–33).
b TG Scriptures, Preservation of.
6*a* TG Scriptures, Writing of.
b See title page of the Book of Mormon. TG Sacred.
c Morm. 8: 17 (13–17); Ether 12: 23 (23–28).
7*a* Num. 15: 31 (30–31); 2 Ne. 33: 2; Jacob 4: 14; D&C 3: 7 (4–13).
b Ezek. 34: 19; D&C 76: 35. TG Blasphemy; Sacrilege.
c TG Disobedience; Prophets, Rejection of.
8*a* TG Jesus Christ, Betrayal of; Jesus Christ, Birth of; Jesus Christ, Prophecies about.
b 1 Ne. 2: 4; 10: 4 (4–11); 2 Ne. 25: 19.
9*a* Isa. 50: 6 (5–6); Matt. 27: 30.
b TG Kindness.
c TG Forbearance.
10*a* 2 Ne. 10: 3; 26: 12; Mosiah 7: 27; 27: 31 (30–31); Alma 11: 39 (38–39); 3 Ne. 11: 14 (14–15).
b Gen. 15: 14 (13–14); Ex. 3: 10 (2–10); 6: 6; 1 Ne. 5: 15; 17: 24 (24, 31, 40); 2 Ne. 25: 20; D&C 136: 22.

[Between 588 and 570 B.C.]

[c]God of Abraham, and of Isaac, and
the God of Jacob, [d]yieldeth himself,
according to the words of the angel,
as a man, into the hands of [e]wicked
men, to be [f]lifted up, according to
the words of [g]Zenock, and to be
[h]crucified, according to the words
of Neum, and to be buried in a
[i]sepulchre, according to the words
of [j]Zenos, which he spake concerning
the three days of [k]darkness, which
should be a sign given of his death
unto those who should inhabit the
isles of the sea, more especially
given unto those who are of the
[l]house of Israel.
11 For thus spake the prophet:
The Lord God surely shall [a]visit all
the house of Israel at that day, some
with his [b]voice, because of their
righteousness, unto their great joy
and salvation, and others with the
[c]thunderings and the lightnings of
his power, by tempest, by fire, and
by [d]smoke, and [e]vapor of [f]darkness,
and by the opening of the [g]earth,
and by [h]mountains which shall be
carried up.
12 And [a]all these things must surely
come, saith the prophet [b]Zenos. And
the [c]rocks of the earth must rend;
and because of the [d]groanings of the
earth, many of the kings of the isles
of the sea shall be wrought upon by
the Spirit of God, to exclaim: The
God of nature suffers.
13 And as for those who are at
Jerusalem, saith the prophet, they
shall be [a]scourged by all people,
because they crucify the God of
Israel, and turn their hearts aside,
rejecting signs and wonders, and
the power and glory of the God of
Israel.
14 And because they turn their
hearts aside, saith the prophet, and
have [a]despised the Holy One of
Israel, they shall wander in the flesh,
and perish, and become a [b]hiss and a
[c]byword, and be [d]hated among all
nations.
15 Nevertheless, when that day
cometh, saith the prophet, that they
[a]no more [b]turn aside their hearts
against the Holy One of Israel, then
will he remember the [c]covenants
which he made to their fathers.
16 Yea, then will he remember
the [a]isles of the sea; yea, and all
the people who are of the house of
Israel, will I [b]gather in, saith the
Lord, according to the words of
the prophet Zenos, from the four
quarters of the earth.
17 Yea, and all the earth shall [a]see
the salvation of the Lord, saith the

10*c* Gen. 32: 9; Matt. 22: 32; Mosiah 7: 19; D&C 136: 21. TG Jesus Christ—Jehovah.
d TG Jesus Christ, Condescension of.
e TG Jesus Christ, Betrayal of.
f 3 Ne. 27: 14; 28: 6.
g BD Lost Books. See also Alma 33: 15; 34: 7; Hel. 8: 20 (19–20); 3 Ne. 10: 16 (15–16).
h Nahum 1: 15; 2 Ne. 6: 9; Mosiah 3: 9. TG Jesus Christ, Crucifixion of.
i Matt. 27: 60; Luke 23: 53; 2 Ne. 25: 13.
j Jacob 5: 1; 6: 1; Hel. 15: 11.
k 1 Ne. 12: 4 (4–5); Hel. 14: 27 (20, 27); 3 Ne. 8: 19 (3, 19–23); 10: 9.
l 3 Ne. 16: 1 (1–4).
11*a* D&C 5: 16.
b 3 Ne. 9: 1 (1–22).
c Hel. 14: 21 (20–27); 3 Ne. 8: 6 (5–23).
d Gen. 19: 28; Ex. 19: 18; Morm. 8: 29 (29–30); D&C 45: 41 (40–41).
e 1 Ne. 12: 5.
f Luke 23: 44 (44–45). TG Darkness, Physical.
g Num. 16: 32; 2 Ne. 26: 5.
h 3 Ne. 10: 13 (13–14).
12*a* Hel. 14: 28 (20–28); 3 Ne. 10: 11.
b Jacob 5: 1.
c Matt. 27: 51 (51–54).
d Moses 7: 56 (48–56).
13*a* Matt. 23: 38 (37–39); Luke 23: 28 (27–30).
14*a* Ps. 22: 6; Mosiah 14: 3 (3–6).
b Jer. 24: 9; 3 Ne. 29: 8 (8–9). TG Israel, Bondage of, in Other Lands.
c Deut. 28: 37; 1 Kgs. 9: 7 (6–7); Joel 2: 17; 3 Ne. 16: 9 (8–9).
d 2 Ne. 10: 6; 25: 15. TG Hate.
15*a* 1 Ne. 15: 19; 22: 12 (11–12).
b TG Israel, Restoration of.
c TG Abrahamic Covenant.
16*a* 1 Ne. 22: 4; 2 Ne. 10: 21.
b Isa. 49: 22 (20–22); 60: 4. TG Israel, Gathering of.
17*a* Isa. 40: 5 (4–5).

[Between 588 and 570 B.C.]

prophet; every nation, kindred,
tongue and people shall be blessed.
18 And I, Nephi, have written
these things unto my people, that
perhaps I might persuade them that
they would [a]remember the Lord
their Redeemer.
19 Wherefore, I speak unto all the
house of Israel, if it so be that they
should obtain [a]these things.
20 For behold, I have workings in
the spirit, which doth [a]weary me
even that all my joints are weak,
for those who are at Jerusalem; for
had not the Lord been merciful, to
show unto me concerning them, even
as he had prophets of old, I should
have perished also.
21 And he surely did show unto
the [a]prophets of old all things [b]con-
cerning them; and also he did show
unto many concerning us; wherefore, it must needs be that we know
concerning them for they are written upon the plates of brass.
22 Now it came to pass that I,
Nephi, did teach my brethren these
things; and it came to pass that I
did read many things to them, which
were engraven upon the [a]plates of
brass, that they might know concerning the doings of the Lord in
other lands, among people of old.
23 And I did read many things
unto them which were written in
the [a]books of Moses; but that I
might more fully persuade them to
believe in the Lord their Redeemer
I did read unto them that which was
written by the prophet [b]Isaiah; for
I did [c]liken all scriptures unto us,
that it might be for our [d]profit and
learning.
24 Wherefore I spake unto them,
saying: Hear ye the words of the
prophet, ye who are a [a]remnant of
the house of Israel, a [b]branch who
have been broken off; [c]hear ye the
words of the prophet, which were
written unto all the house of Israel,
and liken them unto yourselves, that
ye may have hope as well as your
brethren from whom ye have been
broken off; for after this manner
has the prophet written.

CHAPTER 20

The Lord reveals his purposes to Israel—They have been chosen in the furnace of affliction and are to go forth from Babylon—Compare Isaiah 48.

[a]HEARKEN and hear this, O house
of Jacob, who are called by the name
of Israel, and are come forth out of
the waters of Judah, or out of the
waters of [b]baptism, who [c]swear by
the name of the Lord, and make
mention of the God of Israel, yet
they swear [d]not in truth nor in
righteousness.
2 Nevertheless, they call themselves of the [a]holy city, but they do
[b]not stay themselves upon the God
of Israel, who is the Lord of Hosts;
yea, the Lord of Hosts is his name.
3 Behold, I have declared the
[a]former things from the beginning;
and they went forth out of my
mouth, and I showed them. I did
show them suddenly.
4 And I did it because I knew that
thou art obstinate, and thy [a]neck is
an iron sinew, and thy brow brass;
5 And I have even from the beginning declared to thee; before it came

18*a* Mosiah 13:29.
19*a* Enos 1:16; Morm. 5:12; 7:9 (9–10). TG Israel, Restoration of.
20*a* Dan. 10:8 (8–12); 1 Ne. 1:7; Alma 27:17; Moses 1:10 (9–10).
21*a* 2 Kgs. 17:13; Amos 3:7. TG Prophets, Mission of.
b 3 Ne. 10:16 (16–17).
22*a* 1 Ne. 13:23; 22:1.
23*a* Ex. 17:14; 1 Ne. 5:11; Moses 1:41 (40–41).
b Isa. 1:1; 1 Ne. 15:20; 2 Ne. 25:5 (2–6); 3 Ne. 23:1.
c TG Scriptures, Value of.
d 2 Ne. 4:15.
24*a* 2 Kgs. 19:31.
b Gen. 49:22 (22–26); 1 Ne. 15:12 (12, 16); 2 Ne. 3:5 (4–5).
c TG Scriptures, Study of.
20 1*a* Isa. 48:1 (1–22).
b TG Baptism; Conversion.
c Deut. 6:13.
d Jer. 4:2; 5:2.
2*a* Isa. 52:1. TG Jerusalem.
b TG Hypocrisy; Prophets, Rejection of.
3*a* Isa. 42:9; 46:10 (9–10). TG God, Foreknowledge of.
4*a* TG Stiffneckedness.

[Between 588 and 570 B.C.]

to pass I [a]showed them thee; and
I showed them for fear lest thou
shouldst say—Mine idol hath done
them, and my graven image, and
my molten image hath commanded
them.
6 Thou hast seen and heard all this;
and will ye [a]not declare them? And
that I have showed thee new things
from this time, even hidden things,
and thou didst not know them.
7 They are created now, and not
from the beginning, even before the
day when thou heardest them not
they were declared unto thee, lest
thou shouldst say—Behold I knew
them.
8 Yea, and thou heardest not; yea,
thou knewest not; yea, from that
time thine ear was not opened; for I
knew that thou wouldst deal very
treacherously, and wast called a
[a]transgressor from the womb.
9 Nevertheless, for my [a]name's
sake will I defer mine anger, and for
my praise will I refrain from thee,
that I cut thee not off.
10 For, behold, I have refined thee,
I have chosen thee in the furnace of
[a]affliction.
11 For mine own sake, yea, for
mine own sake will I do this, for I
will not suffer my [a]name to be polluted, and I will [b]not give my glory
unto another.
12 Hearken unto me, O Jacob, and
Israel my called, for I am he; I am
the [a]first, and I am also the last.
13 Mine hand hath also [a]laid the
foundation of the earth, and my
right hand hath spanned the
heavens. I [b]call unto them and they
stand up together.
14 All ye, assemble yourselves, and
hear; who among them hath declared these things unto them? The
Lord hath loved him; yea, and he
will [a]fulfil his word which he hath
declared by them; and he will do
his pleasure on [b]Babylon, and his
arm shall come upon the Chaldeans.
15 Also, saith the Lord; I the Lord,
yea, I have spoken; yea, I have
called [a]him to declare, I have
brought him, and he shall make his
way prosperous.
16 Come ye near unto me; I have
not spoken in [a]secret; from the beginning, from the time that it was
declared have I spoken; and the
Lord God, and his [b]Spirit, hath sent
me.
17 And thus saith the Lord, thy
[a]Redeemer, the Holy One of Israel;
I have sent him, the Lord thy God
who teacheth thee to profit, who
[b]leadeth thee by the way thou
shouldst go, hath done it.
18 O that thou hadst hearkened to
my [a]commandments—then had thy
[b]peace been as a river, and thy
righteousness as the waves of the
sea.
19 Thy [a]seed also had been as the
sand; the offspring of thy bowels like
the gravel thereof; his name should
not have been cut off nor destroyed
from before me.
20 [a]Go ye forth of Babylon, flee ye
from the [b]Chaldeans, with a voice of
singing declare ye, tell this, utter to
the end of the earth; say ye: The

5*a* TG God, Omniscience of; Idolatry.
6*a* 1 Cor. 9: 16.
8*a* Ps. 58: 3.
9*a* 1 Sam. 12: 22; Ps. 23: 3; 1 Jn. 2: 12.
10*a* Ex. 1: 11 (10–11); 1 Ne. 17: 25. TG Affliction.
11*a* Jer. 44: 26.
b Isa. 42: 8; Moses 4: 1 (1–4).
12*a* Rev. 1: 17; 22: 13. TG Jesus Christ, Firstborn; Jesus Christ—Jehovah.
13*a* Ps. 102: 25. TG God the Father—Jehovah; Jesus Christ, Creator.
b Ps. 148: 8 (5–10).
14*a* 1 Kgs. 8: 56; D&C 64: 31; 76: 3.
b TG Babylon.
15*a* Isa. 45: 1 (1–4).
16*a* Isa. 45: 19.
b TG God, Spirit of.
17*a* TG Jesus Christ—Jehovah.
b TG Guidance, Divine.
18*a* Eccl. 8: 5.
b TG Israel, Blessings of; Peace of God.
19*a* Gen. 22: 17 (15–19); Isa. 48: 19 (18–22); Hosea 1: 10.
20*a* Jer. 51: 6 (6, 44–45); D&C 133: 5 (5–14).
b TG Israel, Bondage of, in Other Lands.

[Between 588 and 570 B.C.]

Lord hath redeemed his [c]servant
Jacob.
21 And they [a]thirsted not; he led
them through the deserts; he caused
the waters to flow out of the [b]rock
for them; he clave the rock also and
the waters gushed out.
22 And notwithstanding he hath
done all this, and greater also, there is
no [a]peace, saith the Lord, unto the
wicked.

CHAPTER 21

Messiah shall be a light to the Gentiles and shall free the prisoners—Israel shall be gathered with power in the last days—Kings shall be their nursing fathers—Compare Isaiah 49.

[a]AND again: Hearken, O ye house
of Israel, all ye that are broken off
and are driven out because of the
wickedness of the pastors of my
people; yea, all ye that are broken
off, that are scattered abroad, who
are of my people, O house of Israel.
Listen, O [b]isles, unto me, and hearken ye people from [c]far; the Lord
hath called me from the womb; from
the bowels of my mother hath he
made mention of my name.
2 And he hath made my mouth like
a sharp sword; in the shadow of his
hand hath he hid me, and made me a
polished shaft; in his quiver hath he
hid me;
3 And said unto me: Thou art my
[a]servant, O Israel, in whom I will be
glorified.
4 Then I said, I have labored in
[a]vain, I have spent my strength for
naught and in vain; surely my judgment is with the Lord, and my work
with my God.
5 And now, saith the Lord—that
[a]formed me from the womb that I
should be his servant, to bring Jacob
again to him—though Israel be not
gathered, yet shall I be glorious in
the eyes of the Lord, and my God
shall be my [b]strength.
6 And he said: It is a light thing
that thou shouldst be my servant to
raise up the [a]tribes of Jacob, and to
restore the preserved of Israel. I will
also give thee for a [b]light to the
[c]Gentiles, that thou mayest be my
salvation unto the ends of the earth.
7 Thus saith the Lord, the Redeemer of Israel, his Holy One, to
him whom man despiseth, to him
whom the nations abhorreth, to
servant of rulers: Kings shall see and
arise, princes also shall worship, because of the Lord that is faithful.
8 Thus saith the Lord: In an acceptable time have I heard thee, O
isles of the sea, and in a day of salvation have I helped thee; and I will
preserve thee, and give thee [a]my
servant for a covenant of the people,
to establish the earth, to cause to
inherit the desolate heritages;
9 That thou mayest say to the
[a]prisoners: Go forth; to them that
sit in [b]darkness: Show yourselves.
They shall feed in the ways, and
their [c]pastures shall be in all high
places.
10 They shall not hunger nor thirst,
neither shall the heat nor the sun
smite them; for he that hath mercy
on them shall lead them, even by the
springs of water shall he guide them.
11 And I will make all my mountains a way, and my [a]highways shall
be exalted.

20*c* Isa. 44: 1 (1–2, 21); 45: 4.
21*a* Ps. 107: 33 (33–37); Isa. 41: 18 (17–20).
b Ex. 17: 6; Num. 20: 11; 1 Ne. 17: 29; 2 Ne. 25: 20; D&C 133: 26 (26–30).
22*a* Rom. 3: 17. TG Peace of God.
21 1*a* Isa. 49: 1 (1–26).
b 1 Ne. 22: 4; 2 Ne. 10: 21 (20–22).
c D&C 1: 1.
3*a* Lev. 25: 55; Isa. 41: 8; D&C 93: 46 (45–46).
4*a* Isa. 55: 2 (1–2).
5*a* Isa. 44: 24.
b TG Strength.
6*a* TG Israel, Twelve Tribes of.
b Ezek. 5: 5; D&C 103: 9 (8–9); Abr. 2: 11 (6–11).
c 3 Ne. 21: 11. TG Israel, Mission of.
8*a* 2 Ne. 3: 11 (6–15); 3 Ne. 21: 11 (8–11); Morm. 8: 16 (16, 25).
9*a* TG Salvation for the Dead; Spirits in Prison.
b 2 Ne. 3: 5.
c Ezek. 34: 14; 1 Ne. 22: 25.
11*a* Isa. 62: 10; D&C 133: 27 (23–32). TG Jesus Christ, Second Coming.

[Between 588 and 570 B.C.]

12 And then, O house of Israel,
behold, [a]these shall come from far;
and lo, these from the north and
from the west; and these from the
land of Sinim.
13 [a]Sing, O heavens; and be joyful,
O earth; for the feet of those who
are in the east shall be established;
and [b]break forth into singing, O
mountains; for they shall be smitten
no more; for the Lord hath comforted his people, and will have
mercy upon his [c]afflicted.
14 But, behold, Zion hath said:
The Lord hath forsaken me, and
my Lord hath forgotten me—but he
will show that he hath not.
15 For can a [a]woman forget her
sucking child, that she should not
have [b]compassion on the son of her
womb? Yea, they may [c]forget, yet
will I not forget thee, O house of
Israel.
16 Behold, I have graven thee upon
the [a]palms of my hands; thy walls
are continually before me.
17 Thy children shall make haste
against thy destroyers; and they
that made thee [a]waste shall go forth
of thee.
18 Lift up thine eyes round about
and behold; all these [a]gather themselves together, and they shall come
to thee. And as I live, saith the Lord,
thou shalt surely clothe thee with
them all, as with an ornament, and
bind them on even as a bride.
19 For thy waste and thy desolate
places, and the land of thy destruction, shall even now be too narrow
by reason of the inhabitants; and
they that swallowed thee up shall be
far away.
20 The children whom thou shalt
have, after thou hast lost the first,
shall [a]again in thine ears say: The
place is too strait for me; give place
to me that I may dwell.
21 Then shalt thou say in thine
heart: Who hath begotten me these,
seeing I have lost my children, and
am [a]desolate, a captive, and remov-
ing to and fro? And who hath
brought up these? Behold, I was
left alone; these, where have they
been?
22 Thus saith the Lord God: Behold, I will lift up mine hand to the
[a]Gentiles, and set up my [b]standard
to the people; and they shall bring
thy sons in their [c]arms, and thy
daughters shall be carried upon their
shoulders.
23 And [a]kings shall be thy [b]nursing
fathers, and their queens thy nursing mothers; they shall bow down to
thee with their face towards the
earth, and lick up the dust of thy
feet; and thou shalt know that I
am the Lord; for they shall not be
ashamed that [c]wait for me.
24 For shall the prey be taken from
the mighty, or the [a]lawful captives
delivered?
25 But thus saith the Lord, even
the captives of the mighty shall be
taken away, and the prey of the
terrible shall be delivered; for I will
contend with him that contendeth
with thee, and I will save thy
children.
26 And I will [a]feed them that

12*a* Isa. 43: 5 (5–7).
13*a* Isa. 44: 23.
b TG Earth, Renewal of.
c 2 Sam. 22: 28; Ps. 18: 27; Isa. 49: 13.
15*a* TG Woman.
b Ps. 103: 13.
c 2 Kgs. 17: 38; Isa. 41: 17 (15–17); Alma 46: 8; D&C 61: 36; 133: 2.
16*a* Zech. 13: 6.
17*a* 3 Ne. 21: 13 (12–20).
18*a* Micah 4: 11 (11–13).
20*a* TG Israel, Gathering of.
21*a* Isa. 54: 1; Gal. 4: 27.
22*a* Isa. 66: 19 (18–20). TG Israel, Mission of.
b Isa. 11: 12 (10–12); 18: 3; Zech. 9: 16.
c 1 Ne. 22: 8; 2 Ne. 10: 8 (8–9).
23*a* Isa. 60: 16 (14–16).
b 1 Ne. 22: 6.
c Gen. 49: 18; Prov. 27: 18; 2 Ne. 6: 13; D&C 98: 2; 133: 11 (10–11, 45).
24*a* IE the covenant people of the Lord. See also v. 25. JST Isa. 49: 25 reads: "But thus saith the Lord; even the captives of the mighty shall be taken away, and the prey of the terrible shall be delivered, for the mighty God shall deliver his covenant people. . ."
26*a* 1 Ne. 14: 17 (15–17); 22: 13 (13–14); 2 Ne. 6: 14 (14–18).

[Between 588 and 570 B.C.]

oppress thee with their own flesh;
they shall be drunken with their
own blood as with sweet wine; and
all flesh shall [b]know that I, the Lord,
am thy [c]Savior and thy Redeemer,
the [d]Mighty One of Jacob.

CHAPTER 22

Israel shall be scattered upon all the face of the earth—The gentiles shall nurse and nourish Israel with the gospel in the last days—Israel shall be gathered and saved, and the wicked shall burn as stubble—The kingdom of the devil shall be destroyed, and Satan shall be bound.

AND now it came to pass that after
I, Nephi, had read these things
which were engraven upon the
[a]plates of brass, my brethren came
unto me and said unto me: What
[b]meaneth these things which ye have
read? Behold, are they to be understood according to things which are
[c]spiritual, which shall come to pass
according to the spirit and not the
flesh?
2 And I, Nephi, said unto them:
Behold they were [a]manifest unto
the prophet by the voice of the
[b]Spirit; for by the Spirit are all
things made known unto the
[c]prophets, which shall come upon
the children of men according to
the flesh.
3 Wherefore, the things of which I
have read are things pertaining to
things both [a]temporal and spiritual;
for it appears that the house of
Israel, sooner or later, will be [b]scat-
tered upon all the face of the earth,
and also [c]among all nations.
4 And behold, there are many who
are already lost from the knowledge of those who are at Jerusalem.
Yea, the more part of all the [a]tribes
have been [b]led away; and they are
[c]scattered to and fro upon the [d]isles
of the sea; and whither they are
none of us knoweth, save that we
know that they have been led away.
5 And since they have been led
away, these things have been
prophesied concerning them, and
also concerning all those who shall
hereafter be scattered and be confounded, because of the Holy One
of Israel; for against him will they
[a]harden their hearts; wherefore,
they shall be scattered among all
nations and shall be [b]hated of all
men.
6 Nevertheless, after they shall be
[a]nursed by the [b]Gentiles, and the
Lord has lifted up his hand upon
the Gentiles and set them up for a
standard, and their [c]children have
been carried in their arms, and their
daughters have been carried upon
their shoulders, behold these things
of which are spoken are temporal;
for thus are the covenants of the
Lord with our fathers; and it meaneth us in the days to come, and also
all our brethren who are of the
house of Israel.
7 And it meaneth that the time
cometh that after all the house of
Israel have been scattered and confounded, that the Lord God will
raise up a mighty nation among the
[a]Gentiles, yea, even upon the face
of this land; and by them shall our
seed be [b]scattered.
8 And after our seed is scattered the

26*b* Ezek. 26: 6; Mosiah 11: 22 (20–22).
c TG Jesus Christ, Savior.
d TG Jesus Christ—Jehovah.
22 1*a* 1 Ne. 19: 22; 2 Ne. 4: 2.
b TG Interpretation.
c TG Spiritual.
2*a* 2 Pet. 1: 21 (19–21).
b TG God, Spirit of.
c TG Prophecy.
3*a* D&C 29: 34 (31–34).
b 1 Ne. 10: 12 (12–14); 2 Ne. 25: 15 (14–16). TG Israel, Scattering of.
c TG Inspiration.
4*a* TG Israel, Ten Lost Tribes of.
b 2 Ne. 10: 22.
c Ps. 107: 4; Zech. 2: 6.
d Isa. 51: 5; 1 Ne. 21: 1; 2 Ne. 10: 8 (8, 20).
5*a* TG Hardheartedness.
b Luke 23: 28–31; 1 Ne. 19: 14.
6*a* 1 Ne. 21: 23.
b TG Gentiles.
c 1 Ne. 15: 13; 2 Ne. 30: 3 (1–7).
7*a* 3 Ne. 20: 27.
b Isa. 18: 7; 1 Ne. 13: 14 (12–14); 2 Ne. 1: 11.

[Between 588 and 570 B.C.]

Lord God will proceed to do a
[a]marvelous work among the [b]Gen-
tiles, which shall be of great [c]worth
unto our seed; wherefore, it is
likened unto their being nourished
by the [d]Gentiles and being carried
in their arms and upon their
shoulders.
9 And it shall also be of [a]worth unto
the Gentiles; and not only unto the
Gentiles but [b]unto all the [c]house of
Israel, unto the making known of the
[d]covenants of the Father of heaven
unto Abraham, saying: In thy [e]seed
shall all the kindreds of the earth be
[f]blessed.
10 And I would, my brethren, that
ye should know that all the kindreds
of the earth cannot be blessed unless
he shall make [a]bare his arm in the
eyes of the nations.
11 Wherefore, the Lord God will
proceed to make bare his arm in the
eyes of all the [a]nations, in bringing
about his covenants and his gospel
unto those who are of the house of
Israel.
12 Wherefore, he will [a]bring them
again out of [b]captivity, and they
shall be [c]gathered together to the
lands of their [d]inheritance; and they
shall be [e]brought out of obscurity
and out of [f]darkness; and they shall
know that the [g]Lord is their [h]Savior
and their Redeemer, the [i]Mighty
One of Israel.
13 And the blood of that great and
[a]abominable church, which is the
whore of all the earth, shall turn
upon their own heads; for they shall
[b]war among themselves, and the
sword of their [c]own hands shall fall
upon their own heads, and they
shall be drunken with their own
blood.
14 And every [a]nation which shall
war against thee, O house of Israel,
shall be turned one against another,
and they shall [b]fall into the pit
which they digged to ensnare the
people of the Lord. And all that
[c]fight against Zion shall be destroyed,
and that great whore, who hath
perverted the right ways of the Lord,
yea, that great and abominable
church, shall tumble to the [d]dust and
great shall be the fall of it.
15 For behold, saith the prophet,
the time cometh speedily that Satan
shall have no more power over the
hearts of the children of men; for
the day soon cometh that all the
proud and they who do wickedly
shall be as [a]stubble; and the day
cometh that they must be [b]burned.
16 For the time soon cometh that
the fulness of the [a]wrath of God shall
be poured out upon all the children

8*a* Isa. 29: 14; 1 Ne. 14: 7; 2 Ne. 27: 26. TG Restoration of the Gospel.
b 2 Ne. 10: 10; 3 Ne. 16: 6 (4–7); Morm. 5: 19.
c 1 Ne. 15: 14 (13–18); Jacob 3: 6; 3 Ne. 5: 23 (21–26); 21: 7 (4–29).
d TG Mission of Latter-day Saints.
9*a* 1 Ne. 14: 5 (1–5); 2 Ne. 28: 2.
b 1 Ne. 15: 13 (13–17); 2 Ne. 30: 3 (1–7).
c 2 Ne. 29: 14 (13–14).
d Deut. 4: 31.
e TG Abrahamic Covenant; Seed of Abraham.
f Gen. 12: 2; 3 Ne. 20: 25 (25, 27).
10*a* Isa. 52: 10.
11*a* TG Israel, Mission of.
12*a* Ps. 80: 19 (17–19); D&C 35: 25.
b 1 Ne. 21: 25 (24–25).
c TG Israel, Gathering of.
d TG Lands of Inheritance.
e TG Israel, Restoration of.
f TG Darkness, Spiritual.
g 1 Ne. 19: 15; 2 Ne. 6: 11 (10–15).
h TG Jesus Christ, Prophecies about; Jesus Christ, Savior.
i TG Jesus Christ—Jehovah.
13*a* Rev. 17: 16 (16–17). TG Devil, Church of.
b 1 Ne. 14: 16 (3, 15–17); 2 Ne. 6: 15. TG War.
c 1 Ne. 21: 26 (24–26).
14*a* Luke 21: 10.
b Ps. 7: 15; Prov. 26: 27; 28: 10; Isa. 60: 12; Zech. 12: 9; 1 Ne. 14: 3; 2 Ne. 28: 8; D&C 109: 25.
c 2 Ne. 10: 13; 27: 3 (2–3); Morm. 8: 41 (40–41); D&C 136: 36. TG Protection, Divine.
d Isa. 25: 12.
15*a* Joel 2: 5; Mal. 4: 1; 2 Ne. 15: 24; 26: 6 (4–6); D&C 64: 24 (23–24); 133: 64.
b Ps. 21: 9 (8–10); 3 Ne. 25: 1; D&C 29: 9. TG Earth, Cleansing of.
16*a* 1 Ne. 14: 17; 3 Ne. 20: 20 (19–21).

[Between 588 and 570 B.C.]

of men; for he will not suffer that the
wicked shall destroy the righteous.
17 Wherefore, he will [a]preserve the
[b]righteous by his power, even if it
so be that the fulness of his wrath
must come, and the righteous be
preserved, even unto the destruction
of their enemies by fire. Wherefore,
the righteous need not fear; for thus
saith the prophet, they shall be
saved, even if it so be as by fire.
18 Behold, my brethren, I say unto
you, that these things must shortly
come; yea, even blood, and fire, and
vapor of smoke must come; and it
must needs be upon the face of this
earth; and it cometh unto men
according to the flesh if it so be that
they will harden their hearts against
the Holy One of Israel.
19 For behold, the righteous shall
not perish; for the time surely must
come that all they who fight against
Zion shall be cut off.
20 And the Lord will surely [a]pre-
pare a way for his people, unto the
fulfilling of the words of Moses,
which he spake, saying: A [b]prophet
shall the Lord your God raise up
unto you, like unto me; him shall ye
hear in all things whatsoever he shall
say unto you. And it shall come to
pass that all those who will not hear
that prophet shall be [c]cut off from
among the people.
21 And now I, Nephi, declare unto
you, that this [a]prophet of whom
Moses spake was the Holy One of
Israel; wherefore, he shall execute
[b]judgment in righteousness.
22 And the righteous need not fear,
for they are those who shall not be
confounded. But it is the kingdom
of the devil, which shall be built up
among the children of men, which
kingdom is established among them
which are in the flesh—
23 For the time speedily shall come
that all [a]churches which are built up
to get gain, and all those who are
built up to get power over the flesh,
and those who are built up to become [b]popular in the eyes of the
world, and those who seek the lusts
of the flesh and the things of the
world, and to do all manner of
iniquity; yea, in fine, all those who
belong to the kingdom of the [c]devil
are they who need fear, and tremble,
and [d]quake; they are those who must
be brought low in the dust; they
are those who must be [e]consumed as
stubble; and this is according to the
words of the prophet.
24 And the time cometh speedily
that the righteous must be led up as
[a]calves of the stall, and the Holy
One of Israel must reign in dominion,
and might, and power, and great
[b]glory.
25 And he [a]gathereth his children
from the four quarters of the earth;
and he numbereth his [b]sheep, and
they know him; and there shall be
one fold and one shepherd; and he
shall feed his sheep, and in him they
shall find [c]pasture.
26 And because of the [a]righteous-
ness of his people, [b]Satan has no
power; wherefore, he cannot be
loosed for the space of [c]many years;
for he hath no power over the hearts

17*a* 2 Ne. 30: 10; 3 Ne. 22: 13 (13–17); Moses 7: 61. TG Protection, Divine.
b Ps. 55: 22; 1 Ne. 17: 35 (33–38).
20*a* TG Millennium, Preparing a People for.
b John 4: 19; 7: 40.
c D&C 133: 63.
21*a* Deut. 18: 15 (15–19); Acts 3: 22 (20–23); 1 Ne. 10: 4; 3 Ne. 20: 23; Moses 1: 6. TG Jesus Christ, Prophecies about.
b Ps. 98: 9; Moses 6: 57. TG Jesus Christ, Judge.
23*a* 1 Ne. 14: 10 (9–10); 2 Ne. 26: 20. TG Covetousness; Priestcraft.
b Luke 6: 26; Alma 1: 3.
c 1 Ne. 13: 6.
d 2 Ne. 28: 19.
e Zeph. 1: 2 (2–3); 2 Ne. 26: 6.
24*a* Mal. 4: 2; 3 Ne. 25: 2.
b TG Jesus Christ, Glory of.
25*a* Isa. 43: 6 (5–7); Eph. 1: 10. TG Israel, Gathering of.
b TG Jesus Christ, Good Shepherd; Sheep; Shepherd.
c 1 Ne. 21: 9.
26*a* TG Millennium; Righteousness.
b Rev. 20: 2; Alma 48: 17 (16–17); D&C 43: 31; 45: 55; 88: 110; 101: 28. TG Devil.
c Jacob 5: 76.

[Between 588 and 570 B.C.]

of the people, for they dwell in righteousness, and the Holy One of Israel [d]reigneth.

27 And now behold, I, Nephi, say unto you that all these things must come [a]according to the flesh.

28 But, behold, all nations, kindreds, tongues, and people shall dwell safely in the Holy One of Israel if it so be that they will [a]repent.

29 And now I, Nephi, make an end; for I durst not speak further as yet concerning these things.

30 Wherefore, my brethren, I would that ye should consider that the things which have been written upon the [a]plates of brass are true; and they testify that a man must be obedient to the commandments of God.

31 Wherefore, ye need not suppose that I and my father are the only ones that have testified, and also taught them. Wherefore, if ye shall be obedient to the [a]commandments, and endure to the end, ye shall be saved at the last day. And thus it is. Amen.

THE SECOND BOOK OF NEPHI

An account of the death of Lehi. Nephi's brethren rebel against him. The Lord warns Nephi to depart into the wilderness. His journeyings in the wilderness, and so forth.

CHAPTER 1

Lehi prophesies of a land of liberty—His seed shall be scattered and smitten if they reject the Holy One of Israel—He exhorts his sons to put on the armor of righteousness.

AND now it came to pass that after I, Nephi, had made an end of teaching my brethren, our [a]father, Lehi, also spake many things unto them, and rehearsed unto them, how great things the Lord had done for them in bringing them out of the land of Jerusalem.

2 And he spake unto them concerning their [a]rebellions upon the waters, and the mercies of God in sparing their lives, that they were not swallowed up in the sea.

3 And he also spake unto them concerning the land of promise, which they had obtained—how [a]merciful the Lord had been in [b]warning us that we should flee out of the land of Jerusalem.

4 For, behold, said he, I have [a]seen a [b]vision, in which I know that [c]Jerusalem is [d]destroyed; and had we remained in Jerusalem we should also have [e]perished.

5 But, said he, notwithstanding our afflictions, we have obtained a [a]land of promise, a land which is [b]choice above all other lands; a land which the Lord God hath [c]covenant-

26*d* TG Jesus Christ, Millennial Reign.
27*a* IE these things pertain to this mortal world.
28*a* TG Repentance; Forgiveness.
30*a* 1 Ne. 19: 22; 2 Ne. 4: 2.
31*a* Matt. 19: 17. TG Commandments of God.

[2 NEPHI]
1 1*a* TG Patriarch.
2*a* Isa. 65: 2 (1–5); 1 Ne. 18: 9 (9–20); Alma 18: 38.
3*a* Gen. 19: 16.
b TG Warnings.
4*a* 1 Ne. 17: 14.
b TG Vision.
c Jer. 26: 18 (17–19); 1 Ne. 1: 4 (4–18); Hel. 8: 20. TG Jerusalem.
d Jer. 44: 2.
e Alma 9: 22.
5*a* TG Promised Lands.
b Ether 2: 10 (7–12).
c TG Vows.

[Between 588 and 570 B.C.]

ed with me should be a land for the
inheritance of my seed. Yea, the Lord
hath [d]covenanted this land unto me,
and to my children forever, and also
all those who should be [e]led out of
other countries by the hand of the
Lord.
6 Wherefore, I, Lehi, prophesy
according to the workings of the
Spirit which is in me, that there
shall [a]none come into this land save
they shall be brought by the hand of
the Lord.
7 Wherefore, this [a]land is consecrated unto him whom he shall
bring. And if it so be that they shall
serve him according to the commandments which he hath given, it
shall be a land of [b]liberty unto them;
wherefore, they shall never be
brought down into captivity; if so,
it shall be because of iniquity; for if
iniquity shall abound [c]cursed shall be
the land for their sakes, but unto the
righteous it shall be blessed forever.
8 And behold, it is wisdom that this
land should be [a]kept as yet from
the knowledge of other [b]nations; for
behold, many nations would overrun the land, that there would be no
place for an inheritance.
9 Wherefore, I, Lehi, have obtained
a [a]promise, that [b]inasmuch as those
whom the Lord God shall bring out
of the land of Jerusalem shall keep
his commandments, they shall
[c]prosper upon the face of this land;
and they shall be kept from all other
nations, that they may possess this
land unto themselves. And if it so
be that they shall [d]keep his commandments they shall be blessed
upon the face of this land, and there
shall be none to molest them, nor to
take away the land of their [e]in-
heritance; and they shall dwell safely
forever.
10 But behold, when the time
cometh that they shall dwindle in
[a]unbelief, after they have received
so great blessings from the hand of
the Lord—having a knowledge of
the creation of the earth, and all
men, knowing the great and marvelous works of the Lord from the
creation of the world; having power
given them to do all things by faith;
having all the commandments from
the beginning, and having been
brought by his infinite goodness into
this precious land of promise—
behold, I say, if the day shall come
that they will reject the Holy One
of Israel, the true [b]Messiah, their
Redeemer and their God, behold,
the judgments of him that is [c]just
shall rest upon them.
11 Yea, he will bring [a]other nations
unto them, and he will give unto
them power, and he will take away
from them the lands of their possessions, and he will cause them to be
[b]scattered and smitten.
12 Yea, as one generation passeth
to another there shall be [a]blood-
sheds, and great visitations among
them; wherefore, my sons, I would
that ye would remember; yea, I
would that ye would hearken unto
my words.
13 O that ye would awake; awake
from a deep [a]sleep, yea, even from
the sleep of [b]hell, and shake off the
awful [c]chains by which ye are bound,
which are the chains which bind the
children of men, that they are carried away captive down to the
eternal [d]gulf of misery and woe.

5*d* TG Covenants.
e Ezra 8: 22.
6*a* 2 Ne. 10: 22.
7*a* Mosiah 29: 32; Alma 46: 10 (10–28, 34).
b 2 Ne. 10: 11. TG Liberty.
c Alma 45: 16 (10–14, 16); Morm. 1: 17; Ether 2: 11 (8–12).
8*a* 3 Ne. 5: 20.
b TG Nations.
9*a* Jacob 1: 5.
b 2 Ne. 4: 4; Alma 9: 13.
c Deut. 29: 9; 30: 9.
d TG Obedience.
e TG Inheritance.
10*a* TG Unbelief, Unbelievers.
b TG Jesus Christ, Messiah.
c TG Justice.
11*a* 1 Ne. 13: 14 (12–20); Morm. 5: 19 (19–20).
b 1 Ne. 22: 7.
12*a* Morm. 1: 11 (11–19); 4: 1 (1–23); D&C 87: 6 (1–6).
13*a* TG Sleep.
b TG Damnation.
c Isa. 58: 6; Alma 12: 11 (9–11). TG Bondage, Spiritual.
d 1 Ne. 12: 18; 15: 28 (28–30); Alma 26: 20 (19–20); Hel. 3: 29.

[Between 588 and 570 B.C.]

14 Awake! and arise from the dust,
and hear the words of a trembling
[a]parent, whose limbs ye must soon
lay down in the cold and silent
[b]grave, from whence no traveler can
[c]return; a few more [d]days and I go
the [e]way of all the earth.
15 But behold, the Lord hath [a]re-
deemed my soul from hell; I have
beheld his [b]glory, and I am encircled
about eternally in the [c]arms of his
[d]love.
16 And I desire that ye should
remember to observe the [a]statutes
and the judgments of the Lord; behold, this hath been the anxiety of
my soul from the beginning.
17 My heart hath been weighed
down with sorrow from time to
time, for I have feared, lest for the
hardness of your hearts the Lord
your God should come out in the
fulness of his [a]wrath upon you, that
ye be [b]cut off and destroyed forever;
18 Or, that a [a]cursing should come
upon you for the space of [b]many
generations; and ye are visited by
sword, and by famine, and are hated,
and are led according to the will and
captivity of the [c]devil.
19 O my sons, that these things
might not come upon you, but that
ye might be a choice and a [a]favored
people of the Lord. But behold, his
will be done; for his [b]ways are
righteousness forever.
20 And he hath said that: [a]Inas-
much as ye shall keep my [b]com-
mandments ye shall [c]prosper in the
land; but inasmuch as ye will not
keep my commandments ye shall be
cut off from my presence.
21 And now that my soul might
have joy in you, and that my heart
might leave this world with gladness
because of you, that I might not be
brought down with grief and sorrow
to the grave, arise from the dust,
my sons, and be [a]men, and be
determined in [b]one mind and in one
heart, united in all things, that ye
may not come down into captivity;
22 That ye may not be [a]cursed with
a sore cursing; and also, that ye may
not incur the displeasure of a [b]just
God upon you, unto the destruction,
yea, the eternal destruction of both
soul and body.
23 Awake, my sons; put on the
armor of [a]righteousness. Shake off
the [b]chains with which ye are bound,
and come forth out of obscurity, and
arise from the dust.
24 Rebel no more against your
brother, whose views have been
[a]glorious, and who hath kept the
commandments from the time that
we left Jerusalem; and who hath
been an instrument in the hands of
God, in bringing us forth into the
land of promise; for were it not for
him, we must have perished with
[b]hunger in the wilderness; nevertheless, ye sought to [c]take away his

---

14*a* TG Family, Love within.
b TG Death.
c Job 10: 21.
d Gen. 47: 29 (28–29); Jacob 1: 9.
e Josh. 23: 14; 1 Kgs. 2: 2.
15*a* Alma 36: 28. TG Jesus Christ, Atonement through.
b Ex. 24: 16; Lev. 9: 6 (6, 23); Ether 12: 6 (6–18). TG Jesus Christ, Glory of.
c Isa. 59: 16; Jacob 6: 5; Alma 5: 33; 3 Ne. 9: 14.
d Rom. 8: 39. TG God, Love of.
16*a* Deut. 4: 6 (5–8); Ezek. 20: 11; 2 Ne. 5: 10 (10–11).
17*a* 1 Ne. 2: 23; 2 Ne. 5: 21 (21–24); Alma 3: 6 (6–19). TG God, Indignation of.
b Gen. 6: 13; 1 Ne. 17: 31; Mosiah 12: 8; 3 Ne. 9: 9.
18*a* TG Curse.
b 1 Ne. 12: 21 (20–23).
c Rev. 12: 9 (7–9); Moses 1: 12. TG Devil.
19*a* TG Peculiar People.
b Hosea 14: 9.
20*a* Jarom 1: 9; Omni 1: 6; Mosiah 1: 7; Alma 9: 13 (13–14); 36: 30; 37: 13; 3 Ne. 5: 22.
b Lev. 26: 3 (3–14); Joel 2: 25 (23–26); Amos 5: 4 (4–8); Mosiah 26: 30.
c Ps. 67: 6; Prov. 22: 4 (4–5); Mosiah 2: 24 (21–25).
21*a* 1 Sam. 4: 9; 1 Kgs. 2: 2.
b Moses 7: 18.
22*a* TG Curse.
b D&C 3: 4. TG Justice.
23*a* TG Righteousness.
b TG Bondage, Spiritual.
24*a* 1 Ne. 18: 3.
b 1 Ne. 16: 32.
c 1 Ne. 16: 37.

[Between 588 and 570 B.C.]

life; yea, and he hath suffered much sorrow because of you.

25 And I exceedingly fear and tremble because of you, lest he shall suffer again; for behold, ye have [a]accused him that he sought power and [b]authority over you; but I know that he hath not sought for power nor authority over you, but he hath sought the glory of God, and your own eternal welfare.

26 And ye have murmured because he hath been plain unto you. Ye say that he hath used [a]sharpness; ye say that he hath been angry with you; but behold, his [b]sharpness was the sharpness of the power of the word of God, which was in him; and that which ye call anger was the truth, according to that which is in God, which he could not restrain, manifesting boldly concerning your iniquities.

27 And it must needs be that the [a]power of God must be with him, even unto his commanding you that ye must obey. But behold, it was not he, but it was the [b]Spirit of the Lord which was in him, which [c]opened his mouth to utterance that he could not shut it.

28 And now my son, Laman, and also Lemuel and Sam, and also my sons who are the sons of Ishmael, behold, if ye will hearken unto the voice of Nephi ye shall not perish. And if ye will hearken unto him I leave unto you a [a]blessing, yea, even my first blessing.

29 But if ye will not hearken unto him I take away my [a]first blessing, yea, even my blessing, and it shall rest upon him.

30 And now, Zoram, I speak unto you: Behold, thou art the [a]servant of Laban; nevertheless, thou hast been brought out of the land of Jerusalem, and I know that thou art a true [b]friend unto my son, Nephi, forever.

31 Wherefore, because thou hast been faithful thy seed shall be blessed [a]with his seed, that they dwell in prosperity long upon the face of this land; and nothing, save it shall be iniquity among them, shall harm or disturb their prosperity upon the face of this land forever.

32 Wherefore, if ye shall keep the commandments of the Lord, the Lord hath consecrated this land for the security of thy seed with the seed of my son.

CHAPTER 2

Redemption cometh through the Holy Messiah—Freedom of choice (agency) is essential to existence and progression—Adam fell that men might be—Men are free to choose liberty and eternal life.

AND now, Jacob, I speak unto you: Thou art my [a]first-born in the days of my tribulation in the wilderness. And behold, in thy childhood thou hast suffered afflictions and much sorrow, because of the rudeness of thy brethren.

2 Nevertheless, Jacob, my first-born in the wilderness, thou knowest the greatness of God; and he shall consecrate thine [a]afflictions for thy gain.

3 Wherefore, thy soul shall be blessed, and thou shalt dwell safely with thy brother, Nephi; and thy days shall be [a]spent in the service of thy God. Wherefore, I know that thou art redeemed, because of the righteousness of thy Redeemer; for thou hast [b]beheld that in the [c]fulness

---

25*a* 1 Ne. 15: 8 (8–11); Mosiah 10: 14.
b Gen. 37: 10 (9–11); 1 Ne. 2: 22.
26*a* Prov. 15: 10; 1 Ne. 16: 2.
b W of M 1: 17; Moro. 9: 4; D&C 121: 43 (41–43).
27*a* 1 Ne. 17: 48.
b D&C 121: 43.
c D&C 33: 8.
28*a* TG Birthright.
29*a* Gen. 49: 3 (3–4); D&C 68: 17; Abr. 1: 3.
30a 1 Ne. 4: 20 (20, 35).
b TG Friendship.
31*a* 2 Ne. 5: 6.
2 1*a* 1 Ne. 18: 7 (7, 19).
2*a* Micah 4: 13; 2 Ne. 32: 9. TG Affliction.
3*a* Enos 1: 1.
b 2 Ne. 11: 3.
c TG Fulness.

[Between 588 and 570 B.C.]

of time he cometh to bring salvation
unto men.
4 And thou hast [a]beheld in thy
youth his glory; wherefore, thou art
blessed even as they unto whom he
shall minister in the flesh; for the
Spirit is the same, yesterday, today,
and forever. And the way is prepared from the fall of man, and
[b]salvation is [c]free.
5 And men are instructed sufficiently that they [a]know good from
evil. And the [b]law is given unto men.
And by the law no flesh is [c]justified;
or, by the law men are [d]cut off. Yea,
by the temporal law they were cut
off; and also, by the spiritual law
they perish from that which is
good, and become miserable forever.
6 Wherefore, [a]redemption cometh
in and through the [b]Holy [c]Messiah;
for he is full of [d]grace and truth.
7 Behold, he offereth himself a
[a]sacrifice for sin, to answer the ends
of the law, unto all those who have a
broken heart and a contrite spirit;
and unto [b]none else can the [c]ends of
the law be answered.
8 Wherefore, how great the
importance to make these things
known unto the inhabitants of the
earth, that they may know that
there is no flesh that can dwell in the
presence of God, [a]save it be through
the merits, and mercy, and grace of
the Holy Messiah, who [b]layeth down
his life according to the flesh, and
taketh it again by the power of the
Spirit, that he may bring to pass the
[c]resurrection of the dead, being the
first that should rise.
9 Wherefore, he is the firstfruits
unto God, inasmuch as he shall make
[a]intercession for all the children of
men; and they that believe in him
shall be saved.
10 And because of the intercession
for [a]all, all men come unto God;
wherefore, they stand in the presence of him, to be [b]judged of him
according to the truth and [c]holiness
which is in him. Wherefore, the ends
of the law which the Holy One hath
given, unto the inflicting of the
[d]punishment which is affixed, which
punishment that is affixed is in
opposition to that of the happiness
which is affixed, to answer the ends
of the [e]atonement—
11 For it must needs be, that there
is an [a]opposition in all things. If not
so, my first-born in the wilderness,
righteousness could not be brought
to pass, neither wickedness, neither
holiness nor misery, neither good
nor bad. Wherefore, all things must
needs be a compound in one; where-

4a 2 Ne. 10: 3; Jacob 7: 5. TG Jesus Christ, Appearances, Antemortal.
b Jude 1: 3.
c TG Grace.
5a Moro. 7: 16.
b Gal. 2: 16; 3: 2; Mosiah 13: 28 (27–28).
c Rom. 3: 20 (20–24); 7: 5; 2 Ne. 25: 23; Alma 42: 14 (12–16). TG Justification.
d Lev. 7: 20 (20–21); 1 Ne. 10: 6; 2 Ne. 9: 6 (6–38); Alma 11: 42 (40–45); 12: 16 (16, 24, 36); 42: 7 (6–11); Hel. 14: 16 (15–18).
6a 1 Ne. 10: 6; 2 Ne. 25: 20; Mosiah 16: 5 (4–5); Alma 12: 22 (22–25); TG Jesus Christ, Redeemer; Redemption.
b TG Holiness.
c TG Jesus Christ, Messiah.
d John 1: 17 (14, 17); Alma 13: 9; Moses 1: 6. TG Grace.
7a TG Jesus Christ, Atonement through; Sacrifice; Self-sacrifice.
b 1 Sam. 2: 2 (1–10).
c Rom. 10: 4.
8a 2 Ne. 25: 20; 31: 21; Mosiah 4: 8; 5: 8; Alma 21: 9; 38: 9.
b TG Jesus Christ, Prophecies about.
c 1 Cor. 15: 20; Mosiah 13: 35; Alma 7: 12; 12: 25 (24–25); 42: 23. TG Jesus Christ, Resurrection.
9a Isa. 53: 12 (1–12); Mosiah 14: 12; 15: 8; Moro. 7: 28 (27–28). TG Jesus Christ, Mission of.
10a Ps. 65: 2. TG Jesus Christ, Redeemer.
b TG Jesus Christ, Judge.
c TG Holiness.
d TG Punishment.
e 2 Ne. 9: 26 (7, 21–22, 26); Alma 22: 14; 33: 22; 34: 9 (8–16). TG Atonement.
11a Job 2: 10; Matt. 5: 45; D&C 29: 39; 122: 7 (5–9); Moses 6: 55. TG Adversity; Agency; Mortality; Opposition.

[Between 588 and 570 B.C.]

fore, if it should be one body it must
needs remain as dead, having no life
neither death, nor corruption nor
incorruption, happiness nor misery,
neither sense nor insensibility.
12 Wherefore, it must needs have
been created for a thing of naught;
wherefore there would have been
no [a]purpose in the end of its creation.
Wherefore, this thing must needs
destroy the wisdom of God and his
eternal purposes, and also the power,
and the mercy, and the [b]justice of
God.
13 And if ye shall say there is [a]no
law, ye shall also say there is no sin.
If ye shall say there is no sin, ye
shall also say there is no righteousness. And if there be no righteousness there be no happiness. And
if there be no righteousness nor
happiness there be no punishment
nor misery. And if these things are
not [b]there is no God. And if there is
no God we are not, neither the earth;
for there could have been no creation
of things, neither to act nor to be
acted upon; wherefore, all things
must have vanished away.
14 And now, my sons, I speak unto
you these things for your profit and
[a]learning; for there is a God, and he
hath [b]created all things, both the
heavens and the earth, and all things
that in them are, both things to act
and things to be [c]acted upon.
15 And to bring about his eternal
[a]purposes in the end of man, after he
had [b]created our first parents, and
the beasts of the field and the [c]fowls
of the air, and in fine, all things which
are created, it must needs be that
there was an opposition; even the
[d]forbidden [e]fruit in [f]opposition to
the [g]tree of life; the one being sweet
and the other bitter.
16 Wherefore, the Lord God gave
unto man that he should [a]act for
himself. Wherefore, man could not
[b]act for himself save it should be
that he was [c]enticed by the one or
the other.
17 And I, Lehi, according to the
things which I have read, must needs
suppose that an [a]angel of God, according to that which is written,
had [b]fallen from heaven; wherefore,
he became a [c]devil, having sought
that which was evil before God.
18 And because he had fallen from
heaven, and had become miserable
forever, he [a]sought also the misery
of all mankind. Wherefore, he said
unto Eve, yea, even that old serpent,
who is the devil, who is the father of
all [b]lies, wherefore he said: Partake
of the forbidden fruit, and ye shall
not die, but ye shall be as God,
[c]knowing good and evil.
19 And after Adam and Eve had
[a]partaken of the forbidden fruit
they were driven out of the garden
of [b]Eden, to till the earth.
20 And they have brought forth

12*a* D&C 88: 25. TG Earth, Purpose of.
b TG God, Justice of.
13*a* Rom. 4: 15; 5: 13; 2 Ne. 9: 25; 11: 7.
b Alma 42: 13.
14*a* TG Learning.
b TG Creation; God, Creator; Jesus Christ, Creator.
c D&C 93: 30.
15*a* Isa. 45: 18 (17–18); Matt. 5: 48; Rom. 8: 17 (14–21); Eph. 3: 11 (7–12); Alma 42: 26; D&C 29: 43 (42–44); Moses 1: 31, 39. TG Earth, Purpose of.
b TG Man, Physical Creation of.
c Gen. 1: 20.
d Gen. 2: 17 (16–17); Moses 3: 17.
e Gen. 3: 6; Mosiah 3: 26; Alma 12: 22 (21–23).
f TG Opposition.
g Gen. 2: 9; 1 Ne. 15: 36 (22, 28, 36); Alma 12: 26 (21, 23, 26); 32: 40.
16*a* Alma 12: 31. TG Initiative.
b 2 Ne. 10: 23. TG Agency.
c D&C 29: 39 (39–40).
17*a* TG Council in Heaven.
b 2 Ne. 9: 8; Moses 4: 3 (3–4); Abr. 3: 28 (27–28). TG Sons of Perdition.
c TG Adversary; Devil; Lucifer; Satan.
18*a* Luke 22: 31; Rev. 13: 7; 2 Ne. 28: 20 (19–23); 3 Ne. 18: 18; D&C 10: 22 (22–27); 50: 3; 76: 29.
b 2 Ne. 28: 8; Moses 4: 4.
c Gen. 3: 5; Mosiah 16: 3; Alma 29: 5; Moro. 7: 16 (15–19).
19*a* Gen. 2: 17 (16–17); Alma 12: 31. TG Fall of Man.
b TG Eden.

[Between 588 and 570 B.C.]

children; yea, even the [a]family of all
the earth.
21 And the days of the children of
[a]men were prolonged, according to
the [b]will of God, that they might
[c]repent while in the flesh; wherefore,
their state became a state of [d]pro-
bation, and their time was lengthened, according to the commandments which the Lord God gave
unto the children of men. For he
gave commandment that all men
must repent; for he showed unto all
men that they were [e]lost, because of
the transgression of their parents.
22 And now, behold, if Adam had
not transgressed he would not have
fallen, but he would have remained
in the garden of Eden. And all things
which were created must have remained in the same state in which
they were after they were created;
and they must have remained forever, and had no end.
23 And they would have had no
[a]children; wherefore they would
have remained in a state of innocence, having no [b]joy, for they
knew no misery; doing no good, for
they knew no [c]sin.
24 But behold, all things have been
done in the wisdom of him who
[a]knoweth all things.
25 [a]Adam [b]fell that men might be;
and men [c]are, that they might have
[d]joy.
26 And the [a]Messiah cometh in the
fulness of time, that he may [b]redeem
the children of men from the fall.
And because that they are [c]re-
deemed from the fall they have become [d]free forever, knowing good
from evil; to act for themselves and
not to be acted upon, save it be by
the punishment of the [e]law at the
great and last day, according to the
commandments which God hath
given.
27 Wherefore, men are [a]free according to the [b]flesh; and [c]all things are
[d]given them which are expedient
unto man. And they are free to
[e]choose [f]liberty and eternal [g]life,
through the great Mediator of all
men, or to choose captivity and
death, according to the captivity
and power of the devil; for he seeketh that all men might be [h] miserable
like unto himself.
28 And now, my sons, I would that
ye should look to the great [a]Media-
tor, and hearken unto his great commandments; and be faithful unto
his words, and choose eternal life,
according to the will of his Holy
Spirit;
29 And not choose eternal death,
according to the will of the flesh and
the [a]evil which is therein, which
giveth the spirit of the devil power
to [b]captivate, to bring you down to
[c]hell, that he may reign over you in
his own kingdom.
30 I have spoken these few words
unto you all, my sons, in the last
days of my probation; and I have

20*a* 1 Cor. 15: 45 (45–48); D&C 27: 11; 138: 38; Moses 1: 34. TG Adam.
21*a* Job 14: 1; Alma 12: 24; Moses 4: 23 (22–25).
b TG God, Will of.
c Alma 34: 32. TG Repentance.
d TG Mortality; Probation.
e Jacob 7: 12.
23*a* Gen. 3: 16; Moses 5: 11. TG Family,; Marriage, Motherhood.
b TG Joy.
c TG Sin.
24*a* TG God, Foreknowledge of; God, Intelligence of; God, Omniscience of.
25*a* TG Adam.
b Moses 6: 48. TG Fall of Man.
c TG Mortality.
d Moses 5: 10. TG Joy; Man, Potential to Become like Heavenly Father.
26*a* TG Jesus Christ, Messiah.
b TG Salvation, Plan of.
c TG Redemption.
d Gal. 5: 1; Alma 41: 7; 42: 27; Hel. 14: 30.
e TG God, Law of.
27*a* Gal. 5: 1; Hel. 14: 30 (29–30); Moses 6: 56.
b TG Mortality.
c 2 Ne. 26: 24; Jacob 5: 41; Alma 26: 37.
d Alma 29: 8. TG Talents.
e TG Initiative; Opposition.
f TG Liberty.
g Deut. 30: 15.
h D&C 10: 22.
28*a* TG Jesus Christ, Mediator.
29*a* TG Evil; Sin.
b Rom. 6: 14 (14–18); 1 Ne. 14: 7; Alma 12: 11 (9–11). TG Bondage, Spiritual.
c TG Hell.

[Between 588 and 570 B.C.]

chosen the good part, according to
the words of the prophet. And I have
none other object save it be the
everlasting [a]welfare of your souls.
Amen.

CHAPTER 3

Joseph in Egypt saw the Nephites in vision—He prophesied of Joseph Smith, the latter-day seer; of Moses, who would deliver Israel; and of the coming forth of the Book of Mormon.

AND now I speak unto you, Joseph,
my [a]last-born. Thou wast born in
the wilderness of mine afflictions;
yea, in the days of my greatest
sorrow did thy mother bear thee.
2 And may the Lord consecrate
also unto thee this [a]land, which is
a most precious land, for thine inheritance and the inheritance of
thy seed with thy brethren, for thy
security forever, if it so be that ye
shall keep the commandments of the
Holy One of Israel.
3 And now, Joseph, my last-born,
whom I have brought out of the
wilderness of mine afflictions, may
the Lord bless thee forever, for thy
[a]seed shall not utterly be [b]destroyed.
4 For behold, thou art the fruit of
my loins; and I am a descendant
of [a]Joseph who was carried [b]cap-
tive into Egypt. And great were the
[c]covenants of the Lord which he
made unto Joseph.
5 Wherefore, Joseph truly [a]saw
our day. And he obtained a [b]promise
of the Lord, that out of the fruit of
his loins the Lord God would raise
up a [c]righteous [d]branch unto the
house of Israel; not the Messiah, but
a branch which was to be broken off,
nevertheless, to be remembered in
the covenants of the Lord that the
Messiah should be made [e]manifest
unto them in the latter days, in the
spirit of power, unto the bringing
of them out of [f]darkness unto light
—yea, out of hidden darkness and
out of captivity unto freedom.
6 For Joseph truly testified, saying:
A [a]seer shall the Lord my God raise
up, who shall be a choice seer unto
the fruit of my [b]loins.
7 Yea, Joseph truly said: Thus
saith the Lord unto me: A choice
[a]seer will I [b]raise up out of the fruit
of thy loins; and he shall be esteemed
highly among the fruit of thy loins.
And unto him will I give commandment that he shall do a work for
the fruit of thy loins, his brethren,
which shall be of great worth unto
them, even to the bringing of them
to the [c]knowledge of the covenants
which I have made with thy fathers.
8 And I will give unto him a commandment that he shall do [a]none
other work, save the work which I
shall command him. And I will make
him great in mine eyes; for he shall
do my work.
9 And he shall be great like unto
[a]Moses, whom I have said I would
raise up unto you, to [b]deliver my
[c]people, O house of Israel.
10 And [a]Moses will I raise up, to
deliver thy people out of the land of
Egypt.
11 But a [a]seer will I raise up out of
the fruit of thy loins; and unto him

30*a* TG Family, Children, Responsibilities toward.
3 1*a* 1 Ne. 18: 7 (7, 19).
2*a* 1 Ne. 2: 20. TG Promised Lands.
3*a* Gen. 45: 7; 1 Ne. 13: 30.
b Amos 9: 8; 2 Ne. 25: 21; 9: 53.
4*a* Gen. 39: 2; 45: 4; 49: 22 (22–26); Ps. 77: 15; 1 Ne. 5: 14 (14–16).
b Gen. 37: 36 (29–36).
c Amos 5: 15.
5*a* JST Gen. 50: 24–38; 2 Ne. 3: 22; 4: 2 (1–32).
b TG Promise.
c Jacob 2: 25.
d Gen. 45: 7 (5–7); 49: 22 (22–26); 1 Ne. 15: 12 (12, 16); 19: 24; 2 Ne. 14: 2. TG Vineyard of the Lord.
e 2 Ne. 6: 14; D&C 3: 18 (16–20).
f Isa. 42: 16; 1 Jn. 2: 8; 1 Ne. 21: 9.
6*a* 3 Ne. 21: 11 (8–11); Morm. 8: 16 (16, 25); Ether 3: 28 (21–28). TG Seer.
b D&C 132: 30.
7*a* TG Joseph Smith.
b TG Millennium, Preparing a People for.
c TG Book of Mormon.
8*a* D&C 24: 9 (8–9).
9*a* Moses 1: 41.
b Ex. 3: 10 (7–10); 1 Ne. 17: 24.
c 2 Ne. 29: 14.
10*a* TG Foreordination.
11*a* 1 Ne. 21: 8; 3 Ne. 21: 11 (8–11); Morm. 8: 16 (16, 25). TG Prophets, Mission of.

[Between 588 and 570 B.C.]

will I give [b]power to [c]bring forth my
word unto the seed of thy loins—
and not to the bringing forth my
word only, saith the Lord, but to the
convincing them of my word, which
shall have already gone forth among
them.
12 Wherefore, the fruit of thy loins
shall [a]write; and the fruit of the
loins of [b]Judah shall [c]write; and
that which shall be written by the
fruit of thy loins, and also that which
shall be written by the fruit of the
loins of Judah, shall grow together,
unto the [d]confounding of [e]false
doctrines and laying down of contentions, and establishing [f]peace
among the fruit of thy loins, and
[g]bringing them to the [h]knowledge
of their fathers in the latter days,
and also to the knowledge of my
covenants, saith the Lord.
13 And out of weakness he shall be
made strong, in that day when my
work shall commence among all my
people, unto the restoring thee, O
house of Israel, saith the Lord.
14 And thus prophesied Joseph,
saying: Behold, that seer will the
Lord bless; and they that seek to
destroy him shall be confounded;
for this promise, which I have obtained of the Lord, of the fruit of
my loins, shall be fulfilled. Behold,
I am sure of the fulfilling of this
promise;
15 And his [a]name shall be called
after me; and it shall be after the
[b]name of his father. And he shall be
[c]like unto me; for the thing, which
the Lord shall bring forth by his
hand, by the power of the Lord
shall bring [d]my people unto [e]salva-
tion.
16 Yea, thus prophesied Joseph: I
am sure of this thing, even as I am
sure of the promise of Moses; for
the Lord hath said unto me, I will
[a]preserve thy seed forever.
17 And the Lord hath said: I will
raise up a Moses; and I will give
power unto him in a rod; and I will
give judgment unto him in writing.
Yet I will not loose his tongue, that
he shall speak much, for I will not
make him mighty in speaking. But I
will [a]write unto him my law, by the
finger of mine own hand; and I will
make a [b]spokesman for him.
18 And the Lord said unto me also:
I will raise up unto the fruit of thy
loins; and I will make for him a
spokesman. And I, behold, I will
give unto him that he shall write the
writing of the fruit of thy loins, unto
the fruit of thy loins; and the
spokesman of thy loins shall declare
it.
19 And the words which he shall
write shall be the words which are
expedient in my wisdom should go
forth unto the [a]fruit of thy loins.
And it shall be as if the fruit of thy
loins had cried unto them [b]from the
dust; for I know their faith.
20 And they shall [a]cry from the
[b]dust; yea, even repentance unto
their brethren, even after many
generations have gone by them.
And it shall come to pass that their
cry shall go, even according to the
simpleness of their words.
21 Because of their faith their
[a]words shall proceed forth out of

11*b* D&C 5: 4 (3–4).
c TG Scriptures to Come Forth.
12*a* TG Book of Mormon.
b 1 Ne. 13: 23 (23–29); 2 Ne. 29: 12.
c TG Scriptures, Preservation of; Scriptures, Writing of.
d Ezek. 37: 17 (15–20); 1 Ne. 13: 39 (38–41); 2 Ne. 29: 8; 33: 10 (10–11).
e TG False Doctrine.
f TG Peacemakers.
g Moro. 1: 4.
h 1 Ne. 15: 14; 2 Ne. 30: 5; 3 Ne. 5: 23; Morm. 7: 9 (1, 5, 9–10).
15*a* D&C 18: 8.
b JS-H 1: 3.
c D&C 28: 2.
d Enos 1: 13 (12–18); Alma 37: 19 (1–20).
e TG Scriptures, Value of.
16*a* Gen. 45: 7 (1–8); D&C 107: 42.
17*a* Deut. 10: 2 (2, 4); Moses 2: 1. TG Scriptures, Writing of.
b Ex. 4: 16 (14–16).
19*a* D&C 28: 8.
b Isa. 29: 4; 2 Ne. 27: 13; 33: 13 (13–15); Morm. 9: 30; Moro. 10: 27.
20*a* 2 Ne. 26: 16; Morm. 8: 23 (23, 26).
b TG Book of Mormon.
21*a* 2 Ne. 29: 2.

[Between 588 and 570 B.C.]

my mouth unto their brethren who are the fruit of thy loins; and the weakness of their words will I make strong in their faith, unto the remembering of my covenant which I made unto thy fathers.

22 And now, behold, my son Joseph, after this manner did my father of old [a]prophesy.

23 Wherefore, because of this covenant thou art [a]blessed; for thy seed shall not be destroyed, for they shall [b]hearken unto the words of the book.

24 And there shall rise up [a]one mighty among them, who shall do much good, both in word and in deed, being an instrument in the hands of God, with exceeding faith, to work mighty wonders, and do that thing which is great in the sight of God, unto the bringing to pass much [b]restoration unto the house of Israel, and unto the seed of thy brethren.

25 And now, blessed art thou, Joseph. Behold, thou art little; wherefore hearken unto the words of thy brother, Nephi, and it shall be done unto thee even according to the words which I have spoken. Remember the words of thy dying father. Amen.

CHAPTER 4

Lehi counsels and blesses his posterity—He dies and is buried—Nephi glories in the goodness of God to him—Nephi puts his trust in the Lord forever.

AND now, I, Nephi, speak concerning the prophecies of which my father hath spoken, concerning [a]Joseph, who was carried into Egypt.

2 For behold, he truly prophesied concerning all his seed. And the [a]prophecies which he wrote, there are not many greater. And he prophesied concerning us, and our future generations; and they are written upon the [b]plates of brass.

3 Wherefore, after my father had made an end of speaking concerning the prophecies of Joseph, he called the children of Laman, his sons, and his daughters, and said unto them: Behold, my sons, and my daughters, who are the sons and the daughters of my [a]first-born, I would that ye should give ear unto my words.

4 For the Lord God hath said that: [a]Inasmuch as ye shall keep my commandments ye shall prosper in the land; and inasmuch as ye will not keep my commandments ye shall be cut off from my presence.

5 But behold, my sons and my daughters, I cannot go down to my grave save I should leave a [a]blessing upon you; for behold, I know that if ye are [b]brought up in the [c]way ye should go ye will not depart from it.

6 Wherefore, if ye are [a]cursed, behold, I leave my blessing upon you, that the [b]cursing may be taken from you and be answered upon the [c]heads of your parents.

7 Wherefore, because of my blessing the Lord God will [a]not suffer that ye shall perish; wherefore, he will be [b]merciful unto you and unto your seed forever.

8 And it came to pass that after my father had made an end of speaking to the sons and daughters of Laman, he caused the sons and daughters of Lemuel to be brought before him.

9 And he spake unto them, saying:

22*a* 2 Ne. 3: 5.
23*a* TG Birthright.
b TG Obedience.
24*a* TG Joseph Smith.
b TG Dispensations; Israel, Restoration of; Restoration of the Gospel.
4 1*a* Gen. 39: 2.
2*a* 2 Ne. 3: 5.
b 1 Ne. 22: 30; 2 Ne. 5: 12.
3*a* TG Firstborn.
4*a* 2 Ne. 1: 9; Alma 9: 13.
5*a* TG Family, Patriarchal; Patriarchal Blessings.
b TG Family, Children, Responsibilities toward.
c Prov. 22: 6.
6*a* 1 Ne. 2: 23.
b TG Curse.
c D&C 68: 25 (25–29).
7*a* 1 Ne. 22: 7 (7–8); 2 Ne. 30: 3 (3–6); Jacob 1: 5. TG Book of Mormon.
b 1 Ne. 13: 31; 2 Ne. 10: 18 (18–19); Jacob 3: 6 (5–9); Hel. 15: 12 (10–17); Morm. 5: 20 (20–21).

[Between 588 and 570 B.C.]

Behold, my sons and my daughters,
who are the sons and the daughters
of my second son; behold I leave
unto you the same blessing which I
left unto the sons and daughters of
Laman; wherefore, thou shalt not
utterly be destroyed; but in the end
thy seed shall be blessed.
10 And it came to pass that when
my father had made an end of
speaking unto them, behold, he
spake unto the sons of [a]Ishmael, yea,
and even all his household.
11 And after he had made an end
of speaking unto them, he spake
unto Sam, saying: Blessed art thou,
and thy [a]seed; for thou shalt inherit the land like unto thy brother
Nephi. And thy seed shall be
numbered with his seed; and thou
shalt be even like unto thy brother,
and thy seed like unto his seed; and
thou shalt be blessed in all thy
days.
12 And it came to pass after my
father, Lehi, had [a]spoken unto all
his household, according to the feelings of his heart and the Spirit of the
Lord which was in him, he waxed
[b]old. And it came to pass that he
died, and was buried.
13 And it came to pass that not
many days after his death, Laman
and Lemuel and the sons of Ishmael
were [a]angry with me because of the
admonitions of the Lord.
14 For I, Nephi, was constrained to
speak unto them, according to his
word; for I had spoken many things
unto them, and also my father,
before his death; many of which
sayings are written upon mine [a]other
plates; for a more history part are
written upon mine other plates.
15 And upon [a]these I [b]write the
things of my soul, and many of the
scriptures which are engraven upon
the plates of brass. For my soul
[c]delighteth in the scriptures, and
my heart [d]pondereth them, and
writeth them for the [e]learning and
the profit of my children.
16 Behold, my [a]soul delighteth in
the things of the Lord; and my
[b]heart pondereth continually upon
the things which I have seen and
heard.
17 Nevertheless, notwithstanding
the great [a]goodness of the Lord, in
showing me his great and marvelous works, my heart exclaimeth: O
[b]wretched man that I am! Yea, my
heart [c]sorroweth because of my
flesh; my soul grieveth because of
mine iniquities.
18 I am encompassed about,
because of the temptations and the
sins which do so easily [a]beset me.
19 And when I desire to rejoice,
my heart groaneth because of my
sins; nevertheless, I know in whom
I have [a]trusted.
20 My God hath been my [a]support;
he hath led me through mine
[b]afflictions in the wilderness; and he
hath preserved me upon the waters
of the great deep.
21 He hath filled me with his [a]love,
even unto the [b]consuming of my
flesh.
22 He hath confounded mine
[a]enemies, unto the causing of them
to quake before me.
23 Behold, he hath heard my cry by

10*a* 1 Ne. 7: 6.
11*a* Jacob 1: 14 (12–14).
12*a* Gen. 49: 1 (1–27).
b TG Old Age.
13*a* 1 Ne. 7: 6 (6–19); 17: 18 (17–55); 18: 10 (9–22); 2 Ne. 5: 2 (1–25). TG Anger.
14*a* 1 Ne. 1: 17 (16–17); 9: 4; 2 Ne. 5: 33 (29–33); D&C 10: 42.
15*a* 1 Ne. 6: 1 (1–6).
b TG Scriptures, Writing of.
c Ps. 119: 24; Moses 6: 59.
d TG Meditation; Scriptures, Study of.
e 1 Ne. 19: 23. TG Scriptures, Value of.
16*a* TG Spirituality; Thanksgiving.
b TG Heart.
17*a* Ex. 34: 6 (5–7); 2 Ne. 9: 10; D&C 86: 11.
b Rom. 7: 24.
c TG Poor in Spirit; Repentance; Sorrow.
18*a* Rom. 7: 21 (15–25); Heb. 12: 1; Alma 7: 15.
19*a* TG Trust in God.
20*a* 2 Cor. 4: 16.
b 1 Ne. 17: 6. TG Affliction; Comfort.
21*a* TG God, Love of.
b D&C 84: 33.
22*a* Ps. 3: 7 (7–8).

[Between 588 and 570 B.C.]

day, and he hath given me [a]knowl-
edge by [b]visions in the night-
time.
24 And by day have I waxed bold
in mighty [a]prayer before him; yea,
my voice have I sent up on high;
and angels came down and ministered unto me.
25 And upon the wings of his Spirit
hath my body been [a]carried away
upon exceedingly high mountains.
And mine eyes have beheld great
things, yea, even too great for man;
therefore I was bidden that I should
not write them.
26 O then, if I have seen so great
things, if the Lord in his condescension unto the children of men
hath [a]visited men in so much [b]mercy,
[c]why should my [d]heart weep and my
soul linger in the valley of sorrow,
and my flesh waste away, and my
strength slacken, because of mine
afflictions?
27 And why should I [a]yield to sin,
because of my flesh? Yea, why
should I give way to [b]temptations,
that the evil one have place in my
heart to destroy my [c]peace and
afflict my soul? Why am I [d]angry
because of mine enemy?
28 Awake, my soul! No longer
[a]droop in sin. Rejoice, O my heart,
and give place no more for the
[b]enemy of my soul.
29 Do not [a]anger again because of
mine enemies. Do not slacken my
strength because of mine afflictions.
30 Rejoice, O my [a]heart, and cry
unto the Lord, and say: O Lord, I
will praise thee forever; yea, my
soul will rejoice in thee, my God,
and the [b]rock of my salvation.
31 O Lord, wilt thou [a]redeem my
soul? Wilt thou deliver me out of
the hands of mine enemies? Wilt
thou make me that I may shake at
the appearance of [b]sin?
32 May the gates of hell be shut
continually before me, because that
my [a]heart is broken and my spirit is
contrite! O Lord, wilt thou not shut
the gates of thy righteousness before
me, that I may [b]walk in the path of
the low valley, that I may be strict in
the plain road!
33 O Lord, wilt thou encircle me
around in the robe of thy [a]righteous-
ness! O Lord, wilt thou make a way
for mine escape before mine [b]ene-
mies! Wilt thou make my path
straight before me! Wilt thou not
place a stumbling block in my way
—but that thou wouldst clear my
way before me, and hedge not up
my way, but the ways of mine
enemy.
34 O Lord, I have [a]trusted in thee,
and I will [b]trust in thee forever. I
will not put my [c]trust in the arm of
flesh; for I know that cursed is he
that putteth his [d]trust in the arm of
flesh. Yea, cursed is he that putteth
his trust in man or maketh flesh his
arm.
35 Yea, I know that God will give
[a]liberally to him that asketh. Yea,
my God will give me, if I [b]ask [c]not
amiss; therefore I will lift up my
voice unto thee; yea, I will cry unto
thee, my God, the [d]rock of my
[e]righteousness. Behold, my voice

23*a* TG Knowledge.
b 2 Chr. 26: 5. TG Dream; Vision.
24*a* James 5: 16; 1 Ne. 1: 5 (5–8); 10: 17.
25*a* 2 Cor. 12: 2 (1–4); 1 Ne. 11: 1 (1–36); Moses 1: 1.
26*a* Ex. 3: 16; Alma 9: 21; Morm. 1: 15.
b TG Compassion; God, Mercy of.
c Ps. 43: 5.
d TG Heart.
27*a* Rom. 6: 13 (10–16).
b TG Temptation.
c TG Contentment; Peace; Peace of God.
d TG Self-mastery.
28a Ps. 42: 11.
b TG Adversary; Enemy.
29*a* TG Anger.
30*a* TG Heart.
b 1 Cor. 3: 11 (9–13). TG Rock.
31a Ps. 16: 10.
b Rom. 12: 9; Alma 13: 12; 37: 32. TG Sin.
32*a* TG Contrite Heart.
b TG Walking with God.
33*a* TG Righteousness.
b Lev. 26: 7 (1–13); D&C 44: 5.
34*a* TG Trustworthiness.
b TG Trust in God.
c Ps. 33: 16; 44: 6 (6–8). TG Trust Not in the Arm of Flesh.
d Prov. 14: 16; Jer. 17: 5; Morm. 3: 9; 4: 8.
35*a* James 1: 5. TG Abundant Life.
b TG Prayer.
c Hel. 10: 5.
d Deut. 32: 4.
e Ps. 4: 1.

[Between 588 and 570 B.C.]

shall forever ascend up unto thee,
my rock and mine everlasting God.
Amen.

CHAPTER 5

The Nephites separate themselves from the Lamanites, keep the law of Moses, and build a temple—Because of their unbelief, the Lamanites are cursed, receive a skin of blackness, and become a scourge unto the Nephites.

BEHOLD, it came to pass that I,
Nephi, did cry much unto the Lord
my God, because of the [a]anger of
my brethren.
2 But behold, their [a]anger did increase against me, insomuch that
they did seek to take away my life.
3 Yea, they did murmur against
me, saying: Our younger brother
thinks to [a]rule over us; and we have
had much trial because of him;
wherefore, now let us slay him, that
we may not be afflicted more because
of his words. For behold, we will
not have him to be our ruler; for it
belongs unto us, who are the elder
brethren, to [b]rule over this people.
4 Now I do not write upon these
plates all the words which they
murmured against me. But it sufficeth me to say, that they did seek to
take away my life.
5 And it came to pass that the Lord
did [a]warn me, that I, [b]Nephi, should
depart from them and flee into the
wilderness, and all those who would
go with me.
6 Wherefore, it came to pass that I,
Nephi, did take my family, and also
[a]Zoram and his family, and Sam,
mine elder brother and his family,
and Jacob and Joseph, my younger
brethren, and also my sisters, and
all those who would go with me.
And all those who would go with
me were those who believed in the
[b]warnings and the revelations of
God; wherefore, they did hearken
unto my words.
7 And we did take our tents and
whatsoever things were possible for
us, and did journey in the wilderness
for the space of many days. And
after we had journeyed for the space
of many days we did pitch our tents.
8 And my people would that we
should call the name of the place
[a]Nephi; wherefore, we did call it
Nephi.
9 And all those who were with me
did take upon them to call themselves the [a]people of Nephi.
10 And we did observe to keep the
judgments, and the [a]statutes, and
the commandments of the Lord in
all things, according to the [b]law of
Moses.
11 And the Lord was with us; and
we did [a]prosper exceedingly; for we
did sow seed, and we did reap again
in abundance. And we began to
raise flocks, and herds, and animals
of every kind.
12 And I, Nephi, had also brought
the records which were engraven
upon the [a]plates of brass; and also
the [b]ball, or [c]compass, which was
prepared for my father by the hand
of the Lord, according to that which
is written.
13 And it came to pass that we
began to prosper exceedingly, and
to multiply in the land.
14 And I, Nephi, did take the
[a]sword of Laban, and after the man-

---

5 1*a* 2 Ne. 4: 13; Jacob 7: 24; Enos 1: 20; Mosiah 10: 12, 15.
2*a* 1 Ne. 7: 6 (6–19); 17: 18 (17–55); 18: 10 (9–22); 2 Ne. 4: 13 (13–14).
3*a* Num. 16: 13; 1 Ne. 16: 37 (37–38); Mosiah 10: 15.
b Alma 54: 17.
5*a* TG Guidance, Divine.
b Mosiah 10: 13.
6*a* 1 Ne. 4: 35; 16: 7; 2 Ne. 1: 31 (30–32).
b TG Warnings.
8*a* Omni 1: 12 (12, 27); Mosiah 7: 1 (1–7, 21); 9: 1 (1–6, 14); 28: 1 (1, 5); Alma 2: 24; 20: 1; 50: 8 (8, 11).
9*a* Jacob 1: 14.
10*a* Ezek. 20: 11; 2 Ne. 1: 16 (16–17).
b 2 Ne. 11: 4. TG Law of Moses.
11*a* Matt. 6: 33.
12*a* 2 Ne. 4: 2; Mosiah 1: 3 (3–4).
b Mosiah 1: 16.
c 1 Ne. 16: 16 (10, 16, 26); 18: 12 (12, 21); Alma 37: 38 (38–47); D&C 17: 1.
14*a* 1 Ne. 4: 9; Jacob 1: 10; W of M 1: 13; Mosiah 1: 16; D&C 17: 1.

[Between 588 and 570 B.C.]

ner of it did make many [b]swords,
lest by any means the people who
were now called Lamanites should
come upon us and destroy us; for
I knew their [c]hatred towards me
and my children and those who were
called my people.
15 And I did teach my people to
[a]build buildings, and to [b]work in all
[c]manner of wood, and of [d]iron, and
of copper, and of [e]brass, and of steel,
and of [f]gold, and of silver, and of
precious ores, which were in great
abundance.
16 And I, Nephi, did [a]build a
[b]temple; and I did construct it after
the manner of the temple of
[c]Solomon save it were not built of
so many [d]precious things; for they
were not to be found upon the land,
wherefore, it could not be built like
unto Solomon's [e]temple. But the
manner of the construction was like
unto the temple of [f]Solomon; and
the workmanship thereof was exceedingly fine.
17 And it came to pass that I,
Nephi, did cause my people to be
[a]industrious, and to [b]labor with their
[c]hands.
18 And it came to pass that they
would that I should be their [a]king.
But I, Nephi, was desirous that they
should have no king; nevertheless,
I did for them according to that
which was in my power.
19 And behold, the words of the
Lord had been fulfilled unto my
brethren, which he spake concerning
them, that I should be their [a]ruler
and their teacher. Wherefore, I had
been their ruler and their [b]teacher,
according to the commandments of
the Lord, until the time they sought
to take away my life.
20 Wherefore, the word of the Lord
was fulfilled which he spake unto
me, saying that: Inasmuch as they
will [a]not hearken unto thy words
they shall be [b]cut off from the
presence of the Lord. And behold,
they were [c]cut off from his presence.
21 And he had caused the [a]cursing
to come upon them, yea, even a sore
cursing, because of their iniquity.
For behold, they had hardened their
hearts against him, that they had
become like unto a flint; wherefore,
as they were white, and exceedingly
fair and [b]delightsome, that they
might not be [c]enticing unto my
people the Lord God did cause a
[d]skin of [e]blackness to come upon
them.
22 And thus saith the Lord God: I
will cause that they shall be [a]loath-
some unto thy people, save they
shall repent of their iniquities.
23 And cursed shall be the seed of
him that [a]mixeth with their seed;
for they shall be cursed even with
the same cursing. And the Lord
spake it, and it was done.
24 And because of their [a]cursing
which was upon them they did
become an [b]idle people, full of

14*b* Jarom 1: 8; Mosiah 10: 8; Alma 2: 12; Hel. 1: 14; 3 Ne. 3: 26.
c TG Hate.
15*a* TG Skill.
b TG Art.
c Jarom 1: 8.
d Josh. 8: 31; 1 Ne. 18: 25; Jacob 2: 12 (12–13); Hel. 6: 9 (9–11); Ether 9: 17; 10: 23 (12, 23); Moses 5: 46.
e Gen. 4: 22.
f Ex. 31: 4 (4–5); 1 Kgs. 6: 21 (21–22); D&C 124: 26 (26–27).
16*a* 2 Chr. 3: 1 (1–17); D&C 84: 5 (5, 31); 124: 31 (25–55).
b 1 Kgs. 5: 5; Jacob 1: 17; Mosiah 1: 18; 7: 17; 11: 10; Alma 16: 13; Hel. 3: 14 (9, 14); 3 Ne. 11: 1. TG Temple.
c 1 Kgs. 6: 2.
d 1 Kgs. 5: 17.
e 1 Kgs. 9: 1.
f 1 Chr. 18: 8.
17*a* TG Industry; Work, Value of.
b TG Labor.
c Prov. 31: 13.
18*a* 2 Ne. 6: 2; Jacob 1: 9 (9, 11, 15); Jarom 1: 7 (7, 14); Mosiah 1: 10.
19*a* 2 Ne. 1: 25 (25–27).
b TG Teacher.
20*a* 1 Ne. 8: 18.
b 1 Ne. 8: 35 (35–36).
c 1 Ne. 2: 21; Alma 9: 14 (13–15); 38: 1.
21*a* 2 Ne. 1: 17; Alma 3: 6 (6–19).
b Gen. 24: 16; 1 Ne. 13: 15; 4 Ne. 1: 10; Morm. 9: 6.
c TG Marriage, Temporal.
d 2 Ne. 30: 6; 3 Ne. 2: 15 (14–16).
e Moses 7: 8.
22*a* 1 Ne. 12: 23.
23*a* TG Marriage, Interfaith.
24*a* TG Curse.
b Alma 22: 28. TG Idleness.

[Between 588 and 570 B.C.]

mischief and subtlety, and did seek in the wilderness for beasts of prey.

25 And the Lord God said unto me: They shall be a scourge unto thy seed, to [a]stir them up in remembrance of me; and inasmuch as they will not remember me, and hearken unto my words, they shall scourge them even unto destruction.

26 And it came to pass that I, Nephi, did [a]consecrate Jacob and Joseph, that they should be [b]priests and [c]teachers over the land of my people.

27 And it came to pass that we lived after the manner of [a]happiness.

28 *And thirty years had passed away from the time we left Jerusalem.

29 And I, Nephi, had kept the [a]records upon my plates, which I had made, of my people thus far.

30 And it came to pass that the Lord God said unto me: [a]Make other plates; and thou shalt engraven many things upon them which are good in my sight, for the profit of thy people.

31 Wherefore, I, Nephi, to be obedient to the commandments of the Lord, went and made [a]these plates upon which I have engraven these things.

32 And I engraved that which is pleasing unto God. And if my people are pleased with the things of God they will be pleased with mine engravings which are upon these plates.

33 And if my people desire to know the more particular part of the history of my people they must search mine [a]other [b]plates.

34 And it sufficeth me to say that †forty years had passed away, and we had already had wars and contentions with our brethren.

CHAPTER 6

Jacob recounts Jewish history: Their Babylonian captivity and return; the ministry and crucifixion of the Holy One of Israel; the help received from the gentiles; and their latter-day restoration when they believe in the Messiah.

THE [a]words of Jacob, the brother of Nephi, which he spake unto the people of Nephi:

2 Behold, my beloved brethren, I, Jacob, having been called of God, and ordained after the manner of his holy [a]order, and having been consecrated by my brother Nephi, unto whom ye look as a [b]king or a protector, and on whom ye depend for safety, behold ye know that I have spoken unto you exceedingly many things.

3 Nevertheless, I speak unto you again; for I am desirous for the [a]welfare of your souls. Yea, mine anxiety is great for you; and ye yourselves know that it ever has been. For I have exhorted you with all diligence; and I have taught you the words of my father; and I have spoken unto you concerning all things which are [b]written, from the creation of the world.

4 And now, behold, I would speak unto you concerning things which are, and which are to come; wherefore, I will read you the words of [a]Isaiah. And they are the words which my brother has desired that I should speak unto you. And I speak unto you for your sakes, that ye may learn and glorify the name of your God.

5 And now, the words which I shall read are they which Isaiah spake concerning all the house of Israel;

25*a* 1 Ne. 2: 24.
26*a* Lev. 16: 32; Jacob 1: 18 (18–19); Mosiah 23: 17. TG Priesthood, Authority.
b TG Priest.
c TG Teacher.
27*a* Alma 50: 23.
29*a* TG Record Keeping.
30*a* 1 Ne. 19: 5 (1–6); Jacob 3: 14.
31*a* 1 Ne. 19: 3; Jacob 1: 1.
33*a* 1 Ne. 1: 17 (16–17); 2 Ne. 4: 14; D&C 10: 42.
b 1 Ne. 19: 4; Jacob 1: 3.
6 1*a* 2 Ne. 11: 1; Jacob 2: 1.
2*a* TG Priesthood, Melchizedek.
b 2 Ne. 5: 18; Jacob 1: 9 (9, 11, 15); Jarom 1: 7 (7, 14); Mosiah 1: 10.
3*a* Jacob 2: 3; Mosiah 25: 11.
b TG Scriptures, Value of.
4*a* 3 Ne. 23: 1 (1–3).

[*569 B.C. †559 B.C.]

wherefore, they may be [a]likened unto you, for ye are of the house of
Israel. And there are many things
which have been spoken by Isaiah
which may be likened unto you,
because ye are of the house of Israel.
6 And now, these are the words:
[a]Thus saith the Lord God: Behold,
I will lift up mine hand to the
Gentiles, and set up my [b]standard
to the people; and they shall bring
thy sons in their arms, and thy
daughters shall be carried upon
their shoulders.
7 And [a]kings shall be thy nursing
fathers, and their queens thy nursing mothers; they shall bow down
to thee with their faces towards the
earth, and lick up the dust of thy
feet; and thou shalt know that [b]I am
the Lord; for they shall not be
ashamed that [c]wait for me.
8 And now I, Jacob, would speak
somewhat concerning these words.
For behold, the Lord has shown me
that those who were at [a]Jerusalem,
from whence we came, have been
[b]slain and [c]carried away captive.
9 Nevertheless, the Lord has
shown unto me that they should
[a]return again. And he also has shown
unto me that the Lord God, the
Holy One of Israel, should manifest
himself unto them in the flesh; and
after he should manifest himself
they should [b]scourge him and
[c]crucify him, according to the words
of the angel who spake it unto me.
10 And after they have [a]hardened
their hearts and [b]stiffened their
necks against the Holy One of Israel,
behold, the [c]judgments of the Holy
One of Israel shall come upon them.
And the day cometh that they shall
be smitten and afflicted.
11 Wherefore, after they are driven
to and fro, for thus saith the angel,
many shall be afflicted in the flesh,
and shall not be suffered to [a]perish,
because of the prayers of the faithful; they shall be scattered, and
smitten, and hated; nevertheless,
the Lord will be merciful unto them,
that [b]when they shall come to the
[c]knowledge of their Redeemer, they
shall be [d]gathered together again to
the [e]lands of their inheritance.
12 And blessed are the [a]Gentiles,
they of whom the prophet has
written; for behold, if it so be that
they shall repent and fight not
against Zion, and do not unite themselves to that great and [b]abominable
church, they shall be saved; for the
Lord God will fulfil his [c]covenants
which he has made unto his children;
and for this cause the prophet has
written these things.
13 Wherefore, they that fight
against Zion and the covenant
people of the Lord shall lick up the
dust of their feet; and the people of
the Lord shall not be [a]ashamed.
For the people of the Lord are they
who [b]wait for him; for they still wait
for the coming of the Messiah.

5*a* IE applied.
6*a* Isa. 49: 22 (22–26); 2 Ne. 10: 9.
b TG Ensign.
7*a* Isa. 60: 16.
b Isa. 44: 8; 45: 5 (5–22); 46: 9; 3 Ne. 24: 6; Moses 1: 6.
c Lam. 3: 25 (25–26); D&C 133: 45.
8*a* Esth. 2: 6; 1 Ne. 7: 13; 10: 3; 2 Ne. 25: 6, 10; Omni 1: 15; Hel. 8: 20 (20–21).
b Ezek. 23: 25 (24–29).
c 2 Kgs. 24: 14 (10–16); 25: 11 (1–12); Jer. 13: 19 (19, 24). TG Israel, Bondage of, in Other Lands.
9*a* Jer. 29: 10 (9–10); 1 Ne. 10: 3.
b TG Jesus Christ, Betrayal of.
c 1 Ne. 19: 10 (10, 13); Mosiah 3: 9; 3 Ne. 11: 14 (14–15). TG Jesus Christ, Crucifixion of.
10*a* TG Hardheartedness.
b TG Stiffneckedness.
c Matt. 27: 25 (24–25).
11*a* Amos 9: 8 (8–9); 2 Ne. 20: 20 (20–21).
b 1 Ne. 22: 12 (11–12); 2 Ne. 9: 2 (1–2).
c Hosea 3: 5; D&C 113: 10. TG Israel, Restoration of.
d TG Israel, Gathering of.
e TG Lands of Inheritance.
12*a* 1 Ne. 14: 2 (1–5); 2 Ne. 10: 10 (8–14, 18).
b TG Devil, Church of.
c TG Abrahamic Covenant.
13*a* Joel 2: 26 (26–27); 3 Ne. 22: 4; D&C 90: 17.
b Gen. 49: 18; Ps. 25: 5; Prov. 20: 22; 27: 18; Isa. 40: 31; 1 Ne. 21: 23; D&C 98: 2; 133: 11, 45.

[Between 559 and 545 B.C.]

14 And behold, according to the words of the prophet, the Messiah will set himself again the [a]second time to recover them; wherefore, he will [b]manifest himself unto them in power and great glory, unto the [c]destruction of their enemies, when that day cometh when they shall believe in him; and none will he destroy that believe in him.

15 And they that believe not in him shall be [a]destroyed, both by [b]fire, and by tempest, and by earthquakes, and by [c]bloodsheds, and by [d]pestilence, and by [e]famine. And they shall know that the Lord is God, the Holy One of Israel.

16 [a]For shall the prey be taken from the mighty, or the [b]lawful captive delivered?

17 But thus saith the Lord: Even the captives of the mighty shall be taken away, and the prey of the terrible shall be delivered; [a]for the [b]Mighty God shall [c]deliver his covenant people. For thus saith the Lord: I will contend with them that contendeth with thee—

18 And I will feed them that oppress thee, with their own flesh; and they shall be drunken with their own blood as with sweet wine; and all flesh shall know that I the Lord am thy Savior and thy [a]Redeemer, the [b]Mighty One of Jacob.

CHAPTER 7

Isaiah speaks Messianically—Messiah shall have the tongue of the learned—He shall give his back to the smiters—He shall not be confounded—Compare Isaiah 50.

[a]YEA, for thus saith the Lord: Have I put thee away, or have I cast thee off forever? For thus saith the Lord: Where is the [b]bill of your mother's [c]divorcement? To whom have I put thee away, or to which of my [d]creditors have I [e]sold you? Yea, to whom have I sold you? Behold, for your iniquities have ye sold yourselves, and for your transgressions is your mother put away.

2 Wherefore, when I came, there was no man; when I [a]called, yea, there was none to answer. O house of Israel, is my hand shortened at all that it cannot redeem, or have I no power to deliver? Behold, at my rebuke I [b]dry up the [c]sea, I make their [d]rivers a wilderness and their [e]fish to stink because the waters are dried up, and they die because of thirst.

3 I clothe the heavens with [a]blackness, and I make [b]sackcloth their covering.

4 The Lord God hath given me the [a]tongue of the learned, that I should know how to speak a word in season unto thee, O house of Israel. When

---

14*a* 2 Ne. 21: 11; 25: 17; 29: 1.
b 2 Ne. 3: 5; D&C 3: 18 (16–20).
c 1 Ne. 21: 26 (24–26); 22: 13 (13–14).
15*a* 1 Ne. 22: 13 (13–23); 2 Ne. 10: 16 (15–16); 28: 15 (15–32); 3 Ne. 16: 8 (8–15); Ether 2: 9 (8–11). TG Last Days.
b Joel 1: 19 (19–20); Jacob 5: 77; 6: 3.
c TG Blood, Shedding of.
d Luke 21: 11 (10–13); Mosiah 12: 4; D&C 97: 26 (22–26). TG Plague.
e TG Drought.
16*a* Isa. 49: 24 (24–26); 2 Ne. 11: 2.
b HEB righteous captive; i.e., the covenant people of the Lord, as stated in v. 17.
17*a* 1 Ne. 21: 25.
b TG Jesus Christ—Jehovah.
c 2 Kgs. 17: 39; D&C 105: 8. TG Jesus Christ, Prophecies about; Jesus Christ, Savior.
18*a* TG Jesus Christ, Redeemer.
b Gen. 49: 24; Ps. 132: 2; Isa. 1: 24; 60: 16.
7 1*a* Isa. 50: 1 (1–11); 2 Ne. 8: 1.
b Jer. 3: 8.
c TG Divorce.
d 2 Kgs. 4: 1; Matt. 18: 25.
e Judg. 4: 2; Isa. 52: 3. TG Apostasy of Israel.
2*a* Prov. 1: 24 (24–27); Isa. 65: 12; Alma 5: 37.
b Nahum 1: 4.
c Ex. 14: 21 (1–31); Ps. 106: 9; D&C 133: 68.
d Josh. 3: 16 (15–16).
e Ex. 7: 21 (17–21).
3*a* Ex. 10: 21.
b Rev. 6: 12.
4*a* Luke 21: 15.

[Between 559 and 545 B.C.]

ye are weary he waketh morning by
morning. He waketh mine ear to
hear as the learned.
5 The Lord God hath opened mine
[a]ear, and I was not rebellious, neither
turned away back.
6 I gave my back to the [a]smiter,
and my cheeks to them that plucked
off the hair. I hid not my face from
[b]shame and spitting.
7 For the Lord God will help me,
therefore shall I not be confounded.
Therefore have I set my face like a
flint, and I know that I shall not be
[a]ashamed.
8 And the Lord is near, and he
[a]justifieth me. Who will contend
with me? Let us stand together.
Who is mine adversary? Let him
come near me, and I will [b]smite him
with the strength of my mouth.
9 For the Lord God will help me.
And all they who shall [a]condemn
me, behold, all they shall [b]wax old
as a garment, and the moth shall
eat them up.
10 Who is among you that feareth
the Lord, that obeyeth the [a]voice of
his servant, that [b]walketh in darkness and hath no light?
11 Behold all ye that kindle fire,
that compass yourselves about with
sparks, walk in the light of [a]your fire
and in the sparks which ye have
kindled. [b]This shall ye have of mine
hand—ye shall lie down in sorrow.

CHAPTER 8

In the last days, the Lord shall comfort Zion and gather Israel—The redeemed shall come to Zion amid great joy—Compare Isaiah 51 and 52:1–2.

[a]HEARKEN unto me, ye that follow
after righteousness. Look unto the
[b]rock from whence ye are hewn, and
to the hole of the pit from whence ye
are digged.
2 Look unto Abraham, your
[a]father, and unto [b]Sarah, she that
bare you; for I called him alone, and
blessed him.
3 For the Lord shall [a]comfort [b]Zion,
he will comfort all her waste places;
and he will make her [c]wilderness
like [d]Eden, and her desert like the
garden of the Lord. Joy and gladness
shall be found therein, thanksgiving
and the voice of melody.
4 Hearken unto me, my people;
and give ear unto me, O my nation;
for a [a]law shall proceed from me,
and I will make my judgment to rest
for a [b]light for the people.
5 My righteousness is near; my
[a]salvation is gone forth, and mine
arm shall [b]judge the people. The
[c]isles shall wait upon me, and on
mine arm shall they trust.
6 Lift up your eyes to the [a]heavens,
and look upon the earth beneath;
for the heavens shall [b]vanish away
like smoke, and the earth shall [c]wax
old like a garment; and they that
dwell therein shall die in like manner. But my salvation shall be forever, and my righteousness shall not
be abolished.
7 Hearken unto me, ye that know
righteousness, the people in whose
heart I have written my law, [a]fear

5*a* D&C 58:1.
6*a* Isa. 53:4; Matt. 27:26; 2 Ne. 9:5 (4–7).
b TG Shame.
7*a* Rom. 9:33.
8*a* Rom. 8:33 (32–34).
b Isa. 11:4.
9*a* Rom. 8:31.
b Ps. 102:26.
10*a* D&C 1:38.
b TG Walking in Darkness.
11*a* Deut. 12:8; Judg. 17:6.
b D&C 133:70.

8 1*a* Isa. 51:1 (1–23); 2 Ne. 7:1.
b IE Abraham and Sarah; see v. 2. TG Rock.
2*a* Gen. 17:4 (1–8); D&C 109:64; 132:49.
b Gen. 24:36.
3*a* TG Israel, Restoration of.
b TG Zion.
c Isa. 35:2 (1–2, 6–7). TG Israel, Blessings of.
d TG Earth, Renewal of; Eden.

4*a* Isa. 2:3. TG God, Law of.
b TG Light.
5*a* TG Jesus Christ, Savior; Salvation.
b TG Jesus Christ, Judge.
c 2 Ne. 10:20.
6*a* 2 Pet. 3:10.
b Isa. 13:13.
c Ps. 102:26 (25–28).
7*a* Deut. 1:17; Ps. 56:4 (4, 11); 118:6; D&C 122:9. TG Peer Influence.

[Between 559 and 545 B.C.]

ye not the [b]reproach of men, neither
be ye afraid of their [c]revilings.
8 For the [a]moth shall eat them up
like a garment, and the worm shall
eat them like wool. But my righteousness shall be forever, and my
salvation from generation to generation.
9 [a]Awake, awake! Put on [b]strength,
O arm of the Lord; awake as in the
ancient days. Art thou not he that
hath cut [c]Rahab, and wounded the
[d]dragon?
10 Art thou not he who hath dried
the sea, the waters of the great deep;
that hath made the depths of the
sea a [a]way for the ransomed to pass
over?
11 Therefore, the [a]redeemed of the
Lord shall [b]return, and come with
[c]singing unto Zion; and everlasting
joy and holiness shall be upon their
heads; and they shall obtain gladness and joy; sorrow and [d]mourning
shall flee away.
12 [a]I am he; yea, I am he that
comforteth you. Behold, who art
thou, that thou shouldst be [b]afraid
of man, who shall die, and of the son
of man, who shall be made like unto
[c]grass?
13 And [a]forgettest the Lord thy
maker, that hath [b]stretched forth
the heavens, and laid the foundations of the earth, and hast feared
continually every day, because of
the fury of the [c]oppressor, as if he
were ready to destroy? And where is
the fury of the oppressor?
14 The [a]captive exile hasteneth,
that he may be loosed, and that he
should not die in the pit, nor that his
bread should fail.
15 But I am the Lord thy God,
whose [a]waves roared; the Lord of
Hosts is my name.
16 And I have [a]put my words in
thy mouth, and have covered thee
in the shadow of mine hand, that I
may plant the heavens and lay the
foundations of the earth, and say
unto Zion: Behold, thou art my
[b]people.
17 Awake, awake, stand up, O
Jerusalem, which hast drunk at the
hand of the Lord the [a]cup of his
[b]fury—thou hast drunken the dregs
of the cup of trembling wrung out—
18 And none to guide her among
all the sons she hath brought forth;
neither that taketh her by the hand,
of all the sons she hath brought up.
19 These two [a]sons are come unto
thee, who shall be sorry for thee—
thy desolation and destruction, and
the famine and the sword—and by
whom shall I comfort thee?
20 Thy sons have fainted, save
these two; they lie at the head of
all the streets; as a wild bull in a
net, they are full of the fury of the
Lord, the rebuke of thy God.
21 Therefore hear now this, thou
afflicted, and [a]drunken, and not with
wine:
22 Thus saith thy Lord, the Lord
and thy God [a]pleadeth the cause of
his people; behold, I have taken out
of thine hand the cup of trembling,
the dregs of the cup of my fury; thou
shalt no more drink it again.
23 But [a]I will put it into the hand

7*b* TG Reproach.
c TG Hate.
8*a* Isa. 50: 9.
9*a* Isa. 52: 1.
b D&C 113: 8 (7–8).
TG Israel, Restoration of.
c Ps. 89: 10; Isa. 27: 1.
d Ezek. 29: 3.
10*a* Isa. 35: 8 (8–10).
11*a* TG Israel, Restoration of.
b TG Israel, Gathering of.
c Isa. 35: 10; Jer. 31: 12 (12–13).
d Rev. 21: 4 (2–5).
12*a* D&C 133: 47; 136: 22.
b Jer. 1: 8 (7–8).
c Isa. 40: 6 (6–8); 1 Pet. 1: 24 (24–25).
13*a* Jer. 23: 27 (27–39).
b Job 9: 8.
c IE Israel's captors, typifying evil rulers who oppress the righteous; see v. 14. TG Oppression.
14*a* Isa. 52: 2.
15*a* 1 Ne. 4: 2.
16*a* TG Israel, Mission of; Prophets, Mission of.
b 1 Kgs. 8: 51; 2 Ne. 3: 9; 29: 14.
17*a* Jer. 25: 15;
b Luke 21: 24 (22–24).
19*a* Rev. 11: 3 (3–12).
21*a* 2 Ne. 27: 4.
22*a* Jer. 50: 34.
23*a* Joel 3: 16 (9–16); Zech. 12: 9 (2–3, 8–9); 14: 12 (3, 12–15).

[Between 559 and 545 B.C.]

of them that afflict thee; who have
said to thy soul: Bow down, that
we may go over—and thou hast laid
thy body as the ground and as the
street to them that went over.
24 [a]Awake, awake, put on thy
[b]strength, O [c]Zion; put on thy
beautiful garments, O Jerusalem,
the holy city; for henceforth there
shall [d]no more come into thee the
uncircumcised and the unclean.
25 Shake thyself from the dust;
arise, sit down, O Jerusalem; loose
thyself from the [a]bands of thy neck,
O captive daughter of Zion.

CHAPTER 9

Jews shall be gathered in all their lands of promise—Atonement ransoms man from the fall—The bodies of the dead shall come forth from the grave, and their spirits from hell and from paradise—They shall be judged—Atonement saves from death, hell, the devil, and endless torment—The righteous to be saved in the kingdom of God—Penalties for sins set forth—The Holy One of Israel is the keeper of the gate.

AND now, my beloved brethren, I
have read these things that ye might
know concerning the [a]covenants of
the Lord that he has covenanted
with all the house of Israel—
2 That he has spoken unto the Jews,
by the mouth of his holy prophets,
even from the beginning down, from
generation to generation, until the
time comes that they shall be [a]re-
stored to the true church and fold
of God; when they shall be [b]gathered
home to the [c]lands of their inheritance, and shall be established in all
their lands of promise.
3 Behold, my beloved brethren, I
speak unto you these things that ye
may rejoice, and [a]lift up your heads
forever, because of the blessings
which the Lord God shall bestow
upon your children.
4 For I know that ye have searched
much, many of you, to know of
things to come; wherefore I know
that ye know that our [a]flesh must
waste away and die; nevertheless,
in our [b]bodies we shall see God.
5 Yea, I know that ye know that in
the body he shall show himself unto those at Jerusalem, from whence
we came; for it is expedient that it
should be among them; for it behooveth the great [a]Creator that he
[b]suffereth himself to become [c]subject
unto man in the flesh, and [d]die for
[e]all men, that all men might become
subject unto him.
6 For as [a]death hath passed upon
all men, to fulfil the merciful [b]plan
of the great Creator, there must
needs be a power of [c]resurrection,
and the resurrection must needs
come unto man by reason of the
[d]fall; and the fall came by reason
of [e]transgression; and because man
became fallen they were [f]cut off from
the [g]presence of the Lord.
7 Wherefore, it must needs be an
[a]infinite [b]atonement—save it should
be an infinite atonement this corrup-

24*a* Isa. 52: 1 (1–2).
b D&C 113: 8 (7–8). TG Strength.
c TG Zion.
d Joel 3: 17; Zech. 14: 21.
25*a* D&C 113: 10 (9–10).
9 1*a* TG Abrahamic Covenant; Israel, Mission of.
2*a* 2 Ne. 6: 11 (10–15); 10: 7 (5–9). TG Israel, Restoration of; Restoration of the Gospel.
b TG Israel, Gathering of; Mission of Latter-day Saints.
c TG Lands of Inheritance.
3*a* Ps. 24: 7 (7–10).
4*a* Gen. 6: 3; Moses 8 :17.
b Job 19: 26; Alma 11: 41 (41–45); 42: 23; Hel. 14: 15 (15–18); Morm. 9: 13. TG Body, Sanctity of.
5*a* TG Jesus Christ, Creator.
b 2 Ne. 7 : 6 (4–9).
c Mark 10: 44 (43–44).
d TG Jesus Christ, Death of; Jesus Christ, Mission of.
e John 12: 32; 2 Ne. 26: 24; 3 Ne. 27: 14 (14–15).
6*a* Eccl. 8: 8 (6–8).
b TG Salvation, Plan of.
c TG Jesus Christ, Resurrection.
d TG Fall of Man.
e TG Transgression.
f 2 Ne. 2: 5 (5–8); Alma 11: 42 (40–45).
g TG God, Presence of.
7*a* Alma 34: 10.
b Matt. 26: 54 (52–56). TG Jesus Christ, Atonement through.

[Between 559 and 545 B.C.]

tion could not put on incorruption. Wherefore, the [c]first judgment which came upon man must needs have [d]remained to an endless duration. And if so, this flesh must have laid down to rot and to crumble to its mother earth, to rise no more.

8 O the [a]wisdom of God, his [b]mercy and [c]grace! For behold, if the [d]flesh should rise no more our spirits must become subject to that angel who [e]fell from before the presence of the Eternal God, and became the [f]devil, to rise no more.

9 And our spirits must have become [a]like unto him, and we become devils, [b]angels to a [c]devil, to be [d]shut out from the presence of our God, and to remain with the father of [e]lies, in misery, like unto himself; yea, to that being who [f]beguiled our first parents, who [g]transformeth himself nigh unto an [h]angel of light, and [i]stirreth up the children of men unto [j]secret combinations of murder and all manner of secret works of darkness.

10 O how great the [a]goodness of our God, who prepareth a way for our [b]escape from the grasp of this awful monster; yea, that monster, [c]death and [d]hell, which I call the death of the body, and also the death of the spirit.

11 And because of the way of [a]deliverance of our God, the Holy One of Israel, this [b]death, of which I have spoken, which is the temporal, shall deliver up its dead; which death is the grave.

12 And this [a]death of which I have spoken, which is the spiritual death, shall deliver up its dead; which spiritual death is [b]hell; wherefore, death and hell must [c]deliver up their dead, and hell must deliver up its [d]captive [e]spirits, and the grave must deliver up its captive [f]bodies, and the bodies and the [g]spirits of men will be [h]restored one to the other; and it is by the power of the resurrection of the Holy One of Israel.

13 O how great the [a]plan of our God! For on the other hand, the [b]paradise of God must deliver up the spirits of the righteous, and the grave deliver up the body of the righteous; and the spirit and the body is [c]restored to itself again, and all men become incorruptible, and [d]immortal, and they are living souls, having a [e]perfect [f]knowledge like unto us in the flesh, save it be that our knowledge shall be perfect.

14 Wherefore, we shall have a [a]perfect [b]knowledge of all our [c]guilt, and our [d]uncleanness, and our [e]nakedness; and the righteous shall

7*c* Mosiah 16: 4 (4–7); Alma 11: 45; 12: 36; 42: 6 (6, 9, 14).
d Mosiah 15: 19.
8*a* Job 12: 13 (7–25); Abr. 3: 21. TG God, Wisdom of.
b TG God, Mercy of.
c TG Grace.
d D&C 93: 34.
e 2 Ne. 2: 17; Moses 4: 3 (3–4); Abr. 3: 28 (27–28).
f TG Devil.
9*a* 3 Ne. 29: 7.
b Jacob 3: 11; Alma 5: 25, 39; Moro. 9: 13.
c 2 Cor. 11: 14 (13–15).
d Rev. 12: 9 (7–9).
e TG Lying.
f Gen. 3: 13 (1–13); Mosiah 16: 3; Ether 8: 25; Moses 4: 19 (5–19).
g Rev. 16: 14 (13–14); Alma 30: 53.
h D&C 129: 8.
i TG Motivations.
j TG Secret Combinations.
10*a* Ex. 34: 6 (5–7); 2 Ne. 4: 17; D&C 86: 11.
b TG Death, Power over.
c Mosiah 16: 8 (7–8); Alma 42: 15 (6–15).
d TG Hell.
11*a* TG Deliverance.
b TG Death.
12*a* TG Death, Spiritual, First.
b D&C 76: 84.
c D&C 138: 18.
d TG Bondage, Spiritual; Spirits in Prison.
e TG Spirits, Disembodied.
f TG Body, Sanctity of.
g TG Spirit Body.
h TG Resurrection.
13*a* TG Salvation, Plan of.
b D&C 138: 19. TG Paradise.
c Alma 11: 43; 40: 23; 41: 4 (3–5); D&C 138: 17.
d TG Immortality.
e TG Perfection.
f Eccl. 9: 10; D&C 130: 18.
14*a* Mosiah 3: 25.
b Isa. 59: 12; Alma 5: 18; 11: 43.
c TG Guilt.
d TG Uncleanness.
e Gen. 2: 25; Ex. 32: 25; Moses 4: 13 (13, 16–17).

[Between 559 and 545 B.C.]

have a perfect knowledge of their enjoyment, and their [f]righteousness, being [g]clothed with [h]purity, yea, even with the [i]robe of righteousness.

15 And it shall come to pass that when all men shall have passed from this first death unto life, insomuch as they have become immortal, they must appear before the [a]judgment-seat of the Holy One of Israel; and then cometh the [b]judgment, and then must they be judged according to the holy judgment of God.

16 And assuredly, as the Lord liveth, for the Lord God hath spoken it, and it is his eternal [a]word, which cannot [b]pass away, that they who are righteous shall be righteous still, and they who are [c]filthy shall be [d]filthy still; wherefore, they who are filthy are the [e]devil and his angels; and they shall go away into [f]everlasting fire, prepared for them; and their [g]torment is as a [h]lake of fire and brimstone, whose flame ascendeth up forever and ever and has no end.

17 O the greatness and the [a]justice of our God! For he executeth all his words, and they have gone forth out of his mouth, and his law must be [b]fulfilled.

18 But, behold, the [a]righteous, the [b]saints of the Holy One of Israel, they who have believed in the Holy One of Israel, they who have endured the [c]crosses of the world, and despised the shame of it, they shall [d]inherit the [e]kingdom of God, which was prepared for them [f]from the foundation of the world, and their [g]joy shall be full [h]forever.

19 O the greatness of the mercy of our God, the Holy One of Israel! For he [a]delivereth his saints from that [b]awful monster the devil, and death, and [c]hell, and that lake of fire and brimstone, which is endless torment.

20 O how great the [a]holiness of our God! For he [b]knoweth [c]all things, and there is not anything save he knows it.

21 And he cometh into the world that he may [a]save all men if they will hearken unto his voice; for behold, he suffereth the pains of all men, yea, the [b]pains of every living creature, both men, women, and children, who belong to the family of [c]Adam.

22 And he suffereth this that the resurrection might pass upon all men, that all might stand before him at the great and judgment day.

23 And he commandeth all men that they must [a]repent, and be [b]baptized in his name, having perfect [c]faith in the Holy One of Israel, or they cannot be saved in the kingdom of God.

14*f* TG Righteousness.
g Prov. 31: 25.
h TG Purity.
i D&C 109: 76.
15*a* TG Judgment, The Last.
b Job 34: 12; Ps. 19: 9; 2 Ne. 30: 9.
16*a* 1 Kgs. 8: 56; Ps. 33: 11; D&C 1: 38 (37–39); Moses 1: 4.
b D&C 56: 11.
c Prov. 22: 8. TG Filthiness.
d 1 Ne. 15: 33 (33–35); Alma 7: 21; Morm. 9: 14; D&C 88: 35.
e TG Devil.
f Mosiah 27: 28.
g TG Punishment.
h Rev. 19: 20; 21: 8; 2 Ne. 28: 23; D&C 63: 17; 76: 36.
17*a* TG God, Justice of; Justice.
b Ezek. 24: 14.
18*a* Ps. 5: 12. TG Righteousness.
b TG Saints.
c Luke 14: 27.
d Col. 1: 12; D&C 45: 58 (57–58); 84: 38 (33–38).
e TG Exaltation.
f Alma 13: 3 (3, 5, 7–9).
g Matt. 5: 12 (11–12).
h TG Eternal Life.
19*a* Job 23: 7; D&C 108: 8.
b 1 Ne. 15: 35.
c TG Hell.
20*a* HEB *qodesh*—committed, consecrated. TG Holiness.
b Mosiah 24: 12; Alma 26: 35. TG God, Foreknowledge of; God, Intelligence of; God, Omniscience of.
c Prov. 5: 21; D&C 38: 2 (1–2).
21*a* TG Salvation.
b D&C 18: 11; 19: 18 (15–18). TG Jesus Christ, Trials of.
c D&C 107: 54 (53–56); 128: 21. TG Adam.
23*a* TG Repentance.
b Mosiah 26: 22; D&C 76: 52 (50–52); 84: 74; 137: 6. TG Baptism, Essential.
c TG Baptism, Qualifications for; Faith.

[Between 559 and 545 B.C.]

24 And if they will not repent and
believe in his [a]name, and be baptized
in his name, and [b]endure to the end,
they must be [c]damned; for the Lord
God, the Holy One of Israel, has
spoken it.
25 Wherefore, he has given a [a]law;
and where there is [b]no [c]law given
there is no [d]punishment; and where
there is no punishment there is no
condemnation; and where there is
no condemnation the mercies of the
Holy One of Israel have claim upon
them, because of the atonement;
for they are delivered by the power
of him.
26 For the [a]atonement satisfieth
the demands of his [b]justice upon all
those who [c]have not the [d]law given
to them, that they are [e]delivered
from that awful monster, death and
[f]hell, and the devil, and the lake of
fire and brimstone, which is endless
torment; and they are restored to
that God who gave them [g]breath,
which is the Holy One of Israel.
27 But wo unto him that has the
[a]law given, yea, that has all the
commandments of God, like unto us,
and that [b]transgresseth them, and
that [c]wasteth the days of his [d]probation, for awful is his state!
28 O that cunning [a]plan of the evil
one! O the [b]vainness, and the frailties, and the [c]foolishness of men!
When they are [d]learned they think
they are [e]wise, and they [f]hearken not
unto the [g]counsel of God, for they
set it aside, supposing they know of
themselves, wherefore, their [h]wisdom is foolishness and it profiteth
them not. And they shall perish.
29 But to be [a]learned is good if
they [b]hearken unto the [c]counsels of
God.
30 But wo unto the [a]rich, who are
[b]rich as to the things of the [c]world.
For because they are rich they despise the [d]poor, and they persecute
the meek, and their [e]hearts are upon
their treasures; wherefore, their
[f]treasure is their god. And behold,
their [g]treasure shall perish with
them also.
31 And wo unto the deaf that will
not [a]hear; for they shall perish.
32 Wo unto the [a]blind that will not
see; for they shall perish also.
33 Wo unto the [a]uncircumcised
of heart, for a knowledge of their

24*a* TG Jesus Christ, Taking the Name of.
b TG Perseverance.
c TG Damnation.
25*a* TG God, Law of.
b Rom. 4: 15; 5: 13; 2 Ne. 2: 13.
c John 15: 22 (22–24); Acts 17: 30; Rom. 5: 13; James 4: 17; Alma 42: 17 (12–24). TG Accountability.
d TG Punishment.
26*a* Lev. 4: 20; Neh. 10: 33; 2 Ne. 2 : 10. TG Atonement.
b TG God, Justice of; Justice.
c Mosiah 3: 11; Alma 9: 16 (15–16); 42: 21.
d Mosiah 15: 24; D&C 137: 7. TG Ignorance.
e TG Death, Power over.
f TG Spirits in Prison.
g Gen. 2: 7; 6: 17; Mosiah 2: 21; D&C 77: 2; 93: 33; Abr. 5: 7 (7–8).
27*a* Luke 12: 47 (47–48). TG God, Law of.
b TG Disobedience.
c TG Idleness; Procrastination; Waste.
d TG Probation.
28*a* Alma 28: 13.
b Job 11: 12 (11–12); Isa. 9: 9 (9–10). TG Vanity.
c Eccl. 4: 5; 10: 12 (1–3, 12); 2 Ne. 19: 17; D&C 35: 7. TG Foolishness.
d Luke 16: 15; 2 Ne. 26: 20; 28: 4 (4, 15). TG Education; Worldliness.
e Prov. 14: 6; Jer. 8: 8 (8–9); Rom. 1: 22. TG Pride; Wisdom.
f TG Walking in Darkness.
g Prov. 15: 22; Jacob 4: 10; Alma 37: 12. TG Counsel.
h Prov. 23: 4; Eccl. 8: 17 (16–17); Ezek. 28: 5 (4–5); D&C 76: 9. TG Knowledge.
29*a* D&C 67: 6. TG Learning.
b 2 Ne. 28: 26. TG Submissiveness.
c Jacob 4: 10. TG Counsel.
30*a* Jer. 17: 11; Luke 12: 34; D&C 56: 16.
b Matt. 19: 23.
c TG World.
d TG Poor.
e TG Hardheartedness.
f TG Treasure.
g Prov. 27: 24.
31*a* Ezek. 33: 31 (30–33); Matt. 11: 15; 13: 14; Heb. 5: 11 (11–14); Mosiah 26: 28; D&C 1: 14 (2, 11, 14); Moses 6: 27.
32*a* TG Apathy; Spiritual Blindness.
33*a* Rom. 2: 29 (27–29).

[Between 559 and 545 B.C.]

iniquities shall smite them at the last day.

34 Wo unto the [a]liar, for he shall be thrust down to [b]hell.

35 Wo unto the [a]murderer who deliberately [b]killeth, for he shall [c]die.

36 Wo unto them who commit [a]whoredoms, for they shall be thrust down to hell.

37 Yea, wo unto those that [a]worship idols, for the devil of all devils delighteth in them.

38 And, in fine, wo unto all those who die in their [a]sins; for they shall [b]return to God, and behold his face, and remain in their sins.

39 O, my beloved brethren, remember the awfulness in [a]transgressing against that Holy God, and also the awfulness of yielding to the enticings of that [b]cunning one. Remember, to be [c]carnally-minded is [d]death, and to be [e]spiritually-minded is [f]life [g]eternal.

40 O, my beloved brethren, give ear to my words. Remember the greatness of the Holy One of Israel. Do not say that I have spoken hard things against you; for if ye do, ye will [a]revile against the [b]truth; for I have spoken the words of your Maker. I know that the words of truth are [c]hard against all [d]uncleanness; but the [e]righteous fear them not, for they love the truth and are not shaken.

41 O then, my beloved brethren, [a]come unto the Lord, the Holy One. Remember that his paths are righteous. Behold, the [b]way for man is [c]narrow, but it lieth in a straight course before him, and the keeper of the [d]gate is the Holy One of Israel; and he employeth no servant there; and there is none other way save it be by the gate; for he cannot be deceived, for the Lord God is his name.

42 And whoso [a]knocketh, to him will he open; and the [b]wise, and the learned, and they that are rich, who are puffed up because of their [c]learning, and their [d]wisdom, and their riches—yea, they are they whom he despiseth; and save they shall cast these things away, and consider themselves [e]fools before God, and come down in the depths of [f]humility, he will not open unto them.

43 But the things of the wise and the [a]prudent shall be [b]hid from them forever—yea, that happiness which is prepared for the saints.

44 O, my beloved brethren, remember my words. Behold, I take off my garments, and I shake them before you; I pray the God of my salvation that he view me with his

34*a* Prov. 19: 9. TG Gossip; Honesty; Lying.
b TG Hell.
35*a* Num. 35: 16 (16–25).
b Deut. 19: 11; 2 Sam. 12: 9; Mosiah 13: 21.
c TG Capital Punishment.
36*a* 3 Ne. 12: 27 (27–32). TG Chastity; Whoredom.
37*a* Isa. 41: 24 (21–24). TG Idolatry.
38*a* Ezek. 18: 24. TG Sin.
b Alma 40: 11.
39*a* TG Transgression.
b 2 Ne. 28: 21 (20–22); 32: 8; Mosiah 2: 32; 4: 14; Alma 30: 42 (42, 53).
c Rom. 8: 6. TG Carnal Mind.
d TG Death; Death, Spiritual, First; Hell.
e Prov. 15: 24. TG Spirituality.
f Prov. 11: 19.
g TG Eternal Life.
40*a* TG Reviling.
b Prov. 15: 10; Mosiah 13: 7. TG Truth.
c 1 Ne. 16: 2; 2 Ne. 28: 28; 33: 5.
d TG Uncleanness.
e Prov. 28: 1.
41*a* 1 Ne. 6: 4; Jacob 1: 7; Omni 1: 26 (25–26); Alma 29: 2; 3 Ne. 21: 20; Morm. 9: 27; Ether 5: 5; Moro. 10: 30 (30–32).
b Ex. 33: 13 (12–13); 2 Ne. 31: 21 (17–21); Alma 37: 46; D&C 132: 22 (22, 25).
c Luke 13: 24; 2 Ne. 33: 9; Jacob 6: 11; Hel. 3: 29 (29–30).
d 2 Ne. 31: 9 (9, 17–18); 3 Ne. 14: 14 (13–14); D&C 22: 4; 43: 7; 137: 2.
42*a* TG Objectives; Study.
b Matt. 11: 25. TG Wisdom.
c TG Knowledge; Learning; Worldliness.
d Ezek. 28: 5 (4–5).
e 1 Cor. 3: 18 (18–21).
f TG Humility; Teachable.
43*a* TG Prudence.
b 1 Cor. 2: 14 (9–16).

[Between 559 and 545 B.C.]

[a]all-searching eye; wherefore, ye
shall know at the last day, when all
men shall be judged of their works,
that the God of Israel did witness
that I [b]shook your iniquities from
my soul, and that I stand with
brightness before him, and am [c]rid
of your blood.
45 O, my beloved brethren, turn
away from your sins; shake off the
[a]chains of him that would bind you
fast; come unto that God who is the
[b]rock of your salvation.
46 Prepare your souls for that
glorious day when [a]justice shall be
administered unto the righteous,
even the day of [b]judgment, that ye
may not shrink with awful fear; that
ye may not remember your awful
[c]guilt in perfectness, and be constrained to exclaim: Holy, holy are
thy judgments, O Lord God [d]Al-
mighty—but I know my guilt; I
transgressed thy law, and my transgressions are mine; and the devil
hath [e]obtained me, that I am a prey
to his awful misery.
47 But behold, my brethren, is it
expedient that I should awake you
to an awful reality of these things?
Would I harrow up your souls if
your minds were pure? Would I be
plain unto you according to the
plainness of the truth if ye were freed
from sin?
48 Behold, if ye were holy I would
speak unto you of holiness; but as
ye are not holy, and ye look upon
me as a [a]teacher, it must needs be
expedient that I [b]teach you the
consequences of sin.
49 Behold, my soul abhorreth sin,
and my heart [a]delighteth in righteousness; and I will [b]praise the holy
name of my God.
50 Come, my brethren, every one
that [a]thirsteth, come ye to the
[b]waters; and he that hath no
[c]money, come buy and eat; yea,
come buy wine and milk without
money and without price.
51 Wherefore, do not spend
money for that which is of no worth,
nor your [a]labor for that which cannot [b]satisfy. Hearken diligently unto
me, and remember the words which
I have spoken; and come unto the
Holy One of Israel, and [c]feast upon
that which perisheth not, neither
can be corrupted, and let your soul
delight in fatness.
52 Behold, my beloved brethren,
remember the words of your God;
pray unto him continually by day,
and give [a]thanks unto his holy name
by night. Let your hearts [b]rejoice.
53 And behold how great the
[a]covenants of the Lord, and how
great his [b]condescensions unto the
children of men; and because of his
greatness, and his [c]grace and [d]mercy,
he has promised unto us that our
seed shall not utterly be destroyed,
according to the flesh, but that he
would [e]preserve them; and in future
generations they shall become a
righteous [f]branch unto the house of
Israel.
54 And now, my brethren, I would
speak unto you more; but on the
morrow I will declare unto you the
remainder of my words. Amen.

44*a* Jacob 2: 10.
b Jacob 1: 19.
c Jacob 2: 2 (2, 16); Mosiah 2: 28; D&C 61: 34.
45*a* 2 Ne. 28: 22; Alma 36: 18.
b TG Rock.
46*a* TG God, Justice of.
b TG Judgment, The Last.
c Mosiah 3: 25.
d Gen. 48: 3; 1 Ne. 1: 14; 3 Ne. 4: 32; Moses 2: 1.
e TG Apostasy of Individuals.
48*a* 2 Ne. 5: 26. TG Teacher; Teaching.
b Deut. 33: 10; 2 Chr. 15: 3 (1–4); 17: 9. TG Prophets, Mission of.
49*a* TG Desire; Motivations.
b Ezra 3: 11 (11–13); 1 Ne. 18: 16; Alma 36: 28.
50*a* Isa. 44: 3; 55: 1 (1–2).
b TG Living Water.
c Alma 5: 34; 42: 27.
51*a* Isa. 55: 2. TG Work, Value of.
b Eccl. 1: 3.
c Prov. 13: 25; Enos 1: 4; 3 Ne. 12: 6.
52*a* TG Thanksgiving.
b Deut. 26: 11.
53*a* TG Covenants.
b TG Jesus Christ, Condescension of.
c TG Grace.
d TG Compassion; God, Mercy of.
e TG Protection, Divine.
f TG Vineyard of the Lord.

[Between 559 and 545 B.C.]

CHAPTER 10

Jews shall crucify their God—They shall be scattered until they begin to believe in him—America shall be a land of liberty where no king shall rule—Be reconciled to God and gain salvation through his grace.

AND now I, Jacob, speak unto you again, my beloved brethren, concerning this righteous [a]branch of which I have spoken.

2 For behold, the [a]promises which we have obtained are promises unto us according to the flesh; wherefore, as it has been shown unto me that many of our children shall perish in the flesh because of [b]unbelief, nevertheless, God will be merciful unto many; and our children shall be [c]restored, that they may come to that which will give them the true knowledge of their Redeemer.

3 Wherefore, as I said unto you, it must needs be expedient that Christ—for in the last night the [a]angel spake unto me that this should be his name—should [b]come among the [c]Jews, among those who are the more wicked part of the world; and they shall [d]crucify him—for thus it behooveth our God, and there is none other nation on earth that would [e]crucify their [f]God.

4 For should the mighty [a]miracles be wrought among other nations they would repent, and know that he be their God.

5 But because of [a]priestcrafts and iniquities, they at Jerusalem will [b]stiffen their necks against him, that he be [c]crucified.

6 Wherefore, because of their iniquities, destructions, famines, [a]pestilences, and bloodshed shall come upon them; and they who shall not be destroyed shall be [b]scattered among all nations.

7 But behold, thus saith the [a]Lord God: [b]When the day cometh that they shall believe in me, that I am Christ, then have I covenanted with their fathers that they shall be [c]restored in the flesh, upon the earth, unto the [d]lands of their inheritance.

8 And it shall come to pass that they shall be [a]gathered in from their long dispersion, from the [b]isles of the sea, and from the four parts of the earth; and the nations of the Gentiles shall be great in the eyes of me, saith God, in [c]carrying them forth to the lands of their inheritance.

9 [a]Yea, the kings of the Gentiles shall be nursing fathers unto them, and their queens shall become nursing mothers; wherefore, the [b]promises of the Lord are great unto the Gentiles, for he hath spoken it, and who can dispute?

10 But behold, this land, said God, shall be a land of thine inheritance, and the [a]Gentiles shall be blessed upon the land.

11 And this land shall be a land of

10 1*a* 1 Ne. 15: 12 (12–20); 2 Ne. 3: 5; Jacob 5: 45 (43–45); Alma 46: 24 (24–25).
2*a* 1 Ne. 22: 8 (8–12); 3 Ne. 5: 23 (21–26); 21: 7 (4–29). TG Promise.
b TG Doubt.
c TG Restoration of the Gospel.
3*a* 2 Ne. 2: 4; 11: 3; 25: 19; Jacob 7: 5; Moro. 7: 22.
b TG Jesus Christ, Prophecies about.
c TG Israel, Judah, People of.
d Luke 18: 31; 1 Ne. 11: 33; Mosiah 3: 9 (9–10).
e Matt. 27: 22; Luke 22: 2; 23: 23 (20–24).
f 1 Ne. 19: 10 (7, 10); 2 Ne. 26: 12.
4*a* TG Miracles.
5*a* Matt. 27: 20 (11–26); Luke 22: 2; John 11: 47 (47–53). TG Apostasy of Israel; Priestcraft.
b TG Stiffneckedness.
c TG Jesus Christ, Crucifixion of.
6*a* TG Plague.
b 1 Ne. 19: 14 (13–14); 2 Ne. 25: 15. TG Israel, Bondage of, in Other Lands.
7*a* TG Jesus Christ, Lord.
b 2 Ne. 9: 2 (1–2); 25: 16 (16–17).
c Gen. 49: 10. TG Israel, Restoration of.
d TG Lands of Inheritance.
8*a* TG Israel, Gathering of.
b Isa. 51: 5; 1 Ne. 22: 4; 2 Ne. 29: 7; D&C 133: 8.
c Isa. 11: 14; 1 Ne. 21: 22; 22: 8.
9*a* Isa. 49: 22 (22–23); 2 Ne. 6: 6.
b 1 Ne. 22: 8 (1–9); Alma 9: 24; D&C 3: 20.
10*a* 2 Ne. 6: 12; 3 Ne. 16: 6 (4–7).

[Between 559 and 545 B.C.]

[a]liberty unto the Gentiles, and there
shall be no [b]kings upon the land,
who shall raise up unto the Gentiles.
12 And I will fortify this land
[a]against all other nations.
13 And he that [a]fighteth against
Zion shall [b]perish, saith God.
14 For he that raiseth up a [a]king
against me shall perish, for I, the
Lord, the [b]king of heaven, will be
their king, and I will be a [c]light unto them forever, that hear my words.
15 Wherefore, for this cause, that
my [a]covenants may be fulfilled
which I have made unto the children
of men, that I will do unto them
while they are in the flesh, I must
needs destroy the [b]secret works of
[c]darkness, and of murders, and of
abominations.
16 Wherefore, he that [a]fighteth
against [b]Zion, both Jew and Gentile,
both bond and free, both male and
female, [c]shall perish; for [d]they are
they who are the [e]whore of all the
earth; for [f]they who are [g]not for me
are [h]against me, saith our God.
17 For I will [a]fulfil my [b]promises
which I have made unto the children
of men, that I will do unto them
while they are in the flesh—
18 Wherefore, my beloved brethren, thus saith our God: I will afflict
thy seed by the hand of the Gentiles;
nevertheless, I will [a]soften the hearts
of the [b]Gentiles, that they shall be
like unto a father to them; wherefore, the Gentiles shall be [c]blessed
and [d]numbered among the house of
Israel.
19 Wherefore, I will [a]consecrate
this land unto thy seed, and them
who shall be numbered among thy
seed, forever, for the land of their
inheritance; for it is a choice land,
saith God unto me, above all other
lands, wherefore I will have all men
that dwell thereon that they shall
worship me, saith God.
20 And now, my beloved brethren,
seeing that our merciful God has
given us so great knowledge concerning these things, let us remember him, and lay aside our sins,
and not hang down our heads, for
we are not cast off; nevertheless,
we have been [a]driven out of the land
of our inheritance; but we have been
led to a [b]better land, for the Lord
has made the sea our [c]path, and we
are upon an [d]isle of the sea.
21 But great are the promises of
the Lord unto them who are upon
the [a]isles of the sea; wherefore as it
says isles, there must needs be more
than this, and they are inhabited
also by our brethren.
22 For behold, the Lord God has

11*a* TG Liberty.
b 2 Ne. 1: 7; Mosiah 29: 32.
12*a* 1 Ne. 13: 19.
13*a* 1 Ne. 22: 14 (14, 19).
b Isa. 60: 12.
14*a* TG Kings, Earthly.
b Josh. 2: 11; Ps. 44: 4; Matt. 2: 2; Alma 5: 50; D&C 20: 17; 38: 21 (21–22); 128: 22 (22–23); Moses 7: 53.
c TG Jesus Christ, Light of the World.
15*a* TG Abrahamic Covenant; Covenants.
b Lev. 19: 26; Hel. 3: 23; 7: 25 (4–5, 21, 25). TG Secret Combinations.
c TG Darkness, Spiritual.
16*a* TG Protection, Divine.
b TG Zion.
c Isa. 41: 11 (11–12).
d 1 Ne. 13: 5.
e TG Devil, Church of; Whoredom.
f 1 Ne. 14: 10.
g 1 Ne. 22: 13 (13–23); 2 Ne. 6: 15; 28: 15 (15–32); 3 Ne. 16: 8 (8–15); Ether 2: 9 (8–11).
h Matt. 12: 30.
17*a* 1 Kgs. 8: 56; D&C 1: 38; 101: 64.
b TG Promise.
18*a* 1 Ne. 13: 31; 2 Ne. 4: 7; Jacob 3: 6 (5–9); Hel. 15: 12 (10–17); Morm. 5: 20 (20–21).
b Matt. 8: 11 (11–12); 12: 21; Luke 13: 29 (28–30); Acts 10: 45; D&C 45: 9 (7–30).
c Eph. 3: 6 (1–7); 2 Ne. 33: 9; 3 Ne. 21: 14.
d Gal. 3: 7 (7, 29); 1 Ne. 14: 2; 3 Ne. 16: 13; 21: 6 (6, 22, 25); 30: 2; Abr. 2: 10 (9–11).
19*a* 1 Ne. 13: 15.
20*a* 1 Ne. 1: 20 (18–20); 2: 2 (1–4).
b 1 Ne. 2: 20. TG Promised Lands.
c Ps. 8: 8; 1 Ne. 18: 8 (5–23).
d Isa. 11: 11 (11–12); 42: 4; 51: 5; Ezek. 26: 15 (3, 6–7, 15); 39: 6; 2 Ne. 8: 5.
21*a* Isa. 49: 1; 1 Ne. 19: 16; 21: 1; 22: 4.

[Between 559 and 545 B.C.]

[a]led away from time to time from the house of Israel, according to his will and pleasure. And now behold, the Lord remembereth all them who have been broken off, wherefore he remembereth us also.
23 Therefore, [a]cheer up your hearts, and remember that ye are [b]free to [c]act for yourselves—to [d]choose the way of everlasting death or the way of eternal life.
24 Wherefore, my beloved brethren, [a]reconcile yourselves to the [b]will of God, and not to the will of the devil and the flesh; and remember, after ye are reconciled unto God, that it is only in and through the [c]grace of God that ye are [d]saved.
25 Wherefore, may God [a]raise you from death by the power of the resurrection, and also from everlasting death by the power of the [b]atonement, that ye may be received into the [c]eternal kingdom of God, that ye may praise him through grace divine. Amen.

CHAPTER 11

Jacob saw his Redeemer—The law of Moses typifies Christ and proves he shall come.

AND now, [a]Jacob spake many more things to my people at that time; nevertheless only these things have I caused to be [b]written, for the things which I have written sufficeth me.
2 And now I, Nephi, write [a]more of the words of [b]Isaiah, for my soul delighteth in his words. For I will liken his words unto my people, and I will send them forth unto all my children, for he verily [c]saw my [d]Redeemer, even as I have seen him.
3 And my brother, Jacob, also has [a]seen him as I have seen him; wherefore, I will send their words forth unto my children to prove unto them that my words are true. Wherefore, by the words of [b]three, God hath said, I will establish my word. Nevertheless, God sendeth more [c]witnesses, and he proveth all his words.
4 Behold, my soul delighteth in [a]proving unto my people the truth of the [b]coming of Christ; for, for this end hath the [c]law of Moses been given; and all things which have been given of God from the beginning of the world, unto man, are the [d]typifying of him.
5 And also my soul delighteth in the [a]covenants of the Lord which he hath made to our fathers; yea, my soul delighteth in his [b]grace, and in his justice, and power, and mercy in the great and eternal plan of [c]deliverance from death.
6 And my soul delighteth in proving unto my people that [a]save Christ should come all men must perish.
7 For if there be [a]no Christ there be no God; and if there be no God we

---

22*a* 1 Ne. 22: 4 (4–5); 2 Ne. 1: 6. TG Israel, Scattering of; Israel, Ten Lost Tribes of.
23*a* TG Cheerfulness.
b TG Agency.
c 2 Ne. 2: 16.
d Deut. 30: 19 (15, 19).
24*a* TG Reconciliation.
b TG God, Will of.
c TG Grace.
d TG Salvation; Salvation, Plan of.
25*a* TG Death, Power over; Resurrection.
b TG Jesus Christ, Atonement through.
c TG Eternity.

11 1*a* 2 Ne. 6: 1 (1–10)
b 2 Ne. 31: 1.
2*a* 2 Ne. 6: 16 (16–18).
b 3 Ne. 23: 1.
c 2 Ne. 16: 1. TG Jesus Christ, Appearances, Antemortal.
d TG Jesus Christ—Jehovah.
3*a* 2 Ne. 2: 3 (3–4); 10: 3; Jacob 7: 5. TG God, Privilege of Seeing.
b 2 Ne. 27: 12 (12–14); Ether 5: 3 (2–4); D&C 5: 11 (11, 15).
c TG Book of Mormon; Witnesses.
4*a* 2 Ne. 31: 2.
b Jacob 4: 5; Jarom 1: 11; Alma 25: 16 (15–16); Ether 12: 19 (18–19).
c 2 Ne. 5: 10.
d TG Jesus Christ, Types of, in Anticipation; Law of Moses.
5*a* TG Abrahamic Covenant.
b TG Benevolence; Grace.
c TG Deliverance; Jesus Christ, Atonement through.
6*a* Mosiah 3: 15.
7*a* 2 Ne. 2: 13 (13–14).

[Between 559 and 545 B.C.]

are not, for there could have been no
[b]creation. But there is a God, and
[c]he is Christ, and he cometh in the
fulness of his own time.
8 And now I write [a]some of the
words of Isaiah, that whoso of my
people shall see these words may lift
up their hearts and rejoice for all
men. Now these are the words, and
ye may liken them unto you and
unto all men.

CHAPTER 12

Isaiah sees the latter-day temple, gathering of Israel, and millennial judgment and peace—The proud and wicked shall be brought low at the Second Coming—Compare Isaiah 2.

[a]THE word that Isaiah, the son of
Amoz, saw concerning Judah and
Jerusalem:
2 And it shall come to pass in the
last days, [a]when the [b]mountain of
the Lord's [c]house shall be established
in the top of the [d]mountains, and
shall be exalted above the hills, and
all nations shall flow unto it.
3 And many [a]people shall go and
say, Come ye, and let us go up to
the [b]mountain of the Lord, to the
[c]house of the God of Jacob; and he
will teach us of his ways, and we will
[d]walk in his paths; for out of Zion
shall go forth the law, and the word
of the Lord from Jerusalem.
4 And he shall [a]judge among the
nations, and shall rebuke many
people: and they shall beat their
swords into plow-shares, and their
spears into pruning-hooks—nation
shall not lift up sword against
nation, neither shall they learn war
any more.
5 O house of Jacob, come ye and
let us walk in the light of the Lord;
yea, come, for ye have all [a]gone
astray, every one to his [b]wicked
ways.
6 Therefore, O Lord, thou hast
forsaken thy people, the house of
Jacob, because they be replenished
from the east, and hearken unto
[a]soothsayers like the [b]Philistines,
and they please themselves in the
children of strangers.
7 Their land also is full of silver and
gold, neither is there any end of their
[a]treasures; their land is also full of
horses, neither is there any end of
their chariots.
8 Their land is also full of [a]idols;
they worship the work of their own
hands, that which their own fingers
have made.
9 And the mean man [a]boweth [b]not
down, and the great man humbleth
himself not, therefore, forgive him
not.
10 O ye wicked ones, enter into the
rock, and [a]hide thee in the dust, for
the fear of the Lord and the glory of
his majesty shall smite thee.
11 And it shall come to pass that
the [a]lofty looks of man shall be
humbled, and the haughtiness of
men shall be bowed down, and the
Lord alone shall be exalted in that
day.
12 For the [a]day of the Lord of

7*b* Heb. 3: 4 (3–4). TG Creation; God, Creator.
c TG Jesus Christ—Jehovah.
8*a* See the Latter-day Saint edition of the King James Version of the Bible for other notes and cross-references on these chapters from Isaiah.
12 1*a* Isa. 2: 1 (1–22).
2*a* Comparison with the King James Bible in English shows that there are differences in more than half of the 433 verses of Isaiah quoted in the Book of Mormon, while about 200 verses have the same wording as KJV.
b TG Zion.
c 3 Ne. 24: 1.
d Gen. 49: 26; D&C 49: 25; 109: 61; 133: 31 (29–31).
3*a* Zech. 8: 22.
b Joel 2: 1; 2 Ne. 30: 15 (12–18); D&C 133: 13.
c Ps. 122: 1.
d TG Walking with God.
4*a* 2 Ne. 21: 3 (2–5, 9).
5*a* 2 Ne. 28: 14; Mosiah 14: 6; Alma 5: 37.
b Isa. 53: 6.
6*a* TG Sorcery.
b Gen. 10: 14.
7*a* TG Treasure.
8*a* Jer. 2: 28. TG Idolatry.
9*a* Ex. 34: 8; Isa. 2: 9.
b IE unto God; he worships idols instead.
10*a* Amos 9: 3; Rev. 6: 15 (15–16); Alma 12: 14.
11*a* 2 Ne. 15: 15 (15–16).
12*a* TG Day of the Lord.

[Between 559 and 545 B.C.]

Hosts soon cometh upon all nations,
yea, upon every one; yea, upon the
[b]proud and lofty, and upon every
one who is lifted up, and he shall be
brought low.
13 Yea, and the day of the Lord
shall come upon all the [a]cedars of
Lebanon, for they are high and
lifted up; and upon all the oaks of
Bashan;
14 And upon all the [a]high mountains, and upon all the hills, and
upon all the nations which are lifted
up, and upon every people;
15 And upon every [a]high tower,
and upon every fenced wall;
16 And upon all the ships of the
[a]sea, and upon all the ships of Tarshish, and upon all pleasant pictures.
17 And the loftiness of man shall
be bowed down, and the [a]haughtiness of men shall be made low; and
the Lord alone shall be exalted in
[b]that day.
18 And the idols he shall utterly
abolish.
19 And they shall go into the holes
of the rocks, and into the caves of
the earth, for the fear of the Lord
shall come upon them and the [a]glory
of his majesty shall smite them,
when he ariseth to shake terribly
the earth.
20 In that day a man shall cast his
idols of silver, and his idols of gold,
which he hath made for himself to
worship, to the moles and to the
bats;
21 To go into the clefts of the rocks,
and into the tops of the ragged rocks,
for the fear of the Lord shall come
upon them and the majesty of his
glory shall smite them, when he
ariseth to shake terribly the earth.
22 Cease ye from man, whose
breath is in his nostrils; for wherein
is he to be accounted of?

CHAPTER 13

Judah and Jerusalem shall be punished for their disobedience—The Lord pleads for and judges his people—The daughters of Zion are cursed and tormented for their worldliness—Compare Isaiah 3.

[a]FOR behold, the Lord, the Lord
of Hosts, doth take away from
Jerusalem, and from Judah, the
stay and the staff, the whole staff of
bread, and the whole stay of water—
2 The [a]mighty man, and the man
of [b]war, the judge, and the prophet,
and the [c]prudent, and the ancient;
3 The captain of fifty, and the
honorable man, and the counselor,
and the cunning artificer, and the
eloquent orator.
4 And I will give children unto
them to be their princes, and babes
shall rule over them.
5 And the people shall be [a]oppressed, every one by another, and
every one by his neighbor; the
child shall behave himself [b]proudly
against the ancient, and the base
against the honorable.
6 When a man shall take hold of
his brother of the house of his
father, and shall say: Thou hast
clothing, be thou our ruler, and let
not this [a]ruin come under thy
hand—
7 In that day shall he swear, saying: I will not be a healer; for in
my house there is neither bread nor
clothing; make me not a ruler of the
people.
8 For Jerusalem is [a]ruined, and
Judah is [b]fallen, because their

12*b* Job 40: 11; Mal. 4: 1; 2 Ne. 23: 11; D&C 64: 24.
13*a* Isa. 37: 24; Ezek. 31: 3; Zech. 11: 1 (1–2).
14*a* Isa. 30: 25.
15*a* 3 Ne. 21: 15 (15, 18).
16*a* The Greek (Septuagint) has "ships of the sea." The Hebrew has "ships of Tarshish." The Book of Mormon has both, showing that the brass plates had lost neither phrase.
17*a* TG Haughtiness.
b IE the day of the Lord's coming in glory; see v. 17–21.
19*a* TG Jesus Christ, Glory of.
13 1*a* Isa. 3: 1 (1–26).
2*a* 2 Kgs. 24: 14.
b 1 Chr. 28: 3.
c TG Prudence.
5*a* TG Oppression.
b TG Haughtiness.
6*a* Isa. 3: 6.
8*a* Isa. 1: 7; Jer. 9: 11; Ezek. 36: 17 (16–20).
b Lam. 1: 3 (1–3).

[Between 559 and 545 B.C.]

[c]tongues and their doings have been against the Lord, to [d]provoke the eyes of his glory.

9 The show of their countenance doth witness against them, and doth declare their [a]sin to be even as [b]Sodom, and they cannot hide it. Wo unto their souls, for they have rewarded evil unto themselves!

10 Say unto the righteous that it is [a]well with them; for they shall [b]eat the fruit of their doings.

11 Wo unto the wicked, for they shall perish; for the reward of their hands shall be upon them!

12 And my people, children are their oppressors, and women rule over them. O my people, they who [a]lead thee cause thee to err and destroy the way of thy paths.

13 The Lord standeth up to [a]plead, and standeth to judge the people.

14 The Lord will enter into [a]judgment with the ancients of his people and the princes thereof; for ye have eaten up the [b]vineyard and the spoil of the [c]poor in your houses.

15 What mean ye? Ye [a]beat my people to pieces, and grind the faces of the poor, saith the Lord God of Hosts.

16 Moreover, the Lord saith: Because the daughters of Zion are [a]haughty, and [b]walk with stretched-forth necks and wanton eyes, walking and mincing as they go, and making a tinkling with their feet—

17 Therefore the Lord will smite with a [a]scab the crown of the head of the daughters of Zion, and the Lord will [b]discover their secret parts.

18 In that [a]day the Lord will take away the bravery of their tinkling ornaments, and cauls, and round tires like the moon;

19 The chains and the bracelets, and the mufflers;

20 The bonnets, and the ornaments of the legs, and the headbands, and the tablets, and the ear-rings;

21 The rings, and nose jewels;

22 The changeable suits of apparel, and the mantles, and the wimples, and the crisping-pins;

23 The glasses, and the fine linen, and hoods, and the veils.

24 And it shall come to pass, instead of sweet smell there shall be stink; and instead of a girdle, a rent; and instead of well set hair, [a]baldness; and instead of a stomacher, a girding of sackcloth; [b]burning instead of [c]beauty.

25 Thy men shall fall by the sword and thy mighty in the war.

26 And her [a]gates shall lament and [b]mourn; and she shall be desolate, and shall [c]sit upon the ground.

CHAPTER 14

Zion and her daughters shall be redeemed and cleansed in the millennial day—Compare Isaiah 4.

[a]AND in that day, seven women shall take hold of one man, saying: We will eat our own bread, and wear our own apparel; only let us be called by thy name to take away our [b]reproach.

2 In that day shall the [a]branch of the Lord be beautiful and glorious; the fruit of the earth excellent and

8c Ps. 52: 2.
d TG Provoking.
9a TG Apostasy of Israel.
b Gen. 18: 20 (20–21); 19: 5, 24 (24–25); 2 Ne. 23: 19. TG Homosexuality.
10a Deut. 12: 28.
b Ps. 128: 2.
12a Isa. 9: 16. TG Leadership.
13a Micah 6: 2.
14a TG Jesus Christ, Judge.
b Isa. 5: 7.
c Ezek. 18: 12; 2 Ne. 28: 13 (12–13); Hel. 4: 12 (11–13).
15a Micah 3: 3 (2–3).
16a TG Haughtiness.
b TG Walking in Darkness.
17a Deut. 28: 27.
b Jer. 13: 22; Nahum 3: 5.
18a TG Day of the Lord.
24a Isa. 22: 12; Micah 1: 16.
b 2 Ne. 14: 4.
c Lam. 1: 6 (4–6).
26a Jer. 14: 2.
b Lam. 1: 4 (4–6).
c Lam. 2: 10.
14 1a Isa. 4: 1 (1–6).
b TG Reproach.
2a Isa. 60: 21; 61: 3; 2 Ne. 3: 5; Jacob 2: 25.

[Between 559 and 545 B.C.]

comely to them that are escaped of Israel.

3 And it shall come to pass, they that are [a]left in Zion and remain in Jerusalem shall be called holy, every one that is written among the living in Jerusalem—

4 When the Lord shall have [a]washed away the filth of the daughters of Zion, and shall have purged the blood of Jerusalem from the midst thereof by the spirit of judgment and by the spirit of [b]burning.

5 And the [a]Lord will create upon every dwelling-place of mount Zion, and upon her assemblies, a [b]cloud and smoke by day and the shining of a flaming fire by night; for upon all the glory of Zion shall be a defence.

6 And there shall be a tabernacle for a shadow in the daytime from the heat, and for a place of [a]refuge, and a covert from storm and from rain.

CHAPTER 15

The Lord's vineyard (Israel) shall become desolate and his people shall be scattered—Woes shall come upon them in their apostate and scattered state—The Lord shall lift an ensign and gather Israel—Compare Isaiah 5.

[a]AND then will I sing to my well-beloved a song of my beloved, touching his [b]vineyard. My well-beloved hath a vineyard in a very fruitful hill.

2 And he fenced it, and gathered out the stones thereof, and planted it with the choicest [a]vine, and built a tower in the midst of it, and also made a wine-press therein; and he looked that it should bring forth grapes, and it brought forth wild grapes.

3 And now, O inhabitants of Jerusalem, and men of Judah, judge, I pray you, betwixt me and my vineyard.

4 What could have been done more to my vineyard that I have not done in it? Wherefore, when I looked that it should bring forth grapes it brought forth wild grapes.

5 And now go to; I will tell you what I will do to my vineyard—I will [a]take away the hedge thereof, and it shall be eaten up; and I will break down the wall thereof, and it shall be trodden down;

6 And I will lay it waste; it shall not be pruned nor digged; but there shall come up [a]briers and thorns; I will also command the clouds that they [b]rain no rain upon it.

7 For the [a]vineyard of the Lord of Hosts is the house of Israel, and the men of Judah his pleasant plant; and he looked for [b]judgment, and behold, [c]oppression; for righteousness, but behold, a cry.

8 Wo unto them that join [a]house to house, till there can be no place, that they may be placed alone in the midst of the earth!

9 In mine ears, said the Lord of Hosts, of a truth many houses shall be desolate, and great and fair cities without inhabitant.

10 Yea, ten acres of vineyard shall yield one [a]bath, and the seed of a homer shall yield an ephah.

11 Wo unto them that rise up early in the morning, that they may [a]follow strong drink, that continue until night, and [b]wine inflame them!

12 And the harp, and the [a]viol, the tabret, and pipe, and wine are in their feasts; but they [b]regard not

---

3*a* Matt. 13: 43 (41–43).
4*a* 2 Ne. 13: 24 (16–26). TG Washing.
b Mal. 3: 2; 4: 1.
5*a* Isa. 60: 20 (1–3, 19–21). TG God, Presence of.
b Ex. 13: 21; Zech. 2: 5.
6*a* Isa. 25: 4. TG Refuge.
15 1*a* Isa. 5: 1 (1–30).
b TG Vineyard of the Lord.
2*a* Jer. 2: 21.
5*a* Ps. 80: 12 (8–15).
6*a* Isa. 7: 23 (23–24); 32: 13.
b Lev. 26: 4; Jer. 3: 3.
7*a* TG Vineyard of the Lord.
b Amos 5: 24.
c TG Oppression.
8*a* Micah 2: 2.
10*a* BD Weights and Measures. See also Ezek. 45: 11.
11*a* Prov. 23: 30 (29–32).
b TG Drunkenness; Word of Wisdom.
12*a* Amos 6: 5 (5–6).
b Ps. 28: 5. TG Rebellion.

[Between 559 and 545 B.C.]

the work of the Lord, neither consider the operation of his hands.
13 Therefore, my people are gone
into [a]captivity, because they have
no [b]knowledge; and their honorable
men are famished, and their multitude dried up with thirst.
14 Therefore, hell hath enlarged
herself, and opened her mouth without measure; and their glory, and
their multitude, and their pomp,
and he that rejoiceth, shall descend
into it.
15 And the mean man shall be
[a]brought down, and the [b]mighty
man shall be humbled, and the eyes
of the [c]lofty shall be humbled.
16 But the Lord of Hosts shall be
exalted in [a]judgment, and God that
is holy shall be sanctified in righteousness.
17 Then shall the lambs feed after
their manner, and the waste places
of the [a]fat ones shall strangers eat.
18 Wo unto them that draw iniquity with cords of [a]vanity, and sin
as it were with a cart rope;
19 That say: Let him [a]make speed,
[b]hasten his work, that we may [c]see
it; and let the counsel of the Holy
One of Israel draw nigh and come,
that we may know it.
20 Wo unto them that [a]call [b]evil
good, and good evil, that put [c]dark-
ness for light, and light for darkness,
that put bitter for sweet, and sweet
for bitter!
21 Wo unto the [a]wise in their own
eyes and [b]prudent in their own sight!
22 Wo unto the mighty to drink
[a]wine, and men of strength to mingle
strong drink;
23 Who justify the wicked for
[a]reward, and take away the righteousness of the righteous from
him!
24 Therefore, as the [a]fire devoureth the [b]stubble, and the flame
consumeth the [c]chaff, their [d]root
shall be rottenness, and their blossoms shall go up as dust; because
they have cast away the law of the
Lord of Hosts, and [e]despised the
word of the Holy One of Israel.
25 Therefore, is the [a]anger of the
Lord kindled against his people, and
he hath stretched forth his hand
against them, and hath smitten
them; and the hills did tremble, and
their carcasses were torn in the
midst of the streets. For all this his
anger is not turned away, but his
hand is stretched out still.
26 And he will lift up an [a]ensign to
the [b]nations from far, and will hiss
unto them from the [c]end of the
earth; and behold, they shall [d]come
with speed swiftly; none shall be
weary nor stumble among them.
27 None shall slumber nor sleep;
neither shall the girdle of their loins
be loosed, nor the latchet of their
shoes be broken;
28 Whose arrows shall be sharp,
and all their bows bent, and their
horses' hoofs shall be counted like
flint, and their wheels like a whirlwind, their roaring like a lion.
29 They shall roar like young [a]lions;
yea, they shall roar, and lay hold of
the prey, and shall carry away safe,
and none shall deliver.
30 And in that [a]day they shall roar
against them like the roaring of the

13*a* Lam. 1:3 (1–3).
b Isa. 1:3; Hosea 4:6. TG Knowledge.
15*a* Isa. 2:17 (11, 17).
b 2 Ne. 12:11.
c TG Haughtiness.
16*a* TG Jesus Christ, Judge.
17*a* Isa. 10:16.
18*a* TG Vanity.
19*a* Jer. 17:15.
b TG Haste.
c TG Sign Seekers.
20*a* D&C 64:16; 121:16.
b Moro. 7:14 (14, 18).
c 1 Jn. 1:6.
21*a* Prov. 3:7 (5–7); 2 Ne. 28:15.
b TG Prudence.
22*a* Prov. 31:4 (3–9).
23*a* TG Bribery.
24*a* Obad. 1:18; 2 Ne. 20:17; 3 Ne. 20:16.
b Joel 2:5; 1 Ne. 22:15 (15, 23); 2 Ne. 26:6 (4, 6); D&C 64:24 (23–24); 133:64.
c Luke 3:17; Mosiah 7:30 (29–31).
d Job 18:16 (16–21).
e 2 Sam. 12:9 (7–9).
25*a* Deut. 32:21; D&C 63:32; Moses 6:27.
26*a* TG Ensign.
b TG Nations.
c 2 Ne. 29:2.
d TG Israel, Gathering of.
29*a* 3 Ne. 21:12 (12–13).
30*a* TG Day of the Lord.

[Between 559 and 545 B.C.]

sea; and if they look unto the land,
behold, darkness and sorrow, and
the light is darkened in the heavens
thereof.

CHAPTER 16

Isaiah sees the Lord—Isaiah's sins are forgiven—He is called to prophesy—He prophesies of the rejection by the Jews of Christ's teachings—A remnant shall return—Compare Isaiah 6.

[a] IN the [b]year that king Uzziah died,
I [c]saw also the Lord sitting upon a
throne, high and lifted up, and his
train filled the temple.
2 Above it stood the [a]seraphim;
each one had six wings; with twain
he covered his face, and with twain he
covered his feet, and with twain
he did fly.
3 And one cried unto another, and
said: Holy, holy, holy, is the Lord
of Hosts; the whole earth is full of
his [a]glory.
4 And the posts of the door moved
at the voice of him that cried, and
the house was filled with smoke.
5 Then said I: Wo is unto me!
for I am undone; because I am a
man of unclean lips; and I dwell in
the midst of a people of unclean lips;
for mine eyes have [a]seen the King,
the Lord of Hosts.
6 Then flew one of the seraphim
unto me, having a live coal in his
hand, which he had taken with the
tongs from off the altar;
7 And he laid it upon my mouth,
and said: Lo, this has touched thy
lips; and thine [a]iniquity is taken
away, and thy sin purged.
8 Also I heard the voice of the Lord,
saying: [a]Whom shall I send, and
who will go for us? Then I said: Here
am I; send me.
9 And he said: Go and tell this
people—Hear ye indeed, but they
understood not; and see ye indeed,
but they perceived not.
10 Make the heart of this people
fat, and make their ears heavy, and
shut their eyes—lest they see with
their eyes, and [a]hear with their ears,
and understand with their [b]heart,
and be converted and be healed.
11 Then said I: Lord, how long?
And he said: Until the cities be
wasted without inhabitant, and the
houses without man, and the land
be utterly desolate;
12 And the Lord have [a]removed
men far away, for there shall be a
great forsaking in the midst of the
land.
13 But yet there shall be a tenth,
and they shall return, and shall be
eaten, as a teil-tree, and as an oak
whose substance is in them when
they cast their leaves; so the [a]holy
seed shall be the substance thereof.

CHAPTER 17

Ephraim and Syria wage war against Judah—Christ shall be born of a virgin—Compare Isaiah 7.

[a]AND it came to pass in the days of
[b]Ahaz the son of [c]Jotham, the son of
Uzziah, king of Judah, that [d]Rezin,
king of Syria, and [e]Pekah the son of
Remaliah, king of Israel, went up
toward Jerusalem to war against it,
but could not prevail against it.
2 And it was told the house of
David, saying: Syria is confederate
with Ephraim. And his heart was
moved, and the heart of his people,
as the trees of the wood are moved
with the wind.
3 Then said the Lord unto Isaiah:
Go forth now to meet Ahaz, thou

---

16 1*a* Isa. 6: 1 (1–13).
b IE about 750 B.C.
c John 12: 41; 2 Ne. 11: 2.
2*a* BD Seraphim. TG Cherubim.
3*a* Ps. 72: 19 (19–20). TG Jesus Christ, Glory of.
5*a* TG Jesus Christ, Appearances, Antemortal.
7*a* TG Cleanse; Remission of Sins.
8*a* TG Called of God.
10*a* Matt. 13: 14 (14–15); John 12: 40; Acts 28: 26–27; Rom. 11: 8.
b Prov. 2: 2.
12*a* 2 Kgs. 17: 18 (18, 20); 25: 21.
13*a* Ezra 9: 2.
17 1*a* Isa. 7: 1 (1–25).
b 2 Kgs. 16: 5; 2 Chr. 28: 5 (5–6).
c 2 Kgs. 15: 32.
d 2 Kgs. 15: 37 (36–38).
e 2 Kgs. 15: 25.

[Between 559 and 545 B.C.]

and Shearjashub thy son, at the end
of the [a]conduit of the upper pool in
the highway of the fuller's field;
4 And say unto him: Take heed,
and be quiet; fear not, neither be
faint-hearted for the two tails of
these smoking firebrands, for the
fierce anger of Rezin with Syria, and
of the son of Remaliah.
5 Because Syria, Ephraim, and the
son of Remaliah, have taken evil
counsel against thee, saying:
6 Let us go up against Judah and
vex it, and let us make a breach
therein for us, and set a king in the
midst of it, yea, the son of Tabeal.
7 Thus saith the Lord God: [a]It
shall not stand, neither shall it come
to pass.
8 For the head of Syria is Damascus, and the head of Damascus,
Rezin; and within three score and
five years shall Ephraim be [a]broken
that it be not a people.
9 And the head of Ephraim is
Samaria, and the head of Samaria
is Remaliah's son. If ye will [a]not
believe surely ye shall not be
established.
10 Moreover, the Lord spake again
unto Ahaz, saying:
11 Ask thee a [a]sign of the Lord thy
God; ask it either in the depths, or
in the heights above.
12 But Ahaz said: I will not ask,
neither will I [a]tempt the Lord.
13 And he said: Hear ye now, O
house of David; is it a small thing
for you to weary men, but will ye
weary my God also?
14 Therefore, the Lord himself shall
give you a sign—Behold, a [a]virgin
shall conceive, and shall bear a son,
and shall call his name [b]Immanuel.
15 Butter and [a]honey shall he eat,
that he may know to refuse the evil
and to choose the good.
16 For [a]before the child shall know
to refuse the evil and choose the
good, the land that thou abhor-
rest shall be forsaken of [b]both her
kings.
17 The Lord shall [a]bring upon thee,
and upon thy people, and upon thy
father's house, days that have not
come from the day that [b]Ephraim
departed from Judah, the king of
Assyria.
18 And it shall come to pass in that
day that the Lord shall hiss for the
fly that is in the uttermost part of
Egypt, and for the bee that is in the
land of Assyria.
19 And they shall come, and shall
rest all of them in the desolate
valleys, and in the holes of the rocks,
and upon all thorns, and upon all
bushes.
20 In the same day shall the Lord
shave with a [a]razor that is hired, by
them beyond the river, by the king
of Assyria, the head, and the hair of
the feet; and it shall also consume
the beard.
21 And it shall come to pass in that
day, a man shall nourish a young
cow and two sheep;
22 And it shall come to pass, for
the abundance of milk they shall
give he shall eat butter; for butter
and honey shall every one eat that is
left in the land.
23 And it shall come to pass in that
day, every place shall be, where
there were a thousand vines at a
thousand silverlings, which shall be
for briers and thorns.
24 With arrows and with bows shall
men come thither, because all the
land shall become briers and thorns.
25 And all hills that shall be digged
with the mattock, there shall not
come thither the fear of briers and
thorns; but it shall be for the sending
forth of oxen, and the treading of
lesser cattle.

3*a* 2 Kgs. 18:17; Isa. 36:2.
7*a* Prov. 21:30; Isa. 8:10 (9–10).
8*a* TG Israel, Scattering of.
9*a* 2 Chr. 20:20. TG Unbelief, Unbelievers.
11*a* Judg. 6:39 (36–40). TG Signs.
12*a* IE test, try, or prove.
14*a* 2 Ne. 18:8, 10.
b Isa. 8:8.
15*a* 2 Sam. 17:29.
16*a* Isa. 8:4; 2 Ne. 18:4.
b 2 Kgs. 15:30; 16:9.
17*a* 2 Chr. 28:19 (19–21).
b 1 Kgs. 12:19 (16–19).
20*a* 2 Kgs. 16:7 (7–8); 2 Chr. 28:20 (20–21).

[Between 559 and 545 B.C.]

CHAPTER 18

Christ shall be as a stone of stumbling and a rock of offense—Seek the Lord, not peeping wizards—Turn to the law and to the testimony for guidance—Compare Isaiah 8.

MOREOVER, the word of the Lord said unto me: Take thee a great [a]roll, and write in it with a man's pen, concerning [b]Maher-shalal-hash-baz.

2 And I took unto me faithful [a]witnesses to record, Uriah the priest, and Zechariah the son of Jeberechiah.

3 And I went unto the prophetess; and she conceived and bare a son. Then said the Lord to me: [a]Call his name, Maher-shalal-hash-baz.

4 For behold, [a]the child shall [b]not have knowledge to cry, My father, and my mother, before the riches of Damascus and the [c]spoil of [d]Samaria shall be taken away before the king of [e]Assyria.

5 The Lord spake also unto me again, saying:

6 Forasmuch as this people refuseth the waters of [a]Shiloah that go softly, and rejoice in [b]Rezin and Remaliah's son;

7 Now therefore, behold, the Lord bringeth up upon them the waters of the river, strong and many, even the king of [a]Assyria and all his glory; and he shall come up over all his channels, and go over all his banks.

8 And he shall pass through Judah; he shall overflow and go over, he shall [a]reach even to the neck; and the stretching out of his wings shall fill the breadth of thy land, O Immanuel.

9 [a]Associate yourselves, O ye people, and ye shall be broken in pieces; and give ear all ye of far countries; gird yourselves, and ye shall be broken in pieces; gird yourselves, and ye shall be broken in pieces.

10 Take counsel together, and it shall come to naught; speak the word, and it shall not stand; for God is with us.

11 For the Lord spake thus to me with a strong hand, and instructed me that I should not walk in the way of this people, saying:

12 Say ye not, A confederacy, to all to whom this people shall say, A [a]confederacy; neither fear ye their fear, nor be afraid.

13 Sanctify the Lord of Hosts himself, and let him be your fear, and let him be your dread.

14 And he shall be for a sanctuary; but for a [a]stone of [b]stumbling, and for a [c]rock of [d]offense to both the houses of Israel, for a gin and a [e]snare to the inhabitants of Jerusalem.

15 And many among them shall [a]stumble and fall, and be broken, and be snared, and be taken.

16 [a]Bind up the testimony, seal the law among my disciples.

17 And I will wait upon the Lord, that [a]hideth his face from the house of Jacob, and I will look for him.

18 Behold, I and the children whom the Lord hath given me are for [a]signs and for wonders in Israel from the Lord of Hosts, which dwelleth in Mount Zion.

19 And when they shall say unto you: Seek unto them that have [a]familiar spirits, and unto [b]wizards

---

18 1*a* Isa. 8: 1 (1–22).
b IE destruction is imminent.
2*a* TG Witnesses.
3*a* 2 Ne. 18: 18.
4*a* 2 Ne. 17: 16.
b Isa. 8: 4.
c 2 Kgs. 15: 29 (29–30).
d 2 Kgs. 17: 6.
e 2 Kgs. 16: 7 (7–18); 2 Ne. 20: 12. TG Israel, Scattering of.
6*a* Neh. 3: 15; John 9: 7.
b Isa. 7: 1 (1–6).
7*a* Isa. 10: 12.
8*a* Isa. 30: 28.
9*a* Joel 3: 9 (9–14).
12*a* Isa. 31: 1 (1–3).
14*a* Rom. 9: 33 (32–33). TG Cornerstone; Jesus Christ, Prophecies about.
b Isa. 8: 14 (13–15); Luke 2: 34; 1 Pet. 2: 8 (4–8); Jacob 4: 15.
c TG Rock.
d Luke 7: 23.
e Mosiah 7: 29.
15*a* Matt. 21: 44.
16*a* Dan. 12: 9.
17*a* Isa. 54: 8.
18*a* 2 Ne. 18: 3 (1–3).
19*a* Moro. 10: 30. TG Sorcery.
b Lev. 20: 6.

[Between 559 and 545 B.C.]

that peep and mutter—[c]should not a people seek unto their God for the living to hear from the dead?

20 To the [a]law and to the testimony; and if they speak not according to this word, it is because there is no light in them.

21 And they shall pass through it hardly bestead and hungry; and it shall come to pass that when they shall be hungry, they shall fret themselves, and curse their king and their God, and look upward.

22 And they shall look unto the earth and behold trouble, and [a]darkness, dimness of anguish, and shall be driven to darkness.

CHAPTER 19

Isaiah speaks Messianically—The people in darkness to see a great Light—Unto us a child is born—He shall be the Prince of Peace and shall reign on David's throne—Compare Isaiah 9.

[a]NEVERTHELESS, the dimness shall not be such as was in her vexation, when at first he lightly afflicted the [b]land of [c]Zebulun, and the land of [d]Naphtali, and afterwards did more grievously afflict by the way of the Red Sea beyond Jordan in Galilee of the nations.

2 The people that walked in darkness have seen a great light; they that dwell in the land of the shadow of death, upon them hath the light shined.

3 Thou hast multiplied the nation, and [a]increased the joy—they joy before thee according to the joy in harvest, and as men rejoice when they divide the spoil.

4 For thou hast broken the yoke of [a]his burden, and the staff of his shoulder, the rod of his [b]oppressor.

5 For every battle of the warrior is with confused noise, and garments rolled in blood; but [a]this shall be with burning and fuel of fire.

6 For unto us a [a]child is born, unto us a son is given; and the [b]government shall be upon his shoulder; and his name shall be called, Wonderful, Counselor, The [c]Mighty God, The [d]Everlasting Father, The Prince of [e]Peace.

7 Of the increase of [a]government and peace [b]there is no end, upon the throne of [c]David, and upon his kingdom to order it, and to establish it with judgment and with justice from henceforth, even forever. The zeal of the Lord of Hosts will perform this.

8 The Lord sent his word unto Jacob and it hath lighted upon Israel.

9 And all the people shall know, even Ephraim and the inhabitants of Samaria, that say in the pride and stoutness of heart:

10 The bricks are fallen down, but we will build with hewn [a]stones; the sycamores are cut down, but we will change them into [b]cedars.

11 Therefore the Lord shall set up the adversaries of [a]Rezin against him, and join his enemies together;

12 The Syrians before and the Philistines behind; and they shall [a]devour Israel with open mouth. For all this his [b]anger is not turned away, but his hand is stretched out still.

13 For the people turneth not unto [a]him that smiteth them, neither do they seek the Lord of Hosts.

14 Therefore will the Lord cut off

19c 1 Sam. 28: 11 (8–20).
20a Luke 16: 29 (29–31).
22a Isa. 5: 30.
19 1a Isa. 9: 1 (1–21).
b Matt. 4: 15 (15–16).
c Josh. 19: 10 (10–16).
d Josh. 19: 33 (32–39).
3a Isa. 9: 3.
4a IE Israel, the nation mentioned in v. 3.
b TG Oppression.
5a Mal. 4: 1.
6a Isa. 7: 14; Luke 2: 11.
b Matt. 28: 18.
c Titus 2: 13; Mosiah 7: 27. TG Jesus Christ—Jehovah; Jesus Christ, Power of.
d 2 Ne. 26: 12; Mosiah 3: 5; Alma 11: 39 (38–39, 44); Moro. 7: 22; 8: 18.
e Micah 5: 5; D&C 27: 16; 111: 8.
7a TG Kingdom of God, on Earth.
b Dan. 2: 44.
c Ezek. 37: 24.
10a 1 Kgs. 5: 17.
b 1 Kgs. 5: 6.
11a 2 Kgs. 16: 9 (7–9).
12a 2 Kgs. 17: 6 (1–18).
b Isa. 5: 25; 10: 4; Jer. 4: 8.
13a Amos 4: 10 (6–12).

[Between 559 and 545 B.C.]

from Israel head and tail, branch
and rush [a]in one day.
15 The [a]ancient, he is the head; and
the prophet that teacheth lies, he is
the tail.
16 For the [a]leaders of this people
cause them to err; and they that are
[b]led of them are destroyed.
17 Therefore the Lord shall have
no joy in their young men, neither
shall have [a]mercy on their fatherless
and [b]widows; for [c]every one of them
is a hypocrite and an [d]evildoer, and
every mouth speaketh [e]folly. For all
this his anger is not turned away,
but his [f]hand is stretched out still.
18 For [a]wickedness burneth as the
fire; it shall devour the briers and
thorns, and shall kindle in the
thickets of the forests, and they
shall mount up like the lifting up of
smoke.
19 Through the wrath of the Lord
of Hosts is the [a]land darkened, and
the people shall be as the fuel of the
fire; [b]no man shall spare his brother.
20 And he [a]shall snatch on the right
hand and be hungry; and he shall
[b]eat on the left hand and they shall
not be satisfied; they shall eat every
man the flesh of his own arm—
21 Manasseh, [a]Ephraim; and
Ephraim, Manasseh; they together
shall be against [b]Judah. For all this
his anger is not turned away, but
his hand is stretched out still.

CHAPTER 20

Destruction of Assyria is a type of destruction of wicked at the Second Coming—Few people shall be left after the Lord comes again—Remnant of Jacob shall return in that day—Compare Isaiah 10.

[a]Wo unto them that decree [b]un-
righteous decrees, and that write
grievousness which they have pre-
scribed;
2 To turn away the needy from
judgment, and to take away the
right from the [a]poor of my people,
that [b]widows may be their prey, and
that they may rob the fatherless!
3 And what will ye do in the day
of visitation, and in the desolation
which shall come from far? to whom
will ye flee for help? and where will
ye leave your glory?
4 Without me they shall bow down
under the prisoners, and they shall
fall under the slain. For all this his
anger is not turned away, but his
hand is stretched out still.
5 O Assyrian, the rod of mine anger,
and the staff in their hand is [a]their
indignation.
6 I will send him [a]against a hypo-
critical nation, and against the
people of my wrath will I give him a
charge to take the spoil, and to take
the prey, and to tread them down
like the mire of the streets.
7 Howbeit he meaneth not so,
neither doth his heart think so; but
in his heart it is to destroy and cut
off nations not a few.
8 For he saith: Are not my [a]princes
altogether kings?
9 Is not [a]Calno as [b]Carchemish?
Is not Hamath as Arpad? Is not
Samaria as [c]Damascus?
10 As [a]my hand hath founded the

14*a* Isa. 10: 17.
15*a* Isa. 9: 15.
16*a* Isa. 1: 23. TG Leadership.
b TG Trust Not in the Arm of Flesh.
17*a* TG Mercy.
b TG Widows.
c Micah 7: 2 (2–3).
d Prov. 1: 16; D&C 64: 16.
e Eccl. 10: 12 (1–3, 12); 2 Ne. 9: 28 (28–29); D&C 35: 7.
f 2 Ne. 28: 32; Jacob 5: 47; 6: 4.
18*a* Mal. 4: 1.
19*a* Isa. 8: 22.
b Micah 7: 2 (2–6).
20*a* Lev. 26: 26 (26, 29).
b Deut. 28: 53 (53–57).
21*a* TG Israel, Joseph, People of.
b TG Israel, Judah, People of.
20 1*a* Isa. 10: 1 (1–34).
b TG Injustice.
2*a* Amos 4: 1.
b TG Widows.
5*a* Isa. 10: 5.
6*a* IE against Israel. TG Hypocrisy.
8*a* 2 Kgs. 18: 33 (33–35); 19: 10 (10–13).
9*a* Amos 6: 2 (1–2).
b 2 Chr. 35: 20.
c 2 Kgs. 16: 9.
10*a* IE the king of Assyria's hand (v. 10–11).

[Between 559 and 545 B.C.]

kingdoms of the idols, and whose
graven images did excel them of
Jerusalem and of Samaria;
11 Shall I not, as I have done unto
Samaria and her [a]idols, so do to
Jerusalem and to her idols?
12 Wherefore it shall come to pass
that when the Lord hath performed
his whole work upon Mount Zion
and upon Jerusalem, I will punish
the fruit of the stout heart of the
king of [a]Assyria, and the glory of
his high looks.
13 For [a]he saith: By the strength of
[b]my hand and by my wisdom I have
done these things; for I am prudent;
and I have moved the borders of
the people, and have robbed their
treasures, and I have put down the
inhabitants like a valiant man;
14 And my hand hath found as a
nest the riches of the people; and as
one gathereth eggs that are left have
I gathered all the earth; and there
was none that moved the wing, or
opened the mouth, or peeped.
15 Shall the [a]ax boast itself against
him that heweth therewith? Shall
the saw magnify itself against him
that shaketh it? As if the rod should
shake itself against them that lift
it up, or as if the staff should lift up
itself as if it were no wood!
16 Therefore shall the Lord, the
Lord of Hosts, send among his fat
ones, leanness; and under his glory
he shall kindle a burning like the
burning of a fire.
17 And the light of Israel shall be for
a [a]fire, and his Holy One for a flame,
and shall burn and shall devour his
thorns and his briers in one day;
18 And shall consume the glory of
his forest, and of his fruitful field,
both soul and body; and they
shall be as when a standard-bearer
fainteth.
19 And the [a]rest of the trees of his
forest shall be few, that a child may
write them.
20 And it shall come to pass in that
day, that the remnant of Israel, and
such as are escaped of the [a]house of
Jacob, shall no more again [b]stay
upon him that smote them, but shall
stay upon the Lord, the Holy One
of Israel, in truth.
21 The [a]remnant shall return, yea,
even the remnant of Jacob, unto the
mighty God.
22 For though thy people [a]Israel
be as the sand of the sea, yet a
remnant of them shall [b]return; the
[c]consumption decreed shall overflow
with righteousness.
23 For the Lord God of Hosts shall
make a [a]consumption, even determined in all the land.
24 Therefore, thus saith the Lord
God of Hosts: O my people that
dwellest in Zion, [a]be not afraid of
the Assyrian; he shall smite thee
with a rod, and shall lift up his staff
against thee, after the [b]manner of
Egypt.
25 For yet a very little while, and
the [a]indignation shall cease, and
mine anger in their destruction.
26 And the Lord of Hosts shall [a]stir
up a scourge for him according to
the slaughter of [b]Midian at the rock
of Oreb; and as his rod was upon the
sea so shall he lift it up after the
manner of [c]Egypt.

11*a* Ezek. 36: 18 (16–20).
12*a* 2 Kgs. 16: 7 (7–18); Zeph. 2: 13; 2 Ne. 18: 4 (4–7).
13*a* IE the king of Assyria (v. 13–14).
b Isa. 37: 24 (24–38).
15*a* IE the prophet compares the king to a tool.
17*a* Obad. 1: 18; 2 Ne. 15: 24; 3 Ne. 20: 16.
19*a* IE the remnants of the army of Assyria.
20*a* Amos 9: 8 (8–9); 2 Ne. 6: 11 (10–11).
b IE depend upon. 2 Kgs. 16: 8 (7–9); 2 Chr. 28: 21 (20–21).
21*a* Isa. 11: 11. TG Israel, Remnant of.
22*a* Gen. 22: 17; Rom. 9: 27.
b TG Israel, Gathering of.
c Isa. 28: 22. TG World, End of.
23*a* Dan. 9: 27.
24*a* Isa. 37: 6 (6–7).
b TG Israel, Bondage of, in Egypt; Israel, Bondage of, in Other Lands.
25*a* Isa. 10: 25; Dan. 11: 36.
26*a* 2 Kgs. 19: 35.
b Gen. 25: 2 (1–6); Judg. 7: 25; Isa. 9: 4.
c Ex. 14: 27 (26–27).

[Between 559 and 545 B.C.]

27 And it shall come to pass in that day that his [a]burden shall be taken away from off thy shoulder, and his yoke from off thy neck, and the yoke shall be destroyed because of the [b]anointing.

28 [a]He is come to Aiath, he is passed to Migron; at Michmash he hath laid up his carriages.

29 They are gone over the [a]passage; they have taken up their lodging at [b]Geba; Ramath is afraid; [c]Gibeah of Saul is fled.

30 Lift up the voice, O daughter of [a]Gallim; cause it to be heard unto Laish, O poor [b]Anathoth.

31 Madmenah is removed; the inhabitants of Gebim gather themselves to flee.

32 As yet shall he remain at [a]Nob that day; he shall shake his hand against the mount of the daughter of Zion, the hill of Jerusalem.

33 Behold, the Lord, the Lord of Hosts shall lop the bough with terror; and the [a]high ones of stature shall be [b]hewn down; and the [c]haughty shall be humbled.

34 And he shall cut down the thickets of the forests with iron, and Lebanon shall fall by a mighty one.

CHAPTER 21

Stem of Jesse (Christ) shall judge in righteousness—The knowledge of God shall cover the earth in the Millennium—The Lord shall raise an ensign and gather Israel—Compare Isaiah 11.

[a]AND there shall [b]come forth a rod out of the [c]stem of Jesse, and a [d]branch shall grow out of his roots.

2 And the [a]Spirit of the Lord shall rest upon him, the spirit of [b]wisdom and [c]understanding, the spirit of counsel and might, the spirit of knowledge and of the fear of the Lord;

3 And shall make him of quick understanding in the fear of the Lord; and he shall not [a]judge after the sight of his eyes, neither reprove after the hearing of his ears.

4 But with [a]righteousness shall he [b]judge the poor, and reprove with equity for the [c]meek of the earth; and he shall [d]smite the earth with the [e]rod of his mouth, and with the breath of his lips shall he slay the wicked.

5 And [a]righteousness shall be the girdle of his loins, and faithfulness the girdle of his reins.

6 The [a]wolf also shall dwell with the lamb, and the leopard shall lie down with the kid, and the calf and the young lion and fatling together; and a little child shall lead them.

7 And the cow and the bear shall feed; their young ones shall lie down together; and the lion shall eat straw like the ox.

8 And the sucking child shall play on the hole of the asp, and the weaned child shall put his hand on the cockatrice's den.

9 They shall [a]not hurt nor [b]destroy in all my holy mountain, for the [c]earth shall be full of the [d]knowledge

27*a* Isa. 14: 25.
b TG Jesus Christ, Messiah.
28*a* IE the Assyrian invasion forces introduced in v. 5 progress toward Jerusalem, v. 28–32.
29*a* 1 Sam. 13: 23.
b Neh. 11: 31.
c 1 Sam. 11: 4.
30*a* 1 Sam. 25: 44.
b Josh. 21: 18.
32*a* 1 Sam. 21: 1; 22: 19; Neh. 11: 32.
33*a* Obad. 1: 3 (3–4); Hel. 4: 12 (12–13); D&C 101: 42.
b Ezek. 17: 24; Amos 2: 9; D&C 112: 8 (3–8).
c Ps. 18: 27; 3 Ne. 25: 1; D&C 29: 9.

21 1*a* Isa. 11: 1 (1–16).
b Isa. 53: 2; Rev. 5: 5.
c D&C 113: 2 (1–2).
d TG Jesus Christ, Davidic Descent of.
2*a* Isa. 61: 1 (1–3).
b 1 Kgs. 3: 28.
c 1 Kgs. 3: 11 (10–11).
3*a* 2 Ne. 12: 4.
4*a* Ps. 50: 6; Mosiah 29: 12.
b Ps. 72: 4 (2–4). TG Jesus Christ, Judge.
c TG Meekness.
d Ps. 2: 9.
e 2 Thes. 2: 8; Rev. 19: 15.
5*a* TG Jesus Christ, Millennial Reign.
6*a* Isa. 65: 25.
9*a* Isa. 2: 4.
b TG War.
c Hab. 2: 14.
d Ps. 66: 4; D&C 88: 104. TG Knowledge; Millennium.

[Between 559 and 545 B.C.]

of the Lord, as the waters cover the sea.

10 And in that day there shall be a [a]root of Jesse, which shall stand for an ensign of the people; to it shall the [b]Gentiles seek; and his [c]rest shall be glorious.

11 And it shall come to pass in that day that the Lord shall set his hand again the [a]second time to recover the remnant of his people which shall be left, from [b]Assyria, and from Egypt, and from Pathros, and from Cush, and from Elam, and from [c]Shinar, and from Hamath, and from the islands of the sea.

12 And he shall set up an [a]ensign for the nations, and shall assemble the [b]outcasts of Israel, and [c]gather together the dispersed of Judah from the four corners of the earth.

13 The [a]envy of Ephraim also shall depart, and the adversaries of Judah shall be cut off; Ephraim shall not [b]envy [c]Judah, and Judah shall not vex Ephraim.

14 But they shall fly upon the shoulders of the [a]Philistines towards the west; they shall spoil them of the east together; they shall lay their hand upon [b]Edom and [c]Moab; and the children of Ammon shall obey them.

15 And the Lord shall utterly [a]destroy the tongue of the Egyptian sea; and with his mighty wind he shall shake his hand over the river, and shall smite it in the seven streams, and make men go over [b]dry shod.

16 And there shall be a [a]highway for the remnant of his people which shall be left, from Assyria, like as it was to Israel in the day that he came up out of the land of Egypt.

CHAPTER 22

In the millennial day all men shall praise the Lord—He shall dwell among them—Compare Isaiah 12.

[a]AND in that day thou shalt say: O Lord, I will praise thee; though thou wast angry with me thine anger is turned away, and thou comfortedest me.

2 Behold, God is my salvation; I will [a]trust, and not be afraid; for the Lord [b]JEHOVAH is my [c]strength and my [d]song; he also has become my salvation.

3 Therefore, with joy shall ye draw [a]water out of the wells of salvation.

4 And in that day shall ye say: [a]Praise the Lord, call upon his name, declare his doings among the people, make mention that his name is exalted.

5 [a]Sing unto the Lord; for he hath done excellent things; this is known in all the earth.

6 [a]Cry out and shout, thou inhabitant of Zion; for great is the Holy One of Israel in the midst of thee.

CHAPTER 23

Destruction of Babylon is a type of destruction at Second Coming—It shall be a day of wrath and vengeance

10*a* Rom. 15: 12; D&C 113: 5 (5–6).
b D&C 45: 9 (9–10).
c D&C 19: 9. TG Earth, Renewal of.
11*a* 2 Ne. 6: 14; 25: 17; 29: 1.
b Zech. 10: 10.
c Gen. 10: 10.
12*a* TG Ensign.
b 3 Ne. 15: 15; 16: 1 (1–4).
c Neh. 1: 9; 1 Ne. 22: 12 (10–12); D&C 45: 25 (24–25). TG Israel, Gathering of.
13*a* Jer. 3: 18.
b Ezek. 37: 22 (16–22). TG Envy.
c TG Israel, Joseph, People of; Israel, Judah, People of.
14*a* Obad. 1: 19 (18–19).
b Lam. 4: 21.
c Gen. 19: 37 (30–38).
15*a* Zech. 10: 11.
b Rev. 16: 12.
16*a* Isa. 11: 16; 19: 23; 35: 8 (8–10); D&C 133: 27. TG Earth, Renewal of.
22 1*a* Isa. 12: 1 (1–6).
2*a* Ps. 36: 7 (7–8); Mosiah 4: 6; Hel. 12: 1.
b Ex. 15: 2; Ps. 83: 18. TG Jesus Christ—Jehovah.
c TG Strength.
d TG Singing.
3*a* TG Living Water.
4*a* TG Praise; Thanksgiving.
5*a* Ps. 57: 7 (7–11); 108: 1 (1–5); Alma 26: 8; D&C 136: 28.
6*a* Isa. 54: 1 (1–8); Zeph. 3: 14 (14–20); Zech 2: 10 (10–13).

[Between 559 and 545 B.C.]

—Babylon (the world) shall fall for-
ever—Compare Isaiah 13.

[a]THE burden of [b]Babylon, which
Isaiah the son of Amoz did see.
2 Lift ye up a banner upon the
high mountain, exalt the voice unto
them, [a]shake the hand, that they
may go into the gates of the nobles.
3 I have commanded my sanctified
ones, I have also called my [a]mighty
ones, for mine anger is not upon
them that rejoice in my highness.
4 The noise of the multitude in the
mountains like as of a great people,
a tumultuous noise of the [a]kingdoms
of nations [b]gathered together, the
Lord of Hosts mustereth the hosts of
the battle.
5 They come from a far country,
from the end of heaven, yea, the
Lord, and the weapons of his
indignation, to destroy the whole
land.
6 Howl ye, for the [a]day of the Lord
is at hand; it shall come as a destruction from the Almighty.
7 Therefore shall all hands be faint,
every man's heart shall [a]melt;
8 And they shall be afraid; pangs
and sorrows shall take hold of them;
they shall be amazed one at another;
their faces shall be as flames.
9 Behold, the day of the Lord
cometh, cruel both with wrath and
fierce anger, to lay the land desolate;
and he shall [a]destroy the sinners
thereof out of it.
10 For the [a]stars of heaven and the
[b]constellations thereof shall not give
their [c]light; the [d]sun shall be
darkened in his going forth, and the
moon shall not cause her light to
shine.
11 And I will [a]punish the world
for evil, and the [b]wicked for their
iniquity; I will cause the arrogancy
of the [c]proud to cease, and will lay
down the haughtiness of the terrible.
12 I will make a [a]man more precious
than fine gold; even a man than the
golden wedge of Ophir.
13 Therefore, I will [a]shake the
heavens, and the earth shall [b]remove
out of her place, in the wrath of the
Lord of Hosts, and in the day of his
fierce anger.
14 And it shall be as the chased roe,
and as a sheep that no man taketh
up; and they shall every man turn
to his own people, and flee every one
into his own [a]land.
15 Every one that is proud shall be
thrust through; yea, and every one
that is [a]joined to the wicked shall
fall by the sword.
16 Their [a]children also shall be
[b]dashed to pieces before their eyes;
their houses shall be spoiled and
their wives ravished.
17 Behold, I will stir up the [a]Medes
against them, which shall not regard
silver and gold, nor shall they delight
in it.
18 Their bows shall also dash the
young men to pieces; and they shall
have no [a]pity on the fruit of the
womb; their eyes shall not spare
children.
19 And [a]Babylon, the glory of
kingdoms, the beauty of the Chaldees' excellency, shall be as when
God overthrew [b]Sodom and Gomorrah.

23 1*a* Isa. 13: 1 (1–22).
b TG Babylon.
2*a* IE wave the hand, give a signal.
3*a* Joel 3: 11.
4*a* Joel 3: 14 (11, 14); Zeph. 3: 8; Zech. 14: 2 (2–3).
b Zech. 12: 3 (2–9).
6*a* TG Day of the Lord.
7*a* Jer. 9: 7; D&C 133: 41.
9*a* TG Earth, Cleansing of.
10*a* Isa. 24: 23; Ezek. 32: 7 (7–8); Rev. 6: 13 (12–13).
b TG Astronomy.
c Joel 3: 15.
d TG World, End of.
11*a* Isa. 24: 6; Mal. 4: 1.
b Ex. 34: 7; Prov. 21: 12.
c Job 40: 11; 2 Ne. 12: 12; D&C 64: 24.
12*a* Isa. 4: 1 (1–4).
13*a* Hag. 2: 6 (6–7); Heb. 12: 26.
b TG Earth, Renewal of.
14*a* TG Lands of Inheritance.
15*a* Lam. 2: 9; Alma 59: 6 (5–6).
16*a* Job 27: 14 (13–15).
b Ps. 137: 9 (8–9).
17*a* Isa. 21: 2.
18*a* Lam. 2: 2 (2, 17, 21).
19*a* Isa. 14: 15 (4–27).
b Gen. 19: 24 (24–25); Deut. 29: 23; Jer. 49: 18; 2 Ne. 13: 9.

[Between 559 and 545 B.C.]

20 It shall never be [a]inhabited, neither shall it be dwelt in from generation to generation: neither shall the Arabian pitch tent there; neither shall the shepherds make their fold there.

21 But [a]wild beasts of the desert shall lie there; and their houses shall be full of doleful creatures; and owls shall dwell there, and satyrs shall dance there.

22 And the wild beasts of the islands shall cry in their desolate houses, and dragons in their pleasant palaces; and her time is near to come, and her day shall not be prolonged. For I will destroy her speedily; yea, for I will be merciful unto my people, but the wicked shall perish.

CHAPTER 24

Israel shall be gathered and shall enjoy millennial rest—Lucifer cast out of heaven for rebellion—Israel shall triumph over Babylon (the world)—Compare Isaiah 14.

[a]FOR the Lord will have mercy on Jacob, and will yet [b]choose Israel, and set them in their own land; and the [c]strangers shall be joined with them, and they shall cleave to the house of Jacob.

2 And the people shall take them and bring them to their place; yea, from far unto the ends of the earth; and they shall return to their [a]lands of promise. And the house of Israel shall [b]possess them, and the land of the Lord shall be for [c]servants and handmaids; and they shall take them captives unto whom they were captives; and they shall [d]rule over their oppressors.

3 And it shall come to pass in that day that the Lord shall give thee [a]rest, from thy sorrow, and from thy fear, and from the hard bondage wherein thou wast made to serve.

4 And it shall come to pass in that day, that thou shalt take up this proverb [a]against the king of [b]Babylon, and say: How hath the oppressor ceased, the golden city ceased!

5 The Lord hath broken the staff of the [a]wicked, the scepters of the rulers.

6 [a]He who smote the people in wrath with a continual stroke, he that ruled the nations in anger, is persecuted, and none hindereth.

7 The whole earth is at [a]rest, and is quiet; they break forth into [b]singing.

8 Yea, the fir-trees rejoice at thee, and also the cedars of Lebanon, saying: Since thou art laid down no feller is come up against us.

9 [a]Hell from beneath is moved for thee to meet thee at thy coming; it stirreth up the [b]dead for thee, even all the chief ones of the earth; it hath raised up from their thrones all the kings of the nations.

10 All they shall speak and say unto thee: Art thou also become weak as we? Art thou become like unto us?

11 Thy pomp is brought down to the grave; the noise of thy viols is not heard; the worm is spread under thee, and the worms cover thee.

12 [a]How art thou fallen from heaven, O [b]Lucifer, son of the morning! Art thou cut down to the ground, which did weaken the nations!

13 For thou hast said in thy heart: [a]I will ascend into heaven, I will

20*a* Jer. 50: 39 (3, 39–40); 51: 29 (29, 62).
21*a* Isa. 34: 14 (11–15).
24 1*a* Isa. 14: 1 (1–32).
b Zech. 1: 17; 2: 12.
c Isa. 60: 3 (3–5, 10). TG Stranger.
2*a* TG Promised Lands.
b Amos 9: 12.
c Isa. 60: 14 (10–12, 14).
d TG Kingdom of God, on Earth.
3*a* Josh. 1: 13; D&C 84: 24.
4*a* Hab. 2: 6 (6–8).
b TG Babylon.
5*a* TG Earth, Cleansing of; Wickedness.
6*a* IE Babylon.
7*a* TG Earth, Renewal of.
b Isa. 55: 12 (12–13).
9*a* Ezek. 32: 21. TG Hell.
b TG Spirits in Prison.
12*a* IE the fallen king of Babylon is typified by the fallen "son of the morning," Lucifer in v. 12–15. D&C 76: 26.
b TG Devil.
13*a* Moses 4: 1 (1–4).

[Between 559 and 545 B.C.]

exalt my throne above the stars of
God; I will sit also upon the mount
of the congregation, in the sides of
the north;
14 [a]I will ascend above the heights
of the clouds; I will be like the Most
High.
15 Yet thou shalt be brought down
to hell, to the sides of the [a]pit.
16 They that see thee shall narrowly look upon thee, and shall consider
thee, and shall say: Is this the man
that made the earth to tremble, that
did shake kingdoms?
17 And made the world as a wilderness, and destroyed the cities thereof, and opened not the house of his
prisoners?
18 All the kings of the nations, yea,
all of them, lie in glory, every one
of them in his own house.
19 But thou art cast out of thy
grave like an abominable branch,
and the remnant of those that are
slain, thrust through with a sword,
that go down to the stones of the
pit; as a carcass trodden under feet.
20 Thou shalt not be joined with
them in burial, because thou hast
destroyed thy land and slain thy
people; the [a]seed of [b]evil-doers shall
never be renowned.
21 Prepare slaughter for his
children for the [a]iniquities of their
fathers, that they do not rise, nor
possess the land, nor fill the face of
the world with cities.
22 For I will rise up against them,
saith the Lord of Hosts, and cut
off from Babylon the [a]name, and
remnant, and son, and [b]nephew,
saith the Lord.
23 I will also make it a [a]possession
for the bittern, and pools of water;
and I will sweep it with the besom
of destruction, saith the Lord of
Hosts.
24 The Lord of Hosts hath sworn,
saying: Surely as I have thought,
so shall it come to pass; and as I
have purposed, so shall it stand—
25 That I will bring the Assyrian in
my land, and upon my mountains
tread him under foot; then shall his
[a]yoke depart from off them, and
his burden depart from off their
shoulders.
26 This is the purpose that is
purposed upon the whole earth; and
this is the hand that is stretched out
upon all nations.
27 For the Lord of Hosts hath
purposed, and who shall disannul?
And his hand is stretched out, and
who shall turn it back?
28 In the year that king [a]Ahaz died
was this burden.
29 Rejoice not thou, whole Palestina, because the rod of him that
[a]smote thee is broken; for out of the
serpent's root shall come forth a
cockatrice, and his [b]fruit shall be a
[c]fiery flying serpent.
30 And the first-born of the poor
shall feed, and the needy shall lie
down in safety; and I will kill thy
root with famine, and he shall slay
thy remnant.
31 Howl, O gate; cry, O city; thou,
whole Palestina, art dissolved; for
there shall come from the north a
smoke, and none shall be alone in
his appointed times.
32 What shall then answer the
messengers of the nations? That
the Lord hath founded [a]Zion, and
the [b]poor of his people shall trust
in it.

CHAPTER 25

Nephi glories in plainness—Isaiah's prophecies shall be understood in the last days—The Jews shall return from Babylon, crucify the Messiah, and be scattered and scourged—They shall be restored when they believe in the

14*a* 2 Thes. 2: 4.
15*a* Ps. 28: 1; 88: 4; 1 Ne. 14: 3.
20*a* Ps. 21: 10 (10–11); 37: 28; 109: 13.
b TG Wickedness.
21*a* Ex. 20: 5.
22*a* Prov. 10: 7; Jer. 51: 62.
b Job 18: 19.
23*a* Isa. 34: 11 (11–15).
25*a* Isa. 10: 27.
28*a* 2 Kgs. 16: 20.
29*a* 2 Chr. 26: 6.
b 2 Kgs. 18: 8 (1, 8).
c TG Jesus Christ, Types of, in Anticipation.
32*a* TG Zion.
b Zeph. 3: 12.

[Between 559 and 545 B.C.]

Messiah—He shall first come six hundred years after Lehi left Jerusalem—Nephites keep the law of Moses and believe in Christ, who is the Holy One of Israel.

NOW I, Nephi, do speak somewhat concerning the words which I have written, which have been spoken by the mouth of Isaiah. For behold, Isaiah spake many things which were [a]hard for many of my people to understand; for they know not concerning the manner of prophesying among the Jews.
2 For I, Nephi, have not taught them many things concerning the manner of the Jews; for their [a]works were works of darkness, and their doings were doings of abominations.
3 Wherefore, I write unto my people, unto all those that shall receive hereafter these things which I write, [a]that they may know the judgments of God, that they come upon all nations, according to the word which he hath spoken.
4 Wherefore, hearken, O my people, which are of the house of Israel, and give ear unto my words; for because the words of Isaiah are not plain unto you, nevertheless they are plain unto all those that are filled with the [a]spirit of [b]prophecy. But I give unto you a [c]prophecy, according to the spirit which is in me; wherefore I shall prophesy according to the [d]plainness which hath been with me from the time that I came out from Jerusalem with my father; for behold, my soul delighteth in [e]plainness unto my people, that they may learn.
5 Yea, and my soul delighteth in the words of [a]Isaiah, for I came out from Jerusalem, and mine eyes hath beheld the things of the [b]Jews, and I know that the Jews do [c]understand the things of the prophets, and there is none other people that understand the things which were spoken unto the Jews like unto them, save it be that they are taught after the manner of the things of the Jews.
6 But behold, I, Nephi, have not taught my children after the manner of the Jews; but behold, I, of myself, have dwelt at Jerusalem, wherefore I know concerning the regions round about; and I have made mention unto my children concerning the judgments of God, which [a]hath come to pass among the Jews, unto my children, according to all that which Isaiah hath spoken, and I do not write them.
7 But behold, I proceed with mine own prophecy, according to my [a]plainness; in the which I [b]know that no man can err; nevertheless, in the days that the prophecies of Isaiah shall be fulfilled men shall know of a surety, at the times when they shall come to pass.
8 Wherefore, they are of [a]worth unto the children of men, and he that supposeth that they are not, unto them will I speak particularly, and confine the words unto mine [b]own people; for I know that they shall be of great worth unto them in the [c]last days; for in that day shall they understand them; wherefore, for their good have I written them.
9 And as one generation hath been [a]destroyed among the Jews because of iniquity, even so have they been destroyed from generation to

25 1*a* Jacob 4: 14. TG Symbolism.
2*a* 2 Kgs. 17: 13–20.
3*a* TG God, Knowledge about; Prophets, Mission of; Scriptures, Value of.
4*a* TG Holy Ghost, Source of Testimony.
b TG Prophecy.
c 2 Ne. 31: 1.
d 2 Ne. 31: 3; 33: 5; Jacob 2: 11; 4: 13.
e TG Communication; Plainness.
5*a* 1 Ne. 19: 23.
b TG Israel, Judah, People of.
c Matt. 13: 11 (10–17).
6*a* 2 Ne. 6: 8; Hel. 8: 20 (20–21).
7*a* 2 Ne. 32: 7; Alma 13: 23; Ether 12: 39.
b Ezek. 12: 23 (21–25).
8*a* TG Scriptures, Value of.
b 2 Ne. 27: 6; Enos 1: 16 (13–16); Morm. 5: 12; D&C 3: 20 (16–20).
c TG Last Days.
9*a* Lam., chs. 1–5; Matt. 23: 37.

[Between 559 and 545 B.C.]

generation according to their iniquities; and never hath any of them
been destroyed save it were [b]fore-
told them by the prophets of the
Lord.
10 Wherefore, it hath been told
them concerning the destruction
which should come upon them, immediately after my father left [a]Jeru-
salem; nevertheless, they [b]hardened
their hearts; and according to my
prophecy they have been destroyed,
save it be those which are [c]carried
away [d]captive into Babylon.
11 And now this I speak because of
the [a]spirit which is in me. And notwithstanding they have been carried
away they shall return again, and
possess the land of Jerusalem;
wherefore, they shall be [b]restored
again to the [c]land of their inheritance.
12 But, behold, they shall have
[a]wars, and rumors of wars; and
when the day cometh that the [b]Only
Begotten of the Father, yea, even
the Father of heaven and of earth,
shall [c]manifest himself unto them in
the flesh, behold, they will reject
him, because of their iniquities, and
the hardness of their hearts, and the
stiffness of their necks.
13 Behold, they will [a]crucify him;
and after he is laid in a [b]sepulchre
for the space of [c]three days he shall
[d]rise from the dead, with healing in
his wings; and all those who shall
believe on his name shall be saved
in the kingdom of God. Wherefore,
my soul delighteth to prophesy concerning him, for I have [e]seen his day,
and my heart doth magnify his holy
name.
14 And behold it shall come to pass
that after the [a]Messiah hath risen
from the dead, and hath manifested
himself unto his people, unto as
many as will believe on his name,
behold, Jerusalem shall be [b]destroy-
ed again; for [c]wo unto them that
fight against God and the people of
his [d]church.
15 Wherefore, the [a]Jews shall be
[b]scattered among all nations; yea,
and also [c]Babylon shall be destroyed; wherefore, the Jews shall
be scattered by other nations.
16 And after they have been
[a]scattered, and the Lord God hath
scourged them by other nations
for the space of many generations,
yea, even down from generation
to generation until they shall be
persuaded to [b]believe in Christ, the
Son of God, and the atonement,
which is infinite for all mankind—
and when that day shall come that
they shall believe in Christ, and
worship the Father in his name, with
pure hearts and [c]clean hands, and
look not forward any more for
[d]another Messiah, then, at that time,
the day will come that it must needs
be expedient that they should
believe these things.
17 And the Lord will set his hand

9*b* Ezek. 4:3; Amos 3:7; D&C 5:20.
10*a* 1 Ne. 7:13; 2 Ne. 6:8; Omni 1:15; Hel. 8:21 (20–21).
b TG Hardheartedness.
c 2 Kgs. 24:14 (14–15); Jer. 52:15 (3–15); 1 Ne. 1:13; 10:3.
d Lam. 1:3 (1–3).
11*a* TG Teaching with the Spirit.
b Jer. 24:6 (5–7).
c TG Lands of Inheritance.
12*a* TG War.
b TG Jesus Christ, Divine Sonship.
c TG Jesus Christ, Birth of.
13*a* TG Jesus Christ, Crucifixion of.
b Luke 23:53; John 19:41 (41–42); 1 Ne. 19:10.
c Mosiah 3:10.
d Mal. 4:2. TG Jesus Christ, Prophecies about; Jesus Christ, Resurrection; Resurrection.
e 1 Ne. 11:27 (13–34).
14*a* TG Jesus Christ, Messiah.
b Matt. 24:2 (1–2); Luke 21:24.
c Ps. 83:17 (2–17); D&C 71:7; Moses 7:15 (14–16).
d TG Jesus Christ, Head of the Church.
15*a* TG Israel, Judah, People of.
b Neh. 1:8 (7–9); 2 Ne. 10:6; 3 Ne. 16:8. TG Israel, Bondage of, in Other Lands; Israel, Scattering of.
c TG Babylon.
16*a* Ezek. 34:22; Morm. 5:14.
b 2 Ne. 10:7 (5–9); 30:7 (7–8).
c Job 17:9; D&C 88:86.
d TG False Christs.

[Between 559 and 545 B.C.]

again the second time to [a]restore
his people from their lost and fallen
state. Wherefore, he will proceed
to do a [b]marvelous work and a
wonder among the children of
men.
18 Wherefore, he shall bring forth
[a]his [b]words unto them, which words
shall [c]judge them at the last day,
for they shall be given them for the
purpose of [d]convincing them of the
true Messiah, who was rejected by
them; and unto the convincing of
them that they need not look forward any more for a Messiah to
come, for there should not any
come, save it should be a [e]false
Messiah which should deceive the
people; for there is save one [f]Mes-
siah spoken of by the prophets, and
that Messiah is he who should be
rejected of the Jews.
19 For according to the words of
the prophets, the [a]Messiah cometh
in [b]six hundred years from the time
that my father left Jerusalem; and
according to the words of the prophets, and also the word of the [c]angel
of God, his [d]name shall be Jesus
Christ, the [e]Son of God.
20 And now, my brethren, I have
spoken plainly that ye cannot err.
And as the Lord God liveth that
[a]brought Israel up out of the land of
Egypt, and gave unto Moses power
that he should [b]heal the nations
after they had been bitten by the
poisonous serpents, if they would
cast their eyes unto the [c]serpent
which he did raise up before them,
and also gave him power that he
should smite the [d]rock and the water
should come forth; yea, behold I
say unto you, that as these things
are [e]true, and as the Lord God liveth,
there is none other [f]name given
under heaven save it be this Jesus
Christ, of which I have spoken,
whereby man can be saved.
21 Wherefore, for this cause hath
the Lord God promised unto me that
these things which I [a]write shall be
kept and preserved, and handed
down unto my seed, from generation
to generation, that the promise may
be fulfilled unto Joseph, that his
seed should never [b]perish as long as
the earth should stand.
22 Wherefore, these things shall go
from generation to generation as
long as the earth shall stand; and
they shall go according to the will
and pleasure of God; and the nations
who shall possess them shall be
[a]judged of them according to the
words which are written.
23 For we labor diligently to write,
to [a]persuade our children, and also
our brethren, to believe in Christ,
and to be reconciled to God; for we

17*a* Gen. 49: 10; 2 Ne. 21: 11; 29: 1. TG Israel, Gathering of; Israel, Restoration of; Restoration of the Gospel.
b Isa. 29: 14; 2 Ne. 27: 26; 3 Ne. 28: 32 (31–33).
18*a* 3 Ne. 16: 4.
b 2 Ne. 29: 11; 33: 14 (11, 14–15); W of M 1: 11; 3 Ne. 27: 25 (23–27); Ether 5: 4.
c TG Judgment, The Last.
d 2 Ne. 26: 12; Morm. 3: 21.
e TG False Christs.
f TG Jesus Christ, Messiah.
19*a* TG Jesus Christ, Betrayal of; Jesus Christ, Birth of.
b 1 Ne. 10: 4; 19: 8; 3 Ne. 1: 1.
c 2 Ne. 10: 3.
d TG Jesus Christ, Prophecies about.
e TG Jesus Christ, Divine Sonship.
20*a* Ex. 3: 10 (2–10); 1 Ne. 17: 24 (24, 31, 40); 19: 10.
b John 3: 14; 1 Ne. 17: 41.
c 2 Kgs. 18: 4; Alma 33: 19; Hel. 8: 14 (14–15).
d Ex. 17: 6; Num. 20: 11; Neh. 9: 15; 1 Ne. 17: 29; 20: 21.
e 1 Ne. 14: 30; Mosiah 1: 6.
f Hosea 13: 4; Acts 4: 12; 1 Jn. 3: 23 (19–24); 1 Ne. 10: 6; 2 Ne. 2: 6 (5–8); Mosiah 16: 5 (4–5); Alma 12: 22 (22–25). TG Jesus Christ, Savior.
21*a* 2 Ne. 27: 6.
b Amos 5: 15; Alma 46: 24 (24–27).
22*a* 2 Ne. 29: 11; 33: 15 (10–15); 3 Ne. 27: 25 (23–27); Ether 4: 10 (8–10).
23*a* TG Family, Children, Responsibilities toward.

[Between 559 and 545 B.C.]

know that it is by [b]grace that we are saved, after all we can [c]do.

24 And, notwithstanding we believe in Christ, we [a]keep the law of Moses, and look forward with steadfastness unto Christ, until the law shall be fulfilled.

25 For, for this end was the [a]law given; wherefore the law hath become [b]dead unto us, and we are made alive in Christ because of our faith; yet we keep the law because of the commandments.

26 And we [a]talk of Christ, we rejoice in Christ, we preach of Christ, we [b]prophesy of Christ, and we write according to our prophecies, that our [c]children may know to what source they may look for a [d]remission of their sins.

27 Wherefore, we speak concerning the law that our children may know the deadness of the law; and they, by knowing the deadness of the law, may look forward unto that life which is in Christ, and know for what end the law was given. And after the law is fulfilled in Christ, that they need not harden their hearts against him when the law ought to be done away.

28 And now behold, my people, ye are a [a]stiffnecked people; wherefore, I have spoken plainly unto you, that ye cannot misunderstand. And the words which I have spoken shall stand as a [b]testimony against you; for they are sufficient to [c]teach any man the [d]right way; for the right way is to believe in Christ and deny him not; for by denying him ye also deny the prophets and the law.

29 And now behold, I say unto you that the right way is to believe in Christ, and deny him not; and Christ is the Holy One of Israel; wherefore ye must bow down before him, and [a]worship him with all your [b]might, mind, and strength, and your whole soul; and if ye do this ye shall in nowise be cast out.

30 And, inasmuch as it shall be expedient, ye must keep the [a]performances and [b]ordinances of God until the law shall be fulfilled which was given unto Moses.

CHAPTER 26

Christ shall minister to the Nephites—Nephi foresees the destruction of his people—They shall speak from the dust—The gentiles shall build up false churches and secret combinations—The Lord forbids men to practice priestcrafts.

AND after Christ shall have [a]risen from the dead he shall [b]show himself unto you, my children, and my beloved brethren; and the words which he shall speak unto you shall be the [c]law which ye shall do.

2 For behold, I say unto you that I have beheld that many generations shall pass away, and there shall be great wars and contentions among my people.

3 And after the Messiah shall come there shall be [a]signs given unto my people of his [b]birth, and also of his [c]death and resurrection; and great and terrible shall that day be unto the wicked, for they shall perish; and they perish because they cast

23b Ps. 130: 4 (3–4); Rom. 3: 20 (20–24); 7: 5; 2 Ne. 2: 5 (4–10); Mosiah 13: 32; Alma 42: 14 (12–16); D&C 20: 30; 138: 4. TG Grace.
c James 2: 24 (14–26). TG Good Works.
24a Jacob 4: 5.
25a TG Law of Moses.
b Rom. 7: 4 (4–6); D&C 74: 5 (2–6).
26a Jacob 4: 12; Jarom 1: 11; Mosiah 3: 13; 16: 6.
b Luke 10: 24 (23–24).
c TG Family, Children, Responsibilities toward.
d TG Remission of Sins.
28a Mosiah 3: 14; Alma 9: 31. TG Stiffneckedness.
b TG Testimony.
c 1 Kgs. 8: 36; 2 Ne. 33: 10. TG Teaching.
d 1 Sam. 12: 23; Isa. 45: 19; 2 Pet. 2: 15.
29a TG Worship.
b Deut. 6: 5; Mark 12: 30 (29–31).
30a 4 Ne. 1: 12.
b TG Ordinance.
26 1a 3 Ne. 11: 8 (1–12). TG Jesus Christ, Resurrection.
b 1 Ne. 11: 7; 12: 6.
c 3 Ne. 15: 9 (2–10).
3a 1 Ne. 12: 4 (4–6). TG Signs.
b TG Jesus Christ, Birth of.
c TG Jesus Christ, Death of.

[Between 559 and 545 B.C.]

out the [d]prophets, and the saints,
and stone them, and slay them;
wherefore the cry of the [e]blood of the
saints shall ascend up to God from
the ground against them.
4 Wherefore, all those who are
proud, and that do wickedly, the
day that cometh shall [a]burn them
up, saith the Lord of Hosts, for they
shall be as stubble.
5 And they that kill the [a]prophets,
and the saints, the depths of the
earth shall [b]swallow them up, saith
the Lord of Hosts; and [c]mountains
shall cover them, and whirlwinds
shall carry them away, and buildings shall fall upon them and crush
them to pieces and grind them to
powder.
6 And they shall be visited with
thunderings, and lightnings, and
earthquakes, and all manner of
destructions, for the [a]fire of the
anger of the Lord shall be kindled
against them, and they shall be as
stubble, and the day that cometh
shall consume them, saith the Lord
of Hosts.
7 [a]O the pain, and the anguish of
my soul for the loss of the slain of
my people! For I, Nephi, have seen
it, and it well nigh consumeth me
before the presence of the Lord; but
I must cry unto my God: Thy ways
are [b]just.
8 But behold, the righteous that
hearken unto the words of the
prophets, and destroy them not,
but look forward unto Christ with
[a]steadfastness for the signs which
are given, notwithstanding all [b]per-
secution—behold, they are they
which shall [c]not perish.
9 But the Son of righteousness shall
[a]appear unto them; and he shall
[b]heal them, and they shall have
[c]peace with him, until [d]three generations shall have passed away, and
many of the [e]fourth generation shall
have passed away in righteousness.
10 And when these things have
passed away a speedy [a]destruction
cometh unto my people; for, notwithstanding the pains of my soul,
I have seen it; wherefore, I know
that it shall come to pass; and they
sell themselves for naught; for, for
the reward of their pride and their
[b]foolishness they shall reap destruction; for because they yield unto the
devil and [c]choose works of [d]dark-
ness rather than light, therefore they
must go down to [e]hell.
11 For the Spirit of the Lord will
not always [a]strive with man. And
when the Spirit [b]ceaseth to strive
with man then cometh speedy destruction, and this grieveth my soul.
12 And as I spake concerning the
[a]convincing of the [b]Jews, that Jesus
is the [c]very Christ, it must needs be
that the Gentiles be convinced also
that Jesus is the Christ, the [d]Eternal
[e]God;
13 And that he [a]manifesteth himself unto all those who believe in

3*d* TG Prophets, Rejection of.
e Gen. 4:10; 2 Ne. 28:10; Morm. 8:27.
4*a* 3 Ne. 8:14 (14–24); 9:3 (3–9).
5*a* Ps. 105:15.
b Num. 16:32; 1 Ne. 19:11; 3 Ne. 10:14.
c Hosea 10:8; Alma 12:14.
6*a* 3 Ne. 8:8; 9:3–11.
7*a* Morm. 6:17 (17–22).
b Rom. 3:5; Alma 42:1 (1, 13–25).
8*a* TG Steadfastness.
b TG Persecution.
c 3 Ne. 10:12 (12–13).
9*a* Alma 16:20.
b John 12:40; 3 Ne. 9:13 (13–14); 18:32; D&C 112:13.
c TG Peace.
d 1 Ne. 12:11 (11–12); 3 Ne. 27:32 (30–32).
e Alma 45:12 (10–12); Hel. 13:10 (5, 9–10).
10*a* Mosiah 12:8; Alma 45:11 (9–14); Hel. 13:6 (5–6).
b TG Foolishness.
c TG Agency.
d Job 38:15; John 3:19.
e Job 24:24 (17–24). TG Hell.
11*a* Gen. 6:3; Ether 2:15; Moses 8:17.
b TG Holy Ghost, Loss of.
12*a* 2 Ne. 25:18.
b 2 Ne. 30:7 (7–8); Morm. 5:14 (12–14); D&C 19:27. TG Israel, Judah, People of.
c Morm. 3:21.
d 2 Ne. 19:6; Mosiah 3:5; Alma 11:39 (38–39, 44); Moro. 7:22; 8:18.
e 1 Ne. 19:10 (7, 10); 2 Ne. 10:3; Mosiah 7:27; 27:31 (30–31); 3 Ne. 11:14.
13*a* TG God, Access to.

[Between 559 and 545 B.C.]

him, by the power of the [b]Holy
Ghost; yea, unto every nation,
kindred, tongue, and people, working mighty [c]miracles, signs, and
wonders, among the children of men
according to their [d]faith.
14 But behold, I prophesy unto
you concerning the [a]last days; concerning the days when the Lord God
shall [b]bring these things forth unto
the children of men.
15 After my seed and the seed of
my brethren shall have [a]dwindled
in unbelief, and shall have been
smitten by the Gentiles; yea, after
the Lord God shall have [b]camped
against them round about, and shall
have laid siege against them with a
mount, and raised forts against
them; and after they shall have been
brought down low in the dust, even
that they are not, yet the words of
the righteous shall be written, and
the [c]prayers of the faithful shall
be heard, and all those who have
[d]dwindled in unbelief shall not be
forgotten.
16 For those who shall be destroyed
shall [a]speak unto them out of the
ground, and their speech shall be
low out of the dust, and their voice
shall be as one that hath a familiar
spirit; for the Lord God will give
unto him power, that he may
whisper concerning them, even as it
were out of the ground; and their
speech shall whisper out of the dust.
17 For thus saith the Lord God:
They shall [a]write the things which
shall be done among them, and they
shall be written and [b]sealed up in a
book, and those who have dwindled
in [c]unbelief shall not have them, for
they [d]seek to destroy the things of
God.
18 Wherefore, as those who have
been destroyed have been destroyed
speedily; and the multitude of their
[a]terrible ones shall be as [b]chaff that
passeth away—yea, thus saith the
Lord God: It shall be at an instant,
suddenly—
19 And it shall come to pass, that
those who have dwindled in unbelief shall be [a]smitten by the hand
of the Gentiles.
20 And the Gentiles are lifted up
in the [a]pride of their eyes, and have
[b]stumbled, because of the greatness
of their [c]stumbling block, that they
have built up many [d]churches;
nevertheless, they [e]put down the
power and miracles of God, and
preach up unto themselves their
own wisdom and their own [f]learning,
that they may get gain and grind
upon the face of the poor.
21 And there are many churches
built up which cause [a]envyings, and
[b]strifes, and [c]malice.
22 And there are also secret
[a]combinations, even as in times of
old, according to the combinations
of the [b]devil, for he is the founder of

13*b* TG Holy Ghost, Mission of.
c TG Miracle.
d TG Faith.
14*a* TG Last Days.
b TG Restoration of the Gospel.
15*a* 1 Ne. 12: 22 (22–23); 15: 13.
b Isa. 29: 3.
c Ex. 3: 9 (7, 9); Mosiah 21: 15; D&C 109: 49.
d D&C 3: 18.
16*a* Isa. 29: 4; 2 Ne. 3: 20; 33: 13; Morm. 8: 23 (23, 26); 9: 30; Moro. 10: 27. TG Book of Mormon.
17*a* 1 Ne. 13: 40 (39–42); 2 Ne. 27: 6 (6–26); 29: 12.
b TG Scriptures, Preservation of.
c TG Unbelief, Unbelievers.
d Enos 1: 14; Morm. 6: 6.
18*a* Isa. 29: 5.
b Hosea 13: 3 (1–4); Morm. 5: 16 (16–18).
19*a* 1 Ne. 13: 14; 3 Ne. 16: 8 (8–9); 20: 27 (27–28); Morm. 5: 9.
20*a* Prov. 11: 2; D&C 38: 39. TG Pride.
b 1 Ne. 13: 34 (29, 34); 14: 1 (1–3). TG Apostasy of the Early Christian Church.
c Ezek. 3: 20; 14: 4 (3–7).
d 1 Ne. 14: 10 (9–10); 22: 23; Morm. 8: 28 (25–41).
e 2 Ne. 28: 5 (4–6); Morm. 9: 26 (7–26).
f 1 Tim. 6: 20; 2 Ne. 9: 28; 28: 4 (4, 15); D&C 1: 19. TG Learning.
21*a* TG Envy.
b Rom. 16: 17 (17–18). TG Strife.
c TG Malice.
22*a* TG Secret Combinations.
b 2 Ne. 28: 21.

[Between 559 and 545 B.C.]

all these things; yea, the founder
of murder, and [c]works of darkness;
yea, and he leadeth them by the
neck with a flaxen cord, until he
bindeth them with his strong cords
forever.
23 For behold, my beloved brethren, I say unto you that the Lord
God worketh not in [a]darkness.
24 He doeth not [a]anything save it
be for the benefit of the world; for
he [b]loveth the world, even that he
layeth down his own life that he may
draw [c]all men unto him. Wherefore,
he commandeth none that they shall
not partake of his salvation.
25 Behold, doth he cry unto any,
saying: Depart from me? Behold, I
say unto you, Nay; but he saith:
[a]Come unto me all ye [b]ends of the
earth, [c]buy milk and honey, without
money and without price.
26 Behold, hath he commanded
any that they should [a]depart out of
the synagogues, or out of the houses
of worship? Behold, I say unto you,
Nay.
27 Hath he commanded any that
they should not partake of his
[a]salvation? Behold I say unto you,
Nay; but he hath [b]given it free for
all men; and he hath commanded
his people that they should persuade
all men to [c]repentance.
28 Behold, hath the Lord commanded any that they should not
partake of his goodness? Behold I
say unto you, Nay; but [a]all men are
privileged the one [b]like unto the
other, and none are forbidden.
29 He commandeth that there shall
be no [a]priestcrafts; for, behold,
priestcrafts are that men preach and
set [b]themselves up for a light unto
the world, that they may get [c]gain
and [d]praise of the world; but they
seek not the [e]welfare of Zion.
30 Behold, the Lord hath forbidden
this thing; wherefore, the Lord God
hath given a commandment that
all men should have [a]charity, which
[b]charity is [c]love. And except they
should have charity they were
nothing. Wherefore, if they should
have charity they would not suffer
the laborer in Zion to perish.
31 But the [a]laborer in [b]Zion shall
labor for Zion; for if they labor for
[c]money they shall perish.
32 And again, the Lord God hath
[a]commanded that men should not
murder; that they should not lie;
that they should not [b]steal; that
they should not take the name of the
Lord their God in [c]vain; that they
should not [d]envy; that they should
not have [e]malice; that they should
not contend one with another; that
they should not commit [f]whore-
doms; and that they should do none
of these things; for whoso doeth
them shall perish.
33 For none of these iniquities
come of the Lord; for he doeth that
which is good among the children of
men; and he doeth nothing save it
be plain unto the children of men;
and he [a]inviteth them [b]all to [c]come
unto him and partake of his goodness; and he [d]denieth none that come

22c Lev. 19: 26.
23a Isa. 48: 16 (16–18).
24a 2 Ne. 2: 27; Jacob 5: 41; Alma 26: 37.
b John 3: 16.
c John 12: 32; 2 Ne. 9: 5.
25a 1 Ne. 1: 14; Alma 5: 34 (33–36); 3 Ne. 9: 14 (13–14).
b Mark 16: 15–16.
c Isa. 55: 1.
26a Mark 9: 39 (38–40).
27a TG Salvation.
b Eph. 2: 8.
c TG Repentance.
28a Rom. 2: 11; Alma 13: 5.
b 1 Ne. 17: 35 (33–35).
29a Acts 8: 9; Alma 1: 12; 3 Ne. 16: 10. TG Priestcraft.
b TG Unrighteous Dominion.
c Ezek. 22: 27.
d D&C 58: 39; 121: 35 (34–37).
e Ezek. 34: 3.
30a TG Charity.
b Moro. 7: 47 (47–48).
c TG God, Love of; Love.
31a TG Industry.
b TG Zion.
c Jacob 2: 18 (17–19); D&C 11: 7; 38: 39.
32a TG Commandments of God; Law of Moses.
b TG Stealing.
c TG Profanity.
d TG Envy.
e TG Malice.
f TG Chastity; Whoredom.
33a Jude 1: 3.
b Alma 19: 36.
c TG God, Access to.
d Acts 10: 28 (9–35, 44). TG Justice.

[Between 559 and 545 B.C.]

unto him, black and white, [e]bond
and free, male and female; and he
remembereth the [f]heathen; and all
are alike unto God, both Jew and
Gentile.

CHAPTER 27

Darkness and apostasy shall cover the earth in the last days—The Book of Mormon shall come forth—Three witnesses shall testify of the book—The learned man cannot read the sealed book—The Lord shall do a marvelous work and a wonder—Compare Isaiah 29.

BUT, behold, in the [a]last days, or
in the days of the Gentiles—yea,
behold all the nations of the Gentiles
and also the Jews, both those who
shall come upon this land and those
who shall be upon other lands, yea,
even upon all the lands of the earth,
behold, they will be [b]drunken with
iniquity and all manner of abominations—
2 And when that day shall come
they shall be [a]visited of the Lord of
Hosts, with thunder and with earthquake, and with a great noise, and
with storm, and with tempest, and
with the [b]flame of devouring fire.
3 And all the [a]nations that [b]fight
against Zion, and that distress her,
shall be as a dream of a night vision;
yea, it shall be unto them, even as
unto a hungry man which dream-
eth, and behold he eateth but he
awaketh and his soul is empty; or
like unto a thirsty man which dream-
eth, and behold he drinketh but he
awaketh and behold he is faint, and
his soul hath appetite; yea, even so
shall the multitude of all the nations
be that fight against Mount Zion.
4 For behold, all ye that doeth
iniquity, stay yourselves and wonder, for ye shall cry out, and cry;
yea, ye shall be [a]drunken but not
with wine, ye shall stagger but not
with strong drink.
5 For behold, the Lord hath poured
out upon you the spirit of deep
sleep. For behold, ye have closed
your [a]eyes, and ye have [b]rejected
the prophets; and your rulers, and
the seers hath he covered because of
your iniquity.
6 And it shall come to pass that the
Lord God shall bring forth unto [a]you
the words of a [b]book, and they shall
be the words of them which have
slumbered.
7 And behold the book shall be
[a]sealed; and in the book shall be a
[b]revelation from God, from the beginning of the world to the [c]ending
thereof.
8 Wherefore, because of the things
which are [a]sealed up, the things
which are sealed shall not be delivered in the day of the wickedness and abominations of the people.
Wherefore the book shall be kept
from them.
9 But the book shall be delivered
unto a man, and he shall deliver the
words of the book, which are the
words of those who have slumbered
in the dust, and he shall deliver these
words unto [a]another;
10 But the words which are [a]sealed
he shall not deliver, neither shall he
deliver the book. For the book shall

33*e* Rom. 2: 11; 1 Ne. 17: 35 (35–40).
f Jonah 4: 11 (10–11); 2 Ne. 29: 12; Alma 26: 37 (27, 37). TG Heathen.
27 1*a* TG Last Days.
b Isa. 29: 9. TG Abomination; Iniquity; Wickedness.
2*a* Isa. 29: 6 (6–10); Morm. 8: 29.
b Isa. 24: 6; 66: 16; Jacob 6: 3; 3 Ne. 25: 1.
3*a* Isa. 29: 7 (7–8).
b 1 Ne. 22: 14. TG Protection, Divine.
4*a* Rev. 17: 6 (1–6); 2 Ne. 8: 21.
5*a* TG Spiritual Blindness.
b 2 Chr. 24: 19; Jer. 26: 5; 37: 15; Zech. 1: 4 (2–5).
6*a* Jarom 1: 2; Morm. 5: 12 (12–13).
b 2 Ne. 26: 17 (16–17); 29: 12. TG Book of Mormon.
7*a* Isa. 29: 11 (11–12); Ether 3: 27. TG Seal.
b Mosiah 8: 19; Ether 3: 25 (20–28); 4: 4.
c Ether 1: 2–4; 13: 1–13.
8*a* 3 Ne. 26: 9 (7–12, 18); Ether 4: 5; 5: 1; D&C 17: 6.
9*a* JS-H 1: 64.
10*a* Dan. 12: 9; 1 Ne. 14: 26; D&C 35: 18; JS-H 1: 65.

[Between 559 and 545 B.C.]

be sealed by the power of God, and
the revelation which was sealed shall
be kept in the book until the own
due time of the Lord, that they may
come forth; for behold, they [b]reveal
all things from the foundation of
the world unto the end thereof.
11 And the day cometh that the
words of the book which were sealed
shall be read upon the house tops;
and they shall be read by the power
of Christ; and all things shall be
[a]revealed unto the children of men
which ever have been among the
children of men, and which ever
will be even unto the end of the
earth.
12 Wherefore, at that day when
the book shall be delivered unto
the man of whom I have spoken,
the book shall be hid from the eyes
of the world, that the eyes of none
shall behold it save it be that [a]three
[b]witnesses shall behold it, by the
power of God, besides him to whom
the book shall be delivered; and
they shall testify to the truth of the
book and the things therein.
13 And there is [a]none other which
shall view it, save it be a few according to the will of God, to bear
testimony of his word unto the
children of men; for the Lord God
hath said that the words of the
faithful should speak as if it were
[b]from the dead.
14 Wherefore, the Lord God will
proceed to bring forth the words of
the book; and in the mouth of as
many witnesses as seemeth him
good will he establish his word; and
wo be unto him that [a]rejecteth the
word of God!
15 But behold, it shall come to pass
that the Lord God shall say unto
him to whom he shall deliver the
book: Take these words which are
not sealed and deliver them to
another, that he may show them
unto the learned, saying: [a]Read this,
I pray thee. And the learned shall
say: Bring hither the book, and I
will read them.
16 And now, because of the glory
of the world and to get [a]gain will
they say this, and not for the glory
of God.
17 And the man shall say: I cannot
bring the book, for it is sealed.
18 Then shall the learned say: I
cannot read it.
19 Wherefore it shall come to pass,
that the Lord God will [a]deliver again
the book and the words thereof to
him that is not learned; and the
man that is not learned shall say:
I am not learned.
20 Then shall the Lord God say
unto him: The learned shall not
read them, for they have rejected
them, and I am [a]able to do mine
own work; wherefore thou shalt read
the words which I shall give unto
thee.
21 [a]Touch not the things which
are sealed, for I will bring them forth
in mine own due time; for I will
show unto the children of men that
I am able to do mine own work.
22 Wherefore, when thou hast read
the words which I have commanded thee, and obtained the
[a]witnesses which I have promised
unto thee, then shalt thou seal up
the book again, and hide it up unto
me, that I may preserve the words
which thou hast not read, until I
shall see fit in mine own [b]wisdom to
[c]reveal all things unto the children
of men.
23 For behold, I am God; and I am
a God of [a]miracles; and I will show

10*b* Ether 4: 15. TG God, Omniscience of.
11*a* Luke 12: 3; Morm. 5: 8; D&C 121: 26–31.
12*a* 2 Ne. 11: 3; Ether 5: 3 (2–4); D&C 5: 11 (11, 15); 17: 1.
b Deut. 19: 15.
13*a* D&C 5: 14 (3, 14).
b 2 Ne. 3: 19 (19–20); 33: 13 (13–15); Morm. 9: 30; Moro. 10: 27.
14*a* 2 Ne. 28: 29 (29–30); Ether 4: 8.
15*a* Isa. 29: 11.
16*a* TG Priestcraft.
19*a* Isa. 29: 12.
20*a* Ex. 4: 11 (11–12); Jer. 1: 7 (7–9).
21*a* Ether 5: 1.
22*a* TG Witnesses.
b TG God, Wisdom of.
c Ether 4: 7 (6–7). TG Mysteries of Godliness.
23*a* TG Marvelous; Miracle.

[Between 559 and 545 B.C.]

unto the [b]world that I am the same
yesterday, today, and forever; and I
[c]work not among the children of men
save it be [d]according to their faith.
24 And again it shall come to pass
that the Lord shall say unto him
that shall read the words that shall
be delivered him:
25 [a]Forasmuch as this people draw
near unto me with their mouth, and
with their lips do [b]honor me, but
have removed their [c]hearts far from
me, and their fear towards me is
taught by the [d]precepts of men—
26 Therefore, I will proceed to do
a [a]marvelous work among this
people, yea, a [b]marvelous work and
a wonder, for the [c]wisdom of their
wise and [d]learned shall perish, and
the [e]understanding of their [f]prudent
shall be hid.
27 And [a]wo unto them that seek
deep to hide their [b]counsel from the
Lord! And their works are in the
[c]dark; and they say: Who seeth us,
and who knoweth us? And they also
say: Surely, your turning of things
upside down shall be esteemed as
the [d]potter's clay. But behold, I will
show unto them, saith the Lord of
Hosts, that I [e]know all their works.
For shall the work say of him that
made it, he made me not? Or shall
the thing framed say of him that
framed it, he had no understanding?
28 But behold, saith the Lord of
Hosts: I will show unto the children
of men that it is yet a very little
while and Lebanon shall be turned
into a fruitful field; and the [a]fruitful
field shall be esteemed as a forest.
29 [a]And in that day shall the [b]deaf
hear the words of the book, and the
eyes of the blind shall see out of
obscurity and out of darkness.
30 And the [a]meek also shall increase, and their [b]joy shall be in the
Lord, and the poor among men shall
rejoice in the Holy One of Israel.
31 For assuredly as the Lord liveth
they shall see that the [a]terrible one
is brought to naught, and the scorner
is consumed, and all that watch for
iniquity are cut off;
32 And they that make a man an
[a]offender for a word, and lay a snare
for him that reproveth in the [b]gate,
and [c]turn aside the just for a thing
of naught.
33 Therefore, thus saith the Lord,
who redeemed Abraham, concerning the house of Jacob: Jacob shall
[a]not now be ashamed, neither shall
his face now wax pale.
34 But when he [a]seeth his children,
the work of my hands, in the midst
of him, they shall sanctify my name,
and sanctify the Holy One of Jacob,
and shall fear the God of Israel.
35 They also that [a]erred in spirit
shall come to understanding, and
they that murmured shall [b]learn doctrine.

CHAPTER 28

Many false churches shall be built up in the last days—They shall teach false and vain and foolish doctrines—Apostasy shall abound because of false teachers—The devil shall rage in the hearts of men—He shall teach all manner of false doctrines.

AND now, behold, my brethren, I
have spoken unto you, according as

23*b* TG World.
c W of M 1:7.
d Heb., ch. 11; Ether 12: 12 (7–22).
25*a* Isa. 29: 13 (13–24).
b Matt. 15: 8 (7–9). TG Honor; Respect.
c TG Hardheartedness.
d 2 Ne. 28: 31.
26*a* 1 Ne. 22: 8; 2 Ne. 29: 1 (1–2). TG Restoration of the Gospel.
b Isa. 29: 14; 2 Ne. 25: 17.
c TG Wisdom.
d TG Learning.
e TG Knowledge.
f TG Prudence.
27*a* Isa. 29: 15 (15–16).
b TG Conspiracy; Counsel.
c TG Secret Combinations.
d Jer. 18: 6.
e TG God, Omniscience of.
28*a* TG Earth, Renewal of.
29*a* Isa. 29: 18.
b TG Deaf.
30*a* TG Meekness.
b D&C 101: 36.
31*a* Isa. 29: 20.
32*a* Luke 11: 54 (53–54); Acts 22: 22. TG Offense.
b Amos 5: 10 (7, 10).
c 2 Ne. 28: 16.
33*a* TG Israel, Restoration of.
34*a* Isa. 29: 23.
35*a* 2 Ne. 28: 14; D&C 33: 4.
b Dan. 12: 4 (4–10).

[Between 559 and 545 B.C.]

the Spirit hath constrained me; wherefore, I know that they must surely come to pass.

2 And the things which shall be written out of the [a]book shall be of great [b]worth unto the children of men, and especially unto our seed, which is a [c]remnant of the house of Israel.

3 For it shall come to pass in that day that the [a]churches which are built up, and not unto the Lord, when the one shall say unto the other: Behold, I, I am the Lord's; and the others shall say: I, I am the Lord's; and thus shall every one say that hath built up [b]churches, and not unto the Lord—

4 And they shall contend one with another; and their priests shall contend one with another, and they shall teach with their [a]learning, and deny the [b]Holy Ghost, which giveth utterance.

5 And they [a]deny the [b]power of God, the Holy One of Israel; and they say unto the people: Hearken unto us, and hear ye our precept; for behold there is [c]no God today, for the Lord and the Redeemer hath done his work, and he hath given his power unto men;

6 Behold, hearken ye unto my precept; if they shall say there is a miracle wrought by the hand of the Lord, believe it not; for this day he is not a God of [a]miracles; he hath done his work.

7 Yea, and there shall be many which shall say: [a]Eat, drink, and be merry, for tomorrow we die; and it shall be well with us.

8 And there shall also be many which shall say: [a]Eat, drink, and be [b]merry; nevertheless, fear God—he will [c]justify in committing a little [d]sin; yea, [e]lie a little, take the advantage of one because of his words, dig a [f]pit for thy neighbor; there is [g]no harm in this; and do all these things, for tomorrow we die; and if it so be that we are guilty, God will beat us with a few stripes, and at last we shall be saved in the kingdom of God.

9 Yea, and there shall be many which shall teach after this manner, [a]false and vain and [b]foolish [c]doctrines, and shall be puffed up in their hearts, and shall seek deep to hide their counsels from the Lord; and their works shall be in the dark.

10 And the [a]blood of the saints shall cry from the ground against them.

11 Yea, they have all gone out of the [a]way; they have become [b]corrupted.

12 Because of [a]pride, and because of [b]false teachers, and [c]false doctrine, their churches have become corrupted, and their churches are lifted up; because of pride they are puffed up.

13 They [a]rob the [b]poor because of their fine sanctuaries; they rob the poor because of their fine clothing;

28 2*a* TG Book of Mormon; Restoration of the Gospel.
b 1 Ne. 13: 39 (34–42); 14: 5 (1–5); 22: 9; 2 Ne. 30: 3; 3 Ne. 21: 6.
c TG Israel, Remnant of.
3*a* 1 Cor. 1: 13 (10–13); 1 Ne. 22: 23; 4 Ne. 1: 26 (25–29); Morm. 8: 28 (28, 32–38).
b TG Churches, False.
4*a* 2 Ne. 9: 28; 26: 20.
b 1 Cor. 2: 4 (1–9).
5*a* 2 Ne. 26: 20; Morm. 9: 26 (7–26).
b 2 Tim. 3: 5.
c Alma 30: 28.
6*a* 3 Ne. 29: 7; Morm. 8: 26; 9: 15 (15–26).
7*a* Prov. 16: 25; 1 Cor. 15: 32; Alma 30: 17 (17–18).
8*a* Isa. 22: 13.
b TG Worldliness.
c Morm. 8: 31.
d Mal. 2: 17.
e D&C 10: 25; Moses 4: 4. TG Lying.
f Job 6: 27; Prov. 26: 27; 1 Ne. 14: 3; 22: 14; D&C 109: 25.
g Alma 30: 17.
9*a* TG False Doctrine.
b Ezek. 13: 3; Hel. 13: 29.
c Matt. 15: 9; Col. 2: 22 (18–22).
10*a* Gen. 4: 10; Rev. 6: 10 (9–11); 18: 24 (22–24); 19: 2; 2 Ne. 26: 3; Morm. 8: 27; Ether 8: 22 (22–24); D&C 87: 7.
11*a* Hel. 6: 31; D&C 132: 25 (22–25).
b Morm. 8: 28 (28–41); D&C 33: 4.
12*a* Prov. 28: 25. TG Pride.
b Jer. 23: 21 (21–32); 50: 6; 3 Ne. 14: 15. TG False Prophets.
c TG False Doctrine.
13*a* Ezek. 34: 8; Morm. 8: 37 (37–41).
b Ezek. 18: 12; 2 Ne. 13: 14 (14–15); Hel. 4: 12 (11–13).

[Between 559 and 545 B.C.]

and they persecute the meek and
the poor in heart, because in their
[c]pride they are puffed up.
14 They wear [a]stiff necks and high
heads; yea, and because of pride,
and wickedness, and abominations,
and [b]whoredoms, they have all
[c]gone astray save it be a [d]few, who
are the humble followers of Christ;
nevertheless, they are [e]led, that in
many instances they do [f]err because
they are taught by the precepts of
men.
15 O the [a]wise, and the learned,
and the rich, that are puffed up in
the [b]pride of their [c]hearts, and all
those who preach [d]false doctrines,
and all those who commit [e]whore-
doms, and pervert the right way of
the Lord, [f]wo, wo, wo be unto them,
saith the Lord God Almighty, for
they shall be thrust down to hell!
16 Wo unto them that [a]turn aside
the just for a thing of naught and
[b]revile against that which is good,
and say that it is of no worth! For the
day shall come that the Lord God
will speedily visit the inhabitants
of the earth; and in that day that
they are [c]fully ripe in iniquity they
shall perish.
17 But behold, if the inhabitants of
the earth shall repent of their
wickedness and abominations they
shall not be destroyed, saith the
Lord of Hosts.
18 But behold, that great and
[a]abominable church, the [b]whore of
all the earth, must [c]tumble to the
earth, and great must be the fall
thereof.
19 For the kingdom of the devil
must [a]shake, and they which belong
to it must needs be stirred up unto
repentance, or the [b]devil will grasp
them with his everlasting [c]chains,
and they be stirred up to anger, and
perish;
20 For behold, at that day shall he
[a]rage in the [b]hearts of the children
of men, and stir them up to anger
against that which is good.
21 And others will he [a]pacify, and
lull them away into carnal [b]security,
that they will say: All is well in
Zion; yea, Zion prospereth, all is
well—and thus the [c]devil [d]cheateth
their souls, and leadeth them away
carefully down to hell.
22 And behold, others he [a]flattereth
away, and telleth them there is no
[b]hell; and he saith unto them: I am
no devil, for there is none—and thus
he whispereth in their ears, until he
grasps them with his awful [c]chains,
from whence there is no deliverance.
23 Yea, they are grasped with
death, and hell; and death, and hell,
and the devil, and all that have been
seized therewith must stand before
the throne of God, and be [a]judged
according to their works, from
whence they must go into the place
prepared for them, even a [b]lake of
fire and brimstone, which is endless
torment.
24 Therefore, wo be unto him that
is at [a]ease in Zion!

13*c* Alma 5: 53; Morm. 8: 36 (36–39).
14*a* Prov. 21: 4. TG Stiffneckedness.
b TG Whoredom.
c 2 Ne. 12: 5; Mosiah 14: 6; Alma 5: 37.
d Morm. 8: 36.
e 2 Pet. 3: 17.
f Matt. 22: 29; 2 Ne. 27: 35 (34–35); D&C 33: 4.
15*a* Prov. 3: 7 (5–7); 2 Ne. 15: 21.
b TG Pride.
c TG Hardheartedness.
d Matt. 5: 19.
e Mosiah 11: 2.
f 3 Ne. 29: 5 (4–7); Morm. 9: 26.
16*a* 2 Ne. 27: 32.
b Mal. 2: 17. TG Reviling.
c Ether 2: 10 (8–11).
18*a* TG Devil, Church of.
b Rev. 19: 2.
c 1 Ne. 14: 3 (3, 17).
19*a* 1 Ne. 22: 23 (22–23).
b Alma 34: 35.
c Mosiah 23: 12; Alma 12: 11. TG Chain.
20*a* Rev. 13: 7; 2 Ne. 2: 18; D&C 10: 27; 76: 29.
b Alma 8: 9; D&C 10: 20.
21*a* Jacob 3: 11; Alma 5: 7 (6–7); Morm. 8: 31.
b TG Apathy.
c 2 Ne. 9: 39; 32: 8; Alma 30: 42 (42, 53).
d Rev. 13: 14 (11–18).
22*a* TG Flattery.
b Mal. 2: 17.
c 2 Ne. 9: 45; Alma 36: 18. TG Bondage, Spiritual.
23*a* TG Jesus Christ, Judge.
b Rev. 19: 20; 21: 8; 2 Ne. 9: 16 (8–19, 26); Jacob 6: 10.
24*a* Amos 6: 1.

[Between 559 and 545 B.C.]

25 Wo be unto him that crieth: All is well!

26 Yea, wo be unto him that [a]hearkeneth unto the precepts of men, and denieth the power of God, and the gift of the Holy Ghost!

27 Yea, wo be unto him that saith: We have received, and we [a]need no more!

28 And in fine, wo unto all those who tremble, and are [a]angry because of [b]the truth of God! For behold, he that is built upon the [c]rock [d]receiveth it with gladness; and he that is built upon a sandy foundation trembleth lest he shall fall.

29 Wo be unto him that shall say: We have received the word of God, and we [a]need [b]no more of the word of God, for we have enough!

30 For behold, thus saith the Lord God: I will give unto the children of men line upon line, precept upon [a]precept, here a little and there a little; and blessed are those who hearken unto my precepts, and lend an ear unto my counsel, for they shall learn [b]wisdom; for unto him that [c]receiveth I will give [d]more; and from them that shall say, We have enough, from them shall be taken away even that which they have.

31 Cursed is he that putteth his [a]trust in man, or maketh flesh his arm, or shall hearken unto the [b]precepts of men, save their precepts shall be given by the power of the Holy Ghost.

32 [a]Wo be unto the Gentiles, saith the Lord God of Hosts! For notwithstanding I shall lengthen out mine arm unto them from day to day, they will deny me; nevertheless, I will be merciful unto them, saith the Lord God, if they will repent and [b]come unto me; for mine [c]arm is lengthened out all the day long, saith the Lord God of Hosts.

CHAPTER 29

Many gentiles shall reject the Book of Mormon—They shall say: We need no more Bible—The Lord speaks to many nations—He will judge the world out of the books thus written.

BUT behold, there shall be many—at that day when I shall proceed to do a [a]marvelous work among them, that I may remember my [b]covenants which I have made unto the children of men, that I may set my hand again the [c]second time to recover my people, which are of the house of Israel;

2 And also, that I may remember the promises which I have made unto thee, Nephi, and also unto thy father, that I would remember your seed; and that the [a]words of your seed should proceed forth out of my mouth unto your seed; and my words shall [b]hiss forth unto the [c]ends of the earth, for a [d]standard unto my people, which are of the house of Israel;

3 And because my words shall hiss forth—many of the Gentiles shall say: A [a]Bible! A Bible! We have

---

26*a* 2 Ne. 9: 29.
27*a* Alma 12: 10 (10–11); 3 Ne. 26: 10 (9–10); Ether 4: 8.
28*a* 2 Ne. 9: 40; 33: 5. TG Rebellion, Rebel.
b Matt. 7: 25.
c TG Rock.
d TG Teachable.
29*a* 2 Ne. 29: 10 (3–10).
b 2 Ne. 27: 14; Ether 4: 8.
30*a* Prov. 2: 9 (9–11); Isa. 28: 13 (9–13); D&C 98: 12.
b Prov. 14: 8. TG Wisdom.
c Luke 8: 18.
d Alma 12: 10; D&C 50: 24.
31*a* D&C 1: 19 (19–20). TG Trust Not in the Arm of Flesh.
b 2 Ne. 27: 25.
32*a* 1 Ne. 14: 6; 3 Ne. 16: 8.
b TG God, Access to.
c 2 Ne. 19: 17 (17–21); Jacob 5: 47; 6: 4; D&C 133: 67.
29 1*a* 2 Ne. 27: 26. TG Restoration of the Gospel.
b TG Abrahamic Covenant.
c 2 Ne. 6: 14; 21: 11; 25: 17. TG Israel, Gathering of; Israel, Restoration of.
2*a* 2 Ne. 3: 21.
b Isa. 5: 26; Moro. 10: 28.
c 2 Ne. 15: 26.
d Ps. 60: 4. TG Ensign.
3*a* 1 Ne. 13: 24 (23–24). TG Bible; Book of Mormon.

[Between 559 and 545 B.C.]

got a Bible, and there cannot be any
more Bible.
4 But thus saith the Lord God:
O fools, they shall have a [a]Bible;
and it shall proceed forth from
the [b]Jews, mine ancient covenant
people. And what [c]thank they the
[d]Jews for the Bible which they
receive from them? Yea, what do
the Gentiles mean? Do they remember the travails, and the labors, and
the pains of the Jews, and their
diligence unto me, in bringing forth
salvation unto the Gentiles?
5 O ye Gentiles, have ye remembered the Jews, mine ancient
covenant people? Nay; but ye have
[a]cursed them, and have [b]hated them,
and have not sought to recover
them. But behold, I will return all
these things upon your own heads;
for I the Lord have not forgotten
my people.
6 Thou fool, that shall say: A
[a]Bible, we have got a Bible, and we
need no more Bible. Have ye obtained a Bible save it were by the
Jews?
7 Know ye not that there are more
[a]nations than one? Know ye not
that I, the Lord your God, have
created all men, and that I remember those who are upon the
[b]isles of the sea; and that I rule in
the heavens above and in the [c]earth
beneath; and I bring forth my [d]word
unto the children of men, yea, even
upon all the nations of the earth?
8 Wherefore murmur ye, because
that ye shall receive more of my
word? Know ye not that the [a]testi-
mony of [b]two nations is a [c]witness
unto you that I am God, that I remember one [d]nation like unto another? Wherefore, I speak the same
words unto one nation like unto another. And when the two [e]nations
shall run together the testimony of
the two nations shall run together
also.
9 And I do this that I may prove
unto many that I am the [a]same
yesterday, today, and forever; and
that I speak forth my [b]words according to mine own pleasure. And because that I have spoken one [c]word
ye need not suppose that I cannot speak another; for my [d]work
is not yet finished; neither shall it
be until the end of man, neither
from that time henceforth and forever.
10 Wherefore, because that ye
have a Bible ye need not suppose
that it contains all my [a]words;
neither [b]need ye suppose that I have
not caused more to be written.
11 For I command [a]all men, both
in the east and in the west, and in
the north, and in the south, and in
the islands of the sea, that they shall
[b]write the words which I speak unto
them; for out of the [c]books which
shall be written I will [d]judge the
world, every man according to their
works, according to that which is
written.
12 For behold, I shall speak unto
the [a]Jews and they shall [b]write it;
and I shall also speak unto the

4*a* Rom. 3: 2 (1–3).
b Neh. 1: 10; 1 Ne. 13: 25 (23–25); D&C 3: 16.
c TG Ingratitude; Thanksgiving.
d TG Israel, Judah, People of.
5*a* Micah 6: 16. TG Curse.
b 3 Ne. 29: 8. TG Hate.
6*a* 1 Ne. 13: 23, 38.
7*a* TG Jesus Christ, Creator; Man, Physical Creation of; Nations.
b Isa. 51: 5; 1 Ne. 22: 4; 2 Ne. 10: 8 (8, 20); D&C 133: 8.
c Deut. 10: 14; 1 Ne. 11: 6; D&C 55: 1; Moses 6: 44.
d D&C 5: 6.
8*a* TG Testimony.
b Ezek. 37: 17 (15–20); 1 Ne. 13: 39 (38–41); 2 Ne. 3: 12; 33: 10 (10–11).
c Matt. 18: 16.
d 2 Sam. 7: 23; Alma 9: 20.
e Hosea 1: 11.
9*a* Heb. 13: 8.
b TG Word of God; Word of the Lord.
c TG Revelation.
d Moses 1: 4.
10*a* TG Scriptures to Come Forth.
b 2 Ne. 28: 29.
11*a* Alma 29: 8.
b 2 Tim. 3: 16; Moses 1: 40. TG Scriptures, Preservation of; Scriptures, Writing of.
c TG Book of Life.
d 2 Ne. 25: 22 (18, 22); 33: 14 (11, 14–15). TG Jesus Christ, Judge.
12*a* 1 Ne. 13: 23 (23–29); 2 Ne. 3: 12.
b TG Scriptures, Lost.

[Between 559 and 545 B.C.]

Nephites and they shall [c]write it;
and I shall also speak unto the other
tribes of the house of Israel, which I
have led away, and they shall write
it; and I shall also speak unto [d]all
nations of the earth and they shall
write it.
13 And it shall come to pass that
the [a]Jews shall have the words of
the Nephites, and the Nephites shall
have the words of the Jews; and the
Nephites and the Jews shall have
the words of the [b]lost tribes of Israel;
and the lost tribes of Israel shall
have the words of the Nephites and
the Jews.
14 And it shall come to pass that
my people, which are of the [a]house
of Israel, shall be gathered home
unto the [b]lands of their possessions;
and my word also shall be gathered
in [c]one. And I will show unto them
that fight against my word and
against my [d]people, who are of the
[e]house of Israel, that I am God, and
that I [f]covenanted with [g]Abraham
that I would remember his [h]seed
[i]forever.

CHAPTER 30

Converted gentiles shall be numbered with the covenant people—Many Lamanites and Jews shall believe the word and become a delightsome people—Israel shall be restored and the wicked destroyed.

AND now behold, my beloved
brethren, I would speak unto you;
for I, Nephi, would not suffer that
ye should suppose that ye are more
righteous than the Gentiles shall
be. For behold, except ye shall keep
the commandments of God ye shall
all likewise [a]perish; and because of
the words which have been spoken
ye need not suppose that the
Gentiles are utterly destroyed.
2 For behold, I say unto you that
as many of the Gentiles as will
repent are the [a]covenant people of
the Lord; and as many of the [b]Jews
as will not repent shall be [c]cast off;
for the Lord [d]covenanteth with none
save it be with them that [e]repent
and believe in his Son, who is the
Holy One of Israel.
3 And now, I would prophesy
somewhat more concerning the Jews
and the Gentiles. For after the book
of which I have spoken shall come
forth, and be written unto the
Gentiles, and sealed up again unto
the Lord, there shall be many which
shall [a]believe the words which are
written; and [b]they shall carry them
forth unto the [c]remnant of our seed.
4 And then shall the remnant of
our seed know concerning us, how
that we came out from Jerusalem,
and that they are descendants of
the Jews.
5 And the gospel of Jesus Christ
shall be declared among [a]them;
wherefore, [b]they shall be restored
unto the [c]knowledge of their fathers,
and also to the knowledge of Jesus
Christ, which was had among their
fathers.

12c 1 Ne. 13: 40 (39–42); 2 Ne. 26: 17 (16–17); 27: 6 (6–26).
d 2 Ne. 26: 33; Alma 29: 8.
13a Morm. 5: 14 (13–14).
b TG Israel, Ten Lost Tribes of.
14a Jer. 3: 18 (17–19).
b TG Israel, Gathering of; Lands of Inheritance.
c Ezek. 37: 17 (16–17).
d 1 Kgs. 8: 51; 2 Ne. 3: 9; 8: 16.
e 1 Ne. 22: 9; 2 Ne. 30: 7 (7–8).
f Gen. 12: 2 (1–3); 1 Ne. 17: 40; 3 Ne. 20: 27; Abr. 2: 9. TG Abrahamic Covenant.
g Micah 7: 20 (18–20).
h Ps. 102: 28; D&C 132: 30; Moses 7: 52 (50–53). TG Seed of Abraham.
i Gen. 17: 7 (5–7).
30 1a Luke 13: 3 (1–5).
2a Gal. 3: 29 (26–29); Abr. 2: 10 (9–11).
b Matt. 8: 12. TG Israel, Judah, People of.
c Luke 3: 9 (3–9); Rom. 9: 6; Jacob 5: 6.
d Rom. 3: 29.
e TG Repentance.
3a 2 Ne. 28: 2; 3 Ne. 16: 6 (6–13).
b 1 Ne. 22: 9 (5–10); 3 Ne. 5: 25 (20–26).
c 2 Ne. 4: 7 (7–11); Jacob 1: 5. TG Israel, Remnant of.
5a 3 Ne. 21: 5 (3–7, 24–26); Morm. 5: 15.
b D&C 3: 20.
c 1 Ne. 15: 14; 2 Ne. 3: 12; Morm. 7: 9 (1, 9–10).

[Between 559 and 545 B.C.]

6 And then shall they rejoice; for they shall [a]know that it is a blessing unto them from the hand of God; and their [b]scales of darkness shall begin to fall from their eyes; and many generations shall not pass away among them, save they shall be a pure and a [c]delightsome people.

7 And it shall come to pass that the [a]Jews which are scattered also shall [b]begin to believe in Christ; and they shall begin to gather in upon the face of the land; and as many as shall believe in Christ shall also become a delightsome people.

8 And it shall come to pass that the Lord God shall commence his work among all nations, kindreds, tongues, and people, to bring about the [a]restoration of his people upon the earth.

9 And with righteousness shall the [a]Lord God [b]judge the poor, and reprove with equity for the [c]meek of the earth. And he shall smite the earth with the rod of his mouth; and with the breath of his lips shall he slay the wicked.

10 For the [a]time speedily cometh that the Lord God shall cause a great [b]division among the people, and the wicked will he [c]destroy; and he will [d]spare his people, yea, even if it so be that he must [e]destroy the wicked by fire.

11 And [a]righteousness shall be the girdle of his loins, and faithfulness the girdle of his reins.

12 And then shall the wolf [a]dwell with the lamb; and the leopard shall lie down with the kid, and the calf, and the young lion, and the fatling, together; and a little child shall lead them.

13 And the cow and the bear shall feed; their young ones shall lie down together; and the lion shall eat straw like the ox.

14 And the sucking child shall play on the hole of the asp, and the weaned child shall put his hand on the cockatrice's den.

15 They shall not hurt nor destroy in all my holy [a]mountain; for the earth shall be full of the [b]knowledge of the Lord as the waters cover the sea.

16 Wherefore, the things of [a]all nations shall be made known; yea, all things shall be made [b]known unto the children of men.

17 There is nothing which is secret save it shall be [a]revealed; there is no work of darkness save it shall be made manifest in the light; and there is nothing which is sealed upon the earth save it shall be loosed.

18 Wherefore, all things which have been revealed unto the children of men shall at that [a]day be revealed; and Satan shall have power over the hearts of the children of men [b]no more, for a long time. And now, my beloved brethren, I make an end of my sayings.

CHAPTER 31

Nephi tells why Christ was baptized—Men must follow Christ, be baptized, receive the Holy Ghost, and endure to the end to be saved—Repentance and

6*a* Alma 3: 14.
b TG Darkness, Spiritual; Spiritual Blindness.
c W of M 1: 8; D&C 49: 24; 109: 65.
7*a* 2 Ne. 29: 14 (13–14); 3 Ne. 5: 25 (23–26). TG Israel, Judah, People of.
b 2 Ne. 25: 16 (16–17).
8*a* TG Israel, Restoration of; Millennium, Preparing a People for.
9*a* Isa. 11: 4 (4–9).
b Ps. 19: 9; 2 Ne. 9: 15.
c TG Meekness.
10*a* Jacob 5: 29; 6: 2. TG Last Days.
b D&C 63: 54.
c Ps. 73: 17 (3–17); D&C 29: 17; JS-M 1: 55.
d 1 Ne. 22: 17 (15–22); 3 Ne. 22: 13 (13–17); Moses 7: 61.
e 1 Ne. 22: 23 (15–17, 23); Jacob 5: 69. TG Earth, Cleansing of.
11*a* Isa. 11: 5 (5–9). TG Righteousness.
12*a* Isa. 65: 25. TG Earth, Renewal of.
15*a* Joel 2: 1.
b TG God, Knowledge about.
16*a* D&C 101: 32 (32–35); 121: 28 (26–32).
b Ether 4: 7 (6–7, 13–17).
17*a* Luke 12: 2 (2–3); D&C 1: 3 (1–3).
18*a* Acts 3: 21.
b Rev. 20: 2 (2–3); Ether 8: 26.

[Between 559 and 545 B.C.]

baptism are the gate to the strait and narrow path—Eternal life comes to those who keep the commandments after baptism.

AND now I, Nephi, make an end of my [a]prophesying unto you, my beloved brethren. And I cannot write but a few things, which I know must surely come to pass; neither can I write but a few of the [b]words of my brother Jacob.

2 Wherefore, the things which I have written sufficeth me, save it be a few words which I [a]must speak concerning the doctrine of Christ; wherefore, I shall speak unto you plainly, according to the plainness of my prophesying.

3 For my soul delighteth in [a]plainness; for after this manner doth the Lord God work among the children of men. For the Lord God giveth light unto the [b]understanding; for he speaketh unto men according to their [c]language, unto their understanding.

4 Wherefore, I would that ye should remember that I have spoken unto you concerning that [a]prophet which the Lord showed unto me, that should baptize the [b]Lamb of God, which should take away the sins of the world.

5 And now, if the Lamb of God, he being [a]holy, should have need to be [b]baptized by water, to fulfil all righteousness, O then, how much more need have we, being unholy, to be [c]baptized, yea, even by water!

6 And now, I would ask of you, my beloved brethren, wherein the Lamb of God did fulfil all righteousness in being baptized by water?

7 Know ye not that he was holy? But notwithstanding he being holy, he showeth unto the children of men that, according to the flesh he humbleth himself before the Father, and witnesseth unto the Father that he would be [a]obedient unto him in keeping his commandments.

8 Wherefore, after he was baptized with water the Holy Ghost descended upon him in the [a]form of a [b]dove.

9 And again, it showeth unto the children of men the straitness of the path, and the narrowness of the [a]gate, by which they should enter, he having set the [b]example before them.

10 And he said unto the children of men: [a]Follow thou me. Wherefore, my beloved brethren, can we [b]follow Jesus save we shall be willing to keep the commandments of the Father?

11 And the Father said: Repent ye, repent ye, and be baptized in the name of my Beloved Son.

12 And also, the voice of the Son came unto me, saying: He that is baptized in my name, to him will the Father [a]give the Holy Ghost, like unto me; wherefore, [b]follow me, and do the things which ye have seen me do.

13 Wherefore, my beloved brethren, I know that if ye shall [a]follow the Son, with full purpose of heart, acting no [b]hypocrisy and no deception before God, but with real [c]intent, repenting of your sins, witnessing unto the Father that ye are [d]willing to take upon you the [e]name

---

31 1*a* 2 Ne. 25: 4 (1–4).
b 2 Ne. 11: 1.
2*a* 2 Ne. 11: 4 (4–6).
3*a* 2 Ne. 25: 7 (7–8); 32: 7.
b TG Understanding.
c D&C 1: 24. TG Language.
4*a* 1 Ne. 10: 7; 11: 27.
b TG Jesus Christ, Lamb of God.
5*a* 1 Jn. 3: 3.
b Matt. 3: 11 (11–17). TG Jesus Christ, Baptism of.
c TG Baptism, Essential.
7*a* John 5: 30. TG Obedience.
8*a* 1 Ne. 11: 27.
b TG Holy Ghost, Dove, Sign of.
9*a* 2 Ne. 9: 41; 3 Ne. 14: 14 (13–14); D&C 22: 4; 43: 7.
b TG Example.
10*a* Matt. 4: 19; 8: 22; 9: 9.
b Matt. 8: 19; Moro. 7: 11; D&C 56: 2.
12*a* TG Holy Ghost, Gift of.
b Matt. 16: 24 (24–26); Luke 9: 59 (57–62); John 12: 26; 1 Jn. 2: 6. TG God, the Standard of Righteousness.
13*a* TG Jesus Christ, Exemplar.
b TG Hypocrisy.
c TG Integrity; Sincerity.
d TG Agency; Commitment.
e TG Jesus Christ, Taking the Name of.

[Between 559 and 545 B.C.]

of Christ, by [f]baptism—yea, by following your Lord and your Savior
down into the water, according to his
word, behold, then shall ye receive
the Holy Ghost; yea, then cometh
the [g]baptism of fire and of the Holy
Ghost; and then can ye speak with
the [h]tongue of angels, and shout
praises unto the Holy One of Israel.
14 But, behold, my beloved brethren, thus came the voice of the Son
unto me, saying: After ye have repented of your sins, and witnessed
unto the Father that ye are willing
to keep my commandments, by the
baptism of water, and have received
the baptism of fire and of the Holy
Ghost, and can speak with a new
tongue, yea, even with the tongue
of angels, and after this should [a]deny
me, it would have been [b]better for
you that ye had not known me.
15 And I heard a voice from the
Father, saying: Yea, the [a]words of
my Beloved are true and faithful.
He that [b]endureth to the [c]end, the
same shall be saved.
16 And now, my beloved brethren,
I know by this that unless a man
shall [a]endure to the end, in following
the [b]example of the Son of the living
God, he cannot be saved.
17 Wherefore, do the things which
I have told you I have seen that your
Lord and your Redeemer should do;
for, for this cause have they been
shown unto me, that ye might know
the gate by which ye should enter.
For the gate by which ye should
enter is repentance and [a]baptism by
water; and then cometh a [b]remission
of your sins by fire and by the Holy
Ghost.
18 And then are ye in this [a]strait
and narrow [b]path which leads to
eternal life; yea, ye have entered in
by the gate; ye have done according
to the commandments of the Father
and the Son; and ye have received
the Holy Ghost, which [c]witnesses of
the [d]Father and the Son, unto the
fulfilling of the promise which he
hath made, that if ye entered in by
the way ye should receive.
19 And now, my beloved brethren,
after ye have gotten into this strait
and narrow [a]path, I would ask if all
is [b]done? Behold, I say unto you,
Nay; for ye have not come thus far
save it were by the word of Christ
with unshaken [c]faith in him, [d]rely-
ing wholly upon the merits of him
who is mighty to [e]save.
20 Wherefore, ye must press forward with a [a]steadfastness in Christ,
having a perfect brightness of [b]hope,
and a [c]love of God and of all men.
Wherefore, if ye shall press forward,
feasting upon the word of Christ,
and [d]endure to the end, behold, thus
saith the Father: Ye shall have
[e]eternal life.
21 And now, behold, my beloved
brethren, this is the [a]way; and there

13*f* Gal. 3: 27 (26–27).
g TG Holy Ghost, Baptism of.
h 2 Ne. 32: 2 (2–3). TG Holy Ghost, Gifts of.
14*a* Matt. 10: 33 (32–33); Rom. 1: 16 (15–18); 2 Tim. 2: 12 (10–15); Alma 24: 30; D&C 101: 5 (1–5). TG Holy Ghost, Unpardonable Sin against.
b Heb. 6: 4 (4–6); 2 Pet. 2: 21.
15*a* D&C 64: 31; 66: 11.
b Jacob 6: 11 (7–11). TG Endure; Steadfastness.
c Alma 5: 13.
16*a* Mark 13: 13; Alma 38: 2; D&C 20: 29; 53: 7.
b TG Example; Jesus Christ, Exemplar.
17*a* Mosiah 18: 10. TG Baptism.
b TG Holy Ghost, Mission of; Remission of Sins.
18*a* 1 Ne. 8: 20.
b Prov. 4: 18. TG Gate; Path; Way.
c TG Holy Ghost, Mission of; Holy Ghost, Source of Testimony.
d 3 Ne. 28: 11; Moses 6: 66.
19*a* Hosea 14: 9 (8–9).
b Mosiah 4: 10.
c TG Faith.
d Moro. 6: 4; D&C 3: 20; Moses 7: 53.
e TG Jesus Christ, Atonement through.
20*a* TG Commitment; Dedication; Perseverance; Steadfastness; Walking with God.
b TG Hope.
c TG God, Love of; Love.
d James 5: 8 (7–11); Rev. 2: 25 (25–26); 3 Ne. 15: 9.
e 1 Jn. 2: 25; 5: 13 (10–21). TG Objectives.
21*a* Ex. 33: 13 (12–13); Acts 4: 12; 2 Ne. 9: 41; Alma 37: 46; D&C 132: 22 (22, 25).

[Between 559 and 545 B.C.]

is [b]none other way nor [c]name given
under heaven whereby man can be
saved in the kingdom of God. And
now, behold, this is the [d]doctrine
of Christ, and the only and true
doctrine of the [e]Father, and of the
Son, and of the Holy Ghost, which
is [f]one God, without end. Amen.

CHAPTER 32

Angels speak by the power of the Holy Ghost—Men must pray and gain knowledge for themselves from the Holy Ghost.

AND now, behold, my beloved
brethren, I suppose that ye ponder
somewhat in your hearts concerning
that which ye should do after ye
have entered in by the way. But, behold, why do ye ponder these things
in your hearts?
2 Do ye not remember that I said
unto you that after ye had [a]received
the Holy Ghost ye could speak with
the [b]tongue of angels? And now,
how could ye speak with the tongue
of angels save it were by the Holy
Ghost?
3 [a]Angels speak by the power of the
Holy Ghost; wherefore, they speak
the words of Christ. Wherefore, I
said unto you, [b]feast upon the [c]words
of Christ; for behold, the words of
Christ will [d]tell you all things what
ye should do.
4 Wherefore, now after I have
spoken these words, if ye cannot
understand them it will be because
ye [a]ask not, neither do ye knock;
wherefore, ye are not brought into
the light, but must perish in the dark.
5 For behold, again I say unto you
that if ye will enter in by the way,
and receive the Holy Ghost, it will
[a]show unto you all things what ye
should do.
6 Behold, this is the doctrine of
Christ, and there will be no more
doctrine given until after he shall
[a]manifest himself unto you in the
flesh. And when he shall manifest
himself unto you in the flesh, the
things which he shall say unto you
shall ye observe to do.
7 And now I, Nephi, cannot say
more; the Spirit stoppeth mine
utterance, and I am left to mourn
because of the [a]unbelief, and the
wickedness, and the ignorance, and
the [b]stiffneckedness of men; for
they will [c]not search [d]knowledge,
nor understand great knowledge,
when it is given unto them in [e]plain-
ness, even as plain as word can be.
8 And now, my beloved brethren, I
perceive that ye ponder still in your
hearts; and it grieveth me that I
must speak concerning this thing.
For if ye would hearken unto the
[a]Spirit which teacheth a man to
[b]pray ye would know that ye must
[c]pray; for the [d]evil spirit teacheth
not a man to pray, but teacheth him
that he must not pray.
9 But behold, I say unto you that
ye must [a]pray always, and not faint;
that ye must not perform any thing
unto the Lord save in the first place
ye shall [b]pray unto the Father in

21*b* 2 Ne. 25: 20; Mosiah 3: 17.
c TG Jesus Christ, Taking the Name of.
d Matt. 7: 28; John 7: 16.
e TG Godhead.
f Deut. 6: 4; Gal. 3: 20; 1 Ne. 13: 41; 3 Ne. 28: 10; Morm. 7: 7. TG Unity.
32 2*a* Alma 36: 24; 3 Ne. 9: 20.
b 2 Ne. 31: 13.
3*a* TG Angels.
b Jer. 15: 16. TG Bread of Life; Study.
c Col. 3: 16.
d Ex. 4: 15. TG Problem-Solving.
4*a* TG Ask.
5*a* 3 Ne. 16: 6; Ether 4: 11 (11–12); D&C 28: 15; Moses 8: 24. TG Holy Ghost, Gifts of; Revelation.
6*a* 1 Ne. 12: 6.
7*a* TG Doubt; Unbelief, Unbelievers.
b TG Stiffneckedness.
c 2 Pet. 3: 5.
d TG Knowledge.
e 2 Ne. 25: 7 (7–8); 31: 3; Jacob 4: 13; Alma 13: 23; Ether 12: 39.
8*a* TG Discernment, Spiritual.
b TG Prayer.
c Jacob 3: 1.
d 2 Ne. 9: 39; 28: 21 (20–22); Mosiah 2: 32; 4: 14; Alma 30: 42 (42, 53). TG Spirits, Evil or Unclean.
9*a* 1 Sam. 7: 8; Mosiah 26: 39; 3 Ne. 20: 1.
b Job 33: 26; D&C 75: 11.

[Between 559 and 545 B.C.]

the [c]name of Christ, that he will [d]consecrate thy performance unto thee, that thy performance may be for the [e]welfare of thy soul.

CHAPTER 33

Nephi's words are true—They testify of Christ—Those who believe in Christ will believe Nephi's words—They shall stand as a witness before the judgment bar.

AND now I, Nephi, cannot write all the things which were taught among my people; neither am I [a]mighty in writing, like unto speaking; for when a man [b]speaketh by the power of the Holy Ghost the power of the Holy Ghost carrieth it unto the hearts of the children of men.

2 But behold, there are many that [a]harden their [b]hearts against the Holy [c]Spirit, that it hath no place in them; wherefore, they cast many things away which are written and esteem them as things of naught.

3 But I, Nephi, have written what I have written, and I esteem it as of great [a]worth, and especially unto my people. For I [b]pray continually for them by day, and mine [c]eyes water my pillow by night, because of them; and I cry unto my God in faith, and I know that he will hear my cry.

4 And I know that the Lord God will consecrate my prayers for the gain of my people. And the words which I have written in weakness will be made strong unto them; for it [a]persuadeth them to do good; it maketh known unto them of their fathers; and it speaketh of Jesus, and persuadeth them to believe in him, and to endure to the end, which is life [b]eternal.

5 And it speaketh [a]harshly against sin, according to the [b]plainness of the truth; wherefore, no man will be angry at the words which I have written save he shall be of the spirit of the devil.

6 I [a]glory in [b]plainness; I glory in truth; I glory in my Jesus, for he hath [c]redeemed my soul from hell.

7 I have [a]charity for my people, and great faith in Christ that I shall meet many souls spotless at his judgment-seat.

8 I have charity for the [a]Jew—I say Jew, because I mean them from whence I came.

9 I also have charity for the Gentiles. But behold, for none of [a]these can I hope except they shall be [b]reconciled unto Christ, and enter into the [c]narrow [d]gate, and [e]walk in the [f]strait path which leads to life, and continue in the path until the end of the day of [g]probation.

10 And now, my beloved brethren, and also [a]Jew, and all ye ends of the earth, hearken unto these words and [b]believe in Christ; and if ye believe not in these words believe in Christ.

9c Col. 3:17; Moses 5:8.
d Micah 4:13; 2 Ne. 2:2.
e Alma 34:27.
33 1a Ether 12:23 (23–27).
b Rom. 10:17 (13–17); D&C 100:8 (7–8). TG Holy Ghost, Gifts of.
2a Num. 15:31 (30–31); 1 Ne. 19:7; Jacob 4:14; D&C 3:7 (4–13). TG Hardheartedness.
b TG Spiritual Blindness.
c TG Holy Ghost, Loss of.
3a TG Scriptures, Value of.
b Gen. 20:7; Num. 21:7; 1 Sam. 7:5; Jer. 42:4; Enos 1:9 (9–12); W of M 1:8; Moro. 9:22.
c Jer. 13:17; Ps. 6:6; Acts 20:19.
4a Ether 8:26; Moro. 7:13 (12–17). TG Motivations.
b TG Eternal Life.
5a 1 Ne. 16:2 (1–3); 2 Ne. 9:40; 28:28; Enos 1:23; W of M 1:17.
b 2 Ne. 25:4; Jacob 2:11; 4:13.
6a Ps. 44:8 (4–8); D&C 76:61.
b 2 Ne. 31:3.
c Enos 1:27.
7a TG Charity.
8a BD Judah, Kingdom of. TG Israel, Judah, People of.
9a Eph. 3:6 (1–7); 2 Ne. 10:18; 3 Ne. 21:14.
b TG Reconciliation.
c 2 Ne. 9:41; Hel. 3:29 (29–30).
d Matt. 7:14.
e TG Walking with God.
f D&C 132:22.
g TG Probation.
10a TG Israel, Judah, People of.
b TG Believe.

[Between 559 and 545 B.C.]

And if ye shall [c]believe in Christ ye will believe in these [d]words, for they are the [e]words of Christ, and he hath given them unto me; and they [f]teach all men that they should do good.

11 And if they are not the words of Christ, judge ye—for Christ will show unto you, with [a]power and great [b]glory, that they are his words, at the last day; and you and I shall stand face to face before his bar; and ye shall know that I have been commanded of him to write these things, notwithstanding my weakness.

12 And I pray the Father in the name of Christ that many of us, if not all, may be saved in his [a]kingdom at that great and last day.

13 And now, my beloved brethren, all those who are of the house of Israel, and all ye ends of the earth, I speak unto you as the voice of one [a]crying from the dust: Farewell until that great day shall come.

14 And you that will not partake of the goodness of God, and respect the words of the [a]Jews, and also my [b]words, and the words which shall proceed forth out of the mouth of the Lamb of God, behold, I bid you an everlasting farewell, for these words shall [c]condemn you at the last day.

15 For what I seal on earth, shall be brought against you at the [a]judgment bar; for thus hath the Lord commanded me, and I must [b]obey. Amen.

THE BOOK OF JACOB

THE BROTHER OF NEPHI

The words of his preaching unto his brethren. He confoundeth a man who seeketh to overthrow the doctrine of Christ. A few words concerning the history of the people of Nephi.

CHAPTER 1

Jacob and Joseph seek to persuade men to believe in Christ and keep his commandments—Nephi dies—Wickedness prevails among the Nephites.

FOR behold, it came to pass that *fifty and five years had passed away from the time that Lehi left Jerusalem; wherefore, Nephi gave me, Jacob, a [a]commandment concerning the [b]small plates, upon which these things are engraven.

2 And he gave me, Jacob, a commandment that I should [a]write upon [b]these plates a few of the things which I considered to be most precious; that I should not touch, save it were lightly, concerning the history of this people which are called the people of Nephi.

3 For he said that the history of his

10c John 8: 47.
d TG Book of Mormon.
e Isa. 51: 16; Moro. 10: 27 (27–29); D&C 1: 24.
f 1 Kgs. 8: 36; 2 Ne. 25: 28.
11a Ether 5: 4 (4–6); Moro. 7: 35.
b TG Jesus Christ, Glory of.
12a TG Kingdom of God, in Heaven; Kingdom of God, on Earth.
13a Isa. 29: 4; 2 Ne. 27: 13; Morm. 8: 26.
14a TG Bible.
b TG Book of Mormon.
c 2 Ne. 29: 11; W of M 1: 11.
15a 2 Ne. 25: 22; 3 Ne. 27: 25 (23–27); Ether 4: 10 (8–10).
b TG Obedience.

[JACOB]
1 1a Jacob 7: 27; Jarom 1: 15 (1–2, 15); Omni 1: 3.
b 2 Ne. 5: 31 (28–33); Jacob 3: 13 (13–14).
2a TG Scribe; Scriptures, Writing of.
b 1 Ne. 6: 6.

[*544 B.C.]

people should be engraven upon his [a]other plates, and that I should [b]preserve these plates and hand them down unto my seed, from generation to generation.

4 And if there were preaching which was [a]sacred, or revelation which was great, or prophesying, that I should engraven the [b]heads of them upon these plates, and touch upon them as much as it were possible, for Christ's sake, and for the sake of our people.

5 For because of faith and great anxiety, it truly had been made manifest unto us concerning our people, what things should [a]happen unto them.

6 And we also had many revelations, and the spirit of much prophecy; wherefore, we knew of [a]Christ and his kingdom, which should come.

7 Wherefore we labored diligently among our people, that we might persuade them to [a]come unto Christ, and partake of the goodness of God, that they might enter into his [b]rest, lest by any means he should swear in his wrath they should not [c]enter in, as in the [d]provocation in the days of temptation while the children of Israel were in the [e]wilderness.

8 Wherefore, we would to God that we could persuade all men [a]not to rebel against God, to [b]provoke him to anger, but that all men would believe in Christ, and view his death, and suffer his [c]cross and bear the shame of the world; wherefore, I, Jacob, take it upon me to fulfil the commandment of my brother Nephi.

9 Now Nephi began to be old, and he saw that he must soon [a]die; wherefore, he [b]anointed a man to be a king and a ruler over his people now, according to the reigns of the [c]kings.

10 The people having loved Nephi exceedingly, he having been a great protector for them, having wielded the [a]sword of Laban in their defence, and having labored in all his days for their welfare—

11 Wherefore, the people were desirous to retain in remembrance his name. And whoso should reign in his stead were called by the people, second Nephi, third Nephi, and so forth, according to the reigns of the kings; and thus they were called by the people, let them be of whatever name they would.

12 And it came to pass that Nephi died.

13 Now the people which were not [a]Lamanites were Nephites; nevertheless, they were called Nephites, Jacobites, Josephites, [b]Zoramites, Lamanites, Lemuelites, and Ishmaelites.

14 But I, Jacob, shall not hereafter distinguish [a]them by these names, but I shall [b]call them Lamanites that seek to destroy the people of Nephi, and those who are friendly to Nephi I shall call [c]Nephites, or the [d]people of Nephi, according to the reigns of the kings.

3*a* 2 Ne. 5: 33 (29–33); Jacob 3: 13 (13–14).
b TG Scriptures, Preservation of.
4*a* TG Sacred.
b IE the dominant, important items.
5*a* See 1 Nephi, chapters 12–15. See also 1 Ne. 22: 7 (7–8); 2 Ne. 1: 9 (5–10); 4: 7 (7–11); 30: 3 (3–6).
6*a* 1 Ne. 10: 4 (4–11); 19: 8 (8–14).
7*a* 2 Ne. 9: 41 (41, 45, 51); Omni 1: 26 (25–26).
b TG Rest.
c Num. 14: 23; Deut. 1: 35 (35–37); D&C 84: 24 (23–25).
d Heb. 3: 8.
e Num. 26: 65; 1 Ne. 17: 31 (23–31).
8*a* TG Loyalty; Rebellion.
b Num. 14: 11 (11–12); 1 Kgs. 16: 33; 1 Ne. 17: 30 (23–31); Alma 12: 37 (36–37); Hel. 7: 18.
c Luke 14: 27.
9*a* Gen. 47: 29 (28–29); 2 Ne. 1: 14.
b TG Anointing.
c 2 Ne. 6: 2; Jarom 1: 7 (7, 14).
10*a* 1 Ne. 4: 9; 2 Ne. 5: 14; W of M 1: 13; Mosiah 1: 16; D&C 17: 1.
13*a* Enos 1: 13; Alma 23: 17; D&C 3: 18.
b 1 Ne. 4: 35; Alma 54: 23; 4 Ne. 1: 36 (36–37).
14*a* W of M 1: 16.
b Mosiah 25: 12; Alma 2: 11.
c 2 Ne. 4: 11.
d 2 Ne. 5: 9.

[Between 544 and 421 B.C.]

15 And now it came to pass that
the people of Nephi, under the reign
of the second king, began to grow
hard in their hearts, and indulge
themselves somewhat in wicked
practices, such as like unto David
of old desiring many [a]wives and
[b]concubines, and also Solomon, his
son.
16 Yea, and they also began to
search much [a]gold and silver, and
began to be lifted up somewhat in
pride.
17 Wherefore I, Jacob, gave unto
them these words as I taught them in
the [a]temple, having first obtained
mine [b]errand from the Lord.
18 For I, Jacob, and my brother
Joseph had been [a]consecrated priests
and [b]teachers of this people, by the
hand of Nephi.
19 And we did [a]magnify our office
unto the Lord, taking upon us the
[b]responsibility, answering the sins
of the people upon our own heads if
we did not [c]teach them the word of
God with all diligence; wherefore,
by laboring with our might their
[d]blood might not come upon our
garments; otherwise their blood
would come upon our garments,
and we would not be found spotless
at the last day.

CHAPTER 2

Jacob denounces the love of riches, pride, and unchastity—Men should seek riches to help their fellow men—Jacob condemns the unauthorized practice of plural marriage—The Lord delights in the chastity of women.

THE [a]words which Jacob, the
brother of Nephi, spake unto the
people of Nephi, after the death of
Nephi:
2 Now, my beloved brethren, I,
Jacob, according to the [a]responsibility which I am under to God, to
[b]magnify mine office with [c]soberness,
and that I might [d]rid my garments of
your sins, I come up into the temple
this day that I might declare unto
you the word of God.
3 And ye yourselves know that I
have hitherto been diligent in the
office of my calling; but I this day
am weighed down with much more
desire and anxiety for the [a]welfare
of your souls than I have hitherto
been.
4 For behold, as yet, ye have been
obedient unto the word of the Lord,
which I have given unto you.
5 But behold, hearken ye unto me,
and know that by the help of the all-powerful Creator of heaven and
earth I can tell you concerning your
[a]thoughts, how that ye are beginning
to labor in sin, which sin appeareth
very abominable unto me, yea, and
abominable unto God.
6 Yea, it grieveth my soul and
causeth me to shrink with shame
before the presence of my Maker,
that I must testify unto you concerning the wickedness of your
hearts.
7 And also it grieveth me that I
must use so much [a]boldness of
speech concerning you, before your
wives and your children, many of
whose feelings are exceedingly
tender and [b]chaste and delicate

15*a* Deut. 17:17; 1 Sam. 25:43 (42–43); D&C 132:38 (38–39).
b 2 Sam. 20:3; 1 Chr. 3:9.
16*a* Mosiah 2:12.
17*a* 2 Ne. 5:16; Alma 16:13; Hel. 3:14 (9, 14); 3 Ne. 11:1. TG Temple.
b TG Called of God.
18*a* 2 Ne. 5:26. TG Delegation of Responsibility; Setting Apart.
b TG Teacher.
19*a* Jacob 2:2; D&C 24:3. TG Leadership; Priesthood, Magnifying Callings within.
b Ezek. 34:10. TG Accountability; Stewardship.
c 1 Sam. 8:9; Moro. 9:6.
d Lev. 20:27; Acts 20:26; 2 Ne. 9:44; Mosiah 2:27; D&C 88:85; 112:33.
2 1*a* 2 Ne. 6:1.
2*a* TG Stewardship.
b Rom. 11:13; Jacob 1:19; D&C 24:3.
c TG Sincerity.
d Mosiah 2:28.
3*a* 2 Ne. 6:3; Mosiah 25:11.
5*a* Amos 4:13; Alma 12:3 (3–7); D&C 6:16. TG God, Omniscience of.
7*a* Lev. 19:17; D&C 121:43.
b TG Chastity.

[Between 544 and 421 B.C.]

before God, which thing is pleasing
unto God;
8 And it supposeth me that they
have come up hither to hear the
pleasing [a]word of God, yea, the word
which healeth the wounded soul.
9 Wherefore, it burdeneth my soul
that I should be constrained, because of the strict commandment
which I have received from God, to
[a]admonish you according to your
crimes, to enlarge the wounds of
those who are already wounded,
instead of consoling and healing
their wounds; and those who have
not been wounded, instead of feasting upon the pleasing word of God
have daggers placed to pierce their
souls and wound their delicate
minds.
10 But, notwithstanding the greatness of the task, I must do according
to the strict [a]commands of God, and
tell you concerning your wickedness
and abominations, in the presence
of the pure in heart, and the broken
heart, and under the glance of the
[b]piercing eye of the Almighty God.
11 Wherefore, I must tell you the
truth according to the [a]plainness of
the [b]word of God. For behold, as I
inquired of the Lord, thus came the
word unto me, saying: Jacob, get
thou up into the temple on the
morrow, and declare the word which
I shall give thee unto this people.
12 And now behold, my brethren,
this is the word which I declare
unto you, that many of you have
begun to search for gold, and for
silver, and for all manner of precious [a]ores, in the which this land,
which is a [b]land of promise unto
you and to your seed, doth abound
most plentifully.
13 And the hand of providence
hath smiled upon you most pleas-
ingly, that you have obtained many
riches; and because some of you
have obtained more abundantly
than that of your brethren ye are
[a]lifted up in the pride of your hearts,
and wear stiff necks and high heads
because of the costliness of your
apparel, and persecute your brethren because ye suppose that ye are
better than they.
14 And now, my brethren, do ye
suppose that God justifieth you in
this thing? Behold, I say unto you,
Nay. But he condemneth you, and
if ye persist in these things his judgments must speedily come unto you.
15 O that he would show you that
he can pierce you, and with one
glance of his [a]eye he can smite you
to the dust!
16 O that he would rid you from
this iniquity and abomination. And,
O that ye would listen unto the
word of his commands, and let not
this [a]pride of your hearts destroy
your souls!
17 Think of your [a]brethren like
unto yourselves, and be familiar
with all and free with your [b]sub-
stance, that [c]they may be rich like
unto you.
18 But [a]before ye seek for [b]riches,
seek ye for the [c]kingdom of God.
19 And after ye have obtained a
hope in Christ ye shall obtain riches,
if ye seek them; and ye will seek
them for the intent to [a]do good—

8*a* Micah 2: 7; Alma 31: 5; 36: 26; Hel. 3: 29 (29–30). TG Gospel.
9*a* TG Warnings.
10*a* TG Commandments of God.
b 2 Ne. 9: 44. TG God, Omniscience of.
11*a* 2 Ne. 25: 4; 33: 5; Jacob 4: 13.
b Jacob 7: 5.
12*a* 1 Ne. 18: 25; 2 Ne. 5: 15 (14–16); Hel. 6: 9 (9–11); Ether 9: 17; 10: 23 (12, 23).
b 1 Ne. 4: 14; 17: 13 (13–14). TG Promised Lands.
13*a* 2 Kgs. 14: 10; Alma 1: 32; 31: 25; Morm. 8: 28 (28, 36–40).
15*a* TG God, Indignation of; God, Omniscience of.
16*a* TG Pride.
17*a* James 5: 3 (1–6). TG Love.
b TG Almsgiving; Generosity; Welfare.
c Alma 4: 12; 5: 55; 4 Ne. 1: 3 (3, 24–26).
18*a* Mark 10: 24 (17–27).
b 1 Kgs. 3: 11 (11–13); Prov. 27: 24 (24–27); 2 Ne. 26: 31; Alma 39: 14; D&C 6: 7. TG Worldliness.
c Luke 12: 31 (22–31).
19*a* Mosiah 4: 26; 3 Ne. 12: 42; 4 Ne. 1: 3. TG Good Works.

[Between 544 and 421 B.C.]

to clothe the naked, and to feed the
hungry, and to liberate the captive,
and administer relief to the sick and
the afflicted.
20 And now, my brethren, I have
spoken unto you concerning pride;
and those of you which have afflicted
your neighbor, and persecuted him
because ye were proud in your
hearts, of the things which God hath
given you, what say ye of it?
21 Do ye not suppose that such
things are abominable unto him
who created all flesh? And the one
being is as precious in his sight as the
other. And all flesh is of the dust;
and for the selfsame end hath he
created them, that they should keep
his [a]commandments and glorify
him forever.
22 And now I make an end of
speaking unto you concerning this
pride. And were it not that I must
speak unto you concerning a grosser
crime, my heart would rejoice exceedingly because of you.
23 But the word of God burdens
me because of your grosser crimes.
For behold, thus saith the Lord:
This people begin to wax in iniquity;
they understand not the scriptures,
for they seek to excuse themselves in
committing [a]whoredoms, because of
the things which were written concerning David, and Solomon his son.
24 Behold, David and [a]Solomon
truly had many [b]wives and concubines, which thing was [c]abomin-
able before me, saith the Lord.
25 Wherefore, thus saith the Lord,
I have led this people forth out of
the land of Jerusalem, by the power
of mine arm, that I might raise up
unto me a [a]righteous branch from
the fruit of the loins of Joseph.
26 Wherefore, I the Lord God will
not suffer that this people shall do
like unto them of old.
27 Wherefore, my brethren, hear
me, and hearken to the word of the
Lord: For there shall not any [a]man
among you have save it be [b]one
[c]wife; and concubines he shall have
none;
28 For I, the Lord God, delight in
the [a]chastity of women. And [b]whore-
doms are an abomination before me;
thus saith the Lord of Hosts.
29 Wherefore, this people shall
keep my commandments, saith the
Lord of Hosts, or [a]cursed be the land
for their sakes.
30 For if I will, saith the Lord of
Hosts, raise up [a]seed unto me, I
will command my people; otherwise
they shall hearken unto these things.
31 For behold, I, the Lord, have
seen the sorrow, and heard the
mourning of the daughters of my
people in the land of Jerusalem, yea,
and in all the lands of my people,
because of the wickedness and
[a]abominations of their [b]husbands.
32 And I will not suffer, saith the
Lord of Hosts, that the cries of the
fair daughters of this people, which
I have led out of the land of
Jerusalem, shall come up unto me
against the men of my people, saith
the Lord of Hosts.
33 For they shall not lead away
captive the daughters of my people
because of their tenderness, save I
shall visit them with a sore curse,
even unto destruction; for they shall
not commit [a]whoredoms, like unto

21a D&C 11:20; Abr. 3:25 (25–26).
23a TG Whoredom.
24a 1 Kgs. 11:1; Neh. 13:26 (25–27).
b Deut. 17:17 (14–17); 2 Sam. 5:13; D&C 132:39 (38–39).
c Deut. 7:3 (1–4); 1 Kgs. 11:3; Ezra 9:2 (1–2).
25a Gen. 49:22 (22–26); Ezek. 17:22 (22–24); Amos 5:15; 2 Ne. 3:5; 14:2; Alma 26:36. TG Israel, Joseph, People of.
27a TG Marriage, Husbands.
b Jacob 3:5 (5–7); D&C 49:16. TG Marriage, Plural.
c TG Marriage, Wives.
28a TG Chastity.
b TG Sexual Immorality; Whoredom.
29a Ether 2:11 (8–12). TG Curse.
30a Mal. 2:15; D&C 132:63 (61–66).
31a TG Family, Children, Responsibilities toward.
b TG Marriage, Husbands.
33a Ezek. 16:25 (20–34). TG Sensuality.

[Between 544 and 421 B.C.]

them of old, saith the Lord of Hosts.

34 And now behold, my brethren, ye know that these commandments were given to our [a]father, Lehi; wherefore, ye have known them before; and ye have come unto great condemnation; for ye have done these things which ye ought not to have done.

35 Behold, ye have done [a]greater iniquities than the Lamanites, our brethren. Ye have broken the hearts of your tender wives, and lost the confidence of your children, because of your bad examples before them; and the sobbings of their hearts ascend up to God against you. And because of the [b]strictness of the word of God, which cometh down against you, many hearts died, pierced with deep wounds.

CHAPTER 3

The pure in heart receive the pleasing word of God—Lamanite righteousness exceeds that of Nephites—Jacob warns against fornication, lasciviousness, and every sin.

BUT behold, I, Jacob, would speak unto you that are pure in heart. Look unto God with firmness of mind, and [a]pray unto him with exceeding faith, and he will [b]console you in your [c]afflictions, and he will plead your cause, and send down [d]justice upon those who seek your destruction.

2 O all ye that are pure in heart, lift up your heads and receive the pleasing word of God, and feast upon his [a]love; for ye may, if your [b]minds are [c]firm, forever.

3 But, wo, wo, unto you that are not pure in heart, that are filthy this day before God; for except ye repent the land is [a]cursed for your sakes; and the Lamanites, which are not [b]filthy like unto you, nevertheless they are [c]cursed with a sore cursing, shall scourge you even unto destruction.

4 And the time speedily cometh, that except ye repent they shall possess the land of your inheritance, and the Lord God will [a]lead away the righteous out from among you.

5 Behold, the Lamanites your brethren, whom ye hate because of their filthiness and the cursing which hath come upon their skins, are more righteous than you; for they have not [a]forgotten the commandment of the Lord, which was given unto our father—that they should have save it were [b]one wife, and [c]concubines they should have none, and there should not be [d]whoredoms committed among them.

6 And now, this commandment they observe to keep; wherefore, because of this observance, in keeping this commandment, the Lord God will not destroy them, but will be [a]merciful unto them; and one day they shall [b]become a blessed people.

7 Behold, their [a]husbands [b]love their [c]wives, and their wives love their husbands; and their husbands and their wives love their children; and their [d]unbelief and their hatred towards you is because of the iniquity of their fathers; wherefore,

---

34*a* 1 Ne. 1: 16 (16–17).
35*a* Jacob 3: 5 (5–7).
b Gen. 2: 24.
3 1*a* 2 Ne. 32: 8.
b TG Comfort; Consolation; Pure.
c TG Affliction.
d TG Deliverance; Protection, Divine.
2*a* TG God, Love of.
b TG Steadfastness.
c Alma 57: 27.
3*a* TG Earth, Curse of.
b TG Filthiness.
c 1 Ne. 12: 23.
4*a* Omni 1: 12 (5–7, 12–13).
5*a* Jacob 2: 35.
b Jacob 2: 27.
c Mosiah 11: 2 (2–14); Ether 10: 5.
d TG Chastity.
6*a* 1 Ne. 13: 31; 2 Ne. 4: 7; 10: 18 (18–19); Hel. 15: 12 (10–17); Morm. 5: 20 (20–21).
b 1 Ne. 15: 14 (13–18); 22: 8.
7*a* TG Marriage, Husbands.
b TG Family, Love within; Marriage, Continuing Courtship in.
c TG Marriage, Wives.
d D&C 3: 18. TG Unbelief, Unbelievers.

[Between 544 and 421 B.C.]

how much better are you than they,
in the sight of your great Creator?
8 O my brethren, I fear that unless
ye shall repent of your sins that their
skins will be [a]whiter than yours,
when ye shall be brought with them
before the throne of God.
9 Wherefore, a commandment I
give unto you, which is the word of
God, that ye [a]revile no more against
them because of the darkness of
their skins; neither shall ye revile
against them because of their filthiness; but ye shall remember your
own filthiness, and remember that
their filthiness came because of their
fathers.
10 Wherefore, ye shall remember
your [a]children, how that ye have
grieved their hearts because of the
[b]example that ye have set before
them; and also, remember that ye
may, because of your filthiness,
bring your children unto destruction, and their sins be heaped upon
your heads at the last day.
11 O my brethren, hearken unto
my words; [a]arouse the faculties of
your souls; shake yourselves that ye
may [b]awake from the slumber of
death; and loose yourselves from the
pains of [c]hell that ye may not
become [d]angels to the devil, to be
cast into that lake of fire and brimstone which is the second [e]death.
12 And now I, Jacob, spake many
more things unto the people of
Nephi, [a]warning them against
[b]fornication and [c]lasciviousness, and
every kind of sin, telling them the
awful consequences of them.
13 And a hundredth part of the
proceedings of this people, which
now began to be numerous, cannot
be written upon [a]these plates; but
many of their proceedings are
written upon the [b]larger plates, and
their wars, and their contentions,
and the reigns of their kings.
14 [a]These plates are called the
plates of Jacob, and they were
[b]made by the hand of Nephi. And
I make an end of speaking these
words.

CHAPTER 4

All the prophets worshipped the Father in the name of Christ—Abraham's offering of Isaac was in similitude of God and his Only Begotten—Men should reconcile themselves to God through the atonement—The Jews shall reject the foundation stone.

Now behold, it came to pass that
I, Jacob, having ministered much
unto my people in word, (and I cannot write but a [a]little of my words,
because of the [b]difficulty of engrav-
ing our words upon plates) and we
know that the things which we write
upon plates must remain;
2 But whatsoever things we write
upon anything save it be upon
[a]plates must perish and vanish
away; but we can write a few words
upon plates, which will give our
children, and also our beloved
brethren, a small degree of knowledge concerning us, or concerning
their fathers—
3 Now in this thing we do rejoice;
and we labor diligently to engraven
these words upon plates, hoping
that our beloved brethren and our
children will receive them with
thankful hearts, and look upon
them that they may learn with joy
and not with sorrow, neither with
contempt, concerning their first
[a]parents.

8*a* 3 Ne. 2: 15.
9*a* TG Reviling.
10*a* TG Family, Children, Responsibilities toward; Family, Love within.
b TG Example.
11*a* TG Apathy.
b 2 Ne. 28: 21; Alma 5: 7 (6–7).
c TG Hell.
d 2 Ne. 9: 9 (8–9). TG Spirits, Evil or Unclean.
e TG Death, Spiritual, Second.
12*a* TG Warnings.
b TG Fornication.
c TG Lust.
13*a* Jacob 1: 1 (1–4); 4: 1 (1–4).
b Jarom 1: 14.
14*a* Jarom 1: 2 (1–2).
b 1 Ne. 19: 2 (2–3).
4 1*a* 1 Ne. 6: 6; Jarom 1: 14; Omni 1: 30.
b Ether 12: 24 (23–26).
2*a* TG Scriptures, Preservation of.
3*a* TG Scriptures, Value of.

[Between 544 and 421 B.C.]

4 For, for this intent have we
written these things, that they may
know that we [a]knew of Christ, and
we had a hope of his [b]glory many
hundred years before his coming;
and not only we ourselves had a
hope of his glory, but also all the
holy [c]prophets which were before us.
5 Behold, they believed in Christ
and [a]worshiped the Father in his
name, and also we worship the
Father in his [b]name. And for this
intent we [c]keep the [d]law of Moses,
it [e]pointing our souls to him; and
for this cause it is sanctified unto
us for righteousness, even as it was
accounted unto Abraham in the
wilderness to be obedient unto the
commands of God in offering up his
son Isaac, which is a [f]similitude of
God and his [g]Only Begotten Son.
6 Wherefore, we search the prophets, and we have many revelations and the spirit of [a]prophecy;
and having all these [b]witnesses we
obtain a hope, and our faith becometh unshaken, insomuch that
we truly can [c]command in the [d]name
of Jesus and the very trees obey us,
or the mountains, or the waves of
the sea.
7 Nevertheless, the Lord God showeth us our [a]weakness that we may
know that it is by his [b]grace, and his
great condescensions unto the children of men, that we have power to
do these things.
8 Behold, great and marvelous are
the [a]works of the Lord. How [b]un-
searchable are the depths of the
[c]mysteries of him; and it is impossible that man should find out all
his ways. And no man [d]knoweth of
his [e]ways save it be revealed unto
him; wherefore, brethren, despise
not the [f]revelations of God.
9 For behold, by the power of his
[a]word [b]man came upon the face of
the earth, which earth was [c]created
by the power of his word. Wherefore,
if God being able to speak and the
world was, and to speak and man
was created, O then, why not able to
command the [d]earth, or the workmanship of his hands upon the face
of it, according to his will and
pleasure?
10 Wherefore, brethren, seek not
to [a]counsel the Lord, but to take
counsel from his hand. For behold,
ye yourselves know that he counsel-
eth in [b]wisdom, and in justice, and
in great mercy, over all his works.
11 Wherefore, beloved brethren,
be [a]reconciled unto him through the
[b]atonement of Christ, his [c]Only Be-

4*a* TG Jesus Christ, Prophecies about; Testimony.
b TG Jesus Christ, Glory of.
c Luke 24: 27; 1 Pet. 1: 11; Jacob 7: 11 (11–12); Mosiah 13: 33 (33–35); D&C 20: 26.
5*a* Moses 5: 8.
b Gen. 4: 26; Hel. 8: 16 (16–20). TG Name of the Lord.
c 2 Ne. 25: 24; Jacob 7: 7; Mosiah 13: 30.
d Jarom 1: 11; Alma 25: 15 (15–16). TG Law of Moses.
e Gal. 3: 24; Ether 12: 19 (18–19).
f TG Jesus Christ, Types of, in Anticipation.
g Gen. 22: 2 (1–14); John 3: 16 (16–21); Heb. 11: 17. TG Jesus Christ, Divine Sonship.
6*a* TG Prophecy.
b TG Witnesses.
c 3 Ne. 28: 20 (19–22). TG God, Power of.
d Acts 3: 6 (6–16); 3 Ne. 8: 1.
7*a* Ether 12: 27; D&C 66: 3.
b TG Grace.
8*a* Ps. 106: 2.
b Rom. 11: 34 (33–36); Mosiah 4: 9.
c D&C 19: 10; 76: 114 (114–116). TG Mysteries of Godliness.
d Dan. 1: 17; 1 Cor. 2: 11 (9–16); Alma 26: 21 (21–22). TG God, Knowledge about.
e Isa. 55: 8 (8–9).
f D&C 3: 7.
9*a* Morm. 9: 17; Moses 1: 32.
b TG Man, Physical Creation of.
c TG Creation; God, Creator; Jesus Christ, Creator.
d Hel. 12: 16 (8–17).
10*a* Josh. 9: 14; Prov. 15: 22; Isa. 45: 9; 2 Ne. 9: 28–29; Alma 37: 12, 37; D&C 3: 4, 13; 22: 4.
b TG God, Justice of; God, Wisdom of.
11*a* Lev. 6: 30. TG Jesus Christ, Mission of; Reconciliation.
b TG Jesus Christ, Atonement through.
c TG Jesus Christ, Divine Sonship.

[Between 544 and 421 B.C.]

gotten Son, and ye may obtain a
[d]resurrection, according to the
[e]power of the resurrection which is
in Christ, and be presented as the
[f]first-fruits of Christ unto God,
having faith, and obtained a good
hope of glory in him before he
manifesteth himself in the flesh.
12 And now, beloved, marvel not
that I tell you these things; for why
not [a]speak of the atonement of
Christ, and attain to a perfect
knowledge of him, as to attain to
the knowledge of a resurrection and
the world to come?
13 Behold, my brethren, he that
prophesieth, let him prophesy to
the understanding of men; for the
[a]Spirit speaketh the [b]truth and lieth
not. Wherefore, it speaketh of things
as they really [c]are, and of things
as they really will be; wherefore,
these things are manifested unto
us [d]plainly, for the salvation of our
souls. But behold, we are not
witnesses alone in these things; for
God also [e]spake them unto prophets
of old.
14 But behold, the Jews were a
[a]stiffnecked people; and they [b]de-
spised the words of [c]plainness, and
[d]killed the prophets, and sought for
things that they could not understand. Wherefore, because of their
[e]blindness, which [f]blindness came
by looking beyond the [g]mark, they
must needs fall; for God hath taken
away his plainness from them, and
delivered unto them many things
which they [h]cannot understand,
because they desired it. And because
they desired it God hath done it,
that they may [i]stumble.
15 And now I, Jacob, am led on by
the Spirit unto prophesying; for I
perceive by the workings of the
Spirit which is in me, that by the
[a]stumbling of the [b]Jews they will
[c]reject the [d]stone upon which they
might build and have safe foundation.
16 But behold, according to the
scriptures, this [a]stone shall become
the great, and the last, and the only
sure [b]foundation, upon which the
Jews can build.
17 And now, my beloved, how is
it possible that these, after having
rejected the sure foundation, can
[a]ever build upon it, that it may become the head of their corner?
18 Behold, my beloved brethren,
I will unfold this mystery unto
you; if I do not, by any means, get
shaken from my firmness in the
Spirit, and stumble because of my
over anxiety for you.

CHAPTER 5

Jacob quotes Zenos relative to the allegory of the tame and wild olive trees—They are a likeness of Israel and the gentiles—The scattering and gathering of Israel are prefigured—Allusions are made to the Nephites and Lamanites and all the house of Israel—Gentiles shall be grafted into Israel—Eventually the vineyard shall be burned.

11*d* TG Resurrection.
e TG God, Power of.
f Mosiah 15: 21 (21–23); 18: 9; Alma 40: 16 (16–21).
12*a* 2 Ne. 25: 26.
13*a* TG Holy Ghost, Mission of.
b John 17: 17. TG Honesty.
c D&C 93: 24.
d Neh. 8: 8; Jacob 2: 11; Alma 13: 23.
e TG Witness of the Father.
14*a* Deut. 9: 13; Neh. 9: 16; 2 Ne. 25: 2. TG Stiffneckedness.
b Num. 15: 31 (30–31); Ezek. 20: 13 (13–16); 1 Ne. 17: 30 (30–31); 19: 7; 2 Ne. 33: 2; D&C 3: 7 (4–13).
c 2 Cor. 11: 3.
d Zech. 1: 4 (2–5).
e Isa. 44: 18.
f Rom. 11: 25. TG Spiritual Blindness.
g John 7: 47 (45–53).
h 2 Ne. 25: 1.
i Isa. 57: 14.
15*a* Isa. 8: 14 (13–15); 1 Cor. 1: 23; 2 Ne. 18: 14 (13–15).
b TG Israel, Judah, People of.
c Rom. 11: 1, 20 (1–36); 1 Ne. 10: 11; Morm. 5: 14 (14–20).
d TG Cornerstone; Jesus Christ, Prophecies about; Rock.
16*a* Ps. 118: 22 (22–23).
b Isa. 28: 16 (14–17); Hel. 5: 12.
17*a* Matt. 19: 30; Jacob 5: 63 (62–64); D&C 29: 30.

[Between 544 and 421 B.C.]

BEHOLD, my brethren, do ye not remember to have read the words of the prophet [a]Zenos, which he spake unto the house of Israel, saying:

2 Hearken, O ye house of Israel, and hear the words of me, a prophet of the Lord.

3 For behold, thus saith the Lord, I will liken thee, O house of [a]Israel, like unto a tame [b]olive-tree, which a man took and nourished in his [c]vineyard; and it grew, and waxed old, and began to [d]decay.

4 And it came to pass that the master of the vineyard went forth, and he saw that his olive-tree began to decay; and he said: I will [a]prune it, and dig about it, and nourish it, that perhaps it may shoot forth young and tender branches, and it perish not.

5 And it came to pass that he [a]pruned it, and digged about it, and nourished it according to his word.

6 And it came to pass that after many days it began to put forth somewhat a little, young and tender branches; but behold, the main [a]top thereof began to perish.

7 And it came to pass that the master of the vineyard saw it, and he said unto his [a]servant: It grieveth me that I should lose this tree; wherefore, go and pluck the branches from a [b]wild olive-tree, and bring them hither unto me; and we will pluck off those main branches which are beginning to wither away, and we will cast them into the fire that they may be burned.

8 And behold, saith the Lord of the vineyard, I take [a]away many of these young and tender branches, and I will graft them [b]whithersoever I will; and it mattereth not that if it so be that the root of this tree will perish, I may preserve the fruit thereof unto myself; wherefore, I will take these young and tender branches, and I will graft them whithersoever I will.

9 Take thou the branches of the wild olive-tree, and graft them in, in the [a]stead thereof; and these which I have plucked off I will cast into the fire and burn them, that they may not cumber the ground of my vineyard.

10 And it came to pass that the servant of the Lord of the vineyard did according to the word of the Lord of the vineyard, and grafted in the branches of the [a]wild olive-tree.

11 And the Lord of the vineyard caused that it should be digged about, and pruned, and nourished, saying unto his servant: It grieveth me that I should lose this tree; wherefore, that perhaps I might preserve the roots thereof that they perish not, that I might preserve them unto myself, I have done this thing.

12 Wherefore, go thy way; watch the tree, and nourish it, according to my words.

13 And these will I [a]place in the nethermost part of my vineyard, whithersoever I will, it mattereth not unto thee; and I do it that I may preserve unto myself the natural branches of the tree; and also, that I may lay up fruit thereof against the season, unto myself; for it grieveth me that I should lose this tree and the fruit thereof.

14 And it came to pass that the Lord of the vineyard went his way, and hid the natural [a]branches of the

5 1*a* 1 Ne. 19: 12 (12, 16); Jacob 6: 1. TG Scriptures, Lost.
3*a* TG Israel, Twelve Tribes of.
b Ezek. 36: 8 (8–15); Rom. 11: 21 (1–36); 1 Ne. 10: 12; Jacob 6: 1 (1–7). TG Israel, Mission of; Vineyard of the Lord.
c Matt. 21: 33 (33–41); D&C 101: 44.
d TG Apostasy of Israel.
4*a* TG Prophets, Mission of.
5*a* 2 Kgs. 17: 13 (13–18).
6*a* Luke 3: 9 (8–9); 2 Ne. 30: 2. TG Chief Priest.
7*a* TG Servant.
b Rom. 11: 17 (17, 24).
8*a* TG Israel, Scattering of.
b Ezek. 17: 22 (4–10, 22).
9*a* Acts 9: 15; 14: 27; Rom. 1: 13; Gal. 3: 14.
10*a* TG Gentiles.
13*a* Hosea 8: 8; 1 Ne. 10: 12.
14*a* TG Israel, Bondage of, in Other Lands.

[Between 544 and 421 B.C.]

tame olive-tree in the nethermost parts of the vineyard, some in one and some in another, according to his will and pleasure.

15 And it came to pass that a long time passed away, and the Lord of the vineyard said unto his servant: Come, let us go down into the vineyard, that we may [a]labor in the vineyard.

16 And it came to pass that the Lord of the vineyard, and also the servant, went down into the vineyard to labor. And it came to pass that the servant said unto his master: Behold, look here; behold the tree.

17 And it came to pass that the Lord of the vineyard looked and beheld the tree in the which the wild olive branches had been grafted; and it had sprung forth and begun to bear [a]fruit. And he beheld that it was good; and the fruit thereof was like unto the natural fruit.

18 And he said unto the servant: Behold, the branches of the wild tree have taken hold of the moisture of the root thereof, that the root thereof hath brought forth much strength; and because of the much strength of the root thereof the wild branches have brought forth tame fruit. Now, if we had not grafted in these branches, the tree thereof would have perished. And now, behold, I shall lay up much fruit, which the tree thereof hath brought forth; and the fruit thereof I shall lay up against the season, unto mine own self.

19 And it came to pass that the Lord of the vineyard said unto the servant: Come, let us go to the nethermost part of the vineyard, and behold if the natural branches of the tree have not brought forth much fruit also, that I may lay up of the fruit thereof against the season, unto mine own self.

20 And it came to pass that they went forth whither the master had hid the natural branches of the tree, and he said unto the servant: Behold these; and he beheld the [a]first that it had [b]brought forth much fruit; and he beheld also that it was good. And he said unto the servant: Take of the fruit thereof, and lay it up against the season, that I may preserve it unto mine own self; for behold, said he, this long time have I nourished it, and it hath brought forth much fruit.

21 And it came to pass that the servant said unto his master: How comest thou hither to plant this tree, or this branch of the tree? For behold, it was the poorest spot in all the land of thy vineyard.

22 And the Lord of the vineyard said unto him: Counsel me not; I knew that it was a poor spot of ground; wherefore, I said unto thee, I have nourished it this long time, and thou beholdest that it hath brought forth much fruit.

23 And it came to pass that the Lord of the vineyard said unto his servant: Look hither; behold I have planted another branch of the tree also; and thou knowest that this spot of ground was poorer than the first. But, behold the tree. I have nourished it this long time, and it hath brought forth much fruit; therefore, gather it, and lay it up against the season, that I may preserve it unto mine own self.

24 And it came to pass that the Lord of the vineyard said again unto his servant: Look hither, and behold another [a]branch also, which I have planted; behold that I have nourished it also, and it hath brought forth fruit.

25 And he said unto the servant: Look hither and behold the last. Behold, this have I planted in a [a]good spot of ground; and I have

---

15*a* TG Millennium, Preparing a People for.
17*a* Matt. 12:33; John 15:16; Gal. 3:9 (7–9, 29); Col. 1:6 (3–8).
20*a* Jacob 5:39.
b TG Israel, Restoration of.
24*a* Ezek. 17:22 (22–24); Alma 16:17.
25*a* Ezek. 17:8; 1 Ne. 2:20; Jacob 5:43.

[Between 544 and 421 B.C.]

nourished it this long time, and only
a [b]part of the tree hath brought forth
tame fruit, and the [c]other part of
the tree hath brought forth wild
fruit; behold, I have nourished this
tree like unto the others.
26 And it came to pass that the
Lord of the vineyard said unto the
servant: Pluck off the branches that
have not brought forth good [a]fruit,
and cast them into the fire.
27 But behold, the servant said
unto him: Let us prune it, and dig
about it, and nourish it a little
[a]longer, that perhaps it may bring
forth good fruit unto thee, that thou
canst lay it up against the season.
28 And it came to pass that the
Lord of the vineyard and the servant
of the Lord of the vineyard did
nourish all the fruit of the vineyard.
29 And it came to pass that a [a]long
time had passed away, and the Lord
of the vineyard said unto his [b]ser-
vant: Come, let us go down into
the vineyard, that we may labor
again in the vineyard. For behold,
the time draweth near, and the [c]end
soon cometh; wherefore, I must lay
up fruit against the season, unto
mine own self.
30 And it came to pass that the
Lord of the vineyard and the servant
went down into the vineyard; and
they came to the tree whose natural
branches had been broken off, and
the wild branches had been grafted
in; and behold all [a]sorts of fruit did
cumber the tree.
31 And it came to pass that the
Lord of the vineyard did [a]taste of
the fruit, every sort according to its
number. And the Lord of the vineyard said: Behold, this long time
have we nourished this tree, and I
have laid up unto myself against
the season much fruit.
32 But behold, this time it hath
brought forth much [a]fruit, and there
is [b]none of it which is good. And
behold, there are all kinds of bad
fruit; and it profiteth me nothing,
notwithstanding all our labor; and
now it grieveth me that I should lose
this tree.
33 And the Lord of the vineyard
said unto the servant: What shall
we do unto the tree, that I may
preserve again good fruit thereof
unto mine own self?
34 And the servant said unto his
master: Behold, because thou didst
graft in the branches of the wild
olive-tree they have nourished the
roots, that they are alive and they
have not perished; wherefore thou
beholdest that they are yet good.
35 And it came to pass that the
Lord of the vineyard said unto
his servant: The tree profiteth me
nothing, and the roots thereof profit
me nothing so long as it shall bring
forth evil fruit.
36 Nevertheless, I know that the
roots are good, and for mine own
purpose I have preserved them;
and because of their much strength
they have hitherto brought forth,
from the wild branches, good fruit.
37 But behold, the wild branches
have grown and have [a]overrun the
roots thereof; and because that the
wild branches have overcome the
roots thereof it hath brought forth
much evil fruit; and because that it
hath brought forth so much evil
fruit thou beholdest that it beginneth to perish; and it will soon
become ripened, that it may be cast
into the fire, except we should do
something for it to preserve it.
38 And it came to pass that the
Lord of the vineyard said unto his
servant: Let us go down into the
nethermost parts of the vineyard,
and behold if the natural branches
have also brought forth evil fruit.
39 And it came to pass that they

25*b* Hel. 15:3 (3–4).
c Alma 26:36.
26*a* Matt. 7:19 (15–20); Alma 5:36; D&C 97:7.
27*a* Jacob 5:50 (50–51); Alma 42:4.
29*a* TG Last Days.
b D&C 101:55; 103:21.
c 2 Ne. 30:10; Jacob 6:2.
30*a* TG Apostasy.
31*a* TG Jesus Christ, Judge; Judgment.
32*a* Hosea 10:1.
b JS-H 1:19.
37*a* D&C 45:30.

[Between 544 and 421 B.C.]

went down into the nethermost parts of the vineyard. And it came to pass that they beheld that the fruit of the natural branches had become corrupt also; yea, the [a]first and the second and also the last; and they had all become corrupt.

40 And the [a]wild fruit of the last had overcome that part of the tree which brought forth good fruit, even that the branch had withered away and died.

41 And it came to pass that the Lord of the vineyard wept, and said unto the servant: [a]What could I have done more for my vineyard?

42 Behold, I knew that all the fruit of the vineyard, save it were these, had become [a]corrupted. And now these which have once brought forth good fruit have also become corrupted; and now all the trees of my vineyard are good for nothing save it be to be [b]hewn down and cast into the fire.

43 And behold this last, whose branch hath withered away, I did plant in a [a]good spot of ground; yea, even that which was choice unto me above all other parts of the land of my vineyard.

44 And thou beheldest that I also cut down that which [a]cumbered this spot of ground, that I might plant this tree in the stead thereof.

45 And thou beheldest that a [a]part thereof brought forth good fruit, and a part thereof brought forth wild fruit; and because I plucked not the branches thereof and cast them into the fire, behold, they have overcome the good branch that it hath withered away.

46 And now, behold, notwithstanding all the care which we have taken of my vineyard, the trees thereof have become corrupted, that they bring forth no good [a]fruit; and these I had hoped to preserve, to have laid up fruit thereof against the season, unto mine own self. But, behold, they have become like unto the wild olive-tree, and they are of no worth but to be [b]hewn down and cast into the fire; and it grieveth me that I should lose them.

47 But [a]what could I have done more in my vineyard? Have I slackened mine hand, that I have not nourished it? Nay, I have nourished it, and I have digged about it, and I have pruned it, and I have dunged it; and I have [b]stretched forth mine [c]hand almost all the day long, and the [d]end draweth nigh. And it grieveth me that I should hew down all the trees of my vineyard, and cast them into the fire that they should be burned. Who is it that has corrupted my vineyard?

48 And it came to pass that the servant said unto his master: Is it not the [a]loftiness of thy vineyard—have not the branches thereof overcome the roots which are good? And because the branches have overcome the roots thereof, behold they grew faster than the strength of the roots, [b]taking strength unto themselves. Behold, I say, is not this the cause that the trees of thy vineyard have become corrupted?

49 And it came to pass that the Lord of the vineyard said unto the servant: Let us go to and hew down the trees of the vineyard and cast them into the fire, that they shall not cumber the ground of my vineyard, for I have done all. What could I have done more for my vineyard?

50 But, behold, the servant said unto the Lord of the vineyard: Spare it a little [a]longer.

39*a* Jacob 5: 20 (20, 23, 25).
40*a* Hel. 15: 4 (3–4).
41*a* Isa. 5: 4; 2 Ne. 2: 27; 26: 24; Jacob 5: 47; Alma 26: 37.
42*a* TG Apostasy.
b Matt. 3: 10.
43*a* Ezek. 17: 8; Jacob 5: 25.
44*a* Moro. 9: 23.
45*a* 1 Ne. 15: 12 (12–17); 2 Ne. 3: 5; 10: 1; Alma 46: 24 (24–25).
46*a* Luke 3: 9.
b Alma 5: 52; 3 Ne. 27: 11.
47*a* Jacob 5: 41 (41, 49).
b Isa. 9:12 (12, 17, 21).
c 2 Ne. 19: 17 (17–21); 28: 32; Jacob 6: 4.
d TG World, End of.
48*a* TG Haughtiness; Pride.
b D&C 121: 39. TG Unrighteous Dominion.
50*a* Jacob 5: 27.

[Between 544 and 421 B.C.]

51 And the Lord said: Yea, I will
spare it a little longer, for it grieveth
me that I should lose the trees of
my vineyard.
52 Wherefore, let us take of the
[a]branches of these which I have
planted in the nethermost parts of
my vineyard, and let us graft them
into the tree from whence they
came; and let us pluck from the tree
those branches whose fruit is most
bitter, and graft in the natural
branches of the tree in the stead
thereof.
53 And this will I do that the tree
may not perish, that, perhaps, I
may preserve unto myself the roots
thereof for mine [a]own purpose.
54 And, behold, the roots of the
natural branches of the tree which I
planted whithersoever I would are
yet alive; wherefore, that I may
preserve them also for mine own
purpose, I will take of the [a]branches
of this tree, and I will [b]graft them in
unto them. Yea, I will graft in unto
them the branches of their mother
tree, that I may preserve the roots
also unto mine own self, that when
they shall be sufficiently strong
perhaps they may bring forth good
fruit unto me, and I may yet have
glory in the fruit of my vineyard.
55 And it came to pass that they
took from the natural tree which had
become wild, and grafted in unto the
natural trees, which also had become wild.
56 And they also took of the natural
trees which had become wild, and
[a]grafted into their mother tree.
57 And the Lord of the vineyard
said unto the servant: Pluck not
the wild branches from the trees,
save it be those which are most
bitter; and in them ye shall graft
according to that which I have said.
58 And we will nourish again the
trees of the vineyard, and we will
trim up the [a]branches thereof; and
we will pluck from the trees those
branches which are ripened, that
must perish, and cast them into the
fire.
59 And this I do that, perhaps, the
roots thereof may take strength because of their goodness; and because
of the change of the branches,
that the good may [a]overcome the
evil.
60 And because that I have preserved the natural branches and
the roots thereof, and that I have
grafted in the natural branches
again into their mother tree, and
have preserved the roots of their
mother tree, that, perhaps, the
trees of my vineyard may bring
forth again good [a]fruit; and that I
may have joy again in the fruit of
my vineyard, and, perhaps, that I
may rejoice exceedingly that I have
preserved the roots and the branches
of the first fruit—
61 Wherefore, go to, and call
[a]servants, that we may [b]labor diligently with our might in the vineyard, that we may [c]prepare the way,
that I may bring forth again the
natural fruit, which natural fruit is
good and the most precious above
all other fruit.
62 Wherefore, let us go to and labor
with our might this last time, for
behold the end draweth nigh, and
this is for the last time that I shall
[a]prune my vineyard.
63 Graft in the branches; begin
at the [a]last that they may be first,
and that the first may be [b]last, and
dig about the trees, both old and
young, the first and the last; and
the last and the first, that all may be
nourished once again for the last
time.
64 Wherefore, dig about them,

52*a* TG Israel, Gathering of; Israel, Restoration of.
53*a* Ex. 19: 6; Isa. 49: 6.
54*a* 3 Ne. 21: 6 (5–6); Morm. 5: 15.
b 1 Ne. 15: 16.
56*a* Jer. 24: 6.
58*a* Isa. 27: 11.
59*a* TG Triumph.
60*a* Isa. 27: 6.
61*a* Jacob 6:2.
b D&C 24: 19; 39: 17; 95: 4.
c TG Millennium, Preparing a People for.
62*a* D&C 75: 2.
63*a* Matt. 20: 16; Mark 10: 31; Luke 13: 30; 1 Ne. 13: 42; Ether 13: 12 (10–12).
b Matt. 19: 30; Jacob 4: 17; D&C 29: 30.

[Between 544 and 421 B.C.]

and prune them, and dung them
once more, for the last time, for the
end draweth nigh. And if it be so
that these last grafts shall grow, and
bring forth the natural fruit, then
shall ye prepare the way for them,
that they may grow.
65 And as they begin to grow ye
shall [a]clear away the branches which
bring forth bitter fruit, according to
the strength of the good and the size
thereof; and ye shall not clear away
the bad thereof all at once, lest the
roots thereof should be too strong
for the graft, and the graft thereof
shall perish, and I lose the trees of
my vineyard.
66 For it grieveth me that I should
lose the trees of my vineyard;
wherefore ye shall clear away the
bad according as the good shall
grow, that the root and the top may
be equal in strength, until the good
shall overcome the bad, and the bad
be hewn down and cast into the fire,
that they cumber not the ground of
my vineyard; and thus will I sweep
away the bad out of my vineyard.
67 And the branches of the natural
tree will I graft in again into the
natural tree;
68 And the branches of the natural
tree will I graft into the natural
branches of the tree; and thus will I
bring them together again, that they
shall bring forth the natural [a]fruit,
and they shall be one.
69 And the bad shall be [a]cast away,
yea, even out of all the land of my
vineyard; for behold, only this once
will I prune my vineyard.
70 And it came to pass that the
Lord of the vineyard sent his [a]ser-
vant; and the servant went and did
as the Lord had commanded him,
and brought other [b]servants; and
they were [c]few.
71 And the Lord of the vineyard
said unto them: Go to, and [a]labor in
the vineyard, with your might. For
behold, this is the [b]last time that I
shall [c]nourish my vineyard; for the
end is nigh at hand, and the season
speedily cometh; and if ye labor
with your might with me ye shall
have joy in the fruit which I shall
lay up unto myself against the time
which will soon come.
72 And it came to pass that the
servants did go and labor with their
mights; and the Lord of the vineyard labored also with them; and
they did obey the commandments
of the Lord of the vineyard in all
things.
73 And there began to be the
natural fruit again in the vineyard;
and the natural branches began to
grow and thrive exceedingly; and
the wild branches began to be
plucked off and to be cast away;
and they did keep the root and the
top thereof equal, according to the
strength thereof.
74 And thus they labored, with
all diligence, according to the commandments of the Lord of the vineyard, even until the bad had been
cast away out of the vineyard, and
the Lord had preserved unto himself that the trees had become again
the natural fruit; and they became
like unto [a]one body; and the fruits
were equal; and the Lord of the
vineyard had preserved unto himself the natural fruit, which was
most precious unto him from the
beginning.
75 And it came to pass that when
the [a]Lord of the vineyard saw that
his fruit was good, and that his vineyard was no more corrupt, he called
up his servants, and said unto them:
Behold, for this last time have
we nourished my vineyard; and
thou beholdest that I have done
according to my will; and I have
preserved the natural fruit, that it

65*a* D&C 86:6 (6–7).
68*a* TG Israel, Mission of.
69*a* 1 Ne. 22:23 (15–17, 23); 2 Ne. 30:10 (9–10).
70*a* D&C 101:55; 103:21.
b Matt. 9:37 (36–38).
c 1 Ne. 14:12.
71*a* Matt. 21:28; Jacob 6:2 (2–3); D&C 33:3 (3–4).
b D&C 39:17; 43:28 (28–30).
c TG Millennium, Preparing a People for.
74*a* D&C 38:27.
75*a* TG Jesus Christ, Millennial Reign.

[Between 544 and 421 B.C.]

is good, even like as it was in the
beginning. And [b]blessed art thou;
for because ye have been diligent in
laboring with me in my vineyard,
and have kept my commandments,
and have brought unto me again the
[c]natural fruit, that my vineyard is
no more corrupted, and the bad is
cast away, behold ye shall have [d]joy
with me because of the fruit of my
vineyard.
76 For behold, for a [a]long time will
I lay up of the fruit of my vineyard unto mine own self against the
season, which speedily cometh; and
for the last time have I nourished
my vineyard, and pruned it, and
dug about it, and dunged it; wherefore I will lay up unto mine own self
of the fruit, for a long time, according to that which I have spoken.
77 And when the time cometh that
evil fruit shall again come into my
vineyard, then will I cause the [a]good
and the bad to be gathered; and the
good will I preserve unto myself,
and the bad will I cast away into its
own place. And then cometh the
[b]season and the end; and my vineyard will I cause to be [c]burned with
[d]fire.

CHAPTER 6

The Lord shall recover Israel in the last days—Then the world shall be burned with fire—Men must follow Christ to avoid the lake of fire and brimstone.

AND now, behold, my brethren,
as I said unto you that I would
prophesy, behold, this is my prophecy—that the things which this
prophet [a]Zenos spake, concerning
the house of Israel, in the which he
likened them unto a tame [b]olive-
tree, must surely come to pass.
2 And the day that he shall set his
hand again the second time to [a]re-
cover his people, is the day, yea,
even the last time, that the [b]servants
of the Lord shall go forth in his
[c]power, to [d]nourish and prune his
[e]vineyard; and after that the [f]end
soon cometh.
3 And how [a]blessed are they who
have labored [b]diligently in his vineyard; and how [c]cursed are they who
shall be cast out into their own
place! And the [d]world shall be
[e]burned with fire.
4 And how merciful is our God
unto us, for he remembereth the
house of [a]Israel, both roots and
branches; and he stretches forth his
[b]hands unto them all the day long;
and they are a [c]stiffnecked and a
gainsaying people; but as many as
will not harden their hearts shall be
saved in the kingdom of God.
5 Wherefore, my beloved brethren,
I beseech of you in words of soberness that ye would repent, and come
with full purpose of heart, and
[a]cleave unto God as he cleaveth
unto you. And while his [b]arm of
mercy is extended towards you in

75*b* 1 Ne. 13: 37; D&C 21: 9.
c TG Israel, Restoration of.
d D&C 6: 31; 18: 15 (15–16).
76*a* 1 Ne. 22: 26.
77*a* D&C 86: 7.
b Rev. 20: 3 (3–10); D&C 29: 22; 43: 31 (30–31); 88: 111 (110–112).
c TG World, End of.
d Joel 1: 19 (19–20); 2 Ne. 6: 15 (14–15); Jacob 6: 3.
6 1*a* Jacob 5: 1; Alma 33: 13 (13–15). TG Scriptures, Lost.
b Rom. 11: 21 (1–36); 1 Ne. 10: 12; Jacob 5: 3 (3–77).
2*a* 1 Ne. 22: 12 (10–12); D&C 110: 11; 137: 6. TG Israel, Gathering of; Israel, Restoration of.
b Jacob 5: 61.
c 1 Ne. 14: 1, 14.
d Jacob 5: 71; D&C 101: 56.
e Jer. 12: 10; D&C 138: 56. TG Vineyard of the Lord.
f 2 Ne. 30: 10; Jacob 5: 29; D&C 43: 17 (17–20, 28).
3*a* Jacob 5: 71.
b TG Diligence; Perseverance.
c D&C 41: 1.
d TG World.
e Isa. 24: 6; 2 Ne. 27: 2; 3 Ne. 25: 1; Jacob 5: 77. TG World, End of.
4*a* 2 Sam. 7: 24.
b Neh. 9: 19 (18–26); 2 Ne. 19: 17 (17–21); 28: 32; Jacob 5: 47.
c TG Stiffneckedness.
5*a* Deut. 10: 20; Josh. 23: 8; 2 Kgs. 18: 6; Hel. 4: 25; D&C 11: 19.
b Isa. 59: 16; 2 Ne. 1: 15; Alma 5: 33; 3 Ne. 9: 14.

[Between 544 and 421 B.C.]

the light of the day, harden not
your hearts.
6 Yea, today, if ye will hear his
voice, harden not your hearts; for
why will ye [a]die?
7 For behold, after ye have been
nourished by the good [a]word of God
all the day long, will ye bring forth
evil fruit, that ye must be [b]hewn
down and cast into the fire?
8 Behold, will ye reject these
words? Will ye reject the words of
the [a]prophets; and will ye reject all
the words which have been spoken
concerning Christ, after so many
have spoken concerning him; and
[b]deny the good word of Christ, and
the power of God, and the [c]gift of
the Holy Ghost, and quench the
Holy Spirit, and make a [d]mock of
the great plan of redemption, which
hath been laid for you?
9 Know ye not that if ye will do
these things, that the power of the
redemption and the resurrection,
which is in Christ, will bring you
to stand with [a]shame and [b]awful
[c]guilt before the bar of God?
10 And according to the power of
[a]justice, for justice cannot be denied, ye must go away into that
[b]lake of fire and brimstone, whose
flames are unquenchable, and whose
smoke ascendeth up forever and
ever, which lake of fire and brimstone is [c]endless [d]torment.
11 O then, my beloved brethren,
repent ye, and enter in at the [a]strait
gate, and [b]continue in the way which
is narrow, until ye shall obtain
eternal life.
12 O be [a]wise; what can I say more?
13 Finally, I bid you farewell, until
I shall meet you before the [a]pleasing
bar of God, which bar striketh the
wicked with [b]awful dread and fear.
Amen.

CHAPTER 7

Sherem denies Christ, contends with Jacob, demands a sign, and is smitten of God—All of the prophets have spoken of Christ and his atonement—The Nephites lived out their days as wanderers, born in tribulation, and hated by the Lamanites.

AND now it came to pass after
some years had passed away, there
came a man among the people of
Nephi, whose name was [a]Sherem.
2 And it came to pass that he began
to preach among the people, and to
declare unto them that there should
be [a]no Christ. And he preached many
things which were flattering unto
the people; and this he did that he
might [b]overthrow the doctrine of
Christ.
3 And he labored diligently that
he might lead away the hearts of the
people, insomuch that he did lead
away many hearts; and he knowing
that I, Jacob, had faith in Christ
who should come, he sought much
opportunity that he might come
unto me.
4 And he was [a]learned, that he had
a perfect knowledge of the language
of the people; wherefore, he could
use much [b]flattery, and much power
of speech, according to the [c]power of
the devil.
5 And he had hope to shake me
from the faith, notwithstanding the
many [a]revelations and the many
things which I had seen concerning

6a Ezek. 18:28 (26–28, 32).
7a Ps. 119:28.
b Alma 5:52; 3 Ne. 27:11 (11–12).
8a Jer. 26:5.
b TG Holy Ghost, Loss of.
c TG Holy Ghost, Gift of.
d TG Sacrilege.
9a TG Shame.
b Jacob 7:19; Mosiah 15:26.
c TG Guilt; Judgment, The Last.
10a TG God, Justice of; Justice.
b Rev. 19:20; 2 Ne. 28:23; Mosiah 3:27. TG Hell.
c Mosiah 2:33; D&C 19:11 (10–12).
d TG Damnation.
11a 2 Ne. 9:41.
b 2 Ne. 31:15. TG Commitment.
12a Matt. 10:16; Morm. 9:28.
13a Moro. 10:34.
b Alma 40:14.
7 1a TG False Prophets.
2a Alma 21:8; 30:12 (12, 22).
b TG False Doctrine.
4a TG Learning.
b TG Flattery.
c TG False Priesthoods.
5a 2 Ne. 10:3; 11:3; Jacob 2:11.

[Between 544 and 421 B.C.]

these things; for I truly had seen
[b]angels, and they had ministered
unto me. And also, I had [c]heard the
voice of the Lord speaking unto me
in very word, from time to time;
wherefore, I could not be shaken.
6 And it came to pass that he came
unto me, and on this wise did he
speak unto me, saying: Brother
Jacob, I have sought much opportunity that I might speak unto you;
for I have heard and also know that
thou goest about much, preaching
that which ye call the [a]gospel, or
the doctrine of Christ.
7 And ye have led away much of
this people that they pervert the
right way of God, and [a]keep not the
law of Moses which is the right way;
and convert the law of Moses into
the worship of a being which ye say
shall come many hundred years
hence. And now behold, I, Sherem,
declare unto you that this is
[b]blasphemy; for no man knoweth of
such things; for he cannot [c]tell of
things to come. And after this
manner did Sherem contend against
me.
8 But behold, the Lord God poured
in his [a]Spirit into my soul, insomuch
that I did [b]confound him in all his
words.
9 And I said unto him: Deniest
thou the Christ who shall come?
And he said: If there should be a
Christ, I would not deny him; but I
know that there is no Christ, neither
has been, nor ever will be.
10 And I said unto him: Believest
thou the scriptures? And he said,
Yea.
11 And I said unto him: Then ye do
not understand them; for they truly
testify of Christ. Behold, I say unto
you that none of the [a]prophets have
written, nor [b]prophesied, save they
have spoken concerning this Christ.
12 And this is not all—it has been
made manifest unto me, for I have
heard and seen; and it also has been
made manifest unto me by the
[a]power of the Holy Ghost; wherefore, I know if there should be no
atonement made all mankind must
be [b]lost.
13 And it came to pass that he said
unto me: Show me a [a]sign by this
power of the Holy Ghost, in the
which ye know so much.
14 And I said unto him: What am I
that I should [a]tempt God to show
unto thee a sign in the thing which
thou knowest to be [b]true? Yet thou
wilt deny it, because thou art of
the [c]devil. Nevertheless, not my
will be done; but if God shall
smite thee, let that be a [d]sign unto
thee that he has power, both in
heaven and in earth; and also, that
Christ shall come. And thy will, O
Lord, be done, and not mine.
15 And it came to pass that when I,
Jacob, had spoken these words, the
power of the Lord came upon him,
insomuch that he fell to the earth.
And it came to pass that he was
nourished for the space of many
days.
16 And it came to pass that he said
unto the people: Gather together on
the morrow, for I shall die; wherefore, I desire to speak unto the
people before I shall die.
17 And it came to pass that on the
morrow the multitude were gathered together; and he spake plainly
unto them and denied the things
which he had taught them, and
confessed the Christ, and the power

5*b* 2 Ne. 2: 4.
c Ex. 19: 9 (9–13).
6*a* 2 Ne. 31: 2.
7*a* Jacob 4: 5.
b TG Blasphemy.
c Alma 30: 13.
8*a* TG God, Spirit of; Holy Ghost, Mission of.
b Ps. 97: 7. TG Confound.
11*a* 1 Ne. 10: 5; 3 Ne. 20: 24 (23–24). TG Jesus Christ, Prophecies about.
b 1 Pet. 1: 11; Rev. 19: 10; Jacob 4: 4; Mosiah 13: 33 (33–35); D&C 20: 26.
12*a* TG Holy Ghost, Gifts of.
b 2 Ne. 2: 21 (10–30).
13*a* John 6: 30; Alma 30: 43 (43–60); D&C 46: 9 (8–9). TG Sign Seekers.
14*a* TG Test, Try, Prove.
b Mosiah 12: 30; Alma 30: 42 (41–42).
c Alma 30: 53.
d Num. 26: 10; D&C 124: 53 (50–53).

[Between 544 and 421 B.C.]

of the Holy Ghost, and the ministering of angels.
18 And he spake plainly unto them,
that he had been [a]deceived by the
power of the [b]devil. And he spake of
hell, and of [c]eternity, and of eternal
[d]punishment.
19 And he said: I [a]fear lest I have
committed the [b]unpardonable sin,
for I have lied unto God; for I
denied the Christ, and said that I
believed the scriptures; and they
truly testify of him. And because I
have thus lied unto God I greatly
fear lest my case shall be [c]awful; but
I confess unto God.
20 And it came to pass that when
he had said these words he could say
no more, and he [a]gave up the [b]ghost.
21 And when the multitude had
witnessed that he spake these things
as he was about to give up the ghost,
they were astonished exceedingly;
insomuch that the power of God
came down upon them, and they
were [a]overcome that they fell to the
earth.
22 Now, this thing was pleasing
unto me, Jacob, for I had requested
it of my Father who was in heaven;
for he had heard my cry and
answered my prayer.
23 And it came to pass that peace
and the [a]love of God was restored
again among the people; and they
[b]searched the scriptures, and hearkened no more to the words of this
wicked man.
24 And it came to pass that many
means were devised to [a]reclaim
and restore the Lamanites to the
knowledge of the truth; but it all
was [b]vain, for they delighted in [c]wars
and [d]bloodshed, and they had an
eternal [e]hatred against us, their
brethren. And they sought by the
power of their arms to destroy us
continually.
25 Wherefore, the people of Nephi
did fortify against them with their
arms, and with all their might,
trusting in the God and [a]rock of their
salvation; wherefore, they became
as yet, conquerors of their enemies.
26 And it came to pass that I,
Jacob, began to be old; and the
record of this people being kept on
the [a]other plates of Nephi, wherefore, I conclude this record, declaring that I have written according to
the best of my knowledge, by saying
that the time passed away with us,
and also our [b]lives passed away like
as it were unto us a [c]dream, we being
a [d]lonesome and a solemn people,
[e]wanderers, cast out from Jerusalem, born in tribulation, in a
wilderness, and hated of our brethren, which caused wars and contentions; wherefore, we did mourn
out our days.
27 And I, Jacob, saw that I must
soon go down to my grave; wherefore, I said unto my son [a]Enos: Take
these [b]plates. And I told him the
things which my brother Nephi had
[c]commanded me, and he promised
obedience unto the commands. And
I make an end of my writing upon
these plates, which writing has been
[d]small; and to the reader I bid farewell, hoping that many of my brethren may read my words. Brethren,
adieu.

18*a* Gal. 3:1 (1–4); Alma 30:53 (53, 60).
b TG Deceit; Devil.
c TG Eternity.
d TG Punishment.
19*a* TG Despair.
b TG Holy Ghost, Unpardonable Sin against; Sons of Perdition.
c Jacob 6:9; Mosiah 15:26.
20*a* Jer. 28:16 (15–17); Alma 30:59 (12–60).
b Gen. 49:33; Hel. 14:21.
21*a* Alma 19:6 (1–36).
23*a* TG God, Love of.
b Alma 17:2. TG Scriptures, Study of.
24*a* Enos 1:20.
b Enos 1:14.
c Mosiah 1:5; 10:12 (11–18); Alma 3:8; 9:16; D&C 93:39.
d Jarom 1:6; Alma 26:24 (23–25).
e 2 Ne. 5:1 (1–3); Mosiah 28:2. TG Malice.
25*a* TG Rock.
26*a* 1 Ne. 19:1 (1–6); Jarom 1:14 (1, 14–15).
b James 4:14.
c 1 Chr. 29:15; Ps. 144:4.
d Alma 13:23.
e Alma 26:36.
27*a* Enos 1:1.
b Omni 1:3.
c Jacob 1:1 (1–4).
d 1 Ne. 6:3 (1–6); Jarom 1:2 (2, 14).

[Between 544 and 421 B.C.]

THE BOOK OF ENOS

Enos prays mightily and gains a remission of his sins—The voice of the Lord comes into his mind promising salvation for the Lamanites in a future day—Nephites sought to reclaim the Lamanites in their day—Enos rejoices in his Redeemer.

BEHOLD, it came to pass that
I, [a]Enos, knowing my father
that [b]he was a just man—for
he [c]taught me in his language, and
also in the [d]nurture and admonition
of the Lord—and blessed be the
name of my God for it—
2 And I will tell you of the [a]wrestle
which I had before God, before I
received a [b]remission of my sins.
3 Behold, I went to hunt beasts
in the forests; and the words which
I had often heard my father speak
concerning eternal life, and the [a]joy
of the saints, [b]sunk deep into my
heart.
4 And my soul [a]hungered; and I
[b]kneeled down before my Maker,
and I [c]cried unto him in mighty
[d]prayer and supplication for mine
own soul; and all the day long did I
cry unto him; yea, and when the
night came I did still raise my voice
high that it reached the heavens.
5 And there came a [a]voice unto me,
saying: Enos, thy sins are [b]forgiven
thee, and thou shalt be blessed.
6 And I, Enos, knew that God
[a]could not lie; wherefore, my guilt
was swept away.
7 And I said: Lord, how is it
done?
8 And he said unto me: [a]Because of
thy [b]faith in Christ, whom thou hast
never before heard nor seen. And
many years pass away before he
shall manifest himself in the flesh;
wherefore, go to, thy faith hath
made thee [c]whole.
9 Now, it came to pass that when I
had heard these words I began to
feel a [a]desire for the [b]welfare of my
brethren, the Nephites; wherefore,
I did [c]pour out my whole soul unto
God for them.
10 And while I was thus struggling
in the spirit, behold, the voice of
the Lord came into my [a]mind again,
saying: I will visit thy brethren
according to their diligence in keeping my commandments. I have
[b]given unto them this land, and it is
a holy land; and I [c]curse it not save
it be for the cause of iniquity;
wherefore, I will visit thy brethren
according as I have said; and their
[d]transgressions will I bring down
with sorrow upon their own heads.
11 And after I, Enos, had heard
these words, my [a]faith began to
be [b]unshaken in the Lord; and I
[c]prayed unto him with many long

1 1*a* Jacob 7: 27.
b 2 Ne. 2: 3 (2–4).
c 1 Ne. 1: 1; Mosiah 1: 2.
d Eph. 6: 4.
2*a* Gen. 32: 24 (24–32); Alma 8: 10. TG Repentance.
b TG Remission of Sins.
3*a* TG Joy.
b 1 Ne. 10: 17 (17–19); Alma 36: 17. TG Teachable.
4*a* 2 Ne. 9: 51; 3 Ne. 12: 6. TG Meditation; Motivations.
b TG Reverence.
c Ps. 138: 3. TG Perseverance.
d TG Prayer.
5*a* TG Revelation.
b TG Forgiveness.
6*a* TG God, the Standard of Righteousness.
8*a* Ether 3: 13 (12–13).
b TG Faith.
c Matt. 9: 22. TG Man, New, Spiritually Reborn; Steadfastness.
9*a* 1 Ne. 8: 12; Alma 36: 24.
b Alma 19: 29. TG Benevolence.
c Num. 21: 7; 1 Sam. 1: 15; 7: 5; Jer. 42: 4; 2 Ne. 33: 3; Alma 34: 26 (26–27).
10*a* TG Inspiration; Mind.
b 1 Ne. 2: 20.
c Gen. 8: 21 (20–22); Ether 2: 9 (7–12).
d TG Transgression.
11*a* TG Faith.
b TG Steadfastness.
c Gen. 20: 7; 1 Sam. 7: 5; 2 Ne. 33: 3; W of M 1: 8.

[Between 544 and 421 B.C.]

[d]strugglings for my brethren, the Lamanites.

12 And it came to pass that after I had [a]prayed and labored with all diligence, the Lord said unto me: I will grant unto thee according to thy [b]desires, because of thy faith.

13 And now behold, this was the desire which I desired of him—that if it should so be, that my people, the Nephites, should fall into transgression, and by any means be [a]destroyed, and the Lamanites should not be [b]destroyed, that the Lord God would [c]preserve a record of my people, the Nephites; even if it so be by the power of his holy arm, that it might be [d]brought forth at some future day unto the Lamanites, that, perhaps, they might be [e]brought unto salvation—

14 For at the present our strugglings were [a]vain in restoring them to the true faith. And they swore in their wrath that, if it were possible, they would [b]destroy our records and us, and also all the traditions of our fathers.

15 Wherefore, I knowing that the Lord God was able to [a]preserve our records, I cried unto him continually, for he had said unto me: Whatsoever thing ye shall ask in faith, believing that ye shall receive in the name of Christ, ye shall receive it.

16 And I had faith, and I did cry unto God that he would [a]preserve the [b]records; and he covenanted with me that he would [c]bring [d]them forth unto the Lamanites in his own due time.

17 And I, Enos, [a]knew it would be according to the covenant which he had made; wherefore my soul did rest.

18 And the Lord said unto me: Thy fathers have also required of me this thing; and it shall be done unto them according to their faith; for their faith was like unto thine.

19 And now it came to pass that I, Enos, went about among the people of Nephi, prophesying of things to come, and testifying of the things which I had heard and seen.

20 And I bear record that the people of Nephi did seek diligently to [a]restore the Lamanites unto the true faith in God. But our [b]labors were vain; their [c]hatred was fixed, and they were led by their evil nature that they became wild, and ferocious, and a [d]blood-thirsty people, full of [e]idolatry and [f]filthiness; feeding upon beasts of prey; dwelling in [g]tents, and wandering about in the wilderness with a short skin girdle about their loins and their heads shaven; and their skill was in the [h]bow, and in the cimeter, and the ax. And many of them did eat nothing save it was raw meat; and they were continually seeking to destroy us.

21 And it came to pass that the people of Nephi did till the land, and [a]raise all manner of grain, and of fruit, and [b]flocks of herds, and flocks of all manner of cattle of every kind, and goats, and wild goats, and also many horses.

22 And there were exceedingly

11*d* Eph. 6: 18.
12*a* Morm. 5: 21; 8: 25 (24–26); 9: 36 (36–37).
b Ps. 37: 4; 1 Ne. 7: 12; Hel. 10: 5.
13*a* 1 Ne. 15: 5; Morm. 6: 1.
b Lev. 26: 44.
c W of M 1: 7 (6–11); Alma 37: 2.
d 2 Ne. 3: 15; Jacob 1: 13; Alma 37: 19; Morm. 7: 9 (8–10); Ether 12: 22; D&C 3: 18.
e Alma 9: 17; Hel. 15: 16.
14*a* Jacob 7: 24.
b 2 Ne. 26: 17; Morm. 6: 6.
15*a* TG Scriptures, Preservation of.
16*a* 3 Ne. 5: 14 (13–15); D&C 3: 19 (16–20); 10: 47 (46–50).
b TG Book of Mormon.
c 2 Ne. 25: 8; 27: 6; Morm. 5: 12.
d 1 Ne. 19: 19. TG Israel, Restoration of.
17*a* TG Trust in God.
20*a* Jacob 7: 24.
b Moro. 9: 6.
c 2 Ne. 5: 1. TG Hate.
d Jarom 1: 6.
e Mosiah 9: 12. TG Idolatry.
f TG Filthiness.
g Gen. 25: 27.
h Mosiah 10: 8; Alma 3: 5 (4–5); 43: 20 (18–21).
21*a* 1 Ne. 8: 1; Mosiah 9: 9.
b 1 Ne. 18: 25; Ether 9: 19 (18–19).

[Between 544 and 421 B.C.]

many [a]prophets among us. And the people were a [b]stiffnecked people, hard to understand.

23 And there was nothing save it was exceeding [a]harshness, [b]preaching and prophesying of wars, and contentions, and destructions, and continually [c]reminding them of death, and the duration of eternity, and the judgments and the power of God, and all these things—stirring them up [d]continually to keep them in the fear of the Lord. I say there was nothing short of these things, and exceedingly great plainness of speech, would keep them from going down speedily to destruction. And after this manner do I write concerning them.

24 And I saw [a]wars between the Nephites and Lamanites in the course of my days.

25 And it came to pass that I began to be old, *and an hundred and seventy and nine years had passed away from the time that our father Lehi [a]left Jerusalem.

26 And I saw that I [a]must soon go down to my grave, having been wrought upon by the power of God that I must preach and prophesy unto this people, and declare the word according to the truth which is in Christ. And I have declared it in all my days, and have rejoiced in it above that of the world.

27 And I soon go to the place of my [a]rest, which is with my Redeemer; for I know that in him I shall [b]rest. And I rejoice in the day when my [c]mortal shall put on [d]immortality, and shall stand before him; then shall I see his face with pleasure, and he will say unto me: Come unto me, ye blessed, there is a place prepared for you in the [e]mansions of my Father. Amen.

THE BOOK OF JAROM

The Nephites keep the law of Moses, look forward to the coming of Christ, and prosper in the land—Many prophets labor to keep them in the way of truth.

NOW behold, I, Jarom, write a few words according to the commandment of my father, Enos, that our [a]genealogy may be kept.

2 And as [a]these plates are [b]small, and as these things are [c]written for the intent of the benefit of our brethren the [d]Lamanites, wherefore, it must needs be that I write a little; but I shall not write the things of my prophesying, nor of my revelations. For what could I write more than my fathers have written? For have not they revealed the plan of salvation? I say unto you, Yea; and this sufficeth me.

3 Behold, it is expedient that much

22*a* W of M 1: 16.
b Jarom 1: 3.
23*a* 1 Ne. 16: 2 (1–3); 2 Ne. 33: 5; W of M 1: 17.
b TG Preaching.
c Hel. 12: 3.
d Jarom 1: 12; Alma 4: 19; 31: 5.
24*a* 1 Ne. 12: 2 (2–3); Morm. 8: 7 (7–8). TG War.
25*a* 1 Ne. 2: 2 (2–4).
26*a* 1 Cor. 9: 16; Ether 12: 2. TG Duty.
27*a* TG Rest.
b 2 Ne. 33: 6.
c TG Mortality.
d TG Immortality.
e Ps. 65: 4; John 14: 2 (2–3); Ether 12: 32 (32–34); D&C 72: 4; 98: 18.

[JAROM]

1 1*a* 1 Ne. 3: 12; 5: 14.
2*a* Jacob 3: 14 (13–14); Omni 1: 1.
b 1 Ne. 6: 3 (1–6); Jacob 7: 27.
c TG Scriptures, Writing of.
d 2 Ne. 27: 6; Morm. 5: 12 (12–13).

[*420 B.C.]

should be done among this people, because of the hardness of their hearts, and the deafness of their ears, and the blindness of their minds, and the [a]stiffness of their necks; nevertheless, God is exceedingly merciful unto them, and has not as yet [b]swept them off from the face of the land.

4 And there are many among us who have many [a]revelations, for they are not all [b]stiffnecked. And as many as are not stiffnecked and have faith, have [c]communion with the Holy Spirit, which maketh manifest unto the children of men, according to their faith.

5 And now, behold, *two hundred years had passed away, and the people of Nephi had waxed strong in the land. They observed to [a]keep the law of Moses and the [b]sabbath day holy unto the Lord. And they [c]profaned not; neither did they [d]blaspheme. And the [e]laws of the land were exceedingly strict.

6 And they were scattered upon [a]much of the face of the land, and the Lamanites also. And they were exceedingly more [b]numerous than were they of the Nephites; and they loved [c]murder and would drink the [d]blood of beasts.

7 And it came to pass that they came many times against us, the Nephites, to battle. But our [a]kings and our [b]leaders were mighty men in the faith of the Lord; and they taught the people the ways of the Lord; wherefore, we withstood the Lamanites and swept them away out of [c]our lands, and began to fortify our cities, or whatsoever place of our inheritance.

8 And we multiplied exceedingly, and spread upon the face of the land, and became exceedingly rich in [a]gold, and in silver, and in precious things, and in fine [b]workmanship of wood, in buildings, and in [c]machinery, and also in iron and copper, and brass and steel, making all manner of tools of every kind to till the ground, and [d]weapons of war—yea, the sharp pointed arrow, and the quiver, and the dart, and the javelin, and all preparations for war.

9 And thus being prepared to meet the Lamanites, they did not prosper against us. But the word of the Lord was verified, which he spake unto our fathers, saying that: [a]Inasmuch as ye will keep my commandments ye shall [b]prosper in the land.

10 And it came to pass that the prophets of the Lord did threaten the people of Nephi, according to the word of God, that if they did not keep the commandments, but should fall into transgression, they should be [a]destroyed from off the face of the land.

11 Wherefore, the prophets, and the priests, and the [a]teachers, did labor diligently, exhorting with all long-suffering the people to [b]diligence; teaching the [c]law of Moses, and the intent for which it was given; persuading them to [d]look forward unto the Messiah, and believe in him to come [e]as though he already

3*a* Enos 1:22 (22–23).
b Ether 2:8 (8–10).
4*a* Alma 26:22; Hel. 11:23; D&C 107:19 (18–19).
b TG Stiffneckedness.
c TG Holy Ghost; Revelation.
5*a* 2 Ne. 25:24; Mosiah 2:3; Alma 30:3; 34:14 (13–14).
b Ex. 35:2. TG Sabbath.
c TG Profanity.
d TG Blasphemy.
e Alma 1:1.
6*a* Hel. 11:20 (19–20).
b Alma 2:27.
c Jacob 7:24; Enos 1:20; Alma 26:24 (23–25).
d TG Blood, Eating of.
7*a* 2 Ne. 5:18; 6:2; Jacob 1:9 (9, 11, 15); Mosiah 1:10.
b TG Leadership.
c W of M 1:14.
8*a* 2 Ne. 5:15.
b TG Art.
c TG Skill.
d 2 Ne. 5:14; Mosiah 10:8.
9*a* 2 Ne. 1:20; Omni 1:6.
b Josh. 1:7; Ps. 122:6.
10*a* 1 Ne. 12:19 (19–20); Omni 1:5.
11*a* TG Teacher.
b TG Diligence.
c Jacob 4:5; Alma 25:15 (15–16).
d 2 Ne. 11:4; Ether 12:19 (18–19).
e 2 Ne. 25:26 (24–27); Mosiah 3:13; 16:6.

[*399 B.C.]

was. And after this manner did they
teach them.
12 And it came to pass that by
so doing they kept them from being
[a]destroyed upon the face of the
land; for they did [b]prick their hearts
with the word, [c]continually stirring
them up unto repentance.
13 And it came to pass that *two
hundred and thirty and eight years
had passed away—after the manner
of wars, and [a]contentions, and dissensions, for the space of [b]much of
the time.
14 And I, Jarom, do not write more,
for the plates are [a]small. But behold,
my brethren, ye can go to the [b]other
plates of Nephi; for behold, upon
them the records of our wars are
engraven, according to the writings
of the [c]kings, or those which they
caused to be written.
15 And I deliver these plates into
the hands of my son Omni, that they
may be kept according to the [a]com-
mandments of my fathers.

THE BOOK OF OMNI

Omni, Amaron, Chemish, Abinadom, and Amaleki, each in turn, keep the records—Mosiah discovers the people of Zarahemla who came from Jerusalem in the days of Zedekiah—He is made king over them—The Mulekites had discovered Coriantumr, the last of the Jaredites—King Benjamin succeeds Mosiah—Men should offer their souls as an offering to Christ.

BEHOLD, it came to pass that
I, Omni, being commanded
by my father, Jarom, that I
should write somewhat upon [a]these
plates, to preserve our genealogy—
2 Wherefore, in my days, I would
that ye should know that I fought
much with the sword to preserve my
people, the Nephites, from falling
into the hands of their enemies, the
Lamanites. But behold, I of myself
[a]am a wicked man, and I have not
kept the statutes and the commandments of the Lord as I ought to have
done.
3 And it came to pass that †two
hundred and seventy and six years
had passed away, and we had many
seasons of peace; and we had
many [a]seasons of serious war and
bloodshed. Yea, and in fine, ‡two
hundred and eighty and two years
had passed away, and I had kept
these plates according to the [b]com-
mandments of my [c]fathers; and
I [d]conferred them upon my son
Amaron. And I make an end.
4 And now I, Amaron, write the
things whatsoever I write, which are
few, in the book of my father.
5 Behold, it came to pass that
§three hundred and twenty years
had passed away, and the more
wicked part of the Nephites were
[a]destroyed.
6 For the Lord would not suffer,
after he had led them out of the land
of Jerusalem and kept and preserved
them from falling into the hands of
their enemies, yea, he would not
suffer that the words should not be

12*a* Ether 2: 10 (8–10).
b Alma 31: 5.
c Enos 1: 23.
13*a* TG Contention.
b Omni 1: 3.
14*a* Jacob 4: 1 (1–2); Omni 1: 30.
b Jacob 7: 26 (26–27); W of M 1: 3.
c Omni 1: 11; W of M 1: 10.
15*a* Jacob 1:1 (1–4); Omni 1: 3.

[OMNI]
1 1*a* Jarom 1: 2 (1–2); Omni 1: 9.
2*a* TG Confession; Honesty; Humility.
3*a* Jarom 1: 13.
b Jacob 1: 1 (1–4); 7: 27; Jarom 1: 15 (1–2, 15).
c TG Patriarch.
d TG Delegation of Responsibility.
5*a* Jarom 1: 10.

[*361 B.C. †323 B.C. ‡317 B.C. §279 B.C.]

verified, which he spake unto our
fathers, saying that: [a]Inasmuch
as ye will not keep my commandments ye shall not [b]prosper in the
land.
7 Wherefore, the Lord did visit
them in great judgment; nevertheless, he did spare the righteous that
they should not perish, but did
deliver them out of the hands of
their enemies.
8 And it came to pass that I did
deliver the plates unto my brother
Chemish.
9 Now I, Chemish, write what few
things I write, in the same book with
my brother; for behold, I saw the
last which he wrote, that he wrote it
with his own hand; and he wrote it
in the day that he delivered them
unto me. And after this manner we
keep the [a]records, for it is according to the commandments of our
fathers. And I make an end.
10 Behold, I, Abinadom, am the
son of Chemish. Behold, it came
to pass that I saw much war and
contention between my people, the
Nephites, and the Lamanites; and
I, with my own sword, have taken
the lives of many of the Lamanites
in the defence of my brethren.
11 And behold, the [a]record of this
people is engraven upon plates
which is had by the [b]kings, according to the generations; and I know
of no revelation save that which
has been written, neither prophecy;
wherefore, that which is sufficient is
written. And I make an end.
12 Behold, I am Amaleki, the son
of Abinadom. Behold, I will speak
unto you somewhat concerning
[a]Mosiah, who was made king over
the [b]land of Zarahemla; for behold,
he being [c]warned of the Lord that
he should [d]flee out of the [e]land
of [f]Nephi, and as many as would
hearken unto the voice of the Lord
should also [g]depart out of the land
with him, into the wilderness—
13 And it came to pass that he
did according as the Lord had commanded him. And they departed
out of the land into the wilderness,
as many as would hearken unto the
voice of the Lord; and they were led
by many preachings and prophesy-
ings. And they were admonished
continually by the word of God; and
they were led by the power of his
[a]arm, through the wilderness until they came down into the land
which is called the [b]land of Zarahemla.
14 And they discovered a [a]people,
who were called the people of
Zarahemla. Now, there was great
rejoicing among the people of
Zarahemla; and also Zarahemla did
rejoice exceedingly, because the
Lord had sent the people of Mosiah
with the [b]plates of brass which
contained the record of the Jews.
15 Behold, it came to pass that
Mosiah discovered that the people
of [a]Zarahemla came out from Jerusalem at the time that [b]Zedekiah,
king of Judah, was carried away
captive into Babylon.
16 And they [a]journeyed in the
wilderness, and were brought by
the hand of the Lord across the great
waters, into the land where Mosiah
discovered them; and they had
dwelt there from that time forth.
17 And at the time that Mosiah
discovered them, they had become
exceedingly numerous. Nevertheless, they had had many wars and
serious contentions, and had fallen
by the sword from time to time; and

6*a* Jarom 1:9; Mosiah 1:7.
b Deut. 28:29.
9*a* Omni 1:1. TG Record Keeping.
11*a* W of M 1:10.
b Jarom 1:14.
12*a* Omni 1:19.
b Alma 4:1.
c TG Warnings.
d Mosiah 11:13.
e Omni 1:27; W of M 1:13.
f 2 Ne. 5:8; Mosiah 7:6 (6–7).
g Jacob 3:4.
13*a* Isa. 33:2; Mosiah 12:24.
b Mosiah 1:1; 2:4.
14*a* Mosiah 1:10.
b 1 Ne. 3:3 (3, 19–20); 5:10 (10–22).
15*a* Ezek. 17:22 (22–23); Mosiah 25:2 (2–4).
b Jer. 39:4 (1–10); 52:11 (9–11); Hel. 8:21.
16*a* 1 Ne. 16:9.

[Between 279 and 130 B.C.]

their [a]language had become corrupted; and they had brought no [b]re-
cords with them; and they denied
the being of their Creator; and
Mosiah, nor the people of Mosiah,
could understand them.
18 But it came to pass that Mosiah
caused that they should be taught
in his [a]language. And it came to pass
that after they were taught in the
language of Mosiah, Zarahemla gave
a genealogy of his fathers, according
to his memory; and they are written,
but [b]not in these plates.
19 And it came to pass that the
people of Zarahemla, and of Mosiah,
did [a]unite together; and [b]Mosiah
was appointed to be their king.
20 And it came to pass in the days
of Mosiah, there was a large [a]stone
brought unto him with engravings
on it; and he did [b]interpret the
engravings by the gift and power of
God.
21 And they gave an account of
one [a]Coriantumr, and the slain of
his people. And Coriantumr was discovered by the people of Zarahemla;
and he dwelt with them for the space
of nine moons.
22 It also spake a few words concerning his fathers. And his first
parents came out from the [a]tower,
at the time the Lord [b]confounded
the language of the people; and the
severity of the Lord fell upon them
according to his judgments, which
are just; and their [c]bones lay scattered in the land northward.
23 Behold, I, Amaleki, was born in
the days of Mosiah; and I have lived
to see his death; and [a]Benjamin, [b]his
son, reigneth in his stead.
24 And behold, I have seen, in the
days of king Benjamin, a serious
war and much bloodshed between
the Nephites and the Lamanites.
But behold, the Nephites did obtain
much advantage over them; yea,
insomuch that king Benjamin did
drive them out of the land of Zarahemla.
25 And it came to pass that I began
to be old; and, having no seed, and
knowing king [a]Benjamin to be a
just man before the Lord, wherefore,
I shall [b]deliver up [c]these plates unto
him, exhorting all men to come unto God, the Holy One of Israel,
and believe in prophesying, and in
revelations, and in the ministering
of angels, and in the gift of speaking with tongues, and in the gift of
interpreting languages, and in all
things which are [d]good; for there is
nothing which is good save it comes
from the Lord: and that which is
evil cometh from the devil.
26 And now, my beloved brethren,
I would that ye should [a]come unto
Christ, who is the Holy One of Israel,
and partake of his salvation, and
the power of his redemption. Yea,
come unto him, and [b]offer your
whole souls as an [c]offering unto him,
and continue in [d]fasting and praying, and endure to the end; and as
the Lord liveth ye will be saved.
27 And now I would speak somewhat concerning a certain [a]number
who went up into the wilderness to
[b]return to the [c]land of Nephi; for
there was a large number who were
desirous to possess the land of their
inheritance.
28 Wherefore, they went up into

17*a* 1 Ne. 3:19.
TG Language.
b Mosiah 1:3 (2–6).
18*a* Mosiah 24:4.
b 1 Ne. 9:4; W of M 1:10.
19*a* Mosiah 25:13.
b Omni 1:12.
20*a* Mosiah 21:28 (27–28); 28:13.
b Mosiah 8:13 (13–19); 28:17. TG Urim and Thummim.
21*a* Ether 12:1 (1–2); 13:20 (13–31); 15:32.
22*a* Ether 1:3 (1–6).
b Gen. 11:7 (6–9); Mosiah 28:17; Ether 1:33.
c Mosiah 8:8 (8–12).
23*a* W of M 1:3.
b Mosiah 2:11.
25*a* W of M 1:18 (17–18); Mosiah 29:13.
b W of M 1:10.
c 1 Ne. 10:1.
d Alma 5:40; Ether 4:12; Moro. 7:16 (15–17).
26*a* Jacob 1:7; Alma 29:2.
b TG Commitment; Self-sacrifice.
c 3 Ne. 9:20.
d TG Fasting.
27*a* Mosiah 9:3 (1–4).
b Mosiah 7:1.
c Omni 1:12.

[Between 279 and 130 B.C.]

the wilderness. And their leader being a strong and mighty man, and
a stiffnecked man, wherefore he
caused a contention among them;
and they were [a]all slain, save fifty,
in the wilderness, and they returned
again to the land of Zarahemla.
29 And it came to pass that they
also took others to a considerable
number, and took their journey
again into the wilderness.
30 And I, Amaleki, had a brother,
who also went with them; and I
have not since known concerning
them. And I am about to lie down
in my grave; and [a]these plates are
full. And I make an end of my
speaking.

THE WORDS OF MORMON

Mormon abridges their history onto the plates of Mormon—He inserts the plates of Nephi into the abridgment—King Benjamin establishes peace in the land.

AND now I, Mormon, being
about to deliver up the [a]record
which I have been making
into the hands of my son Moroni,
behold I have witnessed almost all
the destruction of my people, the
Nephites.
2 And it is [a]many hundred years
after the coming of Christ *that I
deliver these records into the hands
of my son; and it supposeth me that
he will witness the entire [b]destruc-
tion of my people. But may God
grant that he may survive them,
that he may write somewhat concerning them, and somewhat concerning Christ, that perhaps some
day it may [c]profit them.
3 And now, I speak somewhat
concerning that which I have written; for after I had made an [a]abridg-
ment from the [b]plates of Nephi,
down to the reign of this king
Benjamin, of whom Amaleki spake,
I searched among the [c]records which
had been delivered into my hands,
and I found these plates, which contained this small account of the
prophets, from Jacob down to the
reign of this king [d]Benjamin, and
also many of the words of Nephi.
4 And the things which are upon
these plates [a]pleasing me, because
of the prophecies of the coming of
Christ; and my fathers knowing that
many of them have been fulfilled;
yea, and I also know that as many
things as have been [b]prophesied concerning us down to this day have been
fulfilled, and as many as go beyond
this day must surely come to pass—
5 Wherefore, I chose [a]these things,
to finish my [b]record upon them,
which remainder of my record I
shall take from the [c]plates of Nephi;
and I cannot write the [d]hundredth
part of the things of my people.
6 But behold, I shall take these

28*a* Mosiah 9: 2 (1–4).
30*a* 1 Ne. 6: 3 (3–6); Jacob 4: 1 (1–2); Jarom 1: 14.

[WORDS OF MORMON]

1 1*a* 3 Ne. 5: 12 (9–12); Morm. 1: 4 (1–4); 2: 17 (17–18); 8: 5 (1, 4–5, 14).
2*a* Morm. 6: 5 (5–6).
b 1 Ne. 12: 19.
c D&C 3: 19 (16–20).
3*a* 1 Ne. 1: 17 (16–17); D&C 10: 44.
b Jarom 1: 14; W of M 1: 10; D&C 10: 38 (38–40).
c Mosiah 1: 6 (2–6); Hel. 3: 13 (13–15); Morm. 4: 23.
d Omni 1: 23 (23–25).
4*a* 1 Ne. 6: 5 (3–6).
b TG Jesus Christ, Prophecies about.
5*a* IE the things pleasing to him, mentioned in v. 4.
b 3 Ne. 5: 17 (14–18); Morm. 1: 1.
c 1 Ne. 9: 2.
d Alma 13: 31; 3 Ne. 5: 8 (8–11); 26: 6 (6–12).

[*About A.D. 385]

plates, which contain these proph-
esyings and revelations, and put
them with the remainder of my
record, for they are choice unto me;
and I know they will be choice unto
my brethren.
7 And I do this for a [a]wise [b]purpose;
for thus it whispereth me, according
to the workings of the Spirit of the
Lord which is in me. And now, I do
not know all things; but the Lord
[c]knoweth all things which are to
come; wherefore, he [d]worketh in me
to do according to his [e]will.
8 And my [a]prayer to God is concerning my brethren, that they may
once again come to the knowledge of
God, yea, the redemption of Christ;
that they may once again be a
[b]delightsome people.
9 And now I, Mormon, *proceed to
finish out my record, which I take
from the plates of Nephi; and I make
it according to the knowledge and
the [a]understanding which God has
given me.
10 Wherefore, it came to pass that
after Amaleki had [a]delivered up
these plates into the hands of king
Benjamin, he took them and put
them with the [b]other plates, which
contained records which had been
handed down by the [c]kings, from
generation to generation until the
days of king Benjamin.
11 And they were handed down
from king Benjamin, from generation to generation until they have
fallen into [a]my hands. And I,
Mormon, pray to God that they
may be preserved from this time
henceforth. And I know that they
will be preserved; for there are great
things written upon them, out of
which [b]my people and their brethren shall be [c]judged at the great and
last day, according to the word of
God which is written.
12 And now, concerning this king
Benjamin—he had somewhat of
contentions among his own people.
13 And it came to pass also that
the armies of the Lamanites came
down out of the [a]land of Nephi, to
battle against his people. But behold,
king Benjamin gathered together
his armies, and he did stand against
them; and he did fight with the
strength of his own arm, with the
[b]sword of Laban.
14 And in the [a]strength of the
Lord they did contend against their
enemies, until they had slain many
thousands of the Lamanites. And it
came to pass that they did contend
against the Lamanites until they
had driven them out of all the lands
of their [b]inheritance.
15 And it came to pass that after
there had been false [a]Christs, and
their mouths had been shut, and they
punished according to their crimes;
16 And after there had been [a]false
prophets, and false preachers and
teachers among the people, and all
these having been punished according to their crimes; and after there
having been much contention and
many dissensions away [b]unto the
Lamanites, behold, it came to pass
that king Benjamin, with the assistance of the holy [c]prophets who were
among his people—
17 For behold, king Benjamin was

7a 1 Ne. 9: 5; 19: 3; Enos 1: 13 (13–18); Alma 37: 2; D&C 3: 19 (9–20); 10: 34 (1–19, 30–47).
b D&C 10: 40 (20–46).
c TG God, Foreknowledge of; God, Intelligence of; God, Omniscience of.
d 2 Ne. 27: 23.
e TG God, Will of.
8a 2 Ne. 33: 3; Enos 1: 11 (11–12); Moro. 9: 22.
b 2 Ne. 30: 6.
9a TG Understanding.
10a Omni 1: 25 (25, 30).
b 1 Ne. 9: 4; Omni 1: 11, 18; W of M 1: 3; Mosiah 28: 11.
c Jarom 1: 14.
11a 3 Ne. 5: 12 (8–12); Morm. 1: 4 (1–5).
b Hel. 15: 3 (3–4).
c 2 Ne. 25: 18; 29: 11; 33: 14 (11, 14–15); 3 Ne. 27: 25 (23–27); Ether 5: 4.
13a Omni 1: 12.
b 1 Ne. 4: 9; 2 Ne. 5: 14; Jacob 1: 10; Mosiah 1: 16; D&C 17: 1.
14a TG Strength.
b Jarom 1: 7.
15a TG False Christs.
16a TG False Prophets.
b Jacob 1: 14 (13–14).
c Enos 1: 22.

[*About A.D. 385]

a [a]holy man, and he did reign over
his people in righteousness; and
there were many holy men in the
land, and they did speak the word of
God with [b]power and with authority; and they did use much [c]sharp-
ness because of the stiffneckedness
of the people—
18 Wherefore, with the help of
these, king [a]Benjamin, by laboring
with all the might of his body and
the [b]faculty of his whole soul, and
also the prophets, did once more
establish peace in the land.

THE BOOK OF MOSIAH

CHAPTER 1

King Benjamin teaches his sons the language and prophecies of their fathers—Their religion and civilization have been preserved because of the records kept on the various plates—Mosiah is chosen as king and is given custody of the records and other things.

AND now there was no more
contention in all the [a]land of
Zarahemla, among all the
people who belonged to king Benjamin, so that king Benjamin had
continual peace all the remainder of
his days.
2 And it came to pass that he
had three [a]sons; and he called their
names Mosiah, and Helorum, and
Helaman. And he caused that they
should be [b]taught in all the [c]language
of his fathers, that thereby they
might become men of understanding; and that they might know
concerning the prophecies which
had been spoken by the mouths of
their fathers, which were delivered
them by the hand of the Lord.
3 And he also taught them concerning the records which were engraven on the [a]plates of brass, saying: My sons, I would that ye should
remember that were it not for these
[b]plates, which contain these records
and these commandments, we must
have suffered in [c]ignorance, even at
this present time, not knowing the
mysteries of God.
4 For it were not possible that
our father, Lehi, could have remembered all these things, to have
taught them to his children, except
it were for the help of these plates;
for he having been taught in the
[a]language of the Egyptians therefore he could read these engravings,
and teach them to his children, that
thereby they could teach them to
their children, and so fulfilling the
commandments of God, even down
to this present time.
5 I say unto you, my sons, [a]were
it not for these things, which have
been kept and [b]preserved by the
hand of God, that we might [c]read
and understand of his [d]mysteries,
and have his [e]commandments al-

17*a* Ex. 22:31; Alma 13:26; D&C 49:8; 107:29.
b Alma 17:3 (2–3). TG God, Power of.
c Enos 1:23; Moro. 9:4; D&C 121:43 (41–43).
18*a* Omni 1:25; Mosiah 29:13.
b 1 Ne. 15:25.

[MOSIAH]

1 1*a* Omni 1:13; Alma 2:15.
2*a* 1 Ne. 1:1; D&C 68:25 (25, 28).
b Enos 1:1; Mosiah 4:15 (14–15).
c Morm. 9:32.
3*a* 2 Ne. 5:12; Mosiah 1:16; 28:20.
b 1 Ne. 3:19 (19–20); Omni 1:17.
c Alma 37:8.
4*a* 1 Ne. 1:2; 3:19; Morm. 9:32 (32–33); JS-H 1:64.
5*a* Alma 37:9.
b TG Scriptures, Preservation of.
c Deut. 6:6 (6–8); 2 Chr. 34:21; 1 Ne. 15:24 (23–24). TG Scriptures, Value of.
d TG Mysteries of Godliness.
e 1 Ne. 4:15.

[About 130 B.C.]

ways before our eyes, that even our
fathers would have dwindled in unbelief, and we should have been like
unto our brethren, the Lamanites,
who know nothing concerning these
things, or even do not believe them
when they are taught them, because
of the [f]traditions of their fathers,
which are not correct.
6 O my sons, I would that ye should
remember that these sayings are
true, and also that these records are
[a]true. And behold, also the plates of
Nephi, which contain the records
and the sayings of our fathers from
the time they left Jerusalem until
now, and they are true; and we can
know of their surety because we have
them before our eyes.
7 And now, my sons, I would that
ye should remember to [a]search them
diligently, that ye may profit thereby; and I would that ye should [b]keep
the commandments of God, that ye
may [c]prosper in the land according to the [d]promises which the Lord
made unto our fathers.
8 And many more things did king
Benjamin teach his sons, which are
not written in this book.
9 And it came to pass that after
king Benjamin had made an end of
teaching his sons, that he waxed
[a]old, and he saw that he must very
soon go the way of all the earth;
therefore, he thought it expedient
that he should confer the kingdom
upon one of his sons.
10 Therefore, *he had Mosiah
brought before him; and these are
the words which he spake unto
him, saying: My son, I would that
ye should make a proclamation
throughout all this land among all
this [a]people, or the people of Zarahemla, and the people of Mosiah
who dwell in the land, that thereby
they may be gathered together; for
on the morrow I shall proclaim unto
this my people out of mine own
mouth that thou art a [b]king and a
ruler over this people, whom the
Lord our God hath given us.
11 And moreover, I shall give this
people a [a]name, that thereby they
may be distinguished above all the
people which the Lord God hath
brought out of the land of Jerusalem; and this I do because they
have been a [b]diligent people in keeping the commandments of the Lord.
12 And I give unto them a name
that never shall be blotted out,
except it be through [a]transgression.
13 Yea, and moreover I say unto you, that if this highly favored
people of the Lord should fall into
[a]transgression, and become a wicked
and an adulterous people, that the
Lord will deliver them up, that
thereby they become [b]weak like
unto their brethren; and he will no
more [c]preserve them by his matchless and marvelous power, as he has
hitherto preserved our fathers.
14 For I say unto you, that if he
had not extended his arm in the
preservation of our fathers they
must have fallen into the hands of
the Lamanites, and become victims
to their hatred.
15 And it came to pass that after
king Benjamin had made an end
of these sayings to his son, that he
gave him [a]charge concerning all the
affairs of the kingdom.
16 And moreover, he also gave him
charge concerning the records which

5*f* Jacob 7: 24; Mosiah 10: 12 (11–17).
6*a* 1 Ne. 1: 3; 14: 30; 2 Ne. 25: 20; Alma 3: 12; Ether 5: 3 (1–3).
7*a* TG Scriptures, Study of.
b Lev. 25: 18 (18–19); Mosiah 2: 22; Alma 50: 20 (20–22).
c Josh. 1: 7; Ps. 1: 3 (2–3); 122: 6; 1 Ne. 2: 20.
d Omni 1: 6; Alma 9: 13 (13–14).
9*a* TG Old Age.
10*a* Omni 1: 14; Mosiah 27: 35.
b Gen. 41: 43 (41–43); Jarom 1: 7 (7, 14); Mosiah 2: 30.
11*a* Mosiah 5: 8 (8–12). TG Jesus Christ, Taking the Name of.
b TG Diligence.
12*a* TG Transgression.
13*a* Heb. 6: 6 (4–6).
b Jer. 46: 15 (15-17); Hel. 4: 24 (24, 26).
c D&C 103: 8.
15*a* 1 Kgs. 2: 1; Ps. 72: 1 (1–4).

[*About 124 B.C.]

were engraven on the [a]plates of
brass; and also the plates of Nephi;
and also, the [b]sword of Laban, and
the [c]ball or director, which led
our fathers through the wilderness,
which was prepared by the hand of
the Lord that thereby they might be
led, every one according to the heed
and diligence which they gave unto
him.
17 Therefore, as they were [a]un-
faithful they did not prosper nor
progress in their journey, but were
[b]driven back, and incurred the displeasure of God upon them; and
therefore they were smitten with
famine and sore [c]afflictions, to stir
them up in [d]remembrance of their
duty.
18 And now, it came to pass that
Mosiah went and did as his father
had commanded him, and proclaimed unto all the people who were
in the land of Zarahemla that thereby they might gather themselves
together, to go up to the [a]temple
to hear the words which his father
should speak unto them.

CHAPTER 2

King Benjamin addresses his people—He recounts the equity, fairness, and spirituality of his reign—He counsels them to serve their heavenly King—Those who rebel against God shall suffer anguish like unquenchable fire.

AND it came to pass that after
Mosiah had done as his father had
commanded him, and had made a
proclamation throughout all the
land, that the people [a]gathered
themselves together throughout all
the land, that they might go up
to the [b]temple to [c]hear the [d]words
which king Benjamin should speak
unto them.
2 And there were a great number,
even so many that they did not
number them; for they had multiplied exceedingly and waxed great
in the land.
3 And they also took of the [a]first-
lings of their flocks, that they might
offer [b]sacrifice and [c]burnt [d]offerings
[e]according to the law of Moses;
4 And also that they might give
thanks to the Lord their God, who
had brought them out of the
land of Jerusalem, and who had delivered them out of the hands of
their enemies, and had [a]appointed
just men to be their [b]teachers, and
also a just man to be their king, who
had established peace in the [c]land
of Zarahemla, and who had taught
them to [d]keep the commandments
of God, that they might rejoice and
be filled with [e]love towards God and
all men.
5 And it came to pass that when
they came up to the temple, they
pitched their tents round about,
every man according to his [a]family,
consisting of his wife, and his sons,
and his daughters, and their sons,
and their daughters, from the eldest
down to the youngest, every family
being separate one from another.
6 And they pitched their tents
round about the temple, every man
having his [a]tent with the door thereof towards the temple, that thereby
they might remain in their tents and
hear the words which king Benjamin
should speak unto them;

16*a* Mosiah 1: 3.
b Jacob 1: 10; W of M 1: 13; D&C 17: 1.
c 2 Ne. 5: 12.
17*a* TG Disobedience.
b 1 Ne. 18: 13 (12–13).
c Lam. 1: 5. TG Affliction.
d Judg. 13: 1; Hel. 12: 3 (2–3).
18*a* 2 Ne. 5: 16; Mosiah 2: 1.
2 1*a* TG Assembly for Worship.
b Mosiah 1: 18.
c 2 Chr. 34: 30 (29–33).
d Mosiah 26: 1.
3*a* Gen. 4: 4 (2–7); Ex. 13: 12 (12–13); Deut. 12: 6; Moses 5: 20 (5, 19–23).
b Ezra 6: 10. TG Sacrifice.
c Lev. 1: 3 (2–9); Deut. 33: 10.
d Ezra 3: 2 (2–5); 1 Ne. 5: 9.
e 2 Ne. 25: 24; Jarom 1: 5; Alma 30: 3; 34: 14 (13–14).
4*a* TG Called of God.
b Mosiah 18: 18 (18–22).
c Omni 1: 13 (12–15).
d John 15: 10; D&C 95: 12.
e Deut. 11:1. TG Love.
5*a* TG Family, Patriarchal.
6*a* Ex. 33: 8 (8–10).

[About 124 B.C.]

7 For the multitude being so great
that king Benjamin could not teach
them all within the walls of the
temple, therefore he caused a
[a]tower to be erected, that thereby
his people might hear the words
which he should speak unto them.
8 And it came to pass that he
began to speak to his people from
the tower; and they could not all
hear his words because of the greatness of the multitude; therefore he
caused that the words which he
spake should be written and sent
forth among those that were not
under the sound of his voice, that
they might also receive his words.
9 And these are the words which
he [a]spake and caused to be written,
saying: My brethren, all ye that
have assembled yourselves together,
you that can hear my words which
I shall speak unto you this day; for
I have not commanded you to come
up hither to [b]trifle with the words
which I shall speak, but that you
should [c]hearken unto me, and open
your ears that ye may hear, and your
[d]hearts that ye may understand,
and your [e]minds that the [f]mysteries
of God may be unfolded to your view.
10 I have not commanded you to
come up hither that ye should fear
[a]me, or that ye should think that I of
myself am more than a mortal man.
11 But I am like as yourselves,
subject to all manner of infirmities
in body and mind; yet I have been
chosen by this people, and [a]conse-
crated by [b]my father, and was suffered by the hand of the Lord that
I should be a ruler and a king over
this people; and have been kept and
preserved by his matchless power,
to serve you with all the might,
mind and strength which the Lord
hath granted unto me.
12 I say unto you that as I have
been suffered to [a]spend my days in
your service, even up to this time,
and have not sought [b]gold nor silver
nor any manner of riches of you;
13 Neither have I suffered that ye
should be confined in dungeons, nor
that ye should make slaves one of
another, nor that ye should murder,
or plunder, or steal, or commit adultery; nor even have I suffered that
ye should commit any manner of
wickedness, and have taught you
that ye should keep the commandments of the Lord, in all things
which he hath commanded you—
14 And even I, myself, have
[a]labored with mine own [b]hands that
I might serve you, and that ye
should not be [c]laden with taxes, and
that there should nothing come
upon you which was grievous to be
borne—and of all these things which
I have spoken, ye yourselves are
witnesses this day.
15 Yet, my brethren, I have not
done these things that I might
[a]boast, neither do I tell these things
that thereby I might accuse you;
but I tell you these things that ye
may know that I can answer a clear
[b]conscience before God this day.
16 Behold, I say unto you that
because I said unto you that I had
spent my days in your service, I do
not desire to boast, for I have only
been in the service of God.
17 And behold, I tell you these
things that ye may learn [a]wisdom;
that ye may learn that when ye are
in the [b]service of your [c]fellow beings

7*a* Gen. 35: 21; Neh. 8: 4 (4–5); Mosiah 11: 12 (12–13).
9*a* Mosiah 8: 3.
b D&C 6: 12; 32: 5. TG Mocking.
c TG Teachable.
d Prov. 8:5; Mosiah 12: 27; 3 Ne. 19: 33.
e TG Mind.
f TG Mysteries of Godliness.
10*a* TG Humility.
11*a* TG Setting Apart.
b Omni 1: 23 (23–24). TG Serve; Service.
12*a* 1 Sam. 12: 2 (1–25).
b 2 Kgs. 5: 16; Acts 20: 33 (33–34); Jacob 1: 16.
14*a* Deut. 17: 17; Neh. 5: 14 (14–15); 1 Cor. 9: 18 (4–18). TG Self-sacrifice; Work, Value of.
b Acts 20: 34 (33–35).
c Ezek. 46: 18.
15*a* TG Boasting.
b TG Conscience.
17*a* TG Wisdom.
b Matt. 25: 40; D&C 42: 31 (30–31). TG Service.
c TG Brotherhood and Sisterhood; Fellowshipping; Neighbor.

[About 124 B.C.]

ye are only in the service of your
God.
18 Behold, ye have called me your
king; and if I, whom ye call your
king, do labor to [a]serve you, then
ought not ye to labor to serve one
another?
19 And behold also, if I, whom ye
call your king, who has spent his
days in your service, and yet has
been in the service of God, do merit
any thanks from you, O how you
ought to [a]thank your heavenly
[b]King!
20 I say unto you, my brethren,
that if you should render all the
[a]thanks and [b]praise which your
whole soul has power to possess, to
that God who has created you, and
has kept and [c]preserved you, and
has caused that ye should [d]rejoice,
and has granted that ye should live
in peace one with another—
21 I say unto you that if ye should
[a]serve him who has created you
from the beginning, and is [b]preserv-
ing you from day to day, by lending
you [c]breath, that ye may live and
move and do according to your own
[d]will, and even supporting you from
one moment to another—I say, if
ye should serve him with all your
[e]whole souls yet ye would be [f]un-
profitable servants.
22 And behold, all that he [a]requires
of you is to [b]keep his commandments; and he has [c]promised you
that if ye would keep his commandments ye should prosper in the land;
and he never doth [d]vary from that
which he hath said; therefore, if
ye do [e]keep his [f]commandments he
doth bless you and prosper you.
23 And now, in the first place, he
hath created you, and granted unto
you your lives, for which ye are
indebted unto him.
24 And secondly, he doth [a]require
that ye should do as he hath commanded you; for which if ye do, he
doth immediately [b]bless you; and
therefore he hath paid you. And ye
are still indebted unto him, and are,
and will be, forever and ever; therefore, of what have ye to boast?
25 And now I ask, can ye say
aught of yourselves? I answer you,
Nay. Ye cannot say that ye are even
as much as the dust of the earth;
yet ye were [a]created of the [b]dust of
the earth; but behold, it [c]belongeth
to him who created you.
26 And I, even I, whom ye call
your king, am [a]no better than ye
yourselves are; for I am also of the
dust. And ye behold that I am old,
and am about to yield up this mortal
frame to its mother earth.
27 Therefore, as I said unto you
that I had [a]served you, [b]walking
with a clear conscience before God,
even so I at this time have caused
that ye should assemble yourselves
together, that I might be found
blameless, and that your [c]blood
should not come upon me, when I
shall stand to be judged of God of the
things whereof he hath commanded
me concerning you.
28 I say unto you that I have
caused that ye should assemble
yourselves together that I might

18*a* Luke 22: 26.
19*a* 1 Chr. 16: 8.
TG Thanksgiving.
b TG Kingdom of God, in Heaven.
20*a* Job 1: 21; Ps. 34: 1 (1–3); D&C 59: 21; 62: 7; 78: 19.
b 1 Sam. 12: 24; 1 Ne. 18: 16; D&C 136: 28.
c D&C 63: 3.
d Neh. 12: 43.
21*a* Job 22: 3 (3–4).
b Neh. 9: 6.
c 2 Ne. 9: 26.
d TG Agency.
e TG Dedication.
f Luke 17: 10 (7–10); Rom. 3: 12.
22*a* TG God, the Standard of Righteousness.
b Gen. 4: 7; Lev. 25: 18 (18–19); Mosiah 1: 7; Alma 50: 20 (20–22).
c 1 Ne. 4: 14; Omni 1: 6; Ether 2: 7 (7–12).
d TG God, Perfection of.
e Ps. 19: 11 (9–11); 2 Ne. 1: 20; D&C 14: 7; 58: 2.
f TG Commandments of God.
24*a* TG Duty.
b Prov. 22: 4 (4–5); 2 Ne. 1: 20.
25*a* TG Man, Physical Creation of.
b Jacob 2: 21; Alma 42: 2; Hel. 12: 7 (7–8); Morm. 9: 17.
c 1 Chr. 29: 12; Mosiah 4: 22.
26*a* TG Equal.
27*a* TG Serve; Service.
b TG Walking with God.
c Jacob 1: 19.

[About 124 B.C.]

[a]rid my garments of your blood, at
this period of time when I am about
to go down to my grave, that I might
go down in peace, and my immortal
[b]spirit may join the [c]choirs above in
singing the praises of a just God.
29 And moreover, I say unto you
that I have caused that ye should
assemble yourselves together, that
I might declare unto you that I can
no longer be your teacher, nor your
king;
30 For even at this time, my whole
frame doth tremble exceedingly
while attempting to speak unto you;
but the Lord God doth support me,
and hath suffered me that I should
speak unto you, and hath commanded me that I should declare
unto you this day, that my son
Mosiah is a [a]king and a ruler over you.
31 And now, my brethren, I would
that ye should do as ye have hitherto done. As ye have kept my commandments, and also the commandments of my father, and have
prospered, and have been kept from
falling into the hands of your
enemies, even so if ye shall keep the
commandments of my son, or the
commandments of God which shall
be delivered unto you by him, ye
shall prosper in the land, and your
enemies shall have no power over
you.
32 But, O my people, beware lest
there shall arise [a]contentions among
you, and ye [b]list to [c]obey the evil
spirit, which was spoken of by my
father Mosiah.
33 For behold, there is a wo pronounced upon him who listeth to
[a]obey that spirit; for if he listeth to
obey him, and remaineth and dieth
in his [b]sins, the same drinketh
[c]damnation to his own soul; for he
receiveth for his wages an [d]ever-
lasting [e]punishment, having transgressed the law of God contrary to
his own knowledge.
34 I say unto you, that there are
not any among you, except it be
your little children that have not
been taught concerning these things,
but what knoweth that ye are
eternally [a]indebted to your heavenly
Father, to render to him [b]all that
you have and are; and also have
been taught concerning the [c]records
which contain the prophecies which
have been spoken by the holy prophets, even down to the time our
father, Lehi, left Jerusalem;
35 And also, all that has been
spoken by our fathers until now.
And behold, also, they spake that
which was commanded them of the
Lord; therefore, they are [a]just and
true.
36 And now, I say unto you, my
brethren, that after ye have known
and have been taught all these
things, if ye should transgress and
go [a]contrary to that which has been
spoken, that ye do [b]withdraw yourselves from the Spirit of the Lord,
that it may have no place in you to
guide you in wisdom's paths that
ye may be blessed, prospered, and
preserved—
37 I say unto you, that the man
that doeth this, the same cometh
out in open [a]rebellion against God;
therefore he [b]listeth to obey the evil
spirit, and becometh an enemy to all
righteousness; therefore, the Lord

28*a* 2 Ne. 9: 44; Jacob 2: 2 (2, 16); D&C 61: 34.
b TG Spirit Body.
c Morm. 7: 7.
30*a* Mosiah 1: 10; 6: 3 (3–4). TG Kings, Earthly.
32*a* Eph. 4: 27 (26–27); 3 Ne. 11: 29. TG Contention.
b Alma 3: 27 (26–27); 5: 42 (41–42); 30: 60; D&C 29: 45.
c 2 Ne. 32: 8; Mosiah 4: 14; Alma 5: 20.
33*a* TG Agency.
b TG Accountability.
c TG Damnation.
d Jacob 6: 10; D&C 19: 11 (10–12).
e TG Punishment.
34*a* Philip. 3: 8 (7–10). TG Debt.
b Rom. 12: 1 (1–2).
c 1 Ne. 5: 14; Alma 33: 2.
35*a* Rom. 7: 12; Rev. 15: 3.
36*a* TG Disobedience.
b TG Holy Ghost, Loss of.
37*a* Mosiah 3: 12; Hel. 8: 25 (24–25). TG Holy Ghost, Unpardonable Sin against; Rebellion.
b Prov. 19: 27; 1 Ne. 8: 34 (33–34).

[About 124 B.C.]

has no place in him, for he dwelleth
not in [c]unholy temples.
38 Therefore if that man [a]repenteth
not, and remaineth and dieth an
enemy to God, the demands of
divine [b]justice do awaken his immortal soul to a lively sense of his
own [c]guilt, which doth cause him
to shrink from the [d]presence of the
Lord, and doth fill his breast with
guilt, and [e]pain, and [f]anguish, which
is like an unquenchable [g]fire, whose
flame ascendeth up forever and
ever.
39 And now I say unto you, that
[a]mercy hath no claim on that man;
therefore his final doom is to endure
a never-ending [b]torment.
40 O, all ye [a]old men, and also ye
young men, and you little children
who can understand my words, for
I have spoken plainly unto you that
ye might understand, I pray that ye
should awake to a [b]remembrance of
the awful situation of those that
have fallen into transgression.
41 And moreover, I would desire
that ye should consider on the
blessed and [a]happy state of those
that keep the commandments of
God. For behold, they are [b]blessed
in all things, both temporal and
spiritual; and if they hold out
[c]faithful to the end they are received
into [d]heaven, that thereby they may
dwell with God in a state of never-
ending happiness. O remember,
remember that these things are
true; for the Lord God hath spoken
it.

CHAPTER 3

King Benjamin continues his address—The Lord Omnipotent shall minister among men in a tabernacle of clay—Blood shall come from every pore as he atones for the sins of the world—His is the only name whereby salvation comes—Men can put off the natural man and become saints through the atonement—The torment of the wicked shall be as a lake of fire and brimstone.

AND again my brethren, I would
call your attention, for I have somewhat more to speak unto you; for
behold, I have things to tell you
concerning that which is to come.
2 And the things which I shall tell
you are made known unto me by an
[a]angel from God. And he said unto
me: [b]Awake; and I awoke, and behold he stood before me.
3 And he said unto me: Awake, and
hear the words which I shall tell
thee; for behold, I am come to
declare unto you the [a]glad tidings of
great [b]joy.
4 For the Lord hath heard thy
prayers, and hath judged of thy
[a]righteousness, and hath sent me to
declare unto thee that thou mayest
rejoice; and that thou mayest declare unto thy people, that they may
also be filled with joy.
5 For behold, the time cometh,
and is not far distant, that with
power, the [a]Lord [b]Omnipotent who
[c]reigneth, who was, and is from all
[d]eternity to all eternity, shall come
down from heaven among the

37*c* Alma 7: 21; 34: 36; Hel. 4: 24.
38*a* TG Repentance.
b TG God, Justice of.
c Mosiah 27: 29 (25–29). TG Guilt.
d TG God, Presence of.
e TG Pain.
f TG Sorrow.
g TG Hell.
39*a* TG Mercy.
b TG Damnation; Punishment.
40*a* TG Old Age.
b Alma 5: 18 (7–18).
41*a* Matt. 11: 29 (28–30); Alma 50: 23; 4 Ne. 1: 16 (15–18). TG Happiness; Joy.
b Gen. 39: 3 (1–6); Ps. 37: 25; Matt. 6: 33; 1 Ne. 17: 3 (1–5, 12–14).
c Ps. 31: 23; Ether 4: 19; D&C 6: 13; 63: 47.
d TG Heaven.
3 2*a* Mosiah 4: 1; 5: 5. TG Angels.
b Zech. 4: 1 (1–2).
3*a* Isa. 52: 7 (7–10); Luke 2: 10 (10–11); Rom. 10: 15; D&C 31: 3.
b TG Joy.
4*a* TG Righteousness.
5*a* TG Jesus Christ—Jehovah.
b Rev. 1: 8 (7–8). TG Jesus Christ, Power of.
c TG Jesus Christ, Authority of.
d 2 Ne. 26: 12; Mosiah 16: 15.

[About 124 B.C.]

children of men, and shall dwell in
a [e]tabernacle of clay, and shall go
forth amongst men, working mighty
[f]miracles, such as healing the sick,
raising the dead, causing the lame
to walk, the [g]blind to receive their
sight, and the deaf to hear, and
curing all manner of diseases.
6 And he shall cast out [a]devils, or
the [b]evil spirits which dwell in the
hearts of the children of men.
7 And lo, he shall [a]suffer [b]tempta-
tions, and pain of body, [c]hunger,
thirst, and fatigue, even more than
man can [d]suffer, except it be unto
death; for behold, [e]blood cometh
from every pore, so great shall be
his [f]anguish for the wickedness and
the abominations of his people.
8 And he shall be called [a]Jesus
[b]Christ, the [c]Son of God, the [d]Father
of heaven and earth, the [e]Creator of
all things from the beginning; and
his [f]mother shall be called Mary.
9 And lo, he cometh unto his own,
that [a]salvation might come unto the
children of men even through [b]faith
on his name; and even after all this
they shall consider him a man, and
say that he hath a [c]devil, and shall
[d]scourge him, and shall [e]crucify
him.
10 And he shall [a]rise the [b]third
day from the dead; and behold, he
standeth to [c]judge the world; and
behold, all these things are done that
a righteous judgment might come
upon the children of men.
11 For behold, and also his [a]blood
[b]atoneth for the sins of those who
have [c]fallen by the transgression of
Adam, who have died not knowing
the [d]will of God concerning them, or
who have [e]ignorantly sinned.
12 But wo, wo unto him who
knoweth that he [a]rebelleth against
God! For salvation cometh to none
such except it be through repentance
and faith on the [b]Lord Jesus Christ.
13 And the Lord God hath sent his
holy [a]prophets among all the children of men, to declare these things
to every kindred, nation, and
tongue, that thereby whosoever
should believe that Christ should
come, the same might receive [b]re-
mission of their sins, and rejoice
with exceedingly great joy, even [c]as
though he had already come among
them.

5*e* Mosiah 7: 27; 15: 2 (1–7); Alma 7: 9 (9–13).
f Matt. 4: 24 (23–24); 9: 35; Acts 2: 22; 1 Ne. 11: 31. TG Death, Power over; Healing; Miracle.
g Matt. 9: 28 (28–31); 20: 30 (30–34); John 9: 1 (1–4); 3 Ne. 17: 9 (7–10); D&C 84: 69.
6*a* Mark 1: 34 (32–34); 1 Ne. 11: 31.
b TG Spirits, Evil or Unclean.
7*a* Luke 12: 50. TG Suffering.
b TG Jesus Christ, Temptation of; Temptation.
c Matt. 4: 2 (1–2).
d D&C 19: 16 (15–18).
e Matt. 26: 39 (38–39); Luke 22: 44.
f Isa. 53: 4 (4–5).
8*a* TG Foreordination; Jesus Christ, Prophecies about.
b TG Jesus Christ, Messiah.
c Mosiah 15: 3; Alma 7: 10; 3 Ne. 1: 14.
d Mosiah 15: 4; Hel. 14: 12; 3 Ne. 9: 15; Ether 4: 7.
e TG Jesus Christ, Creator.
f Matt. 1: 16; 1 Ne. 11: 18 (14–21).
9*a* TG Jesus Christ, Mission of.
b TG Faith.
c Luke 11: 15 (14–22); John 8: 48; 12: 37; Hel. 13: 26 (26–27).
d Luke 18: 31; 1 Ne. 11: 33; 2 Ne. 10: 3.
e 1 Ne. 19: 10 (10, 13); 2 Ne. 6: 9; 3 Ne. 11: 14 (14–15, 33). TG Jesus Christ, Crucifixion of.
10*a* TG Jesus Christ, Resurrection.
b 2 Ne. 25: 13; Hel. 14: 20 (20–27).
c TG Jesus Christ, Judge.
11*a* TG Blood, Symbolism of.
b TG Jesus Christ, Redeemer; Redemption.
c TG Fall of Man.
d TG God, Will of.
e Lev. 4: 13 (13–35); Num. 15: 27 (2–29); 2 Ne. 9: 26 (25–26); Alma 9: 16 (15–16); 42: 21; 3 Ne. 6: 18. TG Accountability; Ignorance.
12*a* Mosiah 2: 37 (36–38); Hel. 8: 25 (24–25). TG Rebellion.
b TG Jesus Christ, Lord.
13*a* TG Prophets, Mission of.
b TG Remission of Sins.
c 2 Ne. 25: 26 (24–27); Jarom 1: 11; Mosiah 16: 6.

[About 124 B.C.]

14 Yet the Lord God saw that his
people were a [a]stiffnecked people,
and he appointed unto them a [b]law,
even the [c]law of Moses.
15 And many signs, and wonders,
and [a]types, and shadows showed he
unto them, concerning his coming;
and also holy prophets spake unto
them concerning his coming; and
yet they [b]hardened their hearts, and
understood not that the [c]law of
Moses availeth nothing [d]except it
were through the [e]atonement of his
blood.
16 And even if it were possible that
little [a]children could sin they could
not be saved; but I say unto you
they are [b]blessed; for behold, as in
Adam, or by nature, they fall, even
so the blood of Christ [c]atoneth for
their sins.
17 And moreover, I say unto you,
that there shall be [a]no other name
given nor any other way nor means
whereby [b]salvation can come unto
the children of men, only in and
through the name of Christ, the
[c]Lord Omnipotent.
18 For behold he judgeth, and his
judgment is just; and the infant
perisheth not that dieth in his infancy; but men drink [a]damnation
to their own souls except they
humble themselves and [b]become as
little children, and believe that
[c]salvation was, and is, and is to
come, in and through the [d]atoning
blood of Christ, the Lord Omnipotent.
19 For the [a]natural [b]man is an
[c]enemy to God, and has been from
the [d]fall of Adam, and will be, forever and ever, unless he [e]yields to
the enticings of the Holy [f]Spirit,
and [g]putteth off the [h]natural man
and becometh a [i]saint through the
atonement of Christ the Lord, and
becometh as a [j]child, [k]submissive,
meek, humble, patient, full of love,
willing to submit to all things which
the Lord seeth fit to inflict upon
him, even as a child doth submit to
his father.
20 And moreover, I say unto you,
that the time shall come when the
[a]knowledge of a [b]Savior shall spread
throughout [c]every nation, kindred,
tongue, and people.
21 And behold, when that time
cometh, none shall be found [a]blame-
less before God, except it be little
children, only through repentance
and faith on the name of the Lord
God Omnipotent.
22 And even at this time, when
thou shalt have taught thy people
the things which the Lord thy God
hath commanded thee, even then

14a 2 Ne. 25: 28; Alma 9: 31.
TG Stiffneckedness.
b Josh. 1: 8; Mosiah 13: 29 (29–32); Alma 25: 15 (15–16); D&C 41: 5 (4–5).
c TG Law of Moses.
15a TG Jesus Christ, Types of, in Anticipation; Passover; Symbolism.
b TG Hardheartedness.
c Heb. 10: 1; Mosiah 12: 31; 13: 28 (27–32); Alma 25: 16.
d 2 Ne. 11: 6.
e Lev. 4: 20; Matt. 26: 54 (51–56).
16a TG Conceived in Sin.
b TG Salvation of Little Children.
c Moro. 8: 8 (8–9); Moses 6: 54 (54–56).
TG Jesus Christ, Atonement through.
17a Acts 4: 12 (10–12); 2 Ne. 31: 21; Mosiah 4: 8 (7–8); 3 Ne. 9: 17.
b Matt. 7: 14 (13–14).
TG Jesus Christ, Savior; Salvation, Plan of.
c TG Jesus Christ, Lord.
18a 1 Cor. 11: 29.
b Matt. 18: 3.
c TG Salvation.
d Mosiah 4: 2; Hel. 5: 9.
19a Gen. 8: 21; 1 Cor. 2: 14 (11–14); 2 Pet. 2: 12; Mosiah 16: 3; Alma 41: 11; Ether 3: 2. TG Man, Natural, Not Spiritually Reborn; Worldliness.
b TG Mortality.
c James 4: 4.
TG Enemies.
d TG Fall of Man.
e 2 Chr. 30: 8; Rom. 6: 13 (12–14).
f Rom. 8: 4 (1–9).
TG Guidance, Divine.
g Alma 19: 6.
h Col. 3: 9; D&C 67: 12.
i Luke 22: 32 (31–38).
TG Man, New, Spiritually Reborn; Saints; Spirituality.
j Matt. 18: 3; 1 Pet. 2: 2 (1–3); 3 Ne. 9: 22.
k TG Self-mastery; Submissiveness.
20a D&C 3: 16.
b TG Jesus Christ, Savior.
c Mosiah 16: 1.
TG Missionary Work.
21a Col. 1: 22; D&C 4: 2.
TG Accountability.

[About 124 B.C.]

are they found no more blameless in the sight of God, only according to the words which I have spoken unto thee.

23 And now I have spoken the words which the Lord God hath commanded me.

24 And thus saith the Lord: They shall stand as a bright testimony against this people, at the judgment day; whereof they shall be judged, every man according to his [a]works, whether they be good, or whether they be evil.

25 And if they be evil they are consigned to an awful [a]view of their own guilt and abominations, which doth cause them to shrink from the presence of the Lord into a state of [b]misery and [c]endless torment, from whence they can no more return; therefore they have drunk damnation to their own souls.

26 Therefore, they have drunk out of the [a]cup of the wrath of God, which justice could no more deny unto them than it could deny that [b]Adam should fall because of his partaking of the forbidden [c]fruit; therefore, [d]mercy could have claim on them no more forever.

27 And their [a]torment is as a [b]lake of fire and brimstone, whose flames are unquenchable, and whose smoke ascendeth up [c]forever and ever. Thus hath the Lord commanded me. Amen.

CHAPTER 4

King Benjamin continues his address—Salvation comes because of the atonement—Believe in God to be saved—Retain a remission of your sins through faithfulness—Impart of your substance to the poor—Do all things in wisdom and order.

AND now, it came to pass that when king Benjamin had made an end of speaking the words which had been delivered unto him by the [a]angel of the Lord, that he cast his eyes round about on the multitude, and behold they had [b]fallen to the earth, for the [c]fear of the Lord had come upon them.

2 And they had [a]viewed themselves in their own [b]carnal state, even [c]less than the dust of the earth. And they all cried aloud with one voice, saying: O have mercy, and apply the [d]atoning blood of Christ that we may receive forgiveness of our sins, and our hearts may be [e]purified; for we believe in Jesus Christ, the Son of God, who [f]created heaven and earth, and all things; who shall come down among the children of men.

3 And it came to pass that after they had spoken these words the Spirit of the Lord came upon them, and they were filled with joy, having received a [a]remission of their sins, and having peace of [b]conscience, because of the exceeding [c]faith which they had in Jesus Christ who should come, according to the [d]words which king Benjamin had spoken unto them.

4 And king Benjamin again opened his mouth and began to speak unto them, saying: My friends and my brethren, my kindred and my people, I would again call your attention, that ye may hear and

24*a* TG Good Works.
25*a* 2 Ne. 9: 14, 46; Alma 5: 18; 11: 43; 12: 15 (14–15).
b Rom. 3: 16; Morm. 8: 38.
c TG Punishment.
26*a* Ps. 75: 8; Jer. 25: 15; Lam. 4: 21.
b Morm. 9: 12; Moro. 8: 8.
c Gen. 3: 6; 2 Ne. 2: 15 (15–19); Alma 12: 22 (21–23).
d TG Mercy.
27*a* TG Hell.
b 2 Ne. 9: 16; Jacob 6: 10; Alma 12: 17; D&C 76: 36.
c Mosiah 5: 5.
4 1*a* 1 Chr. 21: 18; Mosiah 3: 2.
b Neh. 8: 9; Alma 19: 17.
c Jer. 36: 16; Heb. 12: 28. TG Reverence.
2*a* TG Poor in Spirit.
b Neh. 9: 1 (1–3). TG Carnal Mind.
c Gen. 18: 27.
d Mosiah 3: 18; Hel. 5: 9.
e TG Purification.
f TG Jesus Christ, Creator.
3*a* TG Remission of Sins.
b TG Conscience.
c TG Faith.
d Neh. 8: 12.

[About 124 B.C.]

understand the remainder of my
words which I shall speak unto you.
5 For behold, if the knowledge of
the goodness of God at this time
has awakened you to a sense of your
[a]nothingness, and your worthless
and fallen state—
6 I say unto you, if ye have come
to a [a]knowledge of the goodness of
God, and his matchless power, and
his wisdom, and his patience, and his
long-suffering towards the children
of men; and also, the [b]atonement
which has been prepared from the
[c]foundation of the world, that thereby salvation might come to him that
should put his [d]trust in the Lord,
and should be diligent in keeping his
commandments, and continue in the
faith even unto the end of his life, I
mean the life of the mortal body—
7 I say, that this is the man who
receiveth salvation, through the
atonement which was prepared from
the foundation of the world for all
mankind, which ever were since the
[a]fall of Adam, or who are, or who
ever shall be, even unto the end of
the world.
8 And this is the means whereby salvation cometh. And there is
[a]none other salvation save this
which hath been spoken of; neither
are there any conditions whereby
man can be saved except the conditions which I have told you.
9 Believe in [a]God; believe that he
is, and that he [b]created all things,
both in heaven and in earth; believe
that he has all [c]wisdom, and all
power, both in heaven and in earth;
believe that man doth not [d]compre-
hend all the things which the Lord
can comprehend.
10 And again, believe that ye must
[a]repent of your sins and forsake
them, and humble yourselves before
God; and ask in [b]sincerity of heart
that he would [c]forgive you; and now,
if you [d]believe all these things see
that ye [e]do them.
11 And again I say unto you as I
have said before, that as ye have
come to the knowledge of the glory
of God, or if ye have known of his
goodness and have [a]tasted of his
love, and have received a [b]remission
of your sins, which causeth such
exceedingly great joy in your souls,
even so I would that ye should
remember, and always retain in remembrance, the greatness of God,
and your own [c]nothingness, and his
[d]goodness and long-suffering towards you, unworthy creatures, and
humble yourselves even in the
depths of [e]humility, [f]calling on the
name of the Lord daily, and standing [g]steadfastly in the faith of that
which is to come, which was spoken
by the mouth of the angel.
12 And behold, I say unto you that
if ye do this ye shall always rejoice,
and be filled with the [a]love of God,
and always [b]retain a remission of
your sins; and ye shall grow in the
[c]knowledge of the glory of him that
created you, or in the knowledge of
that which is just and true.
13 And ye will not have a [a]mind
to injure one another, but to live
[b]peaceably, and to render to every

5*a* Moses 1:10.
6*a* TG God, Attributes of; God, Knowledge about.
b TG Jesus Christ, Atonement through.
c Mosiah 15:19; 18:13.
d Ps. 36:7 (7–8); 2 Ne. 22:2; Hel. 12:1. TG Trust in God.
7*a* TG Fall of Man.
8*a* Acts 4:12; 2 Ne. 31:21; Mosiah 3:17.
9*a* Deut. 4:39.
b TG God, Creator; Jesus Christ, Creator.
c Rom. 11:34 (33–36); Jacob 4:8 (8–13). TG God, Perfection of.
d Isa. 55:9.
10*a* TG Repentance.
b TG Sincerity.
c Ps. 41:4; D&C 61:2.
d Matt. 7:24 (24–27); Acts 16:31 (30–31).
e 2 Ne. 31:19 (19–21).
11*a* Ps. 34:8; Alma 36:24 (24–26).
b TG Remission of Sins.
c Rom. 5:8 (6–8); Moses 1:10.
d Ex. 34:6 (5–7); Moro. 8:3.
e TG Humility.
f TG Prayer.
g TG Steadfastness.
12*a* TG God, Love of.
b Alma 4:14 (13–14); 5:26 (26–35); D&C 20:32 (31–34).
c TG God, Knowledge about.
13*a* TG Man, New, Spiritually Reborn.
b TG Peacemakers.

[About 124 B.C.]

man according to that which is his
due.
14 And ye will not suffer your
[a]children that they go hungry, or
naked; neither will ye [b]suffer that
they transgress the laws of God, and
fight and [c]quarrel one with another,
and serve the devil, who is the
master of sin, or who is the [d]evil
spirit which hath been spoken of by
our fathers, he being an enemy to all
righteousness.
15 But ye will [a]teach them to [b]walk
in the ways of truth and [c]soberness;
ye will teach them to [d]love one
another, and to serve one another.
16 And also, ye yourselves will
[a]succor those that stand in need of
your succor; ye will administer of
your substance unto him that standeth in need; and ye will not suffer
that the [b]beggar putteth up his petition to you in vain, and turn him
out to perish.
17 Perhaps thou shalt [a]say: The
man has brought upon himself his
misery; therefore I will stay my
hand, and will not give unto him of
my food, nor impart unto him of my
substance that he may not suffer,
for his punishments are just—
18 But I say unto you, O man, whosoever doeth this the same hath
great cause to repent; and except he
repenteth of that which he hath
done he perisheth forever, and
hath no interest in the kingdom of
God.
19 For behold, are we not all
[a]beggars? Do we not all depend upon
the same Being, even God, for all the
substance which we have, for both
food and raiment, and for gold, and
for silver, and for all the riches which
we have of every kind?
20 And behold, even at this time,
ye have been calling on his name,
and begging for a [a]remission of your
sins. And has he suffered that ye
have begged in vain? Nay; he has
poured out his [b]Spirit upon you, and
has caused that your hearts should
be filled with [c]joy, and has caused
that your mouths should be stopped
that ye could not find utterance, so
exceedingly great was your joy.
21 And now, if God, who has
created you, on whom you are dependent for your lives and for all
that ye have and are, doth grant
unto you whatsoever ye ask that is
right, in faith, believing that ye
shall receive, O then, how ye ought
to [a]impart of the substance that ye
have one to another.
22 And if ye [a]judge the man who
putteth up his petition to you for
your substance that he perish not,
and condemn him, how much more
just will be your [b]condemnation for
withholding your substance, which
doth not belong to you but to God,
to whom also your life [c]belongeth;
and yet ye put up no petition, nor
repent of the thing which thou hast
done.
23 I say unto you, wo be unto that
man, for his substance shall perish
with him; and now, I say these
things unto those who are [a]rich as
pertaining to the things of this
world.
24 And again, I say unto the poor,
ye who have not and yet have
sufficient, that ye remain from day
to day; I mean all you who deny

14*a* 1 Tim. 5: 8; D&C 83: 4. TG Marriage, Fatherhood.
b Prov. 13: 24.
c TG Contention.
d 2 Ne. 32: 8; Mosiah 2: 32.
15*a* Mosiah 1: 2; Moses 6: 58 (58–63). TG Family, Children, Responsibilities toward.
b TG Walking with God.
c TG Sincere, Sincerity.
d 1 Sam. 18: 1; Mosiah 18: 21. TG Family, Love within.
16*a* Prov. 19: 17. TG Charity; Service; Welfare.
b Prov. 21: 13; Isa. 10: 2; Luke 3: 11; D&C 38: 16.
17*a* Prov. 17: 5.
19*a* Prov. 22: 2; 1 Cor. 4: 7.
20*a* Rom. 2: 4 (1–4).
b TG God, Spirit of.
c TG Joy.
21*a* Dan. 4: 27. TG Generosity; Welfare.
22*a* Matt. 7: 2 (1–2); John 7: 24.
b 1 Jn. 3: 17.
c Mosiah 2: 25.
23*a* Luke 21: 1 (1–4); D&C 56: 16.

[About 124 B.C.]

the beggar, because ye have not; I
would that ye say in your hearts
that: I [a]give not because I [b]have not,
but if I had I would [c]give.
25 And now, if ye say this in your
hearts ye remain guiltless, otherwise
ye are [a]condemned; and your condemnation is just for ye covet that
which ye have not received.
26 And now, for the sake of these
things which I have spoken unto
you—that is, for the sake of retaining a remission of your sins from day
to day, that ye may [a]walk guiltless
before God—I would that ye should
[b]impart of your substance to the
[c]poor, every man according to that
which he hath, such as [d]feeding
the hungry, clothing the naked,
visiting the sick and administering
to their relief, both spiritually
and temporally, according to their
wants.
27 And see that all these things are
done in wisdom and [a]order; for it is
not requisite that a man should run
[b]faster than he has strength. And
again, it is expedient that he should
be diligent, that thereby he might
win the prize; therefore, all things
must be done in order.
28 And I would that ye should
remember, that whosoever among
you [a]borroweth of his neighbor
should return the thing that he
borroweth, according as he doth
agree, or else thou shalt commit sin;
and perhaps thou shalt cause thy
neighbor to commit sin also.
29 And finally, I cannot tell you all
the things whereby ye may commit
sin; for there are divers ways and
means, even so many that I cannot
number them.
30 But this much I can tell you,
that if ye do not [a]watch yourselves,
and your [b]thoughts, and your
[c]words, and your deeds, and observe
the commandments of God, and
[d]continue in the faith of what ye
have heard concerning the coming
of our Lord, even unto the end of
your lives, ye must perish. And now,
O man, remember, and perish not.

CHAPTER 5

The saints become the sons and daughters of Christ through faith—They are then called by the name of Christ—King Benjamin exhorts them to be steadfast and immovable in good works.

AND now, it came to pass that
when king Benjamin had thus spoken to his people, he sent among
them, desiring to know of his people
if they [a]believed the words which he
had spoken unto them.
2 And they all cried with one voice,
saying: Yea, we believe all the
words which thou hast spoken unto
us; and also, we know of their surety
and truth, because of the Spirit of
the Lord Omnipotent, which has
wrought a mighty [a]change in us, or
in our hearts, that we have no more
disposition to do [b]evil, but to do
good continually.
3 And we, ourselves, also, through
the infinite [a]goodness of God, and
the manifestations of his Spirit,
have great views of that which is
to come; and were it expedient, we
could prophesy of all things.
4 And it is the faith which we have
had on the things which our king
has spoken unto us that has brought

24*a* Deut. 16: 17.
b Acts 3: 6 (5–7).
c Mark 12: 44.
25*a* D&C 56: 17.
26*a* TG Walking with God.
b Jacob 2: 19 (17–19); Mosiah 21: 17; Alma 35: 9.
c Job 29: 12; Zech. 7: 10; Luke 18: 22; Alma 1: 27. TG Almsgiving.
d Isa. 58: 10 (9–11); Alma 4: 12 (12–13); 3 Ne. 12: 42.
27*a* TG Order.
b Eccl. 9: 11; Alma 1: 26; D&C 10: 4.
28*a* TG Borrowing; Debt; Honesty.
30*a* Deut. 4: 9; Alma 12: 14. TG Watchfulness.
b Matt. 5: 28 (27–28); Mark 7: 23 (15–23).
c Matt. 15: 18 (18–20). TG Gossip.
d TG Steadfastness.
5 1*a* 1 Ne. 11: 4 (1–5).
2*a* Rom. 8: 2 (1–4); Alma 5: 14; 13: 12. TG Man, New, Spiritually Reborn.
b Alma 19: 33.
3*a* Ex. 34: 6 (5–7).

[About 124 B.C.]

us to this great knowledge, whereby
we do rejoice with such exceedingly
great joy.
5 And we are willing to enter into a
[a]covenant with our God to do his
will, and to be obedient to his commandments in all things that he
shall command us, all the remainder
of our days, that we may not bring
upon ourselves a [b]never-ending torment, as has been spoken by the
[c]angel, that we may not drink out of
the cup of the wrath of God.
6 And now, these are the words
which king Benjamin desired of
them; and therefore he said unto
them: Ye have spoken the words
that I desired; and the covenant
which ye have made is a righteous
covenant.
7 And now, because of the covenant which ye have made ye shall
be called the [a]children of Christ, his
sons, and his daughters; for behold,
this day he hath spiritually begotten
you; for ye say that your hearts are
[b]changed through faith on his name;
therefore, ye are [c]born of him and
have become his [d]sons and his
daughters.
8 And under this head ye are made
[a]free, and there is [b]no other head
whereby ye can be made free. There
is no other [c]name given whereby
salvation cometh; therefore, I would
that ye should take upon you the
name of Christ, all you that have
entered into the covenant with God
that ye should be obedient unto the
end of your lives.
9 And it shall come to pass that
whosoever doeth this shall be found
at the right hand of God, for he
shall know the name by which he is
called; for he shall be called by the
name of Christ.
10 And now it shall come to pass,
that whosoever shall not take upon
him the name of Christ must be
called by some [a]other name; therefore, he findeth himself on the [b]left
hand of God.
11 And I would that ye should
remember also, that this is the
[a]name that I said I should give unto
you that never should be blotted
out, except it be through transgression; therefore, take heed that ye do
not transgress, that the name be not
blotted out of your hearts.
12 I say unto you, I would that
ye should remember to [a]retain the
name written always in your hearts,
that ye are not found on the left
hand of God, but that ye hear and
know the voice by which ye shall be
called, and also, the name by which
he shall call you.
13 For how [a]knoweth a man the
master whom he has not served, and
who is a stranger unto him, and is
far from the thoughts and intents of
his heart?
14 And again, doth a man take an
ass which belongeth to his neighbor,
and keep him? I say unto you, Nay;
he will not even suffer that he shall
feed among his flocks, but will drive
him away, and cast him out. I say
unto you, that even so shall it be
among you if ye know not the name
by which ye are called.
15 Therefore, I would that ye
should be steadfast and immovable,
always abounding in [a]good works,
that Christ, the [b]Lord God Omnipo-

5*a* 2 Chr. 15: 12 (12–15); Neh. 10: 29; Mosiah 6: 3. TG Commitment.
b Mosiah 3: 27 (25–27).
c Mosiah 3: 2.
7*a* 1 Jn. 2: 12; Mosiah 15: 2; 27: 25 (24–26); Moses 6: 68 (64–68).
b TG Sanctification.
c John 1: 13 (12–13); Mosiah 15: 10. TG Man, New, Spiritually Reborn.
d Matt. 12: 49 (49–50); D&C 11: 30.
8*a* Rom. 6: 18 (14–22); 1 Cor. 7: 22; Gal. 5: 1; D&C 88: 86.
b Acts 4: 12; Mosiah 4: 8; Alma 21: 9.
c Gal. 3: 27; Mosiah 1: 11; 26: 18.
10*a* Alma 5: 39 (38–42).
b Matt. 25: 33.
11*a* Mosiah 1: 11 (11–12). TG Jesus Christ, Taking the Name of.
12*a* Ps. 119: 55; Num. 6: 27; D&C 18: 25.
13*a* Jer. 4: 22; Mosiah 26: 25 (24–27).
15*a* TG Good Works.
b TG Jesus Christ—Jehovah; Jesus Christ, Lord.

[About 124 B.C.]

tent, may [c]seal you his, that you
may be brought to heaven, that ye
may have everlasting salvation and
eternal life, through the wisdom,
and power, and justice, and mercy
of him who [d]created all things, in
heaven and in earth, who is God
above all. Amen.

CHAPTER 6

King Benjamin records the names of the people and appoints priests to teach them—Mosiah reigns as a righteous king.

AND now, king Benjamin thought
it was expedient, after having
finished speaking to the people, that
he should [a]take the names of all
those who had entered into a covenant with God to keep his commandments.
2 And it came to pass that there
was not one soul, except it were little
children, but who had entered into
the covenant and had taken upon
them the name of Christ.
3 And again, it came to pass that
when king Benjamin had made an
end of all these things, and had
consecrated his son [a]Mosiah to be a
ruler and a king over his people, and
had given him all the charges concerning the kingdom, and also had
[b]appointed [c]priests to [d]teach the
people, that thereby they might
hear and know the commandments
of God, and to stir them up in remembrance of the [e]oath which they
had made, he dismissed the multitude, and they returned, every one,
according to their [f]families, to their
own houses.
4 And Mosiah began to reign in his
father's stead. *And he began to
reign in the thirtieth year of his
age, making in the whole, about
four hundred and seventy-six years
from the [a]time that Lehi left Jerusalem.
5 And king Benjamin lived three
years† and he died.
6 And it came to pass that king
Mosiah did [a]walk in the ways of the
Lord, and did observe his judgments
and his statutes, and did keep his
commandments in all things whatsoever he commanded him.
7 And king Mosiah did cause his
people that they should till the
earth. And he also, himself, did till
the earth, that thereby he might
[a]not become burdensome to his
people, that he might do according
to that which his father had done in
all things. And there was no contention among all his people for the
space of three years.

CHAPTER 7

Ammon finds the land of Lehi-Nephi where Limhi is king—Limhi's people are in bondage to the Lamanites—Limhi recounts their history—A prophet (Abinadi) had testified that Christ is the God and Father of all things—Those who sow filthiness reap the whirlwind, and those who put their trust in the Lord shall be delivered.

AND now, it came to pass that
after king Mosiah had had continual
peace for the space of three years,
he was desirous to know concerning
the people who [a]went up to dwell in
the land of [b]Lehi-Nephi, or in the
city of Lehi-Nephi; for his people
had heard nothing from them from
the time they left the land of [c]Zara-
hemla; therefore, they wearied him
with their teasings.
2 And it came to pass that ‡king
Mosiah granted that sixteen of their
strong men might go up to the land
of Lehi-Nephi, to inquire concerning
their brethren.

15c TG Election.
d Col. 1: 16; Mosiah 4: 2; Alma 11: 39.
6 1a D&C 128: 8.
3a Mosiah 1: 10; 2: 30.
b TG Priesthood, Ordination.
c Mosiah 29: 42.
d Alma 4: 7.
e Mosiah 5: 5 (5–7).
f Num. 1: 2; Ether 1: 41; D&C 48: 6.
4a 1 Ne. 1: 4; 2: 4.
6a TG Walking with God.
7a 2 Cor. 11: 9.
7 1a Omni 1: 27 (27–30).
b 2 Ne. 5: 8; Mosiah 9: 6.
c Omni 1: 13.

[*About 124 B.C.]
[†About 121 B.C.]
[‡About 121 B.C.]

3 And it came to pass that on the morrow they started to go up, having with them one [a]Ammon, he being a strong and mighty man, and a [b]descendant of Zarahemla; and he was also their leader.

4 And now, they knew not the course they should travel in the wilderness to go up to the land of Lehi-Nephi; therefore they wandered many days in the wilderness, even [a]forty days did they wander.

5 And when they had wandered forty days they came to a [a]hill, which is north of the land of [b]Shilom, and there they pitched their tents.

6 And [a]Ammon took three of his brethren, and their names were Amaleki, Helem, and Hem, and they went down into the land of [b]Nephi.

7 And behold, they met the king of the people who were in the land of Nephi, and in the land of [a]Shilom; and they were surrounded by the king's guard, and were [b]taken, and were [c]bound, and were committed to [d]prison.

8 And it came to pass when they had been in prison two days they were again brought before the king, and their bands were loosed; and they stood before the king, and were permitted, or rather [a]commanded, that they should answer the questions which he should ask them.

9 And he said unto them: Behold, I am [a]Limhi, the son of Noah, who was the son of Zeniff, who came up out of the [b]land of Zarahemla to inherit this land, which was the land of their fathers, who was made a [c]king by the [d]voice of the people.

10 And now, [a]I desire to know the cause whereby ye were so bold as to come near the walls of the city, when I, myself, was with my guards without the [b]gate?

11 And now, for this cause have I suffered that ye should be preserved, that I might inquire of you, or else I should have caused that my guards should have put you to death. Ye are permitted to speak.

12 And now, when Ammon saw that he was permitted to speak, he went forth and [a]bowed himself before the king; and rising again he said: O king, I am very thankful before God this day that I am yet alive, and am permitted to speak; and I will endeavor to speak with boldness;

13 For I am assured that if ye had known me ye would not have suffered that I should have worn these bands. For I am Ammon, and am a [a]descendant of Zarahemla, and have come up out of the [b]land of Zarahemla to inquire concerning our brethren, whom [c]Zeniff brought up out of that land.

14 And now, it came to pass that after Limhi had heard the words of Ammon, he was exceedingly [a]glad, and said: Now, I know of a surety that my brethren who were in the land of Zarahemla are [b]yet alive. And now, I will rejoice; and on the morrow I will cause that my people shall rejoice also.

15 For behold, we are in bondage to the Lamanites, and are [a]taxed with a tax which is grievous to be borne. And now, behold, our brethren will deliver us out of our [b]bondage, or out of the hands of the

3*a* Mosiah 8: 2.
b Omni 1: 14.
4*a* Num. 13: 25 (17–25).
5*a* Mosiah 11: 13.
b Mosiah 9: 14 (6, 8, 14); 11: 12 (12–13); 22: 11 (8, 11); Alma 23: 12.
6*a* Mosiah 21: 22, 26.
b 2 Ne. 5: 8; Omni 1: 12 (12, 27); Mosiah 9: 1 (1, 3–4, 14); 28: 1 (1,5); Alma 50: 8 (8, 11).
7*a* Mosiah 22: 8.
b Mosiah 21: 21.
c Alma 17: 20.
d Mosiah 21: 23 (22–24).
8*a* Alma 14: 19.
9*a* Mosiah 11: 1; 19: 16.
b Omni 1: 13.
c TG Kings, Earthly.
d Mosiah 19: 26.
10*a* Mosiah 21: 23 (23–24).
b Josh. 20: 4.
12*a* Alma 47: 22 (22–23).
13*a* Omni 1: 14.
b Omni 1: 13.
c Mosiah 8: 2; 9: 1.
14*a* Mosiah 21: 24.
b Mosiah 21: 25 (25–26).
15*a* Mosiah 19: 15.
b TG Bondage, Physical.

[About 121 B.C.]

Lamanites, and we will be their
[c]slaves; for it is better that we be
slaves to the Nephites than to pay
tribute to the king of the Lamanites.
16 And now, king Limhi commanded his guards that they should
no more bind Ammon nor his brethren, but caused that they should go
to the hill which was north of
Shilom, and bring their brethren
into the city, that thereby they
might eat, and drink, and rest themselves from the labors of their
journey; for they had suffered many
things; they had suffered hunger,
thirst, and fatigue.
17 And now, it came to pass on the
morrow that king Limhi sent a
proclamation among all his people,
that thereby they might gather
themselves together to the [a]temple,
to hear the words which he should
speak unto them.
18 And it came to pass that when
they had gathered themselves together that he [a]spake unto them in
this wise, saying: O ye, my people,
lift up your heads and be comforted; for behold, the time is at
hand, or is not far distant, when we
shall no longer be in subjection to
our enemies, notwithstanding our
many strugglings, which have been
in vain; yet I trust there [b]remaineth
an effectual struggle to be made.
19 Therefore, lift up your heads,
and rejoice, and put your [a]trust in
[b]God, in that God who was the God
of Abraham, and Isaac, and Jacob;
and also, that God who [c]brought the
children of [d]Israel out of the land of
Egypt, and caused that they should
walk through the Red [e]Sea on dry
ground, and fed them with [f]manna
that they might not perish in the
wilderness; and many more things
did he do for them.
20 And again, that same God has
brought our fathers [a]out of the land
of Jerusalem, and has kept and
preserved his people even until now;
and behold, it is [b]because of our
iniquities and abominations that he
has brought us into bondage.
21 And ye all are witnesses this day,
that Zeniff, who was made king over
this people, he being [a]over-zealous
to inherit the land of his fathers,
therefore being deceived by the
cunning and craftiness of king
Laman, who having entered into a
treaty with king Zeniff, and having
yielded up into his hands the possessions of a part of the land, or even
the city of Lehi-Nephi, and the city
of Shilom; and the land round
about—
22 And all this he did, for the sole
purpose of [a]bringing this people into
subjection or into bondage. And
behold, we at this time do pay
[b]tribute to the king of the Lamanites, to the amount of one half of our
corn, and our barley, and even all
our grain of every kind, and one half
of the increase of our flocks and our
herds; and even one half of all we
have or possess the king of the
Lamanites doth exact of us, or our
lives.
23 And now, is not this grievous
to be borne? And is not this, our
affliction, great? Now behold, how
great reason we have to [a]mourn.
24 Yea, I say unto you, great are
the reasons which we have to
[a]mourn; for behold how many of
our brethren have been slain, and
their blood has been spilt in vain,
and all because of iniquity.
25 For if this people had not fallen
into transgression the Lord would
not have suffered that this great evil
should come upon them. But behold,

15*c* TG Slavery.
17*a* 2 Ne. 5: 16.
18*a* Mosiah 8: 1.
b Mosiah 22: 1 (1–16).
19*a* TG Trust in God.
b Ex. 3: 6 (2–10); 1 Ne. 19: 10; D&C 136: 21.
c Ex. 12: 51; 1 Ne. 17: 40; Mosiah 12: 34; Alma 36: 28.
d TG Israel, Origins of.
e Josh. 2: 10; 1 Ne. 4: 2; 17: 26.
f Ex. 16: 15, 35; Num. 11: 7 (7–8); Josh. 5: 12; John 6: 49; 1 Ne. 17: 28.
20*a* 1 Ne. 2: 2 (1–4).
b Deut. 28: 15 (1–2, 15–68).
21*a* Mosiah 9: 3 (1–3).
22*a* Mosiah 9: 10; 10: 18.
b TG Tribute.
23*a* Prov. 29: 2.
24*a* Ezek. 24: 23; Hel. 9: 22.

[About 121 B.C.]

they would not hearken unto his
words; but there arose contentions
among them, even so much that
they did shed blood among themselves.
26 And a [a]prophet of the Lord have
they [b]slain; yea, a chosen man of
God, who told them of their wickedness and abominations, and prophesied of many things which are to
come, yea, even the coming of
Christ.
27 And because he said unto them
that Christ was the [a]God, the Father
of all things, and said that he should
take upon him the [b]image of man,
and it should be the [c]image after
which man was created in the
beginning; or in other words, he said
that man was created after the
image of [d]God, and that God should
come down among the children of
men, and take upon him flesh and
blood, and go forth upon the face of
the earth—
28 And now, because he said this,
they did [a]put him to death; and
many more things did they do
which brought down the wrath of
God upon them. Therefore, who
wondereth that they are in bondage,
and that they are smitten with sore
afflictions?
29 For behold, the Lord hath said:
I will not [a]succor my people in the
day of their transgression; but I will
hedge up their ways that they
prosper not; and their doings shall
be as a [b]stumbling block before
them.
30 And again, he saith: If my
people shall sow [a]filthiness they shall
[b]reap the [c]chaff thereof in the whirlwind; and the effect thereof is poison.
31 And again he saith: If my
people shall sow filthiness they shall
reap the [a]east wind, which bringeth
immediate destruction.
32 And now, behold, the promise
of the Lord is fulfilled, and ye are
smitten and afflicted.
33 But if ye will [a]turn to the Lord
with full purpose of heart, and put
your trust in him, and serve him
with all [b]diligence of mind, if ye do
this, he will, according to his own
will and pleasure, deliver you out
of bondage.

CHAPTER 8

Ammon teaches the people of Limhi—He learns of the twenty-four Jaredite plates—Ancient records can be translated by seers—The gift of seership exceeds all others.

AND it came to pass that after
king Limhi had made an end of
[a]speaking to his people, for he spake
many things unto them and only a
few of them have I written in this
book, he told his people all the things
concerning their brethren who were
in the land of Zarahemla.
2 And he caused that Ammon
should stand up before the multitude, and rehearse unto them all
that had happened unto their
brethren from the time that [a]Zeniff
went up out of the land even until
the time that he [b]himself came up
out of the land.
3 And he also rehearsed unto them
the last words which king Benjamin
had [a]taught them, and explained
them to the people of king Limhi,
so that they might understand all
the words which he spake.

26*a* Mosiah 17:20 (12–20).
b TG Prophets, Rejection of.
27*a* Isa. 9:6; 2 Ne. 26:12; Mosiah 27:31 (30–31).
b TG God, Body of—Corporeal Nature.
c Gen. 1:26 (26–28); Ether 3:15 (14–17); D&C 20:18 (17–18).
d Mosiah 13:34; 15:2 (1–7); Alma 7:9 (9–13).
28*a* Mosiah 17:13.
29*a* Josh. 24:20; 1 Sam. 12:15; 2 Chr. 24:20.
b Jer. 6:21.
30*a* TG Filthiness.
b Hosea 8:7; Gal. 6:8 (7–8); D&C 6:33. TG Harvest.
c Luke 3:17; 2 Ne. 15:24.
31*a* Gen. 41:23; Jer. 18:17; Ezek. 27:26; Jonah 4:8; Mosiah 12:6.
33*a* Deut. 30:10; Lam. 5:21; Morm. 9:6; D&C 98:47.
b TG Diligence.
8 1*a* Mosiah 7:18 (18–33).
2*a* Mosiah 7:13.
b Mosiah 7:3.
3*a* Mosiah 2:9.

[About 121 B.C.]

4 And it came to pass that after he had done all this, that king Limhi dismissed the multitude, and caused that they should return every one unto his own house.

5 And it came to pass that he caused that the [a]plates which contained the [b]record of his people from the time that they left the [c]land of Zarahemla, should be brought before Ammon, that he might read them.

6 Now, as soon as Ammon had read the record, the king inquired of him to know if he could [a]interpret languages, and Ammon told him that he could not.

7 And the king said unto him: Being grieved for the afflictions of my people, I caused that [a]forty and three of my people should take a journey into the wilderness, that thereby they might find the land of Zarahemla, that we might appeal unto our brethren to deliver us out of bondage.

8 And they were lost in the wilderness for the space of [a]many days, yet they were diligent, and found not the land of Zarahemla but returned to this land, having traveled in a land among many waters, having discovered a land which was covered with [b]bones of men, and of beasts, and was also covered with ruins of buildings of every kind, having discovered a land which had been peopled with a people who were as numerous as the hosts of Israel.

9 And for a testimony that the things that they had said are true they have brought [a]twenty-four plates which are filled with engravings, and they are of pure gold.

10 And behold, also, they have brought [a]breastplates, which are large, and they are of [b]brass and of copper, and are perfectly sound.

11 And again, they have brought swords, the hilts thereof have perished, and the blades thereof were cankered with rust; and there is no one in the land that is able to interpret the language or the engravings that are on the plates. Therefore I said unto thee: Canst thou translate?

12 And I say unto thee again: Knowest thou of any one that can translate? For I am desirous that these records should be translated into our language; for, perhaps, they will give us a knowledge of a remnant of the people who have been destroyed, from whence these records came; or, perhaps, they will give us a knowledge of this very people who have been destroyed; and I am desirous to know the cause of their destruction.

13 Now Ammon said unto him: I can assuredly tell thee, O king, of a man that can [a]translate the records; for he has wherewith that he can look, and translate all records that are of ancient date; and it is a gift from God. And the things are called [b]interpreters, and no man can look in them except he be commanded, lest he should look for that he ought not and he should perish. And whosoever is commanded to look in them, the same is called [c]seer.

14 And behold, the king of the people who are in the land of Zarahemla is the man that is commanded to do these things, and who has this high gift from God.

15 And the king said that a [a]seer is greater than a prophet.

16 And Ammon said that a seer is a revelator and a prophet also; and a gift which is greater can no man

5*a* See Mosiah, chapters 9–22.
b Mosiah 9: 1; 22: 14.
c Omni 1: 13.
6*a* 1 Cor. 12: 10; Mosiah 21: 28.
7*a* Mosiah 21: 25.
8*a* Alma 50: 29; Hel. 3: 4 (3–4); Morm. 6: 4.
b Omni 1: 22; Mosiah 21: 26 (26–27).
9*a* Mosiah 21: 27; 22: 14.
10*a* Ex. 25: 7; Ether 15: 15.
b Ether 10: 23.
13*a* Dan. 5: 16; Omni 1: 20 (20–22); Mosiah 28: 17 (11–17).
b Ex. 28: 30; Mosiah 21: 28 (27–28). TG Urim and Thummim.
c TG Seer.
15*a* 1 Sam. 9: 9; D&C 21: 1.

[About 121 B.C.]

have, except he should possess the power of God, which no man can; yet a man may have great power given him from God.

17 But a seer can know of things which are past, and also of things which are to come, and by them shall all things be revealed, or, rather, shall secret things be made manifest, and hidden things shall come to light, and things which are not known shall be made known by them, and also things shall be made known by them which otherwise could not be known.

18 Thus God has provided a means that man, through faith, might work mighty miracles; therefore he becometh a great benefit to his fellow beings.

19 And now, when Ammon had made an end of speaking these words the king rejoiced exceedingly, and gave thanks to God, saying: Doubtless a [a]great mystery is contained within these plates, and these interpreters were doubtless prepared for the purpose of unfolding all such mysteries to the children of men.

20 O how marvelous are the works of the Lord, and how long doth he suffer with his people; yea, and how [a]blind and impenetrable are the understandings of the children of men; for they will not seek wisdom, neither do they desire that she should rule over them!

21 Yea, they are as a wild flock which fleeth from the shepherd, and scattereth, and are driven, and are devoured by the beasts of the forest.

THE RECORD OF ZENIFF—*An account of his people, from the time they left the land of Zarahemla until the time that they were delivered out of the hands of the Lamanites. Comprising chapters 9 to 22 inclusive.*

CHAPTER 9

Zeniff leads a group from Zarahemla to possess the land of Lehi-Nephi—The Lamanite king permits them to inherit the land—There is war between the Lamanites and Zeniff's people.

[a]I, [b]ZENIFF, having been taught in all the language of the Nephites, and having had a knowledge of the land of [c]Nephi, or of the land of our fathers' first inheritance, *and having been sent as a spy among the Lamanites that I might spy out their forces, that our army might come upon them and destroy them—but when I saw that which was good among them I was desirous that they should not be destroyed.

2 Therefore, I contended with my brethren in the wilderness, for I would that our ruler should make a treaty with them; but he being an austere and a blood-thirsty man commanded that I should be slain; but I was rescued by the shedding of much blood; for father fought against father, and brother against brother, until the greater number of our army was destroyed in the wilderness; and we returned, those of us that were spared, to the land of Zarahemla, to relate that tale to their wives and their children.

3 And yet, I being [a]over-zealous to inherit the land of our fathers, collected as many as were desirous to go up to possess the land, and started again on our [b]journey into the wilderness to go up to the land; but we were smitten with famine and sore afflictions; for we were slow to remember the Lord our God.

4 Nevertheless, after many days' wandering in the wilderness we pitched our tents in the place where our brethren were slain, which was near to the land of our fathers.

5 And it came to pass that I went again with four of my men into the

19*a* Ether 3:26 (21–28); 4:4 (1–8).
20*a* TG Spiritual Blindness.
9 1*a* Mosiah 8:5; 22:14.
b Mosiah 7:13.
c 2 Ne. 5:8; Omni 1:12 (12, 27); Mosiah 7:6 (6–7); 28:1 (1, 5).
3*a* Omni 1:27 (27–29); Mosiah 7:21.
b Mosiah 25:5.

[*About 200 B.C.]

city, in unto the king, that I might
know of the disposition of the king,
and that I might know if I might go
in with my people and possess the
land in peace.
6 And I went in unto the king, and
he covenanted with me that I might
possess the [a]land of Lehi-Nephi, and
the land of Shilom.
7 And he also commanded that his
people should depart out of the land,
and I and my people went into the
land that we might possess it.
8 And we began to build buildings,
and to repair the walls of the city,
yea, even the walls of the city
of Lehi-Nephi, and the city of
Shilom.
9 And we began to till the ground,
yea, even with all manner of [a]seeds,
with seeds of corn, and of wheat,
and of barley, and with neas, and
with sheum, and with seeds of all
manner of fruits; and we did begin
to multiply and prosper in the
land.
10 Now it was the cunning and the
craftiness of king [a]Laman, to [b]bring
my people into bondage, that he
yielded up the land that we might
possess it.
11 Therefore it came to pass, that
after we had dwelt in the land for
the space of *twelve years that king
Laman began to grow uneasy, lest
by any means my people should
[a]wax strong in the land, and that
they could not overpower them and
bring them into bondage.
12 Now they were a [a]lazy and an
[b]idolatrous people; therefore they
were desirous to bring us into bondage, that they might glut themselves with the labors of our hands;
yea, that they might feast themselves upon the flocks of our fields.
13 Therefore it came to pass that
king Laman began to stir up his
people that they should contend
with my people; therefore there
began to be wars and contentions in
the land.
14 For, in the †thirteenth year of
my reign in the land of Nephi, away
on the south of the land of [a]Shilom,
when my people were watering and
[b]feeding their flocks, and tilling their
lands, a numerous host of Lamanites
came upon them and began to slay
them, and to take off their flocks,
and the corn of their fields.
15 Yea, and it came to pass that
they fled, all that were not overtaken, even into the city of Nephi,
and did call upon me for protection.
16 And it came to pass that I did
arm them with bows, and with
arrows, with swords, and with
cimeters, and with clubs, and with
slings, and with all manner of
weapons which we could invent,
and I and my people did go forth
against the Lamanites to battle.
17 Yea, in the [a]strength of the Lord
did we go forth to battle against the
Lamanites; for I and my people did
cry mightily to the Lord that he
would [b]deliver us out of the hands
of our enemies, for we were awakened to a remembrance of the
deliverance of our fathers.
18 And God did [a]hear our cries and
did answer our prayers; and we did
go forth in his might; yea, we did go
forth against the Lamanites, and in
one day and a night we did slay
three thousand and forty-three; we
did slay them even until we had
driven them out of our land.
19 And I, myself, with mine own
hands, did help to bury their dead.
And behold, to our great sorrow and
lamentation, two hundred and
seventy-nine of our brethren were
slain.

6*a* 2 Ne. 5: 8; Mosiah 7: 1 (1–4, 21).
9*a* 1 Ne. 8: 1; Enos 1: 21; Mosiah 10: 4.
10*a* Mosiah 24: 3.
b Mosiah 7: 22; 10: 18.
11*a* Ex. 1: 9 (9–10).
12*a* TG Laziness.
b Enos 1: 20. TG Idolatry.
14*a* Mosiah 7: 5; 11: 12 (12–13).
b Mosiah 10: 21.
17*a* TG Strength.
b Josh. 21: 44; Alma 46: 7.
18*a* Ex. 2: 24 (23–24); Ps. 4: 1 (1, 3); Dan. 10: 12; D&C 35: 3; Abr. 1: 15 (15–16).

[*About 188 B.C.]
[†About 187 B.C.]

CHAPTER 10

King Laman dies—His people are wild and ferocious and believe in false traditions—Zeniff and his people prevail against them.

AND it came to pass that we again began to establish the kingdom and we again began to possess the land in peace. And I caused that there should be [a]weapons of war made of every kind, that thereby I might have weapons for my people against the time the Lamanites should come up again to war against my people.
2 And I set guards round about the land, that the Lamanites might not come upon us again unawares and destroy us; and thus I did guard my people and my flocks, and keep them from falling into the hands of our enemies.
3 And it came to pass that we did inherit the land of our fathers for many years, yea, *for the space of twenty and two years.
4 And I did cause that the men should till the ground, and raise all manner of [a]grain and all manner of fruit of every kind.
5 And I did cause that the women should spin, and toil, and work, and work all manner of fine linen, yea, and [a]cloth of every kind, that we might clothe our nakedness; and thus we did prosper in the land—thus we did have continual peace in the land for the space of twenty and two years.
6 And it came to pass that king [a]Laman died, and his son began to reign in his stead. And he began to stir his people up in rebellion against my people; therefore they began to prepare for war, and to come up to battle against my people.
7 But I had sent my spies out round about the land of [a]Shemlon, that I might discover their preparations, that I might guard against them, that they might not come upon my people and destroy them.
8 And it came to pass that they came up upon the north of the land of Shilom, with their numerous hosts, men [a]armed with [b]bows, and with arrows, and with swords, and with cimeters, and with stones, and with slings; and they had their heads shaved that they were naked; and they were girded with a leathern girdle about their loins.
9 And it came to pass that I caused that the women and children of my people should be hid in the wilderness; and I also caused that all my old men that could bear arms, and also all my young men that were able to bear arms, should gather themselves together to go to battle against the Lamanites; and I did place them in their ranks, every man according to his age.
10 And it came to pass that we did go up to battle against the Lamanites; and I, even I, in my old age, did go up to battle against the Lamanites. And it came to pass that we did go up in the strength of the Lord to battle.
11 Now, the Lamanites knew nothing concerning the Lord, nor the strength of the Lord, therefore they depended upon their own strength. Yet they were a strong people, as to the [a]strength of men.
12 They were a [a]wild, and ferocious, and a blood-thirsty people, believing in the [b]tradition of their fathers, which is this—Believing that they were driven out of the land of Jerusalem because of the iniquities of their fathers, and that they were [c]wronged in the wilderness by their brethren, and they were also wronged while crossing the sea;
13 And again, that they were

10 1*a* TG Weapon.
4*a* Mosiah 9:9.
5*a* Alma 1:29; Hel. 6:13. TG Clothing.
6*a* Mosiah 9:10 (10–11); 24:3.
7*a* Mosiah 11:12.
8*a* 2 Ne. 5:14; Jarom 1:8; Alma 2:12.
b Enos 1:20; Alma 3:5 (4–5).
10*a* TG Strength; Trust in God.
11*a* TG Trust Not in the Arm of Flesh.
12*a* Alma 17:14.
b 2 Ne. 5:1 (1–3); Mosiah 1:5; Alma 3:8.
c TG Injustice.

[*About 178 B.C.]

wronged while in the land of their
[a]first inheritance, after they had
crossed the sea, and all this because
that Nephi was more faithful in
keeping the commandments of the
Lord—therefore [b]he was favored of
the Lord, for the Lord heard his
prayers and answered them, and he
took the lead of their journey in the
wilderness.
14 And his brethren were [a]wroth
with him because they [b]understood
not the dealings of the Lord; they
were also wroth with him upon the
waters because they hardened their
hearts against the Lord.
15 And again, they were [a]wroth
with him when they had arrived in
the promised land, because they
said that he had taken the [b]ruling
of the people out of their hands; and
they sought to kill him.
16 And again, they were wroth
with him because he departed into
the wilderness as the Lord had commanded him, and took the [a]records
which were engraven on the plates
of brass, for they said that he
[b]robbed them.
17 And thus they have taught their
children that they should hate them,
and that they should murder them,
and that they should rob and plunder them, and do all they could to
destroy them; therefore they have
an eternal hatred towards the
children of Nephi.
18 For this very cause has king
Laman, by his [a]cunning, and lying
craftiness, and his fair promises,
deceived me, that I have brought
this my people up into this land,
that they may destroy them; yea,
and we have suffered these many
years in the land.
19 And now I, Zeniff, after having
told all these things unto my people
concerning the Lamanites, I did
stimulate them to go to battle with
their might, putting their trust in
the Lord; therefore, we did contend
with them, face to face.
20 And it came to pass that we did
drive them again out of our land;
and we slew them with a great
slaughter, even so many that we did
not number them.
21 And it came to pass that we
returned again to our own land,
and my people again began to
[a]tend their flocks, and to till their
ground.
22 And now I, being old, *did confer the kingdom upon one of my
sons; therefore, I say no more. And
may the Lord [a]bless my people.
Amen.

CHAPTER 11

King Noah rules in wickedness—He revels in riotous living with his wives and concubines—Abinadi prophesies that the people will be taken into bondage—His life is sought by King Noah.

AND now it came to pass that
Zeniff conferred the kingdom upon
Noah, one of his sons; therefore
Noah began to reign in his stead;
and he did not walk in the ways of
his father.
2 For behold, he did not keep the
commandments of God, but he did
walk after the desires of his own
heart. And he had many wives and
[a]concubines. And he did [b]cause his
people to commit sin, and do that
which was [c]abominable in the sight
of the Lord. Yea, and they did
commit [d]whoredoms and [e]all manner of wickedness.
3 And he laid a [a]tax of one fifth
part of all they possessed, a fifth
part of their gold and of their silver,

13*a* 1 Ne. 18: 23.
b 2 Ne. 5: 5 (5–9).
14*a* 1 Ne. 18: 10 (10–11).
b 1 Ne. 15: 8 (8–11); 2 Ne. 1: 25 (24–27).
15*a* 2 Ne. 5: 1.
b 2 Ne. 5: 3 (1–4).
16*a* 2 Ne. 5: 12; Mosiah 28: 11.
b Alma 20: 10 (10, 13).
18*a* Mosiah 9: 10; 19: 28 (26, 28).
21*a* Mosiah 9: 14 (9, 14).
22*a* Num. 6: 24 (22–27).
11 2*a* Jacob 3: 5; Ether 10: 5.
b 1 Kgs. 14: 16; 15: 26; 16: 2; 21: 22; 2 Kgs. 21: 2 (1–9); Mosiah 23: 12; 29: 31.
c Mosiah 29: 18.
d 2 Ne. 28: 15.
e Mosiah 23: 9.
3*a* Gen. 47: 24; Ether 10: 5 (5–6).

[*Probably about 160 B.C.]

and a fifth part of their [b]ziff, and of their copper, and of their brass and their iron; and a fifth part of their fatlings; and also a fifth part of all their grain.

4 And all this did he take to [a]support himself, and his wives and his [b]concubines; and also his priests, and their wives and their concubines; thus he had changed the affairs of the kingdom.

5 For he put down all the priests that had been consecrated by his father, and consecrated new [a]ones in their stead, such as were lifted up in the pride of their hearts.

6 Yea, and thus they were supported in their laziness, and in their idolatry, and in their whoredoms, by the taxes which king Noah had put upon his people; thus did the people labor exceedingly to support iniquity.

7 Yea, and they also became idolatrous, because they were deceived by the vain and flattering words of the king and priests; for they did speak flattering things unto them.

8 And it came to pass that king Noah built many elegant and spacious buildings; and he ornamented them with fine work of wood, and of all manner of [a]precious things, of gold, and of silver, and of iron, and of brass, and of ziff, and of copper;

9 And he also built him a spacious palace, and a throne in the midst thereof, all of which was of fine wood and was ornamented with gold and silver and with precious things.

10 And he also caused that his workmen should work all manner of fine work within the walls of the [a]temple, of fine wood, and of copper, and of brass.

11 And the seats which were set apart for the [a]high priests, which were above all the other seats, he did ornament with pure gold; and he caused a breastwork to be built before them, that they might rest their bodies and their arms upon while they should speak lying and vain words to his people.

12 And it came to pass that he built a [a]tower near the temple; yea, a very high tower, even so high that he could stand upon the top thereof and overlook the land of [b]Shilom, and also the land of [c]Shemlon, which was possessed by the Lamanites; and he could even look over all the land round about.

13 And it came to pass that he caused many buildings to be built in the land Shilom; and he caused a great tower to be built on the [a]hill north of the land Shilom, which had been a resort for the children of Nephi at the time they [b]fled out of the land; and thus he did do with the riches which he obtained by the taxation of his people.

14 And it came to pass that he placed his heart upon his riches, and he spent his time in [a]riotous living with his wives and his concubines; and so did also his priests spend their time with harlots.

15 And it came to pass that he planted vineyards round about in the land; and he built wine-presses, and made [a]wine in abundance; and therefore he became a wine-bibber, and also his people.

16 And it came to pass that the Lamanites began to come in upon his people, upon small numbers, and to slay them in their fields, and while they were tending their flocks.

17 And king Noah sent guards round about the land to keep them

3*b* HEB related words: adjective, "shining"; verb, "to overlay or plate with metal."
4*a* Prov. 29: 3.
b TG Concubine.
5*a* 1 Kgs. 12: 31; 2 Chr. 11: 14 (13–14); Mosiah 11: 11; 12: 25 (17, 25).
8*a* Esth. 1: 4.
10*a* 2 Ne. 5: 16.
11*a* Mosiah 11: 5 (5, 14); 12: 17.
12*a* Gen. 35: 21; Mosiah 2: 7 (7–8); 19: 5 (5–6).
b Mosiah 9: 14 (6, 8, 14); 22: 11 (8, 11).
c Mosiah 10: 7.
13*a* Mosiah 7: 5.
b Omni 1: 12 (12–13).
14*a* TG Rioting and Reveling.
15*a* TG Drunkenness; Wine.

[Between 160 and 150 B.C.]

off; but he did not send a sufficient number, and the Lamanites came upon them and killed them, and drove many of their flocks out of the land; thus the Lamanites began to destroy them, and to exercise their hatred upon them.

18 And it came to pass that king Noah sent his armies against them, and they were driven back, or they drove them back for a time; therefore, they returned rejoicing in their spoil.

19 And now, because of this great victory they were lifted up in the pride of their hearts; they did [a]boast in their own strength, saying that their fifty could stand against thousands of the Lamanites; and thus they did boast, and did delight in blood, and the shedding of the blood of their brethren, and this because of the wickedness of their king and priests.

20 And it came to pass that there was a man among them whose name was [a]Abinadi; *and he went forth among them, and began to prophesy, saying: Behold, thus saith the Lord, and thus hath he commanded me, saying, Go forth, and say unto this people, thus saith the Lord—Wo be unto this people, for I have seen their abominations, and their wickedness, and their whoredoms; and except they repent I will [b]visit them in mine anger.

21 And except they repent and turn to the Lord their God, behold, I will deliver them into the hands of their enemies; yea, and they shall be brought into [a]bondage; and they shall be afflicted by the hand of their enemies.

22 And it shall come to pass that they shall [a]know that I am the Lord their God, and am a [b]jealous God, visiting the iniquities of my people.

23 And it shall come to pass that except this people repent and turn unto the Lord their God, they shall be brought into bondage; and none shall [a]deliver them, except it be the Lord the Almighty God.

24 Yea, and it shall come to pass that when they shall [a]cry unto me I will be [b]slow to hear their cries; yea, and I will suffer them that they be smitten by their enemies.

25 And except they repent in [a]sackcloth and ashes, and cry mightily to the Lord their God, I will not [b]hear their prayers, neither will I deliver them out of their afflictions; and thus saith the Lord, and thus hath he commanded me.

26 Now it came to pass that when Abinadi had spoken these words unto them they were wroth with him, and sought to take away his life; but the Lord [a]delivered him out of their hands.

27 Now when king Noah had heard of the words which Abinadi had spoken unto the people, he was also wroth; and he said: [a]Who is Abinadi, that I and my people should be judged of him, or [b]who is the Lord, that shall bring upon my people such great affliction?

28 I command you to bring Abinadi hither, that I may slay him, for he has said these things that he might [a]stir up my people to anger one with another, and to raise contentions among my people; therefore I will slay him.

29 Now the eyes of the people were [a]blinded; therefore they [b]hardened their hearts against the words of

19*a* Amos 6: 13; D&C 3: 4. TG Boasting.
20*a* See accounts of Abinadi in Mosiah, chapters 11–17.
b TG Punishment; Reproof.
21*a* Mosiah 12: 2; D&C 101: 79.
22*a* Ezek. 26: 6; 1 Ne. 21: 26 (25–26); D&C 43: 25.
b Ex. 20: 5; Deut. 6: 15; 32: 21; Mosiah 13: 13.
23*a* Hosea 13: 10 (4, 10).
24*a* Micah 3: 4.
b Ps. 10: 1; Jer. 2: 27; Mosiah 21: 15.
25*a* TG Sackcloth.
b Isa. 1: 15 (15–17); 59: 2.
26*a* TG Prophets, Rejection of; Protection, Divine.
27*a* Alma 9: 6 (5–6).
b Ex. 5: 2; Mosiah 12: 13.
28*a* TG Provoking.
29*a* 1 Kgs. 15: 26 (26–34). TG Spiritual Blindness.
b TG Hardheartedness.

[*About 150 B.C.]

Abinadi, and they sought from that time forward to take him. And king Noah hardened his heart against the word of the Lord, and he did not repent of his evil doings.

CHAPTER 12

Abinadi is imprisoned for prophesying the destruction of the people and the death of King Noah—The false priests quote the scriptures and pretend to keep the law of Moses—Abinadi begins to teach them the Ten Commandments.

AND it came to pass that *after the space of two years that Abinadi came among them in disguise, that they knew him not, and began to [a]prophesy among them, saying: Thus has the Lord commanded me, saying—Abinadi, go and prophesy unto this my people, for they have hardened their hearts against my words; they have repented not of their evil doings; therefore, I will [b]visit them in my anger, yea, in my fierce anger will I visit them in their iniquities and abominations.

2 Yea, wo be unto this generation! And the Lord said unto me: Stretch forth thy hand and prophesy, saying: Thus saith the Lord, it shall come to pass that this generation, because of their iniquities, shall be brought into [a]bondage, and shall be smitten on the [b]cheek; yea, and shall be driven by men, and shall be slain; and the vultures of the air, and the dogs, yea, and the wild beasts, shall devour their [c]flesh.

3 And it shall come to pass that the [a]life of king Noah shall be valued even as a garment in a hot [b]furnace; for he shall know that I am the Lord.

4 And it shall come to pass that I will smite this my people with sore afflictions, yea, with famine and with [a]pestilence; and I will cause that they shall [b]howl all the day long.

5 Yea, and I will cause that they shall have [a]burdens lashed upon their backs; and they shall be driven before like a dumb ass.

6 And it shall come to pass that I will send forth [a]hail among them, and it shall smite them; and they shall also be smitten with the [b]east wind; and [c]insects shall pester their land also, and devour their grain.

7 And they shall be smitten with a great pestilence—and all this will I do because of their [a]iniquities and abominations.

8 And it shall come to pass that except they repent I will utterly [a]destroy them from off the face of the earth; yet they shall leave a [b]record behind them, and I will preserve them for other nations which shall possess the land; yea, even this will I do that I may discover the abominations of this people to other nations. And many things did Abinadi prophesy against this people.

9 And it came to pass that they were angry with him; and they took him and carried him bound before the king, and said unto the king: Behold, we have brought a man before thee who has prophesied evil concerning thy people, and saith that God will destroy them.

10 And he also prophesieth evil concerning thy [a]life, and saith that thy life shall be as a garment in a furnace of fire.

11 And again, he saith that thou

---

12 1*a* TG Missionary Work.
b Isa. 65: 6 (6–7, 11); Jer. 9: 9.
2*a* 1 Kgs. 8: 46; Mosiah 11: 21; 20: 21.
b Lam. 3: 30; Mosiah 21: 3 (3–4, 13).
c Deut. 28: 26.
3*a* Amos 7: 11 (10–11); Mosiah 12: 10 (10–12).
b Mosiah 19: 20.
4*a* Luke 21: 11 (10–13); 2 Ne. 6: 15; D&C 97: 26 (22–26).
b Mosiah 21: 9 (1–15).
5*a* Mosiah 21: 3.
6*a* Ex. 9: 18 (13–35); Ezek. 13: 13.
b Jer. 18: 17; Ezek. 27: 26; Mosiah 7: 31.
c Ex. 10: 4 (1–12).
7*a* D&C 3: 18.
8*a* Gen. 6: 13; Isa. 42: 14 (14–15); 2 Ne. 26: 10 (10–11); Alma 45: 11 (9–14).
b Morm. 8: 14 (14–16).
10*a* Amos 7: 11 (10–11); Mosiah 12: 3.

[*About 148 B.C.]

shalt be as a stalk, even as a dry
stalk of the field, which is run over
by the beasts and trodden under
foot.
12 And again, he saith thou shalt
be as the blossoms of a thistle,
which, when it is fully ripe, if the
wind bloweth, it is driven forth
upon the face of the land. And he
pretendeth the Lord hath spoken it.
And he saith all this shall come
upon thee except thou repent, and
this because of thine iniquities.
13 And now, O king, what great
evil hast thou done, or what great
sins have thy people committed,
that we should be [a]condemned of
God or judged of this man?
14 And now, O king, behold, we
are [a]guiltless, and thou, O king,
hast not sinned; therefore, this man
has [b]lied concerning you, and he has
prophesied in vain.
15 And behold, we are strong, we
shall not come into bondage, or be
taken captive by our enemies; yea,
and thou hast prospered in the land,
and thou shalt also prosper.
16 Behold, here is the man, we
deliver him into thy hands; thou
mayest do with him as seemeth thee
good.
17 And it came to pass that king
Noah caused that Abinadi should
be cast into prison; and he commanded that the [a]priests should
gather themselves together that he
might hold a council with them
what he should do with him.
18 And it came to pass that they
said unto the king: Bring him
hither that we may question him;
and the king commanded that he
should be brought before them.
19 And they began to question
him, that they might cross him, that
thereby they might have wherewith
to [a]accuse him; but he answered
them boldly, and withstood all their
questions, yea, to their astonishment; for he did [b]withstand them in
all their questions, and did confound them in all their words.
20 And it came to pass that one of
them said unto him: [a]What meaneth
the words which are written, and
which have been taught by our
fathers, saying:
21 [a]How beautiful upon the mountains are the feet of him [b]that bringeth good tidings; that publisheth
peace; that bringeth good tidings of
good; that publisheth salvation;
that saith unto Zion, Thy God
reigneth;
22 [a]Thy watchmen shall lift up the
voice; with the voice together shall
they sing; for they shall see eye to
eye when the Lord shall bring again
Zion;
23 Break forth into joy; sing together ye waste places of Jerusalem;
for the Lord hath comforted his
people, he hath redeemed Jerusalem;
24 The Lord hath made bare his
holy [a]arm in the eyes of all the
nations, and all the ends of the earth
shall see the salvation of our God?
25 And now Abinadi said unto
them: Are you [a]priests, and pretend
to teach this people, and to understand the spirit of prophesying, and
yet desire to know of me what these
things mean?
26 I say unto you, wo be unto you
for perverting the ways of the Lord!
For if ye understand these things
ye have not taught them; therefore,
ye have perverted the ways of the
Lord.
27 Ye have not applied your
[a]hearts to [b]understanding; therefore, ye have not been wise. Therefore, what teach ye this people?
28 And they said: We teach the
law of Moses.
29 And again he said unto them:

13*a* Mosiah 11:27.
14*a* Jer. 2:35; Alma 21:6.
b Hel. 13:26 (24–28).
17*a* Mosiah 11:11.
19*a* John 8:6.
b D&C 100:5 (5–6).
20*a* Mosiah 13:3.
21*a* Isa. 52:7 (7–10).
b Mosiah 15:14; 27:37 (36–37).
22*a* Mosiah 15:29.
24*a* Isa. 33:2; Omni 1:13.
25*a* John 3:10 (7–10); Mosiah 11:5.
27*a* Prov. 8:5; Mosiah 2:9.
b TG Understanding.

[About 148 B.C.]

If ye teach the [a]law of Moses why do ye not keep it? Why do ye set your hearts upon [b]riches? Why do ye commit whoredoms and [c]spend your strength with harlots, yea, and cause this people to commit sin, that the Lord has cause to send me to prophesy against this people, yea, even a great evil against this people?

30 Know ye not that I speak the [a]truth? Yea, ye know that I speak the truth; and you ought to tremble before God.

31 And it shall come to pass that ye shall be smitten for your iniquities, for ye have said that ye teach the law of Moses. And what know ye concerning the law of Moses? [a]Doth salvation come by the law of Moses? What say ye?

32 And they answered and said that salvation did come by the law of Moses.

33 But now Abinadi said unto them: I know if ye [a]keep the commandments of God ye shall be saved; yea, if ye keep the commandments which the Lord delivered unto Moses in the mount of [b]Sinai, saying:

34 [a]I am the Lord thy God, who hath [b]brought thee out of the land of Egypt, out of the house of bondage.

35 Thou shalt have no [a]other God before me.

36 [a]Thou shalt not make unto thee any graven image, or any likeness of any thing in heaven above, or things which are in the earth beneath.

37 Now Abinadi said unto them, Have ye done all this? I say unto you, Nay, ye have not. And have ye [a]taught this people that they should do all these things? I say unto you, Nay, ye have not.

CHAPTER 13

Abinadi is protected by divine power—He teaches the Ten Commandments—Salvation does not come by the law of Moses alone—God himself shall make an atonement and redeem his people.

AND now when the king had heard these words, he said unto his priests: Away with this fellow, and slay him; for what have we to do with him, for he is [a]mad.

2 And they stood forth and attempted to lay their hands on him; but he withstood them, and said unto them:

3 [a]Touch me not, for God shall smite you if ye lay your hands upon me, for I have not delivered the message which the Lord sent me to deliver; neither have I told you that which ye [b]requested that I should tell; therefore, God will not suffer that I shall be destroyed at this time.

4 But I must fulfil the commandments wherewith God has commanded me; and because I have told you the truth ye are angry with me. And again, because I have spoken the word of God ye have judged me that I am mad.

5 Now it came to pass after Abinadi had spoken these words that the people of king Noah durst not lay their hands on him, for the Spirit of the Lord was upon him; and his face [a]shone with exceeding luster, even as Moses' did while in the mount of Sinai, while speaking with the Lord.

6 And he spake with [a]power and authority from God; and he continued his words, saying:

7 Ye see that ye have not power to

29*a* TG Law of Moses.
b Jer. 48: 7.
c TG Sexual Immorality.
30*a* Jacob 7: 14; Alma 30: 42 (41–42).
31*a* Mosiah 3: 15; 13: 28 (27–32); Alma 25: 16.
33*a* Deut. 27: 1; Neh. 9: 13; 3 Ne. 25: 4.
b Ex. 19: 18 (9, 16–20); Mosiah 13: 5.
34*a* Ex. 20: 2 (2–4).
b Ex. 12: 51; 1 Ne. 17: 40; Mosiah 7: 19.
35*a* Hosea 13: 4. TG Idolatry.
36*a* Mosiah 13: 12.
37*a* Mosiah 13: 25 (25–26).

13 1*a* John 10: 20 (19–20).
3*a* 1 Ne. 17: 48.
b Mosiah 12: 20 (20–24).
5*a* Ex. 34: 29 (29–35).
6*a* TG Priesthood, Power of; Teaching with the Spirit.

[About 148 B.C.]

slay me, therefore I finish my [a]message. Yea, and I perceive that it cuts you to your hearts because I tell you the truth concerning your iniquities.

8 Yea, and my words fill you with wonder and amazement, and with anger.

9 But I finish my message; and then it [a]matters not whither I go, if it so be that I am saved.

10 But this much I tell you, what you [a]do with me, after this, shall be as a [b]type and a shadow of things which are to come.

11 And now I read unto you the remainder of the [a]commandments of God, for I perceive that they are not written in your hearts; I perceive that ye have studied and taught [b]iniquity the most part of your lives.

12 And now, ye remember that I [a]said unto you: Thou shalt not make unto thee any graven image, or any likeness of things which are in heaven above, or which are in the earth beneath, or which are in the water under the earth.

13 And again: Thou shalt not [a]bow down thyself unto them, nor serve them; for I the Lord thy God am a jealous God, visiting the iniquities of the fathers upon the children, unto the third and fourth generations of them that hate me;

14 And showing mercy unto thousands of them that love me and keep my commandments.

15 Thou shalt not take the name of the Lord thy God in vain; for the Lord will not hold him [a]guiltless that taketh his name in vain.

16 Remember the [a]sabbath day, to keep it holy.

17 Six days shalt thou labor, and do all thy work;

18 But the seventh day, the sabbath of the Lord thy God, thou shalt not do any work, thou, nor thy son, nor thy daughter, thy man-servant, nor thy maid-servant, nor thy cattle, nor thy stranger that is within thy gates;

19 For in [a]six days the Lord made heaven and earth, and the sea, and all that in them is; wherefore the Lord blessed the sabbath day, and hallowed it.

20 [a]Honor thy [b]father and thy mother, that thy days may be long upon the land which the Lord thy God giveth thee.

21 Thou shalt not [a]kill.

22 Thou shalt not commit [a]adultery. Thou shalt not [b]steal.

23 Thou shalt not bear [a]false witness against thy neighbor.

24 Thou shalt not [a]covet thy neighbor's house, thou shalt not covet thy neighbor's wife, nor his man-servant, nor his maid-servant, nor his ox, nor his ass, nor anything that is thy neighbor's.

25 And it came to pass that after Abinadi had made an end of these sayings that he said unto them: Have ye [a]taught this people that they should observe to do all these things for to keep these commandments?

26 I say unto you, Nay; for if ye had, the Lord would not have caused me to come forth and to prophesy evil concerning this people.

27 And now ye have said that salvation cometh by the law of Moses. I say unto you that it is expedient that ye should [a]keep the law of Moses as yet; but I say unto you,

---

7*a* Prov. 15: 10; 1 Ne. 16: 2 (1–3); 2 Ne. 9: 40.
9*a* Dan. 3: 16 (16–18).
10*a* Alma 25: 10.
b Jer. 26: 14; Mosiah 17: 18 (13–19).
11*a* Ex. 20: 1 (1–17).
b Micah 2: 1 (1–2).
12*a* Mosiah 12: 36.
13*a* Ex. 20: 5.
15*a* Ex. 20: 7; Morm. 7: 7; D&C 58: 30.
16*a* Mosiah 18: 23. TG Sabbath.
19*a* Gen. 1: 31; Ex. 20: 11.
20*a* TG Honoring Father and Mother.
b Prov. 20: 20.
21*a* Ex. 20: 13; Deut. 5: 17; Matt. 5: 21 (21–37); 3 Ne. 12: 21 (21–37); D&C 42: 18.
22*a* TG Adultery.
b TG Stealing.
23*a* Prov. 24: 28.
24*a* TG Covetousness.
25*a* Mosiah 12: 37.
27*a* 2 Ne. 25: 24.

[About 148 B.C.]

that the time shall come when it shall [b]no more be expedient to keep the law of Moses.

28 And moreover, I say unto you, that [a]salvation doth not come by the [b]law alone; and were it not for the [c]atonement, which God himself shall make for the sins and iniquities of his people, that they must unavoidably perish, notwithstanding the law of Moses.

29 And now I say unto you that it was expedient that there should be a law given to the children of Israel, yea, even a very [a]strict law; for they were a stiffnecked people, [b]quick to do iniquity, and slow to remember the Lord their God;

30 Therefore there was a [a]law given them, yea, a law of performances and of [b]ordinances, a law which they were to [c]observe strictly from day to day, to keep them in remembrance of God and their duty towards him.

31 But behold, I say unto you, that all these things were [a]types of things to come.

32 And now, did they [a]understand the law? I say unto you, Nay, they did not all understand the law; and this because of the hardness of their hearts; for they understood not that there could not any man be saved [b]except it were through the redemption of God.

33 For behold, did not Moses prophesy unto them concerning the coming of the Messiah, and that God should redeem his people? Yea, and even [a]all the prophets who have prophesied ever since the world began—have they not spoken more or less concerning these things?

34 Have they not said that [a]God himself should come down among the children of men, and take upon him the form of man, and go forth in mighty power upon the face of the earth?

35 Yea, and have they not said also that he should bring to pass the [a]resurrection of the dead, and that he, himself, should be oppressed and afflicted?

CHAPTER 14

Isaiah speaks Messianically—Messiah's humiliation and sufferings are set forth—He makes his soul an offering for sin and makes intercession for transgressors—Compare Isaiah 53.

YEA, even doth not Isaiah say: Who hath [a]believed our report, and to whom is the arm of the Lord revealed?

2 For he shall grow up before him as a tender plant, and as a root out of dry ground; he hath no form nor comeliness; and when we shall see him there is no beauty that we should desire him.

3 He is [a]despised and rejected of men; a man of sorrows, and acquainted with grief; and we hid as it were our faces from him; he was despised, and we esteemed him not.

4 Surely he has [a]borne our [b]griefs, and carried our sorrows; yet we did esteem him stricken, smitten of God, and afflicted.

27*b* 3 Ne. 9: 19 (19–20); 15: 4 (2–10).
28*a* Gal. 2: 16; Mosiah 12: 31; Alma 25: 16. TG Redemption; Salvation, Plan of.
b Rom. 7: 4 (4–25); Gal. 2: 21; 3: 2; Heb. 10: 1; 2 Ne. 2: 5; Mosiah 3: 15 (14–15).
c TG Jesus Christ, Atonement through.
29*a* Josh. 1: 8; Heb. 9: 10 (8–10); Mosiah 3: 14 (14–15); Alma 25: 15 (15–16); D&C 41: 5 (4–5).
b 1 Ne. 17: 45; Alma 46: 8.
30*a* Rom. 7: 1 (1–3).
b TG Ordinance.
c 2 Ne. 25: 24; Jacob 4: 5.
31*a* Mosiah 16: 14; Alma 25: 15 (15–16). TG Jesus Christ, Types of, in Anticipation; Symbolism.
32*a* Ps. 111: 10.
b 2 Ne. 25: 23 (23–25).
33*a* 1 Pet. 1: 11; 1 Ne. 10: 5; Jacob 4: 4; 7: 11 (11–12); Alma 25: 16 (10–16); 30: 44. TG Jesus Christ, Prophecies about.
34*a* Mosiah 7: 27; 15: 1; 17: 8; Alma 10: 21. TG Jesus Christ—Jehovah.
35*a* Isa. 26: 19; 2 Ne. 2: 8.
14 1*a* Isa. 53: 1 (1–12).
3*a* Ps. 22: 6; 1 Ne. 19: 14.
4*a* Alma 7: 11.
b Matt. 8: 17.

[About 148 B.C.]

5 But he was [a]wounded for our [b]transgressions, he was bruised for our iniquities; the chastisement of our peace was upon him; and with his stripes we are [c]healed.

6 All we, like [a]sheep, have gone astray; we have turned every one to his own way; and the Lord hath laid on him the iniquities of us all.

7 He was oppressed, and he was afflicted, yet he [a]opened not his mouth; he is brought as a [b]lamb to the slaughter, and as a sheep before her shearers is dumb so he opened not his mouth.

8 He was taken from prison and from judgment; and who shall declare his generation? For he was cut off out of the land of the living; for the transgressions of my people was he stricken.

9 And he made his grave with the wicked, and with the [a]rich in his death; because he had done no [b]evil, neither was any deceit in his mouth.

10 Yet it pleased the Lord to [a]bruise him; he hath put him to grief; when thou shalt make his soul an offering for sin he shall see his [b]seed, he shall prolong his days, and the pleasure of the Lord shall prosper in his hand.

11 He shall see the travail of his soul, and shall be satisfied; by his knowledge shall my righteous servant justify many; for he shall [a]bear their iniquities.

12 Therefore will I divide him a portion with the [a]great, and [b]he shall divide the spoil with the strong; because he hath poured out his soul unto death; and he was numbered with the transgressors; and he bore the sins of many, and made [c]intercession for the transgressors.

CHAPTER 15

How Christ is both the Father and the Son—He shall make intercession and bear the transgressions of his people—They and all the holy prophets are his seed—He bringeth to pass the resurrection—Little children have eternal life.

AND now Abinadi said unto them: I would that ye should understand that [a]God himself shall [b]come down among the children of men, and shall [c]redeem his people.

2 And because he [a]dwelleth in [b]flesh he shall be called the [c]Son of God, and having subjected the flesh to the [d]will of the [e]Father, being the Father and the Son—

3 The Father, [a]because he was [b]conceived by the power of God; and the Son, because of the flesh; thus becoming the Father and Son—

5*a* TG Jesus Christ, Crucifixion of.
b Mosiah 15: 9; Alma 11: 40.
c 1 Pet. 2: 24 (24–25).
6*a* Matt. 9: 36; 2 Ne. 12: 5; 28: 14; Alma 5: 37.
7*a* Isa. 53: 7 (7–8); Mark 15: 3 (2–14); John 19: 9 (9–10); 1 Pet. 2: 23 (22–23); Mosiah 15: 6. TG Jesus Christ, Trial of.
b Jer. 11: 19. TG Passover.
9*a* Matt. 27: 57 (57–60); Mark 15: 46 (27, 43–46). TG Jesus Christ, Death of.
b John 19: 4.
10*a* Gen. 3: 15; Rom. 16: 20.
b Mosiah 15: 10 (10–13).
11*a* Lev. 16: 22 (21–22); 1 Pet. 3: 18; D&C 19: 16 (16–19).
12*a* Luke 24: 26.
b Mosiah 15: 12.
c 2 Ne. 2: 9; Mosiah 15: 8; Moro. 7: 28 (27–28).
15 1*a* Isa. 54: 5; 1 Tim. 3: 16; Mosiah 13: 34 (33–34).
b TG God, Manifestations of.
c TG Jesus Christ, Mission of.
2*a* Mosiah 3: 5; 7: 27; Alma 7: 9 (9–13).
b TG Jesus Christ, Condescension of.
c John 19: 7. TG Jesus Christ, Divine Sonship.
d TG God, Will of.
e Isa. 9: 6; 64: 8; John 10: 30; 14: 10 (8–10); Mosiah 5: 7; Alma 11: 39 (38–39); Ether 3: 14.
3*a* D&C 93: 4.
b Luke 1: 32 (31–33); Mosiah 3: 8 (8–9); Alma 7: 10; 3 Ne. 1: 14. TG Jesus Christ, Divine Sonship.

[About 148 B.C.]

4 And they are [a]one God, yea, the very [b]Eternal [c]Father of heaven and of earth.

5 And thus the flesh becoming subject to the Spirit, or the Son to the Father, being one God, [a]suffereth temptation, and yieldeth not to the temptation, but suffereth himself to be mocked, and [b]scourged, and cast out, and disowned by his [c]people.

6 And after all this, after working many mighty miracles among the children of men, he shall be led, yea, even [a]as Isaiah said, as a sheep before the shearer is dumb, so he [b]opened not his mouth.

7 Yea, even so he shall be led, [a]crucified, and slain, the [b]flesh becoming subject even unto death, the [c]will of the Son being swallowed up in the will of the Father.

8 And thus God breaketh the [a]bands of death, having gained the [b]victory over death; giving the Son power to make [c]intercession for the children of men—

9 Having ascended into heaven, having the bowels of mercy; being filled with compassion towards the children of men; standing betwixt them and justice; having broken the bands of death, taken upon [a]himself their iniquity and their transgressions, having redeemed them, and [b]satisfied the demands of justice.

10 And now I say unto you, who shall declare his [a]generation? Behold, I say unto you, that when his soul has been made an offering for [b]sin he shall see his [c]seed. And now what say ye? And who shall be his seed?

11 Behold I say unto you, that whosoever has heard the words of the [a]prophets, yea, all the holy prophets who have prophesied concerning the coming of the Lord—I say unto you, that all those who have hearkened unto their words, and believed that the Lord would redeem his people, and have looked forward to that day for a remission of their sins, I say unto you, that these are his seed, or they are the heirs of the [b]kingdom of God.

12 For these are they whose sins [a]he has borne; these are they for whom he has died, to redeem them from their transgressions. And now, are they not his seed?

13 Yea, and are not the [a]prophets, every one that has opened his mouth to prophesy, that has not fallen into transgression, I mean all the holy prophets ever since the world began? I say unto you that they are his seed.

14 And these are [a]they who have published peace, who have brought good [b]tidings of good, who have [c]published salvation; and said unto Zion: Thy God reigneth!

4*a* Deut. 6: 4. TG Godhead.
b Alma 11: 39.
c Mosiah 3: 8; Hel. 14: 12; 3 Ne. 9: 15; Ether 4: 7.
5*a* Luke 4: 2; Heb. 4: 15. TG Jesus Christ, Temptation of.
b John 19: 1.
c Matt. 21: 42; Mark 8: 31; Luke 17: 25; 23: 38.
6*a* Isa. 53: 7.
b Luke 23: 9; John 19: 9 (9–10); Mosiah 14: 7. TG Jesus Christ, Trial of.
7*a* TG Jesus Christ, Crucifixion of.
b Isa. 53: 10.
c Luke 22: 42; John 6: 38; 3 Ne. 11: 11.
8*a* Alma 5: 7.
b Hosea 13: 14; 1 Cor. 15: 57 (55–57); Mosiah 16: 7.
c 2 Ne. 2: 9; Mosiah 14: 12; Moro. 7: 28 (27–28).
9*a* Mosiah 14: 5 (5–12). TG Self-sacrifice.
b TG Jesus Christ, Mission of.
10*a* Isa. 53: 8.
b Lev. 6: 25 (25–26).
c Isa. 53: 10; Mosiah 5: 7; 27: 25; Moro. 7: 19. TG God the Father—Jehovah.
11*a* Luke 10: 16; D&C 84: 36 (36–38).
b TG Kingdom of God, in Heaven; Kingdom of God, on Earth.
12*a* Mosiah 14: 12; Alma 7: 13; 11: 40 (40–41).
13*a* Zech. 7: 12; Matt. 11: 13; 1 Ne. 3: 20. TG Sons and Daughters of God.
14*a* Mosiah 12: 21 (21–24); 27: 37.
b Isa. 52: 7.
c TG Missionary Work.

[About 148 B.C.]

15 And O how beautiful upon the mountains were their feet!

16 And again, how beautiful upon the mountains are the feet of those that are still publishing peace!

17 And again, how beautiful upon the mountains are the feet of those who shall hereafter publish peace, yea, from this time henceforth and forever!

18 And behold, I say unto you, this is not all. For O how beautiful upon the mountains are the [a]feet of him that bringeth good tidings, that is the founder of [b]peace, yea, even the Lord, who has redeemed his people; yea, him who has granted salvation unto his people;

19 For were it not for the redemption which he hath made for his people, which was prepared from the [a]foundation of the world, I say unto you, were it not for this, all mankind must have [b]perished.

20 But behold, the bands of death shall be broken, and the Son reigneth, and hath power over the dead; therefore, he bringeth to pass the resurrection of the dead.

21 And there cometh a resurrection, even a [a]first resurrection; yea, even a resurrection of those that have been, and who are, and who shall be, even until the resurrection of Christ—for so shall he be called.

22 And now, the resurrection of all the prophets, and all those that have believed in their words, or all those that have kept the commandments of God, shall come forth in the first resurrection; therefore, they are the first resurrection.

23 They are raised to [a]dwell with God who has redeemed them; thus they have eternal life through Christ, who has [b]broken the bands of death.

24 And these are those who have part in the first resurrection; and these are they that have died before Christ came, in their ignorance, not having [a]salvation declared unto them. And thus the Lord bringeth about the restoration of these; and they have a part in the first resurrection, or have eternal life, being redeemed by the Lord.

25 And little [a]children also have eternal life.

26 But behold, and [a]fear, and tremble before God, for ye ought to tremble; for the Lord redeemeth none such that [b]rebel against him and [c]die in their sins; yea, even all those that have perished in their sins ever since the world began, that have wilfully rebelled against God, that have known the commandments of God, and would not keep them; [d]these are they that have [e]no part in the first [f]resurrection.

27 Therefore ought ye not to tremble? For salvation cometh to none such; for the Lord hath redeemed none such; yea, neither can the Lord redeem such; for he cannot deny himself; for he cannot deny [a]justice when it has its claim.

28 And now I say unto you that the time shall come that the [a]salvation of the Lord shall be declared to every nation, kindred, tongue, and people.

29 Yea, Lord, [a]thy [b]watchmen shall lift up their voice; with the voice together shall they sing; for

18*a* Nahum 1: 15; 3 Ne. 20: 40; D&C 128: 19.
b Micah 5: 5 (4–7); John 16: 33. TG Peace of God.
19*a* Mosiah 4: 6.
b 2 Ne. 9: 7 (6–13).
21*a* Jacob 4: 11; Alma 40: 16 (16–21). TG Firstfruits.
23*a* Ps. 15: 1 (1–5); 24: 3 (3–4); 1 Ne. 15: 33 (33–36); D&C 76: 62 (50–70).
b TG Death, Power over.
24*a* 2 Ne. 9: 26 (25–26); D&C 137: 7.
25*a* D&C 29: 46; 137: 10. TG Salvation of Little Children.
26*a* Deut. 5: 29; Jacob 6: 9; 7: 19.
b Josh. 22: 16; Job 24: 13; Ps. 5: 10; 1 Ne. 2: 23 (21–24).
c Ezek. 18: 26; 1 Ne. 15: 33 (32–33); Moro. 10: 26.
d Alma 40: 19.
e D&C 76: 85.
f TG Telestial Glory.
27*a* Alma 12: 32; 34: 16 (15–16); 42: 1.
28*a* Ps. 67: 2 (1–2). TG Missionary Work.
29*a* Isa. 52: 8 (8–10); Mosiah 12: 22 (22–24).
b TG Watchmen.

[About 148 B.C.]

they shall see eye to eye, when the
Lord shall bring again Zion.
30 Break forth into joy, sing together, ye waste places of Jerusalem; for the Lord hath comforted his people, he hath redeemed Jerusalem.
31 The Lord hath made bare his holy arm in the eyes of all the nations; and all the ends of the earth shall see the [a]salvation of our God.

CHAPTER 16

God redeems men from their lost and fallen state—Those who are carnal remain as though there was no redemption—Christ brings to pass a resurrection to endless life or to endless damnation.

AND now, it came to pass that after Abinadi had spoken these words he stretched forth his hand and said: The time shall come when all shall see the [a]salvation of the Lord; when [b]every nation, kindred, tongue, and people shall see eye to eye and shall [c]confess before God that his [d]judgments are just.
2 And then shall the [a]wicked be [b]cast out, and they shall have cause to howl, and [c]weep, and wail, and gnash their teeth; and this because they would not [d]hearken unto the voice of the Lord; therefore the Lord redeemeth them not.
3 For they are [a]carnal and devilish, and the devil has power over them; yea, even that old serpent that did [b]beguile our first parents, which was the [c]cause of their fall; which was the cause of [d]all mankind becoming carnal, sensual, devilish, [e]knowing evil from good, [f]subjecting themselves to the devil.
4 Thus all mankind were [a]lost; and behold, they would have been endlessly lost were it not that God redeemed his people from their lost and fallen state.
5 But remember that he that persists in his own [a]carnal nature, and goes on in the ways of sin and rebellion against God, remaineth in his fallen state and the [b]devil hath all power over him. Therefore he is as though there was no [c]redemption made, being an enemy to God; and also is the [d]devil an enemy to God.
6 And now if Christ had not come into the world, speaking of things to come [a]as though they had already come, there could have been no redemption.
7 And if Christ had not risen from the dead, or have broken the bands of death that the grave should have no victory, and that death should have no [a]sting, there could have been no resurrection.
8 But there is a [a]resurrection, therefore the grave hath no victory, and the sting of [b]death is swallowed up in Christ.
9 He is the [a]light and the life of the world; yea, a light that is endless,

31*a* TG Salvation.
16 1*a* TG Salvation.
b Mosiah 3: 20 (20–21).
c Mosiah 27: 31; D&C 88: 104.
d TG Justice.
2*a* Ps. 91: 8; Jer. 12: 1; D&C 1: 9 (9–10).
b Ps. 52: 5; D&C 63: 54.
c Matt. 13: 42 (41–42); Luke 13: 28; Alma 40: 13; Moses 1: 22.
d Jer. 44: 16; Ether 11: 13.
3*a* Gal. 5: 19 (16–26); Mosiah 3: 19.
b Gen. 3: 13; 2 Ne. 9: 9; Ether 8: 25; Moses 4: 19 (5–19).
c Moses 5: 13.
d Ps. 14: 3. TG Man, Natural, Not Spiritually Reborn.
e Gen. 3: 5; 2 Ne. 2: 18 (18, 26); Alma 29: 5; Moro. 7: 16 (15–19).
f Alma 5: 41 (41–42); D&C 29: 40.
4*a* 2 Ne. 9: 7; Alma 11: 45; 12: 36; 42: 6 (6, 9, 14). TG Fall of Man.
5*a* TG Carnal Mind; Man, Natural, Not Spiritually Reborn.
b TG Bondage, Spiritual.
c 1 Ne. 10: 6; 2 Ne. 2: 6 (5–8); 25: 20; Alma 12: 22 (22–25).
d TG Devil.
6*a* 2 Ne. 25: 26 (24–27); Jarom 1: 11; Mosiah 3: 13.
7*a* Hosea 13: 14; Mosiah 15: 8 (8, 20).
8*a* 2 Ne. 9: 10; Alma 42: 15 (6–15).
b 1 Cor. 15: 55; Morm. 7: 5.
9*a* Ether 3: 14; Moro. 7: 18; D&C 88: 13 (7–13). TG Jesus Christ, Light of the World.

[About 148 B.C.]

that can never be darkened; yea,
and also a life which is endless, that
there can be no more death.
10 Even this mortal shall put on
[a]immortality, and this [b]corruption
shall put on incorruption, and shall
be brought to [c]stand before the bar
of God, to be judged of him according to their works whether they be
good or whether they be evil—
11 If they be good, to the resurrection of [a]endless life and [b]happiness;
and if they be evil, to the resurrection of [c]endless damnation, being
delivered up to the devil, who hath
subjected them, which is damnation—
12 Having gone according to their
own carnal wills and desires; having
never called upon the Lord while
the arms of mercy were extended
towards them; for the arms of
mercy were extended towards them,
and they would [a]not; they being
warned of their iniquities and yet
they would not depart from them;
and they were commanded to repent and yet they would not repent.
13 And now, ought ye not to
tremble and repent of your sins,
and remember that only in and
through Christ ye can be saved?
14 Therefore, if ye teach the [a]law
of Moses, also teach that it is a
[b]shadow of those things which are
to come—
15 Teach them that redemption
cometh through Christ the Lord,
who is the very [a]Eternal Father.
Amen.

CHAPTER 17

Alma believes and writes the words of Abinadi—Abinadi suffers death by fire—He prophesies disease and death by fire upon his murderers.

AND now it came to pass that
when Abinadi had finished these
sayings, that the king commanded
that the [a]priests should take him
and cause that he should be put to
[b]death.
2 But there was one among them
whose name was [a]Alma, he also
being a descendant of Nephi. And
he was a young man, and he
[b]believed the words which Abinadi
had spoken, for he knew concerning
the iniquity which Abinadi had
testified against them; therefore he
began to plead with the king that
he would not be angry with Abinadi,
but suffer that he might depart in
peace.
3 But the king was more wroth,
and caused that Alma should be
cast out from among them, and
sent his servants after him that they
might slay him.
4 But he fled from before them and
[a]hid himself that they found him
not. And he being concealed for
many days did [b]write all the words
which Abinadi had spoken.
5 And it came to pass that the king
caused that his guards should
surround Abinadi and take him;
and they bound him and cast him
into prison.
6 And after three days, having
counseled with his [a]priests, he
caused that he should again be
brought before him.
7 And he said unto him: Abinadi,
we have found an accusation against
thee, and thou art worthy of death.
8 For thou hast said that [a]God
himself should come down among

10*a* Alma 40:2.
TG Immortality.
b 1 Cor. 15:42.
c 3 Ne. 26:4. TG Jesus Christ, Judge.
11*a* Dan. 12:2 (2–3); John 5:29 (28–29).
b TG Happiness.
c Alma 9:11. TG Damnation.
12*a* TG Prophets, Rejection of.
14*a* TG Law of Moses.
b Mosiah 13:31; Alma 25:15 (15–16). TG Jesus Christ, Types of, in Anticipation.
15*a* Mosiah 3:5.
17 1*a* TG False Priesthoods.
b Jer. 26:11.
2*a* Mosiah 23:9.
b Mosiah 26:15; Alma 5:11.
4*a* 1 Kgs. 17:3 (1–16); Ether 13:13 (13, 22).
b TG Scriptures, Writing of.
6*a* Mosiah 11:5.
8*a* Mosiah 7:27; 13:34.

[About 148 B.C.]

the children of men; and now, for
this cause thou shalt be put to
death unless thou wilt recall all the
words which thou hast spoken evil
concerning me and my people.
9 Now Abinadi said unto him: I
say unto you, I will [a]not recall the
words which I have spoken unto
you concerning this people, for
they are true; and that ye may know
of their surety I have suffered myself
that I have fallen into your hands.
10 Yea, and I will [a]suffer even until
death, and I will not recall my
words, and they shall stand as a
[b]testimony against you. And if ye
slay me ye will shed [c]innocent blood,
and this shall also stand as a testimony against you at the last day.
11 And now king Noah was about
to release him, for he feared his
word; for he feared that the judgments of God would come upon
him.
12 But the [a]priests lifted up their
voices against him, and began to
accuse him, saying: He has reviled
the king. Therefore the king was
stirred up in [b]anger against him,
and he delivered him up that he
might be slain.
13 And it came to pass that they
took him and bound him, and
[a]scourged his skin with faggots, yea,
even unto [b]death.
14 And now when the flames began
to scorch him, he cried unto them,
saying:
15 Behold, even as ye have done
unto me, so shall it come to pass
that thy [a]seed shall cause that
many shall suffer the pains that I
do suffer, even the pains of [b]death
by fire; and this because they
believe in the salvation of the Lord
their God.
16 And it will come to pass that ye
shall be afflicted with all manner of
[a]diseases because of your iniquities.
17 Yea, and ye shall be smitten on
every hand, and shall be driven and
scattered to and fro, even as a wild
flock is driven by wild and ferocious
beasts.
18 And in that day ye shall be
[a]hunted, and ye shall be taken by
the hand of your enemies, and then
ye shall suffer, as I suffer, the pains
of [b]death by fire.
19 Thus God executeth [a]ven-
geance upon those that destroy his
people. O God, [b]receive my soul.
20 And now, *when [a]Abinadi had
said these words, he fell, having
suffered death by fire; yea, having
been put to death because he would
not deny the commandments of
God, having sealed the truth of his
words by his [b]death.

CHAPTER 18

Alma preaches in private—He sets forth the covenant of baptism and baptizes at the waters of Mormon—He organizes the Church of Christ and ordains priests—They support themselves and teach the people—Alma and his people flee from King Noah into the wilderness.

AND now, it came to pass that
Alma, who had fled from the servants of king Noah, [a]repented of his
sins and iniquities, and went about
privately among the people, and
began to teach the words of
Abinadi—
2 Yea, concerning that which was
to come, and also concerning the
resurrection of the dead, and the
[a]redemption of the people, which
was to be brought to pass through

9*a* TG Courage; Integrity.
10*a* TG Persecution.
b TG Testimony.
c Jer. 26: 15 (14–15); Lam. 4: 13; Alma 14: 11; 60: 13.
12*a* Mosiah 11: 5; 12: 25 (17, 25).
b Prov. 20: 2.
13*a* Dan. 3: 6; James 5: 10 (10–11); Alma 14: 26 (20–27).
b Mosiah 7: 28; 21: 30; Alma 25: 11.
15*a* Mosiah 13: 10; Alma 25: 12 (7–12).
b Alma 25: 5.
16*a* Deut. 28: 60 (25–60).
18*a* Alma 25: 8.
b Mosiah 13: 10; 19: 20; Alma 25: 11 (7–12).
19*a* Ps. 125: 3.
b Luke 23: 46; Acts 7: 59.
20*a* Mosiah 7: 26.
b Heb. 9: 16 (16–17).
18 1*a* Mosiah 23: 9.
2*a* TG Jesus Christ, Redeemer.

[*About 148 B.C.]

the power, and sufferings, and
[b]death of Christ, and his resurrection
and ascension into heaven.
3 And as many as would hear his
word he did teach. And he taught
them privately, that it might not
come to the knowledge of the king.
And many did believe his words.
4 And it came to pass that as many
as did believe him did go forth to
a [a]place which was called Mormon,
having received its name from the
king, being in the [b]borders of the
land having been infested, by times
or at seasons, by wild beasts.
5 Now, there was in Mormon a
fountain of pure water, and Alma
resorted thither, there being near
the water a thicket of small trees,
where he did hide himself in the
daytime from the searches of the
king.
6 And it came to pass that as
many as believed him went thither
to hear his words.
7 And it came to pass *after many
days there were a goodly number
gathered together at the place of
Mormon, to hear the words of Alma.
Yea, all were gathered together that
believed on his word, to hear him.
And he did [a]teach them, and did
preach unto them repentance,
and redemption, and faith on the
Lord.
8 And it came to pass that he said
unto them: Behold, here are the
waters of Mormon (for thus were
they called) and now, as ye are
[a]desirous to come into the [b]fold of
God, and to be called his people,
and are willing to bear one another's
burdens, that they may be light;
9 Yea, and are [a]willing to mourn
with those that [b]mourn; yea, and
comfort those that stand in need of
comfort, and to stand as [c]witnesses
of God at all times and in all things,
and in all places that ye may be in,
even until death, that ye may be
redeemed of God, and be numbered
with those of the [d]first resurrection,
that ye may have eternal life—
10 Now I say unto you, if this be
the desire of your hearts, what have
you against being [a]baptized in the
[b]name of the Lord, as a witness
before him that ye have entered
into a [c]covenant with him, that ye
will serve him and keep his commandments,
that he may pour out
his Spirit more abundantly upon
you?
11 And now when the people had
heard these words, they clapped
their hands for joy, and exclaimed:
This is the desire of our hearts.
12 And now it came to pass that
Alma took Helam, he being one of
the first, and went and stood forth
in the water, and cried, saying: O
Lord, pour out thy Spirit upon thy
servant, that he may do this work
with holiness of heart.
13 And when he had said these
words, the [a]Spirit of the Lord was
upon him, and he said: Helam, I
baptize thee, having [b]authority
from the Almighty God, as a testimony
that ye have entered into a
[c]covenant to serve him until you are
dead as to the mortal body; and
may the Spirit of the Lord be
poured out upon you; and may he
grant unto you eternal life, through
the redemption of Christ, whom he
has prepared from the [d]foundation
of the world.
14 And after Alma had said these
words, both Alma and Helam were

2*b* TG Jesus Christ, Ascension of; Jesus Christ, Death of.
4*a* Alma 5: 3; 3 Ne. 5: 12.
b Mosiah 18: 31.
7*a* Alma 5: 13.
8*a* D&C 20: 36–37, 77.
b TG Brotherhood and Sisterhood; Conversion.
9*a* TG Baptism, Qualifications for.
b TG Comfort; Compassion.
c TG Missionary Work; Witnesses.
d Jacob 4: 11.
10*a* 2 Ne. 31: 17; Alma 4: 4.
b TG Jesus Christ, Taking the Name of.
c Neh. 10: 29. TG Commitment.
13*a* TG Holy Ghost, Mission of.
b Mosiah 21: 33; Alma 5: 3; 3 Ne. 11: 25.
c Mosiah 21: 31. TG Covenants.
d Mosiah 4: 6; Alma 12: 30 (25, 30).

[*About 147 B.C.]

[a]buried in the water; and they arose and came forth out of the water rejoicing, being filled with the Spirit.

15 And again, Alma took another, and went forth a second time into the water, and baptized him according to the first, only he did not bury [a]himself again in the water.

16 And after this manner he did baptize every one that went forth to the place of Mormon; and they were in number about two hundred and four souls; yea, and they were [a]baptized in the waters of Mormon, and were filled with the [b]grace of God.

17 And they were called the church of God, or the [a]church of Christ, from that time forward. And it came to pass that whosoever was baptized by the power and authority of God was added to his church.

18 And it came to pass that Alma, having [a]authority from God, [b]ordained priests; even one priest to every fifty of their number did he ordain to preach unto them, and to [c]teach them concerning the things pertaining to the kingdom of God.

19 And he commanded them that [a]they should [b]teach nothing save it were the things which he had taught, and which had been spoken by the mouth of the holy prophets.

20 Yea, even he commanded them that they should [a]preach nothing save it were repentance and faith on the Lord, who had redeemed his people.

21 And he commanded them that there should be no [a]contention one with another, but that they should look forward with [b]one eye, having one faith and one baptism, having their hearts [c]knit together in unity and in love one towards another.

22 And thus he commanded them to preach. And thus they became the [a]children of God.

23 And he commanded them that they should observe the [a]sabbath day, and keep it holy, and also every day they should give thanks to the Lord their God.

24 And he also commanded them that the priests whom he had ordained [a]should [b]labor with their own hands for their support.

25 And there was [a]one day in every week that was set apart that they should [b]gather themselves together to teach the people, and to worship the Lord their God, and also, as often as it was in their power, to [c]assemble themselves together.

26 And the priests were not to depend upon the people for their support; but for their labor they were to receive the [a]grace of God, that they might wax strong in the Spirit, having the [b]knowledge of God, that they might teach with power and authority from God.

27 And again Alma commanded that the people of the church should impart of their substance, [a]every one according to that which he had; if he have more abundantly he should impart more abundantly; and of him that had but little, but

14*a* TG Baptism, Immersion.
15*a* JS-H 1:71 (70–71).
16*a* Mosiah 25:18.
b TG Grace.
17*a* Mosiah 21:34; 25:22 (18–23); 26:4; Alma 4:5 (4–5); 3 Ne. 26:21. TG Jesus Christ, Head of the Church.
18*a* Mosiah 23:16. TG Priesthood, Authority.
b TG Priesthood, History of.
c Mosiah 2:4; 23:14; 24:4 (4–8).
19*a* Mosiah 23:14.
b D&C 5:10.
20*a* TG Preaching; Repentance.
21*a* TG Contention.
b Matt. 6:22; Morm. 8:15; D&C 4:5; 88:68.
c 1 Sam. 18:1; Rom. 15:5 (1–7); Mosiah 4:15; 23:15.
22*a* Moses 6:68.
23*a* Ex. 35:2; Mosiah 13:16 (16–19).
24*a* Acts 20:34 (33–35); Mosiah 27:5 (3–5); Alma 1:3, 26.
b 1 Cor. 9:18 (16–19); Alma 30:32.
25*a* Alma 32:11.
b TG Meetings.
c TG Assembly for Worship.
26*a* TG Blessing; Reward; Wages.
b Neh. 10:28 (28–31). TG God, Knowledge about.
27*a* Alma 16:16; 4 Ne. 1:3.

[About 147 B.C.]

little should be required; and to
him that had not should be given.
28 And thus they should impart of
their [a]substance of their own free
will and good desires towards God,
and to those priests that stood in
need, yea, and to every needy,
naked soul.
29 And this he said unto them,
having been commanded of God;
and they did [a]walk uprightly before
God, imparting to one another both
temporally and spiritually according to their needs and their wants.
30 And now it came to pass that
all this was done in Mormon, yea, by
the [a]waters of Mormon, in the forest
that was near the waters of Mormon; yea, the place of Mormon, the
waters of Mormon, the forest of
Mormon, how beautiful are they to
the eyes of them who there came to
the knowledge of their Redeemer;
yea, and how blessed are they, for
they shall [b]sing to his praise forever.
31 And these things were done in
the [a]borders of the land, that they
might not come to the knowledge
of the king.
32 But behold, it came to pass that
the king, having discovered a move-
ment among the people, sent his
servants to watch them. Therefore
on the day that they were assembling themselves together to hear
the word of the Lord they were
discovered unto the king.
33 And now the king said that
Alma was stirring up the people to
rebellion against him; therefore he
sent his [a]army to destroy them.
34 And it came to pass that Alma
and the people of the Lord were
[a]apprised of the coming of the king's
army; therefore they took their
tents and their families and [b]depart-
ed into the wilderness.
35 And they were in number about
[a]four hundred and fifty souls.

CHAPTER 19

Gideon seeks to slay King Noah—The Lamanites invade the land—King Noah suffers death by fire—Limhi rules as a tributary monarch.

AND it came to pass that the
[a]army of the king returned, having
searched in vain for the people of
the Lord.
2 And now behold, the forces of the
king were small, having been reduced, and there began to be a
division among the remainder of the
people.
3 And the lesser part began to
[a]breathe out threatenings against
the king, and there began to be a
great contention among them.
4 And now there was a man among
them whose name was Gideon, and
he being a strong man and an
enemy to the king, therefore he
drew his sword, and swore in his
wrath that he would slay the king.
5 And it came to pass that he
fought with the king; and when the
king saw that he was about to overpower him, he fled and ran and got
upon the [a]tower which was near
the temple.
6 And Gideon pursued after him
and was about to get upon the tower
to slay the king, and the king cast
his eyes round about towards the
land of [a]Shemlon, and behold, the
army of the Lamanites were within
the borders of the land.
7 And now the king cried out in the
anguish of his soul, saying: Gideon,
[a]spare me, for the Lamanites are
upon us, and they will destroy us;
yea, they will destroy my people.
8 And now the king was not so
much concerned about his people as

28*a* TG Generosity; Initiative.
29*a* TG Walking with God; Welfare.
30*a* Mosiah 26: 15.
b TG Praise; Singing.
31*a* Mosiah 18: 4.
33*a* Mosiah 19: 1.
34*a* Mosiah 23: 1.
b Mosiah 21: 30; 23: 13, 36.
35*a* Mosiah 23: 10.
19 1*a* Mosiah 18: 33.
3*a* Acts 9: 1.
5*a* Judg. 9: 51 (50–55); Mosiah 11: 12.
6*a* Mosiah 10: 7; 11: 12; 20: 1.
7*a* Deut. 13: 8 (6–9).

[About 145 B.C.]

he was about his [a]own life; nevertheless, Gideon did spare his life.

9 And the king commanded the people that they should flee before the Lamanites, and he himself did go before them, and they did flee into the wilderness, with their women and their children.

10 And it came to pass that the Lamanites did pursue them, and did overtake them, and began to slay them.

11 Now it came to pass that the king commanded them that all the men should [a]leave their wives and their children, and flee before the Lamanites.

12 Now there were many that would not leave them, but had rather stay and perish with them. And the rest left their wives and their children and fled.

13 And it came to pass that those who tarried with their wives and their children caused that their fair daughters should stand forth and plead with the Lamanites that they would not slay them.

14 And it came to pass that the Lamanites had compassion on them, for they were charmed with the beauty of their women.

15 Therefore the Lamanites did spare their lives, and took them captives and carried them back to the land of Nephi, and granted unto them that they might possess the land, under the conditions that they would deliver up king Noah into the hands of the Lamanites, and deliver up their property, even [a]one half of all they possessed, one half of their gold, and their silver, and all their precious things, and thus they should pay tribute to the king of the Lamanites from year to year.

16 And now there was one of the sons of the king among those that were taken captive, whose name was [a]Limhi.

17 And now Limhi was desirous that his father should not be destroyed; nevertheless, Limhi was not ignorant of the iniquities of his father, he himself being a just man.

18 And it came to pass that Gideon sent men into the wilderness secretly, to search for the king and those that were with him. And it came to pass that they met the people in the wilderness, all save the king and his priests.

19 Now they had sworn in their hearts that they would return to the land of Nephi, and if their [a]wives and their children were slain, and also those that had tarried with them, that they would seek revenge, and also perish with them.

20 And the king commanded them that they should not return; and they were angry with the king, and caused that he should suffer, even unto [a]death by fire.

21 And they were about to take the priests also and [a]put them to death, and they fled before them.

22 And it came to pass that they were about to return to the land of Nephi, and they met the men of Gideon. And the men of Gideon told them of all that had happened to their wives and their children; and that the Lamanites had granted unto them that they might possess the land by paying a tribute to the Lamanites of one half of all they possessed.

23 And the people told the men of [a]Gideon that they had slain the king, and his [b]priests had fled from them farther into the wilderness.

24 And it came to pass that after they had ended the ceremony, that they returned to the land of Nephi, rejoicing, because their wives and their children were not slain; and they told Gideon what they had done to the king.

25 And it came to pass that the

8*a* TG Selfishness.
11*a* Mosiah 19: 19 (19–23).
15*a* Mosiah 7: 15.
16*a* Mosiah 7: 9; 11: 1.
19*a* Mosiah 19: 11.
20*a* Mosiah 12: 3; 13: 10; 17: 18 (13–19); Alma 25: 11 (7–12).
21*a* Mosiah 20: 3.
23*a* Mosiah 20: 17.
b Mosiah 17: 12 (1, 6, 12–18); 20: 23 (3, 18, 23).

[Between 145 and 122 B.C.]

king of the Lamanites made an [a]oath unto them, that his people should not slay them.

26 And also Limhi, being the son of the king, having the kingdom conferred upon him [a]by the people, made [b]oath unto the king of the Lamanites that his people should pay [c]tribute unto him, even one half of all they possessed.

27 And it came to pass that Limhi began to establish the kingdom and to establish [a]peace among his people.

28 And the king of the Lamanites set [a]guards round about the land, that he might [b]keep the people of Limhi in the land, that they might not depart into the wilderness; and he did support his guards out of the tribute which he did receive from the Nephites.

29 And now king Limhi did have continual peace in his kingdom for the space of two years, that the Lamanites did not molest them nor seek to destroy them.

CHAPTER 20

Lamanite daughters are abducted by the priests of Noah—The Lamanites wage war upon Limhi and his people—They are repulsed and pacified.

Now there was a place in [a]Shemlon where the daughters of the Lamanites did gather themselves together to sing, and to [b]dance, and to make themselves merry.

2 And it came to pass that there was one day a small number of them gathered together to sing and to dance.

3 And now the priests of king Noah, being ashamed to return to the city of Nephi, yea, and also fearing that the people would [a]slay them, therefore they durst not return to their wives and their [b]children.

4 And having tarried in the wilderness, and having discovered the daughters of the Lamanites, they laid and watched them;

5 And when there were but few of them gathered together to dance, they came forth out of their secret places and took them and carried them into the wilderness; yea, twenty and four of the [a]daughters of the Lamanites they carried into the wilderness.

6 And it came to pass that when the Lamanites found that their daughters had been missing, they were angry with the people of Limhi, for they thought it was the people of Limhi.

7 Therefore they sent their armies forth; yea, even the king himself went before his people; and they went up to the land of Nephi to destroy the people of Limhi.

8 And now Limhi had discovered them from the [a]tower, even all their preparations for war did he discover; therefore he gathered his people together, and laid wait for them in the fields and in the forests.

9 And it came to pass that when the Lamanites had come up, that the people of Limhi began to fall upon them from their waiting places, and began to slay them.

10 And it came to pass that the battle became exceedingly sore, for they fought like lions for their prey.

11 And it came to pass that the people of Limhi began to drive the Lamanites before them; yet they were not half so numerous as the Lamanites. But they [a]fought for their lives, and for their [b]wives, and for their children; therefore they exerted themselves and like dragons did they fight.

12 And it came to pass that they found the king of the Lamanites

25a Mosiah 21:3.
26a Mosiah 7:9.
b Mosiah 20:14, 22.
c Mosiah 22:7.
27a TG Peacemakers.
28a Mosiah 21:5; 22:6 (6–10).
b Mosiah 7:22; 9:10.
20 1a Mosiah 19:6.
b Judg. 21:21.
3a Mosiah 19:21.
b Mosiah 25:12.
5a Mosiah 21:20; 23:33 (30–35).
8a Mosiah 11:12.
11a Alma 43:45.
b Alma 46:12.

[Between 145 and 122 B.C.]

among the number of their dead; yet
he was not dead, having been wounded and left upon the ground, so
speedy was the flight of his people.
13 And they took him and bound
up his wounds, and brought him
before Limhi, and said: Behold,
here is the king of the Lamanites;
he having received a wound has
fallen among their dead, and they
have left him; and behold, we have
brought him before you; and now
let us slay him.
14 But Limhi said unto them: Ye
shall not slay him, but bring him
hither that I may see him. And they
brought him. And Limhi said unto
him: What cause have ye to come
up to war against my people? Behold, my people have not broken the
[a]oath that I made unto you; therefore, why should ye break the oath
which ye made unto my people?
15 And now the king said: I have
broken the oath because thy
people did carry away the daughters
of my people; therefore, in my anger
I did cause my people to come up
to war against thy people.
16 And now Limhi had heard
nothing concerning this matter;
therefore he said: I will search
among my people and whosoever
has done this thing shall perish.
Therefore he caused a search to
be made among his people.
17 Now when [a]Gideon had heard
these things, he being the king's
captain, he went forth and said unto
the king: I pray thee forbear, and
do not search this people, and lay
not this thing to their charge.
18 For do ye not remember the
priests of thy father, whom this
people sought to destroy? And are
they not in the wilderness? And are
not they the ones who have stolen
the daughters of the Lamanites?
19 And now, behold, and tell the
king of these things, that he may
tell his people that they may be
pacified towards us; for behold they
are already preparing to come
against us; and behold also there
are but few of us.
20 And behold, they come with
their numerous hosts; and except
the king doth pacify them towards
us we must perish.
21 For are not the words of
Abinadi [a]fulfilled, which he prophesied against us—and all this
because we would not hearken unto
the words of the Lord, and turn
from our iniquities?
22 And now let us pacify the king,
and we fulfil the [a]oath which we
have made unto him; for it is better
that we should be in bondage than
that we should lose our [b]lives;
therefore, let us put a stop to the
shedding of so much blood.
23 And now Limhi told the king all
the things concerning his father,
and the [a]priests that had fled into
the wilderness, and attributed the
carrying away of their daughters to
them.
24 And it came to pass that the
king was pacified towards his
people; and he said unto them: Let
us go forth to meet my people, without arms; and I swear unto you
with an [a]oath that my people shall
not slay thy people.
25 And it came to pass that they
followed the king, and went forth
without arms to meet the Lamanites. And it came to pass that they
did meet the Lamanites; and the
king of the Lamanites did bow himself down before them, and did
plead in behalf of the people of
Limhi.
26 And when the Lamanites saw
the people of Limhi, that they were
without arms, they had [a]compas-
sion on them and were pacified
towards them, and returned with
their king in peace to their own land.

14*a* Mosiah 19: 26 (25–26).
17*a* Mosiah 19: 23 (4–8, 23); 22: 3; Alma 1: 8 (8–9).
21*a* Mosiah 12: 2 (1–8); 21: 4.
22*a* Mosiah 19: 26.
b TG Life, Sanctity of.
23*a* Mosiah 19: 23 (21, 23); 23: 9 (9, 12, 31).
24*a* Mosiah 21: 3.
26*a* TG Compassion.

[Between 145 and 122 B.C.]

CHAPTER 21

Limhi's people are smitten and defeated by the Lamanites—They meet Ammon and are converted—They tell Ammon of the twenty-four Jaredite plates.

AND it came to pass that Limhi
and his people returned to the city
of Nephi, and began to dwell in the
land again in peace.
2 And it came to pass that after
many days the Lamanites began
again to be stirred up in anger
against the Nephites, and they
began to come into the borders of
the land round about.
3 Now they durst not slay them,
because of the [a]oath which their
king had made unto Limhi; but
they would smite them on their
[b]cheeks, and exercise authority
over them; and began to put heavy
[c]burdens upon their backs, and
drive them as they would a dumb
ass—
4 Yea, all this was done that the
[a]word of the Lord might be [b]fulfilled.
5 And now the afflictions of the
Nephites were great, and there was
no way that they could deliver
themselves out of their hands, for
the Lamanites had [a]surrounded
them on every side.
6 And it came to pass that the
people began to murmur with the
king because of their afflictions; and
they began to be desirous to go
against them to battle. And they
did afflict the king sorely with their
complaints; therefore he granted
unto them that they should do
according to their desires.
7 And they gathered themselves
together again, and put on their
armor, and went forth against the
Lamanites to drive them out of their
land.
8 And it came to pass that the
Lamanites did beat them, and drove
them back, and [a]slew many of them.
9 And now there was a great
[a]mourning and lamentation among
the people of Limhi, the widow
mourning for her husband, the son
and the daughter mourning for their
father, and the brothers for their
brethren.
10 Now there were a great many
[a]widows in the land, and they did
cry mightily from day to day, for a
great fear of the Lamanites had
come upon them.
11 And it came to pass that their
continual cries did stir up the
remainder of the people of Limhi to
anger against the Lamanites; and
they went again to battle, but they
were driven back again, suffering
much loss.
12 Yea, they went again even the
third time, and suffered in the like
manner; and those that were not
slain returned again to the city of
Nephi.
13 And they did humble themselves even to the dust, subjecting
themselves to the [a]yoke of bondage,
[b]submitting themselves to be smitten, and to be driven to and fro, and
burdened, according to the desires of
their enemies.
14 And they did [a]humble themselves even in the depths of humility; and they did cry mightily to
God; yea, even all the day long did
they cry unto their God that he
would [b]deliver them out of their
afflictions.
15 And now the Lord was slow to
[a]hear their cry because of their
iniquities; nevertheless the Lord

21 3*a* Mosiah 19:25; 20:24.
b Lam. 3:30; Mosiah 12:2.
c Ex. 1:11 (10–11); Mosiah 12:5; 24:9.
4*a* D&C 3:19.
b Mosiah 20:21.
5*a* Mosiah 19:28; 22:6 (6–10).
8*a* Mosiah 21:29.
9*a* Mosiah 12:4. TG Mourning.
10*a* TG Widows.
13*a* Mosiah 19:28 (26, 28); 21:36.
b TG Submissiveness.
14*a* Mosiah 29:20.
b TG Deliverance; Protection, Divine.
15*a* 1 Sam. 8:18; Prov. 15:29; Isa. 59:2; Jer. 7:16; 14:12 (10–12); Mosiah 11:24 (23–25); D&C 101:7 (7–9).

[Between 145 and 122 B.C.]

did hear their [b]cries, and began to soften the hearts of the Lamanites that they began to ease their burdens; yet the Lord did not see fit to deliver them out of bondage.

16 And it came to pass that they began to prosper by degrees in the land, and began to raise grain more abundantly, and flocks, and herds, that they did not suffer with hunger.

17 Now there was a great number of women, more than there was of men; therefore king Limhi commanded that every man should [a]impart to the support of the [b]widows and their children, that they might not perish with hunger; and this they did because of the greatness of their number that had been slain.

18 Now the people of Limhi kept together in a body as much as it was possible, and secured their grain and their flocks;

19 And the king himself did not trust his person without the walls of the city, unless he took his guards with him, fearing that he might by some means fall into the hands of the Lamanites.

20 And he caused that his people should watch the land round about, that by some means they might take those priests that fled into the wilderness, who had stolen the [a]daughters of the Lamanites, and that had caused such a great destruction to come upon them.

21 For they were desirous to take them that they might [a]punish them; for they had come into the land of Nephi by night, and carried off their grain and many of their precious things; therefore they laid wait for them.

22 And it came to pass that there was no more disturbance between the Lamanites and the people of Limhi, *even until the time that [a]Ammon and his brethren came into the land.

23 And the king having been without the gates of the city with his guard, [a]discovered Ammon and his brethren; and supposing them to be priests of Noah therefore he caused that they should be taken, and bound, and cast into [b]prison. And had they been the priests of Noah he would have caused that they should be put to death.

24 But when he found that they were not, but that they were his brethren, and had come from the [a]land of Zarahemla, he was filled with exceedingly great joy.

25 Now king Limhi had sent, previous to the coming of Ammon, a [a]small number of men to [b]search for the land of Zarahemla; but they could not find it, and they were lost in the wilderness.

26 Nevertheless, they did find a land which had been peopled; yea, a land which was covered with dry [a]bones; yea, a land which had been peopled and which had been destroyed; and they, having supposed it to be the land of Zarahemla, returned to the land of Nephi, having arrived in the borders of the land not many days before the [b]coming of Ammon.

27 And they brought a [a]record with them, even a record of the people whose bones they had found; and it was engraven on plates of ore.

28 And now Limhi was again filled with joy on learning from the mouth of Ammon that king Mosiah had a [a]gift from God, whereby he could [b]interpret such engravings; yea, and Ammon also did rejoice.

29 Yet Ammon and his brethren were filled with sorrow because so

15*b* Ex. 3: 9 (7, 9); 2 Ne. 26: 15; D&C 109: 49.
17*a* Mosiah 4: 26 (16, 26).
b TG Widows.
20*a* Mosiah 20: 5.
21*a* Mosiah 7: 7 (7–11).
22*a* Mosiah 7: 6 (6–13).
23*a* Mosiah 7: 10.
b Mosiah 7: 7 (6–8); Hel. 5: 21.
24*a* Omni 1: 13.
25*a* Mosiah 8: 7.
b Mosiah 7: 14.
26*a* Mosiah 8: 8; Hel. 3: 6 (3–12).
b Mosiah 7: 6 (6–11).
27*a* Mosiah 8: 9; 28: 11.
28*a* Omni 1: 20 (20–22); Mosiah 28: 13 (11–19). TG God, Gifts of.
b 1 Cor. 12: 10; Mosiah 8: 6 (6, 12–13).

[*About 121 B.C.]

many of their brethren had been
[a]slain;
30 And also that king Noah and
his priests had caused the people to
commit so many sins and iniquities
against God; and they also did
mourn for the [a]death of Abinadi;
and also for the [b]departure of Alma
and the people that went with him,
who had formed a church of God
through the strength and power of
God, and faith on the words which
had been spoken by Abinadi.
31 Yea, they did mourn for their
departure, for they knew not
whither they had fled. Now they
would have gladly joined with them,
for they themselves had entered
into a [a]covenant with God to serve
him and keep his commandments.
32 And now since the coming of
Ammon, king Limhi had also entered into a covenant with God, and
also many of his people, to serve
him and keep his commandments.
33 And it came to pass that king
Limhi and many of his people were
desirous to be baptized; but there
was none in the land that had
[a]authority from God. And Ammon
declined doing this thing, considering himself an unworthy servant.
34 Therefore they did not at that
time form themselves into a [a]church,
waiting upon the Spirit of the Lord.
Now they were desirous to become
even as Alma and his brethren, who
had fled into the wilderness.
35 They were desirous to be baptized as a witness and a testimony
that they were willing to serve God
with all their hearts; nevertheless
they did prolong the time; and an
account of their baptism shall be
[a]given hereafter.
36 And now all the study of Ammon and [a]his people, and king
Limhi and his people, was to deliver
themselves out of the hands of the
Lamanites and from [b]bondage.

CHAPTER 22

Plans are made for the people to escape from Lamanite bondage—The Lamanites are made drunk—The people escape, return to Zarahemla, and become subject to King Mosiah.

AND now it came to pass that
Ammon and king Limhi began to
consult with the people how they
should [a]deliver themselves out of
bondage; and even they did cause
that all the people should gather
themselves together; and this they
did that they might have the voice
of the people concerning the matter.
2 And it came to pass that they
could find no way to deliver themselves out of bondage, except it were
to take their women and children,
and their flocks, and their herds,
and their tents, and depart into the
wilderness; for the Lamanites being
so numerous, it was impossible for
the people of Limhi to contend with
them, thinking to deliver themselves out of bondage by the sword.
3 Now it came to pass that
[a]Gideon went forth and stood before
the king, and said unto him: Now
O king, thou hast hitherto hearkened unto my words many times
when we have been contending with
our brethren, the Lamanites.
4 And now O king, if thou hast not
found me to be an unprofitable servant, or if thou hast hitherto
listened to my words in any degree,
and they have been of service to
thee, even so I desire that thou
wouldst listen to my words at this
time, and I will be thy servant and
deliver this people out of bondage.
5 And the king granted unto him
that he might speak. And Gideon
said unto him:
6 Behold the back pass, through
the back wall, on the back side of
the city. The Lamanites, or the

29*a* Mosiah 21:8 (7–14); 25:9.
30*a* Mosiah 17:13 (12–20).
b Mosiah 18:34 (34–35).
31*a* Mosiah 18:13.
33*a* TG Baptism, Essential; Priesthood, Authority.
34*a* Mosiah 18:17.
35*a* Mosiah 25:18 (17–18).
36*a* Mosiah 7:3 (2–3).
b Mosiah 21:13.
22 1*a* Mosiah 7:18.
3*a* Mosiah 20:17; Alma 1:8 (8–9).

[About 121 B.C.]

[a]guards of the Lamanites, by night are [b]drunken; therefore let us send a proclamation among all this people that they gather together their flocks and herds, that they may drive them into the wilderness by night.

7 And I will go according to thy command and pay the last [a]tribute of wine to the Lamanites, and they will be [b]drunken; and we will pass through the secret pass on the left of their camp when they are drunken and asleep.

8 Thus we will depart with our women and our children, our flocks, and our herds into the wilderness; and we will travel around the land of [a]Shilom.

9 And it came to pass that the king hearkened unto the words of Gideon.

10 And king Limhi caused that his people should gather their flocks together; and he sent the tribute of wine to the Lamanites; and he also sent more wine, as a present unto them; and they did drink freely of the wine which king Limhi did send unto them.

11 And it came to pass that the people of king Limhi did [a]depart by night into the wilderness with their flocks and their herds, and they went round about the land of [b]Shilom in the wilderness, and bent their course towards the land of Zarahemla, being led by Ammon and his brethren.

12 And they had taken all their gold, and silver, and their precious things, which they could carry, and also their provisions with them, into the wilderness; and they pursued their journey.

13 And after being many days in the wilderness they [a]arrived in the land of Zarahemla, and joined Mosiah's people, and became his subjects.

14 And it came to pass that Mosiah [a]received them with joy; and he also received their [b]records, and also the [c]records which had been found by the people of Limhi.

15 And now it came to pass when the Lamanites had found that the people of Limhi had departed out of the land by night, that they sent an [a]army into the wilderness to pursue them;

16 And after they had pursued them two days, they could no longer follow their tracks; therefore they were lost in the wilderness.

An account of Alma and the people of the Lord, who were driven into the wilderness by the people of King Noah. Comprising chapters 23 and 24.

CHAPTER 23

Alma refuses to be king—He serves as high priest—The Lord chastens his people, and the Lamanites conquer the land of Helam—Amulon, leader of King Noah's wicked priests, rules subject to the Lamanite monarch.

Now Alma, having been [a]warned of the Lord that the armies of king Noah would come upon them, and having made it known to his people, therefore they gathered together their flocks, and took of their grain, and [b]departed into the wilderness before the armies of king Noah.

2 And the Lord did strengthen them, that the people of king Noah could not overtake them to destroy them.

3 And they fled [a]eight days' journey into the wilderness.

4 And they came to a land, yea, even a very beautiful and pleasant land, a land of pure water.

5 And they pitched their tents, and began to till the ground, and began

6a Mosiah 19: 28; 21: 5.
b Alma 55: 14 (8–17).
7a Mosiah 19: 26.
b TG Drunkenness.
8a Mosiah 7: 7 (5–16).
11a Mosiah 25: 8.
b Mosiah 11: 12 (12–13); Alma 23: 12.
13a Mosiah 25: 5.
14a Mosiah 24: 25.
b Mosiah 8: 5; 9: 1.
c Mosiah 8: 9.
15a Mosiah 23: 30 (30–39).
23 1a Mosiah 18: 34; Alma 5: 4. TG Warnings.
b Mosiah 27: 16.
3a Mosiah 24: 25.

[Between 145 and 121 B.C.]

to build buildings; yea, they were
[a]industrious, and did labor exceedingly.
6 And the people were desirous that
Alma should be their [a]king, for he
was beloved by his people.
7 But he said unto them: Behold,
it is not expedient that we should
have a king; for thus saith the Lord:
Ye shall [a]not esteem one flesh above
another, or one man shall not think
himself above another; therefore I
say unto you it is not expedient that
ye should have a king.
8 Nevertheless, if it [a]were possible
that ye could always have just men
to be your [b]kings it would be well
for you to have a king.
9 But remember the [a]iniquity of
king Noah and his [b]priests; and I
myself was [c]caught in a snare, and
did many things which were abominable in the sight of the Lord,
which caused me sore [d]repentance;
10 Nevertheless, [a]after much [b]trib-
ulation, the Lord did hear my cries,
and did answer my prayers, and has
made me an [c]instrument in his
hands in bringing [d]so many of you
to a knowledge of his truth.
11 Nevertheless, in this I do not
glory, for I am unworthy to glory
of myself.
12 And now I say unto you, ye have
been [a]oppressed by king Noah, and
have been in bondage to him and his
priests, and have been [b]brought into
iniquity by them; therefore ye were
bound with the [c]bands of iniquity.
13 And now as ye have been delivered by the power of God out of
these bonds; yea, even out of the
[a]hands of king Noah and his people,
and also from the [b]bonds of iniquity,
even so I desire that ye should [c]stand
fast in this [d]liberty wherewith ye
have been made free, and that ye
trust [e]no man to be a king over you.
14 And also trust no one to be your
[a]teacher nor your minister, except
he be a man of God, walking in his
ways and keeping his commandments.
15 Thus did Alma teach his people,
that every man should [a]love his
[b]neighbor [c]as himself, that there
should be no [d]contention among
them.
16 And now, Alma was their [a]high
priest, he being the founder of their
church.
17 And it came to pass that none
received [a]authority to preach or to
teach except it were by him from
God. Therefore he [b]consecrated all
their priests and all their teachers;
and none were consecrated except
they were just men.
18 Therefore they did watch over
their people, and did [a]nourish them
with things pertaining to righteousness.
19 And it came to pass that they
began to prosper exceedingly in the
land; and they called the land
[a]Helam.
20 And it came to pass that they
did multiply and prosper exceedingly in the land of Helam; and they
built a city, which they called the
city of Helam.
21 Nevertheless the Lord seeth fit

5*a* TG Industry; Work, Value of.
6*a* 1 Sam. 8: 5; 3 Ne. 6: 30.
7*a* Mosiah 27: 3 (3–5).
8*a* Mosiah 29: 13.
b TG Governments.
9*a* Prov. 16: 12; Mosiah 11: 2 (1–15); 29: 17 (17–19).
b Mosiah 17: 12 (1, 6, 12–18).
c Mosiah 17: 2 (1–4).
d Mosiah 18: 1.
10*a* D&C 58: 4.
b TG Tribulation.
c Alma 17: 9 (9–11); 26: 3.
d Mosiah 18: 35.
12*a* TG Oppression; Unrighteous Dominion.
b Mosiah 11: 2 (1–15).
c Isa. 58: 6; 2 Ne. 28: 19 (19–22); Alma 12: 11.
13*a* Mosiah 18: 34 (34–35).
b TG Bondage, Spiritual.
c Gal. 5: 1.
d TG Liberty.
e Mosiah 29: 13 (5–36).
14*a* Mosiah 2: 4; 18: 18 (18–22).
15*a* TG Love.
b TG Neighbor.
c Mosiah 18: 21.
d 3 Ne. 11: 29 (28–29).
16*a* Mosiah 18: 18; 26: 7.
17*a* TG Priesthood, Authority.
b Lev. 16: 32; 2 Ne. 5: 26.
18*a* Eph. 6: 4; 1 Tim. 4: 6.
19*a* Mosiah 27: 16; Alma 24: 1.

[Between 145 and 121 B.C.]

to [a]chasten his people; yea, he trieth their [b]patience and their faith.

22 Nevertheless—whosoever putteth his [a]trust in him the same shall be [b]lifted up at the last day. Yea, and thus it was with this people.

23 For behold, I will show unto you that they were brought into [a]bondage, and none could deliver them but the Lord their God, yea, even the God of Abraham and Isaac and of Jacob.

24 And it came to pass that he did deliver them, and he did show forth his mighty power unto them, and great were their rejoicings.

25 For behold, it came to pass that while they were in the land of Helam, yea, in the city of Helam, while tilling the land round about, behold an army of the Lamanites was in the borders of the land.

26 Now it came to pass that the brethren of Alma fled from their fields, and gathered themselves together in the city of Helam; and they were much frightened because of the appearance of the Lamanites.

27 But Alma went forth and stood among them, and exhorted them that they should not be frightened, but that they should remember the Lord their God and he would deliver them.

28 Therefore they hushed their fears, and began to cry unto the Lord that he would soften the hearts of the Lamanites, that they would spare them, and their wives, and their children.

29 And it came to pass that the Lord did soften the hearts of the Lamanites. And Alma and his brethren went forth and delivered themselves up into their hands; and the Lamanites took possession of the land of Helam.

30 Now the [a]armies of the Lamanites, which had followed after the people of king Limhi, had been lost in the wilderness for many days.

31 And behold, they had found those priests of king Noah, in a place which they called [a]Amulon; and they had begun to possess the land of Amulon and had begun to till the ground.

32 Now the name of the leader of those priests was [a]Amulon.

33 And it came to pass that Amulon did plead with the Lamanites; and he also sent forth their wives, who were the [a]daughters of the Lamanites, to plead with their brethren, that they should not destroy their husbands.

34 And the Lamanites had [a]compassion on Amulon and his brethren, and did not destroy them, because of their wives.

35 And [a]Amulon and his brethren did join the Lamanites, and they were traveling in the wilderness in search of the land of Nephi when they discovered the land of Helam, which was possessed by Alma and his brethren.

36 And it came to pass that the Lamanites promised unto Alma and his brethren, that if they would show them the [a]way which led to the land of Nephi that they would grant unto them their lives and their liberty.

37 But after Alma had shown them the way that led to the land of Nephi the Lamanites would not keep their promise; but they set [a]guards round about the land of Helam, over Alma and his brethren.

38 And the remainder of them went to the land of Nephi; and a part of them returned to the land of Helam, and also brought with them the wives and the children of the guards who had been left in the land.

21*a* Deut. 11: 2 (1–8); Hel. 12: 3; D&C 98: 21. TG Chastening.
b TG Patience.
22*a* TG Trust in God.
b 1 Ne. 13: 37; Alma 26: 7.
23*a* Alma 36: 2.
30*a* Mosiah 22: 15.
31*a* Mosiah 24: 1; Alma 23: 14.
32*a* Mosiah 24: 8.
33*a* Mosiah 20: 5; 25: 12.
34*a* TG Compassion.
35*a* Alma 25: 4.
36*a* Mosiah 18: 34.
37*a* Mosiah 24: 9 (8–15); Alma 5: 5.

[Between 145 and 121 B.C.]

39 And the king of the Lamanites had granted unto Amulon that he should be a king and a ruler over his people, who were in the land of Helam; nevertheless he should have no power to do anything contrary to the will of the king of the Lamanites.

CHAPTER 24

Amulon persecutes Alma and his people—They are to be put to death if they pray—The Lord makes their burdens seem light—He delivers them from bondage, and they return to Zarahemla.

AND it came to pass that Amulon did gain favor in the eyes of the king of the Lamanites; therefore, the king of the Lamanites granted unto him and his brethren that they should be appointed teachers over his people, yea, even over the people who were in the land of Shemlon, and in the land of Shilom, and in the [a]land of Amulon.

2 For the Lamanites had taken possession of all these lands; therefore, the king of the Lamanites had appointed kings over all these lands.

3 And now the name of the king of the Lamanites was [a]Laman, being called after the name of his father; and therefore he was called king Laman. And he was king over a numerous people.

4 And he appointed [a]teachers of the [b]brethren of Amulon in every land which was possessed by his people; and thus the [c]language of Nephi began to be taught among all the people of the Lamanites.

5 And they were a people friendly one with another; nevertheless they knew not God; neither did the brethren of Amulon teach them anything concerning the Lord their God, neither the law of Moses; nor did they teach them the words of Abinadi;

6 But they taught them that they should keep their record, and that they might write one to another.

7 And thus the Lamanites began to increase in riches, and began to [a]trade one with another and wax great, and began to be a cunning and a wise people, as to the wisdom of the world, yea, a very cunning people, delighting in all manner of wickedness and plunder, except it were among their own brethren.

8 And now it came to pass that [a]Amulon began to exercise [b]authority over Alma and his brethren, and began to persecute him, and cause that his children should persecute their children.

9 For Amulon knew Alma, that he had been [a]one of the king's priests, and that it was he that believed the words of Abinadi and was driven out before the king, and therefore he was wroth with him; for he was subject to king Laman, yet he exercised authority over them, and put [b]tasks upon them, and put [c]taskmasters over them.

10 And it came to pass that so great were their afflictions that they began to cry mightily to God.

11 And Amulon commanded them that they should stop their cries; and he [a]put guards over them to watch them, that whosoever should be found calling upon God should be put to death.

12 And Alma and his people did not raise their voices to the Lord their God, but did pour out their [a]hearts to him; and he did know the [b]thoughts of their hearts.

13 And it [a]came to pass that the voice of the Lord came to them in their afflictions, saying: Lift up

---

24 1*a* Mosiah 23:31; Alma 21:3 (2–4).
3*a* Mosiah 9:10 (10–11); 10:6.
4*a* Mosiah 2:4; 18:18 (18–22); 23:14.
b Mosiah 23:9 (9, 12, 31).
c Omni 1:18.
7*a* Gen. 34:10 (10–21); 4 Ne. 1:46.
8*a* Mosiah 23:32.
b D&C 121:39.
9*a* Mosiah 17:2 (1–4); 23:9.
b Mosiah 21:3 (3–6).
c Mosiah 23:37 (37–39).
11*a* Dan. 6:7 (7–27).
12*a* TG Prayer.
b Ps. 139:2; Matt. 12:25.
13*a* Jer. 33:3 (1–3); Matt. 6:6.

[Between 145 and 121 B.C.]

your heads and be of good comfort, for I know of the covenant which ye have made unto me; and I will covenant with my people and deliver them out of bondage.

14 And I will also ease the [a]burdens which are put upon your shoulders, that even you cannot feel them upon your backs, even while you are in bondage; and this will I do that ye may stand as [b]witnesses for me hereafter, and that ye may know of a surety that I, the Lord God, do visit my people in their [c]afflictions.

15 And now it came to pass that the burdens which were laid upon Alma and his brethren were made light; yea, the Lord did [a]strengthen them that they could bear up their [b]burdens with ease, and they did submit cheerfully and with [c]patience to all the will of the Lord.

16 And it came to pass that so great was their faith and their patience that the voice of the Lord came unto them again, saying: Be of good comfort, for on the morrow I will deliver you out of bondage.

17 And he said unto Alma: Thou shalt go before this people, and I will go [a]with thee and deliver this people out of [b]bondage.

18 Now it came to pass that Alma and his people in the night-time gathered their flocks together, and also of their grain; yea, even all the night-time were they gathering their flocks together.

19 And in the morning the Lord caused a [a]deep sleep to come upon the Lamanites, yea, and all their task-masters were in a profound sleep.

20 And Alma and his people departed into the wilderness; and when they had traveled all day they pitched their tents in a valley, and they called the valley Alma, because he led their way in the wilderness.

21 Yea, and in the valley of Alma they poured out their [a]thanks to God because he had been merciful unto them, and eased their [b]burdens, and had delivered them out of bondage; for they were in bondage, and none could deliver them except it were the Lord their God.

22 And they gave [a]thanks to God, yea, all their men and all their women and all their children that could speak lifted their voices in the praises of their God.

23 And now the Lord said unto Alma: Haste thee and get thou and this people out of this land, for the Lamanites have awakened and do pursue thee; therefore get thee out of this land, and I will stop the Lamanites in this valley that they come no further in pursuit of this people.

24 And it came to pass that they departed out of the valley, and took their journey into the wilderness.

25 And after they had been in the wilderness [a]twelve days *they arrived in the land of Zarahemla; and king Mosiah did also [b]receive them with joy.

CHAPTER 25

The people (the Mulekites) of Zarahemla become Nephites—They learn of the people of Alma and of Zeniff—Alma baptizes Limhi and all his people—Mosiah authorizes Alma to organize the Church of God.

AND now king Mosiah caused that all the people should be gathered together.

2 Now there were not so many of the children of Nephi, or so many of those who were descendants of

14*a* Isa. 46:4 (3–4).
b TG Witnesses.
c TG Adversity; Affliction.
15*a* Matt. 11:28 (28–30).
b Alma 31:38; 33:23.
c 2 Cor. 4:16; D&C 54:10. TG Patience.
17*a* Ex. 3:12; 1 Ne. 17:55; Alma 38:4.
b Mosiah 25:10. TG Bondage, Physical.
19*a* 1 Sam. 26:12; Alma 55:15 (15–16).
21*a* TG Thanksgiving.
b Ps. 81:6 (5–6).
22*a* TG Thanksgiving.
25*a* Mosiah 23:3.
b Mosiah 22:14.

[*About 120 B.C.]

Nephi, as there were of the [a]people
of Zarahemla, who was a descendant of [b]Mulek, and those who came
with him into the wilderness.
3 And there were not so many of
the people of Nephi and of the people
of Zarahemla as there were of the
Lamanites; yea, they were not half
so numerous.
4 And now all the people of Nephi
were assembled together, and also
all the people of Zarahemla, and
they were gathered together in two
bodies.
5 And it came to pass that Mosiah
did read, and caused to be read, the
records of Zeniff to his people; yea,
he read the records of the people
of Zeniff, from the time they [a]left
the land of Zarahemla until they
[b]returned again.
6 And he also read the account of
Alma and his brethren, and all their
afflictions, from the time they left
the land of Zarahemla until the time
they returned again.
7 And now, when Mosiah had made
an end of reading the records, his
people who tarried in the land were
struck with wonder and amazement.
8 For they knew not what to think;
for when they beheld those that had
been delivered [a]out of bondage they
were filled with exceedingly great
joy.
9 And again, when they thought
of their brethren who had been
[a]slain by the Lamanites they were
filled with sorrow, and even shed
many tears of sorrow.
10 And again, when they thought
of the immediate goodness of God,
and his power in delivering Alma
and his brethren out of the hands of
the Lamanites and of [a]bondage,
they did raise their voices and give
thanks to God.
11 And again, when they thought
upon the Lamanites, who were their
brethren, of their sinful and [a]pol-
luted state, they were filled with
[b]pain and anguish for the [c]welfare of
their souls.
12 And it came to pass that those
who [a]were the children of Amulon
and his brethren, who had taken to
wife the [b]daughters of the Lamanites, were displeased with the conduct of their fathers, and they
would no longer be called by the
names of their fathers, therefore
they took upon themselves the
name of Nephi, that they might be
called the children of Nephi and be
numbered among those who were
[c]called Nephites.
13 And now all the people of
Zarahemla were [a]numbered with the
Nephites, and this because the
kingdom had been conferred upon
none but those who were descendants of Nephi.
14 And now it came to pass that
when Mosiah had made an end of
speaking and reading to the people,
he desired that Alma should also
speak to the people.
15 And Alma did speak unto them,
when they were assembled together
in large bodies, and he went from
one body to another, preaching
unto the people repentance and
faith on the Lord.
16 And he did exhort the people of
Limhi and his brethren, all those
that had been delivered out of bondage, that they should remember that
it was the Lord that did deliver
them.
17 And it came to pass that after
Alma had taught the people many
things, and had made an end of
speaking to them, that king Limhi
was desirous that he might be baptized; and all his people were

25 2*a* Hel. 6: 10.
b Ezek. 17: 22 (22–23); Omni 1: 15 (14–19).
5*a* Mosiah 9: 3 (3–4).
b Mosiah 22: 13.
8*a* Mosiah 22: 11 (11–13).
9*a* Mosiah 21: 29 (8, 29).
10*a* Mosiah 24: 17; 27: 16.
11*a* TG Pollution.
b Mosiah 28: 3 (3–4); Alma 13: 27.
c 2 Ne. 6: 3; Jacob 2: 3. TG Worth of Souls.
12*a* Mosiah 20: 3 (3–5).
b Mosiah 23: 33.
c Jacob 1: 14 (13–14); Alma 2: 11.
13*a* Omni 1: 19.

[About 120 B.C.]

desirous that they might be baptized also.

18 Therefore, Alma did go forth into the water and did [a]baptize them; yea, he did baptize them after the manner he did his brethren in the [b]waters of Mormon; yea, and as many as he did baptize did belong to the church of God; and this because of their belief on the words of Alma.

19 And it came to pass that king Mosiah granted unto Alma that he might establish [a]churches throughout all the land of Zarahemla; and gave him power to [b]ordain [c]priests and [d]teachers over every church.

20 Now this was done because there were so many people that they could not all be governed by one teacher; neither could they all hear the word of God in one assembly;

21 Therefore they did [a]assemble themselves together in different bodies, being called churches; every church having their priests and their teachers, and every priest preaching the word according as it was delivered to him by the mouth of Alma.

22 And thus, notwithstanding there being many churches they were all one [a]church, yea, even the church of God; for there was nothing preached in all the churches except it were repentance and faith in God.

23 And now there were seven churches in the land of Zarahemla. And it came to pass that whosoever were desirous to take upon them the [a]name of Christ, or of God, they did join the churches of God;

24 And they were called the [a]people of God. And the Lord did pour out his [b]Spirit upon them, and they were blessed, and prospered in the land.

CHAPTER 26

Many members of the Church are led into sin by unbelievers—Alma is promised eternal life—Those who repent and are baptized gain forgiveness—Church members in sin who repent and confess to Alma and to the Lord shall be forgiven; otherwise they shall be excommunicated.

Now it came to pass that there were many of the rising generation that could not understand the [a]words of king Benjamin, being little children at the time he spake unto his people; and they did [b]not believe the tradition of their fathers.

2 They did not believe what had been said concerning the resurrection of the dead, neither did they believe concerning the coming of Christ.

3 And now because of their [a]unbelief they could not [b]understand the word of God; and their hearts were hardened.

4 And they would not be baptized; neither would they join the [a]church. And they were a separate people as to their faith, and remained so ever after, even in their [b]carnal and sinful state; for they would not call upon the Lord their God.

5 And now in the reign of Mosiah they were not half so numerous as the people of God; but because of the [a]dissensions among the brethren they became more numerous.

6 For it came to pass that they did [a]deceive many with their [b]flattering words, who were in the church, and did cause them to commit many sins; therefore it became expedient

18*a* Mosiah 21:35.
b Mosiah 18:16 (8–17).
19*a* Mosiah 26:17.
b TG Priesthood.
c TG Priest.
d TG Teacher.
21*a* TG Church.
22*a* Mosiah 18:17; 26:4.
23*a* TG Jesus Christ, Taking the Name of.
24*a* TG Sons and Daughters of God.
b TG God, Spirit of; Prosper.
26 1*a* Mosiah 2:1.
b TG Family, Children, Duties of.
3*a* TG Unbelief, Unbelievers.
b TG Understanding.
4*a* Mosiah 25:22 (18–23); Alma 4:5 (4–5).
b TG Man, Natural, Not Spiritually Reborn.
5*a* TG Apostasy.
6*a* Col. 2:18 (16–23). TG Deceit.
b TG Flattery.

[About 120 B.C.]

that those who committed sin, that
were in the church, should be
[c]admonished by the church.
7 And it came to pass that they
were brought before the priests, and
delivered up unto the [a]priests by the
teachers; and the priests brought
them before Alma, who was the
[b]high priest.
8 Now king Mosiah had given
Alma the [a]authority over the
[b]church.
9 And it came to pass that Alma
did not know concerning them; but
there were many [a]witnesses against
them; yea, the people stood and
testified of their iniquity in abundance.
10 Now there had not any such
thing happened before in the
church; therefore Alma was troubled
in his spirit, and he caused that they
should be brought before the king.
11 And he said unto the king:
Behold, here are many whom we
have brought before thee, who are
accused of their brethren; yea, and
they have been taken in divers
iniquities. And they do not repent
of their iniquities; therefore we have
brought them before thee, that thou
mayest judge them according to
their crimes.
12 But king Mosiah said unto
Alma: Behold, I judge them not;
therefore I [a]deliver them into thy
hands to be judged.
13 And now the spirit of Alma was
again troubled; and he went and
inquired of the Lord what he should
do concerning this matter, for he
feared that he should do wrong in
the sight of God.
14 And it came to pass that after
he had poured out his whole soul to
God, the [a]voice of the Lord came to
him, saying:
15 Blessed art thou, Alma, and
blessed are they who were baptized
in the [a]waters of Mormon. Thou art
blessed because of thy exceeding
[b]faith in the words alone of my
servant Abinadi.
16 And blessed are they because of
their exceeding faith in the words
alone which thou hast spoken unto
them.
17 And blessed art thou because
thou hast established a [a]church
among this people; and they shall
be established, and they shall be my
people.
18 Yea, blessed is this people who
are willing to bear my [a]name; for in
my [b]name shall they be called; and
they are mine.
19 And because thou hast inquired
of me concerning the transgressor,
thou art blessed.
20 Thou art my servant; and I
covenant with thee that thou shalt
have [a]eternal life; and thou shalt
serve me and go forth in my name,
and shalt gather together my sheep.
21 And he that will hear my voice
shall be my [a]sheep; and him shall ye
receive into the church, and him
will I also receive.
22 For behold, [a]this is my [b]church;
whosoever is [c]baptized shall be
baptized unto repentance. And
whomsoever ye receive shall [d]believe
in my name; and him will I freely
[e]forgive.
23 For it is I that taketh upon me
the [a]sins of the world; for it is I that
hath [b]created them; and it is I that
granteth unto him that believeth

6*c* Alma 5: 57 (57–58); 6: 3. TG Warnings.
7*a* TG Priest.
b Mosiah 23: 16; 29: 42.
8*a* TG Delegation of Responsibility.
b TG Church Organization.
9*a* TG Witnesses.
12*a* D&C 42: 87 (78–93).
14*a* TG Guidance, Divine.
15*a* Mosiah 18: 30.
b Mosiah 17: 2; D&C 46: 14. TG Faith.
17*a* Mosiah 25: 19 (19–24).
18*a* Mosiah 1: 11; 5: 8. TG Jesus Christ, Taking the Name of.
b Deut. 28: 10.
20*a* TG Election.
21*a* TG Jesus Christ, Good Shepherd.
22*a* Mosiah 27: 13.
b TG Jesus Christ, Head of the Church.
c 2 Ne. 9: 23.
d TG Baptism, Qualifications for.
e TG Remission of Sins.
23*a* TG Jesus Christ, Redeemer.
b TG Jesus Christ, Creator.

[Probably between 120 and 100 B.C.]

unto the end a place at my right hand.

24 For behold, in my name are they called; and if they [a]know me they shall come forth, and shall have a place eternally at my right hand.

25 And it shall come to pass that when the [a]second trump shall sound then shall they that never [b]knew me come forth and shall stand before me.

26 And then shall they know that I am the Lord their God, that I am their Redeemer; but they would not be redeemed.

27 And then I will confess unto them that I never [a]knew them; and they shall [b]depart into [c]everlasting fire prepared for the devil and his angels.

28 Therefore I say unto you, that he that will not [a]hear my voice, the same shall ye not receive into my church, for him I will not receive at the last day.

29 Therefore I say unto you, Go; and whosoever transgresseth against me, him shall ye [a]judge [b]according to the sins which he has committed; and if he [c]confess his sins before thee and me, and [d]repenteth in the sincerity of his heart, him shall ye [e]forgive, and I will forgive him also.

30 Yea, and [a]as often as my people [b]repent will I forgive them their trespasses against me.

31 And ye shall also [a]forgive one another your trespasses; for verily I say unto you, he that forgiveth not his [b]neighbor's trespasses when he says that he repents, the same hath brought himself under condemnation.

32 Now I say unto you, Go; and whosoever will [a]not repent of his sins the same shall not be numbered among my people; and this shall be observed from this time forward.

33 And it came to pass when Alma had heard these words he [a]wrote them down that he might have them, and that he might judge the people of that church according to the commandments of God.

34 And it came to pass that Alma went and judged those that had been taken in iniquity, according to the [a]word of the Lord.

35 And whosoever repented of their sins and did [a]confess them, them he did number among the people of the church;

36 And those that would not confess their sins and repent of their iniquity, the same were not numbered among the people of the church, and their names were [a]blotted out.

37 And it came to pass that Alma did regulate all the affairs of the church; and they began again to have peace and to prosper exceedingly in the affairs of the church, walking circumspectly before God, receiving many, and baptizing many.

38 And now all these things did Alma and his [a]fellow laborers do who were over the church, [b]walking in all diligence, teaching the word of God in all things, suffering all manner of afflictions, being persecuted by all those who did not belong to the church of God.

39 And they did admonish their

24*a* John 17: 3.
25*a* Dan. 12: 2 (1–2).
b 3 Ne. 14: 23 (21–23); D&C 76: 85 (81–86); 112: 26.
27*a* Matt. 7: 23 (21–23).
b Luke 13: 27.
c 1 Ne. 15: 35 (32–36).
28*a* 2 Ne. 9: 31; D&C 1: 14 (2, 11, 14); Moses 6: 27.
29*a* TG Judgment.
b TG Accountability.
c Num. 5: 7 (6–10); Alma 17: 4; 3 Ne. 1: 25. TG Confession.
d TG Repentance.
e TG Forgiveness.
30*a* Moro. 6: 8.
b Ezek. 33: 11 (11, 15–16); Amos 5: 4 (4–8); Acts 3: 19 (19–20); 2 Ne. 1: 20; Mosiah 29: 20.
31*a* Col. 3: 13 (12–14); 3 Ne. 13: 14 (14–15); D&C 64: 10 (9–10).
b TG Neighbor.
32*a* Alma 1: 24. TG Excommunication.
33*a* TG Scriptures, Writing of.
34*a* 2 Ne. 33: 14 (13–15).
35*a* TG Confession.
36*a* Ex. 32: 33; Ps. 9: 5; 109: 13; Alma 1: 24. TG Book of Life.
38*a* TG Church Organization.
b TG Walking with God.

[Probably between 120 and 100 B.C.]

brethren; and they were also
[a]admonished, every one by the word
of God, according to his sins, or to
the sins which he had committed,
being commanded of God to [b]pray
without ceasing, and to give [c]thanks
in all things.

CHAPTER 27

Mosiah forbids persecution and enjoins equality—Alma the younger and the four sons of Mosiah seek to destroy the Church—An angel appears and commands them to cease their evil course—Alma is struck dumb—All mankind must be born again to gain salvation—Alma and the sons of Mosiah declare glad tidings.

AND now it came to pass that the
persecutions which were inflicted
on the church by the unbelievers
became so great that the church
began to murmur, and complain to
their leaders concerning the matter;
and they did complain to Alma.
And Alma laid the case before their
king, Mosiah. And Mosiah [a]consulted with his priests.
2 And it came to pass that king
Mosiah sent a proclamation throughout the land round about that there
should not any unbeliever [a]perse-
cute any of those who belonged to
the church of God.
3 And there was a strict command
throughout all the churches that
there should be no [a]persecutions
among them, that there should be
an [b]equality among all men;
4 That they should let no pride nor
haughtiness disturb their [a]peace;
that every man should [b]esteem his
[c]neighbor as himself, [d]laboring with
their own hands for their support.
5 Yea, and all their priests and
teachers [a]should [b]labor with their
own hands for their support, in all
cases save it were in sickness, or in
much want; and doing these things,
they did abound in the [c]grace of
God.
6 And there began to be much
peace again in the land; and the
people began to be very numerous,
and began to scatter abroad upon
the face of the earth, yea, on the
north and on the south, on the east
and on the west, building large
cities and villages in all quarters of
the land.
7 And the Lord did [a]visit them and
[b]prosper them, and they became a
large and wealthy people.
8 Now the sons of Mosiah were
numbered among the [a]unbelievers;
and also one of the sons of Alma was
numbered among them, he being
called Alma, after his father; nevertheless, he became a very wicked
and an [b]idolatrous man. And he was
a man of many words, and did speak
much [c]flattery to the people; therefore he [d]led many of the people to do
after the manner of his [e]iniquities.
9 And he became a great hinder-
ment to the prosperity of the church
of God; [a]stealing away the hearts of
the people; causing much dissension
among the people; giving a chance
for the enemy of God to exercise his
[b]power over them.
10 And now it came to pass that
while he was going about to [a]destroy
the church of God, for he did go
about secretly with the sons of Mosiah seeking to destroy the church,

39*a* TG Warnings.
b 2 Ne. 32: 9 (8–9).
c TG Thanksgiving.
27 1*a* TG Counsel.
2*a* TG Persecution.
3*a* TG Malice.
b Mosiah 23: 7; 29: 32; Alma 30: 11.
4*a* TG Peace.
b TG Love.
c TG Neighbor.
d TG Industry; Labor.
5*a* Mosiah 18: 24 (24, 26); Alma 1: 3, 26.
b TG Work, Value of.
c TG Grace.
7*a* Ex. 3: 16.
b TG Prosper.
8*a* 1 Sam. 3: 13; 1 Ne. 2: 12 (12–13); Moses 5: 16. TG Unbelief, Unbelievers.
b TG Idolatry.
c TG Flattery.
d TG Peer Influence.
e Mal. 2: 8.
9*a* 2 Sam. 12: 14 (1–14); 15: 6 (1–6). TG Apostasy of Individuals.
b D&C 50: 7; 93: 39 (37, 39).
10*a* Acts 8: 3; Mosiah 28: 4 (3–4).

[Probably between 100 and 92 B.C.]

and to lead astray the people of
the Lord, contrary to the commandments of God, or even the king—
11 And as I said unto you, as they
were going about [a]rebelling against
God, behold, the [b]angel of the Lord
[c]appeared unto them; and he descended as it were in a [d]cloud; and
he spake as it were with a voice of
thunder, which caused the earth to
shake upon which they stood;
12 And so great was their astonishment, that they fell to the earth, and
understood not the words which he
spake unto them.
13 Nevertheless he cried again,
saying: Alma, arise and stand forth,
for why persecutest thou the church
of God? For the Lord hath said:
[a]This is my church, and I will establish it; and nothing shall [b]overthrow
it, save it is the transgression of my
people.
14 And again, the angel said:
Behold, the Lord hath [a]heard the
prayers of his people, and also the
[b]prayers of his servant, Alma, who
is thy father; for he has [c]prayed with
much faith concerning thee that
thou mightest be brought to the
[d]knowledge of the truth; therefore,
for this purpose have I come to
[e]convince thee of the power and
authority of God, that the [f]prayers
of his servants might be answered
according to their faith.
15 And now behold, can ye dispute the power of God? For behold,
doth not my voice shake the earth?
And can ye not also [a]behold me
before you? And I am sent from
God.
16 Now I say unto thee: Go, and
remember the captivity of thy
fathers in the land of [a]Helam, and
in the land of Nephi; and remember
how great things he has done for
them; for they were in [b]bondage,
and he has [c]delivered them. And
now I say unto thee, Alma, go thy
way, and seek to destroy the church
no more, that their prayers may be
answered, and this even if thou wilt
of [d]thyself be [e]cast off.
17 And now it came to pass that
these were the last words which the
angel spake unto Alma, and he
departed.
18 And now Alma and those that
were with him fell again to the earth,
for great was their astonishment;
for with their own eyes they had
beheld an [a]angel of the Lord; and
his voice was as thunder, which
[b]shook the earth; and they knew
that there was nothing save the
power of God that could shake the
earth and cause it to tremble as
though it would part asunder.
19 And now the astonishment of
Alma was so great that he became
[a]dumb, that he could not open his
mouth; yea, and he became weak,
even that he could not move his
hands; therefore he was taken by
those that were with him, and carried helpless, even until he was
laid before his father.
20 And they rehearsed unto his
father all that had happened unto
them; and his father rejoiced, for
he knew that it was the power of
God.
21 And he caused that a multitude
should be gathered together that
they might witness what the Lord

11*a* TG Disobedience; Rebellion.
b Alma 21: 5.
c Acts 9: 3 (1–9); Mosiah 27: 15; Alma 8: 15; 17: 2.
d Ex. 19: 9 (9, 16).
13*a* Mosiah 26: 22. TG Jesus Christ, Head of the Church.
b Hosea 13: 9. TG Apostasy of Individuals.
14*a* Dan. 10: 12; Abr. 1: 16 (15–16).
b 2 Cor. 1: 11; Alma 10: 22.
c TG Family, Love within.
d Hosea 4: 6.
e Alma 29: 10.
f Alma 19: 17; Morm. 9: 36 (36–37).
15*a* Mosiah 27: 11.
16*a* Mosiah 23: 19; Alma 24: 1.
b Mosiah 25: 10; Alma 5: 5 (5–6).
c Mosiah 23: 1 (1–4).
d Alma 30: 47.
e Micah 3: 6 (1–7); Matt. 8: 12 (11–12).
18*a* TG Angels.
b Isa. 6: 4; Alma 36: 7.
19*a* Dan. 10: 15; Luke 1: 20 (20–22).

[Probably between 100 and 92 B.C.]

had done for his son, and also for those that were with him.

22 And he caused that the priests should assemble themselves together; and they began to fast, and to pray to the Lord their God that he would open the mouth of Alma, that he might speak, and also that his limbs might receive their strength—that the eyes of the people might be opened to see and know of the goodness and glory of God.

23 And it came to pass after they had fasted and prayed for the space of [a]two days and two nights, the limbs of Alma received their strength, and he stood up and began to speak unto them, bidding them to be of good comfort:

24 For, said he, I have repented of my sins, and have been [a]redeemed of the Lord; behold I am born of the Spirit.

25 And the Lord said unto me: Marvel not that all mankind, yea, men and women, all nations, kindreds, tongues and people, must be [a]born again; yea, [b]born of God, [c]changed from their carnal and [d]fallen state, to a state of righteousness, being redeemed of God, becoming his [e]sons and daughters;

26 And thus they become new creatures; and unless they do this, they can in [a]nowise inherit the kingdom of God.

27 I say unto you, unless this be the case, they must be cast off; and this I know, because I was like to be cast off.

28 Nevertheless, after [a]wading through much [b]tribulation, repenting nigh unto death, the Lord in mercy hath seen fit to snatch me out of an [c]everlasting burning, and I am born of God.

29 My soul hath been [a]redeemed from the gall of bitterness and [b]bonds of iniquity. I was in the darkest abyss; but now I behold the marvelous light of God. My soul was [c]racked with eternal torment; but I am [d]snatched, and my soul is [e]pained no more.

30 I rejected my Redeemer, and denied that which had been spoken of by our fathers; but now that they may foresee that he will come, and that he remembereth every creature of his creating, he will make himself manifest unto [a]all.

31 Yea, [a]every knee shall bow, and every tongue confess before him. Yea, even at the last day, when all men shall stand to be [b]judged of him, then shall they confess that he is [c]God; then shall they confess, who live [d]without God in the world, that the judgment of an everlasting punishment is just upon them; and they shall quake, and tremble, and shrink beneath the glance of his [e]all-searching eye.

32 And now it came to pass that Alma began from this time forward to teach the people, and those who were with Alma at the time the angel appeared unto them, traveling round about through all the land, publishing to all the people the things which they had heard and seen, and preaching the word of God in much tribulation, being greatly persecuted by those who were unbelievers, being smitten by many of them.

23*a* Alma 36: 10.
24*a* Ps. 49: 15; Alma 27: 25; A of F 3.
25*a* Rom. 6: 3 (3–11). TG Conversion; Man, New, Spiritually Reborn.
b Mosiah 5: 7; Alma 5: 14 (14, 49).
c Moses 6: 65.
d TG Man, Natural, Not Spiritually Reborn.
e Mosiah 15: 10; Moro. 7: 19.
26*a* John 3: 5.
28*a* 1 Kgs. 18: 21.
b TG Tribulation.
c 2 Ne. 9: 16.
29*a* Isa. 38: 17.
b Isa. 58: 6.
c Mosiah 2: 38.
d HEB *natzal*, to snatch away from danger, to save; e.g. 2 Sam. 19: 9.
e TG Pain.
30*a* D&C 84: 46 (45–46).
31*a* Philip. 2: 10 (9–11); Mosiah 16: 1 (1–2); D&C 88: 104; 138: 23.
b TG Jesus Christ, Judge.
c Mosiah 7: 27; Alma 11: 39 (38–39).
d Eph. 2: 12; Alma 41: 11.
e TG God, Omniscience of.

[Probably between 100 and 92 B.C.]

33 But notwithstanding all this, they did impart much consolation to the church, confirming their faith, and exhorting them with long-suffering and much travail to keep the commandments of God.

34 And four of them were the [a]sons of Mosiah; and their names were Ammon, and Aaron, and Omner, and Himni; these were the names of the sons of Mosiah.

35 And they traveled throughout all the land of Zarahemla, and among all the [a]people who were under the reign of king Mosiah, [b]zealously striving to repair all the injuries which they had done to the church, [c]confessing all their sins, and publishing all the things which they had seen, and explaining the prophecies and the scriptures to all who desired to hear them.

36 And thus they were instruments in the hands of God in bringing many to the knowledge of the truth, yea, to the knowledge of their Redeemer.

37 And how blessed are they! For they did [a]publish [b]peace; they did publish good tidings of good; and they did declare unto the people that the Lord reigneth.

CHAPTER 28

The sons of Mosiah shall have eternal life—They go to preach to the Lamanites—Mosiah translates the Jaredite plates with the two seer stones.

Now it came to pass that after the [a]sons of Mosiah had done all these things, *they took a small number with them and returned to their father, the king, and desired of him that he would grant unto them that they might, with these whom they had [b]selected, go up to the land of [c]Nephi that they might preach the things which they had heard, and that they might impart the word of God to their brethren, the Lamanites—

2 [a]That perhaps they might bring them to the knowledge of the Lord their God, and convince them of the iniquity of their fathers; and that perhaps they might cure them of their [b]hatred towards the Nephites, that they might also be brought to rejoice in the Lord their God, that they might become friendly to one another, and that there should be no more contentions in all the land which the Lord their God had given them.

3 Now they were desirous that salvation should be declared to every creature, for they could not [a]bear that any human [b]soul should [c]perish; yea, even the very thoughts that any soul should endure [d]endless torment did cause them to quake and [e]tremble.

4 And thus did the Spirit of the Lord work upon them, for they were the very [a]vilest of sinners. And the Lord saw fit in his infinite [b]mercy to spare them; nevertheless they suffered much anguish of soul because of their iniquities, suffering much and fearing that they should be cast off forever.

5 And it came to pass that they did plead with their father many days that they might go up to the land of Nephi.

6 And king Mosiah went and [a]inquired of the Lord if he should let his sons go up among the Lamanites to preach the word.

34*a* Mosiah 28: 1; 29: 3; Alma 17: 1.
35*a* Mosiah 1: 10; 28: 18.
b TG Zeal.
c Alma 39: 13.
37*a* Mosiah 12: 21; 15: 14 (14–17).
b TG Peace of God.
28 1*a* Mosiah 27: 34.
b Alma 17: 8.
c Mosiah 9: 1 (1, 3–4, 14); Alma 50: 8 (8, 11).
2*a* Alma 17: 16.
b Jacob 7: 24; Mosiah 1: 5; Alma 26: 9.
3*a* 1 Ne. 7: 8; Mosiah 25: 11; Alma 13: 27 (27–30); 31: 2; 3 Ne. 17: 14; Moses 7: 41.
b TG Worth of Souls.
c Matt. 18: 14.
d Jacob 6: 10; Moro. 8: 21; D&C 19: 12 (10–12).
e 1 Cor. 2: 3.
4*a* Mosiah 27: 10; Alma 26: 18 (17–18).
b TG God, Mercy of.
6*a* Ex. 18: 15; Alma 43: 23.

[*About 92 B.C.]

7 And the Lord said unto Mosiah: Let them go up, for many shall believe on their words, and they shall have eternal life; and I will [a]deliver thy sons out of the hands of the Lamanites.

8 And it came to pass that Mosiah granted that they might go and do according to their request.

9 And they [a]took their journey into the wilderness to go up to preach the word among the Lamanites; and I shall give an [b]account of their proceedings hereafter.

10 Now king Mosiah had no one to confer the kingdom upon, for there was not any of his sons who [a]would accept of the kingdom.

11 Therefore he took the records which were engraven on the plates of [a]brass, and also the plates of [b]Nephi, and all the things which he had kept and preserved according to the commandments of God, after having translated and caused to be written the records which were on the [c]plates of gold which had been found by the people of Limhi, which were delivered to him by the hand of Limhi;

12 And this he did because of the great anxiety of his people; for they were desirous beyond measure to know concerning those people [a]who had been destroyed.

13 And now he translated them by the means of those two [a]stones which were fastened into the two rims of a bow.

14 Now these things were prepared from the beginning, and were handed down from generation to generation, for the purpose of interpreting languages;

15 And they have been kept and preserved by the hand of the Lord, that he should discover to every creature who should possess the land the iniquities and abominations of his people;

16 And whosoever has these things is called [a]seer, after the manner of old times.

17 Now after Mosiah had finished [a]translating these [b]records, behold, it gave an account of the people who were [c]destroyed, from the time that they were destroyed back to the building of the [d]great tower, at the time the Lord [e]confounded the language of the people and they were scattered abroad upon the face of all the earth, yea, and even from that time back until the creation of Adam.

18 Now this account did cause the people of Mosiah to mourn exceedingly, yea, they were filled with sorrow; nevertheless it gave them much knowledge, in the which they did rejoice.

19 And this account shall be [a]written hereafter; for behold, it is expedient that all people should know the things which are written in this account.

20 And now, as I said unto you, that after king Mosiah had done these things, he took the plates of [a]brass, and all the things which he had kept, and [b]conferred them upon Alma, who was the son of Alma; yea, all the records, and also the [c]interpreters, and conferred them upon him, and commanded him that he should keep and [d]preserve them, and also keep a record of the people, handing them down from one gen-

7*a* Alma 17: 35; 19: 23 (22–23).
9*a* Alma 17: 6 (6–9); 26: 1.
b IE in Alma, chapters 17–26.
10*a* Mosiah 29: 3 (1–3).
11*a* Mosiah 10: 16.
b W of M 1: 10.
c Mosiah 21: 27; Alma 37: 21 (21–31).
12*a* Mosiah 8: 8.
13*a* Ex. 28: 30; Mosiah 21: 28 (27–28); Abr. 3: 1; JS-H 1: 35.
16*a* Mosiah 8: 13 (13–18). TG Seer.
17*a* Omni 1: 20; Alma 9: 21.
b TG Scriptures, Writing of.
c Mosiah 8: 8 (7–12); Alma 22: 30.
d Ether 1: 3 (1–5).
e Gen. 11: 7 (6–9); Omni 1: 22.
19*a* Ether 1:1.
20*a* Mosiah 1: 3 (3–4); Alma 37: 3 (3–12).
b Alma 37: 1.
c TG Urim and Thummim.
d TG Scriptures, Preservation of.

[About 92 B.C.]

eration to another, even as they had
been handed down from the time
that Lehi left Jerusalem.

CHAPTER 29

Mosiah proposes that judges be chosen in place of a king—Unrighteous kings lead their people into sin—Alma the younger is chosen chief judge by the voice of the people—He is also the high priest over the Church—Alma the elder and Mosiah die.

Now when Mosiah had done this
he sent out throughout all the land,
among all the people, desiring to
know their will concerning who
should be their king.
2 And it came to pass that the
voice of the people came, saying:
We are desirous that Aaron thy son
should be our king and our ruler.
3 Now Aaron had gone up to the
land of Nephi, therefore the king
could not confer the kingdom upon
him; [a]neither would Aaron take
upon him the kingdom; neither
were any of the [b]sons of Mosiah
[c]willing to take upon them the
kingdom.
4 Therefore king Mosiah sent again
among the people; yea, even a
written word sent he among the
people. And these were the words
that were written, saying:
5 Behold, O ye my people, or my
brethren, for I esteem you as such,
I desire that ye should consider the
cause which ye are called to [a]con-
sider—for ye are desirous to have a
king.
6 Now I declare unto you that he
to whom the kingdom doth rightly
belong has declined, and will not
take upon him the kingdom.
7 And now if there should be
another appointed in his stead, behold I fear there would rise [a]con-
tentions among you. And who
knoweth but what my son, to whom
the kingdom doth belong, should
turn to be angry and [b]draw away a
part of this people after him, which
would cause wars and contentions
among you, which would be the
cause of shedding much blood and
perverting the way of the Lord, yea,
and destroy the souls of many
people.
8 Now I say unto you let us be wise
and consider these things, for we
have no right to destroy my son,
neither should we have any right to
destroy another if he should be
appointed in his stead.
9 And if my son should turn again
to his pride and vain things he
would recall the things which he had
said, and claim his right to the
kingdom, which would cause him
and also this people to commit much
sin.
10 And now let us be wise and look
forward to these things, and do that
which will make for the peace of this
people.
11 Therefore I will be your king the
remainder of my days; neverthe-
less, let [a]us appoint [b]judges, to judge
this people according to our law;
and we will newly arrange the affairs
of this people, for we will appoint
wise men to be judges, that will
judge this people according to the
commandments of God.
12 Now it is better that a man
should be [a]judged of God than of
man, for the judgments of God are
always just, but the judgments of
man are not always just.
13 Therefore, [a]if it were possible
that you could have [b]just men to be
your kings, who would establish the
[c]laws of God, and judge this people
according to his commandments,
yea, if ye could have men for your

29 3*a* Alma 17: 6.
b Mosiah 27: 34.
c Mosiah 28: 10.
5*a* 1 Sam. 8: 9 (9–19).
7*a* TG Contention.
b Judg. 8: 23; 9: 2 (1–55).
11*a* Mosiah 29: 25 (25–27, 41).
b Ex. 18: 13; Deut. 16: 18; Ezra 7: 25; Alma 46: 4; D&C 107: 74 (74, 78).
12*a* 2 Sam. 23: 3; 2 Chr. 1: 10; Ps. 50: 6; 75: 7; 2 Ne. 21: 4; D&C 98: 9; Moses 6: 57. TG God, Justice of.
13*a* Mosiah 23: 8, 13.
b 1 Kgs. 15: 14 (11–14).
c Ex. 18: 21; Neh. 7: 2.

[About 92 B.C.]

kings who would do even as my
father [d]Benjamin did for this
people—I say unto you, if this
could always be the case then it
would be expedient that ye should
always have kings to rule over you.
14 And even I myself have labored
with all the power and faculties
which I have possessed, to teach
you the commandments of God, and
to establish peace throughout the
land, that there should be no wars
nor contentions, no stealing, nor
plundering, nor murdering, nor any
manner of iniquity;
15 And whosoever has committed
iniquity, him have I [a]punished
according to the crime which he has
committed, according to the law
which has been given to us by our
fathers.
16 Now I say unto you, that because all men are not just it is not
expedient that ye should have a
[a]king or kings to rule over you.
17 For behold, how much [a]iniquity
doth one [b]wicked king cause to be
committed, yea, and what great
destruction!
18 Yea, remember king Noah, his
[a]wickedness and his abominations,
and also the wickedness and abominations of his people. Behold what
great destruction did come upon
them; and also because of their
iniquities they were brought into
[b]bondage.
19 And were it not for the interposition of their all-wise Creator,
and this because of their sincere
repentance, they must unavoidably
remain in bondage until now.
20 But behold, he did deliver them
because they did [a]humble themselves before him; and because they
[b]cried mightily unto him he did
deliver them out of bondage; and
thus doth the Lord work with his
power in all cases among the children of men, extending the arm of
[c]mercy towards them that put their
[d]trust in him.
21 And behold, now I say unto
you, ye cannot dethrone an iniquitous [a]king save it be through much
contention, and the shedding of
much blood.
22 For behold, he has his [a]friends in
iniquity, and he keepeth his guards
about him; and he teareth up the
laws of those who have reigned in
righteousness before him; and he
trampleth under his feet the commandments of God;
23 And he enacteth laws, and
sendeth them forth among his
people, yea, laws after the manner
of his own wickedness; and whosoever doth not obey his laws he
[a]causeth to be destroyed; and whosoever doth rebel against him he
will send his armies against them to
war, and if he can he will destroy
them; and thus an unrighteous
[b]king doth pervert the ways of all
righteousness.
24 And now behold I say unto you,
it is not expedient that such abominations should come upon you.
25 Therefore, choose you by the
[a]voice of this people, judges, that ye
may be [b]judged according to the
[c]laws which have been given you by
our fathers, which are correct, and
which were given them by the hand
of the Lord.
26 Now it is not common that the
[a]voice of the people desireth any-

13*d* Omni 1:25; W of M 1:18 (17–18).
15*a* Alma 1:32.
16*a* 1 Sam. 8:5 (4–22). TG Kings, Earthly.
17*a* 1 Kgs. 16:26 (25–26); Alma 46:9.
b Prov. 16:12; Mosiah 23:9 (8–10).
18*a* Mosiah 11:2 (1–15).
b 1 Sam. 8:11 (10–18); Mosiah 12:2 (2–8); Ether 6:23.
20*a* Mosiah 21:14.
b Ex. 2:23 (23–25); Alma 43:49 (49–50).
c Ezek. 33:11 (11, 15–16); Mosiah 26:30.
d TG Trust in God.
21*a* 1 Sam. 8:9; Prov. 25:5 (4–5).
22*a* 1 Kgs. 12:8 (8–15).
23*a* TG Tyranny; Unrighteous Dominion.
b TG Kings, Earthly.
25*a* Mosiah 29:11; Alma 2:3 (3–7). TG Citizenship.
b Ex. 18:22 (19–27).
c Deut. 4:8; Alma 34:11.
26*a* 1 Sam. 8:7; Alma 29:4; D&C 26:2. TG Common Consent.

[About 92 B.C.]

thing [b]contrary to that which is right; but it is common for the lesser part of the [c]people to desire that which is not right; therefore this shall ye observe and make it your law—to do your business by the voice of the people.

27 And [a]if the time comes that the voice of the people doth choose iniquity, then is the time that the judgments of God will come upon you; yea, then is the time he will visit you with great destruction even as he has hitherto visited this land.

28 And now if ye have judges, and they do not [a]judge you according to the law which has been given, ye can cause that they may be judged of a higher judge.

29 If your higher judges do not judge righteous judgments, ye shall cause that a small number of your lower judges should be gathered together, and they shall judge your higher judges, according to the voice of the people.

30 And I command you to do these things in the fear of the Lord; and I command you to do these things, and that ye have no king; that if these people commit sins and iniquities they shall be answered upon their own heads.

31 For behold I say unto you, the sins of many people have been [a]caused by the iniquities of their kings; therefore their iniquities are answered upon the heads of their kings.

32 And now I desire that this [a]inequality should be no more in this land, especially among this my people; but I desire that this land be a land of [b]liberty, and [c]every man may enjoy his rights and privileges alike, so long as the Lord sees fit that we may live and inherit the land, yea, even as long as any of our posterity remains upon the face of the land.

33 And many more things did king Mosiah write unto them, unfolding unto them all the trials and [a]troubles of a righteous king, yea, all the travails of soul for their people, and also all the murmurings of the people to their king; and he explained it all unto them.

34 And he told them that these things ought not to be; but that the burden should come upon all the people, that every man might [a]bear his part.

35 And he also unfolded unto them all the disadvantages they labored under, by having an unrighteous [a]king to rule over them;

36 Yea, all [a]his iniquities and abominations, and all the wars, and contentions, and bloodshed, and the stealing, and the plundering, and the committing of whoredoms, and all manner of iniquities which cannot be enumerated—telling them that these things ought not to be, that they were expressly repugnant to the commandments of God.

37 And now it came to pass, after king Mosiah had sent these things forth among the people they were [a]convinced of the truth of his words.

38 Therefore they relinquished their desires for a king, and became exceedingly anxious that every man should have an equal [a]chance throughout all the land; yea, and every man expressed a willingness to answer for his own sins.

39 Therefore, it came to pass that they assembled themselves together in bodies throughout the land, to cast in their [a]voices concerning who should be their [b]judges,

26*b* TG Disobedience.
c TG Governments.
27*a* Alma 2: 4 (3–7); 10: 19; Hel. 4: 21 (20–24); 5: 2.
28*a* Deut. 17: 8 (8–9).
31*a* 1 Kgs. 14: 16; 15: 26; 16: 2; 21: 22; Mosiah 29: 36.
32*a* Mosiah 27: 3; Alma 30: 11. TG Injustice.
b 2 Ne. 1: 7; 10: 11; Alma 46: 17 (10–28, 34). TG Liberty.
c Alma 27: 9.
33*a* TG Stewardship.
34*a* TG Accountability.
35*a* TG Kings, Earthly.
36*a* Mosiah 29: 31.
37*a* 1 Sam. 8: 19.
38*a* TG Agency.
39*a* TG Common Consent.
b Alma 62: 47.

[About 92 B.C.]

to judge them according to the [c]law
which had been given them; and
they were exceedingly rejoiced
because of the [d]liberty which had
been granted unto them.
40 And they did wax strong in love
towards Mosiah; yea, they did
esteem him more than any other
man; for they did not look upon
him as a [a]tyrant who was seeking
for gain, yea, for that [b]lucre which
doth [c]corrupt the soul; for he had
not exacted riches of them, neither
had he delighted in the shedding of
blood; but he had established [d]peace
in the land, and he had granted unto
his people that they should be
delivered from all manner of bondage; therefore they did esteem him,
yea, exceedingly, beyond measure.
41 And it came to pass that they
did [a]appoint [b]judges to rule over
them, or to judge them according
to the law; and this they did
throughout all the land.
42 And it came to pass that Alma
was appointed to be the first [a]chief
judge, he being also the [b]high priest,
his father having conferred the office
upon him, and having given him the
charge concerning all the affairs of
the church.
43 And now it came to pass that
Alma did [a]walk in the ways of the
Lord, and he did keep his commandments, and he did judge
righteous judgments; and there was
continual peace through the land.
44 And thus *commenced the
[a]reign of the judges throughout all
the land of Zarahemla, among all
the people who were called the
Nephites; and Alma was the first
and chief judge.
45 And now it came to pass that his
father died, being eighty and two
years old, having lived to fulfil the
commandments of God.
46 And it came to pass that
Mosiah [a]died also, in the thirty and
third year of his reign, being [b]sixty
and three years old; making in the
whole, five hundred and nine years
from the time Lehi left Jerusalem.
47 And thus ended the reign of the
kings over the people of Nephi; and
thus ended the days of Alma, who
was the founder of their church.

THE BOOK OF ALMA

THE SON OF ALMA

The account of Alma, who was the son of Alma, the first and chief judge over the people of Nephi, and also the high priest over the Church. An account of the reign of the judges, and the wars and contentions among the people. And also an account of a war between the Nephites and the Lamanites, according to the record of Alma, the first and chief judge.

CHAPTER 1

Nehor teaches false doctrines, establishes a church, introduces priestcraft, and slays Gideon—He is executed for his crimes—Priestcrafts and persecutions spread among the people—The priests support themselves, the people care for the poor, and the Church prospers.

39*c* Alma 1:14.
d TG Liberty.
40*a* TG Tyranny.
b Titus 1:11.
c TG Bribery.
d TG Peacemakers.
41*a* Alma 11:4.
b Judg. 2:16; Mosiah 29:11.
42*a* Alma 2:16; 7:1.
b Mosiah 26:7; Alma 4:4.
43*a* TG Walking with God.
44*a* Alma 17:6.
46*a* Alma 1:1.
b Mosiah 6:4.

[*91 B.C.]

NOW it came to pass that in the first year of the reign of the judges over the people of Nephi, from this time forward, king Mosiah having [a]gone the way of all the earth, having warred a good warfare, walking uprightly before God, leaving none to reign in his stead; nevertheless he had established [b]laws, and they were acknowledged by the people; therefore they were obliged to abide by the [c]laws which he had made.

2 And it came to pass that in the first year of the reign of Alma in the judgment-seat, there was a [a]man brought before him to be judged, a man who was large, and was noted for his much strength.

3 And he had gone about among the people, preaching to them that which he [a]termed to be the word of God, bearing down [b]against the church; declaring unto the people that every priest and teacher ought to become [c]popular; and they ought [d]not to labor with their hands, but that they ought to be supported by the people.

4 And he also testified unto the people that [a]all mankind should be saved at the last day, and that they [b]need not fear nor tremble, but that they might lift up their heads and rejoice; for the Lord had [c]created all men, and had also [d]redeemed [e]all men; and, in the end, all men should have eternal life.

5 And it came to pass that he did teach these things so much that many did believe on his words, even so many that they began to support him and give him [a]money.

6 And he began to be lifted up in the pride of his heart, and to wear very costly [a]apparel, yea, and even began to [b]establish a [c]church after the manner of his preaching.

7 And it came to pass as he was going, to preach to those who believed on his word, he met a man who belonged to the church of God, yea, even one of their [a]teachers; and he began to contend with him sharply, that he might lead away the people of the church; but the man withstood him, admonishing him with the [b]words of God.

8 Now the name of the man was [a]Gideon; and it was he who was an instrument in the hands of God in delivering the people of Limhi out of bondage.

9 Now, because Gideon withstood him with the words of God he was wroth with Gideon, and drew his sword and began to smite him. Now Gideon being [a]stricken with many years, therefore he was not able to withstand his blows, therefore he was [b]slain by the sword.

10 And the man who slew him was taken by the people of the church, and was brought before Alma, to be [a]judged according to the crimes which he had committed.

11 And it came to pass that he stood before Alma and pleaded for himself with much boldness.

12 But Alma said unto him: Behold, this is the first time that [a]priestcraft has been introduced among this people. And behold, thou art not only guilty of priestcraft, but hast endeavored to enforce it by the sword; and were

1 1*a* Mosiah 29: 46.
b Jarom 1: 5; Alma 4: 16; 8: 17; Hel. 4: 22.
c TG Citizenship.
2*a* Alma 1: 15.
3*a* Ezek. 13: 3 (1–4).
b TG Antichrist.
c Luke 6: 26; 1 Ne. 22: 23.
d Mosiah 18: 24 (24, 26); 27: 5 (3–5).
4*a* Alma 15: 15; 21: 6; 30: 17; Morm. 8: 31.
b TG Humility; Meekness.
c TG Jesus Christ, Creator; Man, Physical Creation of.
d TG Jesus Christ, Redeemer; Redemption.
e Moses 4: 1 (1–4).
5*a* Acts 8: 18 (17–23).
6*a* TG Apparel.
b TG Unrighteous Dominion.
c TG Devil, Church of.
7*a* TG Teacher.
b TG Word of God; Word of the Lord.
8*a* Mosiah 20: 17; 22: 3; Alma 2: 1.
9*a* Gen. 24: 1; 1 Ne. 18: 17.
b Alma 6: 7.
10*a* Mosiah 29: 42.
12*a* 2 Ne. 26: 29; Alma 2: 20; 14: 16. TG Priestcraft.

[About 91 B.C.]

[b]priestcraft to be enforced among this people it would prove their entire destruction.

13 And thou hast shed the [a]blood of a righteous man, yea, a man who has done much good among this people; and were we to spare thee his blood would come upon us for [b]vengeance.

14 Therefore thou art condemned to [a]die, according to the [b]law which has been given us by Mosiah, our last king; and it has been [c]acknowledged by this people; therefore this people must [d]abide by the law.

15 And it came to pass that they took him; and his name was [a]Nehor; and they carried him upon the top of the hill Manti, and there he was caused, or rather did acknowledge, between the heavens and the earth, that what he had taught to the people was contrary to the word of God; and there he suffered an ignominious [b]death.

16 Nevertheless, this did not put an end to the spreading of priestcraft through the land; for there were many who loved the vain things of the world, and they went forth preaching [a]false doctrines; and this they did for the sake of [b]riches and honor.

17 Nevertheless, they durst not [a]lie, if it were known, for fear of the law, for liars were punished; therefore they pretended to preach according to their belief; and now the law could have no power on any man for [b]his belief.

18 And they durst not [a]steal, for fear of the law, for such were punished; neither durst they rob, nor murder, for he that [b]murdered was punished unto [c]death.

19 But it came to pass that whosoever did not belong to the church of God began to persecute those that did belong to the church of God, and had taken upon them the name of Christ.

20 Yea, they did persecute them, and afflict them with all manner of words, and this because of their humility; because they were not proud in their own eyes, and because they did impart the word of God, one with another, without [a]money and without price.

21 Now there was a strict law among the people of the church, that there should [a]not any man, belonging to the church, arise and persecute those that did not belong to the church, and that there should be no persecution among themselves.

22 Nevertheless, there were many among them who began to be proud, and began to contend warmly with their adversaries, even unto blows; yea, they would smite one another with their [a]fists.

23 Now this was in the *second year of the reign of Alma, and it was a cause of much affliction to the church; yea, it was the cause of much trial with the church.

24 For the hearts of many were hardened, and their names were [a]blotted out, that they were remembered no more among the people of God. And also many [b]withdrew themselves from among them.

25 Now this was a great trial to those that did stand fast in the faith; nevertheless, they were [a]steadfast

---

12*b* Alma 21:4.
13*a* Prov. 28:17. TG Blood, Shedding of.
b Luke 18:7; D&C 121:5. TG Vengeance.
14*a* TG Capital Punishment.
b Mosiah 29:39.
c Hel. 1:8.
d TG Citizenship.
15*a* Alma 1:2; 2:1 (1, 20).
b Deut. 13:5 (1–9).
16*a* TG False Doctrine.
b TG Riches; Vanity.
17*a* TG Honesty; Lying.
b Alma 30:7 (7–12); A of F 11.
18*a* Alma 30:10. TG Stealing.
b TG Murder.
c TG Capital Punishment.
20*a* Isa. 55:1 (1–2).
21*a* Alma 4:8. TG Persecution.
22*a* Ex. 21:18 (18–19); Isa. 58:4.
24*a* Ex. 32:33; Mosiah 26:32, 36; Alma 6:3. TG Excommunication.
b Alma 46:7. TG Apostasy of Individuals.
25*a* TG Commitment; Steadfastness.

[*About 90 B.C.]

and immovable in keeping the commandments of God, and they bore with [b]patience the persecution which was heaped upon them.
26 And when the priests left their [a]labor to impart the word of God unto the people, the people also left their labors to hear the word of God. And when the priest had imparted unto them the word of God they all returned again diligently unto their labors; and the priest, not esteeming himself above his hearers, for the preacher was no better than the hearer, neither was the teacher any better than the learner; and thus they were all equal, and they did all labor, every man [b]according to his strength.
27 And they did [a]impart of their substance, every man according to that which he had, to the [b]poor, and the needy, and the sick, and the afflicted; and they did not wear costly [c]apparel, yet they were neat and comely.
28 And thus they did establish the affairs of the church; and thus they began to have continual peace again, notwithstanding all their persecutions.
29 And now, because of the steadiness of the church they began to be exceedingly [a]rich, having abundance of all things whatsoever they stood in need—an abundance of flocks and herds, and fatlings of every kind, and also abundance of grain, and of gold, and of silver, and of precious things, and abundance of [b]silk and fine-twined linen, and all manner of good homely [c]cloth.
30 And thus, in their [a]prosperous circumstances, they did not send away any who were [b]naked, or that were hungry, or that were athirst, or that were sick, or that had not been nourished; and they did not set their hearts upon [c]riches; therefore they were [d]liberal to all, both old and young, both bond and free, both male and female, whether out of the church or in the church, having no [e]respect to persons as to those who stood in need.
31 And thus they did [a]prosper and become far more wealthy than those who did not belong to their church.
32 For those who did not belong to their church did indulge themselves in [a]sorceries, and in [b]idolatry or [c]idleness, and in [d]babblings, and in [e]envyings and [f]strife; wearing costly apparel; being [g]lifted up in the pride of their own eyes; persecuting, lying, thieving, robbing, committing whoredoms, and murdering, and all manner of wickedness; nevertheless, the law was put in force upon all those who did transgress it, inasmuch as it was possible.
33 And it came to pass that by thus exercising the law upon them, every man suffering according to that which he had done, they became more still, and durst not commit any wickedness if it were known; therefore, there was much peace among the people of Nephi until the fifth year of the reign of the judges.

CHAPTER 2

Amlici seeks to be king and is rejected by the voice of the people—His followers make him king—The Amlicites

25*b* TG Patience.
26*a* Mosiah 18:24 (24, 26); 27:5 (3–5).
b Mosiah 4:27; D&C 10:4.
27*a* TG Almsgiving; Consecration.
b Luke 18:22; Acts 20:35 (33–35); Mosiah 4:26; D&C 42:30 (29–31).
c TG Vanity.
29*a* TG Riches; Treasure.
b Alma 4:6.
c Mosiah 10:5; Hel. 6:13. TG Clothing.
30*a* 2 Cor. 8:14; Jacob 2:19 (17–19).
b TG Poor.
c Job 31:25. TG Wealth.
d TG Generosity.
e Deut. 10:17; Alma 16:14; D&C 1:35.
31*a* TG Prosper.
32*a* TG Sorcery.
b TG Idolatry.
c TG Laziness.
d TG Gossip.
e TG Envy.
f TG Strife.
g 2 Kgs. 14:10; Jacob 2:13; Alma 31:25; Morm. 8:28. TG Pride.

[About 90 B.C.]

make war on the Nephites and are defeated—The Lamanites and Amlicites join forces and are defeated—Alma slays Amlici.

AND it came to pass in the commencement of the *fifth year of their
reign there began to be a contention
among the people; for a certain
[a]man, being called Amlici, he being
a very cunning man, yea, a wise man
as to the wisdom of the world, he
being after the order of the man that
slew [b]Gideon by the sword, who was
executed according to the law—
2 Now this Amlici had, by his cunning, [a]drawn away much people
after him; even so much that they
began to be very powerful; and they
began to endeavor to establish
Amlici to be a king over the people.
3 Now this was alarming to the
people of the church, and also to
all those who had not been drawn
away after the persuasions of
Amlici; for they knew that according to their law that such things
must be established by the [a]voice of
the people.
4 Therefore, if it were possible that
Amlici should gain the voice of the
people, he, being a wicked man,
would [a]deprive them of their rights
and privileges of the church; for
it was his intent to destroy the
church of God.
5 And it came to pass that the
people assembled themselves together throughout all the land,
every man according to his mind,
whether it were for or against
Amlici, in separate bodies, having
much dispute and wonderful [a]con-
tentions one with another.
6 And thus they did assemble
themselves together to cast in their
[a]voices concerning the matter; and
they were laid before the judges.
7 And it came to pass that the
[a]voice of the people came against
Amlici, that he was not made king
over the people.
8 Now this did cause much joy in
the hearts of those who were against
him; but Amlici did stir up those
who were in his favor to anger
against those who were not in his
favor.
9 And it came to pass that they
gathered themselves together, and
did [a]consecrate Amlici to be their
king.
10 Now when Amlici was made
king over them he commanded
them that they should take up arms
against their brethren; and this he
did that he might subject them to
him.
11 Now the people of Amlici were
distinguished by the name of
Amlici, being called [a]Amlicites; and
the remainder were [b]called Nephites, or the people of God.
12 Therefore the people of the
Nephites were aware of the intent
of the Amlicites, and therefore they
did prepare to meet them; yea, they
did arm themselves with swords,
and with cimeters, and with bows,
and with arrows, and with stones,
and with slings, and with all manner of [a]weapons of war, of every
kind.
13 And thus they were prepared to
meet the Amlicites at the time of
their coming. And there were
appointed [a]captains, and higher
captains, and chief captains, according to their numbers.
14 And it came to pass that Amlici
did arm his men with all manner of
weapons of war of every kind; and
he also appointed rulers and leaders
over his people, to lead them to war
against their brethren.
15 And it came to pass that the

2 1*a* Alma 1:15; 16:11; 24:28 (28–30).
b Alma 1:8.
2*a* 2 Sam. 15:6 (1–10).
3*a* Mosiah 29:25 (25–27); Alma 4:16 (16–17).
4*a* Mosiah 29:27; Alma 10:19; Hel. 5:2.
5*a* 3 Ne. 11:29.
6*a* TG Common Consent.
7*a* Mosiah 29:25 (25–27).
9*a* TG Unrighteous Dominion.
11*a* Alma 3:4.
b Jacob 1:14 (13–14); Mosiah 25:12; Alma 3:11 (11, 17).
12*a* Mosiah 10:8; Hel. 1:14.
13*a* Alma 16:5.

[*87 B.C.]

Amlicites came upon the hill Amnihu, which was east of the [a]river Sidon, which ran by the [b]land of Zarahemla, and there they began to make war with the Nephites.
16 Now Alma, being the [a]chief judge and the [b]governor of the people of Nephi, therefore he went up with his people, yea, with his captains, and chief captains, yea, at the head of his armies, against the Amlicites to battle.
17 And they began to slay the Amlicites upon the hill east of Sidon. And the Amlicites did contend with the Nephites with great strength, insomuch that many of the Nephites did fall before the Amlicites.
18 Nevertheless the Lord did strengthen the hand of the Nephites, that they slew the Amlicites with great slaughter, that they began to flee before them.
19 And it came to pass that the Nephites did pursue the Amlicites all that day, and did slay them with much slaughter, insomuch that there were [a]slain of the Amlicites twelve thousand five hundred thirty and two souls; and there were slain of the Nephites six thousand five hundred sixty and two souls.
20 And it came to pass that when Alma could pursue the Amlicites no longer he caused that his people should pitch their tents in the [a]valley of Gideon, the valley being called after that Gideon who was slain by the hand of [b]Nehor with the sword; and in this valley the Nephites did pitch their tents for the night.
21 And Alma sent spies to follow the remnant of the Amlicites, that he might know of their plans and their plots, whereby he might guard himself against them, that he might preserve his people from being destroyed.
22 Now those whom he had sent out to watch the camp of the Amlicites were called Zeram, and Amnor, and Manti, and Limher; these were they who went out with their men to watch the camp of the Amlicites.
23 And it came to pass that on the morrow they returned into the camp of the Nephites in great haste, being greatly astonished, and struck with much fear, saying:
24 Behold, we followed the [a]camp of the [b]Amlicites, and to our great astonishment, in the land of Minon, above the land of Zarahemla, in the course of the land of [c]Nephi, we saw a numerous host of the Lamanites; and behold, the Amlicites have joined them;
25 And they are upon our brethren in that land; and they are fleeing before them with their flocks, and their wives, and their children, towards our city; and except we make haste they obtain possession of our city, and our fathers, and our wives, and our children be slain.
26 And it came to pass that the people of Nephi took their tents, and departed out of the valley of Gideon towards their [a]city, which was the city of [b]Zarahemla.
27 And behold, as they were crossing the river Sidon, the Lamanites and the Amlicites, being as [a]numerous almost, as it were, as the sands of the sea, came upon them to destroy them.
28 Nevertheless, the Nephites being [a]strengthened by the hand of the Lord, having prayed mightily to him that he would deliver them out of the hands of their enemies, therefore the Lord did hear their cries, and did strengthen them, and the Lamanites and the Amlicites did fall before them.
29 And it came to pass that Alma fought with Amlici with the sword,

15*a* Alma 3:3.
b Omni 1:13; Mosiah 1:1.
16*a* Mosiah 29:42.
b Mosiah 1:10.
19*a* Alma 3:1 (1–2, 26); 4:2.
20*a* Alma 6:7; 8:1.
b Alma 1:12 (7–15); 14:16.
24*a* Alma 3:20.
b Alma 3:4 (4, 13–18).
c 2 Ne. 5:8; Alma 20:1.
26*a* Alma 6:4.
b Omni 1:14 (14, 18).
27*a* Jarom 1:6.
28*a* Deut. 31:6.

[87 B.C.]

face to face; and they did contend mightily, one with another.

30 And it came to pass that Alma, being a man of God, being exercised with much [a]faith, cried, saying: O Lord, have mercy and [b]spare my life, that I may be an instrument in thy hands to save and preserve this people.

31 Now when Alma had said these words he contended again with Amlici; and he was strengthened, insomuch that he slew Amlici with the sword.

32 And he also contended with the king of the Lamanites; but the king of the Lamanites fled back from before Alma and sent his guards to contend with Alma.

33 But Alma, with his guards, contended with the guards of the king of the Lamanites until he slew and drove them back.

34 And thus he cleared the ground, or rather the bank, which was on the west of the river Sidon, throwing the bodies of the Lamanites who had been slain into the waters of Sidon, that thereby his people might have room to cross and contend with the Lamanites and the Amlicites on the west side of the river Sidon.

35 And it came to pass that when they had all crossed the river Sidon that the Lamanites and the Amlicites began to flee before them, notwithstanding they were so numerous that they could not be numbered.

36 And they fled before the Nephites towards the wilderness which was west and north, away beyond the borders of the land; and the Nephites did pursue them with their might, and did slay them.

37 Yea, they were met on every hand, and slain and driven, until they were scattered on the west, and on the north, until they had reached the wilderness, which was called Hermounts; and it was that part of the wilderness which was infested by wild and ravenous beasts.

38 And it came to pass that many died in the wilderness of their wounds, and were devoured by those beasts and also the vultures of the air; and their bones have been found, and have been heaped up on the earth.

CHAPTER 3

The Amlicites had marked themselves according to the prophetic word—The Lamanites had been cursed for their rebellion—Men bring their own curses upon themselves—The Nephites defeat another Lamanite army.

AND it came to pass that the Nephites who were not [a]slain by the weapons of war, after having buried those who had been slain—now the number of the slain were not numbered, because of the greatness of their number—after they had finished burying their dead they all returned to their lands, and to their houses, and their wives, and their children.

2 Now many women and children had been slain with the sword, and also many of their flocks and their herds; and also many of their fields of grain were destroyed, for they were trodden down by the hosts of men.

3 And now as many of the Lamanites and the Amlicites who had been slain upon the bank of the river Sidon were cast into the [a]waters of Sidon; and behold their bones are in the depths of the [b]sea, and they are many.

4 And the [a]Amlicites were distinguished from the Nephites, for they had [b]marked themselves with red in their foreheads after the manner of the Lamanites; nevertheless they had not shorn their heads like unto the Lamanites.

5 Now the heads of the Lamanites were shorn; and they were [a]naked,

30*a* TG Faith.
b Alma 3:22.
3 1*a* Alma 2:19; 4:2.
3*a* Alma 2:15; 4:4.
b Alma 44:22.
4*a* Alma 2:11, 24.
b Alma 3:13 (13–19).
5*a* Enos 1:20; Mosiah 10:8; Alma 43:20 (18–21).

[87 B.C.]

save it were skin which was girded
about their loins, and also their
armor, which was girded about
them, and their bows, and their
arrows, and their stones, and their
slings, and so forth.
6 And the skins of the Lamanites
were dark, according to the mark
which was set upon their fathers,
which was a [a]curse upon them because of their transgression and
their rebellion against their brethren, who consisted of Nephi, Jacob,
and Joseph, and Sam, who were
just and holy men.
7 And their brethren sought to
destroy them, therefore they were
cursed; and the Lord God set a
[a]mark upon them, yea, upon Laman
and Lemuel, and also the sons of
Ishmael, and Ishmaelitish women.
8 And this was done that their seed
might be distinguished from the
seed of their brethren, that thereby
the Lord God might preserve his
people, that they might not [a]mix
and believe in incorrect [b]traditions
which would prove their destruction.
9 And it came to pass that whosoever did mingle his seed with that
of the Lamanites did bring the same
curse upon his seed.
10 Therefore, whosoever suffered
himself to be led away by the
Lamanites was called under that
head, and there was a mark set
upon him.
11 And it came to pass that whosoever would not believe in the
[a]tradition of the Lamanites, but
believed those records which were
brought out of the land of Jerusalem, and also in the tradition of
their fathers, which were correct,
who believed in the commandments
of God and kept them, were [b]called
the Nephites, or the people of
Nephi, from that time forth—
12 And it is they who have kept
the records which are [a]true of their
people, and also of the people of the
Lamanites.
13 Now we will return again to the
Amlicites, for they also had a
[a]mark set upon them; yea, they set
the mark upon themselves, yea,
even a mark of red upon their foreheads.
14 Thus the word of God is fulfilled, for these are the words which
he said to Nephi: Behold, the
Lamanites have I cursed, and I will
set a mark on them that they and
their seed may be [a]separated from
thee and thy seed, from this time
henceforth and forever, except they
repent of their wickedness and
[b]turn to me that I may have mercy
upon them.
15 And again: I will set a mark
upon him that mingleth his seed
with thy brethren, that they may
be cursed also.
16 And again: I will set a mark
upon him that fighteth against thee
and thy seed.
17 And again, I say he that
departeth from thee shall no more
be called thy seed; and I will bless
thee, and whomsoever shall be
called thy seed, henceforth and
forever; and these were the promises of the Lord unto Nephi and to
his seed.
18 Now the Amlicites knew not
that they were fulfilling the words
of God when they began to mark
themselves in their foreheads;
nevertheless they had come out in
open [a]rebellion against God; therefore it was expedient that the curse
should fall upon them.
19 Now I would that ye should
see that they brought upon themselves the [a]curse; and even so doth
every man that is cursed bring

6*a* 1 Ne. 2: 23; 2 Ne. 5: 21 (21–24).
7*a* 1 Ne. 12: 23.
8*a* TG Marriage, Interfaith; Separation.
b Mosiah 10: 12 (11–18); Alma 9: 16.
11*a* Alma 17: 9 (9–11).
b Alma 2: 11.
12*a* Mosiah 1: 6; Ether 4: 11 (6–11).
13*a* Alma 3: 4.
14*a* TG Separation.
b 2 Ne. 30: 6 (4–7).
18*a* Josh. 22: 18; 4 Ne. 1: 38. TG Rebellion.
19*a* 2 Ne. 5: 21 (21–25); Alma 17: 15.

upon himself his own condemnation.
20 Now it came to pass that not many days after the battle which was fought in the land of Zarahemla, by the Lamanites and the Amlicites, that there was another army of the Lamanites came in upon the people of Nephi, in the [a]same place where the first army met the Amlicites.
21 And it came to pass that there was an army sent to drive them out of their land.
22 Now Alma himself being afflicted with a [a]wound did not go up to battle at this time against the Lamanites;
23 But he sent up a numerous army against them; and they went up and slew many of the Lamanites, and drove the remainder of them out of the borders of their land.
24 And then they returned again and began to establish peace in the land, being troubled no more for a time with their enemies.
25 Now all these things were done, yea, all these wars and contentions were commenced and ended in the *fifth year of the reign of the judges.
26 And in one year were thousands and tens of thousands of souls sent to the eternal world, that they might reap their [a]rewards according to their works, whether they were good or whether they were bad, to reap eternal happiness or eternal misery, according to the spirit which they listed to obey, whether it be a good spirit or a bad one.
27 For every man receiveth [a]wages of him whom he listeth to [b]obey, and this according to the words of the spirit of prophecy; therefore let it be according to the truth. And thus endeth the fifth year of the reign of the judges.

CHAPTER 4

Alma baptizes thousands of converts—Iniquity enters the Church, and the Church's progress is hindered—Nephihah is appointed chief judge—Alma, as high priest, devotes himself to the ministry.

Now it came to pass in the †sixth year of the reign of the judges over the people of Nephi, there were no contentions nor wars in the [a]land of Zarahemla;
2 But the people were afflicted, yea, greatly afflicted for the loss of their brethren, and also for the [a]loss of their flocks and herds, and also for the loss of their fields of grain, which were trodden under foot and destroyed by the Lamanites.
3 And so great were their afflictions that every soul had cause to mourn; and they believed that it was the judgments of God sent upon them because of their wickedness and their abominations; therefore they were [a]awakened to a remembrance of their duty.
4 And they began to establish the [a]church more fully; yea, and many were [b]baptized in the [c]waters of Sidon and were joined to the church of God; yea, they were baptized by the hand of Alma, who had been consecrated the [d]high priest over the people of the church, by the hand of his father Alma.
5 And it came to pass in the ‡seventh year of the reign of the judges there were about three thousand five hundred souls that united themselves to the [a]church of God and were baptized. And thus ended the seventh year of the reign of the judges over the people

20*a* Alma 2:24.
22*a* Alma 2:30 (29–33).
26*a* Ps. 7:16. TG Agency; Reward.
27*a* Mosiah 2:32 (32–33); Alma 5:42 (41–42). TG Wages.
b Rom. 6:16 (14–18); Hel. 14:31 (29–31).
4 1*a* Omni 1:12 (12–19).
2*a* Alma 2:19; 3:1 (1–2, 26).
3*a* 1 Cor. 15:34 (33–34).
4*a* TG Church Organization.
b Mosiah 18:10 (10–17).
c Alma 3:3; 6:7.
d Mosiah 29:42. TG High Priest.
5*a* Mosiah 25:22 (18–23); 3 Ne. 26:21.

[*87 B.C †86 B.C. ‡85 B.C.]

of Nephi; and there was continual
peace in all that time.
6 And it came to pass in the
*eighth year of the reign of the
judges, that the people of the
church began to wax proud, because of their exceeding [a]riches, and
their [b]fine silks, and their fine-
twined linen, and because of their
many flocks and herds, and their
gold and their silver, and all manner
of precious things, which they had
obtained by their [c]industry; and in
all these things were they lifted up
in the pride of their eyes, for they
began to wear very costly [d]apparel.
7 Now this was the cause of much
affliction to Alma, yea, and to many
of the people whom Alma had
consecrated to be [a]teachers, and
[b]priests, and [c]elders over the
church; yea, many of them were
sorely grieved for the wickedness
which they saw had begun to be
among their people.
8 For they saw and beheld with
great sorrow that the people of the
church began to be lifted up in the
pride of their eyes, and to set their
[a]hearts upon riches and upon the
vain things of the world, that they
began to be scornful, one towards
another, and they began to persecute those that did [b]not believe
according to their own will and
pleasure.
9 And thus, in this eighth year of
the reign of the judges, there began
to be great [a]contentions among the
people of the church; yea, there
were [b]envyings, and [c]strife, and
malice, and persecutions, and pride,
even to exceed the pride of those
who did not belong to the church of
God.
10 And thus ended the eighth year
of the reign of the judges; and the
wickedness of the church was a
great [a]stumbling-block to those
who did not belong to the church;
and thus the church began to fail in
its progress.
11 And it came to pass in the
†commencement of the ninth year,
Alma saw the wickedness of the
church, and he saw also that the
[a]example of the church began to
lead those who were unbelievers on
from one piece of iniquity to
another, thus bringing on the
destruction of the people.
12 Yea, he saw great inequality
among the people, some lifting
themselves up with their pride,
despising others, turning their
backs upon the [a]needy and the
naked and those who were [b]hungry,
and those who were athirst, and
those who were sick and afflicted.
13 Now this was a great cause for
lamentations among the people,
while others were abasing themselves, succoring those who stood
in need of their succor, such as
imparting their substance to the
[a]poor and the needy, feeding the
hungry, and suffering all manner of
[b]afflictions, for Christ's [c]sake, who
should come according to the spirit
of prophecy;
14 Looking forward to that day,
thus [a]retaining a [b]remission of their
sins; being filled with great [c]joy because of the resurrection of the dead,
according to the will and power and
[d]deliverance of Jesus Christ from
the bands of death.
15 And now it came to pass that
Alma, having seen the afflictions of
the humble followers of God, and

6*a* TG Riches.
b Alma 1: 29.
c TG Industry.
d TG Apparel.
7*a* Mosiah 6: 3. TG Teacher.
b TG Church Organization.
c Alma 4: 16. TG Elder.
8*a* TG Pride; Vanity; Worldliness.
b Alma 1: 21.
9*a* TG Contention.
b TG Envy.
c Alma 16: 18. TG Strife.
10*a* TG Stumblingblock.
11*a* 2 Sam. 12: 14; Alma 39: 11. TG Example.
12*a* Isa. 3: 14; Ezek. 22: 12 (6–13); Amos 3: 10; Jacob 2: 17.
b Mosiah 4: 26.
13*a* TG Almsgiving.
b TG Affliction.
c 2 Cor. 12: 10.
14*a* Mosiah 4: 12; Alma 5: 26 (26–35); D&C 20: 32 (31–34).
b TG Justification.
c TG Joy.
d TG Deliverance.

[*84 B.C. †83 B.C.]

the persecutions which were heaped upon them by the remainder of his people, and seeing all their [a]inequality, began to be very sorrowful; nevertheless the Spirit of the Lord did not fail him.

16 And he selected a wise man who was among the [a]elders of the church, and gave him power according to the [b]voice of the people, that he might have power to enact [c]laws according to the laws which had been given, and to put them in force according to the wickedness and the crimes of the people.

17 Now this man's name was [a]Nephihah, and he was appointed [b]chief judge; and he sat in the judgment-seat to judge and to govern the people.

18 Now Alma did not grant unto him the office of being [a]high priest over the church, but he retained the office of high priest unto himself; but he delivered the judgment-seat unto [b]Nephihah.

19 And this he did that he [a]himself might go forth among his people, or among the people of Nephi, that he might [b]preach the [c]word of God unto them, to [d]stir them up in [e]remembrance of their duty, and that he might pull down, by the word of God, all the pride and craftiness and all the contentions which were among his people, seeing no way that he might reclaim them save it were in bearing down in pure [f]testimony against them.

20 And thus in the commencement of the ninth year of the reign of the judges over the people of Nephi, Alma delivered up the judgment-seat to [a]Nephihah, and confined himself wholly to the [b]high priesthood of the holy order of God, to the [c]testimony of the word, according to the spirit of revelation and prophecy.

The words which Alma, the High Priest according to the holy order of God, delivered to the people in their cities and villages throughout the land. Comprising chapter 5.

CHAPTER 5

To gain salvation, men must repent and keep the commandments, be born again, cleanse their garments through the blood of Christ, be humble and strip themselves from pride and envy, and do the works of righteousness—The Good Shepherd calleth his people—Those who do evil works are children of the devil—Alma testifies of the truth of his doctrine and commands men to repent—Names of the righteous shall be written in the book of life.

Now it came to pass that *Alma began to [a]deliver the word of [b]God unto the people, first in the land of Zarahemla, and from thence throughout all the land.

2 And these are the words which he spake to the people in the church which was established in the city of Zarahemla, according to his own record, saying:

3 I, Alma, having been [a]consecrated by my father, Alma, to be a [b]high priest over the church of God, he having power and [c]authority from God to do these things, behold, I say unto you that he began to

15*a* 2 Cor. 8:14; D&C 49:20.
16*a* Alma 4:7.
b Alma 2:3 (3–7); 50:39.
c Alma 1:1 (1, 14, 18).
17*a* Alma 27:20.
b Alma 30:29; 50:37.
18*a* TG High Priest.
b Alma 7:2.
19*a* Alma 7:1.
b Alma 5:1.
c Alma 31:5; D&C 11:2.
d Enos 1:23.
e 2 Chr. 35:6; Alma 16:16; D&C 108:7.
f TG Testimony.
20*a* Alma 8:12.
b Mosiah 29:42; Alma 5:3 (3, 44, 49).
c TG Preaching.

5 1*a* Alma 4:19.
b Alma 5:61.
3*a* TG Priesthood, Authority.
b Alma 4:20 (4, 18, 20); 8:23 (11, 23).
c Mosiah 18:13; 3 Ne. 11:25.

[*About 83 B.C.]

establish a church in the [d]land
which was in the borders of Nephi;
yea, the land which was called the
land of Mormon; yea, and he did
baptize his brethren in the waters
of Mormon.
4 And behold, I say unto you, they
were [a]delivered out of the hands of
the people of king Noah, by the
mercy and power of God.
5 And behold, after that, they
were brought into [a]bondage by the
hands of the Lamanites in the
wilderness; yea, I say unto you,
they were in captivity, and again
the Lord did deliver them out of
[b]bondage by the power of his word;
and we were brought into this land,
and here we began to establish
the church of God throughout this
land also.
6 And now behold, I say unto you,
my brethren, you that belong to
this church, have you sufficiently
retained in [a]remembrance the captivity of your fathers? Yea, and
have you sufficiently retained in
remembrance his mercy and long-
suffering towards them? And moreover, have ye sufficiently retained
in remembrance that he has
[b]delivered their souls from hell?
7 Behold, he changed their hearts;
yea, he awakened them out of a
deep sleep, and they awoke unto
God. Behold, they were in the midst
of darkness; nevertheless, their
souls were illuminated by the light
of the everlasting word; yea, they
were encircled about by the [a]bands
of death, and the [b]chains of hell,
and an everlasting destruction did
await them.
8 And now I ask of you, my
brethren, were they destroyed?
Behold, I say unto you, Nay, they
were not.
9 And again I ask, were the bands
of death broken, and the [a]chains
of hell which encircled them about,
were they loosed? I say unto you,
Yea, they were loosed, and their
souls did expand, and they did [b]sing
redeeming love. And I say unto you
that they are saved.
10 And now I ask of you on what
conditions are they [a]saved? Yea,
what grounds had they to hope for
salvation? What is the cause of
their being loosed from the bands of
death, yea, and also the chains of
hell?
11 Behold, I can tell you—did not
my father Alma believe in the
words which were delivered by the
[a]mouth of Abinadi? And was he not
a holy prophet? Did he not speak
the words of God, and my father
Alma believe them?
12 And according to his faith there
was a mighty [a]change wrought in
his heart. Behold I say unto you
that this is all true.
13 And behold, he [a]preached the
word unto your fathers, and a
mighty change was also wrought in
their hearts, and they humbled
themselves and put their [b]trust in
the true and [c]living God. And
behold, they were faithful until the
[d]end; therefore they were saved.
14 And now behold, I ask of you,
my brethren of the church, have ye
[a]spiritually been [b]born of God?
Have ye received his image in your
countenances? Have ye experienced
this mighty [c]change in your hearts?
15 Do ye exercise faith in the

3*d* Mosiah 18: 4; 3 Ne. 5: 12.
4*a* Mosiah 23: 1 (1–3).
5*a* Mosiah 23: 37 (37–39); 24: 9 (8–15).
b Mosiah 24: 17; 25: 10; 27: 16.
6*a* 2 Pet. 3: 1 (1–2).
b TG Deliverance.
7*a* Mosiah 15: 8. TG Bondage, Spiritual; Man, Natural, Not Spiritually Reborn.
b Alma 12: 11 (9–11); D&C 138: 23. TG Hell.
9*a* Alma 12: 6.
b Ps. 147: 1 (1–7).
10*a* TG Save.
11*a* Mosiah 17: 2 (2–4).
12*a* TG Conversion.
13*a* Mosiah 18: 7 (1–31).
b TG Trust in God.
c 1 Sam. 17: 26; Ps. 42: 2; Morm. 9: 28; D&C 20: 19.
d 2 Ne. 31: 15.
14*a* TG Spirituality.
b Mosiah 27: 25 (24–27); Alma 22: 15.
c Rom. 7: 22; 8: 11 (11–17); Col. 3: 10 (9–10); Mosiah 5: 2; Moses 6: 65. TG Sanctification.

[About 83 B.C.]

redemption of him who [a]created
you? Do you look forward with an
eye of faith, and view this mortal
body raised in immortality, and
this corruption [b]raised in incorruption, to stand before God to
be [c]judged according to the deeds
which have been done in the mortal
body?
16 I say unto you, can you
imagine to yourselves that ye hear
the voice of the Lord, saying unto
you, in that day: Come unto me ye
[a]blessed, for behold, your works
have been the works of righteousness upon the face of the earth?
17 Or do ye [a]imagine to yourselves
that ye can lie unto the Lord in that
day, and [b]say—Lord, our works
have been righteous works upon
the face of the earth—and that he
will save you?
18 Or otherwise, can ye imagine
yourselves brought before the tribunal of God with your souls filled
with guilt and remorse, having a
remembrance of all your guilt, yea,
a perfect [a]remembrance of all your
wickedness, yea, a remembrance
that ye have set at defiance the
commandments of God?
19 I say unto you, can ye look up
to God at that day with a pure heart
and clean hands? I say unto you,
can you look up, having the [a]image
of God engraven upon your countenances?
20 I say unto you, can ye think of
being saved when you have yielded
yourselves to become [a]subjects to
the devil?
21 I say unto you, ye will know at
that day that ye cannot be [a]saved;
for there can no man be saved
except his [b]garments are washed
white; yea, his garments must be
[c]purified until they are cleansed
from all stain, through the blood of
him of whom it has been spoken
by our fathers, who should come
to redeem his people from their
sins.
22 And now I ask of you, my
brethren, how will any of you feel,
if ye shall stand before the bar of
God, having your garments stained
with [a]blood and all manner of
[b]filthiness? Behold, what will these
things testify against you?
23 Behold will they not [a]testify
that ye are murderers, yea, and also
that ye are [b]guilty of all manner of
wickedness?
24 Behold, my brethren, do ye
suppose that such an one can have
a place to sit down in the kingdom
of God, with [a]Abraham, with Isaac,
and with Jacob, and also all the
holy prophets, whose garments are
cleansed and are spotless, pure and
white?
25 I say unto you, Nay; except
ye make our Creator a liar from the
beginning, or suppose that he is a
liar from the beginning, ye cannot
suppose that such can have place in
the kingdom of heaven; but they
shall be cast out for they are the
[a]children of the kingdom of the
devil.
26 And now behold, I say unto
you, my brethren, if ye have experienced a [a]change of heart, and
if ye have felt to sing the [b]song of
redeeming love, I would ask, [c]can
ye feel so now?

15a TG Jesus Christ, Creator.
b TG Immortality; Redemption; Resurrection.
c TG Jesus Christ, Judge; Judgment, The Last.
16a Matt. 25: 34 (31–46).
17a Alma 7: 3.
b 3 Ne. 14: 22 (21–23).
18a Ezek. 20: 43; 2 Ne. 9: 14; Mosiah 2: 40; 3: 25; Alma 11: 43.
19a 1 Jn. 3: 2 (1–3).
20a Mosiah 2: 32.
21a TG Salvation, Plan of.
b 1 Ne. 12: 10; Alma 13: 11 (11–13); 3 Ne. 27: 19 (19–20).
c D&C 138: 59. TG Purification.
22a Isa. 59: 3.
b TG Filthiness.
23a Isa. 59: 12.
b TG Guilt.
24a Luke 13: 28.
25a Deut. 32: 5; 2 Ne. 9: 9.
26a TG Change; Conversion; Man, New, Spiritually Reborn.
b Alma 26: 13.
c Mosiah 4: 12; Alma 4: 14 (13–14); D&C 20: 32 (31–34).

[About 83 B.C.]

27 Have ye walked, keeping yourselves [a]blameless before God? Could
ye say, if ye were called to die at
this time, within yourselves, that ye
have been sufficiently [b]humble?
That your garments have been
[c]cleansed and made white through
the blood of Christ, who will come
to [d]redeem his people from their
sins?
28 Behold, are ye stripped of
[a]pride? I say unto you, if ye are not
ye are not prepared to meet God.
Behold ye must prepare quickly;
for the kingdom of heaven is soon
at hand, and such an one hath not
eternal life.
29 Behold, I say, is there one
among you who is not stripped of
[a]envy? I say unto you that such an
one is not prepared; and I would
that he should prepare [b]quickly,
for the hour is close at hand, and
he knoweth not when the time shall
come; for such an one is not found
guiltless.
30 And again I say unto you, is
there one among you that doth
make a [a]mock of his brother, or that
heapeth upon him persecutions?
31 Wo unto such an one, for he is
not prepared, and the [a]time is at
hand that he must repent or he cannot be saved!
32 Yea, even wo unto all ye
[a]workers of iniquity; repent, repent,
for the Lord God hath spoken it!
33 Behold, he sendeth an invitation unto [a]all men, for the [b]arms of
mercy are extended towards them,
and he saith: Repent, and I will
receive you.
34 Yea, he saith: [a]Come unto me
and ye shall partake of the [b]fruit
of the tree of life; yea, ye shall eat
and drink of the [c]bread and the
waters of life [d]freely;
35 Yea, come unto me and bring
forth works of righteousness, and
ye shall not be hewn down and cast
into the fire—
36 For behold, the time is at hand
that whosoever [a]bringeth forth not
good fruit, or whosoever doeth not
the works of righteousness, the
same have cause to wail and mourn.
37 O ye workers of iniquity; ye
that are [a]puffed up in the vain
things of the world, ye that have
professed to have known the ways
of righteousness nevertheless have
gone [b]astray, as [c]sheep having no
[d]shepherd, notwithstanding a shepherd hath [e]called after you and is
still calling after you, but ye will
not [f]hearken unto his voice!
38 Behold, I say unto you, that
the good [a]shepherd doth call you;
yea, and in his own name he doth
call you, which is the name of
Christ; and if ye will not [b]hearken
unto the voice of the [c]good shepherd, to the [d]name by which ye are
called, behold, ye are not the sheep
of the good shepherd.
39 And now if ye are not the [a]sheep
of the good shepherd, of what fold
are ye? Behold, I say unto you,
that the [b]devil is your shepherd,
and ye are of his fold; and now,

27*a* 1 Jn. 3: 21 (19–24). TG Justification.
b TG Humility.
c Rev. 19: 8.
d 1 Cor. 15: 3. TG Jesus Christ, Mission of.
28*a* TG Pride.
29*a* TG Envy.
b TG Procrastination.
30*a* TG Backbiting; Mocking.
31*a* TG Procrastination.
32*a* Ps. 5: 5 (4–6).
33*a* Alma 19: 36; 3 Ne. 18: 25.
b Isa. 59: 16; 2 Ne. 1: 15; Jacob 6: 5; 3 Ne. 9: 14.
34*a* 1 Ne. 1: 14; 2 Ne. 26: 25 (24–28); 3 Ne. 9: 14 (13–14).
b 1 Ne. 8: 11; 15: 36.
c TG Bread of Life.
d 2 Ne. 9: 50 (50–51); Alma 42: 27.
36*a* Matt. 3: 10; 7: 19 (15–20); Jacob 5: 26 (26–60); 3 Ne. 14: 19; D&C 97: 7.
37*a* TG Worldliness.
b 2 Ne. 12: 5; 28: 14; Mosiah 14: 6.
c Matt. 9: 36.
d TG Shepherd.
e Prov. 1: 24 (24–27); Isa. 65: 12; 1 Ne. 17: 13; 2 Ne. 7: 2.
f 2 Chr. 33: 10; Jer. 26: 4; Alma 10: 6 (5–6).
38*a* TG Jesus Christ, Good Shepherd.
b Lev. 26: 14 (14–20); D&C 101: 7.
c 3 Ne. 15: 24; 18: 31.
d Mosiah 5: 8; Alma 34: 38.
39*a* Matt. 6: 24; Luke 16: 13.
b Mosiah 5: 10. TG Devil, Church of.

[About 83 B.C.]

who can deny this? Behold, I say
unto you, whosoever denieth this
is a [c]liar and a [d]child of the devil.
40 For I say unto you that whatsoever is [a]good cometh from God,
and whatsoever is [b]evil cometh from
the devil.
41 Therefore, if a man bringeth
forth [a]good works he hearkeneth
unto the voice of the good shepherd,
and he doth follow him; but whosoever bringeth forth evil works,
the same becometh a [b]child of the
devil, for he hearkeneth unto his
voice, and doth follow him.
42 And whosoever doeth this must
receive his [a]wages of him; therefore,
for his [b]wages he receiveth [c]death,
as to things pertaining unto
righteousness, being dead unto all
good works.
43 And now, my brethren, I would
that ye should hear me, for I speak
in the [a]energy of my soul; for
behold, I have spoken unto you
plainly that ye cannot err, or have
spoken according to the commandments of God.
44 For I am called to speak after
this manner, according to the [a]holy
order of God, which is in Christ
Jesus; yea, I am commanded to
stand and testify unto this people
the things which have been spoken
by our fathers concerning the things
which are to come.
45 And this is not all. Do ye not
suppose that I [a]know of these things
myself? Behold, I testify unto you
that I do know that these things
whereof I have spoken are true.
And how do ye suppose that I know
of their surety?
46 Behold, I say unto you they
are made [a]known unto me by the
Holy Spirit of God. Behold, I have
[b]fasted and prayed many days that
I might know these things of myself. And now I do know of myself
that they are true; for the Lord God
hath made them manifest unto me
by his Holy Spirit; and this is the
spirit of [c]revelation which is in me.
47 And moreover, I say unto you
that it has thus been revealed unto
me, that the words which have been
spoken by our fathers are true, even
so according to the spirit of
prophecy which is in me, which is
also by the manifestation of the
Spirit of God.
48 I say unto you, that I know of
myself that whatsoever I shall say
unto you, concerning that which is
to come, is true; and I say unto
you, that I know that Jesus Christ
shall come, yea, the Son, the Only
Begotten of the Father, full of
grace, and mercy, and truth. And
behold, it is he that cometh to take
away the sins of the world, yea, the
sins of every man who steadfastly
believeth on his name.
49 And now I say unto you that
this is the [a]order after which I am
called, yea, to preach unto my
beloved brethren, yea, and every
one that dwelleth in the land; yea,
to preach unto all, both old and
young, both bond and free; yea, I
say unto you the aged, and also the
middle aged, and the rising generation; yea, to cry unto them that
they must repent and be [b]born
again.
50 Yea, thus saith the Spirit:
Repent, all ye ends of the earth,
for the kingdom of heaven is soon
at hand; yea, the Son of God
cometh in his [a]glory, in his might,

39*c* 1 Jn. 2: 22.
d 2 Ne. 9: 9.
40*a* Ezra 3: 11; Ps. 85: 12; Omni 1: 25; Ether 4: 12; Moro. 7: 16 (15–17).
b Isa. 45: 7; Amos 3: 6; Moro. 7: 12.
41*a* 3 Ne. 14: 17 (16–20). TG Good Works.
b Mosiah 16: 3 (3–5); Alma 11: 23.
42*a* Alma 3: 27 (26–27); D&C 29: 45.
b Rom. 6: 23.
c Hel. 14: 18 (16–18).
43*a* Alma 7: 5.
44*a* Mosiah 29: 42.
45*a* Alma 36: 4.
46*a* 1 Cor. 2: 10 (9–16).
b Alma 10: 7.
c Rev. 19: 10.
49*a* TG Called of God; Priesthood.
b TG Man, New, Spiritually Reborn.
50*a* Ps. 24: 8; 72: 19. TG Jesus Christ, Glory of.

[About 83 B.C.]

majesty, power, and dominion. Yea, my beloved brethren, I say unto you, that the Spirit saith: Behold the glory of the [b]King of all the earth; and also the King of heaven shall very soon shine forth among all the children of men.

51 And also the Spirit saith unto me, yea, crieth unto me with a mighty voice, saying: Go forth and say unto this people—Repent, for except ye repent ye can in nowise inherit the [a]kingdom of [b]heaven.

52 And again I say unto you, the Spirit saith: Behold, the [a]ax is laid at the root of the tree; therefore every tree that bringeth not forth good fruit shall be [b]hewn down and cast into the fire, yea, a fire which cannot be consumed, even an unquenchable fire. Behold, and remember, the Holy One hath spoken it.

53 And now my beloved brethren, I say unto you, can ye withstand these sayings; yea, can ye lay aside these things, and [a]trample the Holy One under your feet; yea, can ye be [b]puffed up in the pride of your hearts; yea, will ye still persist in the wearing of [c]costly apparel and setting your hearts upon the vain things of the world, upon your [d]riches?

54 Yea, will ye persist in supposing that ye are better one than another; yea, will ye persist in the persecution of your brethren, who humble themselves and do walk after the holy order of God, wherewith they have been brought into this church, having been [a]sanctified by the Holy Spirit, and they do bring forth works which are meet for repentance—

55 Yea, and will you persist in turning your backs upon the [a]poor, and the needy, and in withholding your substance from them?

56 And finally, all ye that will persist in your wickedness, I say unto you that these are they who shall be hewn down and cast into the fire except they speedily repent.

57 And now I say unto you, all you that are desirous to follow the voice of the [a]good shepherd, come ye out from the wicked, and be ye [b]separate, and touch not their unclean things; and behold, their names shall be [c]blotted out, that the names of the wicked shall not be numbered among the names of the righteous, that the word of God may be fulfilled, which saith: The names of the wicked shall not be mingled with the names of my people;

58 For the names of the righteous shall be written in the [a]book of life, and unto them will I grant an inheritance at my right hand. And now, my brethren, what have ye to say against this? I say unto you, if ye speak against it, it matters not, for the word of God must be fulfilled.

59 For what shepherd is there among you having many sheep doth not watch over them, that the wolves enter not and devour his flock? And behold, if a wolf enter his [a]flock doth he not drive him out? Yea, and at the last, if he can, he will destroy him.

60 And now I say unto you that the good shepherd doth call after you; and if you will hearken unto his voice he will bring you into his

50*b* Ps. 74: 12; 149: 2; Matt. 2: 2; Luke 23: 2; 2 Ne. 10: 14; D&C 38: 21 (21–22); 128: 22 (22–23); Moses 7: 53. TG Jesus Christ, King; Kingdom of God, on Earth.
51*a* TG Kingdom of God, in Heaven.
b TG Heaven.
52*a* Luke 3: 9; D&C 97: 7.
b Jacob 5: 46; 6: 7; 3 Ne. 27: 11 (11–12).
53*a* TG Sacrilege.
b 1 Cor. 5: 2.
c 2 Ne. 28: 13 (11–14); Morm. 8: 36 (36–39).
d Ps. 62: 10; D&C 56: 16 (16–18).
54*a* TG Sanctification.
55*a* Ps. 109: 16 (15–16); Jacob 2: 17; Hel. 6: 39 (39–40); D&C 56: 16.
57*a* TG Jesus Christ, Good Shepherd.
b Ezra 6: 21; 9: 1; Neh. 9: 2; 2 Thes. 3: 6; D&C 133: 5 (5, 14).
c Deut. 29: 20; Ps. 109: 13.
58*a* TG Book of Life.
59*a* Prov. 27: 23.

[About 83 B.C.]

fold, and ye are his sheep; and he commandeth you that ye suffer no ravenous wolf to enter among you, that ye may not be destroyed.

61 And now I, Alma, do command you in the language of [a]him who hath commanded me, that ye observe to do the words which I have spoken unto you.

62 I speak by way of command unto you that belong to the church; and unto those who do not belong to the church I speak by way of invitation, saying: Come and be baptized unto repentance, that ye also may be partakers of the fruit of the [a]tree of life.

CHAPTER 6

The Church in Zarahemla is cleansed and set in order—Alma goes to Gideon to preach.

AND now it came to pass that after Alma had made an end of speaking unto the people of the church, which was established in the city of Zarahemla, he [a]ordained priests and [b]elders, by laying on his [c]hands according to the order of God, to preside and [d]watch over the church.

2 And it came to pass that whosoever did not belong to the church who [a]repented of their sins were baptized unto repentance, and were received into the church.

3 And it also came to pass that whosoever did belong to the church that did not [a]repent of their wickedness and humble themselves before God—I mean those who were lifted up in the [b]pride of their hearts—the same were rejected, and their names were [c]blotted out, that their names were not numbered among those of the righteous.

4 And thus they began to establish the order of the church in the [a]city of Zarahemla.

5 Now I would that ye should understand that the word of God was liberal unto all, that none were deprived of the privilege of assembling themselves together to hear the word of God.

6 Nevertheless the children of God were commanded that they should gather themselves together oft, and join in [a]fasting and mighty prayer in behalf of the welfare of the souls of those who knew not God.

7 And now it came to pass that when Alma had made these regulations he departed from them, yea, from the church which was in the city of Zarahemla, and went over upon the east of the [a]river Sidon, into the [b]valley of Gideon, there having been a city built, which was called the city of Gideon, which was in the valley that was called Gideon, being called after the man who was [c]slain by the hand of Nehor with the sword.

8 And Alma went and began to declare the word of God unto the church which was established in the valley of Gideon, according to the revelation of the truth of the word which had been spoken by his fathers, and according to the spirit of prophecy which was in him, according to the [a]testimony of Jesus Christ, the Son of God, who should come to redeem his people from their sins, and the holy order by which he was called. And thus it is written. Amen.

The words of Alma which he delivered to the people in Gideon, according to his own record. Comprising chapter 7.

61*a* Alma 5: 1 (1, 44).
62*a* 1 Ne. 8: 10; 11: 21 (21–23).
6 1*a* TG Ordination; Priesthood.
b TG Elder; Priest.
c TG Hands, Laying on of.
d D&C 52: 39.
2*a* TG Baptism, Qualifications for.
3*a* Mosiah 26: 6.
b 1 Cor. 5: 2.
c Ex. 32: 33; Mosiah 26: 36; Alma 1: 24; 5: 57 (57–58).
TG Excommunication.
4*a* Alma 2: 26.
6*a* TG Fasting.
7*a* Alma 4: 4; 8: 3.
b Alma 2: 20.
c Alma 1: 9.
8*a* Rev. 19: 10.

[About 83 B.C.]

CHAPTER 7

Christ shall be born of Mary—He shall loose the bands of death and bear the sins of his people—Those who repent, are baptized, and keep the commandments shall have eternal life—Filthiness cannot inherit the kingdom of God—Humility, faith, hope, and charity are required.

BEHOLD my beloved brethren,
seeing that I have been permitted
to come unto you, therefore I
attempt to address you in my
language; yea, by my [a]own mouth,
seeing that it is the first time that I
have spoken unto you by the words
of my mouth, I having been wholly
confined to the [b]judgment-seat,
having had much business that I
could not come unto you.
2 And even I could not have come
now at this time were it not that
the judgment-seat hath been [a]given
to another, to reign in my stead;
and the Lord in much mercy hath
granted that I should come unto you.
3 And behold, I have come having
great hopes and much desire that I
should find that ye had humbled
yourselves before God, and that ye
had continued in the supplicating
of his grace, that I should find that
ye were blameless before him, that
I should find that ye were not in the
awful [a]dilemma that our brethren
were in at Zarahemla.
4 But blessed be the name of God,
that he hath given me to know, yea,
hath given unto me the exceedingly
great joy of knowing that they are
established again in the way of his
righteousness.
5 And I trust, according to the
Spirit of God which is in me, that I
shall also have joy over you; nevertheless I do not desire that my joy
over you should come by the cause
of so much afflictions and sorrow
which I have had for the brethren
at Zarahemla, for behold, my joy
cometh over them after wading
through much affliction and sorrow.
6 But behold, I trust that ye are
not in a state of so much unbelief as
were your brethren; I trust that ye
are not lifted up in the pride of your
hearts; yea, I trust that ye have not
set your hearts upon riches and the
vain things of the world; yea, I
trust that you do not worship [a]idols,
but that ye do worship the true and
the [b]living God, and that ye look
forward for the remission of your
sins, with an everlasting faith,
which is to come.
7 For behold, I say unto you there
be many things to come; and
behold, there is one thing which is
of more importance than they all—
for behold, the [a]time is not far
distant that the Redeemer liveth
and cometh among his people.
8 Behold, I do not say that he will
come among us at the [a]time of his
dwelling in his mortal tabernacle;
for behold, the Spirit hath not said
unto me that this should be the case.
Now as to this thing I do not know;
but this much I do know, that the
Lord God hath power to do all
things which are according to his
word.
9 But behold, the Spirit hath said
this much unto me, saying: Cry
unto this people, saying—[a]Repent
ye, and prepare the way of the
Lord, and walk in his paths, which
are straight; for behold, the kingdom of heaven is at hand, and the
Son of God [b]cometh upon the face of
the earth.
10 And behold, he shall be [a]born
of Mary, at [b]Jerusalem which is the
[c]land of our forefathers, she being a
[d]virgin, a precious and chosen

7 1*a* Alma 4: 19.
b Mosiah 29: 42.
2*a* Alma 4: 18 (16–18).
3*a* Alma 5: 17 (16–17).
6*a* 2 Ne. 9: 37; Hel. 6: 31.
b Dan. 6: 26.
7*a* Alma 9: 26.
8*a* 1 Ne. 12: 6 (4–8); Alma 16: 20.
9*a* Matt. 3: 2 (2–3); Alma 9: 25 (25–26).
b Mosiah 3: 5; 7: 27; 15: 2 (1–7).
10*a* Isa. 7: 14; Luke 1: 27; Mosiah 3: 8.
b Luke 2: 4.
c 1 Chr. 9: 3; 2 Chr. 15: 9; 1 Ne. 1: 4; 3 Ne. 20: 29.
d 1 Ne. 11: 13 (13–21).

[About 83 B.C.]

vessel, who shall be overshadowed
and [e]conceive by the power of the
Holy Ghost, and bring forth a son,
yea, even the Son of God.
11 And he shall go forth, suffering
pains and [a]afflictions and [b]tempta-
tions of every kind; and this that
the word might be fulfilled which
saith he will [c]take upon him the
pains and the sicknesses of his
people.
12 And he will take upon him
[a]death, that he may [b]loose the
bands of death which bind his
people; and he will take upon him
their infirmities, that his bowels
may be filled with mercy, according to the flesh, that he may know
according to the flesh how to
[c]succor his people according to their
infirmities.
13 Now the Spirit [a]knoweth all
things; nevertheless the Son of God
suffereth according to the [b]flesh
that he might [c]take upon him the
sins of his people, that he might
blot out their transgressions according to the power of his deliverance;
and now behold, this is the testimony which is in me.
14 Now I say unto you that ye
must [a]repent, and be born again;
for the Spirit saith if ye are not
born again ye cannot inherit the
kingdom of heaven; therefore come
and be baptized unto repentance,
that ye may be washed from your
sins, that ye may have faith on the
Lamb of God, who taketh away the
sins of the world, who is mighty to
save and to cleanse from all unrighteousness.
15 Yea, I say unto you come and
fear not, and lay aside every sin,
which easily doth [a]beset you, which
doth bind you down to destruction,
yea, come and go forth, and show
unto your God that ye are willing to
repent of your sins and enter into a
covenant with him to keep his
commandments, and witness it unto him this day by going into the
waters of baptism.
16 And whosoever doeth this, and
keepeth the commandments of God
from thenceforth, the same will
[a]remember that I say unto him,
yea, he will remember that I have
said unto him, he shall have eternal
life, according to the testimony of
the Holy Spirit, which testifieth in
me.
17 And now my beloved brethren,
do you believe these things? Behold, I say unto you, yea, I know
that ye believe them; and the way
that I know that ye believe them is
by the manifestation of the Spirit
which is in me. And now because
your faith is strong concerning that,
yea, concerning the things which I
have spoken, great is my joy.
18 For as I said unto you from the
beginning, that I had much desire
that ye were not in the state of
[a]dilemma like your brethren, even
so I have found that my desires
have been gratified.
19 For I perceive that ye are in
the paths of righteousness; I
perceive that ye are in the path
which leads to the kingdom of God;
yea, I perceive that ye are making
his [a]paths straight.
20 I perceive that it has been
made known unto you, by the
testimony of his word, that he cannot [a]walk in crooked paths; neither
doth he vary from that which he
hath said; neither hath he a shadow
of turning from the right to the left,
or from that which is right to that
which is wrong; therefore, his
course is one eternal round.

10*e* Matt. 1: 20; Mosiah 15: 3.
11*a* Isa. 53: 5 (3–5).
b TG Jesus Christ, Temptation of.
c Mosiah 14: 4 (3–5).
12*a* TG Jesus Christ, Death of.
b Ps. 116: 16 (15–16); 2 Ne. 2: 8; Alma 12: 25 (24–25); 42: 23.
c Heb. 2: 18; 4: 15; D&C 62: 1.
13*a* TG God, Omniscience of.
b TG Jesus Christ, Condescension of.
c Mosiah 15: 12.
14*a* TG Purification.
15*a* 2 Ne. 4: 18.
16*a* Ether 12: 4; Moro. 7: 3.
18*a* James 1: 8.
19*a* Matt. 3: 3.
20*a* 1 Ne. 10: 19; Alma 37: 12; D&C 3: 2.

[About 83 B.C.]

21 And he doth not dwell in [a]unholy temples; neither can filthiness or anything which is unclean be received into the kingdom of God; therefore I say unto you the time shall come, yea, and it shall be at the last day, that he who is [b]filthy shall remain in his filthiness.

22 And now my beloved brethren, I have said these things unto you that I might awaken you to a sense of your duty to God, that ye may walk blameless before him, that ye may walk after the holy order of God, after which ye have been received.

23 And now I would that ye should be [a]humble, and be [b]submissive and gentle; easy to be entreated; full of patience and long-suffering; being temperate in all things; being diligent in keeping the commandments of God at all times; asking for whatsoever things ye stand in need, both spiritual and temporal; always returning thanks unto God for whatsoever things ye do receive.

24 And see that ye have [a]faith, hope, and charity, and then ye will always abound in good works.

25 And may the Lord bless you, and keep your garments spotless, that ye may at last be brought to sit down with [a]Abraham, Isaac, and Jacob, and the holy prophets who have been ever since the world began, having your garments [b]spotless even as their garments are spotless, in the kingdom of heaven to go no more out.

26 And now my beloved brethren, I have spoken these words unto you according to the Spirit which testifieth in me; and my soul doth exceedingly rejoice, because of the exceeding diligence and heed which ye have given unto my word.

27 And now, may the [a]peace of God rest upon you, and upon your houses and lands, and upon your flocks and herds, and all that you possess, your women and your children, according to your faith and good works, from this time forth and forever. And thus I have spoken. Amen.

CHAPTER 8

Alma preaches and baptizes in Melek—He is rejected in Ammonihah and leaves—An angel commands him to return and cry repentance unto the people—He is received by Amulek, and the two of them preach in Ammonihah.

AND now it came to pass that Alma returned from the [a]land of Gideon, after having taught the people of Gideon many things which cannot be written, having established the [b]order of the church, according as he had before done in the land of Zarahemla, yea, he returned to his own house at Zarahemla to rest himself from the labors which he had performed.

2 And thus ended the ninth year of the reign of the judges over the people of Nephi.

3 And it came to pass in the commencement of the *tenth year of the reign of the judges over the people of Nephi, that Alma departed from thence and took his journey over into the land of [a]Melek, on the west of the [b]river Sidon, on the west by the borders of the wilderness.

4 And he began to teach the people in the land of Melek according to the [a]holy order of God, by which he had been called; and he began to teach the people throughout all the land of Melek.

5 And it came to pass that the people came to him throughout all

21*a* 1 Cor. 3: 17 (16–17); 6: 19; Mosiah 2: 37; Alma 34: 36.
b 1 Ne. 15: 33 (33–35); 2 Ne. 9: 16; Morm. 9: 14; D&C 88: 35.
23*a* Prov. 18: 12.
b TG Submissiveness.
24*a* 1 Cor. 13: 13 (1–13); Ether 12: 31 (30–35); Moro. 7: 44 (33–48).
25*a* D&C 27: 10.
b 2 Pet. 3: 14.
27*a* TG Peace of God.
8 1*a* Alma 2: 20; 6: 7.
b TG Church Organization.
3*a* Alma 31: 6.
b Alma 6: 7; 16: 6 (6–7).
4*a* D&C 107: 3 (2–4).
TG Priesthood.

[*82 B.C.]

the borders of the land which was by
the wilderness side. And they were
baptized throughout all the land;
6 So that when he had finished his
work at Melek he departed thence,
and traveled three days' journey on
the north of the land of Melek; and
he came to a city which was called
[a]Ammonihah.
7 Now it was the custom of the
people of Nephi to call their lands,
and their cities, and their villages,
yea, even all their small villages,
after the [a]name of him who first
possessed them; and thus it was with
the land of Ammonihah.
8 And it came to pass that when
Alma had come to the city of Ammonihah he began to preach the
word of God unto them.
9 Now Satan had gotten great
[a]hold upon the hearts of the people
of the city of Ammonihah; therefore
they would not hearken unto the
words of Alma.
10 Nevertheless Alma [a]labored
much in the spirit, [b]wrestling with
God in [c]mighty prayer, that he
would pour out his Spirit upon the
people who were in the city; that he
would also grant that he might
baptize them unto repentance.
11 Nevertheless, they hardened
their hearts, saying unto him: Behold, we know that thou art Alma;
and we know that thou art high
priest over the church which thou
hast established in many parts of
the land, according to your tradition; and we are not of thy church,
and we do not believe in such foolish
traditions.
12 And now we know that because
we are not of thy church we know
that thou hast no power over us; and
thou hast delivered up the judgment-
seat unto [a]Nephihah; therefore thou
art not the chief judge over us.
13 Now when the people had said
this, and withstood all his words,
and [a]reviled him, and spit upon him,
and caused that he should be [b]cast
out of their city, he departed thence
and took his journey towards the
city which was called Aaron.
14 And it came to pass that while
he was journeying thither, being
weighed down with sorrow, wading
through much [a]tribulation and
anguish of soul, because of the
wickedness of the people who were
in the city of Ammonihah, it came
to pass while Alma was thus weighed
down with sorrow, behold an [b]angel
of the Lord appeared unto him,
saying:
15 Blessed art thou, Alma; therefore, lift up thy head and rejoice,
for thou hast great cause to rejoice;
for thou hast been faithful in keeping the commandments of God from
the time which thou receivedst thy
first message from him. Behold, I
am he that [a]delivered it unto you.
16 And behold, I am sent to [a]com-
mand thee that thou return to the
city of Ammonihah, and preach
again unto the people of the city;
yea, preach unto them. Yea, say
unto them, except they repent the
Lord God will [b]destroy them.
17 For behold, they do study at
this time that they may destroy the
liberty of thy people, (for thus saith
the Lord) which is contrary to the
[a]statutes, and judgments, and commandments which he has given unto
his people.
18 Now it came to pass that after
Alma had received his message from
the angel of the Lord he returned
speedily to the land of Ammonihah.
And he entered the city by another
way, yea, by the way which is on the
south of the city of Ammonihah.
19 And as [a]he entered the city he

6a Alma 9:1.
7a Ether 2:13.
9a 2 Ne. 28:20 (19–22); D&C 10:20.
10a Alma 17:5.
b Enos 1:2 (1–12).
c 3 Ne. 27:1; 5:24; 29:2.
12a Alma 4:20.
13a 1 Cor. 4:12.
b Alma 8:24.
14a TG Tribulation.
b Mosiah 3:2 (2–3); Alma 10:20 (7–10, 20).
15a Mosiah 27:11 (11–16).
16a Gal. 2:2; Hel. 13:3.
b Alma 9:12 (4, 12, 18, 24).
17a Alma 1:1 (1, 14). TG Commandments of God.
19a Alma 10:8.

[About 82 B.C.]

was an hungered, and he said to a
man: Will ye give to an humble
servant of God something to eat?
20 And the man said unto him:
I am a Nephite, and I know that
thou art a holy prophet of God, for
thou art the man whom an [a]angel
said in a vision: Thou shalt receive.
Therefore, go with me into my house
and I will impart unto thee of my
[b]food; and I know that thou wilt be
a blessing unto me and my house.
21 And it came to pass that the
man received him into his house;
and the man was called Amulek;
and he brought forth bread and
meat and set before Alma.
22 And it came to pass that Alma
ate bread and was filled; and he
[a]blessed Amulek and his house, and
he gave thanks unto God.
23 And after he had eaten and was
filled he said unto Amulek: I am
Alma, and am the [a]high priest over
the church of God throughout the
land.
24 And behold, I have been called
to preach the word of God among
all this people, according to the
spirit of revelation and prophecy;
and I was in this land and they
would not receive me, but they [a]cast
me out and I was about to set my
back towards this land forever.
25 But behold, I have been commanded that I should turn again
and prophesy unto this people, yea,
and to testify against them concerning their iniquities.
26 And now, Amulek, because thou
hast fed me and taken me in, thou
art blessed; for I was an hungered,
for I had fasted many days.
27 And Alma [a]tarried many days
with Amulek before he began to
preach unto the people.
28 And it came to pass that the
people did wax more gross in their
iniquities.
29 And the word came to Alma,
saying: Go; and also say unto my
servant [a]Amulek, go forth and
prophesy unto this people, saying—
Repent ye, for thus saith the Lord,
except ye repent I will visit this
people in mine anger; yea, and I
will not turn my [b]fierce anger
away.
30 And Alma went forth, and also
Amulek, among the people, to
declare the words of God unto them;
and they were filled with the Holy
Ghost.
31 And they had [a]power given unto
them, insomuch that they could not
be confined in dungeons; neither
was it possible that any man could
slay them; nevertheless they did not
exercise their [b]power until they were
bound in bands and cast into prison.
Now, this was done that the Lord
might show forth his power in them.
32 And it came to pass that they
went forth and began to preach and
to prophesy unto the people, according to the spirit and power which the
Lord had given them.

The words of Alma, and also the words of Amulek, which were declared unto the people who were in the land of Ammonihah. And also they are cast into prison, and delivered by the miraculous power of God which was in them, according to the record of Alma. Comprising chapters 9 to 14 inclusive.

CHAPTER 9

Alma commands the people of Ammonihah to repent—The Lord will be merciful to the Lamanites in the last days—If the Nephites forsake the light, they shall be destroyed by the Lamanites—The Son of God soon cometh—He shall redeem those who repent and are baptized and have faith in his name.

20*a* Alma 10: 7 (7–9).
b 1 Kgs. 17: 11 (8–13).
22*a* Alma 10: 11.
23*a* Alma 5: 3 (3, 44, 49); 13: 1 (1–20).
24*a* Alma 8: 13.
27*a* Alma 10: 10.
29*a* Alma 10: 1.
b Alma 9: 12, 18.
31*a* Alma 14: 10.
b Alma 14: 25 (17–29).

[About 82 B.C.]

AND again, I, Alma, having been
commanded of God that I should
take Amulek and go forth and
preach again unto this people, or the
people who were in the city of
[a]Ammonihah, it came to pass as
I began to preach unto them,
they began to contend with me,
saying:
2 Who art thou? Suppose ye that
we shall believe the testimony of
[a]one man, although he should preach
unto us that the earth should pass
away?
3 Now they understood not the
words which they spake; for they
knew not that the earth should pass
away.
4 And they said also: We will not
believe thy words if thou shouldst
prophesy that this great city should
be destroyed in [a]one day.
5 Now they knew not that God
could do such marvelous [a]works,
for they were a hard-hearted and a
stiffnecked people.
6 And they said: [a]Who is God, that
sendeth [b]no more authority than
one man among this people, to
declare unto them the truth of such
great and marvelous things?
7 And they stood forth to lay their
hands on me; but behold, they did
not. And I stood with boldness to
declare unto them, yea, I did boldly
testify unto them, saying:
8 Behold, O ye wicked and perverse
[a]generation, how have ye forgotten
the [b]tradition of your fathers; yea,
how soon ye have forgotten the
commandments of God.
9 Do ye not remember that our
father, Lehi, was brought out of
Jerusalem by the [a]hand of God? Do
ye not remember that they were all
led by him through the wilderness?
10 And have ye forgotten so soon
how many times he [a]delivered our
fathers out of the hands of their
enemies, and preserved them from
being destroyed, even by the hands
of their own brethren?
11 Yea, and if it had not been for
his matchless power, and his mercy,
and his [a]long-suffering towards us,
we should unavoidably have been
cut off from the face of the earth
long before this period of time, and
perhaps been consigned to a state of
[b]endless misery and woe.
12 Behold, now I say unto you that
he commandeth you to repent; and
except ye repent, ye can in nowise
inherit the kingdom of God. But
behold, this is not all—he has commanded you to repent, or he will
utterly [a]destroy you from off the
face of the earth; yea, he will visit
you in his [b]anger, and in his [c]fierce
anger he will not turn away.
13 Behold, do ye not remember the
words which he spake unto Lehi,
saying that: [a]Inasmuch as ye shall
keep my commandments, ye shall
prosper in the land? And again it is
said that: Inasmuch as ye will not
keep my commandments ye shall
be cut off from the presence of the
Lord.
14 Now I would that ye should
remember, that inasmuch as the
Lamanites have not kept the commandments of God, they have been
[a]cut off from the presence of the
Lord. Now we see that the word of
the Lord has been verified in this
thing, and the Lamanites have been
cut off from his presence, from the
beginning of their transgressions in
the land.
15 Nevertheless I say unto you,
that it shall be more [a]tolerable for
them in the day of judgment than
for you, if ye remain in your sins,

9 1*a* Alma 8: 6.
2*a* Deut. 17: 6.
4*a* Alma 16: 10 (9–10).
5*a* TG God, Works of.
6*a* Ex. 5: 2; Mosiah 11: 27; Moses 5: 16.
b Alma 10: 12.
8*a* Matt. 3: 7; Alma 10: 17 (17–25).
b TG Birthright.
9*a* 1 Ne. 2: 2 (1–7).
10*a* TG Deliver, Deliverance.
11*a* TG Longsuffering.
b Mosiah 16: 11.
12*a* Alma 8: 16; 10: 27 (19, 23, 27).
b Jer. 18: 10 (6–10).
c Alma 8: 29.
13*a* 2 Ne. 1: 20; Mosiah 1: 7; Alma 37: 13.
14*a* 2 Ne. 5: 20 (20–24); Alma 38: 1.
15*a* Matt. 11: 22 (22, 24).

[About 82 B.C.]

yea, and even more tolerable for
them in this life than for you, except
ye repent.
16 For there are many promises
which are [a]extended to the Lamanites; for it is because of the [b]tradi-
tions of their fathers that caused
them to remain in their state of
[c]ignorance; therefore the Lord will
be merciful unto them and [d]prolong
their existence in the land.
17 And at some period of time they
will be [a]brought to believe in his
word, and to know of the incorrectness of the traditions of their fathers;
and many of them will be saved, for
the Lord will be merciful unto all
who [b]call on his name.
18 But behold, I say unto you that
if ye persist in your wickedness that
your days shall not be [a]prolonged in
the land, for the [b]Lamanites shall be
sent upon you; and if ye repent not
they shall come in a time when you
know not, and ye shall be visited
with [c]utter destruction; and it shall
be according to the fierce [d]anger of
the Lord.
19 For he will not suffer you that
ye shall live in your iniquities, to
[a]destroy his people. I say unto you,
Nay; he would rather suffer that the
Lamanites might destroy all his
people who are called the people
of Nephi, if it were possible that
they could [b]fall into sins and transgressions, after having had so
much light and so much knowledge
given unto them of the Lord their
God;
20 Yea, after having been such a
highly favored people of the Lord;
yea, after having been favored
above every other [a]nation, kindred,
tongue, or people; after having had
all things [b]made known unto them,
according to their desires, and their
faith, and prayers, of that which
has been, and which is, and which is
to come;
21 Having been [a]visited by the
Spirit of God; having conversed
with angels, and having been spoken
unto by the voice of the Lord; and
having the spirit of prophecy, and
the spirit of revelation, and also
many gifts, the gift of speaking with
tongues, and the gift of preaching,
and the gift of the Holy Ghost, and
the gift of [b]translation;
22 Yea, and after having been
[a]delivered of God out of the land of
Jerusalem, by the hand of the Lord;
having been [b]saved from famine,
and from sickness, and all manner of
diseases of every kind; and they
having waxed strong in battle, that
they might not be destroyed; having been brought out of [c]bondage
time after time, and having been
kept and preserved until now;
and they have been prospered until they are rich in all manner of
things—
23 And now behold I say unto
you, that if this people, who have
received so many blessings from the
hand of the Lord, should transgress
[a]contrary to the light and knowledge
which they do have, I say unto you
that if this be the case, that if they
should fall into transgression, it
would be far more [b]tolerable for the
Lamanites than for them.
24 For behold, the [a]promises of the
Lord are extended to the Lamanites,
but they are not unto you if ye transgress; for has not the Lord expressly

16*a* Alma 17: 15.
b Alma 3: 8; 17: 15.
c 2 Ne. 9: 26 (25–26); Mosiah 3: 11; Alma 42: 21.
d Deut. 11: 9 (8–9); 32: 47; Hel. 15: 11 (10–11); D&C 5: 33.
17*a* Enos 1: 13.
b Ps. 81: 7; Alma 38: 5; D&C 3: 8.
18*a* Deut. 6: 2.
b Alma 16: 3.
c Alma 16: 9.
d Alma 8: 29.
19*a* 1 Ne. 12: 19 (15, 19–20); Alma 45: 11 (10–14).
b Alma 24: 30.
20*a* 2 Sam. 7: 23; Abr. 2: 9.
b TG Prophets, Mission of.
21*a* Ex. 3: 16; 2 Ne. 4: 26; Morm. 1: 15.
b Omni 1: 20; Mosiah 8: 13 (13–19); 28: 17 (11–17).
22*a* 2 Ne. 1: 4.
b TG Protection, Divine.
c Mosiah 27: 16.
23*a* TG Disobedience.
b Matt. 11: 22 (22–24).
24*a* 2 Ne. 30: 6 (4–7); D&C 3: 20.

[About 82 B.C.]

promised and firmly decreed, that if ye will rebel against him that ye shall [b]utterly be destroyed from off the face of the earth?

25 And now for this cause, that ye may not be destroyed, the Lord has sent his angel to visit many of his people, declaring unto them that they must go forth and cry mightily unto this people, saying: [a]Repent ye, for the kingdom of heaven is nigh at hand;

26 And [a]not many days hence the Son of God shall come in his [b]glory; and his glory shall be the glory of the Only Begotten of the Father, full of [c]grace, equity, and truth, full of patience, [d]mercy, and long-suffering, quick to [e]hear the cries of his people and to answer their prayers.

27 And behold, he cometh to [a]redeem those who will be [b]baptized unto repentance, through faith on his name.

28 Therefore, prepare ye the way of the Lord, for the time is at hand that all men shall reap a [a]reward of their [b]works, according to that which they have been—if they have been righteous they shall [c]reap the salvation of their souls, according to the power and deliverance of Jesus Christ; and if they have been evil they shall reap the [d]damnation of their souls, according to the power and captivation of the devil.

29 Now behold, this is the voice of the angel, crying unto the people.

30 And now, my [a]beloved brethren, for ye are my brethren, and ye ought to be beloved, and ye ought to bring forth works which are meet for repentance, seeing that your hearts have been grossly hardened against the word of God, and seeing that ye are a [b]lost and a fallen people.

31 Now it came to pass that when I, Alma, had spoken these words, behold, the people were wroth with me because I said unto them that they were a hard-hearted and a [a]stiffnecked people.

32 And also because I said unto them that they were a lost and a fallen people they were angry with me, and sought to lay their hands upon me, that they might cast me into prison.

33 But it came to pass that the Lord did not suffer them that they should take me [a]at that time and cast me into prison.

34 And it came to pass that Amulek went and stood forth, and began to preach unto them also. And now the [a]words of Amulek are not all written, nevertheless a part of his words are written in this book.

CHAPTER 10

Lehi descended from Manasseh—Amulek recounts the angelic command that he care for Alma—The prayers of the righteous cause the people to be spared—Unrighteous lawyers and judges lay the foundation of the destruction of the people.

Now these are the [a]words which [b]Amulek preached unto the people who were in the land of Ammonihah, saying:

2 I am Amulek; I am the son of Giddonah, who was the son of Ishmael, who was a descendant of Aminadi; and it was that same Aminadi who interpreted the [a]writing which was upon the wall of the temple, which was written by the finger of God.

24*b* Alma 16: 9 (2–9); Morm. 6: 15 (15–22).
25*a* Matt. 3: 2 (2–3); Alma 7: 9; Hel. 5: 32.
26*a* Alma 7: 7.
b TG Jesus Christ, Glory of.
c TG Grace.
d TG God, Mercy of.
e Deut. 26: 7; Isa. 65: 24.
27*a* TG Redemption.
b TG Baptism, Essential.
28*a* TG Reward.
b Job 34: 11; D&C 1: 10; 6: 33.
c Ps. 7: 16.
d TG Damnation.
30*a* 1 Jn. 4: 11.
b Alma 12: 22.
31*a* 2 Ne. 25: 28; Mosiah 3: 14.
33*a* Alma 14: 17 (17–18).
34*a* Alma 10: 1 (1–11).
10 1*a* Alma 9: 34.
b Alma 8: 29 (21–29).
2*a* Dan. 5: 16.

[About 82 B.C.]

3 And Aminadi was a descendant of Nephi, who was the son of Lehi, who came out of the land of Jerusalem, who was a descendant of [a]Manasseh, who was the son of [b]Joseph who was [c]sold into Egypt by the hands of his brethren.

4 And behold, I am also a man of no small [a]reputation among all those who know me; yea, and behold, I have many kindreds and [b]friends, and I have also acquired much riches by the hand of my [c]industry.

5 Nevertheless, after all this, I never have known much of the ways of the Lord, and his [a]mysteries and marvelous power. I said I never had known much of these things; but behold, I mistake, for I have seen much of his mysteries and his marvelous power; yea, even in the preservation of the lives of this people.

6 Nevertheless, I did harden my heart, for I was [a]called many times and I would not [b]hear; therefore I knew concerning these things, yet I would not know; therefore I went on rebelling [c]against God, in the wickedness of my heart, even until the fourth day of this seventh month, which is in the tenth year of the reign of the judges.

7 As I was journeying to see a very near kindred, behold an [a]angel of the Lord appeared unto me and said: Amulek, return to thine own house, for thou shalt feed a prophet of the Lord; yea, a holy man, who is a chosen man of God; for he has [b]fasted many days because of the sins of this people, and he is an hungered, and thou shalt [c]receive him into thy house and feed him, and he shall bless thee and thy house; and the blessing of the Lord shall rest upon thee and thy house.

8 And it came to pass that I obeyed the voice of the angel, and returned towards my house. And as I was going thither I found the [a]man whom the angel said unto me: Thou shalt receive into thy house—and behold it was this same man who has been speaking unto you concerning the things of God.

9 And the angel said unto me he is a [a]holy man; wherefore I know he is a holy man because it was said by an angel of God.

10 And again, I know that the things whereof he hath testified are true; for behold I say unto you, that as the Lord liveth, even so has he sent his [a]angel to make these things manifest unto me; and this he has done while this Alma hath [b]dwelt at my house.

11 For behold, he hath [a]blessed mine house, he hath blessed me, and my women, and my children, and my father and my kinsfolk; yea, even all my kindred hath he blessed, and the blessing of the Lord hath rested upon us according to the words which he spake.

12 And now, when Amulek had spoken these words the people began to be astonished, seeing there was [a]more than one witness who testified of the things whereof they were accused, and also of the things which were to come, according to the spirit of prophecy which was in them.

13 Nevertheless, there were some among them who thought to question them, that by their cunning [a]devices they might catch them in their words, that they might [b]find

3*a* Gen. 41: 51; Josh. 17: 1; 1 Chr. 7: 14; 9: 3; 1 Ne. 5: 14.
b TG Israel, Joseph, People of.
c Gen. 37: 36 (29–36).
4*a* Acts 5: 34 (34–39).
b Alma 15: 16.
c TG Industry; Work, Value of.
5*a* TG Mysteries of Godliness.
6*a* 2 Chr. 33: 10; Isa. 50: 2; Alma 5: 37.
b D&C 39: 9.
c Acts 9: 5.
7*a* Alma 8: 20.
b Alma 5: 46; 6: 6.
c Acts 10: 30 (30–35). TG Hospitality.
8*a* Alma 8:19 (19–21).
9*a* TG Holiness.
10*a* Mosiah 3: 2 (2–3); Alma 11: 31.
b Alma 8: 27.
11*a* 1 Sam. 2: 20; Alma 8: 22.
12*a* Alma 9: 6.
13*a* Jer. 11: 19; Lam. 3: 62 (60–62); Alma 11: 21.
b Mark 14: 55 (55–60).

[About 82 B.C.]

witness against them, that they might deliver them to their judges that they might be judged according to the law, and that they might be slain or cast into prison, according to the crime which they could make appear or witness against them.

14 Now it was those men who sought to destroy them, who were [a]lawyers, who were hired or appointed by the people to administer the law at their times of trials, or at the trials of the crimes of the people before the judges.

15 Now these lawyers were learned in all the arts and [a]cunning of the people; and this was to enable them that they might be skilful in their profession.

16 And it came to pass that they began to question Amulek, that thereby they might make him [a]cross his words, or contradict the words which he should speak.

17 Now they knew not that Amulek could [a]know of their designs. But it came to pass as they began to question him, he [b]perceived their thoughts, and he said unto them: O ye wicked and perverse [c]generation, ye lawyers and hypocrites, for ye are laying the foundations of the devil; for ye are laying [d]traps and snares to catch the holy ones of God.

18 Ye are laying plans to [a]pervert the ways of the righteous, and to bring down the wrath of God upon your heads, even to the utter destruction of this people.

19 Yea, well did Mosiah say, who was our last king, when he was about to deliver up the kingdom, having no one to confer it upon, causing that this people should be governed by their own voices—yea, well did he say that if the time should come that the voice of this people should [a]choose iniquity, that is, if the time should come that this people should fall into transgression, they would be ripe for destruction.

20 And now I say unto you that well doth the Lord [a]judge of your iniquities; well doth he cry unto this people, by the voice of his [b]angels: Repent ye, repent, for the kingdom of heaven is at hand.

21 Yea, well doth he cry, by the voice of his angels that: [a]I will come down among my people, with equity and justice in my hands.

22 Yea, and I say unto you that if it were not for the [a]prayers of the righteous, who are now in the land, that ye would even now be visited with utter destruction; yet it would not be by [b]flood, as were the people in the days of [c]Noah, but it would be by famine, and by pestilence, and the [d]sword.

23 But it is by the [a]prayers of the righteous that ye are spared; now therefore, if ye will [b]cast out the righteous from among you then will not the Lord stay his hand; but in his fierce anger he will come out against you; then ye shall be smitten by famine, and by pestilence, and by the sword; and the [c]time is soon at hand except ye repent.

24 And now it came to pass that the people were more angry with Amulek, and they cried out, saying: This man doth revile against our laws which are just, and our wise [a]lawyers whom we have selected.

25 But Amulek stretched forth his hand, and cried the mightier unto them, saying: O ye wicked and

14*a* Alma 10: 24; 11: 21 (20–37); 14: 18 (18, 23); 3 Ne. 6: 11.
15*a* Luke 20: 23.
16*a* Mark 12: 13.
17*a* Luke 5: 22.
b Alma 12: 3; D&C 6: 16.
c Matt. 3: 7; Alma 9: 8.
d D&C 10: 25 (21–27).
18*a* Acts 13: 10.
19*a* Mosiah 29: 27; Alma 2: 4 (3–7); Hel. 5: 2.
20*a* TG Jesus Christ, Judge.
b Alma 8: 14 (14–16, 20); 13: 22.
21*a* Mosiah 13: 34 (28–35).
22*a* 1 Sam. 7: 9 (7–10); Mosiah 27: 14 (14–16).
b Gen. 8: 21; 3 Ne. 22: 9 (8–10). TG Flood.
c TG Earth, Cleansing of.
d Deut. 32: 25; JS-H 1: 45.
23*a* TG Prayer.
b 2 Chr. 13: 9; Moro. 9: 14.
c TG Procrastination.
24*a* Alma 10: 14.

[About 82 B.C.]

perverse generation, why hath Satan got such great hold upon your hearts? Why will ye yield yourselves unto him that he may have power over you, to [a]blind your eyes, that ye will not understand the words which are spoken, according to their truth?

26 For behold, have I testified against your law? Ye do not understand; ye say that I have spoken against your law; but I have not, but I have spoken in favor of your law, to your condemnation.

27 And now behold, I say unto you, that the foundation of the [a]destruction of this people is beginning to be laid by the [b]unrighteousness of your [c]lawyers and your judges.

28 And now it came to pass that when Amulek had spoken these words the people cried out against him, saying: Now we know that this man is a [a]child of the devil, for he hath [b]lied unto us; for he hath spoken against our law. And now he says that he has not spoken against it.

29 And again, he has reviled against our lawyers, and our judges.

30 And it came to pass that the lawyers put it into their hearts that they should remember these things against him.

31 And there was one among them whose name was Zeezrom. Now he was the foremost to [a]accuse Amulek and Alma, he being one of the most expert among them, having much business to do among the people.

32 Now the object of these lawyers was to get gain; and they got gain [a]according to their employ.

CHAPTER 11

Nephite coinage set forth—Amulek contends with Zeezrom—Christ will not save people in their sins—Only those who inherit the kingdom of heaven are saved—All men shall rise in immortality—There is no death after the resurrection.

Now it was in the law of Mosiah that every man who was a judge of the law, or those who were appointed to be judges, should receive [a]wages [b]according to the time which they labored to judge those who were brought before them to be judged.

2 Now if a man owed another, and he would not [a]pay that which he did owe, he was complained of to the judge; and the judge executed authority, and sent forth officers that the man should be brought before him; and he judged the man according to the law and the evidences which were brought against him, and thus the man was compelled to pay that which he owed, or be stripped, or be cast out from among the people as a thief and a robber.

3 And the judge received for his wages [a]according to his time—a [b]senine of gold for a day, or a senum of silver, which is equal to a senine of gold; and this is according to the law which was given.

4 Now these are the names of the different pieces of their gold, and of their silver, according to their value. And the names are given by the Nephites, for they did not reckon after the [a]manner of the Jews who were at Jerusalem; neither did they measure after the manner of the Jews; but they altered their reckoning and their measure, according to the minds and the circumstances of the people, in every generation, until the reign of the judges, they having been [b]established by king Mosiah.

25*a* 2 Cor. 4: 4 (3–4); Alma 14: 6; Moses 6: 27.
27*a* Alma 8: 16; 9: 12 (4, 12, 18, 24).
b TG Injustice.
c Luke 11: 46 (45–52); 2 Ne. 28: 16.
28*a* John 7: 20.
b Alma 14: 2.
31*a* Alma 11: 21 (20–36).
32*a* Alma 11: 1 (1–3).
11 1*a* TG Wages.
b Alma 10: 32.
2*a* TG Justice.
3*a* Alma 10: 32.
b Alma 30: 33; 3 Ne. 12: 26.
4*a* BD Money.
b Mosiah 29: 41 (40–44).

[About 82 B.C.]

5 Now the reckoning is thus—a
senine of gold, a seon of gold, a shum
of gold, and a limnah of gold.
6 A senum of silver, an amnor of
silver, an ezrom of silver, and an
onti of silver.
7 A senum of silver was equal to a
senine of gold, and either for a
measure of barley, and also for a
measure of every kind of grain.
8 Now the amount of a seon of gold
was twice the value of a senine.
9 And a shum of gold was twice the
value of a seon.
10 And a limnah of gold was the
value of them all.
11 And an amnor of silver was as
great as two senums.
12 And an ezrom of silver was as
great as four senums.
13 And an onti was as great as them
all.
14 Now this is the value of the
lesser numbers of their reckoning—
15 A shiblon is half of a senum;
therefore, a shiblon for half a
measure of barley.
16 And a shiblum is a half of a
shiblon.
17 And a leah is the half of a
shiblum.
18 Now this is their number,
according to their reckoning.
19 Now an antion of gold is equal
to three shiblons.
20 Now, it was for the sole purpose
to get [a]gain, because they received
their wages according to their
[b]employ, therefore, they did [c]stir up
the people to [d]riotings, and all
manner of disturbances and wickedness, that they might have more
employ, that they might [e]get
[f]money according to the suits which
were brought before them; therefore they did stir up the people
against Alma and Amulek.
21 And this Zeezrom began to
question Amulek, saying: Will ye
answer me a few questions which I
shall ask you? Now Zeezrom was a
man who was [a]expert in the [b]devices
of the devil, that he might destroy
that which was good; therefore, he
said unto Amulek: Will ye answer
the questions which I shall put unto
you?
22 And Amulek said unto him:
Yea, if it be according to the [a]Spirit
of the Lord, which is in me; for I
shall say nothing which is contrary
to the Spirit of the Lord. And
Zeezrom said unto him: Behold,
here are six onties of silver, and all
these will I [b]give thee if thou wilt
deny the existence of a Supreme
Being.
23 Now Amulek said: O thou [a]child
of hell, why [b]tempt ye me? Knowest
thou that the righteous yieldeth to
no such temptations?
24 Believest thou that there is no
God? I say unto you, Nay, thou
knowest that there is a God, but
thou lovest that [a]lucre more than
him.
25 And now thou hast lied before
God unto me. Thou saidst unto me—
Behold these six onties, which are of
great worth, I will give unto thee—
when thou hadst it in thy heart to
retain them from me; and it was
only thy desire that I should deny
the true and living God, that thou
mightest have cause to destroy me.
And now behold, for this great evil
thou shalt have thy reward.
26 And Zeezrom said unto him:
Thou sayest there is a true and
living God?
27 And Amulek said: Yea, there
is a true and living God.
28 Now Zeezrom said: Is there
more than one God?

20*a* TG Selfishness.
b Prov. 28: 8.
c TG Provoking.
d TG Rioting and Reveling.
e Alma 10: 32.
f Luke 11: 52 (45–54).
21*a* Alma 10: 31; 14: 7 (6–7, 18, 23).
b Lam. 3: 62 (60–62); Alma 10: 13.
22*a* TG Holy Ghost, Mission of; God, Spirit of.
b TG Bribery.
23*a* Acts 13: 10 (8–12); Alma 5: 41.
b TG Temptation; Test, Try, Prove.
24*a* Luke 16: 14; John 12: 43 (42–43); Acts 19: 27 (27, 36–38); Titus 1: 11.

[About 82 B.C.]

29 And he answered, No.
30 Now Zeezrom said unto him
again: How knowest thou these
things?
31 And he said: An [a]angel hath
made them known unto me.
32 And Zeezrom said again: Who
is he that shall come? Is it the Son
of God?
33 And he said unto him, Yea.
34 And Zeezrom said again: Shall
he save his people [a]in their sins? And
Amulek answered and said unto
him: I say unto you he shall not,
for it is impossible for him to deny
his word.
35 Now Zeezrom said unto the
people: See that ye remember these
things; for he said there is but one
God; yet he saith that the Son of
God shall come, but he shall [a]not
save his people—as though he had
authority to command God.
36 Now Amulek saith again unto
him: Behold thou hast [a]lied, for
thou sayest that I spake as though
I had authority to command God
because I said he shall not save his
people in their sins.
37 And I say unto you again that
he cannot save them in their [a]sins;
for I cannot deny his word, and he
hath said that [b]no unclean thing can
inherit the [c]kingdom of heaven;
therefore, how can ye be saved,
except ye inherit the kingdom of
heaven? Therefore, ye cannot be
saved in your sins.
38 Now Zeezrom saith again unto
him: Is the Son of God the very
Eternal Father?
39 And Amulek said unto him:
Yea, he is the very [a]Eternal Father
of heaven and of earth, and [b]all
things which in them are; he is the
beginning and the end, the first and
the last;
40 And he shall come into the
[a]world to [b]redeem his people; and
he shall [c]take upon him the transgressions of those who believe on
his name; and these are they that
shall have eternal life, and salvation
cometh to none else.
41 Therefore the wicked remain as
though there had been [a]no redemption made, except it be the loosing
of the bands of death; for behold,
the day cometh that [b]all shall rise
from the dead and stand before God,
and be [c]judged according to their
works.
42 Now, there is a death which is
called a temporal death; and the
death of Christ shall loose the
[a]bands of this temporal death, that
all shall be raised from this temporal
death.
43 The spirit and the body shall be
[a]reunited again in its [b]perfect form;
both limb and joint shall be restored
to its proper frame, even as we now
are at this time; and we shall be
brought to stand before God,
[c]knowing even as we know now, and
have a bright [d]recollection of all our
[e]guilt.
44 Now, this restoration shall
come to all, both old and young,
both bond and free, both male and
female, both the wicked and the
righteous; and even there shall not
so much as a hair of their heads be
lost; but every thing shall be
[a]restored to its perfect frame, as it is
now, or in the body, and shall be

31*a* Alma 10: 10.
34*a* Hel. 5: 10 (10–11).
35*a* Alma 14: 5.
36*a* Alma 12: 1.
37*a* 1 Cor. 6: 9 (9–10).
b 1 Ne. 15: 33; Alma 40: 26; 3 Ne. 27: 19. TG Uncleanness.
c TG Kingdom of God, in Heaven.
39*a* Isa. 9: 6; 64: 8; Mosiah 15: 4 (2–4); Moro. 7: 22; 8: 18.
b Col. 1: 16; Mosiah 4: 2.
40*a* TG World.
b Luke 2: 34; Rom. 11: 26 (26–27).
c Ex. 34: 7; 1 Jn. 2: 2; Mosiah 14: 5 (5, 8); 15: 12; D&C 19: 17 (16–18); 29: 17.
41*a* Alma 12: 18; D&C 88: 33.
b Rev. 20: 13 (12–13); Alma 28: 12; 42: 23.
c TG Judgment, The Last.
42*a* Alma 12: 16 (16, 24, 36).
43*a* 2 Ne. 9: 13; Alma 40: 23.
b TG Perfection.
c D&C 130: 18.
d 2 Ne. 9: 14; Mosiah 3: 25; Alma 5: 18.
e Matt. 12: 36 (36–37). TG Guilt.
44*a* Rev. 20: 12 (12–15).

[About 82 B.C.]

brought and be arraigned before
the bar of Christ the Son, and God
the [b]Father, and the Holy Spirit,
which is [c]one Eternal God, to be
[d]judged according to their works,
whether they be good or whether
they be evil.
45 Now, behold, I have spoken
unto you concerning the [a]death of
the mortal body, and also concerning the [b]resurrection of the mortal
body. I say unto you that this mortal
body is [c]raised to an [d]immortal body,
that is from death, even from the
first death unto life, that they can
[e]die no more; their spirits uniting
with their bodies, never to be
divided; thus the whole becoming
[f]spiritual and immortal, that they
can no more see corruption.
46 Now, when Amulek had finished
these words the people began again
to be astonished, and also Zeezrom
began to tremble. And thus ended
the words of Amulek, or this is all
that I have written.

CHAPTER 12

Alma contends with Zeezrom—The mysteries of God can be given only to the faithful—Men are judged by their thoughts, beliefs, words, and works—The wicked shall suffer a spiritual death—This mortal life is a probationary state—The plan of redemption brings to pass the resurrection and, through faith, a remission of sins—The repentant have a claim on mercy through the Only Begotten Son.

Now Alma, seeing that the words
of Amulek had silenced Zeezrom,
for he beheld that Amulek had
caught him in his [a]lying and de-
ceiving to destroy him, and seeing
that he began to tremble under a
[b]consciousness of his guilt, he opened
his mouth and began to speak unto
him, and to establish the words
of Amulek, and to explain things
beyond, or to unfold the scriptures
beyond that which Amulek had
done.
2 Now the words that Alma spake
unto Zeezrom were heard by the
people round about; for the multitude was great, and he spake on this
wise:
3 Now Zeezrom, seeing that thou
hast been taken in thy lying and
craftiness, for thou hast not lied
unto men only but thou hast lied
unto God; for behold, he knows all
thy [a]thoughts, and thou seest that
thy [b]thoughts are made known unto
us by his Spirit;
4 And thou seest that we know that
thy plan was a very [a]subtle plan,
as to the subtlety of the devil, for to
lie and to deceive this people that
thou mightest set them against us,
to [b]revile us and to cast us out—
5 Now this was a plan of thine
[a]adversary, and he hath exercised
his power in thee. Now I would that
ye should remember that what I say
unto thee I say unto all.
6 And behold I say unto you all
that this was a [a]snare of the adversary, which he has laid to catch
this people, that he might bring you
into subjection unto him, that he
might encircle you about with his
[b]chains, that he might chain you
down to everlasting destruction,
according to the power of his
captivity.
7 Now when Alma had spoken
these words, Zeezrom began to
tremble more exceedingly, for he
was convinced more and more of
the power of God; and he was also

44*b* TG Godhead.
c 3 Ne. 11: 27 (27–28, 36). TG God, Eternal Nature of.
d 2 Pet. 2: 9. TG Jesus Christ, Judge.
45*a* Alma 12: 12.
b Alma 40: 23; D&C 88: 16.
c TG Death, Power over.
d TG Immortality.
e Rev. 21: 4; Alma 12: 18 (18, 20); D&C 63: 49; 88: 116.
f 1 Cor. 15: 44.
12 1*a* Alma 11: 36 (20–38).
b Alma 62: 45; D&C 6: 11; 18: 44. TG Conscience.
3*a* Jacob 2: 5; D&C 6: 16.
b Alma 10: 17.
4*a* D&C 123: 12.
b TG Slander.
5*a* TG Devil.
6*a* Prov. 29: 6 (3–8).
b Alma 5: 9 (7–10).

[About 82 B.C.]

convinced that Alma and Amulek
had a knowledge of him, for he was
convinced that they [a]knew the
thoughts and intents of his heart;
for power was given unto them that
they might know of these things
according to the spirit of prophecy.
8 And Zeezrom began to inquire of
them diligently, that he might know
more concerning the kingdom of
God. And he said unto Alma: What
does this mean which Amulek hath
spoken concerning the resurrection
of the dead, that all shall rise from
the dead, both the [a]just and the
unjust, and are brought to stand
before God to be [b]judged according
to their works?
9 And now Alma began to expound
these things unto him, saying: It
is given unto many to [a]know the
[b]mysteries of God; nevertheless they
are laid under a strict command that
they shall not impart [c]only according
to the portion of his word which
he doth grant unto the children of
men, according to the heed and diligence
which they give unto him.
10 And therefore, he that will
[a]harden his heart, the same receiveth
the [b]lesser portion of the word;
and he that will [c]not harden his
heart, to him is [d]given the greater
portion of the word, until it is given
unto him to know the mysteries of
God until he know them in full.
11 And they that will harden their
hearts, to them is given the lesser
[a]portion of the word until they
[b]know nothing concerning his mysteries;
and then they are taken
captive by the devil, and led by his
will down to destruction. Now this
is what is meant by the [c]chains of
[d]hell.
12 And Amulek hath spoken
plainly concerning [a]death, and
being raised from this mortality to
a state of immortality, and being
brought before the bar of God, to
be [b]judged according to our works.
13 Then if our hearts have been
hardened, yea, if we have hardened
our hearts against the word, insomuch
that it has not been found in
us, then will our state be awful, for
then we shall be condemned.
14 For our [a]words will condemn us,
yea, all our works will condemn us;
we shall not be found spotless; and
our thoughts will also condemn us;
and in this awful state we shall not
dare to look up to our God; and we
would fain be glad if we could command
the rocks and the [b]mountains
to fall upon us to [c]hide us from his
presence.
15 But this cannot be; we must
come forth and stand before him in
his glory, and in his power, and in
his might, majesty, and dominion,
and acknowledge to our everlasting
[a]shame that all his [b]judgments are
just; that he is just in all his works,
and that he is merciful unto the
children of men, and that he has all
power to save every man that
believeth on his name and bringeth
forth fruit meet for repentance.
16 And now behold, I say unto you
then cometh a death, even a second
[a]death, which is a spiritual death;

7*a* Alma 14: 2.
8*a* Dan. 12: 2.
b TG Judgment, The Last.
9*a* Dan. 1: 17.
b Alma 26: 22. TG Mysteries of Godliness.
c John 16: 12; Alma 29: 8; 3 Ne. 26: 10 (6–11); Ether 4: 7 (1–7).
10*a* 2 Ne. 28: 27; 3 Ne. 26: 10 (9–10); Ether 4: 8.
b D&C 93: 39.
c TG Teachable.
d Dan. 2: 21; 2 Ne. 28: 30; D&C 50: 24; 71: 5.
11*a* Matt. 25: 29 (29–30).
b TG Apostasy of Individuals.
c Prov. 5: 22; John 8: 34 (31–36); 2 Ne. 28: 19 (19–22); Mosiah 23: 12; Alma 26: 14. TG Bondage, Spiritual.
d Prov. 9: 18; 1 Ne. 14: 7; 2 Ne. 2: 29 (26–29). TG Hell.
12*a* Alma 11: 45 (41–45).
b TG Judgment, The Last.
14*a* Prov. 18: 21; Matt. 12: 36; James 3: 6 (1–13); Mosiah 4: 30 (29–30).
b Hosea 10: 8; 2 Ne. 26: 5.
c Job 34: 22; Amos 9: 3; 2 Ne. 12: 10.
15*a* Mosiah 3: 25. TG Shame.
b 2 Pet. 2: 9. TG Justice.
16*a* TG Death, Spiritual, Second.

[About 82 B.C.]

then is a time that whosoever dieth
in his sins, as to a temporal [b]death,
shall also [c]die a spiritual death; yea,
he shall die as to things pertaining
unto righteousness.
17 Then is the time when their
torments shall be as a [a]lake of fire
and brimstone, whose flame ascendeth up forever and ever; and then is
the time that they shall be chained
down to an everlasting destruction,
according to the power and captivity
of Satan, he having subjected them
according to his will.
18 Then, I say unto you, they shall
be as though there had been [a]no
redemption made; for they cannot
be redeemed according to God's
justice; and they cannot [b]die, seeing
there is no more corruption.
19 Now it came to pass that when
Alma had made an end of speaking
these words, the people began to be
more astonished;
20 But there was one Antionah,
who was a chief ruler among them,
came forth and said unto him: What
is this that thou hast said, that man
should rise from the dead and be
changed from this mortal to an
[a]immortal state, that the soul can
never die?
21 What does the scripture mean,
which saith that God placed [a]cheru-
bim and a flaming sword on the east
of the garden of [b]Eden, lest our first
parents should enter and partake of
the fruit of the tree of life, and live
forever? And thus we see that there
was no possible chance that they
should live forever.
22 Now Alma said unto him: This
is the thing which I was about to
explain. Now we see that Adam did
[a]fall by the partaking of the forbidden [b]fruit, according to the word
of God; and thus we see, that by his
fall, all mankind became a [c]lost and
fallen people.
23 And now behold, I say unto you
that if it had been possible for Adam
to have [a]partaken of the fruit of the
tree of life at that time, there would
have been no death, and the word
would have been void, making God
a liar, for he said: [b]If thou eat thou
shalt surely die.
24 And we see that [a]death comes
upon mankind, yea, the death which
has been spoken of by Amulek,
which is the temporal death;
nevertheless there was a space
granted unto [b]man in which he
might repent; therefore this life
became a [c]probationary state; a
time to [d]prepare to meet God; a
time to prepare for that endless state
which has been spoken of by us,
which is after the resurrection of
the dead.
25 Now, if it had not been for the
plan of redemption, which was laid
from the foundation of the world,
there could have been no [a]resurrec-
tion of the dead; but there was a
plan of [b]redemption laid, which shall
bring to pass the resurrection of the
dead, of which has been spoken.
26 And now behold, if it were
possible that our first parents could
have gone forth and partaken of the
[a]tree of life they would have been
forever miserable, having no preparatory state; and thus the [b]plan

16*b* Alma 11:42 (40–45).
c 1 Ne. 15:33; Alma 40:26.
17*a* Rev. 19:20; 21:8; Mosiah 3:27; Alma 14:14.
18*a* Alma 11:41.
b Rev. 21:4; Alma 11:45; D&C 63:49; 88:116.
20*a* TG Immortality.
21*a* Gen. 3:24; Alma 42:2; Moses 4:31.
TG Cherubim.
b TG Eden.
22*a* TG Fall of Man.
b Gen. 3:6; 2 Ne. 2:15 (15–19); Mosiah 3:26.
c Mosiah 16:5 (4–5); Alma 9:30 (30–32).
23*a* Alma 42:5 (2–9).
b Gen. 2:17.
24*a* TG Death.
b 2 Ne. 2:21; Moses 5:8–12.
c 1 Pet. 2:20 (20–21).
TG Earth, Purpose of; Probation.
d Alma 34:32 (32–35).
25*a* 2 Ne. 2:8; Alma 7:12; 42:23.
b TG Redemption.
26*a* Gen. 2:9; 1 Ne. 15:36 (22, 28, 36); 2 Ne. 2:15; Alma 32:40.
b Alma 34:9 (8–16); 42:8 (6–28); Moses 6:62.

[About 82 B.C.]

of redemption would have been
frustrated, and the word of God
would have been void, taking none
effect.
27 But behold, it was not so; but
it was [a]appointed unto men that
they must die; and after death,
they must come to [b]judgment, even
that same judgment of which we
have spoken, which is the end.
28 And after God had appointed
that these things should come unto
man, behold, then he saw that it
was expedient that man should
know concerning the things whereof
he had appointed unto them;
29 Therefore he sent [a]angels to
converse with them, who caused
men to behold of his glory.
30 And they began from that time
forth to call on his name; therefore
God [a]conversed with men, and
made known unto them the [b]plan of
redemption, which had been prepared from the [c]foundation of the
world; and this he made known unto
them according to their faith and
repentance and their [d]holy works.
31 Wherefore, he gave [a]command-
ments unto men, they having first
transgressed the [b]first commandments as to things which were
temporal, and becoming as Gods,
[c]knowing good from evil, placing
themselves in a state to [d]act, or
being placed in a state to act
according to their wills and
pleasures, whether to do evil or to
do good—
32 Therefore God gave unto them
commandments, after having made
[a]known unto them the plan of
redemption, that they should not
do evil, the penalty thereof being a
second [b]death, which was an everlasting [c]death as to things pertaining unto righteousness; for on such
the plan of redemption could have
no power, for the works of [d]justice
could not be destroyed, according
to the supreme [e]goodness of God.
33 But God did call on men, in the
name of his Son, (this being the [a]plan
of redemption which was laid) saying: If ye will [b]repent, and harden
not your hearts, then will I have
mercy upon you, through mine
Only Begotten Son;
34 Therefore, whosoever repenteth,
and hardeneth not his heart, he
shall have claim on [a]mercy through
mine Only Begotten Son, unto a
[b]remission of his sins; and these shall
enter into my [c]rest.
35 And whosoever will harden his
heart and will do [a]iniquity, behold,
I swear in my wrath that he shall
not enter into my rest.
36 And now, my brethren, behold
I say unto you, that if ye will
harden your hearts ye shall not
enter into the rest of the Lord;
therefore your iniquity [a]provoketh
him that he sendeth down his [b]wrath
upon you as in the [c]first provocation,
yea, according to his word in the
last provocation as well as the first,
to the everlasting [d]destruction of
your souls; therefore, according to
his word, unto the last death, as
well as the first.
37 And now, my brethren, seeing
we know these things, and they are
true, let us repent, and harden not

27*a* Job 7: 1; Heb. 9: 27; D&C 42: 48; 121: 25.
b TG Judgment, The Last.
29*a* Moro. 7: 25 (25, 31); D&C 29: 42.
30*a* Moses 1: 1; 5: 4 (4–5); 6: 51 (4, 51–68).
b TG Salvation, Plan of.
c Gen. 2: 16 (16–17); Mosiah 18: 13; Alma 13: 3 (3, 5, 7–8); Abr. 3: 26 (24–26).
d Luke 8: 15 (14–15).
31*a* TG Commandments of God.
b Gen. 2: 17 (16–17); 2 Ne. 2: 19 (18–19).
c Gen. 3: 22; Moses 4: 11.
d 2 Ne. 2: 16. TG Agency.
32*a* Moses 5: 9 (4–9).
b TG Death, Spiritual, Second.
c TG Damnation.
d Mosiah 15: 27; Alma 34: 16 (15–16); 42: 15.
e TG Goodness.
33*a* TG Salvation, Plan of.
b Moses 5: 8.
34*a* 2 Cor. 4: 1.
b TG Remission of Sins.
c D&C 84: 24. TG Rest.
35*a* Moses 5: 15.
36*a* 1 Kgs. 16: 33. TG Provoking.
b TG God, Indignation of.
c Heb. 3: 8; 2 Ne. 9: 7; Jacob 1: 7 (7–8); Mosiah 16: 4 (4–7); Alma 11: 45; 42: 6 (6, 9, 14).
d TG Damnation.

[About 82 B.C.]

our hearts, that we [a]provoke not the Lord our God to pull down his wrath upon us in these his second commandments which he has given unto us; but let us enter into the [b]rest of God, which is prepared according to his word.

CHAPTER 13

Men are called as high priests because of their exceeding faith and good works —They are to teach the commandments—Through righteousness they are sanctified and enter into the rest of the Lord—Melchizedek was one of these—Angels are declaring glad tidings throughout the land—They will reveal the actual coming of Christ.

AND again, my brethren, I would cite your minds forward to the time when the Lord God gave these commandments unto his children; and I would that ye should remember that the Lord God [a]ordained priests, after his holy order, which was after the order of his Son, to teach these things unto the people.
2 And those priests were ordained after the [a]order of his Son, in a [b]manner that thereby the people might know in what manner to look forward to his Son for redemption.
3 And this is the manner after which they were ordained—being [a]called and [b]prepared from the [c]foundation of the world according to the [d]foreknowledge of God, on account of their exceeding faith and good works; in the first place being left to [e]choose good or evil; therefore they having chosen good, and exercising exceedingly great [f]faith, are [g]called with a holy calling, yea, with that holy calling which was prepared with, and according to, a preparatory redemption for such.
4 And thus they have been [a]called to this holy calling on account of their faith, while others would reject the Spirit of God on account of the hardness of their hearts and [b]blindness of their minds, while, if it had not been for this they might have had as great [c]privilege as their brethren.
5 Or in fine, in the first place they were on the [a]same standing with their brethren; thus this holy calling being prepared from the foundation of the world for such as would not harden their hearts, being in and through the atonement of the Only Begotten Son, who was prepared—
6 And thus being called by this holy calling, and ordained unto the high priesthood of the holy order of God, to teach his commandments unto the children of men, that they also might enter into his [a]rest—
7 This high priesthood being after the order of his Son, which order was from the foundation of the world; or in other words, being [a]without beginning of days or end of years, being prepared from [b]eternity to all eternity, according to his [c]foreknowledge of all things—
8 Now they were [a]ordained after this manner—being called with a holy calling, and ordained with a holy ordinance, and taking upon them the high priesthood of the holy order, which calling, and ordinance,

37*a* Num. 14:11 (11–12); 1 Ne. 17:30 (23–31); Jacob 1:8; Hel. 7:18.
b Alma 13:6 (6–29); 16:17; D&C 84:24.
13 1*a* Alma 8:23 (11, 23); D&C 84:17 (17–19); Moses 6:7; Abr. 2:9 (9, 11).
2*a* D&C 107:3 (2–4).
b Alma 13:16.
3*a* D&C 127:2. TG Election; Foreordination.
b D&C 138:56.
c Alma 12:30 (25, 30); 22:13. TG Man, Antemortal Existence of.
d TG God, Foreknowledge of.
e TG Agency.
f TG Priesthood, Qualifying for.
g TG Called of God.
4*a* Ether 12:10.
b TG Spiritual Blindness.
c 1 Ne. 17:35 (32–35).
5*a* Rom. 2:11; 2 Ne. 26:28.
6*a* Alma 12:37; 16:17. TG Rest.
7*a* Heb. 7:3; Abr. 1:3 (2–4).
b TG Eternity.
c TG God, Foreknowledge of; God, Omniscience of.
8*a* TG Priesthood, Melchizedek; Priesthood, Oath and Covenant.

[About 82 B.C.]

and high priesthood, is without
beginning or end—
9 Thus they become [a]high priests
forever, after the order of the Son,
the Only Begotten of the Father, who
is without beginning of days or end
of years, who is full of [b]grace, equity,
and truth. And thus it is. Amen.
10 Now, as I said concerning the
holy order, or this [a]high priesthood,
there were many who were ordained
and became high priests of God;
and it was on account of their
exceeding [b]faith and [c]repentance,
and their righteousness before God,
they choosing to repent and work
righteousness rather than to perish;
11 Therefore they were called after
this holy order, and were [a]sanctified,
and their [b]garments were washed
white through the blood of the
Lamb.
12 Now they, after being [a]sanctified
by the [b]Holy Ghost, having their
garments made white, being [c]pure
and spotless before God, could not
look upon [d]sin save it were with
[e]abhorrence; and there were many,
exceedingly great many, who were
made pure and entered into the rest
of the Lord their God.
13 And now, my brethren, I would
that ye should humble yourselves
before God, and bring forth [a]fruit
meet for repentance, that ye may
also enter into that rest.
14 Yea, humble yourselves even as
the people in the days of [a]Melchize-
dek, who was also a high priest after
this same order which I have spoken,
who also took upon him the high
priesthood forever.
15 And it was this same Melchizedek
to whom Abraham paid [a]tithes; yea,
even our father Abraham paid tithes
of one-tenth part of all he possessed.
16 Now these [a]ordinances were
given after this [b]manner, that thereby the people might look forward
on the Son of God, it being a [c]type of
his order, or it being his order, and
this that they might look forward
to him for a remission of their sins,
that they might enter into the rest of
the Lord.
17 Now this Melchizedek was a
king over the land of Salem; and his
people had waxed strong in iniquity
and abomination; yea, they had all
gone astray; they were full of all
manner of wickedness;
18 But Melchizedek having exercised mighty faith, and received the
office of the high priesthood according to the [a]holy order of God, did
preach repentance unto his people.
And behold, they did repent; and
Melchizedek did establish peace in
the land in his days; therefore he
was called the prince of peace, for he
was the king of Salem; and he did
reign under his father.
19 Now, there were [a]many before
him, and also there were many
afterwards, but [b]none were greater;
therefore, of him they have more
particularly made mention.
20 Now I need not rehearse the
matter; what I have said may
suffice. Behold, the [a]scriptures are

9*a* TG High Priest.
b John 1: 17 (14, 17); 2 Ne. 2: 6; Moses 1: 6. TG Grace.
10*a* D&C 84: 18 (6–22); 107: 53 (40–55).
b TG Priesthood, Magnifying Callings within.
c TG Spirituality.
11*a* Lev. 8: 30; Moses 6: 60 (59–60).
b 1 Ne. 12: 10; Alma 5: 21 (21–27); 3 Ne. 27: 19 (19–20).
12*a* Rom. 8: 1 (1–9); D&C 11: 12 (12–13).
TG Sanctification.
b TG Holy Ghost, Baptism of.
c TG Purity.
d Rom. 12: 9; 2 Ne. 4: 31; Mosiah 5: 2; Alma 19: 33.
e Prov. 8: 13; Alma 37: 29.
13*a* Luke 3: 8.
14*a* D&C 84: 14. JST Gen. 14: 25–40 (in Appendix, Latter-day Saint edition of King James Bible). TG Priesthood, History of.
15*a* Gen. 14: 20 (18–20); Mal. 3: 10 (8–10). TG Tithing.
16*a* A of F 5. TG Ordinance.
b Alma 13: 2.
c TG Jesus Christ, Types of, in Anticipation.
18*a* TG Priesthood.
19*a* Hel. 8: 18; D&C 84: 14 (6–16); 107: 53 (40–55).
b D&C 107: 2 (1–4).
20*a* Alma 14: 1 (1, 8, 14). TG Scriptures, Value of.

[About 82 B.C.]

before you; if ye will [b]wrest them it
shall be to your own destruction.
21 And now it came to pass that
when Alma had said these words
unto them, he stretched forth his
hand unto them and cried with a
mighty voice, saying: [a]Now is the
time to repent, for the day of salvation draweth nigh;
22 Yea, and the voice of the Lord,
by the [a]mouth of angels, doth
declare it unto all nations; yea,
doth declare it, that they may have
glad tidings of great joy; yea, and he
doth sound these glad tidings among
all his people, yea, even to them that
are scattered abroad upon the face
of the earth; wherefore they have
come unto us.
23 And they are made known unto
us in [a]plain terms, that we may
understand, that we cannot err;
and this because of our being
[b]wanderers in a strange land; therefore, we are thus highly favored, for
we have these glad tidings declared
unto us in all parts of our vineyard.
24 For behold, [a]angels are declaring
it unto many at this time in our
land; and this is for the purpose of
preparing the hearts of the children
of men to receive his word at the
time of his coming in his glory.
25 And now we only wait to hear
the joyful news declared unto us by
the mouth of angels, of his coming;
for the time cometh, we [a]know not
how soon. Would to God that it
might be in my day; but let it be
sooner or later, in it I will rejoice.
26 And it shall be made known unto
[a]just and holy men, by the mouth of
angels, at the time of his coming,
that the words of our fathers may be
fulfilled, according to that which
they have spoken concerning him,
which was according to the spirit of
prophecy which was in them.
27 And now, my brethren, I [a]wish
from the inmost part of my heart,
yea, with great [b]anxiety even unto
pain, that ye would hearken unto
my words, and cast off your sins,
and not [c]procrastinate the day of
your repentance;
28 But that ye would humble
yourselves before the Lord, and call
on his holy name, and [a]watch and
pray continually, that ye may not
be [b]tempted above that which ye
can bear, and thus be [c]led by the
Holy Spirit, becoming humble,
[d]meek, submissive, patient, full of
love and all long-suffering;
29 [a]Having faith on the Lord;
having a hope that ye shall receive
eternal life; having the [b]love of God
always in your hearts, that ye may
be lifted up at the last day and enter
into his [c]rest.
30 And may the Lord grant unto
you repentance, that ye may not
bring down his wrath upon you,
that ye may not be [a]bound down by
the chains of [b]hell, that ye may not
suffer the second [c]death.
31 And Alma spake many more
words unto the people, which are
not written in [a]this book.

CHAPTER 14

Alma and Amulek are imprisoned and smitten—The believers and their holy scriptures are burned by fire—These martyrs are received by the Lord

20*b* 2 Pet. 3: 16; Alma 41: 1.
21*a* TG Procrastination.
22*a* Alma 10: 20 (7–10, 20).
23*a* 2 Ne. 25: 7 (7–8); 31: 3; 32: 7; Jacob 4: 13; Ether 12: 39.
b Jacob 7: 26.
24*a* Alma 10: 10; 39: 19.
25*a* 1 Ne. 10: 4; 3 Ne. 1: 1.
26*a* Ex. 22: 31; Amos 3: 7; W of M 1: 17; D&C 49: 8; 107: 29.
27*a* Mosiah 28: 3 (3–4).
b Mosiah 25: 11.
c TG Apathy; Procrastination.
28*a* TG Prayer; Watchfulness.
b Rom. 7: 23 (23–24); 1 Cor. 10: 13; D&C 64: 20.
c Alma 22: 1; Morm. 5: 17.
d TG Forbearance; Love; Meekness.
29*a* Alma 7: 24.
b Ps. 18: 1; D&C 20: 31; 76: 116. TG God, Love of.
c D&C 84: 24.
30*a* TG Bondage, Spiritual.
b TG Damnation; Hell.
c TG Death, Spiritual, Second.
31*a* W of M 1: 5; 3 Ne. 5: 9 (8–12).

[About 82 B.C.]

in glory—The prison walls are rent and fall—Alma and Amulek are delivered and their persecutors are slain.

AND it came to pass after he had made an end of speaking unto the people many of them did believe on his words, and began to repent, and to search the [a]scriptures.

2 But the more part of them were desirous that they might destroy Alma and Amulek; for they were angry with Alma, because of the [a]plainness of his words unto Zeezrom; and they also said that Amulek had [b]lied unto them, and had reviled against their law and also against their lawyers and judges.

3 And they were also angry with Alma and Amulek; and because they had [a]testified so plainly against their wickedness, they sought to [b]put them away privily.

4 But it came to pass that they did not; but they took them and bound them with strong cords, and took them before the chief judge of the land.

5 And the people went forth and witnessed against them—testifying that they had reviled against the law, and their lawyers and judges of the land, and also of all the people that were in the land; and also testified that there was but one God, and that he should send his Son among the people, but he should [a]not save them; and many such things did the people testify against Alma and Amulek. Now this was done before the chief judge of the land.

6 And it came to pass that Zeezrom was astonished at the words which had been spoken; and he also knew concerning the [a]blindness of the minds, which he had caused among the people by his [b]lying words; and his soul began to be [c]harrowed up under a [d]consciousness of his own guilt; yea, he began to be encircled about by the pains of hell.

7 And it came to pass that he began to cry unto the people, saying: Behold, I am [a]guilty, and these men are spotless before God. And he began to plead for them from that time forth; but they reviled him, saying: Art thou also possessed with the devil? And they spit upon him, and [b]cast him out from among them, and also all those who believed in the words which had been spoken by Alma and Amulek; and they cast them out, and sent men to cast stones at them.

8 And they brought their wives and children together, and whosoever believed or had been taught to believe in the word of God they caused that they should be [a]cast into the fire; and they also brought forth their records which contained the holy scriptures, and cast them into the fire also, that they might be [b]burned and destroyed by fire.

9 And it came to pass that they took Alma and Amulek, and carried them forth to the place of [a]martyrdom, that they might witness the destruction of those who were consumed by fire.

10 And when Amulek saw the pains of the women and children who were consuming in the fire, he also was pained; and he said unto Alma: How can we witness this awful scene? Therefore let us stretch forth our hands, and exercise the [a]power of God which is in us, and save them from the flames.

11 But Alma said unto him: The Spirit constraineth me that I must not stretch forth mine hand; for behold the Lord receiveth them up

14 1*a* 2 Kgs. 22:11 (8–13); Acts 17:2 (2–3, 11); Alma 13:20.
2*a* Alma 12:7 (3–7).
b Alma 10:28 (24–32).
3*a* Prov. 26:26; Alma 37:21.
b Acts 23:12 (12–15).
5*a* Alma 11:35 (33–37).
6*a* TG Spiritual Blindness.
b Alma 10:31 (25–31).
c Alma 15:5.
d TG Conscience.
7*a* Alma 10:31; 11:21 (21–36); 15:3.
b Alma 15:1.
8*a* Alma 15:2.
b Jer. 36:23 (21–28).
9*a* TG Martyrdom.
10*a* Alma 8:31 (30–31).

[About 82 B.C.]

unto himself, in [a]glory; and he doth
suffer that they may do this thing,
or that the people may do this thing
unto them, according to the hardness of their hearts, that the [b]judg-
ments which he shall exercise upon
them in his wrath may be just; and
the [c]blood of the [d]innocent shall
stand as a witness against them,
yea, and cry mightily against them
at the last day.
12 Now Amulek said unto Alma:
Behold, perhaps they will burn us
also.
13 And Alma said: Be it according
to the will of the Lord. But, behold,
our work is not finished; therefore
they burn us not.
14 Now it came to pass that when
the bodies of those who had been
cast into the fire were consumed,
and also the records which were cast
in with them, the chief judge of the
land came and stood before Alma
and Amulek, as they were bound;
and he smote them with his hand
upon their [a]cheeks, and said unto
them: After what ye have seen, will
ye preach again unto this people,
that they shall be cast into a [b]lake
of fire and brimstone?
15 Behold, ye see that ye had not
power to save those who had been
cast into the fire; neither has God
saved them because they were of
thy faith. And the judge smote
them again upon their cheeks, and
asked: What say ye for yourselves?
16 Now this judge was after the
order and faith of [a]Nehor, who slew
Gideon.
17 And it came to pass that Alma
and Amulek answered him [a]nothing;
and he smote them again, and
delivered them to the officers to be
[b]cast into prison.
18 And when they had been cast
into prison three days, there came
many [a]lawyers, and judges, and
priests, and teachers, who were of
the profession of Nehor; and they
came in unto the prison to see them,
and they questioned them about
many words; but they answered
them nothing.
19 And it came to pass that the
judge stood before them, and said:
Why do ye not answer the words of
this people? Know ye not that I
have [a]power to deliver you up unto
the flames? And he [b]commanded
them to speak; but they answered
nothing.
20 And it came to pass that they
departed and went their ways, but
came again on the morrow; and the
judge also smote them again on their
cheeks. And many came forth also,
and smote them, saying: Will ye
stand again and judge this people,
and condemn our law? If ye have
such great power why do ye not
[a]deliver yourselves?
21 And many such things did they
say unto them, gnashing their teeth
upon them, and spitting upon them,
and saying: How shall we look when
we are damned?
22 And many such things, yea, all
manner of such things did they say
unto them; and thus they did [a]mock
them for many days. And they did
withhold food from them that they
might hunger, and water that they
might thirst; and they also did take
from them their clothes that they
were naked; and thus they were
[b]bound with strong cords, and confined in [c]prison.
23 And it came to pass after they
had thus suffered for many days,
(and it was on the twelfth day, in
the tenth month, *in the tenth year
of the reign of the judges over the

11a TG Exaltation.
b Ex. 23: 7; Ps. 37: 9 (8–13); Alma 60: 13; D&C 103: 3. TG Justice.
c TG Cruelty; Martyrdom.
d Lam. 4: 13; Mosiah 17: 10.
14a 1 Kgs. 22: 24 (14–27).
b Alma 12: 17. TG Damnation.
16a Alma 1: 12 (7–15); 2: 20; 21: 4.
17a Matt. 27: 12 (12–14).
b Alma 9: 33.
18a Alma 10: 14; 11: 21 (20–37).
19a John 19: 10 (9–10).
b Mosiah 7: 8.
20a Matt. 27: 40 (39–43).
22a TG Mocking.
b Acts 16: 23 (23–40); D&C 122: 6.
c Gen. 39: 20; Mosiah 7: 7.

[*81 B.C.]

people of Nephi) that the chief judge over the land of [a]Ammonihah and many of their teachers and their lawyers went in unto the prison where Alma and Amulek were bound with cords.

24 And the chief judge stood before them, and smote them again, and said unto them: If ye have the [a]power of God deliver yourselves from these bands, and then we will believe that the Lord will destroy this people according to your words.

25 And it came to pass that they all went forth and smote them, saying the same words, even until the last; and when the last had spoken unto them the [a]power of God was upon Alma and Amulek, and they rose and stood upon their feet.

26 And Alma cried, saying: How long shall we suffer these great [a]afflictions, O Lord? O Lord, [b]give us strength according to our faith which is in Christ, even unto [c]deliverance. And they broke the cords with which they were bound; and when the people saw this, they began to flee, for the fear of destruction had come upon them.

27 And it came to pass that so great was their fear that they fell to the earth, and did not obtain the outer door of the [a]prison; and the earth shook mightily, and the walls of the prison were rent in twain, so that they fell to the earth; and the chief judge, and the lawyers, and priests, and teachers, who smote upon Alma and Amulek, were slain by the fall thereof.

28 And Alma and Amulek came forth out of the prison, and they were not hurt; for the Lord had granted unto them [a]power, according to their faith which was in Christ. And they straightway came forth out of the prison; and they were [b]loosed from their [c]bands; and the prison had fallen to the earth, and every soul within the walls thereof, save it were Alma and Amulek, was slain; and they straightway came forth into the city.

29 Now the people having heard a great noise came running together by multitudes to know the cause of it; and when they saw Alma and Amulek coming forth out of the prison, and the walls thereof had fallen to the earth, they were struck with great fear, and fled from the presence of Alma and Amulek even as a goat fleeth with her young from two lions; and thus they did flee from the presence of Alma and Amulek.

CHAPTER 15

Alma and Amulek go to Sidom and establish a church—Alma heals Zeezrom, who joins the Church—Many are baptized and the Church prospers—Alma and Amulek go to Zarahemla.

AND it came to pass that Alma and Amulek were commanded to depart out of that city; and they departed, and came out even into the land of Sidom; and behold, there they found all the people who had departed out of the land of [a]Ammonihah, who had been [b]cast out and stoned, because they believed in the words of Alma.

2 And they related unto them all that had happened unto their [a]wives and children, and also concerning themselves, and of their [b]power of deliverance.

3 And also Zeezrom lay sick at Sidom, with a burning fever, which was caused by the great tribulations

23*a* Alma 8: 6; 15: 1 (1, 15–16).
24*a* TG Sign Seekers.
25*a* Alma 8: 31.
26*a* James 5: 10 (10–11); Mosiah 17: 13 (10–20); JS-H 1: 22.
b Ps. 69: 14 (1–2, 14); D&C 121: 3.
c TG Deliverance.
27*a* Acts 12: 4 (4–6); 16: 26; Hel. 5: 21 (21–50); 3 Ne. 28: 19 (19–20); 4 Ne. 1: 30; Ether 12: 13.
28*a* Alma 15: 2.
b 1 Ne. 7: 17 (17–18); Jacob 4: 6; 3 Ne. 28: 20 (19–22).
c Alma 36: 27.
15 1*a* Alma 14: 23; 16: 2 (2–3, 9, 11).
b Alma 14: 7.
2*a* Alma 14: 8 (8–14).
b Alma 14: 28 (26–29).

[About 81 B.C.]

of his mind on account of his [a]wickedness, for he supposed that Alma and Amulek were no more; and he supposed that they had been slain because of his iniquity. And this great sin, and his many other sins, did harrow up his mind until it did become exceedingly sore, having no deliverance; therefore he began to be scorched with a burning heat.

4 Now, when he heard that Alma and Amulek were in the land of Sidom, his heart began to take courage; and he sent a message immediately unto them, desiring them to come unto him.

5 And it came to pass that they went immediately, obeying the message which he had sent unto them; and they went in unto the house unto Zeezrom; and they found him upon his bed, sick, being very low with a burning fever; and his mind also was [a]exceedingly sore because of his iniquities; and when he saw them he stretched forth his hand, and besought them that they would heal him.

6 And it came to pass that Alma said unto him, taking him by the hand: [a]Believest thou in the power of Christ unto salvation?

7 And he answered and said: Yea, I believe all the words that thou hast taught.

8 And Alma said: If thou believest in the redemption of Christ thou canst be [a]healed.

9 And he said: Yea, I believe according to thy words.

10 And then Alma cried unto the Lord, saying: O Lord our God, have [a]mercy on this man, and [b]heal him according to his faith which is in Christ.

11 And when Alma had said these words, [a]Zeezrom leaped upon his feet, and began to walk; and this was done to the great astonishment of all the people; and the knowledge of this went forth throughout all the land of Sidom.

12 And Alma baptized Zeezrom unto the Lord; and he began from that time forth to preach unto the people.

13 And Alma established a church in the land of Sidom, and consecrated [a]priests and [b]teachers in the land, to baptize unto the Lord whosoever were desirous to be baptized.

14 And it came to pass that they were many; for they did flock in from all the region round about Sidom, and were baptized.

15 But as to the people that were in the land of Ammonihah, they yet remained a hard-hearted and a stiffnecked people; and they repented not of their sins, [a]ascribing all the power of Alma and Amulek to the devil; for they were of the profession of [b]Nehor, and did not believe in the repentance of their sins.

16 And it came to pass that Alma and Amulek, Amulek having [a]forsaken all his gold, and silver, and his precious things, which were in the land of Ammonihah, for the word of God, he being [b]rejected by those who were once his friends and also by his father and his kindred;

17 Therefore, after Alma having established the church at Sidom, seeing a great [a]check, yea, seeing that the people were checked as to the pride of their hearts, and began to [b]humble themselves before God, and began to assemble themselves together at their [c]sanctuaries to [d]worship God before the [e]altar, [f]watching and praying continually, that they might be delivered from Satan, and from [g]death, and from destruction—

3*a* Alma 14:7 (6–7).
5*a* Alma 14:6.
6*a* Mark 9:23.
8*a* TG Administrations to the Sick; Healing.
10*a* TG Mercy.
b Mark 2:11 (1–12).
11*a* Acts 3:8 (1–11).
13*a* Alma 4:20 (7, 16, 18, 20); 16:18.
b TG Teacher.
15*a* Matt. 12:24 (24–27).
b Alma 1:15 (2–15).
16*a* Luke 14:33; Alma 10:4.
b TG Prophets, Rejection of.
17*a* Alma 16:21.
b Ezra 10:1 (1–5).
c Ps. 150:1; Alma 16:13.
d TG Worship.
e Ex. 27:1 (1–8).
f TG Watchfulness.
g TG Death, Spiritual, First.

[About 81 B.C.]

18 Now as I said, Alma having seen all these things, therefore he took Amulek and came over to the land of Zarahemla, and took him to his [a]own house, and did administer unto him in his tribulations, and [b]strengthened him in the Lord.

19 And thus ended the tenth year of the reign of the judges over the people of Nephi.

CHAPTER 16

The Lamanites destroy the people of Ammonihah—Zoram leads the Nephites to victory over the Lamanites—Alma and Amulek and many others preach the word—They teach that after his resurrection Christ will appear to the Nephites.

AND it came to pass in the *eleventh year of the reign of the judges over the people of Nephi, on the fifth day of the second month, there having been much peace in the land of Zarahemla, there having been no wars nor contentions for a certain number of years, even until the fifth day of the second month in the eleventh year, there was a cry of war heard throughout the land.

2 For behold, the armies of the Lamanites had come in upon the wilderness side, into the borders of the land, even into the city of [a]Ammonihah, and began to slay the people and destroy the city.

3 And now it came to pass, before the Nephites could raise a sufficient army to drive them out of the land, they had [a]destroyed the people who were in the city of Ammonihah, and also some around the borders of Noah, and taken others captive into the wilderness.

4 Now it came to pass that the Nephites were desirous to obtain those who had been carried away captive into the wilderness.

5 Therefore, he that had been appointed chief captain over the armies of the Nephites, (and his name was Zoram, and he had two sons, Lehi and Aha)—now Zoram and his two sons, knowing that Alma was high priest over the church, and having heard that he had the spirit of prophecy, therefore they went unto him and desired of him to know whither the Lord would that they should go into the wilderness in search of their brethren, who had been taken captive by the Lamanites.

6 And it came to pass that Alma [a]inquired of the Lord concerning the matter. And Alma returned and said unto them: Behold, the Lamanites will cross the river Sidon in the south wilderness, away up beyond the borders of the land of [b]Manti. And behold there shall ye meet them, on the east of the river Sidon, and there the Lord will deliver unto thee thy brethren who have been taken captive by the Lamanites.

7 And it came to pass that Zoram and his sons crossed over the river Sidon, with their armies, and marched away beyond the borders of Manti into the south wilderness, which was on the east side of the river Sidon.

8 And they came upon the armies of the Lamanites, and the Lamanites were scattered and driven into the wilderness; and they took their brethren who had been taken captive by the Lamanites, and there was not one soul of them had been lost that were taken captive. And they were brought by their brethren to possess their own lands.

9 And thus ended the eleventh year of the judges, the Lamanites having been driven out of the land, and the people of Ammonihah were [a]destroyed; yea, [b]every living soul

---

18*a* Alma 27: 20.
b Zech. 10: 12 (11–12).
16 2*a* Alma 15: 1 (1, 15–16); 49: 3 (1–15).
3*a* Alma 9: 18.
6*a* 2 Kgs. 6: 8–12; Alma 43: 23 (23–24); 48: 16; 3 Ne. 3: 20 (18–21).
b Alma 17: 1; 22: 27; 56: 14.
9*a* Alma 8: 16; 9: 24 (18–24); Morm. 6: 15 (15–22).
b Alma 14: 11.

[*81 B.C.]

of the Ammonihahites was [c]destroyed, and also their [d]great city, which they said God could not destroy, because of its greatness.

10 But behold, in [a]one day it was left desolate; and the [b]carcases were mangled by dogs and wild beasts of the wilderness.

11 Nevertheless, after many days their [a]dead bodies were heaped up upon the face of the earth, and they were covered with a shallow covering. And now so great was the scent thereof that the people did not go in to possess the land of Ammonihah for many years. And it was called Desolation of [b]Nehors; for they were of the profession of Nehor, who were slain; and their lands remained desolate.

12 And the Lamanites did not come again to war against the Nephites *until the fourteenth year of the reign of the judges over the people of Nephi. And thus for three years did the people of Nephi have continual peace in all the land.

13 And Alma and Amulek went forth preaching repentance to the people in their [a]temples, and in their [b]sanctuaries, and also in their [c]synagogues, which were built after the manner of the Jews.

14 And as many as would hear their words, unto them they did impart the word of God, without any [a]respect of persons, continually.

15 And thus did Alma and Amulek go forth, and also many more who had been chosen for the work, to preach the word throughout all the land. And the establishment of the church became general throughout the land, in all the region round about, among all the people of the Nephites.

16 And there was [a]no inequality among them; the Lord did pour out his Spirit on all the face of the land to prepare the minds of the children of men, or to prepare their [b]hearts to receive the word which should be taught among them at the time of his coming—

17 That they might not be hardened against the word, that they might not be unbelieving, and go on to destruction, but that they might receive the word with joy, and as a [a]branch be grafted into the true vine, that they might enter into the [b]rest of the Lord their God.

18 Now those [a]priests who did go forth among the people did preach against all [b]lyings, and [c]deceivings, and [d]envyings, and [e]strifes, and malice, and revilings, and stealing, robbing, plundering, murdering, committing adultery, and all manner of lasciviousness, crying that these things ought not so to be—

19 Holding forth things which must shortly come; yea, holding forth the [a]coming of the Son of God, his sufferings and death, and also the resurrection of the dead.

20 And many of the people did inquire concerning the place where the Son of God should come; and they were taught that he would [a]appear unto them [b]after his resurrection; and this the people did hear with great joy and gladness.

21 And now after the church had been established throughout all the land—having got the [a]victory over

9c Alma 25: 2.
d Alma 49: 3.
10a Alma 9: 4.
b Jer. 19: 7.
11a Alma 28: 11.
b Alma 1: 15; 2: 1 (1, 20); 24: 28 (28–30).
13a 2 Ne. 5: 16; Hel. 3: 14 (9, 14).
b Alma 15: 17; 21: 6.
c Alma 21: 20 (4–6, 20).
14a Deut. 10: 17; Alma 1: 30.
16a Mosiah 18: 27 (19–29); 4 Ne. 1: 3.
b Acts 16: 14. TG Teachable.
17a Jacob 5: 24. TG Vineyard of the Lord.
b Alma 12: 37; 13: 6 (6–29).
18a Alma 15: 13; 30: 20 (20–23, 31).
b 3 Ne. 30: 2.
c TG Deceit.
d TG Envy.
e Alma 4: 9 (8–9). TG Strife.
19a TG Jesus Christ, Prophecies about.
20a 2 Ne. 26: 9; 3 Ne. 11: 8 (7–14).
b 1 Ne. 12: 6 (4–8); Alma 7: 8.
21a Alma 15: 17.

[*About 78 B.C.]

the devil, and the word of God being
preached in its purity in all the land,
and the Lord pouring out his blessings upon the people—thus ended
the fourteenth year of the reign of
the judges over the people of Nephi.

An account of the sons of Mosiah, who rejected their rights to the kingdom for the word of God, and went up to the land of Nephi to preach to the Lamanites; their sufferings and deliverance—according to the record of Alma. Comprising chapters 17 to 26 inclusive.

CHAPTER 17

The sons of Mosiah have the spirit of prophecy and of revelation—They go their several ways to declare the word to the Lamanites—Ammon goes to the land of Ishmael and becomes the servant of King Lamoni—Ammon saves the king's flocks and slays his enemies at the waters of Sebus.

AND now it came to pass that as
Alma was journeying from the land
of Gideon southward, away to the
land of [a]Manti, behold, to his
astonishment, he [b]met with the
[c]sons of Mosiah journeying towards
the land of Zarahemla.
2 Now these sons of Mosiah were
with Alma at the time the angel
[a]first appeared unto him; therefore
Alma did rejoice exceedingly to see
his brethren; and what added more
to his joy, they were still his brethren in the Lord; yea, and they had
waxed strong in the knowledge of
the truth; for they were men of a
sound understanding and they had
[b]searched the scriptures diligently,
that they might know the word of
God.
3 But this is not all; they had given
themselves to much prayer, and
[a]fasting; therefore they had the
spirit of prophecy, and the spirit of
revelation, and when they taught,
they taught with [b]power and
authority of God.
4 And they had been teaching the
word of God *for the space of four-
teen years among the Lamanites,
having had much [a]success in bringing many to the [b]knowledge of the
truth; yea, by the power of their
words many were brought before
the altar of God, to call on his name
and [c]confess their sins before him.
5 Now these are the circumstances
which attended them in their
journeyings, for they had many
afflictions; they did suffer much,
both in body and in mind, such as
hunger, thirst and fatigue, and also
much [a]labor in the spirit.
6 Now these were their journeyings: Having [a]taken leave of their
father, Mosiah, in the [b]first year of
the judges; having [c]refused the
kingdom which their father was
desirous to confer upon them, and
also this was the minds of the people;
7 Nevertheless they departed out
of the land of Zarahemla, and took
their swords, and their spears, and
their bows, and their arrows, and
their slings; and this they did that
they might [a]provide food for themselves while in the wilderness.
8 And thus they departed into the
wilderness with their numbers which
they had [a]selected, to go up to the
land of Nephi, to preach the word of
God unto the Lamanites.
9 And it came to pass that they
journeyed many days in the wilderness, and they fasted much and
[a]prayed much that the Lord would
grant unto them a portion of his

17 1*a* Alma 16: 6.
b Alma 27: 16.
c Mosiah 27: 34.
2*a* Mosiah 27: 11 (11–17).
b Jacob 7: 23; D&C 84: 85. TG Scriptures, Study of.
3*a* TG Fasting.
b W of M 1: 17. TG Authority; Teaching with the Spirit.
4*a* Alma 29: 14.
b TG Missionary Work.
c Num. 5: 7 (6–10); Mosiah 26: 29 (29, 35); 3 Ne. 1: 25.
5*a* Alma 8: 10.
6*a* Mosiah 28: 9 (1, 5–9); Alma 26: 1.
b Mosiah 29: 44 (41–44).
c Mosiah 29: 3.
7*a* 1 Ne. 16: 15 (15–32).
8*a* Mosiah 28: 1.
9*a* Alma 25: 17. TG Guidance, Divine.

[*From about 91 to 77 B.C.]

Spirit to go with them, and abide
with them, that they might be an
[b]instrument in the hands of God to
bring, if it were possible, their
brethren, the Lamanites, to the
knowledge of the truth, to the
knowledge of the baseness of the
[c]traditions of their fathers, which
were not correct.
10 And it came to pass that the
Lord did [a]visit them with his [b]Spirit,
and said unto them: Be [c]comforted.
And they were comforted.
11 And the Lord said unto them
also: Go forth among the Lamanites,
thy brethren, and establish my
word; yet ye shall be [a]patient in
long-suffering and afflictions, that
ye may show forth good [b]examples
unto them in me, and I will make an
instrument of thee in my hands unto
the salvation of many souls.
12 And it came to pass that the
hearts of the sons of Mosiah, and
also those who were with them,
took courage to go forth unto the
Lamanites to declare unto them the
word of God.
13 And it came to pass when they
had arrived in the borders of the
land of the Lamanites, that they
[a]separated themselves and departed
one from another, trusting in the
Lord that they should meet again
at the close of their [b]harvest; for
they supposed that great was the
work which they had undertaken.
14 And assuredly it was great, for
they had undertaken to preach the
word of God to a [a]wild and a hardened and a ferocious people; a people
who delighted in murdering the
Nephites, and robbing and plundering them; and their hearts were set
upon riches, or upon gold and silver,
and precious stones; yet they sought
to obtain these things by murdering
and plundering, that they might not
labor for them with their own
hands.
15 Thus they were a very indolent
people, many of whom did worship
idols, and the [a]curse of God had
fallen upon them because of the
[b]traditions of their fathers; notwithstanding the promises of the
Lord were extended unto them on
the conditions of repentance.
16 Therefore, this was the [a]cause
for which the sons of Mosiah had
undertaken the work, that perhaps
they might bring them unto repentance; that perhaps they might bring
them to know of the plan of redemption.
17 Therefore they separated themselves one from another, and went
forth among them, every man alone,
according to the word and power of
God which was given unto him.
18 Now Ammon being the chief
among them, or rather he did
administer unto them, and he
departed from them, after having
[a]blessed them according to their
several stations, having imparted
the word of God unto them, or
administered unto them before his
departure; and thus they took their
several journeys throughout the
land.
19 And Ammon went to the land of
[a]Ishmael, the land being called after
the sons of [b]Ishmael, who also became Lamanites.
20 And as Ammon entered the
land of Ishmael, the Lamanites took
him and [a]bound him, as was their
custom to bind all the Nephites who
fell into their hands, and carry them
before the king; and thus it was left
to the pleasure of the king to slay
them, or to retain them in captivity,
or to cast them into prison, or to

9*b* Mosiah 23: 10; Alma 26: 3.
c Alma 3: 11.
10*a* 1 Ne. 2: 16; D&C 5: 16.
b TG God, Spirit of.
c Alma 26: 27.
11*a* Alma 20: 29; 26: 27. TG Forbearance; Patience.
b TG Example.
13*a* Alma 21: 1.
b Matt. 9: 37.
14*a* Mosiah 10: 12.
15*a* Alma 3: 19 (6–19); 3 Ne. 2: 15 (15–16).
b Alma 9: 16 (16–24); 18: 5.
16*a* Mosiah 28: 2 (1–3).
18*a* TG Blessing.
19*a* Alma 21: 18 (18, 20); 22: 1 (1, 4); 25: 13.
b 1 Ne. 7: 6 (4–6).
20*a* Mosiah 7: 7 (7–10).

[About 90 B.C.]

cast them out of his land, according to his will and pleasure.

21 And thus Ammon was carried before the king who was over the land of Ishmael; and his name was Lamoni; and he was a descendant of Ishmael.

22 And the king inquired of Ammon if it were his desire to dwell in the land among the Lamanites, or among his people.

23 And Ammon said unto him: Yea, I desire to [a]dwell among this people for a time; yea, and perhaps until the day I die.

24 And it came to pass that king Lamoni was much pleased with Ammon, and caused that his bands should be loosed; and he would that Ammon should take one of his daughters to wife.

25 But Ammon said unto him: Nay, but I will be thy servant. Therefore Ammon became a [a]servant to king Lamoni. And it came to pass that he was set among other servants to watch the flocks of Lamoni, according to the custom of the Lamanites.

26 And after he had been in the service of the king three days, as he was with the Lamanitish servants going forth with their flocks to the place of [a]water, which was called the water of Sebus, and all the Lamanites drive their flocks hither, that they may have water—

27 Therefore, as Ammon and the servants of the king were driving forth their flocks to this place of water, behold, a certain number of the Lamanites, who had been with their flocks to water, stood and [a]scattered the flocks of Ammon and the servants of the king, and they scattered them insomuch that they fled many ways.

28 Now the servants of the king began to murmur, saying: Now the king will slay us, as he has our brethren because their flocks were scattered by the wickedness of these men. And they began to weep exceedingly, saying: Behold, our flocks are scattered already.

29 Now they wept because of the fear of being slain. Now when Ammon saw this his heart was swollen within him with joy; for, said he, I will show forth my power unto these my fellow-servants, or the power which is in me, in restoring these flocks unto the king, that I may win the hearts of these my fellow-servants, that I may lead them to [a]believe in my words.

30 And now, these were the thoughts of Ammon, when he saw the afflictions of those whom he termed to be his brethren.

31 And it came to pass that he flattered them by his words, saying: My brethren, be of good cheer and let us go in search of the flocks, and we will gather them together and bring them back unto the place of water; and thus we will preserve the flocks unto the king and he will not slay us.

32 And it came to pass that they went in search of the flocks, and they did follow Ammon, and they rushed forth with much swiftness and did head the flocks of the king, and did gather them together again to the place of water.

33 And those men again stood to scatter their flocks; but Ammon said unto his brethren: Encircle the flocks round about that they flee not; and I go and contend with these men who do scatter our flocks.

34 Therefore, they did as Ammon commanded them, and he went forth and stood to contend with those who stood by the waters of Sebus; and they were in number not a few.

35 Therefore they did not fear Ammon, for they supposed that one of their men could slay him according to their pleasure, for they knew not that the Lord had promised Mosiah that he would [a]deliver

23*a* Alma 19: 19.
25*a* Alma 21: 19.
26*a* Ex. 2: 17 (15–20).
27*a* Alma 18: 3 (3–7); 19: 21 (20–21).
29*a* 2 Kgs. 5: 8.
35*a* Mosiah 28: 7; Alma 19: 23 (22–23).

[About 90 B.C.]

his sons out of their hands; neither
did they know anything concerning the Lord; therefore they delighted in the destruction of their
brethren; and for this cause they
stood to scatter the flocks of the
king.
36 But [a]Ammon stood forth and
began to cast stones at them with
his sling; yea, with mighty power
he did sling stones amongst them;
and thus he slew a [b]certain number
of them insomuch that they began
to be astonished at his power;
nevertheless they were angry because of the slain of their brethren,
and they were determined that he
should fall; therefore, seeing that
they [c]could not hit him with their
stones, they came forth with clubs
to slay him.
37 But behold, every man that
lifted his club to smite Ammon, he
smote off their arms with his sword;
for he did withstand their blows by
smiting their arms with the edge of
his sword, insomuch that they began
to be astonished, and began to flee
before him; yea, and they were
not few in number; and he caused
them to flee by the strength of his
arm.
38 Now six of them had fallen by
the sling, but he [a]slew none save it
were their leader with his sword;
and he smote off as many of their
arms as were lifted against him, and
they were not a few.
39 And when he had driven them
afar off, he returned and they
watered their flocks and returned
them to the pasture of the king, and
then went in unto the king, bearing
the arms which had been smitten off
by the sword of Ammon, of those
who sought to slay him; and they
were carried in unto the king for a
testimony of the things which they
had done.

CHAPTER 18

King Lamoni supposes that Ammon is the Great Spirit—Ammon teaches the king of the creation, of God's dealings with men, and of the redemption that comes through Christ—Lamoni believes and falls to the earth as if dead.

AND it came to pass that king
Lamoni caused that his [a]servants
should stand forth and testify to all
the things which they had seen concerning the matter.
2 And when they had all testified
to the things which they had seen,
and he had learned of the faithfulness of Ammon in preserving his
flocks, and also of his [a]great power
in contending against those who
sought to slay him, he was astonished exceedingly, and said: Surely,
this is more than a man. Behold, is
not this the Great Spirit who doth
send such great punishments upon
this people, because of their
murders?
3 And they answered the king, and
said: Whether he be the Great Spirit
or a man, we know not; but this
much we do know, that he [a]cannot
be slain by the enemies of the king;
neither can they [b]scatter the king's
flocks when he is with us, because of
his expertness and [c]great strength;
therefore, we know that he is a friend
to the king. And now, O king, we do
not believe that a man has such great
power, for we know he cannot be
slain.
4 And now, when the king heard
these words, he said unto them:
Now I know that it is the Great
Spirit; and he has come down at this
time to preserve your lives, that I
might not [a]slay you as I did your
brethren. Now this is the Great
Spirit of whom our fathers have
spoken.
5 Now this was the [a]tradition of
Lamoni, which he had received from

36*a* Ether 12: 15.
b Alma 18: 16 (16, 20).
c Alma 18: 3.
38*a* Alma 19: 22.

18 1*a* Alma 19: 15.
2*a* Alma 22: 9 (9–11).
3*a* Alma 17: 36 (34–38).
b Alma 17: 27; 19: 21 (20–21).
c Alma 22: 20.
4*a* Alma 17: 28 (28–31).
5*a* Alma 17: 15; 60: 32.

[About 90 B.C.]

his father, that there was a [b]Great
Spirit. Notwithstanding they believed in a Great Spirit, they supposed that [c]whatsoever they did
was right; nevertheless, Lamoni
began to fear exceedingly, with fear
lest he had done wrong in slaying
his servants;
6 For he had slain many of them
because their brethren had scattered
their flocks at the place of water;
and thus, because they had had
their flocks scattered they were
slain.
7 Now it was the practice of these
Lamanites to stand by the [a]waters
of Sebus to scatter the flocks of the
people, that thereby they might
drive away many that were scattered
unto their own land, it being a
practice of plunder among them.
8 And it came to pass that king
Lamoni inquired of his servants,
saying: Where is this man that has
such great power?
9 And they said unto him: Behold,
he is feeding thy [a]horses. Now the
king had commanded his servants,
previous to the time of the watering
of their flocks, that they should
prepare his horses and chariots, and
conduct him forth to the land of
Nephi; for there had been a [b]great
[c]feast appointed at the land of
Nephi, by the father of Lamoni,
who was king over all the land.
10 Now when king Lamoni heard
that Ammon was preparing his
horses and his [a]chariots he was more
astonished, because of the faithfulness of Ammon, saying: Surely there
has not been any servant among all
my servants that has been so faithful as this man; for even he doth
remember all my commandments to
execute them.
11 Now I surely know that this is
the Great Spirit, and I would desire
him that he come in unto me, but I
durst not.
12 And it came to pass that when
Ammon had made ready the horses
and the chariots for the king and his
servants, he went in unto the king,
and he saw that the [a]countenance of
the king was changed; therefore he
was about to return out of his
presence.
13 And one of the king's servants
said unto him, [a]Rabbanah, which is,
being interpreted, powerful or great
king, considering their kings to be
powerful; and thus he said unto him:
Rabbanah, the king desireth thee
to stay.
14 Therefore Ammon turned himself unto the king, and said unto
him: What wilt thou that I should
do for thee, O king? And the king
answered him not for the space of
an [a]hour, according to their time,
for he knew not what he should say
unto him.
15 And it came to pass that Ammon
said unto him again: What desirest
thou of me? But the king answered
him not.
16 And it came to pass that Ammon, being filled with the [a]Spirit of
God, therefore he perceived the
[b]thoughts of the king. And he said
unto him: Is it because thou hast
heard that I defended thy servants
and thy flocks, and slew [c]seven of
their brethren with the sling and
with the sword, and smote off the
arms of others, in order to defend
thy flocks and thy servants; behold,
is it this that causeth thy marvelings?
17 I say unto you, what is it, that
thy marvelings are so great? Behold,
I am a [a]man, and am thy servant;
therefore, whatsoever thou desirest
which is right, that will I do.
18 Now when the king had heard

5*b* Alma 19:25 (25–27). TG God, Knowledge about.
c Alma 30:17.
7*a* Alma 17:26; 19:20 (20–21).
9*a* Enos 1:21; Alma 20:6.
b Alma 20:9 (9, 12).
c Esth. 1:3.
10*a* Alma 20:6; 3 Ne. 3:22.
12*a* Dan. 5:6.
13*a* John 20:16.
14*a* 3 Ne. 8:19.
16*a* Gen. 41:38; 1 Ne. 1:12; Mosiah 27:24.
b Alma 12:3.
c Alma 17:36.
17*a* Dan. 2:30.

[About 90 B.C.]

these words, he marveled again,
for he beheld that Ammon could
[a]discern his thoughts; but notwithstanding this, king Lamoni did
open his mouth, and said unto him:
Who art thou? Art thou that Great
Spirit, who [b]knows all things?
19 Ammon answered and said unto
him: I am not.
20 And the king said: How knowest
thou the thoughts of my heart?
Thou mayest speak boldly, and tell
me concerning these things; and
also tell me by what power ye slew
and smote off the arms of my
brethren that scattered my flocks—
21 And now, [a]if thou wilt tell me
concerning these things, whatsoever thou desirest I will give unto
thee; and if it were needed, I would
guard thee with my armies; but I
know that thou art more powerful
than all they; nevertheless, whatsoever thou desirest of me I will
grant it unto thee.
22 Now Ammon being [a]wise, yet
harmless, he said unto Lamoni:
Wilt thou hearken unto my words,
if I tell thee by what power I do
these things? And this is the thing
that I desire of thee.
23 And the king answered him, and
said: Yea, I [a]will believe all thy
words. And thus he was caught with
[b]guile.
24 And Ammon began to speak
unto him with [a]boldness, and said
unto him: Believest thou that there
is a God?
25 And he answered, and said unto
him: I do not know what that
meaneth.
26 And then Ammon said: Believest thou that there is a [a]Great Spirit?
27 And he said, Yea.
28 And Ammon said: This is God.
And Ammon said unto him again:
Believest thou that this Great Spirit,
who is God, created all things which
are in heaven and in the earth?
29 And he said: Yea, I believe that
he created all things which are in
the earth; but I do not know the
heavens.
30 And Ammon said unto him:
The heavens is a place where God
dwells and all his holy angels.
31 And king Lamoni said: Is it
above the earth?
32 And Ammon said: Yea, and he
looketh down upon all the children
of men; and he [a]knows all the
thoughts and [b]intents of the heart;
for by his hand were they all created
from the beginning.
33 And king Lamoni said: I believe
all these things which thou hast
spoken. Art thou [a]sent from God?
34 Ammon said unto him: I am a
[a]man; and man in the beginning was
created after the image of God, and
I am called by his Holy [b]Spirit to
teach these things unto this people,
that they may be brought to a knowledge of that which is just and true;
35 And a portion of that [a]Spirit
dwelleth in me, which giveth me
[b]knowledge, and also power according to my faith and desires which
are in God.
36 Now when Ammon had said
these words, he began at the creation
of the world, and also the creation of
Adam, and told him all the things
concerning the fall of man, and
[a]rehearsed and laid before him the
[b]records and the holy scriptures of
the people, which had been spoken
by the [c]prophets, even down to the
time that their father, Lehi, left
Jerusalem.
37 And he also rehearsed unto

18*a* TG Discernment, Spiritual.
b TG God, Omniscience of.
21*a* Dan. 5:16.
22*a* Gen. 41:39; Alma 48:11 (11–17).
23*a* Alma 18:40.
b Josh. 9:22.
24*a* Alma 38:12.
26*a* Alma 22:9 (9–10).
32*a* TG God, Omniscience of.
b Amos 4:13; 3 Ne. 28:6.
33*a* 2 Chr. 24:19.
34*a* Mosiah 7:27; Ether 3:15 (13–16).
b TG Teaching with the Spirit.
35*a* TG Inspiration.
b TG Knowledge.
36*a* Mosiah 1:4; Alma 22:12; 36:1; 37:9; Hel. 5:13 (1–13); Moses 6:58.
b Alma 63:12. TG Scriptures, Value of.
c Acts 3:18 (18–21); 28:23.

[About 90 B.C.]

them (for it was unto the king and
to his servants) all the journeyings
of their fathers in the wilderness, and
all their sufferings with hunger and
thirst, and their travail, and so forth.
38 And he also rehearsed unto them
concerning the [a]rebellions of Laman
and Lemuel, and the sons of Ishmael,
yea, all their rebellions did he relate
unto them; and he expounded unto
them all the [b]records and scriptures
from the time that Lehi left Jerusalem down to the present time.
39 But this is not all; for he [a]ex-
pounded unto them the [b]plan of
redemption, which was prepared
from the foundation of the world;
and he also made known unto them
concerning the coming of Christ, and
all the works of the Lord did he make
known unto them.
40 And it came to pass that after he
had said all these things, and expounded them to the king, that the
king [a]believed all his words.
41 And he began to cry unto the
Lord, saying: O Lord, have mercy;
according to thy abundant [a]mercy
which thou hast had upon the people
of Nephi, have upon me, and my
people.
42 And now, when he had said this,
he [a]fell unto the earth, [b]as if he were
dead.
43 And it came to pass that his
[a]servants took him and carried him
in unto his wife, and laid him upon a
bed; and he lay as if he were dead
for the space of two days and two
nights; and his wife, and his sons,
and his daughters mourned over
him, after the manner of the Lamanites, greatly lamenting his loss.

CHAPTER 19

Lamoni receives the light of everlasting life and sees the Redeemer—His household fall into a trance, and some see angels—Ammon is preserved miraculously—He baptizes many and establishes a church among them.

AND it came to pass that after two
days and two nights they were about
to take his [a]body and lay it in a
sepulchre, which they had made for
the purpose of burying their dead.
2 Now the queen having heard of
the fame of Ammon, therefore she
sent and desired that he should come
in unto her.
3 And it came to pass that Ammon
did as he was commanded, and went
in unto the queen, and desired to
know what she would that he should
do.
4 And she said unto him: The
[a]servants of my husband have made
it known unto me that thou art a
[b]prophet of a holy God, and that
thou hast [c]power to do many mighty
works in his name;
5 Therefore, if this is the case, I
would that ye should go in and see
my husband, for he has been laid
upon his bed for the space of two
days and two nights; and some say
that he is not dead, but others say
that he is dead and that he [a]stinketh,
and that he ought to be placed in
the sepulchre; but as for myself, to
me he doth not stink.
6 Now, this was what Ammon
desired, for he knew that king
Lamoni was under the power of
God; he knew that the dark [a]veil of
[b]unbelief was being cast away from
his mind, and the [c]light which did
light up his mind, which was the
light of the glory of God, which was
a marvelous light of his goodness—
yea, this light had infused such joy
into his soul, the cloud of darkness
having been dispelled, and that the
light of everlasting life was lit up in

38*a* 2 Ne. 1: 2.
b 1 Ne. 9: 2.
39*a* Alma 19: 31.
TG Missionary Work.
b TG Salvation, Plan of.
40*a* Alma 18: 23.
41*a* TG God, Mercy of.
42*a* Alma 19: 1 (1,5–12).
b Alma 22: 18.
43*a* Alma 19: 4 (4–5).
19 1*a* Alma 18: 42 (42–43).
4*a* Alma 18: 43.
b TG Prophets, Mission of.
c D&C 3: 4.
5*a* John 11: 39.
6*a* 2 Cor. 4: 4 (3–4).
TG Veil.
b TG Unbelief, Unbelievers.
c TG Light.

[About 90 B.C.]

his soul, yea, he knew that this had [d]overcome his natural frame, and he was carried away in God—

7 Therefore, what the queen desired of him was his only desire. Therefore, he went in to see the king according as the queen had desired him; and he saw the king, and he knew that he was not dead.

8 And he said unto the queen: He is not dead, but he sleepeth in God, and on the morrow he shall rise again; therefore bury him not.

9 And Ammon said unto her: [a]Believest thou this? And she said unto him: I have had no witness save thy word, and the word of our servants; nevertheless I [b]believe that it shall be according as thou hast said.

10 And Ammon said unto her: Blessed art thou because of thy exceeding faith; I say unto thee, woman, there has not been such great faith among all the people of the [a]Nephites.

11 And it came to pass that she watched over the bed of her husband, from that time even until that time on the morrow which Ammon had appointed that he should rise.

12 And it came to pass that he arose, according to the words of Ammon; and as he arose, he stretched forth his hand unto the woman, and said: Blessed be the name of God, and blessed art thou.

13 For as sure as thou livest, behold, I have [a]seen my Redeemer; and he shall come forth, and be [b]born of a [c]woman, and he shall redeem all mankind who believe on his name. Now, when he had said these words, his heart was swollen within him, and he sunk again with joy; and the queen also sunk down, being overpowered by the Spirit.

14 Now Ammon seeing the Spirit of the Lord poured out according to his [a]prayers upon the Lamanites, his brethren, who had been the cause of so much mourning among the Nephites, or among all the people of God because of their iniquities and their [b]traditions, he fell upon his knees, and began to pour out his soul in prayer and thanksgiving to God for what he had done for his brethren; and he was also overpowered with [c]joy; and thus they all three had [d]sunk to the earth.

15 Now, when the servants of the king had seen that they had fallen, they also began to cry unto God, for the fear of the Lord had come upon them also, for it was [a]they who had stood before the king and testified unto him concerning the great power of Ammon.

16 And it came to pass that they did call on the name of the Lord, in their might, even until they had all fallen to the earth, save it were one of the Lamanitish [a]women, whose name was Abish, she having been converted unto the Lord for many years, on account of a remarkable vision of her father—

17 Thus, having been converted to the Lord, and never having made it [a]known, therefore, when she saw that all the servants of Lamoni had [b]fallen to the earth, and also her mistress, the queen, and the king, and Ammon lay [c]prostrate upon the earth, she knew that it was the power of God; and supposing that this opportunity, by making known unto the people what had happened among them, that by beholding this scene it would [d]cause them to believe in the power of God, therefore she ran forth from house to house, making it known unto the people.

18 And they began to assemble themselves together unto the house

6*d* Jacob 7:21; Mosiah 3:19.
9*a* John 11:26 (22–45).
b Mosiah 26:15 (15–16).
10*a* Luke 7:9.
13*a* TG God, Privilege of Seeing; Jesus Christ, Appearances, Antemortal.
b TG Jesus Christ, Birth of.
c 1 Ne. 11:18 (13–21).
14*a* D&C 42:14.
b Mosiah 1:5.
c TG Joy.
d Alma 27:17.
15*a* Alma 18:1 (1–2).
16*a* Alma 19:28.
17*a* JS-H 1:74.
b Mosiah 4:1.
c Moses 1:9 (9–10).
d Mosiah 27:14.

[About 90 B.C.]

of the king. And there came a
multitude, and to their astonishment, they beheld the king, and the
queen, and their servants prostrate
upon the earth, and they all lay
there as though they were dead; and
they also saw Ammon, and behold,
he was a Nephite.
19 And now the people began to
murmur among themselves; some
saying that it was a great evil that
had come upon them, or upon the
king and his house, because he had
suffered that the Nephite should
[a]remain in the land.
20 But others rebuked them, saying: The king hath brought this evil
upon his house, because he slew his
servants who had had their flocks
scattered at the [a]waters of Sebus.
21 And they were also rebuked by
those men who had stood at the
waters of Sebus and [a]scattered the
flocks which belonged to the king,
for they were angry with Ammon
because of the number which he had
slain of their brethren at the waters
of Sebus, while defending the flocks
of the king.
22 Now, one of them, whose
brother had been [a]slain with the
sword of Ammon, being exceedingly
angry with Ammon, drew his sword
and went forth that he might let it
fall upon Ammon, to slay him; and
as he lifted the sword to smite him,
behold, he fell dead.
23 Now we see that Ammon could
not be slain, for the [a]Lord had said
unto Mosiah, his father: I will spare
him, and it shall be unto him
according to thy faith—therefore,
Mosiah [b]trusted him unto the Lord.
24 And it came to pass that when
the multitude beheld that the man
had fallen dead, who lifted the
sword to slay Ammon, [a]fear came
upon them all, and they durst not
put forth their hands to touch him
or any of those who had fallen; and
they began to marvel again among
themselves what could be the cause
of this great power, or what all these
things could mean.
25 And it came to pass that there
were many among them who said
that Ammon was the [a]Great Spirit,
and others said he was sent by the
Great Spirit;
26 But others rebuked them all,
saying that he was a [a]monster, who
had been sent from the Nephites to
torment them.
27 And there were some who said
that Ammon was sent by the Great
Spirit to afflict them because of their
iniquities; and that it was the Great
Spirit that had always attended the
Nephites, who had ever delivered
them out of their hands; and they
said that it was this Great Spirit
who had destroyed so many of their
brethren, the Lamanites.
28 And thus the contention began
to be exceedingly sharp among
them. And while they were thus
contending, the [a]woman servant
who had caused the multitude to be
gathered together came, and when
she saw the contention which was
among the multitude she was
exceedingly sorrowful, even unto
tears.
29 And it came to pass that she
went and took the queen by the
[a]hand, that perhaps she might raise
her from the ground; and as soon as
she touched her hand she arose and
stood upon her feet, and cried with a
loud voice, saying: O blessed Jesus,
who has saved me from an [b]awful
hell! O blessed God, have [c]mercy on
this people!
30 And when she had said this, she
clasped her hands, being filled with
joy, speaking many words which
were not understood; and when she
had done this, she took the king,

19*a* Alma 17:23 (22–23).
20*a* Alma 17:26; 18:7.
21*a* Alma 17:27; 18:3.
22*a* Alma 17:38.
23*a* Mosiah 28:7; Alma 17:35.
b TG Family, Love within; Trust in God.
24*a* Luke 7:16; Moses 6:39 (37–40).
25*a* Alma 18:5 (2–5).
26*a* Moses 6:38 (37–39).
28*a* Alma 19:16.
29*a* Alma 22:22.
b 1 Ne. 14:3.
c Enos 1:9; Alma 36:24.

[About 90 B.C.]

Lamoni, by the hand, and behold he arose and stood upon his feet.

31 And he, immediately, seeing the contention among his people, went forth and began to rebuke them, and to teach them the [a]words which he had heard from the mouth of Ammon; and as many as heard his words believed, and were converted unto the Lord.

32 But there were [a]many among them who would not hear his words; therefore they went their way.

33 And it came to pass that when Ammon arose he also administered unto them, and also did all the servants of Lamoni; and they did all declare unto the people the selfsame thing—that their hearts had been [a]changed; that they had no more desire to do [b]evil.

34 And behold, many did declare unto the people that they had seen [a]angels and had conversed with them; and thus they had told them things of God, and of his righteousness.

35 And it came to pass that there were many that did [a]believe in their words; and as many as did believe were baptized; and they became a righteous people, and they did establish a church among them.

36 And thus the work of the Lord did commence among the Lamanites; thus the Lord did begin to pour out his [a]Spirit upon them; and we see that his arm is extended to [b]all people who will repent and believe on his name.

CHAPTER 20

The Lord sends Ammon to Middoni to deliver his imprisoned brethren—Ammon and Lamoni meet Lamoni's father, who is king over all the land—Ammon compels the old king to approve the release of his brethren.

AND it came to pass that when they had established a church in that [a]land, that king Lamoni desired that Ammon should go with him to the land of Nephi, that he might show him unto his father.

2 And the voice of the Lord came to Ammon, saying: Thou shalt not go up to the land of Nephi, for behold, the king will seek thy life; but thou shalt go to the land of [a]Middoni; for behold, thy brother Aaron, and also Muloki and Ammah are in prison.

3 Now it came to pass that when Ammon had heard this, he said unto Lamoni: Behold, my brother and brethren are in prison at Middoni, and I go that I may deliver them.

4 Now Lamoni said unto Ammon: I know, in the [a]strength of the Lord thou canst do all things. But behold, I will go with thee to the land of Middoni; for the king of the land of Middoni, whose name is Antiomno, is a friend unto me; therefore I go to the land of Middoni, that I may flatter the king of the land, and he will cast thy brethren out of [b]prison. Now Lamoni said unto him: Who told thee that thy brethren were in prison?

5 And Ammon said unto him: No one hath told me, save it be God; and he said unto me—Go and deliver thy brethren, for they are in prison in the land of Middoni.

6 Now when Lamoni had heard this he caused that his servants should make ready his [a]horses and his chariots.

7 And he said unto Ammon: Come, I will go with thee down to the land of Middoni, and there I will plead with the king that he will cast thy brethren out of prison.

8 And it came to pass that as Ammon and Lamoni were journey-

31*a* Alma 18: 39 (36–39).
32*a* John 12: 37 (35–37).
33*a* TG Man, New, Spiritually Reborn.
b Jonah 3: 8; Mosiah 5: 2; Alma 13: 12; 3 Ne. 20: 26.
34*a* TG Angels; Vision.
35*a* TG Baptism, Qualifications for.
36*a* TG God, Spirit of.
b 2 Ne. 26: 33; Alma 5: 33; 3 Ne. 18: 25.
20 1*a* 2 Ne. 5: 8; Alma 2: 24.
2*a* Alma 21: 12 (12–13, 18); 23: 10.
4*a* TG Strength.
b Alma 20: 22; 22: 2.
6*a* Alma 18: 9.

[About 90 B.C.]

ing thither, they met the father of
Lamoni, who was king [a]over all the
land.
9 And behold, the father of
Lamoni said unto him: Why did ye
[a]not come to the [b]feast on that great
day when I made a feast unto my
sons, and unto my people?
10 And he also said: Whither art
thou going with this Nephite, who
is one of the children of a [a]liar?
11 And it came to pass that
Lamoni rehearsed unto him whither
he was going, for he feared to offend
him.
12 And he also told him all the
cause of his tarrying in his own
kingdom, that he did not go unto
his father to the feast which he had
prepared.
13 And now when Lamoni had
rehearsed unto him all these things,
behold, to his astonishment, his
father was angry with him, and said:
Lamoni, thou art going to deliver
these Nephites, who are sons of a
liar. Behold, he robbed our fathers;
and now his children are also come
amongst us that they may, by their
cunning and their lyings, deceive us,
that they again may rob us of our
property.
14 Now the father of Lamoni commanded
him that he should slay
Ammon with the sword. And he also
commanded him that he should not
go to the land of Middoni, but that
he should return with him to the
land of [a]Ishmael.
15 But Lamoni said unto him: I
will not slay Ammon, neither will I
return to the land of Ishmael, but I
go to the land of Middoni that I may
release the brethren of Ammon, for
I know that they are just men and
holy prophets of the true God.
16 Now when his father had heard
these words, he was angry with him,
and he drew his sword that he might
smite him to the earth.
17 But Ammon stood forth and
said unto him: Behold, thou shalt
not slay thy son; nevertheless, it
were [a]better that he should fall
than thee, for behold, he has
[b]repented of his sins; but if thou
shouldst fall at this time, in thine
anger, thy soul could not be saved.
18 And again, it is expedient that
thou shouldst forbear; for if thou
shouldst [a]slay thy son, he being an
innocent man, his blood would cry
from the ground to the Lord his
God, for vengeance to come upon
thee; and perhaps thou wouldst
lose thy [b]soul.
19 Now when Ammon had said
these words unto him, he answered
him, saying: I know that if I should
slay my son, that I should shed
innocent blood; for it is thou that
hast sought to destroy him.
20 And he stretched forth his hand
to slay Ammon. But Ammon withstood
his blows, and also smote his
arm that he could not use it.
21 Now when the king saw that
Ammon could slay him, he began to
plead with Ammon that he would
spare his life.
22 But Ammon raised his sword,
and said unto him: Behold, I will
smite thee except thou wilt grant
unto me that my brethren may be
[a]cast out of prison.
23 Now the king, fearing he should
lose his life, said: If thou wilt spare
me I will grant unto thee whatsoever
thou wilt ask, even to half of
the kingdom.
24 Now when Ammon saw that he
had wrought upon the old king
according to his desire, he said unto
him: If thou wilt grant that my
brethren may be cast out of prison,
and also that Lamoni may retain his
kingdom, and that ye be not displeased
with him, but grant that he
may do according to his own desires
in [a]whatsoever thing he thinketh,

8*a* Alma 22: 1.
9*a* 1 Sam. 20: 27.
b Alma 18: 9.
10*a* Mosiah 10: 16 (12–17).
14*a* Alma 17: 19.
17*a* Alma 48: 23.
b Alma 22: 6.
18*a* TG Murder.
b D&C 42: 18.
22*a* Alma 20: 4.
24*a* Alma 21: 21 (21–22); 22: 1.

[About 90 B.C.]

then will I spare thee; otherwise I will smite thee to the earth.

25 Now when Ammon had said these words, the king began to rejoice because of his life.

26 And when he saw that Ammon had no desire to destroy him, and when he also saw the great [a]love he had for his son Lamoni, he was astonished exceedingly, and said: Because this is all that thou hast desired, that I would [b]release thy brethren, and suffer that my son Lamoni should retain his kingdom, behold, I will grant unto you that my son may retain his kingdom from this time and forever; and I will govern him no more—

27 And I will also grant unto thee that thy brethren may be cast out of prison, and thou and thy brethren may come unto me, in my kingdom; for I shall greatly desire to see thee. For the king was greatly astonished at the words which he had spoken, and also at the words which had been spoken by his son Lamoni, therefore he was [a]desirous to learn them.

28 And it came to pass that Ammon and Lamoni proceeded on their journey towards the land of Middoni. And Lamoni found favor in the eyes of the king of the land; therefore the brethren of Ammon were brought forth out of prison.

29 And when Ammon did meet them he was exceedingly sorrowful, for behold they were naked, and their skins were worn exceedingly because of being bound with strong cords. And they also had [a]suffered hunger, thirst, and all kinds of afflictions; nevertheless they were [b]patient in all their sufferings.

30 And, as it happened, it was their lot to have fallen into the hands of a more hardened and a more [a]stiffnecked people; therefore they would not hearken unto their words, and they had cast them out, and had smitten them, and had driven them from house to house, and from place to place, even until they had arrived in the land of Middoni; and there they were taken and cast into prison, and bound with [b]strong cords, and kept in prison for many days, and were delivered by Lamoni and Ammon.

An account of the preaching of Aaron, and Muloki, and their brethren, to the Lamanites. Comprising chapters 21 to 26 inclusive.

CHAPTER 21

Aaron teaches the Amalekites about Christ and his atonement—Aaron and his brethren are imprisoned in Middoni—After their deliverance they teach in the synagogues and make many converts—Lamoni grants religious freedom to the people in the land of Ishmael.

Now when Ammon and his brethren [a]separated themselves in the borders of the land of the Lamanites, behold Aaron took his journey towards the land which was called by the Lamanites, [b]Jerusalem, calling it after the land of their fathers' nativity; and it was away joining the borders of Mormon.

2 Now the Lamanites and the Amalekites and the people of [a]Amulon had built a great city, which was called Jerusalem.

3 Now the Lamanites of themselves were sufficiently hardened, but the Amalekites and the Amulonites were still harder; therefore they did cause the Lamanites that they should harden their hearts, that they should wax strong in wickedness and their abominations.

4 And it came to pass that Aaron came to the city of Jerusalem, and

26*a* 2 Sam. 1:26. TG Loyalty.
b Alma 22:2.
27*a* TG Teachable.
29*a* Alma 21:14.
b Alma 17:11.
30*a* TG Stiffneckedness.
b Alma 26:29.
21 1*a* Alma 17:13 (13, 17).
b Alma 24:1; 3 Ne. 9:7.
2*a* Mosiah 23:31; 24:1; Alma 24:1 (1, 28–30); 25:7 (4–9).

[About 90 B.C.]

first began to preach to the Amalekites. And he began to preach to them in their [a]synagogues, for they had built synagogues after the [b]order of the Nehors; for many of the Amalekites and the Amulonites were after the order of the Nehors.

5 Therefore, as Aaron entered into one of their [a]synagogues to preach unto the people, and as he was speaking unto them, behold there arose an Amalekite and began to contend with him, saying: What is that thou hast testified? Hast thou seen an [b]angel? Why do not angels appear unto us? Behold [c]are not this people as good as thy people?

6 Thou also sayest, except we repent we shall perish. How knowest thou the thought and intent of our hearts? How knowest thou that we have cause to repent? How knowest thou that we are not a [a]righteous people? Behold, we have built [b]sanctuaries, and we do assemble ourselves together to worship [c]God. We do believe that God will save all men.

7 Now Aaron said unto him: Believest thou that the Son of God shall come to redeem mankind from their sins?

8 And the man said unto him: We do not [a]believe that thou knowest any such thing. We do not believe in these foolish traditions. We do not believe that thou knowest of things to come, neither do we believe that thy fathers and also that our fathers did know concerning the things which they spake, of that which is to come.

9 Now Aaron began to open the [a]scriptures unto them concerning the coming of Christ, and also concerning the resurrection of the dead, and that there could be [b]no redemption for mankind [c]save it were through the [d]death and sufferings of Christ, and the atonement of his blood.

10 And it came to pass as he began to expound these things unto them they were angry with him, and began to [a]mock him; and they would not hear the words which he spake.

11 Therefore, when he saw that they would not hear his words, he departed out of their synagogue, and came over to a village which was called Ani-Anti, and there he found Muloki preaching the word unto them; and also Ammah and his brethren. And they contended with many about the word.

12 And it came to pass that they saw that the people would harden their hearts, therefore they departed and came over into the land of [a]Middoni. And they did preach the word unto many, and [b]few believed on the words which they taught.

13 Nevertheless, Aaron and a certain number of his brethren were taken and cast into [a]prison, and the remainder of them fled out of the land of Middoni unto the regions round about.

14 And those who were cast into prison [a]suffered many things, and they were delivered by the hand of Lamoni and Ammon, and they were fed and clothed.

15 And they went forth again to declare the word, and thus they were delivered for the first time out of prison; and thus they had suffered.

16 And they went forth whithersoever they were led by the [a]Spirit of the Lord, preaching the word of God in every synagogue of the Amalekites, or in every assembly of the Lamanites where they could be admitted.

17 And it came to pass that the

4*a* D&C 66:7.
b Alma 1:12 (2–15); 14:16; 24:28.
5*a* Alma 16:13.
b Mosiah 27:11 (11–15).
c Moses 8:21.
6*a* Jer. 2:35; Mosiah 12:14 (9–15).
b Alma 15:17; 16:13; 23:2; Hel. 3:14 (9, 14).
c Alma 1:4.
8*a* Jacob 7:2 (1–7).
9*a* Alma 25:6.
b Alma 22:14 (13–14).
c Mosiah 5:8; Alma 38:9.
d TG Jesus Christ, Death of.
10*a* TG Mocking.
12*a* Alma 23:10.
b Matt. 7:14.
13*a* Alma 20:2.
14*a* Alma 20:29.
16*a* Acts 16:6; Alma 22:1 (1–4).

[Between 90 and 77 B.C.]

Lord began to bless them, insomuch that they brought many to the knowledge of the truth; yea, they did [a]convince many of their sins, and of the traditions of their fathers, which were not correct.

18 And it came to pass that Ammon and Lamoni returned from the land of Middoni to the land of [a]Ishmael, which was the land of their inheritance.

19 And king Lamoni would not suffer that Ammon should serve him, or be his [a]servant.

20 But he caused that there should be [a]synagogues built in the land of Ishmael; and he caused that his people, or the people who were under his reign, should assemble themselves together.

21 And he did rejoice over them, and he did teach them many things. And he did also declare unto them that they were a people who were under him, and that they were a [a]free people, that they were free from the oppressions of the king, his father; for that his father had granted unto him that he might reign over the people who were in the land of Ishmael, and in all the land round about.

22 And he also declared unto them that they might have the [a]liberty of worshiping the Lord their God according to their desires, in whatsoever place they were in, if it were in the land which was under the reign of king Lamoni.

23 And Ammon did preach unto the people of king Lamoni; and it came to pass that he did teach them all things concerning things pertaining to righteousness. And he did exhort them daily, with all diligence; and they gave heed unto his word, and they were [a]zealous for keeping the commandments of God.

CHAPTER 22

Aaron teaches Lamoni's father about the creation, the fall of Adam, and the plan of redemption through Christ—The king and all his household are converted—How the land was divided between the Nephites and the Lamanites.

Now, as Ammon was thus teaching the people of Lamoni continually, we will return to the account of Aaron and his brethren; for after he departed from the land of Middoni he was [a]led by the Spirit to the land of Nephi, even to the house of the king which was [b]over all the land [c]save it were the land of Ishmael; and he was the father of Lamoni.

2 And it came to pass that he went in unto him into the king's palace, with his brethren, and bowed himself before the king, and said unto him: Behold, O king, we are the brethren of Ammon, whom thou hast [a]delivered out of [b]prison.

3 And now, O king, if thou wilt spare our lives, we will be thy servants. And the king said unto them: Arise, for I will grant unto you your lives, and I will not suffer that ye shall be my servants; but I will insist that ye shall administer unto me; for I have been somewhat [a]troubled in mind because of the [b]generosity and the greatness of the words of thy brother Ammon; and I desire to know the cause why he has not come up out of Middoni with thee.

4 And Aaron said unto the king: Behold, the Spirit of the Lord has called him another way; he has gone [a]to the land of Ishmael, to teach the people of Lamoni.

5 Now the king said unto them: What is this that ye have said concerning the Spirit of the Lord?

17*a* Alma 62:45; D&C 18:44.
18*a* Alma 17:19; 22:1 (1, 4); 25:13.
19*a* Alma 17:25.
20*a* Alma 16:13.
21*a* Alma 20:24; 22:1.
22*a* Luke 4:8; D&C 93:19; 134:4 (1–4); A of F 11. TG Liberty.
23*a* TG Zeal, Zealous.
22 1*a* Gen. 24:27; Acts 16:6; Alma 21:16 (16–17).
b Alma 20:8.
c Alma 20:24; 21:21 (21–22).
2*a* Alma 20:26.
b Alma 20:4.
3*a* Acts 2:37 (37–38).
b Alma 20:26.
4*a* Alma 21:18.

[Between 90 and 77 B.C.]

Behold, this is the thing which doth
trouble me.
6 And also, what is this that Ammon said—[a]If ye will repent ye shall
be saved, and if ye will not repent,
ye shall be cast off at the last day?
7 And Aaron answered him and
said unto him: Believest thou that
there is a God? And the king said:
I know that the Amalekites say
that there is a God, and I have
granted unto them that they should
build sanctuaries, that they may
assemble themselves together to
worship him. And if now thou sayest
there is a God, behold I will [a]believe.
8 And now when Aaron heard this,
his heart began to rejoice, and he
said: Behold, assuredly as thou
livest, O king, there is a God.
9 And the king said: Is God that
[a]Great Spirit that brought our
fathers out of the land of Jerusalem?
10 And Aaron said unto him: Yea,
he is that Great Spirit, and he
[a]created all things both in heaven
and in earth. Believest thou this?
11 And he said: Yea, I believe that
the Great Spirit created all things,
and I desire that ye should tell me
concerning all these things, and I
will [a]believe thy words.
12 And it came to pass that when
Aaron saw that the king would
believe his words, he began from the
creation of Adam, [a]reading the
scriptures unto the king—how God
[b]created man after his own image,
and that God gave him commandments, and that because of transgression, man had fallen.
13 And Aaron did expound unto
him the scriptures from the [a]crea-
tion of Adam, laying the fall of man
before him, and their carnal state
and also the [b]plan of [c]redemption,
which was prepared [d]from the
foundation of the world, through
Christ, for all whosoever would
believe on his name.
14 And since man had [a]fallen he
could not [b]merit anything of himself; but the sufferings and [c]death of
Christ [d]atone for their sins, through
faith and repentance, and so forth;
and that he breaketh the bands of
death, that the [e]grave shall have
no victory, and that the sting of
death should be swallowed up in
the hopes of glory; and Aaron did
expound all these things unto the
king.
15 And it came to pass that after
Aaron had expounded these things
unto him, the king said: [a]What shall
I do that I may have this eternal life
of which thou hast spoken? Yea,
what shall I do that I may be [b]born
of God, having this wicked spirit
[c]rooted out of my breast, and receive
his Spirit, that I may be filled with
joy, that I may not be cast off at the
last day? Behold, said he, I will give
up [d]all that I possess, yea, I will forsake my kingdom, that I may
receive this great joy.
16 But Aaron said unto him: If
thou desirest this thing, if thou wilt
[a]bow down before God, yea, if thou
wilt repent of all thy sins, and will
bow down before God, and call on
his name in faith, believing that ye
shall receive, then shalt thou receive
the [b]hope which thou desirest.
17 And it came to pass that when
Aaron had said these words, the
king did [a]bow down before the Lord,
upon his knees; yea, even he did

6*a* Alma 20:17 (17–18).
7*a* D&C 46:14 (13–14).
9*a* Alma 18:2, 26 (18–28).
10*a* TG Creation.
11*a* TG Believe.
12*a* 1 Ne. 5:18 (10–18); Alma 18:36; 37:9.
b TG Man, Physical Creation of.
13*a* Gen. 1:26 (26–28); 2:7.
b TG Salvation, Plan of.
c TG Redemption.
d 2 Ne. 9:18; Alma 13:3 (3, 5, 7–9).
14*a* TG Fall of Man.
b Eph. 2:8 (8–9); Alma 42:14 (10–25).
c TG Jesus Christ, Death of.
d 2 Ne. 2:10; Alma 33:22; 34:9 (8–16).
e Isa. 25:8; 1 Cor. 15:55 (34–57).
15*a* Acts 2:37.
b Alma 5:14 (14, 49); 36:23 (23, 26).
c Rom. 7:18.
d Matt. 13:46 (44–46); 19:21 (16–22).
16*a* TG Conversion.
b Ether 12:4.
17*a* D&C 5:24.

[Between 90 and 77 B.C.]

prostrate himself upon the earth, and cried [b]mightily, saying:
18 O God, Aaron hath told me that there is a God; and if there is a God, and if thou art God, wilt thou make thyself known unto me, and I will give away all my sins to know thee, and that I may be raised from the dead, and be saved at the last day. And now when the king had said these words, he was struck [a]as if he were dead.
19 And it came to pass that his servants ran and told the queen all that had happened unto the king. And she came in unto the king; and when she saw him lay as if he were dead, and also Aaron and his brethren standing as though they had been the cause of his fall, she was angry with them, and commanded that her servants, or the servants of the king, should take them and slay them.
20 Now the servants had seen the cause of the king's fall, therefore they durst not lay their hands on Aaron and his brethren; and they pled with the queen saying: Why commandest thou that we should slay these men, when behold one of them is [a]mightier than us all? Therefore we shall fall before them.
21 Now when the queen saw the fear of the servants she also began to fear exceedingly, lest there should some evil come upon her. And she commanded her servants that they should go and call the people, that they might slay Aaron and his brethren.
22 Now when Aaron saw the determination of the queen, he, also knowing the hardness of the hearts of the people, feared lest that a multitude should assemble themselves together, and there should be a great contention and a disturbance among them; therefore he put forth his [a]hand and raised the king from the earth, and said unto him: Stand. And he stood upon his feet, receiving his strength.
23 Now this was done in the presence of the queen and many of the servants. And when they saw it they greatly marveled, and began to fear. And the king stood forth, and began to [a]minister unto them. And he did minister unto them, insomuch that his [b]whole household were [c]converted unto the Lord.
24 Now there was a multitude gathered together because of the commandment of the queen, and there began to be great murmurings among them because of Aaron and his brethren.
25 But the king stood forth among them and administered unto them. And they were [a]pacified towards Aaron and those who were with him.
26 And it came to pass that when the king saw that the people were pacified, he caused that Aaron and his brethren should stand forth in the midst of the multitude, and that they should preach the word unto them.
27 And it came to pass that the king sent a [a]proclamation throughout all the land, amongst all his people who were in all his land, who were in all the regions round about, which was bordering even to the sea, on the east and on the [b]west, and which was divided from the land of [c]Zarahemla by a narrow strip of wilderness, which ran from the sea east even to the sea west, and round about on the borders of the seashore, and the borders of the wilderness which was on the north by the land of Zarahemla, through the borders of [d]Manti, by the head of the [e]river Sidon, running from the east towards the west—and thus were the Lamanites and the Nephites divided.

17*b* TG Prayer.
18*a* Alma 18: 42 (42–43).
20*a* Alma 18: 3 (1–3).
22*a* Alma 19: 29.
23*a* TG Minister; Ministration; Ministry.
b Alma 23: 3.
c TG Conversion.
25*a* TG Peace; Peacemakers.
27*a* Alma 23: 1 (1–4).
b Hel. 3: 8; 11: 20.
c Omni 1: 13.
d Alma 17: 1; 56: 14.
e Alma 16: 6 (6–7); 43: 22 (22–53).

[Between 90 and 77 B.C.]

28 Now, the more [a]idle part of the
Lamanites lived in the wilderness,
and dwelt in tents; and they were
spread through the wilderness on
the west, in the land of Nephi; yea,
and also on the west of the land
of Zarahemla, in the borders by the
seashore, and on the west in the
land of Nephi, in the place of their
fathers' first inheritance, and thus
bordering along by the seashore.
29 And also there were many
Lamanites on the east by the seashore, whither the Nephites had
driven them. And thus the Nephites
were nearly surrounded by the
Lamanites; nevertheless the Nephites had taken possession of all the
northern parts of the land bordering
on the wilderness, at the head of the
river Sidon, from the east to the
west, round about on the wilderness
side; on the north, even until they
came to the land which they called
[a]Bountiful.
30 And it bordered upon the land
which they called [a]Desolation, it
being so far northward that it came
into the land which had been
peopled and been destroyed, of
whose [b]bones we have spoken, which
was discovered by the [c]people of
Zarahemla, it being the place of
their [d]first landing.
31 And they came from there [a]up
into the south wilderness. Thus the
[b]land on the northward was called
[c]Desolation, and the land on the
southward was called Bountiful, it
being the wilderness which is filled
with all manner of wild animals of
every kind, a part of which had
come from the land northward for
food.
32 And now, it was only the
[a]distance of a day and a half's
journey for a Nephite, on the line
Bountiful and the land Desolation,
from the east to the west sea; and
thus the land of Nephi and the
land of Zarahemla were nearly surrounded by water, there being a
small [b]neck of land between the land
northward and the land southward.
33 And it came to pass that the
Nephites had inhabited the land
Bountiful, even from the east unto
the west sea, and thus the Nephites
in their wisdom, with their guards
and their armies, had hemmed in the
Lamanites on the south, that thereby they should have no more
possession on the north, that they
might not overrun the land northward.
34 Therefore the Lamanites could
have no more possessions only in
the land of Nephi, and the wilderness round about. Now this was
wisdom in the Nephites—as the
Lamanites were an enemy to them,
they would not suffer their afflictions on every hand, and also that
they might have a country whither
they might flee, according to their
desires.
35 And now I, after having said
this, return again to the account of
Ammon and Aaron, Omner and
Himni, and their brethren.

CHAPTER 23

Religious freedom is proclaimed—The Lamanites in seven lands and cities are converted—They call themselves Anti-Nephi-Lehies and are freed from the curse—The Amalekites and the Amulonites reject the truth.

1 BEHOLD, now it came to pass that
the king of the Lamanites sent a
[a]proclamation among all his people,
that they should not lay their hands
on Ammon, or Aaron, or Omner, or
Himni, nor either of their brethren
who should go forth preaching the
word of God, in whatsoever place

28*a* 2 Ne. 5:24 (22–25).
29*a* Alma 52:9, 17, 27; 63:5.
30*a* Alma 46:17; 50:34; Morm. 3:5 (5, 7); 4:3 (1–3).
b Mosiah 8:8 (7–12); 28:17 (11–19).
c Omni 1:21 (20–22).
d Ether 6:12; 7:6.
31*a* Hel. 6:10.
b Alma 46:17; 63:4.
c Hel. 3:6 (5–6).
32*a* Hel. 4:7.
b Alma 50:34; 52:9.
23 1*a* Alma 22:27.

[Between 90 and 77 B.C.]

they should be, in any part of their
land.
2 Yea, he sent a decree among
them, that they should not lay
their hands on them to bind them,
or to cast them into prison; neither
should they spit upon them, nor
smite them, nor cast them out of
their [a]synagogues, nor scourge them;
neither should they cast stones at
them, but that they should have
free access to their houses, and also
their temples, and their [b]sanctuaries.
3 And thus they might go forth and
preach the word according to their
desires, for the king had been converted unto the Lord, and [a]all his
[b]household; therefore he sent his
proclamation throughout the land
unto his people, that the word of
God might have no obstruction, but
that it might go forth throughout
all the land, that his people might
be convinced concerning the wicked
[c]traditions of their fathers, and that
they might be convinced that they
were all brethren, and that they
ought not to murder, nor to plunder,
nor to steal, nor to commit adultery,
nor to commit any manner of
wickedness.
4 And now it came to pass that
when the king had sent forth this
proclamation, that Aaron and his
brethren went forth from [a]city to
city, and from one house of worship
to another, establishing churches,
and consecrating [b]priests and teachers throughout the land among the
Lamanites, to preach and to teach
the word of God among them; and
thus they began to have great
success.
5 And [a]thousands were brought to
the knowledge of the Lord, yea,
thousands were brought to believe
in the [b]traditions of the Nephites;
and they were taught the [c]records
and prophecies which were handed
down even to the present time.
6 And as sure as the Lord liveth, so
sure as many as believed, or as many
as were brought to the knowledge of
the truth, through the preaching of
Ammon and his brethren, according
to the spirit of revelation and of
prophecy, and the power of God
working [a]miracles in them—yea, I
say unto you, as the Lord liveth, as
many of the Lamanites as believed
in their preaching, and were [b]con-
verted unto the Lord, [c]never did fall
away.
7 For they became a righteous
people; they did lay down the
weapons of their rebellion, that they
did not fight against God any more,
neither against any of their brethren.
8 Now, these are [a]they who were
converted unto the Lord:
9 The people of the Lamanites who
were in the land of Ishmael;
10 And also of the people of the
Lamanites who were in the land of
[a]Middoni;
11 And also of the people of the
Lamanites who were in the city of
Nephi;
12 And also of the people of the
Lamanites who were in the land of
[a]Shilom, and who were in the land of
Shemlon, and in the city of Lemuel,
and in the city of Shimnilom.
13 And these are the names of the
cities of the Lamanites which were
[a]converted unto the Lord; and these
are they that laid down the weapons
of their rebellion, yea, all their
weapons of war; and they were all
Lamanites.
14 And the Amalekites were not

2*a* Alma 21: 20 (4–6, 20); 26: 29.
b Hel. 3: 14 (9, 14).
3*a* Alma 22: 23.
b Gen. 18: 19.
c Alma 26: 24.
4*a* Luke 8: 1; D&C 66: 5; 75: 18.
b Alma 30: 31.
5*a* Alma 26: 4.
b Alma 37: 19.
c Alma 63: 12. TG Scriptures, Value of.
6*a* Ex. 8: 19; 1 Ne. 19: 22; D&C 84: 3; 121: 12.
b TG Commitment; Conversion.
c Alma 27: 27.
8*a* Alma 26: 3, 31.
10*a* Alma 20: 2; 21: 12 (12–13, 18).
12*a* Mosiah 22: 11 (8, 11).
13*a* Alma 53: 10.

[Between 90 and 77 B.C.]

[a]converted, save only one; neither were any of the [b]Amulonites; but they did harden their hearts, and also the hearts of the Lamanites in that part of the land wheresoever they dwelt, yea, and all their villages and all their cities.

15 Therefore, we have named all the cities of the Lamanites in which they did repent and come to the knowledge of the truth, and were converted.

16 And now it came to pass that the king and those who were converted were desirous that they might have a name, that thereby they might be distinguished from their brethren; therefore the king consulted with Aaron and many of their priests, concerning the name that they should take upon them, that they might be distinguished.

17 And it came to pass that they called their names [a]Anti-Nephi-Lehies; and they were called by this name and were no more called [b]Lamanites.

18 And they began to be a very [a]industrious people; yea, and they were friendly with the Nephites; therefore, they did [b]open a correspondence with them, and the [c]curse of God did no more follow them.

CHAPTER 24

The Lamanites come against the people of God—The Anti-Nephi-Lehies rejoice in Christ and are visited by angels—They choose to suffer death rather than to defend themselves—More Lamanites are converted.

AND it came to pass that the Amalekites and the Amulonites and the Lamanites who were in the land of [a]Amulon, and also in the land of [b]Helam, and who were in the land of [c]Jerusalem, and in fine, in all the land round about, who had not been converted and had not taken upon them the name of [d]Anti-Nephi-Lehi, were stirred up by the Amalekites and by the Amulonites to anger against their brethren.

2 And their hatred became exceedingly sore against them, even insomuch that they began to rebel against their king, insomuch that they would not that he should be their king; therefore, they took up arms against the people of Anti-Nephi-Lehi.

3 Now the king conferred the kingdom upon his son, and he called his name Anti-Nephi-Lehi.

4 And the king died in that selfsame year that the Lamanites began to make preparations for war against the people of God.

5 Now when Ammon and his brethren and all those who had come up with him saw the preparations of the Lamanites to destroy their brethren, they came forth to the land of Midian, and there Ammon met all his brethren; and from thence they came to the land of Ishmael that they might hold a [a]council with Lamoni and also with his brother Anti-Nephi-Lehi, what they should do to defend themselves against the Lamanites.

6 Now there was not one soul among all the people who had been converted unto the Lord that would take up arms against their brethren; nay, they would not even make any preparations for war; yea, and also their king commanded them that they should not.

7 Now, these are the words which he said unto the people concerning the matter: I thank my God, my beloved people, that our great God has in goodness sent these our brethren, the Nephites, unto us to

14*a* Alma 24: 29.
b Mosiah 23: 31 (31–39).
17*a* Alma 24: 1 (1–3, 5, 20).
b Jacob 1: 13.
18*a* TG Industry.
b Alma 24: 8.
c 1 Ne. 2: 23; 2 Ne. 30: 6 (5–6); 3 Ne. 2: 15 (14–16).
24 1*a* Alma 21: 3 (2–4); 25: 7 (4–9).
b Mosiah 23: 19; 27: 16.
c Alma 21: 1.
d Alma 23: 17; 25: 13 (1, 13).
5*a* Alma 27: 4.

[Between 90 and 77 B.C.]

preach unto us, and to convince us of
the [a]traditions of our wicked fathers.
8 And behold, I thank my great
God that he has given us a portion of
his Spirit to soften our hearts, that
we have [a]opened a correspondence
with these brethren, the Nephites.
9 And behold, I also thank my God,
that by opening this correspondence
we have been convinced of our [a]sins,
and of the many murders which we
have committed.
10 And I also thank my God, yea,
my great God, that he hath granted
unto us that we might repent of
these things, and also that he hath
[a]forgiven us of those our many sins
and murders which we have committed, and taken away the [b]guilt
from our hearts, through the merits
of his Son.
11 And now behold, my brethren,
since it has been all that we could
do, (as we were the most lost of all
mankind) to repent of all our sins
and the many murders which we
have committed, and to get God to
[a]take them away from our hearts,
for it was all we could do to repent
sufficiently before God that he
would take away our stain—
12 Now, my best beloved brethren,
since God hath taken away our
stains, and our swords have become
bright, then let us stain our swords
no more with the blood of our
brethren.
13 Behold, I say unto you, Nay,
let us retain our swords that they be
not stained with the blood of our
brethren; for perhaps, if we should
stain our swords [a]again they can no
more be [b]washed bright through
the blood of the Son of our great
God, which shall be shed for the
atonement of our sins.
14 And the great God has had
mercy on us, and made these things
known unto us that we might not
perish; yea, and he has made these
things known unto us beforehand,
because he loveth our [a]souls as well
as he loveth our children; therefore,
in his mercy he doth visit us by his
angels, that the [b]plan of salvation
might be made known unto us as
well as unto future generations.
15 Oh, how merciful is our God!
And now behold, since it has been
as much as we could do to get our
stains taken away from us, and our
swords are made bright, let us [a]hide
them away that they may be kept
bright, as a testimony to our God
at the last day, or at the day that
we shall be brought to stand before
him to be judged, that we have not
stained our swords in the blood of
our brethren since he imparted his
word unto us and has made us [b]clean
thereby.
16 And now, my brethren, if our
brethren seek to destroy us, behold,
we will hide away our swords, yea,
even we will bury them deep in the
earth, that they may be kept bright,
as a testimony that we have never
used them, at the last day; and if
our brethren destroy us, behold, we
shall [a]go to our God and shall be
saved.
17 And now it came to pass that
when the king had made an end of
these sayings, and all the people
were assembled together, they took
their swords, and all the weapons
which were used for the shedding of
man's blood, and they did [a]bury
them up deep in the earth.
18 And this they did, it being in
their view a testimony to God, and
also to men, that they [a]never would
use weapons again for the shedding
of man's blood; and this they did,
vouching and [b]covenanting with
God, that rather than shed the

7*a* Mosiah 1:5.
8*a* Alma 23:18.
9*a* Micah 3:8; Hel. 13:26; D&C 18:44.
10*a* Dan. 9:9.
b TG Guilt.
11*a* Isa. 53:6 (4–6).
13*a* D&C 42:26.
b Rev. 1:5.
14*a* TG Worth of Souls.
b TG Jesus Christ, Prophecies about; Salvation, Plan of.
15*a* Alma 25:14; 26:32.
b TG Purification.
16*a* Alma 40:11 (11–15).
17*a* Hel. 15:9.
18*a* Alma 53:11.
b TG Covenants.

[Between 90 and 77 B.C.]

blood of their brethren they would
[c]give up their own lives; and rather
than take away from a brother they
would give unto him; and rather
than spend their days in idleness
they would labor abundantly with
their hands.
19 And thus we see that, when
these Lamanites were brought to
[a]believe and to know the truth, they
were [b]firm, and would suffer even
unto death rather than commit sin;
and thus we see that they buried
their weapons of peace, or they
buried the weapons of war, for peace.
20 And it came to pass that their
brethren, the Lamanites, made preparations for war, and came up to
the land of Nephi for the purpose of
destroying the king, and to place
[a]another in his stead, and also of
destroying the people of Anti-
Nephi-Lehi out of the land.
21 Now when the people saw that
they were coming against them they
went out to meet them, and [a]pros-
trated themselves before them to
the earth, and began to call on the
name of the Lord; and thus they were
in this attitude when the Lamanites began to fall upon them, and
began to slay them with the sword.
22 And thus without meeting any
resistance, they did slay a [a]thousand
and five of them; and we know that
they are blessed, for they have gone
to dwell with their God.
23 Now when the Lamanites saw
that their brethren would not flee
from the sword, neither would they
turn aside to the right hand or to the
left, but that they would lie down
and [a]perish, and [b]praised God even
in the very act of perishing under
the sword—
24 Now when the Lamanites saw
this they did [a]forbear from slaying
them; and there were many whose
hearts had [b]swollen in them for those
of their brethren who had fallen
under the sword, for they repented
of the things which they had done.
25 And it came to pass that they
threw down their weapons of war,
and they would not take them
again, for they were stung for the
murders which they had committed; and they came down even
as their brethren, relying upon the
mercies of those whose arms were
lifted to slay them.
26 And it came to pass that the
people of God were joined that day
by more than the number who had
been slain; and those who had been
slain were righteous people, therefore we have no reason to doubt but
what they were [a]saved.
27 And there was not a wicked man
slain among them; but there were
more than a thousand brought to
the knowledge of the truth; thus we
see that the Lord worketh in many
[a]ways to the salvation of his people.
28 Now the greatest number of
those of the Lamanites who slew so
many of their brethren were Amalekites and Amulonites, the greatest
number of whom were after the
[a]order of the [b]Nehors.
29 Now, among those who joined
the people of the Lord, there were
[a]none who were Amalekites or
Amulonites, or who were of the order
of Nehor, but they were actual
descendants of Laman and Lemuel.
30 And thus we can plainly discern,
that after a people have been once
[a]enlightened by the [b]Spirit of God,
and have had great [c]knowledge of
things pertaining to righteousness,
and then have [d]fallen away into

18*c* TG Self-sacrifice.
19*a* TG Faith.
b TG Integrity.
20*a* Isa. 7:6.
21*a* Alma 27:3.
22*a* Alma 26:34.
23*a* Alma 26:32.
b Mosiah 16:7.
24*a* Alma 25:1.
b TG Compassion; Repentance.
26*a* Isa. 57:1; Rev. 14:13.
27*a* 2 Kgs. 5:15; Isa. 55:8 (8–9); Alma 37:7 (6–7).
28*a* Alma 21:4.
b Alma 1:15; 2:1 (1, 20); 16:11.
29*a* Alma 23:14.
30*a* Matt. 12:45.
b TG God, Spirit of.
c Heb. 10:26 (26–27); Alma 47:36.
d 2 Ne. 31:14; Alma 9:19; 31:8; D&C 93:19. TG Apostasy of Individuals; Holy Ghost, Loss of.

[Between 90 and 77 B.C.]

sin and transgression, they become
more [e]hardened, and thus their state
becomes [f]worse than though they
had never known these things.

CHAPTER 25

Lamanite aggressions spread—The seed of the priests of Noah perish as Abinadi prophesied—Many Lamanites are converted and join the people of Anti-Nephi-Lehi—They believe in Christ and keep the law of Moses.

AND behold, now it came to pass
that those Lamanites were more
angry because they had slain their
brethren; therefore they swore
vengeance upon the Nephites; and
they did [a]no more attempt to slay
the people of [b]Anti-Nephi-Lehi at
that time.
2 But they took their armies and
went over into the borders of the
land of Zarahemla, and fell upon
the people who were in the land of
Ammonihah and [a]destroyed them.
3 And after that, they had [a]many
battles with the Nephites, in the
which they were driven and slain.
4 And among the Lamanites who
were slain were almost all the [a]seed
of Amulon and his brethren, who
were the priests of Noah, and they
were slain by the hands of the
Nephites;
5 And the remainder, having fled
into the east wilderness, and having
usurped the power and [a]authority
over the Lamanites, caused that
many of the Lamanites should
[b]perish by fire because of their
belief—
6 For many of [a]them, after having
suffered much loss and so many
afflictions, began to be stirred up in
remembrance of the [b]words which
Aaron and his brethren had
preached to them in their land;
therefore they began to disbelieve
the [c]traditions of their fathers, and
to believe in the Lord, and that he
gave great power unto the Nephites;
and thus there were many of them
converted in the wilderness.
7 And it came to pass that those
rulers who were the remnant of the
children of [a]Amulon caused that
they should be put to [b]death, yea,
all those that believed in these
things.
8 Now this martyrdom caused that
many of their brethren should be
stirred up to anger; and there began
to be contention in the wilderness;
and the Lamanites began to [a]hunt
the seed of Amulon and his brethren
and began to slay them; and they
fled into the east wilderness.
9 And behold they are hunted at
this day by the Lamanites. Thus
the words of Abinadi were brought
to pass, which he said concerning
the seed of the priests who caused
that he should suffer death by fire.
10 For he said unto them: What
ye shall [a]do unto me shall be a type
of things to come.
11 And now Abinadi was the first
that suffered [a]death by fire because
of his belief in God; now this is what
he meant, that many should suffer
death by fire, according as he had
suffered.
12 And he said unto the priests of
Noah that their seed should cause
many to be put to death, in the like
manner as he was, and that they
should be scattered abroad and
slain, even as a sheep having no
shepherd is driven and slain by wild
beasts; and now behold, these words
were verified, for they were driven
by the Lamanites, and they were
hunted, and they were smitten.
13 And it came to pass that when

30*e* TG Hardheartedness.
f 2 Chr. 33:9; Ezek. 5:6; 2 Pet. 2:20 (20–21).
25 1*a* Alma 24:24 (20–25).
b Alma 27:2.
2*a* Alma 8:16; 16:9.
3*a* Alma 27:1.
4*a* Mosiah 23:35.
5*a* TG Authority.
b Mosiah 17:15.
6*a* IE the Lamanites.
b Alma 21:9 (5–12).
c Alma 26:24.
7*a* Alma 21:3 (2–4); 24:1 (1, 28–30).
b TG Martyrdom.
8*a* Mosiah 17:18.
10*a* Mosiah 13:10.
11*a* Mosiah 17:13 (13–20).

[Between 90 and 77 B.C.]

the Lamanites saw that they could
not overpower the Nephites they
returned again to their own land;
and many of them came over to
dwell in the land of [a]Ishmael and
the land of Nephi, and did join
themselves to the people of God,
who were the people of [b]Anti-Nephi-
Lehi.
14 And they did also [a]bury their
weapons of war, according as their
brethren had, and they began to be a
righteous people; and they did walk
in the ways of the Lord, and did
observe to keep his commandments
and his statutes.
15 Yea, and they did keep the law
of Moses; for it was expedient that
they should keep the law of Moses
as yet, for it was not all fulfilled.
But notwithstanding the [a]law of
Moses, they did look forward to the
coming of Christ, considering that
the law of Moses was a [b]type of his
coming, and believing that they
must keep those [c]outward [d]per-
formances until the time that he
should be revealed unto them.
16 Now they did not suppose that
[a]salvation came by the [b]law of
Moses; but the law of Moses did
serve to strengthen their faith in
Christ; and thus they did retain a
[c]hope through faith, unto eternal
salvation, relying upon the spirit of
prophecy, which spake of those
things to come.
17 And now behold, Ammon, and
Aaron, and Omner, and Himni, and
their brethren did rejoice exceedingly, for the success which they
had had among the Lamanites,
seeing that the Lord had granted
unto them according to their
[a]prayers, and that he had also verified his word unto them in every
particular.

CHAPTER 26

Ammon glories in the Lord—The faithful are strengthened by the Lord and are given knowledge—By faith men may bring thousands of souls unto repentance—God has all power and comprehendeth all things.

AND now, these are the words of
Ammon to his brethren, which say
thus: My brothers and my brethren,
behold I say unto you, how great
reason have we to rejoice; for could
we have supposed when we [a]started
from the land of Zarahemla that
God would have granted unto us
such great blessings?
2 And now, I ask, what great
blessings has he bestowed upon us?
Can ye tell?
3 Behold, I answer for you; for
our brethren, the Lamanites, were
in darkness, yea, even in the
darkest abyss, but behold, how
[a]many of them are brought to
behold the marvelous light of God!
And this is the blessing which hath
been bestowed upon us, that we
have been made [b]instruments in the
hands of God to bring about this
great work.
4 Behold, [a]thousands of them do
rejoice, and have been brought into
the fold of God.
5 Behold, the [a]field was ripe, and
blessed are ye, for ye did thrust in
the [b]sickle, and did reap with your
might, yea, all the day long did ye
labor; and behold the number of
your [c]sheaves! And they shall be

13*a* Alma 22:1 (1, 4).
b Alma 24:1 (1–3, 5, 20); 27:21 (2, 21, 25).
14*a* Alma 24:15; 26:32.
15*a* Jacob 4:5; Jarom 1:11.
b Mosiah 16:14. TG Jesus Christ, Types of, in Anticipation.
c Josh. 1:8; Mosiah 3:14 (14–15); 13:29 (29–32); D&C 41:5 (4–5).
d TG Ordinance.
16*a* Mosiah 3:15; 12:31; 13:28 (27–33).
b 2 Ne. 11:4; Jacob 4:5; Jarom 1:11; Ether 12:19 (18–19).
c Alma 33:22 (19–23); 37:46 (45–46).
17*a* Alma 17:9 (7–11).
26 1*a* Mosiah 28:9; Alma 17:6 (6–11).
3*a* Alma 23:8 (8–13).
b 2 Cor. 4:5; Mosiah 23:10.
4*a* Alma 23:5; 26:31.
5*a* John 4:35; D&C 4:4.
b Joel 3:13.
c D&C 33:9; 75:5. TG Reward.

[Between 90 and 77 B.C.]

gathered into the garners, that they are not wasted.

6 Yea, they shall not be beaten down by the storm at the last day; yea, neither shall they be harrowed up by the whirlwinds; but when the [a]storm cometh they shall be gathered together in their place, that the storm cannot penetrate to them; yea, neither shall they be driven with fierce winds whithersoever the enemy listeth to carry them.

7 But behold, they are in the hands of the Lord of the [a]harvest, and they are his; and he will [b]raise them up at the last day.

8 [a]Blessed be the name of our God; let us [b]sing to his praise, yea, let us give [c]thanks to his holy name, for he doth work righteousness forever.

9 For if we had not come up out of the land of Zarahemla, these our dearly beloved brethren, who have so dearly beloved us, would still have been racked with [a]hatred against us, yea, and they would also have been [b]strangers to God.

10 And it came to pass that when Ammon had said these words, his brother Aaron rebuked him, saying: Ammon, I fear that thy joy doth carry thee away unto boasting.

11 But Ammon said unto him: I do not [a]boast in my own strength, nor in my own wisdom; but behold, my [b]joy is full, yea, my heart is brim with [c]joy, and I will rejoice in my God.

12 Yea, I know that I am [a]nothing; as to my strength I am weak; therefore I will [b]not boast of myself, but I will [c]boast of my God, for in his [d]strength I can do all [e]things; yea, behold, many mighty miracles we have wrought in this land, for which we will praise his name forever.

13 Behold, how many thousands of our brethren has he loosed from the pains of [a]hell; and they are brought to [b]sing redeeming love, and this because of the power of his word which is in us, therefore have we not great reason to rejoice?

14 Yea, we have reason to praise him forever, for he is the Most High God, and has loosed our brethren from the [a]chains of hell.

15 Yea, they were encircled about with everlasting [a]darkness and destruction; but behold, he has brought them into his everlasting [b]light, yea, into everlasting salvation; and they are encircled about with the matchless bounty of his love; yea, and we have been instruments in his hands of doing this great and marvelous work.

16 Therefore, let us [a]glory, yea, we will [b]glory in the Lord; yea, we will rejoice, for our joy is full; yea, we will praise our God forever. Behold, who can glory too much in the Lord? Yea, who can say too much of his great power, and of his [c]mercy, and of his long-suffering towards the children of men? Behold, I say unto you, I cannot say the smallest part which I feel.

17 Who could have supposed that our God would have been so merciful as to have snatched us from our awful, sinful, and [a]polluted state?

18 Behold, we went forth even in

6*a* Hel. 5: 12; 3 Ne. 14: 25 (25, 27).
7*a* TG Harvest.
b Mosiah 23: 22; Alma 36: 28.
8*a* Ps. 41: 13.
b Ps. 57: 7 (7–11); 108: 1 (1–5); 2 Ne. 22: 5 (5–6).
c TG Thanksgiving.
9*a* Mosiah 28: 2.
b TG Stranger.
11*a* 2 Cor. 7: 14 (13–16).
b 1 Thes. 3: 9; D&C 18: 16 (14–16).
c TG Joy.
12*a* TG Poor in Spirit.
b Alma 29: 9.
c Jer. 9: 24; Rom. 15: 17.
d Isa. 45: 24; Philip. 4: 13 (12–13); 1 Ne. 17: 3.
e Ps. 18: 32 (32–40); 1 Ne. 7: 12.
13*a* TG Hell.
b Alma 5: 26.
14*a* Alma 12: 11.
15*a* Prov. 20: 20.
b TG Light.
16*a* Rom. 15: 17; 1 Cor. 1: 31.
b Ps. 44: 8 (4–8); 2 Cor. 10: 17 (15–18); D&C 76: 61.
c Ps. 36: 5 (5–6); Morm. 6: 22; D&C 97: 6.
17*a* TG Pollution.

[Between 90 and 77 B.C.]

wrath, with mighty threatenings to [a]destroy his church.

19 Oh then, why did he not consign us to an awful destruction, yea, why did he not let the sword of his justice fall upon us, and doom us to eternal [a]despair?

20 Oh, my soul, almost as it were, fleeth at the thought. Behold, he did not exercise his justice upon us, but in his great mercy hath brought us over that everlasting [a]gulf of death and misery, even to the salvation of our souls.

21 And now behold, my brethren, what [a]natural man is there that knoweth these things? I say unto you, there is [b]none that [c]knoweth these things, save it be the penitent.

22 Yea, he that [a]repenteth and exerciseth faith, and bringeth forth good [b]works, and prayeth continually without ceasing—unto such it is given to know the [c]mysteries of God; yea, unto such it shall be [d]given to [e]reveal things which never have been revealed; yea, and it shall be given unto such to bring thousands of souls to repentance, even as it has been given unto us to bring these our brethren to repentance.

23 Now do ye remember, my brethren, that we said unto our brethren in the land of Zarahemla, we go up to the land of Nephi, to preach unto our brethren, the Lamanites, and they [a]laughed us to scorn?

24 For they said unto us: Do ye suppose that ye can bring the Lamanites to the knowledge of the truth? Do ye suppose that ye can convince the Lamanites of the [a]incorrectness of the [b]traditions of their fathers, as [c]stiffnecked a people as they are; whose hearts delight in the [d]shedding of blood; whose days have been spent in the grossest iniquity; whose ways have been the ways of a transgressor from the beginning? Now my brethren, ye remember that this was their language.

25 And moreover they did say: Let us take up arms against them, that we destroy them and their iniquity out of the land, lest they overrun us and destroy us.

26 But behold, my beloved brethren, we came into the wilderness not with the intent to destroy our brethren, but with the intent that perhaps we might save some few of their souls.

27 Now when our hearts were depressed, and we were about to [a]turn back, behold, the Lord [b]comforted us, and said: Go amongst thy brethren, the Lamanites, and bear with [c]patience thine [d]afflictions, and I will give unto you success.

28 And now behold, we have come, and been forth amongst them; and we have been patient in our sufferings, and we have suffered every privation; yea, we have traveled from house to house, relying upon the mercies of the world—not upon the mercies of the world alone but upon the mercies of God.

29 And we have entered into their houses and taught them, and we have taught them in their streets; yea, and we have taught them upon their hills; and we have also entered into their temples and their [a]synagogues and taught them; and we have been cast out, and mocked, and spit upon, and smote upon our

18*a* Mosiah 27: 10; 28: 4 (3–4); Alma 36: 6 (6–11).
19*a* TG Despair.
20*a* 2 Ne. 1: 13; Hel. 3: 29.
21*a* TG Man, Natural, Not Spiritually Reborn.
b Alma 36: 5.
c 1 Cor. 2: 11 (9–16); Jacob 4: 8 (8–10, 13).
22*a* TG Repentance.
b TG Good Works.
c Luke 8: 10; Alma 12: 9. TG Mysteries of Godliness.
d Dan. 2: 22 (19–22, 28).
e Jarom 1: 4; Hel. 11: 23; D&C 107: 19 (18–19).
23*a* 2 Chr. 30: 10; Neh. 2: 19; Luke 8: 53. TG Laughter.
24*a* Mosiah 1: 5; 28: 2.
b Alma 23: 3; 25: 6.
c TG Stiffneckedness.
d Jacob 7: 24; Jarom 1: 6.
27*a* Hel. 13: 2 (2–3).
b Alma 17: 10.
c Alma 17: 11. TG Patience.
d Alma 7: 5. TG Affliction.
29*a* Alma 23: 2 (2, 4).

[Between 90 and 77 B.C.]

cheeks; and we have been [b]stoned,
and taken and bound with [c]strong
cords, and cast into prison; and
through the power and wisdom of
God we have been delivered again.
30 And we have suffered all manner
of afflictions, and all this, that
perhaps we might be the means of
saving some soul; and we supposed
that our [a]joy would be full if perhaps
we could be the means of saving some.
31 Now behold, we can look forth
and see the [a]fruits of our labors; and
are they few? I say unto you, Nay,
they are [b]many; yea, and we can
witness of their sincerity, because
of their love towards their brethren
and also towards us.
32 For behold, they had rather
[a]sacrifice their lives than even to
take the life of their enemy; and
they have [b]buried their weapons of
war deep in the earth, because of
their love towards their brethren.
33 And now behold I say unto you,
has there been so great love in all
the land? Behold, I say unto you,
Nay, there has not, even among the
Nephites.
34 For behold, they would take up
arms against their brethren; they
would not suffer themselves to be
slain. But behold how [a]many of these
have laid down their lives; and we
know that they have gone to their
God, because of their love and of
their hatred to sin.
35 Now have we not reason to
rejoice? Yea, I say unto you, there
never were men that had so great
reason to rejoice as we, since the
world began; yea, and my joy is
carried away, even unto boasting
in my God; for he has all [a]power,
[b]all wisdom, and all understanding;
he comprehendeth all things, and
he is a [c]merciful Being, even unto
salvation, to those who will repent
and believe on his name.
36 Now if this is [a]boasting, even so
will I boast; for this is my life and
my light, my joy and my salvation,
and my redemption from everlasting
wo. Yea, blessed is the name of my
God, who has been mindful of this
people, who are a [b]branch of the
tree of Israel, and has been [c]lost from
its body in a strange land; yea, I
say, blessed be the name of my God,
who has been mindful of us,
[d]wanderers in a strange land.
37 Now my brethren, we see that
God is [a]mindful of every [b]people,
whatsoever land they may be in;
yea, he numbereth his people, and
his bowels of mercy are over all the
earth. Now this is my joy, and my
great thanksgiving; yea, and I will
give thanks unto my God forever.
Amen.

CHAPTER 27

The Lord commands Ammon to lead the people of Anti-Nephi-Lehi to safety—Upon meeting Alma, Ammon's joy exhausts his strength—The Nephites give them the land of Jershon—They are called the people of Ammon.

Now it came to pass that when
those Lamanites who had gone to
war against the Nephites had
found, after their [a]many struggles to
destroy them, that it was in vain to
seek their destruction, they returned
again to the land of Nephi.
2 And it came to pass that the
Amalekites, because of their loss,
were exceedingly angry. And when
they saw that they could not seek
revenge from the Nephites, they
began to [a]stir up the people in anger

29*b* 2 Cor. 11: 23 (23–29).
c Alma 20: 30 (29–30).
30*a* D&C 18: 15 (15–16).
31*a* Acts 21: 19 (19–20).
b Alma 23: 8 (8–13); 26: 4.
32*a* Alma 24: 23 (20–24).
b Alma 24: 15; 25: 14.
34*a* Alma 24: 22.
35*a* TG God, Intelligence of; God, Perfection of; God, Wisdom of.
b D&C 88: 41.
c TG God, Mercy of.
36*a* Rom. 3: 27.
b Gen. 49: 22 (22–26); Ezek. 17: 22; Jacob 2: 25.
c Jacob 5: 25 (25, 40–45).
d Jacob 7: 26.
37*a* 2 Ne. 2: 27; 26: 24; Jacob 5: 41.
b Jonah 4: 11 (10–11); Acts 10: 35 (9–35, 44); 2 Ne. 26: 33.
27 1*a* Alma 25: 3.
2*a* Acts 13: 50.

[Between 90 and 77 B.C.]

against their [b]brethren, the people
of [c]Anti-Nephi-Lehi; therefore they
began again to destroy them.
3 Now this people [a]again refused to
take their arms, and they suffered
themselves to be slain according to
the desires of their enemies.
4 Now when Ammon and his
brethren saw this work of destruction among those whom they so
dearly beloved, and among those
who had so dearly beloved them—
for they were treated as though
they were angels sent from God to
save them from everlasting destruction—therefore, when Ammon and
his brethren saw this great work of
destruction, they were moved with
compassion, and they [a]said unto the
king:
5 Let us gather together this people
of the Lord, and let us go down to
the land of Zarahemla to our brethren the Nephites, and flee out of the
hands of our enemies, that we be not
destroyed.
6 But the king said unto them:
Behold, the Nephites will destroy
us, because of the many murders and
sins we have committed against
them.
7 And Ammon said: I will go and
inquire of the Lord, and if he say
unto us, go down unto our brethren,
will ye go?
8 And the king said unto him: Yea,
if the Lord saith unto us go, we will
go down unto our brethren, and we
will be their slaves until we repair
unto them the many murders and
sins which we have committed
against them.
9 But Ammon said unto him: It is
against the law of our brethren,
which was established by my father,
that there should be any [a]slaves
among them; therefore let us go
down and rely upon the mercies of
our brethren.
10 But the king said unto him:
Inquire of the Lord, and if he saith
unto us go, we will go; otherwise we
will perish in the land.
11 And it came to pass that Ammon
went and inquired of the Lord, and
the Lord said unto him:
12 Get this people [a]out of this land,
that they perish not; for Satan has
great hold on the hearts of the
Amalekites, who do stir up the
Lamanites to anger against their
brethren to slay them; therefore get
thee out of this land; and blessed
are this people in this generation,
for I will [b]preserve them.
13 And now it came to pass that
Ammon went and told the king all
the words which the Lord had said
unto him.
14 And they gathered together all
their people, yea, all the people of
the Lord, and did gather together
all their flocks and herds, and
departed out of the land, and came
into the wilderness which divided
the land of Nephi from the land of
Zarahemla, and came over near the
borders of the land.
15 And it came to pass that Ammon
said unto them: Behold, I and my
brethren will go forth into the land
of Zarahemla, and ye shall remain
here until we return; and we will
[a]try the hearts of our brethren,
whether they will that ye shall come
into their land.
16 And it came to pass that as
Ammon was going forth into the
land, that he and his brethren met
Alma, over in the [a]place of which
has been spoken; and behold, this
was a joyful meeting.
17 Now the [a]joy of Ammon was so
great even that he was full; yea, he
was swallowed up in the joy of his
God, even to the [b]exhausting of his
strength; and he fell [c]again to the
earth.

2*b* Alma 43: 11.
c Alma 25: 1.
3*a* Alma 24: 21 (21–26).
4*a* Alma 24: 5 (3–5).
9*a* Mosiah 29: 32 (32, 38, 40).
12*a* TG Separation.
b TG Protection, Divine.
15*a* Judg. 7: 4.
16*a* Alma 17: 1 (1–4).
17*a* TG Joy.
b Dan. 10: 8 (8–12); 1 Ne. 1: 7.
c Alma 19: 14 (14, 17).

[Between 90 and 77 B.C.]

18 Now was not this [a]exceeding
joy? Behold, this is joy which none
receiveth save it be the truly
penitent and humble seeker of
[b]happiness.
19 Now the joy of Alma in meeting
his [a]brethren was truly great, and
also the joy of Aaron, of Omner, and
Himni; but behold their joy was not
that to exceed their strength.
20 And now it came to pass that
Alma conducted his brethren back
to the land of Zarahemla; even to
his [a]own house. And they went and
told the [b]chief judge all the things
that had happened unto them in
the land of Nephi, among their
brethren, the Lamanites.
21 And it came to pass that the
chief judge sent a proclamation
throughout all the land, desiring the
voice of the people concerning the
admitting their brethren, who were
the people of [a]Anti-Nephi-Lehi.
22 And it came to pass that the
voice of the people came, saying:
Behold, we will give up the [a]land of
[b]Jershon, which is on the east by
the sea, which joins the land
Bountiful, which is on the south of
the land Bountiful; and this land
Jershon is the land which we will
give unto our brethren for an
inheritance.
23 And behold, we will set our
armies between the land Jershon
and the land Nephi, that we may
[a]protect our brethren in the land
Jershon; and this we do for our
brethren, on account of their fear
to take up arms against their
brethren lest they should commit
sin; and this their great fear came
because of their sore repentance
which they had, on account of their
many murders and their awful
wickedness.
24 And now behold, this will we do
unto our brethren, that they may
inherit the land Jershon; and we will
guard them from their enemies with
our armies, on condition that they
will give us a [a]portion of their substance to assist us that we may
maintain our armies.
25 Now, it came to pass that when
Ammon had heard this, he returned
to the people of Anti-Nephi-Lehi,
and also Alma with him, into the
wilderness, where they had pitched
their tents, and made known unto
them all these things. And Alma also
related unto them his [a]conversion,
with Ammon and Aaron, and his
brethren.
26 And it came to pass that it did
cause great joy among them. And
they went down into the land of
Jershon, and took possession of the
land of Jershon; and they were
called by the Nephites the [a]people
of Ammon; therefore they were
distinguished by that name ever
after.
27 And they were among the
people of Nephi, and also numbered
among the people who were of the
church of God. And they were also
distinguished for their [a]zeal towards
God, and also towards men; for
they were perfectly [b]honest and upright in all things; and they were
[c]firm in the faith of Christ, even unto
the end.
28 And they did look upon shedding the blood of their brethren with
the greatest abhorrence; and they
never could be prevailed upon to
take up arms against their brethren;
and they never did look upon death
with any degree of terror, for their
hope and views of Christ and the
resurrection; therefore, death was
swallowed up to them by the victory
of Christ over it.
29 Therefore, they would suffer

18*a* Alma 28: 8.
b TG Happiness; Objectives.
19*a* TG Friendship.
20*a* Alma 15: 18.
b Alma 4: 17 (16–18).
21*a* Alma 25: 13 (1, 13); 43: 11.
22*a* Alma 43: 12.
b Alma 28: 1 (1, 8).
23*a* Alma 43: 12.
24*a* Alma 43: 13.
25*a* Mosiah 27: 24 (10–25).
26*a* Alma 30: 1.
27*a* TG Zeal.
b Prov. 19: 1; D&C 124: 20 (15, 20). TG Honesty.
c Alma 23: 6; Hel. 15: 8 (6–10).

[Between 90 and 77 B.C.]

[a]death in the most aggravating and distressing manner which could be inflicted by their brethren, before they would take the sword or cimeter to smite them.

30 And thus they were a zealous and beloved people, a highly favored people of the Lord.

CHAPTER 28

The Lamanites are defeated in a tremendous battle—Tens of thousands are slain—The wicked are consigned to a state of endless woe; the righteous attain a never-ending happiness.

AND now it came to pass that after the people of Ammon were established in the land of [a]Jershon, and a church also established in the land of Jershon, and the armies of the Nephites were set round about the land of Jershon, yea, in all the borders round about the land of Zarahemla; behold the armies of the Lamanites had followed their brethren into the wilderness.

2 And thus there was a tremendous battle; yea, even such an one as never had been known among all the people in the land from the time Lehi left Jerusalem; yea, and tens of thousands of the Lamanites were slain and scattered abroad.

3 Yea, and also there was a tremendous slaughter among the people of Nephi; nevertheless, the Lamanites were [a]driven and scattered, and the people of Nephi returned again to their land.

4 And now this was a time that there was a great [a]mourning and lamentation heard throughout all the land, among all the people of Nephi—

5 Yea, the cry of [a]widows mourning for their husbands, and also of fathers mourning for their sons, and the daughter for the brother, yea, the brother for the father; and thus the cry of mourning was heard among all of them, mourning for their kindred who had been slain.

6 And now surely this was a sorrowful day; yea, a time of solemnity, and a time of much [a]fasting and prayer.

7 And thus endeth the fifteenth year of the reign of the judges over the people of Nephi;

8 And [a]this is the account of Ammon and his brethren, their journeyings in the land of Nephi, their sufferings in the land, their sorrows, and their afflictions, and their [b]incomprehensible joy, and the reception and safety of the brethren in the land of Jershon. And now may the Lord, the Redeemer of all men, bless their souls forever.

9 And this is the account of the wars and contentions among the Nephites, and also the wars between the Nephites and the Lamanites; *and the fifteenth year of the reign of the judges is ended.

10 And from the [a]first year to the fifteenth has brought to pass the destruction of many thousand lives; yea, it has brought to pass an awful scene of bloodshed.

11 And the bodies of many thousands are laid low in the earth, while the bodies of many thousands are [a]moldering in heaps upon the face of the earth; yea, and many thousands are [b]mourning for the loss of their kindred, because they have reason to fear, according to the promises of the Lord, that they are consigned to a state of endless wo.

12 While many thousands of others truly [a]mourn for the loss of their kindred, yet they rejoice and exult in the hope, and even know, according to the [b]promises of the Lord, that

29*a* Alma 24: 23 (20–23).
28 1*a* Alma 27: 22; 30: 19 (1, 19).
3*a* Alma 30: 1.
4*a* TG Mourning.
5*a* TG Widows.
6*a* Matt. 5: 4; Alma 30: 2; 3 Ne. 12: 4.
8*a* IE the account covered in Alma, chapters 17–28.
b Alma 27: 18 (16–19).
10*a* IE the years recounted in Alma, chapters 1–28.
11*a* Alma 16: 11.
b Alma 48: 23; D&C 42: 45.
12*a* Gen. 50: 10.
b Alma 11: 41.

[*76 B.C.]

they are raised to dwell at the right
hand of God, in a state of never-
ending [c]happiness.
13 And thus we see how great the
[a]inequality of man is because of sin
and [b]transgression, and the power
of the devil, which comes by the
cunning [c]plans which he hath
devised to ensnare the hearts of men.
14 And thus we see the great call of
[a]diligence of men to labor in the
vineyards of the Lord; and thus we
see the great reason of sorrow, and
also of rejoicing—sorrow because of
death and destruction among men,
and joy because of the [b]light of
Christ unto life.

CHAPTER 29

Alma desires to cry repentance with angelic zeal—The Lord grants teachers for all nations—Alma glories in the Lord's work and in the success of Ammon and his brethren.

O THAT I were an angel, and could
have the wish of mine heart, that I
might go forth and speak with the
[a]trump of God, with a voice to shake
the earth, and cry repentance unto
every people!
2 Yea, I would declare unto every
soul, as with the voice of thunder,
repentance and the plan of redemption, that they should repent and
[a]come unto our God, that there
might not be more sorrow upon all
the face of the earth.
3 But behold, I am a man, and do
sin in my wish; for I ought to be
content with the things which the
Lord hath allotted unto me.
4 I ought not to harrow up in my
desires, the firm decree of a just
God, for I know that he granteth
unto men according to their [a]desire,
whether it be unto death or unto
life; yea, I know that he allotteth
unto men, yea, decreeth unto them
decrees which are unalterable, according to their [b]wills, whether they
be unto salvation or unto destruction.
5 Yea, and I know that good and
evil have come before all men; he
that knoweth not good from evil is
[a]blameless; but he that [b]knoweth
good and evil, to him it is given
according to his desires, whether he
desireth good or evil, life or death,
joy or remorse of [c]conscience.
6 Now, seeing that I know these
things, why should I desire more
than to [a]perform the work to which
I have been called?
7 Why should I desire that I were
an angel, that I could speak unto
all the ends of the earth?
8 For behold, the Lord doth [a]grant
unto [b]all nations, of their own nation
and [c]tongue, to teach his word, yea,
in wisdom, all that he [d]seeth fit that
they should have; therefore we see
that the Lord doth counsel in
wisdom, according to that which is
just and true.
9 I know that which the Lord hath
commanded me, and I glory in it.
I do [a]not [b]glory of myself, but I glory
in that which the Lord hath commanded me; yea, and this is my
glory, that perhaps I may be an
instrument in the hands of God to
bring some soul to repentance; and
this is my joy.
10 And behold, when I see many of
my brethren truly penitent, and
coming to the Lord their God, then
is my soul filled with joy; then do I
remember [a]what the Lord has done

12*c* Alma 56:11.
13*a* 1 Ne. 17:35.
b TG Transgression.
c 2 Ne. 9:28.
14*a* TG Diligence; Vineyard of the Lord.
b TG Light of Christ.
29 1*a* Isa. 58:1; D&C 29:4.
2*a* Omni 1:26 (25–26); 3 Ne. 21:20.
4*a* Ps. 21:2; 37:4.
b TG Agency.
5*a* TG Accountability.
b Gen. 3:5; 2 Ne. 2:18 (18, 26); Mosiah 16:3; Moro. 7:16 (15–19). TG Discernment, Spiritual.
c Job 27:6. TG Conscience.
6*a* TG Stewardship.
8*a* 3 Ne. 26:8 (7–10); D&C 11:22.
b 2 Ne. 2:27; 29:12.
c D&C 90:11.
d Alma 12:9 (9–11).
9*a* Alma 26:12.
b TG Glory.
10*a* Mosiah 27:14 (11–31).

[About 76 B.C.]

for me, yea, even that he hath heard
my prayer; yea, then do I remember
his merciful arm which he extended
towards me.
11 Yea, and I also remember the
captivity of my fathers; for I surely
do know that the [a]Lord did deliver them out of bondage, and by
this did establish his church; yea,
the Lord God, the God of Abraham,
the God of Isaac, and the God
of Jacob, did deliver them out of
bondage.
12 Yea, I have always remembered
the captivity of my fathers; and
that same God who [a]delivered them
out of the hands of the Egyptians
did deliver them out of [b]bondage.
13 Yea, and that same God did
establish his church among them;
yea, and that same God hath called
me by a [a]holy calling, to [b]preach the
word unto this people, and hath
given me much success, in the which
my joy is full.
14 But I do not joy in my own
[a]success alone, but my joy is more
full because of the success of my
brethren, who have been up to the
land of Nephi.
15 Behold, they have labored
exceedingly, and have brought forth
much fruit; and how great shall be
their reward!
16 Now, when I think of the success
of these my brethren my soul is
carried away, even to the separation
of it from the body, as it were, so
great is my [a]joy.
17 And now may God grant unto
these, my brethren, that they may
sit down in the kingdom of God;
yea, and also all those who are the
fruit of their labors that they may
go no more out, but that they may
praise him forever. And may God
grant that it may be done according
to my words, even as I have spoken.
Amen.

CHAPTER 30

Korihor, the antichrist, ridicules Christ, the atonement, and the spirit of prophecy—He teaches that there is no God, no fall of man, no penalty for sin, and no Christ—Alma testifies that Christ shall come and that all things denote there is a God—Korihor demands a sign and is struck dumb—The devil had appeared to Korihor as an angel and taught him what to say—He is trodden down and dies.

BEHOLD, now it came to pass that
after the [a]people of Ammon were
established in the land of Jershon,
yea, and also after the Lamanites
were [b]driven out of the land, and
their dead were buried by the people
of the land—
2 Now their dead were not numbered because of the greatness of
their numbers; neither were the dead
of the Nephites numbered—but it
came to pass after they had buried
their dead, and also after the days of
[a]fasting, and [b]mourning, and prayer,
(and it was in the sixteenth year of
the reign of the judges over the people of Nephi) there began to be continual peace throughout all the land.
3 Yea, and the people did observe
to keep the commandments of the
Lord; and they were strict in observing the [a]ordinances of God, according to the law of Moses; for they
were taught to [b]keep the law of
Moses until it should be fulfilled.
4 And thus the people did have no
disturbance in all the sixteenth year
of the reign of the judges over the
people of Nephi.
5 And it came to pass that in the
commencement of the seventeenth
year of the reign of the judges, there
was continual peace.
6 But it came to pass in the *latter
end of the seventeenth year, there
came a man into the land of Zara-

11*a* Ex. 3: 6; Alma 36: 2.
12*a* Micah 6: 4.
b Alma 5: 5 (5–6); 36: 29 (2, 29).
13*a* Alma 5: 3.
b TG Preaching.
14*a* Alma 17: 4 (1–4).
16*a* TG Joy.
30 1*a* Alma 27: 26.
b Alma 28: 3 (2–3).
2*a* Alma 28: 6.
b TG Mourning.
3*a* TG Ordinance.
b 2 Ne. 25: 24; Jarom 1: 5; Mosiah 2: 3; Alma 34: 14 (13–14).

[*74 B.C.]

hemla, and he was [a]Anti-Christ, for he began to preach unto the people [b]against the prophecies which had been spoken by the prophets, concerning the coming of Christ.

7 Now there was no law against a [a]man's [b]belief; for it was strictly contrary to the commands of God that there should be a law which should bring men on to unequal grounds.

8 For thus saith the scripture: [a]Choose ye this day, whom ye will serve.

9 Now if a man desired to serve God, it was his privilege; or rather, if he believed in God it was his privilege to serve him; but if he did not believe in him there was no law to punish him.

10 But if he [a]murdered he was punished unto [b]death; and if he [c]robbed he was also punished; and if he stole he was also punished; and if he committed [d]adultery he was also punished; yea, for all this wickedness they were punished.

11 For there was a law that men should be judged according to their crimes. Nevertheless, there was no law against a man's belief; therefore, a man was punished only for the crimes which he had done; therefore all men were on [a]equal grounds.

12 And this [a]Anti-Christ, whose name was Korihor, (and the law could have no hold upon him) began to preach unto the people that there should be [b]no Christ. And after this manner did he preach, saying:

13 O ye that are bound down under a [a]foolish and a vain hope, why do ye yoke yourselves with such foolish things? Why do ye look for a Christ? For no man can [b]know of anything which is to come.

14 Behold, these things which ye call prophecies, which ye say are handed down by holy prophets, behold, they are foolish traditions of your fathers.

15 How do ye know of their surety? Behold, ye cannot know of things which ye do not [a]see; therefore ye cannot know that there shall be a Christ.

16 Ye look forward and say that ye see a remission of your sins. But behold, it is the effect of a [a]frenzied mind; and this derangement of your minds comes because of the traditions of your fathers, which lead you away into a belief of things which are not so.

17 And many more such things did he say unto them, telling them that there could be no atonement made for the sins of men, but every man [a]fared in this life according to the management of the creature; therefore every man prospered according to his genius, and that every man conquered according to his strength; and [b]whatsoever a man did was [c]no crime.

18 And thus he did preach unto them, leading away the hearts of many, causing them to lift up their heads in their wickedness, yea, leading away many women, and also men, to commit whoredoms—telling them that when a man was dead, that was the end thereof.

19 Now this man went over to the land of [a]Jershon also, to preach these things among the people of Ammon, who were once the people of the Lamanites.

20 But behold they were more wise than many of the Nephites; for they took him, and bound him, and carried him before Ammon, who was a [a]high priest over that people.

6*a* TG Antichrist; False Prophets.
b TG False Doctrine; Prophets, Rejection of.
7*a* Alma 1: 17.
b Acts 18: 13.
8*a* Josh. 24: 15. TG Agency.
10*a* TG Murder.
b TG Capital Punishment.
c Alma 1: 18.
d TG Adultery.
11*a* Mosiah 27: 3; 29: 32.
12*a* TG Antichrist.
b Jacob 7: 2 (2, 9); Alma 31: 16 (16, 29); 34: 5.
13*a* 1 Cor. 1: 25 (18–25).
b Jacob 7: 7.
15*a* Hel. 16: 20; Ether 12: 5 (5–6, 19).
TG Spiritual Blindness.
16*a* Acts 26: 24 (24–25).
17*a* Prov. 16: 25; 2 Ne. 28: 7 (5–9).
b Alma 18: 5.
c Alma 1: 4; Morm. 8: 31.
19*a* Alma 28: 1 (1, 8); 31: 3.
20*a* Alma 46: 38.

[About 74 B.C.]

21 And it came to pass that he
caused that he should be carried out
of the land. And he came over into
the land of Gideon, and began to
preach unto them also; and here he
did not have much success, for he
was taken and bound and carried
before the high priest, and also the
chief judge over the land.
22 And it came to pass that the
high priest said unto him: Why do
ye go about perverting the ways of
the Lord? Why do ye teach this
people that there shall be no Christ,
to interrupt their rejoicings? Why
do ye speak against all the prophecies of the holy prophets?
23 Now the high priest's name was
Giddonah. And Korihor said unto
him: Because I do not teach the
foolish traditions of your fathers,
and because I do not teach this
people to bind themselves down
under the foolish ordinances and
performances which are laid down
by ancient priests, to usurp power
and authority over them, to keep
them in ignorance, that they may
not lift up their heads, but be
brought down according to thy
words.
24 Ye say that this people is a free
people. Behold, I say they are in
bondage. Ye say that those ancient
prophecies are true. Behold, I say
that ye do not know that they are
true.
25 Ye say that this people is a
guilty and a fallen people, because
of the transgression of a parent.
Behold, I say that a child is not
guilty because of its parents.
26 And ye also say that Christ shall
come. But behold, I say that ye do
not know that there shall be a Christ.
And ye say also that he shall be slain
for the [a]sins of the world—
27 And thus ye lead away this
people after the foolish traditions of
your fathers, and according to your
own desires; and ye keep them down,
even as it were in bondage, that ye
may glut yourselves with the labors
of their hands, that they durst not
look up with boldness, and that they
durst not enjoy their rights and
privileges.
28 Yea, they durst not make use of
that which is their own lest they
should offend their priests, who do
yoke them according to their desires,
and have brought them to believe,
by their traditions and their dreams
and their whims and their visions
and their pretended mysteries, that
they should, if they did not do
according to their words, offend
some unknown being, who they say
is God—a being who [a]never has been
seen or known, who [b]never was nor
ever will be.
29 Now when the high priest and
the [a]chief judge saw the hardness of
his heart, yea, when they saw that
he would [b]revile even against God,
they would not make any reply to
his words; but they caused that he
should be bound; and they delivered
him up into the hands of the officers,
and sent him to the land of Zarahemla, that he might be brought
before Alma, and the chief judge
who was governor over all the land.
30 And it came to pass that when
he was brought before Alma and
the chief judge, he did go on in the
same manner as he did in the land of
Gideon; yea, he went on to [a]blas-
pheme.
31 And he did rise up in great
[a]swelling words before Alma, and
did revile against the [b]priests and
teachers, accusing them of leading
away the people after the silly traditions of their fathers, for the sake of
glutting on the labors of the people.
32 Now Alma said unto him: Thou
knowest that we do not glut ourselves upon the labors of this people;
for behold I have [a]labored even from

26a Isa. 53: 6 (4–12).
28a 2 Ne. 28: 5.
b Alma 30: 53.
29a Alma 4: 17.
b TG Reviling.
30a TG Blasphemy.
31a Hel. 13: 22.
TG Boasting.
b Alma 23: 4.
32a TG Labor; Self-sacrifice.

[About 74 B.C.]

the commencement of the reign of
the judges until now, with mine
[b]own hands for my support, notwithstanding my many travels
round about the land to declare the
word of God unto my people.
33 And notwithstanding the many
labors which I have performed in
the church, I have never received
so much as even one [a]senine for my
labor; neither has any of my brethren, save it were in the judgment-
seat; and then we have received only
according to law for our time.
34 And now, if we do not receive
anything for our labors in the church,
what doth it profit us to labor in the
church save it were to declare the
truth, that we may have rejoicings
in the [a]joy of our brethren?
35 Then why sayest thou that we
preach unto this people to get gain,
when thou, of thyself, knowest that
we receive no gain? And now,
believest thou that we deceive this
people, that [a]causes such joy in their
hearts?
36 And Korihor answered him,
Yea.
37 And then Alma said unto him:
Believest thou that there is a God?
38 And he answered, Nay.
39 Now Alma said unto him: Will
ye deny again that there is a God,
and also deny the Christ? For behold, I say unto you, I know there
is a God, and also that Christ shall
come.
40 And now what evidence have ye
that there is no [a]God, or that Christ
cometh not? I say unto you that ye
have none, save it be your word only.
41 But, behold, I have all things as
a [a]testimony that these things are
true; and ye also have all things as a
testimony unto you that they are
true; and will ye deny them?
Believest thou that these things are
true?
42 Behold, I know that thou
[a]believest, but thou art possessed
with a [b]lying spirit, and ye have put
[c]off the Spirit of God that it may
have no place in you; but the devil
has power over you, and he doth
carry you about, working devices
that he may destroy the children of
God.
43 And now Korihor said unto
Alma: If thou wilt show me a [a]sign,
that I may be convinced that there
is a God, yea, show unto me that he
hath power, and then will I be
convinced of the truth of thy words.
44 But Alma said unto him: Thou
hast had signs enough; will ye tempt
your God? Will ye say, Show unto
me a sign, when ye have the testimony of [a]all these thy brethren, and
also all the holy prophets? The
scriptures are laid before thee, yea,
and all things denote there is a God;
yea, even the [b]earth, and [c]all things
that are upon the face of it, yea, and
its [d]motion, yea, and also all the
[e]planets which move in their regular
form do witness that there is a
Supreme Creator.
45 And yet do ye go about, leading
away the hearts of this people,
testifying unto them there is no
God? And yet will ye deny against
all these [a]witnesses? And he said:
Yea, I will deny, except ye shall show
me a sign.
46 And now it came to pass that
Alma said unto him: Behold, I am
grieved because of the hardness of
your heart, yea, that ye will still
resist the spirit of the truth, that thy
soul may be destroyed.
47 But behold, it is [a]better that thy

32*b* Acts 20: 34 (33–35); 1 Thes. 2: 9; Mosiah 18: 24.
33*a* Alma 11: 3.
34*a* TG Joy.
35*a* Matt. 7: 16.
40*a* Ps. 14: 1.
41*a* TG Testimony.
42*a* Acts 26: 27; Jacob 7: 14; Mosiah 12: 30; Alma 30: 52.
b Jer. 27: 10; Rom. 3: 3–4; Mosiah 2: 32.
c 1 Sam. 16: 14.
43*a* John 6: 30; Jacob 7: 13 (13–21); D&C 46: 9 (8–9). TG Sign Seekers.
44*a* Mosiah 13: 33 (33–34).
b Job 12: 8 (7–10). TG Nature.
c D&C 88: 47.
d Hel. 12: 15 (11–15).
e Moses 6: 63. TG Astronomy.
45*a* TG Witnesses.
47*a* 1 Ne. 4: 13.

[About 74 B.C.]

soul should be [b]lost than that thou
shouldst be the means of bringing
many souls down to destruction, by
thy lying and by thy flattering
words; therefore if thou shalt deny
again, behold God shall smite thee,
that thou shalt become dumb, that
thou shalt never open thy mouth
any more, that thou shalt not
deceive this people any more.
48 Now Korihor said unto him: I
do not deny the existence of a God,
but I do not believe that there is a
God; and I say also, that ye do not
know that there is a God; and except
ye show me a sign, I will not believe.
49 Now Alma said unto him: This
will I give unto thee for a sign, that
thou shalt be [a]struck dumb, according to my words; and I say, that in
the name of God, ye shall be struck
dumb, that ye shall no more have
utterance.
50 Now when Alma had said these
words, Korihor was struck dumb,
that he could not have utterance,
according to the words of Alma.
51 And now when the chief judge
saw this, he put forth his hand and
wrote unto Korihor, saying: Art
thou convinced of the power of God?
In whom did ye desire that Alma
should show forth his sign? Would
ye that he should afflict others, to
show unto thee a sign? Behold, he
has showed unto you a sign; and
now will ye dispute more?
52 And Korihor put forth his hand
and wrote, saying: I know that I
am dumb, for I cannot speak; and I
know that nothing save it were the
[a]power of God could bring this upon
me; yea, and I always [b]knew that
there was a God.
53 But behold, the devil hath
[a]deceived me; for he [b]appeared unto
me in the [c]form of an angel, and said
unto me: Go and reclaim this people,
for they have all gone astray after
an unknown God. And he said unto
me: There is [d]no God; yea, and he
taught me that which I should say.
And I have taught his words; and
I taught them because they were
pleasing unto the [e]carnal mind; and
I taught them, even until I had
much success, insomuch that I verily
believed that they were true; and
for this cause I withstood the truth,
even until I have brought this great
[f]curse upon me.
54 Now when he had said this, he
besought that Alma should pray
unto God, that the [a]curse might be
taken from him.
55 But Alma said unto him: If this
curse should be taken from thee thou
wouldst again lead away the hearts
of this people; therefore, it shall be
unto thee even as the Lord will.
56 And it came to pass that the
curse was not taken off of Korihor;
but he was [a]cast out, and went about
from house to house begging for his
food.
57 Now the knowledge of what had
happened unto Korihor was immediately published throughout all the
land; yea, the proclamation was
sent forth by the chief judge to all
the people in the land, declaring unto those who had believed in the
words of Korihor that they must
speedily repent, [a]lest the same judgments would come unto them.
58 And it came to pass that they
were all convinced of the wickedness of Korihor; therefore they were
all converted again unto the Lord;
and this put an end to the iniquity
after the manner of Korihor. And
Korihor did go about from house to
house, begging food for his support.
59 And it came to pass that as he
went forth among the people, yea,
among a people who had separated
themselves from the Nephites and
called themselves [a]Zoramites, being

47*b* Mosiah 27:16.
49*a* Luke 1:20; Acts 13:11 (8–12).
52*a* 2 Chr. 13:20.
b Alma 30:42 (41–42).
53*a* Jacob 7:14 (14, 18).
b 2 Ne. 9:9.
c 2 Cor. 11:14.
d Ps. 10:4 (2–11); Alma 30:28.
e TG Carnal Mind.
f TG Curse.
54*a* Num. 12:13 (9–15).
56*a* Dan. 5:21.
57*a* John 5:14.
59*a* Alma 31:7 (7–8).

[About 74 B.C.]

led by a man whose name was
Zoram—and as he went forth
amongst them, behold, he was run
upon and trodden down, even until
he was [b]dead.
60 And thus we see the end of him
who [a]perverteth the ways of the
Lord; and thus we see that the devil
will not [b]support his children at the
last day, but doth speedily drag
them down to [c]hell.

CHAPTER 31

Alma heads a mission to reclaim the apostate Zoramites—The Zoramites deny Christ, believe in a false concept of election, and worship with set prayers—The missionaries are filled with the Holy Spirit—Their afflictions are swallowed up in the joy of Christ.

Now it came to pass that after the
end of Korihor, Alma having
received tidings that the Zoramites
were perverting the ways of the
Lord, and that Zoram, who was their
leader, was leading the hearts of the
people to [a]bow down to dumb [b]idols,
his heart again began to [c]sicken
because of the iniquity of the people.
2 For it was the cause of great
[a]sorrow to Alma to know of iniquity
among his people; therefore his
heart was exceedingly [b]sorrowful
because of the separation of the
Zoramites from the Nephites.
3 Now the Zoramites had gathered
themselves together in a land which
they called [a]Antionum, which was
east of the land of Zarahemla, which
lay nearly bordering upon the seashore, which was south of the land
of [b]Jershon, which also bordered
upon the wilderness south, which
wilderness was full of the Lamanites.
4 Now the Nephites greatly feared
that the Zoramites would enter into
a [a]correspondence with the Lamanites, and that it would be the means
of great loss on the part of the
Nephites.
5 And now, as the [a]preaching of
the [b]word had a great tendency to
[c]lead the people to do that which
was just—yea, it had had more
powerful effect upon the minds of
the people than the sword, or anything else, which had happened
unto them—therefore Alma thought
it was expedient that they should
try the virtue of the word of God.
6 Therefore he took Ammon, and
Aaron, and Omner; and Himni he
did leave in the church in Zarahemla; but the former three he took
with him, and also [a]Amulek and
Zeezrom, who were at [b]Melek; and
he also took two of his sons.
7 Now the eldest of his sons he took
not with him, and his name was
Helaman; but the names of those
whom he took with him were
[a]Shiblon and [b]Corianton; and these
are the names of those who went
with him among the [c]Zoramites, to
preach unto them the word.
8 Now the Zoramites were [a]dis-
senters from the Nephites; therefore they had had the word of God
preached unto them.
9 But they had [a]fallen into great
errors, for they would not observe
to keep the commandments of God,

59*b* Jer. 28:16 (15–17); Jacob 7:20 (1–20).
60*a* TG Lying.
b Alma 3:27 (26–27); 5:42 (41–42); D&C 29:45.
c TG Hell.
31 1*a* Ex. 20:5; Mosiah 13:13.
b 2 Ne. 9:37. TG Idolatry.
c Alma 35:15.
2*a* 1 Ne. 7:8; Mosiah 28:3; 3 Ne. 17:14; Moses 7:41.
b Isa. 22:4.
3*a* Alma 43:5 (5, 15, 22).
b Alma 27:22.
4*a* TG Conspiracy.
5*a* Ex. 24:7; Jonah 3:5; Rom. 10:17; Enos 1:23; Alma 4:19. TG Preaching.
b 2 Kgs. 22:11; Heb. 4:12; Jacob 2:8; Alma 36:26.
c Jarom 1:12; Alma 45:21; Hel. 5:51 (50–52); D&C 11:2. TG Gospel.
6*a* Hel. 5:41.
b Alma 8:3; 35:13; 45:18.
7*a* Alma 31:32; 35:14.
b Alma 39:1.
c Alma 30:59; 38:3.
8*a* Alma 24:30; 53:8; Hel. 1:15; D&C 93:19.
9*a* TG Apostasy of Individuals.

[About 74 B.C.]

and his statutes, according to the law of Moses.

10 Neither would they observe the [a]performances of the church, to continue in prayer and supplication to God daily, that they might not enter into temptation.

11 Yea, in fine, they did pervert the ways of the Lord in very many instances; therefore, for this cause, Alma and his brethren went into the land to preach the word unto them.

12 Now, when they had come into the land, behold, to their astonishment they found that the Zoramites had built synagogues, and that they did gather themselves together on one day of the week, which day they did call the day of the Lord; and they did [a]worship after a manner which Alma and his brethren had never beheld;

13 For they had a place built up in the center of their synagogue, a place for standing, which was high above the head; and the top thereof would only admit one person.

14 Therefore, whosoever desired to [a]worship must go forth and stand upon the top thereof, and stretch forth his hands towards heaven, and cry with a loud voice, saying:

15 Holy, holy God; we believe that thou art God, and we believe that thou art holy, and that thou wast a [a]spirit, and that thou art a spirit, and that thou wilt be a spirit forever.

16 Holy God, we believe that thou hast separated us from our brethren; and we do not believe in the tradition of our brethren, which was handed down to them by the childishness of their fathers; but we believe that thou hast [a]elected us to be thy [b]holy children; and also thou hast made it known unto us that [c]there shall be [d]no Christ.

17 But thou art the same yesterday, today, and forever; and thou hast [a]elected us that we shall be saved, whilst all around us are elected to be cast by thy wrath down to hell; for the which holiness, O God, we thank thee; and we also thank thee that thou hast elected us, that we may not be led away after the foolish traditions of our brethren, which doth [b]bind them down to a belief of Christ, which doth lead their hearts to wander far from thee, our God.

18 And again we thank thee, O God, that we are a chosen and a holy people. Amen.

19 Now it came to pass that after Alma and his brethren and his sons had heard these prayers, they were astonished beyond all measure.

20 For behold, every man did go forth and offer up these same [a]prayers.

21 Now the place was called by them Rameumptom, which, being interpreted, is the holy stand.

22 Now, from this stand they did offer up, every man, the selfsame prayer unto God, thanking their God that they were chosen of him, and that he did not lead them away after the tradition of their brethren, and that their hearts were not stolen away to believe in things to come, which they knew nothing about.

23 Now, after the people had all offered up thanks after this manner, they returned to their homes, [a]never speaking of their God again until they had assembled themselves together again to the holy stand, to offer up thanks after their manner.

24 Now when Alma saw this his heart was [a]grieved; for he saw that they were a wicked and a perverse people; yea, he saw that their hearts were set upon gold, and upon silver, and upon all manner of fine goods.

10*a* TG Ordinance.
12*a* TG Worship.
14*a* Matt. 6: 5 (1–7).
15*a* Alma 18: 4 (4–5).
16*a* Luke 18: 11; Alma 38: 14 (13–14).
b Isa. 65: 5 (1–5).
c Alma 34: 5.
d Jacob 7: 2 (2, 9); Alma 30: 12 (12, 22).
17*a* TG Conceit; Pride.
b TG False Doctrine.
20*a* Matt. 6: 7.
23*a* James 1: 22 (21–25).
24*a* Gen. 6: 6; 1 Ne. 2: 18.

[About 74 B.C.]

25 Yea, and he also saw that their
hearts were [a]lifted up unto great
boasting, in their pride.
26 And he lifted up his voice to
heaven, and [a]cried, saying: O, how
long, O Lord, wilt thou suffer that
thy servants shall dwell here below
in the flesh, to behold such gross
wickedness among the children of
men?
27 Behold, O God, they [a]cry unto
thee, and yet their hearts are
swallowed up in their pride. Behold,
O God, they cry unto thee with their
mouths, while they are [b]puffed up,
even to greatness, with the vain
things of the [c]world.
28 Behold, O my God, their costly
apparel, and their ringlets, and their
[a]bracelets, and their ornaments of
gold, and all their precious things
which they are ornamented with;
and behold, their hearts are set upon
them, and yet they cry unto thee
and say—We thank thee, O God, for
we are a chosen people unto thee,
while others shall perish.
29 Yea, and they say that thou hast
made it known unto them that
there shall be no Christ.
30 O Lord God, how long wilt thou
suffer that such wickedness and in-
fidelity shall be among this people?
O Lord, wilt thou give me strength,
that I may [a]bear with mine infirmities. For I am infirm, and such
wickedness among this people doth
pain my soul.
31 O Lord, my heart is exceedingly
sorrowful; wilt thou comfort my
soul [a]in Christ. O Lord, wilt thou
grant unto me that I may have
strength, that I may suffer with
patience these [b]afflictions which
shall come upon me, because of the
iniquity of this people.
32 O Lord, wilt thou comfort my
soul, and give unto me success, and
also my fellow laborers who are with
me—yea, Ammon, and Aaron, and
Omner, and also [a]Amulek and
Zeezrom, and also my [b]two sons—
yea, even all these wilt thou comfort,
O Lord. Yea, wilt thou comfort
their souls in Christ.
33 Wilt thou grant unto them that
they may have strength, that they
may [a]bear their afflictions which
shall come upon them because of the
iniquities of this people.
34 O Lord, wilt thou grant [a]unto
us that we may have success in
bringing them again unto thee in
Christ.
35 Behold, O Lord, their [a]souls
are precious, and many of them are
our brethren; therefore, give unto
us, O Lord, power and wisdom that
we may bring these, our brethren,
again unto thee.
36 Now it came to pass that when
Alma had said these words, that he
[a]clapped his [b]hands upon all them
who were with him. And behold, as
he clapped his hands upon them,
they were filled with the Holy
Spirit.
37 And after that they did separate
themselves one from another, [a]tak-
ing no thought for themselves
what they should eat, or what they
should drink, or what they should
put on.
38 And the Lord provided for them
that they should hunger not,
neither should they thirst; yea, and
he also gave them strength, that
they should suffer no manner of
[a]afflictions, save it were swallowed
up in the joy of Christ. Now this was
according to the prayer of Alma;
and this because he prayed in [b]faith.

25*a* 2 Kgs. 14: 10; Jacob 2: 13; Alma 1: 32.
26*a* Moses 7: 44 (41–58).
27*a* Isa. 29: 13. TG Hypocrisy.
b TG Pride; Selfishness.
c TG Worldliness.
28*a* Isa. 3: 19 (16–24).
30*a* Num. 11: 14.
31*a* John 16: 33. TG Comfort; Peace of God.
b TG Affliction.
32*a* Alma 8: 21; 34: 1.
b Alma 31: 7.
33*a* Rom. 15: 1.
34*a* 2 Ne. 26: 33.
35*a* TG Worth of Souls.
36*a* 3 Ne. 18: 37.
b TG Hands, Laying on of.
37*a* Matt. 6: 25 (25–34); 3 Ne. 13: 25 (25–34).
38*a* Matt. 5: 10 (10–12); Mosiah 24: 15 (13–15); Alma 33: 23.
b TG Faith.

[About 74 B.C.]

CHAPTER 32

Alma teaches the poor whose afflictions had humbled them—Faith is a hope in that which is not seen which is true—Alma testifies that angels minister to men, women, and children—Alma compares the word unto a seed—It must be planted and nourished—Then it grows into a tree from which the fruit of eternal life is picked.

AND it came to pass that they did go forth, and began to preach the word of God unto the people, entering into their synagogues, and into their houses; yea, and even they did preach the word in their streets.

2 And it came to pass that after much labor among them, they began to have success among the [a]poor class of people; for behold, they were cast out of the synagogues because of the coarseness of their apparel—

3 Therefore they were not permitted to enter into their synagogues to worship God, being esteemed as filthiness; therefore they were poor; yea, they were esteemed by their brethren as [a]dross; therefore they were [b]poor as to things of the world; and also they were poor in heart.

4 Now, as Alma was teaching and speaking unto the people upon the hill [a]Onidah, there came a great [b]multitude unto him, who were those of whom we have been speaking, of whom were [c]poor in heart, because of their poverty as to the things of the world.

5 And they came unto Alma; and the one who was the foremost among them said unto him: Behold, [a]what shall these my brethren do, for they are [b]despised of all men because of their poverty, yea, and more especially by our priests; for they have [c]cast us out of our synagogues which we have labored abundantly to build with our own hands; and they have cast us out because of our exceeding poverty; and we have [d]no place to worship our God; and behold, [e]what shall we do?

6 And now when Alma heard this, he turned him about, his face immediately towards him, and he beheld with great joy; for he beheld that their [a]afflictions had truly [b]humbled them, and that they were in a [c]preparation to hear the word.

7 Therefore he did say no more to the other multitude; but he stretched forth his hand, and cried unto those whom he beheld, who were truly penitent, and said unto them:

8 I behold that ye are [a]lowly in heart; and if so, blessed are ye.

9 Behold thy brother hath said, What shall we do?—for we are cast out of our synagogues, that we cannot worship our God.

10 Behold I say unto you, do ye suppose that ye [a]cannot worship God save it be in your synagogues only?

11 And moreover, I would ask, do ye suppose that ye must not worship God only [a]once in a week?

12 I say unto you, it is well that ye are cast out of your synagogues, that ye may be humble, and that ye may learn [a]wisdom; for it is necessary that ye should learn wisdom; for it is because that ye are cast out, that ye are despised of your brethren because of your exceeding [b]poverty, that ye are brought to a lowliness of heart; for ye are necessarily brought to be humble.

32 2*a* Luke 6:20; 7:22. TG Poor.
3*a* Luke 18:9.
b Alma 34:40.
4*a* Alma 47:5.
b TG Assembly for Worship.
c TG Poor in Spirit.
5*a* Prov. 18:23.
b TG Oppression.
c Alma 33:10.
d Alma 33:2.
e Acts 2:37 (37–38); Alma 34:3.
6*a* TG Adversity.
b TG Humility; Teachable.
c Prov. 16:1; Alma 16:16 (16–17); D&C 101:8.
8*a* Matt. 5:5 (3–5).
10*a* TG Worship.
11*a* Mosiah 18:25.
12*a* Eccl. 4:13.
b Prov. 16:8; 28:11.

[About 74 B.C.]

13 And now, because ye are compelled to be humble blessed are ye; for a man sometimes, if he is compelled to be humble, seeketh [a]repentance; and now surely, whosoever repenteth shall find mercy; and he that findeth mercy and [b]endureth to the end the same shall be saved.

14 And now, as I said unto you, that because ye were compelled to be [a]humble ye were blessed, do ye not suppose that they are more blessed who truly humble themselves because of the word?

15 Yea, he that truly humbleth himself, and repenteth of his sins, and endureth to the end, the same shall be blessed—yea, much more blessed than they who are compelled to be humble because of their exceeding poverty.

16 Therefore, blessed are they who [a]humble themselves without being [b]compelled to be humble; or rather, in other words, blessed is he that believeth in the word of God, and is baptized without [c]stubbornness of heart, yea, without being brought to know the word, or even compelled to know, before they will believe.

17 Yea, there are many who do say: If thou wilt show unto us a [a]sign from heaven, then we shall know of a surety; then we shall believe.

18 Now I ask, is this faith? Behold, I say unto you, Nay; for if a man knoweth a thing he hath no cause to [a]believe, for he knoweth it.

19 And now, how much [a]more [b]cursed is he that [c]knoweth the [d]will of God and doeth it not, than he that only believeth, or only hath cause to believe, and falleth into [e]transgression?

20 Now of this thing ye must judge. Behold, I say unto you, that it is on the one hand even as it is on the other; and it shall be unto every man according to his work.

21 And now as I said concerning faith—[a]faith is not to have a perfect knowledge of things; therefore if ye have faith ye [b]hope for things which are [c]not seen, which are true.

22 And now, behold, I say unto you, and I would that ye should remember, that God is [a]merciful unto all who believe on his name; therefore he desireth, in the first place, that ye should believe, yea, even on his word.

23 And now, he imparteth his word by angels unto men, yea, [a]not only men but women also. Now this is not all; little [b]children do have words given unto them many times, which [c]confound the wise and the learned.

24 And now, my beloved brethren, as ye have desired to know of me what ye shall do because ye are afflicted and cast out—now I do not desire that ye should suppose that I mean to judge you only according to that which is true—

25 For I do not mean that ye all of you have been compelled to humble yourselves; for I verily believe that there are some among you who [a]would humble themselves, let them be in whatsoever circumstances they might.

26 Now, as I said concerning faith—that it was not a perfect knowledge—even so it is with my words. Ye cannot know of their surety at first, unto perfection, any more than faith is a perfect knowledge.

27 But behold, if ye will awake and arouse your faculties, even to an experiment upon my words, and

13*a* TG Objectives.
b Alma 38:2; 3 Ne. 15:9; 27:6 (6–17). TG Perseverance; Steadfastness.
14*a* 2 Kgs. 22:19.
16*a* TG Humility.
b TG Initiative.
c TG Stubbornness.
17*a* TG Sign Seekers; Signs.
18*a* Luke 16:30 (27–31); Ether 12:12 (12, 18).
19*a* D&C 41:1.
b TG Curse.
c John 15:24 (22–24).
d TG God, Will of.
e TG Transgression.
21*a* John 20:29; Heb. 11:1 (1–40).
b TG Hope.
c Ether 12:6.
22*a* TG God, Mercy of.
23*a* Joel 2:29 (28–29).
b Matt. 11:25; Luke 10:21; 3 Ne. 26:14 (14–16); D&C 128:18.
c D&C 133:58.
25*a* TG Initiative; Sincerity.

[About 74 B.C.]

exercise a particle of faith, yea,
even if ye can no more than [a]desire
to believe, let this desire work in
you, even until ye believe in a
manner that ye can give place for a
portion of my words.
28 Now, we will compare the word
unto a [a]seed. Now, if ye give place,
that a [b]seed may be planted in your
[c]heart, behold, if it be a true seed, or
a good seed, if ye do not cast it out
by your [d]unbelief, that ye will resist
the Spirit of the Lord, behold, it will
begin to swell within your breasts;
and when you feel these swelling
motions, ye will begin to say within
yourselves—It must needs be that
this is a good seed, or that the word
is good, for it beginneth to enlarge
my soul; yea, it beginneth to [e]en-
lighten my [f]understanding, yea, it
beginneth to be delicious to me.
29 Now behold, would not this increase your faith? I say unto you,
Yea; nevertheless it hath not grown
up to a perfect knowledge.
30 But behold, as the seed swelleth,
and sprouteth, and beginneth to
grow, then you must needs say that
the seed is good; for behold it swelleth, and sprouteth, and beginneth
to grow. And now, behold, will not
this strengthen your faith? Yea, it
will strengthen your faith: for ye
will say I know that this is a good
seed; for behold it sprouteth and
beginneth to grow.
31 And now, behold, are ye sure
that this is a good seed? I say unto
you, Yea; for every seed bringeth
forth unto its own [a]likeness.
32 Therefore, if a seed groweth it is
good, but if it groweth not, behold
it is not good, therefore it is cast
away.
33 And now, behold, because ye
have tried the experiment, and
planted the seed, and it swelleth and
sprouteth, and beginneth to grow,
ye must needs know that the seed is
good.
34 And now, behold, is your [a]knowl-
edge [b]perfect? Yea, your knowledge
is perfect in that thing, and your
[c]faith is dormant; and this because
you know, for ye know that the
word hath swelled your souls, and
ye also know that it hath sprouted
up, that your understanding doth
begin to be enlightened, and your
[d]mind doth begin to expand.
35 O then, is not this real? I say
unto you, Yea, because it is [a]light;
and whatsoever is light, is [b]good,
because it is discernible, therefore
ye must know that it is good; and
now behold, after ye have tasted
this light is your knowledge perfect?
36 Behold I say unto you, Nay;
neither must ye lay aside your faith,
for ye have only exercised your faith
to plant the seed that ye might try
the experiment to know if the seed
was good.
37 And behold, as the tree beginneth to grow, ye will say: Let us
nourish it with great care, that it
may get root, that it may grow up,
and bring forth fruit unto us. And
now behold, if ye nourish it with
much care it will get root, and grow
up, and bring forth fruit.
38 But if ye [a]neglect the tree, and
take no thought for its nourishment,
behold it will not get any root; and
when the heat of the sun cometh and
scorcheth it, because it hath no root
it withers away, and ye pluck it up
and cast it out.
39 Now, this is not because the
seed was not good, neither is it
because the fruit thereof would not
be desirable; but it is because your
[a]ground is [b]barren, and ye will not
nourish the tree, therefore ye cannot
have the fruit thereof.

27*a* TG Motivations; Teachable.
28*a* Alma 33: 1.
b Luke 8: 11 (11–15).
c TG Heart.
d TG Doubt; Unbelief, Unbelievers.
e TG Discernment, Spiritual; Edification.
f TG Intelligence; Testimony; Understanding.
31*a* Gen. 1: 12 (11–12).
34*a* TG Knowledge.
b Ps. 19: 7.
c Ether 3: 19.
d TG Mind.
35*a* TG Light.
b Gen. 1: 4.
38*a* TG Apostasy of Individuals.
39*a* Matt. 13: 5 (3–8).
b TG Barrenness.

[About 74 B.C.]

40 And thus, if ye will not nourish
the word, looking forward with an
eye of faith to the fruit thereof, ye
can never pluck of the fruit of the
[a]tree of life.
41 But if ye will nourish the word,
yea, nourish the tree as it beginneth
to grow, by your faith with great
diligence, and with [a]patience, looking forward to the fruit thereof, it
shall take root; and behold it shall
be a tree [b]springing up unto everlasting life.
42 And because of your [a]diligence
and your faith and your patience
with the word in nourishing it, that
it may take root in you, behold, by
and by ye shall pluck the [b]fruit
thereof, which is most precious,
which is sweet above all that is
sweet, and which is white above all
that is white, yea, and pure above
all that is pure; and ye shall feast
upon this fruit even until ye are
filled, that ye hunger not, neither
shall ye thirst.
43 Then, my brethren, ye shall
[a]reap the [b]rewards of your faith, and
your diligence, and patience, and
long-suffering, waiting for the tree
to bring forth [c]fruit unto you.

CHAPTER 33

Zenos taught that men should pray and worship in all places, and that judgments are turned away because of the Son—Zenock taught that mercy is bestowed because of the Son—Moses had lifted up in the wilderness a type of the Son of God.

Now after Alma had spoken these
words, they sent forth unto him
desiring to know whether they
should believe in [a]one God, that they
might obtain this fruit of which he
had spoken, or [b]how they should
plant the [c]seed, or the word of which
he had spoken, which he said must
be planted in their hearts; or in what
manner they should begin to exercise their faith.
2 And Alma said unto them: Behold, ye have said that ye [a]could not
[b]worship your God because ye are
cast out of your synagogues. But
behold, I say unto you, if ye suppose
that ye cannot worship God, ye do
greatly err, and ye ought to search
the [c]scriptures; if ye suppose that
they have taught you this, ye do not
understand them.
3 Do ye remember to have read
what [a]Zenos, the prophet of old, has
said concerning prayer or [b]worship?
4 For he said: Thou art merciful,
O God, for thou hast heard my
prayer, even when I was [a]in the
wilderness; yea, thou wast merciful
when I prayed concerning those who
were mine [b]enemies, and thou didst
turn them to me.
5 Yea, O God, and thou wast merciful unto me when I did cry unto thee
in my [a]field; when I did cry unto
thee in my prayer, and thou didst
hear me.
6 And again, O God, when I did
turn to my house thou didst hear me
in my prayer.
7 And when I did turn unto my
[a]closet, O Lord, and prayed unto
thee, thou didst hear me.
8 Yea, thou art merciful unto thy
children when they cry unto thee, to
be heard of thee and not of men, and
thou [a]wilt hear them.
9 Yea, O God, thou hast been merciful unto me, and heard my cries in
the midst of thy congregations.

40*a* Gen. 2:9; 1 Ne. 15:36 (22, 28, 36).
41*a* TG Patience.
b Alma 33:23; D&C 63:23.
42*a* TG Diligence.
b Matt. 13:23; Col. 1:6; 1 Ne. 8:10 (10–18); 3 Ne. 14:16; D&C 52:34 (18, 34).
43*a* TG Harvest.
b TG Reward.
c Alma 33:23.
33 1*a* 2 Ne. 31:21; Mosiah 15:4; Alma 11:28 (28–35).
b Alma 33:23.
c Alma 32:28 (28–43).
2*a* Alma 32:5.
b TG Worship.
c Mosiah 2:34; Alma 37:8 (3–10). TG Prayer.
3*a* Alma 34:7. TG Scriptures, Lost.
b TG Worship.
4*a* 1 Kgs. 8:47 (44–52).
b Matt. 5:44.
5*a* Alma 34:20 (20–25).
7*a* Matt. 6:6 (5–6); Alma 34:26 (17–27).
8*a* TG God, Access to.

[About 74 B.C.]

10 Yea, and thou hast also heard me when I have been [a]cast out and have been despised by mine enemies; yea, thou didst hear my cries, and wast angry with mine enemies, and thou didst [b]visit them in thine anger with speedy destruction.

11 And thou didst hear me because of mine afflictions and my [a]sincerity; and it is because of thy Son that thou hast been thus merciful unto me, therefore I will cry unto thee in all mine [b]afflictions, for in thee is my joy; for thou hast turned thy judgments away from me, [c]because of thy Son.

12 And now Alma said unto them: Do ye [a]believe those scriptures which have been written by them of old?

13 Behold, if ye do, ye must believe what [a]Zenos said; for, behold he said: Thou hast turned away thy judgments because of thy Son.

14 Now behold, my brethren, I would ask if ye have read the scriptures? If ye have, how can ye [a]disbelieve on the Son of God?

15 For it is [a]not written that Zenos alone spake of these things, but [b]Zenock also spake of these things—

16 For behold, he said: Thou art angry, O Lord, with this people, because they [a]will not understand thy mercies which thou hast bestowed upon them because of thy Son.

17 And now, my brethren, ye see that a second prophet of old has testified of the Son of God, and because the people would not understand his words they [a]stoned him to death.

18 But behold, this is not all; these are not the only ones who have spoken concerning the Son of God.

19 Behold, he was spoken of by [a]Moses; yea, and behold a [b]type was [c]raised up in the wilderness, that whosoever would look upon it might live. And many did look and live.

20 But few understood the meaning of those things, and this because of the hardness of their hearts. But there were many who were so hardened that they would not look, therefore they perished. Now the reason they would not look is because they did not believe that it would [a]heal them.

21 O my brethren, if ye could be healed by merely casting about your eyes that ye might be healed, would ye not behold quickly, or would ye rather harden your hearts in [a]unbelief, and be [b]slothful, that ye would not cast about your eyes, that ye might perish?

22 If so, wo shall come upon you; but if not so, then cast about your eyes and [a]begin to believe in the Son of God, that he will come to redeem his people, and that he shall suffer and die to [b]atone for their sins; and that he shall [c]rise again from the dead, which shall bring to pass the [d]resurrection, that all men shall stand before him, to be [e]judged at the last and judgment day, according to their [f]works.

23 And now, my brethren, I desire that ye shall [a]plant this word in your hearts, and as it beginneth to swell even so nourish it by your faith. And behold, it will become a tree, [b]springing up in you unto [c]ever-

10*a* Alma 32: 5.
b Ps. 3: 7; 18: 17.
11*a* TG Sincerity.
b TG Affliction.
c TG Jesus Christ, Atonement through.
12*a* TG Scriptures, Value of.
13*a* Jacob 6: 1; Alma 34: 7.
14*a* John 5: 39.
15*a* Jacob 4: 4; Mosiah 15: 11 (11–13).
b 1 Ne. 19: 10; Alma 34: 7.
16*a* 2 Pet. 3: 5 (4–5).
17*a* TG Martyrdom.
19*a* Deut. 18: 15 (15, 18); Alma 34: 7.
b Num. 21: 9; 1 Ne. 17: 41; 2 Ne. 25: 20. TG Jesus Christ, Types of, in Anticipation; Symbolism.
c John 3: 14; Hel. 8: 14.
20*a* Hosea 11: 3; 1 Ne. 17: 41 (40–41).
21*a* TG Doubt; Unbelief, Unbelievers.
b TG Apathy; Laziness.
22*a* Alma 25: 16; 37: 46 (45–46).
b 2 Ne. 2: 10; Alma 22: 14; 34: 9 (8–16).
c TG Jesus Christ, Resurrection.
d Alma 11: 44. TG Resurrection.
e TG Jesus Christ, Judge.
f TG Good Works.
23*a* Alma 33: 1; 34: 4.
b Alma 32: 41; D&C 63: 23.
c Alma 32: 43.

[About 74 B.C.]

lasting life. And then may God grant unto you that your [d]burdens may be light, through the joy of his Son. And even all this can ye do if ye [e]will. Amen.

CHAPTER 34

Amulek testifies that the word is in Christ unto salvation—Unless an atonement is made, all mankind must perish—The whole law of Moses points toward the sacrifice of the Son of God—The eternal plan of redemption is based on faith and repentance—Pray for temporal and spiritual blessings—This life is the time for men to prepare to meet God—Work out your salvation with fear and trembling.

AND now it came to pass that after Alma had spoken these words unto them he sat down upon the ground, and [a]Amulek arose and began to teach them, saying:

2 My brethren, I think that it is impossible that ye should be ignorant of the things which have been spoken concerning the coming of Christ, who is taught by us to be the Son of God; yea, I know that [a]these things were taught unto you bountifully before your dissension from among us.

3 And as ye have desired of my beloved brother that he should make known unto you [a]what ye should do, because of your afflictions; and he hath spoken somewhat unto you to prepare your minds; yea, and he hath exhorted you unto faith and to patience—

4 Yea, even that ye would have so much faith as even to [a]plant the word in your hearts, that ye may try the experiment of its goodness.

5 And we have beheld that the great question which is in your minds is whether the word be in the Son of God, or whether there shall be [a]no Christ.

6 And ye also beheld that my brother has proved unto you, in many instances, that the [a]word is in Christ unto salvation.

7 My brother has called upon the words of [a]Zenos, that redemption cometh through the Son of God, and also upon the words of [b]Zenock; and also he has appealed unto [c]Moses, to prove that these things are true.

8 And now, behold, I will [a]testify unto you of myself that these things are true. Behold, I say unto you, that I do know that Christ shall come among the children of men, to take upon him the [b]transgressions of his people, and that he shall [c]atone for the sins of the world; for the Lord God hath spoken it.

9 For it is expedient that an [a]atonement should be made; for according to the great [b]plan of the Eternal God there must be an atonement made, or else all mankind must unavoidably perish; yea, all are hardened; yea, all are [c]fallen and are lost, and must perish except it be through the atonement which it is expedient should be made.

10 For it is expedient that there should be a great and last [a]sacrifice; yea, not a [b]sacrifice of man, neither of beast, neither of any manner of fowl; for it shall not be a human sacrifice; but it must be an [c]infinite and [d]eternal [e]sacrifice.

23*d* Mosiah 24: 15 (13–15); Alma 31: 38.
e TG Agency.
34 1*a* Alma 8: 21; 31: 32.
2*a* Alma 16: 15 (13–21).
3*a* Alma 32: 5.
4*a* Alma 33: 23.
5*a* Jacob 7: 2 (2, 9); Alma 30: 12 (12, 22); 31: 16 (16, 29).
6*a* John 1: 14 (1, 14).
7*a* Alma 33: 13; Hel. 8: 19.
b Alma 33: 15; Hel. 8: 20 (19–20).
c Alma 33: 19.
8*a* TG Testimony; Witnesses.
b TG Jesus Christ, Redeemer.
c TG Jesus Christ, Atonement through.
9*a* 2 Ne. 2: 10; 9: 7 (7–9); Alma 22: 14; 33: 22.
b Alma 12: 26 (22–33); 42: 8 (6–28); Moses 6: 62.
c TG Fall of Man.
10*a* 1 Chr. 6: 49; Moses 5: 7 (6–7).
b TG Blood, Symbolism of.
c 2 Ne. 9: 7.
d Isa. 45: 17; Heb. 5: 9.
e TG Sacrifice.

[About 74 B.C.]

11 Now there is not any man that
can sacrifice his own blood which
will atone for the sins of another.
Now, if a man murdereth, behold
will our law, which is [a]just, take the
life of his brother? I say unto you,
Nay.
12 But the law requireth the [a]life
of him who hath [b]murdered; therefore there can be nothing which
is short of an infinite atonement
which will suffice for the sins of the
world.
13 Therefore, it is expedient that
there should be a great and last
sacrifice, and then shall there be, or
it is expedient there should be, a
[a]stop to the shedding of [b]blood; then
shall the [c]law of Moses be fulfilled;
yea, it shall be all fulfilled, every jot
and tittle, and none shall have
passed away.
14 And behold, this is the whole
[a]meaning of the [b]law, every whit
[c]pointing to that great and last
[d]sacrifice; and that great and last
[e]sacrifice will be the Son of God, yea,
[f]infinite and eternal.
15 And thus he shall bring [a]salva-
tion to all those who shall believe on
his name; this being the intent of
this last sacrifice, to bring about the
bowels of mercy, which over-
powereth justice, and bringeth
about means unto men that they
may have faith unto repentance.
16 And thus [a]mercy can satisfy the
demands of [b]justice, and encircles
them in the arms of safety, while he
that exercises no faith unto repentance is exposed to the whole law of
the demands of [c]justice; therefore
only unto him that has faith unto
repentance is brought about the
great and eternal [d]plan of [e]redemp-
tion.
17 Therefore may God grant unto
you, my brethren, that ye may
begin to exercise your [a]faith unto
repentance, that ye begin to [b]call
upon his holy name, that he would
have mercy upon you;
18 Yea, cry unto him for mercy;
for he is [a]mighty to save.
19 Yea, humble yourselves, and
continue in [a]prayer unto him.
20 Cry unto him when ye are
in your [a]fields, yea, over all your
flocks.
21 [a]Cry unto him in your houses,
yea, over all your household, both
morning, mid-day, and evening.
22 Yea, cry unto him against the
power of your [a]enemies.
23 Yea, [a]cry unto him against the
[b]devil, who is an enemy to all
[c]righteousness.
24 Cry unto him over the crops of
your fields, that ye may prosper in
them.
25 Cry over the flocks of your fields,
that they may increase.
26 But this is not all; ye must [a]pour
out your souls in your [b]closets, and
your secret places, and in your
wilderness.
27 Yea, and when you do not cry
unto the Lord, let your [a]hearts be
[b]full, drawn out in prayer unto him
continually for your [c]welfare, and
also for the welfare of [d]those who
are around you.

11*a* Deut. 24: 16; Mosiah 29: 25.
12*a* TG Blood, Shedding of; Life, Sanctity of.
b TG Capital Punishment; Murder.
13*a* 3 Ne. 9: 19.
b TG Blood, Symbolism of.
c 3 Ne. 1: 24; 15: 5.
14*a* 2 Ne. 25: 24; Jarom 1: 5; Mosiah 2: 3; Alma 30: 3.
b TG Law of Moses.
c TG Jesus Christ, Types of, in Anticipation.
d Ex. 12: 21 (1–30).
e D&C 138: 35.
f D&C 20: 17 (17, 28).
15*a* TG Salvation.
16*a* TG Mercy.
b TG God, Justice of.
c Mosiah 15: 27; Alma 12: 32.
d TG Salvation, Plan of.
e TG Redemption.
17*a* TG Faith.
b TG God, Access to; Prayer.
18*a* Heb. 7: 25 (24–25).
19*a* TG Prayer.
20*a* Alma 33: 5 (4–5).
21*a* Ps. 5: 3 (1–3); Dan. 6: 10; 3 Ne. 18: 21.
22*a* TG Enemies.
23*a* 3 Ne. 18: 15 (15, 18).
b TG Devil.
c TG Righteousness.
26*a* 1 Sam. 1: 15; Enos 1: 9.
b Matt. 6: 6 (5–6); Alma 33: 7 (4–11).
27*a* TG Heart.
b TG Meditation.
c 2 Ne. 32: 9. TG Welfare.
d D&C 108: 7.

[About 74 B.C.]

28 And now behold, my beloved brethren, I say unto you, do not suppose that this is all; for after ye have done all these things, if ye [a]turn away the [b]needy, and the [c]naked, and visit not the sick and afflicted, and [d]impart of your substance, if ye have, to those who stand in need—I say unto you, if ye do not any of these things, behold, your [e]prayer is [f]vain, and availeth you nothing, and ye are as [g]hypocrites who do deny the faith.
29 Therefore, if ye do not remember to be [a]charitable, ye are as dross, which the refiners do cast out, (it being of no worth) and is trodden under foot of men.
30 And now, my brethren, I would that, after ye have [a]received so many witnesses, seeing that the holy scriptures testify of these things, ye come forth and bring [b]fruit unto repentance.
31 Yea, I would that ye would come forth and [a]harden not your hearts any longer; for behold, now is the time and the [b]day of your [c]salvation; and therefore, if ye will repent and [d]harden not your hearts, immediately shall the great plan of redemption be brought about unto you.
32 For behold, this [a]life is the time for men to [b]prepare to meet God; yea, behold the day of [c]this life is the day for men to perform their [d]labors.
33 And now, as I said unto you before, as ye have had so many [a]witnesses, therefore, I beseech of you that ye do not [b]procrastinate the day of your [c]repentance until the end; for after this day of life, which is given us to prepare for eternity, behold, if we do not improve our time while in this life, then cometh the [d]night of [e]darkness wherein there can be no labor performed.
34 Ye cannot say, when ye are brought to that awful [a]crisis, that I will repent, that I will return to my God. Nay, ye cannot say this; for that same spirit which doth [b]possess your bodies at the time that ye go out of this life, that same spirit will have power to possess your body in that eternal world.
35 For behold, if ye have procrastinated the day of your repentance even until death, behold, ye have become [a]subjected to the spirit of the devil, and he doth [b]seal you his; therefore, the Spirit of the Lord hath withdrawn from you, and hath no place in you, and the devil hath all power over you; and this is the final state of the wicked.
36 And this I know, because the Lord hath said he dwelleth not in [a]unholy temples, but in the [b]hearts of the [c]righteous doth he dwell; yea, and he has also said that the righteous shall sit down in his kingdom, to go no more out; but their garments should be made white through the [d]blood of the Lamb.
37 And now, my beloved brethren, I desire that ye should remember

28a TG Apathy.
b TG Poor.
c Ezek. 18: 7 (5–9).
d TG Almsgiving; Good Works.
e Ezek. 33: 31; Matt. 15: 8 (7–8).
f Isa. 58: 3; Moro. 7: 6 (6–8).
g TG Hypocrisy.
29a TG Charity; Generosity.
30a TG Witnesses.
b Matt. 3: 8; Alma 13: 13.
31a TG Self-mastery.
b Rom. 13: 12 (11–12).
c Matt. 11: 20; 3 Ne. 9: 3; D&C 84: 114.
d TG Hardheartedness.
32a TG Mortality.
b 2 Cor. 6: 2; 2 Ne. 2: 21; Alma 12: 24; 42: 4 (4–6). TG Self-mastery.
c D&C 138: 57.
d TG Good Works; Industry.
33a TG Witnesses.
b Job 27: 8; Hel. 13: 38; D&C 45: 2. TG Apathy; Idleness; Procrastination.
c TG Repentance.
d Eccl. 9: 10; John 9: 4.
e TG Darkness, Spiritual.
34a Alma 40: 14 (13–14); Ether 9: 34.
b Rom. 6: 16 (14–18).
35a 2 Ne. 28: 19 (19–23).
b 2 Ne. 9: 9; 3 Ne. 2: 10. TG Devil; Sealing.
36a Mosiah 2: 37; Alma 7: 21; Hel. 4: 24. TG Cleanliness.
b D&C 130: 3.
c TG Righteousness.
d Rev. 12: 11.

[About 74 B.C.]

these things, and that ye should [a]work out your salvation with fear before God, and that ye should no more deny the coming of Christ;

38 That ye [a]contend no more against the Holy Ghost, but that ye receive it, and take upon you the [b]name of Christ; that ye humble yourselves even to the dust, and [c]worship God, in whatsoever place ye may be in, in spirit and in truth; and that ye live in [d]thanksgiving daily, for the many [e]mercies and blessings which he doth bestow upon you.

39 Yea, and I also [a]exhort you, my brethren, that ye be [b]watchful unto prayer continually, that ye may not be led away by the [c]temptations of the devil, that he may not overpower you, that ye may not become his subjects at the last day; for behold, he rewardeth you [d]no good thing.

40 And now my beloved brethren, I would exhort you to have [a]patience, and that ye bear with all manner of [b]afflictions; that ye do not [c]revile against those who do cast you out because of your [d]exceeding poverty, lest ye become sinners like unto them;

41 But that ye have [a]patience, and bear with those [b]afflictions, with a firm hope that ye shall one day rest from all your afflictions.

CHAPTER 35

The preaching of the word destroys the craft of the Zoramites—They expel the converts, who then join the people of Ammon in Jershon—Alma sorrows because of the wickedness of the people.

Now it came to pass that after Amulek had made an end of these words, they withdrew themselves from the multitude and came over into the land of [a]Jershon.

2 Yea, and the rest of the brethren, after they had preached the word unto the [a]Zoramites, also came over into the land of Jershon.

3 And it came to pass that after the more popular part of the Zoramites had consulted together concerning the words which had been preached unto them, they were angry because of the word, for it did destroy their [a]craft; therefore they would not hearken unto the words.

4 And they sent and gathered together throughout all the land all the people, and consulted with them concerning the words which had been spoken.

5 Now their rulers and their priests and their teachers did not let the people know concerning their desires; therefore they found out privily the minds of all the people.

6 And it came to pass that after they had found out the minds of all the people, those who were in favor of the words which had been spoken by Alma and his brethren were cast out of the land; and they were [a]many; and they came over also into the land of Jershon.

7 And it came to pass that Alma and his brethren did minister unto them.

8 Now the [a]people of the Zoramites were angry with the people of Ammon who were in Jershon, and the [b]chief ruler of the Zoramites, being a very wicked man, sent over unto the people of Ammon desiring them that they should cast out of their land all those who came over from them into their land.

9 And he breathed out many

37*a* Philip. 2: 12 (12–16).
38*a* TG Holy Ghost, Loss of.
b Mosiah 5: 8; Alma 5: 38. TG Jesus Christ, Taking the Name of.
c TG Worship.
d Ps. 69: 30 (30–31); D&C 46: 7. TG Thanksgiving.
e Gen. 32: 10; 1 Ne. 1: 20; D&C 46: 15.
39*a* Heb. 3: 13.
b TG Watchfulness.
c TG Temptation.
d Alma 30: 60.
40*a* TG Patience; Steadfastness.
b TG Affliction.
c TG Reviling.
d Alma 32: 3.
41*a* TG Patience.
b Job 23: 2 (2–5).
35 1*a* Alma 28: 1.
2*a* Alma 30: 59.
3*a* TG Priestcraft.
6*a* Alma 35: 14.
8*a* Alma 27: 26.
b Alma 30: 59.

[About 74 B.C.]

threatenings against them. And
now the people of Ammon did not
fear their words; therefore they did
not cast them out, but they did
receive all the poor of the Zoramites
that came over unto them; and they
did [a]nourish them, and did clothe
them, and did give unto them lands
for their inheritance; and they did
administer unto them according to
their wants.
10 Now this did [a]stir up the Zoramites to [b]anger against the people of
Ammon, and they began to mix
with the Lamanites and to stir them
up also to anger against them.
11 And thus the Zoramites and the
Lamanites began to make preparations for war against the people of
Ammon, and also against the Nephites.
12 And thus ended the *seventeenth year of the reign of the judges
over the people of Nephi.
13 And the people of Ammon departed out of the land of Jershon,
and came over into the land of
Melek, and gave place in the land of
Jershon for the armies of the
Nephites, that they might contend
with the armies of the Lamanites
and the armies of the Zoramites;
and thus commenced a war betwixt
the Lamanites and the Nephites, in
the eighteenth year of the reign of
the judges; and an [a]account shall be
given of their wars hereafter.
14 And Alma, and Ammon, and
their brethren, and also the [a]two
sons of Alma returned to the land of
Zarahemla, after having been instruments in the hands of God of
bringing [b]many of the [c]Zoramites to
repentance; and as many as were
brought to repentance were driven
out of their land; but they have
lands for their inheritance in the
land of Jershon, and they have
taken up arms to defend themselves,
and their wives, and children, and
their lands.
15 Now Alma, being [a]grieved for
the iniquity of his people, yea for
the wars, and the bloodsheds, and
the contentions which were among
them; and having been to declare
the word, or sent to declare the
word, among all the people in every
city; and seeing that the hearts of
the people began to wax hard, and
that they began to be [b]offended
because of the strictness of the word,
his heart was exceedingly sorrowful.
16 Therefore, he caused that his
sons should be gathered together,
that he might give unto them every
one his [a]charge, separately, concerning the things pertaining unto
righteousness. And we have an
account of his commandments,
which he gave unto them according
to his own record.

The commandments of Alma to his son Helaman. Comprising chapters 36 and 37.

CHAPTER 36

Alma testifies to Helaman of his conversion by an angel—He suffered the pains of a damned soul; he called upon the name of Jesus, and was then born of God—Sweet joy filled his soul—He saw concourses of angels praising God—His converts have tasted and seen as he did.

MY [a]son, give ear to my words;
for I swear unto you, that inasmuch
as ye shall keep the commandments
of God ye shall prosper in the land.
2 I would that ye should do as I
have done, in remembering the
captivity of our fathers; for they
were in [a]bondage, and none could

9*a* Mosiah 4:26; D&C 42:43. TG Nourish; Welfare.
10*a* Alma 47:1; Hel. 1:17.
b TG Anger; War.
13*a* Alma 43:3.
14*a* Alma 31:7.
b Alma 35:6.
c Alma 30:59.
15*a* Alma 31:1.
b TG Prophets, Rejection of.
16*a* TG Stewardship.
36 1*a* Hel. 5:13 (1–13); Moses 6:58.
2*a* Mosiah 23:23; 24:17 (17–21). TG Israel, Bondage of, in Egypt.

[* 74 B.C.]

[b]deliver them except it was the
[c]God of Abraham, and the God of
Isaac, and the God of Jacob; and
he surely did deliver them in their
afflictions.
3 And now, O my son Helaman,
behold, thou art in thy youth, and
therefore, I beseech of thee that
thou wilt hear my words and learn
of me; for I do know that whosoever
shall put their [a]trust in God shall be
supported in their [b]trials, and their
troubles, and their afflictions, and
shall be [c]lifted up at the last day.
4 And I would not that ye think
that I [a]know of myself—not of the
temporal but of the spiritual, not of
the [b]carnal mind but of God.
5 Now, behold, I say unto you, if I
had not been [a]born of God I should
[b]not have known these things; but
God has, by the mouth of his holy
[c]angel, made these things known
unto me, not of any [d]worthiness of
myself;
6 For I went about with the
sons of Mosiah, seeking to [a]destroy
the church of God; but behold, God
sent his holy angel to stop us by the
way.
7 And behold, he spake unto us, as
it were the voice of thunder, and the
whole earth did [a]tremble beneath
our feet; and we all fell to the earth,
for the [b]fear of the Lord came upon
us.
8 But behold, the voice said unto
me: Arise. And I arose and stood up,
and beheld the angel.
9 And he said unto me: If thou wilt
of thyself be destroyed, seek no
more to destroy the church of God.
10 And it came to pass that I fell to
the earth; and it was for the space
of [a]three days and three nights that
I could not open my mouth, neither
had I the use of my limbs.
11 And the angel spake more things
unto me, which were heard by my
brethren, but I did [a]not hear them;
for when I heard the words—If thou
wilt be destroyed of thyself, seek no
more to destroy the church of God—
I was struck with such great fear
and amazement lest perhaps I
should be destroyed, that I fell to
the earth and I did hear no more.
12 But I was racked with [a]eternal
[b]torment, for my soul was [c]harrowed
up to the greatest degree and racked
with all my sins.
13 Yea, I did remember all my sins
and iniquities, for which I was
[a]tormented with the [b]pains of hell;
yea, I saw that I had [c]rebelled
against my God, and that I had not
kept his holy commandments.
14 Yea, and I had [a]murdered many
of his children, or rather led them
away unto destruction; yea, and in
fine so great had been my iniquities,
that the very thought of coming
into the presence of my God did rack
my soul with inexpressible horror.
15 Oh, thought I, that I [a]could be
banished and become extinct both
soul and body, that I might not be
brought to stand in the presence of
my God, to be judged of my [b]deeds.
16 And now, for three days and for
three nights was I racked, even with
the [a]pains of a [b]damned soul.
17 And it came to pass that as I was
thus [a]racked with torment, while I

2*b* Deut. 26: 8.
c Ex. 3: 6; Alma 29: 11.
3*a* TG Trust in God.
b Rom. 8: 28.
c Mosiah 23: 22 (21–22).
4*a* 1 Cor. 2: 11; Alma 5: 45 (45–46). TG Knowledge.
b TG Carnal Mind.
5*a* TG Man, New, Spiritually Reborn.
b Alma 26: 21 (21–22).
c Mosiah 27: 11 (11–18).
d TG Worthiness.
6*a* Mosiah 27: 10; 28: 4 (3–4).
7*a* Isa. 6: 4; Mosiah 27: 18.
b Prov. 2: 5. TG Fear of God.
10*a* Mosiah 27: 23 (19–23); Alma 38: 8.
11*a* Dan. 10: 7; Acts 9: 7 (3–7).
12*a* D&C 19: 11 (11–15).
b TG Despair.
c TG Poor in Spirit; Repentance; Sorrow.
13*a* TG Guilt.
b Moses 1: 20.
c TG Disobedience.
14*a* Matt. 10: 28.
15*a* Rev. 6: 16 (15–17); Alma 12: 14.
b Isa. 59: 18; Alma 41: 3 (2–5); 42: 27; D&C 1: 10 (9–10).
16*a* TG Pain.
b TG Damnation.
17*a* Ps. 119: 67.

[About 73 B.C.]

was [b]harrowed up by the [c]memory of my many sins, behold, I [d]remembered also to have heard my father prophesy unto the people concerning the coming of one Jesus Christ, a Son of God, to atone for the sins of the world.

18 Now, as my mind caught hold upon this thought, I cried within my heart: O Jesus, thou Son of God, [a]have mercy on me, who am [b]in the [c]gall of bitterness, and am encircled about by the everlasting [d]chains of [e]death.

19 And now, behold, when I thought this, I could remember my [a]pains [b]no more; yea, I was harrowed up by the memory of my sins no more.

20 And oh, what [a]joy, and what marvelous light I did behold; yea, my soul was filled with joy as exceeding as was my pain!

21 Yea, I say unto you, my son, that there could be nothing so exquisite and so bitter as were my pains. Yea, and again I say unto you, my son, that on the other hand, there can be nothing so exquisite and sweet as was my joy.

22 Yea, methought I saw, even as our father [a]Lehi saw, God sitting upon his throne, surrounded with numberless concourses of angels, in the attitude of singing and [b]praising their God; yea, and my soul did long to be there.

23 But behold, my limbs did receive their [a]strength again, and I stood upon my feet, and did manifest unto the people that I had been [b]born of God.

24 Yea, and from that time even until now, I have labored without ceasing, that I might bring souls unto [a]repentance; that I might bring them to [b]taste of the exceeding joy of which I did taste; that they might also be [c]born of God, and be [d]filled with the Holy Ghost.

25 Yea, and now behold, O my son, the Lord doth [a]give me exceedingly great joy in the fruit of my [b]labors;

26 For because of the [a]word which he has imparted unto me, behold, many have been born of God, and have [b]tasted as I have tasted, and have seen eye to eye as I have seen; therefore they do know of these things of which I have spoken, as I do know; and the knowledge which I have is of God.

27 And I have been supported under trials and troubles of every kind, yea, and in all manner of afflictions; yea, God has [a]delivered me from prison, and from bonds, and from death; yea, and I do put my trust in him, and he will still [b]deliver me.

28 And I know that he will [a]raise me up at the last day, to dwell with him in [b]glory; yea, and I will [c]praise him forever, for he has [d]brought our fathers out of Egypt, and he has swallowed up the [e]Egyptians in the Red Sea; and he led them by his power into the promised land; yea, and he has delivered them out of

17*b* 2 Cor. 7: 10 (8–11).
c Alma 11: 43; D&C 18: 44.
d 1 Ne. 10: 17 (17–19); Enos 1: 3.
18*a* Matt. 15: 22.
b IE in extreme remorse.
c Jonah 2: 2; Acts 8: 23.
d Prov. 5: 22; 2 Ne. 9: 45; 28: 22; Alma 12: 11 (10–11); Moses 7: 26.
e TG Death, Spiritual, First.
19*a* TG Peace of God.
b Jer. 31: 34; D&C 19: 16.
20*a* Moses 5: 11. TG Forgiveness; Joy.
22*a* 1 Ne. 1: 8. TG God, Manifestations of.
b Isa. 6: 3 (1–4).
23*a* Moses 1: 10.
b Alma 22: 15; 38: 6. TG Conversion.
24*a* Alma 19: 29.
b Ps. 34: 8; 1 Ne. 8: 12; Mosiah 4: 11.
c TG Holy Ghost, Baptism of.
d 2 Ne. 32: 2 (2, 5); 3 Ne. 9: 20. TG Holy Ghost, Mission of.
25*a* TG Reward.
b TG Work, Value of.
26*a* Prov. 10: 11; Jacob 2: 8; Alma 31: 5; D&C 108: 7.
b 1 Pet. 2: 3 (1–3).
27*a* Alma 14: 28 (26–29).
b Ps. 34: 17.
28*a* Alma 26: 7; 3 Ne. 15: 1.
b TG Exaltation.
c Ezra 3: 11 (11–13); 2 Ne. 9: 49.
d Mosiah 12: 34; D&C 103: 16.
e Ex. 14: 27 (26–27).

[About 73 B.C.]

bondage and captivity from time to time.

29 Yea, and he has also brought our fathers out of the land of Jerusalem; and he has also, by his everlasting power, delivered them out of [a]bondage and captivity, from time to time even down to the present day; and I have always retained in remembrance their captivity; yea, and ye also ought to retain in remembrance, as I have done, their captivity.

30 But behold, my son, this is not all; for ye ought to know as I do know, that [a]inasmuch as ye shall keep the commandments of God ye shall [b]prosper in the land; and ye ought to know also, that inasmuch as ye will not keep the commandments of God ye shall be cut off from his presence. Now this is according to his word.

CHAPTER 37

The plates of brass and other scriptures are preserved to bring souls to salvation—The Jaredites were destroyed because of their wickedness—Their secret oaths and covenants must be kept from the people—Counsel with the Lord in all thy doings—As the Liahona guided the Nephites, so the word of Christ leads men to eternal life.

AND now, my son Helaman, I command you that ye take the [a]records which have been [b]entrusted with me;

2 And I also command you that ye keep a [a]record of this people, according as I have done, upon the plates of Nephi, and keep all these things sacred which I have kept, even as I have kept them; for it is for a [b]wise purpose that they are kept.

3 And these [a]plates of brass, which contain these engravings, which have the records of the holy scriptures upon them, which have the [b]genealogy of our forefathers, even from the beginning—

4 Behold, it has been prophesied by our fathers, that they should be kept and [a]handed down from one generation to another, and be kept and preserved by the hand of the Lord until they should go forth unto every nation, kindred, tongue, and people, that they shall know of the [b]mysteries contained thereon.

5 And now behold, if they are kept they must retain their brightness; yea, and they will retain their brightness; yea, and also shall all the plates which do contain that which is holy writ.

6 Now ye may suppose that this is [a]foolishness in me; but behold I say unto you, that by [b]small and simple things are great things brought to pass; and small means in many instances doth confound the wise.

7 And the Lord God doth work by [a]means to bring about his great and eternal purposes; and by very [b]small means the Lord doth [c]confound the wise and bringeth about the salvation of many souls.

8 And now, it has hitherto been wisdom in God that these things should be preserved; for behold, [a]they have [b]enlarged the memory of this people, yea, and convinced many of the error of their ways, and brought them to the [c]knowledge of

29*a* Mosiah 24: 17; 25: 10; 27: 16; Alma 5: 5 (5–6); 29: 12 (11–12).
30*a* 2 Ne. 1: 20.
b Mosiah 1: 7; Alma 37: 13; 50: 20.
37 1*a* Alma 45: 2 (2–8); 50: 38; 63: 1.
b Mosiah 28: 20.
2*a* TG Record Keeping.
b Enos 1: 13 (13–18); W of M 1: 7 (6–11); Alma 37: 12. TG Restoration of the Gospel.
3*a* Mosiah 28: 20; Alma 63: 12 (1, 11–14).
b 1 Ne. 5: 14.
4*a* 1 Ne. 5: 19 (16–19); Alma 63: 13; Hel. 3: 16.
b TG Mysteries of Godliness.
6*a* 1 Cor. 2: 14.
b 1 Ne. 16: 29; D&C 64: 33; 123: 16.
7*a* Isa. 55: 8 (8–9); Alma 24: 27.
b 2 Kgs. 5: 13; Alma 37: 41.
c 1 Cor. 1: 27; D&C 133: 58 (58–59).
8*a* Mosiah 2: 34; Alma 33: 2.
b Mosiah 1: 3 (3–5).
c TG Education; Scriptures, Value of.

[About 73 B.C.]

their God unto the salvation of their
souls.
9 Yea, I say unto you, [a]were it not
for these things that these records
do contain, which are on these
plates, Ammon and his brethren
could not have [b]convinced so many
thousands of the Lamanites of the
incorrect tradition of their fathers;
yea, these records and their [c]words
brought them unto repentance;
that is, they brought them to the
knowledge of the Lord their God,
and to rejoice in Jesus Christ their
Redeemer.
10 And who knoweth but what
they will be the [a]means of bringing
many thousands of them, yea, and
also many thousands of our [b]stiff-
necked brethren, the Nephites, who
are now hardening their hearts in
sin and iniquities, to the knowledge
of their Redeemer?
11 Now these mysteries are not yet
fully made known unto me; therefore I shall forbear.
12 And it may suffice if I only say
they are preserved for a [a]wise purpose, which purpose is known unto
God; for he doth [b]counsel in wisdom
over all his works, and his paths are
straight, and his course is [c]one
eternal round.
13 O remember, remember, my
son Helaman, how [a]strict are the
commandments of God. And he
said: [b]If ye will keep my commandments ye shall [c]prosper in the land—
but if ye keep not his commandments ye shall be cut off from his
presence.
14 And now remember, my son,
that God has [a]entrusted you with
these things, which are [b]sacred,
which he has kept sacred, and also
which he will keep and [c]preserve for
a [d]wise purpose in him, that he may
show forth his power unto future
generations.
15 And now behold, I tell you by
the spirit of prophecy, that if ye
transgress the commandments of
God, behold, these things which are
sacred shall be taken away from
you by the power of God, and ye
shall be delivered up unto Satan,
that he may sift you as chaff before
the wind.
16 But if ye keep the commandments of God, and do with these
things which are sacred according
to that which the Lord doth command you, (for you must appeal
unto the Lord for all things whatsoever ye must do with them) behold,
no power of earth or hell can [a]take
them from you, for God is powerful
to the fulfilling of all his words.
17 For he will fulfil all his [a]prom-
ises which he shall make unto you,
for he has fulfilled his promises
which he has made unto our fathers.
18 For he promised unto them that
he would [a]preserve these things for
a wise purpose in him, that he might
show forth his power unto future
generations.
19 And now behold, one purpose
hath he fulfilled, even to the restoration of [a]many thousands of the
Lamanites to the knowledge of the
truth; and he hath shown forth his
power in them, and he will also still
show forth his power in them unto
[b]future generations; therefore they
shall be preserved.
20 Therefore I command you, my
son Helaman, that ye be diligent in
fulfilling all my words, and that ye
be diligent in keeping the commandments of God as they are written.
21 And now, I will speak unto

9*a* Mosiah 1:5.
b Alma 18:36; 22:12.
c TG Gospel.
10*a* 2 Ne. 3:15.
b TG Stiffneckedness.
12*a* Alma 37:2.
b Prov. 15:22; 2 Ne. 9:28; Jacob 4:10.
c 1 Ne. 10:19; Alma 7:20.
13*a* Luke 13:24 (22–30).
b Alma 9:13 (13–14); 3 Ne. 5:22.
c Ps. 122:6; Mosiah 1:7; Alma 36:30; 50:20.
14*a* D&C 3:5.
b TG Sacred.
c TG Scriptures, Preservation of.
d 1 Ne. 9:5 (3–6).
16*a* JS-H 1:59.
17*a* 2 Kgs. 10:10. TG Promise.
18*a* D&C 5:9.
19*a* Alma 23:5 (5–13).
b 2 Ne. 3:15; Enos 1:13 (12–18); Morm. 7:9 (8–10).

[About 73 B.C.]

you concerning those [a]twenty-four plates, that ye keep them, that the [b]mysteries and the works of darkness, and their secret works, or the secret works of those people who have been destroyed, may be made [c]manifest unto this people; yea, all their murders, and robbings, and their plunderings, and all their wickedness and abominations, may be made manifest unto this people; yea, and that ye preserve these [d]interpreters.

22 For behold, the Lord saw that his people began to work in darkness, yea, work secret murders and abominations; therefore the Lord said, if they did not repent they should be destroyed from off the face of the earth.

23 And the Lord said: I will prepare unto my servant Gazelem, a [a]stone, which shall shine forth in darkness unto light, that I may [b]discover unto my people who serve me, that I may discover unto them the works of their brethren, yea, their secret works, their works of darkness, and their wickedness and abominations.

24 And now, my son, these [a]interpreters were prepared that the word of God might be fulfilled, which he spake, saying:

25 I will [a]bring forth out of darkness unto light all their secret works and their abominations; and except they repent I will [b]destroy them from off the face of the earth; and I will bring to light all their secrets and abominations, unto every nation that shall hereafter possess the land.

26 And now, my son, we see that they did not repent; therefore they have been destroyed, and thus far the word of God has been fulfilled; yea, their [a]secret abominations have been brought out of darkness and made known unto us.

27 And now, my son, I command you that ye retain all their oaths, and their covenants, and their agreements in their secret abominations; yea, and all their [a]signs and their wonders ye shall [b]keep from this people, that they know them not, lest peradventure they should fall into darkness also and be destroyed.

28 For behold, there is a [a]curse upon all this land, that destruction shall come upon all those workers of darkness, according to the power of God, when they are fully ripe; therefore I desire that this people might not be destroyed.

29 Therefore ye shall keep these secret plans of their [a]oaths and their covenants from this people, and only their wickedness and their murders and their abominations shall ye make known unto them; and ye shall teach them to [b]abhor such wickedness and abominations and murders; and ye shall also teach them that these people were destroyed on account of their wickedness and abominations and their murders.

30 For behold, they [a]murdered all the prophets of the Lord who came among them to declare unto them concerning their iniquities; and the blood of those whom they murdered did cry unto the Lord their God for vengeance upon those who were their murderers; and thus the judgments of God did come upon these workers of darkness and secret [b]combinations.

31 Yea, and [a]cursed be the land forever and ever unto those workers of

---

21*a* Mosiah 8: 9; 21: 27; 28: 11; Ether 1: 2 (1–5); 15: 33.
b TG Secret Combinations.
c Prov. 26: 26; Alma 14: 3 (2–3).
d TG Urim and Thummim.
23*a* Mosiah 8: 13.
b IE reveal, make known.
24*a* TG Urim and Thummim.
25*a* Ps. 64: 5 (4–6); D&C 88: 108 (108–109).
b Mosiah 21: 26.
26*a* 2 Ne. 10: 15.
27*a* Hel. 6: 22. TG Signs.
b Alma 63: 12.
28*a* Ether 2: 8 (7–12).
29*a* Hel. 6: 25.
b Deut. 32: 19; Alma 13: 12. TG Hate.
30*a* TG Prophets, Rejection of.
b TG Secret Combinations.
31*a* Alma 45: 16. TG Earth, Curse of.

[About 73 B.C.]

darkness and secret combinations,
even unto destruction, except they
repent before they are fully [b]ripe.
32 And now, my son, remember the
words which I have spoken unto
you; trust not those secret plans
unto this people, but teach them an
everlasting [a]hatred against sin and
iniquity.
33 [a]Preach unto them repentance,
and faith on the Lord Jesus Christ;
teach them to humble themselves
and to be [b]meek and lowly in heart;
teach them to [c]withstand every
[d]temptation of the devil, with their
faith on the Lord Jesus Christ.
34 Teach them to never be weary of
good works, but to be meek and
lowly in heart; for such shall find
[a]rest to their souls.
35 O, remember, my son, and
[a]learn [b]wisdom in thy [c]youth; yea,
learn in thy youth to keep the
commandments of God.
36 Yea, and [a]cry unto God for all
thy support; yea, let all thy [b]doings
be unto the Lord, and whithersoever thou goest let it be in the Lord;
yea, let all thy [c]thoughts be directed
unto the Lord; yea, let the affec-
tions of thy heart be placed upon
the Lord forever.
37 [a]Counsel with the Lord in all thy
doings, and he will direct thee for
[b]good; yea, when thou liest down at
night lie down unto the Lord, that
he may watch over you in your
sleep; and when thou risest in the
[c]morning let thy heart be full of
thanks unto God; and if ye do these
things, ye shall be lifted up at the
last day.
38 And now, my son, I have somewhat to say concerning the thing
which our fathers call a ball, or
director—or our fathers called it
[a]Liahona, which is, being interpreted, a compass; and the Lord
prepared it.
39 And behold, there cannot any
man work after the manner of
so curious a workmanship. And
behold, it was prepared to show unto
our fathers the course which they
should travel in the wilderness.
40 And it did work for them
according to their [a]faith in God;
therefore, if they had faith to believe that God could cause that
those spindles should point the way
they should go, behold, it was done;
therefore they had this miracle,
and also many other miracles
wrought by the power of God, day
by day.
41 Nevertheless, because those
miracles were worked by [a]small
means it did show unto them marvelous works. They were [b]slothful,
and forgot to exercise their faith
and diligence and then those marvelous works ceased, and they did
not progress in their journey;
42 Therefore, they tarried in the
wilderness, or did [a]not travel a
direct course, and were afflicted
with hunger and thirst, because of
their transgressions.
43 And now, my son, I would that
ye should understand that these
things are not without a [a]shadow;
for as our fathers were slothful to
give heed to this compass (now
these things were temporal) they

31*b* Gen. 15: 16; Hel. 13: 14; D&C 61: 31; 101: 11.
32*a* Prov. 3: 5 (5–6); 2 Ne. 4: 31; Alma 43: 7.
33*a* TG Mission of Early Saints; Preaching.
b TG Meekness.
c TG Perseverance; Self-mastery.
d TG Temptation.
34*a* Matt. 11: 29 (28–30).
35*a* TG Education; Learning.
b TG Wisdom.
c Eccl. 12: 1; Lam. 3: 27.
36*a* TG Prayer.
b Ps. 37: 5 (4–7).
c TG Motivations.
37*a* Josh. 9: 14; Ps. 34: 4 (4, 6, 10); Lam. 3: 25; Heb. 11: 6; Jacob 4: 10; D&C 3: 4.
b TG Abundant Life.
c Ps. 5: 3; 1 Chr. 16: 8 (7–36); Ether 6: 9; D&C 46: 32.
38*a* 1 Ne. 16: 10 (10, 16, 26); 18: 12 (12, 21); 2 Ne. 5: 12; D&C 17: 1.
40*a* 1 Ne. 16: 28.
41*a* 1 Ne. 16: 29; Alma 37: 7 (6–8).
b TG Apathy; Laziness.
42*a* 1 Ne. 16: 28.
43*a* Col. 2: 17; Heb. 8: 5; Mosiah 3: 15.

[About 73 B.C.]

did not prosper; even so it is with
things which are spiritual.
44 For behold, it is as easy to give
heed to the [a]word of Christ, which
will point to you a straight course to
eternal bliss, as it was for our fathers
to give heed to this compass, which
would point unto them a straight
course to the promised land.
45 And now I say, is there not a
[a]type in this thing? For just as
surely as this director did bring our
fathers, by following its course, to
the promised land, shall the words
of Christ, if we follow their course,
carry us beyond this vale of sorrow
into a far better land of promise.
46 O my son, do not let us be [a]slothful
because of the [b]easiness of the
[c]way; for so was it with our fathers;
for so was it prepared for them, that
if they would [d]look they might [e]live;
even so it is with us. The way is prepared,
and if we will look we may
live forever.
47 And now, my son, see that ye
take [a]care of these sacred things, yea,
see that ye [b]look to God and live.
Go unto this people and declare the
word, and be sober. My son, farewell.

The commandments of Alma to his son Shiblon.

CHAPTER 38

Shiblon was persecuted for righteousness' sake—Salvation is in Christ, who is the life and the light of the world—Bridle all your passions.

My [a]son, give ear to my words, for
I say unto you, even as I said unto
Helaman, that [b]inasmuch as ye
shall keep the commandments of
God ye shall prosper in the land;
and [c]inasmuch as ye will not keep
the commandments of God ye shall
be [d]cut off from his [e]presence.
2 And now, my son, I trust that I
shall have great joy in you, because
of your [a]steadiness and your
faithfulness unto God; for as you
have commenced in your youth
to look to the Lord your God, even
so I hope that you will continue in
keeping his commandments; for
blessed is he that [b]endureth to the
end.
3 I say unto you, my son, that I
have had great joy in thee already,
because of thy faithfulness and thy
diligence, and thy patience and thy
long-suffering among the people of
the [a]Zoramites.
4 For I know that thou wast in
bonds; yea, and I also know that
thou wast stoned for the word's
sake; and thou didst bear all these
things with [a]patience because the
Lord was [b]with thee; and now thou
knowest that the Lord did deliver
thee.
5 And now my son, Shiblon, I
would that ye should remember,
that as much as ye shall put your
[a]trust in God even so much ye shall
be [b]delivered out of your trials, and
your [c]troubles, and your afflictions,
and ye shall be lifted up at the last
day.
6 Now, my son, I would not that ye

44*a* Ps. 119: 105.
45*a* TG Jesus Christ, Types of, in Anticipation.
46*a* Luke 6: 46 (46–49); 1 Ne. 17: 41 (40–41).
b Matt. 11: 30.
c Ex. 33: 13 (12–13); 2 Ne. 9: 41; 31: 21 (17–21); D&C 132: 22 (22, 25).
d Alma 25: 16; 33: 22 (19–23).
e John 11: 25; Hel. 8: 15; 3 Ne. 15: 9.
47*a* TG Scriptures, Preservation of.
b Amos 5: 6; Ether 12: 41.
38 1*a* Alma 31: 7; 63: 1.
b Alma 60: 16.
c Alma 44: 3.
d 1 Ne. 2: 21; 2 Ne. 5: 20 (20–24); Alma 9: 14 (13–15).
e TG God, Presence of.
2*a* TG Commitment.
b Matt. 10: 22; Mark 13: 13; 2 Ne. 31: 16 (15–20); Alma 32: 13 (13–15); 3 Ne. 15: 9; 27: 6 (6–17); D&C 20: 29; 53: 7.
3*a* Alma 31: 7; 39: 2.
4*a* TG Patience.
b Ex. 3: 12; 1 Ne. 17: 55; Mosiah 24: 17.
5*a* Ps. 50: 15; D&C 100: 17.
b Matt. 11: 28 (28–30).
c Ps. 81: 7; Alma 9: 17; D&C 3: 8.

[About 73 B.C.]

should think that I know these things of myself, but it is the Spirit of God which is in me which maketh these things known unto me; for if I had not been [a]born of God I should not have known these things.

7 But behold, the Lord in his great mercy sent his [a]angel to declare unto me that I must stop the work of [b]destruction among his people; yea, and I have seen an angel face to face, and he spake with me, and his voice was as thunder, and it shook the whole earth.

8 And it came to pass that I was [a]three days and three nights in the most bitter [b]pain and [c]anguish of soul; and never, until I did cry out unto the Lord Jesus Christ for mercy, did I receive a [d]remission of my sins. But behold, I did cry unto him and I did find peace to my soul.

9 And now, my son, I have told you this that ye may learn wisdom, that ye may learn of me that there is [a]no other way or means whereby man can be saved, only in and through Christ. Behold, he is the life and the [b]light of the world. Behold, he is the word of truth and [c]righteousness.

10 And now, as ye have begun to teach the word even so I would that ye should continue to teach; and I would that ye would be diligent and [a]temperate in all things.

11 See that ye are not lifted up unto pride; yea, see that ye do not [a]boast in your own wisdom, nor of your much strength.

12 Use [a]boldness, but not overbearance; and also see that ye [b]bridle all your passions, that ye may be filled with love; see that ye refrain from idleness.

13 Do not [a]pray as the Zoramites do, for ye have seen that they pray to be heard of men, and to be praised for their wisdom.

14 Do not say: O God, I thank thee that we are [a]better than our brethren; but rather say: O Lord, forgive my [b]unworthiness, and remember my brethren in mercy—yea, acknowledge your unworthiness before God at all times.

15 And may the Lord bless your soul, and receive you at the last day into his kingdom, to sit down in peace. Now go, my son, and teach the word unto this people. Be [a]sober. My son, farewell.

The commandments of Alma to his son Corianton. Comprising chapters 39 to 42 inclusive.

CHAPTER 39

Sexual sin is an abomination—Corianton's sins kept the Zoramites from receiving the word—Christ's redemption is retroactive in saving the faithful who preceded it.

AND now, my [a]son, I have somewhat more to say unto thee than what I said unto thy brother; for behold, have ye not observed the steadiness of thy brother, his faithfulness, and his diligence in keeping the commandments of God? Behold, has he not set a good [b]example for thee?

2 For thou didst not give so much heed unto my words as did thy brother, among the people of the [a]Zoramites. Now this is what I have against thee; thou didst go on unto

6*a* Alma 36:23 (23, 26); D&C 5:16. TG Holy Ghost, Baptism of; Man, Natural, Not Spiritually Reborn; Man, New, Spiritually Reborn.
7*a* Mosiah 27:11 (11–17).
b Mosiah 28:4 (3–4); Alma 26:18 (17–18); 36:6 (6–11).
8*a* Alma 36:10 (10, 16).
b TG Pain.
c TG Sorrow.
d TG Remission of Sins.
9*a* Alma 21:9.
b TG Jesus Christ, Light of the World.
c Ether 4:12.
10*a* TG Temperance.
11*a* TG Boasting; Pride.
12*a* Alma 18:24.
b TG Priesthood, Magnifying Callings within; Self-mastery.
13*a* TG Hypocrisy.
14*a* Alma 31:16.
b Luke 18:13 (10–14). TG Ingratitude; Poor in Spirit.
15*a* 1 Pet. 5:8.
39 1*a* Alma 31:7.
b TG Example.
2*a* Alma 38:3.

[About 73 B.C.]

boasting in thy strength and thy
wisdom.
3 And this is not all, my son. Thou
didst do that which was grievous
unto me; for thou didst forsake the
ministry, and did go over into the
land of Siron among the borders of
the Lamanites, after the [a]harlot
Isabel.
4 Yea, *she* did [a]steal away the
hearts of many; but this was no excuse for thee, my son. Thou shouldst
have tended to the ministry wherewith thou wast entrusted.
5 Know ye not, my son, that these
things are an abomination in the
sight of the Lord; yea, most [a]abom-
inable above all sins save it be
the shedding of innocent [b]blood or
denying the Holy Ghost?
6 For behold, if ye [a]deny the Holy
Ghost when it once has had place
in you, and ye know that ye deny it,
behold, this is a sin which is [b]un-
pardonable; yea, and whosoever
murdereth against the light and
knowledge of God, it is not easy for
him to obtain [c]forgiveness; yea, I
say unto you, my son, that it is
not easy for him to obtain a forgiveness.
7 And now, my son, I would to God
that ye had not been [a]guilty of so
great a crime. I would not dwell
upon your crimes, to harrow up your
soul, if it were not for your good.
8 But behold, ye cannot [a]hide
your crimes from God; and except
ye repent they will stand as a testimony against you at the last day.
9 Now my son, I would that ye
should repent and forsake your sins,
and go no more after the [a]lusts of
your eyes, but [b]cross yourself in all
these things; for except ye do this
ye can in nowise inherit the kingdom of God. Oh, remember, and take
it upon you, and [c]cross yourself in
these things.
10 And I command you to take it
upon you to counsel with your elder
brothers in your undertakings; for
behold, thou art in thy youth, and
ye stand in need to be nourished by
your brothers. And give heed to
their counsel.
11 Suffer not yourself to be led
away by any vain or foolish thing;
suffer not the devil to lead away
your heart again after those wicked
harlots. Behold, O my son, how
great [a]iniquity ye brought upon the
[b]Zoramites; for when they saw your
[c]conduct they would not believe in
my words.
12 And now the Spirit of the Lord
doth say unto me: [a]Command thy
children to do good, lest they [b]lead
away the hearts of many people to
destruction; therefore I command
you, my son, in the fear of God, that
ye [c]refrain from your iniquities;
13 That ye turn to the Lord with all
your mind, might, and strength;
that ye lead away the hearts of no
more to do wickedly; but rather
return unto them, and [a]acknowl-
edge your faults and that wrong
which ye have done.
14 [a]Seek not after riches nor the
vain things of this world; for behold,
you cannot carry them with you.

3*a* 1 Sam. 2: 22 (22–25); Prov. 5: 3. TG Sensuality.
4*a* Prov. 7: 18 (6–27).
5*a* TG Adultery; Fornication; Sexual Immorality.
b TG Life, Sanctity of.
6*a* Moro. 8: 28; D&C 76: 35. TG Holy Ghost, Loss of.
b TG Holy Ghost, Unpardonable Sin against.
c Rom. 9: 18; D&C 64: 10. TG Forgiveness.
7*a* TG Guilt.
8*a* TG God, Omniscience of.
9*a* Prov. 5: 8. TG Carnal Mind; Chastity; Covetousness; Lust.
b TG Self-mastery.
c 3 Ne. 12: 30.
11*a* 1 Sam. 2: 24 (22–25).
b Alma 35: 14 (2–14); 43: 4 (4–6, 13).
c 2 Sam. 12: 14; Ezek. 5: 5; Rom. 2: 21 (21–23); 14: 13; 1 Cor. 9: 14 (13–14); 1 Ne. 21: 6; Alma 4: 11; D&C 103: 9 (8–9). TG Example.
12*a* TG Commandments of God; Teaching.
b TG Peer Influence.
c TG Abstinence.
13*a* Mosiah 27: 35.
14*a* Matt. 6: 33 (25–34); Jacob 2: 18 (18–19); D&C 6: 7 (6–7); 68: 31 (31–32). TG Treasure.

[About 73 B.C.]

15 And now, my son, I would say somewhat unto you concerning the [a]coming of Christ. Behold, I say unto you, that it is he that surely shall come to take away the sins of the world; yea, he cometh to declare glad tidings of salvation unto his people.

16 And now, my son, this was the ministry unto which ye were called, to declare these glad tidings unto this people, to prepare their minds; or rather that salvation might come unto them, that they may prepare the minds of their [a]children to hear the word at the time of his coming.

17 And now I will ease your mind somewhat on this subject. Behold, you marvel why these things should be known so long beforehand. Behold, I say unto you, is not a soul at this time as precious unto God as a soul will be at the time of his coming?

18 Is it not as necessary that the plan of redemption should be [a]made known unto this people as well as unto their children?

19 Is it not as easy at this time for the Lord to [a]send his angel to declare these glad tidings unto us as unto our children, or as after the time of his coming?

CHAPTER 40

Christ bringeth to pass the resurrection of all men—The righteous dead go to paradise and the wicked to outer darkness to await the day of their resurrection—All things shall be restored to their proper and perfect frame in the resurrection.

Now my son, here is somewhat more I would say unto thee; for I perceive that thy mind is worried concerning the resurrection of the dead.

2 Behold, I say unto you, that there is no resurrection—or, I would say, in other words, that this mortal does not put on [a]immortality, this corruption does not [b]put on incorruption—[c]until after the coming of Christ.

3 Behold, he bringeth to pass the [a]resurrection of the dead. But behold, my son, the resurrection is not yet. Now, I unfold unto you a mystery; nevertheless, there are many [b]mysteries which are [c]kept, that no one knoweth them save God himself. But I show unto you one thing which I have inquired diligently of God that I might know—that is concerning the resurrection.

4 Behold, there is a time appointed that all shall [a]come forth from the dead. Now when this time cometh no one knows; but God knoweth the time which is appointed.

5 Now, whether there shall be one time, or a [a]second time, or a third time, that men shall come forth from the dead, it mattereth not; for God [b]knoweth all these things; and it sufficeth me to know that this is the case—that there is a time appointed that all shall rise from the dead.

6 Now there must needs be a space betwixt the time of death and the time of the resurrection.

7 And now I would inquire what becometh of the [a]souls of men [b]from this time of death to the time appointed for the resurrection?

8 Now whether there is more than one [a]time appointed for men to rise it mattereth not; for all do not die at once, and this mattereth not; all is

15*a* TG Jesus Christ, Mission of.
16*a* TG Family, Children, Responsibilities toward.
18*a* Jacob 4: 4 (4–6).
19*a* Mosiah 3: 2 (2–3).
40 2*a* Mosiah 16: 10 (10–13). TG Immortality.
b 1 Cor. 15: 53 (42–54).
c 1 Cor. 15: 20 (20–23).
3*a* TG Resurrection.
b TG Mysteries of Godliness.
c D&C 25: 4; 121: 26; 124: 41.
4*a* John 5: 29 (28–29).
5*a* 1 Thes. 4: 16; Mosiah 26: 25 (24–25); D&C 43: 18; 76: 85.
b TG God, Omniscience of.
7*a* TG Soul.
b TG Spirits, Disembodied.
8*a* 2 Pet. 3: 8. TG Time.

[About 73 B.C.]

as one day with God, and time only is measured unto men.

9 Therefore, there is a time appointed unto men that they shall rise from the dead; and there is a space between the time of death and the resurrection. And now, concerning this space of time, what becometh of the souls of men is the thing which I have inquired diligently of the Lord to know; and this is the thing of which I do know.

10 And when the time cometh when all shall rise, then shall they know that God [a]knoweth all the [b]times which are appointed unto man.

11 Now, concerning the [a]state of the soul between [b]death and the resurrection—Behold, it has been made known unto me by an angel, that the spirits of all men, as soon as they are departed from this mortal body, yea, the spirits of all men, whether they be good or evil, are [c]taken [d]home to that God who gave them life.

12 And then shall it come to pass, that the spirits of those who are righteous are received into a state of [a]happiness, which is called [b]paradise, a state of rest, a state of [c]peace, where they shall rest from all their troubles and from all care, and sorrow.

13 And then shall it come to pass, that the [a]spirits of the wicked, yea, who are evil— for behold, they have no part nor portion of the Spirit of the Lord; for behold, they chose evil works rather than good; therefore the spirit of the [b]devil did enter into them, and take possession of their house—and these shall be cast out into outer [c]darkness; there shall be [d]weeping, and wailing, and gnashing of teeth, and this because of their own iniquity, being led captive by the will of the devil.

14 Now this is the state of the [a]souls of the [b]wicked, yea, in darkness, and a state of awful, [c]fearful looking for the fiery [d]indignation of the wrath of God upon them; thus they remain in this [e]state, as well as the righteous in paradise, until the time of their resurrection.

15 Now, there are some that have understood that this state of happiness and this state of misery of the soul, before the resurrection, was a first resurrection. Yea, I admit it may be termed a resurrection, the [a]raising of the spirit or the soul and their consignation to happiness or misery, according to the words which have been spoken.

16 And behold, again it hath been spoken, that there is a [a]first [b]resurrection, a resurrection of all those who have been, or who are, or who shall be, down to the resurrection of Christ from the dead.

17 Now, we do not suppose that this first resurrection, which is spoken of in this manner, can be the resurrection of the souls and their [a]consignation to happiness or misery. Ye cannot suppose that this is what it meaneth.

18 Behold, I say unto you, Nay; but it meaneth the [a]reuniting of the

---

10*a* TG God, Foreknowledge of.
b Acts 17: 26.
11*a* John 20: 17.
b Job 14: 10; Luke 16: 22 (22–26); 1 Ne. 15: 31 (31–36); Alma 11: 45; D&C 76: 73 (71–74).
c Alma 40: 15.
d Eccl. 12: 5; 2 Ne. 9: 38; Alma 24: 16; Hel. 8: 23.
12*a* Isa. 51: 11; Luke 16: 22; D&C 138: 15. TG Happiness.
b TG Paradise.
c 2 Kgs. 22: 20; Alma 7: 27; D&C 45: 46. TG Peace of God.
13*a* TG Spirits in Prison.
b TG Bondage, Spiritual.
c TG Damnation; Darkness, Spiritual; Hell.
d Matt. 8: 12; Mosiah 16: 2.
14*a* TG Spirits in Prison.
b D&C 138: 20.
c Jacob 6: 13; Moses 7: 1.
d TG God, Indignation of.
e Alma 34: 34.
15*a* Alma 40: 11.
16*a* Jacob 4: 11; Mosiah 15: 21 (21–23); 18: 9.
b TG Jesus Christ, Resurrection.
17*a* D&C 76: 17 (17, 32, 50). TG Judgment, The Last.
18*a* Matt. 27: 52.

[About 73 B.C.]

soul with the body, of those from the days of Adam down to the resurrection of Christ.

19 Now, whether the souls and the bodies of those of whom has been spoken shall all be reunited at once, the wicked as well as the righteous, I do not say; let it suffice, that I say that they all come forth; or in other words, their resurrection cometh to pass [a]before the resurrection of those who die after the resurrection of Christ.

20 Now, my son, I do not say that their resurrection cometh at the resurrection of Christ; but behold, I give it as my opinion, that the souls and the bodies are reunited, of the righteous, at the resurrection of Christ, and his [a]ascension into heaven.

21 But whether it be at his resurrection or after, I do not say; but this much I say, that there is a [a]space between death and the resurrection of the body, and a state of the soul in [b]happiness or in [c]misery until the time which is appointed of God that the dead shall come forth, and be reunited, both soul and body, and be [d]brought to stand before God, and be judged according to their works.

22 Yea, this bringeth about the restoration of those things of which has been spoken by the mouths of the prophets.

23 The [a]soul shall be [b]restored to the [c]body, and the body to the soul; yea, and every limb and joint shall be restored to its body; yea, even a [d]hair of the head shall not be lost; but all things shall be restored to their proper and [e]perfect frame.

24 And now, my son, this is the restoration of which has been [a]spoken by the mouths of the prophets—

25 And then shall the [a]righteous shine forth in the kingdom of God.

26 But behold, an awful [a]death cometh upon the wicked; for they die as to things pertaining to things of righteousness; for they are unclean, and [b]no unclean thing can inherit the kingdom of God; but they are cast out, and consigned to partake of the fruits of their labors or their works, which have been evil; and they drink the dregs of a bitter [c]cup.

CHAPTER 41

In the resurrection men come forth to a state of endless happiness or endless misery—Wickedness never was happiness—Carnal men are without God in the world—Every person receives again in the restoration the characteristics and attributes acquired in mortality.

AND now, my son, I have somewhat to say concerning the restoration of which has been spoken; for behold, some have [a]wrested the scriptures, and have gone far [b]astray because of this thing. And I perceive that thy mind has been [c]worried also concerning this thing. But behold, I will explain it unto thee.

2 I say unto thee, my son, that the plan of restoration is requisite with the justice of God; for it is requisite that all things should be restored to their proper order. Behold, it is requisite and just, according to the power and resurrection of Christ,

19*a* Mosiah 15: 26.
20*a* TG Jesus Christ, Ascension of.
21*a* Luke 23: 43 (39–43).
b TG Paradise.
c TG Spirits in Prison.
d Alma 42: 23.
23*a* Ezek. 37: 14 (6–14); D&C 88: 15 (15–17). TG Soul.
b 2 Ne. 9: 13; Alma 11: 45 (40–45).
c TG Body, Sanctity of.
d Luke 21: 18; Alma 41: 2; D&C 29: 25.
e Philip. 3: 21. TG Perfection.
24*a* Isa. 26: 19. TG Resurrection.
25*a* Dan. 12: 3; Matt. 13: 43.
26*a* Ps. 94: 3 (1–11); 1 Cor. 6: 9 (9–10); 1 Ne. 15: 33; Alma 12: 16; D&C 29: 41. TG Hell.
b Eph. 5: 5; Alma 11: 37. TG Uncleanness.
c Ps. 75: 8.
41 1*a* 2 Pet. 1: 20; Alma 13: 20.
b TG Apostasy of Individuals.
c TG Problem-Solving.

[About 73 B.C.]

that the soul of man should be restored to its body, and that every [a]part of
the body should be restored to itself.
3 And it is requisite with the
[a]justice of God that men should be
[b]judged according to their [c]works;
and if their works were good in this
life, and the desires of their hearts
were good, that they should also, at
the last day, be [d]restored unto that
which is good.
4 And if their works are evil they
shall be [a]restored unto them for evil.
Therefore, all things shall be [b]re-
stored to their proper order, every
thing to its natural frame—[c]mor-
tality raised to [d]immortality, [e]cor-
ruption to incorruption—raised to
[f]endless happiness to [g]inherit the
kingdom of God, or to endless
misery to inherit the kingdom of the
devil, the one on one hand, the
other on the other—
5 The one raised to [a]happiness
according to his desires of happiness,
or good according to his desires of
good; and the other to evil according
to his desires of evil; for as he has
desired to do evil all the day long
even so shall he have his reward of
evil when the night cometh.
6 And so it is on the other hand. If
he hath repented of his sins, and
desired righteousness until the end
of his days, even so he shall be
rewarded unto righteousness.
7 [a]These are they that are redeemed
of the Lord; yea, these are they that
are taken out, that are delivered
from that endless night of darkness;
and thus they stand or fall; for
behold, they are their own [b]judges,
whether to do good or do evil.
8 Now, the decrees of God are
[a]unalterable; therefore, the way is
prepared that [b]whosoever will may
[c]walk therein and be saved.
9 And now behold, my son, do not
risk [a]one more offense against your
God upon those points of doctrine,
which ye have hitherto risked to
commit sin.
10 Do not suppose, because it has
been spoken concerning restoration,
that ye shall be restored from sin to
happiness. Behold, I say unto you,
[a]wickedness never was [b]happiness.
11 And now, my son, all men that
are in a state of [a]nature, or I would
say, in a [b]carnal state, are in the [c]gall
of bitterness and in the [d]bonds of
iniquity; they are [e]without God in
the world, and they have gone
[f]contrary to the nature of God;
therefore, they are in a state
contrary to the nature of happiness.
12 And now behold, is the meaning
of the word restoration to take a
thing of a natural state and place it
in an unnatural state, or to place it
in a state opposite to its nature?
13 O, my son, this is not the case;
but the meaning of the word
restoration is to bring back again
[a]evil for evil, or carnal for carnal, or
devilish for devilish—good for that
which is good; righteous for that
which is righteous; just for that
which is just; merciful for that which
is merciful.

2*a* Alma 40: 23.
3*a* TG God, Justice of; Justice.
b TG Accountability; Judgment, The Last.
c Isa. 59: 18; Alma 36: 15; 42: 27; D&C 1: 10 (9–10).
d Hel. 14: 31.
4*a* Alma 42: 28.
b 2 Ne. 9: 13 (10–13); D&C 138: 17. TG Resurrection.
c TG Mortality.
d TG Immortality.
e 1 Cor. 15: 50 (50–53).
f TG Eternal Life.
g TG Exaltation.
5*a* TG Happiness.
7*a* D&C 76: 65.
b 2 Ne. 2: 26; Alma 42: 27; Hel. 14: 30. TG Agency.
8*a* Morm. 9: 19.
b Alma 42: 27.
c TG Walking with God.
9*a* Prov. 26: 11; Matt. 12: 45 (43–45); D&C 42: 26 (23–28).
10*a* Ps. 32: 10; Isa. 57: 21; Hel. 13: 38. TG Evil; Wickedness.
b Alma 50: 21; Morm. 2: 13. TG Happiness; Peace of God.
11*a* Mosiah 3: 19. TG Man, Natural, Not Spiritually Reborn.
b TG Carnal Mind; Fall of Man.
c Acts 8: 23; Morm. 8: 31.
d TG Bondage, Spiritual.
e Eph. 2: 12; Mosiah 27: 31.
f Hel. 13: 38.
13*a* Dan. 12: 10; Rev. 22: 12 (6–16).

[About 73 B.C.]

14 Therefore, my son, see that you
are merciful unto your brethren;
deal [a]justly, [b]judge righteously, and
do [c]good continually; and if ye do all
these things then shall ye receive
your [d]reward; yea, ye shall have
[e]mercy restored unto you again; ye
shall have justice restored unto you
again; ye shall have a righteous
judgment restored unto you again;
and ye shall have good rewarded
unto you again.
15 For that which ye do [a]send out
shall return unto you again, and be
restored; therefore, the word restoration more fully condemneth the
sinner, and justifieth him not at all.

CHAPTER 42

Mortality is a probationary time to enable man to repent and serve God—The fall brought temporal and spiritual death upon all mankind—Redemption comes through repentance—God himself atoneth for the sins of the world—Mercy is for those who repent—All others are subject to God's justice—Mercy cometh because of the atonement—Only the truly penitent are saved.

AND now, my son, I perceive there
is somewhat more which doth worry
your mind, which ye cannot understand—which is concerning the
[a]justice of God in the [b]punishment
of the sinner; for ye do try to suppose
that it is [c]injustice that the sinner
should be consigned to a state of
misery.
2 Now behold, my son, I will explain this thing unto thee. For
behold, after the Lord God sent our
first parents forth from the garden
of [a]Eden, to till the [b]ground, from
whence they were taken—yea, he
drew out the man, and he placed at
the east end of the garden of Eden,
[c]cherubim, and a flaming sword
which turned every way, to keep
the tree of life—
3 Now, we see that the man had
become as God, knowing good and
evil; and lest he should put forth his
hand, and take also of the tree of
life, and eat and live forever, the
Lord God placed [a]cherubim and the
flaming sword, that he should not
partake of the fruit—
4 And thus we see, that there was a
[a]time granted unto man to repent,
yea, a [b]probationary time, a time to
repent and serve God.
5 For behold, if Adam had put
forth his hand immediately, and
[a]partaken of the [b]tree of life, he
would have lived forever, according
to the word of God, having no space
for repentance; yea, and also the
word of God would have been void,
and the great plan of salvation
would have been frustrated.
6 But behold, it was appointed
unto man to [a]die—therefore, as
they were cut off from the tree of
life they should be cut off from the
face of the earth—and man became
[b]lost forever, yea, they became
[c]fallen man.
7 And now, ye see by this that our
first parents were [a]cut off both
temporally and spiritually from the
[b]presence of the Lord; and thus we
see they became subjects to follow
after their own [c]will.
8 Now behold, it was not expedient

14*a* TG Honesty.
b Matt. 7:1 (1–5); D&C 11:12.
c TG Benevolence.
d TG Reward.
e TG Mercy.
15*a* Prov. 19:17; Eccl. 11:1; Alma 42:27 (27–28).
42 1*a* Mosiah 15:27. TG God, Justice of.
b TG Punishment.
c Rom. 3:5; 2 Ne. 26:7. TG Injustice.
2*a* TG Eden.
b Jacob 2:21; Mosiah 2:25; Morm. 9:17.
c Gen. 3:24; Alma 12:21; Moses 4:31.
3*a* TG Cherubim.
4*a* Jacob 5:27.
b Alma 34:32. TG Earth, Purpose of; Probation.
5*a* Alma 12:23; Moses 4:28.
b Gen. 2:9; 3:24 (22–24); 1 Ne. 8:10 (10–12); Moses 3:9.
6*a* TG Death.
b 2 Ne. 9:7; Mosiah 16:4 (4–7); Alma 11:45; 12:36.
c TG Fall of Man.
7*a* 2 Ne. 2:5; 9:6 (6–15); Hel. 14:16 (15–18).
b TG God, Presence of.
c TG Agency.

[About 73 B.C.]

that man should be reclaimed from
this [a]temporal death, for that would
destroy the great [b]plan of happiness.
9 Therefore, as the soul could
never die, and the [a]fall had brought
upon all mankind a spiritual [b]death
as well as a temporal, that is, they
were cut off from the presence of the
Lord, it was expedient that mankind
should be reclaimed from this
spiritual death.
10 Therefore, as they had become
[a]carnal, sensual, and devilish, by
[b]nature, this [c]probationary state
became a state for them to prepare;
it became a preparatory state.
11 And now remember, my son, if
it were not for the plan of redemption, (laying it aside) as soon as they
were dead their souls were [a]miser-
able, being cut off from the presence
of the Lord.
12 And now, there was no means to
reclaim men from this fallen state,
which [a]man had brought upon himself because of his own [b]disobedience;
13 Therefore, according to justice,
the [a]plan of [b]redemption could not
be brought about, only on conditions
of repentance of men in this probationary state, yea, this preparatory state; for except it were for
these conditions, mercy could not
take effect except it should destroy
the work of justice. Now the work of
justice could not be destroyed; if so,
God would [c]cease to be God.
14 And thus we see that all mankind were [a]fallen, and they were in
the grasp of [b]justice; yea, the
justice of God, which consigned
them forever to be cut off from his
presence.
15 And now, the plan of mercy
could not be brought about except
an atonement should be made;
therefore God himself [a]atoneth for
the sins of the world, to bring about
the plan of [b]mercy, to appease the
demands of [c]justice, that God might
be a [d]perfect, just God, and a
[e]merciful God also.
16 Now, repentance could not
come unto men except there were
a [a]punishment, which also was
[b]eternal as the life of the soul
should be, affixed [c]opposite to the
plan of happiness, which was as
[d]eternal also as the life of the soul.
17 Now, how could a man repent
except he should [a]sin? How could
he sin if there was no [b]law? How
could there be a law save there was
a punishment?
18 Now, there was a punishment
affixed, and a just law given, which
brought remorse of [a]conscience unto
man.
19 Now, if there was no law given—
if a man [a]murdered he should [b]die—
would he be afraid he would die if
he should murder?
20 And also, if there was no law
given against sin men would not be
afraid to sin.
21 And if there was [a]no law given,
if men sinned what could justice do,
or mercy either, for they would have
no claim upon the creature?
22 But there is a law given, and a

8*a* Gen. 3:22 (22–24).
b Alma 12:26 (22–33); 34:9 (8–16); Moses 6:62.
9*a* TG Fall of Man.
b Moses 5:4. TG Death, Spiritual, First.
10*a* TG Carnal Mind.
b TG Man, Natural, Not Spiritually Reborn.
c TG Mortality; Probation.
11*a* 2 Ne. 9:9 (7–9).
12*a* 1 Cor. 15:22.
b TG Disobedience.
13*a* TG Salvation, Plan of.
b TG Redemption; Repentance.
c 2 Ne. 2:13 (13–14).
14*a* Eph. 2:8 (8–9); Alma 22:14 (13–14).
b Rom. 7:5; 2 Ne. 2:5 (4–10); 25:23.
15*a* 2 Ne. 9:10; Mosiah 16:8 (7–8). TG Atonement; Jesus Christ, Redeemer.
b TG Jesus Christ, Mission of.
c Alma 12:32. TG Justice.
d TG God, Perfection of.
e TG God, Mercy of.
16*a* TG Punishment.
b D&C 19:11 (10–12).
c TG Opposition.
d TG Eternity.
17*a* Rom. 7:8 (1–25). TG Sin.
b Rom. 4:15; 5:13; 2 Ne. 9:25.
18*a* TG Conscience.
19*a* TG Murder.
b TG Blood, Shedding of.
21*a* 2 Ne. 9:26 (25–26); Mosiah 3:11; Alma 9:16 (15–16).

[About 73 B.C.]

[a]punishment affixed, and a [b]repent-
ance granted; which repentance,
mercy claimeth; otherwise, justice
claimeth the creature and executeth the [c]law, and the law inflicteth the punishment; if not so,
the works of justice would be destroyed, and God would cease to be
God.
23 But God ceaseth not to be God,
and [a]mercy claimeth the penitent,
and mercy cometh because of the
[b]atonement; and the atonement
bringeth to pass the [c]resurrection of
the dead; and the [d]resurrection of
the dead bringeth [e]back men into
the presence of God; and thus they
are restored into his presence, to be
[f]judged according to their works,
according to the law and justice.
24 For behold, justice exerciseth
all his demands, and also [a]mercy
claimeth all which is her own; and
thus, none but the truly penitent
are saved.
25 What, do ye suppose that
[a]mercy can rob [b]justice? I say unto
you, Nay; not one whit. If so, God
would cease to be God.
26 And thus God bringeth about
his great and eternal [a]purposes,
which were prepared [b]from the
foundation of the world. And thus
cometh about the salvation and the
redemption of men, and also their
destruction and misery.
27 Therefore, O my son, [a]whoso-
ever will come may come and partake of the waters of life freely; and
whosoever will not come the same
is not compelled to come; but in the
last day it shall be [b]restored unto
him according to his [c]deeds.
28 If he has desired to do [a]evil, and
has not repented in his days, behold, evil shall be done unto him,
according to the restoration of God.
29 And now, my son, I desire that
ye should let these things [a]trouble
you no more, and only let your sins
trouble you, with that trouble
which shall bring you down unto
repentance.
30 O my son, I desire that ye should
deny the [a]justice of God no more.
Do not endeavor to excuse yourself
in the least point because of your
sins, by denying the justice of God;
but do you let the justice of God,
and his [b]mercy, and his long-suffering have full sway in your heart;
and let it bring you down to the
dust in [c]humility.
31 And now, O my son, ye are
called of God to [a]preach the word
unto this people. And now, my son,
go thy way, declare the word with
truth and soberness, that thou
mayest [b]bring souls unto repentance, that the great plan of mercy
may have claim upon them. And
may God grant unto you even
according to my words. Amen.

CHAPTER 43

Alma and his sons preach the word—The Zoramites and other Nephite dissenters become Lamanites—The Lamanites come against the Nephites in war—Moroni arms the Nephites with defensive armor—The Lord

22a TG Punishment.
b TG Repentance.
c Gal. 3: 13; D&C 76: 48.
23a TG God, Mercy of.
b TG Jesus Christ, Atonement through.
c 2 Ne. 2: 8; Alma 7: 12; 12: 25 (24–25).
d 2 Ne. 9: 4; Alma 11: 41 (41–45); Hel. 14: 15 (15–18); Morm. 9: 13.
e Alma 40: 21 (21–24).
f TG Jesus Christ, Judge.
24a TG God, Mercy of.
25a TG Mercy.
b TG Justice.
26a Matt. 5: 48; Rom. 8: 17 (14–21); 2 Ne. 2: 15 (14–30); D&C 29: 43 (42–44); Moses 1: 39. TG Earth, Purpose of.
b Alma 13: 3 (3, 5, 7–8); 3 Ne. 1: 14.
27a Alma 5: 34; 41: 7 (7–8); Hel. 14: 30. TG Agency.
b Alma 41: 15.
c Isa. 59: 18; Alma 36: 15; D&C 1: 10 (9–10).
28a Alma 41: 4 (2–5).
29a 2 Cor. 7: 10 (8–11); Morm. 2: 13.
30a TG Justice.
b TG God, Mercy of.
c TG Humility.
31a D&C 11: 15.
b TG Mission of Early Saints.

[About 73 B.C.]

reveals to Alma the strategy of the Lamanites—The Nephites defend their homes, liberties, families, and religion—The armies of Moroni and Lehi surround the Lamanites.

AND now it came to pass that the sons of Alma did go forth among the people, to declare the word unto them. And Alma, also, himself, could not [a]rest, and he also went forth.

2 Now [a]we shall say no more concerning their preaching, except that they preached the word, and the truth, according to the spirit of prophecy and revelation; and they preached after the [b]holy order of God by which they were called.

3 And now [a]I return to an [b]account of the wars between the Nephites and the Lamanites, in the *eighteenth year of the reign of the judges.

4 For behold, it came to pass that the [a]Zoramites became Lamanites; therefore, in the commencement of the eighteenth year the people of the Nephites saw that the Lamanites were coming upon them; therefore they made preparations for war; yea, they gathered together their armies in the land of Jershon.

5 And it came to pass that the Lamanites came with their thousands; and they came into the land of [a]Antionum, which is the land of the Zoramites; and a man by the name of [b]Zerahemnah was their leader.

6 And now, as the [a]Amalekites were of a more wicked and murderous disposition than the Lamanites were, in and of themselves, therefore, Zerahemnah appointed chief [b]captains over the Lamanites, and they were all Amalekites and [c]Zoramites.

7 Now this he did that he might preserve their [a]hatred towards the Nephites, that he might bring them into subjection to the accomplishment of his designs.

8 For behold, his [a]designs were to [b]stir up the Lamanites to anger against the Nephites; this he did that he might usurp great power over them, and also that he might gain power over the Nephites by bringing them into [c]bondage.

9 And now the design of the Nephites was to support their lands, and their houses, and their [a]wives, and their children, that they might preserve them from the hands of their enemies; and also that they might preserve their [b]rights and their privileges, yea, and also their [c]liberty, that they might worship God according to their desires.

10 For they knew that if they should fall into the hands of the Lamanites, that whosoever should [a]worship God in [b]spirit and in truth, the true and the living God, the Lamanites would [c]destroy.

11 Yea, and they also knew the extreme hatred of the Lamanites towards their [a]brethren, who were the [b]people of Anti-Nephi-Lehi, who were called the people of Ammon—and they would not take up arms, yea, they had entered into a covenant and they would not break it—therefore, if they should fall into the hands of the Lamanites they would be destroyed.

12 And the Nephites would not suffer that they should be destroyed; therefore they gave them lands for their inheritance.

43 1*a* Ether 12:2 (2–3).
2*a* W of M 1:9 (1–9).
b Alma 30:20 (20–23, 31); 46:38. TG Priesthood.
3*a* Morm. 5:9.
b Alma 35:13.
4*a* Alma 30:59; 35:14 (2–14); 52:33 (20, 33).
5*a* Alma 31:3.
b Alma 44:1.
6*a* Alma 21:4 (2–16).
b Alma 48:5.
c Alma 43:44.
7*a* Alma 37:32.
8*a* Alma 43:29.
b Alma 27:12; 47:1.
c Alma 44:2.
9*a* Alma 44:5; 46:12; 48:10 (10, 24).
b TG Citizenship.
c TG Liberty.
10*a* TG Worship.
b John 4:23 (23–24).
c Dan. 6:7 (4–17).
11*a* Alma 23:17; 24:1 (1–3, 5, 20); 25:13 (1, 13); 27:2 (2, 21–26).
b Alma 47:29.

[*About 74 B.C.]

13 And the people of Ammon did give unto the Nephites a large portion of their substance to [a]support their armies; and thus the Nephites were compelled, alone, to withstand against the Lamanites, who were a compound of Laman and Lemuel, and the sons of Ishmael, and all those who had dissented from the Nephites, who were Amalekites and Zoramites, and the [b]descendants of the priests of Noah.

14 Now those descendants were as numerous, nearly, as were the Nephites; and thus the Nephites were obliged to contend with their brethren, even unto bloodshed.

15 And it came to pass as the armies of the Lamanites had gathered together in the [a]land of Antionum, behold, the armies of the Nephites were prepared to meet them in the land of Jershon.

16 Now, the leader of the Nephites, or the man who had been [a]appointed to be the [b]chief captain over the Nephites—now the chief captain took the command of all the armies of the Nephites—and his name was Moroni;

17 And Moroni took all the command, and the government of their wars. And he was only twenty and five years old when he was appointed chief captain over the armies of the Nephites.

18 And it came to pass that he met the Lamanites in the borders of Jershon, and his people were armed with swords, and with cimeters, and all manner of [a]weapons of war.

19 And when the armies of the Lamanites saw that the people of Nephi, or that Moroni, had [a]prepared his people with [b]breastplates and with arm-shields, yea, and also shields to defend their heads, and also they were dressed with thick clothing—

20 Now the army of Zerahemnah was not prepared with any such thing; they had only their [a]swords and their cimeters, their bows and their arrows, their [b]stones and their slings; and they were [c]naked, save it were a skin which was girded about their loins; yea, all were naked, save it were the Zoramites and the Amalekites;

21 But they were not armed with breastplates, nor shields—therefore, they were exceedingly afraid of the armies of the Nephites because of their armor, notwithstanding their number being so much greater than the Nephites.

22 Behold, now it came to pass that they durst not come against the Nephites in the borders of Jershon; therefore they departed out of the land of Antionum into the wilderness, and took their journey round about in the wilderness, away by the head of the river Sidon, that they might come into the land of [a]Manti and take possession of the land; for they did not suppose that the armies of Moroni would know whither they had gone.

23 But it came to pass, as soon as they had departed into the wilderness Moroni sent spies into the wilderness to watch their camp; and Moroni, also, knowing of the prophecies of Alma, sent certain men unto him, desiring him that he should [a]inquire of the Lord [b]whither the armies of the Nephites should go to defend themselves against the Lamanites.

24 And it came to pass that the [a]word of the Lord came unto Alma, and Alma informed the messengers of Moroni, that the armies of the

13*a* Alma 57: 27.
b Alma 25: 4.
15*a* Alma 27: 26.
16*a* Alma 46: 34.
b Alma 46: 11.
18*a* TG Weapon.
19*a* TG Skill.
b Alma 49: 24.
20*a* Mosiah 10: 8; Alma 3: 5 (4–5); 44: 8.
b 1 Ne. 16: 15; Alma 49: 2.
c Enos 1: 20.
22*a* Alma 22: 27; 56: 14.
23*a* Ex. 18: 15; 2 Kgs. 6: 12 (8–18); Mosiah 28: 6.
b Alma 16: 6 (5–8); 48: 16; 3 Ne. 3: 20 (18–21).
24*a* Isa. 31: 5; Alma 43: 47; D&C 134: 11. TG Guidance, Divine.

[About 74 B.C.]

Lamanites were marching round about in the wilderness, that they might come over into the land of Manti, that they might commence an attack upon the weaker part of the people. And those messengers went and delivered the message unto Moroni.

25 Now Moroni, leaving a part of his army in the land of Jershon, lest by any means a part of the Lamanites should come into that land and take possession of the city, took the remaining part of his army and marched over into the land of Manti.

26 And he caused that all the people in that quarter of the land should gather themselves together to battle against the Lamanites, to defend their lands and their country, their rights and their liberties; therefore they were prepared against the time of the coming of the Lamanites.

27 And it came to pass that Moroni caused that his army should be secreted in the valley which was near the bank of the river Sidon, which was on the west of the river Sidon in the wilderness.

28 And Moroni placed spies round about, that he might know when the camp of the Lamanites should come.

29 And now, as Moroni knew the [a]intention of the Lamanites, that it was their intention to destroy their brethren, or to [b]subject them and bring them into bondage that they might establish a kingdom unto themselves over all the land;

30 And he also knowing that it was the [a]only desire of the Nephites to preserve their lands, and their [b]liberty, and their church, therefore he thought it no sin that he should defend them by [c]stratagem; therefore, he found by his spies which course the Lamanites were to take.

31 Therefore, he divided his army and brought a part over into the valley, and [a]concealed them on the east, and on the south of the hill Riplah;

32 And the remainder he concealed in the west [a]valley, on the west of the river Sidon, and so down into the borders of the land Manti.

33 And thus having placed his army according to his desire, he was prepared to meet them.

34 And it came to pass that the Lamanites came up on the north of the hill, where a part of the army of Moroni was concealed.

35 And as the Lamanites had passed the hill Riplah, and came into the valley, and began to cross the river Sidon, the army which was concealed on the south of the hill, which was led by a man whose name was [a]Lehi, and he led his army forth and encircled the Lamanites about on the east in their rear.

36 And it came to pass that the Lamanites, when they saw the Nephites coming upon them in their rear, turned them about and began to contend with the army of Lehi.

37 And the work of death commenced on both sides, but it was more dreadful on the part of the Lamanites, for their [a]nakedness was exposed to the heavy blows of the Nephites with their swords and their cimeters, which brought death almost at every stroke.

38 While on the other hand, there was now and then a man fell among the Nephites, by their swords and the loss of blood, they being shielded from the more vital parts of the body, or the more vital parts of the body being shielded from the strokes of the Lamanites, by their [a]breastplates, and their armshields, and their head-plates; and thus the Nephites did carry on the work of death among the Lamanites.

29*a* Alma 43: 8.
b Alma 49: 7.
30*a* Alma 44: 5; 46: 12 (12–20); 48: 10 (10–16).
b Alma 46: 35.
c Judg. 7: 16 (15–25).
31*a* Josh. 8: 13; Alma 52: 21 (21–31); 58: 16 (15–21).
32*a* Alma 43: 41.
35*a* Alma 49: 16.
37*a* Alma 3: 5.
38*a* Alma 44: 9.

[About 74 B.C.]

39 And it came to pass that the
Lamanites became frightened, because of the great destruction
among them, even until they began
to flee towards the river Sidon.
40 And they were pursued by Lehi
and his men; and they were driven
by Lehi into the waters of Sidon,
and they crossed the waters of
Sidon. And Lehi retained his armies
upon the bank of the river Sidon
that they should not cross.
41 And it came to pass that Moroni
and his army met the Lamanites in
the [a]valley, on the other side of the
river Sidon, and began to fall upon
them and to slay them.
42 And the Lamanites did flee
again before them, towards the land
of Manti; and they were met again
by the armies of Moroni.
43 Now in this case the Lamanites
did fight exceedingly; yea, never
had the Lamanites been known to
fight with such exceedingly great
strength and courage, no, not even
from the beginning.
44 And they were inspired by the
[a]Zoramites and the Amalekites, who
were their chief captains and leaders,
and by Zerahemnah, who was their
chief captain, or their chief leader
and commander; yea, they did
fight like dragons, and many of the
Nephites were slain by their hands,
yea, for they did smite in two
many of their head-plates, and they
did pierce many of their breastplates, and they did smite off many
of their arms; and thus the Lamanites did smite in their fierce anger.
45 Nevertheless, the Nephites
were inspired by a [a]better cause, for
they were not [b]fighting for mon-
archy nor power but they were
fighting for their homes and their
[c]liberties, their wives and their
children, and their all, yea, for their
rites of worship and their church.
46 And they were doing that which
they felt was the [a]duty which they
owed to their God; for the Lord had
said unto them, and also unto their
fathers, that: [b]Inasmuch as ye are
not guilty of the [c]first offense,
neither the second, ye shall not
suffer yourselves to be slain by the
hands of your enemies.
47 And again, the Lord has said
that: Ye shall [a]defend your families
even unto [b]bloodshed. Therefore for
this cause were the Nephites contending with the Lamanites, to
defend themselves, and their families, and their lands, their country,
and their rights, and their religion.
48 And it came to pass that when
the men of Moroni saw the fierceness
and the anger of the Lamanites,
they were about to shrink and flee
from them. And Moroni, perceiving
their intent, sent forth and inspired
their hearts with these thoughts—
yea, the thoughts of their lands,
their liberty, yea, their freedom
from bondage.
49 And it came to pass that they
turned upon the Lamanites, and
they [a]cried with one voice [b]unto the
Lord their God, for their [c]liberty
and their freedom from bondage.
50 And they [a]began to stand
against the Lamanites with power;
and in that selfsame hour that they
cried unto the Lord for their freedom, the Lamanites began to flee
before them; and they fled even to
the waters of Sidon.
51 Now, the Lamanites were more
[a]numerous, yea, by more than
double the number of the Nephites;
nevertheless, they were driven inso-

41*a* Alma 43: 32.
44*a* Alma 43: 6.
45*a* Alma 44: 1.
b Mosiah 20: 11; Alma 44: 5.
c TG Liberty.
46*a* TG Duty.
b Alma 48: 14 (14–16); D&C 98: 33 (23–36).
c Luke 6: 29; 3 Ne. 3: 21 (20–21); Morm. 3: 10 (10–11); D&C 98: 23 (22–48).
47*a* Isa. 31: 5; Alma 43: 24; 61: 14; Morm. 7: 4; D&C 134: 11. TG Family, Children, Responsibilities toward; War.
b Josh 1: 18.
49*a* Ex. 2: 23 (23–25); Mosiah 29: 20.
b Ps. 59: 1 (1–5).
c TG Liberty.
50*a* Ex. 17: 11 (8–13).
51*a* Alma 46: 30.

[About 74 B.C.]

much that they were gathered together in one body in the valley, upon the bank by the river Sidon.

52 Therefore the armies of Moroni encircled them about, yea, even on both sides of the river, for behold, on the east were the men of Lehi.

53 Therefore when Zerahemnah saw the men of Lehi on the east of the river Sidon, and the armies of Moroni on the west of the river Sidon, that they were encircled about by the Nephites, they were struck with terror.

54 Now Moroni, when he saw their [a]terror, commanded his men that they should stop shedding their blood.

CHAPTER 44

Moroni commands the Lamanites to make a covenant of peace or be destroyed—Zerahemnah rejects the offer, and the battle resumes—Moroni's armies defeat the Lamanites.

AND it came to pass that they did stop and withdrew a pace from them. And Moroni said unto [a]Zerahemnah: Behold, Zerahemnah, that we do [b]not desire to be men of blood. Ye know that ye are in our hands, yet we do not desire to slay you.

2 Behold, we have not come out to battle against you that we might shed your blood for power; neither do we desire to bring any one to the [a]yoke of bondage. But this is the [b]very cause for which ye have come against us; yea, and ye are angry with us because of our religion.

3 But now, ye behold that the Lord is with us; and ye behold that he has delivered you into our hands. And now I would that ye should understand that this is done unto us [a]because of our religion and our faith in Christ. And now ye see that ye cannot destroy this our faith.

4 Now ye see that this is the true faith of God; yea, ye see that God will support, and keep, and preserve us, so long as we are [a]faithful unto him, and unto our faith, and our religion; and never will the Lord suffer that we shall be destroyed except we should fall into transgression and deny our faith.

5 And now, Zerahemnah, I command you, in the name of that all-powerful God, who has strengthened our arms that we have gained power over you, [a]by our faith, by our religion, and by our [b]rites of worship, and by our church, and by the sacred support which we owe to our [c]wives and our children, by that [d]liberty which binds us to our lands and our country; yea, and also by the maintenance of the sacred word of God, to which we owe all our happiness; and by all that is most dear unto us—

6 Yea, and this is not all; I command you by all the desires which ye have for life, that ye [a]deliver up your weapons of war unto us, and we will seek not your blood, but we will [b]spare your lives, if ye will go your way and come not again to war against us.

7 And now, if ye do not this, behold, ye are in our hands, and I will command my men that they shall fall upon you, and [a]inflict the wounds of death in your bodies, that ye may become extinct; and then we will see who shall have power over this people; yea, we will see who shall be brought into bondage.

8 And now it came to pass that when Zerahemnah had heard these sayings he came forth and delivered up his [a]sword and his cimeter, and his bow into the hands of Moroni, and said unto him: Behold, here are

54*a* Alma 47: 2.
44 1*a* Alma 43: 5.
b Alma 43: 45.
2*a* TG Bondage, Physical.
b Alma 43: 8.
3*a* Alma 38: 1.
TG Protection, Divine.
4*a* Mark 4: 40 (35–41).
5*a* Alma 43: 45 (9, 45); 46: 12 (12–20).
b TG Ordinance.
c Gen. 2: 24 (23–24).
d TG Liberty.
6*a* Alma 52: 25 (25, 32).
b TG Benevolence.
7*a* Alma 62: 11.
8*a* Alma 43: 20.

[About 74 B.C.]

our weapons of war; we will deliver
them up unto you, but we will not
suffer ourselves to take an [b]oath
unto you, which we know that we
shall break, and also our children;
but take our weapons of war, and
suffer that we may depart into the
wilderness; otherwise we will retain
our swords, and we will perish or
conquer.
9 Behold, we are [a]not of your faith;
we do not believe that it is God that
has delivered us into your hands;
but we believe that it is your cunning that has preserved you from
our swords. Behold, it is your
[b]breastplates and your shields that
have preserved you.
10 And now when Zerahemnah had
made an end of speaking these
words, Moroni returned the sword
and the weapons of war, which he
had received, unto Zerahemnah,
saying: Behold, we will end the
conflict.
11 Now I cannot recall the words
which I have spoken, therefore as
the Lord liveth, ye shall not depart
except ye depart with an oath that
ye will not return again against us
to war. Now as ye are in our hands
we will spill your blood upon the
ground, or ye shall submit to
the conditions which I have pro-
posed.
12 And now when Moroni had said
these words, Zerahemnah retained
his sword, and he was angry with
Moroni, and he rushed forward that
he might slay Moroni; but as he
raised his sword, behold, one of
Moroni's soldiers smote it even to
the earth, and it broke by the hilt;
and he also smote Zerahemnah that
he took off his scalp and it fell to
the earth. And Zerahemnah withdrew from before them into the
midst of his soldiers.
13 And it came to pass that the
soldier who stood by, who smote off
the scalp of Zerahemnah, took up
the scalp from off the ground by the
hair, and laid it upon the point of
his sword, and stretched it forth
unto them, saying unto them with a
loud voice:
14 Even as this scalp has fallen to
the earth, which is the scalp of your
chief, so shall ye fall to the earth
except ye will deliver up your
weapons of war and depart with a
covenant of peace.
15 Now there were many, when
they heard these words and saw
the scalp which was upon the sword,
that were struck with fear; and
many came forth and threw down
their weapons of war at the feet of
Moroni, and entered into a [a]cove-
nant of peace. And as many as
entered into a covenant they
suffered to [b]depart into the wilderness.
16 Now it came to pass that
Zerahemnah was exceedingly wroth,
and he did stir up the remainder of
his soldiers to anger, to contend
more powerfully against the
Nephites.
17 And now Moroni was angry,
because of the stubbornness of the
Lamanites; therefore he commanded his people that they should
fall upon them and slay them. And
it came to pass that they began to
slay them; yea, and the Lamanites
did contend with their swords and
their might.
18 But behold, their naked skins
and their bare heads were exposed
to the sharp swords of the Nephites;
yea, behold they were pierced and
smitten, yea, and did fall exceedingly fast before the swords of the
Nephites; and they began to be
swept down, even as the soldier of
Moroni had prophesied.
19 Now Zerahemnah, when he
saw that they were all about to be
destroyed, cried mightily unto
Moroni, promising that he would
covenant and also his people with
them, if they would spare the
remainder of their lives, that they

8*b* TG Oath.
9*a* TG Unbelief, Unbelievers.
b Alma 43:38; 46:13.
15*a* 1 Ne. 4:37; Alma 50:36.
b Hel. 1:33.

[About 74 B.C.]

[a]never would come to war again
against them.
20 And it came to pass that Moroni
caused that the work of death
should [a]cease again among the
people. And he took the weapons of
war from the Lamanites; and after
they had entered into a [b]covenant
with him of peace they were suffered
to depart into the wilderness.
21 Now the number of their dead
was not numbered because of the
greatness of the number; yea, the
number of their dead was exceedingly great, both on the Nephites
and on the Lamanites.
22 And it came to pass that they
did cast their dead into the waters of
Sidon, and they have gone forth and
are buried in the depths of the [a]sea.
23 And the armies of the Nephites,
or of Moroni, returned and came to
their houses and their lands.
24 And thus *ended the eighteenth
year of the reign of the judges over
the people of Nephi. And thus ended
the record of Alma, which was written upon the plates of Nephi.

The account of the people of Nephi, and their wars and dissensions, in the days of Helaman, according to the record of Helaman, which he kept in his days. Comprising chapters 45 to 62 inclusive.

CHAPTER 45

Helaman believes the words of Alma—Alma prophesies the destruction of the Nephites—He blesses and curses the land—Alma is taken up by the Spirit, even as Moses—Dissension grows in the Church.

BEHOLD, now it came to pass that
the people of Nephi were exceedingly rejoiced, because the Lord had
again [a]delivered them out of the
hands of their enemies; therefore
they gave thanks unto the Lord
their God; yea, and they did [b]fast
much and pray much, and they did
worship God with exceedingly great
joy.
2 And it came to pass in the nineteenth year of the reign of the judges
over the people of Nephi, that Alma
came unto his son Helaman and
said unto him: Believest thou the
words which I spake unto thee concerning those [a]records which have
been kept?
3 And Helaman said unto him:
Yea, I [a]believe.
4 And Alma said again: Believest
thou in Jesus Christ, who shall
come?
5 And he said: Yea, I believe all
the words which thou hast spoken.
6 And Alma said unto him again:
Will ye [a]keep my commandments?
7 And he said: Yea, I will keep thy
commandments with all my heart.
8 Then Alma said unto him:
Blessed art thou; and the Lord
shall [a]prosper thee in this land.
9 But behold, I have somewhat to
[a]prophesy unto thee; but what I
prophesy unto thee ye shall not
make known; yea, what I prophesy
unto thee shall not be made known,
even until the prophecy is fulfilled;
therefore write the words which I
shall say.
10 And these are the words: Behold, I perceive that this very
people, the Nephites, according to
the spirit of revelation which is in
me, in [a]four hundred years from the
time that Jesus Christ shall manifest himself unto them, shall dwindle
in [b]unbelief.
11 Yea, and then shall they see
wars and pestilences, yea, famines
and bloodshed, even until the

19*a* Alma 47: 6.
20*a* Alma 46: 7.
b Alma 55: 28; 62: 16 (16–17).
22*a* Alma 3: 3.
45 1*a* TG Deliverance.
b TG Fasting.
2*a* Alma 37: 1 (1–32); 50: 38.
3*a* 1 Ne. 11: 5.
6*a* TG Commandments of God; Obedience.
8*a* 1 Ne. 4: 14; Alma 48: 15, 25.
9*a* TG Prophecy.
10*a* 1 Ne. 12: 12 (10–15); Hel. 13: 9; Morm. 8: 6.
b TG Apostasy of Individuals.

[*73 B.C.]

people of Nephi shall become
[a]extinct—
12 Yea, and this because they
shall dwindle in unbelief and fall
into the works of darkness, and
[a]lasciviousness, and all manner of
iniquities; yea, I say unto you, that
because they shall sin against so
great light and knowledge, yea, I
say unto you, that from that day,
even the [b]fourth generation shall
not all pass away before this great
iniquity shall come.
13 And when that great day
cometh, behold, the time very soon
cometh that those who are now, or
the seed of those who are now
numbered among the people of
Nephi, shall [a]no more be numbered
among the people of Nephi.
14 But whosoever remaineth, and
is not destroyed in that great and
dreadful day, shall be [a]numbered
among the [b]Lamanites, and shall
become like unto them, all, save it
be a few who shall be called the
disciples of the Lord; and them
shall the Lamanites pursue even
[c]until they shall become extinct.
And now, because of iniquity, this
prophecy shall be fulfilled.
15 And now it came to pass that
after Alma had said these things to
Helaman, he [a]blessed him, and also
his other sons; and he also blessed
the earth for the [b]righteous' sake.
16 And he said: Thus saith the
Lord God—[a]Cursed shall be the
land, yea, this land, unto every
nation, kindred, tongue, and people,
unto destruction, which do [b]wicked-
ly, when they are fully ripe; and as I
have said so shall it be; for this is
the cursing and the [c]blessing of God
upon the land, for the Lord cannot
look upon sin with the [d]least degree
of allowance.
17 And now, when Alma had said
these words he blessed the [a]church,
yea, all those who should stand fast
in the faith from that time henceforth.
18 And when Alma had done this
he [a]departed out of the land of
Zarahemla, as if to go into the land
of [b]Melek. And it came to pass that
he was never heard of more; as to
his death or burial we know not of.
19 Behold, this we know, that he
was a righteous man; and the saying
went abroad in the church that he
was taken up by the [a]Spirit, or
[b]buried by the hand of the Lord,
even as Moses. But behold, the
scriptures saith the Lord took
Moses unto himself; and we suppose that he has also received Alma
in the spirit, unto himself; therefore, for this cause we know nothing
concerning his death and burial.
20 And now it came to pass in the
*commencement of the nineteenth
year of the reign of the judges over
the people of Nephi, that Helaman
went forth among the people to
declare the [a]word unto them.
21 For behold, because of their
wars with the Lamanites and the
many little dissensions and disturbances which had been among
the people, it became expedient that
the [a]word of God should be declared
among them, yea, and that a
[b]regulation should be made throughout the church.
22 Therefore, [a]Helaman and his
brethren went forth to establish the
church again in all the land, yea, in
every city throughout all the land
which was possessed by the people

11*a* Jarom 1:10; Hel. 13:6 (5–19).
12*a* TG Lust.
b 2 Ne. 26:9; 3 Ne. 27:32.
13*a* Hel. 3:16.
14*a* Moro. 9:24.
b 1 Ne. 13:30; D&C 3:17.
c Moro. 1:2 (1–3).
15*a* Gen. 49:1 (1–27); Alma 8:22.
b Alma 46:10; 62:40.
16*a* 2 Ne. 1:7; Alma 37:31; Morm. 1:17; Ether 2:11 (8–12). TG Earth, Curse of.
b Jer. 44:5 (5–6).
c D&C 130:21.
d D&C 1:31.
17*a* TG Church.
18*a* 3 Ne. 1:3 (2–3).
b Alma 35:13.
19*a* 2 Kgs. 2:16.
b Deut. 34:6 (5–6). TG Translated Beings.
20*a* Alma 46:1.
21*a* Alma 31:5.
b Alma 6:7; 62:44 (44–47).
22*a* Alma 48:19.

[*73 B.C.]

of Nephi. And it came to pass that
they did appoint [b]priests and
[c]teachers throughout all the land,
over all the churches.
23 And now it came to pass that
after Helaman and his brethren had
appointed priests and teachers over
the churches that there arose a
[a]dissension among them, and they
would not give heed to the words of
Helaman and his brethren;
24 But they grew proud, being lifted up in their hearts, because of their
exceedingly great [a]riches; therefore
they grew rich in their own eyes,
and would not give heed to their
words, to [b]walk uprightly before
God.

CHAPTER 46

Amalickiah conspires to be king—Moroni raises the title of liberty—He rallies the people to defend their religion—True believers are called Christians—A remnant of Joseph shall be preserved—Amalickiah and the dissenters flee to the land of Nephi—Those who will not support the cause of freedom are put to death.

AND it came to pass that as many
as would not hearken to the [a]words
of Helaman and his brethren were
gathered together against their
brethren.
2 And now behold, they were
exceedingly wroth, insomuch that
they were determined to slay them.
3 Now the leader of those who were
wroth against their brethren was a
large and a strong man; and his
name was [a]Amalickiah.
4 And Amalickiah was desirous to
be a [a]king; and those people who
were wroth were also desirous that
he should be their king; and they
were the greater part of them the
lower [b]judges of the land, and they
were seeking for power.
5 And they had been led by the
[a]flatteries of Amalickiah, that if they
would support him and establish
him to be their king that he would
make them rulers over the people.
6 Thus they were led away by
Amalickiah to dissensions, notwithstanding the preaching of Helaman and his brethren, yea, notwithstanding their exceedingly great
care over the church, for they were
[a]high priests over the church.
7 And there were many in the
church who believed in the [a]flatter-
ing words of Amalickiah, therefore
they [b]dissented even from the
church; and thus were the affairs of
the people of Nephi exceedingly
precarious and dangerous, notwithstanding their great [c]victory
which they had had over the
Lamanites, and their great rejoicings which they had had because of
their [d]deliverance by the hand of
the Lord.
8 Thus we see how [a]quick the
children of men do [b]forget the Lord
their God, yea, how quick to do
[c]iniquity, and to be led away by the
evil one.
9 Yea, and we also see the great
[a]wickedness one very wicked man
can cause to take place among the
children of men.
10 Yea, we see that Amalickiah,
because he was a man of cunning
device and a man of many flattering words, that he led away the
hearts of many people to do wickedly; yea, and to seek to [a]destroy
the church of God, and to destroy
the foundation of [b]liberty which

22*b* TG Church Organization.
c TG Teacher.
23*a* 3 Ne. 11: 29 (28–29).
24*a* TG Treasure.
b TG Pride; Walking in Darkness.
46 1*a* Alma 45: 20.
3*a* Alma 49: 25.
4*a* Alma 2: 2.
b Mosiah 29: 11 (11–44).
5*a* Prov. 29: 5.
6*a* Alma 46: 38.
7*a* TG Flattery.
b Alma 1: 24.
c Alma 44: 20.
d Josh. 21: 44; 1 Kgs. 5: 3; Mosiah 9: 17. TG Deliverance.
8*a* Ex. 32: 8; Judg. 2: 17; Hel. 4: 26; 6: 32; 12: 2 (2, 4–5).
b Deut. 6: 12.
c Mosiah 13: 29.
9*a* 2 Kgs. 10: 29; Mosiah 29: 17 (17–18).
10*a* TG Tyranny.
b 2 Ne. 1: 7; Mosiah 29: 32. TG Liberty.

[73 B.C.]

God had granted unto them, or
which blessing God had sent upon
the face of the land for the [c]right-
eous' sake.
11 And now it came to pass that
when Moroni, who was the [a]chief
commander of the armies of the
Nephites, had heard of these dissensions, he was angry with
Amalickiah.
12 And it came to pass that he
rent his coat; and he took a piece
thereof, and wrote upon it—[a]In
memory of our God, our religion,
and freedom, and our peace, our
wives, and our children—and he
fastened it upon the end of a pole.
13 And he fastened on his head-
plate, and his [a]breastplate, and his
shields, and girded on his armor
about his loins; and he took the
pole, which had on the end thereof
his rent coat, (and he called it the
[b]title of liberty) and he [c]bowed himself to the earth, and he prayed
mightily unto his God for the blessings of liberty to rest upon his
brethren, so long as there should a
band of [d]Christians remain to
possess the land—
14 For thus were all the true
believers of Christ, who belonged
to the church of God, called by those
who did not belong to the church.
15 And those who did belong to the
church were [a]faithful; yea, all those
who were true believers in Christ
[b]took upon them, gladly, the name
of Christ, or [c]Christians as they were
called, because of their belief in
Christ who should come.
16 And therefore, at this time,
Moroni prayed that the cause of the
Christians, and the [a]freedom of the
land might be favored.
17 And it came to pass that when
he had poured out his soul to God,
he named all the land which was
[a]south of the land [b]Desolation, yea,
and in fine, all the land, both on the
[c]north and on the south—A chosen
land, and the land of [d]liberty.
18 And he said: Surely God shall
not [a]suffer that we, who are despised
because we take upon us the name
of Christ, shall be trodden down and
destroyed, until we bring it upon us
by our own [b]transgressions.
19 And when Moroni had said
these words, he went forth among
the people, waving the [a]rent part of
his garment in the air, that all might
see the writing which he had written
upon the rent part, and crying with
a loud voice, saying:
20 Behold, whosoever will maintain this title upon the land, let
them come forth in the strength of
the Lord, and [a]enter into a covenant
that they will [b]maintain their rights,
and their religion, that the Lord
God may bless them.
21 And it came to pass that when
Moroni had proclaimed these words,
behold, the people came running
[a]together with their armor girded
about their loins, [b]rending their
garments in token, or as a [c]covenant,
that they would not forsake the
Lord their God; or, in other words,
if they should transgress the commandments of God, or fall into
transgression, and be [d]ashamed to
take upon them the name of Christ,
the Lord should rend them even as
they had rent their garments.

10*c* Alma 45: 15 (15–16); 62: 40.
11*a* Alma 43: 16.
12*a* 2 Sam. 10: 12; Neh. 4: 14 (10–14); Alma 44: 5; 48: 10 (10, 24).
13*a* Alma 44: 9; 49: 6 (6, 24).
b Alma 51: 20. TG Citizenship.
c TG Reverence.
d Alma 48: 10.
15*a* TG Faithful; Loyalty.
b TG Jesus Christ, Taking the Name of.
c Acts 11: 26.
16*a* Alma 51: 13.
17*a* 3 Ne. 3: 24; Morm. 3: 5.
b Alma 22: 30; 50: 34.
c Alma 22: 31; 63: 4.
d 2 Ne. 1: 7; Mosiah 29: 32.
18*a* TG Protection, Divine.
b TG Transgression.
19*a* TG Ensign.
20*a* Alma 48: 13.
b TG Citizenship.
21*a* 2 Sam. 20: 14 (11–14).
b TG Rend, Rent.
c TG Commitment.
d Jer. 17: 13; Rom. 1: 16; 2 Tim. 1: 8; 1 Ne. 8: 25; Morm. 8: 38.

[73 B.C.]

22 Now this was the covenant
which they made, and they [a]cast
their garments at the feet of Moroni,
saying: We [b]covenant with our God,
that we shall be destroyed, even as
our brethren in the land northward,
if we shall fall into transgression;
yea, he may cast us at the feet of our
enemies, even as we have cast our
garments at thy feet to be trodden
under foot, if we shall fall into
transgression.
23 Moroni said unto them: Behold,
we are a [a]remnant of the seed of
Jacob; yea, we are a remnant of the
seed of [b]Joseph, whose [c]coat was rent
by his brethren into many pieces;
yea, and now behold, let us remember to keep the commandments of
God, or our garments shall be rent
by our brethren, and we be cast
into prison, or be sold, or be slain.
24 Yea, let us preserve our liberty
as a [a]remnant of Joseph; yea, let us
remember the words of Jacob,
before his death, for behold, he saw
that a [b]part of the [c]remnant of the
coat of Joseph was [d]preserved and
had not decayed. And he said—
Even as this remnant of garment of
my son hath been preserved, so shall
a [e]remnant of the seed of my son be
preserved by the hand of God, and
be taken unto himself, while the
remainder of the seed of Joseph
shall perish, even as the remnant of
his garment.
25 Now behold, this giveth my
soul sorrow; nevertheless, my soul
hath joy in my son, because of that
part of his seed which shall be taken
unto God.
26 Now behold, this was the
language of Jacob.
27 And now who knoweth but what
the remnant of the seed of Joseph,
which shall perish as his garment,
are those who have dissented from
us? Yea, and even it shall be ourselves if we do not stand fast in the
faith of Christ.
28 And now it came to pass that
when Moroni had said these words
he went forth, and also sent forth in
all the parts of the land where there
were dissensions, and gathered together all the people who were
desirous to maintain their liberty,
to stand against Amalickiah and
those who had dissented, who were
called Amalickiahites.
29 And it came to pass that when
Amalickiah saw that the people of
Moroni were more numerous than
the Amalickiahites—and he also
saw that his people were [a]doubtful
concerning the justice of the cause
in which they had undertaken—
therefore, fearing that he should not
gain the point, he took those of his
people who would and departed into
the [b]land of Nephi.
30 Now Moroni thought it was
not expedient that the Lamanites
should have any more [a]strength;
therefore he thought to cut off the
people of Amalickiah, or to take
them and bring them back, and put
Amalickiah to death; yea, for he
knew that he would stir up the
Lamanites to anger against them,
and cause them to come to battle
against them; and this he knew that
Amalickiah would do that he might
obtain his purposes.
31 Therefore Moroni thought it
was expedient that he should take
his armies, who had gathered themselves together, and armed themselves, and entered into a covenant
to keep the peace—and it came to
pass that he took his army and
marched out with his tents into the
wilderness, to cut off the course of
Amalickiah in the wilderness.
32 And it came to pass that he did

22*a* Acts 7: 58; 22: 20.
b TG Commitment.
23*a* TG Israel, Remnant of.
b TG Israel, Joseph, People of.
c Gen. 37: 3 (3, 31–36).
24*a* 2 Ne. 10: 1; Jacob 5: 45 (43–45).
b Gen. 44: 28.
c 3 Ne. 5: 23 (23–24); 10: 17.
d 2 Ne. 3: 5 (5–24); 25: 21; Ether 13: 7.
e Ether 13: 6.
29*a* TG Doubt.
b Alma 47: 20.
30*a* Alma 43: 51.

[73 B.C.]

according to his desires, and marched forth into the wilderness, and
headed the armies of Amalickiah.
33 And it came to pass that
Amalickiah [a]fled with a small number of his men, and the remainder
were delivered up into the hands of
Moroni and were taken back into
the land of Zarahemla.
34 Now, Moroni being a man who
was [a]appointed by the chief judges
and the voice of the people, therefore he had power according to his
will with the armies of the Nephites,
to establish and to exercise authority over them.
35 And it came to pass that whomsoever of the Amalickiahites that
would not enter into a covenant to
support the [a]cause of freedom, that
they might maintain a free [b]govern-
ment, he caused to be put to death;
and there were but few who denied
the covenant of freedom.
36 And it came to pass also, that
he caused the [a]title of liberty to be
hoisted upon every tower which
was in all the land, which was possessed by the Nephites; and thus
Moroni planted the standard of
liberty among the Nephites.
37 And they began to have peace
again in the land; and thus they did
maintain peace in the land until
nearly the *end of the nineteenth
year of the reign of the judges.
38 And Helaman and the [a]high
priests did also maintain order in
the church; yea, even for the space
of four years did they have much
peace and rejoicing in the church.
39 And it came to pass that there
were many who died, firmly [a]believ-
ing that their souls were redeemed
by the Lord Jesus Christ; thus they
went out of the world rejoicing.
40 And there were some who died
with fevers, which at some seasons
of the year were very frequent in
the land—but not so much so with
fevers, because of the excellent
qualities of the many [a]plants and
roots which God had prepared to
remove the cause of [b]diseases, to
which men were subject by the
nature of the climate—
41 But there were many who died
with [a]old age; and those who died
in the faith of Christ are [b]happy in
him, as we must needs suppose.

CHAPTER 47

Amalickiah uses treachery, murder, and intrigue to become king of the Lamanites—The Nephite dissenters are more wicked and ferocious than the Lamanites.

Now we will return in our record to
Amalickiah and those who had [a]fled
with him into the wilderness; for,
behold, he had taken those who
went with him, and went up in the
[b]land of Nephi among the Lamanites, and did [c]stir up the Lamanites
to anger against the people of Nephi,
insomuch that the king of the
Lamanites sent a proclamation
throughout all his land, among all
his people, that they should gather
themselves together again to go to
battle against the Nephites.
2 And it came to pass that when
the proclamation had gone forth
among them they were exceedingly
afraid; yea, they [a]feared to dis-
please the king, and they also feared
to go to battle against the Nephites
lest they should lose their lives. And
it came to pass that they would not,
or the more part of them would not,
obey the commandments of the
king.
3 And now it came to pass that the

33*a* Alma 47:1.
34*a* Alma 43:16.
35*a* Alma 43:30.
b TG Governments.
36*a* Alma 62:4.
38*a* Alma 43:2; 46:6; 49:30.
39*a* Moro. 7:41 (3, 41).
40*a* D&C 59:17 (17–20); 89:10.
b Ezek. 47:12. TG Health; Sickness.
41*a* TG Old Age.
b Rev. 14:13.
47 1*a* Alma 46:33.
b 2 Ne. 5:8; Omni 1:12; Alma 49:10.
c Alma 27:12; 35:10; 43:8; Hel. 1:17. TG Provoking.
2*a* Alma 43:54 (49–54).

[*72 B.C.]

king was wroth because of their disobedience; therefore he gave Amalickiah the command of that part of his army which was obedient unto his commands, and commanded him that he should go forth and [a]compel them to arms.

4 Now behold, this was the desire of Amalickiah; for he being a very [a]subtle man to do evil therefore he laid the plan in his heart to [b]dethrone the king of the Lamanites.

5 And now he had got the command of those parts of the Lamanites who were in favor of the king; and he sought to gain favor of those who were not obedient; therefore he went forward to the place which was called [a]Onidah, for thither had all the Lamanites fled; for they discovered the army coming, and, supposing that they were coming to destroy them, therefore they fled to Onidah, to the place of arms.

6 And they had appointed a man to be a king and a leader over them, being fixed in their minds with a determined resolution that they would [a]not be subjected to go against the Nephites.

7 And it came to pass that they had gathered themselves together upon the top of the mount which was called Antipas, in preparation to battle.

8 Now it was not Amalickiah's intention to give them battle according to the commandments of the king; but behold, it was his intention to gain favor with the armies of the Lamanites, that he might place himself at their head and dethrone the king and take possession of the kingdom.

9 And behold, it came to pass that he caused his army to pitch their tents in the valley which was near the mount Antipas.

10 And it came to pass that when it was night he sent a secret embassy into the mount Antipas, desiring that the leader of those who were upon the mount, whose name was Lehonti, that he should come down to the foot of the mount, for he desired to speak with him.

11 And it came to pass that when Lehonti received the message he durst not go down to the foot of the mount. And it came to pass that Amalickiah sent again the second time, desiring him to come down. And it came to pass that Lehonti would not; and he sent again the third time.

12 And it came to pass that when Amalickiah found that he could not get Lehonti to come down off from the mount, he went up into the mount, nearly to Lehonti's camp; and he sent again the fourth time his message unto Lehonti, desiring that he would come down, and that he would bring his guards with him.

13 And it came to pass that when Lehonti had come down with his guards to Amalickiah, that Amalickiah desired him to come down with his army in the night-time, and surround those men in their camps over whom the king had given him command, and that he would deliver them up into Lehonti's hands, if he would make him (Amalickiah) a second [a]leader over the whole army.

14 And it came to pass that Lehonti came down with his men and surrounded the men of Amalickiah, so that before they awoke at the dawn of day they were surrounded by the armies of Lehonti.

15 And it came to pass that when they saw that they were surrounded, they plead with Amalickiah that he would suffer them to fall in with their brethren, that they might not be destroyed. Now this was the very thing which Amalickiah desired.

16 And it came to pass that he delivered his men, [a]contrary to the commands of the king. Now this was the thing that Amalickiah

3*a* Alma 47: 16 (16, 21).
4*a* 2 Sam. 13: 3 (3–14).
b Alma 47: 35 (8, 35).
5*a* Alma 32: 4.
6*a* Alma 44: 19 (8, 19).
13*a* Alma 49: 10.
16*a* Alma 47: 3.

desired, that he might accomplish
his designs in dethroning the king.
17 Now it was the custom among
the Lamanites, if their chief leader
was killed, to appoint the second
leader to be their chief leader.
18 And it came to pass that
Amalickiah caused that one of his
servants should administer [a]poison
by degrees to Lehonti, that he died.
19 Now, when Lehonti was dead,
the Lamanites appointed Amalickiah to be their leader and their
chief commander.
20 And it came to pass that
Amalickiah marched with his armies
(for he had gained his desires) to the
[a]land of Nephi, to the city of Nephi,
which was the chief city.
21 And the king came out to meet
him with his guards, for he supposed that Amalickiah had [a]ful-
filled his commands, and that
Amalickiah had gathered together
so great an army to go against the
Nephites to battle.
22 But behold, as the king came
out to meet him Amalickiah caused
that his servants should go forth
to meet the king. And they went
and [a]bowed themselves before the
king, as if to reverence him because
of his greatness.
23 And it came to pass that the
king put forth his hand to raise
them, as was the custom with the
Lamanites, as a token of peace,
which custom they had taken from
the Nephites.
24 And it came to pass that when
he had raised the first from the
ground, behold he stabbed the king
to the heart; and he fell to the earth.
25 Now the servants of the king
fled; and the servants of Amalickiah
raised a cry, saying:
26 Behold, the servants of the king
have stabbed him to the heart, and
he has fallen and they have fled;
behold, come and see.
27 And it came to pass that
Amalickiah commanded that his
armies should march forth and see
what had happened to the king; and
when they had come to the spot,
and found the king lying in his gore,
Amalickiah pretended to be wroth,
and said: Whosoever loved the king,
let him go forth, and pursue his
servants that they may be slain.
28 And it came to pass that all they
who loved the king, when they
heard these words, came forth and
pursued after the servants of the
king.
29 Now when the [a]servants of the
king saw an army pursuing after
them, they were frightened again,
and fled into the wilderness, and
came over into the land of Zarahemla and joined the [b]people of
Ammon.
30 And the army which pursued
after them returned, having pursued after them in vain; and thus
Amalickiah, by his [a]fraud, gained
the hearts of the people.
31 And it came to pass on the
morrow he entered the city Nephi
with his armies, and took possession
of the city.
32 And now it came to pass that the
queen, when she had heard that the
king was slain—for Amalickiah had
sent an embassy to the queen in-
forming her that the king had been
slain by his servants, that he had
pursued them with his army, but
it was in vain, and they had made
their escape—
33 Therefore, when the queen had
received this message she sent unto
Amalickiah, desiring him that he
would spare the people of the city;
and she also desired him that he
should come in unto her; and she
also desired him that he should
bring [a]witnesses with him to testify
concerning the death of the king.
34 And it came to pass that
Amalickiah took the same servant
that slew the king, and all them who

18*a* Alma 54: 7.
20*a* Alma 46: 29.
21*a* Alma 47: 3.
22*a* Mosiah 7: 12.
29*a* Alma 55: 5.
b Alma 43: 11; 62: 17.
30*a* Alma 55: 1. TG Fraud.
33*a* TG Witnesses.

[72 B.C.]

were with him, and went in unto
the queen, unto the place where she
sat; and they all [a]testified unto her
that the king was slain by his own
servants; and they said also: They
have fled; does not this testify
against them? And thus they satisfied the queen concerning the death
of the king.
35 And it came to pass that
Amalickiah sought the [a]favor of the
queen, and took her unto him to
wife; and thus by his [b]fraud, and
by the assistance of his cunning
servants, he [c]obtained the kingdom;
yea, he was acknowledged king
throughout all the land, among
all the people of the Lamanites,
who were [d]composed of the
Lamanites and the Lemuelites
and the Ishmaelites, and all the
dissenters of the Nephites, from the
reign of Nephi down to the present
time.
36 Now these [a]dissenters, having
the same instruction and the same
information of the Nephites, yea,
having been instructed in the same
[b]knowledge of the Lord, nevertheless, it is strange to relate, not long
after their dissensions they became
more hardened and [c]impenitent, and
more wild, wicked and ferocious
than the Lamanites—drinking in
with the [d]traditions of the Lamanites; giving way to [e]indolence, and
all manner of lasciviousness; yea,
entirely forgetting the Lord their
God.

CHAPTER 48

Amalickiah incites the Lamanites against the Nephites—Moroni prepares his people to defend the cause of the Christians—He rejoiced in liberty and freedom and was a mighty man of God.

AND now it came to pass that, as
soon as [a]Amalickiah had obtained
the kingdom he began to [b]inspire the
hearts of the Lamanites against the
people of Nephi; yea, he did appoint
men to speak unto the Lamanites
from their [c]towers, against the
Nephites.
2 And thus he did inspire their
hearts against the Nephites, insomuch that in the *latter end of the
[a]nineteenth year of the reign of the
judges, he having accomplished his
designs thus far, yea, having been
made king over the Lamanites, he
[b]sought also to [c]reign over all the
land, yea, and all the people who
were in the land, the Nephites as
well as the Lamanites.
3 Therefore he had accomplished
his design, for he had hardened the
hearts of the Lamanites and blinded
their minds, and stirred them up to
anger, insomuch that he had gathered together a numerous host to
go to battle against the Nephites.
4 For he was determined, because
of the greatness of the number of
his people, to [a]overpower the
Nephites and to bring them into
bondage.
5 And thus he did appoint [a]chief
captains of the [b]Zoramites, they
being the most acquainted with the
strength of the Nephites, and their
places of resort, and the weakest
parts of their cities; therefore he
appointed them to be chief captains
over his armies.
6 And it came to pass that they
took their camp, and moved forth
toward the land of Zarahemla in the
wilderness.
7 Now it came to pass that while
Amalickiah had thus been obtaining
power by fraud and deceit, Moroni,
on the other hand, had been [a]pre-

34*a* TG False; Lying.
35*a* Prov. 19:6 (6–7).
b TG Conspiracy; Tyranny.
c Alma 47:4.
d Jacob 1:13 (13–14).
36*a* TG Apostasy of Individuals.
b Heb. 10:26 (26–27); Alma 24:30.
c Jer. 8:12.
d TG Peer Influence.
e 3 Ne. 4:5.
48 1*a* Alma 52:3 (1–3); 54:5.
b Alma 62:35.
c Mosiah 2:8.
2*a* Alma 48:21.
b D&C 121:39.
c Alma 54:24.
4*a* TG Tyranny.
5*a* Alma 43:6; 49:5 (5, 23).
b Alma 52:20 (20, 33).
7*a* Alma 49:8.

[*72 B.C.]

paring the minds of the people to
be faithful unto the Lord their God.
8 Yea, he had been strengthening
the armies of the Nephites, and
erecting small [a]forts, or places of
resort; throwing up banks of earth
round about to enclose his armies,
and also building [b]walls of stone to
encircle them about, round about
their cities and the borders of their
lands; yea, all round about the land.
9 And in their weakest fortifications he did place the greater number of men; and thus he did fortify
and strengthen the land which was
possessed by the Nephites.
10 And thus he was preparing to
[a]support their liberty, their lands,
their wives, and their children, and
their peace, and that they might
live unto the Lord their God, and
that they might maintain that
which was called by their enemies
the cause of [b]Christians.
11 And Moroni was a [a]strong and
a mighty man; he was a man of a
perfect [b]understanding; yea, a man
that did not delight in bloodshed;
a man whose soul did joy in the
liberty and the freedom of his
country, and his brethren from
bondage and slavery;
12 Yea, a man whose heart did
swell with thanksgiving to his God,
for the many privileges and blessings which he bestowed upon his
people; a man who did labor
exceedingly for the [a]welfare and
safety of his people.
13 Yea, and he was a man who was
firm in the faith of Christ, and he
had [a]sworn with an oath to defend
his people, his rights, and his
country, and his religion, even to
the loss of his blood.
14 Now the Nephites were taught
to defend themselves against their
enemies, even to the shedding of
blood if it were necessary; yea, and
they were also taught [a]never to give
an offense, yea, and never to raise
the sword except it were against an
enemy, except it were to preserve
their lives.
15 And this was their [a]faith, that
by so doing God would [b]prosper
them in the land, or in other words,
if they were faithful in keeping the
commandments of God that he
would prosper them in the land;
yea, warn them to flee, or to prepare for war, according to their
danger;
16 And also, that God would make
it known unto them [a]whither they
should go to defend themselves
against their enemies, and by so
doing, the Lord would deliver them;
and this was the faith of Moroni,
and his heart did glory in it; not in
the [b]shedding of blood but in doing
good, in preserving his people, yea,
in keeping the commandments of
God, yea, and resisting iniquity.
17 Yea, verily, verily I say unto
you, if all men had been, and were,
and ever would be, like unto
[a]Moroni, behold, the very powers of
hell would have been shaken forever; yea, the [b]devil would never
have power over the hearts of the
children of men.
18 Behold, he was a man like unto
[a]Ammon, the son of Mosiah, yea,
and even the other sons of Mosiah,
yea, and also Alma and his sons, for
they were all men of God.
19 Now behold, Helaman and his
brethren were no less [a]serviceable
unto the people than was Moroni;
for they did preach the word of God,
and they did baptize unto repent-

8*a* Alma 49: 13 (2–13, 18–24).
b Deut. 3: 5.
10*a* Alma 44: 5; 46: 12.
b Alma 46: 13.
11*a* TG Strength.
b Alma 18: 22. TG Understanding.
12*a* TG Welfare.
13*a* Alma 46: 20 (20–22). TG Dependability.
14*a* Alma 43: 46 (46–47); 3 Ne. 3: 21 (20–21); Morm. 3: 10 (10–11); D&C 98: 16.
15*a* TG Steadfastness.
b Alma 45: 8.
16*a* Alma 16: 6 (5–8); 43: 23 (23–24); 3 Ne. 3: 20 (18–21). TG Guidance, Divine.
b Alma 55: 19.
17*a* Alma 53: 2.
b 1 Ne. 22: 26; 3 Ne. 6: 15; D&C 35: 24.
18*a* Alma 28: 8.
19*a* Alma 45: 22.

[72 B.C.]

ance all men whosoever would
hearken unto their words.
20 And thus they went forth, and
the people did [a]humble themselves
because of their [b]words, insomuch
that they were highly [c]favored of the
Lord, and thus they were free from
wars and contentions among themselves, yea, even for the space of
four years.
21 But, as I have said, in the
[a]latter end of the nineteenth year,
yea, notwithstanding their peace
amongst themselves, they were
compelled reluctantly to contend
with their brethren, the Lamanites.
22 Yea, and in fine, their wars
never did cease for the space of
many years with the Lamanites, notwithstanding their much reluctance.
23 Now, they were [a]sorry to take
up arms against the Lamanites,
because they did not delight in the
shedding of blood; yea, and this
was not all—they were [b]sorry to be
the means of sending so many of
their brethren out of this world into
an eternal world, [c]unprepared to
meet their God.
24 Nevertheless, they could not
suffer to lay down their lives, that
their [a]wives and their children
should be [b]massacred by the barbarous [c]cruelty of those who were
once their brethren, yea, and had
[d]dissented from their church, and
had left them and had gone to
destroy them by joining the Lamanites.
25 Yea, they could not bear that
their brethren should rejoice over
the blood of the Nephites, so long
as there were any who should keep
the commandments of God, for the
promise of the Lord was, if they
should keep his commandments
they should [a]prosper in the land.

CHAPTER 49

The invading Lamanites are unable to take the fortified cities of Ammonihah and Noah—Amalickiah curses God and swears to drink the blood of Moroni—Helaman and his brethren continue to strengthen the Church.

AND now it came to pass in the
*eleventh month of the nineteenth
year, on the tenth day of the
month, the armies of the Lamanites
were seen approaching towards the
land of [a]Ammonihah.
2 And behold, the city had been
rebuilt, and Moroni had stationed
an army by the borders of the city,
and they had [a]cast up dirt round
about to shield them from the
arrows and the [b]stones of the Lamanites; for behold, they fought
with stones and with arrows.
3 Behold, I said that the city of
[a]Ammonihah had been rebuilt. I
say unto you, yea, that it was in
part rebuilt; and because the
Lamanites had destroyed it once
because of the iniquity of the
people, they supposed that it would
again become an easy prey for
them.
4 But behold, how great was their
disappointment; for behold, the
Nephites had dug up a [a]ridge of
earth round about them, which was
so high that the Lamanites could
not cast their stones and their
arrows at them that they might
take effect, neither could they come
upon them save it was by their
place of [b]entrance.
5 Now at this time the chief [a]cap-
tains of the Lamanites were astonished exceedingly, because of the
wisdom of the Nephites in preparing their places of security.
6 Now the leaders of the Laman-

20*a* TG Humility.
b 1 Ne. 15: 20; Hel. 6: 5.
c 1 Ne. 17: 35.
21*a* Alma 48: 2.
23*a* Alma 28: 11 (11–12); D&C 42: 45.
b 3 Ne. 12: 44.
c Amos 4: 12; Alma 20: 17.
24*a* Alma 46: 12.
b TG Martyrdom.
c TG Cruelty.
d TG Apostasy of Individuals.
25*a* Alma 45: 8.
49 1*a* Alma 8: 6.
2*a* Alma 48: 8.
b 1 Ne. 16: 15; Alma 43: 20.
3*a* Alma 16: 2 (2–3, 9, 11).
4*a* Alma 48: 8; 50: 1.
b Alma 49: 20.
5*a* Alma 52: 19.

[*72 B.C.]

ites had supposed, because of the
greatness of their numbers, yea,
they supposed that they should be
privileged to come upon them as
they had hitherto done; yea, and
they had also prepared themselves
with shields, and with [a]breastplates;
and they had also prepared themselves with garments of skins, yea,
very thick garments to cover their
nakedness.
7 And being thus prepared they
supposed that they should easily
overpower and [a]subject their brethren to the yoke of bondage, or slay
and massacre them according to
their pleasure.
8 But behold, to their uttermost
astonishment, they were [a]prepared
for them, in a manner which never
had been known among the children of Lehi. Now they were prepared for the Lamanites, to battle
after the manner of the instructions
of Moroni.
9 And it came to pass that the
Lamanites, or the Amalickiahites,
were exceedingly astonished at
their manner of preparation for
war.
10 Now, if king Amalickiah had
come down out of the [a]land of
Nephi, at the head of his army,
perhaps he would have caused the
Lamanites to have attacked the
Nephites at the city of Ammonihah; for behold, he did care not for
the blood of his people.
11 But behold, Amalickiah did not
come down himself to battle. And
behold, his chief captains durst not
attack the Nephites at the city of
Ammonihah, for Moroni had altered
the management of affairs among
the Nephites, insomuch that the
Lamanites were disappointed in
their places of retreat and they
could not come upon them.
12 Therefore they retreated into
the wilderness, and took their
camp and marched towards the
land of [a]Noah, supposing that to be
the next best place for them to
come against the Nephites.
13 For they knew not that Moroni
had fortified, or had built [a]forts of
security, for every city in all the
land round about; therefore, they
marched forward to the land of
Noah with a firm determination;
yea, their chief captains came forward and took an [b]oath that they
would destroy the people of that
city.
14 But behold, to their astonishment, the city of Noah, which had
hitherto been a weak place, had
now, by the means of Moroni, become strong, yea, even to exceed
the strength of the city Ammonihah.
15 And now, behold, this was wisdom in Moroni; for he had supposed
that they would be frightened at
the city Ammonihah; and as the
city of Noah had hitherto been the
weakest part of the land, therefore
they would march thither to battle;
and thus it was according to his
desires.
16 And behold, Moroni had
appointed Lehi to be chief captain
over the men of that city; and it
was that [a]same Lehi who fought
with the Lamanites in the valley on
the east of the river Sidon.
17 And now behold it came to
pass, that when the Lamanites had
found that Lehi commanded the
city they were again disappointed,
for they feared Lehi exceedingly;
nevertheless their chief captains
had [a]sworn with an oath to attack
the city; therefore, they brought
up their armies.
18 Now behold, the Lamanites
could not get into their forts of
security by any other way save by
the entrance, because of the highness of the bank which had been
thrown up, and the depth of the

6*a* Alma 46:13; Hel. 1:14.
7*a* Alma 43:29.
8*a* Alma 48:7 (7–10).
10*a* 2 Ne. 5:8; Omni 1:12; Alma 47:1 (1, 13–24).
12*a* Alma 16:3.
13*a* Alma 48:8; 50:10 (1–6, 10).
b Alma 49:17.
16*a* Alma 43:35.
17*a* Alma 49:13.

[72 B.C.]

ditch which had been dug round
about, save it were by the entrance.
19 And thus were the Nephites
prepared to destroy all such as
should attempt to climb up to enter
the fort by any other way, by casting over stones and arrows at them.
20 Thus they were prepared, yea,
a body of their strongest men, with
their swords and their slings, to
smite down all who should attempt
to come into their place of security
by the place of [a]entrance; and thus
were they prepared to defend themselves against the Lamanites.
21 And it came to pass that the
captains of the Lamanites brought
up their armies before the place of
entrance, and began to contend with
the Nephites, to get into their place
of security; but behold, they were
driven back from time to time,
insomuch that they were slain with
an immense slaughter.
22 Now when they found that they
could not obtain power over the
Nephites by the pass, they began to
dig down their banks of earth that
they might obtain a pass to their
armies, that they might have an
equal chance to fight; but behold,
in these attempts they were swept
off by the stones and arrows which
were thrown at them; and instead of
filling up their ditches by pulling
down the banks of earth, they were
filled up in a measure with their
dead and wounded bodies.
23 Thus the Nephites had all power
over their enemies; and thus the
Lamanites did attempt to destroy
the Nephites until their [a]chief captains were all slain; yea, and more
than a thousand of the Lamanites
were slain; while, on the other hand,
there was not a single soul of the
Nephites which was slain.
24 There were about fifty who were
wounded, who had been exposed to
the arrows of the Lamanites through
the pass, but they were shielded by
their [a]shields, and their breastplates,
and their head-plates, insomuch
that their wounds were upon their
legs, many of which were very
severe.
25 And it came to pass, that when
the Lamanites saw that their chief
captains were all slain they fled into
the wilderness. And it came to pass
that they returned to the land of
Nephi, to inform their king, Amalickiah, who was a [a]Nephite by
birth, concerning their great [b]loss.
26 And it came to pass that he was
exceedingly angry with his people,
because he had not obtained his
desire over the Nephites; he had not
subjected them to the yoke of
bondage.
27 Yea, he was exceedingly wroth,
and he did [a]curse God, and also
Moroni, swearing with an [b]oath that
he would drink his blood; and this
because Moroni had kept the commandments of God in preparing for
the safety of his people.
28 And it came to pass, that on the
other hand, the people of Nephi did
[a]thank the Lord their God, because
of his matchless power in delivering
them from the hands of their
enemies.
29 And thus ended the nineteenth
year of the reign of the judges over
the people of Nephi.
30 Yea, and there was continual
peace among them, and exceedingly
great prosperity in the church because of their heed and diligence
which they gave unto the word of
God, which was declared unto them
by Helaman, and Shiblon, and
Corianton, and Ammon and his
brethren, yea, and by all those who
had been ordained by the [a]holy
order of God, being baptized unto
repentance, and sent forth to preach
among the people.

20*a* Alma 49: 4 (4, 18, 21, 24).
23*a* Alma 48: 5.
24*a* Alma 43: 19.
25*a* Alma 46: 3.
b Alma 51: 11.
27*a* TG Blasphemy.
b Acts 23: 12; Alma 51: 9.
28*a* TG Thanksgiving.
30*a* Alma 30: 20 (20–23, 31); 43: 2; 46: 38.

[72 B.C.]

CHAPTER 50

Moroni fortifies the lands of the Nephites—They build many new cities—Wars and destructions befell the Nephites in the days of their wickedness and abominations—Morianton and his dissenters are defeated by Teancum—Nephihah dies and his son Pahoran fills the judgment-seat.

AND now it came to pass that Moroni did not stop making preparations for war, or to defend his people against the Lamanites; for he caused that his armies should commence in the *commencement of the twentieth year of the reign of the judges, that they should commence in digging up [a]heaps of earth round about all the cities, throughout all the land which was possessed by the Nephites.

2 And upon the top of these ridges of earth he caused that there should be [a]timbers, yea, works of timbers built up to the height of a man, round about the cities.

3 And he caused that upon those works of timbers there should be a frame of pickets built upon the timbers round about; and they were strong and high.

4 And he caused towers to be erected that overlooked those works of pickets, and he caused places of security to be built upon those [a]towers, that the stones and the arrows of the Lamanites could not hurt them.

5 And they were prepared that they could cast stones from the top thereof, according to their pleasure and their strength, and slay him who should attempt to approach near the walls of the city.

6 Thus Moroni did prepare strongholds against the coming of their enemies, round about every city in all the land.

7 And it came to pass that Moroni caused that his armies should go forth into the east wilderness; yea, and they went forth and drove all the Lamanites who were in the east wilderness into their own lands, which were [a]south of the land of Zarahemla.

8 And the land of [a]Nephi did run in a straight course from the east sea to the west.

9 And it came to pass that when Moroni had driven all the Lamanites out of the east wilderness, which was north of the lands of their own possessions, he caused that the inhabitants who were in the land of Zarahemla and in the land round about should go forth into the east wilderness, even to the borders by the seashore, and possess the land.

10 And he also placed armies on the south, in the borders of their possessions, and caused them to erect [a]fortifications that they might secure their armies and their people from the hands of their enemies.

11 And thus he cut off all the strongholds of the Lamanites in the east wilderness, yea, and also on the west, fortifying the line between the Nephites and the Lamanites, between the land of Zarahemla and the land of Nephi, from the west sea, running by the head of the [a]river Sidon—the Nephites possessing all the land [b]northward, yea, even all the land which was northward of the land Bountiful, according to their pleasure.

12 Thus Moroni, with his armies, which did increase daily because of the assurance of protection which his works did bring forth unto them, did seek to cut off the strength and the power of the Lamanites from off the lands of their possessions, that they should have no power upon the lands of their possession.

13 And it came to pass that the Nephites began the foundation of a

---

50 1*a* Alma 48: 8; 49: 4; 52: 6.
2*a* Alma 53: 4.
4*a* 2 Chr. 14: 7 (7–8).
7*a* Alma 22: 32.
8*a* 2 Ne. 5: 8; Omni 1: 12 (12, 27); Mosiah 7: 6 (6–7); 9: 1 (1, 3–4, 14).
10*a* Alma 49: 13 (13, 18–24); 53: 3 (3–7).
11*a* Alma 2: 15; 22: 29.
b Morm. 2: 3.

[*72 B.C.]

city, and they called the name of the
city [a]Moroni; and it was by the east
sea; and it was on the south by the
line of the possessions of the
Lamanites.
14 And they also began a foundation for a city between the city of
Moroni and the city of Aaron, joining the borders of Aaron and
Moroni; and they called the name
of the city, or the land, [a]Nephihah.
15 And they also began in that
same year to build many cities on the
north, one in a particular manner
which they called [a]Lehi, which was
in the north by the borders of the
seashore.
16 And thus ended the twentieth
year.
17 And in these prosperous circumstances were the people of
Nephi in the *commencement of the
twenty and first year of the reign of
the judges over the people of Nephi.
18 And they did prosper [a]exceed-
ingly, and they became exceedingly
rich; yea, and they did multiply and
wax strong in the land.
19 And thus we see how merciful
and just are all the dealings of the
Lord, to the fulfilling of all his words
unto the children of men; yea, we
can behold that his words are verified, even at this time, which he
spake unto Lehi, saying:
20 Blessed art thou and thy children; and they shall be blessed, inasmuch as they shall keep my [a]com-
mandments they shall prosper in
the land. But remember, inasmuch
as they will not keep my commandments they shall be [b]cut off from
the presence of the Lord.
21 And we see that these promises
have been verified to the people of
Nephi; for it has been their quarrel-
ings and their contentions, yea, their
murderings, and their plunderings,
their idolatry, their whoredoms,
and their abominations, which were
among themselves, which [a]brought
upon them their wars and their
destructions.
22 And those who were faithful in
keeping the commandments of the
Lord were delivered at all times,
whilst thousands of their wicked
brethren have been consigned to
bondage, or to perish by the sword,
or to dwindle in unbelief, and mingle
with the Lamanites.
23 But behold there never was a
[a]happier time among the people of
Nephi, since the days of Nephi, than
in the days of Moroni, yea, even at
this time, in the twenty and first
year of the reign of the judges.
24 And it came to pass that the
twenty and second year of the reign
of the judges also ended in peace;
yea, and also the twenty and third
year.
25 And it came to pass that in the
†commencement of the twenty and
fourth year of the reign of the
judges, there would also have been
peace among the people of Nephi
had it not been for a [a]contention
which took place among them concerning the land of [b]Lehi, and the
land of [c]Morianton, which joined
upon the borders of Lehi; both of
which were on the borders by the
seashore.
26 For behold, the people who
possessed the land of Morianton did
claim a part of the land of Lehi;
therefore there began to be a warm
[a]contention between them, insomuch that the people of Morianton
took up arms against their brethren, and they were determined by
the sword to slay them.
27 But behold, the people who
possessed the land of Lehi fled to the
camp of Moroni, and appealed unto

13*a* Alma 51:22 (22–24); 62:32 (32, 34); 3 Ne. 8:9.
14*a* Alma 51:24 (24–26); 59:5; 62:18 (14, 18, 26).
15*a* Alma 51:26 (24–26); 62:30.
18*a* Alma 1:29.
20*a* Lev. 25:18 (18–19); Ps. 1:3 (2–3); Alma 37:13; 62:48.
b Ps. 37:2; D&C 1:14.
21*a* Alma 41:10.
23*a* 2 Ne. 5:27; Mosiah 2:41; 4 Ne. 1:16 (15–18).
25*a* TG Contention.
b Hel. 6:10.
c Alma 51:26.
26*a* 3 Ne. 11:29.

[*71 B.C. †68 B.C.]

him for assistance; for behold they
were not in the wrong.
28 And it came to pass that when
the people of Morianton, who were
led by a man whose name was
Morianton, found that the people of
Lehi had fled to the camp of Moroni,
they were exceedingly fearful lest
the army of Moroni should come
upon them and destroy them.
29 Therefore, Morianton put it into
their hearts that they should flee to
the land which was northward,
which was covered with [a]large
bodies of water, and take possession
of the land which was [b]northward.
30 And behold, they would have
carried this plan into effect, (which
would have been a cause to have
been lamented) but behold, Morianton being a man of much passion,
therefore he was angry with one of
his maid servants, and he fell upon
her and beat her much.
31 And it came to pass that she
fled, and came over to the camp of
Moroni, and told Moroni all things
concerning the matter, and also concerning their intentions to flee into
the land northward.
32 Now behold, the people who
were in the land Bountiful, or
rather Moroni, feared that they
would hearken to the words of
Morianton and unite with his people,
and thus he would obtain possession
of those parts of the land, which
would lay a foundation for serious
consequences among the people of
Nephi, yea, which [a]consequences
would lead to the overthrow of their
[b]liberty.
33 Therefore Moroni sent an army,
with their camp, to head the people
of Morianton, to stop their flight
into the land northward.
34 And it came to pass that they
did not [a]head them until they had
come to the borders of the land
[b]Desolation; and there they did
head them, by the narrow pass
which led by the sea into the land
northward, yea, by the sea, on the
west and on the east.
35 And it came to pass that the
army which was sent by Moroni,
which was led by a man whose name
was Teancum, did meet the people
of Morianton; and so stubborn were
the people of Morianton, (being
inspired by his wickedness and his
[a]flattering words) that a battle commenced between them, in the which
Teancum did [b]slay Morianton and
defeat his army, and took them
prisoners, and returned to the camp
of Moroni. And thus ended the
twenty and fourth year of the reign
of the judges over the people of
Nephi.
36 And thus were the people of
Morianton brought back. And upon
their [a]covenanting to keep the
peace they were restored to the land
of Morianton, and a union took
place between them and the people
of Lehi; and they were also restored
to their lands.
37 And it came to pass that in the
same year that the people of Nephi
had peace restored unto them, that
Nephihah, the [a]second chief judge,
died, having filled the judgment-
seat with [b]perfect uprightness before
God.
38 Nevertheless, he had refused
Alma to take possession of those
[a]records and those things which were
esteemed by Alma and his fathers
to be most sacred; therefore Alma
had conferred [b]them upon his son,
Helaman.
39 Behold, it came to pass that the
son of Nephihah was appointed to
fill the judgment-seat, in the stead
of his father; yea, he was appointed

29*a* Mosiah 8:8; Hel. 3:4 (3–4).
b Alma 22:31 (29–31); 51:30.
32*a* TG Contention; Division.
b TG Liberty.
34*a* Hel. 1:28 (28–30).
b Alma 46:17; Morm. 3:5 (5, 7).
35*a* Mosiah 27:8; Hel. 1:7; 2:5.
b Alma 51:29.
36*a* 1 Ne. 4:37; Alma 44:15.
37*a* Alma 4:17 (16–18).
b TG Perfection.
38*a* Alma 37:1 (1–5); 45:2 (2–8).
b 3 Ne. 1:2.

[About 67 B.C.]

chief judge and [a]governor over the people, with an [b]oath and sacred ordinance to judge righteously, and to keep the peace and the [c]freedom of the people, and to grant unto them their sacred privileges to worship the Lord their God, yea, to support and maintain the cause of God all his days, and to bring the wicked to justice according to their crime.

40 Now behold, his name was [a]Pahoran. And Pahoran did fill the seat of his father, and did commence his reign in the end of the twenty and fourth year, over the people of Nephi.

CHAPTER 51

The king-men seek to change the law and set up a king—Pahoran and the freemen are supported by the voice of the people—Moroni compels the king-men to defend their liberty or be put to death—Amalickiah and the Lamanites capture many fortified cities—Teancum repels the Lamanite invasion and slays Amalickiah in his tent.

AND now it came to pass in the *commencement of the twenty and fifth year of the reign of the judges over the people of Nephi, they having established peace between the people of Lehi and the people of Morianton concerning their lands, and having commenced the twenty and fifth year in [a]peace;

2 Nevertheless, they did not long maintain an entire peace in the land, for there began to be a contention among the people concerning the chief judge Pahoran; for behold, there were a part of the people who desired that a few particular points of the [a]law should be altered.

3 But behold, Pahoran would not alter nor suffer the law to be altered; therefore, he did not hearken to those who had sent in their voices with their petitions concerning the altering of the law.

4 Therefore, those who were desirous that the law should be altered were angry with him, and desired that he should no longer be chief judge over the land; therefore there arose a warm [a]dispute concerning the matter, but not unto bloodshed.

5 And it came to pass that those who were desirous that Pahoran should be dethroned from the judgment-seat were called [a]king-men, for they were desirous that the law should be altered in a manner to overthrow the free government and to establish a [b]king over the land.

6 And those who were desirous that Pahoran should remain chief judge over the land took upon them the name of [a]freemen; and thus was the [b]division among them, for the freemen had sworn or [c]covenanted to maintain their rights and the privileges of their religion by a free government.

7 And it came to pass that this matter of their contention was settled by the [a]voice of the people. And it came to pass that the voice of the people came in favor of the freemen, and Pahoran retained the judgment-seat, which caused much rejoicing among the brethren of Pahoran and also many of the people of liberty, who also put the king-men to silence, that they durst not oppose but were obliged to maintain the cause of freedom.

8 Now those who were in favor of kings were those of [a]high birth, and they sought to be [b]kings; and they were supported by those who sought power and authority over the people.

39*a* Alma 60: 1.
b TG Oath; Ordinance.
c Alma 4: 16 (16–17); Hel. 1: 5 (3–5, 13).
40*a* Alma 59: 3; 61: 1; Hel. 1: 2.
51 1*a* TG Peacemakers.
2*a* Alma 1: 1.
4*a* TG Disputations.
5*a* Alma 60: 16; 62: 9. TG Kings, Earthly; Unrighteous Dominion.
b 3 Ne. 6: 30.
6*a* Alma 61: 3 (3–4); 62: 6.
b 1 Kgs. 16: 21 (21–22).
c Alma 48: 13; 60: 25 (25–27).
7*a* Alma 4: 16; Hel. 1: 5.
8*a* TG Haughtiness; Pride.
b TG Tyranny.

[*67 B.C.]

9 But behold, this was a critical time for such contentions to be among the people of Nephi; for behold, Amalickiah had again [a]stirred up the hearts of the people of the Lamanites against the people of the Nephites, and he was gathering together soldiers from all parts of his land, and arming them, and preparing for war with all diligence; for he had [b]sworn to drink the blood of Moroni.

10 But behold, we shall see that his promise which he made was [a]rash; nevertheless, he did prepare himself and his armies to come to battle against the Nephites.

11 Now his armies were not so great as they had hitherto been, because of the many thousands who had been [a]slain by the hand of the Nephites; but notwithstanding their great loss, Amalickiah had gathered together a wonderfully great army, insomuch that he feared not to come down to the land of Zarahemla.

12 Yea, even Amalickiah did himself come down, at the head of the Lamanites. And it was in the twenty and fifth year of the reign of the judges; and it was at the same time that they had begun to settle the affairs of their contentions concerning the chief judge, Pahoran.

13 And it came to pass that when the men who were called king-men had heard that the Lamanites were coming down to battle against them, they were glad in their hearts; and they refused to take up arms, for they were so wroth with the chief judge, and also with the [a]people of [b]liberty, that they would not take up arms to defend their country.

14 And it came to pass that when Moroni saw this, and also saw that the Lamanites were coming into the borders of the land, he was exceedingly wroth because of the [a]stubbornness of those people whom he had labored with so much diligence to preserve; yea, he was exceedingly wroth; his soul was filled with anger against them.

15 And it came to pass that he sent a petition, with the voice of the people, unto the governor of the land, desiring that he should read it, and give him (Moroni) power to compel those dissenters to defend their country or to put them to death.

16 For it was his first care to put an end to such contentions and dissensions among the people; for behold, this had been hitherto a cause of all their destruction. And it came to pass that it was granted according to the voice of the people.

17 And it came to pass that Moroni commanded that his army should go against those king-men, to pull down their pride and their nobility and level them with the earth, or they should take up arms and support the cause of liberty.

18 And it came to pass that the armies did march forth against them; and they did pull down their pride and their nobility, insomuch that as they did lift their weapons of war to fight against the men of Moroni they were hewn down and leveled to the earth.

19 And it came to pass that there were four thousand of those [a]dissenters who were hewn down by the sword; and those of their leaders who were not slain in battle were taken and [b]cast into prison, for there was no time for their trials at this period.

20 And the remainder of those dissenters, rather than be smitten down to the earth by the sword, yielded to the standard of liberty, and were compelled to hoist the [a]title of liberty upon their towers, and in their cities, and to take up arms in defence of their country.

9*a* Alma 63: 14.
b Acts 23: 12; Alma 49: 27 (26–27).
10*a* TG Rashness.
11*a* Alma 49: 25 (22–25).
13*a* Alma 46: 16 (10–16).
b TG Liberty.
14*a* TG Stubbornness.
19*a* Alma 60: 16.
b Alma 62: 9.
20*a* Alma 46: 13 (12–13).

[About 67 B.C.]

21 And thus Moroni put an end to those king-men, that there were not any known by the appellation of king-men; and thus he put an end to the stubbornness and the pride of those people who professed the blood of nobility; but they were brought down to humble themselves like unto their brethren, and to fight [a]valiantly for their freedom from bondage.

22 Behold, it came to pass that while [a]Moroni was thus breaking down the wars and contentions among his own people, and subjecting them to peace and civilization, and making regulations to prepare for war against the Lamanites, behold, the Lamanites had come into the land of Moroni, which was in the borders by the seashore.

23 And it came to pass that the Nephites were not sufficiently strong in the city of Moroni; therefore Amalickiah did drive them, slaying many. And it came to pass that Amalickiah took possession of the city, yea, possession of all their fortifications.

24 And those who fled out of the [a]city of Moroni came to the city of Nephihah; and also the people of the city of Lehi gathered themselves together, and made preparations and were ready to receive the Lamanites to battle.

25 But it came to pass that Amalickiah would not suffer the Lamanites to go against the city of Nephihah to battle, but kept them down by the seashore, leaving men in every city to maintain and defend it.

26 And thus he went on, taking possession of [a]many cities, the city of [b]Nephihah, and the city of [c]Lehi, and the city of [d]Morianton, and the city of Omner, and the city of [e]Gid, and the city of [f]Mulek, all of which were on the east borders by the seashore.

27 And thus had the Lamanites obtained, by the cunning of Amalickiah, so many cities, by their numberless hosts, all of which were strongly fortified after the manner of the [a]fortifications of Moroni; all of which afforded strongholds for the Lamanites.

28 And it came to pass that they marched to the [a]borders of the land Bountiful, driving the Nephites before them and slaying many.

29 But it came to pass that they were met by Teancum, who had [a]slain Morianton and had [b]headed his people in his flight.

30 And it came to pass that he headed Amalickiah also, as he was marching forth with his numerous army that he might take possession of the land Bountiful, and also the land [a]northward.

31 But behold he met with a disappointment by being repulsed by Teancum and his men, for they were great warriors; for every man of Teancum did exceed the Lamanites in their strength and in their skill of war, insomuch that they did gain advantage over the Lamanites.

32 And it came to pass that they did harass them, insomuch that they did slay them even until it was dark. And it came to pass that Teancum and his men did pitch their tents in the borders of the land Bountiful; and Amalickiah did pitch his tents in the borders on the beach by the seashore, and after this manner were they driven.

33 And it came to pass that when the night had come, Teancum and his servant stole forth and went out by night, and went into the camp of Amalickiah; and behold, sleep

21*a* TG Courage.
22*a* Alma 50: 13; 62: 32 (32, 34); 3 Ne. 8: 9.
24*a* Alma 50: 14.
26*a* Alma 58: 31.
b Alma 50: 14; 62: 18 (14, 18, 26).
c Alma 50: 15; 62: 30.
d Alma 50: 25; 55: 33.
e Alma 55: 7.
f Alma 52: 2 (2, 16, 22); 53: 6 (2, 6).
27*a* Alma 48: 8 (8–9).
28*a* Alma 52: 12.
29*a* Alma 50: 35.
b Hel. 1: 28 (28–30).
30*a* Alma 50: 29; 52: 9.

[About 67 B.C.]

had overpowered them because of
their much fatigue, which was
caused by the labors and heat of the
day.
34 And it came to pass that Teancum stole privily into the tent of the
king, and [a]put a javelin to his heart;
and he did cause the [b]death of the
king immediately that he did not
awake his servants.
35 And he returned again privily
to his own camp, and behold, his
men were asleep, and he awoke them
and told them all the things that he
had done.
36 And he caused that his armies
should stand in [a]readiness, lest the
Lamanites had awakened and
should come upon them.
37 And thus endeth the twenty and
fifth year of the reign of the judges
over the people of Nephi; and thus
endeth the days of Amalickiah.

CHAPTER 52

Ammoron succeeds Amalickiah as king of the Lamanites—Moroni, Teancum, and Lehi lead the Nephites in a victorious war against the Lamanites—The city of Mulek is retaken, and Jacob the Lamanite is slain.

AND now, it came to pass in the
*twenty and sixth year of the reign
of the judges over the people of
Nephi, behold, when the Lamanites
awoke on the first morning of the
first month, behold, they found
Amalickiah was dead in his own
tent; and they also saw that Teancum was [a]ready to give them battle
on that day.
2 And now, when the Lamanites
saw this they were affrighted; and
they abandoned their design in
marching into the land northward,
and retreated with all their army
into the city of [a]Mulek, and sought
protection in their fortifications.
3 And it came to pass that the
[a]brother of Amalickiah was appointed king over the people; and his
name was [b]Ammoron; thus king
Ammoron, the brother of king
Amalickiah, was appointed to reign
in his stead.
4 And it came to pass that he did
command that his people should
maintain those cities, which they
had taken by the shedding of blood;
for they had not taken any cities
save they had lost much blood.
5 And now, Teancum saw that the
Lamanites were determined to
maintain those cities which they
had taken, and those parts of the
land which they had obtained possession of; and also seeing the
enormity of their number, Teancum
thought it was not expedient that he
should attempt to attack them in
their forts.
6 But he kept his men round about,
as if making preparations for war;
yea, and truly he was preparing to
defend himself against them, by
[a]casting up walls round about and
preparing places of resort.
7 And it came to pass that he kept
thus preparing for war until Moroni
had sent a large number of men to
strengthen his army.
8 And Moroni also sent orders
unto him that he should retain all
the prisoners who fell into his hands;
for as the Lamanites had taken
many prisoners, that he should
retain all the prisoners of the Lamanites as a [a]ransom for those whom
the Lamanites had taken.
9 And he also sent orders unto
him that he should fortify the land
[a]Bountiful, and secure the [b]narrow
pass which led into the land [c]north-
ward, lest the Lamanites should
obtain that point and should have
power to harass them on every
side.

34*a* Alma 62:36.
b Alma 54:16.
36*a* Alma 52:1.
52 1*a* Alma 51:36.
2*a* Alma 51:26.
3*a* Alma 48:1 (1–6); 54:5.
b Alma 54:1; Hel. 1:16.
6*a* Alma 50:1; 53:3.
8*a* Alma 54:2 (1–2).
9*a* Alma 22:29; 53:3 (3–4); 63:5; Hel. 1:23.
b Alma 22:32; Morm. 2:29.
c Alma 51:30.

[*66 B.C.]

10 And Moroni also sent unto him, desiring him that he would be [a]faithful in maintaining that quarter of the land, and that he would seek every opportunity to scourge the Lamanites in that quarter, as much as was in his power, that perhaps he might take again by stratagem or some other way those cities which had been taken out of their hands; and that he also would fortify and strengthen the cities round about, which had not fallen into the hands of the Lamanites.

11 And he also said unto him, I would come unto you, but behold, the Lamanites are upon us in the borders of the land by the west sea; and behold, I go against them, therefore I cannot come unto you.

12 Now, the king (Ammoron) had [a]departed out of the land of Zarahemla, and had made known unto the queen concerning the death of his brother, and had gathered together a large number of men, and had marched forth against the Nephites on the borders by the west sea.

13 And thus he was endeavoring to harass the Nephites, and to draw away a part of their forces to that part of the land, while he had commanded those whom he had left to possess the cities which he had taken, that they should also harass the Nephites on the borders by the east sea, and should take possession of their lands as much as it was in their power, according to the power of their armies.

14 And thus were the Nephites in those dangerous circumstances in the ending of the twenty and sixth year of the reign of the judges over the people of Nephi.

15 But behold, it came to pass in the *twenty and seventh year of the reign of the judges, that Teancum, by the command of Moroni—who had established armies to protect the south and the west borders of the land, and had begun his march towards the land Bountiful, that he might assist Teancum with his men in retaking the cities which they had lost—

16 And it came to pass that Teancum had received orders to make an attack upon the city of Mulek, and retake it if it were possible.

17 And it came to pass that Teancum made preparations to make an attack upon the city of Mulek, and march forth with his army against the Lamanites; but he saw that it was impossible that he could overpower them while they were in their fortifications; therefore he abandoned his designs and returned again to the city Bountiful, to wait for the coming of Moroni, that he might receive strength to his army.

18 And it came to pass that Moroni did arrive with his army at the land of Bountiful, in the latter end of the twenty and seventh year of the reign of the judges over the people of Nephi.

19 And in the †commencement of the twenty and eighth year, Moroni and Teancum and many of the chief [a]captains held a council of war—what they should do to cause the Lamanites to come out against them to battle; or that they might by some means flatter them out of their strongholds, that they might gain advantage over them and take again the city of Mulek.

20 And it came to pass they sent embassies to the army of the Lamanites, which protected the city of Mulek, to their leader, whose name was Jacob, desiring him that he would come out with his armies to meet them upon the plains between the two cities. But behold, Jacob, who was a [a]Zoramite, would not come out with his army to meet them upon the plains.

21 And it came to pass that Moroni, having no hopes of meeting them upon fair grounds, therefore, he resolved upon a plan that he might

10*a* TG Trustworthiness.
12*a* Alma 51: 28.
19*a* Alma 49: 5; 55: 23.
20*a* Alma 48: 5.

[*65 B.C. †64 B.C.]

[a]decoy the Lamanites out of their strongholds.
22 Therefore he caused that Teancum should take a small number of men and march down near the seashore; and Moroni and his army, by night, marched in the wilderness, on the west of the city [a]Mulek; and thus, on the morrow, when the guards of the Lamanites had discovered Teancum, they ran and told it unto Jacob, their leader.
23 And it came to pass that the armies of the Lamanites did march forth against Teancum, supposing by their numbers to overpower Teancum because of the smallness of his numbers. And as Teancum saw the armies of the Lamanites coming out against him he began to retreat down by the seashore, northward.
24 And it came to pass that when the Lamanites saw that he began to flee, they took courage and pursued them with vigor. And while Teancum was thus leading away the Lamanites who were pursuing them in vain, behold, Moroni commanded that a part of his army who were with him should march forth into the city, and take possession of it.
25 And thus they did, and slew all those who had been left to protect the city, yea, all those who would not [a]yield up their weapons of war.
26 And thus Moroni had obtained possession of the city Mulek with a part of his army, while he marched with the remainder to meet the Lamanites when they should return from the pursuit of Teancum.
27 And it came to pass that the Lamanites did pursue Teancum until they came near the city Bountiful, and then they were met by Lehi and a small army, which had been left to protect the city Bountiful.
28 And now behold, when the chief captains of the Lamanites had beheld Lehi with his army coming against them, they fled in much confusion, lest perhaps they should not obtain the city Mulek before Lehi should overtake them; for they were wearied because of their march, and the men of Lehi were fresh.
29 Now the Lamanites did not know that Moroni had been in their rear with his army; and all they feared was Lehi and his men.
30 Now Lehi was not desirous to overtake them till they should meet Moroni and his army.
31 And it came to pass that before the Lamanites had retreated far they were surrounded by the Nephites, by the men of Moroni on one hand, and the men of Lehi on the other, all of whom were fresh and full of strength; but the Lamanites were wearied because of their long march.
32 And Moroni commanded his men that they should fall upon them until they had given up their weapons of war.
33 And it came to pass that Jacob, being their leader, being also a [a]Zoramite, and having an unconquerable spirit, he led the Lamanites forth to battle with exceeding fury against Moroni.
34 Moroni being in their course of march, therefore Jacob was determined to slay them and cut his way through to the city of Mulek. But behold, Moroni and his men were more powerful; therefore they did not give way before the Lamanites.
35 And it came to pass that they fought on both hands with exceeding fury; and there were many slain on both sides; yea, and Moroni was wounded and Jacob was killed.
36 And Lehi pressed upon their rear with such fury with his strong men, that the Lamanites in the rear delivered up their weapons of war; and the remainder of them, being much confused, knew not whither to go or to strike.
37 Now Moroni seeing their con-

21*a* Josh. 8: 13; Alma 43: 31 (30–43); 56: 30.
22*a* Alma 51: 26; 53: 6 (2, 6).
25*a* Alma 44: 6.
33*a* Alma 30: 59.

[About 64 B.C.]

fusion, he said unto them: If ye
will bring forth your weapons of war
and deliver them up, behold we will
forbear shedding your blood.
38 And it came to pass that when
the Lamanites had heard these
words, their chief captains, all those
who were not slain, came forth and
threw down their weapons of war
[a]at the feet of Moroni, and also commanded their men that they should
do the same.
39 But behold, there were many
that would not; and those who
would not deliver up their swords
were taken and bound, and their
weapons of war were taken from
them, and they were compelled to
march with their brethren forth
into the land Bountiful.
40 And now the number of prisoners who were taken exceeded
more than the number of those who
had been slain, yea, more than those
who had been slain on both sides.

CHAPTER 53

The Lamanite prisoners are used to fortify the city Bountiful—Dissensions among the Nephites give rise to Lamanite victories—Helaman takes command of the two thousand stripling sons of the people of Ammon.

AND it came to pass that they did
set guards over the prisoners of the
Lamanites, and did compel them to
go forth and bury their dead, yea,
and also the dead of the Nephites
who were slain; and Moroni placed
men over them to guard them while
they should perform their labors.
2 And [a]Moroni went to the city of
Mulek with Lehi, and took command of the city and gave it unto
Lehi. Now behold, this Lehi was a
man who had been with Moroni in
the more part of all his battles; and
he was a man like unto Moroni, and
they rejoiced in each other's safety;
yea, they were beloved by each
other, and also beloved by all the
people of Nephi.
3 And it came to pass that after
the Lamanites had finished burying
their dead and also the dead of the
Nephites, they were marched back
into the land Bountiful; and Teancum, by the orders of Moroni,
caused that they should commence
laboring in [a]digging a ditch round
about the land, or the city, [b]Bounti-
ful.
4 And he caused that they should
build a [a]breastwork of timbers upon
the inner bank of the ditch; and they
cast up dirt out of the ditch against
the breastwork of timbers; and thus
they did cause the Lamanites to
labor until they had encircled the
city of Bountiful round about with
a strong wall of timbers and earth,
to an exceeding height.
5 And this city became an exceeding stronghold ever after; and in
this city they did guard the prisoners of the Lamanites; yea, even
within a wall which they had caused
them to [a]build with their own hands.
Now Moroni was compelled to
cause the Lamanites to labor, because it was easy to guard them
while at their labor; and he desired
all his forces when he should make
an attack upon the Lamanites.
6 And it came to pass that Moroni
had thus gained a victory over one
of the greatest of the armies of the
Lamanites, and had obtained possession of the city of [a]Mulek, which
was one of the strongest holds of the
Lamanites in the land of Nephi; and
thus he had also built a stronghold
to retain his prisoners.
7 And it came to pass that he did
no more attempt a battle with the
Lamanites in that year, but he did
employ his men in preparing for war,
yea, and in making fortifications to
guard against the Lamanites, yea,
and also delivering their women and
their children from famine and

38*a* Alma 55: 23.
53 2*a* Alma 48: 17.
3*a* Alma 52: 6.
b Alma 52: 9 (9, 17, 27); 63: 5.
4*a* Alma 50: 2 (2–3).
5*a* Alma 55: 25 (25–26).
6*a* Alma 51: 26; 52: 22.

[About 64 B.C.]

affliction, and providing food for their armies.

8 And now it came to pass that the armies of the Lamanites, on the west sea, south, while in the absence of Moroni on account of some intrigue amongst the Nephites, which caused [a]dissensions amongst them, had gained some ground over the Nephites, yea, insomuch that they had obtained possession of a number of their cities in that part of the land.

9 And thus because of [a]iniquity amongst themselves, yea, because of dissensions and intrigue among themselves they were placed in the most dangerous circumstances.

10 And now behold, I have somewhat to say concerning the [a]people of Ammon, who, in the beginning, were Lamanites; but by Ammon and his brethren, or rather by the power and word of God, they had been [b]converted unto the Lord; and they had been brought down into the land of Zarahemla, and had ever since been protected by the Nephites.

11 And because of their oath they had been kept from taking up arms against their brethren; for they had taken an oath that they [a]never would shed blood more; and according to their oath they would have perished; yea, they would have suffered themselves to have fallen into the hands of their brethren, had it not been for the pity and the exceeding love which Ammon and his brethren had had for them.

12 And for this cause they were brought down into the land of Zarahemla; and they ever had been [a]protected by the Nephites.

13 But it came to pass that when they saw the danger, and the many [a]afflictions and tribulations which the Nephites bore for them, they were moved with compassion and were [b]desirous to take up arms in the defence of their country.

14 But behold, as they were about to take their weapons of war, they were overpowered by the persuasions of Helaman and his brethren, for they were about to [a]break the [b]oath which they had made.

15 And Helaman feared lest by so doing they should lose their souls; therefore all those who had entered into this covenant were compelled to behold their brethren wade through their afflictions, in their dangerous circumstances at this time.

16 But behold, it came to pass they had many [a]sons, who had not entered into a covenant that they would not take their weapons of war to defend themselves against their enemies; therefore they did assemble themselves together at this time, as many as were able to take up arms, and they called themselves Nephites.

17 And they entered into a covenant to fight for the liberty of the Nephites, yea, to protect the land unto the [a]laying down of their lives; yea, even they covenanted that they never would give up their [b]liberty, but they would fight in all cases to protect the Nephites and themselves from bondage.

18 Now behold, there were two thousand of those young men, who entered into this covenant and took their weapons of war to defend their country.

19 And now behold, as they never had hitherto been a disadvantage to the Nephites, they became now at this period of time also a great support; for they took their weapons of war, and they would that Helaman should be their leader.

20 And they were all young men,

8*a* Alma 31:8; Hel. 1:15.
9*a* Josh. 7:4.
10*a* Alma 27:26.
b Alma 23:13 (8–13).
11*a* Alma 24:18 (17–19).
12*a* Alma 27:23.
13*a* TG Affliction; Tribulation.
b Alma 24:18 (17–19); 56:7.
14*a* Num. 30:2.
b TG Oath.
16*a* Alma 57:6.
17*a* TG Self-sacrifice.
b Alma 56:47.
TG Liberty.

[About 64 B.C.]

and they were exceedingly valiant for [a]courage, and also for strength and activity; but behold, this was not all—they were men who were true at all times in whatsoever thing they were entrusted.

21 Yea, they were men of truth and [a]soberness, for they had been taught to keep the commandments of God and to [b]walk uprightly before him.

22 And now it came to pass that Helaman did march at the head of his [a]two thousand stripling soldiers, to the support of the people in the borders of the land on the south by the west sea.

23 And thus ended the twenty and eighth year of the reign of the judges over the people of Nephi.

CHAPTER 54

Ammoron and Moroni negotiate for the exchange of prisoners—Moroni demands that the Lamanites withdraw and cease their murderous attacks—Ammoron demands that the Nephites lay down their arms and become subject to the Lamanites.

AND now it came to pass in the *commencement of the twenty and ninth year of the judges, that [a]Ammoron sent unto Moroni desiring that he would exchange prisoners.

2 And it came to pass that Moroni felt to [a]rejoice exceedingly at this request, for he desired the provisions which were imparted for the support of the Lamanite prisoners for the support of his own people; and he also desired his own people for the strengthening of his army.

3 Now the Lamanites had taken many women and children, and there was not a woman nor a child among all the prisoners of Moroni, or the prisoners whom Moroni had taken; therefore Moroni resolved upon a stratagem to obtain as many prisoners of the Nephites from the Lamanites as it were possible.

4 Therefore he wrote an epistle, and sent it by the servant of Ammoron, the same who had brought an epistle to Moroni. Now these are the words which he wrote unto Ammoron, saying:

5 Behold, Ammoron, I have written unto you somewhat concerning this war which ye have waged against my people, or rather which thy [a]brother hath waged against them, and which ye are still determined to carry on after his death.

6 Behold, I would tell you somewhat concerning the [a]justice of God, and the sword of his almighty wrath, which doth hang over you except ye repent and withdraw your armies into your own lands, or the land of your possessions, which is the land of Nephi.

7 Yea, I would tell you these things if ye were capable of hearkening unto them; yea, I would tell you concerning that awful [a]hell that awaits to receive such [b]murderers as thou and thy brother have been, except ye repent and withdraw your murderous purposes, and return with your armies to your own lands.

8 But as ye have once rejected these things, and have fought against the people of the Lord, even so I may expect you will do it again.

9 And now behold, we are prepared to receive you; yea, and except you withdraw your purposes, behold, ye will pull down the [a]wrath of that God whom you have rejected upon you, even to your utter destruction.

10 But, as the Lord liveth, our armies shall come upon you except ye withdraw, and ye shall soon be visited with [a]death, for we will retain our cities and our lands; yea,

20*a* TG Courage; Dependability; Integrity.
21*a* TG Sobriety.
b TG Walking with God.
22*a* Alma 56: 3 (1–9).
54 1*a* Alma 52: 3.
2*a* Alma 52: 8.
5*a* Alma 48: 1 (1–6); 52: 3 (1–3).
6*a* TG God, Indignation of; God, Justice of.
7*a* TG Hell.
b Alma 47: 18 (18, 22–34). TG Murder.
9*a* TG Punishment.
10*a* Alma 43: 47.

[*63 B.C.]

and we will maintain our religion
and the cause of our God.
11 But behold, it supposeth me
that I talk to you concerning these
things in vain; or it supposeth me
that thou art a [a]child of hell; therefore I will close my epistle by telling
you that I will not exchange prisoners, save it be on conditions that ye
will deliver up a man and his wife
and his children, for one prisoner;
if this be the case that ye will do it,
I will exchange.
12 And behold, if ye do not this,
I will come against you with my
armies; yea, even I will arm my
women and my children, and I will
come against you, and I will follow
you even into your own land, which
is the land of [a]our first inheritance;
yea, and it shall be blood for blood,
yea, life for life; and I will give you
battle even until you are destroyed
from off the face of the earth.
13 Behold, I am in my anger, and
also my people; ye have sought to
[a]murder us, and we have only sought
to defend ourselves. But behold, if
ye seek to destroy us more we will
seek to destroy you; yea, and we
will seek our land, the land of our
first inheritance.
14 Now I close my epistle. I am
Moroni; I am a leader of the people
of the Nephites.
15 Now it came to pass that
Ammoron, when he had received
this epistle, was angry; and he
wrote another epistle unto Moroni,
and these are the words which he
wrote, saying:
16 I am Ammoron, the king of the
Lamanites; I am the brother of
Amalickiah whom ye have [a]mur-
dered. Behold, I will avenge his
blood upon you, yea, and I will come
upon you with my armies for I fear
not your threatenings.
17 For behold, your fathers did
wrong their brethren, insomuch that
they did rob them of their [a]right to
the [b]government when it rightly
belonged unto them.
18 And now behold, if ye will lay
down your arms, and subject yourselves to be governed by those to
whom the government doth rightly
belong, then will I cause that my
people shall lay down their weapons and shall be at war no more.
19 Behold, ye have breathed out
many threatenings against me and
my people; but behold, we fear not
your threatenings.
20 Nevertheless, I will grant to
exchange prisoners according to
your request, gladly, that I may
preserve my food for my men of
war; and we will wage a war which
shall be eternal, either to the subjecting the Nephites to our authority or to their eternal extinction.
21 And as concerning that God
whom ye say we have rejected,
behold, we [a]know not such a being;
neither do ye; but if it so be that
there is such a being, we know not but
that he hath made us as well as you.
22 And if it so be that there is a
devil and a hell, behold will he not
send you there to dwell with my
brother whom ye have murdered,
whom ye have hinted that he hath
gone to such a place? But behold
these things matter not.
23 I am Ammoron, and a descendant of [a]Zoram, whom your fathers
pressed and brought out of Jerusalem.
24 And behold now, I am a bold
Lamanite; behold, this war hath
been waged to avenge their wrongs,
and [a]to maintain and to obtain their
rights to the government; and I
close my epistle to Moroni.

CHAPTER 55

*Moroni refuses to exchange prison-
ers—The Lamanite guards are en-*

11*a* John 8: 44 (43–44).
12*a* 2 Ne. 5: 8 (5–8).
13*a* Alma 55: 2.
16*a* Alma 51: 34.
17*a* 2 Ne. 5: 3 (1–4); Mosiah 10: 15 (12–17).
b TG Governments.
21*a* TG Unbelief, Unbelievers.
23*a* 1 Ne. 4: 35; Jacob 1: 13; 4 Ne. 1: 36 (36–37).
24*a* Alma 48: 2 (1–4).

[About 63 B.C.]

ticed to become drunk, and the Nephite prisoners are freed—The city of Gid is taken without bloodshed.

Now it came to pass that when Moroni had received this epistle he was more angry, because he knew that Ammoron had a perfect knowledge of his [a]fraud; yea, he knew that Ammoron knew that it was not a just cause that had caused him to wage a war against the people of Nephi.

2 And he said: Behold, I will not exchange prisoners with Ammoron save he will withdraw his [a]purpose, as I have stated in my epistle; for I will not grant unto him that he shall have any more power than what he hath got.

3 Behold, I know the place where the Lamanites do guard my people whom they have taken prisoners; and as Ammoron would not grant unto me mine epistle, behold, I will give unto him according to my words; yea, I will seek death among them until they shall sue for peace.

4 And now it came to pass that when Moroni had said these words, he caused that a search should be made among his men, that perhaps he might find a man who was a descendant of Laman among them.

5 And it came to pass that they found one, whose name was Laman; and he was [a]one of the servants of the king who was murdered by Amalickiah.

6 Now Moroni caused that Laman and a small number of his men should go forth unto the guards who were over the Nephites.

7 Now the Nephites were guarded in the city of [a]Gid; therefore Moroni appointed Laman and caused that a small number of men should go with him.

8 And when it was evening Laman went to the guards who were over the Nephites, and behold, they saw him coming and they hailed him; but he saith unto them: Fear not; behold, I am a Lamanite. Behold, we have escaped from the Nephites, and they sleep; and behold we have taken of their wine and brought with us.

9 Now when the Lamanites heard these words they received him with joy; and they said unto him: Give us of your wine, that we may drink; we are glad that ye have thus taken wine with you for we are weary.

10 But Laman said unto them: Let us keep of our wine till we go against the Nephites to battle. But this saying only made them more desirous to drink of the wine;

11 For, said they: We are weary, therefore let us take of the wine, and by and by we shall receive wine for our rations, which will strengthen us to go against the Nephites.

12 And Laman said unto them: You may do according to your desires.

13 And it came to pass that they did take of the wine freely; and it was pleasant to their taste, therefore they took of it more freely; and it was strong, having been prepared in its [a]strength.

14 And it came to pass they did drink and were merry, and by and by they were all [a]drunken.

15 And now when Laman and his men saw that they were all drunken, and were in a [a]deep sleep, they returned to Moroni and told him all the things that had happened.

16 And now this was according to the design of Moroni. And Moroni had prepared his men with weapons of war; and he went to the city Gid, while the Lamanites were in a deep sleep and drunken, and cast in [a]weapons of war unto the prisoners, insomuch that they were all armed;

17 Yea, even to their women, and all those of their children, as many as were able to use a weapon of war,

---

55 1*a* Neh. 6: 8; Alma 47: 30 (12–35).
2*a* Alma 54: 13.
5*a* Alma 47: 29.
7*a* Alma 51: 26.
13*a* Prov. 20: 1. TG Wine.
14*a* Mosiah 22: 6 (6–11).
15*a* 1 Sam. 26: 12; Mosiah 24: 19.
16*a* Alma 62: 22 (21–23).

[About 63 B.C.]

when Moroni had armed all those prisoners; and all those things were done in a profound silence.
18 But had they awakened the Lamanites, behold they were drunken and the Nephites could have slain them.
19 But behold, this was not the desire of Moroni; he did not [a]delight in murder or bloodshed, but he delighted in the saving of his people from destruction; and for this cause he might not bring upon him injustice, he would not fall upon the Lamanites and destroy them in their drunkenness.
20 But he had obtained his desires; for he had armed those prisoners of the Nephites who were within the wall of the city, and had given them power to gain possession of those parts which were within the walls.
21 And then he caused the men who were with him to withdraw a pace from them, and surround the armies of the Lamanites.
22 Now behold this was done in the night-time, so that when the Lamanites awoke in the morning they beheld that they were surrounded by the Nephites without, and that their prisoners were armed within.
23 And thus they saw that the Nephites had power over them; and in these circumstances they found that it was not expedient that they should fight with the Nephites; therefore their chief [a]captains demanded their weapons of war, and they brought them forth and [b]cast them at the feet of the Nephites, pleading for mercy.
24 Now behold, this was the desire of Moroni. He took them prisoners of war, and took possession of the city, and caused that all the prisoners should be liberated, who were Nephites; and they did join the army of Moroni, and were a great strength to his army.
25 And it came to pass that he did cause the Lamanites, whom he had taken prisoners, that they should commence a [a]labor in strengthening the fortifications round about the city Gid.
26 And it came to pass that when he had fortified the city Gid, according to his desires, he caused that his prisoners should be taken to the city Bountiful; and he also guarded that city with an exceedingly strong force.
27 And it came to pass that they did, notwithstanding all the intrigues of the Lamanites, keep and protect all the prisoners whom they had taken, and also maintain all the ground and the advantage which they had retaken.
28 And it came to pass that the Nephites began [a]again to be victorious, and to reclaim their rights and their privileges.
29 Many times did the Lamanites attempt to encircle them about by night, but in these attempts they did lose many prisoners.
30 And many times did they attempt to administer of their wine to the Nephites, that they might destroy them with poison or with drunkenness.
31 But behold, the Nephites were not slow to [a]remember the Lord their God in this their time of affliction. They could not be taken in their snares; yea, they would not partake of their wine, save they had first given to some of the Lamanite prisoners.
32 And they were thus cautious that no poison should be administered among them; for if their wine would poison a Lamanite it would also poison a Nephite; and thus they did try all their liquors.
33 And now it came to pass that it was expedient for Moroni to make preparations to attack the city [a]Morianton; for behold, the Laman-

19*a* Alma 48:16; 55:30 (30–32).
23*a* Alma 52:19; 56:12.
b Alma 52:38.
25*a* Alma 53:5 (3–5).
28*a* Alma 44:20 (12–23).
31*a* Hosea 5:15; Alma 62:49 (49–51).
33*a* Alma 50:25; 51:26.

[About 63 B.C.]

ites had, by their labors, fortified
the city Morianton until it had
become an exceeding stronghold.
34 And they were continually
bringing new forces into that city,
and also new supplies of provisions.
35 And thus ended the twenty and
ninth year of the reign of the judges
over the people of Nephi.

CHAPTER 56

Helaman sends an epistle to Moroni recounting the state of the war with the Lamanites—Antipus and Helaman gain a great victory over the Lamanites—Helaman's two thousand stripling sons fight with miraculous power and none of them are slain.

AND now it came to pass in the
*commencement of the thirtieth
year of the reign of the judges, on the
second day in the first month,
[a]Moroni received an [b]epistle from
Helaman, stating the affairs of the
people in [c]that quarter of the land.
2 And these are the words which he
wrote, saying: My dearly beloved
brother, Moroni, as well in the Lord
as in the tribulations of our warfare;
behold, my beloved brother, I
have somewhat to tell you concerning
our warfare in this part of the
land.
3 Behold, [a]two thousand of the
sons of those men whom Ammon
brought down out of the land of
Nephi—now ye have known that
these were descendants of Laman,
who was the eldest son of our father
Lehi;
4 Now I need not rehearse unto
you concerning their traditions or
their unbelief, for thou knowest concerning
all these things—
5 Therefore it sufficeth me that I
tell you that two thousand of these
young men have taken their weapons
of war, and would that I should
be their leader; and we have come
forth to defend our country.
6 And now ye also know concerning
the [a]covenant which their
fathers made, that they would not
take up their weapons of war against
their brethren to shed blood.
7 But in the twenty and sixth year,
when they saw our afflictions and
our tribulations for them, they were
about to [a]break the covenant which
they had made and take up their
weapons of war in our defence.
8 But I would not suffer them that
they should break this [a]covenant
which they had made, supposing
that God would strengthen us,
insomuch that we should not suffer
more because of the fulfilling the
[b]oath which they had taken.
9 But behold, here is one thing in
which we may have great joy. For
behold, in the †twenty and sixth
year, I, Helaman, did march at the
head of these [a]two thousand young
men to the city of [b]Judea, to assist
Antipus, whom ye had appointed a
leader over the people of that part
of the land.
10 And I did join my two thousand
[a]sons, (for they are worthy to be
called sons) to the army of Antipus,
in which strength Antipus did rejoice
exceedingly; for behold, his
army had been reduced by the
Lamanites because their forces
had slain a vast number of our
men, for which cause we have to
mourn.
11 Nevertheless, we may console
ourselves in this point, that they
have died in the cause of their
country and of their God, yea, and
they are [a]happy.
12 And the Lamanites had also
retained many prisoners, all of
whom are chief [a]captains, for none
other have they spared alive. And
we suppose that they are now at this

56 1*a* Alma 58: 35.
b Alma 59: 1.
c Alma 53: 22 (8, 22).
3*a* Alma 53: 22.
6*a* TG Covenants.
7*a* Alma 24: 18 (17–19); 53: 13 (13–15).
8*a* TG Honesty.
b TG Vows.
9*a* Alma 53: 22.
b Alma 57: 11.
10*a* Alma 56: 17.
11*a* Alma 28: 12.
12*a* Alma 52: 19.

[*62 B.C. †66 B.C.]

time in the land of Nephi; it is so if
they are not slain.
13 And now these are the cities of
which the Lamanites have obtained
possession by the shedding of the
blood of so many of our valiant
men;
14 The land of [a]Manti, or the city of
Manti, and the city of Zeezrom, and
the city of [b]Cumeni, and the city of
Antiparah.
15 And these are the cities which
they possessed when I arrived at the
city of Judea; and I found Antipus
and his men toiling with their might
to fortify the city.
16 Yea, and they were depressed in
body as well as in spirit, for they
had fought valiantly by day and
toiled by night to maintain their
cities; and thus they had suffered
great afflictions of every kind.
17 And now they were determined
to conquer in this place or die; therefore
you may well suppose that this
little force which I brought with me,
yea, those [a]sons of mine, gave them
great hopes and much joy.
18 And now it came to pass that
when the Lamanites saw that
Antipus had received a greater
strength to his army, they were
compelled by the orders of Ammoron
to not come against the city of
Judea, or against us, to battle.
19 And thus were we favored of the
Lord; for had they come upon us in
this our weakness they might have
perhaps destroyed our little army;
but thus were we preserved.
20 They were commanded by
Ammoron to maintain those cities
which they had taken. And thus
ended the twenty and sixth year.
And in the *commencement of the
twenty and seventh year we had
prepared our city and ourselves for
defence.
21 Now we were desirous that the
Lamanites should come upon us;
for we were not desirous to make an
attack upon them in their strongholds.
22 And it came to pass that we
kept spies out round about, to
watch the movements of the Lamanites,
that they might not pass
us by night nor by day to make an
attack upon our other cities which
were on the northward.
23 For we knew in those cities they
were not sufficiently strong to meet
them; therefore we were desirous,
if they should pass by us, to fall upon
them in their rear, and thus bring
them up in the rear at the same time
they were met in the front. We
supposed that we could overpower
them; but behold, we were disappointed
in this our desire.
24 They durst not pass by us with
their whole army, neither durst they
with a part, lest they should not be
sufficiently strong and they should
fall.
25 Neither durst they march down
against the city of Zarahemla;
neither durst they cross the head of
Sidon, over to the city of Nephihah.
26 And thus, with their forces, they
were determined to maintain those
cities which they had taken.
27 And now it came to pass in the
second month of this year, there
was brought unto us many provisions
from the fathers of those my
two thousand sons.
28 And also there were sent two
thousand men unto us from the land
of Zarahemla. And thus we were
prepared with ten thousand men,
and provisions for them, and also
for their wives and their children.
29 And the Lamanites, thus seeing
our forces increase daily, and provisions
arrive for our support, they
began to be fearful, and began to
sally forth, if it were possible to put
an end to our receiving provisions
and strength.
30 Now when we saw that the
Lamanites began to grow uneasy
on this wise, we were desirous to
bring a stratagem into effect upon
them; therefore Antipus ordered
that I should march forth with my

14*a* Alma 43:22.
b Alma 57:7 (7–34).
17*a* Alma 56:10.

[*65 B.C.]

little sons to a neighboring city, [a]as
if we were carrying provisions to a
neighboring city.
31 And we were to march near the
city of Antiparah, as if we were
going to the city beyond, in the
borders by the seashore.
32 And it came to pass that we did
march forth, as if with our provisions, to go to that city.
33 And it came to pass that
Antipus did march forth with a
part of his army, leaving the
remainder to maintain the city. But
he did not march forth until I had
gone forth with my little army, and
came near the city Antiparah.
34 And now, in the city Antiparah
were stationed the strongest army
of the Lamanites; yea, the most
numerous.
35 And it came to pass that when
they had been informed by their
spies, they came forth with their
army and marched against us.
36 And it came to pass that we did
flee before them, northward. And
thus we did lead away the most
powerful army of the Lamanites;
37 Yea, even to a considerable
distance, insomuch that when they
saw the army of Antipus pursuing
them, with their might, they did not
turn to the right nor to the left, but
pursued their march in a straight
course after us; and, as we suppose,
it was their intent to slay us before
Antipus should overtake them, and
this that they might not be surrounded by our people.
38 And now Antipus, beholding
our danger, did speed the march of
his army. But behold, it was night;
therefore they did not overtake us,
neither did Antipus overtake them;
therefore we did camp for the night.
39 And it came to pass that before
the dawn of the morning, behold,
the Lamanites were pursuing us.
Now we were not sufficiently strong
to contend with them; yea, I would
not suffer that my little sons should
fall into their hands; therefore we
did continue our march, and we
took our march into the wilderness.
40 Now they durst not turn to the
right nor to the left lest they should
be surrounded; neither would I turn
to the right nor to the left lest they
should overtake me, and we could
not stand against them, but be slain,
and they would make their escape;
and thus we did flee all that day into
the wilderness, even until it was
dark.
41 And it came to pass that again,
when the light of the morning came
we saw the Lamanites upon us, and
we did flee before them.
42 But it came to pass that they
did not pursue us far before they
halted; and it was in the morning
of the third day of the seventh
month.
43 And now, whether they were
overtaken by Antipus we knew not,
but I said unto my men: Behold,
we know not but they have halted
for the purpose that we should come
against them, that they might
catch us in their snare;
44 Therefore what say ye, my sons,
will ye go against them to battle?
45 And now I say unto you, my
beloved brother Moroni, that never
had I seen [a]so great [b]courage, nay,
not amongst all the Nephites.
46 For as I had ever called them
my sons (for they were all of them
very young) even so they said unto
me: Father, behold our God is with
us, and he will [a]not suffer that we
should fall; then let us go forth; we
would not slay our brethren if they
would let us alone; therefore let us
go, lest they should overpower the
army of Antipus.
47 Now they never had fought,
yet they did not fear death; and
they did think more upon the
[a]liberty of their [b]fathers than they
did upon their lives; yea, they had

30*a* Alma 52:21; 58:1.
45*a* Alma 19:10.
b TG Courage.
46*a* Alma 61:10 (10–11).
47*a* TG Birthright; Liberty.
b Alma 53:17 (15–18).
TG Honoring Father and Mother.

[About 64 B.C.]

been taught by their [c]mothers, that if they did not doubt, God would deliver them.

48 And they rehearsed unto me the words of their [a]mothers, saying: We [b]do not doubt our mothers knew it.

49 And it came to pass that I did return with my two thousand against these Lamanites who had pursued us. And now behold, the armies of Antipus had overtaken them, and a terrible battle had commenced.

50 The army of Antipus being weary, because of their long march in so short a space of time, were about to fall into the hands of the Lamanites; and had I not returned with my two thousand they would have obtained their purpose.

51 For Antipus had fallen by the sword, and many of his leaders, because of their weariness, which was occasioned by the speed of their march—therefore the men of Antipus, being confused because of the fall of their leaders, began to give way before the Lamanites.

52 And it came to pass that the Lamanites took courage, and began to pursue them; and thus were the Lamanites pursuing them with great vigor when [a]Helaman came upon their rear with his two thousand, and began to slay them exceedingly, insomuch that the whole army of the Lamanites halted and turned upon Helaman.

53 Now when the people of Antipus saw that the Lamanites had turned them about, they gathered together their men and came again upon the rear of the Lamanites.

54 And now it came to pass that we, the people of Nephi, the people of Antipus, and I with my two thousand, did surround the Lamanites, and did slay them; yea, insomuch that they were compelled to deliver up their weapons of war and also themselves as prisoners of war.

55 And now it came to pass that when they had surrendered themselves up unto us, behold, I numbered those young men who had fought with me, fearing lest there were many of them slain.

56 But behold, to my great joy, there had [a]not one soul of them fallen to the earth; yea, and they had fought as if with the [b]strength of God; yea, never were men known to have fought with such miraculous strength; and with such mighty power did they fall upon the Lamanites, that they did frighten them; and for this cause did the Lamanites deliver themselves up as prisoners of war.

57 And as we had no place for our prisoners, that we could guard them to keep them from the armies of the Lamanites, therefore we sent them to the land of Zarahemla, and a part of those men who were not slain of Antipus, with them; and the remainder I took and joined them to my stripling [a]Ammonites, and took our march back to the city of Judea.

CHAPTER 57

Helaman recounts the taking of Antiparah and the surrender and later the defense of Cumeni—His Ammonite striplings fight valiantly and all are wounded, but none are slain—Gid reports the slaying and the escape of the Lamanite prisoners.

AND now it came to pass that I received an epistle from Ammoron, the king, stating that if I would deliver up those prisoners of war whom we had taken that he would deliver up the city of Antiparah unto us.

2 But I sent an epistle unto the king, that we were sure our forces were sufficient to take the city of

47*c* Alma 57:21. TG Marriage, Motherhood.
48*a* TG Family, Love within.
b D&C 46:14.
52*a* Morm. 6:6. IE Mormon here abridges some of the material in the letter of Helaman.
56*a* Alma 57:25; 58:39.
b TG Strength.
57*a* Alma 27:26.

[About 64 B.C.]

Antiparah by our force; and by
delivering up the prisoners for that
city we should suppose ourselves
unwise, and that we would only
deliver up our prisoners on exchange.
3 And Ammoron refused mine
epistle, for he would not exchange
prisoners; therefore we began to
make preparations to go against the
city of Antiparah.
4 But the people of Antiparah did
leave the city, and fled to their other
cities, which they had possession of,
to fortify them; and thus the city
of Antiparah fell into our hands.
5 And thus ended the twenty and
eighth year of the reign of the
judges.
6 And it came to pass that in the
*commencement of the twenty and
ninth year, we received a supply of
provisions, and also an addition to
our army, from the land of Zarahemla, and from the land round
about, to the number of six thousand men, besides sixty of the [a]sons
of the Ammonites who had come to
join their brethren, my little band
of two thousand. And now behold,
we were strong, yea, and we had also
plenty of provisions brought unto us.
7 And it came to pass that it was
our desire to wage a battle with the
army which was placed to protect
the city [a]Cumeni.
8 And now behold, I will show unto
you that we soon accomplished our
desire; yea, with our strong force,
or with a part of our strong force,
we did surround, by night, the city
Cumeni, a little before they were to
receive a supply of provisions.
9 And it came to pass that we did
camp round about the city for many
nights; but we did sleep upon our
swords, and keep guards, that the
Lamanites could not come upon us
by night and slay us, which they
attempted many times; but as
many times as they attempted this
their blood was spilt.
10 At length their provisions did
arrive, and they were about to enter
the city by night. And we, instead of
being Lamanites, were Nephites;
therefore, we did take them and
their provisions.
11 And notwithstanding the Lamanites being cut off from their support after this manner, they were
still determined to maintain the
city; therefore it became expedient
that we should take those provisions
and send them to [a]Judea, and our
prisoners to the land of Zarahemla.
12 And it came to pass that not
many days had passed away before
the Lamanites began to lose all
hopes of succor; therefore they
yielded up the city unto our hands;
and thus we had accomplished our
designs in obtaining the city
Cumeni.
13 But it came to pass that our
prisoners were so numerous that,
notwithstanding the enormity of
our numbers, we were obliged to
employ all our force to keep them,
or to put them to death.
14 For behold, they would break
out in great numbers, and would
fight with stones, and with clubs, or
whatsoever thing they could get
into their hands, insomuch that we
did slay upwards of two thousand
of them after they had surrendered
themselves prisoners of war.
15 Therefore it became expedient
for us, that we should put an end to
their lives, or guard them, sword in
hand, down to the land of Zarahemla; and also our provisions were
not any more than sufficient for our
own people, notwithstanding that
which we had taken from the
Lamanites.
16 And now, in those critical circumstances, it became a very
serious matter to determine concerning these prisoners of war;
nevertheless, we did resolve to send
them down to the land of Zarahemla; therefore we selected a part
of our men, and gave them charge
over our prisoners to go down to the
land of Zarahemla.

57 6*a* Alma 53:16.
7*a* Alma 56:14.
11*a* Alma 56:9.

[*63 B.C.]

17 But it came to pass that on the
morrow they did return. And now
behold, we did not [a]inquire of them
concerning the prisoners; for behold,
the Lamanites were upon us, and
they returned in season to save us
from falling into their hands. For
behold, Ammoron had sent to their
support a new supply of provisions
and also a numerous army of men.
18 And it came to pass that those
men whom we sent with the prisoners did arrive in season to check
them, as they were about to overpower us.
19 But behold, my little band of
two thousand and sixty fought most
desperately; yea, they were firm
before the Lamanites, and did
[a]administer death unto all those who
opposed them.
20 And as the remainder of our
army were about to give way before
the Lamanites, behold, those two
thousand and sixty were firm and
undaunted.
21 Yea, and they did [a]obey and
observe to perform every word of
command with exactness; yea, and
even according to their faith it was
done unto them; and I did remember the words which they said unto
me that their [b]mothers had taught
them.
22 And now behold, it was these
my sons, and those men who had
been selected to convey the prisoners, to whom we owe this great
victory; for it was they who did
beat the Lamanites; therefore they
were driven back to the city of
Manti.
23 And we retained our city
Cumeni, and were not all destroyed
by the sword; nevertheless, we had
suffered great loss.
24 And it came to pass that after
the Lamanites had fled, I immediately gave orders that my men who
had been wounded should be taken
from among the dead, and caused
that their wounds should be dressed.
25 And it came to pass that there
were two hundred, out of my two
thousand and sixty, who had
fainted because of the loss of blood;
nevertheless, according to the goodness of God, and to our great
astonishment, and also the joy of
our whole army, there was [a]not one
soul of them who did perish; yea,
and neither was there one soul
among them who had not received
many wounds.
26 And now, their [a]preservation
was astonishing to our whole army,
yea, that they should be spared
while there was a thousand of our
brethren who were slain. And we do
justly ascribe it to the miraculous
[b]power of God, because of their
exceeding [c]faith in that which they
had been taught to believe—that
there was a just God, and whosoever did not doubt, that they should
be preserved by his marvelous
power.
27 Now this was the [a]faith of these
of whom I have spoken; they are
young, and their minds are [b]firm,
and they do put their trust in God
continually.
28 And now it came to pass that
after we had thus taken care of our
wounded men, and had buried our
dead and also the dead of the
Lamanites, who were many, behold,
we did inquire of Gid concerning the
[a]prisoners whom they had started
to go down to the land of Zarahemla
with.
29 Now Gid was the chief captain
over the band who was appointed
to guard them down to the land.
30 And now, these are the words
which Gid said unto me: Behold,
we did start to go down to the land
of Zarahemla with our prisoners.
And it came to pass that we did
meet the spies of our armies, who

17*a* Alma 57:28.
19*a* Alma 62:11.
21*a* TG Trustworthiness.
b Alma 56:47 (47–48).
25*a* Alma 56:56.
26*a* 1 Chr. 5:20 (18–22).
b TG God, Power of.
c TG Faith.
27*a* Alma 43:13.
b Jacob 3:2.
28*a* Alma 57:17 (16–17).

[About 63 B.C.]

had been sent out to watch the camp of the Lamanites.

31 And they cried unto us, saying—Behold, the armies of the Lamanites are marching towards the city of Cumeni; and behold, they will fall upon them, yea, and will destroy our people.

32 And it came to pass that our prisoners did hear their cries, which caused them to take courage; and they did rise up in rebellion against us.

33 And it came to pass because of their rebellion we did cause that our swords should come upon them. And it came to pass that they did in a body run upon our swords, in the which, the greater number of them were slain; and the remainder of them broke through and fled from us.

34 And behold, when they had fled and we could not overtake them, we took our march with speed towards the city Cumeni; and behold, we did arrive in time that we might assist our brethren in preserving the city.

35 And behold, we are again delivered out of the hands of our enemies. And blessed is the name of our God; for behold, it is he that has delivered us; yea, that has done this great thing for us.

36 Now it came to pass that when I, Helaman, had heard these words of Gid, I was filled with exceeding joy because of the goodness of God in preserving us, that we might not all perish; yea, and I trust that the souls of them who have been slain have [a]entered into the rest of their God.

CHAPTER 58

Helaman, Gid, and Teomner take the city of Manti by a stratagem—The Lamanites withdraw—The sons of the people of Ammon are preserved as they stand fast in defense of their liberty and faith.

AND behold, now it came to pass that our next object was to obtain the city of Manti; but behold, there was no way that we could lead them out of the city by our small bands. For behold, they remembered that which we had hitherto done; therefore we could not [a]decoy them away from their strongholds.

2 And they were so much more numerous than was our army that we durst not go forth and attack them in their strongholds.

3 Yea, and it became expedient that we should employ our men to the maintaining those parts of the land which we had regained of our possessions; therefore it became expedient that we should wait, that we might receive more strength from the land of Zarahemla and also a new supply of provisions.

4 And it came to pass that I thus did send an embassy to the governor of our land, to acquaint him concerning the affairs of our people. And it came to pass that we did wait to receive provisions and strength from the land of Zarahemla.

5 But behold, this did profit us but little; for the Lamanites were also receiving great strength from day to day, and also many provisions; and thus were our circumstances at this period of time.

6 And the Lamanites were sallying forth against us from time to time, resolving by stratagem to destroy us; nevertheless we could not come to battle with them, because of their [a]retreats and their strongholds.

7 And it came to pass that we did wait in these difficult circumstances for the space of many months, even until we were about to [a]perish for the want of food.

8 But it came to pass that we did receive food, which was guarded to us by an army of two thousand men to our assistance; and this is all the assistance which we did receive, to defend ourselves and our country

36*a* Alma 12:34.
58 1*a* Alma 52:21; 56:30.
6*a* 1 Sam. 24:22; 3 Ne. 4:1.
7*a* Alma 60:9.

from falling into the hands of our
enemies, yea, to contend with an
enemy which was innumerable.
9 And now the cause of these our
embarrassments, or the cause why
they did not send more strength
unto us, we knew not; therefore we
were grieved and also filled with
fear, lest by any means the judgments of God should come upon our
land, to our overthrow and utter
destruction.
10 Therefore we did pour out our
souls in prayer to God, that he
would strengthen us and deliver us
out of the hands of our enemies, yea,
and also give us strength that we
might retain our cities, and our
lands, and our possessions, for the
support of our people.
11 Yea, and it came to pass that
the Lord our God did visit us with
assurances that he would deliver
us; yea, insomuch that he did speak
peace to our souls, and did grant
unto us great faith, and did cause us
that we should hope for our [a]deliver-
ance in him.
12 And we did take courage with
our small force which we had
received, and were fixed with a
determination to conquer our
enemies, and to [a]maintain our
lands, and our possessions, and our
wives, and our children, and the
cause of our [b]liberty.
13 And thus we did go forth with all
our might against the Lamanites,
who were in the city of Manti; and
we did pitch our tents by the wilderness side, which was near to the city.
14 And it came to pass that on the
morrow, that when the Lamanites
saw that we were in the borders by
the wilderness which was near the
city, that they sent out their spies
round about us that they might
discover the number and the
strength of our army.
15 And it came to pass that when
they saw that we were not strong,
according to our numbers, and
fearing that we should cut them off
from their support except they
should come out to battle against
us and kill us, and also supposing
that they could easily destroy
us with their numerous hosts,
therefore they began to make
preparations to come out against us
to battle.
16 And when we saw that they
were making preparations to come
out against us, behold, I caused that
Gid, with a small number of men,
should [a]secrete himself in the
wilderness, and also that Teomner
and a small number of men should
secrete themselves also in the
wilderness.
17 Now Gid and his men were on
the right and the others on the left;
and when they had thus secreted
themselves, behold, I remained,
with the remainder of my army, in
that same place where we had first
pitched our tents against the time
that the Lamanites should come
out to battle.
18 And it came to pass that the
Lamanites did come out with their
numerous army against us. And
when they had come and were about
to fall upon us with the sword, I
caused that my men, those who were
with me, should retreat into the
wilderness.
19 And it came to pass that the
Lamanites did follow after us with
great speed, for they were exceedingly desirous to overtake us that
they might slay us; therefore they
did follow us into the wilderness;
and we did pass by in the midst of
Gid and Teomner, insomuch that
they were not discovered by the
Lamanites.
20 And it came to pass that when
the Lamanites had passed by, or
when the army had passed by, Gid
and Teomner did rise up from their
secret places, and did cut off the
spies of the Lamanites that they
should not return to the city.

11*a* TG Deliverance.
12*a* Alma 46:12; 3 Ne. 2:12; Morm. 2:23.
b TG Liberty.
16*a* Josh. 8:13; Alma 43:31 (30–43); 52:21 (21–31).

[About 63 B.C.]

21 And it came to pass that when they had cut them off, they ran to the city and fell upon the guards who were left to guard the city, insomuch that they did destroy them and did take possession of the city.

22 Now this was done because the Lamanites did suffer their whole army, save a few guards only, to be led away into the wilderness.

23 And it came to pass that Gid and Teomner by this means had obtained possession of their strongholds. And it came to pass that we took our course, after having traveled much in the wilderness towards the land of Zarahemla.

24 And when the Lamanites saw that they were marching towards the land of Zarahemla, they were exceedingly afraid, lest there was a plan laid to lead them on to destruction; therefore they began to retreat into the wilderness again, yea, even back by the same way which they had come.

25 And behold, it was night and they did pitch their tents, for the chief [a]captains of the Lamanites had supposed that the Nephites were weary because of their march; and supposing that they had driven their whole army therefore they took no thought concerning the city of Manti.

26 Now it came to pass that when it was night, I caused that my men should not sleep, but that they should march forward by another way towards the land of Manti.

27 And because of this our march in the night-time, behold, on the morrow we were beyond the Lamanites, insomuch that we did arrive before them at the city of Manti.

28 And thus it came to pass, that by this stratagem we did take possession of the city of Manti without the shedding of blood.

29 And it came to pass that when the armies of the Lamanites did arrive near the city, and saw that we were prepared to meet them, they were astonished exceedingly and struck with great fear, insomuch that they did [a]flee into the wilderness.

30 Yea, and it came to pass that the armies of the Lamanites did flee out of all this quarter of the land. But behold, they have carried with them many women and children out of the land.

31 And [a]those cities which had been taken by the Lamanites, all of them are at this period of time in our possession; and our fathers and our women and our children are returning to their homes, all save it be those who have been taken prisoners and carried off by the Lamanites.

32 But behold, our armies are small to maintain so great a number of cities and so great possessions.

33 But behold, we [a]trust in our God who has given us victory over those lands, insomuch that we have obtained those cities and those lands, which were our own.

34 Now we do not know the [a]cause that the government does not grant us more strength; neither do those men who came up unto us know why we have not received greater strength.

35 Behold, we do not know but what [a]ye are unsuccessful, and ye have drawn away the forces into that quarter of the land; if so, we do not desire to murmur.

36 And if it is not so, behold, we fear that there is some [a]faction in the government, that they do not send more men to our assistance; for we know that they are more numerous than that which they have sent.

37 But, behold, it mattereth not—we trust God will [a]deliver us, notwithstanding the weakness of our

25*a* Alma 59: 12.
29*a* Alma 59: 6.
31*a* Alma 51: 26 (25–27); 59: 1.
33*a* TG Trust in God.
34*a* Alma 59: 13.
35*a* Alma 56: 1.
36*a* Alma 61: 3.
37*a* 2 Kgs. 17: 39.

[About 63 B.C.]

armies, yea, and deliver us out of
the hands of our enemies.
38 Behold, this is the twenty and
ninth year, in the latter end, and
we are in the possession of our lands;
and the Lamanites have fled to the
land of Nephi.
39 And those sons of the people of
Ammon, of whom I have so highly
spoken, are with me in the city of
Manti; and the Lord has supported
them, yea, and kept them from
falling by the sword, insomuch that
even [a]one soul has not been slain.
40 But behold, they have received
many wounds; nevertheless they
[a]stand fast in that [b]liberty wherewith God has made them free; and
they are strict to remember the
Lord their God from day to day;
yea, they do observe to keep his
statutes, and his judgments, and
his commandments continually;
and their faith is strong in the
prophecies concerning that which is
to come.
41 And now, my beloved brother,
Moroni, may the Lord our God, who
has redeemed us and made us free,
keep you continually in his presence; yea, and may he favor this
people, even that ye may have success in obtaining the possession of all
that which the Lamanites have
taken from us, which was for our
support. And now, behold, I close
mine epistle. I am Helaman, the
son of Alma.

CHAPTER 59

Moroni asks Pahoran to strengthen the forces of Helaman—The Lamanites take the city of Nephihah—Moroni is angry with the government.

Now it came to pass in the *thirtieth year of the reign of the judges
over the people of Nephi, after
Moroni had received and had read
Helaman's [a]epistle, he was exceedingly rejoiced because of the welfare,
yea, the exceeding success which
Helaman had had, in obtaining
[b]those lands which were lost.
2 Yea, and he did make it known
unto all his people, in all the land
round about in that part where he
was, that they might rejoice also.
3 And it came to pass that he immediately sent [a]an epistle to [b]Pahor-
an, desiring that he should cause
men to be gathered together to
strengthen Helaman, or the armies
of Helaman, insomuch that he
might with ease maintain that part
of the land which he had been so
miraculously prospered in regaining.
4 And it came to pass when
Moroni had sent this epistle to the
land of Zarahemla, he began again
to lay a plan that he might obtain
the remainder of those possessions
and cities which the Lamanites had
taken from them.
5 And it came to pass that while
Moroni was thus making preparations to go against the Lamanites to
battle, behold, the people of [a]Nephi-
hah, who were gathered together
from the city of Moroni and the city
of Lehi and the city of Morianton,
were attacked by the Lamanites.
6 Yea, even those who had been
[a]compelled to flee from the land of
Manti, and from the land round
about, had come over and joined the
Lamanites in this part of the land.
7 And thus being exceedingly
numerous, yea, and receiving
strength from day to day, by the
command of Ammoron they came
forth against the people of Nephihah, and they did begin to slay
them with an exceedingly great
slaughter.
8 And their armies were so numerous that the remainder of the
people of [a]Nephihah were [b]obliged
to flee before them; and they came
even and joined the army of Moroni.

39*a* Alma 56: 56.
40*a* Alma 61: 21.
TG Trustworthiness.
b TG Liberty.
59 1*a* Alma 56: 1.
b Alma 58: 31 (31, 41).
3*a* Alma 60: 1 (1–3).
b Alma 50: 40.
5*a* Alma 50: 14.
6*a* Alma 58: 29 (29–30).
8*a* Alma 62: 26.
b Alma 60: 17.

[*62 B.C.]

9 And now as Moroni had supposed that there [a]should be men sent to the city of Nephihah, to the assistance of the people to maintain that city, and knowing that it was easier to keep the city from falling into the hands of the Lamanites than to retake it from them, he supposed that they would easily maintain that city.

10 Therefore he retained all his force to maintain those places which he had recovered.

11 And now, when Moroni saw that the city of Nephihah was [a]lost he was exceedingly sorrowful, and began to doubt, because of the wickedness of the people, whether they should not fall into the hands of their brethren.

12 Now this was the case with all his chief captains. They doubted and marveled also because of the wickedness of the people, and this because of the success of the Lamanites over them.

13 And it came to pass that Moroni was angry with the government, because of their [a]indifference concerning the freedom of their country.

CHAPTER 60

Moroni complains to Pahoran of the government's neglect of the armies—The Lord suffers the righteous to be slain—The Nephites must use all of their power and means to deliver themselves from their enemies—Moroni threatens to fight against the government unless help is supplied to his armies.

AND it came to pass that he wrote [a]again to the governor of the land, who was Pahoran, and these are the words which he wrote, saying: Behold, I direct mine epistle to Pahoran, in the city of Zarahemla, who is the chief judge and the [b]governor over the land, and also to all those who have been chosen by this people to govern and manage the affairs of this war.

2 For behold, I have somewhat to say unto them by the way of [a]condemnation; for behold, ye yourselves know that ye have been appointed to gather together men, and arm them with swords, and with cimeters, and all manner of weapons of war of every kind, and send forth against the Lamanites, in whatsoever parts they should come into our land.

3 And now behold, I say unto you that myself, and also my men, and also Helaman and his men, have suffered exceedingly great [a]sufferings; yea, even hunger, thirst, and fatigue, and all manner of afflictions of every kind.

4 But behold, were this all we had suffered we would not murmur nor complain.

5 But behold, great has been the slaughter among our people; yea, thousands have fallen by the sword, while it might have otherwise been if ye had rendered unto our armies sufficient strength and succor for them. Yea, great has been your neglect towards us.

6 And now behold, we desire to know the cause of this exceedingly great neglect; yea, we desire to know the cause of your thoughtless state.

7 Can you think to sit upon your thrones in a state of thoughtless [a]stupor, while your enemies are spreading the work of death around you? Yea, while they are murdering thousands of your brethren—

8 Yea, even they who have looked up to you for protection, yea, have placed you in a situation that ye might have succored them, yea, ye might have sent armies unto them, to have strengthened them, and have saved thousands of them from falling by the sword.

9*a* Alma 60: 15.
11*a* Alma 62: 14.
13*a* Alma 58: 34; 61: 3.

60 1*a* Alma 59: 3.
b Alma 50: 39.
2*a* TG Reproof.

3*a* Alma 61: 2.
7*a* TG Apathy.

[About 62 B.C.]

9 But behold, this is not all—ye
have withheld your provisions from
them, insomuch that many have
fought and bled out their lives
because of their great desires which
they had for the welfare of this
people; yea, and this they have done
when they were about to [a]perish
with hunger, because of your exceedingly great neglect towards them.
10 And now, my beloved brethren—for ye ought to be beloved;
yea, and ye ought to have stirred
yourselves more diligently for the
welfare and the freedom of this
people; but behold, ye have neglected them insomuch that the
blood of thousands shall come upon
your heads for vengeance; yea, for
[a]known unto God were all their
cries, and all their sufferings—
11 Behold, could ye suppose that
ye could sit upon your thrones, and
because of the exceeding goodness
of God ye could do nothing and he
would deliver you? Behold, if ye
have supposed this ye have supposed in vain.
12 Do ye [a]suppose that, because so
many of your brethren have been
killed it is because of their wickedness? I say unto you, if ye have supposed this ye have supposed in vain;
for I say unto you, there are many
who have fallen by the sword; and
behold it is to your condemnation;
13 For the Lord suffereth the
[a]righteous to be slain that his justice
and [b]judgment may come upon the
wicked; therefore ye need not suppose that the righteous are lost
because they are slain; but behold,
they do enter into the rest of the
Lord their God.
14 And now behold, I say unto
you, I fear exceedingly that the
judgments of God will come upon
this people, because of their exceeding [a]slothfulness, yea, even the
slothfulness of our government, and
their exceedingly great neglect towards their brethren, yea, towards
those who have been slain.
15 For were it not for the wickedness which first commenced at our
head, we [a]could have withstood our
enemies that they could have gained
no power over us.
16 Yea, had it not been for the war
which broke out [a]among ourselves;
yea, were it not for these [b]king-men,
who caused so much bloodshed
among ourselves; yea, at the time
we were contending among ourselves, if we had united our strength
as we hitherto have done; yea, had it
not been for the desire of power and
authority which those king-men
had over us; had they been true to
the cause of our freedom, and united
with us, and gone forth against our
enemies, instead of taking up their
swords against us, which was the
cause of so much bloodshed among
ourselves; yea, if we had gone forth
against them in the strength of the
Lord, we should have dispersed our
enemies, for it would have been
done, according to the [c]fulfilling of
his word.
17 But behold, now the Lamanites
are coming upon us, taking [a]pos-
session of our lands, and they are
murdering our people with the
sword, yea, our women and our
children, and also carrying them
away captive, causing them that
they should suffer all manner of
afflictions, and this because of the
great wickedness of those who are
seeking for power and authority,
yea, even those king-men.
18 But why should I say much concerning this matter? For we know
not but what ye yourselves are
seeking for authority. We know not
but what ye are also [a]traitors to your
country.

9*a* Alma 58: 7 (7–9).
10*a* Ex. 3: 9; Ps. 9: 12.
12*a* Luke 13: 2 (1–2).
13*a* Lam. 4: 13; D&C 42: 46.
b Alma 14: 11 (10–11); D&C 103: 3.
14*a* TG Laziness.
15*a* Alma 59: 9.
16*a* Alma 51: 19 (5–7, 13–27).
b Alma 62: 9.
c Alma 38: 1.
17*a* Alma 59: 8 (5–8).
18*a* Alma 62: 1.

[About 62 B.C.]

19 Or is it that ye have neglected us because ye are in the heart of our country and ye are [a]surrounded by security, that ye do not cause food to be sent unto us, and also men to strengthen our armies?
20 Have ye forgotten the commandments of the Lord your God? Yea, have ye forgotten the captivity of our fathers? Have ye forgotten the many times we have been delivered out of the hands of our enemies?
21 Or do ye suppose that the Lord [a]will still deliver us, while we sit upon our thrones and do not make use of the means which the Lord has provided for us?
22 Yea, will ye sit in idleness while ye are surrounded with thousands of those, yea, and tens of thousands, who do also sit in idleness, while there are thousands round about in the borders of the land who are falling by the sword, yea, wounded and bleeding?
23 Do ye suppose that God will look upon you as guiltless while ye sit still and behold these things? Behold I say unto you, Nay. Now I would that ye should remember that God has said that the [a]inward vessel shall be [b]cleansed first, and then shall the outer vessel be cleansed also.
24 And now, except ye do repent of that which ye have done, and begin to be up and doing, and send forth food and men unto us, and also unto Helaman, that he may support those parts of our country which he has regained, and that we may also recover the remainder of our possessions in these parts, behold it will be expedient that we contend no more with the Lamanites until we have first cleansed our inward vessel, yea, even the great head of our government.
25 And except ye grant mine epistle, and come out and show unto me a true [a]spirit of freedom, and strive to strengthen and fortify our armies, and grant unto them food for their support, behold I will leave a part of my freemen to maintain this part of our land, and I will leave the strength and the blessings of God upon them, that none other power can operate against them—
26 And this because of their exceeding faith, and their patience in their [a]tribulations—
27 And I will come unto you, and if there be any among you that has a desire for freedom, yea, if there be even a spark of freedom remaining, behold I will stir up insurrections among you, even until those who have desires to usurp power and authority shall become extinct.
28 Yea, behold I do not fear your power nor your authority, but it is my [a]God whom I fear; and it is according to his commandments that I do take my sword to defend the cause of my country, and it is because of your iniquity that we have suffered so much loss.
29 Behold it is time, yea, the time is now at hand, that except ye do bestir yourselves in the defence of your country and your little ones, the [a]sword of justice doth hang over you; yea, and it shall fall upon you and visit you even to your utter destruction.
30 Behold, I wait for assistance from you; and, except ye do administer unto our relief, behold, I come unto you, even in the land of Zarahemla, and smite you with the sword, insomuch that ye can have no more power to impede the progress of this people in the cause of our freedom.
31 For behold, the Lord will not suffer that ye shall live and wax strong in your iniquities to destroy his righteous people.
32 Behold, can you suppose that the Lord will spare you and come

19*a* TG Apathy.
21*a* 1 Ne. 17: 23 (23–35).
23*a* Matt. 23: 26 (25–26).
b TG Purification.
25*a* Alma 51: 6 (6–7); 61: 15.
26*a* TG Tribulation.
28*a* Acts 5: 29 (26–29).
29*a* Isa. 1: 20 (19–20); Hel. 13: 5; 3 Ne. 2: 19.

[About 62 B.C.]

out in judgment against the Lamanites, when it is the [a]tradition of their fathers that has caused their hatred, yea, and it has been redoubled by those who have dissented from us, while your iniquity is for the cause of your love of glory and the vain things of the world?
33 Ye know that ye do transgress the laws of God, and ye do know that ye do trample them under your feet. Behold, the Lord saith unto me: If those whom ye have appointed your governors do not repent of their sins and [a]iniquities, ye shall [b]go up to battle against them.
34 And now behold, I, Moroni, am constrained, according to the covenant which I have made to keep the commandments of my God; therefore I would that ye should adhere to the word of God, and send speedily unto me of your provisions and of your men, and also to Helaman.
35 And behold, if ye will not do this I come unto you speedily; for behold, God will not suffer that we should perish with hunger; therefore he will give unto us of your food, even if it must be by the sword. Now see that ye fulfil the word of God.
36 Behold, I am Moroni, your chief captain. I [a]seek not for power, but to pull it down. I [b]seek not for honor of the world, but for the glory of my God, and the freedom and welfare of my country. And thus I close mine epistle.

CHAPTER 61

Pahoran tells Moroni of the insurrection and rebellion against the government—The king-men take Zarahemla and are in league with the Lamanites—Pahoran asks for military aid against the rebels.

BEHOLD, now it came to pass that soon after Moroni had sent his epistle unto the chief governor, he received an epistle from [a]Pahoran, the chief governor. And these are the words which he received:
2 I, Pahoran, who am the chief governor of this land, do send these words unto Moroni, the chief captain over the army. Behold, I say unto you, Moroni, that I do not joy in your great [a]afflictions, yea, it grieves my soul.
3 But behold, there are those who do joy in your afflictions, yea, insomuch that they have risen up in [a]rebellion against me, and also those of my people who are [b]freemen, yea, and those who have risen up are exceedingly numerous.
4 And it is those who have sought to take away the judgment-seat from me that have been the cause of this great iniquity; for they have used great [a]flattery, and they have [b]led away the hearts of many people, which will be the cause of sore affliction among us; they have withheld our provisions, and have daunted our [c]freemen that they have not come unto you.
5 And behold, they have driven me out before them, and I have fled to the land of Gideon, with as many men as it were possible that I could get.
6 And behold, I have sent a proclamation throughout this part of the land; and behold, they are [a]flocking to us [b]daily, to their arms, in the defence of their country and their [c]freedom, and to avenge our [d]wrongs.
7 And they have come unto us, insomuch that those who have risen up in rebellion against us are set at defiance, yea, insomuch that they do fear us and durst not come out against us to battle.

32*a* Alma 17:15.
33*a* Alma 61:18.
b Alma 61:20.
36*a* Alma 61:9; D&C 121:39.
b TG Motivations.

61 1*a* Alma 50:40.
2*a* Alma 60:3 (3–9).
3*a* Alma 58:36; 59:13.
b Alma 51:6 (6–7).
4*a* TG Flattery.
b TG Peer Influence.
c Alma 51:6 (6–7); 62:6.
6*a* Alma 62:5.
b Acts 2:47.
c TG Liberty.
d TG Injustice.

[About 62 B.C.]

8 They have [a]got possession of the land, or the city, of Zarahemla; they have appointed a [b]king over them, and he hath written unto the king of the Lamanites, in the which he hath joined an alliance with him; in the which alliance he hath agreed to maintain the city of Zarahemla, which maintenance he supposeth will enable the Lamanites to conquer the remainder of the land, and he shall be placed king over this people when they shall be conquered [c]under the Lamanites.

9 And now, in your epistle you have [a]censured me, but it mattereth not; I am not angry, but do rejoice in the greatness of your heart. I, Pahoran, do not [b]seek for power, save only to retain my judgment-seat that I may preserve the rights and the liberty of my people. My soul standeth fast in that liberty in the which God hath made us [c]free.

10 And now, behold, we will resist wickedness even unto bloodshed. We would [a]not shed the blood of the Lamanites if they would stay in their own land.

11 We would not shed the blood of our brethren if they would not rise up in rebellion and take the sword against us.

12 We would subject ourselves to the [a]yoke of bondage if it were requisite with the justice of God, or if he should command us so to do.

13 But behold he doth not command us that we shall subject ourselves to our enemies, but that we should put our [a]trust in him, and he will deliver us.

14 Therefore, my beloved brother, Moroni, let us resist evil, and whatsoever evil we cannot resist with our [a]words, yea, such as rebellions and dissensions, let us [b]resist them with our swords, that we may retain our freedom, that we may rejoice in the great privilege of our church, and in the cause of our Redeemer and our God.

15 Therefore, come unto me speedily with a few of your men, and leave the remainder in the charge of Lehi and Teancum; give unto them power to conduct the [a]war in that part of the land, according to the [b]Spirit of God, which is also the [c]spirit of freedom which is in them.

16 Behold I have sent a few provisions unto them, that they may not perish until ye can come unto me.

17 Gather together whatsoever force ye can upon your march hither, and we will go speedily against those dissenters, in the strength of our God according to the faith which is in us.

18 And we will [a]take possession of the city of Zarahemla, that we may obtain more food to send forth unto Lehi and Teancum; yea, we will go forth against them in the strength of the Lord, and we will put an end to this great iniquity.

19 And now, Moroni, I do joy in receiving your epistle, for I was somewhat worried concerning what we should do, whether it should be just in us to go against our brethren.

20 But ye have said, except they repent the Lord [a]hath commanded you that ye should go against them.

21 See that ye [a]strengthen Lehi and Teancum in the Lord; tell them to fear not, for God will deliver them, yea, and also all those who [b]stand fast in that liberty wherewith God hath made them free. And now I close mine epistle to my beloved brother, Moroni.

8*a* Alma 61: 18.
b Alma 62: 6. TG Tyranny.
c Mosiah 7: 21.
9*a* D&C 101: 5. TG Reproof.
b Alma 60: 36; D&C 121: 39.
c John 8: 36; Gal. 5: 1; D&C 88: 86.
10*a* Alma 56: 46.
12*a* TG Bondage, Physical; Submissiveness.
13*a* TG Trust in God.
14*a* TG Reproof.
b Alma 43: 47.
15*a* TG War.
b 2 Cor. 3: 17. TG God, Spirit of.
c Alma 60: 25.
18*a* Alma 61: 8.
20*a* Alma 60: 33.
21*a* Zech. 10: 12.
b Alma 58: 40.

[About 62 B.C.]

CHAPTER 62

Moroni marches to the aid of Pahoran in the land of Gideon—The king-men who refuse to defend their country are put to death—Pahoran and Moroni retake Nephihah—Many Lamanites join the people of Ammon—Teancum slays Ammoron and is in turn slain—The Lamanites are driven from the land, and peace is established—Helaman returns to the ministry and builds up the Church.

AND now it came to pass that when Moroni had received this epistle his heart did take courage, and was filled with exceedingly great joy because of the faithfulness of Pahoran, that he was not also a [a]traitor to the freedom and cause of his country.

2 But he did also mourn exceedingly because of the iniquity of those who had driven Pahoran from the judgment-seat, yea, in fine because of those who had rebelled against their country and also their God.

3 And it came to pass that Moroni took a small number of men, according to the desire of Pahoran, and gave Lehi and Teancum command over the remainder of his army, and took his march towards the land of Gideon.

4 And he did raise the [a]standard of [b]liberty in whatsoever place he did enter, and gained whatsoever force he could in all his march towards the land of Gideon.

5 And it came to pass that thousands did [a]flock unto his standard, and did take up their swords in the defence of their freedom, that they might not come into bondage.

6 And thus, when Moroni had gathered together whatsoever men he could in all his march, he came to the land of Gideon; and uniting his forces with those of Pahoran they became exceedingly strong, even stronger than the men of Pachus, who was the [a]king of those dissenters who had driven the [b]freemen out of the land of Zarahemla and had taken possession of the land.

7 And it came to pass that Moroni and Pahoran went down with their armies into the land of Zarahemla, and went forth against the city, and did meet the men of Pachus, insomuch that they did come to battle.

8 And behold, Pachus was slain and his men were taken prisoners, and Pahoran was restored to his judgment-seat.

9 And the men of Pachus received their trial, according to the law, and also those king-men who had been taken and [a]cast into prison; and they were [b]executed according to the law; yea, those men of Pachus and those [c]king-men, whosoever would not take up arms in the defence of their country, but would fight against it, were put to death.

10 And thus it became expedient that this law should be strictly observed for the safety of their country; yea, and whosoever was found denying their freedom was speedily [a]executed according to the law.

11 And thus ended the thirtieth year of the reign of the judges over the people of Nephi; Moroni and Pahoran having restored peace to the land of Zarahemla, among their own people, having [a]inflicted death upon all those who were not true to the cause of freedom.

12 And it came to pass in the *commencement of the thirty and first year of the reign of the judges over the people of Nephi, Moroni immediately caused that provisions should be sent, and also an army of six thousand men should be sent unto Helaman, to assist him in preserving that part of the land.

13 And he also caused that an

62 1*a* Alma 60: 18.
4*a* Alma 46: 36 (12–13, 36).
b TG Liberty.
5*a* Alma 61: 6.
6*a* Alma 61: 8 (4–8).
b Alma 51: 6 (6–7).
9*a* Alma 51: 19.
b TG Capital Punishment.
c Alma 51: 5 (5, 17, 21); 60: 16.
10*a* 1 Kgs. 2: 46.
11*a* Alma 44: 7; 57: 19.

[*61 B.C.]

army of six thousand men, with a
sufficient quantity of food, should
be sent to the armies of Lehi and
Teancum. And it came to pass that
this was done to fortify the land
against the Lamanites.
14 And it came to pass that Moroni
and Pahoran, leaving a large body
of men in the land of Zarahemla,
took their march with a large body
of men towards the land of Nephihah, being determined to [a]over-
throw the Lamanites in that city.
15 And it came to pass that as they
were marching towards the land,
they took a large body of men of
the Lamanites, and slew many of
them, and took their provisions and
their weapons of war.
16 And it came to pass after they
had taken them, they caused them
to enter into a [a]covenant that they
would no more take up their weapons
of war against the Nephites.
17 And when they had entered into
this covenant they sent them to
[a]dwell with the people of Ammon,
and they were in number about four
thousand who had not been slain.
18 And it came to pass that when
they had sent them away they
pursued their march towards the
land of [a]Nephihah. And it came to
pass that when they had come to
the city of Nephihah, they did pitch
their tents in the plains of Nephihah,
which is near the city of Nephihah.
19 Now Moroni was desirous that
the Lamanites should come out to
battle against them, upon the
plains; but the Lamanites, knowing
of their exceedingly great courage,
and beholding the greatness of
their numbers, therefore they durst
not come out against them; therefore they did not come to battle in
that day.
20 And when the night came,
Moroni went forth in the darkness of
the night, and came upon the top of
the wall to spy out in what part of
the city the Lamanites did camp
with their army.
21 And it came to pass that they
were on the east, by the entrance;
and they were all asleep. And now
Moroni returned to his army, and
caused that they should prepare in
haste strong cords and ladders, to
be let down from the top of the [a]wall
into the inner part of the wall.
22 And it came to pass that Moroni
caused that his men should march
forth and come upon the top of the
wall, and let [a]themselves down into
that part of the city, yea, even on
the west, where the Lamanites did
not camp with their armies.
23 And it came to pass that they
were all let down into the city by
night, by the means of their strong
cords and their ladders; thus when
the morning came they were all
within the walls of the city.
24 And now, when the Lamanites
awoke and saw that the armies of
Moroni were within the walls, they
were affrighted exceedingly, insomuch that they did flee out by the
pass.
25 And now when Moroni saw that
they were fleeing before him, he did
cause that his men should march
forth against them, and slew many,
and surrounded many others, and
took them prisoners; and the
remainder of them fled into the land
of Moroni, which was in the borders
by the seashore.
26 Thus had Moroni and Pahoran
obtained the [a]possession of the city
of Nephihah without the loss of one
soul; and there were many of the
Lamanites who were slain.
27 Now it came to pass that many
of the Lamanites that were prisoners
were desirous to [a]join the people of
Ammon and become a free people.
28 And it came to pass that as many
as were desirous, unto them it was
granted according to their desires.
29 Therefore, all the prisoners of

14*a* Alma 59: 11 (5–11).
16*a* Alma 44: 15, 20; 3 Ne. 5: 4.
17*a* Alma 47: 29.
18*a* Alma 50: 14; 51: 26 (24–26).
21*a* Alma 49: 13 (13,18–24).
22*a* Alma 55: 16.
26*a* Alma 59: 8.
27*a* Alma 24: 26 (25–27).

[About 61 B.C.]

the Lamanites did join the people of Ammon, and did begin to labor exceedingly, tilling the ground, raising all manner of grain, and flocks and herds of every kind; and thus were the Nephites relieved from a great burden; yea, insomuch that they were relieved from all the prisoners of the Lamanites.
30 Now it came to pass that Moroni, after he had obtained possession of the city of Nephihah, having taken many prisoners, which did reduce the armies of the Lamanites exceedingly, and having regained many of the Nephites who had been taken prisoners, which did strengthen the army of Moroni exceedingly; therefore Moroni went forth from the land of Nephihah to the land of [a]Lehi.
31 And it came to pass that when the Lamanites saw that Moroni was coming against them, they were again frightened and fled before the army of Moroni.
32 And it came to pass that [a]Moroni and his army did pursue them from city to city, until they were met by Lehi and Teancum; and the Lamanites fled from Lehi and Teancum, even down upon the borders by the seashore, until they came to the land of Moroni.
33 And the armies of the Lamanites were all gathered together, insomuch that they were all in one body in the land of Moroni. Now Ammoron, the king of the Lamanites, was also with them.
34 And it came to pass that Moroni and Lehi and Teancum did encamp with their armies round about in the borders of the land of Moroni, insomuch that the Lamanites were encircled about in the borders by the wilderness on the south, and in the borders by the wilderness on the east.
35 And thus they did encamp for the night. For behold, the Nephites and the Lamanites also were weary because of the greatness of the march; therefore they did not resolve upon any stratagem in the night-time, save it were Teancum; for he was exceedingly angry with Ammoron, insomuch that he considered that Ammoron, and Amalickiah his brother, had been the [a]cause of this great and lasting war between them and the Lamanites, which had been the cause of so much war and bloodshed, yea, and so much famine.
36 And it came to pass that Teancum in his anger did go forth into the camp of the Lamanites, and did let himself down over the walls of the city. And he went forth with a cord, from place to place, insomuch that he did find the king; and he did [a]cast a javelin at him, which did pierce him near the heart. But behold, the king did awaken his servants before he died, insomuch that they did pursue Teancum, and slew him.
37 Now it came to pass that when Lehi and Moroni knew that Teancum was dead they were exceedingly sorrowful; for behold, he had been a man who had [a]fought valiantly for his country, yea, a true friend to liberty; and he had suffered very many exceedingly sore afflictions. But behold, he was dead, and had gone the way of all the earth.
38 Now it came to pass that Moroni marched forth on the morrow, and came upon the Lamanites, insomuch that they did slay them with a great slaughter; and they did drive them out of the land; and they did flee, even that they did not return at that time against the Nephites.
39 And thus *ended the thirty and first year of the reign of the judges over the people of Nephi; and thus they had had wars, and bloodsheds, and famine, and affliction, for the space of many years.
40 And there had been murders,

30*a* Alma 50: 15; 51: 26 (24–26).
32*a* Alma 50: 13; 51: 22 (22–23); 3 Ne. 8: 9.
35*a* Alma 48: 1.
36*a* Alma 51: 34.
37*a* IE throughout the Amalickiah–Ammoron wars, Alma 50: 35; 51: 29–34; 52; 61; 62: 3–37.

[*60 B.C.]

and contentions, and dissensions,
and all manner of iniquity among
the people of Nephi; nevertheless
for the [a]righteous' sake, yea, because
of the prayers of the righteous, they
were spared.
41 But behold, because of the
exceedingly great length of the war
between the Nephites and the
Lamanites many had become hardened, because of the exceedingly
great length of the war; and many
were softened because of their
[a]afflictions, insomuch that they did
humble themselves before God, even
in the depth of humility.
42 And it came to pass that after
Moroni had fortified those parts of
the land which were most exposed
to the Lamanites, until they were
sufficiently strong, he returned to
the city of Zarahemla; and also
Helaman returned to the place of
his inheritance; and there was once
more peace established among the
people of Nephi.
43 And Moroni yielded up the
[a]command of his armies into the
hands of his son, whose name was
[b]Moronihah; and he retired to his
own house that he might spend the
remainder of his days in peace.
44 And Pahoran did return to his
judgment-seat; and Helaman did
take upon him again to preach unto
the people the word of God; for
because of so many wars and contentions it had become expedient
that a [a]regulation should be made
again in the church.
45 Therefore, Helaman and his
brethren went forth, and did declare
the word of God with much power
unto the [a]convincing of many people
of their wickedness, which did cause
them to repent of their sins and to
be baptized unto the Lord their
God.
46 And it came to pass that they
did establish again the church of
God, throughout all the land.
47 Yea, and regulations were made
concerning the law. And their
[a]judges, and their chief judges were
chosen.
48 And the people of Nephi began
to [a]prosper again in the land, and
began to multiply and to wax
exceedingly strong again in the land.
And they began to grow exceedingly
rich.
49 But notwithstanding their
riches, or their strength, or their
prosperity, they were not lifted up
in the pride of their eyes; neither
were they [a]slow to remember the
Lord their God; but they did humble
themselves exceedingly before him.
50 Yea, they did remember how
great things the Lord had done for
them, that he had [a]delivered them
from death, and from bonds, and
from prisons, and from all manner of
[b]afflictions, and he had [c]delivered
them out of the hands of their
enemies.
51 And they did pray unto the Lord
their God continually, insomuch
that the Lord did bless them, according to his word, so that they did wax
strong and [a]prosper in the land.
52 And it came to pass that all
these things were done. And [a]Hela-
man died, in the *thirty and fifth
year of the reign of the judges over
the people of Nephi.

CHAPTER 63

Shiblon and later Helaman take possession of the sacred records—Many Nephites travel to the land northward—Hagoth builds ships, which sail forth in the west sea—Moronihah defeats the Lamanites in battle.

40*a* Alma 45: 15 (15–16); 46: 10.
41*a* TG Adversity; Affliction.
43*a* Hel. 4: 16 (10, 16).
b Alma 63: 15.
44*a* Alma 45: 21.
45*a* Alma 21: 17; D&C 18: 44.
47*a* Mosiah 29: 39.
48*a* Alma 50: 20.
49*a* Alma 55: 31.
50*a* 2 Cor. 11: 26 (24–33).
b TG Adversity.
c TG Deliver, Deliverance.
51*a* Gen. 26: 22. TG Prosper.
52*a* His great career spans Alma chapters 31–62.

[*57 B.C.]

AND it came to pass in the *commencement of the thirty and sixth
year of the reign of the judges over
the people of Nephi, that [a]Shiblon
took possession of those [b]sacred
things which had been delivered unto Helaman by Alma.
2 And he was a just man, and he
did walk uprightly before God; and
he did observe to do good continually, to keep the commandments of
the Lord his God; and also did his
brother.
3 And it came to pass that [a]Moroni
died also. And thus ended the thirty
and sixth year of the reign of the
judges.
4 And it came to pass that in the
†thirty and seventh year of the reign
of the judges, there was a large
company of men, even to the
amount of five thousand and four
hundred men, with their wives and
their children, departed out of the
land of Zarahemla into the land
which was [a]northward.
5 And it came to pass that Hagoth,
he being an [a]exceedingly curious
man, therefore he went forth and
built him an exceedingly large ship,
on the borders of the land [b]Bountiful,
by the land Desolation, and launched it forth into the west sea, by the
[c]narrow neck which led into the land
northward.
6 And behold, there were many of
the Nephites who did enter therein
and did sail forth with much provisions, and also many women and
children; and they took their course
northward. And thus ended the
thirty and seventh year.
7 And in the thirty and eighth
year, this man built [a]other ships.
And the first ship did also return,
and many more people did enter
into it; and they also took much
provisions, and set out again to the
land northward.
8 And it came to pass that they
were never heard of more. And we
suppose that they were drowned in
the depths of the sea. And it came to
pass that one other ship also did sail
forth; and whither she did go we
know not.
9 And it came to pass that in this
year there were many people who
went forth into the land [a]northward. And thus ended the thirty
and eighth year.
10 And it came to pass in the
‡thirty and ninth year of the reign
of the judges, [a]Shiblon died also,
and Corianton had gone forth to
the land northward in a ship, to
carry forth provisions unto the
people who had gone forth into that
land.
11 Therefore it became expedient
for [a]Shiblon to confer those sacred
things, before his death, upon the
son of [b]Helaman, who was called
[c]Helaman, being called after the
name of his father.
12 Now behold, all those [a]engravings which were in the possession of
Helaman were written and sent
forth among the children of men
throughout all the land, save it were
those parts which had been commanded by Alma should [b]not go
forth.
13 Nevertheless, these things were
to be kept sacred, and [a]handed
down from one generation to another; therefore, in this year, they
had been conferred upon Helaman,
before the death of Shiblon.
14 And it came to pass also in this
year that there were some dissenters
who had gone forth unto the

63 1*a* Alma 38:1 (1–2); 49:30.
b Mosiah 1:3; Alma 37:1 (1–12). TG Sacred.
3*a* See Alma chapters 43–63 for his great contributions.
4*a* Alma 22:31; 46:17; Hel. 3:3.
5*a* Hel. 3:10 (10, 14).
b Alma 53:3 (3–4); Hel. 1:23.
c Alma 22:32; Morm. 2:29; Ether 10:20.
7*a* Hel. 3:10.
9*a* Hel. 3:12 (11–12); 6:6.
10*a* Alma 31:7.
11*a* Alma 63:1.
b See heading to the book of Helaman.
c Hel. 3:37.
12*a* Alma 18:36; 3 Ne. 1:2.
b Alma 37:27 (27–32).
13*a* Alma 37:4.

[*56 B.C. †55 B.C. ‡53 B.C.]

Lamanites; and they were [a]stirred up again to anger against the Nephites.
15 And also in this same year they came down with a numerous army to war against the people of [a]Moronihah, or against the army of Moronihah, in the which they were beaten and driven back again to their own lands, suffering great loss.
16 And thus ended the thirty and ninth year of the reign of the judges over the people of Nephi.
17 And thus ended the account of [a]Alma, and Helaman his son, and also Shiblon, who was his son.

THE BOOK OF HELAMAN

An account of the Nephites. Their wars and contentions, and their dissensions. And also the prophecies of many holy prophets, before the coming of Christ, according to the records of Helaman, who was the son of Helaman, and also according to the records of his sons, even down to the coming of Christ. And also many of the Lamanites are converted. An account of their conversion. An account of the righteousness of the Lamanites, and the wickedness and abominations of the Nephites, according to the record of Helaman and his sons, even down to the coming of Christ, which is called the book of Helaman.

CHAPTER 1

Pahoran the second becomes chief judge and is murdered by Kishkumen—Pacumeni fills the judgment-seat—Coriantumr leads the Lamanite armies, takes Zarahemla, and slays Pacumeni—Moronihah defeats the Lamanites and retakes Zarahemla, and Coriantumr is slain.

AND now behold, it came to pass in the *commencement of the fortieth year of the reign of the judges over the people of Nephi, there began to be a serious difficulty among the people of the Nephites.
2 For behold, [a]Pahoran had died, and gone the way of all the earth; therefore there began to be a serious contention concerning who should have the judgment-seat among the brethren, who were the sons of Pahoran.
3 Now these are their names who did contend for the judgment-seat, who did also cause the people to contend: Pahoran, Paanchi, and Pacumeni.
4 Now these are not all the sons of Pahoran (for he had many), but these are they who did contend for the judgment-seat; therefore, they did cause three [a]divisions among the people.
5 Nevertheless, it came to pass that Pahoran was appointed by the [a]voice of the people to be chief judge and a governor over the people of Nephi.
6 And it came to pass that Pacumeni, when he saw that he could not obtain the judgment-seat, he did [a]unite with the voice of the people.
7 But behold, Paanchi, and that part of the people that were desirous that he should be their governor, was exceedingly wroth; therefore,

14a Alma 51: 9; Hel. 4: 4.
15a Alma 62: 43.
17a Alma 1: 2 (1–2).

[HELAMAN]
1 2a Alma 50: 40.
4a Matt. 12: 25.

5a Mosiah 29: 11; Alma 51: 7; Hel. 5: 2.
6a TG Unity.

[*52 B.C.]

he was about to [a]flatter away those people to rise up in rebellion against their brethren.

8 And it came to pass as he was about to do this, behold, he was taken, and was tried according to the [a]voice of the people, and condemned unto death; for he had raised up in rebellion and sought to destroy the [b]liberty of the people.

9 Now when those people who were desirous that he should be their governor saw that he was condemned unto death, therefore they were angry, and behold, they sent forth one [a]Kishkumen, even to the judgment-seat of Pahoran, and murdered Pahoran as he sat upon the judgment-seat.

10 And he was pursued by the servants of Pahoran; but behold, so speedy was the flight of Kishkumen that no man could overtake him.

11 And he went unto those that sent him, and they all entered into a covenant, yea, [a]swearing by their everlasting Maker, that they would tell no man that Kishkumen had murdered Pahoran.

12 Therefore, Kishkumen was not known among the people of Nephi, for he was in disguise at the time that he murdered Pahoran. And Kishkumen and his band, who had covenanted with him, did mingle themselves among the people, in a manner that they all could not be found; but as many as were found were condemned unto [a]death.

13 And now behold, Pacumeni was appointed, according to the [a]voice of the people, to be a chief judge and a governor over the people, to reign in the stead of his brother Pahoran; and it was according to his right. And all this was done in the fortieth year of the reign of the judges; and it had an end.

14 And it came to pass in the *forty and first year of the reign of the judges, that the Lamanites had gathered together an innumerable army of men, and [a]armed them with swords, and with cimeters and with bows, and with arrows, and with head-plates, and with breastplates, and with all manner of shields of every kind.

15 And they came down again that they might pitch battle against the Nephites. And they were led by a man whose name was [a]Coriantumr; and he was a descendant of Zarahemla; and he was a [b]dissenter from among the Nephites; and he was a large and a mighty man.

16 Therefore, the king of the Lamanites, whose name was Tubaloth, who was the son of [a]Ammoron, supposing that Coriantumr, being a mighty man, could stand against the Nephites, with his strength and also with his great [b]wisdom, insomuch that by sending him forth he should gain power over the Nephites—

17 Therefore he did [a]stir them up to anger, and he did gather together his armies, and he did appoint Coriantumr to be their leader, and did cause that they should march down to the land of Zarahemla to battle against the Nephites.

18 And it came to pass that because of so much contention and so much difficulty in the government, that they had not kept sufficient guards in the land of Zarahemla; for they had supposed that the Lamanites durst not come into the heart of their lands to attack that great city Zarahemla.

19 But it came to pass that Coriantumr did march forth at the head of his numerous host, and came upon the inhabitants of the city, and their march was with such exceedingly great speed that there

---

7*a* Mosiah 27: 8; Alma 50: 35; Hel. 2: 5; Ether 8: 2.
8*a* Alma 1: 14 (10–15).
b TG Liberty.
9*a* Hel. 2: 3.
11*a* Gen. 24: 3; Ether 8: 14 (13–14).
12*a* TG Capital Punishment.
13*a* Hel. 1: 5; 2: 2.
14*a* Alma 2: 12; 49: 6 (6, 24).
15*a* Hel. 1: 30.
b Alma 31: 8; 53: 8; Hel. 4: 8.
16*a* Alma 52: 3.
b Ezek. 28: 5 (4–5).
17*a* Alma 35: 10; 47: 1.

[*51 B.C.]

was no time for the Nephites to
gather together their armies.
20 Therefore Coriantumr did cut
down the watch by the entrance of
the city, and did march forth with
his whole army into the city, and
they did slay every one who did
oppose them, insomuch that they
did take possession of the whole
city.
21 And it came to pass that Pacumeni,
who was the chief judge, did
flee before Coriantumr, even to the
walls of the city. And it came to pass
that Coriantumr did smite him
against the wall, insomuch that he
died. And thus ended the days of
Pacumeni.
22 And now when Coriantumr saw
that he was in possession of the city
of Zarahemla, and saw that the
Nephites had fled before them, and
were slain, and were taken, and were
cast into prison, and that he had
obtained the possession of the
strongest hold in all the land, his
heart [a]took courage insomuch that
he was about to go forth against all
the land.
23 And now he did not tarry in the
land of Zarahemla, but he did march
forth with a large army, even towards
the city of [a]Bountiful; for it
was his determination to go forth
and cut his way through with the
sword, that he might obtain the
north parts of the land.
24 And, supposing that their
greatest strength was in the center
of the land, therefore he did march
forth, giving them no time to
assemble themselves together save
it were in small bodies; and in this
manner they did fall upon them and
cut them down to the earth.
25 But behold, this march of
Coriantumr through the center of
the land gave Moronihah great
advantage over them, notwithstanding
the greatness of the number
of the Nephites who were slain.
26 For behold, Moronihah had
supposed that the Lamanites durst
not come into the center of the land,
but that they would attack the cities
round about in the borders as they
had hitherto done; therefore
Moronihah had caused that their
strong armies should maintain those
parts round about by the borders.
27 But behold, the Lamanites
were not frightened according to his
desire, but they had come into the
center of the land, and had taken
the capital city which was the city of
Zarahemla, and were marching
through the most capital parts of
the land, slaying the people with a
great slaughter, both men, women,
and children, taking possession of
many cities and of many strongholds.
28 But when Moronihah had discovered
this, he immediately sent
forth Lehi with an army round about
to [a]head them before they should
come to the land Bountiful.
29 And thus he did; and he did
head them before they came to the
land Bountiful, and gave unto them
battle, insomuch that they began to
retreat back towards the land of
Zarahemla.
30 And it came to pass that
Moronihah did head them in their
retreat, and did give unto them
battle, insomuch that it became an
exceedingly bloody battle; yea,
many were slain, and among the
number who were slain [a]Coriantumr
was also found.
31 And now, behold, the Lamanites
could not retreat either way, neither
on the north, nor on the south, nor
on the east, nor on the west, for they
were surrounded on every hand by
the Nephites.
32 And thus had Coriantumr
plunged the Lamanites into the
midst of the Nephites, insomuch
that they were in the power of the
Nephites, and he himself was slain,
and the Lamanites did [a]yield themselves
into the hands of the Nephites.

22*a* TG Pride.
23*a* Alma 22: 29.
28*a* Alma 50: 34; 51: 29 (29–30).
30*a* Hel. 1: 15.
32*a* Hel. 4: 3.

[About 51 B.C.]

33 And it came to pass that Moronihah took possession of the city of
Zarahemla again, and caused that
the Lamanites who had been taken
prisoners should depart out of the
land in [a]peace.
34 And thus ended the forty and
first year of the reign of the judges.

CHAPTER 2

Helaman the second becomes chief judge—Gadianton leads the band of Kishkumen — Helaman's servant slays Kishkumen, and the Gadianton band flees into the wilderness.

AND it came to pass in the *forty
and second year of the reign of the
judges, after Moronihah had established again peace between the
Nephites and the Lamanites, behold
there was no one to fill the judgment-
seat; therefore there began to be a
contention again among the people
concerning who should fill the
judgment-seat.
2 And it came to pass that [a]Hela-
man, who was the son of Helaman,
was appointed to fill the judgment-
seat, by the [b]voice of the people.
3 But behold, [a]Kishkumen, who
had murdered Pahoran, did lay wait
to destroy Helaman also; and he
was upheld by his band, who had
entered into a covenant that no one
should know his wickedness.
4 For there was one [a]Gadianton,
who was exceedingly expert in many
words, and also in his craft, to carry
on the secret work of murder and of
robbery; therefore he became the
leader of the band of Kishkumen.
5 Therefore he did [a]flatter them,
and also Kishkumen, that if they
would place him in the judgment-
seat he would grant unto those who
belonged to his band that they
should be placed in power and
authority among the people; therefore Kishkumen sought to destroy
Helaman.
6 And it came to pass as he went
forth towards the judgment-seat to
destroy Helaman, behold one of the
servants of Helaman, having been
out by night, and having obtained,
through disguise, a knowledge of
those plans which had been laid by
this band to destroy Helaman—
7 And it came to pass that he met
Kishkumen, and he gave unto him a
sign; therefore Kishkumen made
known unto him the object of his
desire, desiring that he would conduct him to the judgment-seat that
he might murder Helaman.
8 And when the servant of Helaman had known all the heart of
Kishkumen, and how that it was his
[a]object to murder, and also that it
was the object of all those who
belonged to his band to murder, and
to rob, and to gain power, (and this
was their [b]secret plan, and their
combination) the servant of Helaman said unto Kishkumen: Let us
go forth unto the judgment-seat.
9 Now this did please Kishkumen
exceedingly, for he did suppose that
he should accomplish his design;
but behold, the servant of Helaman,
as they were going forth unto the
judgment-seat, did stab Kishkumen
even to the heart, that he fell dead
without a groan. And he ran and
told Helaman all the things which
he had seen, and heard, and done.
10 And it came to pass that Helaman did send forth to take this
band of robbers and [a]secret murderers, that they might be executed
according to the law.
11 But behold, when Gadianton
had found that Kishkumen did not
return he feared lest that he should
be destroyed; therefore he caused
that his band should follow him.
And they took their flight out of

33*a* Alma 44: 15.
2 2*a* Hel. 3: 20.
b Hel. 1: 13.
3*a* Hel. 1: 9.
4*a* Hel. 3: 23; 6: 18 (18, 29).
5*a* Mosiah 27: 8; Alma 50: 35; Hel. 1: 7; Ether 8: 2. TG Flattery.
8*a* TG Conspiracy.
b 2 Ne. 10: 15; Moses 5: 31 (18–31). TG Secret Combinations.
10*a* Hel. 3: 23.

[*50 B.C.]

the land, by a secret way, into the wilderness; and thus when Helaman sent forth to take them they could nowhere be found.

12 And more of this Gadianton shall be spoken hereafter. And thus ended the forty and second year of the reign of the judges over the people of Nephi.

13 And behold, in the end of this book ye shall see that this [a]Gadianton did prove the overthrow, yea, almost the entire destruction of the people of Nephi.

14 Behold I do not mean the end of the [a]book of Helaman, but I mean the end of the book of Nephi, from which I have taken all the account which I have written.

CHAPTER 3

Many Nephites migrate to the land northward—They build houses of cement and keep many records—Tens of thousands are converted and baptized—The word of God leads men to salvation—Nephi the son of Helaman fills the judgment seat.

AND now it came to pass in the *forty and third year of the reign of the judges, there was no contention among the people of Nephi save it were a little pride which was in the church, which did cause some little dissensions among the people, which affairs were settled in the ending of the forty and third year.

2 And there was no contention among the people in the forty and fourth year; neither was there much contention in the forty and fifth year.

3 And it came to pass in the †forty and sixth, yea, there was much contention and many dissensions; in the which there were an exceedingly great many who departed out of the land of Zarahemla, and went forth unto the land [a]northward to inherit the land.

4 And they did travel to an exceedingly great distance, insomuch that they came to [a]large bodies of water and many rivers.

5 Yea, and even they did spread forth into all parts of the land, into whatever parts it had not been rendered desolate and without timber, because of the many inhabitants who had before inherited the land.

6 And now no part of the land was desolate, save it were for timber; but because of the greatness of the [a]destruction of the people who had before inhabited the land it was called [b]desolate.

7 And there being but little timber upon the face of the land, nevertheless the people who went forth became exceedingly [a]expert in the working of cement; therefore they did build houses of cement, in the which they did dwell.

8 And it came to pass that they did multiply and spread, and did go forth from the land southward to the land northward, and did spread insomuch that they began to cover the face of the whole earth, from the sea south to the sea north, from the sea [a]west to the sea east.

9 And the people who were in the land northward did dwell in [a]tents, and in houses of cement, and they did suffer whatsoever tree should spring up upon the face of the land that it should grow up, that in time they might have timber to build their houses, yea, their cities, and their temples, and their [b]synagogues, and their sanctuaries, and all manner of their buildings.

10 And it came to pass as timber was exceedingly scarce in the land northward, they did send forth much by the way of [a]shipping.

13*a* Hel. 6: 18; 3 Ne. 4: 1.
14*a* W of M 1: 9; 3 Ne. 5: 10.
3 3*a* Alma 63: 4.
4*a* Mosiah 8: 8; Alma 50: 29; Morm. 6: 4.
6*a* Mosiah 8: 8; 21: 26 (26–27).
b Alma 22: 31.
7*a* TG Skill.
8*a* Alma 22: 27 (27, 32–33); Hel. 11: 20.
9*a* Gen. 25: 27; Ether 2: 13.
b Alma 16: 13.
10*a* Alma 63: 7 (5–8).

[*49 B.C. †46 B.C.]

11 And thus they did enable the
people in the land northward that
they might build many cities, both
of wood and of cement.
12 And it came to pass that there
were many of the [a]people of Ammon,
who were Lamanites by birth, did
also go forth into this land.
13 And now there are many
[a]records kept of the proceedings of
this people, by many of this people,
which are particular and very large,
concerning them.
14 But behold, a [a]hundredth part
of the proceedings of this people,
yea, the account of the Lamanites
and of the Nephites, and their wars,
and contentions, and dissensions,
and their preaching, and their
prophecies, and their shipping and
their building of ships, and their
building of [b]temples, and of synagogues and their [c]sanctuaries, and
their righteousness, and their
wickedness, and their murders, and
their robbings, and their plundering, and all manner of abominations
and whoredoms, cannot be contained in this work.
15 But behold, there are many
books and many [a]records of every
kind, and they have been kept
chiefly by the Nephites.
16 And they have been [a]handed
down from one generation to another
by the Nephites, even until they
have fallen into transgression and
have been murdered, plundered, and
hunted, and driven forth, and slain,
and [b]scattered upon the face of the
earth, and mixed with the Lamanites until they are [c]no more called
the Nephites, becoming wicked, and
wild, and ferocious, yea, even becoming Lamanites.
17 And now I return again to mine
account; therefore, what I have
spoken had passed after there had
been great contentions, and disturbances, and wars, and dissensions,
among the people of Nephi.
18 The forty and sixth year of the
reign of the judges ended;
19 And it came to pass that there
was still great contention in the
land, yea, even in the *forty and
seventh year, and also in the forty
and eighth year.
20 Nevertheless [a]Helaman did fill
the judgment-seat with justice and
equity; yea, he did observe to keep
the statutes, and the judgments,
and the commandments of God; and
he did do that which was right in the
sight of God continually; and he did
walk after the ways of his father, insomuch that he did prosper in the
land.
21 And it came to pass that he had
two sons. He gave unto the eldest the
name of [a]Nephi, and unto the
youngest, the name of [b]Lehi. And
they began to grow up unto the Lord.
22 And it came to pass that the wars
and contentions began to cease, in a
small degree, among the people of
the Nephites, in the latter end of the
forty and eighth year of the reign of
the judges over the people of Nephi.
23 And it came to pass in the †forty
and ninth year of the reign of the
judges, there was continual peace
established in the land, all save it
were the [a]secret combinations which
[b]Gadianton the robber had established in the more settled parts of
the land, which at that time were
not known unto those who were at
the head of government; therefore
they were not destroyed out of the
land.
24 And it came to pass that in this
same year there was exceedingly
great prosperity in the church, insomuch that there were thousands
who did [a]join themselves unto the

12*a* Alma 27: 26; 63: 9 (4–9); Hel. 6: 6.
13*a* W of M 1: 3 (1–11).
14*a* 3 Ne. 5: 8; 26: 6 (6–11).
b 2 Ne. 5: 16; Jacob 1: 17; 3 Ne. 11: 1.
c Alma 23: 2.
15*a* 3 Ne. 5: 9; 4 Ne. 1: 48.
16*a* 1 Ne. 5: 18 (16–19); Alma 37: 4.
b Ezek. 36: 19 (16–20).
c Alma 45: 13 (12–14).
20*a* Hel. 2: 2.
21*a* Hel. 4: 14; 5: 5; 3 Ne. 1: 2.
b Hel. 3: 37.
23*a* 2 Ne. 10: 15; Hel. 2: 10 (8–10); 7: 25 (4–5, 21, 25).
b Hel. 2: 4; 6: 18.
24*a* Mosiah 25: 23.

[*45 B.C. †43 B.C.]

church and were baptized unto
repentance.
25 And so great was the prosperity
of the church, and so many the
blessings which were poured out
upon the people, that even the high
priests and the teachers were themselves astonished beyond measure.
26 And it came to pass that the
work of the Lord did prosper unto
the baptizing and uniting to the
church of God, many souls, yea,
even tens of thousands.
27 Thus we may see that the Lord
is merciful unto all who will, in the
sincerity of their hearts, call upon
his holy name.
28 Yea, thus we see that the [a]gate
of heaven is open unto [b]all, even to
those who will believe on the name
of Jesus Christ, who is the Son of
God.
29 Yea, we see that whosoever will
may lay hold upon the [a]word of God,
which is [b]quick and powerful, which
shall [c]divide asunder all the cunning
and the snares and the wiles of the
devil, and lead the man of Christ in a
strait and [d]narrow course across that
everlasting [e]gulf of misery which is
prepared to engulf the wicked—
30 And land their souls, yea, their
immortal souls, at the [a]right hand of
God in the kingdom of heaven, to
sit down with Abraham, and Isaac,
and with Jacob, and with all our
holy fathers, to go no more out.
31 And in this year there was continual rejoicing in the land of
Zarahemla, and in all the regions
round about, even in all the land
which was possessed by the Nephites.
32 And it came to pass that there
was peace and exceedingly great joy
in the remainder of the forty and
ninth year; yea, and also there was
continual peace and great joy in the
fiftieth year of the reign of the judges.
33 And in the *fifty and first year
of the reign of the judges there was
peace also, save it were the pride
which began to enter into the church
—not into the church of God, but
into the hearts of the people who
[a]professed to belong to the church
of God—
34 And they were lifted up in [a]pride,
even to the persecution of many of
their brethren. Now this was a great
evil, which did cause the more
humble part of the people to suffer
great persecutions, and to wade
through much affliction.
35 Nevertheless they did [a]fast and
[b]pray oft, and did wax stronger
and stronger in their [c]humility,
and firmer and firmer in the faith
of Christ, unto the filling their
souls with joy and consolation, yea,
even to the [d]purifying and the
[e]sanctification of their hearts, which
sanctification cometh because of
their [f]yielding their hearts unto God.
36 And it came to pass that the fifty
and second year ended in peace also,
save it were the exceedingly great
pride which had gotten into the
hearts of the people; and it was
because of their exceedingly great
[a]riches and their prosperity in the
land; and it did grow upon them
from day to day.
37 And it came to pass in the †fifty
and third year of the reign of the
judges, [a]Helaman died, and his
eldest son [b]Nephi began to reign in
his stead. And it came to pass that
he did fill the judgment-seat with
justice and equity; yea, he did keep

28a Isa. 26: 2.
b Acts 10: 28 (9–35, 44); Rom. 2: 11 (10–11).
29a Micah 2: 7; Jacob 2: 8; D&C 11: 2; 33: 1. TG Gospel.
b Heb. 4: 12; D&C 27: 1.
c D&C 6: 2.
d 2 Ne. 9: 41; 33: 9.
e 1 Ne. 12: 18; 15: 28 (28–30).
30a Matt. 25: 34 (31–46).
33a D&C 112: 26.
34a TG Pride.
35a TG Fasting.
b TG Prayer.
c TG Humility.
d TG Cleanliness; Purification; Purity.
e TG Sanctification.
f 2 Chr. 30: 8; Rom. 6: 13 (12–14). TG Submissiveness; Teachable.
36a TG Treasure.
37a Alma 63: 11; Hel. 16: 25.
b Hel. 3: 21; 5: 1.

[*41 B.C. †39 B.C.]

the commandments of God, and did walk in the ways of his father.

CHAPTER 4

Nephite dissenters and the Lamanites join forces and take the land of Zarahemla—The Nephites' defeats come because of their wickedness—The Church dwindles and the people become weak like the Lamanites.

AND it came to pass in the *fifty and fourth year there were many dissensions in the church, and there was also a [a]contention among the people, insomuch that there was much bloodshed.

2 And the rebellious part were slain and driven out of the land, and they did go unto the king of the Lamanites.

3 And it came to pass that they did endeavor to stir up the Lamanites to [a]war against the Nephites; but behold, the Lamanites were [b]exceedingly afraid, insomuch that they would not hearken to the words of those dissenters.

4 But it came to pass in the fifty and sixth year of the reign of the judges, there were [a]dissenters who went up from the Nephites unto the Lamanites; and they succeeded with those others in [b]stirring them up to anger against the Nephites; and they were all that year preparing for war.

5 And in the †fifty and seventh year they did come down against the Nephites to battle, and they did commence the work of death; yea, insomuch that in the fifty and eighth year of the reign of the judges they succeeded in obtaining [a]possession of the land of Zarahemla; yea, and also all the lands, even unto the land which was near the land Bountiful.

6 And the Nephites and the armies of Moronihah were driven even into the land of Bountiful;

7 And there they did fortify against the Lamanites, from the west sea, even unto the east; it being a [a]day's journey for a Nephite, on the line which they had fortified and stationed their armies to defend their north country.

8 And thus those [a]dissenters of the Nephites, with the help of a numerous army of the Lamanites, had obtained all the possession of the Nephites which was in the land southward. And all this was done in the fifty and eighth and ninth years of the reign of the judges.

9 And it came to pass in the sixtieth year of the reign of the judges, Moronihah did succeed with his armies in obtaining many parts of the land; yea, they regained many cities which had fallen into the hands of the Lamanites.

10 And it came to pass in the ‡sixty and first year of the reign of the judges they succeeded in regaining even the half of all their possessions.

11 Now this great loss of the Nephites, and the great slaughter which was among them, [a]would not have happened had it not been for their [b]wickedness and their abomination which was among them; yea, and it was among those also who professed to belong to the church of God.

12 And it was because of the [a]pride of their hearts, because of their exceeding [b]riches, yea, it was because of their oppression to the [c]poor, withholding their food from the hungry, withholding their clothing from the naked, and smiting their humble brethren upon the cheek, making a [d]mock of that which was sacred, denying the spirit of prophecy and of revelation, murdering, plundering, lying, stealing,

4 1*a* 3 Ne. 11: 29.
3*a* Hel. 11: 24.
b Hel. 1: 32 (30–33).
4*a* Hel. 5: 17.
b Alma 63: 14.
5*a* Hel. 5: 16, 52.
7*a* Alma 22: 32.
8*a* Hel. 1: 15.
11*a* D&C 82: 10.
b Mosiah 27: 13.
12*a* Obad. 1: 3 (3–4); 2 Ne. 20: 33; D&C 101: 42.
b 1 Tim. 6: 17; 2 Ne. 9: 42; 3 Ne. 6: 12 (10–16).
c Ezek. 18: 12; Zech. 7: 10; D&C 42: 30 (30–39, 71).
d TG Mocking; Sacrilege.

[*38 B.C. †35 B.C. ‡31 B.C.]

committing adultery, rising up in great contentions, and deserting away into the land of Nephi, among the Lamanites—

13 And because of this their great wickedness, and their [a]boastings in their own strength, they were left in their own strength; therefore they did not prosper, but were afflicted and smitten, and driven before the Lamanites, until they had lost possession of almost all their lands.

14 But behold, Moronihah did [a]preach many things unto the people because of their iniquity, and also [b]Nephi and Lehi, who were the sons of Helaman, did preach many things unto the people, yea, and did prophesy many things unto them concerning their iniquities, and what should come unto them if they did not repent of their sins.

15 And it came to pass that they did repent, and inasmuch as they did repent they did begin to prosper.

16 For when Moronihah saw that they did repent he did venture to [a]lead them forth from place to place, and from city to city, even until they had regained the one-half of their property and the one-half of all their lands.

17 And thus ended the sixty and first year of the reign of the judges.

18 And it came to pass in the *sixty and second year of the reign of the judges, that Moronihah could obtain no more possessions over the Lamanites.

19 Therefore they did abandon their design to obtain the remainder of their lands, for so numerous were the Lamanites that it became impossible for the Nephites to obtain more power over them; therefore Moronihah did employ all his armies in maintaining those parts which he had taken.

20 And it came to pass, because of the greatness of the number of the Lamanites the Nephites were in great fear, lest they should be overpowered, and trodden down, and slain, and destroyed.

21 Yea, they began to remember the [a]prophecies of Alma, and also the [b]words of Mosiah; and they saw that they had been a [c]stiffnecked people, and that they had set at [d]naught the commandments of God;

22 And that they had altered and trampled under their feet the [a]laws of Mosiah, or that which the Lord commanded him to give unto the people; and they saw that their laws had become corrupted, and that they had become a wicked people, insomuch that they were wicked even like unto the Lamanites.

23 And because of their iniquity the church had begun to [a]dwindle; and they began to disbelieve in the spirit of prophecy and in the spirit of revelation; and the judgments of God did stare them in the face.

24 And they saw that they had become [a]weak, like unto their brethren, the Lamanites, and that the Spirit of the Lord did no more preserve them; yea, it had withdrawn from them because the Spirit of the Lord doth not [b]dwell in [c]unholy [d]temples—

25 Therefore the Lord did cease to preserve them by his miraculous and matchless power, for they had fallen into a state of [a]unbelief and awful wickedness; and they saw that the Lamanites were exceedingly more numerous than they, and except they should [b]cleave unto the Lord their God they must unavoidably perish.

26 For behold, they saw that the strength of the Lamanites was as

13a Ezek. 35: 13.
b TG Boasting; Trust Not in the Arm of Flesh.
14a Hel. 5: 17 (14–20).
b Hel. 3: 21.
16a Alma 62: 43.
21a Alma 5: 53 (1–62).
b Mosiah 29: 27.
c TG Stiffneckedness.
d Prov. 1: 25.
22a Alma 1: 1.
23a TG Apostasy.
24a Jer. 46: 15 (15–17); Mosiah 1: 13.
b TG Holy Ghost, Loss of.
c Mosiah 2: 37; Alma 7: 21; 34: 36.
d TG Temple.
25a TG Unbelief, Unbelievers.
b Josh. 23: 8; Jacob 6: 5; D&C 11: 19.

[*30 B.C.]

great as their strength, even man
for man. And thus had they fallen
into this great transgression; yea,
thus had they become [a]weak, because of their transgression, in the
space of [b]not many years.

CHAPTER 5

Nephi and Lehi devote themselves to preaching—Their names invite them to pattern their lives after their forebears—Christ redeems those who repent—Nephi and Lehi make many converts and are imprisoned, and fire encircles them—A cloud of darkness overshadows three hundred people—The earth shakes and a voice commands men to repent—Nephi and Lehi converse with angels, and the multitude are encircled by fire.

AND it came to pass that in this
*same year, behold, [a]Nephi [b]de-
livered up the judgment-seat to a
man whose name was [c]Cezoram.
2 For as their laws and their
governments were established by the
[a]voice of the people, and they who
[b]chose evil were [c]more numerous
than they who chose good, therefore
they were [d]ripening for destruction,
for the laws had become corrupted.
3 Yea, and this was not all; they
were a [a]stiffnecked people, insomuch
that they could not be governed by
the law nor justice, save it were to
their destruction.
4 And it came to pass that Nephi
had become weary because of their
iniquity; and he yielded up the
judgment-seat, and took it upon
him to preach the word of God all
the remainder of his days, and his
brother Lehi also, all the remainder
of his days;
5 For they remembered the words
which their [a]father Helaman spake
unto them. And these are the words
which he spake:
6 Behold, my sons, I desire that ye
should remember to keep the commandments of God; and I would
that ye should declare unto the
people these words. Behold, I have
given unto you the names of our
first [a]parents who came out of the
land of Jerusalem; and this I have
done that when you remember your
names ye may remember them; and
when ye remember them ye may
remember their works; and when ye
remember their works ye may know
how that it is said, and also written,
that they were [b]good.
7 Therefore, my sons, I would that
ye should do that which is good,
that it may be said of you, and also
written, even as it has been said and
written of them.
8 And now my sons, behold I have
somewhat more to desire of you,
which desire is, that ye may not do
these things that ye may boast, but
that ye may do these things to lay
up for yourselves a [a]treasure in
heaven, yea, which is eternal, and
which fadeth not away; yea, that
ye may have that [b]precious gift of
eternal life, which we have reason to
suppose hath been given to our
fathers.
9 O remember, remember, my sons,
the [a]words which king Benjamin
spake unto his people; yea, remember that there is no other way
nor means whereby man can be
saved, only through the [b]atoning
blood of Jesus Christ, who shall
come; yea, remember that he cometh to [c]redeem the [d]world.

26*a* Ezek. 19: 8 (6–9).
TG Weak, Weaker.
b Alma 46: 8; Hel. 6: 32; 7: 6; 11: 26; 12: 2.
5 1*a* Hel. 3: 37.
b Alma 4: 20 (15–20).
c Hel. 6: 15.
2*a* Mosiah 29: 25 (25–27); Hel. 1: 5 (3–5, 13).
b Alma 10: 19.
c 4 Ne. 1: 40.
d Hel. 6: 40; 10: 11; D&C 18: 6; 61: 31.
3*a* TG Stiffneckedness.
5*a* Hel. 3: 21 (21, 37).
6*a* 1 Ne. 1: 4 (1, 4).
b 2 Ne. 4: 12; 33: 3 (1–15); Jacob 1: 10 (9–12).
8*a* Hel. 8: 25; 3 Ne. 13: 20 (19–21).
TG Treasure.
b 1 Ne. 15: 36.
9*a* Mosiah 2: 9.
b Mosiah 3: 18; 4: 2.
TG Jesus Christ, Atonement through.
c TG Jesus Christ, Redeemer.
d TG World.

[*30 B.C.]

10 And remember also the words
which Amulek spake unto Zeezrom,
[a]in the city of Ammonihah; for he
said unto him that the Lord surely
should come to redeem his people,
but that he should not come to
redeem them in their sins, but to
redeem them from their sins.
11 And he hath power given unto
him from the Father to redeem them
from their sins because of repentance; therefore he hath [a]sent his
angels to declare the tidings of the
conditions of repentance, which
bringeth unto the power of the
Redeemer, unto the salvation of
their souls.
12 And now, my sons, remember,
remember that it is upon the [a]rock
of our Redeemer, who is Christ, the
Son of God, that ye must build your
[b]foundation; that when the devil
shall send forth his mighty winds,
yea, his shafts in the whirlwind,
yea, when all his hail and his mighty
[c]storm shall beat upon you, it shall
have no power over you to drag
you down to the gulf of misery and
endless wo, because of the rock
upon which ye are built, which is
a sure foundation, a foundation
whereon if men build they cannot
fall.
13 And it came to pass that these
were the words which Helaman
[a]taught to his sons; yea, he did
teach them many things which are
not written, and also many things
which are written.
14 And they did remember his
words; and therefore they went
forth, keeping the commandments
of God, to teach the word of God
among all the people of Nephi,
beginning at the city Bountiful;
15 And from thenceforth to the
city of Gid; and from the city of Gid
to the city of Mulek;
16 And even from one city to
another, until they had gone forth
[a]among all the people of Nephi who
were in the land southward; and
from thence into the land of Zarahemla, among the Lamanites.
17 And it came to pass that they
did [a]preach with great [b]power, insomuch that they did confound
many of those [c]dissenters who had
gone over from the Nephites, insomuch that they came forth and did
confess their sins and were baptized
unto repentance, and immediately
returned to the Nephites to endeavor to repair unto them the
wrongs which they had done.
18 And it came to pass that Nephi
and Lehi did preach unto the
Lamanites with such great power
and authority, for they had power
and authority given unto them that
they might [a]speak, and they also
had what they should speak given
unto them—
19 Therefore they did speak unto
the great astonishment of the
Lamanites, to the convincing them,
insomuch that there were eight
thousand of the Lamanites who
were in the land of Zarahemla and
round about [a]baptized unto repentance, and were convinced of the
[b]wickedness of the [c]traditions of
their fathers.
20 And it came to pass that Nephi
and Lehi did proceed from thence
to go to the [a]land of Nephi.
21 And it came to pass that they
were taken by an army of the
Lamanites and cast into [a]prison;
yea, even in that same prison in
which Ammon and his brethren
were cast by the servants of Limhi.

10*a* Alma 11: 34.
11*a* Alma 13: 24 (24–25); 39: 19.
12*a* Ps. 71: 3; Matt. 7: 24 (24–27); D&C 6: 34; Moses 7: 53. TG Cornerstone; Rock.
b Isa. 28: 16 (14–17); Jacob 4:16.
c Alma 26: 6; 3 Ne. 14: 25 (25, 27).
13*a* Mosiah 1: 4; Alma 18: 36; 36: 1; Moses 6: 58.
16*a* Hel. 4: 5.
17*a* Hel. 4: 14.
b TG Teaching with the Spirit.
c Hel. 4: 4 (2, 4).
18*a* D&C 24: 6; 100: 5 (5–8). TG Prophets, Mission of.
19*a* TG Missionary Work.
b Mal. 2: 6.
c Hel. 15: 4.
20*a* Alma 22: 1.
21*a* Mosiah 7: 7 (6–8); 21: 23 (22–24).

[About 30 B.C.]

22 And after they had been cast into prison many days without food,
behold, they went forth into the
prison to take them that they might
slay them.
23 And it came to pass that Nephi
and Lehi were encircled about [a]as if
by [b]fire, even insomuch that they
durst not lay their hands upon them
for fear lest they should be burned.
Nevertheless, Nephi and Lehi were
not burned; and they were as standing in the midst of fire and were not
burned.
24 And when they saw that they
were encircled about with a [a]pillar
of fire, and that it burned them not,
their hearts did take courage.
25 For they saw that the Lamanites
durst not lay their hands upon them;
neither durst they come near unto
them, but stood as if they were
struck dumb with amazement.
26 And it came to pass that Nephi
and Lehi did stand forth and began
to speak unto them, saying: [a]Fear
not, for behold, it is God that has
shown unto you this marvelous
thing, in the which is shown unto
you that ye cannot lay your hands
on us to slay us.
27 And behold, when they had said
these words, the earth shook exceedingly, and the walls of the prison
did shake as if they were about to
tumble to the earth; but behold,
they did not fall. And behold, they
that were in the prison were Lamanites and Nephites who were dissenters.
28 And it came to pass that they
were overshadowed with a cloud of
[a]darkness, and an awful solemn fear
came upon them.
29 And it came to pass that there
came a [a]voice as if it were above the
cloud of darkness, saying: Repent
ye, repent ye, and seek no more to
destroy my [b]servants whom I have
sent unto you to declare good tidings.
30 And it came to pass when they
heard this [a]voice, and beheld that it
was not a voice of thunder, neither
was it a voice of a great tumultuous
noise, but behold, it was a [b]still
voice of perfect mildness, as if it had
been a whisper, and it did pierce
even to the very soul—
31 And notwithstanding the mildness of the voice, behold the earth
shook exceedingly, and the walls of
the prison trembled again, as if it
were about to tumble to the earth;
and behold the cloud of darkness,
which had overshadowed them, did
not disperse—
32 And behold the voice came
again, saying: [a]Repent ye, repent
ye, for the kingdom of heaven is at
hand; and seek no more to destroy
my servants. And it came to pass
that the earth shook again, and the
walls trembled.
33 And also again the third time
the voice came, and did speak unto
them marvelous words which [a]can-
not be uttered by man; and the walls
did tremble again, and the earth
shook as if it were about to divide
asunder.
34 And it came to pass that the
Lamanites could not flee because of
the cloud of darkness which did
overshadow them; yea, and also
they were immovable because of the
fear which did come upon them.
35 Now there was one among them
who was a Nephite by birth, who
had once belonged to the church of
God but had dissented from them.
36 And it came to pass that he
turned him about, and behold, he
saw through the cloud of darkness
the faces of Nephi and Lehi; and
behold, they did [a]shine exceedingly,

23*a* Ex. 24: 17; D&C 137: 2.
b Ex. 3: 2; Dan. 3: 25 (25, 27).
24*a* Ex. 14: 24; 1 Ne. 1: 6; D&C 29: 12; JS-H 1: 16. TG Protection, Divine.
26*a* Dan. 10: 12.
28*a* Ex. 14: 20.
29*a* Deut. 4: 33; 3 Ne. 11: 3 (3–14).
b TG Servant.
30*a* Moses 1: 25.
b 1 Kgs. 19: 12; D&C 85: 6 (6–7).
32*a* Matt. 3: 2 (2–3); Alma 7: 9; 9: 25 (25–26).
33*a* Rom. 8: 26.
36*a* Ex. 34: 29 (29–35); Acts 6: 15.

[About 30 B.C.]

even as the faces of angels. And he beheld that they did lift their eyes to heaven; and they were in the attitude as if talking or lifting their voices to some being whom they beheld.

37 And it came to pass that this man did cry unto the multitude, that they might turn and look. And behold, there was power given unto them that they did turn and look; and they did behold the faces of Nephi and Lehi.

38 And they said unto the man: Behold, what do all these things mean, and who is it with whom these men do converse?

39 Now the man's name was Aminadab. And Aminadab said unto them: They do converse with the angels of God.

40 And it came to pass that the Lamanites said unto him: [a]What shall we do, that this cloud of darkness may be removed from overshadowing us?

41 And Aminadab said unto them: You must [a]repent, and cry unto the voice, even until ye shall have [b]faith in Christ, who was taught unto you by Alma, and [c]Amulek, and Zeezrom; and when ye shall do this, the cloud of darkness shall be removed from overshadowing you.

42 And it came to pass that they all did begin to cry unto the voice of him who had shaken the earth; yea, they did cry even until the cloud of darkness was dispersed.

43 And it came to pass that when they cast their eyes about, and saw that the cloud of darkness was dispersed from overshadowing them, behold, they saw that they were [a]encircled about, yea every soul, by a pillar of fire.

44 And [a]Nephi and [b]Lehi were in the midst of them; yea, they were encircled about; yea, they were as if in the midst of a flaming fire, yet it did harm them not, neither did it take hold upon the walls of the prison; and they were filled with that [c]joy which is unspeakable and full of glory.

45 And behold, the [a]Holy Spirit of God did come down from heaven, and did enter into their hearts, and they were filled as if with fire, and they could [b]speak forth marvelous words.

46 And it came to pass that there came a voice unto them, yea, a pleasant voice, as if it were a whisper, saying:

47 [a]Peace, peace be unto you, because of your faith in my Well Beloved, who was from the foundation of the world.

48 And now, when they heard this they cast up their eyes as if to behold from whence the voice came; and behold, they saw the [a]heavens open; and angels came down out of heaven and ministered unto them.

49 And there were about three hundred souls who saw and heard these things; and they were bidden to go forth and marvel not, neither should they doubt.

50 And it came to pass that they did go forth, and did minister unto the people, declaring throughout all the regions round about all the things which they had heard and seen, insomuch that the more part of the Lamanites were [a]convinced of them, because of the greatness of the evidences which they had received.

51 And as many as were [a]convinced did lay down their weapons of war, and also their hatred and the tradition of their fathers.

52 And it came to pass that they did [a]yield up unto the Nephites the lands of their possession.

40*a* Acts 2: 37 (37–39).
41*a* TG Repentance.
b TG Faith.
c Alma 31: 6 (5–38).
43*a* 3 Ne. 17: 24; 19: 14.
44*a* Hel. 6: 6.
b Hel. 11: 19.
c TG Joy.
45*a* 3 Ne. 9: 20; 19: 14 (13–14); Ether 12: 14.
b TG Holy Ghost, Gifts of.
47*a* TG Peace of God.
48*a* Acts 7: 56 (55–56); 1 Ne. 1: 8.
50*a* Ether 12: 14.
51*a* Alma 31: 5.
52*a* Hel. 4: 5 (5, 18–19).

[About 30 B.C.]

CHAPTER 6

The righteous Lamanites preach to the wicked Nephites—Both peoples prosper during an era of peace and plenty—Lucifer, the author of sin, guides the Gadianton robbers in their murders and wickedness—They take over the Nephite government.

AND it came to pass that when the sixty and second year of the reign of the judges *had ended, all these things had happened and the Lamanites had become, the more part of them, a righteous people, insomuch that their [a]righteousness did exceed that of the Nephites, because of their firmness and their steadiness in the faith.
2 For behold, there were many of the Nephites who had become [a]hardened and impenitent and grossly wicked, insomuch that they did reject the word of God and all the preaching and prophesying which did come among them.
3 Nevertheless, the people of the church did have great joy because of the conversion of the Lamanites, yea, because of the church of God, which had been established among them. And they did [a]fellowship one with another, and did rejoice one with another, and did have great joy.
4 And it came to pass that many of the Lamanites did come down into the land of Zarahemla, and did declare unto the people of the Nephites the manner of their [a]conversion, and did exhort them to faith and repentance.
5 Yea, and many did [a]preach with exceedingly great power and authority, unto the bringing down many of them into the depths of humility, to be the humble followers of God and the Lamb.
6 And it came to pass that many of the Lamanites did go into the land northward; and also [a]Nephi and [b]Lehi went into the [c]land northward, to preach unto the people. And thus ended the sixty and third year.
7 And behold, there was peace in all the land, insomuch that the Nephites did go into whatsoever part of the land they would, whether among the Nephites or the Lamanites.
8 And it came to pass that the Lamanites did also go whithersoever they would, whether it were among the Lamanites or among the Nephites; and thus they did have free intercourse one with another, to [a]buy and to sell, and to get gain, according to their desire.
9 And it came to pass that they became exceedingly rich, both the Lamanites and the Nephites; and they did have an exceeding plenty of [a]gold, and of silver, and of all manner of precious metals, both in the land south and in the land north.
10 Now the land south was called [a]Lehi, and the land north was called [b]Mulek, which was after the [c]son of Zedekiah; for the Lord did bring Mulek into the land north, and Lehi into the land south.
11 And behold, there was all manner of gold in both these lands, and of silver, and of precious ore of every kind; and there were also curious workmen, who did [a]work all kinds of ore and did refine it; and thus they did become rich.
12 They did raise grain in abundance, both in the north and in the south; and they did flourish exceedingly, both in the north and in the

6 1*a* Hel. 13: 1.
2*a* Rom. 1: 28 (28–32); Hel. 6: 21. TG Hardheartedness.
3*a* TG Fellowshipping.
4*a* TG Conversion, Convert.
5*a* 1 Ne. 15: 20; Alma 48: 20.
6*a* Hel. 7: 1.
b Hel. 5: 44 (36–44); 11: 19.
c Alma 63: 9 (4–9); Hel. 3: 12 (11–12).
8*a* 3 Ne. 6: 11.
9*a* 1 Ne. 18: 25; 2 Ne. 5: 15 (14–16); Jacob 2: 12 (12–13); Ether 9: 17; 10: 23 (12, 23).
10*a* Alma 50: 25.
b Omni 1: 14; Mosiah 25: 2 (2–4); Hel. 8: 21.
c Jer. 39: 6; 52: 10; Ezek. 17: 22 (22–23); Alma 22: 31.
11*a* TG Industry.

[*29 B.C.]

south. And they did multiply and
wax exceedingly strong in the land.
And they did raise many flocks and
herds, yea, many fatlings.
13 Behold their women did toil
and spin, and did [a]make all manner
of [b]cloth, of fine-twined linen and
cloth of every kind, to clothe their
nakedness. And thus the sixty and
fourth year did pass away in
peace.
14 And in the *sixty and fifth year
they did also have great joy and
peace, yea, much preaching and
many prophecies concerning that
which was to come. And thus passed
away the sixty and fifth year.
15 And it came to pass that in the
†sixty and sixth year of the reign of
the judges, behold, [a]Cezoram was
murdered by an unknown hand as
he sat upon the judgment-seat. And
it came to pass that in the same year,
that his son, who had been appointed by the people in his stead,
was also murdered. And thus ended
the sixty and sixth year.
16 And in the ‡commencement of
the sixty and seventh year the
people began to grow exceedingly
wicked again.
17 For behold, the Lord had
blessed them so long with the [a]riches
of the world that they had not been
stirred up to anger, to wars, nor to
bloodshed; therefore they began to
set their hearts upon their riches;
yea, they began to seek to get gain
that they might be lifted up one
above another; therefore they began
to commit [b]secret murders, and to
rob and to plunder, that they might
get gain.
18 And now behold, those murderers and plunderers were a band who
had been formed by Kishkumen
and [a]Gadianton. And now it had
come to pass that there were many,
even among the Nephites, of
Gadianton's band. But behold, they
were more numerous among the
more wicked part of the Lamanites.
And they were called Gadianton's
robbers and murderers.
19 And it was they who did murder
the chief judge [a]Cezoram, and his
son, while in the judgment-seat;
and behold, they were not found.
20 And now it came to pass that
when the Lamanites found that
there were robbers among them they
were exceedingly sorrowful; and
they did use every means in their
power to destroy them off the face
of the earth.
21 But behold, Satan did stir up
the [a]hearts of the more part of the
Nephites, insomuch that they did
unite with those bands of robbers,
and did enter into their covenants
and their oaths, that they would
protect and preserve one another in
whatsoever difficult circumstances
they should be placed, that they
should not suffer for their murders,
and their plunderings, and their
[b]stealings.
22 And it came to pass that they
did have their signs, yea, their
[a]secret signs, and their [b]secret
words; and this that they might
distinguish a brother who had
entered into the covenant, that
whatsoever wickedness his brother
should do he should not be injured
by his brother, nor by those who did
belong to his band, who had taken
this covenant.
23 And thus they might murder,
and plunder, and steal, and commit
[a]whoredoms and all manner of
wickedness, contrary to the laws of
their country and also the laws of
their God.
24 And whosoever of those who
belonged to their band should reveal
unto the world of their [a]wickedness
and their abominations, should be

13*a* TG Art.
b Mosiah 10: 5; Alma 1: 29.
15*a* Hel. 5: 1; 6: 19.
17*a* TG Treasure.
b 3 Ne. 6: 23; 9: 9.
18*a* Hel. 2: 4 (4, 12–13, 23).
19*a* Hel. 6: 15.
21*a* Hel. 6: 2.
b TG Stealing.
22*a* Alma 37: 27. TG Secret Combinations.
b Hel. 11: 2; 3 Ne. 3: 7.
23*a* TG Whoredom.
24*a* TG Wickedness.

[*27 B.C. †26 B.C. ‡25 B.C.]

tried, not according to the laws of their country, but according to the laws of their wickedness, which had been given by Gadianton and Kishkumen.
25 Now behold, it is these secret [a]oaths and covenants which Alma commanded his son should not go forth unto the world, lest they should be a means of bringing down the people unto destruction.
26 Now behold, those [a]secret oaths and covenants did not come forth unto Gadianton from the [b]records which were delivered unto Helaman; but behold, they were put into the heart of [c]Gadianton by that [d]same being who did entice our first parents to partake of the forbidden fruit—
27 Yea, that same being who did plot with [a]Cain, that if he would murder his brother Abel it should not be known unto the world. And he did plot with Cain and his followers from that time forth.
28 And also it is that same being who put it into the hearts of the people to [a]build a tower sufficiently high that they might get to heaven. And it was that same being who led on the people who came from that tower into this land; who spread the works of darkness and abominations over all the face of the land, until he dragged the people down to an [b]entire destruction, and to an everlasting hell.
29 Yea, it is that same being who put it into the heart of [a]Gadianton to still carry on the work of darkness, and of secret murder; and he has brought it forth from the beginning of man even down to this time.
30 And behold, it is he who is the [a]author of all sin. And behold, he doth carry on his works of darkness and secret murder, and doth hand down their plots, and their oaths, and their covenants, and their plans of awful wickedness, from generation to generation according as he can get hold upon the hearts of the children of men.
31 And now behold, he had got great hold upon the hearts of the Nephites; yea, insomuch that they had become exceedingly wicked; yea, the more part of them had turned out of the [a]way of righteousness, and did [b]trample under their feet the commandments of God, and did turn unto their own ways, and did build up unto themselves [c]idols of their gold and their silver.
32 And it came to pass that all these iniquities did come unto them in the space of [a]not many years, insomuch that a more part of it had come unto them in the sixty and seventh year of the reign of the judges over the people of Nephi.
33 And they did grow in their iniquities in the *sixty and eighth year also, to the great sorrow and lamentation of the righteous.
34 And thus we see that the [a]Nephites did begin to dwindle in unbelief, and grow in wickedness and abominations, while the Lamanites began to grow exceedingly in the knowledge of their God; yea, they did begin to keep his statutes and commandments, and to walk in truth and uprightness before him.
35 And thus we see that the Spirit of the Lord began to [a]withdraw from the Nephites, because of the wickedness and the hardness of their hearts.
36 And thus we see that the Lord began to pour out his [a]Spirit upon the Lamanites, because of their easi-

25*a* Alma 37: 29 (27–32).
26*a* 3 Ne. 3: 9; Ether 8: 9 (9–19); Moses 5: 29 (29, 49–52).
b 3 Ne. 6: 28.
c Hel. 8: 28.
d Moses 4: 6 (6–12).
27*a* Moses 5: 25 (18–33).
28*a* Gen. 11: 4 (1–4); Ether 1: 3.
b Ether 8: 21 (9, 15–25).
29*a* Hel. 2: 4 (4–13).
30*a* Alma 5: 40 (39–42); Moro. 7: 12 (12, 17); Moses 4: 4.
31*a* Gen. 6: 12; 2 Ne. 28: 11.
b 1 Ne. 19: 7.
c Judg. 2: 17; 2 Ne. 9: 37; Alma 7: 6.
32*a* Alma 46: 8; Hel. 4: 26; 7: 6; 11: 26.
34*a* Moro. 9: 20.
35*a* Matt. 13: 15; Mosiah 2: 36; D&C 121: 37.
36*a* TG God, Spirit of.

[*24 B.C.]

ness and [b]willingness to believe in his words.

37 And it came to pass that the Lamanites did hunt the band of robbers of Gadianton; and they did preach the word of God among the more wicked part of them, insomuch that this band of robbers was utterly destroyed from among the Lamanites.

38 And it came to pass on the other hand, that the Nephites did build them up and support them, beginning at the more wicked part of them, until they had overspread all the land of the Nephites, and had seduced the more part of the righteous until they had come down to believe in their works and partake of their spoils, and to join with them in their secret murders and combinations.

39 And thus they did obtain the sole management of the government, insomuch that they did trample under their feet and smite and rend and turn their backs upon the [a]poor and the meek, and the humble followers of God.

40 And thus we see that they were in an awful state, and [a]ripening for an everlasting destruction.

41 And it came to pass that thus ended the sixty and eighth year of the reign of the judges over the people of Nephi.

THE PROPHECY OF NEPHI, THE SON OF HELAMAN—*God threatens the people of Nephi that he will visit them in his anger, to their utter destruction except they repent of their wickedness. God smiteth the people of Nephi with pestilence; they repent and turn unto him. Samuel, a Lamanite, prophesies unto the Nephites. Comprising chapters 7 to 16 inclusive.*

CHAPTER 7

Nephi is rejected in the north and returns to Zarahemla—He prays upon his garden tower and then calls upon the people to repent or perish.

BEHOLD, now it came to pass in the *sixty and ninth year of the reign of the judges over the people of the Nephites, that Nephi, the son of Helaman, [a]returned to the land of Zarahemla from the land northward.

2 For he had been forth among the people who were in the land northward, and did preach the word of God unto them, and did prophesy many things unto them;

3 And they did [a]reject all his words, insomuch that he could not stay among them, but returned again unto the land of his nativity.

4 And seeing the people in a state of such awful wickedness, and those Gadianton robbers filling the judgment-seats—having [a]usurped the power and authority of the land; laying aside the commandments of God, and not in the least aright before him; doing no justice unto the children of men;

5 Condemning the righteous because of their righteousness; letting the guilty and the wicked go [a]unpunished because of their [b]money; and moreover to be held in office at the head of government, to rule and do according to their wills, that they might get gain and glory of the [c]world, and, moreover, that they might the more easily commit adultery, and steal, and kill, and do according to their own wills—

6 Now this great iniquity had come upon the Nephites, in the space of [a]not many years; and when Nephi saw it, his heart was swollen with sorrow within his breast; and he did exclaim in the agony of his soul:

36*b* Ex. 25: 2 (1–7).
39*a* Ps. 109: 16 (15–16); Ezek. 22: 7 (7–13); Amos 5: 12; Alma 5: 55 (54–56); D&C 56: 16.
40*a* Hel. 5: 2; 11: 37; D&C 18: 6; 61: 31.
7 1*a* Hel. 6: 6.
3*a* TG Prophets, Rejection of.
4*a* TG Tyranny; Unrighteous Dominion.
5*a* Job 12: 6; 21: 7; Ps. 73: 12.
b TG Bribery.
c Matt. 13: 22; D&C 39: 9.
6*a* IE six years; see Hel. 4: 26; 6: 6, 32; 11: 26.

[*23 B.C.]

7 Oh, that I could have had my
days in the days when my father
Nephi first came out of the land of
Jerusalem, that I could have [a]joyed
with him in the promised land; then
were his people easy to be entreated,
[b]firm to keep the commandments of
God, and slow to be led to do iniquity;
and they were quick to hearken
unto the words of the Lord—
8 Yea, if my days could have been
in those days, then would my soul
have had joy in the righteousness of
my brethren.
9 But behold, I am consigned that
these are my days, and that my soul
shall be filled with [a]sorrow because of
this the wickedness of my brethren.
10 And behold, now it came to pass
that it was upon a tower, which was
in the [a]garden of Nephi, which was
by the highway which led to the chief
market, which was in the city of
Zarahemla; therefore, Nephi had
bowed himself upon the tower which
was in his garden, which tower was
also near unto the garden gate by
which led the highway.
11 And it came to pass that there
were certain men passing by and
saw Nephi as he was pouring out his
soul unto God upon the [a]tower; and
they ran and told the people what
they had seen, and the people came
together in multitudes that they
might know the cause of so great
mourning for the wickedness of the
people.
12 And now, when Nephi arose he
beheld the multitudes of people who
had gathered together.
13 And it came to pass that he
opened his mouth and said unto
them: Behold, [a]why have ye
gathered yourselves together? That
I may tell you of your iniquities?
14 Yea, because I have got upon
my tower that I might pour out my
soul unto my God, because of the
exceeding sorrow of my heart, which
is because of your iniquities!
15 And because of my [a]mourning
and lamentation ye have gathered
yourselves together, and do marvel;
yea, and ye have great need to
marvel; yea, ye ought to marvel
because ye are given away that the
devil has got so great hold upon your
hearts.
16 Yea, how could you have given
way to the enticing of him who is
seeking to hurl away your souls
down to [a]everlasting misery and
endless wo?
17 O repent ye, repent ye! [a]Why
will ye die? Turn ye, turn ye unto
the Lord your God. Why has he forsaken
you?
18 It is because you have hardened
your hearts; yea, ye will not
[a]hearken unto the voice of the [b]good
shepherd; yea, ye have [c]provoked
him to anger against you.
19 And behold, instead of [a]gathering
you, except ye will repent, behold,
he shall scatter you forth that
ye shall become meat for dogs and
wild beasts.
20 O, how could you have [a]forgotten
your God in the very day that
he has delivered you?
21 But behold, it is to get [a]gain, to
be [b]praised of men, yea, and that ye
might get gold and silver. And ye
have set your hearts upon the [c]riches
and the vain things of this world,
for the which ye do murder, and
plunder, and steal, and bear [d]false
witness against your neighbor, and
do all manner of iniquity.
22 And for this cause [a]wo shall
come unto you except ye shall re-

7*a* 2 Ne. 5:27 (26–28).
b D&C 5:22.
9*a* Jer. 9:1 (1–3).
10*a* Hel. 9:8.
11*a* Alma 50:4.
13*a* Matt. 3:7 (5–8).
15*a* TG Mourning.
16*a* Alma 26:20.
17*a* Isa. 1:5 (5–6); Ezek. 18:23 (23, 32).
18*a* TG Disobedience.
b Ezek. 34:12; John 10:14; Alma 5:60 (38–60). TG Jesus Christ, Good Shepherd.
c Num. 14:11 (11–12); 1 Ne. 17:30 (23–31); Jacob 1:8; Alma 12:37 (36–37).
19*a* 3 Ne. 10:4 (4–7).
20*a* Isa. 17:10 (4–11).
21*a* TG Selfishness.
b TG Peer Influence.
c TG Treasure.
d Matt. 15:19 (19–20). TG Slander.
22*a* Rev. 8:13; D&C 5:5.

[Between 23 and 20 B.C.]

pent. For if ye will not repent, behold, this [b]great city, and also all those great cities which are round about, which are in the land of our possession, shall be taken away that ye shall have no place in them; for behold, the Lord will not grant unto you [c]strength, as he has hitherto done, to withstand against your enemies.

23 For behold, thus saith the Lord: I will not show unto the wicked of my strength, to one more than the other, save it be unto those who repent of their sins, and hearken unto my words. Now therefore, I would that ye should behold, my brethren, that it shall be [a]better for the Lamanites than for you except ye shall repent.

24 For behold, they are more righteous than you, for they have not sinned against that great knowledge which ye have received; therefore the Lord will be merciful unto them; yea, he will [a]lengthen out their days and increase their seed, even when thou shalt be utterly [b]destroyed except thou shalt repent.

25 Yea, wo be unto you because of that great abomination which has come among you; and ye have united yourselves unto it, yea, to that [a]secret band which was established by Gadianton!

26 Yea, [a]wo shall come unto you because of that pride which ye have suffered to enter your hearts, which has lifted you up beyond that which is good because of your exceedingly great riches!

27 Yea, wo be unto you because of your wickedness and abominations!

28 And except ye repent ye shall perish; yea, even your lands shall be taken from you, and ye shall be destroyed from off the face of the earth.

29 Behold now, I do not say that these things shall be, of myself, because it is not of myself that I [a]know these things; but behold, I [b]know that these things are true because the Lord God has made them known unto me, therefore I testify that they shall be.

CHAPTER 8

Corrupt judges seek to incite the people against Nephi—Abraham, Moses, Zenos, Zenock, Ezias, Isaiah, Jeremiah, Lehi, and Nephi all testified of Christ—By inspiration Nephi announces the murder of the chief judge.

AND now it came to pass that when Nephi had said these words, behold, there were men who were judges, who also belonged to the secret band of Gadianton, and they were angry, and they cried out against him, saying unto the people: Why do ye not seize upon this man and bring him forth, that he may be condemned according to the crime which he has done?

2 Why seest thou this man, and hearest him revile against this people and against our law?

3 For behold, Nephi had spoken unto them concerning the corruptness of their law; yea, many things did Nephi speak which cannot be written; and nothing did he speak which was contrary to the commandments of God.

4 And those judges were angry with him because he [a]spake plainly unto them concerning their secret works of darkness; nevertheless, they durst not lay their own hands upon him, for they feared the people lest they should cry out against them.

5 Therefore they did cry unto the people, saying: Why do you suffer this man to revile against us? For behold he doth condemn all this

22*b* Hel. 8: 5.
c Mosiah 7: 29.
23*a* Hel. 15: 14 (11–15).
24*a* Ex. 20: 12; 1 Ne. 17: 55; Alma 9: 16; D&C 5: 33.
b Alma 9: 19; Hel. 10: 14.
25*a* 2 Ne. 10: 15; Hel. 3: 23.
26*a* Isa. 5: 8 (8–25).
29*a* Hel. 8: 8.
b Hel. 8: 12.
8 4*a* 1 Ne. 16: 2 (2–3).

[Between 23 and 20 B.C.]

people, even unto destruction; yea, and also that these our [a]great cities shall be taken from us, that we shall have no place in them.

6 And now we know that this is impossible, for behold, we are [a]powerful, and our cities great, therefore our enemies can have no power over us.

7 And it came to pass that thus they did [a]stir up the people to anger against Nephi, and raised contentions among them; for there were some who did cry out: [b]Let this man alone, for he is a good man, and those things which he saith will surely come to pass except we repent;

8 Yea, behold, all the judgments will come upon us which he has testified unto us; for we know that he has testified aright unto us concerning our iniquities. And behold they are many, and he [a]knoweth as well all things which shall befall us as he knoweth of our iniquities;

9 Yea, and behold, if he had not been a prophet he could not have [a]testified concerning those things.

10 And it came to pass that those people who sought to destroy Nephi were compelled because of their fear, that they did not lay their hands on him; therefore he began again to speak unto them, seeing that he had gained favor in the eyes of some, insomuch that the remainder of them did fear.

11 Therefore he was constrained to speak more unto them saying: Behold, my brethren, have ye not read that God gave power unto one man, even Moses, to smite upon the waters of the Red [a]Sea, and they parted hither and thither, insomuch that the Israelites, who were our fathers, came through upon dry ground, and the waters closed upon the armies of the Egyptians and swallowed them up?

12 And now behold, if God gave unto this man such power, then why should ye dispute among yourselves, and say that he hath given unto me no power whereby I may [a]know concerning the judgments that shall come upon you except ye repent?

13 But, behold, ye not only deny my words, but ye also deny all the words which have been spoken by our fathers, and also the words which were spoken by this man, Moses, who had such great power given unto him, yea, the words which he hath spoken concerning the coming of the Messiah.

14 Yea, did he not bear record that the Son of God should come? And as he [a]lifted up the brazen serpent in the wilderness, even so shall he be lifted up who should come.

15 And as many as should look upon that serpent should [a]live, even so as many as should look upon the Son of God with faith, having a contrite spirit, might [b]live, even unto that life which is eternal.

16 And now behold, Moses did not only testify of these things, but also [a]all the holy prophets, from his days even to the days of Abraham.

17 Yea, and behold, [a]Abraham saw of his coming, and was filled with gladness and did rejoice.

18 Yea, and behold I say unto you, that Abraham not only knew of these things, but there were [a]many before the days of Abraham who were called by the [b]order of God;

5*a* Hel. 7: 22.
6*a* Moses 8: 21 (20–22).
7*a* TG Provoking.
b Acts 5: 38 (37–40).
8*a* Hel. 7: 29. TG God, Foreknowledge of.
9*a* TG Testimony.
11*a* Ex. 14: 16; Josh. 2: 10; Neh. 9: 11; 1 Ne. 17: 26; Mosiah 7: 19; D&C 8: 3; Moses 1: 25.
12*a* Hel. 7: 29 (28–29).
14*a* Num. 21: 9 (6–9); 2 Ne. 25: 20; Alma 33: 19 (19–22). TG Jesus Christ, Types of, in Anticipation.
15*a* 1 Ne. 17: 41; Alma 37: 46 (46–47); 3 Ne. 15: 9.
b John 11: 25.
16*a* Luke 24: 27; Rev. 19: 10; Jacob 4: 4 (4–5); 7: 11.
17*a* Gen. 22: 8 (8–14); John 8: 56 (53, 56).
18*a* Alma 13: 19; D&C 84: 14 (6–16); 136: 37.
b TG Priesthood.

[Between 23 and 20 B.C.]

yea, even after the order of his Son;
and this that it should be shown unto
the people, a great many thousand
years before his coming, that even
redemption should come unto
them.
19 And now I would that ye should
know, that even since the days of
Abraham there have been many
prophets that have testified these
things; yea, behold, the prophet
[a]Zenos did testify boldly; for the
which he was slain.
20 And behold, also [a]Zenock, and
also [b]Ezias, and also [c]Isaiah, and
[d]Jeremiah, (Jeremiah being that
same prophet who testified of the
destruction of [e]Jerusalem) and now
we know that Jerusalem was
destroyed according to the words
of Jeremiah. O then why not the
Son of God come, according to his
prophecy?
21 And now will you dispute that
[a]Jerusalem was destroyed? Will ye
say that the [b]sons of Zedekiah were
not slain, all except it were [c]Mulek?
Yea, and do ye not behold that the
seed of Zedekiah are with us, and
they were driven out of the land of
Jerusalem? But behold, this is not
all—
22 Our father Lehi was driven out
of Jerusalem because he [a]testified of
these things. Nephi also testified of
these things, and also almost all of
our fathers, even down to this time;
yea, they have testified of the
[b]coming of Christ, and have looked
forward, and have rejoiced in his day
which is to come.
23 And behold, he is God, and he is
[a]with them, and he did manifest
himself unto them, that they were
redeemed by him; and they gave
unto him glory, because of that
which is to come.
24 And now, seeing ye know these
things and cannot deny them except
ye shall lie, therefore in this ye have
sinned, for ye have rejected all these
things, notwithstanding so many
[a]evidences which ye have received;
yea, even ye have received [b]all
things, both things in heaven, and
all things which are in the earth, as
a witness that they are true.
25 But behold, ye have rejected the
truth, and [a]rebelled against your
holy God; and even at this time,
instead of laying up for yourselves
[b]treasures in heaven, where nothing
doth corrupt, and where nothing
can come which is unclean, ye are
heaping up for yourselves wrath
against the day of [c]judgment.
26 Yea, even at this time ye are
ripening, because of your murders
and your [a]fornication and wickedness, for everlasting destruction;
yea, and except ye repent it will
come unto you soon.
27 Yea, behold it is now even at
your doors; yea, go ye in unto the
judgment-seat, and search; and
behold, your judge is murdered, and
he [a]lieth in his blood; and he hath
been murdered [b]by his brother, who
seeketh to sit in the judgment-seat.
28 And behold, they both belong
to your secret band, whose [a]author
is Gadianton and the evil one who
seeketh to destroy the souls of
men.

19*a* Alma 34: 7; Hel. 15: 11.
20*a* 1 Ne. 19: 10; Alma 33: 15; 34: 7; 3 Ne. 10: 16 (15–16).
b TG Scriptures, Lost.
c Isa. 53: 2 (1–12).
d 1 Ne. 5: 13; 7: 14.
e Jer. 26: 18 (17–19); 1 Ne. 1: 4 (4–18); 2 Ne. 6: 8; 25: 6.
21*a* Omni 1: 15.
b 2 Kgs. 25: 7; Jer. 39: 6; 52: 10.
c Ezek. 17: 22 (22–23); Hel. 6: 10; Morm. 7: 2.
22*a* D&C 138: 49.
b TG Jesus Christ, Prophecies about.
23*a* Alma 40: 11 (11–12).
24*a* 2 Kgs. 17: 13; 1 Ne. 10: 5.
b Alma 30: 44; Moses 6: 63.
25*a* Ps. 5: 10; Mosiah 2: 37 (36–38); 3: 12.
b Hel. 5: 8; 3 Ne. 13: 20 (19–21). TG Treasure.
c Ps. 109: 7 (3–7); D&C 10: 23 (20–23); 121: 24 (23–25).
26*a* TG Fornication.
27*a* Hel. 9: 3, 15.
b Hel. 9: 6 (6, 26–38).
28*a* Hel. 6: 26 (26–30).

[Between 23 and 20 B.C.]

CHAPTER 9

Messengers find the chief judge dead at the judgment seat—They are imprisoned and later released—By inspiration Nephi identifies Seantum as the murderer—Nephi is accepted by some as a prophet.

BEHOLD, now it came to pass that
when Nephi had spoken these words,
certain men who were among them
ran to the judgment-seat; yea, even
there were [a]five who went, and they
said among themselves, as they
went:
2 Behold, now we will know of a
surety whether this man be a
prophet and God hath commanded
him to prophesy such marvelous
things unto us. Behold, we do not
[a]believe that he hath; yea, we do not
believe that he is a prophet; nevertheless, if this thing which he has
said concerning the chief judge be
true, that he be dead, then will we
believe that the other words which
he has spoken are true.
3 And it came to pass that they ran
in their might, and came in unto the
judgment-seat; and behold, the
chief judge had fallen to the earth,
and did [a]lie in his blood.
4 And now behold, when they saw
this they were astonished exceedingly, insomuch that they fell to the
earth; for they had not believed the
words which Nephi had spoken concerning the chief judge.
5 But now, when they saw they
believed, and fear came upon them
lest all the judgments which Nephi
had spoken [a]should come upon the
people; therefore they did quake,
and had fallen to the earth.
6 Now, immediately when the
judge had been murdered—he being
stabbed by his brother by a garb of
secrecy, and he fled, and the servants
ran and told the people, raising the
cry of murder among them;
7 And behold the people did gather
themselves together unto the place
of the judgment-seat—and behold,
to their astonishment they saw
those [a]five men who had fallen to
the earth.
8 And now behold, the people knew
nothing concerning the multitude
who had gathered together at the
[a]garden of Nephi; therefore they
said among themselves: These men
are they who have murdered the
judge, and God has smitten them
that they could not flee from us.
9 And it came to pass that they laid
hold on them, and bound them and
cast them into prison. And there
was a proclamation sent abroad that
the judge was slain, and that the
murderers had been taken and were
cast into prison.
10 And it came to pass that on the
morrow the people did assemble
themselves together to [a]mourn and
to [b]fast, at the burial of the great
chief judge who had been slain.
11 And thus also those judges who
were at the garden of Nephi, and
heard his words, were also gathered
together at the burial.
12 And it came to pass that they
inquired among the people, saying:
Where are the five who were sent to
inquire concerning the chief judge
whether he was dead? And they
answered and said: Concerning this
five whom ye say ye have sent, we
know not; but there are five who
are the murderers, whom we have
cast into prison.
13 And it came to pass that the
judges desired that they should be
brought; and they were brought,
and behold they were the five who
were sent; and behold the judges
inquired of them to know concerning the matter, and they told them
all that they had done, saying:
14 We ran and came to the place
of the judgment-seat, and when we
saw all things even as Nephi had
testified, we were astonished inso-

9 1*a* Hel. 9: 7 (7, 12).
2*a* Dan. 2: 9.
3*a* Hel. 8: 27.
5*a* 2 Kgs. 22: 13 (8–20).
7*a* Hel. 9: 1.
8*a* Hel. 7: 10 (10–11, 14).
10*a* TG Mourning.
b TG Fasting.

[Between 23 and 20 B.C.]

much that we fell to the earth; and when we were recovered from our astonishment, behold they cast us into [a]prison.

15 Now, as for the murder of this man, we know not who has done it; and only this much we know, we ran and came [a]according as ye desired, and behold he was dead, according to the words of Nephi.

16 And now it came to pass that the judges did expound the matter unto the people, and did cry out against Nephi, saying: Behold, we know that this Nephi must have agreed with some one to slay the judge, and then he might declare it unto us, that he might convert us unto his faith, that he might raise himself to be a great man, chosen of God, and a prophet.

17 And now behold, we will detect this man, and he shall confess his fault and make known unto us the true murderer of this judge.

18 And it came to pass that the five were liberated on the day of the burial. Nevertheless, they did rebuke the judges in the words which they had spoken against Nephi, and did contend with them one by one, insomuch that they did confound them.

19 Nevertheless, they caused that Nephi should be taken and bound and brought before the multitude, and they began to question him in divers ways that they might cross him, that they might accuse him to death—

20 Saying unto him: Thou art confederate; who is this man that hath done this murder? Now tell us, and acknowledge thy fault; saying, Behold here is [a]money; and also we will grant unto thee thy life if thou wilt tell us, and acknowledge the agreement which thou hast made with him.

21 But Nephi said unto them: O ye [a]fools, ye uncircumcised of heart, ye blind, and ye [b]stiffnecked people, do ye know how long the Lord your God will suffer you that ye shall go on in this your way of sin?

22 O ye ought to begin to howl and [a]mourn, because of the great destruction which at this time doth await you, except ye shall repent.

23 Behold ye say that I have agreed with a man that he should murder Seezoram, our chief judge. But behold, I say unto you, that this is because I have testified unto you that ye might know concerning this thing; yea, even for a witness unto you, that I did know of the wickedness and abominations which are among you.

24 And because I have done this, ye say that I have agreed with a man that he should do this thing; yea, because I showed unto you this sign ye are angry with me, and seek to destroy my life.

25 And now behold, I will show unto you another sign, and see if ye will in this thing seek to destroy me.

26 Behold I say unto you: Go to the house of Seantum, who is the [a]brother of Seezoram, and say unto him—

27 Has Nephi, the pretended prophet, who doth prophesy so much evil concerning this people, agreed with thee, in the which ye have murdered Seezoram, who is your brother?

28 And behold, he shall say unto you, Nay.

29 And ye shall say unto him: Have ye murdered your brother?

30 And he shall stand with fear, and wist not what to say. And behold, he shall deny unto you; and he shall make as if he were astonished; nevertheless, he shall declare unto you that he is innocent.

31 But behold, ye shall examine

14*a* Gen. 39:20.
15*a* Hel. 8:27.
20*a* 1 Sam. 8:3 (1–4); Ether 9:11.
TG Bribery.
21*a* Ps. 75:4; Luke 24:25; Acts 7:51.
b TG Stiffneckedness.
22*a* Ezek. 24:23; Mosiah 7:24.
26*a* Hel. 8:27.

[Between 23 and 20 B.C.]

him, and ye shall find blood upon
the skirts of his cloak.
32 And when ye have seen this, ye
shall say: From whence cometh this
blood? Do we not know that it is the
blood of your brother?
33 And then shall he tremble, and
shall look pale, even as if death had
come upon him.
34 And then shall ye say: Because
of this fear and this paleness which
has come upon your face, behold,
we know that thou art guilty.
35 And then shall greater fear come
upon him; and then shall he confess
unto you, and deny no more that he
has done this murder.
36 And then shall he say unto you,
that I, Nephi, know nothing concerning the matter save it were given
unto me by the power of God. And
then shall ye know that I am an
honest man, and that I am sent unto
you from God.
37 And it came to pass that they
went and did, even according as
Nephi had said unto them. And
behold, the words which he had said
were true; for according to the words
he did deny; and also according to
the words he did confess.
38 And he was brought to prove
that he himself was the very
murderer, insomuch that the five
were set at liberty, and also was
Nephi.
39 And there were some of the
Nephites who believed on the words
of Nephi; and there were some also,
who believed because of the testimony of the five, for they had been
converted while they were in prison.
40 And now there were some among
the people, who said that Nephi was
a prophet.
41 And there were others who said:
Behold, he is a god, for except he
was a god he could not [a]know of all
things. For behold, he has told us
the thoughts of our hearts, and also
has told us things; and even he has
brought unto our knowledge the
true murderer of our chief judge.

CHAPTER 10

The Lord gives Nephi the sealing power—He is empowered to bind and loose on earth and in heaven—He commands the people to repent or perish—The Spirit carries him from congregation to congregation.

AND it came to pass that there
arose a division among the people,
insomuch that they divided hither
and thither and went their ways,
leaving Nephi alone, as he was
standing in the midst of them.
2 And it came to pass that Nephi
went his way towards his own house,
[a]pondering upon the things which
the Lord had shown unto him.
3 And it came to pass as he was
thus pondering—being much cast
down because of the wickedness of
the people of the Nephites, their
secret works of darkness, and their
murderings, and their plunderings,
and all manner of iniquities—and it
came to pass as he was thus pondering in his heart, behold, a [a]voice
came unto him saying:
4 [a]Blessed art thou, Nephi, for
those things which thou hast done;
for I have beheld how thou hast with
[b]unwearyingness declared the word,
which I have given unto thee, unto
this people. And thou hast not
feared them, and hast not sought
thine [c]own life, but hast sought my
[d]will, and to keep my commandments.
5 And now, because thou hast done
this with such unwearyingness, behold, I will bless thee forever; and I
will make thee mighty in word and
in deed, in faith and in works; yea,
even that [a]all things shall be [b]done

41*a* TG God, Omniscience of.
10 2*a* TG Meditation.
3*a* TG Guidance, Divine.
4*a* Acts 23: 11.
b Acts 20: 31.
TG Dedication; Dependability; Priesthood, Magnifying Callings within; Steadfastness.
c TG Self-sacrifice.
d Mosiah 24: 15; 3 Ne. 11: 11.
5*a* 3 Ne. 18: 20; D&C 88: 64 (63–65).
b Ex. 33: 17.

[Between 23 and 20 B.C.]

unto thee according to thy [c]word, for thou shalt [d]not ask that which is contrary to my will.

6 Behold, thou art Nephi, and I am God. Behold, I declare it unto thee in the presence of mine angels, that ye shall have power over this people, and shall smite the earth with [a]famine, and with pestilence, and destruction, according to the wickedness of this people.

7 Behold, I give unto you [a]power, that whatsoever ye shall [b]seal on earth shall be sealed in heaven; and whatsoever ye shall loose on earth shall be loosed in heaven; and thus shall ye have power among this people.

8 And thus, if ye shall say unto this temple it shall be rent in twain, it shall be done.

9 And if ye shall say unto this [a]mountain, Be thou cast down and become smooth, it shall be done.

10 And behold, if ye shall say that God shall smite this people, it shall come to pass.

11 And now behold, I command you, that ye shall go and declare unto this people, that thus saith the Lord God, who is the Almighty: Except ye repent ye shall be smitten, even unto [a]destruction.

12 And behold, now it came to pass that when the Lord had spoken these words unto Nephi, he did stop and did not go unto his own house, but did return unto the multitudes who were scattered about upon the face of the land, and began to declare unto them the word of the Lord which had been spoken unto him, concerning their destruction if they did not repent.

13 Now behold, [a]notwithstanding that great miracle which Nephi had done in telling them concerning the death of the chief judge, they did harden their hearts and did not hearken unto the words of the Lord.

14 Therefore Nephi did declare unto them the word of the Lord, saying: Except ye repent, thus saith the Lord, ye shall be [a]smitten even unto destruction.

15 And it came to pass that when Nephi had declared unto them the word, behold, they did still harden their hearts and would not hearken unto his words; therefore they did [a]revile against him, and did seek to lay their hands upon him that they might cast him into prison.

16 But behold, the power of God was with him, and they could not take him to cast him into prison, for he was taken by the Spirit and [a]conveyed away out of the midst of them.

17 And it came to pass that thus he did go forth in the Spirit, from multitude to multitude, declaring the word of God, even until he had declared it unto them all, or sent it forth among all the people.

18 And it came to pass that they would not hearken unto his words; and there began to be contentions, insomuch that they were divided against themselves and began to slay one another with the sword.

19 And thus ended the seventy and first year of the reign of the judges over the people of Nephi.

CHAPTER 11

Nephi persuades the Lord to replace their war with a famine—Many people perish—They repent, and Nephi importunes the Lord for rain—Nephi and Lehi receive many revelations—The Gadianton robbers entrench themselves in the land.

5*c* 1 Kgs. 17: 1; Enos 1: 12.
d James 4: 3 (1–3); 2 Ne. 4: 35; D&C 46: 30.
6*a* Hel. 11: 4 (4–18). TG Drought.
7*a* Hel. 11: 18.
b Matt. 16: 19. TG Priesthood, Authority.
9*a* Matt. 17: 20; Jacob 4: 6; Morm. 8: 24; Ether 12: 30.
11*a* Hel. 5: 2; 11: 8.
13*a* Mark 6: 6 (4–6).
14*a* Hel. 7: 24.
15*a* TG Reviling.
16*a* Acts 8: 39 (39–40).

[Between 23 and 20 B.C.]

AND now it came to pass in the
*seventy and second year of the
reign of the judges that the contentions did increase, insomuch that
there were wars throughout all the
land among all the people of Nephi.
2 And it was this [a]secret band of
robbers who did carry on this work
of destruction and wickedness. And
this war did last all that year; and
in the †seventy and third year it did
also last.
3 And it came to pass that in this
year Nephi did cry unto the Lord,
saying:
4 O Lord, do not suffer that this
people shall be destroyed by the
sword; but O Lord, rather [a]let there
be a [b]famine in the land, to stir them
up in remembrance of the Lord their
God, and perhaps they will repent
and turn unto thee.
5 And so it was done, according to
the words of Nephi. And there was a
great famine upon the land, among
all the people of Nephi. And thus in
the ‡seventy and fourth year the
famine did continue, and the work
of destruction did cease by the
sword but became sore by famine.
6 And this work of destruction did
also continue in the §seventy and
fifth year. For the earth was smitten
that it was [a]dry, and did not yield
forth grain in the season of grain;
and the whole earth was smitten,
even among the Lamanites as well
as among the Nephites, so that they
were smitten that they did perish by
thousands in the more wicked parts
of the land.
7 And it came to pass that the
people saw that they were about to
perish by famine, and they began
to [a]remember the Lord their God;
and they began to remember the
words of Nephi.
8 And the people [a]began to plead
with their chief judges and their
leaders, that they would say unto
Nephi: Behold, we know that thou
art a man of God, and therefore cry
unto the Lord our God that he turn
away from us this famine, lest all the
words which thou hast spoken concerning our [b]destruction be fulfilled.
9 And it came to pass that the
judges did say unto Nephi, according to the words which had been
desired. And it came to pass that
when Nephi saw that the people had
[a]repented and did humble themselves in sackcloth, he cried again
unto the Lord, saying:
10 O Lord, behold this people
repenteth; and they have swept
away the band of Gadianton from
amongst them insomuch that they
have become extinct, and they have
concealed their secret plans in the
earth.
11 Now, O Lord, because of this
their humility wilt thou turn away
thine anger, and let thine anger be
appeased in the destruction of those
wicked men whom thou hast already
destroyed.
12 O Lord, wilt thou turn away
thine anger, yea, thy fierce anger,
and cause that this famine may cease
in this land.
13 O Lord, wilt thou hearken unto
me, and cause that it may be done
according to my words, and send
forth [a]rain upon the face of the earth,
that she may bring forth her fruit,
and her grain in the season of grain.
14 O Lord, thou didst hearken unto
[a]my words when I said, Let there be
a famine, that the pestilence of the
sword might cease; and I know that
thou wilt, even at this time, hearken
unto my words, for thou saidst that:
If this people repent I will spare
them.
15 Yea, O Lord, and thou seest that
they have repented, because of the
famine and the pestilence and

11 2*a* Hel. 6: 22 (18–24); 11: 26 (25–26).
4*a* Hel. 11: 14.
b 1 Kgs. 8: 35; 1 Chr. 21: 12; Hel. 10: 6. TG Famine.
6*a* TG Drought.
7*a* Amos 4: 7 (6–10); Hel. 12: 3.
8*a* Ex. 10: 7.
b Hel. 10: 11 (11–14).
9*a* Morm. 2: 12.
13*a* 1 Kgs. 18: 41 (1, 41–46).
14*a* Hel. 11: 4.

[*20 B.C. †19 B.C. ‡18 B.C. §17 B.C.]

destruction which has come unto
them.
16 And now, O Lord, wilt thou turn
away thine anger, and try again if
they will serve thee? And if so, O
Lord, thou canst bless them according
to thy words which thou hast
said.
17 And it came to pass that in the
*seventy and sixth year the Lord
did turn away his anger from the
people, and caused that [a]rain should
fall upon the earth, insomuch that
it did bring forth her fruit in the
season of her fruit. And it came to
pass that it did bring forth her grain
in the season of her grain.
18 And behold, the people did rejoice
and glorify God, and the whole
face of the land was filled with rejoicing;
and they did no more seek
to destroy Nephi, but they did
esteem him as a [a]great prophet, and a
man of God, having great power and
authority given unto him from God.
19 And behold, Lehi, his brother,
was not a [a]whit behind him as to
things pertaining to righteousness.
20 And thus it did come to pass
that the people of Nephi began to
prosper again in the land, and began
to build up their waste places,
and began to multiply and spread,
even until they did [a]cover the
whole face of the land, both on the
northward and on the southward,
from the sea west to the sea east.
21 And it came to pass that the
seventy and sixth year did end in
peace. And the seventy and seventh
year began in peace; and the [a]church
did spread throughout the face of all
the land; and the more part of the
people, both the Nephites and the
Lamanites, did belong to the church;
and they did have exceedingly great
peace in the land; and thus ended
the seventy and seventh year.
22 And also they had peace in the
seventy and eighth year, save it
were a few contentions concerning
the points of doctrine which had
been laid down by the prophets.
23 And in the †seventy and ninth
year there began to be much strife.
But it came to pass that Nephi and
Lehi, and many of their brethren
who knew concerning the true points
of doctrine, having many [a]revelations
daily, therefore they did
preach unto the people, insomuch
that they did put an end to their
strife in that same year.
24 And it came to pass that in the
‡eightieth year of the reign of the
judges over the people of Nephi,
there were a certain number of the
dissenters from the people of Nephi,
who had some years before gone
over unto the Lamanites, and taken
upon themselves the name of
Lamanites, and also a certain number
who were real descendants of
the Lamanites, being stirred up to
anger by them, or by those dissenters,
therefore they commenced a
[a]war with their brethren.
25 And they did commit murder
and plunder; and then they would
retreat back into the mountains,
and into the wilderness and secret
places, hiding themselves that they
could not be discovered, receiving
daily an addition to their numbers,
inasmuch as there were dissenters
that went forth unto them.
26 And thus in time, yea, even in
the space of [a]not many years, they
became an exceedingly great band
of robbers; and they did search out
all the [b]secret plans of Gadianton;
and thus they became robbers of
Gadianton.
27 Now behold, these robbers did
make great havoc, yea, even great
destruction among the people of
Nephi, and also among the people
of the Lamanites.

17*a* Deut. 11: 14 (13–17); Ether 2: 24; D&C 117: 1.
18*a* Hel. 10: 7 (5–11).
19*a* Hel. 5: 44 (36–44); 6: 6.
20*a* Jarom 1: 6; Alma 22: 27 (27, 32–33); Hel. 3: 8; 3 Ne. 1: 17.
21*a* TG Church; Peace.
23*a* Jarom 1: 4; Alma 26: 22; D&C 107: 19.
24*a* Hel. 4: 3.
26*a* Hel. 4: 26; 6: 32; 7: 6.
b Hel. 11: 2.

[*16 B.C. †13 B.C. ‡12 B.C.]

28 And it came to pass that it was
expedient that there should be a
stop put to this work of destruction;
therefore they sent an army of
strong men into the wilderness and
upon the mountains to search out
this band of robbers, and to destroy
them.
29 But behold, it came to pass that
in that same year they were driven
back even into their own lands. And
thus ended the eightieth year of the
reign of the judges over the people
of Nephi.
30 And it came to pass in the
*commencement of the eighty and
first year they did go forth again
against this band of robbers, and
did destroy many; and they were
also visited with much destruction.
31 And they were again obliged to
return out of the wilderness and out
of the [a]mountains unto their own
lands, because of the exceeding
greatness of the numbers of those
robbers who infested the mountains
and the wilderness.
32 And it came to pass that thus
ended this year. And the robbers did
still increase and wax strong, insomuch that they did defy the whole
armies of the Nephites, and also of
the Lamanites; and they did cause
great fear to come unto the people
upon all the face of the land.
33 Yea, for they did visit many
parts of the land, and did do great
destruction unto them; yea, did kill
many, and did carry away others
captive into the wilderness, yea,
and more especially their women
and their children.
34 Now this great evil, which came
unto the people because of their
iniquity, did stir them up again in
[a]remembrance of the Lord their God.
35 And thus ended the eighty and
first year of the reign of the judges.
36 And in the eighty and second
year they began again to [a]forget the
Lord their God. And in the eighty
and third year they began to wax
strong in iniquity. And in the eighty
and fourth year they did not mend
their ways.
37 And it came to pass in the
†eighty and fifth year they did wax
stronger and stronger in their pride,
and in their wickedness; and thus
they were [a]ripening again for
destruction.
38 And thus ended the eighty and
fifth year.

CHAPTER 12

Men are unstable and foolish and quick to do evil—The Lord chastens his people—The nothingness of men compared with the power of God—In the day of judgment men shall gain everlasting life or everlasting damnation.

AND thus we can behold how false,
and also the unsteadiness of the
hearts of the children of men; yea,
we can see that the Lord in his great
infinite goodness doth bless and
[a]prosper those who put their [b]trust
in him.
2 Yea, and we may see at the very
[a]time when he doth [b]prosper his
people, yea, in the increase of their
fields, their flocks and their herds,
and in gold, and in silver, and in all
manner of [c]precious things of every
kind and art; sparing their lives,
and delivering them out of the hands
of their enemies; softening the
hearts of their enemies that they
should not declare wars against
them; yea, and in fine, doing all
things for the welfare and happiness
of his people; yea, then is the time
that they do [d]harden their hearts,
and do [e]forget the Lord their God,
and do [f]trample under their feet the

31*a* 3 Ne. 1: 27.
34*a* Hosea 5: 15.
36*a* Mosiah 13: 29.
37*a* Hel. 6: 40.
12 1*a* 2 Chr. 26: 5; Ps. 1: 3 (2–3).
b Ps. 36: 7 (7–8); 2 Ne. 22: 2; Mosiah 4: 6. TG Trust in God.
2*a* Alma 46: 8; Hel. 4: 26; 6: 32.
b Ps. 62: 10.
c TG Treasure.
d TG Apostasy of Individuals.
e Deut. 8: 11 (10–20).
f Alma 5: 53; 3 Ne. 28: 35. TG Sacrilege.

[*11 B.C. †7 B.C.]

Holy One—yea, and this because of
their ease, and their exceedingly
great prosperity.
3 And thus we see that except the
Lord doth [a]chasten his people with
many afflictions, yea, except he doth
visit them with [b]death and with
terror, and with famine and with all
manner of pestilence, they will not
[c]remember him.
4 O how [a]foolish, and how vain,
and how evil, and devilish, and how
[b]quick to do iniquity, and how slow
to do good, are the children of men;
yea, how quick to hearken unto the
words of the evil one, and to set their
[c]hearts upon the vain things of the
world!
5 Yea, how quick to be lifted up in
[a]pride; yea, how quick to [b]boast,
and do all manner of that which is
iniquity; and how slow are they to
remember the Lord their God, and
to give ear unto his counsels, yea,
how slow to [c]walk in wisdom's paths!
6 Behold, they do not desire that
the Lord their God, who hath
[a]created them, should [b]rule and reign
over them; notwithstanding his
great goodness and his mercy
towards them, they do set at
[c]naught his counsels, and they will
not that he should be their guide.
7 O how great is the [a]nothingness of
the children of men; yea, even they
are [b]less than the dust of the earth.
8 For behold, the dust of the earth
moveth hither and thither, to the
dividing asunder, at the command
of our great and everlasting God.
9 Yea, behold at his [a]voice do the
hills and the mountains tremble and
[b]quake.
10 And by the [a]power of his voice
they are broken up, and become
smooth, yea, even like unto a valley.
11 Yea, by the power of his voice
doth the [a]whole earth shake;
12 Yea, by the power of his voice,
do the foundations rock, even to the
very center.
13 Yea, and if he say unto the
earth—Move—it is moved.
14 Yea, if he say unto the [a]earth—
Thou shalt [b]go back, that it [c]lengthen
out the day for many hours—it is
done;
15 And thus, according to his word
the [a]earth goeth back, and it
appeareth unto man that the [b]sun
standeth still; yea, and behold, this
is so; for surely it is the earth that
moveth and not the sun.
16 And behold, also, if he say unto
the [a]waters of the great deep—[b]Be
thou dried up—it is done.
17 Behold, if he say unto this
mountain—Be thou raised up, and
[a]come over and fall upon that city,
that it be buried up—behold it is
done.
18 And behold, if a man [a]hide up a
treasure in the earth, and the Lord
shall say—Let it be [b]accursed,
because of the iniquity of him who
hath hid it up—behold, it shall be
accursed.
19 And if the Lord shall say—Be
thou accursed, that no man shall
find thee from this time henceforth
and forever—behold, no man get-
teth it henceforth and forever.

3*a* Deut. 11: 2 (1–8); Ezek. 20: 26; Mosiah 23: 21; D&C 98: 21; 101: 8.
b Ps. 78: 34.
c Amos 4: 6 (6–11); Jonah 2: 7; Mosiah 1: 17.
4*a* TG Foolishness.
b Ex. 32: 8; Judg. 2: 17; Isa. 59: 7; Jer. 4: 22.
c Gen. 6: 5; Matt. 15: 19; Heb. 3: 12.
5*a* Prov. 29: 23.
b TG Boasting.
c TG Walking in Darkness; Walking with God.
6*a* Isa. 45: 9 (9–10); D&C 58: 30.
b Judg. 8: 23 (22–23); D&C 60: 4.
c Jer. 8: 7.
7*a* Isa. 40: 17 (15, 17); Dan. 4: 35; Moses 1: 10.
b Gen. 18: 27.
9*a* Ezek. 1: 24.
b Judg. 5: 5; 3 Ne. 22: 10.
10*a* 1 Ne. 17: 46.
11*a* Morm. 5: 23; Ether 4: 9.
14*a* Josh. 10: 12 (12–14).
b Isa. 38: 8 (7–8).
c 2 Kgs. 20: 9 (8–11).
15*a* Alma 30: 44.
b Hab. 3: 11.
16*a* Matt. 8: 27 (23–27); Jacob 4: 9.
b Isa. 44: 27; 51: 10.
17*a* 3 Ne. 8: 10 (10, 25); 9: 8 (5–6, 8).
18*a* Hel. 13: 18 (18–23); Morm. 1: 18 (17–19).
b Hel. 13: 17.

[About 7 B.C.]

20 And behold, if the Lord shall
say unto a man—Because of thine
iniquities, thou shalt be accursed
[a]forever—it shall be done.
21 And if the Lord shall say—
Because of thine iniquities thou
shalt be [a]cut off from my presence—
he will cause that it shall be so.
22 And wo unto him to whom he
shall say this, for it shall be unto him
that will do iniquity, and he cannot
be [a]saved; therefore, for this cause,
that men might be saved, hath
repentance been declared.
23 Therefore, blessed are they who
will repent and hearken unto the
voice of the Lord their God; for
these are they that shall be saved.
24 And may God grant, in his great
fulness, that men might be brought
unto repentance and good works,
that they might be restored unto
grace for [a]grace, according to their
works.
25 And I would that all men might
be saved. But we read that in the
[a]great and last day there are some
who shall be cast out, yea, who shall
be cast off from the [b]presence of the
Lord;
26 Yea, who shall be consigned to a
state of endless misery, fulfilling the
words which say: They that have
done good shall have [a]everlasting
life; and they that have done evil
shall have everlasting [b]damnation.
And thus it is. Amen.

The prophecy of Samuel, the Lamanite, to the Nephites. Comprising chapters 13 to 15 inclusive.

CHAPTER 13

Samuel the Lamanite prophesies the destruction of the Nephites unless they repent—They and their riches are cursed—They reject and stone the prophets, are encircled about by demons, and seek for happiness in doing iniquity.

AND now it came to pass in the
*eighty and sixth year, the Nephites
did still remain in wickedness, yea,
in great wickedness, while the
[a]Lamanites did observe strictly to
keep the commandments of God,
according to the law of Moses.
2 And it came to pass that in this
year there was one [a]Samuel, a
[b]Lamanite, came into the land of
Zarahemla, and began to preach
unto the people. And it came to pass
that he did preach, many days,
repentance unto the people, and
they did [c]cast him out, and he was
about to [d]return to his own land.
3 But behold, the [a]voice of the
Lord came unto him, that he should
return again, and prophesy unto
the people whatsoever things should
come into his [b]heart.
4 And it came to pass that they
would not suffer that he should enter
into the city; therefore he went and
got upon the [a]wall thereof, and
stretched forth his hand and cried
with a loud voice, and [b]prophesied
unto the people whatsoever things
the Lord put into his heart.
5 And he said unto them: Behold,
I, Samuel, a Lamanite, do speak the
words of the Lord which he doth put
into my heart; and behold he hath
put it into my heart to say unto this
people that the [a]sword of justice
hangeth over this people; and four
hundred years pass not away save
the sword of justice falleth upon this
people.
6 Yea, heavy [a]destruction awaiteth

20*a* Mosiah 27: 31.
21*a* Jer. 23: 39 (39–40); D&C 63: 4.
22*a* TG Salvation.
24*a* TG Grace.
25*a* Mal. 4: 5; 3 Ne. 26: 4.
b TG God, Presence of.
26*a* Dan. 12: 2 (2–3); D&C 19: 7.
b TG Damnation.
13 1*a* Hel. 6: 1; 15: 5.
2*a* Hel. 14: 1; 3 Ne. 23: 9 (9–10).
b Hel. 16: 7.
c Hel. 14: 10.
d Alma 26: 27.
3*a* Gal. 2: 2; Alma 8: 16; 20: 2; 3 Ne. 1: 12.
b D&C 100: 5.
4*a* Hel. 14: 11; 16: 1.
b TG Teaching with the Spirit.
5*a* Alma 60: 29; 3 Ne. 2: 19.
6*a* Alma 45: 11 (10–14); Hel. 15: 17.

[*6 B.C.]

this people, and it surely cometh
unto this people, and nothing can
save this people save it be repentance and faith on the Lord Jesus
Christ, who surely shall come into
the world, and shall suffer many
things and shall be slain for his
people.
7 And behold, an [a]angel of the Lord
hath declared it unto me, and he did
bring [b]glad tidings to my soul. And
behold, I was sent unto you to
declare it unto you also, that ye
might have glad tidings; but behold
ye would [c]not receive me.
8 Therefore, thus saith the Lord:
Because of the hardness of the hearts
of the people of the Nephites, except
they repent I will take away my
word from them, and I will [a]with-
draw my Spirit from them, and I
will suffer them no longer, and I will
turn the hearts of their brethren
against them.
9 And [a]four hundred years shall
not pass away before I will cause
that they shall be smitten; yea, I
will visit them with the sword and
with famine and with pestilence.
10 Yea, I will visit them in my
fierce anger, and there shall be those
of the [a]fourth generation who shall
live, of your enemies, to behold your
utter destruction; and this shall
surely come except ye repent, saith
the Lord; and those of the fourth
generation shall visit your destruction.
11 But if ye will repent and [a]return
unto the Lord your God I will turn
away mine anger, saith the Lord;
yea, thus saith the Lord, blessed are
they who will repent and turn unto
me, but wo unto him that repenteth
not.
12 Yea, [a]wo unto this great city of
Zarahemla; for behold, it is because
of those who are righteous that it is
saved; yea, wo unto this great city,
for I perceive, saith the Lord, that
there are many, yea, even the more
part of this great city, that will
harden their hearts against me,
saith the Lord.
13 But blessed are they who will
repent, for them will I spare. But
behold, if it were not for the righteous who are in this great city,
behold, I would cause that [a]fire
should come down out of heaven
and [b]destroy it.
14 But behold, it is for the righteous' sake that it is spared. But
behold, the time cometh, saith the
Lord, that when ye shall cast out
the righteous from among you, then
shall ye be [a]ripe for destruction; yea,
wo be unto this great city, because
of the wickedness and abominations
which are in her.
15 Yea, and wo be unto the city of
Gideon, for the wickedness and
abominations which are in her.
16 Yea, and wo be unto all the
cities which are in the land round
about, which are possessed by the
Nephites, because of the wickedness
and abominations which are in them.
17 And behold, a [a]curse shall come
upon the land, saith the Lord of
Hosts, because of the peoples' sake
who are upon the land, yea, because
of their wickedness and their
abominations.
18 And it shall come to pass, saith
the Lord of Hosts, yea, our great
and true God, that whoso shall
[a]hide up treasures in the earth shall
find them again no more, because of
the great curse of the land, save he be
a righteous man and shall hide it up
unto the Lord.
19 For I will, saith the Lord, that
they shall hide up their [a]treasures

7*a* Alma 13: 26; Hel. 14: 26 (9, 26, 28).
b Isa. 52: 7.
c TG Prophets, Rejection of.
8*a* Ex. 23: 21 (20–21).
9*a* Alma 45: 10.
10*a* 1 Ne. 12: 12; 2 Ne. 26: 9; Alma 45: 12; 3 Ne. 27: 32.
11*a* 1 Sam. 7: 3; 3 Ne. 10: 6 (5–7).
12*a* 3 Ne. 8: 24 (8, 24); 9: 3.
13*a* 2 Kgs. 1: 10 (9–16); 3 Ne. 9: 11.
b Gen. 18: 23; 1 Ne. 22: 16; D&C 64: 24.
14*a* Gen. 15: 16; Alma 37: 31; D&C 61: 31; 101: 11.
17*a* Hel. 12: 18.
18*a* Morm. 1: 18 (17–19).
19*a* Prov. 13: 11.

[About 6 B.C.]

unto me; and cursed be they who
hide not up their treasures unto me;
for none hideth up their treasures
unto me save it be the righteous;
and he that hideth not up his
treasures unto me, cursed is he, and
also the treasure, and none shall
redeem it because of the curse of the
land.
20 And the day shall come that
they shall hide up their treasures,
because they have set their hearts
upon riches; and because they have
set their hearts upon their riches,
and will hide up their treasures
when they shall flee before their
enemies; because they will not hide
them up unto me, cursed be they
and also their treasures; and in that
day shall they be smitten, saith the
Lord.
21 Behold ye, the people of this
great city, and hearken unto my
words; yea, hearken unto the words
which the Lord saith; for behold, he
saith that ye are [a]cursed because of
your riches, and also are your riches
cursed because ye have set your
hearts upon them, and have not
[b]hearkened unto the words of him
who gave them unto you.
22 Ye do not remember the Lord
your God in the things with which he
hath blessed you, but ye do always
remember your [a]riches, not to thank
the Lord your God for them; yea,
your hearts are not drawn out unto
the Lord, but they do swell with
great pride, unto [b]boasting, and
unto great [c]swelling, [d]envyings,
strifes, malice, persecutions, and
murders, and all manner of iniquities.
23 For this cause hath the Lord
God caused that a curse should come
upon the land, and also upon your
riches, and this because of your
iniquities.
24 Yea, wo unto this people,
because of this time which has
arrived, that ye do [a]cast out the
prophets, and do mock them, and
cast stones at them, and do slay
them, and do all manner of iniquity
unto them, even as they did of old
time.
25 And now when ye talk, ye say:
If our days had been in the days of
our [a]fathers of old, we would not
have [b]slain the prophets; we would
not have stoned them, and cast
them out.
26 Behold ye are worse than they;
for as the Lord liveth, if a [a]prophet
come among you and declareth unto
you the word of the Lord, which
testifieth of your [b]sins and iniquities,
ye are [c]angry with him, and cast him
out and seek all manner of ways to
destroy him; yea, you will say that
he is a [d]false [e]prophet, and that he is
a sinner, and of the devil, because
he [f]testifieth that your deeds are
evil.
27 But behold, if a man shall come
among you and shall say: Do this,
and there is no iniquity; do that
and ye shall not suffer; yea, he will
say: [a]Walk after the pride of your
own hearts; yea, walk after the pride
of your eyes, and do whatsoever
your heart desireth—and if a man
shall come among you and say this,
ye will receive him, and say that he
is a [b]prophet.
28 Yea, ye will lift him up, and ye
will give unto him of your substance;
ye will give unto him of your gold,
and of your silver, and ye will clothe
him with costly apparel; and because he speaketh [a]flattering words
unto you, and he saith that all is

21*a* TG Curse.
b TG Disobedience.
22*a* Luke 12: 34.
b TG Boasting.
c Alma 30: 31.
d TG Envy.
24*a* 2 Chr. 36: 16 (15–16); Neh. 9: 26; Jer. 20: 2; 1 Ne. 1: 20; Hel. 16: 6.
25*a* Matt. 23: 32; Acts 7: 51 (51–52).
b TG Prophets, Rejection of.
26*a* 2 Chr. 18: 7; Luke 16: 31 (19–31).
b Micah 3: 8.
c Isa. 30: 9 (9–10).
d Mosiah 12: 14.
e Luke 11: 15 (14–22); Mosiah 3: 9 (9–12).
f Gal. 4: 16.
27*a* TG Walking in Darkness.
b Lam. 2: 14; 4: 13; Micah 2: 11. TG False Prophets.
28*a* 2 Tim. 4: 3 (3–4).

[About 6 B.C.]

well, then ye will not find fault with
him.
29 O ye wicked and ye perverse
generation; ye hardened and ye
[a]stiffnecked people, how long will
ye suppose that the Lord will suffer
you? Yea, how long will ye suffer
yourselves to be led by [b]foolish and
[c]blind guides? Yea, how long will
ye [d]choose darkness rather than
[e]light?
30 Yea, behold, the anger of the
Lord is already kindled against you;
behold, he hath cursed the land
because of your iniquity.
31 And behold, the time cometh
that he curseth your riches, that
they become [a]slippery, that ye cannot hold them; and in the days of
your poverty ye cannot retain them.
32 And in the days of your poverty
ye shall cry unto the Lord; and in
vain shall ye cry, for your desolation
is already come upon you, and your
destruction is made sure; and then
shall ye weep and howl in that day,
saith the Lord of Hosts. And then
shall ye lament, and say:
33 O [a]that I had repented, and had
not killed the prophets, and [b]stoned
them, and cast them out. Yea, in
that day ye shall say: O that we had
remembered the Lord our God in
the day that he gave us our riches,
and then they would not have become slippery that we should lose
them; for behold, our riches are
gone from us.
34 Behold, we lay a tool here and
on the morrow it is gone; and behold,
our swords are taken from us in the
day we have sought them for battle.
35 Yea, we have hid up our
[a]treasures and they have slipped
away from us, because of the curse
of the land.
36 O that we had repented in the
day that the word of the Lord came
unto us; for behold the land is
cursed, and all things are become
slippery, and we cannot hold them.
37 Behold, we are surrounded by
[a]demons, yea, we are encircled
about by the angels of him who hath
sought to destroy our souls. Behold,
our iniquities are great. O Lord,
canst thou not turn away thine
anger from us? And this shall be
your language in those days.
38 But behold, your [a]days of probation are past; ye have [b]procrastinated the day of your salvation until it is everlastingly too late,
and your destruction is made sure;
yea, for ye have sought all the days
of your lives for that which ye could
not obtain; and ye have sought for
[c]happiness in doing iniquity, which
thing is [d]contrary to the nature of
that righteousness which is in our
great and Eternal Head.
39 O ye people of the land, that ye
would hear my words! And I pray
that the anger of the Lord be turned
away from you, and that ye would
repent and be saved.

CHAPTER 14

Samuel predicts light during the night and a new star at Christ's birth—Christ redeems men from temporal and spiritual death—The signs of his death include three days of darkness, the rending of the rocks, and great upheavals of nature.

AND now it came to pass that
[a]Samuel, the Lamanite, did prophesy a great many more things which
cannot be written.
2 And behold, he said unto them:
Behold, I give unto you a sign; for
[a]five years more cometh, and behold,
then cometh the Son of God to

29a TG Stiffneckedness.
b Ezek. 13: 3; 2 Ne. 28: 9.
c Matt. 15: 14; 23: 16.
d John 3: 19.
e Job 24: 13 (2–16).
31a Jer. 48: 36 (35–36); Morm. 1: 18 (17–19).
33a Morm. 2: 10 (10–15).
b Matt. 23: 37.
35a TG Treasure.
37a Mosiah 2: 32.
38a Morm. 2: 15 (10–15). TG Probation.
b Alma 34: 33 (33–34). TG Apathy; Procrastination.
c Alma 41: 10. TG Abundant Life; Happiness.
d Alma 41: 11 (10–12).
14 1a Hel. 13: 2; 3 Ne. 23: 9 (9–10).
2a Hel. 16: 4; 3 Ne. 1: 5 (5–21).

[About 6 B.C.]

redeem all those who shall believe
on his name.
3 And behold, this will I give unto
you for a [a]sign at the time of his
coming; for behold, there shall be
great lights in heaven, insomuch
that in the night before he cometh
there shall be no darkness, insomuch
that it shall appear unto man as if it
was day.
4 Therefore, there shall be one [a]day
and a night and a day, as if it were
one day and there were no night;
and this shall be unto you for a
sign; for ye shall know of the rising
of the sun and also of its setting;
therefore they shall know of a surety
that there shall be two days and a
night; nevertheless the night shall
not be darkened; and it shall be the
night before he is [b]born.
5 And behold, there shall a new
[a]star arise, such an one as ye never
have beheld; and this also shall be a
sign unto you.
6 And behold this is not all, there
shall be many [a]signs and wonders in
heaven.
7 And it shall come to pass that ye
shall all be amazed, and wonder, insomuch that ye shall [a]fall to the earth.
8 And it shall come to pass that
whosoever shall [a]believe on the Son
of God, the same shall have everlasting life.
9 And behold, thus hath the Lord
commanded me, by his angel, that
I should come and tell this thing
unto you; yea, he hath commanded
that I should prophesy these things
unto you; yea, he hath said unto
me: Cry unto this people, repent
and prepare the way of the Lord.
10 And now, because I am a
Lamanite, and have spoken unto
you the words which the Lord hath
commanded me, and because it was
hard against you, ye are angry with
me and do seek to destroy me, and
have [a]cast me out from among you.
11 And ye shall [a]hear my words,
for, for this intent have I come up
upon the walls of this city, that ye
might hear and know of the judgments of God which do await you
because of your iniquities, and also
that ye might know the conditions
of repentance;
12 And also that ye might know of
the coming of Jesus Christ, the Son
of God, the [a]Father of heaven and
of earth, the Creator of all things
from the beginning; and that ye
might know of the signs of his
coming, to the intent that ye might
believe on his name.
13 And if ye [a]believe on his name
ye will repent of all your sins, that
thereby ye may have a remission of
them through his [b]merits.
14 And behold, again, another
sign I give unto you, yea, a sign of
his [a]death.
15 For behold, he surely must die
that [a]salvation may come; yea, it
behooveth him and becometh expedient that he [b]dieth, to bring to
pass the [c]resurrection of the dead,
that thereby men may be brought
into the [d]presence of the Lord.
16 Yea, behold, this death bringeth
to pass the [a]resurrection, and
[b]redeemeth all mankind from the
first death—that spiritual death;
for all mankind, by the [c]fall of Adam
being [d]cut off from the presence of

3a Hel. 16: 13; 3 Ne. 1: 15 (8–20).
4a 3 Ne. 1: 8.
b TG Jesus Christ, Birth of.
5a Matt. 2: 2 (1–2); 3 Ne. 1: 21. TG Astronomy.
6a 3 Ne. 2: 1.
7a 3 Ne. 1: 16 (16–17).
8a John 3: 16.
10a Hel. 13: 2 (2–7).
11a Ezek. 2: 7 (6–7).
12a Mosiah 3: 8; 15: 4; 3 Ne. 9: 15; Ether 4: 7. TG Jesus Christ, Creator.
13a Acts 16: 31 (30–31).
b D&C 19: 16 (16–20).
14a TG Jesus Christ, Death of.
15a TG Jesus Christ, Savior.
b 1 Cor. 15: 36.
c 2 Ne. 9: 4; Alma 42: 23; Morm. 9: 13. TG Resurrection.
d TG God, Presence of.
16a John 20: 9; D&C 18: 12 (11–12).
b TG Salvation, Plan of.
c TG Fall of Man.
d 2 Ne. 2: 5; 9: 6 (6–15); Alma 11: 42 (40–45); 12: 16 (16, 24, 36); 42: 7 (6–11).

[About 6 B.C.]

the Lord, are considered as [e]dead,
both as to things temporal and to
things spiritual.
17 But behold, the resurrection of
Christ [a]redeemeth mankind, yea,
even all mankind, and bringeth
them back into the presence of the
Lord.
18 Yea, and it bringeth to pass the
condition of repentance, that whosoever repenteth the same is not
[a]hewn down and cast into the fire;
but whosoever repenteth not is
hewn down and cast into the fire;
and there cometh upon them again
a [b]spiritual death, yea, a second
death, for they are cut off again as
to things pertaining to righteousness.
19 Therefore repent ye, repent ye,
lest by knowing these things and
not doing them ye shall suffer yourselves to come under condemnation,
and ye are brought down unto this
second death.
20 But behold, as I said unto you
concerning another [a]sign, a sign of
his death, behold, in that day that he
shall suffer death the sun shall be
darkened and refuse to give his
[b]light unto you; and also the moon
and the stars; and there shall be no
light upon the face of this land, even
from the time that he shall suffer
death, for the space of [c]three days,
to the time that he shall rise again
from the dead.
21 Yea, at the time that he shall
yield up the [a]ghost there shall be
[b]thunderings and lightnings for the
space of many hours, and the earth
shall shake and tremble; and the
[c]rocks which are upon the face of this
earth, which are both above the
earth and beneath, which ye know
at this time are solid, or the more
part of it is one solid mass, shall be
[d]broken up;
22 Yea, they shall be rent in twain,
and shall ever after be [a]found in
seams and in cracks, and in broken
fragments upon the face of the whole
earth, yea, both above the earth and
beneath.
23 And behold, there shall be great
[a]tempests, and there shall be many
mountains laid low, like unto a
valley, and there shall be many
places which are now called [b]valleys
which shall become mountains,
whose height is great.
24 And [a]many highways shall be
broken up, and many cities shall
become desolate.
25 And many [a]graves shall be
opened, and shall yield up many of
their dead; and many saints shall
appear unto many.
26 And behold, thus hath the [a]angel
spoken unto me; for he said unto
me that there should be thunderings
and lightnings for the space of many
hours.
27 And he said unto me that while
the thunder and the lightning lasted,
and the tempest, that these things
should be, and that [a]darkness should
cover the face of the whole earth for
the space of three days.
28 And the angel said unto me that
many shall see greater things than
these, to the intent that they might
believe that [a]these signs and these
wonders should come to pass upon
all the face of this land, to the intent
that there should be no cause for
unbelief among the children of
men—
29 And this to the intent that whosoever will believe might be saved,

16*e* TG Death, Spiritual, First.
17*a* TG Redemption.
18*a* Luke 13: 7.
b TG Death, Spiritual, Second.
20*a* 3 Ne. 8: 5 (5–25); 11: 2.
b Luke 23: 44.
c Mosiah 3: 10.
21*a* Matt. 27: 50 (50–54).
b 1 Ne. 19: 11; 3 Ne. 8: 6 (5–23).
c 3 Ne. 10: 9.
d Gen. 7: 11; 1 Ne. 12: 4.
22*a* 3 Ne. 8: 18.
23*a* 3 Ne. 10: 14.
b Isa. 40: 4; Luke 3: 5; D&C 49: 23; 109: 74.
24*a* 3 Ne. 8: 14 (8–10, 14); 9: 12 (3–12); 10: 7.
25*a* Matt. 27: 52 (52–53); 3 Ne. 23: 11 (7–13).
26*a* Alma 13: 26; Hel. 13: 7.
27*a* 1 Ne. 19: 10; 3 Ne. 8: 3; 10: 9.
28*a* 1 Ne. 12: 4 (4–5); 19: 12 (10–12); 3 Ne. 10: 11.

[About 6 B.C.]

and that whosoever will not believe,
a [a]righteous judgment might come
upon them; and also if they are
condemned they bring upon themselves their own condemnation.
30 And now remember, remember,
my brethren, that whosoever perisheth, perisheth unto [a]himself; and
whosoever doeth iniquity, doeth it
unto himself; for behold, ye are [b]free;
ye are permitted to act for yourselves; for behold, God hath given
unto you a [c]knowledge and he hath
made you free.
31 He hath given unto you that ye
might [a]know good from evil, and he
hath given unto you that ye might
[b]choose life or death; and ye can do
good and be [c]restored unto that
which is good, or have that which is
good restored unto you; or ye can
do evil, and have that which is evil
restored unto you.

CHAPTER 15

The Lord chastened the Nephites because he loved them—Converted Lamanites are firm and steadfast in the faith—The Lord will be merciful unto the Lamanites in the latter days.

AND now, my beloved brethren,
behold, I declare unto you that
except ye shall repent your houses
shall be left unto you [a]desolate.
2 Yea, except ye repent, your
women shall have great cause to
mourn in the day that they shall
give suck; for ye shall attempt to
flee and there shall be no place for
[a]refuge; yea, and wo unto them
which are [b]with child, for they shall
be heavy and cannot flee; therefore,
they shall be trodden down and shall
be left to perish.
3 Yea, wo unto this [a]people who
are called the [b]people of Nephi
except they shall repent, when they
shall see all these signs and wonders
which shall be showed unto them;
for behold, they have been a chosen
people of the Lord; yea, the people
of Nephi hath he loved, and also
hath he [c]chastened them; yea, in
the days of their iniquities hath he
chastened them because he loveth
them.
4 But behold my brethren, the
[a]Lamanites hath he hated because
their deeds have been evil continually, and this because of the iniquity
of the [b]tradition of their fathers.
But behold, salvation hath come
unto them through the preaching of
the Nephites; and for this intent
hath the Lord [c]prolonged their
days.
5 And I would that ye should behold that the [a]more part of them
are in the path of their duty, and
they do walk circumspectly before
God, and they do observe to keep
his commandments and his statutes
and his judgments according to the
law of Moses.
6 Yea, I say unto you, that the
more part of them are doing this,
and they are striving with [a]un-
wearied diligence that they may
bring the remainder of their brethren to the knowledge of the truth;
therefore there are many who do
add to their numbers daily.
7 And behold, ye do know of yourselves, for ye have witnessed it, that
as many of them as are brought to
the knowledge of the truth, and to
know of the wicked and abominable
traditions of their fathers, and are
led to believe the holy scriptures,
yea, the prophecies of the holy
prophets, which are written, which

29*a* TG Judgment.
30*a* 3 Ne. 3: 11.
b Gal. 5: 1; 2 Ne. 2: 27 (26–27); Alma 41: 7; Moses 6: 56. TG Agency.
c TG Knowledge.
31*a* Moro. 7: 16.
b Rom. 6: 16 (14–18); Alma 3: 27 (26–27).
c Alma 41: 3 (1–15).
15 1*a* Isa. 5: 9; Matt. 23: 38.
2*a* TG Refuge.
b Matt. 24: 19.
3*a* W of M 1: 11.
b Jacob 5: 25.
c Prov. 3: 12; Heb. 12: 6 (5–11); D&C 95: 1.
4*a* Jacob 5: 40.
b Ezek. 20: 18; Hel. 5: 19. TG Traditions of Men.
c Alma 9: 16.
5*a* Hel. 13: 1; 16: 6.
6*a* TG Dedication.

[About 6 B.C.]

leadeth them to faith on the Lord, and unto repentance, which faith and repentance bringeth a [a]change of heart unto them—

8 Therefore, as many as have come to this, ye know of yourselves are [a]firm and steadfast in the faith, and in the thing wherewith they have been made free.

9 And ye know also that they have [a]buried their weapons of war, and they fear to take them up lest by any means they should sin; yea, ye can see that they fear to sin—for behold they will suffer themselves that they be trodden down and slain by their enemies, and will not lift their swords against them, and this because of their [b]faith in Christ.

10 And now, because of their [a]steadfastness when they do believe in that thing which they do believe, for because of their firmness when they are once enlightened, behold, the Lord shall bless them and prolong their days, notwithstanding their iniquity—

11 Yea, even if they should dwindle in unbelief the Lord shall [a]prolong their days, until the time shall come which hath been spoken of by our fathers, and also by the prophet [b]Zenos, and many other prophets, concerning the [c]restoration of our brethren, the Lamanites, again to the knowledge of the truth—

12 Yea, I say unto you, that in the latter times the [a]promises of the Lord have been extended to our brethren, the Lamanites; and notwithstanding the many afflictions which they shall have, and notwithstanding they shall be [b]driven to and fro upon the face of the earth, and be hunted, and shall be smitten and scattered abroad, having no place for [c]refuge, the Lord shall be [d]merciful unto them.

13 And this is according to the prophecy, that they shall again be [a]brought to the true knowledge, which is the knowledge of their Redeemer, and their great and true [b]shepherd, and be numbered among his [c]sheep.

14 Therefore I say unto you, it shall be [a]better for them than for you except ye repent.

15 For behold, [a]had the mighty works been shown unto them which have been shown unto you, yea, unto them who have dwindled in unbelief because of the traditions of their fathers, ye can see of yourselves that they never would again have dwindled in unbelief.

16 Therefore, saith the Lord: I will not utterly destroy them, but I will cause that in the day of my wisdom they shall [a]return again unto me, saith the Lord.

17 And now behold, saith the Lord, concerning the people of the Nephites: If they will not repent, and observe to do my will, I will utterly [a]destroy them, saith the Lord, because of their unbelief notwithstanding the many mighty works which I have done among them; and as surely as the Lord liveth shall these things be, saith the Lord.

CHAPTER 16

The Nephites who believe Samuel are baptized by Nephi—Samuel cannot be slain with their arrows and stones—Some harden their hearts, and others see angels—The unbelievers say it is not reasonable to believe in Christ and his coming in Jerusalem.

7*a* TG Conversion.
8*a* Alma 23:6; 27:27; 3 Ne. 6:14.
9*a* Alma 24:17 (17–26).
b Mark 5:34 (34–36).
10*a* TG Steadfastness.
11*a* Deut. 11:9 (8–9); Alma 9:16.
b Hel. 8:19; 3 Ne. 10:16.
c Morm. 5:12 (9, 12); 7:1.
12*a* Enos 1:13 (12–13).
b Morm. 5:15.
c TG Refuge.
d 1 Ne. 13:31; 2 Ne. 4:7; 10:18 (18–19); Jacob 3:6 (5–9); Morm. 5:20 (20–21).
13*a* 3 Ne. 16:12.
b TG Jesus Christ, Good Shepherd.
c TG Sheep.
14*a* Hel. 7:23.
15*a* Matt. 11:21 (20–24).
16*a* Enos 1:13.
17*a* Hel. 13:6 (5–10); Morm. 3:2.

[About 6 B.C.]

AND now, it came to pass that there
were many who heard the words of
Samuel, the Lamanite, which he
spake upon the [a]walls of the city.
And as many as believed on his
word went forth and sought for
Nephi; and when they had come
forth and found him they confessed
unto him their sins and denied not,
desiring that they might be [b]bap-
tized unto the Lord.
2 But as many as there were who
did not believe in the words of
Samuel were [a]angry with him; and
they cast stones at him upon the
wall, and also many shot arrows at
him as he stood upon the wall; but
the Spirit of the Lord was with him,
insomuch that they could not hit
him with their stones neither with
their arrows.
3 Now when they saw that they
could not hit him, there were many
more who did believe on his words,
insomuch that they went away unto
Nephi to be baptized.
4 For behold, Nephi was baptizing,
and prophesying, and preaching,
crying repentance unto the people,
showing signs and wonders, working
[a]miracles among the people, that
they might know that the Christ
must [b]shortly come—
5 Telling them of things which
must shortly come, that they might
know and remember at the time of
their coming that they had been
made known unto them beforehand,
to the intent that they might
believe; therefore as many as
believed on the words of Samuel
went forth unto him to be baptized,
for they came repenting and con-
fessing their sins.
6 But the [a]more part of them did
not believe in the words of Samuel;
therefore when they saw that they
could not hit him with their stones
and their arrows, they cried unto
their captains, saying: [b]Take this
fellow and bind him, for behold he
[c]hath a devil; and because of the
power of the devil which is in him
we cannot hit him with our stones
and our arrows; therefore take him
and bind him, and away with him.
7 And as they went forth to lay
their hands on him, behold, he did
cast himself down from the wall,
and did flee out of their lands, yea,
even unto his own country, and
began to preach and to prophesy
[a]among his own people.
8 And behold, he was never heard
of more among the Nephites; and
thus were the affairs of the people.
9 And thus ended the eighty and
sixth year of the reign of the judges
over the people of Nephi.
10 And thus ended also the *eighty
and seventh year of the reign of the
judges, the more part of the people
remaining in their pride and wickedness, and the lesser part walking
more circumspectly before God.
11 And these were the conditions
also, in the eighty and eighth year of
the reign of the judges.
12 And there was but little altera-
tion in the affairs of the people, save
it were the people began to be more
hardened in iniquity, and do more
and more of that which was [a]con-
trary to the commandments of God,
in the eighty and ninth year of the
reign of the judges.
13 But it came to pass in the †nine-
tieth year of the reign of the judges,
there were [a]great signs given unto the
people, and wonders; and the words
of the prophets [b]began to be fulfilled.
14 And [a]angels did appear unto
men, wise men, and did declare unto
them glad tidings of great joy; thus
in this year the scriptures began to
be fulfilled.
15 Nevertheless, the people began
to harden their hearts, all save it
were the most believing part of them,
both of the Nephites and also of the

16 1*a* Hel. 13:4.
b Alma 9:27.
2*a* Prov. 29:10.
4*a* TG Miracle.
b Hel. 14:2.
6*a* Hel. 15:5; 3 Ne. 1:22.
b Hel. 13:24.
c John 7:20.
7*a* Hel. 13:2.
12*a* TG Disobedience.
13*a* 3 Ne. 1:4.
b Hel. 14:3 (3–7).
14*a* Alma 13:26.

[*5 B.C. †2 B.C.]

Lamanites, and began to depend upon their [a]own strength and upon their own wisdom, saying:
16 Some things they may have guessed right, among so many; but behold, we know that all these great and marvelous works cannot come to pass, of which has been spoken.
17 And they began to reason and to contend among themselves, saying:
18 That it is [a]not reasonable that such a being as a Christ shall come; if so, and he be the Son of God, the Father of heaven and of earth, as it has been spoken, why will he not show himself unto us as well as unto them who shall be at Jerusalem?
19 Yea, why will he not show himself in this land as well as in the land of Jerusalem?
20 But behold, we know that this is a wicked [a]tradition, which has been handed down unto us by our fathers, to cause us that we should believe in some great and marvelous thing which should come to pass, but not among us, but in a land which is far distant, a land which we know not; therefore they can keep us in ignorance, for we cannot [b]witness with our own eyes that they are true.
21 And they will, by the cunning and the mysterious arts of the evil one, work some great mystery which we cannot understand, which will keep us down to be servants to their words, and also servants unto them, for we depend upon them to teach us the word; and thus will they keep us in ignorance if we will yield ourselves unto them, all the days of our lives.
22 And many more things did the people [a]imagine up in their hearts, which were foolish and [b]vain; and they were much disturbed, for Satan did stir them up to do iniquity continually; yea, he did go about spreading [c]rumors and contentions upon all the face of the land, that he might harden the hearts of the people against that which was good and against that which should come.
23 And notwithstanding the signs and the wonders which were wrought among the people of the Lord, and the many miracles which they did, Satan did get great hold upon the hearts of the people upon all the face of the land.
24 And thus *ended the ninetieth year of the reign of the judges over the people of Nephi.
25 [a]And thus ended the book of Helaman, according to the record of Helaman and his sons.

THIRD NEPHI

THE BOOK OF NEPHI

THE SON OF NEPHI, WHO WAS THE SON OF HELAMAN

And Helaman was the son of Helaman, who was the son of Alma, who was the son of Alma, being a descendant of Nephi who was the son of Lehi, who came out of Jerusalem in the first year of the reign of Zedekiah, the king of Judah.

CHAPTER 1

Nephi the son of Helaman departs out of the land, and his son Nephi keeps the records—Though signs and wonders abound, the wicked plan to slay the righteous—The night of Christ's birth arrives—The sign is

15a Isa. 5: 21.
18a Alma 30: 53.
20a TG Traditions of Men.
b Alma 30: 15; Ether 12: 5 (5–6, 19).
22a Gen. 6: 5.
b 4 Ne. 1: 43.
c Prov. 6: 18 (16–19).
25a Hel. 3: 37.

[*1 B.C.]

given and a new star arises—Lyings
and deceivings increase, and the
Gadianton robbers slaughter many.

NOW it came to pass that the
*ninety and first year had
passed away and it was [a]six
hundred years from the time that
Lehi left Jerusalem; and it was in
the year that [b]Lachoneus was the
chief judge and the governor over
the land.
2 And [a]Nephi, the son of Helaman,
had departed out of the land of
Zarahemla, giving charge unto his
son [b]Nephi, who was his eldest son,
concerning the [c]plates of brass, and
[d]all the records which had been
kept, and all those things which had
been kept sacred from the departure of Lehi out of Jerusalem.
3 Then he [a]departed out of the
land, and [b]whither he went, no man
knoweth; and his son Nephi did
keep the records in his stead, yea,
the record of this people.
4 And it came to pass that in the
commencement of the ninety and
second year, behold, the prophecies
of the prophets began to be fulfilled
more fully; for there began to be
[a]greater signs and greater miracles
wrought among the people.
5 But there were some who began
to say that the time was past for the
words to be fulfilled, which were
[a]spoken by Samuel, the Lamanite.
6 And they began to [a]rejoice over
their brethren, saying: Behold the
time is past, and the words of
Samuel are not fulfilled; therefore,
your joy and your faith concerning
this thing hath been vain.
7 And it came to pass that they
did make a great uproar throughout the land; and the people who
believed began to be very sorrowful,
lest by any means those things
which had been spoken might not
come to pass.
8 But behold, they did watch
steadfastly for [a]that day and that
night and that day which should be
as one day as if there were no night,
that they might know that their
faith had not been vain.
9 Now it came to pass that there
was a day set apart by the [a]un-
believers, that all those who believed in those traditions should be
[b]put to death except the [c]sign
should come to pass, which had
been given by Samuel the prophet.
10 Now it came to pass that when
Nephi, the son of Nephi, saw this
wickedness of his people, his heart
was exceedingly sorrowful.
11 And it came to pass that he
went out and bowed himself down
upon the earth, and cried mightily
to his God in behalf of his people,
yea, those who were about to be
destroyed because of their faith in
the tradition of their fathers.
12 And it came to pass that he
cried mightily unto the Lord [a]all
that day; and behold, the [b]voice of
the Lord came unto him, saying:
13 Lift up your head and be of
good cheer; for behold, the time is
at hand, and on this night shall the
[a]sign be given, and on the [b]morrow
come I into the world, to show unto
the world that I will fulfil all that
which I have caused to be [c]spoken
by the mouth of my holy prophets.
14 Behold, I [a]come unto my own,
to [b]fulfil all things which I have
made known unto the children of
men from the [c]foundation of the

1 1*a* 2 Ne. 25: 19;
Alma 13: 25.
b 3 Ne. 3: 1; 6: 19.
2*a* Hel. 3: 21 (20–21).
b 3 Ne. 7: 15 (15, 20, 23).
c Alma 37: 3 (3–12);
63: 12 (1, 11–14).
d Alma 50: 38.
3*a* Alma 45: 18 (18–19).
b 3 Ne. 2: 9.
4*a* Hel. 16: 13 (13, 23).
5*a* Hel. 14: 2.
6*a* TG Mocking.
8*a* Hel. 14: 4 (3–4).
9*a* TG Unbelief,
Unbelievers.
b 3 Ne. 1: 16.
TG Martyrdom.
c Hel. 14: 3 (2–7).
12*a* Enos 1: 4; Alma 5: 46.
b Alma 20: 2; Hel. 13: 3.
13*a* Matt. 2: 2.
b Luke 2: 11 (10–11).
c TG Jesus Christ,
Prophecies about.
14*a* John 1: 11.
b Matt. 5: 17 (17–18);
Luke 24: 44.
c Alma 42: 26; 3 Ne.
26: 5.

[*A.D. 1]

world, and to do the [d]will, [e]both [f]of the Father and of the Son—of the Father because of me, and of the Son because of my flesh. And behold, the time is at hand, and this night shall the sign be given.

15 And it came to pass that the words which came unto Nephi were fulfilled, according as they had been spoken; for behold, at the going down of the [a]sun there was [b]no darkness; and the people began to be astonished because there was no darkness when the night came.

16 And there were many, who had not believed the words of the prophets, who [a]fell to the earth and became as if they were dead, for they knew that the great [b]plan of destruction which they had laid for those who believed in the words of the prophets had been frustrated; for the sign which had been given was already at hand.

17 And they began to know that the Son of God must shortly appear; yea, in fine, all the people upon the face of the whole earth from the [a]west to the east, both in the land north and in the land south, were so exceedingly astonished that they fell to the earth.

18 For they knew that the prophets had testified of these things for many years, and that the sign which had been given was already at hand; and they began to fear because of their iniquity and their unbelief.

19 And it came to pass that there was no darkness in all that night, but it was as light as though it was mid-day. And it came to pass that the sun did rise in the morning again, according to its proper order; and they knew that it was the day that the Lord should be [a]born, because of the [b]sign which had been given.

20 And it had come to pass, yea, all things, every whit, according to the words of the prophets.

21 And it came to pass also that a new [a]star did appear, according to the word.

22 And it came to pass that from this time forth there began to be [a]lyings sent forth among the people, by Satan, to harden their hearts, to the intent that they might not believe in those [b]signs and wonders which they had seen; but notwithstanding these lyings and deceivings the [c]more part of the people did believe, and were converted unto the Lord.

23 And it came to pass that Nephi went forth among the people, and also many others, baptizing unto repentance, in the which there was a great [a]remission of sins. And thus the people began again to have peace in the land.

24 And there were no contentions, save it were a few that began to preach, endeavoring to prove by the [a]scriptures that it was no more expedient to observe the law of Moses. Now in this thing they did err, having not understood the scriptures.

25 But it came to pass that they soon became converted, and were convinced of the error which they were in, for it was made known unto them that the law was not yet [a]fulfilled, and that it must be fulfilled in every whit; yea, the word came unto them that it must be fulfilled; yea, that one jot or tittle should not pass away till it should all be fulfilled; therefore in this same year were they brought to a knowledge of their error and did [b]confess their faults.

26 And thus the ninety and second

14*d* TG God, Will of.
e D&C 93: 4 (4, 14).
f Mosiah 15: 3.
15*a* Josh. 10: 13.
b Hel. 14:3.
16*a* Hel. 14: 7.
b 3 Ne. 1: 9 (9, 11).
17*a* Hel. 11: 20.
19*a* TG Jesus Christ, Birth of.
b Hel. 14: 3.
21*a* Matt. 2: 2 (1–2); Hel. 14: 5.
22*a* Moses 5: 13.
b TG Signs.
c Hel. 16: 6.
23*a* TG Remission of Sins.
24*a* Alma 34: 13.
25*a* Matt. 5: 18; 2 Ne. 25: 24.
b Num. 5: 7 (6–10); Mosiah 26: 29 (29, 35); Alma 17: 4.

year did pass away, bringing [a]glad
tidings unto the people because of
the signs which did come to pass,
according to the words of the
prophecy of all the holy prophets.
27 And it came to pass that the
ninety and third year did also pass
away in peace, save it were for the
Gadianton robbers, who dwelt upon
the [a]mountains, who did infest the
land; for so strong were their holds
and their secret places that the
people could not overpower them;
therefore they did commit many
murders, and did do much slaughter
among the people.
28 And it came to pass that in the
ninety and fourth year they began
to increase in a great degree, because
there were many dissenters of the
Nephites who did flee unto them,
which did cause much sorrow unto
those Nephites who did remain in
the land.
29 And there was also a cause of
much sorrow among the Lamanites; for behold, they had many
children who did grow up and began
to wax strong in years, that they
became for themselves, and were
[a]led away by some who were
[b]Zoramites, by their lyings and their
flattering words, to join those
Gadianton robbers.
30 And thus were the Lamanites
afflicted also, and began to decrease
as to their faith and righteousness,
because of the wickedness of the
[a]rising generation.

CHAPTER 2

Wickedness and abominations increase among the people—The Nephites and Lamanites unite to defend themselves against the Gadianton robbers—Converted Lamanites become white and are called Nephites.

AND it came to pass that thus
passed away the ninety and fifth
year also, and the people began to
forget those [a]signs and wonders
which they had heard, and began to
be less and less astonished at a sign
or a wonder from heaven, insomuch that they began to be hard in
their hearts, and blind in their
minds, and began to disbelieve all
which they had heard and seen—
2 [a]Imagining up some vain thing
in their hearts, that it was wrought
by men and by the power of the
devil, to lead away and [b]deceive the
hearts of the people; and thus did
Satan get possession of the hearts
of the people again, insomuch that he
did blind their eyes and lead them
away to believe that the doctrine of
Christ was a [c]foolish and a vain thing.
3 And it came to pass that the
people began to wax strong in
wickedness and abominations; and
they did not believe that there
should be any more signs or wonders
given; and Satan did [a]go about,
leading away the hearts of the
people, tempting them and causing
them that they should do great
wickedness in the land.
4 And thus did pass away the
ninety and sixth year; and also the
ninety and seventh year; and also
the ninety and eighth year; and also
the ninety and ninth year;
5 And also an hundred years had
passed away since the days of
[a]Mosiah, who was king over the
people of the Nephites.
6 And six hundred and nine years
had passed away since Lehi left
Jerusalem.
7 And nine years had passed away
from the time when the sign was
given, which was spoken of by the
prophets, that Christ should come
into the world.
8 Now the Nephites began to
[a]reckon their time from this period

26*a* Luke 2: 10.
27*a* Hel. 11: 31 (25–31); 3 Ne. 2: 11.
29*a* TG Peer Influence.
b Alma 30: 59; 43: 4.
30*a* Judg. 2: 10.
2 1*a* Hel. 14: 6.
2*a* Heb. 3: 12.
b TG Deceit.
c 1 Cor. 1: 23 (23–25); Alma 30: 13 (12–18).
3*a* Job 1: 7; D&C 10: 27.
5*a* Mosiah 29: 46 (46–47).
8*a* 3 Ne. 5: 7; 8: 2.

[A.D. 3—9]

when the sign was given, or from
the coming of Christ; therefore,
nine years had passed away.
9 And Nephi, who was the father
of Nephi, who had the charge of the
records, [a]did not return to the land
of Zarahemla, and could nowhere
be found in all the land.
10 And it came to pass that the
people did still [a]remain in wickedness, notwithstanding the much
preaching and prophesying which
was sent among them; and thus
passed away the tenth year also;
and the eleventh year also passed
away in iniquity.
11 And it came to pass in the
thirteenth year there began to be
wars and contentions throughout
all the land; for the [a]Gadianton robbers had become so [b]numerous, and
did slay so many of the people, and
did lay waste so many cities,
and did spread so much death
and carnage throughout the land,
that it became expedient that all
the people, both the Nephites and
the Lamanites, should take up
arms against them.
12 Therefore, all the Lamanites
who had become converted unto the
Lord did unite with their brethren,
the Nephites, and were compelled,
for the [a]safety of their lives and their
women and their children, to take
up arms against those Gadianton
robbers, yea, and also to maintain
their rights, and the privileges of
their church and of their worship,
and their freedom and their [b]liberty.
13 And it came to pass that before
this thirteenth year had passed
away the Nephites were threatened
with utter destruction because of
this war, which had become exceedingly sore.
14 And it came to pass that those
Lamanites who had united with the
Nephites were numbered among the
Nephites;
15 And their [a]curse was taken
from them, and their skin became
[b]white like unto the Nephites;
16 And their young men and their
daughters became exceedingly fair,
and they were numbered among
the Nephites, and were called Nephites. And thus ended the thirteenth year.
17 And it came to pass in the commencement of the fourteenth year,
the war between the robbers and
the people of Nephi did continue
and did become exceedingly sore;
nevertheless, the people of Nephi
did gain some advantage of the
robbers, insomuch that they did
drive them back out of their lands
into the mountains and into their
secret places.
18 And thus ended the fourteenth
year. And in the *fifteenth year they
did come forth against the people of
Nephi; and because of the wickedness of the people of Nephi, and
their many contentions and dissensions, the Gadianton robbers did
gain many advantages over them.
19 And thus ended the fifteenth
year, and thus were the people in a
state of many afflictions; and the
[a]sword of destruction did hang over
them, insomuch that they were
about to be smitten down by it, and
this because of their iniquity.

CHAPTER 3

Giddianhi, the Gadianton leader, demands that Lachoneus and the Nephites surrender themselves and their lands—Lachoneus appoints Gidgiddoni as chief captain of the armies—The Nephites assemble in Zarahemla and Bountiful to defend themselves.

AND now it came to pass that in the
sixteenth year from the coming of
Christ, [a]Lachoneus, the governor of
the land, received an epistle from

9*a* 3 Ne. 1: 3 (2–3).
10*a* Alma 34: 35.
11*a* 3 Ne. 1: 27.
b Morm. 2: 8.
12*a* Alma 58: 12;
3 Ne. 3: 2.
b TG Liberty.
15*a* Alma 17: 15; 23: 18.
b 2 Ne. 5: 21; 30: 6;
Jacob 3: 8.
19*a* Alma 60: 29; Hel.
13: 5; 3 Ne. 3: 3.
3 1*a* 3 Ne. 1: 1; 6: 6.

[*A.D. 15]

the leader and the governor of this
band of robbers; and these were the
words which were written, saying:
2 Lachoneus, most noble and chief
governor of the land, behold, I write
this epistle unto you, and do give
unto you exceedingly great praise
because of your firmness, and also
the firmness of your people, in
[a]maintaining that which ye suppose
to be your right and [b]liberty; yea,
ye do stand well, as if ye were supported by the hand of a god, in the
defence of your liberty, and your
property, and your country, or that
which ye do call so.
3 And it seemeth a pity unto me,
most noble Lachoneus, that ye
should be so foolish and vain as to
suppose that ye can stand against
so many brave men who are at my
command, who do now at this time
stand in their arms, and do await
with great anxiety for the word—
Go down upon the Nephites and
[a]destroy them.
4 And I, knowing of their unconquerable spirit, having proved them
in the field of battle, and knowing of
their everlasting hatred towards you
because of the many wrongs which
ye have done unto them, therefore
if they should come down against
you they would visit you with utter
destruction.
5 Therefore I have written this
epistle, sealing it with mine own
hand, feeling for your welfare,
because of your firmness in that
which ye believe to be right, and
your noble spirit in the field of
battle.
6 Therefore I write unto you,
desiring that ye would yield up unto
this my people, your cities, your
lands, and your possessions, rather
than that they should visit you
with the sword and that destruction
should come upon you.
7 Or in other words, yield yourselves up unto us, and unite with
us and become acquainted with
our [a]secret works, and become our
brethren that ye may be like unto
us—not our slaves, but our brethren
and partners of all our substance.
8 And behold, I [a]swear unto you,
if ye will do this, with an oath, ye
shall not be destroyed; but if ye
will not do this, I swear unto you
with an oath, that on the morrow
month I will command that my
armies shall come down against
you, and they shall not stay their
hand and shall spare not, but shall
slay you, and shall let fall the sword
upon you even until ye shall become
extinct.
9 And behold, I am [a]Giddianhi;
and I am the governor of this the
[b]secret society of Gadianton; which
society and the works thereof I
know to be [c]good; and they are of
[d]ancient date and they have been
handed down unto us.
10 And I write this epistle unto
you, Lachoneus, and I hope that ye
will deliver up your lands and your
possessions, without the shedding
of blood, that this my people may
recover their rights and [a]govern-
ment, who have dissented away
from you because of your wickedness in retaining from them their
rights of government, and except ye
do this, I will avenge their wrongs.
I am Giddianhi.
11 And now it came to pass when
Lachoneus received this epistle he
was exceedingly astonished, because of the boldness of Giddianhi
demanding the possession of the
land of the Nephites, and also of
threatening the people and avenging
the wrongs of those that had received no wrong, save it were they
had [a]wronged themselves by dis-
senting away unto those wicked and
abominable robbers.
12 Now behold, this Lachoneus,

2*a* 3 Ne. 2: 12.
b TG Liberty.
3*a* 3 Ne. 2: 19.
7*a* Hel. 6: 22 (22–26).
8*a* Hel. 1: 11; Ether 8: 14 (13–14).
9*a* 3 Ne. 4: 14.
b TG Secret Combinations.
c Alma 30: 53.
d Hel. 6: 26 (26–30); Ether 8: 9 (9–19); Moses 5: 29 (29, 49–52).
10*a* TG Governments.
11*a* Hel. 14: 30.

[A.D. 16]

the governor, was a just man, and
could not be frightened by the demands and the threatenings of a
[a]robber; therefore he did not
hearken to the epistle of Giddianhi,
the governor of the robbers, but he
did cause that his people should cry
unto the Lord for [b]strength against
the time that the robbers should
come down against them.
13 Yea, he sent a proclamation
among all the people, that they
should [a]gather together their women,
and their children, their flocks and
their herds, and all their substance,
save it were their land, unto one
place.
14 And he caused that [a]fortifica-
tions should be built round about
them, and the strength thereof
should be exceedingly great. And
he caused that armies, both of the
Nephites and of the Lamanites, or
of all them who were numbered
among the Nephites, should be
placed as guards round about to
watch them, and to guard them
from the robbers day and night.
15 Yea, he said unto them: As the
Lord liveth, except ye repent of all
your iniquities, and cry unto the
Lord, ye will in nowise be [a]delivered
out of the hands of those Gadianton
robbers.
16 And so great and marvelous
were the words and prophecies of
Lachoneus that they did cause
fear to come upon all the people;
and they did exert themselves in
their might to do according to the
words of Lachoneus.
17 And it came to pass that
Lachoneus did appoint chief captains over all the armies of the Nephites, to command them at the
time that the robbers should come
down out of the wilderness against
them.
18 Now the chiefest among all the
chief captains and the great commander of all the armies of the
Nephites was appointed, and his
name was [a]Gidgiddoni.
19 Now it was the custom among
all the Nephites to appoint for their
chief captains, (save it were in their
times of wickedness) some one that
had the [a]spirit of revelation and also
prophecy; therefore, this Gidgiddoni was a great prophet among
them, as also was the chief judge.
20 Now the people said unto
Gidgiddoni: [a]Pray unto the Lord,
and let us go up upon the mountains
and into the wilderness, that we
may fall upon the robbers and
destroy them in their own lands.
21 But Gidgiddoni saith unto
them: The Lord [a]forbid; for if we
should go up against them the Lord
would [b]deliver us into their hands;
therefore we will prepare ourselves
in the center of our lands, and we
will gather all our armies together,
and we will not go against them,
but we will wait till they shall come
against us; therefore as the Lord
liveth, if we do this he will deliver
them into our hands.
22 And it came to pass in the
*seventeenth year, in the latter end
of the year, the proclamation of
Lachoneus had gone forth throughout all the face of the land, and they
had taken their [a]horses, and their
chariots, and their cattle, and all
their flocks, and their herds, and
their grain, and all their substance,
and did march forth by thousands
and by tens of thousands, until they
had all gone forth to the [b]place
which [c]had been appointed that
they should gather themselves together, to defend themselves against
their enemies.
23 And the [a]land which was ap-

12*a* 1 Kgs. 20: 3 (2–3); Alma 54: 7 (5–11).
b TG Strength.
13*a* 3 Ne. 3: 22; 4: 1.
14*a* Morm. 2: 4.
15*a* TG Deliver, Deliverance; Protection, Divine.
18*a* 3 Ne. 4: 13 (13, 24, 26); 6: 6.
19*a* TG Guidance, Divine.
20*a* Alma 16: 6 (5–8); 43: 23 (23–24); 48: 16.
21*a* Alma 43: 46 (46–47); 48: 14; Morm. 3: 10 (10–11).
b 1 Sam. 14: 12; 2 Kgs. 3: 18; 1 Ne. 3: 29.
22*a* 3 Ne. 4: 4.
b Morm. 2: 7.
c 3 Ne. 3: 13.
23*a* 3 Ne. 4: 16.

[*A.D. 17]

pointed was the land of Zarahemla,
and the land which was between
the land Zarahemla and the land
[b]Bountiful, yea, to the line which
was between the [c]land Bountiful and
the land Desolation.
24 And there were a great many
thousand people who were called
Nephites, who did gather themselves together in this land. Now
Lachoneus did cause that they
should gather themselves together
in the land [a]southward, because of
the great curse which was upon the
[b]land northward.
25 And they did fortify themselves
against their enemies; and they did
dwell in one land, and in one body,
and they did fear the words which
had been spoken by Lachoneus,
insomuch that they did repent of all
their sins; and they did put up their
[a]prayers unto the Lord their God,
that he would deliver them in the
time that their enemies should come
down against them to battle.
26 And they were exceedingly
sorrowful because of their enemies.
And Gidgiddoni did cause that they
should make [a]weapons of war of
every kind, and they should be
strong with armor, and with shields,
and with bucklers, after the manner
of his instruction.

CHAPTER 4

The Nephite armies defeat the Gadianton robbers—Giddianhi is slain, and his successor, Zemnarihah, is hanged—The Nephites praise the Lord for their victories.

AND it came to pass that in the
latter end of the eighteenth year
those armies of [a]robbers had prepared for battle, and began to come
down and to sally forth from the
hills, and out of the mountains, and
the wilderness, and their strongholds, and their [b]secret places, and
began to take possession of the
lands, both which were in the land
south and which were in the land
north, and began to take possession
of all the lands which had been
[c]deserted by the Nephites, and
the cities which had been left desolate.
2 But behold, there were no wild
beasts nor [a]game in those lands
which had been deserted by the
Nephites, and there was no game
for the robbers save it were in the
wilderness.
3 And the robbers could not exist
save it were in the wilderness, for
the want of food; for the Nephites
had left their lands desolate, and
had gathered their flocks and their
herds and all their substance, and
they were in one body.
4 Therefore, there was no chance
for the robbers to plunder and to
obtain food, save it were to come up
in open battle against the Nephites;
and the Nephites being in one body,
and having so great a number, and
having reserved for themselves provisions, and [a]horses and cattle, and
flocks of every kind, that they might
subsist for the space of [b]seven years,
in the which time they did hope to
destroy the robbers from off the face
of the land; and thus the eighteenth
year did pass away.
5 And it came to pass that in the
nineteenth year Giddianhi found
that it was expedient that he should
go up to battle against the Nephites,
for there was [a]no way that they
could subsist save it were to plunder
and rob and murder.
6 And they durst not spread themselves upon the face of the land insomuch that they could raise grain,
lest the Nephites should come upon

23*b* Alma 22: 29; 3 Ne. 11: 1.
c Morm. 3: 7; 4: 2.
24*a* Alma 46: 17; Morm. 3: 5.
b Alma 22: 31 (30–31).
25*a* TG Trust in God.
26*a* 2 Ne. 5: 14; Jarom 1: 8; Mosiah 10: 8; Alma 2: 12; Hel. 1: 14.

4 1*a* Hel. 2: 13 (11–13).
b Alma 58: 6.
c 3 Ne. 3: 13 (13–14, 22).
2*a* 1 Ne. 18. 25; 2 Ne. 5: 24; 3 Ne. 4: 20.
4*a* 3 Ne. 3: 22; 6: 1 (1–2).
b Gen. 41: 36 (29–36); 3 Ne. 4: 18.
5*a* Alma 47: 36.

[A.D. 18—19]

them and slay them; therefore
Giddianhi gave commandment unto
his armies that in this year they
should go up to battle against the
Nephites.
7 And it came to pass that they did
come up to battle; and it was in the
sixth month; and behold, great and
terrible was the day that they did
come up to battle; and they were
girded about after the manner of
robbers; and they had a lamb-skin
about their loins, and they were
dyed in blood, and their heads were
shorn, and they had headplates
upon them; and great and terrible
was the appearance of the armies of
Giddianhi, because of their armor,
and because of their being dyed in
blood.
8 And it came to pass that the
armies of the Nephites, when they
saw the appearance of the army of
Giddianhi, had all fallen to the
earth, and did lift their cries to the
Lord their God, that he would spare
them and deliver them out of the
hands of their enemies.
9 And it came to pass that when
the armies of Giddianhi saw this
they began to shout with a loud
voice, because of their joy, for they
had supposed that the Nephites had
fallen with fear because of the terror
of their armies.
10 But in this thing they were disappointed, for the Nephites did not
[a]fear them; but they did fear their
God and did supplicate him for
[b]protection; therefore, when the
armies of Giddianhi did rush upon
them they were prepared to meet
them; yea, in the strength of the
Lord they did receive them.
11 And the battle commenced in
this the sixth month; and great and
terrible was the battle thereof, yea,
great and terrible was the [a]slaughter
thereof, insomuch that there never
was known so great a slaughter
among all the people of Lehi since
he left Jerusalem.
12 And notwithstanding the
[a]threatenings and the oaths which
Giddianhi had made, behold, the
Nephites did beat them, insomuch
that they did fall back from before
them.
13 And it came to pass that
[a]Gidgiddoni commanded that his
armies should pursue them as far
as the borders of the wilderness, and
that they should not spare any that
should fall into their hands by the
way; and thus they did pursue them
and did slay them, to the borders of
the wilderness, even until they had
fulfilled the commandment of Gidgiddoni.
14 And it came to pass that Giddianhi, who had stood and fought
with boldness, was pursued as he
fled; and being weary because of his
much fighting he was overtaken and
slain. And thus was the end of
Giddianhi the robber.
15 And it came to pass that the
armies of the Nephites did return
again to their place of security. And
it came to pass that this nineteenth
year did pass away, and the robbers did not come again to battle;
neither did they come again in the
twentieth year.
16 And in the *twenty and first
year they did not come up to battle,
but they came up on all sides to lay
siege round about the people of
Nephi; for they did suppose that if
they should cut off the people of
Nephi from their [a]lands, and should
hem them in on every side, and if
they should cut them off from all
their outward privileges, that they
could cause them to yield themselves
up according to their wishes.
17 Now they had appointed unto
themselves another leader, whose
name was Zemnarihah; therefore it
was Zemnarihah that did cause that
this siege should take place.
18 But behold, this was an advantage to the Nephites; for it was
impossible for the robbers to lay

10*a* TG Reverence.
b Jer. 17:17 (17–18).
11*a* Alma 28:11 (8–12).
12*a* 3 Ne. 3:8 (4–10).
13*a* 3 Ne. 3:18.
16*a* 3 Ne. 3:23.

[*A.D. 21]

siege sufficiently long to have any
effect upon the Nephites, because of
their [a]much [b]provision which they
had laid up in store,
19 And because of the scantiness of
provisions among the robbers; for
behold, they had nothing save it
were meat for their subsistence,
which meat they did obtain in the
wilderness;
20 And it came to pass that the
[a]wild game became scarce in the
wilderness insomuch that the robbers were about to perish with
hunger.
21 And the Nephites were continually marching out by day and by
night, and falling upon their armies,
and cutting them off by thousands
and by tens of thousands.
22 And thus it became the desire
of the people of Zemnarihah to
withdraw from their design, because
of the great destruction which came
upon them by night and by day.
23 And it came to pass that
Zemnarihah did give command unto
his people that they should withdraw themselves from the siege, and
march into the furthermost parts of
the land northward.
24 And now, Gidgiddoni being
aware of their design, and knowing
of their weakness because of the
want of food, and the great slaughter
which had been made among them,
therefore he did send out his armies
in the night-time, and did cut off the
way of their retreat, and did place
his armies in the way of their retreat.
25 And this did they do in the
night-time, and got on their march
beyond the robbers, so that on the
morrow, when the robbers began
their march, they were met by the
armies of the Nephites both in their
front and in their rear.
26 And the robbers who were on
the south were also cut off in their
places of retreat. And all these
things were done by command of
Gidgiddoni.
27 And there were many thousands
who did yield themselves up prisoners unto the Nephites, and the
remainder of them were slain.
28 And their leader, Zemnarihah,
was taken and hanged upon a tree,
yea, even upon the top thereof until
he was dead. And when they had
hanged him until he was dead they
did fell the tree to the earth, and did
cry with a loud voice, saying:
29 May the Lord preserve his
people in righteousness and in
holiness of heart, that they may
cause to be felled to the earth all who
shall seek to slay them because of
power and secret combinations,
even as this man hath been felled
to the earth.
30 And they did rejoice and cry
again with one voice, saying: May
the [a]God of Abraham, and the God
of Isaac, and the God of Jacob, protect this people in righteousness, so
long as they shall [b]call on the name
of their God for [c]protection.
31 And it came to pass that they
did break forth, all as one, in singing,
and [a]praising their God for the great
thing which he had done for them,
in preserving them from falling into
the hands of their enemies.
32 Yea, they did cry: Hosanna to
the Most High God. And they did
cry: Blessed be the name of the Lord
God [a]Almighty, the Most High
God.
33 And their hearts were swollen
with joy, unto the gushing out of
many tears, because of the great
goodness of God in delivering them
out of the hands of their enemies;
and they knew it was because of
their repentance and their humility
that they had been delivered from
an everlasting destruction.

18*a* 3 Ne. 4: 4.
b Gen. 41: 36 (33–57); D&C 4: 4.
20*a* 1 Ne. 18: 25; 2 Ne. 5: 24; 3 Ne. 4: 2.
30*a* Alma 29: 11.
b Gen. 4: 26; Ether 4: 15; Moro. 2: 2.
c TG Protection, Divine.
31*a* Alma 26: 8. TG Thanksgiving.
32*a* 1 Ne. 1: 14.

[A.D. 21—22]

CHAPTER 5

The Nephites repent and forsake their sins—Mormon writes the history of his people and declares the everlasting word to them—Israel shall be gathered in from her long dispersion.

AND now behold, there was not a
living soul among all the people of
the Nephites who did [a]doubt in the
least the words of all the holy
prophets who had spoken; for they
knew that it must needs be that they
must be fulfilled.
2 And they knew that it must be
expedient that Christ had come,
because of the many signs which
had been given, according to the
words of the prophets; and because
of the things which had come to
pass already they knew that it must
needs be that all things should come
to pass according to that which had
been spoken.
3 Therefore they did forsake all
their sins, and their abominations,
and their whoredoms, and did serve
God with all diligence day and night.
4 And now it came to pass that
when they had taken all the robbers prisoners, insomuch that none
did escape who were not slain, they
did cast their prisoners into prison,
and did cause the word of God to be
preached unto them; and as many
as would repent of their sins and
[a]enter into a [b]covenant that they
would murder no more were set at
[c]liberty.
5 But as many as there were who
did not enter into a covenant, and
who did still continue to have those
[a]secret murders in their hearts, yea,
as many as were found breathing
out threatenings against their brethren were condemned and punished
according to the law.
6 And thus they did put an end to
all those wicked, and secret, and
abominable combinations, in the
which there was so much wickedness, and so many murders committed.
7 And thus had the [a]twenty and
second year passed away, and the
twenty and third year also, and the
twenty and fourth, and the twenty
and fifth; and thus had *twenty
and five years passed away.
8 And there had many things
transpired which, in the eyes of
some, would be great and marvelous; nevertheless, they cannot all
be written in this book; yea, this
book cannot contain even a [a]hun-
dredth part of what was done
among so many people in the space
of twenty and five years;
9 But behold there are [a]records
which do contain [b]all the proceedings of this people; and a [c]shorter
but true account was given by
Nephi.
10 Therefore I have made my
[a]record of these things according to
the record of Nephi, which was
engraven on the plates which were
called the [b]plates of Nephi.
11 And behold, I do make the
record on plates which I have made
with mine own hands.
12 And behold, I am called
[a]Mormon, being called after the
[b]land of Mormon, the land in which
Alma did establish the church
among the people, yea, the first
church which was established among
them after their transgression.
13 Behold, I am a disciple of Jesus
Christ, the Son of God. I have been
[a]called of him to declare his word
among his people, that they might
have everlasting life.
14 And it hath become expedient
that I, according to the will of God,
that the prayers of those who have

5 1*a* TG Doubt.
4*a* 3 Ne. 6: 3.
b Alma 44: 15; 62: 16 (16–17).
c TG Liberty.
5*a* 2 Ne. 10: 15.
7*a* 3 Ne. 2: 8.
8*a* W of M 1: 5; 3 Ne. 26: 6 (6–12).
9*a* Hel. 3: 15 (13–15).
b W of M 1: 5; Alma 13: 31.
c Morm. 2: 18.
10*a* Hel. 2: 14.
b W of M 1: 1; Morm. 1: 4 (1–4); 2: 17 (17–18); 8: 5 (1, 4–5, 14).
12*a* W of M 1: 11.
b Mosiah 18: 4; Alma 5: 3.
13*a* 3 Ne. 30: 1; Moro. 7: 2.

[*A.D. 21—26]

gone hence, who were the holy ones,
should be fulfilled according to their
faith, should make a [a]record of these
things which have been done—
15 Yea, a [a]small record of that
which hath taken place from the
time that Lehi left Jerusalem, even
down until the present time.
16 Therefore I do make my record
from the accounts which have been
given by those who were before me,
until the commencement of my day;
17 And then I do make a [a]record of
the things which I have seen with
mine own eyes.
18 And I know the record which I
make to be a just and a true record;
nevertheless there are many things
which, according to our [a]language,
we are not able to [b]write.
19 And now I make an end of my
saying, which is of myself, and proceed to give my account of the things
which have been before me.
20 I am Mormon, and a pure
[a]descendant of Lehi. I have reason
to bless my God and my Savior
Jesus Christ, that he brought our
fathers out of the land of Jerusalem,
(and [b]no one knew it save it were
himself and those whom he brought
out of that land) and that he hath
given me and my people so much
knowledge unto the salvation of
our souls.
21 Surely he hath [a]blessed the
house of [b]Jacob, and hath been
[c]merciful unto the seed of Joseph.
22 And [a]insomuch as the children
of Lehi have kept his commandments he hath blessed them and
prospered them according to his
word.
23 Yea, and surely shall he again
bring a [a]remnant of the seed of
Joseph to the [b]knowledge of the
Lord their God.
24 And as surely as the Lord liveth,
will he [a]gather in from the four
quarters of the earth all the remnant of the [b]seed of Jacob, who are
scattered abroad upon all the face
of the earth.
25 And as he hath [a]covenanted
with all the house of Jacob, even so
shall the covenant wherewith he
hath covenanted with the house of
Jacob be fulfilled in his own due
time, unto the [b]restoring all the
house of Jacob unto the knowledge
of the covenant that he hath
covenanted with them.
26 And then shall they [a]know their
Redeemer, who is Jesus Christ, the
Son of God; and then shall they be
gathered in from the four quarters
of the earth unto their own lands,
from whence they have been dispersed; yea, as the Lord liveth so
shall it be. Amen.

CHAPTER 6

The Nephites prosper—Pride, wealth, and class distinctions arise—The Church is rent with dissensions—Satan leads the people in open rebellion—Many prophets cry repentance and are slain—Their murderers conspire to take over the government.

AND now it came to pass that the
people of the Nephites did all return
to their own lands in the *twenty
and sixth year, every man, with
his family, his flocks and his herds,
his [a]horses and his cattle, and all

14*a* Enos 1:16 (13–18); D&C 3:19; 10:47 (46–50).
15*a* Morm. 7:9; 8:12.
17*a* W of M 1:5; Morm. 1:1.
18*a* TG Language.
b 3 Ne. 19:32 (32–34); Morm. 9:33 (32–33); Ether 12:25 (24–25); D&C 76:116.
20*a* Morm. 1:5; 8:13.
b 1 Ne. 4:36; 3 Ne. 15:14.
21*a* TG Israel, Blessings of.
b Gen. 32:28 (24–32); Ps. 135:4; D&C 49:24 (23–25).
c Ps. 98:3.
22*a* 2 Ne. 1:20; Jarom 1:9; Omni 1:6; Mosiah 1:7; Alma 9:13 (13–14); 37:13.
23*a* Alma 46:24; 3 Ne. 10:17.
b 2 Ne. 3:12; Morm. 7:5 (5, 10).
24*a* TG Israel, Gathering of.
b Gen. 46:8.
25*a* 3 Ne. 15:8; 16:5.
b 2 Ne. 30:3 (1–6); 3 Ne. 16:13 (6–13).
26*a* 2 Ne. 30:7 (7–8); 3 Ne. 20:31 (29–34).
6 1*a* 3 Ne. 3:22 (21–23).

[*A.D. 26]

things whatsoever did belong unto
them.
2 And it came to pass that they
had [a]not eaten up all their provisions; therefore they did take with
them all that they had not devoured,
of all their grain of every kind, and
their gold, and their silver, and all
their precious things, and they did
return to their own lands and their
possessions, both on the north and
on the south, both on the land
northward and on the land southward.
3 And they granted unto those
robbers who had [a]entered into a
covenant to keep the peace of the
land, who were desirous to remain
Lamanites, lands, according to their
numbers, that they might have,
with their labors, wherewith to
subsist upon; and thus they did
establish peace in all the land.
4 And they began again to prosper
and to wax great; and the twenty
and sixth and seventh years passed
away, and there was great [a]order in
the land; and they had formed their
laws according to equity and justice.
5 And now there was nothing in all
the land to hinder the people from
prospering continually, except they
should fall into transgression.
6 And now it was [a]Gidgiddoni, and
the judge, [b]Lachoneus, and those
who had been appointed leaders,
who had established this great
peace in the land.
7 And it came to pass that there
were many cities built anew, and
there were many old cities repaired.
8 And there were many [a]highways
cast up, and many roads made,
which led from city to city, and
from land to land, and from place
to place.
9 And thus passed away the
twenty and eighth year, and the
people had continual peace.
10 But it came to pass in the
twenty and ninth year there began
to be some disputings among the
people; and some were lifted up
unto pride and [a]boastings because
of their exceedingly great riches,
yea, even unto great persecutions;
11 For there were many [a]mer-
chants in the land, and also many
[b]lawyers, and many officers.
12 And the people began to be distinguished by ranks, according to
their [a]riches and their chances for
learning; yea, some were [b]ignorant
because of their poverty, and others
did receive great [c]learning because
of their riches.
13 Some were lifted up in pride,
and others were exceedingly humble; some did return railing for
railing, while others would receive
railing and [a]persecution and all
manner of [b]afflictions, and would
not turn and [c]revile again, but were
humble and penitent before God.
14 And thus there became a great
inequality in all the land, insomuch
that the church began to be broken
up; yea, insomuch that in the
thirtieth year the church was
broken up in all the land save it were
among a few of the Lamanites who
were converted unto the true faith;
and [a]they would not depart from it,
for they were firm, and steadfast,
and immovable, willing with all
[b]diligence to keep the commandments of the Lord.
15 Now the cause of this iniquity
of the people was this—[a]Satan had
great [b]power, unto the stirring up
of the people to do all manner of
iniquity, and to the puffing them up

2a 3 Ne. 4: 4.
3a 3 Ne. 5: 4.
4a TG Order.
6a 3 Ne. 3: 18.
b 3 Ne. 3: 1.
8a 3 Ne. 8: 13.
10a TG Boasting.
11a Hel. 6: 8.
b Alma 10: 14 (14–17, 27); 14: 5 (5, 18–27).
12a 1 Tim. 6: 17; Hel. 4: 12 (11–13).
b TG Ignorance.
c TG Learning.
13a TG Persecution.
b TG Affliction.
c 3 Ne. 12: 39; 4 Ne. 1: 34; D&C 98: 23 (23–27).
TG Reviling.
14a Alma 23: 6; 27: 27; Hel. 15: 8 (5–16).
b TG Dedication; Diligence.
15a Moses 6: 15.
b 1 Ne. 22: 26; Alma 48: 17.

[A.D. 29—30]

with pride, tempting them to seek for
power, and authority, and [c]riches,
and the vain things of the world.
16 And thus Satan did lead away
the hearts of the people to do all
manner of iniquity; therefore they
had enjoyed peace but a few years.
17 And thus, in the commencement of the thirtieth year—the
people having been [a]delivered up for
the space of a long time to be carried
about by the [b]temptations of the
devil whithersoever he desired to
carry them, and to do whatsoever
iniquity he desired they should—
and thus in the commencement of
this, the thirtieth year, they were
in a state of awful wickedness.
18 Now they did not sin [a]igno-
rantly, for they knew the [b]will of
God concerning them, for it had been
taught unto them; therefore they
did wilfully [c]rebel against God.
19 And now it was in the days of
Lachoneus, the son of [a]Lachoneus,
for Lachoneus did fill the seat of
his father and did govern the people
that year.
20 And there began to be men
[a]inspired from heaven and sent
forth, standing among the people in
all the land, preaching and testifying boldly of the sins and iniquities
of the people, and testifying unto
them concerning the redemption
which the Lord would make for his
people, or in other words, the
resurrection of Christ; and they did
testify boldly of his [b]death and
sufferings.
21 Now there were many of the
people who were exceedingly angry
because of those who testified of
these things; and those who were
angry were chiefly the chief judges,
and they who [a]had been high priests
and lawyers; yea, all those who were
lawyers were angry with those who
testified of these things.
22 Now there was no lawyer nor
judge nor high priest that could
have power to condemn any one to
death save their condemnation was
signed by the governor of the land.
23 Now there were many of those
[a]who testified of the things pertaining to Christ who testified
boldly, who were taken and put to
death [b]secretly by the judges, that
the knowledge of their death came
not unto the governor of the land
until after their death.
24 Now behold, this was contrary to the laws of the land, that
any man should be put to death
except they had power from the
governor of the land—
25 Therefore a complaint came up
unto the land of Zarahemla, to the
governor of the land, against these
judges who had condemned the
prophets of the Lord unto [a]death,
not according to the law.
26 Now it came to pass that they
were taken and brought up before
the judge, to be judged of the crime
which they had done, according to
the [a]law which had been given by
the people.
27 Now it came to pass that those
judges had many friends and kindreds; and the remainder, yea, even
almost all the lawyers and the high
priests, did gather themselves together, and unite with the kindreds
of those judges who were to be tried
according to the law.
28 And they did enter into a
[a]covenant one with another, yea,
even into that covenant which was
given by them of old, which covenant was given and administered by
the [b]devil, to combine against all
righteousness.

15c TG Selfishness.
17a Moses 5:23.
b TG Temptation.
18a Num. 15:27 (2–29); Mosiah 3:11. TG Ignorance.
b TG God, Will of.
c TG Rebellion.
19a 3 Ne. 1:1.
20a TG Inspiration; Prophets, Mission of.
b TG Jesus Christ, Death of.
21a D&C 121:37. TG Apostasy of Individuals.
23a 3 Ne. 7:14.
b Hel. 6:17 (17–38).
25a 3 Ne. 9:9.
26a Mosiah 29:25; Alma 1:14.
28a TG Secret Combinations.
b Hel. 6:26; Ether 8:9 (9, 15–16).

[A.D. 29—30]

29 Therefore they did combine against the people of the Lord, and enter into a covenant to destroy them, and to deliver those who were guilty of murder from the grasp of justice, which was about to be administered according to the law.

30 And they did set at defiance the law and the rights of their country; and they did covenant one with another to destroy the governor, and to establish a [a]king over the land, that the land should no more be at [b]liberty but should be subject unto kings.

CHAPTER 7

The chief judge is murdered, the government is overthrown, and the people divide into tribes—Jacob, an antichrist, becomes king of a league of tribes—Nephi preaches repentance and faith in Christ—Angels minister to him daily, and he raises his brother from the dead—Many repent and are baptized.

Now behold, I will show unto you that they did not establish a king over the land; but in this same year, yea, the thirtieth year, they did destroy upon the judgment-seat, yea, did murder the chief judge of the land.

2 And the people were divided one against another; and they did [a]separate one from another into tribes, every man according to his family and his kindred and friends; and thus they did destroy the government of the land.

3 And every tribe did appoint a chief or a leader over them; and thus they became tribes and leaders of tribes.

4 Now behold, there was no man among them save he had much family and many kindreds and friends; therefore their tribes became exceedingly great.

5 Now all this was done, and there were no wars as yet among them; and all this iniquity had come upon the people [a]because they did [b]yield themselves unto the power of Satan.

6 And the regulations of the government were destroyed, because of the [a]secret combination of the friends and kindreds of those who murdered the prophets.

7 And they did cause a great contention in the land, insomuch that the more righteous part of the people had nearly all become wicked; yea, there were but few righteous men among them.

8 And thus six years had not passed away since the more part of the people had turned from their righteousness, like the dog to his [a]vomit, or like the sow to her wallowing in the mire.

9 Now this secret combination, which had brought so great iniquity upon the people, did gather themselves together, and did place at their head a man whom they did call Jacob;

10 And they did call him their king; therefore he became a king over this wicked band; and he was one of the chiefest who had given his voice against the prophets who testified of Jesus.

11 And it came to pass that they were not so strong in number as the tribes of the people, who were united together save it were their leaders did establish their laws, every one according to his tribe; nevertheless they were enemies; notwithstanding they were not a righteous people, yet they were united in the hatred of those who had entered into a covenant to [a]destroy the government.

12 Therefore, Jacob seeing that their enemies were more numerous than they, he being the king of the band, therefore he commanded his

30*a* 1 Sam. 8: 5; Alma 51: 5; 3 Ne. 7: 12. TG Tyranny.
b TG Liberty.
7 2*a* TG Unity.
5*a* Moses 4: 6.
b Rom. 6: 16 (13–20); Alma 10: 25.
6*a* 2 Ne. 9: 9.
8*a* Prov. 26: 11; 2 Pet. 2: 22.
11*a* 3 Ne. 9: 9.

people that they should take their
flight into the northernmost part of
the land, and there build up unto
themselves a [a]kingdom, until they
were joined by dissenters, (for he
flattered them that there would be
many dissenters) and they become
sufficiently strong to contend with
the tribes of the people; and they
did so.
13 And so speedy was their march
that it could not be impeded until
they had gone forth out of the reach
of the people. And thus ended the
thirtieth year; and thus were the
affairs of the people of Nephi.
14 And it came to pass in the thirty
and first year that they were divided into tribes, every man according to his family, kindred and
friends; nevertheless they had come
to an agreement that they would
not go to war one with another; but
they were not united as to their
laws, and their manner of government, for they were established
according to the minds of those who
were their chiefs and their leaders.
But they did establish very strict
laws that one tribe should not trespass against another, insomuch that
in some degree they had peace in
the land; nevertheless, their hearts
were turned from the Lord their
God, and they did stone the
[a]prophets and did cast them out
from among them.
15 And it came to pass that
[a]Nephi—having been visited by
angels and also the voice of the
Lord, therefore having seen angels,
and being eye-witness, and having
had power given unto him that he
might know concerning the ministry of Christ, and also being eye-
witness to their quick return from
righteousness unto their wickedness
and abominations;
16 Therefore, being [a]grieved for
the hardness of their hearts and the
blindness of their minds—went
forth among them in that same year,
and began to testify, boldly, repentance and remission of sins
through faith on the Lord Jesus
Christ.
17 And he did minister many things
unto them; and all of them cannot
be written, and a part of them
would not suffice, therefore they are
not written in this book. And Nephi
did minister with [a]power and with
great authority.
18 And it came to pass that they
were angry with him, even because
he had greater power than they, for
it were [a]not possible that they
could disbelieve his words, for so
great was his faith on the Lord
Jesus Christ that angels did minister
unto him daily.
19 And in the name of Jesus did he
cast out devils and [a]unclean spirits;
and even his [b]brother did he [c]raise
from the dead, after he had been
stoned and suffered death by the
people.
20 And the people saw it, and did
witness of it, and were angry with
him because of his power; and he
did also do [a]many more miracles, in
the sight of the people, in the name
of Jesus.
21 And it came to pass that the
thirty and first year did pass away,
and there were but few who were
converted unto the Lord; but as
many as were converted did truly
signify unto the people that they
had been [a]visited by the power and
[b]Spirit of God, which was in Jesus
Christ, in whom they believed.
22 And as many as had devils cast
out from them, and were [a]healed of
their sicknesses and their infirmities, did truly manifest unto the

12*a* 3 Ne. 6: 30.
14*a* 3 Ne. 6: 23 (23–25).
15*a* 3 Ne. 1: 2 (2–3, 10); 11: 18.
16*a* Gen. 6: 6; 1 Ne. 2: 18; Alma 31: 24; Moses 8: 25.
17*a* TG Priesthood, Power of.
18*a* Alma 4: 19.
19*a* TG Spirits, Evil or Unclean.
b 3 Ne. 19: 4.
c TG Death, Power over.
20*a* 3 Ne. 8: 1.
21*a* TG God, Manifestations of.
b TG God, Spirit of.
22*a* Mark 2: 11 (11–12); Acts 8: 7.

people that they had been wrought
upon by the Spirit of God, and had
been healed; and they did show
forth signs also and did do some
miracles among the people.
23 Thus passed away the thirty
and second year also. And Nephi
did cry unto the people in the commencement of the thirty and third
year; and he did preach unto them
repentance and remission of sins.
24 Now I would have you to
remember also, that there were none
who were brought unto [a]repent-
ance who were not baptized with
water.
25 Therefore, there were ordained
of Nephi, men unto this ministry,
that all such as should come unto
them should be [a]baptized with
water, and this as a witness and a
testimony before God, and unto the
people, that they had repented and
received a [b]remission of their sins.
26 And there were many in the
commencement of this year that
were baptized unto repentance; and
thus the more part of the year did
pass away.

CHAPTER 8

Tempests, earthquakes, fires, whirlwinds, and physical upheavals attest the crucifixion of Christ—Many people are destroyed—Darkness covers the land for three days—Those who remain bemoan their fate.

AND now it came to pass that
according to our record, and we
know our record to be [a]true, for
behold, it was a [b]just man who did
keep the record—for he truly did
[c]many [d]miracles in the [e]name of
Jesus; and there was not any man
who could do a miracle in the name
of Jesus save he were cleansed every
whit from his iniquity—
2 And now it came to pass, if there
was no mistake made by this man
in the reckoning of our time, the
[a]thirty and third year had passed
away;
3 And the people began to look
with great earnestness for the sign
which had been given by the
prophet Samuel, the Lamanite, yea,
for the time that there should be
[a]darkness for the space of three
days over the face of the land.
4 And there began to be great
[a]doubtings and [b]disputations among
the people, notwithstanding so
many signs had been given.
5 And it came to pass in the [a]thirty
and fourth year, in the first month,
on the fourth day of the month,
there arose a great [b]storm, such an
one as never had been known in all
the land.
6 And there was also a great and
terrible tempest; and there was
terrible [a]thunder, insomuch that it
did [b]shake the whole earth as if it
was about to divide asunder.
7 And there were exceedingly
sharp lightnings, such as never had
been known in all the land.
8 And the [a]city of Zarahemla did
take fire.
9 And the city of [a]Moroni did
[b]sink into the depths of the sea,
and the inhabitants thereof were
drowned.
10 And the earth was carried up
upon the city of [a]Moronihah, that
in the place of the city there became a great [b]mountain.

24*a* TG Baptism, Qualifications for.
25*a* TG Baptism.
b D&C 20: 37. TG Remission of Sins.
8 1*a* John 21: 24.
b 3 Ne. 23: 7.
c 3 Ne. 7: 20 (19–20).
d John 6: 14; Morm. 9: 18 (18–19).
e Acts 3: 6 (6–16); Jacob 4: 6.
2*a* 3 Ne. 2: 8.
3*a* 1 Ne. 19: 10; Hel. 14: 27 (20, 27); 3 Ne. 10: 9. TG Darkness, Physical.
4*a* TG Doubt.
b TG Disputations.
5*a* Hel. 14: 20 (20–27); 3 Ne. 11: 2.
b TG Jesus Christ, Crucifixion of; Jesus Christ, Death of.
6*a* 1 Ne. 19: 11; Hel. 14: 21 (20–27).
b Matt. 27: 51 (45, 50–51).
8*a* 4 Ne. 1: 8.
9*a* Alma 50: 13.
b 3 Ne. 9: 4 (4–5).
10*a* 3 Ne. 8: 25.
b Hel. 12: 17; 3 Ne. 9: 8 (6–8).

11 And there was a great and terrible destruction in the land southward.

12 But behold, there was a more great and terrible destruction in the land northward; for behold, the [a]whole face of the land was changed, because of the tempest and the whirlwinds, and the thunderings and the lightnings, and the exceedingly great quaking of the whole earth;

13 And the [a]highways were broken up, and the level roads were spoiled, and many smooth places became rough.

14 And many [a]great and notable cities were [b]sunk, and many were [c]burned, and many were shaken till the buildings thereof had fallen to the earth, and the inhabitants thereof were slain, and the places were left desolate.

15 And there were some cities which remained; but the damage thereof was exceedingly great, and there were many in them who were slain.

16 And there were some who were carried away in the [a]whirlwind; and whither they went no man knoweth, save they know that they were carried away.

17 And thus the face of the whole earth became deformed, because of the tempests, and the thunderings, and the lightnings, and the quaking of the earth.

18 And behold, the rocks were rent in twain; they were broken up upon the face of the whole earth, insomuch that they were [a]found in broken fragments, and in seams and in cracks, upon all the face of the land.

19 And it came to pass that when the thunderings, and the lightnings, and the storm, and the tempest, and the quakings of the earth did cease—for behold, they did last for about the space of [a]three [b]hours; and it was said by some that the time was greater; nevertheless, all these great and terrible things were done in about the space of three hours—and then behold, there was [c]darkness upon the face of the land.

20 And it came to pass that there was thick darkness upon all the face of the land, insomuch that the inhabitants thereof who had not fallen could [a]feel the [b]vapor of darkness;

21 And there could be no light, because of the darkness, neither candles, neither torches; neither could there be fire kindled with their fine and exceedingly dry wood, so that there could not be any light at all;

22 And there was not any light seen, neither fire, nor glimmer, neither the sun, nor the moon, nor the stars, for so great were the mists of darkness which were upon the face of the land.

23 And it came to pass that it did last for the space of three days that there was no light seen; and there was great mourning and [a]howling and weeping among all the people continually; yea, great were the groanings of the people, because of the darkness and the great destruction which had come upon them.

24 And in one place they were heard to cry, saying: O that we had repented [a]before this great and terrible day, and then would our brethren have been spared, and they would not have been [b]burned in that great city Zarahemla.

25 And in another place they were heard to cry and mourn, saying: O that we had repented before this great and terrible day, and had not killed and stoned the prophets, and cast them out; then would our

12*a* 3 Ne. 11: 1.
13*a* Hel. 14: 24; 3 Ne. 6: 8.
14*a* 3 Ne. 9: 12; 10: 4.
b 1 Ne. 12: 4.
c 2 Ne. 26: 4; 3 Ne. 9: 3 (3–9).
16*a* Dan. 11: 40; 3 Ne. 10: 13 (13–14).
18*a* Hel. 14: 22 (21–22).
19*a* Luke 23: 44 (44–45).
b Alma 18: 14.
c 1 Ne. 19: 10; 3 Ne. 10: 9.
20*a* Ex. 10: 21.
b 1 Ne. 12: 5; 19: 11.
23*a* 3 Ne. 10: 8 (2, 8).
24*a* TG Procrastination.
b Hel. 13: 12; 3 Ne. 9: 3.

[A.D. 34]

mothers and our fair daughters, and
our children have been spared, and
not have been buried up in that
great city [a]Moronihah. And thus
were the howlings of the people
great and terrible.

CHAPTER 9

In the darkness the voice of Christ proclaims the destruction of many people and cities for their wickedness—He also proclaims his divinity, announces that the law of Moses is fulfilled, and invites men to come unto him and be saved.

AND it came to pass that there was
a [a]voice heard among all the inhabitants of the earth, upon all the
face of this land, crying:
2 Wo, wo, wo unto this people;
wo unto the inhabitants of the whole
earth except they shall [a]repent; for
the devil [b]laugheth, and his angels
rejoice, because of the slain of the
fair sons and daughters of my
people; and it is because of their
iniquity and abominations that they
are fallen!
3 Behold, that great city Zarahemla have I [a]burned with fire, and
the inhabitants thereof.
4 And behold, that great city
Moroni have I caused to be [a]sunk
in the depths of the sea, and the
inhabitants thereof to be drowned.
5 And behold, that great city
[a]Moronihah have I covered with
earth, and the inhabitants thereof,
to hide their iniquities and their
abominations from before my face,
that the blood of the prophets and
the saints shall not come any more
unto me against them.
6 And behold, the city of Gilgal
have I caused to be sunk, and the
inhabitants thereof to be buried up
in the depths of the earth;
7 Yea, and the city of Onihah and
the inhabitants thereof, and the
city of Mocum and the inhabitants
thereof, and the city of [a]Jerusalem
and the inhabitants thereof; and
[b]waters have I caused to come up
in the stead thereof, to hide their
wickedness and abominations from
before my face, that the [c]blood of
the prophets and the saints shall
[d]not come up any more unto me
against them.
8 And behold, the city of Gadiandi,
and the city of Gadiomnah, and the
city of Jacob, and the city of Gimgimno, all these have I caused to be
sunk, and made [a]hills and valleys in
the places thereof; and the inhabitants thereof have I [b]buried up in
the depths of the earth, to hide their
wickedness and abominations from
before my face, that the blood of the
prophets and the saints should not
come up any more unto me against
them.
9 And behold, that great city
Jacobugath, which was inhabited
by the people of king Jacob, have
I caused to be burned with fire
because of their sins and their
[a]wickedness, which was above all
the wickedness of the whole earth,
because of their [b]secret murders
and combinations; for it was
they that did [c]destroy the peace
of my people and the government
of the land; therefore I did cause
them to be burned, to [d]destroy them
from before my face, that the blood
of the prophets and the saints should
not come up unto me any more
against them.

25*a* 3 Ne. 8: 10; 9: 5.
9 1*a* 1 Ne. 19: 11.
2*a* TG Repentance.
b Moses 7: 26.
3*a* Matt. 11: 20; Hel. 13: 12; 3 Ne. 8: 14 (14–24).
4*a* 3 Ne. 8: 9; 4 Ne. 1: 9.
5*a* 3 Ne. 8: 25 (10, 25).
7*a* Alma 21: 1; 24: 1.
b Ezek. 26: 19.
c Rev. 16: 6 (5–7).
d Jonah 1: 2.
8*a* 1 Ne. 19: 11; 3 Ne. 10: 13 (13–14); Moses 7: 14.
b Num. 16: 32; Hel. 12: 17; 3 Ne. 8: 10 (10, 25).
9*a* Gen. 6: 5 (5–6); Morm. 4: 12 (10–12); D&C 112: 23; Moses 7: 36 (36–37); 8: 22 (22, 28–30).
b Hel. 6: 17 (17–38); 3 Ne. 6: 23.
c 3 Ne. 7: 11 (9–13).
d Gen. 6: 13; 1 Ne. 17: 31; 2 Ne. 1: 17; Mosiah 12: 8.

10 And behold, the city of Laman,
and the city of Josh, and the city of
Gad, and the city of Kishkumen,
have I caused to be burned with fire,
and the inhabitants thereof, because of their wickedness in casting
out the prophets, and stoning those
whom I did send to declare unto
them concerning their wickedness
and their abominations.
11 And because they did cast them
all out, that there were none
righteous among them, I did send
down [a]fire and destroy them, that
their wickedness and abominations
might be hid from before my [b]face,
that the blood of the prophets and
the saints whom I sent among them
might not cry unto me [c]from the
ground against them.
12 And [a]many great destructions
have I caused to come upon this
land, and upon this people, because
of their wickedness and their
abominations.
13 O all ye that are [a]spared because
ye were more [b]righteous than they,
will ye not now return unto me, and
repent of your sins, and be converted, that I may [c]heal you?
14 Yea, verily I say unto you, if ye
will [a]come unto me ye shall have
[b]eternal life. Behold, mine [c]arm of
mercy is extended towards you, and
whosoever will come, him will I
receive; and blessed are those who
come unto me.
15 Behold, I am Jesus Christ the
Son of God. I [a]created the heavens
and the earth, and all thin
them are. I was with the
from the beginning. [b]I am in the
Father, and the Father in me; and
in me hath the Father glorified his
name.
16 I came unto my own, and my
own [a]received me not. And the
scriptures [b]concerning my coming
are fulfilled.
17 And as many as have received
me, to them have I [a]given to become
the sons of God; and even so will I
to as many as shall believe on my
name, for behold, by me [b]redemp-
tion cometh, and [c]in me is the [d]law
of Moses fulfilled.
18 I am the [a]light and the life of the
world. I am [b]Alpha and Omega, the
beginning and the end.
19 And ye shall offer up unto me
[a]no more the shedding of blood;
yea, your sacrifices and your burnt
offerings shall be done away, for I
will accept none of your sacrifices
and your burnt offerings.
20 And ye shall offer for a [a]sacrifice
unto me a broken heart and a contrite spirit. And whoso cometh unto
me with a broken heart and a contrite spirit, him will I [b]baptize with
fire and with the Holy Ghost, even as
the Lamanites, because of their faith
in me at the time of their conversion,
were baptized with fire and with the
Holy Ghost, and they knew it not.
21 Behold, I have come unto the
world to bring [a]redemption unto the
world, to save the world from sin.

11*a* 2 Kgs. 1: 10 (9–16); Hel. 13: 13.
b Deut. 31: 18.
c Gen. 4: 10.
12*a* Hel. 14: 24; 3 Ne. 8: 14 (8–10, 14); 10: 7 (4–7).
13*a* 3 Ne. 10: 6 (6, 12); 27: 31.
b Gen. 18: 26.
c Jer. 3: 22; 17: 14; Matt. 13: 15; 3 Ne. 18: 32.
14*a* 1 Ne. 1: 14; 2 Ne. 26: 25 (24–28); Alma 5: 34 (33–36).
b John 3: 16.
c Isa. 59: 16; Alma 19: 36.
15*a* John 1: 3 (1–3); Col. 1: 16; Heb. 1: 2 (1–3); Mosiah 15: 4; Hel. 14: 12; Ether 4: 7; D&C 14: 9.
b 3 Ne. 11: 27 (7, 11, 27); 19: 23 (23, 29).
16*a* John 1: 11; D&C 6: 21.
b 3 Ne. 15: 5.
17*a* John 1: 12. TG Man, Potential to Become like Heavenly Father; Sons and Daughters of God.
b Ps. 107: 2. TG Jesus Christ, Redeemer.
c 3 Ne. 15: 8 (2–8).
d Heb. 8: 13; 3 Ne. 12: 19 (19, 46–47).
18*a* TG Jesus Christ, Light of the World.
b Rev. 1: 8. TG Jesus Christ, Firstborn.
19*a* Mosiah 13: 27; Alma 34: 13; 3 Ne. 15: 4 (2–10).
20*a* Ps. 51: 17; Omni 1: 26; 3 Ne. 12: 19; D&C 64: 34.
b TG Holy Ghost, Baptism of.
21*a* TG Jesus Christ, Atonement through.

[A.D. 34]

22 Therefore, whoso [a]repenteth
and cometh unto me [b]as a [c]little
child, him will I receive, for of such
is the kingdom of God. Behold, for
such I have [d]laid down my life, and
have taken it up again; therefore
repent, and come unto me ye ends
of the earth, and be saved.

CHAPTER 10

There is silence in the land for many hours—The voice of Christ promises to gather his people as a hen gathereth her chickens—The more righteous part of the people had been preserved.

AND now behold, it came to pass
that all the people of the land did
[a]hear these sayings, and did witness
of it. And after these sayings there
was silence in the land for the space
of many hours;
2 For so great was the astonishment of the people that they did
cease lamenting and howling for the
loss of their kindred which had been
slain; therefore there was silence in
all the land for the space of many
hours.
3 And it came to pass that there
came a voice again unto the people,
and all the people did hear, and did
witness of it, saying:
4 O ye people of these [a]great cities
which have fallen, who are descendants of Jacob, yea, who are of the
house of Israel, how oft have I
[b]gathered you as a hen gathereth her
chickens under her wings, and have
[c]nourished you.
5 And again, how oft would I have
gathered you as a hen gathereth her
chickens under her wings, yea, O
[a]ye people of the house of Israel,
who have fallen; yea, O ye people
of the house of Israel, ye that dwell
at Jerusalem, as ye that have fallen;
yea, how oft would I have gathered
you as a hen gathereth her chickens,
and ye would not.
6 O ye house of Israel whom I have
[a]spared, how oft will I gather you
as a hen gathereth her chickens
under her wings, if ye will repent
and [b]return unto me with full
purpose of [c]heart.
7 But if not, O house of Israel, the
places of your dwellings shall become [a]desolate until the time of the
fulfilling of the [b]covenant to your
fathers.
8 And now it came to pass that
after the people had heard these
words, behold, they began to weep
and howl [a]again because of the loss
of their kindred and friends.
9 And it came to pass that thus did
the three days pass away. And it
was in the morning, and the [a]dark-
ness dispersed from off the face of
the land, and the earth did cease to
tremble, and the [b]rocks did cease
to rend, and the dreadful groanings
did cease, and all the tumultuous
noises did pass away.
10 And the earth did cleave together again, that it stood; and the
[a]mourning, and the weeping, and
the wailing of the people who were
spared alive did cease; and their
mourning was turned into joy, and
their lamentations into the [b]praise
and thanksgiving unto the Lord
Jesus Christ, their Redeemer.
11 And thus far were the [a]scrip-
tures [b]fulfilled which had been
spoken by the prophets.
12 And it was the [a]more righteous
part of the people who were saved,
and it was they who received the

22*a* TG Repentance.
b Mark 10:15.
c Mosiah 3:19; 3 Ne. 11:37 (37–38).
d John 10:15 (15–18). TG Jesus Christ, Death of; Self-sacrifice.
10 1*a* 1 Ne. 19:11.
4*a* 3 Ne. 8:14 (8–16); 9:12 (3–12).
b Hel. 7:19.
c Luke 16:29 (29–31); 1 Ne. 17:3; Jacob 5:25.
5*a* Matt. 23:37; D&C 43:24 (24–25).
6*a* 3 Ne. 9:13.
b 1 Sam. 7:3; Hel. 13:11; 3 Ne. 24:7.
c Ezek. 36:26.
7*a* Ezek. 26:19.
b Enos 1:16 (12–18).
8*a* 3 Ne. 8:23 (23–25).
9*a* 3 Ne. 8:19 (3, 19–23).
b Hel. 14:21.
10*a* TG Mourning.
b Acts 16:25.
11*a* 1 Ne. 19:12 (10–12).
b Acts 3:18 (18–21).
12*a* 2 Ne. 26:8; 3 Ne. 9:13 (11–13); 27:31.

[A.D. 34]

prophets and stoned them not; and it
was they who had not shed the blood
of the saints, who were spared—
13 And they were spared and were
not sunk and buried up in the earth;
and they were not drowned in the
depths of the sea; and they were not
burned by fire, neither were they
fallen upon and crushed to death;
and they were not carried away in
the whirlwind; neither were they
overpowered by the vapor of smoke
and of darkness.
14 And now, whoso readeth, let
him understand; he that hath the
scriptures, let him [a]search them,
and see and behold if all these
deaths and destructions by fire,
and by smoke, and by [b]tempests,
and by whirlwinds, and by the
[c]opening of the earth to receive
them, and all these things are not
unto the fulfilling of the prophecies
of many of the holy prophets.
15 Behold, I say unto you, Yea,
many have testified of these things
at the coming of Christ, and were
[a]slain because they testified of these
things.
16 Yea, the prophet [a]Zenos did
testify of these things, and also
Zenock spake [b]concerning these
things, because they testified particularly concerning us, who are the
remnant of their seed.
17 Behold, our father Jacob also
testified concerning a [a]remnant of
the seed of Joseph. And behold, are
not we a remnant of the seed of
Joseph? And these things which
testify of us, are they not written
upon the plates of brass which our
father Lehi brought out of Jerusalem?
18 And it came to pass that in the
ending of the thirty and fourth year,
behold, I will show unto you that
the people of Nephi who were
spared, and also those who had been
called [a]Lamanites, who had been
spared, did have great favors shown
unto them, and great [b]blessings
poured out upon their heads, insomuch that soon after the [c]ascension
of Christ into heaven he did truly
manifest himself unto them—
19 [a]Showing his body unto them,
and ministering unto them; and
an account of his ministry shall be
given hereafter. Therefore for this
time I make an end of my sayings.

Jesus Christ did show himself unto the people of Nephi, as the multitude were gathered together in the land Bountiful, and did minister unto them; and on this wise did he show himself unto them. Comprising chapters 11 to 26 inclusive.

CHAPTER 11

The Father testifies of his Beloved Son—Christ appears and proclaims his atonement—The people feel the wound marks in his hands and feet and side—They cry Hosanna—He sets forth the mode and manner of baptism—The spirit of contention is of the devil—Christ's doctrine is that men should believe and be baptized and receive the Holy Ghost.

AND now it came to pass that there
were a great multitude [a]gathered
together, of the people of Nephi,
round about the temple which was
in the land [b]Bountiful; and they
were marveling and wondering one
with another, and were showing one
to another the [c]great and marvelous
change which had taken place.
2 And they were also conversing
about this Jesus Christ, of whom the
[a]sign had been given concerning his
death.

14*a* TG Scriptures, Study of.
b Hel. 14: 23.
c Num. 16: 32; 1 Ne. 19: 11; 2 Ne. 26: 5.
15*a* TG Martyrdom.
16*a* Hel. 8: 20 (19–20).
b 1 Ne. 19: 21.
17*a* Alma 46: 24; 3 Ne. 5: 23 (23–24).
18*a* 4 Ne. 1: 20.
b TG Blessing.
c Acts 1: 9 (9–11).
19*a* 3 Ne. 11: 12 (12–15).
11 1*a* Hel. 3: 14 (9, 14).
b Alma 22: 29; 3 Ne. 3: 23.
c 3 Ne. 8: 12 (11–14).
2*a* Hel. 14: 20 (20–27); 3 Ne. 8: 5 (5–25).

[A.D. 34]

3 And it came to pass that while they were thus conversing one with another, they heard a [a]voice as if it came out of heaven; and they cast their eyes round about, for they understood not the voice which they heard; and it was not a harsh voice, neither was it a loud voice; nevertheless, and notwithstanding it being a [b]small voice it did [c]pierce them that did hear to the center, insomuch that there was no part of their frame that it did not cause to quake; yea, it did pierce them to the very soul, and did cause their hearts to burn.

4 And it came to pass that again they heard the voice, and they [a]understood it not.

5 And again the third time they did hear the voice, and did [a]open their ears to hear it; and their eyes were towards the sound thereof; and they did look steadfastly towards heaven, from whence the sound came.

6 And behold, the third time they did understand the voice which they heard; and it said unto them:

7 Behold my [a]Beloved Son, [b]in whom I am well pleased, in whom I have glorified my name—hear ye him.

8 And it came to pass, as they understood they cast their eyes up again towards heaven; and behold, they [a]saw a Man [b]descending out of heaven; and he was clothed in a white robe; and he came down and stood in the midst of them; and the eyes of the whole multitude were turned upon him, and they durst not open their mouths, even one to another, and wist not what it meant, for they thought it was an angel that had appeared unto them.

9 And it came to pass that he stretched forth his hand and spake unto the people, saying:

10 Behold, I am Jesus Christ, whom the prophets testified shall come into the world.

11 And behold, I am the [a]light and the life of the world; and I have drunk out of that bitter [b]cup which the Father hath given me, and have glorified the Father in [c]taking upon me the sins of the world, in the which I have suffered the [d]will of the Father in all things from the beginning.

12 And it came to pass that when Jesus had spoken these words the whole multitude [a]fell to the earth; for they remembered that it had been [b]prophesied among them that Christ should [c]show himself unto them after his ascension into heaven.

13 And it came to pass that the [a]Lord spake unto them saying:

14 Arise and come forth unto me, that ye may [a]thrust your hands into my side, and also that ye may [b]feel the prints of the nails in my hands and in my feet, that ye may know that I am the [c]God of Israel, and the God of the whole [d]earth, and have been slain for the sins of the world.

15 And it came to pass that the multitude went forth, and thrust their hands into his side, and [a]did feel the prints of the nails in his hands and in his feet; and this they

3*a* Deut. 4: 33; Ezek. 1: 24; Hel. 5: 29 (28–36).
b 1 Kgs. 19: 12 (11–13); D&C 85: 6.
c 1 Sam. 3: 11; Jer. 20: 9.
4*a* Ezek. 1: 24 (24–28); 1 Cor. 14: 2.
5*a* Job 36: 15; D&C 101: 92.
7*a* Matt. 3: 17; 17: 5; JS-H 1: 17. TG Witness of the Father.
b 3 Ne. 9: 15.
8*a* 1 Ne. 12: 6; 2 Ne. 26: 1 (1, 9); Alma 16: 20; Ether 3: 17 (17–18).
b Acts 1: 9 (9–11).
11*a* TG Jesus Christ, Light of the World.
b John 18: 11.
c John 1: 29.
d Mark 14: 36 (32–42); Luke 22: 42; John 6: 38; Hel. 10: 4; D&C 19: 2.
12*a* TG Reverence.
b Alma 16: 20.
c 3 Ne. 10: 19.
13*a* TG Jesus Christ, Lord.
14*a* John 20: 27.
b Luke 24: 39 (36–39).
c Isa. 45: 3; 3 Ne. 15: 5; D&C 36: 1; 127: 3.
d Ex. 9: 29; 1 Ne. 11: 6.
15*a* 3 Ne. 18: 25. TG Jesus Christ, Appearances, Postmortal.

did do, going forth one by one until they had all gone forth, and did see with their eyes and did feel with their hands, and did know of a surety and did bear record, that it was he, of whom it was written by the prophets, that should come.

16 And when they had all gone forth and had witnessed for themselves, they did cry out with one accord, saying:

17 Hosanna! Blessed be the name of the Most High God! And they did fall down at the feet of Jesus, and did [a]worship him.

18 And it came to pass that he spake unto [a]Nephi (for Nephi was among the multitude) and he commanded him that he should come forth.

19 And Nephi arose and went forth, and [a]bowed himself before the Lord and did [b]kiss his feet.

20 And the Lord commanded him that he should [a]arise. And he arose and stood before him.

21 And the Lord said unto him: I give unto you [a]power that ye shall [b]baptize this people when I am again ascended into heaven.

22 And again the Lord called [a]others, and said unto them likewise; and he gave unto them power to baptize. And he said unto them: On this wise shall ye baptize; and there shall be [b]no disputations among you.

23 Verily I say unto you, that whoso repenteth of his sins through your [a]words, and [b]desireth to be baptized in my name, on this wise shall ye baptize them—Behold, ye shall go down and [c]stand in the water, and in my name shall ye baptize them.

24 And now behold, these are the words which ye shall say, calling them by name, saying:

25 Having [a]authority given me of Jesus Christ, I baptize you in the name of the [b]Father, and of the Son, and of the Holy Ghost. Amen.

26 And then shall ye [a]immerse them in the water, and come forth again out of the water.

27 And after this manner shall ye [a]baptize in my name; for behold, verily I say unto you, that the Father, and the Son, and the Holy Ghost are [b]one; and I am in the Father, and the Father in me, and the Father and I are one.

28 And according as I have commanded you thus shall ye baptize. And there shall be no [a]disputations among you, as there have hitherto been; neither shall there be disputations among you concerning the points of my doctrine, as there have hitherto been.

29 For verily, verily I say unto you, he that hath the spirit of [a]contention is not of me, but is of the [b]devil, who is the father of contention, and he stirreth up the hearts of men to contend with anger, one with another.

30 Behold, this is not my doctrine, to stir up the hearts of men with anger, one against another; but this

17*a* TG Worship.
18*a* 3 Ne. 1: 2 (2–3, 10); 7: 15 (15, 20, 23).
19*a* Ex. 34: 8; Ether 6: 12.
b 3 Ne. 17: 10.
20*a* Josh. 7: 10; Ezek. 2: 1 (1–2).
21*a* TG Church Organization; Priesthood, Authority.
b TG Baptism, Essential.
22*a* 1 Ne. 12: 7; 3 Ne. 12: 1.
b 1 Cor. 11: 16 (16–19); 3 Ne. 18: 34. TG Disputations.
23*a* Mosiah 26: 15 (15–16); 3 Ne. 12: 2.
b TG Baptism, Qualifications for.
c 3 Ne. 19: 11 (10–13).
25*a* Mosiah 18: 13; Alma 5: 3; D&C 20: 73. TG Delegation of Responsibility; Priesthood, Authority.
b TG Godhead.
26*a* Moses 6: 52. TG Baptism, Immersion; Jesus Christ, Types of, in Memory.
27*a* TG Baptism.
b Alma 11: 44; 3 Ne. 28: 10; Morm. 7: 7; D&C 20: 28.
28*a* Acts 4: 32; 1 Cor. 1: 10 (10–13); Eph. 4: 13 (11–14); D&C 38: 27. TG Disputations.
29*a* 2 Tim. 2: 24 (23–24); Mosiah 23: 15. TG Contention.
b Eph. 4: 27 (26–27); Mosiah 2: 32 (32–33); Alma 2: 5; 45: 23; Hel. 4: 1.

[A.D. 34]

is my doctrine, that such things [a]should be done away.

31 Behold, verily, verily, I say unto you, I will declare unto you my [a]doctrine.

32 And this is my [a]doctrine, and it is the doctrine which the Father hath given unto me; and I bear [b]record of the Father, and the Father beareth record of me, and the [c]Holy Ghost beareth record of the Father and me; and I bear record that the Father commandeth all men, everywhere, to repent and believe in me.

33 And whoso believeth in me, and is [a]baptized, the same shall be [b]saved; and they are they who shall [c]inherit the kingdom of God.

34 And whoso believeth not in me, and is not [a]baptized, shall be damned.

35 Verily, verily, I say unto you, that this is my doctrine, and I bear record of it from the Father; and whoso [a]believeth in me believeth in the Father also; and unto him will the Father bear record of me, for he will visit him [b]with fire and with the [c]Holy Ghost.

36 And thus will the Father bear record of me, and the [a]Holy Ghost will bear record unto him of the Father and me; for the Father, and I, and the Holy Ghost are [b]one.

37 And again I say unto you, ye must repent, and [a]become as a [b]little child, and be baptized in my name, or ye can in nowise receive these things.

38 And again I say unto you, ye must repent, and be baptized in my name, and become as a little [a]child, or ye can in nowise inherit the kingdom of God.

39 Verily, verily, I say unto you, that this is my [a]doctrine, and whoso [b]buildeth upon this buildeth upon my rock, and the [c]gates of hell shall not prevail against them.

40 And whoso shall [a]declare more or less than this, and establish it for my doctrine, the same cometh of evil, and is not built upon my rock; but he buildeth upon a [b]sandy foundation, and the gates of hell stand open to receive such when the floods come and the winds beat upon them.

41 Therefore, go forth unto this people, and declare the words which I have spoken, unto the ends of the earth.

CHAPTER 12

Jesus calls and commissions the Twelve—He delivers to the Nephites a discourse similar to the Sermon on the Mount—He speaks the Beatitudes—His teachings transcend and take precedence over the law of Moses—Men are commanded to be perfect even as he and his Father are perfect—Compare Matthew 5.

[a]AND it came to pass that when Jesus had spoken these words unto Nephi, and to those who had been called, (now the number of them who had been called, and received power and authority to [b]baptize, was [c]twelve) and behold, he stretched forth his hand unto the multi-

30*a* Mark 9: 50; John 16: 33.
31*a* John 18: 37; 2 Ne. 31: 21 (2–21).
32*a* TG Jesus Christ, Teaching Mode of.
b 1 Jn. 5: 7 (6–9). TG Jesus Christ, Relationships with the Father.
c 3 Ne. 28: 11; Ether 5: 4; Moses 1: 24.
33*a* Mark 16: 16. TG Baptism, Essential.
b TG Salvation, Plan of.
c TG Exaltation.
34*a* TG Baptism.
35*a* Ether 4: 12.
b 3 Ne. 9. 20; 12: 2.
c TG Holy Ghost, Baptism of.
36*a* TG Holy Ghost, Source of Testimony.
b TG Godhead; Unity.
37*a* Mark 10: 15; Luke 18: 17.
b 3 Ne. 9: 22.
38*a* TG Baptism, Qualifications for.
39*a* Mark 4: 2.
b Matt. 7: 24 (24–29); 1 Pet. 2: 6 (4–8); 1 Ne. 13: 36. TG Rock.
c Matt. 16: 18; 3 Ne. 18: 13 (12–13); D&C 17: 8.
40*a* Rom. 16: 17 (17–19); 1 Tim. 1: 3.
b 3 Ne. 14: 26 (24–27).
12 1*a* Matt. 5: 1 (1–48).
b Mark 16: 16 (15–16); John 4: 2 (1–2).
c 3 Ne. 11: 22; 13: 25.

[A.D. 34]

tude, and cried unto them, saying: [d]Blessed are ye if ye shall give heed unto the words of these twelve whom I have [e]chosen from among you to minister unto you, and to be your servants; and unto them I have given power that they may baptize you with water; and after that ye are baptized with water, behold, I will baptize you with fire and with the Holy Ghost; therefore blessed are ye if ye shall believe in me and be baptized, after that ye have seen me and know that I am.

2 And again, more blessed are they who shall [a]believe in your words because that ye shall testify that ye have seen me, and that ye know that I am. Yea, blessed are they who shall [b]believe in your [c]words, and [d]come down into the depths of humility and be baptized, for they shall be visited [e]with fire and with the Holy Ghost, and shall receive a remission of their sins.

3 Yea, blessed are the [a]poor in spirit who [b]come unto me, for theirs is the kingdom of heaven.

4 And again, blessed are all they that [a]mourn, for they shall be [b]comforted.

5 And blessed are the [a]meek, for they shall inherit the [b]earth.

6 And blessed are all they who do [a]hunger and [b]thirst after [c]righteousness, for they shall be [d]filled with the Holy Ghost.

7 And blessed are the [a]merciful, for they shall obtain mercy.

8 And blessed are all the [a]pure in heart, for they shall [b]see God.

9 And blessed are all the [a]peacemakers, for they shall be called the [b]children of God.

10 And blessed are all they who are [a]persecuted for my name's sake, for theirs is the kingdom of heaven.

11 And blessed are ye when men shall [a]revile you and persecute, and shall say all manner of evil against you falsely, for my sake;

12 For [a]ye shall have great joy and be exceedingly glad, for great shall be your [b]reward in heaven; for so [c]persecuted they the prophets who were before you.

13 Verily, verily, I say unto you, I give unto you to be the [a]salt of the earth; but if the salt shall lose its savor wherewith shall the earth be salted? The salt shall be thenceforth good for nothing, but to be cast out and to be trodden under foot of men.

14 Verily, verily, I say unto you, I give unto you to be the light of this people. A city that is set on a hill cannot be hid.

15 Behold, do men light a [a]candle and put it under a bushel? Nay, but on a candlestick, and it giveth light to all that are in the house;

16 Therefore let your [a]light so shine before this people, that they may see your good works and [b]glorify your Father who is in heaven.

17 Think not that I am come to destroy the law or the prophets.

1*d* TG Blessing.
e TG Called of God.
2*a* TG Teachable.
b Mosiah 26: 15 (15–16); D&C 46: 14.
c 3 Ne. 11: 23.
d Ether 4: 13.
e 3 Ne. 11: 35; 19: 13 (13–14).
3*a* Ps. 86: 1; Eccl. 4: 13 (13–14); Matt. 5: 3; D&C 56: 18 (17–18). TG Poor in Spirit.
b Matt. 11: 28 (28–30).
4*a* Morm. 2: 11 (11–14). TG Mourning.
b Matt. 5: 4; Alma 28: 6. TG Comfort.
5*a* Zeph. 2: 3 (1–3); Rom. 12: 16. TG Meekness.
b TG Earth, Destiny of.
6*a* Matt. 5: 6; 2 Ne. 9: 51; Enos 1: 4.
b Jer. 29: 13.
c Prov. 21: 21.
d TG Spirituality.
7*a* TG Mercy.
8*a* TG Purity.
b TG God, Privilege of Seeing.
9*a* TG Peacemakers.
b TG Sons and Daughters of God.
10*a* Matt. 5: 10; D&C 122: 5 (5–9).
11*a* TG Reviling.
12*a* Matt. 5: 12.
b TG Reward.
c 2 Cor. 7: 4. TG Prophets, Rejection of.
13*a* 2 Chr. 13: 5; Matt. 5: 13; D&C 101: 39 (39–40). TG Mission of Early Saints; Salt.
15*a* Luke 8: 16.
16*a* 3 Ne. 18: 24. TG Example.
b John 11: 4 (1–4); Ether 12: 4.

I am not come to destroy but to fulfil;

18 For verily I say unto you, one jot nor one tittle [a]hath not passed away from the [b]law, but in me it hath all been fulfilled.

19 And behold, I have given you the law and the commandments of my Father, that ye shall believe in me, and that ye shall repent of your sins, and come unto me with a [a]broken heart and a contrite spirit. Behold, ye have the commandments before you, and the [b]law is fulfilled.

20 Therefore [a]come unto me and be ye saved; for verily I say unto you, that except ye shall keep my [b]commandments, which I have commanded you at this time, ye shall in no case enter into the kingdom of heaven.

21 Ye have heard that it hath been said by them of old time, and it is also written before you, that thou shalt not [a]kill, and whosoever shall kill shall be in danger of the judgment of God;

22 But I say unto you, that whosoever is [a]angry with his brother shall be in danger of his judgment. And whosoever shall say to his brother, Raca, shall be in danger of the council; and whosoever shall say, Thou fool, shall be in danger of hell fire.

23 Therefore, [a]if ye shall come unto me, or shall desire to come unto me, and rememberest that thy brother hath aught against thee—

24 Go thy way unto thy brother, and first be [a]reconciled to thy brother, and then come unto me with full [b]purpose of heart, and I will receive you.

25 [a]Agree with thine adversary quickly while thou art in the way with him, lest at any time he shall get thee, and thou shalt be cast into prison.

26 Verily, verily, I say unto thee, thou shalt by no means come out thence until thou hast paid the uttermost senine. And while ye are in prison can ye pay even one [a]senine? Verily, verily, I say unto you, Nay.

27 Behold, it is written by them of old time, that thou shalt not commit [a]adultery;

28 But I say unto you, that whosoever looketh on a woman, to [a]lust after her, hath committed adultery already in his heart.

29 Behold, I give unto you a commandment, that ye suffer [a]none of these things to enter into your [b]heart;

30 For it is better that ye should deny yourselves of these things, wherein ye will take up your [a]cross, than that ye should be cast into hell.

31 It hath been written, that whosoever shall put away his wife, let him give her a writing of [a]divorcement.

32 Verily, verily, I say unto you, that whosoever shall [a]put away his wife, saving for the cause of [b]fornication, causeth her to commit [c]adultery; and whoso shall marry her who is divorced committeth adultery.

33 And again it is written, thou shalt not [a]forswear thyself, but

---

18*a* Matt. 5: 18.
b TG Law of Moses.
19*a* 3 Ne. 9: 20.
TG Contrite Heart.
b 3 Ne. 9: 17.
20*a* Isa. 55: 3.
b 3 Ne. 15: 10.
21*a* Ex. 20: 13 (13–17); Deut. 5: 17 (17–21); Matt. 5: 21; Mosiah 13: 21 (21–24); D&C 42: 18.
TG Life, Sanctity of.
22*a* Matt. 5: 22.
23*a* Matt. 5: 23.
24*a* TG Forgiveness; Reconciliation.
b 3 Ne. 18: 29 (28–33); D&C 46: 4.
25*a* Matt. 5: 25 (25–26).
26*a* Alma 11: 3; 30: 33.
27*a* Matt. 5: 27; 2 Ne. 9: 36; D&C 59: 6.
28*a* TG Lust.
29*a* D&C 42: 23.
b Acts 8: 22.
30*a* Matt. 10: 38; 16: 24; Luke 9: 23; 14: 27; D&C 23: 6.
31*a* TG Divorce.
32*a* Matt. 5: 32; Mark 10: 11 (11–12); Luke 16: 18.
b TG Fornication.
c TG Adultery.
33*a* TG Swearing.

[A.D. 34]

shalt [b]perform unto the Lord thine [c]oaths;
34 But verily, verily, I say unto
you, [a]swear not at all; neither by
heaven, for it is God's throne;
35 Nor by the earth, for it is his
footstool;
36 Neither shalt thou swear by thy
head, because thou canst not make
one hair black or white;
37 But let your [a]communication
be [b]Yea, yea; Nay, nay; for whatsoever
cometh of more than these
is evil.
38 And behold, it is written, an
[a]eye for an eye, and a tooth for a
tooth;
39 But I say unto you, that ye
shall not [a]resist evil, but whosoever
shall smite thee on thy right [b]cheek,
[c]turn to him the other also;
40 And if any man will sue thee at
the law and take away thy coat,
[a]let him have thy cloak also;
41 And whosoever shall compel thee
to [a]go a mile, go with him twain.
42 [a]Give to him that asketh thee,
and from him that would [b]borrow
of thee turn thou not away.
43 And behold it is written also,
that thou shalt love thy neighbor
and hate thine enemy;
44 But behold I say unto you, love
your [a]enemies, bless them that
curse you, do [b]good to them that
hate you, and [c]pray for them who
despitefully use you and persecute
you;
45 That ye may be the children of
your Father who is in heaven; for
he maketh his sun to rise [a]on the
evil and on the good.
46 Therefore those things which
were of old time, which were under
the law, in me are all [a]fulfilled.
47 [a]Old things are done away, and
all things have become [b]new.
48 Therefore I would that ye
should be [a]perfect even as I, or your
Father who is in heaven is perfect.

CHAPTER 13

Jesus teaches the Nephites the Lord's Prayer—They are to lay up treasures in heaven—The Twelve in their ministry are commanded to take no thought for temporal things—Compare Matthew 6.

[a]VERILY, verily, I say that I would
that ye should do alms unto the
poor; but take heed that ye do not
your alms before men to be seen of
them; otherwise ye have no reward
of your Father who is in heaven.
2 Therefore, when ye shall do your
alms do not sound a trumpet before
you, as will hypocrites do in the
synagogues and in the streets, that
they may have [a]glory of men.
Verily I say unto you, they have
their reward.
3 But when thou doest alms let not
thy left hand know what thy right
hand doeth;
4 That thine alms may be in secret;
and thy Father who seeth in secret,
himself shall reward thee openly.
5 And when thou [a]prayest thou
shalt not do as the [b]hypocrites, for

33*b* TG Dependability.
c TG Oath.
34*a* Lev. 5: 4; Morm. 3: 14. TG Profanity.
37*a* TG Communication.
b TG Honesty.
38*a* Lev. 24: 20; Matt. 5: 38 (38–42). TG Punishment.
39*a* 3 Ne. 6: 13; 4 Ne. 1: 34; D&C 98: 23 (23–27). TG Submissiveness.
b Lam. 3: 30.
c TG Forbearance; Patience.
40*a* TG Charity; Initiative.
41*a* TG Generosity.
42*a* Jacob 2: 19 (17–19); Mosiah 4: 26.
b TG Borrowing.
44*a* Prov. 24: 17; 25: 21 (21–22); Alma 48: 23. TG Enemies.
b TG Benevolence.
c Acts 7: 60 (59–60); 2 Tim. 4: 16.
45*a* Matt. 5: 45.
46*a* Heb. 8: 13.
47*a* 3 Ne. 9: 17; 15: 2 (2, 7); D&C 22: 1.
b Jer. 31: 31 (31–33); Ether 13: 9.
48*a* Matt. 5: 48; 3 Ne. 19: 29 (28–29); 27: 27. TG God, Perfection of; God, the Standard of Righteousness; Jesus Christ, Exemplar; Man, New, Spiritually Reborn; Man, Potential to Become like Heavenly Father.
13 1*a* Matt. 6: 1 (1–34). TG Almsgiving.
2*a* D&C 121: 35 (34–35).
5*a* TG Prayer.
b TG Hypocrisy.

[A.D. 34]

they love to pray, standing in the
synagogues and in the corners of
the streets, that they may be seen
of men. Verily I say unto you, they
have their reward.
6 But thou, when thou prayest,
enter into thy closet, and when thou
hast [a]shut thy door, pray to thy
Father who is in secret; and thy
Father, who [b]seeth in secret, shall
reward thee openly.
7 But when ye pray, use not [a]vain
repetitions, as the [b]heathen, for they
think that they shall be heard for
their much speaking.
8 Be not ye therefore like unto
them, for your Father [a]knoweth
what things ye have need of before
ye [b]ask him.
9 After this [a]manner therefore
[b]pray ye: Our [c]Father who art in
heaven, hallowed be thy name.
10 Thy will be done on earth as it
is in heaven.
11 And forgive us our debts, as we
forgive our debtors.
12 And [a]lead us not into temptation, but deliver us from evil.
13 For thine is the kingdom, and the
power, and the glory, forever. Amen.
14 For, if ye [a]forgive men their
trespasses your heavenly Father
will also forgive you;
15 But if ye forgive not men their
trespasses neither will your Father
forgive your trespasses.
16 Moreover, when ye [a]fast be not
as the [b]hypocrites, of a sad countenance, for they disfigure their faces
that they may appear unto men to
fast. Verily I say unto you, they
have their reward.
17 But thou, when thou fastest,
anoint thy head, and [a]wash thy face;
18 That thou appear not unto
men to fast, but unto thy Father,
who is in [a]secret; and thy Father,
who seeth in secret, shall reward thee
openly.
19 Lay not up for yourselves
treasures upon earth, where [a]moth
and rust doth corrupt, and thieves
break through and steal;
20 But lay up for yourselves
[a]treasures in heaven, where neither
moth nor rust doth corrupt, and
where thieves do not break through
nor steal.
21 For where your treasure is,
there will your heart be also.
22 The [a]light of the body is the
[b]eye; if, therefore, thine eye be
[c]single, thy whole body shall be full
of light.
23 But if thine eye be evil, thy
whole body shall be full of darkness.
If, therefore, the light that is in thee
be darkness, how great is that
darkness!
24 No man can [a]serve [b]two
masters; for either he will hate the
one and love the other, or else he
will hold to the one and despise the
other. Ye cannot serve God and
Mammon.
25 And now it came to pass that
when Jesus had spoken these words
he looked upon the [a]twelve whom
he had chosen, and said unto them:
Remember the words which I have
spoken. For behold, ye are they
whom I have chosen to [b]minister
unto this people. Therefore I say
unto you, [c]take no thought for your

6*a* 2 Kgs. 4: 33.
b TG God, Omniscience of.
7*a* TG Sincerity.
b TG Heathen.
8*a* D&C 84: 83.
b Ezek. 36: 37.
9*a* Matt. 6: 9 (9–13).
b TG Prayer.
c TG God the Father—Elohim.
12*a* See JST Matt. 6: 14 in footnote for Matt. 6: 13.
14*a* Mosiah 26: 31.
TG Forgiveness.
16*a* Isa. 58: 5 (5–7); Zech. 7: 5 (5–6).
TG Fasting.
b TG Hypocrisy.
17*a* TG Washing.
18*a* Isa. 45: 15; D&C 38: 7.
19*a* 3 Ne. 27: 32.
20*a* Hel. 5: 8; 8: 25.
TG Treasure.
22*a* Ezra 9: 8.
b Matt. 6: 22 (20–25).
c D&C 88: 67.
TG Dedication.
24*a* 1 Sam. 7: 3; Alma 5: 41 (39–42); Moses 1: 15.
b Hosea 10: 2.
25*a* Matt. 6: 25; 3 Ne. 12: 1; 15: 11.
b TG Church Organization; Delegation of Responsibility.
c Alma 31: 37; D&C 84: 81 (79–85).

[A.D. 34]

life, what ye shall eat, or what ye
shall drink; nor yet for your body,
what ye shall put on. Is not the life
more than meat, and the body than
[d]raiment?
26 Behold the [a]fowls of the air, for
they sow not, neither do they reap
nor gather into barns; yet your
heavenly Father feedeth them. Are
ye not much better than they?
27 Which of you by taking thought
can add one cubit unto his stature?
28 And why take ye thought for
raiment? Consider the [a]lilies of the
field how they grow; they toil not,
neither do they spin;
29 And yet I say unto you, that
even Solomon, in all his glory, was
not arrayed like one of these.
30 Wherefore, if God so clothe the
grass of the field, which today is,
and tomorrow is cast into the oven,
even so will he clothe you, if ye are
not of little faith.
31 Therefore take no thought, saying, What shall we eat? or, What
shall we drink? or, Wherewithal
shall we be clothed?
32 For your heavenly Father
knoweth that ye have need of all
these things.
33 But [a]seek ye first the [b]kingdom
of God and his righteousness, and
all these things shall be added unto
you.
34 Take therefore no thought for
the morrow, for the morrow shall
take thought for the things of itself.
[a]Sufficient is the day unto the evil
thereof.

CHAPTER 14

Jesus commands: Judge not; ask of God; beware of false prophets—He promises salvation to those who do the will of the Father—Compare Matthew 7.

[a]AND now it came to pass that when
Jesus had spoken these words he
turned again to the multitude,
and did open his mouth unto them
again, saying: Verily, verily, I say
unto you, Judge not, that ye be not
judged.
2 [a]For with what judgment ye
judge, ye shall be judged; and with
what measure ye mete, it shall be
measured to you again.
3 And why beholdest thou the
mote that is in thy brother's eye,
but considerest not the beam that
is in thine own eye?
4 Or how wilt thou say to thy
brother: Let me pull the mote out
of thine eye—and behold, a beam is
in thine own eye?
5 Thou [a]hypocrite, first cast the
[b]beam out of thine own eye; and
then shalt thou see clearly to cast
the mote out of thy brother's eye.
6 Give not that which is [a]holy unto
the dogs, neither cast ye your pearls
before swine, lest they trample
them under their feet, and turn
again and rend you.
7 [a]Ask, and it shall be given unto
you; [b]seek, and ye shall find; knock,
and it shall be opened unto you.
8 For every one that asketh, receiveth; and he that seeketh, findeth; and to him that knocketh, it
shall be opened.
9 Or what man is there of you, who,
if his son ask bread, will give him a
stone?
10 Or if he ask a fish, will he give
him a serpent?
11 If ye then, being evil, know how
to give good gifts unto your children,
how much more shall your Father
who is in heaven give good things to
them that ask him?
12 Therefore, all things whatsoever ye would that men should do
to you, [a]do ye even so to them, for
this is the law and the prophets.

25*d* Job 27:16 (16–17).
26*a* D&C 117:6.
28*a* TG Nature.
33*a* TG Commitment.
b Luke 12:31 (22–34). TG Objectives.
34*a* Matt. 6:34.

14 1*a* Matt. 7:1 (1–27). See also footnote to Matt. 7:1.
2*a* Morm. 8:19.
5*a* TG Hypocrisy.
b John 8:7 (3–11).
6*a* TG Holiness.
7*a* 3 Ne. 27:29. TG Prayer.
b TG Initiative; Objectives.
12*a* TG Benevolence; Compassion; Courtesy.

[A.D. 34]

13 Enter ye in at the [a]strait gate; for wide is the gate, and [b]broad is the way, which leadeth to destruction, and many there be who go in thereat;

14 Because strait is the [a]gate, and [b]narrow is the way, which leadeth unto life, and [c]few there be that find it.

15 Beware of [a]false prophets, who come to you in sheep's clothing, but inwardly they are ravening wolves.

16 Ye shall know them by their [a]fruits. Do men gather grapes of thorns, or figs of thistles?

17 Even so every [a]good tree bringeth forth good fruit; but a corrupt tree bringeth forth evil fruit.

18 A good tree cannot bring forth evil fruit, neither a corrupt tree bring forth good fruit.

19 Every tree that [a]bringeth not forth good fruit is hewn down, and cast into the fire.

20 Wherefore, by their [a]fruits ye shall know them.

21 Not every one that saith unto me, Lord, Lord, shall [a]enter into the kingdom of heaven; but he that doeth the will of my Father who is in heaven.

22 Many will [a]say to me in that day: Lord, Lord, have we not prophesied in thy name, and in thy name have cast out devils, and in thy name done many wonderful works?

23 And then will [a]I profess unto them: I never [b]knew you; [c]depart from me, ye that work iniquity.

24 Therefore, whoso heareth these sayings of mine and doeth them, I will liken him unto a wise man, who built his house upon a [a]rock—

25 And the [a]rain descended, and the floods came, and the winds blew, and beat upon that house; and it [b]fell not, for it was founded upon a rock.

26 And every one that heareth these sayings of mine and doeth them not shall be likened unto a [a]foolish man, who built his house upon the [b]sand—

27 And the rain descended, and the floods came, and the winds blew, and beat upon that house; and it fell, and great was the fall of it.

CHAPTER 15

Jesus announces that the law of Moses is fulfilled in him—The Nephites are the other sheep of whom he spake in Jerusalem—Because of iniquity the Lord's people in Jerusalem do not know of the scattered sheep of Israel.

AND now it came to pass that when Jesus had ended these sayings he cast his eyes round about on the multitude, and said unto them: Behold, ye have heard the things which I [a]taught before I ascended to my Father; therefore, whoso remembereth these sayings of mine and [b]doeth them, him will I [c]raise up at the last day.

2 And it came to pass that when Jesus had said these words he perceived that there were some among them who marveled, and wondered what he would concerning the law

---

13*a* Luke 13: 24; 3 Ne. 27: 33.
b D&C 132: 25.
14*a* 2 Ne. 9: 41; 31: 9 (9, 17–18); D&C 22: 4.
b 1 Ne. 8: 20.
c Matt. 7: 14; 1 Ne. 14: 12.
15*a* Jer. 23: 21 (21–32); 2 Ne. 28: 12 (9, 12, 15). TG False Prophets.
16*a* Col. 1: 6; Alma 32: 42 (28–42); D&C 52: 34 (18, 34).
17*a* Alma 5: 41.
19*a* Matt. 3: 10; Alma 5: 36 (36–41); D&C 97: 7.
20*a* Matt. 7: 17 (16–20); 12: 33; Luke 6: 43 (43–45); Moro. 7: 5.
21*a* 1 Jn. 2: 17.
22*a* Alma 5: 17.
23*a* Matt. 7: 23.
b Mosiah 5: 13; 26: 25 (24–27); D&C 112: 26.
c Ps. 119: 115; Luke 13: 27.
24*a* TG Rock.
25*a* Alma 26: 6; Hel. 5: 12.
b Prov. 12: 7.
26*a* TG Foolishness.
b 3 Ne. 11: 40.
15 1*a* IE in Galilee and Judea.
b James 1: 22 (22–24).
c John 6: 39; 1 Ne. 13: 37; Mosiah 23: 22; Alma 26: 7; D&C 5: 35.

[A.D. 34]

of Moses; for they understood not the saying that [a]old things had passed away, and that all things had become new.

3 And he said unto them: Marvel not that I said unto you that old things had passed away, and that all things had become [a]new.

4 Behold, I say unto you that the [a]law is fulfilled that was given unto Moses.

5 Behold, [a]I am he that gave the law, and I am he who covenanted with my people Israel; therefore, the law in me is fulfilled, for I have come to [b]fulfil the law; therefore it hath an end.

6 Behold, I do [a]not destroy the prophets, for as many as have not been fulfilled in me, verily I say unto you, shall all be fulfilled.

7 And because I said unto you that old things have passed away, I do not destroy that which hath been spoken concerning things which are to come.

8 For behold, the [a]covenant which I have made with my people is not all fulfilled; but the law which was given unto Moses hath an end in me.

9 Behold, I am the [a]law, and the [b]light. Look unto me, and endure to the end, and ye shall [c]live; for unto him that [d]endureth to the end will I give eternal life.

10 Behold, I have given unto you the [a]commandments; therefore keep my commandments. And this is the law and the prophets, for they truly [b]testified of me.

11 And now it came to pass that when Jesus had spoken these words, he [a]said unto those twelve whom he had chosen:

12 Ye are my [a]disciples; and ye are a [b]light unto this people, who are a remnant of the house of [c]Joseph.

13 And behold, this is the [a]land of your inheritance; and the Father hath given it unto you.

14 And not at any time hath the Father given me commandment that I should [a]tell it unto your brethren at Jerusalem.

15 Neither at any time hath the Father given me commandment that I should tell unto them concerning the [a]other tribes of the house of Israel, whom the Father hath led away out of the land.

16 This much did the Father [a]command me, that I should tell unto them:

17 That other sheep I have which are not of this fold; them also I must bring, and they shall hear my voice; and there shall be one fold, and one [a]shepherd.

18 And now, because of [a]stiffneckedness and [b]unbelief they [c]understood not my word; therefore I was commanded to say no more of the [d]Father concerning this thing unto them.

19 But, verily, I say unto you that the Father hath commanded me, and I tell it unto you, that ye were [a]separated from among them because of their iniquity; therefore it

---

2*a* 3 Ne. 12: 47 (46–47).
3*a* Heb. 8: 13; Ether 13: 9.
4*a* Mosiah 13: 27 (27–31); 3 Ne. 9: 17 (17–20).
5*a* 1 Cor. 10: 4 (1–4); 3 Ne. 11: 14. TG Jesus Christ—Jehovah.
b Alma 34: 13. TG Jesus Christ, Mission of.
6*a* 3 Ne. 20: 11 (11–12); 23: 3 (1–3).
8*a* 3 Ne. 5: 25 (24–26); 16: 5. TG Covenants; Restoration of the Gospel.
9*a* 2 Ne. 26: 1.
b TG Jesus Christ, Light of the World.
c Lev. 18: 5; John 11: 25; D&C 84: 44.
d Matt. 10: 22 (22–33); Mark 13: 13; 2 Ne. 31: 20; Alma 32: 13 (13–15); 3 Ne. 27: 6 (6–17).
10*a* 3 Ne. 12: 20.
b Mosiah 13: 33.
11*a* 3 Ne. 13: 25; Moro. 2: 1.
12*a* TG Church Organization.
b TG Example; Leadership.
c TG Israel, Joseph, People of.
13*a* 1 Ne. 18: 23; 3 Ne. 16: 16.
14*a* 3 Ne. 5: 20.
15*a* 2 Ne. 21: 12; 3 Ne. 16: 1 (1–4). TG Israel, Ten Lost Tribes of.
16*a* John 15: 15; 16: 12.
17*a* TG Shepherd.
18*a* TG Stiffneckedness.
b TG Doubt; Unbelief, Unbelievers.
c D&C 10: 59.
d John 12: 50.
19*a* 1 Kgs. 8: 53; John 17: 6 (6–22).

[A.D. 34]

is because of their iniquity that they know not of you.

20 And verily, I say unto you again that the other tribes hath the Father separated from them; and it is because of their iniquity that they know not of them.

21 And verily I say unto you, that ye are they of whom I said: [a]Other sheep I have which are not of this fold; them also I must bring, and they shall hear my voice; and there shall be one fold, and one [b]shepherd.

22 And they understood me not, for they supposed it had been the [a]Gentiles; for they understood not that the Gentiles should be [b]converted through their preaching.

23 And they understood me not that I said they shall hear my voice; and they understood me not that the [a]Gentiles should not at any time hear my voice—that I should not manifest myself unto them save it were by the [b]Holy Ghost.

24 But behold, ye have both heard [a]my voice, and seen me; and ye are my sheep, and ye are numbered among those whom the Father hath [b]given me.

CHAPTER 16

Jesus will visit others of the lost sheep of Israel—In the latter days the gospel will go to the Gentiles and then to the house of Israel—The Lord's people shall see eye to eye when he brings again Zion.

AND verily, verily, I say unto you that I have [a]other sheep, which are not of this land, neither of the land of Jerusalem, neither in any parts of that land round about whither I have been to minister.

2 For they of whom I speak are they who have not as yet heard my voice; neither have I at any time manifested myself unto them.

3 But I have received a [a]commandment of the Father that I shall go unto them, and that they shall [b]hear my voice, and shall be numbered among my sheep, that there may be one fold and one shepherd; therefore I go to show myself unto them.

4 And I command you that ye shall [a]write these sayings after I am gone, that if it so be that my people at Jerusalem, they who have seen me and been with me in my ministry, do not ask the Father in my name, that they may receive a knowledge of you by the Holy Ghost, and also of the other tribes whom they know not of, that these sayings which ye shall write shall be kept and shall be manifested unto the [b]Gentiles, that through the fulness of the Gentiles, the remnant of their seed, who shall be scattered forth upon the face of the earth because of their [c]unbelief, may be brought in, or may be brought to a [d]knowledge of me, their Redeemer.

5 And then will I [a]gather them in from the four quarters of the earth; and then will I fulfil the [b]covenant which the Father hath made unto all the people of the [c]house of Israel.

6 And blessed are the [a]Gentiles, because of their belief in me, in and of the Holy Ghost, which [b]wit-

21*a* John 10: 16 (14–16).
b TG Jesus Christ, Good Shepherd.
22*a* TG Gentiles.
b Acts 10: 45 (34–48).
23*a* Matt. 15: 24.
b 1 Ne. 10: 11. TG Holy Ghost, Mission of.
24*a* Alma 5: 38; 3 Ne. 16: 3 (1–5); 18: 31.
b John 6: 37; D&C 27: 14.
16 1*a* 1 Ne. 19: 10; 2 Ne. 21: 12; 3 Ne. 15: 15. TG Israel, Ten Lost Tribes of.
3*a* 3 Ne. 18: 27.
b 3 Ne. 17: 4.
4*a* 2 Ne. 25: 18. TG Scriptures to Come Forth.
b 1 Ne. 10: 14; 3 Ne. 21: 6 (1–11).
c TG Unbelief, Unbelievers.
d Ezek. 20: 42 (42–44); Micah 7: 9 (8–9); 3 Ne. 20: 13. TG Israel, Restoration of.
5*a* TG Israel, Gathering of.
b 3 Ne. 5: 25 (24–26); 15: 8.
c 1 Ne. 22: 9; 3 Ne. 21: 27 (26–29).
6*a* 1 Ne. 13: 39 (23, 30–42); 2 Ne. 30: 3; 3 Ne. 20: 27.
b 2 Ne. 32: 5; 3 Ne. 11: 32 (32, 35–36). TG Holy Ghost, Source of Testimony.

nesses unto them of me and of the
Father.
7 Behold, because of their belief
in me, saith the Father, and because
of the unbelief of you, O house of
Israel, in the [a]latter day shall the
truth come unto the [b]Gentiles, that
the fulness of these things shall be
made known unto them.
8 But wo, saith the Father, unto
the [a]unbelieving of the Gentiles—
for notwithstanding they have come
forth upon the face of this land, and
have [b]scattered my people who are
of the house of Israel; and my people
who are of the house of Israel have
been [c]cast out from among them,
and have been trodden under feet
by them;
9 And because of the mercies of the
Father unto the Gentiles, and also
the judgments of the Father upon
my people who are of the house of
Israel, verily, verily, I say unto you,
that after all this, and I have caused
my people who are of the house of
Israel to be smitten, and to be
afflicted, and to be [a]slain, and to be
cast out from among them, and to
become [b]hated by them, and to
become a hiss and a byword among
them—
10 And thus commandeth the
Father that I should say unto you:
At that day when the Gentiles shall
[a]sin against my gospel, and shall
reject the fulness of my gospel, and
shall be [b]lifted up in the pride of
their hearts above all nations, and
above all the people of the whole
earth, and shall be filled with all
manner of lyings, and of deceits,
and of mischiefs, and all manner
of hypocrisy, and [c]murders, and
[d]priestcrafts, and whoredoms, and
of secret abominations; and if they
shall do all those things, and shall
[e]reject the fulness of my gospel,
behold, saith the Father, I will bring
the fulness of my gospel from among
them.
11 And then will I [a]remember my
covenant which I have made unto
my people, O house of Israel, and I
will bring my gospel unto them.
12 And I will show unto thee, O
house of Israel, that the Gentiles
shall not have power over you; but
I will remember my covenant unto
you, O house of Israel, and ye shall
come unto the [a]knowledge of the
fulness of my gospel.
13 But if the Gentiles will repent
and return unto me, saith the
Father, behold they shall be [a]numbered among my people, O house of
Israel.
14 And I will not suffer my people,
who are of the house of Israel, to go
through among them, and tread
them down, saith the Father.
15 But if they will not turn unto
me, and hearken unto my voice, I
will suffer them, yea, I will suffer
my people, O house of Israel, that
they shall go through among them,
and shall [a]tread them down, and
they shall be as salt that hath lost
its savor, which is thenceforth good
for nothing but to be cast out, and
to be trodden under foot of my
people, O house of Israel.
16 Verily, verily, I say unto you,
thus hath the Father commanded

7*a* TG Restoration of the Gospel.
b D&C 19: 27; 107: 33. TG Mission of Latter-day Saints.
8*a* 2 Ne. 6: 15; 28: 15 (15–32); Ether 2: 9 (8–11).
b 1 Ne. 13: 14; 2 Ne. 26: 19; Morm. 5: 9 (9, 15).
c 3 Ne. 20: 28.
9*a* Amos 9: 1 (1–4).
b Jer. 23: 40; Lam. 2: 16 (15–16); Joel 2: 17; 1 Ne. 19: 14.
10*a* 3 Ne. 20: 15.
b Morm. 8: 36 (35–41).
c 3 Ne. 30: 2; Morm. 8: 31.
d 2 Ne. 26: 29. TG Priestcraft.
e 3 Ne. 20: 28 (27–28); D&C 6: 31.
11*a* Isa. 44: 21; 3 Ne. 20: 29 (28–31); 21: 4 (1–11); Morm. 5: 20.
12*a* Hel. 15: 13. TG Israel, Restoration of; Knowledge.
13*a* Gal. 3: 7 (7, 29); 1 Ne. 15: 13 (13–17); 22: 9 (5–10); 2 Ne. 10: 18 (18–19); 3 Ne. 30: 2; Abr. 2: 10 (9–11).
15*a* Micah 5: 8 (8–15); 3 Ne. 20: 16; 21: 12 (12–21); D&C 87: 5.

[A.D. 34]

me—that I should give unto [a]this
people this land for their inheritance.
17 And then the [a]words of the
prophet Isaiah shall be fulfilled,
which say:
18 [a]Thy [b]watchmen shall lift up the
voice; with the voice together shall
they sing, for they shall see eye to
eye when the Lord shall bring again
Zion.
19 Break forth into joy, sing together,
ye waste places of Jerusalem;
for the Lord hath comforted
his people, he hath redeemed
Jerusalem.
20 The Lord hath made bare his
holy arm in the eyes of all the
nations; and all the ends of the
earth shall see the salvation of God.

CHAPTER 17

Jesus directs the people to ponder his words and pray for understanding—He heals their sick—He prays for the people, using language that cannot be written—Angels minister to and fire encircles their little ones.

BEHOLD, now it came to pass that
when Jesus had spoken these words
he looked round about again on the
multitude, and he said unto them:
Behold, my [a]time is at hand.
2 I [a]perceive that ye are weak,
that ye cannot [b]understand all my
words which I am commanded of
the Father to speak unto you at
this time.
3 Therefore, go ye unto your
homes, and [a]ponder upon the things
which I have said, and ask of the
Father, in my name, that ye may
understand, and [b]prepare your
minds for the [c]morrow, and I come
unto you again.
4 But now I [a]go unto the Father,
and also to [b]show myself unto the
lost tribes of Israel, for they are not
[c]lost unto the Father, for he knoweth
whither he hath taken them.
5 And it came to pass that when
Jesus had thus spoken, he cast
his eyes round about again on the
multitude, and beheld they were [a]in
tears, and did look steadfastly upon
him as if they would ask him to tarry
a little longer with them.
6 And he said unto them: Behold,
my bowels are filled with [a]compassion
towards you.
7 Have ye any that are [a]sick among
you? Bring them hither. Have ye
any that are lame, or blind, or halt,
or maimed, or [b]leprous, or that are
withered, or that are deaf, or that
are afflicted in any manner? Bring
them hither and I will [c]heal them,
for I have compassion upon you; my
bowels are filled with mercy.
8 For I perceive that ye desire that
I should show unto you what I have
done unto your brethren at Jerusalem,
for I see that your [a]faith is
[b]sufficient that I should heal you.
9 And it came to pass that when he
had thus spoken, all the multitude,
with one accord, did go forth with
their sick and their afflicted, and
their lame, and with their [a]blind, and
with their dumb, and with all them
that were afflicted in any manner;
and he did heal them every one
as they were brought forth unto
him.

16*a* 3 Ne. 15: 13.
17*a* 3 Ne. 20: 11.
18*a* Isa. 52: 8 (8–10); 3 Ne. 20: 32.
b Ezek. 33: 2 (2, 7); D&C 101: 45 (45, 53–54). TG Watchmen.
17 1*a* IE to return to the Father. See v. 4.
2*a* TG Jesus Christ, Teaching Mode of.
b John 16: 12; D&C 50: 40; 78: 18 (17–18).
3*a* TG Meditation.
b Ezra 7: 10; D&C 29: 8; 132: 3.
c 3 Ne. 19: 2.
4*a* 3 Ne. 18: 39.
b 3 Ne. 16: 3. TG Jesus Christ, Appearances, Postmortal.
c TG Israel, Ten Lost Tribes of.
5*a* TG God, Love of.
6*a* TG Compassion.
7*a* TG Sickness.
b TG Leprosy.
c TG Administrations to the Sick; Healing.
8*a* Matt. 8: 10 (1–17); Luke 18: 42.
b 2 Ne. 27: 23; Ether 12: 12.
9*a* Matt. 9: 28 (28–31); Mosiah 3: 5; 3 Ne. 26: 15; D&C 84: 69.

10 And they did all, both they who had been healed and they who were whole, bow down at his feet, and did worship him; and as many as could come for the multitude did [a]kiss his feet, insomuch that they did bathe his feet with their tears.

11 And it came to pass that he commanded that their [a]little children should be brought.

12 So they brought their little children and set them down upon the ground round about him, and Jesus stood in the midst; and the multitude gave way till they had all been brought unto him.

13 And it came to pass that when they had all been brought, and Jesus stood in the midst, he commanded the multitude that they should [a]kneel down upon the ground.

14 And it came to pass that when they had knelt upon the ground, Jesus groaned within himself, and said: Father, I am [a]troubled because of the wickedness of the people of the house of Israel.

15 And when he had said these words, he himself also [a]knelt upon the earth; and behold he [b]prayed unto the Father, and the things which he prayed cannot be written, and the multitude did bear record who heard him.

16 And after this manner do they bear record: The [a]eye hath never seen, neither hath the ear heard, before, so great and marvelous things as we saw and heard Jesus speak unto the Father;

17 And no [a]tongue can speak, neither can there be written by any man, neither can the hearts of men conceive so great and marvelous things as we both saw and heard Jesus speak; and no one can conceive of the joy which filled our souls at the time we heard him pray for us unto the Father.

18 And it came to pass that when Jesus had made an end of praying unto the Father, he arose; but so great was the [a]joy of the multitude that they were overcome.

19 And it came to pass that Jesus spake unto them, and bade them arise.

20 And they arose from the earth, and he said unto them: Blessed are ye because of your faith. And [a]now behold, my joy is full.

21 And when he had said these words, he [a]wept, and the multitude bare record of it, and he took their little children, one by one, and [b]blessed them, and prayed unto the Father for them.

22 And when he had done this he wept again;

23 And he spake unto the multitude, and said unto them: Behold your little ones.

24 And as they looked to behold they cast their eyes towards heaven, and they saw the heavens open, and they saw angels descending out of heaven as it were in the midst of fire; and they came down and [a]encircled those little ones about, and they were encircled about with fire; and the angels did minister unto them.

25 And the multitude did see and [a]hear and bear record; and they know that their record is true for they all of them did see and hear, every man for himself; and they were in number about two thousand and five hundred souls; and they did consist of men, women, and children.

10*a* Luke 7: 38 (38, 45); 3 Ne. 11: 19.
11*a* Matt. 19: 13 (13–14); Mark 10: 13; 3 Ne. 26: 14 (14, 16). TG Children.
13*a* Acts 9: 40; 20: 36; 3 Ne. 19: 6 (6, 16–17).
14*a* Mosiah 28: 3; Alma 31: 2; 3 Ne. 17: 20; 27: 32; Moses 7: 41.
15*a* 3 Ne. 19: 19 (19, 27).
b TG Jesus Christ, Relationships with the Father.
16*a* Isa. 64: 4; 1 Cor. 2: 9; 3 Ne. 19: 32 (30–36); D&C 76: 10, 116 (114–119).
17*a* 2 Cor. 12: 4; 3 Ne. 19: 34 (32–34).
18*a* TG Joy.
20*a* 3 Ne. 17: 14.
21*a* John 11: 35. TG Sincerity.
b Mark 10: 16 (14–16).
24*a* Hel. 5: 43 (23–24, 43–45); 3 Ne. 19: 14. TG Transfiguration.
25*a* Ex. 19: 9 (9–13).

CHAPTER 18

Jesus institutes the sacrament among the Nephites—They are commanded to pray always in his name—Those who eat his flesh and drink his blood unworthily are damned—The disciples are given power to confer the Holy Ghost.

AND it came to pass that Jesus commanded his disciples that they should bring forth some [a]bread and wine unto him.

2 And while they were gone for bread and wine, he commanded the multitude that they should sit themselves down upon the earth.

3 And when the disciples had come with [a]bread and wine, he took of the bread and brake and blessed it; and he gave unto the disciples and commanded that they should eat.

4 And when they had eaten and were filled, he commanded that they should give unto the multitude.

5 And when the multitude had eaten and were filled, he said unto the disciples: Behold there shall one be [a]ordained among you, and to him will I give power that he shall [b]break [c]bread and bless it and give it unto the people of my [d]church, unto all those who shall believe and be baptized in my name.

6 And this shall ye always observe to [a]do, even as I have done, even as I have broken bread and blessed it and given it unto you.

7 And this shall ye do in [a]remembrance of my [b]body, which I have shown unto you. And it shall be a testimony unto the Father that ye do always remember me. And if ye do always remember me ye shall have my Spirit to be with you.

8 And it came to pass that when he said these words, he commanded his disciples that they should take of the [a]wine of the cup and drink of it, and that they should also give unto the multitude that they might drink of it.

9 And it came to pass that they did so, and did drink of it and were filled; and they gave unto the multitude, and they did drink, and they were filled.

10 And when the disciples had done this, Jesus said unto them: Blessed are ye for this thing which ye have done, for this is fulfilling my commandments, and this doth witness unto the Father that ye are [a]willing to do that which I have commanded you.

11 And this shall ye always do to those who repent and are baptized in my name; and ye shall do it in [a]remembrance of my [b]blood, which I have shed for you, that ye may witness unto the Father that ye do always remember me. And if ye do always remember me ye shall have my Spirit to be with you.

12 And I give unto you a commandment that ye shall do these things. And if ye shall always do these things blessed are ye, for ye are built upon my [a]rock.

13 But whoso among you shall do [a]more or less than these are not built upon my rock, but are built upon a sandy foundation; and when the rain descends, and the floods come, and the winds blow, and beat upon them, they shall [b]fall, and the [c]gates of hell are ready open to receive them.

14 Therefore blessed are ye if ye shall keep my commandments, which the Father hath commanded me that I should give unto you.

18 1*a* Matt. 26:26; 3 Ne. 20:3 (3–9); 26:13.
3*a* TG Jesus Christ, Types of, in Memory.
5*a* TG Church Organization.
b Moro. 4:1.
c Matt. 14:19 (19–21); 3 Ne. 20:6 (6–7).
d TG Church.
6*a* TG Jesus Christ, Exemplar.
7*a* 3 Ne. 20:8; Moro. 4:3. TG Sacrament.
b TG Bread of Life.
8*a* Matt. 26:27 (27–29). TG Jesus Christ, Types of, in Memory.
10*a* TG Commitment.
11*a* Moro. 5:1.
b TG Blood, Symbolism of.
12*a* TG Rock.
13*a* Josh. 1:7; D&C 3:2.
b TG Apostasy of Individuals.
c Matt. 16:18; 3 Ne. 11:39.

[A.D. 34]

15 Verily, verily, I say unto you,
ye must watch and [a]pray always,
lest ye be tempted by the devil, and
ye be led away captive by him.
16 And as I have prayed among
you even so shall ye pray in my
[a]church, among my people who do
repent and are baptized in my name.
Behold I am the [b]light; I have set
an [c]example for you.
17 And it came to pass that when
Jesus had spoken these words unto
his disciples, he turned again unto
the multitude and said unto them:
18 Behold, verily, verily, I say
unto you, ye must watch and pray
always lest ye enter into temptation;
for [a]Satan desireth to have
you, that he may sift you as wheat.
19 Therefore ye must always pray
unto the Father in my name;
20 And [a]whatsoever ye shall ask the
Father in my name, which is right,
believing that ye shall receive, behold
it shall be given unto you.
21 [a]Pray in your families unto the
Father, always in my name, that
your wives and your children may
be blessed.
22 And behold, ye shall [a]meet
together oft; and ye shall not forbid
any man from coming unto you
when ye shall meet together, but
suffer them that they may come
unto you and forbid them not;
23 But ye shall [a]pray for them, and
shall not cast them out; and if it so
be that they come unto you oft ye
shall pray for them unto the Father,
in my name.
24 Therefore, hold up your [a]light
that it may shine unto the world.
Behold I am the [b]light which ye
shall hold up—that which ye have
seen me do. Behold ye see that I
have prayed unto the Father, and
ye all have witnessed.
25 And ye see that I have commanded
that [a]none of you should go
away, but rather have commanded
that ye should come unto me, that
ye might [b]feel and see; even so shall
ye do unto the world; and whosoever
breaketh this commandment
suffereth himself to be led into
temptation.
26 And now it came to pass that
when Jesus had spoken these words,
he turned his eyes again upon the
[a]disciples whom he had chosen, and
said unto them:
27 Behold verily, verily, I say unto
you, I give unto you another commandment,
and then I must go unto
my [a]Father that I may fulfil [b]other
commandments which he hath given
me.
28 And now behold, this is the
commandment which I give unto
you, that ye shall not suffer any one
knowingly to [a]partake of my flesh
and blood [b]unworthily, when ye
shall minister it;
29 For whoso eateth and drinketh
my flesh and [a]blood [b]unworthily
eateth and drinketh damnation to
his soul; therefore if ye know that a
man is unworthy to eat and drink
of my flesh and blood ye shall forbid
him.
30 Nevertheless, ye shall not [a]cast
him out from among you, but ye

15a Alma 34:23; D&C 93:49.
16a TG Jesus Christ, Head of the Church.
b TG Jesus Christ, Light of the World.
c TG God, the Standard of Righteousness; Jesus Christ, Exemplar.
18a Luke 22:31; 2 Ne. 2:18 (17–18); D&C 10:22 (22–27).
20a Isa. 58:9 (8–9); Matt. 21:22 (21–22); Mark 11:24; Hel. 10:5; Morm. 9:21; Moro. 7:26; D&C 88:64 (63–65).
21a Alma 34:21. TG Family, Children, Responsibilities toward.
22a TG Meetings.
23a 3 Ne. 18:30. TG Missionary Work.
24a TG Jesus Christ, Light of the World.
b Matt. 5:16; Mark 4:21; 3 Ne. 12:16.
25a Alma 5:33; 19:36.
b 3 Ne. 11:15 (14–16).
26a 3 Ne. 13:25.
27a TG God the Father—Elohim.
b 3 Ne. 16:3.
28a Ex. 12:43; 1 Cor. 11:27 (27–30); 4 Ne. 1:27.
b Lev. 7:18; Morm. 9:29.
29a TG Blood, Symbolism of.
b 3 Ne. 12:24 (23–26); D&C 46:4.
30a D&C 46:3.

[A.D. 34]

shall [b]minister unto him and shall
pray for him unto the Father, in
my name; and if it so be that he
repenteth and is baptized in my
name, then shall ye receive him,
and shall minister unto him of my
flesh and blood.
31 But if he repent not he shall not
be numbered among my people, that
he may not destroy my people, for
behold I [a]know [b]my sheep, and they
are numbered.
32 Nevertheless, ye shall not cast
him out of your [a]synagogues, or
your places of worship, for unto such
shall ye continue to minister; for ye
know not but what they will return
and repent, and come unto me with
full purpose of heart, and I shall [b]heal
them; and ye shall be the means
of bringing salvation unto them.
33 Therefore, keep these sayings
which I have commanded you that
ye come not under [a]condemnation;
for wo unto him whom the Father
condemneth.
34 And I give you these commandments because of the disputations which have been among you.
And blessed are ye if ye have [a]no
disputations among you.
35 And now I go unto the Father,
because it is expedient that I should
go unto the Father [a]for your sakes.
36 And it came to pass that when
Jesus had made an end of these
sayings, he touched with his [a]hand
the [b]disciples whom he had chosen,
one by one, even until he had
touched them all, and spake unto
them as he touched them.
37 And the multitude heard not
the words which he spake, therefore
they did not bear record; but the
disciples bare record that he gave
them [a]power to give the [b]Holy
Ghost. And I will show unto you
[c]hereafter that this record is true.
38 And it came to pass that when
Jesus had touched them all, there
came a [a]cloud and overshadowed the
multitude that they could not see
Jesus.
39 And while they were overshadowed he [a]departed from them,
and ascended into heaven. And the
disciples saw and did bear record
that he ascended again into heaven.

CHAPTER 19

The Twelve Disciples minister unto the people and pray for the Holy Ghost—They are baptized and receive the Holy Ghost and the ministering of angels—Jesus prays using words that cannot be written—He attests to the exceedingly great faith of these Nephites.

AND now it came to pass that when
Jesus had ascended into heaven, the
multitude did disperse, and every
man did take his wife and his children and did return to his own
home.
2 And it was noised abroad among
the people immediately, before it
was yet dark, that the multitude had
seen Jesus, and that he had ministered unto them, and that he would
also show himself on the [a]morrow
unto the multitude.
3 Yea, and even all the night it was
noised abroad concerning Jesus;
and insomuch did they send forth
unto the people that there were
many, yea, an exceedingly great
number, did labor exceedingly all
that night, that they might be on
the morrow in the place where
Jesus should show himself unto the
multitude.

30*b* 3 Ne. 18: 23.
31*a* D&C 27: 14.
b John 10: 14; Alma 5: 38; 3 Ne. 15: 24.
32*a* Alma 16: 13; Moro. 7: 1.
b Jer. 3: 22; 3 Ne. 9: 13 (13–14); D&C 112: 13.
33*a* TG Condemnation.
34*a* 3 Ne. 11: 28 (28–30). TG Disputations.
35*a* 1 Jn. 2: 1; 2 Ne. 2: 9; Moro. 7: 28 (27–28); D&C 29: 5.
36*a* TG Hands, Laying on of.
b 1 Ne. 12: 7; 3 Ne. 15: 11; 19: 4 (4–12).
37*a* TG Holy Ghost, Gift of; Priesthood, Authority.
b Alma 31: 36.
c Moro. 2: 2 (2–3).
38*a* Ex. 19: 9 (9, 16); 2 Chr. 5: 14 (11–14).
39*a* 3 Ne. 17: 4.
19 2*a* 3 Ne. 17: 3.

[A.D. 34]

4 And it came to pass that on the morrow, when the multitude was gathered together, behold, Nephi and his [a]brother whom he had raised from the [b]dead, whose name was Timothy, and also his son, whose name was Jonas, and also Mathoni, and Mathonihah, his brother, and Kumen, and Kumenonhi, and Jeremiah, and Shemnon, and Jonas, and Zedekiah, and Isaiah—now these were the names of the [d]disciples whom Jesus had chosen—and it came to pass that they went forth and stood in the midst of the multitude.

5 And behold, the multitude was [a]so great that they did cause that they should be separated into twelve bodies.

6 And the twelve did teach the multitude; and behold, they did cause that the multitude should [a]kneel down upon the face of the earth, and should pray unto the Father in the name of Jesus.

7 And the disciples did pray unto the Father also in the name of Jesus. And it came to pass that they arose and ministered unto the people.

8 And when they had ministered those same words which Jesus had spoken—nothing varying from the words which Jesus had spoken—behold, they knelt again and prayed to the Father in the name of Jesus.

9 And they did pray for that which they most desired; and they desired that the [a]Holy Ghost should be given unto them.

10 And when they had thus prayed they went down unto the water's edge, and the multitude followed them.

11 And it came to pass that Nephi went down [a]into the water and was [b]baptized.

12 And he came up out of the water and began to baptize. And he baptized all those whom Jesus had chosen.

13 And it came to pass when they were all baptized and had come [a]up out of the water, the [b]Holy Ghost did fall upon them, and they were filled with the Holy Ghost and with fire.

14 And behold, they were [a]encircled about as if it were by fire; and it came down from heaven, and the multitude did witness it, and did bear record; and angels did come down out of heaven and did minister unto them.

15 And it came to pass that while the angels were ministering unto the disciples, behold, Jesus came and stood in the midst and ministered unto them.

16 And it came to pass that he spake unto the multitude, and commanded them that they should kneel down again upon the earth, and also that his disciples should kneel down upon the earth.

17 And it came to pass that when they had all knelt down upon the earth, he commanded his disciples that they should pray.

18 And behold, they began to pray; and they did pray unto Jesus, calling him their Lord and their God.

19 And it came to pass that Jesus departed out of the midst of them, and went a little way off from them and [a]bowed himself to the earth, and he said:

20 Father, I thank thee that thou hast given the Holy Ghost unto these whom I have [a]chosen; and it is because of their belief in me that I have chosen them out of the world.

21 Father, I pray thee that thou wilt give the Holy Ghost unto all them that shall believe in their words.

4*a* 3 Ne. 7: 19.
b TG Death, Power over.
c 3 Ne. 28: 25.
d 3 Ne. 18: 36 (36–37); 26: 17.
5*a* Mosiah 2: 7.
6*a* 3 Ne. 17: 13.
9*a* 3 Ne. 9: 20.
11*a* 3 Ne. 11: 23.
b Matt. 3: 14 (13–15); JS-H 1: 71 (70–71).
13*a* TG Baptism, Immersion.
b 3 Ne. 12: 2; Morm. 7: 10. TG Holy Ghost, Baptism of.
14*a* Hel. 5: 43 (23–24, 43–45); 3 Ne. 17: 24.
19*a* 3 Ne. 17: 15.
20*a* TG Church Organization.

22 Father, thou hast given them the Holy Ghost because they believe in [a]me; and thou seest that they believe in me because thou hearest them, and they pray unto me; and they pray unto me because I am with them.

23 And now Father, I [a]pray unto thee for them, and also for all those who shall believe on their words, that they may believe in me, that I may be in them [b]as thou, Father, art in me, that we may be [c]one.

24 And it came to pass that when Jesus had thus prayed unto the Father, he came unto his disciples, and behold, they did still continue, without ceasing, to pray unto him; and they did not [a]multiply many words, for it was given unto them what they should [b]pray, and they were filled with desire.

25 And it came to pass that Jesus blessed them as they did pray unto him; and his [a]countenance did smile upon them, and the light of his [b]countenance did [c]shine upon them, and behold they were as [d]white as the countenance and also the garments of Jesus; and behold the whiteness thereof did exceed all the whiteness, yea, even there could be nothing upon earth so white as the whiteness thereof.

26 And Jesus said unto them: Pray on; nevertheless they did not cease to pray.

27 And he turned from them again, and went a little way off and bowed himself to the earth; and he prayed again unto the Father, saying:

28 Father, I thank thee that thou hast [a]purified those whom I have chosen, because of their faith, and I pray for them, and also for them who shall believe on their words, that they may be purified in me, through faith on their words, even as they are purified in me.

29 Father, I pray not for the world, but for those whom thou hast given me [a]out of the world, because of their faith, that they may be purified in me, that I may be in them as thou, Father, art in me, that we may be one, that I may be glorified in them.

30 And when Jesus had spoken these words he came again unto his disciples; and behold they did pray steadfastly, without ceasing, unto him; and he did smile upon them again; and behold they were [a]white, even as Jesus.

31 And it came to pass that he went again a little way off and prayed unto the Father;

32 And tongue cannot speak the words which he prayed, neither can be [a]written by man the words which he prayed.

33 And the multitude did hear and do bear record; and their [a]hearts were open and they did understand in their hearts the words which he prayed.

34 Nevertheless, so great and marvelous were the words which he prayed that they cannot be written, neither can they be [a]uttered by man.

35 And it came to pass that when Jesus had made an end of praying he came again to the disciples, and said unto them: [a]So great [b]faith have I never seen among all the Jews; wherefore I could not show unto them so great [c]miracles, because of their [d]unbelief.

22*a* Acts 7: 59.
23*a* TG Jesus Christ, Relationships with the Father.
b 3 Ne. 9: 15; 11: 27.
c John 17: 22 (1–22); 1 Cor. 6: 17.
24*a* Matt. 6: 7.
b Hel. 10: 5; D&C 46: 30.
25*a* Num. 6: 25 (23–27).
b Ps. 4: 6.
c Dan. 9: 17.
d TG Transfiguration.
28*a* Neh. 12: 30; Moro. 7: 48; D&C 50: 29 (28–29); 88: 74 (74–75). TG Purity.
29*a* John 17: 6.
30*a* Matt. 17: 2.
32*a* 3 Ne. 5: 18; D&C 76: 116.
33*a* Prov. 2: 2; 8: 5; Isa. 44: 18; Mosiah 2: 9; 12: 27.
34*a* 2 Cor. 12: 4; 3 Ne. 17: 17.
35*a* Matt. 8: 10.
b TG Faith.
c John 11: 47 (47–48).
d Matt. 13: 58. TG Doubt; Unbelief, Unbelievers.

36 Verily I say unto you, there are none of them that have seen so great things as ye have seen; neither have they heard so great things as ye have heard.

CHAPTER 20

Jesus provides bread and wine miraculously and again administers the sacrament unto them—The remnant of Jacob shall come to the knowledge of the Lord their God and shall inherit the Americas—Jesus is the prophet like unto Moses, and the Nephites are children of the prophets—Others of the Lord's people shall be gathered to Jerusalem.

AND it came to pass that he commanded the multitude that they should [a]cease to [b]pray, and also his disciples. And he commanded them that they should not cease to pray in their hearts.

2 And he commanded them that they should arise and stand up upon their feet. And they arose up and stood upon their feet.

3 And it came to pass that he [a]brake [b]bread again and blessed it, and gave to the disciples to eat.

4 And when they had eaten he commanded them that they should break bread, and give unto the multitude.

5 And when they had given unto the multitude he also gave them wine to drink, and commanded them that they should give unto the multitude.

6 Now, there had been no [a]bread, neither wine, brought by the disciples, neither by the multitude;

7 But he truly [a]gave unto them bread to eat, and also wine to drink.

8 And he said unto them: He that eateth this bread eateth of [a]my body to his soul; and he that drinketh of this wine drinketh of my blood to his soul; and his soul shall never hunger nor thirst, but shall be filled.

9 Now, when the multitude had all eaten and drunk, behold, they were filled with the Spirit; and they did cry out with one voice, and gave glory to Jesus, whom they both saw and heard.

10 And it came to pass that when they had all given glory unto Jesus, he said unto them: Behold now I finish the commandment which the Father hath commanded me concerning this people, who are a remnant of the house of Israel.

11 Ye remember that I spake unto you, and said that when the [a]words of [b]Isaiah should be fulfilled—behold they are written, ye have them before you, therefore search them—

12 And verily, verily, I say unto you, that when they shall be fulfilled then is the fulfilling of the [a]covenant which the Father hath made unto his people, O house of Israel.

13 And then shall the [a]remnants, which shall be [b]scattered abroad upon the face of the earth, be [c]gathered in from the east and from the west, and from the south and from the north; and they shall be brought to the [d]knowledge of the Lord their God, who hath redeemed them.

14 And the Father hath [a]commanded me that I should give unto you this [b]land, for your inheritance.

15 And I say unto you, that if the Gentiles do not [a]repent after the

20 1*a* 1 Sam. 7: 8; 2 Ne. 32: 9.
b Mosiah 24: 12.
3*a* Mark 6: 41 (36–44).
b 3 Ne. 18: 1; 26: 13.
6*a* Matt. 14: 19 (19–21).
7*a* John 6: 14.
8*a* John 6: 51 (50–58); 1 Cor. 11: 24 (20–26); 3 Ne. 18: 7; Moro. 4: 3.
11*a* 3 Ne. 16: 17 (17–20); 23: 3 (1–3).
b 2 Ne. 25: 5 (1–5); Morm. 8: 23.
12*a* Gen. 17: 11 (9–12); 3 Ne. 15: 7.
13*a* 3 Ne. 16: 13 (6–13); 21: 3 (2–7).
b TG Israel, Scattering of.
c Jer. 46: 27 (2–28); 3 Ne. 22: 7 (6–17). TG Israel, Gathering of.
d Ezek. 20: 42 (42–44); 3 Ne. 16: 4 (4–5).
14*a* TG Jesus Christ, Authority of.
b TG Promised Lands.
15*a* 3 Ne. 16: 10 (10–14).

[A.D. 34]

[b]blessing which they shall receive, after they have scattered my people—

16 Then shall ye, who are a [a]remnant of the house of Jacob, go forth among them; and ye shall be in the midst of them who shall be many; and ye shall be among them as a lion among the beasts of the forest, and as a young [b]lion among the flocks of sheep, who, if he goeth through both [c]treadeth down and teareth in pieces, and none can deliver.

17 Thy hand shall be lifted up upon thine adversaries, and all thine enemies shall be cut off.

18 And I will [a]gather my people together as a man gathereth his sheaves into the floor.

19 For I will make my [a]people with whom the Father hath covenanted, yea, I will make thy [b]horn iron, and I will make thy hoofs brass. And thou shalt [c]beat in pieces many people; and I will consecrate their gain unto the Lord, and their substance unto the Lord of the whole earth. And behold, I am he who doeth it.

20 And it shall come to pass, saith the Father, that the [a]sword of my justice shall hang over them at that day; and except they repent it shall fall upon them, saith the Father, yea, even upon all the nations of the Gentiles.

21 And it shall come to pass that I will establish my [a]people, O house of Israel.

22 And behold, this [a]people will I establish in this land, unto the fulfilling of the [b]covenant which I made with your father Jacob; and it shall be a [c]New Jerusalem. And the [d]powers of heaven shall be in the midst of this people; yea, even [e]I will be in the midst of you.

23 Behold, I am he of whom Moses spake, saying: [a]A prophet shall the Lord your God raise up unto you of your brethren, like unto me; him shall ye hear in all things whatsoever he shall say unto you. And it shall come to pass that every soul who will not hear that prophet shall be cut off from among the people.

24 Verily I say unto you, yea, and [a]all the prophets from Samuel and those that follow after, as many as have spoken, have testified of me.

25 And behold, ye are the [a]children of the prophets; and ye are of the house of Israel; and ye are of the [b]covenant which the Father made with your fathers, saying unto Abraham: And [c]in thy seed shall all the kindreds of the earth be blessed.

26 The Father having raised me up unto you first, and sent me to [a]bless you in [b]turning away every one of you from his iniquities; and this because ye are the children of the covenant—

27 And after that ye were blessed then fulfilleth the Father the covenant which he made with Abraham, saying: [a]In thy seed shall all the kindreds of the earth be blessed—unto the pouring out of the Holy

15*b* 3 Ne. 20: 27.
16*a* TG Israel, Remnant of.
b Gen. 49: 9; Morm. 5: 24; D&C 87: 5 (4–5); 109: 65 (65–67). TG Israel, Deliverance of.
c Micah 5: 8 (8–9); 3 Ne. 16: 15 (14–15); 21: 12 (11–21).
18*a* Micah 4: 12.
19*a* Lev. 26: 12; D&C 63: 1 (1–6).
b TG Last Days.
c Micah 4: 13.
20*a* 1 Ne. 14: 17; 22: 16 (15–16); 3 Ne. 29: 4.
21*a* 1 Kgs. 8: 51; 3 Ne. 16: 8 (8–15); 21: 23 (12–24).
22*a* TG Israel, Joseph, People of.
b Gen. 49: 26 (22–26).
c Isa. 2: 3 (2–5); 3 Ne. 21: 23 (23–24); Ether 13: 3 (1–12); D&C 84: 2 (2–4). TG Jerusalem, New.
d 3 Ne. 21: 25.
e Isa. 59: 20 (20–21); 3 Ne. 24: 1.
23*a* Deut. 18: 15 (15–19); Acts 3: 22 (22–23); 1 Ne. 22: 20 (20–21); D&C 133: 63.
24*a* Acts 3: 24 (24–26); 1 Ne. 10: 5; Jacob 7: 11.
25*a* Rom. 4: 24 (23–24).
b TG Abrahamic Covenant.
c Gen. 12: 3 (1–3); 22: 18 (9, 18). TG Seed of Abraham.
26*a* TG Israel, Blessings of.
b Prov. 16: 6; Alma 19: 33.
27*a* Gen. 12: 2 (1–3); Gal. 3: 8 (7–29); 2 Ne. 29: 14; Abr. 2: 9.

Ghost through me upon the Gentiles, which [b]blessing upon the
[c]Gentiles shall make them mighty
above all, unto the [d]scattering of
my people, O house of Israel.
28 And they shall be a [a]scourge
unto the people of this land. Nevertheless, when they shall have received the fulness of my gospel, then
if they shall harden their hearts
against me I will return their
[b]iniquities upon their own heads,
saith the Father.
29 And I will [a]remember the
covenant which I have made with
my people; and I have covenanted
with them that I would [b]gather
them together in mine own due
time, that I would give unto them
again the [c]land of their fathers for
their inheritance, which is the land
of Jerusalem, which is the promised
land unto them forever, saith the
Father.
30 And it shall come to pass that
the time cometh, when the fulness
of my gospel shall be preached unto
them;
31 And they shall [a]believe in me,
that I am Jesus Christ, the Son of
God, and shall pray unto the
Father in my name.
32 Then shall their [a]watchmen lift
up their voice, and with the voice
together shall they sing; for they
shall see eye to eye.
33 Then will the Father gather
them together again, and give unto
them [a]Jerusalem for the [b]land of
their inheritance.
34 Then shall they break forth into
joy—[a]Sing together, ye waste places
of Jerusalem; for the Father hath
comforted his people, he hath
redeemed Jerusalem.
35 The Father hath made bare his
holy arm in the eyes of all the
nations; and all the ends of the
earth shall see the salvation of the
Father; and the Father and I are one.
36 And then shall be brought to
pass that which is written: [a]Awake,
awake again, and put on thy
strength, O Zion; put on thy beautiful garments, O Jerusalem, the holy
city, for henceforth there shall no
more come into thee the uncircumcised and the unclean.
37 Shake thyself from the dust;
arise, sit down, O Jerusalem; loose
thyself from the bands of thy neck,
O captive daughter of Zion.
38 For thus saith the Lord: Ye
have sold yourselves for naught,
and ye shall be redeemed without
money.
39 Verily, verily, I say unto you,
that my people shall know my
name; yea, in that day they shall
know that I am he that doth speak.
40 And then shall they say: [a]How
beautiful upon the mountains are
the feet of him that bringeth good
tidings unto them, that [b]publisheth
peace; that bringeth good tidings
unto them of good, that publisheth
salvation; that saith unto Zion:
Thy God reigneth!
41 And then shall a cry go forth:
[a]Depart ye, depart ye, go ye out
from thence, touch not that which
is [b]unclean; go ye out of the midst
of her; be ye [c]clean that bear the
vessels of the Lord.

27*b* 3 Ne. 20: 15.
c 3 Ne. 16: 6 (6–7); Morm. 5: 19.
d 3 Ne. 16: 8 (8–9); Morm. 5: 9.
28*a* Josh. 23: 13; 1 Ne. 2: 24; 3 Ne. 16: 8 (8–10).
b Isa. 51: 23.
29*a* Isa. 44: 21; 3 Ne. 16: 11 (11–12).
b TG Israel, Gathering of.
c Amos 9: 15; Alma 7: 10; D&C 133: 24. TG Israel, Land of.
31*a* 3 Ne. 5: 26 (21–26); 21: 26 (26–29).
32*a* Isa. 52: 8 (8–9); 3 Ne. 16: 18 (18–20). TG Watchmen.
33*a* Isa. 18: 7; D&C 84: 2. TG Jerusalem.
b Deut. 11: 11. TG Israel, Land of; Lands of Inheritance.
34*a* Isa. 54: 1.
36*a* Isa. 52: 1 (1–3); D&C 113: 7 (7–10). TG Priesthood, Power of.
40*a* Isa. 52: 7; Nahum 1: 15; Mosiah 15: 18 (13–18); D&C 128: 19.
b Mark 13: 10; 1 Ne. 13: 37.
41*a* Isa. 52: 11 (11–15).
b TG Uncleanness.
c D&C 133: 5. TG Cleanliness.

[A.D. 34]

42 For ye shall [a]not go out with
[b]haste nor go by flight; for the Lord
will go before you, and the God of
Israel shall be your rearward.
43 Behold, my servant shall deal
prudently; he shall be exalted and
extolled and be very high.
44 As many were astonished at
thee—his visage was so marred,
more than any man, and his form
more than the sons of men—
45 So shall he [a]sprinkle many
nations; the kings shall shut their
mouths at him, for that which had
not been told them shall they see;
and that which they had not heard
shall they [b]consider.
46 Verily, verily, I say unto you,
all these things shall surely come,
even as the Father hath commanded
me. Then shall this covenant
which the Father hath covenanted
with his people be fulfilled;
and then shall [a]Jerusalem be inhabited
again with my people,
and it shall be the land of their inheritance.

CHAPTER 21

Israel shall be gathered when the Book of Mormon comes forth—The Gentiles shall be established as a free people in America—They shall be saved if they believe and obey; otherwise they shall be cut off and destroyed—Israel shall build the New Jerusalem, and the lost tribes shall return.

AND verily I say unto you, I give
unto you a [a]sign, that ye may know
the [b]time when these things shall be
about to take place—that I shall
gather in, from their long dispersion,
my people, O house of Israel, and
shall establish again among them
my Zion;
2 And behold, this is the thing
which I will give unto you for a sign—
for verily I say unto you that [a]when
these things which I declare unto
you, and which I shall declare
unto you hereafter of myself, and
by the power of the Holy Ghost
which shall be given unto you of the
Father, shall be made known unto
the Gentiles that they may know
concerning this people who are a
remnant of the house of Jacob, and
concerning this my people who
shall be scattered by them;
3 Verily, verily, I say unto you,
when these things shall be made
[a]known unto them of the Father,
and shall come forth of the Father,
[b]from them unto you;
4 For it is wisdom in the Father
that they should be established in
this land, and be set up as a [a]free
people by the power of the Father,
that these things might come forth
from them unto a remnant of your
seed, that the [b]covenant of the
Father may be fulfilled which he
hath covenanted with his people, O
house of Israel;
5 Therefore, when these works and
the works which shall be wrought
among you hereafter shall come
forth [a]from the Gentiles, unto your
[b]seed which shall dwindle in unbelief
because of iniquity;
6 For thus it behooveth the Father
that it should come forth from the
[a]Gentiles, that he may show forth
his power unto the Gentiles, for this
cause that the Gentiles, if they will
not harden their hearts, that they
may repent and come unto me and

42*a* 3 Ne. 21: 29.
b TG Haste; Rashness.
45*a* Lev. 1: 5; Isa. 52: 15; Ezek. 36: 25.
b 3 Ne. 21: 8; D&C 101: 94.
46*a* Joel 2: 18; Ether 13: 5 (5, 11).
21 1*a* Isa. 66: 19.
b TG Last Days.
2*a* 1 Ne. 10: 14; Ether 4: 17; D&C 20: 9 (8–11); JS-H 1: 34.
3*a* TG Witness of the Father.
b 3 Ne. 20: 13; Morm. 5: 15 (10–21).
4*a* John 8: 32 (32–36); 1 Ne. 13: 19 (17–19); D&C 101: 77 (77–80).
b Ps. 89: 35; 3 Ne. 16: 11 (8–12); Morm. 5: 20. TG Abrahamic Covenant.
5*a* 3 Ne. 26: 8.
b 2 Ne. 30: 5; Morm. 5: 15; D&C 3: 18.
6*a* 1 Ne. 10: 14; Jacob 5: 54; 3 Ne. 16: 4 (4–7); 21: 24 (24–26); Morm. 5: 15.

be baptized in my name and know
of the true points of my doctrine,
that they may be [b]numbered among
my people, O house of Israel;
7 And when these things come to
pass that thy [a]seed shall begin to
know these things—it shall be a
sign unto them, that they may know
that the work of the Father hath
already commenced unto the fulfilling of the covenant which he
hath made unto the people who are
of the house of Israel.
8 And when that day shall come,
it shall come to pass that kings
shall shut their mouths; for that
which had not been told them shall
they see; and that which they had
not heard shall they [a]consider.
9 For in that day, for my sake shall
the Father [a]work a work, which
shall be a great and a [b]marvelous
[c]work among them; and there shall
be among them those who will not
believe it, although a man shall
declare it unto them.
10 But behold, the life of my servant shall be in my hand; therefore
they shall not hurt him, although
he shall be [a]marred because of them.
Yet I will heal him, for I will show unto them that [b]my wisdom is greater
than the cunning of the devil.
11 Therefore it shall come to pass
that whosoever will not believe in
my words, who am Jesus Christ,
which the Father shall cause [a]him
to bring forth unto the [b]Gentiles,
and shall give unto him power that
he shall bring them forth unto the
Gentiles, (it shall be done even as
Moses said) they shall be [c]cut off
from among my people who are of
the covenant.
12 And my people who are a remnant of Jacob shall be among the
Gentiles, yea, in the midst of them
as a [a]lion among the beasts of the
forest, as a young lion among the
flocks of sheep, who, if he go through
both treadeth down and teareth in
pieces, and none can deliver.
13 Their hand shall be lifted up
upon their [a]adversaries, and all their
enemies shall be cut off.
14 Yea, wo be unto the Gentiles
except they [a]repent; for it shall
come to pass in that day, saith the
Father, that I will cut off thy horses
out of the midst of thee, and I will
destroy thy [b]chariots;
15 And I will cut off the cities of
thy land, and throw down all thy
[a]strongholds;
16 And I will cut off [a]witchcrafts
out of thy land, and thou shalt have
no more soothsayers;
17 Thy [a]graven images I will also
cut off, and thy standing images out
of the midst of thee, and thou shalt
no more worship the works of thy
hands;
18 And I will pluck up thy [a]groves
out of the midst of thee; so will I
destroy thy cities.
19 And it shall come to pass that
all [a]lyings, and deceivings, and
envyings, and strifes, and priestcrafts, and whoredoms, shall be
done away.
20 For it shall come to pass, saith
the Father, that at that [a]day whosoever will not repent and come
unto my Beloved Son, them will I

6*b* Gal. 3: 7 (7, 29); 2 Ne. 30: 3; 3 Ne. 16: 13; Abr. 2: 10 (9–11).
7*a* 3 Ne. 5: 23 (21–26); 21: 26.
8*a* 3 Ne. 20: 45.
9*a* TG God, Works of.
b 1 Ne. 22: 8. TG Restoration of the Gospel.
c Acts 13: 41 (40–41).
10*a* D&C 135: 1 (1–3).
b D&C 10: 43.
11*a* 2 Ne. 3: 11 (6–15); Morm. 8: 16 (16, 25); Ether 3: 28 (21–28).
b 1 Ne. 21: 6.
c D&C 1: 14; 133: 63.
12*a* Isa. 5: 29; Micah 5: 8 (8–15); Mal. 4: 3; 2 Ne. 15: 29; 3 Ne. 16: 15 (7–15); 20: 16; 25: 3; D&C 87: 5.
13*a* 1 Ne. 21: 17 (17–19).
14*a* Eph. 3: 6 (1–7); 2 Ne. 10: 18; 33: 9.
b Lev. 26: 22 (21–22); Hel. 14: 24.
15*a* 2 Ne. 12: 15.
16*a* TG Sorcery; Superstitions.
17*a* Ex. 20: 4 (3–4, 23); Isa. 41: 29 (24, 29); Mosiah 13: 12; D&C 1: 16. TG Idolatry.
18*a* 1 Kgs. 16: 33 (32–33).
19*a* 3 Ne. 30: 2; D&C 109: 30.
20*a* Amos 5: 18; Alma 29: 2; Morm. 9: 27.

[A.D. 34]

[b]cut off from among my people, O
house of Israel;
21 And I will execute [a]vengeance
and [b]fury upon them, even as upon
the heathen, such as they have not
heard.
22 But if they will repent and
hearken unto my words, and
[a]harden not their hearts, I will
[b]establish my church among them,
and they shall come in unto the
covenant and be [c]numbered among
this the remnant of Jacob, unto
whom I have given this land for
their [d]inheritance;
23 And they shall assist my
[a]people, the remnant of Jacob, and
also as many of the house of Israel
as shall come, that they may build
a city, which shall be called the
[b]New Jerusalem.
24 And then shall [a]they assist my
people that they may be gathered
in, who are scattered upon all the
face of the land, in unto the New
Jerusalem.
25 And then shall the [a]power of
heaven come down among them;
and [b]I also will be in the midst.
26 And then shall the work of the
Father commence at that day, even
[a]when this gospel shall be preached
among the remnant of [b]this people.
Verily I say unto you, at that day
shall the work of the Father commence among all the dispersed of my
people, yea, even the tribes which
have been [c]lost, which the Father
hath led away out of Jerusalem.
27 Yea, the work shall commence
among all the [a]dispersed of my
people, with the Father to prepare
the way whereby they may [b]come
unto me, that they may call on the
Father in my name.
28 Yea, and then shall the work
commence, with the Father among
all nations in preparing the way
whereby his people may be [a]gath-
ered home to the land of their
inheritance.
29 And they shall go out from all
nations; and they shall [a]not go out
in [b]haste, nor go by flight, for I will
go before them, saith the Father,
and I will be their rearward.

CHAPTER 22

In the last days, Zion and her stakes shall be established, and Israel shall be gathered in mercy and tenderness—They shall triumph—Compare Isaiah 54.

AND then shall that which is written come to pass: Sing, O [a]barren,
thou that didst not bear; break
forth into [b]singing, and cry aloud,
thou that didst not travail with
child; for more are the children of
the [c]desolate than the children of
the married wife, saith the Lord.
2 Enlarge the place of thy tent, and
let them stretch forth the curtains
of thy habitations; spare not,
lengthen thy cords and strengthen
thy [a]stakes;
3 For thou shalt break forth on the
right hand and on the left, and thy
seed shall [a]inherit the [b]Gentiles and
make the desolate cities to be
inhabited.

20*b* Jer. 44: 8 (6–8).
21*a* Isa. 34: 8; 61: 2; Jer. 23: 19 (19–20); Mal. 4: 1 (1, 3); D&C 97: 26 (25–28).
b Ezek. 21: 17 (14–17).
22*a* TG Hardheartedness.
b 1 Ne. 14: 12 (12, 14). TG Dispensations; Millennium, Preparing a People for.
c 2 Ne. 10: 18 (18–19); 3 Ne. 16: 13; 30: 2.
d TG Lands of Inheritance.
23*a* 3 Ne. 16: 8 (8–15).
b 3 Ne. 20: 22 (21–22, 39); Ether 13: 3 (1–12). TG Jerusalem, New.
24*a* 3 Ne. 21: 6.
25*a* 1 Ne. 13: 37; 3 Ne. 20: 22.
b Isa. 2: 2 (2–4); 59: 20 (20–21); 3 Ne. 24: 1.
26*a* 3 Ne. 20: 31 (29–34); Morm. 5: 14.
b 1 Ne. 14: 17; 3 Ne. 21: 6 (6–7).
c TG Israel, Ten Lost Tribes of.
27*a* 3 Ne. 16: 5 (4–5).
b TG Israel, Restoration of.
28*a* TG Israel, Gathering of.
29*a* 3 Ne. 20: 42.
b Isa. 52: 12 (11–12).
22 1*a* Isa. 54: 1 (1–17).
b TG Singing.
c Isa. 49: 21.
2*a* TG Stakes.
3*a* Obad. 1: 19 (19–21).
b TG Gentiles.

[A.D. 34]

4 Fear not, for thou shalt not be ashamed; neither be thou confounded, for thou shalt not be put to [a]shame; for thou shalt forget the [b]shame of thy youth, and shalt not remember the [c]reproach of thy youth, and shalt not remember the reproach of thy widowhood any more.

5 For thy maker, thy [a]husband, the Lord of Hosts is his name; and thy Redeemer, the Holy One of Israel—the God of the whole earth shall he be called.

6 For the Lord hath called thee [a]as a woman forsaken and grieved in spirit, and a wife of youth, when thou wast refused, saith thy God.

7 For a small moment have I [a]forsaken thee, but with great mercies will I gather thee.

8 In a little wrath I hid my face from thee for a moment, but with everlasting [a]kindness will I have [b]mercy on thee, saith the Lord thy Redeemer.

9 For this, the [a]waters of Noah unto me, for as I have sworn that the waters of Noah should no more go over the earth, so have I sworn that I would not be wroth with thee.

10 For the [a]mountains shall depart and the hills be removed, but my [b]kindness shall not [c]depart from thee, neither shall the covenant of my peace be removed, saith the Lord that hath mercy on thee.

11 O thou afflicted, tossed with tempest, and not comforted! Behold, I will lay thy [a]stones with fair colors, and lay thy foundations with sapphires.

12 And I will make thy windows of agates, and thy gates of carbuncles, and all thy borders of pleasant stones.

13 And [a]all thy children shall be taught of the Lord; and great shall be the [b]peace of thy children.

14 In [a]righteousness shalt thou be established; thou shalt be far from oppression for thou shalt not fear, and from terror for it shall not come near thee.

15 Behold, they shall surely gather together [a]against thee, not by me; whosoever shall gather together against thee shall fall for thy sake.

16 Behold, I have created the smith that bloweth the coals in the fire, and that bringeth forth an instrument for his work; and I have created the waster to destroy.

17 No weapon that is formed against thee shall prosper; and every tongue that shall revile against thee in judgment thou shalt condemn. This is the heritage of the [a]servants of the Lord, and their righteousness is of me, saith the Lord.

CHAPTER 23

Jesus approves the words of Isaiah—He commands the people to search the prophets—The words of Samuel the Lamanite concerning the resurrection are added to their records.

AND now, behold, I say unto you, that ye ought to [a]search these things. Yea, a commandment I give unto you that ye search these things diligently; for great are the words of [b]Isaiah.

2 For surely he spake as touching all things concerning my people which are of the house of Israel;

4*a* Joel 2: 26 (26–27); 2 Ne. 6: 13 (7, 13).
b TG Shame.
c TG Reproach.
5*a* Hosea 3: 5 (4–5).
6*a* Isa. 62: 4.
7*a* Jer. 46: 27 (2–28); 3 Ne. 20: 13 (11–13).
8*a* TG Kindness.
b TG God, Mercy of.
9*a* Gen. 8: 21; Matt. 24: 37 (36–38); Alma 10: 22. TG Earth, Cleansing of.
10*a* Isa. 40: 4 (4–5). TG Earth, Renewal of.
b TG Israel, Blessings of.
c Ps. 94: 14; D&C 35: 25.
11*a* Rev. 21: 19 (18–21). TG Rock.
13*a* Isa. 60: 21; Jer. 31: 34 (33–34).
b 1 Ne. 22: 17 (15–22); 2 Ne. 30: 10; Moses 7: 61.
14*a* TG Righteousness.
15*a* 1 Ne. 22: 14.
17*a* TG Servant.
23 1*a* TG Scriptures, Study of.
b Isa. 1: 1; 2 Ne. 25: 5 (1–5); 3 Ne. 20: 11; Morm. 8: 23.

[A.D. 34]

[a]therefore it must needs be that he must speak also to the Gentiles.

3 And all things that he spake have been and [a]shall be, even according to the words which he spake.

4 Therefore give heed to my words; write the things which I have told you; and according to the time and the will of the Father [a]they shall go forth unto the Gentiles.

5 And whosoever will hearken unto my words and repenteth and is baptized, the same shall be saved. Search the [a]prophets, for many there be that testify of these things.

6 And now it came to pass that when Jesus had said these words he said unto them again, after he had expounded all the scriptures unto them which they had received, he said unto them: Behold, other scriptures I would that ye should write, that ye have not.

7 And it came to pass that he said unto [a]Nephi: Bring forth the record which ye have kept.

8 And when Nephi had brought forth the records, and laid them before him, he cast his eyes upon them and said:

9 Verily I say unto you, I commanded my servant [a]Samuel, the Lamanite, that he should testify unto this people, that at the day that the Father should glorify his name in me that there were [b]many [c]saints who should [d]arise from the dead, and should appear unto many, and should minister unto them. And he said unto them: Was it not so?

10 And his disciples answered him and said: Yea, Lord, Samuel did prophesy according to thy words, and they were all fulfilled.

11 And Jesus said unto them: How be it that ye have not [a]written this thing, that many [b]saints did arise and appear unto many and did minister unto them?

12 And it came to pass that Nephi remembered that this thing had not been written.

13 And it came to pass that Jesus commanded that it should be [a]written; therefore it was written according as he commanded.

14 And now it came to pass that when Jesus had [a]expounded all the scriptures in one, which they had written, he commanded them that they should [b]teach the things which he had expounded unto them.

CHAPTER 24

The Lord's messenger shall prepare the way for the Second Coming—Christ shall sit in judgment—Israel is commanded to pay tithes and offerings—A book of remembrance is kept—Compare Malachi 3.

AND it came to pass that he commanded them that they should write the words which the Father had given unto Malachi, which he should tell unto them. And it came to pass that after they were written he expounded them. And these are the words which he did tell unto them, saying: Thus said the Father unto Malachi—Behold, I will [a]send my [b]messenger, and he shall prepare the way before me, and the Lord whom ye seek shall suddenly [c]come to his temple, even the [d]messenger of the covenant, whom ye delight in; behold, he shall come, saith the Lord of Hosts.

2 But who may [a]abide the day of his coming, and who shall stand when he appeareth? For he is like

2*a* Isa. 49: 6.
3*a* 3 Ne. 15: 6; 20: 11 (11–12).
4*a* Morm. 8: 26.
5*a* Luke 24: 27 (25–27).
7*a* 3 Ne. 8: 1; 4 Ne. 1: 19.
9*a* Hel. 13: 2.
b Hel. 14: 25 (1, 21–26).
c TG Saints.
d TG Resurrection.
11*a* TG Jesus Christ, Teaching Mode of.
b Matt. 27: 52 (52–53).
13*a* TG Record Keeping.
14*a* Luke 24: 44 (27, 44).
b TG Scriptures, Study of; Teaching.
24 1*a* Mal. 3: 1 (1–18).
b D&C 45: 9.
c Isa. 59: 20 (20–21); 3 Ne. 20: 22; 21: 25.
d TG Jesus Christ, Messenger of the Covenant.
2*a* 3 Ne. 25: 1.

a [b]refiner's fire, and like fuller's
soap.
3 And he shall sit as a refiner and
purifier of silver; and he shall
[a]purify the [b]sons of Levi, and purge
them as gold and silver, that they
may [c]offer unto the Lord an offering in righteousness.
4 Then shall the offering of Judah
and Jerusalem be pleasant unto the
Lord, as in the days of old, and as in
former years.
5 And I will come [a]near to you to
judgment; and I will be a swift witness against the [b]sorcerers, and
against the adulterers, and against
false [c]swearers, and against those
that [d]oppress the hireling in his
wages, the widow and the [e]father-
less, and that turn aside the
[f]stranger, and fear not me, saith the
Lord of Hosts.
6 For [a]I am the Lord, I change
not; therefore ye sons of Jacob are
not consumed.
7 Even from the days of your
fathers ye are gone away from mine
[a]ordinances, and have not kept
them. [b]Return unto me and I will
return unto you, saith the Lord of
Hosts. But ye say: Wherein shall
we return?
8 Will a man rob God? Yet ye have
robbed me. But ye say: Wherein
have we robbed thee? In [a]tithes and
[b]offerings.
9 Ye are cursed with a curse, for ye
have robbed me, even this whole
nation.
10 Bring ye all the [a]tithes into the
storehouse, that there may be
[b]meat in my house; and prove me
now herewith, saith the Lord of
Hosts, if I will not open you the
[c]windows of heaven, and pour you
out a [d]blessing that there shall not
be room enough to receive it.
11 And I will rebuke the [a]devourer
for your sakes, and he shall not
destroy the fruits of your ground;
neither shall your vine cast her fruit
before the time in the fields, saith
the Lord of Hosts.
12 And all nations shall call you
blessed, for ye shall be a delightsome land, saith the Lord of
Hosts.
13 Your words have been stout
against me, saith the Lord. Yet ye
say: What have we spoken against
thee?
14 Ye have [a]said: It is [b]vain to
serve God, and what doth it profit
that we have kept his [c]ordinances
and that we have walked mourn-
fully before the Lord of Hosts?
15 And now we call the proud
happy; yea, they that work wickedness are set up; yea, they that tempt
God are even delivered.
16 Then they that feared the Lord
[a]spake often one to another, and the
Lord hearkened and heard; and a
book of [b]remembrance was written
before him for them that feared the
Lord, and that thought upon his
name.
17 And they shall be [a]mine, saith
the Lord of Hosts, in that day when
I [b]make up my jewels; and I will

2*b* Deut. 4:24; Zech. 13:9; D&C 128:24. TG Earth, Cleansing of; Jesus Christ, Second Coming.
3*a* TG Purification.
b Deut. 10:8; D&C 84:31 (31–34); 128:24.
c D&C 13:1.
5*a* Ezek. 43:7 (1–7).
b TG Sorcery.
c Hosea 10:4; D&C 104:5 (4–5). TG Swearing.
d Ps. 94:6. TG Oppression.
e Ps. 10:14; 68:5; James 1:27; D&C 136:8.
f TG Stranger.
6*a* 2 Ne. 6:7; Moses 1:6.
7*a* TG Ordinance.
b 1 Sam. 7:3; Hel. 13:11; 3 Ne. 10:6 (5–7); Moro. 9:22.
8*a* TG Tithing.
b Neh. 10:32. TG Sacrifice.
10*a* D&C 64:23; 119:4 (1–7).
b TG Food.
c Gen. 7:11.
d TG Blessing.
11*a* D&C 85:3.
14*a* Job 16:11 (11–17); Jer. 20:7 (7–8); Hab. 1:2 (1–4).
b Mal. 3:14 (14–15).
c TG Ordinance.
16*a* 4 Ne. 1:12; Moro. 6:5 (5–6).
b D&C 85:9 (7–9); Moses 6:5. TG Book of Remembrance.
17*a* Lev. 20:26.
b D&C 101:3.

spare them as a man spareth his own son that serveth him.

18 Then shall ye return and [a]discern between the righteous and the wicked, between him that serveth God and him that serveth him not.

CHAPTER 25

At the Second Coming the proud and wicked shall be burned as stubble—Elijah shall return before that great and dreadful day—Compare Malachi 4.

[a]FOR behold, the day cometh that shall [b]burn as an oven; and all the [c]proud, yea, and all that do wickedly, shall be stubble; and the day that cometh shall burn them up, saith the Lord of Hosts, that it shall leave them neither root nor branch.

2 But unto you that fear my name, shall the [a]Son of Righteousness arise with healing in his wings; and ye shall go forth and [b]grow up as [c]calves in the stall.

3 And ye shall [a]tread down the wicked; for they shall be ashes under the soles of your feet in the day that I shall do this, saith the Lord of Hosts.

4 Remember ye the law of Moses, my servant, which I commanded unto him in [a]Horeb for all Israel, with the statutes and judgments.

5 Behold, I will send you [a]Elijah the prophet before the coming of the great and dreadful [b]day of the Lord;

6 And he shall [a]turn the heart of the [b]fathers to the children, and the heart of the children to their fathers, lest I come and [c]smite the earth with a curse.

CHAPTER 26

Jesus expounds all things from the beginning to the end—Babes and children utter marvelous things which cannot be written—Those in the Church of Christ have all things in common among them.

AND now it came to pass that when Jesus had told these things he expounded them unto the multitude; and he did expound all things unto them, both great and small.

2 And he saith: [a]These scriptures, which ye had not with you, the Father commanded that I should give unto you; for it was wisdom in him that they should be given unto future generations.

3 And he did expound all things, even from the beginning until the [a]time that he should come in his [b]glory—yea, even all things which should come upon the face of the earth, even until the [c]elements should melt with fervent heat, and the earth should be [d]wrapt together as a scroll, and the heavens and the earth should pass away;

4 And even unto the [a]great and last day, when all people, and all kindreds, and all nations and tongues shall [b]stand before God, to be

18*a* TG Discernment, Spiritual.
25 1*a* Mal. 4: 1 (1–6).
b Ps. 21: 9 (8–10); Isa. 24: 6; 66: 16; 1 Ne. 22: 15; 3 Ne. 24: 2; D&C 29: 9; 64: 23 (23–24); 133: 64; JS-H 1: 37. TG Earth, Cleansing of.
c Ps. 18: 27; 2 Ne. 20: 33. TG Pride.
2*a* Ps. 84: 11; Mal. 4: 2; Ether 9: 22.
b D&C 45: 58.
c 1 Ne. 22: 24.
3*a* 3 Ne. 21: 12.
4*a* Ex. 3: 1; 19: 18 (9, 16–20); 1 Kgs. 19: 8; Neh. 9: 13; Mosiah 12: 33; 13: 5.
5*a* 2 Kgs. 2: 2; D&C 2: 1; 35: 4; 110: 13 (13–16); 128: 17 (17–18). TG Genealogy and Temple Work.
b TG Day of the Lord.
6*a* D&C 98: 16 (16–17).
b TG Family, Eternal; Salvation for the Dead.
c Mal. 4: 6; D&C 110: 15 (13–16).
26 2*a* IE Mal. chapters 3 and 4, quoted in 3 Ne. chapters 24 and 25.
3*a* TG Day of the Lord.
b Ps. 72: 19. TG Jesus Christ, Glory of.
c Amos 9: 13; 2 Pet. 3: 10 (10, 12); Morm. 9: 2. TG Earth, Cleansing of; Earth, Destiny of; World, End of.
d Morm. 5: 23.
4*a* Mal. 4: 5; Hel. 12: 25; 3 Ne. 28: 31.
b Mosiah 16: 10 (1–2, 10–11). TG Judgment, The Last.

judged of their works, whether they
be good or whether they be evil—
5 If they be good, to the [a]resur-
rection of everlasting life; and if
they be evil, to the resurrection of
damnation; being on a parallel, the
one on the one hand and the other
on the other hand, according to the
mercy, and the [b]justice, and the
holiness which is in Christ, who was
[c]before the world began.
6 And now there cannot be written
in this book even a [a]hundredth part
of the things which Jesus did truly
teach unto the people;
7 But behold the [a]plates of Nephi
do contain the more part of the
things which he taught the people.
8 And these things have I written,
which are a [a]lesser part of the things
which he taught the people; and I
have written them to the intent
that they may be brought again
unto this people, [b]from the Gentiles,
according to the words which Jesus
hath spoken.
9 And when they shall have received this, which is expedient that
they should have first, to try their
faith, and if it shall so be that they
shall believe these things then shall
the [a]greater things be made manifest unto them.
10 And if it so be that they will not
believe these things, then shall the
[a]greater things be [b]withheld from
them, unto their condemnation.
11 Behold, I was about to write
them, all which were engraven upon
the plates of Nephi, but the Lord
[a]forbade it, saying: I will [b]try the
faith of my people.
12 Therefore I, [a]Mormon, do write
the things which have been commanded me of the Lord. And now
I, [b]Mormon, make an end of my
sayings, and proceed to write the
things which have been commanded me.
13 Therefore, I would that ye
should behold that the Lord truly
did teach the people, for the space
of three days; and after that he did
[a]show himself unto them oft, and
did break [b]bread oft, and bless it,
and give it unto them.
14 And it came to pass that he did
teach and minister unto the [a]chil-
dren of the multitude of whom hath
been spoken, and he did [b]loose their
[c]tongues, and they did speak unto
their fathers great and marvelous
things, even greater than he had
revealed unto the people; and he
loosed their tongues that they
could utter.
15 And it came to pass that after he
had ascended into heaven—the
second time that he showed himself
unto them, and had gone unto the
Father, after having [a]healed all their
sick, and their lame, and opened the
eyes of their blind and unstopped
the ears of the deaf, and even had
done all manner of cures among
them, and raised a man from the
[b]dead, and had shown forth his
power unto them, and had ascended
unto the Father—
16 Behold, it came to pass on the
morrow that the multitude gathered
themselves together, and they both
saw and heard these children; yea,
even [a]babes did open their mouths

5*a* Dan. 12: 2.
b TG God, Justice of; Justice.
c 3 Ne. 1: 14; Ether 3: 14. TG Man, Antemortal Existence of.
6*a* John 21: 25; W of M 1: 5; 3 Ne. 5: 8 (8–11); Ether 15: 33.
7*a* Jarom 1: 14; 4 Ne. 1: 19.
8*a* 3 Ne. 28: 33; D&C 11: 22.
b 3 Ne. 21: 5 (5–6).
9*a* John 16: 12; 2 Ne. 27: 8 (7–11, 21); Morm. 8: 12; Ether 4: 8 (4–10).
10*a* Ether 4: 7 (1–8).
b 2 Ne. 28: 27; Alma 12: 10 (9–11); D&C 6: 26 (26–27).
11*a* 3 Ne. 26: 18.
b Ether 12: 6.
12*a* 3 Ne. 28: 24.
b W of M 1: 1 (1–2).
13*a* John 21· 14; 3 Ne. 27: 2.
b 3 Ne. 18: 1; 20: 3 (3–9). TG Bread; Sacrament.
14*a* Luke 10: 21; Alma 32: 23; 3 Ne. 17: 11; D&C 128: 18.
b D&C 23: 3.
c 3 Ne. 19: 32; 28: 14 (14, 16).
15*a* 3 Ne. 17: 9. TG Administrations to the Sick; Healing.
b TG Death, Power over.
16*a* Matt. 11: 25.

and utter marvelous things; and
the things which they did utter were
[b]forbidden that there should not
any man write them.
17 And it came to pass that the
[a]disciples whom Jesus had chosen
began [b]from that time forth to
[c]baptize and to teach as many as did
come unto them; and as many as
were baptized in the name of Jesus
were filled with the Holy Ghost.
18 And many of them saw and
heard unspeakable things, which
are [a]not lawful to be written.
19 And they taught, and did
[a]minister one to another; and they
had [b]all things [c]common among
them, every man dealing justly, one
with another.
20 And it came to pass that they
did do all things even as Jesus had
commanded them.
21 And they who were baptized in
the name of Jesus were called the
[a]church of Christ.

CHAPTER 27

Jesus commands them to call the Church in his name—His mission and atoning sacrifice constitute his gospel—Men are commanded to repent and be baptized that they may be sanctified by the Holy Ghost—They are to be even as Jesus is.

AND it came to pass that as the
disciples of Jesus were journeying
and were preaching the things which
they had both heard and seen, and
were baptizing in the name of Jesus,
it came to pass that the disciples
were gathered together and were
[a]united in [b]mighty prayer and
[c]fasting.
2 And Jesus again [a]showed himself unto them, for they were praying unto the Father in his name;
and Jesus came and stood in the
midst of them, and said unto them:
What will ye that I shall give unto
you?
3 And they said unto him: Lord,
we will that thou wouldst tell us the
[a]name whereby we shall call this
church; for there are disputations
among the people concerning this
matter.
4 And the Lord said unto them:
Verily, verily, I say unto you, why
is it that the people should murmur
and dispute because of this thing?
5 Have they not read the scriptures, which say ye must take upon
you the [a]name of Christ, which is
my name? For by this name shall
ye be called at the last day;
6 And whoso taketh upon him my
name, and [a]endureth to the end, the
same shall be saved at the last day.
7 Therefore, whatsoever ye shall
do, ye shall do it in my name; therefore ye shall call the church in my
name; and ye shall call upon the
Father in my name that he will bless
the church for my sake.
8 And how be it [a]my [b]church save
it be called in my name? For if a
church be called in Moses' name
then it be Moses' church; or if it be
called in the name of a man then
it be the church of a man; but if it be
called in my name then it is my
church, if it so be that they are built
upon my gospel.
9 Verily I say unto you, that ye are
built upon my gospel; therefore ye
shall call whatsoever things ye do
call, in my name; therefore if ye call
upon the Father, for the church, if
it be in my name the Father will
hear you;
10 And if it so be that the church

16*b* 3 Ne. 27: 23.
17*a* 3 Ne. 19: 4 (4–12); 4 Ne. 1: 14.
b Ether 12: 31.
c 4 Ne. 1: 1.
18*a* 3 Ne. 26: 11.
19*a* TG Benevolence.
b 4 Ne. 1: 3 (3, 25–26).
c TG Consecration.
21*a* Mosiah 18: 17; Alma 4: 5 (4–5). TG Church.
27 1*a* D&C 29: 6; 84: 1.
b Alma 8: 10; D&C 5: 24; 29: 2.
c Mosiah 27: 22; Alma 5: 46; 6: 6. TG Fasting.
2*a* 3 Ne. 26: 13. TG Jesus Christ, Appearances, Postmortal.
3*a* D&C 1: 1; 20: 1.
5*a* TG Jesus Christ, Taking the Name of.
6*a* Alma 32: 13 (13–15); 38: 2; 3 Ne. 15: 9.
8*a* 1 Cor. 1: 12 (11–13); D&C 115: 4.
b TG Jesus Christ, Head of the Church.

is built upon my gospel then will the
Father show forth his own works
in it.
11 But if it be not built upon my
gospel, and is built upon the works
of men, or upon the works of the
devil, verily I say unto you they
have joy in their works for a season,
and by and by the end cometh, and
they are [a]hewn down and cast into
the [b]fire, from whence there is no
return.
12 For their works do [a]follow them,
for it is because of their works that
they are hewn down; therefore
remember the things that I have
told you.
13 Behold I have given unto you
my [a]gospel, and this is the gospel
which I have given unto you—that
I came into the world to do the [b]will
of my Father, because my Father
sent me.
14 And my Father sent me that I
might be [a]lifted up upon the [b]cross;
and after that I had been lifted up
upon the [c]cross, that I might [d]draw
all men unto me, that as I have
been lifted up by men even so
should men be lifted up by the
Father, to stand before me, to be
[e]judged of their works, whether they
be good or whether they be evil—
15 And for this cause have I been
[a]lifted up; therefore, according to
the power of the Father I will draw
all men unto me, that they may be
judged according to their [b]works.
16 And it shall come to pass, that
whoso [a]repenteth and is baptized in
my [b]name shall be filled; and if he
[c]endureth to the end, behold, him
will I hold guiltless before my
Father at that day when I shall
stand to judge the world.
17 And he that endureth not unto
the end, the same is he that is also
hewn down and cast into the fire,
from whence they can no more
return, because of the [a]justice of the
Father.
18 And this is the word which he
hath given unto the children of men.
And for this cause he fulfilleth the
words which he hath given, and he
lieth not, but fulfilleth all his words.
19 And [a]no unclean thing can enter
into his kingdom; therefore nothing
entereth into his [b]rest save it be
those who have [c]washed their garments in my blood, because of their
faith, and the repentance of all their
sins, and their faithfulness unto the
end.
20 Now this is the commandment:
[a]Repent, all ye ends of the earth,
and come unto me and be [b]baptized
in my name, that ye may be [c]sancti-
fied by the reception of the Holy
Ghost, that ye may stand [d]spotless
before me at the last day.
21 Verily, verily, I say unto you,
this is my [a]gospel; and ye know the
things that ye must [b]do in my
church; for the works which ye have
seen me do that shall ye also do;
for that which ye have seen me do
even that shall ye do;

11*a* Jacob 5: 46; 6: 7; Alma 5: 52; D&C 132: 13.
b TG Hell.
12*a* Rev. 14: 13; D&C 59: 2.
13*a* Acts 10: 36 (36–40); D&C 76: 40 (40–42). TG Gospel.
b John 6: 39. TG Jesus Christ, Mission of.
14*a* 3 Ne. 15: 1; Morm. 2: 19.
b Moses 7: 55.
c Luke 9: 44 (44–45); 1 Ne. 11: 32.
d John 6: 44; 2 Ne. 9: 5; D&C 17: 8; 27: 18.
e TG Jesus Christ, Judge.
15*a* TG Jesus Christ, Atonement through.
b 1 Sam. 2: 3.
16*a* TG Repentance.
b TG Baptism, Qualifications for.
c 1 Ne. 13: 37. TG Endure; Steadfastness.
17*a* TG God, Justice of.
19*a* Alma 11: 37. TG Uncleanness.
b D&C 84: 24. TG Rest.
c Rev. 1: 5 (1–6); 7: 14; 1 Ne. 12: 10; Alma 5: 21 (21–27); 13: 11 (11–13).
20*a* Ether 4: 18; Moro. 7: 34.
b TG Baptism, Essential.
c TG Sanctification.
d 1 Cor. 1: 8; D&C 4: 2.
21*a* 1 Ne. 13: 36. TG Gospel; Salvation, Plan of.
b TG Jesus Christ, Exemplar.

[A.D. 34—35]

22 Therefore, if ye do these things
blessed are ye, for ye shall be lifted
up at the last day.
23 [a]Write the things which ye have
seen and heard, save it be those
which are [b]forbidden.
24 Write the works of this people,
which shall be, even as hath been
written, of that which hath been.
25 For behold, out of the books
which have been written, and which
shall be written, shall this people be
[a]judged, for by them shall their
[b]works be known unto men.
26 And behold, all things are
[a]written by the Father; therefore
out of the books which shall be
written shall the world be judged.
27 And know ye that [a]ye shall be
[b]judges of this people, according to
the judgment which I shall give unto you, which shall be just. Therefore, what [c]manner of men ought ye
to be? Verily I say unto you, even
[d]as I am.
28 And now I [a]go unto the Father.
And verily I say unto you, whatsoever things ye shall ask the Father
in my name shall be given unto you.
29 Therefore, [a]ask, and ye shall
receive; knock, and it shall be
opened unto you; for he that asketh,
receiveth; and unto him that knocketh, it shall be opened.
30 And now, behold, my joy is
great, even unto fulness, because of
you, and also this generation; yea,
and even the Father rejoiceth, and
also all the holy angels, because of
you and this generation; for [a]none
of them are lost.
31 Behold, I would that ye should
understand; for I mean them who
are [a]now alive of [b]this generation;
and none of them are lost; and in
them I have fulness of [c]joy.
32 But behold, it [a]sorroweth me
because of the [b]fourth generation
from this generation, for they are
led away captive by him even as
was the [c]son of perdition; for they
will sell me for silver and for gold,
and for that which [d]moth doth
corrupt and which thieves can break
through and steal. And in that day
will I visit them, even in turning
their works upon their own heads.
33 And it came to pass that when
Jesus had ended these sayings he
said unto his disciples: Enter ye in
at the [a]strait gate; for strait is the
gate, and narrow is the way that
leads to life, and few there be that
find it; but wide is the gate, and
broad the way which leads to death,
and many there be that travel therein, until the night cometh, wherein
no man can work.

CHAPTER 28

Nine of the Twelve desire and are promised an inheritance in Christ's kingdom when they die—The Three Nephites desire and are given power over death so as to remain on the earth until Jesus comes again—They are translated and see things not lawful to utter, and they are now ministering among men.

1 AND it came to pass when Jesus had
said these words, he spake unto
his disciples, one by one, saying unto them: What is it that ye [a]desire of

23*a* TG Record Keeping.
b 3 Ne. 26: 16 (16, 18).
25*a* 2 Ne. 33: 15 (10–15); W of M 1: 11.
b Ps. 33: 15 (13–15); 1 Ne. 15: 33 (26–36).
26*a* 3 Ne. 24: 16. TG Book of Life.
27*a* 1 Ne. 12: 10 (9–10); Morm. 3: 19.
b Rev. 20: 4 (4–6).
c 2 Pet. 3: 11. TG Godliness; Jesus Christ, Exemplar; Man, Potential to Become like Heavenly Father.
d Matt. 5: 48; 3 Ne. 12: 48.
28*a* John 16: 10; 20: 17.
29*a* Matt. 7: 7; 3 Ne. 14: 7.
30*a* John 17: 12.
31*a* 3 Ne. 9: 13 (11–13); 10: 12.
b 3 Ne. 28: 23.
c TG Joy.
32*a* Gen. 6: 6; 3 Ne. 17: 14.
b 1 Ne. 12: 11 (11–12); 2 Ne. 26: 9 (9–10); Alma 45: 12 (10, 12); Hel. 13: 6 (5–19).
c John 17: 12; 3 Ne. 29: 7.
d Matt. 6: 19; 3 Ne. 13: 19 (19–21).
33*a* Matt. 7: 13 (13–14); Luke 13: 24; 3 Ne. 14: 13; D&C 22: 4 (1–4).
28 1*a* 2 Chr. 1: 7(7–12); D&C 7: 1 (1–8).

[A.D. 34—35]

me, after that I am gone to the
Father?
2 And they all spake, save it were
three, saying: We desire that after
we have lived unto the age of man,
that our ministry, wherein thou
hast called us, may have an end, that
we may speedily come unto thee in
thy kingdom.
3 And he said unto them: Blessed
are ye because ye desired this thing
of me; therefore, after that ye are
[a]seventy and two years old ye shall
come unto me in my [b]kingdom; and
with me ye shall find [c]rest.
4 And when he had spoken unto
them, he turned himself unto the
three, and said unto them: What
will ye that I should do unto you,
when I am gone unto the Father?
5 And they sorrowed in their hearts,
for they durst not speak unto him
the thing which they desired.
6 And he said unto them: Behold,
I [a]know your thoughts, and ye have
desired the thing which [b]John,
my beloved, who was with me in
my ministry, before that I was lifted
up by the Jews, desired of me.
7 Therefore, more blessed are ye,
for ye shall [a]never taste of [b]death;
but ye shall live to behold all the
doings of the Father unto the
children of men, even until all things
shall be fulfilled according to the
will of the Father, when I shall come
in my glory with the [c]powers of
heaven.
8 And ye shall never endure the
pains of death; but when I shall
come in my glory ye shall be changed
in the twinkling of an eye from
[a]mortality to [b]immortality; and
then shall ye be blessed in the kingdom of my Father.
9 And again, ye shall not have pain
while ye shall dwell in the flesh,
neither sorrow save it be for the [a]sins
of the world; and all *this* will I do
because of the thing which ye have
desired of me, for ye have desired
that ye might [b]bring the souls of
men unto me, while the world shall
stand.
10 And for this cause ye shall have
[a]fulness of joy; and ye shall sit down
in the kingdom of my Father; yea,
your joy shall be full, even as the
Father hath given me fulness of joy;
and ye shall be even as I am, and I
am even as the Father; and the
Father and I are [b]one;
11 And the [a]Holy Ghost beareth
record of the Father and me; and the
Father giveth the Holy Ghost unto
the children of men, because of me.
12 And it came to pass that when
Jesus had spoken these words, he
touched every one of them with his
finger save it were the [a]three who
were to tarry, and then he departed.
13 And behold, the heavens were
opened, and they were [a]caught up
into heaven, and saw and heard unspeakable things.
14 And it was [a]forbidden them that
they should utter; neither was it
given unto them [b]power that they
could utter the things which they
saw and heard;
15 And whether they were in the
body or out of the body, they could
not tell; for it did seem unto them
like a [a]transfiguration of them, that

3*a* 4 Ne. 1: 14.
b TG Election.
c TG Rest.
6*a* Amos 4: 13; Alma 18: 32.
b John 21: 22 (21–23); D&C 7: 3 (1–8).
7*a* 4 Ne. 1: 37 (14, 37); Morm. 8: 10 (10–12); Ether 12: 17.
b Luke 9: 27. TG Translated Beings.
c 3 Ne. 20: 22.
8*a* 3 Ne. 28: 36 (36–40). TG Mortality.
b TG Immortality.
9*a* 4 Ne. 1: 44; Morm. 8: 10.
b Philip. 1: 24 (23–24); 3 Ne. 28: 27; D&C 7: 5 (1–8).
10*a* John 16: 15; D&C 76: 59; 84: 38 (37–38).
b Deut. 6: 4; Gal. 3: 20; 2 Ne. 31: 21; 3 Ne. 11: 27 (27–28, 36); Morm. 7: 7; D&C 20: 28.
11*a* 2 Ne. 31: 18 (17–21); 3 Ne. 11: 32; Ether 5: 4; Moses 6: 66.
12*a* 4 Ne. 1: 14 (14, 37); Morm. 1: 13.
13*a* 2 Cor. 12: 4 (2–4).
14*a* D&C 76: 115.
b 3 Ne. 19: 32; 26: 14.
15*a* Moses 1: 11. TG Transfiguration.

they were changed from this body of flesh into an immortal state, that they could *behold* the things of God.

16 But it came to pass that they did again minister upon the face of the earth; nevertheless they did not minister of the things which they had heard and seen, because of the commandment which was given them in heaven.

17 And now, whether they were mortal or immortal, from the day of their transfiguration, I know not;

18 But this much I know, according to the record which hath been given—they did go forth upon the face of the land, and did minister unto all the people, uniting as many to the church as would believe in their preaching; baptizing them, and as many as were baptized did receive the Holy Ghost.

19 And they were cast *into* prison by them who did not belong to the church. And the [a]prisons could not hold them, for they were rent in twain.

20 And they were cast down into the earth; but they did smite the earth with the word of God, insomuch that by his [a]power they were delivered out of the depths of the earth; and therefore they could not dig pits sufficient to hold them.

21 And thrice they were cast into a [a]furnace and received no harm.

22 And twice were they cast into a [a]den of wild beasts; and behold they did play with the beasts as a child with a suckling lamb, and received no harm.

23 And it came to pass that thus they did go forth among all the people of Nephi, and did preach the [a]gospel of Christ unto all people upon the face of the land; and they were converted unto the Lord, and were united unto the church of Christ, *and thus* the people of [b]that generation were blessed, according to the word of Jesus.

24 And now I, [a]Mormon, make an end of speaking concerning these things for a time.

25 Behold, I was about to write the [a]names of those who were never to taste of death, but the Lord forbade; therefore I write them not, for they are hid from the world.

26 But behold, [a]I have seen them, and they have ministered unto me.

27 And behold they will be [a]among the Gentiles, and the Gentiles shall know them not.

28 They will also be among the Jews, and the Jews shall know them not.

29 And it shall come to pass, when the Lord seeth fit in his wisdom that they shall minister unto all the [a]scattered tribes of Israel, and unto all nations, kindreds, tongues and people, and shall bring out of them unto Jesus many souls, that their desire may be fulfilled, and also because of the convincing power of God which is in them.

30 And they are as the [a]angels of God, and if they shall pray unto the Father in the name of Jesus they can show themselves unto whatsoever man it seemeth them good.

31 Therefore, great and marvelous works shall be wrought by them, before the [a]great and coming day when all people must surely stand before the judgment-seat of Christ;

32 Yea even among the Gentiles shall there be a [a]great and marvelous work wrought by them, before that judgment day.

33 And if ye had [a]all the scriptures which give an account of all the

19*a* Acts 16:26; Alma 14:27 (26–28); 4 Ne. 1:30; Morm. 8:24.
20*a* 1 Ne. 7:17 (17–18); Jacob 4:6.
21*a* Dan. 3:25; 4 Ne. 1:32; Morm. 8:24.
22*a* Dan. 6:16 (16–27); 4 Ne. 1:33.
23*a* TG Gospel.
b 3 Ne. 27:31 (30–31).
24*a* 3 Ne. 26:12.
25*a* 3 Ne. 19:4.
26*a* Morm. 8:11.
27*a* 3 Ne. 28:9.
29*a* TG Israel, Scattering of; Israel, Ten Lost Tribes of.
30*a* TG Angels.
31*a* Mal. 4:5; Hel. 12:25; 3 Ne. 26:4; Morm. 9:2.
32*a* 2 Ne. 25:17.
33*a* 3 Ne. 26:8 (6–12).

marvelous works of Christ, ye would, according to the words of Christ, know that these things must surely come.

34 And wo be unto him that will [a]not hearken unto the words of Jesus, and also to them whom he hath chosen and [b]sent among them; for whoso [c]receiveth not the words of Jesus and the words of those whom he hath sent receiveth not him; and therefore he will not receive them at the last day;

35 And it would be better for them if they had not been born. For do ye suppose that ye can get rid of the justice of an [a]offended God, who hath been [b]trampled under feet of men, that thereby salvation might come?

36 And now behold, as I spake concerning those whom the Lord hath chosen, yea, even three who were caught up into the heavens, that I knew not whether they were [a]cleansed from [b]mortality to immortality—

37 But behold, since I wrote, I have inquired of the Lord, and he hath made it manifest unto me that there must needs be a change wrought upon their bodies, or else it needs be that they must taste of death;

38 Therefore, that they might not taste of death there was a [a]change wrought upon their bodies, that they might not [b]suffer pain nor sorrow save it were for the sins of the world.

39 Now this change was not equal to that which shall take place at the last day; but there was a change wrought upon them, insomuch that Satan could have no power over them, that he could not [a]tempt them; and they were [b]sanctified in the flesh, that they were [c]holy, and that the powers of the earth could not hold them.

40 And in this state they were to remain until the judgment day of Christ; and at that day they were to receive a greater change, and to be received into the kingdom of the Father to go no more out, but to dwell with God eternally in the heavens.

CHAPTER 29

The coming forth of the Book of Mormon is a sign that the Lord has commenced to gather Israel and fulfill his covenants—Those who reject his latter-day revelations and gifts shall be cursed.

AND now behold, I say unto you that when the Lord shall see fit, in his wisdom, that these sayings shall [a]come unto the Gentiles according to his word, then ye may know that the [b]covenant which the Father hath made with the children of Israel, concerning their restoration to the [c]lands of their inheritance, is already beginning to be fulfilled.

2 And ye may know that the words of the Lord, which have been spoken by the holy prophets, shall all be fulfilled; and ye need not say that the Lord [a]delays his coming unto the children of Israel.

3 And ye need not imagine in your hearts that the words which have been spoken are vain, for behold, the Lord will remember his covenant which he hath made unto his people of the house of Israel.

4 And when ye shall see these sayings coming forth among you, then ye need not any longer spurn at the doings of the Lord, for the [a]sword of his [b]justice is in his right hand;

34*a* Ether 4: 8 (8–12).
b Matt. 10: 5 (5–42).
c TG Prophets, Rejection of.
35*a* TG Blasphemy.
b Hel. 12: 2.
36*a* TG Purification.
b 3 Ne. 28: 8 (8–9). TG Immortality; Mortality.
38*a* TG Translated Beings.
b TG Suffering.
39*a* TG Temptation; Test, Try, Prove.
b TG Sanctification.
c TG Holiness.
29 1*a* 2 Ne. 30: 3 (3–8); Morm. 3: 17.
b Ezek. 20: 37; Morm. 5: 14 (14, 20).
c TG Lands of Inheritance.
2*a* Matt. 24: 48; Luke 12: 45.
4*a* 3 Ne. 20: 20.
b TG Justice.

[A.D. 34—35]

and behold, at that day, if ye shall
spurn at his doings he will cause that
it shall soon overtake you.
5 [a]Wo unto him that [b]spurneth at
the doings of the Lord; yea, wo unto
him that shall [c]deny the Christ and
his works!
6 Yea, [a]wo unto him that shall deny
the revelations of the Lord, and that
shall say the Lord no longer worketh
by revelation, or by prophecy, or
by [b]gifts, or by tongues, or by heal-
ings, or by the power of the Holy
Ghost!
7 Yea, and wo unto him that shall
say at that day, to get [a]gain, that
there can be [b]no miracle wrought by
Jesus Christ; for he that doeth this
shall become [c]like unto the son of
perdition, for whom there was no
mercy, according to the word of
Christ!
8 Yea, and ye need not any longer
[a]hiss, nor [b]spurn, nor make game of
the [c]Jews, nor any of the remnant of
the house of Israel; for behold, the
Lord remembereth his covenant
unto them, and he will do unto them
according to that which he hath
sworn.
9 Therefore ye need not suppose
that ye can turn the right hand of
the Lord unto the left, that he may
not execute judgment unto the fulfilling of the covenant which he hath
made unto the house of Israel.

CHAPTER 30

The latter-day Gentiles are commanded to repent and come unto Christ and be numbered with the house of Israel.

HEARKEN, O ye Gentiles, and hear
the words of Jesus Christ, the Son
of the living God, which he hath
[a]commanded me that I should speak
concerning you, for, behold he commandeth me that I should write,
saying:
2 Turn, all ye [a]Gentiles, from your
wicked ways; and [b]repent of your
evil doings, of your [c]lyings and
deceivings, and of your whoredoms,
and of your secret abominations,
and your idolatries, and of your
[d]murders, and your [e]priestcrafts,
and your [f]envyings, and your strifes,
and from all your wickedness and
abominations, and come unto me,
and be baptized in my name, that ye
may receive a remission of your sins,
and be filled with the Holy Ghost,
that ye may be [g]numbered with my
people who are of the house of Israel.

5*a* 2 Ne. 28: 15; Morm. 9: 26.
b Morm. 8: 17; Ether 4: 8 (8–10).
c Matt. 10: 33 (32–33); Moro. 1: 3.
6*a* Morm. 9: 7 (7–11, 15).
b TG Holy Ghost, Gifts of.
7*a* TG Priestcraft.
b 2 Ne. 28: 6 (4–6); Morm. 8: 26; 9: 15 (15–26).
c 2 Ne. 9: 9; 3 Ne. 27: 32. TG Sons of Perdition.
8*a* 1 Ne. 19: 14.
b 2 Ne. 29: 5 (4–5). TG Backbiting.
c TG Israel, Judah, People of.
30 1*a* 3 Ne. 5: 13 (12–13).
2*a* Rom. 15: 10 (8–21).
b TG Repentance.
c Alma 16: 18; 3 Ne. 21: 19 (19–21).
d 3 Ne. 16: 10; Morm. 8: 31.
e TG Priestcraft.
f TG Envy.
g Gal. 3: 29 (27–29); 2 Ne. 10: 18 (18–19); 3 Ne. 21: 22 (22–25); Abr. 2: 10.

[A.D. 34—35]

FOURTH NEPHI

THE BOOK OF NEPHI

WHO IS THE SON OF NEPHI—ONE OF THE DISCIPLES OF JESUS CHRIST

An account of the people of Nephi, according to his record.

The Nephites and the Lamanites are all converted to the Church of Christ—They have all things in common, work miracles, and prosper in the land—After two centuries divisions, evils, false churches, and persecutions arise—After three hundred years both the Nephites and the Lamanites are wicked—Ammaron hides up the sacred records.

AND it came to pass that the thirty and fourth year passed away, and also the thirty and fifth, and behold the disciples of Jesus had formed a church of Christ in all the lands round about. And as many as did come unto them, and did truly repent of their sins, were [a]baptized in the name of Jesus; and they did also receive the Holy Ghost.

2 And it came to pass in the thirty and sixth year, the people were all converted unto the Lord, upon all the face of the land, both Nephites and Lamanites, and there were no contentions and disputations among them, and every man did deal justly one with another.

3 And they had [a]all things common among them; therefore there were not rich and poor, bond and free, but they were all made free, and partakers of the heavenly [b]gift.

4 And it came to pass that the thirty and seventh year passed away also, and there still continued to be [a]peace in the land.

5 And there were great and marvelous works wrought by the disciples of Jesus, insomuch that they did [a]heal the sick, and [b]raise the dead, and cause the lame to walk, and the blind to receive their sight, and the deaf to hear; and all manner of [c]miracles did they work among the children of men; and in nothing did they work miracles save it were in the name of Jesus.

6 And thus did the thirty and eighth year pass away, and also the thirty and ninth, and forty and first, and the forty and second, yea, even until forty and nine years had passed away, and also the fifty and first, and the fifty and second; yea, and even until fifty and nine years had passed away.

7 And the Lord did prosper them exceedingly in the land; yea, insomuch that they did build cities again where there had been cities burned.

8 Yea, even that great [a]city Zarahemla did they cause to be built again.

9 But there were many cities which had been [a]sunk, and waters came up in the stead thereof; therefore these cities could not be renewed.

10 And now, behold, it came to pass that the people of Nephi did wax strong, and did multiply exceedingly fast, and became an exceedingly [a]fair and delightsome people.

---

1 1*a* 3 Ne. 26: 17.
3*a* Jacob 2: 19 (17–19); Mosiah 4: 26; 18: 27 (19–29); Alma 16: 16; 3 Ne. 12: 42; 26: 19. TG Consecration.
b TG God, Gifts of.
4*a* TG Peace.
5*a* TG Healing.
b TG Death, Power over.
c John 14: 12 (12–14). TG Miracle.
8*a* 3 Ne. 8: 8 (8, 24).
9*a* 3 Ne. 9: 4 (4, 7).
10*a* 1 Ne. 13: 15; 2 Ne. 5: 21; Morm. 9: 6.

11 And they were married, and given in marriage, and were blessed according to the multitude of the [a]promises which the Lord had made unto them.

12 And they did not walk any more after the [a]performances and [b]ordinances of the [c]law of Moses; but they did walk after the commandments which they had received from their Lord and their God, continuing in [d]fasting and prayer, and in meeting together oft both to pray and to hear the word of the Lord.

13 And it came to pass that there was no contention among all the people, in all the land; but there were mighty miracles wrought among the disciples of Jesus.

14 And it came to pass that the *seventy and first year passed away, and also the seventy and second year, yea, and in fine, till the seventy and ninth year had passed away; yea, even an hundred years had passed away, and the [a]disciples of Jesus, whom he had chosen, had all gone to the [b]paradise of God, save it were the [c]three who should tarry; and there were other [d]disciples [e]ordained in their stead; and also many of that [f]generation had passed away.

15 And it came to pass that there was no [a]contention in the land, because of the [b]love of God which did dwell in the hearts of the people.

16 And there were no [a]envyings, nor [b]strifes, nor [c]tumults, nor whoredoms, nor lyings, nor murders, nor any manner of [d]lasciviousness; and surely there could not be a [e]happier people among all the people who had been created by the hand of God.

17 There were no robbers, nor murderers, neither were there Lamanites, nor any manner of -ites; but they were in [a]one, the children of Christ, and heirs to the kingdom of God.

18 And how blessed were they! For the Lord did bless them in all their doings; yea, even they were blessed and prospered until †an hundred and ten years had passed away; and the first generation from Christ had passed away, and there was no contention in all the land.

19 And it came to pass that [a]Nephi, he that kept this last record, (and he kept it upon the [b]plates of Nephi) died, and his son Amos kept it in his stead; and he kept it upon the plates of Nephi also.

20 And he kept it eighty and four years, and there was still peace in the land, save it were a small part of the people who had revolted from the church and taken upon them the name of Lamanites; therefore there began to be [a]Lamanites again in the land.

21 And it came to pass that [a]Amos died also, (and it was an hundred and ninety and four years from the coming of Christ) and his son Amos kept the record in his stead; and he also kept it upon the plates of Nephi; and it was also written in the book of Nephi, which is this book.

22 And it came to pass that ‡two hundred years had passed away; and the second generation had all passed away save it were a few.

23 And now I, Mormon, would that ye should know that the people had multiplied, insomuch that they were spread upon all the face of the land,

---

11*a* TG Promise.
12*a* 2 Ne. 25: 30.
b TG Ordinance.
c 3 Ne. 9: 19; 15: 4 (2–8). TG Law of Moses.
d Moro. 6: 5; D&C 88: 76.
14*a* 3 Ne. 28: 3; Morm. 3: 19.
b TG Paradise.
c 3 Ne. 28: 12. TG Translated Beings.
d TG Apostles.
e TG Priesthood, History of.
f 1 Ne. 12: 12.
15*a* TG Contention.
b TG God, Love of.
16*a* TG Envy.
b TG Strife.
c TG Rioting and Reveling.
d TG Lust.
e Prov. 14: 34; Mosiah 2: 41; Alma 50: 23. TG Happiness.
17*a* John 17: 21 (21–23). TG Zion.
19*a* 3 Ne. 23: 7.
b 3 Ne. 26: 7.
20*a* 3 Ne. 10: 18; Morm. 1: 9.
21*a* 4 Ne. 1: 47.

[*A.D. 72 †A.D. 111 ‡A.D. 201]

and that they had become exceedingly [a]rich, because of their prosperity in Christ.
24 And now, in this *two hundred
and first year there began to be
among them those who were lifted
up in [a]pride, such as the wearing of
costly apparel, and all manner of
fine pearls, and of the fine things of
the world.
25 And from that time forth they
did have their goods and their
substance no more [a]common among
them.
26 And they began to be divided
into classes; and they began to build
up [a]churches unto themselves to get
[b]gain, and began to deny the true
church of Christ.
27 And it came to pass that when
†two hundred and ten years had
passed away there were many
churches in the land; yea, there
were many churches which professed
to know the Christ, and yet they did
[a]deny the more parts of his gospel,
insomuch that they did receive all
manner of wickedness, and did
administer that which was sacred
unto him to whom it had been [b]for-
bidden because of unworthiness.
28 And this church did multiply
exceedingly because of iniquity, and
because of the power of [a]Satan who
did get hold upon their [b]hearts.
29 And again, there was another
church which denied the Christ; and
they did [a]persecute the true [b]church
of Christ, because of their humility
and their belief in Christ; and they
did despise them because of the
many miracles which were wrought
among them.
30 Therefore they did exercise
power and authority over the
disciples of Jesus who did tarry with
them, and they did cast them into
[a]prison; but by the power of the
word of God, which was in them,
the prisons were rent in twain, and
they went forth doing mighty
miracles among them.
31 Nevertheless, and notwithstanding all these miracles, the
people did harden their hearts, and
did seek to kill them, even as the
Jews at Jerusalem sought to kill
Jesus, according to his word.
32 And they did cast them into
[a]furnaces of [b]fire, and they came
forth receiving no harm.
33 And they also cast them into
[a]dens of wild beasts, and they did
play with the wild beasts even as a
child with a lamb; and they did come
forth from among them, receiving
no harm.
34 Nevertheless, the people did
harden their hearts, for they were
led by many priests and [a]false
prophets to build up many churches,
and to do all manner of iniquity.
And they did [b]smite upon the people
of Jesus; but the people of Jesus did
not smite again. And thus they did
dwindle in unbelief and wickedness,
from year to year, even until two
hundred and thirty years had passed
away.
35 And now it came to pass in this
year, yea, in the ‡two hundred and
thirty and first year, there was a
great division among the people.
36 And it came to pass that in this
year there arose a people who were
called the [a]Nephites, and they were
true believers in Christ; and among
them there were those who were
called by the Lamanites—Jacobites,
and Josephites, and [b]Zoramites;
37 Therefore the true believers in
Christ, and the true worshipers of

23*a* TG Treasure.
24*a* TG Pride; Selfishness.
25*a* TG Consecration.
26*a* 1 Ne. 22: 23; 2 Ne. 28: 3 (3–32); Morm. 8: 28 (28, 32–38).
b Ezek. 22: 27; D&C 10: 56. TG Priestcraft.
27*a* TG Apostasy of Individuals.
b 3 Ne. 18: 28 (28–29).
28*a* TG Devil, Church of.
b TG Hardheartedness.
29*a* TG Persecution.
b TG Jesus Christ, Head of the Church.
30*a* 3 Ne. 28: 19 (19–20).
32*a* 3 Ne. 28: 21.
b Dan. 3: 27.
33*a* 3 Ne. 28: 22.
34*a* TG False Prophets.
b 3 Ne. 6: 13; 12: 39; D&C 98: 23 (23–27).
36*a* Morm. 1: 8.
b Jacob 1: 13.

[*A.D. 201 †A.D. 211 ‡A.D. 231]

Christ, (among whom were the [a]three disciples of Jesus who should tarry) were called Nephites, and Jacobites, and Josephites, and Zoramites.

38 And it came to pass that they who rejected the gospel were called Lamanites, and Lemuelites, and Ishmaelites; and they did not dwindle in [a]unbelief, but they did [b]wilfully rebel against the gospel of Christ; and they did teach their children that they should not believe, even as their fathers, from the beginning, did dwindle.

39 And it was because of the wickedness and abomination of their fathers, even as it was in the beginning. And they were [a]taught to hate the children of God, even as the Lamanites were taught to [b]hate the children of Nephi from the beginning.

40 And it came to pass that *two hundred and forty and four years had passed away, and thus were the affairs of the people. And the [a]more wicked part of the people did wax strong, and became exceedingly more numerous than were the people of God.

41 And they did still continue to build up churches unto themselves, and adorn them with all manner of precious things. And thus did two hundred and fifty years pass away, and also two hundred and sixty years.

42 And it came to pass that the wicked part of the people began again to build up the secret oaths and [a]combinations of Gadianton.

43 And also the people who were called the people of Nephi began to be proud in their hearts, because of their exceeding riches, and become [a]vain like unto their brethren, the Lamanites.

44 And from this time the disciples began to sorrow for the [a]sins of the world.

45 And it came to pass that when three hundred years had passed away, both the people of Nephi and the Lamanites had become exceedingly wicked one like unto another.

46 And it came to pass that the robbers of [a]Gadianton did spread over all the face of the land; and there were none that were righteous save it were the disciples of Jesus. And gold and silver did they lay up in store in abundance, and did [b]traffic in all manner of traffic.

47 And it came to pass that after †three hundred and five years had passed away, (and the people did still remain in wickedness) [a]Amos died; and his brother, Ammaron, did keep the record in his stead.

48 And it came to pass that when ‡three hundred and twenty years had passed away, [a]Ammaron, being constrained by the Holy Ghost, did [b]hide up the [c]records which were [d]sacred—yea, even all the sacred records which had been handed down from generation to generation, which were sacred—even until the three hundred and twentieth year from the coming of Christ.

49 And he did hide them up unto the Lord, that they might [a]come again unto the remnant of the house of Jacob, according to the prophecies and the promises of the Lord. And thus is the end of the record of Ammaron.

37*a* 3 Ne. 28: 7; Morm. 8: 10 (10–12).
38*a* TG Unbelief, Unbelievers.
b Josh. 22: 18; Morm. 1: 16.
39*a* Mosiah 10: 17.
b TG Hate; Malice.
40*a* Hel. 5: 2.
42*a* TG Secret Combinations.
43*a* Hel. 16: 22.
44*a* Eccl. 3: 16 (16–17); 3 Ne. 28: 9; Morm. 8: 10 (9–10).
46*a* Morm. 2: 8; Ether 8: 20.
b Mosiah 24: 7; Ether 10: 22.
47*a* 4 Ne. 1: 21.
48*a* Morm. 1: 2.
b Morm. 2: 17.
c TG Scriptures, Preservation of.
d Hel. 3: 15 (13, 15–16).
49*a* Enos 1: 13; Morm. 5: 9.

[*A.D. 245 †A.D. 306 ‡A.D. 321]

THE BOOK OF MORMON

CHAPTER 1

Ammaron instructs Mormon concerning the sacred records—War commences between the Nephites and the Lamanites—The Three Nephites are taken away—Wickedness, unbelief, sorceries, and witchcraft prevail.

AND now I, Mormon, make a
[a]record of the things which I
have both seen and heard, and
call it the [b]Book of Mormon.
2 And about the time that [a]Ammaron
hid up the records unto the
Lord, he came unto me, (I being
about ten years of age, and I began
to be [b]learned somewhat after the
manner of the learning of my people)
and Ammaron said unto me: I
perceive that thou art a [c]sober child,
and art quick to observe;
3 Therefore, when ye are about
twenty and four years old I would
that ye should remember the things
that ye have observed concerning
this people; and when ye are of that
age go to the [a]land Antum, unto a
hill which shall be called [b]Shim; and
there have I deposited unto the Lord
all the sacred engravings concerning
this people.
4 And behold, ye shall take the
[a]plates of Nephi unto yourself, and
the remainder shall ye leave in the
place where they are; and ye shall
engrave on the plates of Nephi all
the things that ye have observed
concerning this people.
5 And I, Mormon, being a descendant
of [a]Nephi, (and my father's
name was Mormon) I remembered
the things which Ammaron commanded
me.
6 And it came to pass that I, being
*eleven years old, was carried by
my father into the land southward,
even to the land of Zarahemla.
7 The whole face of the land had
become covered with buildings, and
the people were as numerous almost,
as it were the sand of the sea.
8 And it came to pass in this year
there began to be a war between the
[a]Nephites, who consisted of the
Nephites and the Jacobites and the
Josephites and the Zoramites; and
this war was between the Nephites,
and the Lamanites and the Lemuelites
and the Ishmaelites.
9 Now the [a]Lamanites and the
Lemuelites and the Ishmaelites
were called Lamanites, and the two
parties were Nephites and Lamanites.
10 And it came to pass that the
war began to be among them in the
borders of Zarahemla, by the waters
of Sidon.
11 And it came to pass that the
Nephites had gathered together a
great number of men, even to
exceed the number of thirty thousand.
And it came to pass that they
did have in this same year a number
of [a]battles, in which the Nephites
did beat the Lamanites and did slay
many of them.
12 And it came to pass that the
Lamanites withdrew their design,
and there was peace settled in the
land; and peace did remain for the
space of about four years, that there
was no bloodshed.
13 But wickedness did prevail upon
the face of the whole land, insomuch
that the Lord did take away his
[a]beloved disciples, and the work of
miracles and of healing did cease
because of the iniquity of the people.
14 And there were no [a]gifts from

1 1*a* 3 Ne. 5: 11 (11–18); Morm. 8: 5.
b W of M 1: 5; Morm. 5: 9.
2*a* 4 Ne. 1: 48 (47–49).
b Enos 1: 1; Mosiah 1: 3 (3–5).
c TG Sobriety, Sober, Soberness; Trustworthiness.
3*a* Morm. 2: 17.
b Morm. 4: 23; Ether 9: 3.
4*a* W of M 1: 1 (1, 11); 3 Ne. 5: 10 (9–12); Morm. 2: 17 (17–18); 8: 5 (1, 4–5, 14).
5*a* 3 Ne. 5: 20 (12, 20).
8*a* 4 Ne. 1: 36.
9*a* 4 Ne. 1: 20.
11*a* 2 Ne. 1: 12; Morm. 4: 1 (1–23).
13*a* 3 Ne. 28: 12 (2, 12).
14*a* 1 Sam. 3: 1.

[*About A.D. 322]

the Lord, and the [b]Holy Ghost did
not come upon any, because of their
wickedness and [c]unbelief.
15 And I, *being [a]fifteen years of
age and being somewhat of a [b]sober
mind, therefore I was [c]visited of the
Lord, and [d]tasted and knew of the
goodness of Jesus.
16 And I did endeavor to preach
unto this people, but my mouth was
shut, and I was forbidden that I
should preach unto them; for behold
they had [a]wilfully rebelled against
their God; and the beloved disciples
were [b]taken away out of the land,
because of their iniquity.
17 But I did remain among them,
but I was forbidden to [a]preach unto
them, because of the hardness of
their hearts; and because of the
hardness of their hearts the land
was [b]cursed for their sake.
18 And these Gadianton robbers,
who were among the Lamanites, did
infest the land, insomuch that the
inhabitants thereof began to [a]hide
up their [b]treasures in the earth; and
they became slippery, because the
Lord had cursed the land, that they
could not hold them, nor retain
them again.
19 And it came to pass that there
were [a]sorceries, and witchcrafts,
and magics; and the power of the
evil one was wrought upon all the
face of the land, even unto the fulfilling
of all the words of Abinadi,
and also [b]Samuel the Lamanite.

CHAPTER 2

Mormon leads the Nephite armies—Blood and carnage sweep the land—The Nephites lament and mourn with the sorrowing of the damned—Their day of grace is passed—Mormon obtains the plates of Nephi—Wars continue.

AND it came to pass in that same
year there began to be a war again
between the Nephites and the
Lamanites. And notwithstanding I
being [a]young, was large in stature;
therefore the people of Nephi
appointed me that I should be
their leader, or the leader of their
armies.
2 Therefore it came to pass that
†in my sixteenth year I did go forth
at the head of an army of the
Nephites, against the Lamanites;
therefore three hundred and twenty
and six years had passed away.
3 And it came to pass that in the
three hundred and twenty and
seventh year the Lamanites did
come upon us with [a]exceedingly
great power, insomuch that they
did frighten my armies; therefore
they would not fight, and they began
to retreat towards the [b]north
countries.
4 And it came to pass that we did
come to the city of Angola, and we
did take possession of the city, and
make preparations to defend ourselves
against the Lamanites. And
it came to pass that we did [a]fortify
the city with our might; but notwithstanding
all our fortifications
the Lamanites did come upon us and
did drive us out of the city.
5 And they did also drive us forth
out of the land of David.
6 And we marched forth and came
to the land of Joshua, which was in
the borders west by the seashore.
7 And it came to pass that we did
gather in our people as fast as it were

14*b* TG Holy Ghost, Loss of.
c TG Unbelief, Unbelievers.
15*a* Morm. 2: 1 (1–2).
b TG Sobriety.
c Ex. 3: 16; 2 Ne. 4: 26; Alma 9: 21.
d Ps. 34: 8.
16*a* 4 Ne. 1: 38. TG Rebellion.
b Morm. 8: 10.
17*a* Micah 3: 6 (5–7).
b 2 Ne. 1: 7; Alma 45: 16 (10–14, 16); Ether 2: 11 (8–12).
18*a* Hel. 12: 18; Morm. 2: 10 (10–14); Ether 14: 1 (1–2).
b Hel. 13: 18–23, 30–37. TG Treasure.
19*a* TG Sorcery.
b Morm. 2: 10 (10–15).
2 1*a* Morm. 1: 15 (12, 15–16).
3*a* Morm. 4: 13 (13–17); 5: 6.
b Alma 50: 11; Morm. 2: 29.
4*a* 3 Ne. 3: 14 (14, 25); Morm. 2: 21.

[*About A.D. 326
†A.D. 327—328]

possible, that we might get them together in [a]one body.

8 But behold, the land was [a]filled with [b]robbers and with Lamanites; and notwithstanding the great destruction which hung over my people, they did not repent of their evil doings; therefore there was blood and carnage spread throughout all the face of the land, both on the part of the Nephites and also on the part of the Lamanites; and it was one complete revolution throughout all the face of the land.

9 And now, the Lamanites had a king, and his name was [a]Aaron; and he came against us with an army of forty and four thousand. And behold, I withstood him with forty and two thousand. And it came to pass that I beat him with my army that he fled before me. And behold, all this was done, and *three hundred and thirty years had passed away.

10 And it came to pass that the Nephites began to repent of their iniquity, and began to cry even as had been prophesied by Samuel the prophet; for behold no man could [a]keep that which was his own, for the thieves, and the robbers, and the murderers, and the magic art, and the witchcraft which was in the land.

11 Thus there began to be a [a]mourning and a lamentation in all the land because of these things, and more especially among the people of Nephi.

12 And it came to pass that when I, Mormon, saw their lamentation and their [a]mourning and their sorrow before the Lord, my heart did begin to rejoice within me, knowing the mercies and the long-suffering of the Lord, therefore supposing that he would be merciful unto them that they would [b]again become a righteous people.

13 But behold this my joy was vain, for their [a]sorrowing was not unto repentance, because of the goodness of God; but it was rather the [b]sorrowing of the [c]damned, because the Lord would not always suffer them to take [d]happiness in sin.

14 And they did not come unto Jesus with broken [a]hearts and contrite spirits, but they did [b]curse God, and wish to die. Nevertheless they would struggle with the sword for their lives.

15 And it came to pass that my sorrow did return unto me again, and I saw that the [a]day of [b]grace [c]was passed with them, both temporally and spiritually; for I saw thousands of them hewn down in open [d]rebellion against their God, and heaped up as [e]dung upon the face of the land. And thus †three hundred and forty and four years had passed away.

16 And it came to pass that in the three hundred and forty and fifth year the Nephites did begin to flee before the Lamanites; and they were pursued until they came even to the land of Jashon, before it was possible to stop them in their retreat.

17 And now, the city of Jashon was near the [a]land where Ammaron had [b]deposited the records unto the Lord, that they might not be destroyed. And behold I had gone according to the word of Ammaron, and taken the [c]plates of Nephi, and did make a record according to the words of Ammaron.

18 And upon the plates of Nephi I

7*a* 3 Ne. 3: 22 (22–25).
8*a* 3 Ne. 2: 11.
b 4 Ne. 1: 46; Morm. 8: 9; Ether 8: 20.
9*a* Moro. 9: 17.
10*a* Hel. 12: 18; 13: 18 (17–23); Morm. 1: 18 (17–19); Ether 14: 1 (1–2).
11*a* 3 Ne. 12: 4.
12*a* TG Mourning.
b Hel. 11: 9 (8–17).
13*a* 2 Cor. 7: 10; Alma 42: 29.
b Hosea 7: 14; Ether 8: 7.
c TG Damnation.
d Alma 41: 10.
14*a* TG Contrite Heart.
b TG Blasphemy.
15*a* Hel. 13: 38.
b TG Grace.
c Jer. 8: 20.
d TG Rebellion.
e Jer. 8: 2 (1–3).
17*a* Morm. 1: 3 (1–4).
b 4 Ne. 1: 48 (48–49).
c Morm. 8: 5 (1, 4–5, 14).

[*A.D. 331 †A.D. 345]

did make a full account of all the wickedness and abominations; but upon [a]these plates I did forbear to make a full account of their wickedness and abominations, for behold, a continual scene of wickedness and abominations has been before mine eyes ever since I have been sufficient to behold the ways of man.

19 And wo is me because of their wickedness; for my heart has been filled with sorrow because of their wickedness, all my days; nevertheless, I know that I shall be [a]lifted up at the last day.

20 And it came to pass that in this year the people of Nephi again were hunted and driven. And it came to pass that we were driven forth until we had come northward to the land which was called Shem.

21 And it came to pass that we did [a]fortify the city of Shem, and we did gather in our people as much as it were possible, that perhaps we might save them from destruction.

22 And it came to pass in the *three hundred and forty and sixth year they began to come upon us again.

23 And it came to pass that I did speak unto my people, and did urge them with great energy, that they would stand boldly before the Lamanites and [a]fight for their [b]wives, and their children, and their houses, and their homes.

24 And my words did arouse them somewhat to vigor, insomuch that they did not flee from before the Lamanites, but did stand with boldness against them.

25 And it came to pass that we did contend with an army of thirty thousand against an army of fifty thousand. And it came to pass that we did stand before them with such firmness that they did flee from before us.

26 And it came to pass that when they had fled we did pursue them with our armies, and did meet them again, and did [a]beat them; nevertheless the [b]strength of the Lord was not with us; yea, we were left to ourselves, that the Spirit of the Lord did not abide in us; therefore we had become weak like unto our brethren.

27 And my heart did sorrow because of this the great calamity of my people, because of their wickedness and their abominations. But behold, we did go forth against the Lamanites and the robbers of Gadianton, until we had again taken possession of the lands of our inheritance.

28 And the †three hundred and forty and ninth year had passed away. And in the three hundred and fiftieth year we made a treaty with the Lamanites and the robbers of Gadianton, in which we did get the lands of our inheritance divided.

29 And the Lamanites did give unto us the land [a]northward, yea, even to the [b]narrow passage which led into the land southward. And we did give unto the Lamanites all the land southward.

CHAPTER 3

Mormon cries repentance unto the Nephites—They gain a great victory and glory in their own strength—Mormon refuses to lead them, and his prayers for them are without faith—The Book of Mormon invites the twelve tribes of Israel to believe the gospel.

AND it came to pass that the Lamanites did not come to battle again ‡until ten years more had passed away. And behold, I had employed my people, the Nephites, in preparing their lands and their arms against the time of battle.

2 And it came to pass that the Lord did say unto me: Cry unto this

18*a* 3 Ne. 5: 15 (8–20).
19*a* Mosiah 23: 22; Ether 4: 19.
21*a* Morm. 2: 4.
23*a* Alma 58: 12.
b Ether 14: 2.
26*a* Morm. 3: 8 (7–8, 13).
b TG God, Spirit of; Strength.
29*a* Morm. 2: 3.
b Alma 22: 32; 52: 9; 63: 5.

[*A.D. 346 †A.D. 350 ‡A.D. 360]

people—Repent ye, and come unto me, and be ye baptized, and build up again my church, and ye shall be [a]spared.

3 And I did cry unto this people, but it was [a]in vain; and they did [b]not realize that it was the Lord that had spared them, and granted unto them a chance for repentance. And behold they did harden their hearts against the Lord their God.

4 And it came to pass that after this tenth year had passed away, making, in the whole, three hundred and sixty years from the coming of Christ, the king of the Lamanites sent an epistle unto me, which gave unto me to know that they were preparing to come again to battle against us.

5 And it came to pass that I did cause my people that they should gather themselves together at the land [a]Desolation, to a city which was in the borders, by the narrow pass which led into the land [b]southward.

6 And there we did place our armies, that we might stop the armies of the Lamanites, that they might not get possession of any of our lands; therefore we did fortify against them with all our force.

7 And it came to pass that in the three hundred and sixty and first year the Lamanites did come down to the [a]city of Desolation to battle against us; and it came to pass that in that year we did beat them, insomuch that they did return to their own lands again.

8 And in the *three hundred and sixty and second year they did come down [a]again to battle. And we did beat them again, and did slay a great number of them, and their dead were cast into the sea.

9 And now, because of this great thing which my people, the Nephites, had done, they began to [a]boast in their own strength, and began to swear before the heavens that they would avenge themselves of the blood of their brethren who had been slain by their enemies.

10 And they did [a]swear by the heavens, and also by the throne of God, that they [b]would go up to battle against their enemies, and would cut them off from the face of the land.

11 And it came to pass that I, Mormon, did utterly [a]refuse from this time forth to be a commander and a leader of this people, because of their wickedness and abomination.

12 Behold, I had led them, notwithstanding their wickedness I had led them many times to battle, and had loved them, according to the [a]love of God which was in me, with all my heart; and my soul had been poured out in prayer unto my God all the day long for them; nevertheless, it was [b]without faith, because of the [c]hardness of their hearts.

13 And [a]thrice have I delivered them out of the hands of their enemies, and they have repented not of their sins.

14 And when they had sworn by all that had been [a]forbidden them by our Lord and Savior Jesus Christ, that they would go up unto their enemies to battle, and avenge themselves of the blood of their brethren, behold the voice of the Lord came unto me, saying:

15 [a]Vengeance is mine, and I will

3 2*a* Hel. 15: 17 (16–17); Morm. 6: 11 (11–15).
3*a* Morm. 4: 18.
b TG Hardheartedness; Ingratitude.
5*a* Alma 50: 34; Morm. 4: 3 (1–3).
b Ether 9: 31 (31–32); 10: 21.
7*a* 3 Ne. 3: 23; Morm. 4: 2 (2, 19).
8*a* Morm. 2: 26; 3: 13.
9*a* Prov. 14: 16; 2 Ne. 4: 34; Morm. 4: 8.
10*a* TG Swearing.
b Alma 43: 46 (46–47); 48: 14; 3 Ne. 3: 21 (20–21); Morm. 4: 4.
11*a* Morm. 5: 1.
12*a* TG God, Love of.
b James 1: 6; Morm. 5: 2.
c Neh. 9: 16 (16–17).
13*a* Morm. 2: 26; 3: 8 (7–8).
14*a* 3 Ne. 12: 34.
15*a* Isa. 35: 4; Rom. 12: 19. TG Vengeance.

[*A.D. 362]

[b]repay; and because this people repented not after I had delivered them, behold, they shall be cut off from the face of the earth.

16 And it came to pass that I utterly refused to go up against mine enemies; and I did even as the Lord had commanded me; and I did stand as an idle witness to manifest unto the world the things which I saw and heard, according to the manifestations of the Spirit which had testified of things to come.

17 Therefore I write [a]unto you, Gentiles, and also unto you, house of Israel, when the work shall commence, that ye shall be about to prepare to return to the land of your inheritance;

18 Yea, behold, I write unto all the ends of the earth; yea, unto you, twelve tribes of Israel, who shall be [a]judged according to your works by the twelve whom Jesus chose to be his disciples in the land of Jerusalem.

19 And I write also unto the remnant of this people, who shall also be judged by the [a]twelve whom Jesus chose in this land; and they shall be judged by the other twelve whom Jesus chose in the land of Jerusalem.

20 And these things doth the Spirit manifest unto me; therefore I write unto you all. And for this cause I write unto you, that ye may know that ye must all stand before the [a]judgment-seat of Christ, yea, every soul who belongs to the whole human [b]family of Adam; and ye must stand to be judged of your works, whether they be good or evil;

21 And also that ye may [a]believe the gospel of Jesus Christ, which ye shall [b]have among you; and also that the [c]Jews, the covenant people of the Lord, shall have other [d]witness besides him whom they saw and heard, that Jesus, whom they slew, was the [e]very Christ and the very God.

22 And I would that I could persuade [a]all ye ends of the earth to repent and prepare to stand before the judgment-seat of Christ.

CHAPTER 4

War and carnage continue—The wicked punish the wicked—Greater wickedness prevails than ever before in all Israel—Women and children are sacrificed to idols—The Lamanites begin to sweep the Nephites before them.

AND now it came to pass that in the *three hundred and sixty and third year the Nephites did go up with their armies to [a]battle against the Lamanites, out of the land Desolation.

2 And it came to pass that the armies of the Nephites were driven back again to the land of Desolation. And while they were yet weary, a fresh army of the Lamanites did come upon them; and they had a sore battle, insomuch that the Lamanites did take possession of the [a]city Desolation, and did slay many of the Nephites, and did take many prisoners.

3 And the remainder did flee and join the inhabitants of the city Teancum. Now the city Teancum lay in the borders by the seashore; and it was also near the city [a]Desolation.

4 And it was [a]because the armies of the Nephites went up unto the Lamanites that they began to be

---

15*b* 2 Sam. 16: 12 (9–12); D&C 82: 23. TG God, Justice of.
17*a* 2 Ne. 30: 3 (3–8); 3 Ne. 29: 1.
18*a* Matt. 19: 28; Luke 22: 30 (29–30); D&C 29: 12.
19*a* 1 Ne. 12: 10 (9–10); 3 Ne. 27: 27.
20*a* TG Jesus Christ, Judge; Judgment, The Last.
b D&C 27: 11.
21*a* D&C 3: 20.
b 1 Ne. 13: 23 (20–29, 41).
c TG Israel, Judah, People of.
d 2 Ne. 25: 18.
e 2 Ne. 26: 12; Mosiah 7: 27.
22*a* Alma 29: 1.
4 1*a* 2 Ne. 1: 12; Morm. 1: 11 (11–19).
2*a* 3 Ne. 3: 23; Morm. 3: 7.
3*a* Morm. 3: 5.
4*a* Morm. 3: 10 (10–11).

[*A.D. 363]

smitten; for were it not for that, the
Lamanites could have had no power
over them.
5 But, behold, the judgments of
God will overtake the [a]wicked; and
it is by the wicked that the wicked
are [b]punished; for it is the wicked
that stir up the hearts of the children
of men unto bloodshed.
6 And it came to pass that the
Lamanites did make preparations
to come against the city Teancum.
7 And it came to pass in the three
hundred and sixty and fourth year
the Lamanites did come against the
city Teancum, that they might take
possession of the city Teancum also.
8 And it came to pass that they
were repulsed and driven back by
the Nephites. And when the Nephites saw that they had driven the
Lamanites they did again [a]boast of
their own strength; and they went
forth in their own might, and took
possession again of the city Desolation.
9 And now all these things had
been done, and there had been
thousands slain on both sides, both
the Nephites and the Lamanites.
10 And it came to pass that the
three hundred and sixty and sixth
year had passed away, and the
Lamanites came again upon the
Nephites to battle; and yet the
Nephites repented not of the evil
they had done, but persisted in their
wickedness continually.
11 And it is impossible for the
tongue to describe, or for man to
write a perfect description of the
horrible scene of the blood and
carnage which was among the
people, both of the Nephites and of
the Lamanites; and every heart
was hardened, so that they [a]de-
lighted in the shedding of blood
continually.
12 And there never had been so
great [a]wickedness among all the
children of Lehi, nor even among
all the house of Israel, according to
the words of the Lord, as was among
this people.
13 And it came to pass that the
Lamanites did take possession of
the city Desolation, and this because
their [a]number did exceed the number of the Nephites.
14 And they did also march forward against the city Teancum, and
did drive the inhabitants forth out
of her, and did take many prisoners
both women and children, and did
offer them up as [a]sacrifices unto
their idol gods.
15 And it came to pass that in the
three hundred and sixty and seventh
year, the Nephites being angry
because the Lamanites had sacrificed their women and their children,
that they did go against the Lamanites with exceedingly great anger,
insomuch that they did beat again
the Lamanites, and drive them out
of their lands.
16 And the Lamanites did not
come again against the Nephites
until the three hundred and seventy
and fifth year.
17 And in this year they did come
down against the Nephites with all
their powers; and they were not
numbered because of the greatness
of their number.
18 And [a]from this time forth did
the Nephites gain no power over the
Lamanites, but began to be swept
off by them even as a dew before the
sun.
19 And it came to pass that the
Lamanites did come down against
the [a]city Desolation; and there was
an exceedingly sore battle fought in
the land Desolation, in the which
they did beat the Nephites.

5*a* Nahum 1: 3.
b 2 Pet. 2: 12; D&C 63: 33.
8*a* Morm. 3: 9.
11*a* Moro. 9: 5 (5, 23). TG Blood, Shedding of.
12*a* Gen. 6: 5 (5–6); 3 Ne. 9: 9; D&C 112: 23; Moses 7: 36 (36–37); 8: 22 (22, 28–30).
13*a* Morm. 2: 3; 5: 6.
14*a* Jer. 19: 5; Alma 17: 15; Abr. 1: 8 (6–14). TG Idolatry; Sacrifice.
18*a* Morm. 3: 3.
19*a* Morm. 3: 7.

20 And they fled again from before them, and they came to the city Boaz; and there they did stand against the Lamanites with exceeding boldness, insomuch that the Lamanites did not beat them until they had come again the second time.

21 And when they had come the second time, the Nephites were driven and slaughtered with an exceedingly great slaughter; their women and their [a]children were again sacrificed unto idols.

22 And it came to pass that the Nephites did again flee from before them, taking all the inhabitants with them, both in towns and villages.

23 And now I, Mormon, seeing that the Lamanites were about to overthrow the land, therefore I did go to the hill [a]Shim, and did take up all the [b]records which Ammaron had hid up unto the Lord.

CHAPTER 5

Mormon again leads the Nephite armies in battles of blood and carnage—The Book of Mormon shall come forth to convince all Israel that Jesus is the Christ—The Lamanites shall be a dark, filthy, and loathsome people—They shall receive the gospel from the Gentiles in the latter days.

AND it came to pass that I did go forth among the Nephites, and did repent of the [a]oath which I had made that I would no more assist them; and they gave me command again of their armies, for they looked upon me as though I could deliver them from their afflictions.

2 But behold, I was [a]without hope, for I knew the judgments of the Lord which should come upon them; for they repented not of their iniquities, but did struggle for their lives without calling upon that Being who created them.

3 And it came to pass that the Lamanites did come against us as we had fled to the city of Jordan; but behold, they were driven back that they did not take the city at that time.

4 And it came to pass that they came against us again, and we did maintain the city. And there were also other cities which were maintained by the Nephites, which strongholds did cut them off that they could not get into the country which lay before us, to destroy the inhabitants of our land.

5 But it came to pass that whatsoever lands we had passed by, and the inhabitants thereof were not gathered in, were destroyed by the Lamanites, and their towns, and villages, and cities were burned with fire; and thus three hundred and seventy and nine years passed away.

6 And it came to pass that in the three hundred and eightieth year the Lamanites did come again against us to battle, and we did stand against them boldly; but it was all in vain, for so [a]great were their numbers that they did tread the people of the Nephites under their feet.

7 And it came to pass that we did again take to flight, and those whose flight was swifter than the Lamanites' did escape, and those whose flight did not exceed the Lamanites' were swept down and destroyed.

8 And now behold, I, Mormon, do not desire to harrow up the souls of men in casting before them such an awful scene of blood and carnage as was laid before mine eyes; but I, knowing that these things must surely be made known, and that all things which are hid must be [a]revealed upon the house-tops—

9 And also that a knowledge of these things must [a]come unto the remnant of these people, and also

21*a* 2 Kgs. 17: 31.
TG Idolatry.
23*a* Morm. 1: 3; Ether 9: 3.
b W of M 1: 3.
5 1*a* Morm. 3: 11 (11, 16).
TG Vows.
2*a* Morm. 3: 12.
6*a* Morm. 2: 3; 4: 13 (13–17).
8*a* Matt. 10: 26 (26–33); Luke 12: 3; 2 Ne. 27: 11; D&C 1: 3; 88: 108.
9*a* 4 Ne. 1: 49.

[A.D. 375—380]

unto the Gentiles, who the Lord hath
said should [b]scatter this people, and
this people should be counted as
naught among them—therefore [c]I
write a [d]small abridgment, daring
not to give a full account of the
things which I have seen, because
of the commandment which I have
received, and also that ye might not
have too great sorrow because of
the wickedness of this people.
10 And now behold, this I speak
unto their seed, and also to the
Gentiles who have care for the house
of Israel, that realize and know from
whence their blessings come.
11 For I know that such will sorrow
for the calamity of the house of
Israel; yea, they will sorrow for the
destruction of this people; they will
sorrow that this people had not
repented that they might have been
clasped in the arms of Jesus.
12 Now [a]these things are [b]written
unto the [c]remnant of the house of
Jacob; and they are written after
this manner, because it is known of
God that wickedness will not bring
them forth unto them; and they are
to be [d]hid up unto the Lord that they
may come forth in his own due time.
13 And this is the commandment
which I have received; and behold,
they [a]shall come forth according to
the commandment of the Lord,
when he shall see fit, in his wisdom.
14 And behold, they shall go unto
the [a]unbelieving of the [b]Jews; and
for this intent shall they go—that
they may be [c]persuaded that Jesus
is the Christ, the Son of the living
God; that the Father may bring
about, through his most Beloved,
his great and eternal purpose, in
restoring the Jews, or all the house
of Israel, to the [d]land of their inheritance, which the Lord their God
hath given them, unto the fulfilling
of his [e]covenant;
15 And also that the seed of [a]this
people may more fully believe his
gospel, which shall [b]go forth unto
them from the Gentiles; for this
people shall be [c]scattered, and shall
[d]become a dark, a filthy, and a loathsome people, beyond the description
of that which ever hath been a-
mongst us, yea, even that which
hath been among the Lamanites,
and this because of their unbelief
and idolatry.
16 For behold, the Spirit of the
Lord hath already ceased to [a]strive
with their fathers; and they are
without Christ and God in the world;
and they are driven about as [b]chaff
before the wind.
17 They were once a delightsome
people, and they had Christ for their
[a]shepherd; yea, they were led even
by God the Father.
18 But now, behold, they are [a]led
about by Satan, even as chaff is
driven before the wind, or as a vessel
is tossed about upon the waves,
without sail or anchor, or without
anything wherewith to steer her;
and even as she is, so are they.
19 And behold, the Lord hath
reserved their blessings, which they

9*b* 3 Ne. 16: 8 (8–9).
c Alma 43: 3.
d Morm 1: 1.
12*a* 1 Ne. 19: 19; Enos 1: 16; Hel. 15: 11 (11–13); Morm. 7: 1 (1, 9–10).
b TG Book of Mormon; Scriptures to Come Forth.
c 2 Ne. 25: 8; 27: 6; Jarom 1: 2; D&C 3: 20 (16–20).
d Morm. 8: 4 (4, 13–14); Moro. 10: 2 (1–2). TG Scriptures, Preservation of.
13*a* 2 Ne. 3: 18.
14*a* Rom. 11: 20 (1–36); 1 Ne. 10: 11; Jacob 4: 15 (15–18). TG Unbelief, Unbelievers.
b 2 Ne. 26: 12; 29: 13; 30: 7 (7–8). TG Israel, Judah, People of.
c John 20: 31; 2 Ne. 25: 16 (16–17). TG Israel, Restoration of.
d TG Lands of Inheritance.
e Ezek. 20: 37; 3 Ne. 29: 1 (1–2).
15*a* 2 Ne. 30: 5; 3 Ne. 21: 5 (3–7, 24–26).
b 1 Ne. 13: 38 (20–29, 38); Morm. 7: 8 (8–9).
c 1 Ne. 10: 12 (12–14); 3 Ne. 16: 8.
d 1 Ne. 2: 23; Alma 3: 19 (6–19).
16*a* Gen. 6: 3; Ether 2: 15; Moro. 8: 28.
b Ps. 1: 4 (1–4); Hosea 13: 3 (1–4).
17*a* TG Jesus Christ, Good Shepherd.
18*a* 2 Ne. 28: 21.

[A.D. 380—384]

might have received in the land, for the [a]Gentiles who shall possess the land.

20 But behold, it shall come to pass that they shall be driven and scattered by the Gentiles; and after they have been driven and scattered by the Gentiles, behold, then will the Lord [a]remember the [b]covenant which he made unto Abraham and unto all the house of Israel.

21 And also the Lord will remember the [a]prayers of the righteous, which have been put up unto him for them.

22 And then, O ye Gentiles, how can ye stand before the power of God, except ye shall repent and turn from your evil ways?

23 Know ye not that ye are in the [a]hands of God? Know ye not that he hath all power, and at his great command the [b]earth shall be [c]rolled together as a scroll?

24 Therefore, repent ye, and humble yourselves before him, lest he shall come out in justice against you—lest a [a]remnant of the seed of Jacob shall go forth among you as a [b]lion, and tear you in pieces, and there is none to deliver.

CHAPTER 6

The Nephites gather to the land of Cumorah for the final battles—Mormon hides the sacred records in the hill Cumorah—The Lamanites are victorious, and the Nephite nation is destroyed—Hundreds of thousands are slain with the sword.

AND now I finish my record concerning the [a]destruction of my people, the Nephites. And it came to pass that we did march forth before the Lamanites.

2 And I, Mormon, wrote an epistle unto the king of the Lamanites, and desired of him that he would grant unto us that we might gather together our people unto the [a]land of [b]Cumorah, by a hill which was called Cumorah, and there we could give them battle.

3 And it came to pass that the king of the Lamanites did grant unto me the thing which I desired.

4 And it came to pass that we did march forth to the land of Cumorah, and we did pitch our tents round about the hill Cumorah; and it was in a land of [a]many waters, rivers, and fountains; and here we had hope to gain advantage over the Lamanites.

5 And *when [a]three hundred and eighty and four years had passed away, we had gathered in all the remainder of our people unto the land Cumorah.

6 And it came to pass that when we had gathered in all our people in one to the land of Cumorah, behold I, Mormon, began to be old; and knowing it to be the last struggle of my people, and having been commanded of the Lord that I should not suffer the records which had been handed down by our fathers, which were [a]sacred, to fall into the hands of the Lamanites, (for the Lamanites would [b]destroy them) therefore I made [c]this record out of the plates of Nephi, and [d]hid up in the hill Cumorah all the records which had been entrusted to me by the hand of the Lord, save it were [e]these few plates which I gave unto my son [f]Moroni.

19*a* 3 Ne. 20: 27.
20*a* 1 Ne. 13: 31; 3 Ne. 16: 11 (8–12).
b TG Abrahamic Covenant.
21*a* Enos 1: 12 (12–18); Morm. 8: 25 (24–26); 9: 36 (36–37).
23*a* Ether 1: 1; D&C 87: 6 (6–7).
b Hel. 12: 11 (8–18); Morm. 9: 2.
c 3 Ne. 26: 3.
24*a* TG Israel, Remnant of.
b 3 Ne. 20: 16 (15–16).
6 1*a* 1 Ne. 12: 19 (19–20); Jarom 1: 10; Alma 45: 11 (9–14); Hel. 13: 5 (5–11).
2*a* Ether 9: 3.
b Morm. 8: 2; D&C 128: 20.
4*a* Mosiah 8: 8; Alma 50: 29; Hel. 3: 4 (3–4).
5*a* W of M 1: 2.
6*a* TG Sacred.
b 2 Ne. 26: 17; Enos 1: 14.
c Morm. 2: 18.
d Ether 15: 11.
e Moro. 9: 24; 10: 2; D&C 17: 1; JS-H 1: 52.
f Morm. 8: 1.

[*A.D. 385]

7 And it came to pass that my
people, with their wives and their
children, did now behold the [a]armies
of the Lamanites marching towards
them; and with that awful [b]fear of
death which fills the breasts of all
the wicked, did they await to receive
them.
8 And it came to pass that they
came to battle against us, and every
soul was filled with terror because
of the greatness of their numbers.
9 And it came to pass that they did
fall upon my people with the sword,
and with the bow, and with the
arrow, and with the ax, and with all
manner of weapons of war.
10 And it came to pass that my
men were hewn down, yea, even my
[a]ten thousand who were with me,
and I fell wounded in the midst;
and they passed by me that they did
not put an end to my life.
11 And when they had gone
through and hewn down [a]all my
people save it were twenty and four
of us, (among whom was my son
Moroni) and we having survived the
dead of our people, did behold on
the morrow, when the Lamanites
had returned unto their camps, from
the top of the hill Cumorah, the ten
thousand of my people who were
hewn down, being led in the front
by me.
12 And we also beheld the ten
thousand of my people who were
led by my son Moroni.
13 And behold, the ten thousand of
Gidgiddonah had fallen, and he also
in the midst.
14 And Lamah had fallen with his
ten thousand; and Gilgal had fallen
with his ten thousand; and Limhah
had fallen with his ten thousand;
and Jeneum had fallen with his ten
thousand; and Cumenihah, and
Moronihah, and Antionum, and
Shiblom, and Shem, and Josh, had
fallen with their ten thousand
each.
15 And it came to pass that there
were ten more who did fall by the
sword, with their ten thousand
each; yea, even [a]all my people, save
it were those twenty and four who
were with me, and also a [b]few who
had escaped into the south countries,
and a few who had deserted over
unto the Lamanites, had fallen; and
their flesh, and bones, and blood lay
upon the face of the earth, being
left by the hands of those who slew
them to molder upon the land, and
to crumble and to return to their
mother earth.
16 And my soul was rent with
[a]anguish, because of the slain of my
people, and I cried:
17 [a]O ye fair ones, how could ye
have departed from the ways of the
Lord! O ye fair ones, how could ye
have rejected that Jesus, who stood
with open arms to receive you!
18 Behold, if ye had not done this,
ye would not have fallen. But behold,
ye are fallen, and I [a]mourn your loss.
19 O ye [a]fair sons and daughters,
ye fathers and mothers, ye husbands
and wives, ye fair ones, how is it that
ye could have [b]fallen!
20 But behold, ye are gone, and my
sorrows cannot bring your return.
21 And the day soon cometh that
your mortal must put on immortality, and these bodies which
are now moldering in corruption
must soon become [a]incorruptible
bodies; and then ye must stand
before the judgment-seat of Christ,
to be judged according to your
works; and if it so be that ye are
righteous, then are ye blessed with
your fathers who have gone before
you.
22 O that ye had repented before
this great [a]destruction had come
upon you. But behold, ye are gone,

7*a* 1 Ne. 12: 15.
b TG Fearfulness.
10*a* Judg. 1: 4.
11*a* 1 Ne. 12: 19 (19–20); Hel. 15: 17 (16–17); Morm. 3: 2.
15*a* Alma 9: 24.
b Morm. 8: 2.
16*a* TG Despair; Mourning; Sorrow.
17*a* 2 Ne. 26: 7.
18*a* Lam. 2: 11.
19*a* Ether 13: 17.
b 1 Ne. 13: 15.
21*a* 1 Cor. 15: 53 (53–54).
22*a* 2 Sam. 1: 27 (17–27).

[A.D. 385]

and the Father, yea, the Eternal Father of heaven, [b]knoweth your state; and he doeth with you according to his [c]justice and [d]mercy.

CHAPTER 7

Mormon invites the Lamanites of the latter days to believe in Christ, accept his gospel, and be saved—All who believe the Bible will also believe the Book of Mormon.

AND now, behold, I would speak somewhat unto the [a]remnant of this people who are spared, if it so be that God may give unto them my words, that they may know of the things of their fathers; yea, I speak unto you, ye remnant of the house of Israel; and these are the words which I speak:

2 Know ye that ye are of the [a]house of Israel.

3 Know ye that ye must come unto repentance, or ye cannot be saved.

4 Know ye that ye must lay down your weapons of war, and delight no more in the shedding of blood, and take them not again, save it be that God shall [a]command you.

5 Know ye that ye must come to the [a]knowledge of your fathers, and repent of all your sins and iniquities, and [b]believe in Jesus Christ, that he is the Son of God, and that he was slain by the Jews, and by the power of the Father he hath risen again, whereby he hath gained the [c]victory over the grave; and also in him is the sting of death swallowed up.

6 And he bringeth to pass the [a]resurrection of the dead, whereby man must be raised to stand before his [b]judgment-seat.

7 And he hath brought to pass the [a]redemption of the [b]world, whereby he that is found [c]guiltless before him at the judgment day hath it given unto him to [d]dwell in the presence of God in his kingdom, to sing ceaseless praises with the [e]choirs above, unto the Father, and unto the Son, and unto the Holy Ghost, which are [f]one God, in a state of [g]happiness which hath no end.

8 Therefore repent, and be baptized in the name of Jesus, and lay hold upon the [a]gospel of Christ, which shall be set before you, not only in this record but also in the record which shall come unto the Gentiles [b]from the Jews, which record shall come from the Gentiles [c]unto you.

9 For behold, [a]this is [b]written for the intent that ye may [c]believe that; and if [d]ye believe that ye will believe this also; and if ye believe this ye will know concerning your fathers, and also the marvelous works which were wrought by the power of God among them.

10 And ye will also know that ye are a [a]remnant of the seed of Jacob; therefore ye are numbered among the people of the first covenant; and if it so be that ye believe in Christ, and are baptized, first [b]with water, then with fire and with the Holy Ghost, following the [c]example of

22*b* 2 Sam. 7: 20; D&C 6: 16.
c TG God, Justice of.
d Ps. 36: 5 (5–6); Alma 26: 16; D&C 97: 6.
7 1*a* Hel. 15: 11 (11–13); Morm. 5: 12 (9, 12).
2*a* 1 Ne. 5: 14; Alma 10: 3; Hel. 6: 10; 8: 21.
4*a* Alma 43: 47.
5*a* 2 Ne. 3: 12; 3 Ne. 5: 23.
b TG Faith.
c Mosiah 16: 8 (7–8); Alma 24: 23.
6*a* TG Resurrection.
b TG Jesus Christ, Judge.
7*a* TG Redemption.
b TG World.
c Mosiah 13: 15; D&C 58: 30. TG Justification.
d Ps. 27: 4; 1 Ne. 10: 21; D&C 76: 62 (50–62); Moses 6: 57.
e Mosiah 2: 28.
f Deut. 6: 4; Gal. 3: 20; D&C 20: 28.
g TG Happiness.
8*a* TG Gospel.
b 2 Ne. 29: 4 (4–13).
c 1 Ne. 13: 38 (20–29, 38); Morm. 5: 15.
9*a* 1 Ne. 19: 19; Enos 1: 16 (12–18); 3 Ne. 5: 15 (12–17); Morm. 5: 12. TG Israel, Restoration of.
b TG Book of Mormon.
c 1 Ne. 13: 40 (38–42).
d 2 Ne. 3: 15 (12–15); Alma 37: 19 (1–20).
10*a* TG Israel, Remnant of.
b 3 Ne. 19: 13 (13–14); Ether 12: 14.
c TG God, the Standard of Righteousness.

[About A.D. 385]

our Savior, according to that which
he hath commanded us, it shall
be well with you in the day of
judgment. Amen.

CHAPTER 8

The Lamanites seek out and destroy the Nephites—The Book of Mormon shall come forth by the power of God—Woes pronounced upon those who breathe out wrath and strife against the work of the Lord—The Nephite record shall come forth in a day of wickedness, degeneracy, and apostasy.

BEHOLD I, [a]Moroni, do finish the
[b]record of my father, Mormon. Behold, I have but few things to write,
which things I have been commanded by my father.
2 And now it came to pass that after
the [a]great and tremendous battle at
Cumorah, behold, the Nephites who
had escaped into the country southward were hunted by the [b]Laman-
ites, until they were all destroyed.
3 And my father also was killed by
them, and I even [a]remain [b]alone to
write the sad tale of the destruction
of my people. But behold, they are
gone, and I fulfil the commandment
of my father. And whether they will
slay me, I know not.
4 Therefore I will write and [a]hide
up the records in the earth; and
whither I go it mattereth not.
5 Behold, my father hath made
[a]this record, and he hath written
the intent thereof. And behold, I
would write it also if I had room
upon the [b]plates, but I have not;
and ore I have none, for I am alone.
My father hath been slain in battle,
and all my kinsfolk, and I have not
friends nor whither to go; and [c]how
long the Lord will suffer that I may
live I know not.
6 Behold, [a]*four hundred years
have passed away since the coming
of our Lord and Savior.
7 And behold, the Lamanites have
hunted my people, the Nephites,
down from city to city and from
place to place, even until they are
no more; and great has been their
[a]fall; yea, great and marvelous is
the destruction of my people, the
Nephites.
8 And behold, it is the hand of the
Lord which hath done it. And behold also, the Lamanites are at [a]war
one with another; and the whole face
of this land is one continual round
of murder and bloodshed; and no
one knoweth the end of the war.
9 And now, behold, I say no more
concerning them, for there are none
save it be the Lamanites and
[a]robbers that do exist upon the face
of the land.
10 And there are none that do
know the true God save it be the
[a]disciples of Jesus, who did tarry
in the land until the wickedness of
the people was so great that the
Lord would not suffer them to
[b]remain with the people; and
whether they be upon the face of the
land no man knoweth.
11 But behold, my [a]father and I
have seen [b]them, and they have
ministered unto us.
12 And whoso receiveth [a]this
record, and shall not condemn it
because of the imperfections which
are in it, the same shall know of
[b]greater things than these. Behold, I
am Moroni; and were it possible, I
would make all things known unto
you.

8 1*a* Morm. 6: 6; Moro. 9: 24.
b TG Record Keeping.
2*a* Morm. 6: 15 (2–15).
b D&C 3: 18.
3*a* Moro. 9: 22.
b Ether 4: 3.
4*a* Morm. 5: 12; Moro. 10: 2 (1–2).
5*a* Morm. 2: 17 (17–18).
b Morm. 6: 6.
c Moro. 1: 1; 10: 1 (1–2).
6*a* Alma 45: 10.
7*a* 1 Ne. 12: 2 (2–3); Enos 1: 24.
8*a* 1 Ne. 12: 21 (20–23).
9*a* 4 Ne. 1: 46; Morm. 2: 8 (8, 28); Ether 8: 20.
10*a* 3 Ne. 28: 7; 4 Ne. 1: 37 (14, 37); Ether 12: 17.
b Morm. 1: 16.
11*a* 3 Ne. 28: 26.
b TG Translated Beings.
12*a* 3 Ne. 5: 15 (8–18).
b John 16: 12; 3 Ne. 26: 9 (6–11); D&C 42: 15.

[*A.D. 401]

13 Behold, I make an end of speaking concerning this people. I am the son of Mormon, and my father was a [a]descendant of Nephi.

14 And I am the same who [a]hideth up this record unto the Lord; the plates thereof are of no worth, because of the commandment of the Lord. For he truly saith that no one shall have them [b]to get gain; but the record thereof is of [c]great worth; and whoso shall bring it to light, him will the Lord bless.

15 For none can have power to bring it to light save it be given him of God; for God wills that it shall be done with an [a]eye single to his glory, or the welfare of the ancient and long dispersed covenant people of the Lord.

16 And blessed be [a]he that shall bring this thing to light; for it shall be [b]brought out of darkness unto light, according to the word of God; yea, it shall be brought out of the earth, and it shall shine forth out of darkness, and come unto the knowledge of the people; and it shall be done by the power of God.

17 And if there be [a]faults they be the faults of a man. But behold, we know no fault; nevertheless God knoweth all things; therefore, he that [b]condemneth, let him be aware lest he shall be in danger of hell fire.

18 And he that saith: Show unto me, or ye shall be [a]smitten—let him beware lest he commandeth that which is forbidden of the Lord.

19 For behold, the same that [a]judgeth [b]rashly shall be judged rashly again; for according to his works shall his wages be; therefore, he that smiteth shall be smitten again, of the Lord.

20 Behold what the scripture says —man shall not [a]smite, neither shall he [b]judge; for judgment is mine, saith the Lord, and vengeance is mine also, and I will repay.

21 And he that shall breathe out [a]wrath and [b]strifes against the work of the Lord, and against the [c]covenant people of the Lord who are the house of Israel, and shall say: We will destroy the work of the Lord, and the Lord will not remember his covenant which he hath made unto the house of Israel—the same is in danger to be hewn down and cast into the fire;

22 For the eternal [a]purposes of the Lord shall roll on, until all his promises shall be fulfilled.

23 Search the prophecies of [a]Isaiah. Behold, I cannot write them. Yea, behold I say unto you, that those saints who have gone before me, who have possessed this land, shall [b]cry, yea, even from the dust will they cry unto the Lord; and as the Lord liveth he will remember the covenant which he hath made with them.

24 And he knoweth their [a]prayers, that they were in behalf of their brethren. And he knoweth their faith, for in his name could they remove [b]mountains; and in his name could they cause the earth to shake; and by the power of his word did they cause [c]prisons to tumble to the earth; yea, even the fiery furnace could not harm them, neither wild

13*a* Alma 10: 3; 3 Ne. 5: 20.
14*a* Ether 4: 3; Moro. 10: 2 (1–2).
b JS-H 1: 53. TG Scriptures, Preservation of.
c 2 Ne. 3: 7 (6–9).
15*a* Matt. 6: 22; D&C 4: 5.
16*a* 3 Ne. 21: 11 (8–11); Ether 3: 28 (21–28).
b TG Scriptures to Come Forth.
17*a* 1 Ne. 19: 6; Morm. 9: 31 (31, 33); Ether 12: 23 (22–28, 35).
b 3 Ne. 29: 5 (1–9); Ether 4: 8 (8–10).
18*a* JS-H 1: 60 (60–61).
19*a* 3 Ne. 14: 2; Moro. 7: 14. TG Gossip.
b TG Rashness.
20*a* TG Violence.
b James 4: 12 (11–12).
21*a* Prov. 19: 19.
b TG Strife.
c 1 Ne. 14: 17.
22*a* D&C 3: 3.
23*a* Isa. 29: 4; 3 Ne. 20: 11; 23: 1 (1–3).
b 2 Ne. 3: 20; 26: 16.
24*a* Enos 1: 13 (12–18); Morm. 9: 36 (34–37); D&C 10: 46 (46–49).
b Jacob 4: 6; Hel. 10: 9.
c 3 Ne. 28: 19 (19–21).

[Between A.D. 400 and 421]

beasts nor poisonous serpents, because of the power of his word.
25 And behold, their [a]prayers were
also in behalf of him that the Lord
should suffer to bring these things
forth.
26 And no one need say they shall
not come, for they surely shall, for
the Lord hath spoken it; for [a]out of
the earth shall they come, by the
hand of the Lord, and none can stay
it; and it shall come in a day when it
shall be said that [b]miracles are done
away; and it shall come even as if
one should speak [c]from the dead.
27 And it shall come in a day when
the [a]blood of saints shall cry unto
the Lord, because of secret [b]combi-
nations and the works of darkness.
28 Yea, it shall come in a day when
the power of God shall be [a]denied,
and [b]churches become defiled and
be [c]lifted up in the pride of their
hearts; yea, even in a day when
leaders of churches and teachers
shall rise in the pride of their hearts,
even to the envying of them who
belong to their churches.
29 Yea, it shall come in a day when
[a]there shall be heard of fires, and
tempests, and [b]vapors of smoke in
foreign lands;
30 And there shall also be heard of
[a]wars, rumors of wars, and earthquakes in divers places.
31 Yea, it shall come in a day when
there shall be great [a]pollutions upon
the face of the earth; there shall be
[b]murders, and robbing, and lying,
and deceivings, and whoredoms,
and all manner of abominations;
when there shall be many who will
say, Do this, or do that, and it
[c]mattereth not, for the Lord will
[d]uphold such at the last day. But
wo unto such, for they are in the
[e]gall of bitterness and in the [f]bonds
of iniquity.
32 Yea, it shall come in a day when
there shall be [a]churches built up
that shall say: Come unto me, and
for your money you shall be forgiven of your sins.
33 O ye wicked and perverse and
[a]stiffnecked people, why have ye
built up churches unto yourselves to
get [b]gain? Why have ye [c]trans-
figured the holy word of God, that
ye might bring [d]damnation upon
your souls? Behold, look ye unto
the [e]revelations of God; for behold,
the time cometh at that day when
all these things must be fulfilled.
34 Behold, the Lord hath shown
unto me great and marvelous things
concerning that which must shortly
come, at that day when these things
shall come forth among you.
35 Behold, I speak unto you as if
ye were present, and yet ye are not.
But behold, Jesus Christ hath shown
you unto me, and I know your doing.
36 And I know that ye do [a]walk in
the pride of your hearts; and there
are none save a few only who do not
[b]lift themselves up in the pride of
their hearts, unto the wearing of
[c]very fine apparel, unto envying,

25*a* Morm. 5: 21.
26*a* 3 Ne. 23: 4.
b 3 Ne. 29: 7; Morm. 9: 15 (15–26); Moro. 7: 37 (27–37).
c 2 Ne. 26: 16 (15–16); 33: 13; Morm. 9: 30; Moro. 10: 27.
27*a* Gen. 4: 10; Rev. 6: 10 (1, 10); 2 Ne. 28: 10; Ether 8: 22 (22–24); D&C 87: 7.
b TG Secret Combinations.
28*a* TG Unbelief, Unbelievers.
b 2 Tim. 3: 1 (1–7); 1 Ne. 14: 10 (9–10); 2 Ne. 28: 3 (3–32); D&C 33: 4.
c 2 Kgs. 14: 10; Jacob 2: 13.
29*a* Joel 2: 30 (28–32); 2 Ne. 27: 2 (1–3).
b 1 Ne. 19: 11; D&C 45: 41 (40–41).
30*a* Matt. 24: 6; 1 Ne. 14: 16 (15–17).
31*a* TG Pollution.
b 3 Ne. 16: 10; 30: 2.
c 2 Ne. 28: 21; Alma 1: 4; 30: 17.
d 2 Ne. 28: 8.
e Acts 8: 23; Alma 41: 11.
f TG Bondage, Spiritual.
32*a* TG Devil, Church of.
33*a* D&C 5: 8.
b TG Priestcraft.
c 1 Ne. 13: 26 (20–41). TG Apostasy of the Early Christian Church.
d TG Damnation.
e 1 Ne. 14: 23 (18–27); Ether 4: 16.
36*a* TG Walking in Darkness.
b Jacob 2: 13; 3 Ne. 16: 10.
c 2 Ne. 28: 13 (11–14); Alma 5: 53.

[Between A.D. 400 and 421]

and strifes, and malice, and persecutions, and all manner of iniquities;
and your churches, yea, even every
one, have become polluted because
of the pride of your hearts.
37 For behold, ye do love [a]money,
and your substance, and your fine
apparel, and the adorning of your
churches, more than ye love the
poor and the needy, the sick and the
afflicted.
38 O ye pollutions, ye hypocrites,
ye teachers, who sell yourselves for
that which will canker, why have
ye polluted the holy church of God?
Why are ye [a]ashamed to take upon
you the name of Christ? Why do ye
not think that greater is the value of
an endless happiness than that
[b]misery which never dies—because
of the [c]praise of the world?
39 Why do ye adorn yourselves
with that which hath no life, and
yet suffer the hungry, and the needy,
and the naked, and the sick and the
afflicted to pass by you, and notice
them not?
40 Yea, why do ye build up your
[a]secret abominations to get gain,
and cause that widows should mourn
before the Lord, and also orphans
to mourn before the Lord, and also
the blood of their fathers and their
husbands to cry unto the Lord from
the ground, for vengeance upon
your heads?
41 Behold, the sword of vengeance
hangeth over you; and the time
soon cometh that he avengeth the
[a]blood of the saints upon you, for he
will not suffer their cries any longer.

CHAPTER 9

*Moroni calls upon those who do not
believe in Christ to repent—He proclaims a God of miracles, who gives
revelations and pours out gifts and
signs upon the faithful—Miracles
cease because of unbelief—Signs
follow those who believe—Men are
exhorted to be wise and keep the
commandments.*

AND now, I speak also concerning
those who do not believe in Christ.
2 Behold, will ye believe in the day
of your visitation—behold, when
the Lord shall come, yea, even that
[a]great day when the [b]earth shall be
rolled together as a scroll, and the
elements shall [c]melt with fervent
heat, yea, in that great day when ye
shall be brought to stand before the
Lamb of God—then will ye say that
there is no God?
3 Then will ye longer deny the
Christ, or can ye behold the Lamb of
God? Do ye suppose that ye shall
dwell with him under a [a]conscious-
ness of your guilt? Do ye suppose
that ye could be happy to dwell with
that holy Being, when your souls
are racked with a consciousness of
guilt that ye have ever abused his
laws?
4 Behold, I say unto you that ye
would be more miserable to dwell
with a holy and just God, under a
consciousness of your [a]filthiness
before him, than ye would to dwell
with the [b]damned souls in [c]hell.
5 For behold, when ye shall be
brought to see your [a]nakedness before God, and also the glory of God,
and the [b]holiness of Jesus Christ, it
will kindle a flame of unquenchable
fire upon you.
6 O then ye [a]unbelieving, [b]turn ye
unto the Lord; cry mightily unto
the Father in the name of Jesus, that
perhaps ye may be found spotless,

37*a* Ezek. 34: 8; 1 Ne. 13: 7; 2 Ne. 28: 13 (9–16).
38*a* Rom. 1: 16; 2 Tim. 1: 8; 1 Ne. 8: 25; Alma 46: 21.
b Rom. 3: 16; Mosiah 3: 25.
c 1 Ne. 13: 9.
40*a* TG Secret Combinations.
41*a* 1 Ne. 22: 14; D&C 136: 36.
9 2*a* Mal. 4: 5; 3 Ne. 28: 31.
b Morm. 5: 23; D&C 63: 21 (20–21). TG World, End of.
c Amos 9: 13; 3 Ne. 26: 3.
3*a* TG Conscience; Guilt.
4*a* TG Filthiness.
b TG Damnation.
c TG Hell.
5*a* Ex. 32: 25; 2 Ne. 9: 14.
b TG Holiness.
6*a* TG Unbelief, Unbelievers.
b Ezek. 18: 23, 32; D&C 98: 47.

[Between A.D. 400 and 421]

[c]pure, fair, and white, having been
cleansed by the blood of the [d]Lamb,
at that great and last day.
7 And again I speak unto you who
[a]deny the revelations of God, and
say that they are done away, that
there are no revelations, nor prophecies, nor gifts, nor healing, nor
speaking with tongues, and the
[b]interpretation of tongues;
8 Behold I say unto you, he that
denieth these things knoweth not
the [a]gospel of Christ; yea, he has
not read the scriptures; if so, he does
not [b]understand them.
9 For do we not read that God is the
[a]same [b]yesterday, today, and forever, and in him there is no [c]variable-
ness neither shadow of changing?
10 And now, if ye have imagined
up unto yourselves a god who doth
vary, and in whom there is shadow
of changing, then have ye imagined
up unto yourselves a god who is not
a God of miracles.
11 But behold, I will show unto
you a God of [a]miracles, even the
God of Abraham, and the God of
Isaac, and the God of Jacob; and it
is that same [b]God who created the
heavens and the earth, and all
things that in them are.
12 Behold, he created Adam, and
by [a]Adam came the [b]fall of man. And
because of the fall of man came Jesus
Christ, even the Father and the
Son; and because of Jesus Christ
came the [c]redemption of man.
13 And because of the redemption
of man, which came by Jesus Christ,
they are brought back into the
[a]presence of the Lord; yea, this is
wherein all men are redeemed,
because the death of Christ bringeth
to pass the [b]resurrection, which
bringeth to pass a redemption from
an endless [c]sleep, from which sleep
all men shall be awakened by the
power of God when the trump shall
sound; and they shall come forth,
both small and great, and all shall
stand before his bar, being redeemed
and loosed from this eternal [d]band
of death, which death is a temporal
death.
14 And then cometh the [a]judgment
of the Holy One upon them; and
then cometh the time that he that is
[b]filthy shall be filthy still; and he
that is righteous shall be righteous
still; he that is happy shall be happy
still; and he that is unhappy shall
be unhappy still.
15 And now, O all ye that have
imagined up unto yourselves a god
who can do [a]no miracles, I would ask
of you, have all these things passed,
of which I have spoken? Has the
end come yet? Behold I say unto
you, Nay; and God has not ceased
to be a God of miracles.
16 Behold, are not the things that
God hath wrought marvelous in our
eyes? Yea, and who can comprehend
the marvelous [a]works of God?
17 Who shall say that it was not a
miracle that by his [a]word the heaven
and the earth should be; and by the
power of his word man was [b]created
of the [c]dust of the earth; and by the
power of his word have miracles
been wrought?

6c TG Cleanliness; Purification.
d TG Jesus Christ, Lamb of God.
7a 3 Ne. 29: 6.
b 1 Cor. 12: 10; A of F 7.
8a TG Gospel.
b Matt. 22: 29.
9a Heb. 13: 8; 1 Ne. 10: 18 (18–19); Alma 7: 20; Moro. 8:18; D&C 20: 12.
b TG God, Eternal Nature of.
c TG God, Perfection of.
11a TG God, Power of.
b Gen. 1: 1; Mosiah 4: 2; D&C 76: 24 (20–24).
12a Mosiah 3: 26; Moro. 8: 8.
b TG Fall of Man.
c TG Jesus Christ, Redeemer.
13a TG God, Presence of.
b Hel. 14: 15 (15–18).
c Dan. 12: 2; D&C 43: 18.
d Alma 36: 18; D&C 138: 16.
14a TG Judgment, The Last.
b Alma 7: 21; D&C 88: 35.
15a Morm. 8: 26; Moro. 7: 35; D&C 35: 8. TG Miracle.
16a Ps. 40: 5; 92: 5; D&C 76: 114; Moses 1: 4 (3–5).
17a Jacob 4: 9.
b TG Man, Physical Creation of.
c Gen. 2: 7; Mosiah 2: 25; D&C 77: 12; 93: 35 (33–35).

[Between A.D. 400 and 421]

18 And who shall say that Jesus
Christ did not do many mighty
[a]miracles? And there were many
[b]mighty miracles wrought by the
hands of the apostles.
19 And if there were [a]miracles
wrought then, why has God ceased
to be a God of miracles and yet be an
unchangeable Being? And behold, I
say unto you he [b]changeth not; if so
he would cease to be God; and he
ceaseth not to be God, and is a God
of miracles.
20 And the reason why he ceaseth
to do [a]miracles among the children
of men is because that they dwindle
in unbelief, and depart from the
right way, and know not the God in
whom they should [b]trust.
21 Behold, I say unto you that
whoso believeth in Christ, doubting
nothing, [a]whatsoever he shall ask
the Father in the name of Christ it
shall be granted him; and this
[b]promise is unto all, even unto the
ends of the earth.
22 For behold, thus said Jesus
Christ, the Son of God, unto his
disciples who should tarry, yea, and
also to [a]all his disciples, in the hearing of the multitude: Go ye into all
the world, and preach the gospel to
every creature;
23 And he that [a]believeth and is
baptized shall be saved, but he that
believeth not shall be [b]damned;
24 And [a]these signs shall follow
them that believe—in my name
shall they cast out [b]devils; they shall
speak with new tongues; they shall
take up serpents; and if they drink
any deadly thing it shall not hurt
them; they shall lay [c]hands on the
sick and they shall recover;
25 And whosoever shall believe in
my name, doubting nothing, unto
him will I [a]confirm all my words,
even unto the ends of the earth.
26 And now, behold, who can stand
[a]against the works of the Lord?
[b]Who can deny his sayings? Who
will rise up against the almighty
power of the Lord? Who will despise
the works of the Lord? Who will
despise the children of Christ? Behold, all ye who are [c]despisers of the
works of the Lord, for ye shall
wonder and perish.
27 O then despise not, and wonder
not, but hearken unto the words of
the Lord, and ask the Father in the
name of Jesus for what things
soever ye shall stand in need. [a]Doubt
not, but be believing, and begin as
in times of old, and [b]come unto the
Lord with all your [c]heart, and [d]work
out your own salvation with fear
and trembling before him.
28 Be [a]wise in the days of your
[b]probation; strip yourselves of all
uncleanness; ask not, that ye may
consume it on your [c]lusts, but ask
with a firmness unshaken, that ye
will yield to no temptation, but that
ye will serve the true and [d]living
God.
29 See that ye are not baptized
[a]unworthily; see that ye partake
not of the sacrament of Christ [b]un-
worthily; but see that ye do all

18*a* John 6: 14; 3 Ne. 8: 1.
b Mark 6: 5.
19*a* Rom. 15: 19 (18–19); D&C 63: 10 (7–10).
b TG God, Perfection of.
20*a* Judg. 6: 13 (11–13); Ether 12: 12 (12–18); Moro. 7: 37.
b TG Trust in God.
21*a* Matt. 21: 22 (18–22); 3 Ne. 18: 20.
b TG Promise.
22*a* Mark 16: 15. TG Missionary Work; World.
23*a* Mark 16: 16.
b TG Damnation.
24*a* Mark 16: 17 (17–18). TG Signs.
b Mark 5: 15 (15–20); 1 Ne. 11: 31.
c TG Administrations to the Sick; Hands, Laying on of.
25*a* TG Testimony.
26*a* 2 Ne. 26: 20; 28: 5 (4–6, 15).
b 3 Ne. 29: 5 (4–7).
c Prov. 13: 13.
27*a* TG Doubt.
b 3 Ne. 21: 20; Ether 5: 5; Moro. 10: 30 (30–32).
c Josh 22: 5; D&C 64: 34 (22, 34). TG Commitment.
d Philip. 2: 12 (12–16).
28*a* Matt. 10: 16; Jacob 6: 12.
b TG Probation.
c TG Covetousness; Lust.
d Alma 5: 13.
29*a* TG Baptism, Qualifications for.
b Lev. 22: 3; 1 Cor. 11: 27 (27–30); 3 Ne. 18: 29 (28–32).

[Between A.D. 400 and 421]

things in [c]worthiness, and do it in the name of Jesus Christ, the Son of the living God; and if ye do this, and endure to the end, ye will in nowise be cast out.

30 Behold, I speak unto you as though I [a]spake from the dead; for I know that ye shall have my words.

31 Condemn me not because of mine [a]imperfection, neither my father, because of his imperfection, neither them who have written before him; but rather give thanks unto God that he hath made manifest unto you our imperfections, that ye may learn to be more wise than we have been.

32 And now, behold, we have written this record according to our knowledge, in the characters which are called among us the [a]reformed Egyptian, being handed down and altered by us, according to our manner of speech.

33 And if our plates had been [a]sufficiently large we should have written in Hebrew; but the Hebrew hath been altered by us also; and if we could have written in Hebrew, behold, ye would have had no [b]imperfection in our record.

34 But the Lord knoweth the things which we have written, and also that none other people knoweth our language; and because that none other people knoweth our language, therefore he hath prepared [a]means for the interpretation thereof.

35 And these things are written that we may rid our garments of the blood of our [a]brethren, who have dwindled in unbelief.

36 And behold, these things which we have [a]desired concerning our brethren, yea, even their restoration to the knowledge of Christ, are according to the prayers of all the saints who have dwelt in the land.

37 And may the Lord Jesus Christ grant that their prayers may be answered according to their faith; and may God the Father remember the covenant which he hath made with the house of Israel; and may he bless them forever, through faith on the name of Jesus Christ. Amen.

THE BOOK OF ETHER

The record of the Jaredites, taken from the twenty-four plates found by the people of Limhi in the days of king Mosiah.

CHAPTER 1

Moroni abridges the writings of Ether—Ether's genealogy set forth—The language of the Jaredites is not confounded at the Tower of Babel—The Lord promises to lead them to a choice land and make them a great nation.

AND now I, Moroni, proceed to give an [a]account of those ancient inhabitants who were destroyed by the [b]hand of the Lord upon the face of this north country.

2 And I take mine account from the [a]twenty and four plates which

---

29c TG Worthiness.
30a Morm. 8: 26; Moro. 10: 27.
31a Morm. 8: 17; Ether 12: 23 (22–28, 35).
32a 1 Ne. 1: 2; Mosiah 1: 2 (2–4).
33a Jarom 1: 14 (2, 14).
b 3 Ne. 5: 18.
34a Mosiah 8: 13 (13–18); Ether 3: 23 (23, 28); D&C 17: 1.
35a 2 Ne. 26: 15.
36a Morm. 5: 21; 8: 24 (24–26); D&C 10: 46 (46–49).

[ETHER]
1 1a Mosiah 28: 19.
b 1 Sam. 5: 9; Morm. 5: 23; D&C 87: 6 (6–7).
2a Alma 37: 21 (21–31); Ether 15: 33.

were found by the people of Limhi, which is called the Book of Ether.

3 And as I suppose that the [a]first part of this record, which speaks concerning the creation of the world, and also of Adam, and an account from that time even to the great [b]tower, and whatsoever things transpired among the children of men until that time, is had among the Jews—

4 Therefore I do not write those things which transpired from the days of [a]Adam until that time; but they are had upon the plates; and whoso findeth them, the same will have power that he may get the full account.

5 But behold, I give not the full account, but a [a]part of the account I give, from the tower down until they were destroyed.

6 And on this wise do I give the account. He that wrote this record was [a]Ether, and he was a descendant of Coriantor.

7 Coriantor was the son of Moron.

8 And Moron was the son of Ethem.

9 And Ethem was the son of Ahah.

10 And Ahah was the son of Seth.

11 And Seth was the son of Shiblon.

12 And Shiblon was the son of Com.

13 And Com was the son of Coriantum.

14 And Coriantum was the son of Amnigaddah.

15 And Amnigaddah was the son of Aaron.

16 And Aaron was a descendant of Heth, who was the son of Hearthom.

17 And Hearthom was the son of Lib.

18 And Lib was the son of Kish.

19 And Kish was the son of Corom.

20 And Corom was the son of Levi.

21 And Levi was the son of Kim.

22 And Kim was the son of Morianton.

23 And Morianton was a descendant of Riplakish.

24 And Riplakish was the son of Shez.

25 And Shez was the son of Heth.

26 And Heth was the son of Com.

27 And Com was the son of Coriantum.

28 And Coriantum was the son of Emer.

29 And Emer was the son of Omer.

30 And Omer was the son of Shule.

31 And Shule was the son of Kib.

32 And [a]Kib was the son of [b]Orihah, who was the son of Jared;

33 Which [a]Jared came forth with his brother and their families, with some others and their families, from the great tower, at the time the Lord [b]confounded the language of the people, and swore in his wrath that they should be scattered upon all the [c]face of the earth; and according to the word of the Lord the people were scattered.

34 And the [a]brother of Jared being a large and mighty man, and a man highly favored of the Lord, Jared, his brother, said unto him: Cry unto the Lord, that he will not confound us that we may not [b]understand our words.

35 And it came to pass that the brother of Jared did cry unto the Lord, and the Lord had compassion upon Jared; therefore he did not confound the [a]language of Jared; and Jared and his brother were not confounded.

36 Then Jared said unto his brother: Cry again unto the Lord, and it may be that he will turn away his anger from them who are our [a]friends, that he confound not their language.

37 And it came to pass that the brother of Jared did cry unto the Lord, and the Lord had compassion

3*a* Ether 8: 9.
b Gen. 11: 4 (1–9); Omni 1: 22; Mosiah 28: 17; Hel. 6: 28.
4*a* IE covering same period as Genesis, chapters 1–10.
5*a* Ether 3: 17; 15: 33.
6*a* Ether 11: 23; 12: 2; 15: 34.
32*a* Ether 7: 3.
b Ether 6: 27.
33*a* Gen. 11: 9 (6–9).
b Omni 1: 22.
c Mosiah 28: 17.
34*a* Alma 8: 7; Ether 2: 13; 6:1.
b TG Communication.
35*a* Zeph. 3: 9; Ether 3: 24; Moses 6: 6 (5–6).
36*a* Ether 2:1.

upon their friends and their families also, that they were not confounded.

38 And it came to pass that Jared spake again unto his brother, saying: Go and [a]inquire of the Lord whether he will drive us out of the land, and if he will drive us out of the land, cry unto him whither we shall go. And who knoweth but the Lord will carry us forth into a land which is [b]choice above all the earth? And if it so be, let us be faithful unto the Lord, that we may receive it for our inheritance.

39 And it came to pass that the brother of Jared did cry unto the Lord according to that which had been spoken by the mouth of Jared.

40 And it came to pass that the Lord did hear the brother of Jared, and [a]had compassion upon him, and said unto him:

41 Go to and gather together thy [a]flocks, both male and female, of every kind; and also of the [b]seed of the earth of every kind; and [c]thy [d]families; and also Jared thy brother and his family; and also thy [e]friends and their families, and the friends of Jared and their families.

42 And when thou hast done this thou shalt [a]go at the head of them down into the valley which is northward. And there will I meet thee, and I will go [b]before thee into a land which is [c]choice above all the lands of the earth.

43 And there will I bless thee and thy seed, and raise up unto me of thy seed, and of the seed of thy brother, and they who shall go with thee, a great nation. And [a]there shall be none [b]greater than the nation which I will raise up unto me of thy seed, upon all the face of the earth. And thus I will do unto thee because this long time ye have cried unto me.

CHAPTER 2

The Jaredites prepare for their journey to a promised land—It is a choice land whereon men must serve Christ or be swept off—The Lord talks to the brother of Jared for three hours—They build barges—The Lord asks the brother of Jared to propose how the barges shall be lighted.

AND it came to pass that Jared and his brother, and their families, and also the [a]friends of Jared and his brother and their families, went down into the valley which was northward, (and the name of the valley was [b]Nimrod, being called after the mighty hunter) with their [c]flocks which they had gathered together, male and female, of every kind.

2 And they did also lay snares and catch [a]fowls of the air; and they did also prepare a vessel, in which they did carry with them the fish of the waters.

3 And they did also carry with them deseret, which, by interpretation, is a honey bee; and thus they did carry with them [a]swarms of bees, and all manner of that which was upon the face of the land, [b]seeds of every kind.

4 And it came to pass that when they had come down into the valley of Nimrod the Lord came down and talked with the brother of Jared; and he was in a [a]cloud, and the brother of Jared saw him not.

5 And it came to pass that the Lord commanded them that they should [a]go forth into the wilderness, yea,

---

38*a* 2 Chr. 18: 4 (4–7).
b 1 Ne. 2: 20. TG Lands of Inheritance.
40*a* Ether 3: 3.
41*a* Ether 2: 1 (1–3).
b 1 Ne. 8: 1; 16: 11; Ether 9: 17.
c Ether 6: 20.
d Num. 1: 2; Mosiah 6: 3; D&C 48: 6.
e Ether 6: 16.
42*a* Gen. 12: 1; Num. 9: 17; 1 Ne. 2: 2; Ether 2: 5; Abr. 2: 3.
b Judg. 4: 14; D&C 84: 88 (87–88).
c 1 Ne. 13: 30.
43*a* Gen. 26: 3; Deut. 28: 8.
b Ether 15: 2.
2 1*a* Ether 1: 36.
b Gen. 10: 8; 1 Chr. 1: 10.
c Ether 1: 41; 6: 4; 9: 18 (18–19).
2*a* Gen. 7: 3 (1–3).
3*a* 1 Ne. 17: 5; 18: 6.
b 1 Ne. 16: 11.
4*a* Num. 11: 25; D&C 34: 7 (7–9); JS-H 1: 68 (68–71).
5*a* Num. 9: 17; Ether 1: 42.

into that quarter where there never
had man been. And it came to pass
that the Lord did go before them,
and did talk with them as he stood
in a [b]cloud, and gave [c]directions
whither they should travel.
6 And it came to pass that they
did travel in the wilderness, and
did [a]build [b]barges, in which they did
cross many waters, being directed
continually by the hand of the Lord.
7 And the Lord would not suffer
that they should stop beyond the
sea in the wilderness, but he would
that they should come forth even
unto the [a]land of promise, which
was choice above all other lands,
which the Lord God had [b]preserved
for a righteous people.
8 And he had sworn in his wrath
unto the brother of Jared, that
whoso should possess this land of
promise, from that time henceforth
and forever, should [a]serve him, the
true and only God, or they should be
[b]swept off when the fulness of his
wrath should come upon them.
9 And now, we can behold the
decrees of God concerning this land,
that it is a land of promise; and
whatsoever nation shall possess it
shall serve God, or they shall be
[a]swept off when the fulness of his
[b]wrath shall come upon them. And
the fulness of his wrath cometh
upon them when they are [c]ripened
in iniquity.
10 For behold, this is a land which
is choice above all other lands;
wherefore he that doth possess it
shall serve God or shall be [a]swept
off; for it is the everlasting decree of
God. And it is not until the [b]fulness
of iniquity among the children of the
land, that they are [c]swept off.
11 And this cometh unto you, O ye
[a]Gentiles, that ye may know the
decrees of God—that ye may repent,
and not continue in your iniquities
until the fulness come, that ye may
not bring down the fulness of the
[b]wrath of God upon you as the inhabitants of the land have hitherto
done.
12 Behold, this is a choice land,
and whatsoever nation shall possess
it shall be [a]free from bondage, and
from captivity, and from all other
nations under heaven, if they will
but [b]serve the God of the land, who
is Jesus Christ, who hath been
manifested by the things which we
have written.
13 And now I proceed with my
record; for behold, it came to pass
that the Lord did bring Jared and
his brethren forth even to that great
sea which divideth the lands. And
as they came to the sea they pitched
their tents; and they called the name
of the place [a]Moriancumer; and
they dwelt in [b]tents, and dwelt in
tents upon the seashore for the space
of four years.
14 And it came to pass at the end of
four years that the Lord came again
unto the brother of Jared, and stood
in a cloud and [a]talked with him. And
for the space of three hours did the
Lord talk with the brother of Jared,
and [b]chastened him because he
remembered not to [c]call upon the
name of the Lord.
15 And the brother of Jared repented of the evil which he had done,
and did call upon the name of the
Lord for his brethren who were with
him. And the Lord said unto him:
I will forgive thee and thy brethren
of their sins; but thou shalt not sin

5*b* Ex. 13: 21.
c TG Guidance, Divine.
6*a* TG Skill.
b Gen. 6: 14 (14–15); Ether 2: 16.
7*a* TG Promised Lands.
b 1 Ne. 4: 14.
8*a* Ether 13: 2.
b Jarom 1: 3 (3, 10); Alma 37: 28; Ether 9: 20.
9*a* 2 Ne. 6: 15.
b TG God, Indignation of.
c Gen. 15: 16; 1 Ne. 14: 6.
10*a* Jarom 1: 12.
b 2 Ne. 28: 16.
c 1 Ne. 17: 37.
11*a* 1 Ne. 14: 6; 2 Ne. 28: 32.
b Alma 45: 16 (10–14, 16); Morm. 1: 17.
12*a* 1 Ne. 13: 19. TG Liberty.
b Isa. 60: 12.
13*a* Alma 8: 7; Ether 1: 34.
b Gen. 25: 27; Hel. 3: 9.
14*a* Ex. 25: 22.
b 1 Ne. 16: 25. TG Chastening; Reproof.
c TG Prayer.

any more, for ye shall remember that
my [a]Spirit will not always [b]strive
with man; wherefore, if ye will sin
until ye are fully ripe ye shall be cut
off from the presence of the Lord.
And these are my [c]thoughts upon the
land which I shall give you for your
inheritance; for it shall be a land
[d]choice above all other lands.
16 And the Lord said: Go to work
and build, after the manner of
[a]barges which ye have hitherto built.
And it came to pass that the brother
of Jared did go to work, and also his
brethren, and built barges after the
manner which they had built,
according to the [b]instructions of the
Lord. And they were small, and they
were light upon the water, even like
unto the lightness of a fowl upon the
water.
17 And they were built after a
manner that they were exceedingly
[a]tight, even that they would hold
water like unto a dish; and the
bottom thereof was tight like unto a
dish; and the sides thereof were
tight like unto a dish; and the ends
thereof were peaked; and the top
thereof was tight like unto a dish;
and the length thereof was the
length of a tree; and the door
thereof, when it was shut, was tight
like unto a dish.
18 And it came to pass that the
brother of Jared cried unto the Lord,
saying: O Lord, I have performed
the work which thou hast commanded me, and I have made the
barges according as thou hast
directed me.
19 And behold, O Lord, in them
there is no light; whither shall we
steer? And also we shall perish, for
in them we cannot breathe, save it
is the air which is in them; therefore
we shall perish.
20 And the Lord said unto the
brother of Jared: Behold, thou shalt
make a hole in the top, and also in
the bottom; and when thou shalt
suffer for air thou shalt unstop the
hole and receive air. And if it be so
that the water come in upon thee,
behold, ye shall stop the hole, that
ye may not perish in the flood.
21 And it came to pass that the
brother of Jared did so, according as
the Lord had commanded.
22 And he cried again unto the
Lord saying: O Lord, behold I have
done even as thou hast commanded
me; and I have prepared the vessels
for my people, and behold there is
no light in them. Behold, O Lord,
wilt thou suffer that we shall cross
this great water in darkness?
23 And the Lord said unto the
brother of Jared: What will ye that
I should do that ye may have light
in your vessels? For behold, ye cannot have [a]windows, for they will be
dashed in pieces; neither shall ye
take fire with you, for ye shall not go
by the light of fire.
24 For behold, ye shall be as a
[a]whale in the midst of the sea; for
the mountain waves shall dash upon
you. Nevertheless, I will bring you
up again out of the depths of the
sea; for the [b]winds have gone forth
[c]out of my mouth, and also the
[d]rains and the floods have I sent
forth.
25 And behold, I prepare you
against these things; for ye cannot
cross this great deep save I prepare
you against the waves of the sea, and
the winds which have gone forth,
and the floods which shall come.
Therefore what will ye that I should
prepare for you that ye may have
light when ye are swallowed up in
the depths of the sea?

15*a* TG God, Spirit of.
b Gen. 6:3; 2 Ne. 26:11; Morm. 5:16; Moses 8:17.
c TG Earth, Purpose of.
d Ether 9:20.
16*a* Ether 2:6.
b Ex. 25:40; Prov. 16:9; 1 Ne. 17:51 (50–51).
17*a* Ether 6:7.
23*a* Gen. 6:16.
24*a* Gen. 1:21; Ether 6:10.
b Ether 6:5.
c Job 37:2 (2–13).
d Ps. 148:8; D&C 117:1.

CHAPTER 3

The brother of Jared sees the finger of the Lord as he touches the sixteen stones—Christ shows his spirit body to the brother of Jared—Those who have a perfect knowledge cannot be kept from within the veil—Interpreters are provided to bring the Jaredite record to light.

AND it came to pass that the brother of Jared, (now the number of the vessels which had been prepared was eight) went forth unto the [a]mount, which they called the mount [b]Shelem, because of its exceeding height, and did [c]molten out of a rock sixteen small stones; and they were white and clear, even as transparent [d]glass; and he did carry them in his hands upon the top of the mount, and cried again unto the Lord, saying:

2 O Lord, thou hast said that we must be encompassed about by the floods. Now behold, O Lord, and do not be [a]angry with thy servant because of his weakness before thee; for we know that thou art holy and dwellest in the heavens, and that we are [b]unworthy before thee; because of the [c]fall our [d]natures have become evil continually; nevertheless, O Lord, thou hast given us a commandment that we must call upon thee, that from thee we may receive according to our desires.

3 Behold, O Lord, thou hast smitten us because of our iniquity, and hast driven us forth, and for these many years we have been in the wilderness; nevertheless, thou hast been [a]merciful unto us. O Lord, look upon me in pity, and turn away thine anger from this thy people, and suffer not that they shall go forth across this raging deep in darkness; but behold these [b]things which I have molten out of the rock.

4 And I know, O Lord, that thou hast all [a]power, and can do whatsoever thou wilt for the benefit of man; therefore touch these stones, O Lord, with thy [b]finger, and prepare them that they may shine forth in darkness; and they shall shine forth unto us in the vessels which we have prepared, that we may have [c]light while we shall cross the sea.

5 Behold, O Lord, thou canst do this. We know that thou art able to show forth great power, which [a]looks small unto the understanding of men.

6 And it came to pass that when the brother of Jared had said these words, behold, the [a]Lord stretched forth his hand and touched the stones one by one with his [b]finger. And the [c]veil was taken from off the eyes of the brother of Jared, and he saw the finger of the Lord; and it was as the finger of a man, like unto flesh and blood; and the brother of Jared [d]fell down before the Lord, for he was struck with [e]fear.

7 And the Lord saw that the brother of Jared had fallen to the earth; and the Lord said unto him: Arise, why hast thou fallen?

8 And he saith unto the Lord: I saw the finger of the Lord, and I feared lest he should [a]smite me; for I knew not that the Lord had flesh and blood.

9 And the Lord said unto him: Because of thy faith thou hast seen that I shall take upon me [a]flesh and blood; and never has man come before me with [b]such exceeding faith as thou hast; for were it not so ye

3 1*a* Ex. 24: 13 (12–13); Deut. 10: 1; 1 Ne. 11: 1.
b Ether 4: 1.
c TG Skill.
d Rev. 21: 21.
2*a* Gen. 18: 32 (25–33).
b Moses 1: 10.
c TG Fall of Man.
d Mosiah 3: 19.
3*a* Ether 1: 40 (34–43).
b Ether 6: 2 (2–3, 10).
4*a* TG God, Power of.
b Ether 12: 20 (19–21).
c TG Light.
5*a* Isa. 55: 8 (8–9).
6*a* TG Jesus Christ, Lord.
b Dan. 5: 5; Abr. 3: 12 (11–12).
c Ether 12: 19 (19, 21).
d Ezek. 1: 28; Acts 9: 4 (3–5).
e Ex. 3: 6; JS-H 1: 32.
8*a* Moses 1: 11.
9*a* TG Flesh and Blood; Jesus Christ, Condescension of.
b Matt. 8: 10; Alma 19: 10.

could not have seen my finger.
Sawest thou more than this?
10 And he answered: Nay; Lord,
[a]show thyself unto me.
11 And the Lord said unto him:
[a]Believest thou the words which I
shall speak?
12 And he answered: Yea, Lord, I
know that thou speakest the truth,
for thou art a God of truth, and
[a]canst not lie.
13 And when he had said these
words, behold, the Lord [a]showed
himself unto him, and said: [b]Because
thou knowest these things ye are
redeemed from the fall; therefore
ye are brought back into my
[c]presence; therefore I [d]show myself
unto you.
14 Behold, I am he who was [a]pre-
pared from the foundation of the
world to [b]redeem my people. Behold,
I am Jesus Christ. I am the [c]Father
and the Son. In me shall all mankind
have [d]life, and that eternally, even
they who shall believe on my name;
and they shall become my [e]sons and
my daughters.
15 And never have I [a]showed myself unto man whom I have created,
for never has man [b]believed in me
as thou hast. Seest thou that ye are
created after mine own [c]image? Yea,
even all men were created in the
beginning after mine own image.
16 Behold, this [a]body, which ye
now [b]behold, is the [c]body of my
[d]spirit; and man have I created after
the body of my spirit; and even as I
appear unto thee to be in the spirit
will I appear unto my people in the
flesh.
17 And now, as I, Moroni, said I
could [a]not make a full account of
these things which are written,
therefore it sufficeth me to say that
Jesus showed himself unto this
man in the spirit, even after the
manner and in the likeness of the
same body even as he [b]showed himself unto the Nephites.
18 And he ministered unto him
even as he ministered unto the
Nephites; and all this, that this man
might know that he was God, because of the many great works which
the Lord had showed unto him.
19 And because of the [a]knowledge
of this man he could not be kept
from beholding within the [b]veil;
and he saw the finger of Jesus, which,
when he saw, he fell with fear; for he
knew that it was the finger of the
Lord; and he had [c]faith no longer,
for he knew, nothing [d]doubting.
20 Wherefore, having this perfect
knowledge of God, he could [a]not be
kept from within the veil; therefore
he [b]saw Jesus; and he did minister
unto him.
21 And it came to pass that the
Lord said unto the brother of Jared:
Behold, thou shalt not suffer these
things which ye have seen and heard
to go forth unto the world, until
the [a]time cometh that I shall glorify
my name in the flesh; wherefore, ye
shall [b]treasure up the things which
ye have seen and heard, and show
it to no man.

10*a* Ex. 33: 18 (17–18).
11*a* 1 Ne. 11: 4 (4–5).
12*a* Num. 23: 19; Heb. 6: 18.
13*a* 1 Sam. 3: 21; D&C 67: 11 (11–12).
b Enos 1: 8 (6–8).
c TG God, Presence of; God, Privilege of Seeing.
d TG Jesus Christ, Appearances, Antemortal.
14*a* TG Jesus Christ, Foreordained.
b TG Jesus Christ, Redeemer.
c Mosiah 15: 2.
d Mosiah 16: 9; D&C 88: 13 (7–13).
e TG Sons and Daughters of God.
15*a* Ex. 3: 6; 33: 20 (11–23); John 1: 18; D&C 107: 54; Moses 1: 2. TG God, Privilege of Seeing.
b TG Faith.
c Gen. 1: 26 (26–28); Mosiah 7: 27; D&C 20: 18 (17–18). TG God, Body of—Corporeal Nature.
16*a* TG God, Manifestations of.
b D&C 17: 1.
c TG Spirit Body.
d TG Man, Antemortal Existence of.
17*a* Ether 1: 5; 15: 33.
b 3 Ne. 11: 8 (8–16).
19*a* TG Knowledge.
b TG Veil.
c Alma 32: 34.
d TG Doubt.
20*a* Ether 12: 21 (19–21).
b TG Jesus Christ, Appearances, Antemortal.
21*a* Ether 4: 1.
b Luke 2: 19 (17–20).

22 And behold, when ye shall come
unto me, ye shall write them and
shall seal them up, that no one can
interpret them; for ye shall write
them in a [a]language that they cannot be read.
23 And behold, these [a]two stones
will I give unto thee, and ye shall
seal them up also with the things
which ye shall write.
24 For behold, the [a]language which
ye shall write I have confounded;
wherefore I will cause in my own
due time that these stones shall
magnify to the eyes of men these
things which ye shall write.
25 And when the Lord had said
these words, he [a]showed unto the
brother of Jared [b]all the inhabitants
of the earth which had been, and
also all that would be; and he [c]with-
held them not from his sight, even
unto the ends of the earth.
26 For he had said unto him in
times before, that [a]if he would
[b]believe in him that he could show
unto him [c]all things—it should be
shown unto him; therefore the Lord
could not withhold anything from
him, for he knew that the Lord
could show him all things.
27 And the Lord said unto him:
Write these things and [a]seal them
up; and I will show them in mine
own due time unto the children of
men.
28 And it came to pass that the
Lord commanded him that he
should seal up the two [a]stones
which he had received, and show
them not, until the Lord should show
them unto the children of [b]men.

CHAPTER 4

Moroni is commanded to seal up the writings of the brother of Jared—They shall not be revealed until men have faith even as the brother of Jared—Christ commands men to believe his words and those of his disciples—Men are commanded to repent and believe the gospel and be saved.

1 AND the Lord commanded the
brother of Jared to go down out of
the [a]mount from the presence of the
Lord, and [b]write the things which
he had seen; and they were forbidden to come unto the children of
men [c]until after that he should be
lifted up upon the cross; and for this
cause did king Mosiah keep them,
that they should not come unto the
world until after Christ should show
himself unto his people.
2 And after Christ truly had showed himself unto his people he commanded that they should be made
manifest.
3 And now, after that, they have
all dwindled in unbelief; and there
is [a]none save it be the Lamanites,
and they have rejected the gospel
of Christ; therefore I am commanded that I should [b]hide them up
again in the earth.
4 Behold, I have written upon these
plates the [a]very things which the
brother of Jared saw; and there
never were [b]greater things made
manifest than those which were
made manifest unto the brother of
Jared.
5 Wherefore the Lord hath commanded me to write them; and I
have written them. And he com-

22*a* Mosiah 8: 11 (11–12). TG Language.
23*a* Mosiah 8: 13 (13–18); Morm. 9: 34; D&C 17: 1. TG Urim and Thummim.
24*a* Ether 1: 35.
25*a* 2 Ne. 27: 7. TG God, Omniscience of; Revelation.
b Moses 1: 8.
c Luke 24: 16 (10–24); D&C 25: 4.
26*a* Ether 3: 11–13.
b TG Believe.
c 2 Ne. 27: 7 (7–8, 10–11); Mosiah 8: 19; Ether 4: 4 (1–8).
27*a* 2 Ne. 27: 7 (6–23).
28*a* D&C 17: 1.
b 2 Ne. 3: 6; 3 Ne. 21: 11 (8–11); Morm. 8: 16 (16, 25).
4 1*a* Ether 3: 1.
b Ether 12: 24. TG Record Keeping; Scriptures, Writing of.
c Ether 3: 21.
3*a* Morm. 8: 3 (2–3).
b Morm. 8: 14. TG Scriptures, Preservation of.
4*a* Ether 5: 1.
b 2 Ne. 27: 7 (7–8, 10–11); Mosiah 8: 19; Ether 3: 26 (21–28).

manded me that I should [a]seal them
up; and he also hath commanded
that I should seal up the interpretation thereof; wherefore I have sealed
up the [b]interpreters, according to
the commandment of the Lord.
6 For the Lord said unto me: They
shall not go forth unto the Gentiles
until the day that they shall repent
of their iniquity, and become clean
before the Lord.
7 And in that day that they shall
exercise [a]faith in me, saith the Lord,
even as the brother of Jared did,
that they may become [b]sanctified
in me, then will I [c]manifest unto
them the things which the brother
of Jared saw, even to the unfolding
unto them all my [d]revelations, saith
Jesus Christ, the Son of God, the
[e]Father of the heavens and of the
earth, and all things that in them
are.
8 And he that will [a]contend against
the word of the Lord, let him be
accursed; and he that shall [b]deny
these things, let him be accursed;
for unto them will I show [c]no greater
things, saith Jesus Christ; for I am
he who speaketh.
9 And at my command the heavens
are opened and are [a]shut; and at my
word the [b]earth shall shake; and at
my command the inhabitants thereof shall pass away, even so as by fire.
10 And he that believeth not my
words believeth not my disciples;
and if it so be that I do not speak,
judge ye; for ye shall know that it is
I that speaketh, at the [a]last day.
11 But he that [a]believeth these
things which I have spoken, him
will I visit with the manifestations
of my Spirit, and he shall [b]know and
bear record. For because of my
Spirit he shall [c]know that these
things are [d]true; for it persuadeth
men to do good.
12 And whatsoever thing persuadeth men to do good is of me; for
[a]good cometh of none save it be of
me. I am the same that leadeth men
to all good; he that will [b]not believe
my words will not believe me—that
I am; and he that will not believe
me will not believe the Father who
sent me. For behold, I am the
Father, I am the [c]light, and the
[d]life, and the [e]truth of the world.
13 [a]Come unto me, O ye Gentiles,
and I will show unto you the greater
things, the knowledge which is hid
up because of unbelief.
14 Come unto me, O ye house of
Israel, and it shall be made [a]mani-
fest unto you how great things the
Father hath laid up for you, from
the foundation of the world; and it
hath not come unto you, because of
unbelief.
15 Behold, when ye shall rend that
veil of unbelief which doth cause
you to remain in your awful state of
wickedness, and hardness of heart,
and blindness of mind, then shall
the great and marvelous things
which have been [a]hid up from the
foundation of the world from you—
yea, when ye shall [b]call upon the
Father in my name, with a broken
heart and a contrite spirit, then
shall ye know that the Father hath

5a Dan. 12:9; 3 Ne. 26:9 (7–12, 18); Ether 5:1; D&C 17:6; 35:18; JS-H 1:65.
b Morm. 6:6; D&C 17:1; JS-H 1:52. TG Urim and Thummim.
7a D&C 5:28.
b TG Sanctification.
c 2 Ne. 30:16; Alma 12:9; 3 Ne. 26:10 (6–11).
d 2 Ne. 27:22.
e Mosiah 3:8.
8a Job 9:3 (1–4); 3 Ne. 29:5 (1–9); Morm. 8:17.
b 2 Ne. 27:14; 28:29 (29–30, 34).
c Alma 12:10 (10–11); 3 Ne. 26:10 (9–10).
9a 1 Kgs. 8:35; D&C 77:8.
b Hel. 12:11 (8–18); Morm. 5:23.
10a 2 Ne. 25:22; 33:15 (10–15); 3 Ne. 27:25 (23–27).
11a D&C 5:16.
b 2 Ne. 32:5; 3 Ne. 16:6.
c TG Testimony.
d Alma 3:12; Ether 5:3 (1–4); Moro. 10:4 (1–5).
12a Omni 1:25; Alma 5:40; Moro. 7:16 (12–17).
b 3 Ne. 11:35; 28:34.
c TG Jesus Christ, Light of the World.
d Col. 3:4.
e Alma 38:9.
13a 3 Ne. 12:2 (2–3).
14a D&C 121:26 (26–29).
15a 2 Ne. 27:10.
b Gen. 4:26; Moro. 2:2.

remembered the covenant which he made unto your fathers, O house of Israel.

16 And then shall my [a]revelations which I have caused to be written by my servant John be unfolded in the eyes of all the people. Remember, when ye see these things, ye shall know that the time is at hand that they shall be made manifest in very deed.

17 Therefore, [a]when ye shall receive this record ye may know that the work of the Father has commenced upon all the face of the land.

18 Therefore, [a]repent all ye ends of the earth, and come unto me, and believe in my gospel, and be [b]baptized in my name; for he that believeth and is baptized shall be saved; but he that believeth not shall be damned; and [c]signs shall follow them that believe in my name.

19 And blessed is he that is found [a]faithful unto my name at the last day, for he shall be [b]lifted up to dwell in the kingdom prepared for him [c]from the foundation of the world. And behold it is I that hath spoken it. Amen.

CHAPTER 5

Three witnesses and the work itself shall stand as a testimony of the truthfulness of the Book of Mormon.

AND now I, Moroni, have written the words which were commanded me, according to my memory; and I have told you the things which I have [a]sealed up; therefore touch them not in order that ye may translate; for that thing is forbidden you, except by and by it shall be wisdom in God.

2 And behold, ye may be privileged that ye may show the plates unto [a]those who shall assist to bring forth this work;

3 And unto [a]three shall they be shown by the power of God; wherefore they shall [b]know of a surety that these things are [c]true.

4 And in the mouth of three [a]witnesses shall these things be established; and the [b]testimony of three, and this work, in the which shall be shown forth the power of God and also his word, of which the Father, and the Son, and the Holy Ghost bear record—and all this shall stand as a testimony against the world at the last day.

5 And if it so be that they repent and [a]come unto the Father in the name of Jesus, they shall be received into the kingdom of God.

6 And now, if I have no authority for these things, judge ye; for ye shall know that I have authority when ye shall see me, and we shall stand before God at the last day. Amen.

CHAPTER 6

The Jaredite barges are driven by the winds to the promised land—The people praise the Lord for his goodness—Orihah is appointed king over them—Jared and his brother pass away in death.

AND now I, Moroni, proceed to give the record of [a]Jared and his brother.

2 For it came to pass after the Lord had prepared the [a]stones which the brother of Jared had carried up into the mount, the brother of Jared

---

16*a* Rev. 1: 1; 1 Ne. 14: 23 (18–27).
17*a* 3 Ne. 21: 2 (1–11, 28).
18*a* 3 Ne. 27: 20; Moro. 7: 34.
b John 3: 5 (3–5). TG Baptism, Essential.
c TG Holy Ghost, Gifts of.
19*a* Ps. 31: 23; Mosiah 2: 41; D&C 6: 13; 63: 47. TG Jesus Christ, Taking the Name of.
b Morm. 2: 19.
c 2 Ne. 9: 18; Alma 42: 26; Ether 3: 14.
5 1*a* 2 Ne. 27: 8 (7–11, 21); Ether 4: 5 (4–7); D&C 17: 6.
2*a* 2 Ne. 27: 14 (13–14); D&C 5: 15 (1–16).
3*a* 2 Ne. 11: 3; 27: 12 (12–14); D&C 17: 3 (3–5).
b D&C 5: 25.
c Ether 4: 11 (6–11); Moro. 10: 4 (1–4).
4*a* 2 Ne. 27: 12 (12–14); D&C 14: 8; 17: 1.
b 2 Ne. 25: 18; 29: 11.
5*a* Morm. 9: 27; Moro. 10: 30 (30–32).
6 1*a* Ether 1: 34.
2*a* Ether 3: 3.

came down out of the mount, and he
did put forth the stones into the
vessels which were prepared, one in
each end thereof; and behold, they
did give light unto the vessels.
3 And thus the Lord caused stones
to shine in darkness, to give light
unto men, women, and children,
that they might not cross the great
waters in darkness.
4 And it came to pass that when
they had prepared all manner of
[a]food, that thereby they might subsist upon the water, and also food
for their flocks and herds, and [b]whatsoever beast or animal or fowl that
they should carry with them—and
it came to pass that when they had
done all these things they got aboard
of their vessels or barges, and set
forth into the sea, commending
themselves unto the Lord their
God.
5 And it came to pass that the Lord
God caused that there should be a
[a]furious wind blow upon the face of
the waters, [b]towards the promised
land; and thus they were tossed
upon the waves of the sea before the
wind.
6 And it came to pass that they
were many times buried in the
depths of the sea, because of the
mountain waves which broke upon
them, and also the great and terrible
tempests which were caused by the
fierceness of the wind.
7 And it came to pass that when
they were buried in the deep there
was no water that could hurt them,
their vessels being [a]tight like unto a
dish, and also they were tight like
unto the [b]ark of Noah; therefore
when they were encompassed about
by many waters they did cry unto
the Lord, and he did bring them
forth again upon the top of the
waters.
8 And it came to pass that the wind
did never cease to blow towards the
promised land while they were upon
the waters; and thus they were
[a]driven forth before the wind.
9 And they did [a]sing praises unto
the Lord; yea, the brother of Jared
did sing praises unto the Lord, and
he did [b]thank and praise the Lord all
the day long; and when the night
came, they did not cease to praise
the Lord.
10 And thus they were driven
forth; and no monster of the sea
could break them, neither [a]whale
that could mar them; and they did
have light continually, whether it
was above the water or under the
water.
11 And thus they were driven forth,
[a]three hundred and forty and four
days upon the water.
12 And they did [a]land upon the
shore of the [b]promised land. And
when they had set their feet upon
the shores of the promised land they
bowed themselves down upon the
face of the land, and did humble
themselves before the Lord, and did
shed tears of joy before the Lord,
because of the multitude of his
[c]tender mercies over them.
13 And it came to pass that they
went forth upon the face of the land,
and began to till the earth.
14 And Jared had four [a]sons; and
they were called Jacom, and Gilgah,
and Mahah, and Orihah.
15 And the brother of Jared also
begat sons and daughters.
16 And the [a]friends of Jared and
his brother were in number about
twenty and two souls; and they also
begat sons and daughters before
they came to the promised land;
and therefore they began to be
many.
17 And they were taught to [a]walk

4a TG Food.
b Ether 2: 1; 9: 18 (18–19).
5a Ether 2: 24 (24–25).
b 1 Ne. 18: 9.
7a Ether 2: 17.
b Gen. 6: 14; Moses 7: 43.
8a 1 Ne. 18: 13 (8–13).
9a TG Singing.
b 1 Chr. 16: 8 (7–36); Ps. 34: 1 (1–3); Alma 37: 37; D&C 46: 32.
10a Gen. 1: 21; Ether 2: 24.
11a Gen. 7: 11; 8: 13.
12a Ether 7: 16.
b Alma 22: 30 (29–34); Ether 7: 6.
c Ether 7: 27; 10: 2.
14a Ether 6: 27.
16a Ether 1: 41.
17a TG Walking with God.

humbly before the Lord; and they were also [b]taught from on high.

18 And it came to pass that they began to spread upon the face of the land, and to multiply and to till the earth; and they did wax strong in the land.

19 And the brother of Jared began to be old, and saw that he must soon go down to the grave; wherefore he said unto Jared: Let us gather together our people that we may number them, that we may know of them what they will desire of us before we go down to our graves.

20 And accordingly the people were gathered together. Now the number of the sons and the daughters of the brother of Jared were twenty and two souls; and the number of sons and daughters of Jared were twelve, he having four sons.

21 And it came to pass that they did number their people; and after that they had numbered them, they did desire of them the things which they would that they should do before they went down to their graves.

22 And it came to pass that the people desired of them that they should [a]anoint one of their sons to be a king over them.

23 And now behold, this was grievous unto them. And the brother of Jared said unto them: Surely this thing [a]leadeth into captivity.

24 But Jared said unto his brother: Suffer them that they may have a king. And therefore he said unto them: Choose ye out from among our sons a king, even whom ye will.

25 And it came to pass that they chose even the firstborn of the brother of Jared; and his name was Pagag. And it came to pass that he refused and would not be their [a]king. And the people would that his father should constrain him, but his father would not; and he commanded them that they should constrain no man to be their king.

26 And it came to pass that they chose all the brothers of Pagag, and they would not.

27 And it came to pass that neither would the [a]sons of Jared, even all save it were one; and [b]Orihah was anointed to be king over the people.

28 And he began to reign, and the people began to [a]prosper; and they became exceedingly rich.

29 And it came to pass that Jared died, and his brother also.

30 And it came to pass that Orihah did walk humbly before the Lord, and did remember how great things the Lord had done for his father, and also taught his people how great things the Lord had done for their fathers.

CHAPTER 7

Orihah reigns in righteousness—Amid usurpation and strife the rival kingdoms of Shule and Cohor are set up—Prophets condemn the wickedness and idolatry of the people, who then repent.

AND it came to pass that Orihah did execute judgment upon the land in righteousness all his days, whose days were exceedingly many.

2 And he begat sons and daughters; yea, he begat thirty and one, among whom were twenty and three sons.

3 And it came to pass that he also begat [a]Kib in his [b]old age. And it came to pass that Kib reigned in his stead; and Kib begat Corihor.

4 And when Corihor was thirty and two years old he rebelled against his father, and went over and dwelt in the land of Nehor; and he begat sons and daughters, and they became exceedingly fair; wherefore Corihor drew away many people after him.

5 And when he had gathered together an army he came up unto the

17*b* TG Guidance, Divine; Revelation.
22*a* TG Anointing.
23*a* 1 Sam. 8: 11 (10–18); Mosiah 29: 18 (16–23); Ether 7: 5.
25*a* TG Kings, Earthly.
27*a* Ether 6: 14.
b Ether 1: 32.
28*a* TG Prosper.
7 3*a* Ether 1: 32 (31–32).
b Gen. 18: 12 (11–12); Ether 7: 26; 9: 23.

land of [a]Moron where the king
dwelt, and took him captive, which
[b]brought to pass the saying of the
brother of Jared that they would be
brought into captivity.
6 Now the [a]land of Moron, where
the king dwelt, was near the land
which is called Desolation by the
Nephites.
7 And it came to pass that Kib
dwelt in [a]captivity, and his people
under Corihor his son, until he became exceedingly old; nevertheless
Kib begat Shule in his old age, while
he was yet in captivity.
8 And it came to pass that Shule
was angry with his brother; and
Shule waxed strong, and became
mighty as to the strength of a man;
and he was also mighty in judgment.
9 Wherefore, he came to the hill
Ephraim, and he did molten out of
the hill, and made swords out of
[a]steel for those whom he had drawn
away with him; and after he had
armed them with swords he returned
to the city Nehor, and gave battle
unto his brother Corihor, by which
means he obtained the kingdom and
restored it unto his father Kib.
10 And now because of the thing
which Shule had done, his father bestowed upon him the kingdom;
therefore he began to reign in the
stead of his father.
11 And it came to pass that he did
execute judgment in righteousness;
and he did spread his kingdom upon
all the face of the land, for the people
had become exceedingly numerous.
12 And it came to pass that Shule
also begat many sons and daughters.
13 And Corihor repented of the
many evils which he had done;
wherefore Shule gave him power in
his kingdom.
14 And it came to pass that Corihor
had many sons and daughters. And
among the sons of Corihor there was
one whose name was Noah.
15 And it came to pass that Noah
rebelled against Shule, the king, and
also his father Corihor, and drew
away Cohor his brother, and also all
his brethren and many of the people.
16 And he gave battle unto Shule,
the king, in which he did obtain the
land of their [a]first inheritance; and
he became a king over that part of
the land.
17 And it came to pass that he gave
battle again unto Shule, the king;
and he took Shule, the king, and carried him away captive into Moron.
18 And it came to pass as he was
about to put him to death, the sons
of Shule crept into the house of
Noah by night and slew him, and
broke down the door of the prison
and brought out their father, and
placed him upon his throne in his
own kingdom.
19 Wherefore, the son of Noah did
build up his kingdom in his stead;
nevertheless they did not gain power
any more over Shule the king, and
the people who were under the reign
of Shule the king did prosper exceedingly and wax great.
20 And the country was [a]divided;
and there were two kingdoms, the
kingdom of Shule, and the kingdom
of Cohor, the son of Noah.
21 And Cohor, the son of Noah,
caused that his people should give
battle unto Shule, in which Shule did
beat them and did slay Cohor.
22 And now Cohor had a son who
was called Nimrod; and Nimrod
gave up the kingdom of Cohor unto
Shule, and he did gain favor in the
eyes of Shule; wherefore Shule did
bestow great favors upon him, and
he did do in the kingdom of Shule
according to his desires.
23 And also in the reign of Shule
there came [a]prophets among the
people, who were sent from the Lord,
prophesying that the wickedness and
[b]idolatry of the people was bringing a
curse upon the land, and they should
be destroyed if they did not repent.

5*a* Ether 14: 6 (6, 11).
b Ether 6: 23.
6*a* Ether 6: 12.
7*a* Ether 8: 4 (3–4); 10: 14.
9*a* 1 Ne. 16: 18.
16*a* Ether 6: 12.
20*a* 2 Ne. 5: 7 (1–14).
23*a* Ether 9: 28; 11: 1 (1, 12, 20).
b TG Idolatry.

24 And it came to pass that the
people did [a]revile against the prophets, and did mock them. And it
came to pass that king Shule did
execute judgment against all those
who did revile against the prophets.
25 And he did execute a law
throughout all the land, which gave
power unto the prophets that they
should go whithersoever they would;
and by this cause the people were
brought unto repentance.
26 And because the people did
repent of their iniquities and idolatries the Lord did spare them, and
they began to prosper again in the
land. And it came to pass that Shule
[a]begat sons and daughters in his
old age.
27 And there were no more wars in
the days of Shule; and he remembered the great things that the Lord
had done for his fathers in bringing
them [a]across the great deep into the
promised land; wherefore he did
execute judgment in righteousness
all his days.

CHAPTER 8

There is strife and contention over the kingdom—Akish forms an oath-bound secret combination to slay the king—Secret combinations are of the devil and result in the destruction of nations—Modern Gentiles are warned against the secret combination which shall seek to overthrow the freedom of all lands, nations, and countries.

AND it came to pass that he begat
Omer, and Omer reigned in his stead.
And Omer begat Jared; and Jared
begat sons and daughters.
2 And Jared rebelled against his
father, and came and dwelt in the
land of Heth. And it came to pass
that he did [a]flatter many people, because of his cunning words, until he
had gained the half of the kingdom.
3 And when he had gained the half
of the kingdom he gave battle unto
his father, and he did carry away his
father into captivity, and did make
him serve in captivity;
4 And now, in the days of the reign
of Omer he was in [a]captivity the
half of his days. And it came to pass
that he begat sons and daughters,
among whom were Esrom and
Coriantumr;
5 And they were exceedingly
angry because of the doings of Jared
their brother, insomuch that they
did raise an army and gave battle
unto Jared. And it came to pass that
they did give battle unto him by
night.
6 And it came to pass that when
they had slain the army of Jared
they were about to slay him also;
and he plead with them that they
would not slay him, and he would
give up the kingdom unto his father.
And it came to pass that they did
grant unto him his life.
7 And now Jared became exceedingly [a]sorrowful because of the loss
of the kingdom, for he had set his
heart upon the kingdom and upon
the glory of the world.
8 Now the daughter of Jared being
exceedingly expert, and seeing the
sorrows of her father, thought to
devise a plan whereby she could redeem the kingdom unto her father.
9 Now the daughter of Jared was
exceedingly fair. And it came to pass
that she did talk with her father,
and said unto him: Whereby hath
my father so much sorrow? Hath
he not read the [a]record which our
fathers brought across the great
deep? Behold, is there not an
[b]account concerning them of [c]old,
that they by their [d]secret plans did
obtain kingdoms and great glory?
10 And now, therefore, let my
father send for Akish, the son of

24*a* Mosiah 27: 2 (1–3). TG Prophets, Rejection of; Reviling.
26*a* Ether 7: 3 (3, 7); 9: 23.
27*a* Ether 6: 12 (1–12).
8 2*a* Hel. 1: 7; 2: 5.
4*a* Ether 7: 7 (5–7); 10: 14.
7*a* Morm. 2: 13.
9*a* Ether 1: 3.
b 3 Ne. 6: 28.
c Hel. 6: 26 (26–30); 3 Ne. 3: 9.
d Hel. 6: 27; Ether 13: 18; Moses 5: 30 (18–52).

Kimnor; and behold, I am fair, and I will dance before him, and I will please him, that he will desire me to wife; wherefore if he shall desire of thee that ye shall give unto him me to wife, then shall ye say: I will give her if ye will bring unto me the [a]head of my father, the king.

11 And now Omer was a friend to Akish; wherefore, when Jared had sent for Akish, the daughter of Jared danced before him that she pleased him, insomuch that he desired her to wife. And it came to pass that he said unto Jared: Give her unto me to wife.

12 And Jared said unto him: I will give her unto you, if ye will bring unto me the head of my father, the king.

13 And it came to pass that Akish gathered in unto the house of Jared all his kinsfolk, and said unto them: Will ye swear unto me that ye will be faithful unto me in the thing which I shall desire of you?

14 And it came to pass that they all [a]sware unto him, by the God of heaven, and also by the heavens, and also by the earth, and by their heads, that whoso should vary from the assistance which Akish desired should lose his head; and whoso should divulge whatsoever thing Akish made known unto them, the same should lose his life.

15 And it came to pass that thus they did agree with [a]Akish. And Akish did administer unto them the oaths which were given by them of old who also sought power, which had been handed down even from [b]Cain, who was a murderer from the beginning.

16 And they were kept up by the [a]power of the devil to administer these oaths unto the people, to keep them in darkness, to help such as sought power to gain power, and to murder, and to plunder, and to lie, and to commit all manner of wickedness and whoredoms.

17 And it was the daughter of Jared who put it into his heart to search up these things of old; and Jared put it into the heart of Akish; wherefore, Akish administered it unto his kindred and friends, leading them away by fair promises to do whatsoever thing he desired.

18 And it came to pass that they formed a secret [a]combination, even as they of old; which combination is most abominable and wicked above all, in the sight of God;

19 For the Lord worketh not in secret combinations, neither doth he will that man should shed blood, but in all things hath forbidden it, from the beginning of man.

20 And now I, Moroni, do not write the manner of their oaths and combinations, for it hath been made known unto me that they are had [a]among all people, and they are had among the Lamanites.

21 And they have caused the [a]destruction of this people of whom I am now speaking, and also the destruction of the people of Nephi.

22 And whatsoever [a]nation shall uphold such secret combinations, to get power and gain, until they shall spread over the nation, behold, they shall be destroyed; for the Lord will not suffer that the [b]blood of his saints, which shall be shed by them, shall always cry unto him from the ground for [c]vengeance upon them and yet he avenge them not.

23 Wherefore, O ye Gentiles, it is wisdom in God that these things should be shown unto you, that thereby ye may repent of your sins, and suffer not that these murderous combinations shall get above you,

10*a* Mark 6: 24 (22–28).
14*a* Hel. 1: 11; 3 Ne. 3: 8. TG Swearing.
15*a* Ether 9: 1.
b Gen. 4: 7 (7–8); Moses 5: 25.
16*a* Moses 4: 6; 5: 13.
18*a* TG Secret Combinations.
20*a* 4 Ne. 1: 46; Morm. 2: 8; 8: 9.
21*a* Hel. 6: 28; D&C 38: 13 (13–16).
22*a* TG Governments.
b Rev. 6: 10 (1–11); 19: 2; 2 Ne. 28: 10; Morm. 8: 27 (27, 40–41); D&C 87: 7.
c TG God, Justice of; Vengeance.

which are built up to get [a]power and gain—and the work, yea, even the work of [b]destruction come upon you, yea, even the sword of the justice of the Eternal God shall fall upon you, to your overthrow and destruction if ye shall suffer these things to be.

24 Wherefore, the Lord commandeth you, when ye shall see these things come among you that ye shall awake to a sense of your awful situation, because of this [a]secret combination which shall be among you; or wo be unto it, because of the blood of them who have been slain; for they cry from the dust for vengeance upon it, and also upon those who built it up.

25 For it cometh to pass that whoso buildeth it up seeketh to overthrow the [a]freedom of all lands, nations, and countries; and it bringeth to pass the destruction of all people, for it is built up by the devil, who is the father of all lies; even that same liar who [b]beguiled our first parents, yea, even that same liar who hath caused man to commit murder from the beginning; who hath [c]hardened the hearts of men that they have [d]murdered the prophets, and stoned them, and cast them out from the beginning.

26 Wherefore, I, Moroni, am commanded to write these things that evil may be done away, and that the time may come that Satan may have [a]no power upon the hearts of the children of men, but that they may be [b]persuaded to do good continually, that they may come unto the fountain of all [c]righteousness and be saved.

CHAPTER 9

The kingdom passes from one to another by descent and intrigue and murder—Emer saw the Son of Righteousness—Many prophets cry repentance—A famine and poisonous serpents plague the people.

AND now I, Moroni, proceed with my record. Therefore, behold, it came to pass that because of the [a]secret combinations of Akish and his friends, behold, they did overthrow the kingdom of Omer.

2 Nevertheless, the Lord was merciful unto Omer, and also to his sons and to his daughters who did not seek his destruction.

3 And the Lord [a]warned Omer in a dream that he should depart out of the land; wherefore Omer [b]departed out of the land with his family, and traveled many days, and came over and passed by the hill of [c]Shim, and came over by the place [d]where the Nephites were destroyed, and from thence eastward, and came to a place which was called Ablom, by the seashore, and there he pitched his tent, and also his sons and his daughters, and all his household, save it were Jared and his family.

4 And it came to pass that Jared was anointed king over the people, by the hand of wickedness; and he gave unto Akish his daughter to wife.

5 And it came to pass that Akish [a]sought the life of his father-in-law; and he applied unto those whom he had sworn by the [b]oath of the ancients, and they obtained the head of his father-in-law, as he sat upon his throne, giving audience to his people.

6 For so great had been the spreading of this wicked and secret society that it had corrupted the hearts of all the people; therefore Jared was murdered upon his throne, and Akish reigned in his stead.

23*a* Moses 6: 15.
b Luke 13: 3 (1–5).
24*a* D&C 42: 64.
25*a* TG Liberty.
b Gen. 3: 13 (1–13); 2 Ne. 9: 9; Mosiah 16: 3; Moses 4: 19 (5–19).
c TG Hardheartedness.
d TG Prophets, Rejection of.
26*a* 2 Ne. 30: 18.
b 2 Ne. 33: 4; Moro. 7: 13 (12–17).
c TG Righteousness.
9 1*a* Ether 8: 15 (13–17).
3*a* TG Dream; Warnings.
b Ether 9: 13.
c Morm. 1: 3; 4: 23.
d Morm. 6: 2 (1–15).
5*a* Esth. 2: 21.
b TG Oath.

7 And it came to pass that Akish began to be [a]jealous of his son, therefore he shut him up in prison, and kept him upon little or no food until he had suffered death.

8 And now the brother of him that suffered death, (and his name was Nimrah) was angry with his father because of that which his father had done unto his brother.

9 And it came to pass that Nimrah gathered together a small number of men, and fled out of the land, and came over and dwelt with Omer.

10 And it came to pass that Akish begat other sons, and they won the hearts of the people, notwithstanding they had sworn unto him to do all manner of iniquity according to that which he desired.

11 Now the people of Akish were desirous for gain, even as Akish was desirous for [a]power; wherefore, the sons of Akish did offer them [b]money, by which means they drew away the more part of the people after them.

12 And there began to be a war between the sons of Akish and Akish, which lasted for the space of many years, yea, unto the destruction of nearly all the people of the kingdom, yea, even all, save it were thirty souls, and they who fled with the house of Omer.

13 Wherefore, Omer was restored again to the [a]land of his inheritance.

14 And it came to pass that Omer began to be old; nevertheless, in his old age he begat Emer; and he anointed Emer to be king to reign in his stead.

15 And after that he had anointed Emer to be king he saw peace in the land for the space of two years, and he died, having seen exceedingly many days, which were full of sorrow. And it came to pass that Emer did reign in his stead, and did fill the steps of his father.

16 And the Lord began again to take the curse from off the land, and the house of Emer did prosper exceedingly under the reign of Emer; and in the space of sixty and two years they had become exceedingly strong, insomuch that they became exceedingly rich—

17 Having [a]all manner of fruit, and of grain, and of [b]silks, and of fine linen, and of [c]gold, and of silver, and of precious things;

18 And also [a]all manner of cattle, of oxen, and cows, and of sheep, and of swine, and of goats, and also many other kinds of animals which were useful for the food of man.

19 And they also had [a]horses, and asses, and there were elephants and cureloms and cumoms; all of which were useful unto man, and more especially the elephants and cureloms and cumoms.

20 And thus the Lord did pour out his blessings upon this land, which was [a]choice above all other lands; and he commanded that whoso should possess the land should possess it unto the Lord, or they should be [b]destroyed when they were ripened in iniquity; for upon such, saith the Lord: I will pour out the fulness of my wrath.

21 And Emer did execute judgment in righteousness all his days, and he begat many sons and daughters; and he begat Coriantum, and he anointed Coriantum to reign in his stead.

22 And after he had anointed Coriantum to reign in his stead he lived four years, and he saw peace in the land; yea, and he even saw the [a]Son of Righteousness, and did rejoice and glory in his day; and he died in peace.

23 And it came to pass that Coriantum did walk in the steps of his father, and did build many mighty cities, and did administer that which was good unto his people in all his

---

7*a* TG Jealousy.
11*a* TG Tyranny.
b 1 Sam. 8: 3 (1–4); Hel. 9: 20. TG Bribery.
13*a* Ether 9: 3.
17*a* Ether 1: 41.
b Ether 10: 24.
c Hel. 6: 9 (9–11); Ether 10: 12 (12, 23).
18*a* Ether 6: 4.
19*a* 1 Ne. 18: 25; Enos 1: 21; 3 Ne. 6: 1.
20*a* Ether 2: 15.
b Deut. 31: 4 (4–5); Ether 2: 8 (8–11).
22*a* 3 Ne. 25: 2.

days. And it came to pass that he
had no children even until he was
exceedingly [a]old.
24 And it came to pass that his wife
died, being an hundred and two
years old. And it came to pass that
Coriantum took to wife, in his old
age, a young maid, and begat sons
and daughters; wherefore he lived
until he was an hundred and forty
and two years old.
25 And it came to pass that he
begat Com, and Com reigned in his
stead; and he reigned forty and nine
years, and he begat Heth; and he
also begat other sons and daughters.
26 And the people had spread
again over all the face of the land,
and there began again to be an
exceedingly great wickedness upon
the face of the land, and [a]Heth
began to embrace the secret plans
again of old, to destroy his father.
27 And it came to pass that he did
dethrone his father, for he slew him
with his own sword; and he did
reign in his stead.
28 And there came prophets in the
land [a]again, crying repentance unto
them—that they must prepare the
way of the Lord or there should
come a curse upon the face of the
land; yea, even there should be a
great famine, in which they should
be destroyed if they did not repent.
29 But the people believed not the
words of the prophets, but they cast
them out; and some of them they
cast into [a]pits and left them to
perish. And it came to pass that they
did all these things according to the
commandment of the king, Heth.
30 And it came to pass that there
began to be a great [a]dearth upon the
land, and the inhabitants began to
be destroyed exceedingly fast because of the dearth, for there was no
rain upon the face of the earth.
31 And there came forth [a]poisonous
serpents also upon the face of the
land, and did poison many people.
And it came to pass that their flocks
began to flee before the poisonous
serpents, towards the land [b]south-
ward, which was called by the
Nephites [c]Zarahemla.
32 And it came to pass that there
were many of them which did perish
by the way; nevertheless, there
were some which fled into the land
southward.
33 And it came to pass that the
Lord did cause the [a]serpents that
they should pursue them no more,
but that they should hedge up the
way that the people could not pass,
that whoso should attempt to pass
might fall by the poisonous serpents.
34 And it came to pass that the
people did follow the course of the
beasts, and did devour the [a]car-
casses of them which fell by the
way, until they had devoured them
all. Now when the people saw that
they must [b]perish they began to
[c]repent of their iniquities and cry
unto the Lord.
35 And it came to pass that when
they had [a]humbled themselves
sufficiently before the Lord he did
send rain upon the face of the earth;
and the people began to revive
again, and there began to be fruit in
the north countries, and in all the
countries round about. And the
Lord did show forth his power unto
them in preserving them from
famine.

CHAPTER 10

One king succeeds another—Some of the kings are righteous; others are wicked—When righteousness prevails, the people are blessed and prospered by the Lord.

AND it came to pass that Shez, who
was a descendant of Heth—for

23*a* Ether 7:3 (3, 7).
26*a* Ether 10:1.
28*a* Ether 7:23; 11:1 (1, 12, 20).
29*a* Jer. 38:6 (4–13).
30*a* TG Drought; Famine.
31*a* Ether 10:19.
b Morm. 3:5; Ether 10:21.
c Omni 1:13.
33*a* Deut. 8:15; 1 Ne. 17:41. TG Plague.
34*a* Jer. 7:33 (32–33).
b Alma 34:34.
c D&C 101:8.
35*a* D&C 5:24.

[a]Heth had perished by the famine,
and all his household save it were
Shez—wherefore, Shez began to
build up again a broken people.
2 And it came to pass that Shez
did remember the destruction of his
fathers, and he did build up a
righteous kingdom; for he remembered what the Lord had done in
bringing Jared and his brother
[a]across the deep; and he did walk in
the ways of the Lord; and he begat
sons and daughters.
3 And his eldest son, whose name
was Shez, did [a]rebel against him;
nevertheless, Shez was smitten by
the hand of a robber, because of his
exceeding riches, which brought
peace again unto his father.
4 And it came to pass that his
father did build up many cities upon
the face of the land, and the people
began again to spread over all the
face of the land. And Shez did live
to an exceedingly old age; and he
begat Riplakish. And he died, and
Riplakish reigned in his stead.
5 And it came to pass that Riplakish did not do that which was
right in the sight of the Lord, for
he did have many wives and [a]con-
cubines, and did lay that upon men's
shoulders which was grievous to be
borne; yea, he did [b]tax them with
heavy taxes; and with the taxes he
did build many spacious buildings.
6 And he did erect him an exceedingly beautiful throne; and he did
build many prisons, and whoso
would not be subject unto taxes he
did [a]cast into prison; and whoso was
not able to pay taxes he did cast into
prison; and he did cause that they
should labor continually for their
support; and whoso refused to labor
he did cause to be put to death.
7 Wherefore he did obtain all his
fine work, yea, even his fine [a]gold
he did cause to be refined in prison;
and all manner of fine [b]workmanship
he did cause to be wrought in prison.
And it came to pass that he did
afflict the people with his whoredoms and abominations.
8 And when he had reigned for the
space of forty and two years the
people did rise up in rebellion against
him; and there began to be war
again in the land, insomuch that
Riplakish was killed, and his descendants were driven out of the
land.
9 And it came to pass after the
space of many years, Morianton,
(he being a descendant of Riplakish)
gathered together an army of outcasts, and went forth and gave
battle unto the people; and he
gained power over many cities; and
the war became exceedingly sore,
and did last for the space of many
years; and he did gain power over
all the land, and did establish himself king over all the land.
10 And after that he had established himself king he did ease the
burden of the people, by which he
did gain favor in the eyes of the
people, and they did anoint him to
be their king.
11 And he did do justice unto the
people, but not unto himself because of his many [a]whoredoms;
wherefore he was cut off from the
presence of the Lord.
12 And it came to pass that Morianton built up many cities, and the
people became exceedingly rich
under his reign, both in buildings,
and in [a]gold and silver, and in
raising grain, and in flocks, and
herds, and such things which had
been restored unto them.
13 And Morianton did live to an
exceedingly great age, and then he
begat Kim; and Kim did reign in
the stead of his father; and he did
reign eight years, and his father
died. And it came to pass that Kim
did [a]not reign in righteousness,

10 1*a* Ether 9:26 (25–29).
2*a* Ether 6:12 (1–12).
3*a* Mosiah 10:6.
5*a* Esth. 2:14; Jacob 3:5; Mosiah 11:2 (2–14).
b Gen. 47:24.
6*a* TG Oppression; Tyranny.
7*a* Esth. 1:4.
b TG Art.
11*a* TG Whoredom.
12*a* Ether 9:17 (17–18).
13*a* 1 Ne. 17:35 (34–35).

wherefore he was not favored of the
Lord.
14 And his brother did rise up in
rebellion against him, by which he
did bring him into [a]captivity; and
he did remain in captivity all his
days; and he begat sons and
daughters in captivity, and in his
old age he begat Levi; and he died.
15 And it came to pass that Levi
did serve in captivity after the
death of his father, for the space of
forty and two years. And he did
make war against the king of the
land, by which he did obtain unto
himself the kingdom.
16 And after he had obtained unto
himself the kingdom he did that
which was right in the sight of the
Lord; and the people did prosper in
the land; and he did live to a good
[a]old age, and begat sons and
daughters; and he also begat Corom,
whom he anointed king in his stead.
17 And it came to pass that
Corom did that which was good in
the sight of the Lord all his days;
and he begat many sons and
daughters; and after he had seen
many days he did pass away, even
like unto the rest of the earth; and
Kish reigned in his stead.
18 And it came to pass that Kish
passed away also, and Lib reigned
in his stead.
19 And it came to pass that Lib
also did that which was good in the
sight of the Lord. And in the days
of Lib the [a]poisonous serpents were
destroyed. Wherefore they did go
into the land southward, to hunt
food for the people of the land, for
the land was covered with animals
of the forest. And Lib also himself
became a great [b]hunter.
20 And they built a great city by
the [a]narrow neck of land, by the
place where the sea divides the
land.
21 And they did preserve the land
[a]southward for a wilderness, to get
game. And the whole face of the
land northward was covered with
inhabitants.
22 And they were exceedingly
[a]industrious, and they did buy and
sell and [b]traffic one with another,
that they might get gain.
23 And they did [a]work in all manner of [b]ore, and they did make gold,
and silver, and [c]iron, and [d]brass,
and all manner of metals; and they
did dig it out of the earth; wherefore, they did cast up mighty heaps
of earth to get ore, of gold, and of
silver, and of iron, and of copper.
And they did [e]work all manner of
fine work.
24 And they did have [a]silks, and
fine-twined [b]linen; and they did
work all manner of [c]cloth, that they
might clothe themselves from their
nakedness.
25 And they did make all manner
of tools to till the earth, both to
plow and to sow, to reap and to hoe,
and also to thrash.
26 And they did make all manner
of tools with which they did work
their beasts.
27 And they did make all manner
of [a]weapons of war. And they did
work all manner of work of exceedingly curious workmanship.
28 And never could be a people
more blessed than were they, and
more prospered by the hand of the
Lord. And they were in a land that
was choice above all lands, for the
Lord had spoken it.
29 And it came to pass that Lib
did live many years, and begat sons
and daughters; and he also begat
Hearthom.

14*a* Ether 7: 7; 8: 4 (3–4); 10: 30 (30–31).
16*a* TG Old Age.
19*a* Ether 9: 31.
b Gen. 25: 27; Ether 2: 1.
20*a* Alma 63: 5.
21*a* Morm. 3: 5; Ether 9: 31 (31–32).
22*a* TG Industry.
b Gen. 34: 10 (10–21); Mosiah 24: 7; 4 Ne. 1: 46.
23*a* TG Skill.
b Hel. 6: 9 (9–11); Ether 9: 17.
c 2 Ne. 5: 15; Moses 5: 46.
d Gen. 4: 22; Mosiah 8: 10.
e TG Art.
24*a* Ether 9: 17.
b Ex. 25: 4 (4–5); 1 Ne. 13: 7 (7–8).
c TG Clothing.
27*a* Ether 15: 15.

30 And it came to pass that Hearthom reigned in the stead of his father. And when Hearthom had reigned twenty and four years, behold, the kingdom was taken away from him. And he served many years in [a]captivity, yea, even all the remainder of his days.

31 And he begat Heth, and Heth lived in captivity all his days. And Heth begat Aaron, and Aaron dwelt in captivity all his days; and he begat Amnigaddah, and Amnigaddah also dwelt in captivity all his days; and he begat Coriantum, and Coriantum dwelt in captivity all his days; and he begat Com.

32 And it came to pass that Com drew away the half of the kingdom. And he reigned over the half of the kingdom forty and two years; and he went to battle against the king, Amgid, and they fought for the space of many years, during which time Com gained power over Amgid, and obtained power over the remainder of the kingdom.

33 And in the days of Com there began to be robbers in the land; and they adopted the old plans, and administered [a]oaths after the manner of the ancients, and sought again to destroy the kingdom.

34 Now Com did fight against them much; nevertheless, he did not prevail against them.

CHAPTER 11

Wars, dissensions, and wickedness dominate Jaredite life—Their prophets predict the utter destruction of the Jaredites unless they repent—The people reject the words of the prophets.

AND there came also in the days of Com many [a]prophets, and prophesied of the destruction of that great people except they should repent, and turn unto the Lord, and forsake their murders and wickedness.

2 And it came to pass that the prophets were [a]rejected by the people, and they fled unto Com for protection, for the people sought to destroy them.

3 And they prophesied unto Com many things; and he was blessed in all the remainder of his days.

4 And he lived to a good old age, and begat Shiblom; and Shiblom reigned in his stead. And the brother of Shiblom rebelled against him, and there began to be an exceedingly great war in all the land.

5 And it came to pass that the brother of Shiblom caused that all the prophets who prophesied of the destruction of the people should be put to [a]death;

6 And there was great calamity in all the land, for they had testified that a great curse should come upon the land, and also upon the people, and that there should be a great destruction among them, such an one as never had been upon the face of the earth, and their bones should become as [a]heaps of earth upon the face of the land except they should repent of their wickedness.

7 And they hearkened not unto the voice of the Lord, because of their wicked combinations; wherefore, there began to be wars and [a]contentions in all the land, and also many famines and pestilences, insomuch that there was a great destruction, such an one as never had been known upon the face of the earth; and all this came to pass in the days of Shiblom.

8 And the people began to repent of their iniquity; and inasmuch as they did the Lord did have [a]mercy on them.

9 And it came to pass that Shiblom was slain, and Seth was brought into [a]captivity, and did dwell in captivity all his days.

10 And it came to pass that Ahah,

30*a* Ether 10: 14; 11: 9.
33*a* TG Secret Combinations.
11 1*a* Ether 7: 23; 9: 28.
2*a* TG Prophets, Rejection of.
5*a* TG Persecution.
6*a* Omni 1: 22; Ether 14: 21.
7*a* TG Contention.
8*a* TG Mercy.
9*a* Ether 10: 30; 11: 18 (18–19).

his son, did obtain the kingdom;
and he did reign over the people all
his days. And he did do all manner
of iniquity in his days, by which he
did cause the shedding of much
blood; and few were his days.
11 And Ethem, being a descendant
of Ahah, did obtain the kingdom;
and he also did do that which was
wicked in his days.
12 And it came to pass that in the
days of Ethem there came many
prophets, and prophesied again unto
the people; yea, they did prophesy
that the Lord would utterly [a]de-
stroy them from off the face of the
earth except they repented of their
iniquities.
13 And it came to pass that the
people hardened their hearts, and
would not [a]hearken unto their
words; and the prophets [b]mourned
and withdrew from among the
people.
14 And it came to pass that Ethem
did execute judgment in wickedness
all his days; and he begat Moron.
And it came to pass that Moron did
reign in his stead; and Moron did
that which was wicked before the
Lord.
15 And it came to pass that there
arose a [a]rebellion among the people,
because of that secret [b]combination
which was built up to get power and
gain; and there arose a mighty man
among them in iniquity, and gave
battle unto Moron, in which he did
overthrow the half of the kingdom;
and he did maintain the half of the
kingdom for many years.
16 And it came to pass that Moron
did overthrow him, and did obtain
the kingdom again.
17 And it came to pass that there
arose another mighty man; and he
was a descendant of the brother of
Jared.
18 And it came to pass that he
did overthrow Moron and obtain
the kingdom; wherefore, Moron
dwelt in [a]captivity all the remainder of his days; and he begat Coriantor.
19 And it came to pass that
Coriantor dwelt in captivity all his
days.
20 And in the days of Coriantor
there also came many prophets, and
prophesied of great and marvelous
things, and cried repentance unto
the people, and except they should
repent the Lord God would execute
[a]judgment against them to their
utter destruction;
21 And that the Lord God would
send or bring forth [a]another people
to possess the [b]land, by his power,
after the manner by which he
brought their fathers.
22 And they did [a]reject all the
words of the prophets, because of
their [b]secret society and wicked
abominations.
23 And it came to pass that Coriantor begat [a]Ether, and he died,
having dwelt in captivity all his
days.

CHAPTER 12

The prophet Ether exhorts the people to believe in God—Moroni recounts the wonders and marvels done by faith—Faith enabled the brother of Jared to see Christ—The Lord gives men weaknesses that they may be humble—The brother of Jared moved Mount Zerin by faith—Faith, hope, and charity are essential to salvation—Moroni saw Jesus face to face.

AND it came to pass that the days
of Ether were in the days of
[a]Coriantumr; and Coriantumr was
king over all the land.
2 And [a]Ether was a prophet of the
Lord; wherefore Ether came forth

12a Ether 12:3.
13a Jer. 44:16; Mosiah 16:2.
b TG Mourning.
15a TG Rebellion.
b TG Secret Combinations.
18a Ether 11:9.
20a TG Judgment.
21a Omni 1:21; Ether 13:21 (20–21).
b Deut. 29:28.
22a TG Prophets, Rejection of.
b TG Secret Combinations.
23a Ether 1:6; 12:2; 15:34 (33–34).
12 1a Omni 1:21; Ether 13:20 (13–31).
2a Ether 1:6; 11:23; 15:34 (33–34).

in the days of Coriantumr, and
began to prophesy unto the people,
for he could not be [b]restrained
because of the Spirit of the Lord
which was in him.
3 For he did [a]cry from the [b]morning,
even until the going down of the
sun, exhorting the people to believe
in God unto repentance lest they
should be [c]destroyed, saying unto
them that [d]by [e]faith all things are
fulfilled—
4 Wherefore, whoso believeth in
God might with [a]surety [b]hope for a
better world, yea, even a place at
the right hand of God, which [c]hope
cometh of [d]faith, maketh an [e]anchor
to the souls of men, which would
make them sure and steadfast,
always abounding in [f]good works,
being led to [g]glorify God.
5 And it came to pass that Ether
did prophesy great and marvelous
things unto the people, which they
did not believe, because they [a]saw
them not.
6 And now, I, Moroni, would speak
somewhat concerning these things;
I would show unto the world that
[a]faith is things which are [b]hoped for
and [c]not seen; wherefore, dispute
not because ye see not, for ye
receive no [d]witness until after the
[e]trial of your faith.
7 For it was by faith that Christ
showed himself unto our fathers,
after he had risen from the dead;
and he showed not himself unto
them until after they had faith in
him; wherefore, it must needs be
that some had faith in him, for
he showed himself [a]not unto the
world.
8 But because of the faith of men
he has shown himself unto the
world, and glorified the name of the
Father, and prepared a way that
thereby others might be partakers
of the heavenly gift, that they
might hope for those things which
they have not seen.
9 Wherefore, ye may also have
hope, and be partakers of the gift,
if ye will but have faith.
10 Behold it was by faith that
they of old were [a]called after the
holy order of God.
11 Wherefore, by faith was the
law of Moses given. But in the [a]gift
of his Son hath God prepared a
more [b]excellent way; and it is by
faith that it hath been fulfilled.
12 For if there be no [a]faith among
the children of men God can do no
[b]miracle among them; wherefore,
he showed not himself until after
their faith.
13 Behold, it was the faith of Alma
and Amulek that caused the [a]prison
to tumble to the earth.
14 Behold, it was the faith of
Nephi and Lehi that wrought the
[a]change upon the Lamanites, that
they were baptized with fire and
with the [b]Holy Ghost.
15 Behold, it was the faith of
[a]Ammon and his brethren which
[b]wrought so great a miracle among
the Lamanites.
16 Yea, and even all they who

2*b* Jer. 20: 9; Enos 1: 26; Alma 43: 1.
3*a* D&C 112: 5.
b Jer. 26: 5.
c Ether 11: 12 (12, 20–22).
d Heb. 11: 7 (1–40).
e 1 Cor. 13: 13 (1–13); Moro. 7: 1; 8: 14; 10: 20 (20–23).
4*a* Heb. 7: 22.
b Alma 7: 16; 22: 16; Moro. 7: 3; D&C 25: 10; 138: 14.
c Heb. 11: 1; Moro. 7: 40.
d Luke 7: 50.
e Heb. 6: 19.
f 1 Cor. 15: 58; 1 Tim. 2: 10.
g John 11: 4 (1–4); 3 Ne. 12: 16.
5*a* Heb. 11: 3; Alma 30: 15; Hel. 16: 20.
6*a* Heb. 11: 1.
b Rom. 8: 25 (24–25).
c Alma 32: 21.
d Lev. 9: 6 (6, 23); 2 Ne. 1: 15. TG Sign Seekers.
e 3 Ne. 26: 11. TG Test, Try, Prove.
7*a* Acts 10: 41.
10*a* Alma 13: 4 (3–4). TG Authority.
11*a* TG God, Gifts of.
b 1 Cor. 12: 31.
12*a* Luke 16: 30 (27–31); Alma 32: 18 (17–18); Moro. 7: 37.
b Ps. 78: 41; Matt. 13: 58; Morm. 9: 20.
13*a* Alma 14: 27 (26–29).
14*a* Hel. 5: 50 (50–52).
b Hel. 5: 45; 3 Ne. 9: 20.
15*a* Alma 17: 29 (29–39).
b IE as told in Alma, chapters 17–26.

wrought [a]miracles wrought them by
[b]faith, even those who were before
Christ and also those who were after.
17 And it was by faith that the
three disciples obtained a promise
that they should [a]not taste of
death; and they obtained not the
promise until after their faith.
18 And neither at any time hath
any wrought miracles until after
their faith; wherefore they first
believed in the Son of God.
19 And there were many whose
faith was so exceedingly strong,
even [a]before Christ came, who could
not be kept from within the [b]veil,
but truly saw with their eyes the
things which they had beheld with
an eye of faith, and they were glad.
20 And behold, we have seen in
this record that one of these was the
brother of Jared; for so great was
his faith in God, that when God put
forth his [a]finger he could not hide
it from the sight of the brother of
Jared, because of his word which
he had spoken unto him, which
word he had obtained by faith.
21 And after the brother of Jared
had beheld the finger of the Lord,
because of the [a]promise which the
brother of Jared had obtained by
faith, the Lord could not withhold
anything from his sight; wherefore
he showed him all things, for he could
no longer be kept without the [b]veil.
22 And it is by faith that my
fathers have obtained the [a]promise
that these things should come unto
their brethren through the Gentiles;
therefore the Lord hath commanded
me, yea, even Jesus Christ.
23 And I said unto him: Lord, the
Gentiles will [a]mock at these things,
because of our [b]weakness in writing;
for Lord thou hast made us [c]mighty
in word by faith, but thou hast not
made us mighty in writing; for thou
hast made all this people that they
could speak much, because of the
Holy Ghost which thou hast given
them;
24 And thou hast made us that we
could write but little, because of the
[a]awkwardness of our hands. Behold,
thou hast not made us mighty in
[b]writing like unto the brother of
Jared, for thou madest him that the
things which he [c]wrote were mighty
even as thou art, unto the overpowering of man to read them.
25 Thou hast also made our words
powerful and great, even that we
[a]cannot write them; wherefore, when
we write we behold our [b]weakness,
and stumble because of the placing
of our words; and I fear lest the
Gentiles shall [c]mock at our words.
26 And when I had said this, the
Lord spake unto me, saying: [a]Fools
[b]mock, but they shall mourn; and
my grace is sufficient for the meek,
that they shall take no advantage
of your weakness;
27 And if men come unto me I will
show unto them their [a]weakness. I
[b]give unto men weakness that they
may be humble; and my [c]grace is
sufficient for all men that [d]humble
themselves before me; for if they
humble themselves before me, and
have faith in me, then will I make
[e]weak things become strong unto
them.

16*a* TG Miracle.
b Heb. 11: 7 (7–40).
17*a* 3 Ne. 28: 7; 4 Ne. 1: 37 (14, 37); Morm. 8: 10 (10–12).
19*a* 2 Ne. 11: 4; Jacob 4: 5; Jarom 1: 11; Alma 25: 16 (15–16).
b Ether 3: 6. TG Veil.
20*a* Ether 3: 4.
21*a* Ether 3: 26 (25–26).
b Ether 3: 20; D&C 67: 10 (10–13).
22*a* Enos 1: 13.
23*a* Ether 12: 36.
b 1 Cor. 2: 3 (1–5); 1 Ne. 19: 6; Morm. 8: 17 (13–17); 9: 31 (31, 33).
c 2 Ne. 33: 1.
24*a* Jacob 4: 1.
b TG Language.
c Ether 4: 1.
25*a* 3 Ne. 5: 18.
b Ether 12: 37.
c 1 Cor. 2: 14.
26*a* Prov. 14: 9; 20: 3.
b Gal. 6: 7; D&C 124: 71. TG Mocking; Offense.
27*a* Jacob 4: 7.
b Ex. 4: 11; 1 Cor. 1: 27 (26–31).
c TG Grace.
d D&C 1: 28. TG Humility; Teachable.
e Deut. 11: 8; Joel 3: 10; Luke 9: 48 (46–48); 18: 14 (10–14); 2 Cor. 12: 9 (7–10); Heb. 11: 34; 1 Ne. 14: 1.

28 Behold, I will show unto the
Gentiles their weakness, and I will
show unto them that [a]faith, hope
and charity bringeth unto me—the
fountain of all [b]righteousness.
29 And I, Moroni, having heard
these words, was [a]comforted, and
said: O Lord, thy righteous will be
done, for I know that thou workest
unto the children of men according
to their faith;
30 For the brother of Jared said
unto the mountain Zerin, [a]Remove—and it was removed. And if
he had not had faith it would not
have moved; wherefore thou workest after men have faith.
31 For thus didst thou manifest
thyself unto thy disciples; for [a]after
they had [b]faith, and did speak in
thy name, thou didst show thyself
unto them in great power.
32 And I also remember that thou
hast said that thou hast prepared a
house for man, yea, even among the
[a]mansions of thy Father, in which
man might have a more excellent
[b]hope; wherefore man must hope,
or he cannot receive an inheritance
in the place which thou hast
prepared.
33 And again, I remember that
thou hast said that thou hast [a]loved
the world, even unto the laying
down of thy life for the world, that
thou mightest take it again to prepare a place for the children of men.
34 And now I know that this
[a]love which thou hast had for the
children of men is charity; wherefore, except men shall have charity
they cannot inherit that place
which thou hast prepared in the
mansions of thy Father.
35 Wherefore, I know by this thing
which thou hast said, that if the
Gentiles have not [a]charity, because
of our weakness, that thou wilt
prove them, and [b]take away their
[c]talent, yea, even that which they
have received, and give unto them
who shall have more abundantly.
36 And it came to pass that I
prayed unto the Lord that he would
give unto the Gentiles [a]grace, that
they might have charity.
37 And it came to pass that the
Lord said unto me: If they have not
charity it mattereth not unto thee,
thou hast been faithful; wherefore,
thy garments shall be made [a]clean.
And because thou hast seen thy
[b]weakness thou shalt be made
strong, even unto the sitting down
in the place which I have prepared
in the mansions of my Father.
38 And now I, Moroni, bid farewell unto the Gentiles, yea, and also
unto my brethren whom I love,
until we shall meet before the
[a]judgment-seat of Christ, where all
men shall know that my [b]garments
are not spotted with your blood.
39 And then shall ye know that I
have [a]seen Jesus, and that he hath
talked with me [b]face to face, and
that he told me in [c]plain humility,
even as a man telleth another in
mine own language, concerning
these things;
40 And only a few have I written,
because of my weakness in writing.
41 And now, I would commend
you to [a]seek this Jesus of whom the

28*a* Alma 7: 24.
b TG God, the Standard of Righteousness.
29*a* TG Comfort.
30*a* Matt. 17: 20; Jacob 4: 6; Hel. 10: 9. TG God, Power of.
31*a* 3 Ne. 26: 17 (17–21).
b 1 Cor. 13: 13 (1–13); Moro. 7: 44 (33–48).
32*a* John 14: 2; Enos 1: 27; D&C 72: 4; 98: 18.
b TG Hope.
33*a* John 3: 16 (16–18).
34*a* Moro. 7: 47. TG Love.
35*a* 1 Cor. 13: 2 (1–2).
b Matt. 25: 28 (14–30).
c TG Talents.
36*a* Ether 12: 23. TG Grace.
37*a* Job 15: 14; 25: 4; D&C 38: 42; 88: 74 (74–75); 135: 5 (4–5). TG Cleanliness; Purification.
b Ether 12: 25 (25–27).
38*a* TG Jesus Christ, Judge.
b Acts 20: 26; Jacob 1: 19.
39*a* TG Jesus Christ, Appearances, Postmortal.
b Gen. 32: 30; Ex. 33: 11; Num. 12: 8.
c 2 Ne. 32: 7; Alma 13: 23.
41*a* Ezra 8: 22 (22–23); Ps. 27: 8; Amos 5: 6; Alma 37: 47; D&C 88: 63; 101: 38.

prophets and apostles have written, that the grace of God the Father, and also the Lord Jesus Christ, and the Holy Ghost, which beareth [b]record of them, may be and abide in you forever. Amen.

CHAPTER 13

Ether speaks of a New Jerusalem to be built in America by the seed of Joseph—He prophesies, is cast out, writes the Jaredite history, and foretells the destruction of the Jaredites—War rages over all the land.

AND now I, Moroni, proceed to finish my record concerning the destruction of the people of whom I have been writing.

2 For behold, they rejected all the words of Ether; for he truly told them of all things, from the beginning of man; and that after the waters had [a]receded from off the face of this [b]land it became a choice land above all other lands, a chosen land of the Lord; wherefore the Lord would have that all men should [c]serve him who dwell upon the face thereof;

3 And that it was the place of the [a]New Jerusalem, which should [b]come down out of heaven, and the holy sanctuary of the Lord.

4 Behold, Ether saw the days of Christ, and he spake concerning a [a]New Jerusalem upon this land.

5 And he spake also concerning the house of Israel, and the [a]Jerusalem from whence [b]Lehi should come—after it should be destroyed it should be built up again, a [c]holy city unto the Lord; wherefore, it could not be a new Jerusalem for it had been in a time of old; but it should be built up again, and become a holy city of the Lord; and it should be built unto the house of Israel—

6 And that a [a]New Jerusalem should be built up upon this land, unto the remnant of the seed of [b]Joseph, for which things there has been a [c]type.

7 For as Joseph brought his father down into the land of [a]Egypt, even so he died there; wherefore, the Lord brought a remnant of the seed of Joseph out of the land of Jerusalem, that he might be merciful unto the seed of Joseph that they should [b]perish not, even as he was merciful unto the father of Joseph that he should perish not.

8 Wherefore, the remnant of the house of Joseph shall be built upon this [a]land; and it shall be a land of their inheritance; and they shall build up a holy [b]city unto the Lord, like unto the Jerusalem of old; and they shall [c]no more be confounded, until the end come when the earth shall pass away.

9 And there shall be a [a]new heaven and a new earth; and they shall be like unto the old save the old have passed away, and all things have become new.

10 And then cometh the New Jerusalem; and blessed are they who dwell therein, for it is they whose garments are [a]white through the blood of the Lamb; and they are they who are numbered among the remnant of the seed of Joseph, who were of the house of Israel.

11 And then also cometh the [a]Jerusalem of old; and the inhabitants thereof, blessed are they, for

---

41*b* 3 Ne. 11: 32 (32, 36).
13 2*a* Gen. 8: 3; 7: 19 (11–24).
b TG Earth, Dividing of.
c Ether 2: 8.
3*a* 3 Ne. 20: 22; 21: 23 (23–24). TG Jerusalem, New.
b Rev. 3: 12; 21: 2.
4*a* TG Zion.
5*a* TG Jerusalem.
b 1 Ne. 1: 18 (18–20); 2: 2.
c Joel 2: 18; Rev. 21: 10 (10–27); 3 Ne. 20: 46 (29–36, 46).
6*a* D&C 42: 9; 45: 66 (66–67); 84: 2 (2–5); A of F 10.
b Ezek. 48: 5 (4–5); D&C 28: 8. TG Israel, Joseph, People of.
c Alma 46: 24 (24–26). TG Symbolism.
7*a* Gen. 46: 6 (2–7); 47: 6.
b 2 Ne. 3: 5 (5–24).
8*a* TG Promised Lands.
b Rev. 21: 10 (10–27).
c Moro. 10: 31.
9*a* Heb. 8: 13; 2 Pet. 3: 13 (10–13); Rev. 21: 1; 3 Ne. 12: 47 (46–47); 15: 3 (2–10); D&C 101: 25 (23–25).
10*a* Rev. 7: 14.
11*a* TG Israel, Gathering of; Israel, Land of; Jerusalem.

they have been washed in the blood of the Lamb; and they are they who were scattered and gathered in from the four quarters of the earth, and from the [b]north countries, and are partakers of the fulfilling of the covenant which God made with their father, [c]Abraham.

12 And when these things come, bringeth to pass the scripture which saith, there are they who were [a]first, who shall be last; and there are they who were last, who shall be first.

13 And I was about to write more, but I am forbidden; but great and marvelous were the prophecies of Ether; but they esteemed him as naught, and cast him out; and he [a]hid himself in the cavity of a rock by day, and by night he went forth viewing the things which should come upon the people.

14 And as he dwelt in the cavity of a rock he made the [a]remainder of this record, viewing the destructions which came upon the people, by night.

15 And it came to pass that in that same year in which he was cast out from among the people there began to be a great war among the people, for there were many who rose up, who were mighty men, and sought to destroy Coriantumr by their secret plans of wickedness, of which hath been spoken.

16 And now Coriantumr, having studied, himself, in all the arts of war and all the cunning of the world, wherefore he gave battle unto them who sought to destroy him.

17 But he repented not, neither his [a]fair sons nor daughters; neither the fair sons and daughters of Cohor; neither the fair sons and daughters of Corihor; and in fine, there were none of the fair sons and daughters upon the face of the whole earth who repented of their sins.

18 Wherefore, it came to pass that in the first year that Ether dwelt in the cavity of a rock, there were many people who were slain by the sword of those [a]secret combinations, fighting against Coriantumr that they might obtain the kingdom.

19 And it came to pass that the sons of Coriantumr fought much and bled much.

20 And in the second year the word of the Lord came to Ether, that he should go and [a]prophesy unto [b]Coriantumr that, if he would repent, and all his household, the Lord would give unto him his kingdom and spare the people—

21 Otherwise they should be destroyed, and all his household save it were himself. And he should only live to see the fulfilling of the prophecies which had been spoken concerning [a]another people receiving the land for their inheritance; and Coriantumr should receive a burial by them; and every soul should be destroyed save it were [b]Coriantumr.

22 And it came to pass that Coriantumr repented not, neither his household, neither the people; and the wars ceased not; and they sought to [a]kill Ether, but he fled from before them and hid again in the cavity of the rock.

23 And it came to pass that there arose up Shared, and he also gave battle unto Coriantumr; and he did beat him, insomuch that in the third year he did bring him into captivity.

24 And the sons of Coriantumr, in the fourth year, did beat Shared, and did obtain the kingdom again unto their father.

25 Now there began to be a war

11*b* D&C 133: 26 (26–35).
TG Israel, Ten Lost Tribes of.
c Isa. 27: 6.
12*a* Mark 10: 31; Luke 13: 30; 1 Ne. 13: 42; Jacob 5: 63; D&C 18: 26 (26–27); 90: 9.
13*a* 1 Kgs. 17: 3 (1–16); 1 Ne. 3: 27; Mosiah 17: 4 (1–4).
14*a* Ether 15: 33 (13, 33).
17*a* Morm. 6: 19 (16–22).
18*a* Ether 8: 9 (9–26).
20*a* Ether 15: 1.
b Omni 1: 21; Ether 12: 1 (1–2).
21*a* Ether 11: 21.
b Ether 14: 24; 15: 29 (29–32).
22*a* Prov. 29: 10.

upon all the face of the land, [a]every
man with his band fighting for that
which he desired.
26 And there were robbers, and in
fine, all manner of wickedness upon
all the face of the land.
27 And it came to pass that Coriantumr was exceedingly angry with
Shared, and he went against him
with his armies to battle; and they
did meet in great anger, and they
did meet in the valley of Gilgal; and
the battle became exceedingly sore.
28 And it came to pass that Shared
fought against him for the space of
three days. And it came to pass that
Coriantumr beat him, and did pursue him until he came to the plains
of Heshlon.
29 And it came to pass that Shared
gave him battle again upon the
plains; and behold, he did beat
Coriantumr, and drove him back
again to the valley of Gilgal.
30 And Coriantumr gave Shared
battle again in the valley of Gilgal, in
which he beat Shared and slew him.
31 And Shared wounded Coriantumr in his thigh, that he did not go
to battle again for the space of two
years, in which time all the people
upon the face of the land were
shedding blood, and there was none
to restrain them.

CHAPTER 14

The iniquity of the people brings a curse upon the land—Coriantumr engages in warfare against Gilead, then Lib, and then Shiz—Blood and carnage cover the land.

AND now there began to be a great
[a]curse upon all the land because of
the iniquity of the people, in which,
if a man should lay his tool or his
sword upon his shelf, or upon the
place whither he would keep it,
behold, upon the morrow, he could
not find it, so great was the curse
upon the land.
2 Wherefore every man did cleave
unto that which was his own, with
his hands, and would not borrow
neither would he lend; and every
man kept the hilt of his sword in his
right hand, in the [a]defence of his
property and his own life and of his
wives and children.
3 And now, after the space of two
years, and after the death of Shared,
behold, there arose the brother of
Shared and he gave battle unto
Coriantumr, in which Coriantumr
did beat him and did pursue him to
the wilderness of Akish.
4 And it came to pass that the
brother of Shared did give battle
unto him in the wilderness of Akish;
and the battle became exceedingly
sore, and many thousands fell by
the sword.
5 And it came to pass that Coriantumr did lay siege to the wilderness;
and the brother of Shared did march
forth out of the wilderness by night,
and slew a part of the army of
Coriantumr, as they were drunken.
6 And he came forth to the land of
[a]Moron, and placed himself upon
the throne of Coriantumr.
7 And it came to pass that Coriantumr dwelt with his army in the
wilderness for the space of two
years, in which he did receive great
strength to his army.
8 Now the brother of Shared, whose
name was Gilead, also received
great strength to his army, because
of secret combinations.
9 And it came to pass that his high
priest murdered him as he sat upon
his throne.
10 And it came to pass that one of
the secret combinations murdered
him in a secret pass, and obtained
unto himself the kingdom; and his
name was Lib; and Lib was a man
of great stature, more than any
other man among all the people.
11 And it came to pass that in the
first year of Lib, Coriantumr came
up unto the land of Moron, and gave
battle unto Lib.

25*a* TG Covetousness; Selfishness.
14 1*a* Hel. 12: 18; 13: 18 (17–23); Morm. 1: 18 (17–19); 2: 10 (10–14).
2*a* Morm. 2: 23.
6*a* Ether 7: 5.

12 And it came to pass that he fought with Lib, in which Lib did smite upon his arm that he was wounded; nevertheless, the army of Coriantumr did press forward upon Lib, that he fled to the borders upon the seashore.

13 And it came to pass that Coriantumr pursued him; and Lib gave battle unto him upon the seashore.

14 And it came to pass that Lib did smite the army of Coriantumr, that they fled again to the wilderness of Akish.

15 And it came to pass that Lib did pursue him until he came to the plains of Agosh. And Coriantumr had taken all the people with him as he fled before Lib in that quarter of the land whither he fled.

16 And when he had come to the plains of Agosh he gave battle unto Lib, and he smote upon him until he died; nevertheless, the brother of Lib did come against Coriantumr in the stead thereof, and the battle became exceedingly sore, in the which Coriantumr fled again before the army of the brother of Lib.

17 Now the name of the brother of Lib was called Shiz. And it came to pass that Shiz pursued after Coriantumr, and he did overthrow many cities, and he did slay both women and children, and he did burn the cities.

18 And there went a fear of Shiz throughout all the land; yea, a cry went forth throughout the land—Who can stand before the army of Shiz? Behold, he sweepeth the earth before him!

19 And it came to pass that the people began to flock together in armies, throughout all the face of the land.

20 And they were divided; and a part of them fled to the army of Shiz, and a part of them fled to the army of Coriantumr.

21 And so great and lasting had been the war, and so long had been the scene of bloodshed and carnage, that the whole face of the land was covered with the [a]bodies of the [b]dead.

22 And so swift and speedy was the war that there was none left to bury the dead, but they did march forth from the shedding of [a]blood to the shedding of blood, leaving the bodies of both men, women, and children strewed upon the face of the land, to become a prey to the [b]worms of the flesh.

23 And the [a]scent thereof went forth upon the face of the land, even upon all the face of the land; wherefore the people became troubled by day and by night, because of the scent thereof.

24 Nevertheless, Shiz did [a]not cease to pursue Coriantumr; for he had sworn to avenge himself upon Coriantumr of the blood of his brother, who had been slain, and the word of the Lord which came to Ether that Coriantumr should not fall by the sword.

25 And thus we see that the Lord did visit them in the fulness of his [a]wrath, and their wickedness and abominations had prepared a way for their everlasting destruction.

26 And it came to pass that Shiz did pursue Coriantumr eastward, even to the borders by the seashore, and there he gave battle unto Shiz for the space of three days.

27 And so terrible was the destruction among the armies of Shiz that the people began to be frightened, and began to flee before the armies of Coriantumr; and they fled to the land of Corihor, and swept off the inhabitants before them, all them that would not join them.

28 And they pitched their tents in the valley of Corihor; and Coriantumr pitched his tents in the valley of Shurr. Now the valley of Shurr was near the hill Comnor; where-

21*a* Ether 11: 6.
b Ezek. 35: 8.
22*a* Hosea 4: 2 (1–3).
b Isa. 14: 11 (9–11).
23*a* Alma 16: 11 (9–11).
24*a* Ether 13: 21.
25*a* TG God, Indignation of.

fore, Coriantumr did gather his armies together upon the hill Comnor, and did sound a trumpet unto the armies of Shiz to invite them forth to battle.

29 And it came to pass that they came forth, but were driven again; and they came the second time, and they were driven again the second time. And it came to pass that they came again the third time, and the battle became exceedingly sore.

30 And it came to pass that Shiz smote upon Coriantumr that he gave him many deep wounds; and Coriantumr, having lost his blood, fainted, and was carried away as though he were dead.

31 Now the loss of men, women and children on both sides was so great that Shiz commanded his people that they should not pursue the armies of Coriantumr; wherefore, they returned to their camp.

CHAPTER 15

Millions of the Jaredites are slain in battle—Shiz and Coriantumr assemble all the people to mortal combat—The Spirit of the Lord ceases to strive with them—The Jaredite nation is utterly destroyed—Only Coriantumr remains.

AND it came to pass when Coriantumr had recovered of his wounds, he began to remember the [a]words which Ether had spoken unto him.

2 He saw that there had been slain by the sword already nearly [a]two millions of his people, and he began to sorrow in his heart; yea, there had been slain two millions of mighty men, and also their wives and their children.

3 He began to repent of the evil which he had done; he began to remember the words which had been spoken by the mouth of all the prophets, and he saw them that they were fulfilled thus far, every whit; and his soul [a]mourned and refused to be [b]comforted.

4 And it came to pass that he wrote an epistle unto Shiz, desiring him that he would spare the people, and he would give up the kingdom for the sake of the lives of the people.

5 And it came to pass that when Shiz had received his epistle he wrote an epistle unto Coriantumr, that if he would give himself up, that he might slay him with his own sword, that he would spare the lives of the people.

6 And it came to pass that the people repented not of their iniquity; and the people of Coriantumr were stirred up to anger against the people of Shiz; and the people of Shiz were stirred up to anger against the people of Coriantumr; wherefore, the people of Shiz did give battle unto the people of Coriantumr.

7 And when Coriantumr saw that he was about to fall he fled again before the people of Shiz.

8 And it came to pass that he came to the waters of Ripliancum, which, by interpretation, is large, or to exceed all; wherefore, when they came to these waters they pitched their tents; and Shiz also pitched his tents near unto them; and therefore on the morrow they did come to battle.

9 And it came to pass that they fought an exceedingly sore battle, in which Coriantumr was wounded again, and he fainted with the loss of blood.

10 And it came to pass that the armies of Coriantumr did press upon the armies of Shiz that they beat them, that they caused them to flee before them; and they did flee southward, and did pitch their tents in a place which was called Ogath.

11 And it came to pass that the army of Coriantumr did pitch their tents by the hill Ramah; and it was that same hill where my father Mormon did [a]hide up the records unto the Lord, which were sacred.

---

15 1*a* Ether 13: 20 (20–21).
2*a* Ether 1: 43.
3*a* TG Mourning.
b Gen. 37: 35; Moses 7: 44. TG Comfort.
11*a* Morm. 6: 6.

12 And it came to pass that they did gather together all the people upon all the face of the land, who had not been slain, save it was Ether.

13 And it came to pass that Ether did [a]behold all the doings of the people; and he beheld that the people who were for Coriantumr were gathered together to the army of Coriantumr; and the people who were for Shiz were gathered together to the army of Shiz.

14 Wherefore, they were for the space of four years gathering together the people, that they might get all who were upon the face of the land, and that they might receive all the strength which it was possible that they could receive.

15 And it came to pass that when they were all gathered together, every one to the army which he would, with their wives and their children—both men, women and children being armed with [a]weapons of war, having shields, and [b]breastplates, and head-plates, and being clothed after the manner of war—they did march forth one against another to battle; and they fought all that day, and conquered not.

16 And it came to pass that when it was night they were weary, and retired to their camps; and after they had retired to their camps they took up a howling and a [a]lamentation for the loss of the slain of their people; and so great were their cries, their howlings and lamentations, that they did rend the air exceedingly.

17 And it came to pass that on the morrow they did go again to battle, and great and terrible was that day; nevertheless, they conquered not, and when the night came again they did rend the air with their cries, and their howlings, and their mournings, for the loss of the slain of their people.

18 And it came to pass that Coriantumr wrote again an epistle unto Shiz, desiring that he would not come again to battle, but that he would take the kingdom, and spare the lives of the people.

19 But behold, the [a]Spirit of the Lord had ceased striving with them, and [b]Satan had full power over the [c]hearts of the people; for they were given up unto the hardness of their hearts, and the blindness of their minds that they might be destroyed; wherefore they went again to battle.

20 And it came to pass that they fought all that day, and when the night came they slept upon their swords.

21 And on the morrow they fought even until the night came.

22 And when the night came they were [a]drunken with anger, even as a man who is drunken with wine; and they slept again upon their swords.

23 And on the morrow they fought again; and when the night came they had all fallen by the sword save it were fifty and two of the people of Coriantumr, and sixty and nine of the people of Shiz.

24 And it came to pass that they slept upon their swords that night, and on the morrow they fought again, and they contended in their might with their swords and with their shields, all that day.

25 And when the night came there were thirty and two of the people of Shiz, and twenty and seven of the people of Coriantumr.

26 And it came to pass that they ate and slept, and prepared for death on the morrow. And they were large and mighty men as to the strength of men.

27 And it came to pass that they fought for the space of three hours, and they fainted with the loss of blood.

28 And it came to pass that when the men of Coriantumr had received

13a Ether 13: 14.
15a Ether 10: 27.
b Mosiah 8: 10.
16a TG Mourning.
19a TG God, Spirit of; Holy Ghost, Loss of.
b TG Devil.
c TG Hardheartedness.
22a Moro. 9: 23.

sufficient strength that they could
walk, they were about to flee for
their lives; but behold, Shiz arose,
and also his men, and he swore in
his wrath that he would slay
Coriantumr or he would perish by
the sword.
29 Wherefore, he did pursue them,
and on the morrow he did overtake
them; and they fought again with
the sword. And it came to pass that
when they had [a]all fallen by the
sword, save it were Coriantumr and
Shiz, behold Shiz had fainted with
the loss of blood.
30 And it came to pass that when
Coriantumr had leaned upon his
sword, that he rested a little, he
smote off the head of Shiz.
31 And it came to pass that after
he had smitten off the head of Shiz,
that Shiz raised up on his hands and
[a]fell; and after that he had strug-
gled for breath, he died.
32 And it came to pass that
[a]Coriantumr fell to the earth, and
became as if he had no life.
33 And the Lord spake unto Ether,
and said unto him: Go forth. And
he went forth, and beheld that the
words of the Lord had all been fulfilled; and he [a]finished his [b]record;
(and the [c]hundredth part I have not
written) and he hid them in a manner that the people of Limhi did
find them.
34 Now the last words which are
written by [a]Ether are these:
Whether the Lord will that I be
translated, or that I suffer the will
of the Lord in the flesh, it mattereth
not, if it so be that I am [b]saved in
the kingdom of God. Amen.

THE BOOK OF MORONI

CHAPTER 1

Moroni writes for the benefit of the Lamanites—The Nephites who will not deny Christ are put to death.

NOW I, Moroni, after having
made an end of abridging the
account of the people of
Jared, I had supposed [a]not to have
written more, but I have not as yet
perished; and I make not myself
known to the Lamanites lest they
should destroy me.
2 For behold, their [a]wars are
exceedingly fierce among themselves; and because of their [b]hatred
they [c]put to death every Nephite
that will not deny the Christ.
3 And I, Moroni, will not [a]deny
the Christ; wherefore, I wander
whithersoever I can for the safety
of mine own life.
4 Wherefore, I write a few more
things, contrary to that which I had
supposed; for I had supposed not to
have written any more; but I write
a few more things, that perhaps
they may be of [a]worth unto my
brethren, the Lamanites, in some
future day, according to the will of
the Lord.

CHAPTER 2

Jesus gave the Nephite apostles power to confer the gift of the Holy Ghost.

29a Ether 13: 21.
31a Judg. 5: 27 (26–27).
32a Omni 1: 21 (20–22).
33a Ether 13: 14.
b Mosiah 8: 9; 21: 27; 28: 11; Alma 37: 21 (21–31); Ether 1: 2 (1–5).
c 3 Ne. 26: 6; Ether 3: 17.
34a Ether 1: 6; 11: 23; 12: 2.
b Mosiah 13: 9.

[MORONI]
1 1a Morm. 8: 5; Moro. 10: 1 (1–2).
2a 1 Ne. 12: 21 (20–23).
b TG Hate.
c Alma 45: 14.
3a Matt. 10: 33 (32–33); 3 Ne. 29: 5.
4a 2 Ne. 3: 12 (11–12, 19).

[Between A.D. 400 and 421]

THE words of Christ, which he
spake unto his [a]disciples, the twelve
whom he had chosen, as he laid his
hands upon them—
2 And he called them by name,
saying: Ye shall [a]call on the Father
in my name, in mighty prayer; and
after ye have done this ye shall
have [b]power that to him upon
whom ye shall lay your [c]hands, [d]ye
shall give the Holy Ghost; and in
my name shall ye give it, for thus
do mine apostles.
3 Now Christ spake these words
unto them at the time of his first
appearing; and the multitude heard
it not, but the disciples heard it;
and on as many as they [a]laid their
hands, fell the Holy Ghost.

CHAPTER 3

Elders ordain priests and teachers by the laying on of hands.

THE manner which the disciples,
who were called the [a]elders of the
church, [b]ordained [c]priests and
teachers—
2 After they had prayed unto the
Father in the name of Christ, they
[a]laid their hands upon them, and
said:
3 In the name of Jesus Christ I
ordain you to be a priest, (or, if he
be a [a]teacher) I ordain you to be a
teacher, to preach repentance and
[b]remission of sins through Jesus
Christ, by the endurance of faith on
his name to the end. Amen.
4 And after this manner did they
[a]ordain priests and teachers, according to the [b]gifts and callings of God
unto men; and they ordained them
by the [c]power of the Holy Ghost,
which was in them.

CHAPTER 4

How the elders and priests administer the sacramental bread.

THE [a]manner of their [b]elders and
[c]priests administering the flesh and
blood of Christ unto the church;
and they administered it [d]accord-
ing to the commandments of Christ;
wherefore we know the manner to
be true; and the elder or priest did
minister it—
2 And they did kneel down with the
[a]church, and pray to the Father in
the name of Christ, saying:
3 O God, the Eternal Father, we
ask thee in the name of thy Son,
Jesus Christ, to bless and [a]sanctify
this [b]bread to the souls of all those
who partake of it; that they may
eat in [c]remembrance of the body of
thy Son, and witness unto thee,
O God, the Eternal Father, that
they are willing to take upon them
the [d]name of thy Son, and always
remember him, and keep his commandments which he hath given
them, that they may always have
his [e]Spirit to be with them. Amen.

CHAPTER 5

The mode of administering the sacramental wine is set forth.

THE [a]manner of administering the
wine—Behold, they took the cup,
and said:
2 O God, the Eternal Father, we

2 1*a* 3 Ne. 13: 25; 15: 11.
2*a* Gen. 4: 26; Ether 4: 15.
b Matt. 10: 1. TG Priesthood, Melchizedek.
c TG Hands, Laying on of.
d 3 Ne. 18: 37.
3*a* Acts 19: 6.
3 1*a* Alma 6: 1. TG Elder.
b TG Church Organization.
c Mosiah 6: 3. TG Priest.
2*a* TG Hands, Laying on of.
3*a* TG Teacher.
b TG Remission of Sins.
4*a* D&C 18: 32; 20: 39 (39, 60). TG Priesthood; Priesthood, History of.
b TG God, Gifts of.
c 1 Ne. 13: 37; Moro. 6: 9.
4 1*a* 3 Ne. 18: 5 (1–7).
b TG Elder.
c TG Priest.
d D&C 20: 76.
2*a* TG Church.
3*a* 1 Sam. 21: 4.
b TG Sacrament.
c Luke 22: 19; 3 Ne. 18: 7; 20: 8.
d TG Jesus Christ, Taking the Name of.
e TG God, Spirit of.
5 1*a* 3 Ne. 18: 11 (8–11); D&C 20: 78.

[Between A.D. 400 and 421]

ask thee, in the name of thy Son,
Jesus Christ, to bless and sanctify
this [a]wine to the souls of all those
who drink of it, that they may do it
in [b]remembrance of the [c]blood of thy
Son, which was shed for them; that
they may witness unto thee, O God,
the Eternal Father, that they do
always remember him, that they
may have his [d]Spirit to be with
them. Amen.

CHAPTER 6

Repentant persons are baptized and fellowshipped—Church members who repent are forgiven—Meetings are conducted by the power of the Holy Ghost.

AND now I speak concerning baptism. Behold, elders, priests, and
teachers were baptized; and they
were not baptized save they brought
forth [a]fruit meet that they were
[b]worthy of it.
2 Neither did they receive any
unto baptism save they came forth
with a [a]broken [b]heart and a contrite
spirit, and witnessed unto the
church that they truly repented of
all their sins.
3 And none were received unto
baptism save they [a]took upon them
the name of Christ, having a determination to serve him to the end.
4 And after they had been received
unto baptism, and were wrought
upon and [a]cleansed by the power of
the Holy Ghost, they were numbered among the people of the
[b]church of Christ; and their [c]names
were taken, that they might be
remembered and nourished by the
good word of God, to keep them in
the right way, to keep them continually [d]watchful unto prayer,
[e]relying alone upon the merits of
Christ, who was the author and the
finisher of their faith.
5 And the [a]church did meet together [b]oft, to [c]fast and to pray, and
to speak one with another concerning the welfare of their souls.
6 And they did [a]meet together oft
to partake of bread and wine, in
[b]remembrance of the Lord Jesus.
7 And they were strict to observe
that there should be [a]no iniquity
among them; and whoso was found
to commit iniquity, and [b]three witnesses of the church did condemn
them before the [c]elders, and if they
repented not, and [d]confessed not,
their names were [e]blotted out, and
they were not [f]numbered among the
people of Christ.
8 But [a]as oft as they repented and
sought forgiveness, with real [b]intent,
they were [c]forgiven.
9 And their meetings were [a]con-
ducted by the church after the
manner of the workings of the
Spirit, and by the [b]power of
the Holy Ghost; for as the power
of the Holy Ghost led them whether
to preach, or to exhort, or to pray,
or to supplicate, or to sing, even so
it was done.

2a TG Sacrament.
b Luke 22: 20; 1 Cor. 11: 25.
c D&C 27: 2 (2–4).
d TG Spirituality.
6 1a TG Baptism, Qualifications for.
b TG Worthiness.
2a TG Poor in Spirit.
b TG Contrite Heart.
3a 2 Ne. 9: 23. TG Jesus Christ, Taking the Name of.
4a TG Purification.
b TG Jesus Christ, Head of the Church.
c D&C 20: 82; 47: 1 (1–4).
d D&C 20: 53. TG Watchfulness.
e 2 Ne. 31: 19; D&C 3: 20.
5a Acts 1: 14 (13–14). TG Church.
b 3 Ne. 24: 16.
c 4 Ne. 1: 12; D&C 88: 76.
6a TG Assembly for Worship; Meetings.
b TG Sacrament.
7a D&C 20: 54.
b D&C 42: 80 (80–81). TG Witnesses.
c Ex. 4: 29; Josh. 20: 4; Alma 6: 1. TG Elder.
d TG Confession.
e Ex. 32: 33; D&C 20: 83. TG Excommunication.
f TG Book of Life.
8a Mosiah 26: 30 (30–31).
b TG Sincerity.
c TG Forgiveness.
9a D&C 20: 45; 46: 2.
b 1 Ne. 13: 37; Moro. 3: 4. TG Holy Ghost, Gifts of; Teaching with the Spirit.

[Between A.D. 400 and 421]

CHAPTER 7

An invitation to enter into the rest of the Lord—Pray with real intent—The Spirit of Christ enables men to know good from evil—Satan persuades men to deny Christ and do evil—The prophets manifest the coming of Christ—By faith miracles are wrought and angels minister—Men should hope for eternal life and cleave unto charity.

AND now I, Moroni, write a few of
the words of my father Mormon,
which he spake concerning [a]faith,
hope, and charity; for after this
manner did he speak unto the
people, as he taught them in the
[b]synagogue which they had built
for the place of worship.
2 And now I, Mormon, speak unto
you, my beloved brethren; and it is
by the [a]grace of God the Father,
and our Lord Jesus Christ, and his
holy will, because of the gift of his
[b]calling unto me, that I am permitted to speak unto you at this
time.
3 Wherefore, I would speak unto
you that are of the [a]church, that are
the [b]peaceable followers of Christ,
and that have obtained a sufficient
[c]hope by which ye can enter into
the [d]rest of the Lord, from this time
henceforth until ye shall rest with
him in heaven.
4 And now my brethren, I judge
these things of you because of your
peaceable [a]walk with the children
of men.
5 For I remember the word of God
which saith by their [a]works ye shall
know them; for if their works be
good, then they are good also.
6 For behold, God hath said a man
being [a]evil cannot do that which is
good; for if he [b]offereth a gift, or
[c]prayeth unto God, except he shall
do it with real [d]intent it profiteth
him nothing.
7 For behold, it is not counted
unto him for righteousness.
8 For behold, if a man being [a]evil
giveth a gift, he doeth it [b]grudgingly; wherefore it is counted unto
him the same as if he had retained
the gift; wherefore he is counted
evil before God.
9 And likewise also is it counted
evil unto a man, if he shall pray and
not with [a]real intent of heart; yea,
and it profiteth him nothing, for
God receiveth none such.
10 Wherefore, a man being evil
cannot do that which is good;
neither will he give a good gift.
11 For behold, a bitter [a]fountain
cannot bring forth good water;
neither can a good fountain bring
forth bitter water; wherefore, a
man being a servant of the devil
cannot follow Christ; and if he
[b]follow Christ he cannot be a
[c]servant of the devil.
12 Wherefore, all things which are
[a]good cometh of God; and that
which is [b]evil cometh of the devil;
for the devil is an enemy unto God,
and fighteth against him continually, and inviteth and enticeth

7 1*a* 1 Cor. 13: 13 (1–13); Ether 12: 3 (3–37); Moro. 8: 14; 10: 20 (20–23).
b Alma 16: 13; 3 Ne. 18: 32.
2*a* TG Grace.
b 3 Ne. 5: 13. TG Called of God.
3*a* TG Jesus Christ, Head of the Church.
b Acts 13: 16; Rom. 16: 20.
c Alma 7: 16; Ether 12: 4; D&C 138: 14.
d TG Rest.
4*a* 1 Jn. 2: 6; D&C 19: 23.
5*a* 3 Ne. 14: 20 (15–20).
6*a* Matt. 7: 16 (15–18).
b Lev. 17: 8 (8–9); D&C 132: 9.
c Prov. 28: 9; Alma 34: 28. TG Prayer.
d Lev. 19: 5. TG Hypocrisy; Motivations; Sincerity.
8*a* Prov. 15: 8.
b 1 Chr. 29: 9; D&C 64: 34.
9*a* James 1: 6 (6–7); 5: 16; Moro. 10: 4. TG Sincerity.
11*a* Prov. 13: 14; James 3: 11.
b Matt. 6: 24; 8: 19; 2 Ne. 31: 10 (10–13); D&C 56: 2.
c TG Servant.
12*a* Gen. 1: 31; James 1: 17 (17–21); 1 Jn. 4: 1 (1–6); 3 Jn. 1: 11 (1–14); Ether 4: 12; D&C 59: 17 (16–20); Moses 2: 31.
b Isa. 45: 7; 2 Cor. 4: 4. TG Evil.

[Between A.D. 400 and 421]

to [c]sin, and to do that which is evil
continually.
13 But behold, that which is of
God inviteth and enticeth to do
[a]good continually; wherefore, every
thing which inviteth and [b]enticeth
to do [c]good, and to love God, and to
serve him, is [d]inspired of God.
14 Wherefore, take heed, my beloved brethren, that ye do not
judge that which is [a]evil to be of
God, or that which is good and of
God to be of the devil.
15 For behold, my brethren, it is
given unto you to [a]judge, that ye
may know good from evil; and the
way to judge is as plain, that ye may
know with a perfect knowledge,
as the daylight is from the dark
night.
16 For behold, the [a]Spirit of Christ
is given to every [b]man, that he may
[c]know good from evil; wherefore, I
show unto you the way to judge;
for every thing which inviteth to
do good, and to persuade to believe
in Christ, is sent forth by the power
and gift of Christ; wherefore ye may
know with a perfect knowledge it is
of God.
17 But whatsoever thing persuadeth men to do [a]evil, and believe not
in Christ, and deny him, and serve
not God, then ye may know with a
perfect knowledge it is of the devil;
for after this manner doth the devil
work, for he persuadeth no man to
do good, no, not one; neither do his
angels; neither do they who subject
themselves unto him.
18 And now, my brethren, seeing
that ye know the [a]light by which ye
may judge, which light is the light
of Christ, see that ye do not judge
wrongfully; for with that same
[b]judgment which ye judge ye shall
also be judged.
19 Wherefore, I beseech of you,
brethren, that ye should search
diligently in the [a]light of Christ
that ye may know good from evil;
and if ye will lay hold upon every
good thing, and condemn it not,
ye certainly will be a [b]child of
Christ.
20 And now, my brethren, how is it
possible that ye can lay hold upon
every good thing?
21 And now I come to that faith,
of which I said I would speak; and
I will tell you the way whereby ye
may lay hold on every good thing.
22 For behold, God [a]knowing all
things, being from [b]everlasting to
everlasting, behold, he sent [c]angels
to minister unto the children of
men, to make manifest concerning the coming of Christ; and in
Christ there should come every
good thing.
23 And God also declared unto
prophets, by his own mouth, that
Christ should come.
24 And behold, there were divers
ways that he did manifest things
unto the children of men, which
were good; and all things which are
good cometh of Christ; otherwise
men were [a]fallen, and there could
no good thing come unto them.

12*c* Alma 5: 40 (39–42); Hel. 6: 30. TG Sin.
13*a* D&C 35: 12; 84: 47 (47–51).
b 2 Ne. 33: 4; Ether 8: 26.
c TG Benevolence.
d TG Inspiration.
14*a* Isa. 5: 20; 2 Ne. 15: 20; D&C 64: 16; 121: 16.
15*a* Ezek. 44: 24. TG Discernment, Spiritual.
16*a* TG Conscience; God, Spirit of; Light of Christ.
b TG Mortality.
c Gen. 3: 5; Amos 5: 14 (14–15); Matt. 12: 33 (33–37); 2 Ne. 2: 5 (5, 18, 26); Mosiah 16: 3; Alma 29: 5; Hel. 14: 31; Ether 4: 12 (11–12).
17*a* TG Sin.
18*a* Mosiah 16: 9; Ether 3: 14; D&C 50: 24; 88: 13 (7–13). TG Light of Christ.
b Luke 6: 37.
19*a* D&C 84: 45; 88: 7 (6–13).
b Mosiah 15: 10; 27: 25. TG Sons and Daughters of God.
22*a* TG God, Foreknowledge of; God, Omniscience of.
b 2 Ne. 19: 6; 26: 12; Mosiah 3: 5; Alma 11: 39 (38–39, 44); Moro. 8: 18. TG God, Eternal Nature of.
c Acts 10: 3 (3, 22); 2 Ne. 10: 3; 11: 3; Jacob 7: 5.
24*a* 2 Ne. 2: 5.

[Between A.D. 400 and 421]

25 Wherefore, by the ministering of [a]angels, and by every word which proceeded forth out of the mouth of God, men began to exercise faith in Christ; and thus by faith, they did lay hold upon every good thing; and thus it was until the coming of Christ.

26 And after that he came men also were [a]saved by faith in his name; and by faith, they become the [b]sons of God. And as surely as Christ liveth he spake these words unto our fathers, saying: [c]Whatsoever thing ye shall ask the Father in my name, which is good, in faith believing that ye shall receive, behold, it shall be done unto you.

27 Wherefore, my beloved brethren, have [a]miracles ceased because Christ hath ascended into heaven, and hath sat down on the right hand of God, to [b]claim of the Father his rights of mercy which he hath upon the children of men?

28 For he hath answered the ends of the law, and he claimeth all those who have faith in him; and they who have faith in him will [a]cleave unto every good thing; wherefore he [b]advocateth the cause of the children of men; and he dwelleth eternally in the heavens.

29 And because he hath done this, my beloved brethren, have miracles ceased? Behold I say unto you, Nay; neither have [a]angels ceased to minister unto the children of men.

30 For behold, they are subject unto him, to minister according to the word of his command, showing themselves unto them of strong faith and a firm mind in every form of [a]godliness.

31 And the office of their ministry is to call men unto repentance, and to fulfil and to do the work of the covenants of the Father, which he hath made unto the children of men, to prepare the way among the children of men, by declaring the word of Christ unto the [a]chosen vessels of the Lord, that they may bear testimony of him.

32 And by so doing, the Lord God prepareth the way that the [a]residue of men may have [b]faith in Christ, that the Holy Ghost may have place in their hearts, according to the power thereof; and after this manner bringeth to pass the Father, the covenants which he hath made unto the children of men.

33 And Christ hath said: [a]If ye will have [b]faith in me ye shall have power to do whatsoever thing is [c]expedient in me.

34 And he hath said: [a]Repent all ye ends of the earth, and come unto me, and be baptized in my name, and have faith in me, that ye may be saved.

35 And now, my beloved brethren, if this be the case that these things are true which I have spoken unto you, and God will show unto you, with [a]power and great glory at the last [b]day, that they are true, and if they are true has the day of miracles ceased?

36 Or have angels ceased to appear unto the children of men? Or has he [a]withheld the power of the Holy Ghost from them? Or will he, so

25*a* Alma 12: 29 (28–30); Moses 5: 58.
26*a* D&C 3: 20.
b TG Sons and Daughters of God.
c 3 Ne. 18: 20. TG Prayer.
27*a* TG Miracle.
b Isa. 53: 12 (11–12); 2 Ne. 2: 9.
28*a* TG Motivations.
b 1 Jn. 2: 1; 2 Ne. 2: 9; Mosiah 14: 12; 15: 8; 3 Ne. 18: 35. TG Jesus Christ, Relationships with the Father.
29*a* Judg. 13: 3; Luke 1: 26; Acts 5: 19 (19–20). TG Angels; Miracle.
30*a* TG Godliness.
31*a* D&C 20: 10.
32*a* Acts 15: 17; Moses 7: 28.
b Acts 16: 5; D&C 46: 14.
33*a* Moro. 10: 23.
b Gal. 2: 16. TG Faith.
c D&C 88: 64 (64–65).
34*a* 3 Ne. 27: 20; Ether 4: 18.
35*a* 2 Ne. 33: 11; Ether 5: 4 (4–6).
b Morm. 9: 15; D&C 35: 8.
36*a* 1 Ne. 10: 17 (17–19); Moro. 10: 7 (4–5, 7, 19).

[Between A.D. 400 and 421]

long as time shall last, or the earth shall stand, or there shall be one man upon the face thereof to be saved?

37 Behold I say unto you, Nay; for it is by faith that [a]miracles are wrought; and it is by faith that angels appear and minister unto men; wherefore, if these things have ceased wo be unto the children of men, for it is because of [b]unbelief, and all is vain.

38 For no man can be saved, according to the words of Christ, save they shall have faith in his name; wherefore, if these things have ceased, then has faith ceased also; and awful is the state of man, for they are as though there had been no redemption made.

39 But behold, my beloved brethren, I judge better things of you, for I judge that ye have faith in Christ because of your meekness; for if ye have not faith in him then ye are not [a]fit to be numbered among the people of his church.

40 And again, my beloved brethren, I would speak unto you concerning [a]hope. How is it that ye can attain unto faith, save ye shall have hope?

41 And what is it that ye shall [a]hope for? Behold I say unto you that ye shall have [b]hope through the atonement of Christ and the power of his resurrection, to be raised unto life [c]eternal, and this because of your faith in him according to the promise.

42 Wherefore, if a man have [a]faith he [b]must needs have hope; for without faith there cannot be any hope.

43 And again, behold I say unto you that he cannot have faith and hope, save he shall be [a]meek, and lowly of heart.

44 If so, his [a]faith and hope is vain, for none is [b]acceptable before God, save the [c]meek and lowly in heart; and if a man be meek and lowly in heart, and [d]confesses by the power of the Holy Ghost that Jesus is the Christ, he must needs have charity; for if he have not charity he is nothing; wherefore he must needs have charity.

45 And [a]charity suffereth long, and is [b]kind, and [c]envieth not, and is not puffed up, seeketh not her own, is not easily [d]provoked, thinketh no evil, and rejoiceth not in iniquity but rejoiceth in the truth, beareth all things, believeth all things, hopeth all things, endureth all things.

46 Wherefore, my beloved brethren, if ye have not charity, ye are nothing, for charity never faileth. Wherefore, cleave unto charity, which is the greatest of all, for all things must fail—

47 But [a]charity is the pure [b]love of Christ, and it endureth [c]forever; and whoso is found possessed of it at the last day, it shall be well with him.

48 Wherefore, my beloved brethren, [a]pray unto the Father with all the energy of heart, that ye may be filled with this love, which he hath bestowed upon all who are true [b]followers of his Son, Jesus Christ; that ye may become the sons of God; that when he shall appear we

37*a* Matt. 13: 58; Morm. 8: 26; 9: 20; Ether 12: 12 (12–18).
b Moro. 10: 19 (19–27).
39*a* TG Worthiness.
40*a* Heb. 11: 1; Ether 12: 4. TG Hope.
41*a* D&C 138: 14.
b Zech. 9: 12 (11–12); Titus 1: 2; Jacob 2: 19; Alma 46: 39.
c TG Eternal Life.
42*a* TG Faith.
b Moro. 10: 20.
43*a* TG Humility.
44*a* 1 Cor. 13: 13 (1–13); Alma 7: 24; Ether 12: 31 (28–35).
b Lev. 10: 19.
c TG Meekness.
d Luke 12: 8 (8–9). TG Holy Ghost, Gifts of; Testimony.
45*a* 1 Cor. 13: 4 (1–13).
b TG Kindness.
c TG Envy.
d TG Provoking.
47*a* Rom. 13: 10; 2 Ne. 26: 30. TG Charity.
b Josh. 22: 5; Ether 12: 34; Moro. 7: 48. TG Love.
c TG Eternity.
48*a* TG Communication; Prayer.
b TG Jesus Christ, Exemplar.

[Between A.D. 400 and 421]

shall [c]be like him, for we shall see
him as he is; that we may have this
hope; that we may be [d]purified even
as he is pure. Amen.

CHAPTER 8

Infant baptism is an evil abomination—Little children are alive in Christ because of the atonement—Faith, repentance, meekness and lowliness of heart, receiving the Holy Ghost, and enduring to the end lead to salvation.

AN epistle of my [a]father Mormon,
written to me, Moroni; and it was
written unto me soon after my calling to the ministry. And on this
wise did he write unto me, saying:
2 My beloved son, Moroni, I
rejoice exceedingly that your Lord
Jesus Christ hath been mindful of
you, and hath called you to his
ministry, and to his holy work.
3 I am mindful of you always in my
prayers, continually praying unto
God the Father in the name of his
Holy Child, Jesus, that he, through
his infinite [a]goodness and [b]grace,
will keep you through the endurance
of faith on his name to the end.
4 And now, my son, I speak unto
you concerning that which grieveth
me exceedingly; for it grieveth me
that there should [a]disputations rise
among you.
5 For, if I have learned the truth,
there have been disputations among
you concerning the baptism of your
little children.
6 And now, my son, I desire that
ye should labor diligently, that this
gross error should be removed from
among you; for, for this intent I
have written this epistle.
7 For immediately after I had
learned these things of you I inquired of the Lord concerning the
matter. And the [a]word of the Lord
came to me by the power of the
Holy Ghost, saying:
8 [a]Listen to the words of Christ,
your Redeemer, your Lord and your
God. Behold, I came into the world
not to call the righteous but sinners
to repentance; the [b]whole need no
physician, but they that are sick;
wherefore, little [c]children are [d]whole,
for they are not capable of committing [e]sin; wherefore the curse of
[f]Adam is taken from them in me,
that it hath no power over them;
and the law of [g]circumcision is done
away in me.
9 And after this manner did the
Holy Ghost manifest the word of
God unto me; wherefore, my
beloved son, I know that it is
solemn [a]mockery before God, that
ye should baptize little children.
10 Behold I say unto you that this
thing shall ye teach—repentance
and baptism unto those who are
[a]accountable and capable of committing sin; yea, teach parents that
they must repent and be baptized,
and humble themselves as their
little [b]children, and they shall all be
saved with their little children.
11 And their little [a]children need
no repentance, neither baptism.
Behold, baptism is unto repentance
to the fulfilling the commandments
unto the [b]remission of sins.
12 But little [a]children are alive in
Christ, even from the foundation of
the world; if not so, God is a partial

48c 1 Jn. 3: 2 (1–3); 3 Ne. 27: 27.
d 3 Ne. 19: 28 (28–29). TG Cleanliness; Purity.
8 1a W of M 1: 1.
3a Ex. 34: 6 (5–7); Mosiah 4: 11.
b TG Grace.
4a TG Disputations.
7a TG Word of the Lord.
8a D&C 15: 1.
b Mark 2: 17.
c Mark 10: 14 (13–16). TG Conceived in Sin.
d Mosiah 3: 16; D&C 29: 46; 74: 7.
e TG Sin.
f Mosiah 3: 26; Morm. 9: 12.
g Gen. 17: 11 (10–27); Acts 15: 24. TG Circumcision.
9a 2 Ne. 31: 13.
10a TG Accountability.
b TG Family, Children, Responsibilities toward; Family, Love within.
11a TG Baptism, Qualifications for; Children.
b TG Remission of Sins.
12a D&C 29: 46; 93: 38.

[Between A.D. 400 and 421]

God, and also a changeable God,
and a [b]respecter to persons; for how
many little children have died
without baptism!
13 Wherefore, if little children
could not be saved without baptism,
these must have gone to an endless
hell.
14 Behold I say unto you, that he
that supposeth that little children
need baptism is in the gall of bitterness and in the bonds of iniquity;
for he hath neither [a]faith, hope,
nor charity; wherefore, should he
be cut off while in the thought, he
must go down to hell.
15 For awful is the wickedness to
suppose that God saveth one child
because of baptism, and the other
must perish because he hath no
baptism.
16 Wo be unto them that shall
pervert the ways of the Lord after
this manner, for they shall perish
except they repent. Behold, I speak
with boldness, having [a]authority
from God; and I fear not what man
can do; for [b]perfect [c]love [d]casteth
out all fear.
17 And I am filled with [a]charity,
which is everlasting love; wherefore, all children are alike unto me;
wherefore, I love little children with
a perfect love; and they are all alike
and [b]partakers of salvation.
18 For I know that God is not a
partial God, neither a changeable
being; but he is [a]unchangeable from
[b]all eternity to all eternity.
19 Little [a]children cannot repent;
wherefore, it is awful wickedness to
deny the pure mercies of God unto
them, for they are all alive in him
because of his [b]mercy.
20 And he that saith that little
children need baptism denieth the
mercies of Christ, and setteth at
naught the [a]atonement of him and
the power of his redemption.
21 Wo unto such, for they are in
danger of death, [a]hell, and an [b]end-
less torment. I speak it boldly; God
hath commanded me. Listen unto
them and give heed, or they stand
against you at the [c]judgment-seat
of Christ.
22 For behold that all little children are [a]alive in Christ, and also all
they that are without the [b]law. For
the power of [c]redemption cometh
on all them that have [d]no law;
wherefore, he that is not condemned, or he that is under no condemnation, cannot repent; and unto
such baptism availeth nothing—
23 But it is mockery before God,
denying the mercies of Christ, and
the power of his Holy Spirit, and
putting trust in [a]dead works.
24 Behold, my son, this thing
ought not to be; for [a]repentance is
unto them that are under condemnation and under the curse of a
broken law.
25 And the first fruits of [a]repen-
tance is [b]baptism; and baptism
cometh by faith unto the fulfilling
the commandments; and the fulfilling the commandments bringeth
[c]remission of sins;
26 And the remission of sins
bringeth [a]meekness, and lowliness of
heart; and because of meekness and
lowliness of heart cometh the visita-

12*b* Eph. 6: 9; D&C 38: 16.
14*a* 1 Cor. 13: 13 (1–13); Ether 12: 3 (3–37); Moro. 7: 1; 10: 20 (20–23).
16*a* TG Authority.
b TG Perfection.
c TG Love.
d 1 Jn. 4: 18.
17*a* TG Charity.
b Mosiah 3: 16 (16–19).
18*a* Alma 7: 20; Morm. 9: 9. TG God, Perfection of.
b Moro. 7: 22.
19*a* Luke 18: 16 (15–17).
b TG God, Mercy of.
20*a* TG Jesus Christ, Atonement through; Salvation, Plan of.
21*a* TG Hell.
b Jacob 6: 10; Mosiah 28: 3; D&C 19: 12 (10–12).
c TG Jesus Christ, Judge.
22*a* TG Salvation of Little Children.
b Acts 17: 30.
c TG Redemption.
d TG Accountability.
23*a* D&C 22: 2.
24*a* TG Repentance.
25*a* TG Baptism, Qualifications for.
b Moses 6: 60.
c D&C 76: 52. TG Remission of Sins.
26*a* TG Meekness.

[Between A.D. 400 and 421]

tion of the [b]Holy Ghost, which
[c]Comforter [d]filleth with hope and
perfect [e]love, which love endureth
by [f]diligence unto [g]prayer, until
the end shall come, when all the
[h]saints shall dwell with God.
27 Behold, my son, I will write
unto you again if I go not out soon
against the Lamanites. Behold, the
[a]pride of this nation, or the people
of the Nephites, hath proven their
destruction except they should
repent.
28 Pray for them, my son, that
repentance may come unto them.
But behold, I fear lest the Spirit
hath [a]ceased [b]striving with them;
and in this part of the land they are
also seeking to put down all power
and authority which cometh from
God; and they are [c]denying the
Holy Ghost.
29 And after rejecting so great a
knowledge, my son, they must perish
soon, unto the fulfilling of the
prophecies which were spoken by
the prophets, as well as the words of
our Savior himself.
30 Farewell, my son, until I shall
write unto you, or shall meet you
again. Amen.

CHAPTER 9

The second epistle of Mormon to his son Moroni.

Both the Nephites and the Lamanites are depraved and degenerate—They torture and murder each other—Mormon prays that grace and goodness may rest upon Moroni forever.

My beloved son, I write unto you
again that ye may know that I am
yet alive; but I write somewhat of
that which is grievous.
2 For behold, I have had a sore
battle with the Lamanites, in which
we did not conquer; and Archeantus
has fallen by the sword, and also
Luram and Emron; yea, and we
have lost a great number of our
choice men.
3 And now behold, my son, I fear
lest the Lamanites shall destroy
this people; for they do not repent,
and Satan stirreth them up continually
to [a]anger one with another.
4 Behold, I am laboring with them
continually; and when I speak the
word of God with [a]sharpness they
tremble and anger against me; and
when I use no sharpness they [b]harden
their hearts against it; wherefore,
I fear lest the Spirit of the Lord hath
ceased [c]striving with them.
5 For so exceedingly do they anger
that it seemeth me that they have
no fear of death; and they have lost
their love, one towards another;
and they [a]thirst after blood and
revenge continually.
6 And now, my beloved son, notwithstanding
their hardness, let us
labor [a]diligently; for if we should
cease to [b]labor, we should be brought
under condemnation; for we have a
labor to perform whilst in this
tabernacle of clay, that we may conquer
the enemy of all righteousness,
and rest our souls in the kingdom
of God.
7 And now I write somewhat concerning
the sufferings of this people.

26*b* TG Holy Ghost, Baptism of.
c TG Holy Ghost, Comforter; Holy Ghost, Mission of.
d 1 Ne. 11:22 (22–25). TG Hope.
e 1 Pet. 1:22.
f TG Diligence; Perseverance.
g TG Prayer.
h TG Saints.
27*a* D&C 38:39. TG Pride.
28*a* TG Holy Ghost, Loss of.
b Morm. 5:16; Moro. 9:4.
c Alma 39:6. TG Holy Ghost, Unpardonable Sin against.
9 3*a* TG Anger.
4*a* 2 Ne. 1:26 (26–27); W of M 1:17; D&C 121:43 (41–43).
b TG Hardheartedness.
c Moro. 8:28; D&C 1:33.
5*a* Morm. 4:11 (11–12).
6*a* TG Dedication; Diligence; Perseverance.
b 1 Sam. 8:9; 2 Cor. 5:9; Jacob 1:19; Enos 1:20. TG Duty; Priesthood, Magnifying Callings within.

[Between A.D. 400 and 421]

For according to the knowledge
which I have received from Amoron,
behold, the Lamanites have many
prisoners, which they took from
the tower of Sherrizah; and there
were men, women, and children.
8 And the husbands and fathers of
those women and children they have
slain; and they feed the women
upon the [a]flesh of their husbands,
and the children upon the flesh of
their fathers; and no water, save a
little, do they give unto them.
9 And notwithstanding this great
[a]abomination of the Lamanites, it
doth not exceed that of our people
in Moriantum. For behold, many of
the daughters of the Lamanites have
they taken prisoners; and after [b]de-
priving them of that which was most
dear and precious above all things,
which is [c]chastity and [d]virtue—
10 And after they had done this
thing, they did murder them in a
most [a]cruel manner, torturing their
bodies even unto death; and after
they have done this, they devour
their flesh like unto wild beasts,
because of the hardness of their
hearts; and they do it for a token
of bravery.
11 O my beloved son, how can a
people like this, that are without
civilization—
12 (And only a few years have
passed away, and they were a civil
and a delightsome people)
13 But O my son, how can a people
like this, whose [a]delight is in so
much abomination—
14 How can we expect that God
will [a]stay his hand in judgment
against us?
15 Behold, my heart cries: Wo
unto this people. Come out in
judgment, O God, and hide their
sins, and wickedness, and abominations from before thy face!
16 And again, my son, there are
many [a]widows and their daughters
who remain in Sherrizah; and that
part of the provisions which the
Lamanites did not carry away, behold, the army of Zenephi has carried away, and left them to wander
whithersoever they can for food;
and many old women do faint by the
way and die.
17 And the army which is with me
is weak; and the armies of the Lamanites are betwixt Sherrizah and
me; and as many as have fled to the
army of [a]Aaron have fallen victims
to their awful brutality.
18 O the depravity of my people!
They are without [a]order and without mercy. Behold, I am but a man,
and I have but the [b]strength of a
man, and I cannot any longer
enforce my commands.
19 And they have become strong
in their perversion; and they are
alike brutal, sparing none, neither
old nor young; and they delight in
everything save that which is good;
and the suffering of our women and
our children upon all the face of this
land doth exceed everything; yea,
tongue cannot tell, neither can it be
written.
20 And now, my son, I dwell no
longer upon this horrible scene.
Behold, thou knowest the wickedness of this people; thou knowest
that they are without principle,
and past feeling; and their wickedness doth [a]exceed that of the
Lamanites.
21 Behold, my son, I cannot recom-
mend them unto God lest he should
smite me.
22 But behold, my son, I recom-
mend thee unto God, and I trust in
Christ that thou wilt be saved; and
I [a]pray unto God that he will [b]spare
thy life, to witness the return of his

8*a* Lev. 26:29; 1 Ne. 21:26.
9*a* TG Body, Sanctity of.
b TG Sensuality.
c TG Chastity.
d TG Virtue.
10*a* TG Cruelty.
13*a* 2 Ne. 9:9 (8–9); Jacob 3:11.
14*a* 2 Sam. 24:16; Alma 10:23.
16*a* Mosiah 21:10 (10, 17). TG Widows.
17*a* Morm. 2:9.
18*a* TG Order.
b TG Strength.
20*a* Hel. 6:34 (18–35).
22*a* W of M 1:8.
b Morm. 8:3.

[Between A.D. 400 and 421]

people unto him, or their utter
destruction; for I know that they
must perish except they [c]repent and
return unto him.
23 And if they perish it will be like
unto the [a]Jaredites, because of the
wilfulness of their hearts, [b]seeking
for blood and [c]revenge.
24 And if it so be that they perish,
we know that many of our brethren have [a]deserted over unto the
Lamanites, and many more will also
desert over unto them; wherefore,
write somewhat a few things, if
thou art spared and I shall perish
and not see thee; but I trust that I
may see thee soon; for I have sacred
records that I would [b]deliver up unto
thee.
25 My son, be faithful in Christ;
and may not the things which I have
written grieve thee, to weigh thee
down unto [a]death; but may Christ
lift thee up, and may his sufferings
and death, and the showing his body
unto our fathers, and his mercy and
[b]long-suffering, and the hope of his
glory and of eternal life, rest in your
[c]mind forever.
26 And may the grace of God the
Father, whose throne is high in the
heavens, and our Lord Jesus Christ,
who sitteth on the [a]right hand of his
power, until all things shall become
subject unto him, be, and abide
with you forever. Amen.

CHAPTER 10

A testimony of the Book of Mormon comes by the power of the Holy Ghost—The gifts of the Spirit are dispensed to the faithful—Spiritual gifts always accompany faith—Moroni's words speak from the dust—Come unto Christ, be perfected in him, and sanctify your souls.

Now I, Moroni, write somewhat
as seemeth me good; and I write
unto my brethren, the [a]Lamanites;
and I would that they should know
that *more than [b]four hundred and
twenty years have passed away
since the sign was given of the
coming of Christ.
2 And I [a]seal up [b]these records,
after I have spoken a few words by
way of exhortation unto you.
3 Behold, I would exhort you that
when ye shall read these things, if it
be wisdom in God that ye should
read them, that ye would remember
how [a]merciful the Lord hath been
unto the children of men, from the
creation of Adam even down until
the time that ye shall receive these
things, and [b]ponder it in your
[c]hearts.
4 And when ye shall receive these
things, I would exhort you that ye
would [a]ask God, the Eternal Father,
in the name of Christ, if these things
are not [b]true; and if ye shall ask
with a [c]sincere heart, with [d]real intent, having [e]faith in Christ, he will
[f]manifest the [g]truth of it unto you,
by the power of the Holy Ghost.
5 And by the power of the Holy
Ghost ye may [a]know the [b]truth of
all things.
6 And whatsoever thing is good is

22c 1 Sam. 7: 3; Hel. 13: 11; 3 Ne. 10: 6 (5–7); 24: 7.
23a Jacob 5: 44.
b Morm. 4: 11 (11–12).
c Ether 15: 22 (15–31).
24a Alma 45: 14.
b Morm. 6: 6; 8: 1.
25a TG Jesus Christ, Death of.
b TG Forbearance.
c TG Mind.
26a TG Jesus Christ, Relationships with the Father.

10 1a D&C 10: 48.
b Morm. 8: 5; Moro. 1: 1.
2a Morm. 5: 12; 8: 4 (4, 13–14). TG Scriptures, Preservation of; Seal.
b Morm. 6: 6.
3a Gen. 19: 16.
b Deut. 11: 18. TG Meditation; Study.
c Deut. 6: 6.
4a TG Prayer.
b 1 Ne. 13: 39; 14: 30; Mosiah 1: 6; Alma 3: 12; Ether 4: 11 (6–11); 5: 3 (1–4). TG Book of Mormon.
c TG Honesty; Sincerity.
d James 1: 6 (6–7); Moro. 7: 9.
e TG Faith.
f TG Revelation.
g Ps. 145: 18. TG Guidance, Divine; Truth.
5a D&C 35: 19. TG Discernment, Spiritual; Holy Ghost, Source of Testimony.
b John 8: 32.

[*About A.D. 421]

just and true; wherefore, nothing
that is good denieth the Christ, but
acknowledgeth that he is.
7 And ye may [a]know that he is,
by the power of the Holy Ghost;
wherefore I would exhort you that
ye deny not the power of God; for
he worketh by power, [b]according to
the faith of the children of men, the
same today and tomorrow, and
forever.
8 And again, I exhort you, my
brethren, that ye deny not the
[a]gifts of God, for they are many;
and they come from the same God.
And there are [b]different ways that
these gifts are administered; but it
is the same God who worketh all in
all; and they are given by the manifestations of the [c]Spirit of God unto
men, to profit them.
9 [a]For behold, to one is given by
the Spirit of God, that he may
[b]teach the word of wisdom;
10 And to another, that he may
[a]teach the word of [b]knowledge by
the same Spirit;
11 And to another, exceedingly
great [a]faith; and to another, the
gifts of [b]healing by the same Spirit;
12 And again, to another, that he
may work mighty [a]miracles;
13 And again, to another, that he
may prophesy concerning all things;
14 And again, to another, the beholding of angels and ministering
spirits;
15 And again, to another, all kinds
of tongues;
16 And again, to another, the
interpretation of [a]languages and of
divers kinds of tongues.
17 And all these gifts come by the
Spirit of Christ; and they come unto
every man severally, according as
he will.
18 And I would exhort you, my
beloved brethren, that ye remember
that [a]every good [b]gift cometh of
Christ.
19 And I would exhort you, my
beloved brethren, that ye remember
that he is the [a]same yesterday, today, and forever, and that all these
gifts of which I have spoken, which
are spiritual, never will be done
away, even as long as the world
shall stand, only according to the
[b]unbelief of the children of men.
20 Wherefore, there must be
[a]faith; and if there must be faith
there must also be hope; and if
there must be hope there must also
be charity.
21 And except ye have [a]charity ye
can in nowise be saved in the kingdom of God; neither can ye be
saved in the kingdom of God if ye
have not faith; neither can ye if ye
have no hope.
22 And if ye have no hope ye must
needs be in [a]despair; and despair
cometh because of iniquity.
23 And Christ truly said unto our
fathers: [a]If ye have faith ye can do
all things which are expedient unto
me.
24 And now I speak unto all the
ends of the earth—that if the day
cometh that the power and gifts
of God shall be done away among
you, it shall be [a]because of [b]unbelief.
25 And wo be unto the children of
men if this be the case; for there
shall be [a]none that doeth good
among you, no not one. For if there

7*a* TG Testimony.
b 1 Ne. 10: 17 (17–19); Moro. 7: 36.
8*a* TG God, Gifts of; Holy Ghost, Gifts of.
b D&C 46: 15.
c TG God, Spirit of.
9*a* 1 Cor. 12: 8 (8–11); D&C 46: 12 (8–30).
b Ex. 35: 34; D&C 38: 23; 88: 77 (77–79, 118); 107: 85 (85–89).
10*a* TG Education.
b 1 Cor. 12: 8. TG Learning.
11*a* TG Faith.
b TG Healing.
12*a* TG Miracle.
16*a* TG Language.
18*a* James 1: 17.
b TG Talents.
19*a* Heb. 13: 8.
b Moro. 7: 37. TG Doubt.
20*a* 1 Cor. 13: 13 (1–13); Ether 12: 3 (3–37); Moro. 7: 1, 42 (42–44); 8: 14.
21*a* TG Charity.
22*a* TG Despair.
23*a* Moro. 7: 33.
24*a* Moro. 7: 37.
b TG Doubt; Unbelief, Unbelievers.
25*a* Ps. 14: 3; Rom. 3: 12.

[About A.D. 421]

be one among you that doeth good,
he shall work by the power and
gifts of God.
26 And wo unto them who shall
do these things away and die, for
they [a]die in their [b]sins, and they
cannot be saved in the kingdom of
God; and I speak it according to
the words of Christ; and I lie not.
27 And I exhort you to remember
these things; for the time speedily
cometh that ye shall know that I
lie not, for ye shall see me at the
bar of God; and the Lord God will
say unto you: Did I not declare my
[a]words unto you, which were written by this man, like as one [b]crying
from the dead, yea, even as one
speaking out of the [c]dust?
28 I declare these things unto the
fulfilling of the prophecies. And
behold, they shall proceed forth out
of the mouth of the everlasting
God; and his word shall [a]hiss forth
from generation to generation.
29 And God shall show unto you,
that that which I have written is
[a]true.
30 And again I would exhort you
that ye would [a]come unto Christ,
and lay hold upon every good [b]gift,
and [c]touch not the evil gift, nor the
[d]unclean thing.
31 And [a]awake, and arise from the
dust, O Jerusalem; yea, and put on
thy beautiful garments, O daughter
of [b]Zion; and [c]strengthen thy
[d]stakes and enlarge thy borders forever, that thou mayest [e]no more be
confounded, that the covenants of
the Eternal Father which he hath
made unto thee, O house of Israel,
may be fulfilled.
32 Yea, [a]come unto Christ, and be
[b]perfected in him, and [c]deny yourselves of all ungodliness; and if ye
shall deny yourselves of all ungodliness, and [d]love God with all your
might, mind and strength, then is
his grace sufficient for you, that by
his grace ye may be [e]perfect in
Christ; and if by the grace of God ye
are perfect in Christ, ye can in
nowise deny the power of God.
33 And again, if ye by the grace of
God are perfect in Christ, and deny
not his power, then are ye [a]sancti-
fied in Christ by the grace of God,
through the shedding of the [b]blood
of Christ, which is in the covenant
of the Father unto the remission of
your [c]sins, that ye become [d]holy,
without spot.
34 And now I bid unto all, farewell. I soon go to [a]rest in the
[b]paradise of God, until my [c]spirit
and body shall again [d]reunite, and
I am brought forth triumphant
through the [e]air, to meet you before the [f]pleasing bar of the great
[g]Jehovah, the Eternal [h]Judge of
both quick and dead. Amen.

26*a* Ezek. 18: 26; 1 Ne. 15: 33 (32–33); Mosiah 15: 26.
b John 8: 21 (21–24).
27*a* Isa. 51: 16; 2 Ne. 33: 10 (10–11); D&C 1: 24.
b 2 Ne. 3: 19 (19–20); 27: 13; 33: 13 (13–15); Morm. 9: 30.
c Isa. 29: 4.
28*a* 2 Ne. 29: 2.
29*a* TG Book of Mormon.
30*a* 1 Ne. 6: 4; Morm. 9: 27; Ether 5: 5.
b TG Talents.
c 2 Ne. 18: 19.
d TG Uncleanness.
31*a* Isa. 52: 1 (1–2). TG Israel, Restoration of.
b TG Zion.
c Isa. 54: 2. TG Priesthood, Power of.
d TG Stakes.
e Ether 13: 8.
32*a* Rev. 22: 17 (17–21). TG Teachable.
b Gal. 3: 24; Philip. 3: 15 (14–15). TG Man, New, Spiritually Reborn; Worthiness.
c Rom. 12: 1 (1–3). TG Perseverance.
d Deut. 11: 1; Mosiah 2: 4; D&C 20: 19; 59: 5 (5–6). TG Commitment; Dedication.
e Rom. 6: 6 (1–7). TG Perfection.
33*a* TG Sanctification.
b TG Jesus Christ, Atonement through.
c Ex. 34: 7.
d TG Holiness.
34*a* TG Rest.
b TG Paradise.
c TG Spirit Body.
d TG Resurrection.
e 1 Thes. 4: 17.
f Jacob 6: 13.
g TG Jesus Christ—Jehovah.
h TG Jesus Christ, Judge.

[About A.D. 421]

THE END

PRONOUNCING GUIDE

KEY TO SYMBOLS USED

a	*a*bout	ĭ	*i*t, h*i*m, m*i*rror
ă	*a*sk, p*a*t, m*a*p	ī	*i*dle, f*i*ne, den*y*
ā	*a*ble, b*a*ke, w*ay*	ō	*o*ver, b*o*ne, kn*ow*
ä	*a*lms, f*a*ther, c*a*ll	ou	ab*ou*t
ĕ	*e*bb, m*e*t, s*e*cond	u	j*u*mp
ē	*ea*t, m*e*te, m*e*	ū	r*u*le, b*oo*t, tw*o*
er	p*er*mit		

Aaron ĕr′an
Abel ā′bul
Abinadi a-bĭn′a-dī
Abinadom a-bĭn′a-dum
Abish ā′bĭsh
Ablom ăb′lum
Abraham ā′bra-hăm
Adam ăd′um
Agosh ā′gäsh
Aha ā′hä
Ahah ā′hä
Ahaz ā′hăz
Aiath ī′uth
Akish ā′kĭsh
Alma ăl′ma
Alpha ăl′fa
Amaleki a-măl′a-kī
Amalekite a-măl′a-kīt
Amalickiah a-măl′a-kĭ′a
Amalickiahite a-măl′a-kī′a-īt
Amaron a-mā′rän
Amgid ăm′gĭd
Aminadab a-mĭn′a-dăb
Aminadi a-mĭn′a-dī
Amlici ăm′lĭ-sī
Amlicite ăm′lĭ-sīt
Ammaron ăm′a-rän
Ammon ăm′un
Ammonite ăm′a-nīt
Ammonihah ăm-a-nī′hä
Ammonihahite ăm-a-nī′hä-īt
Ammoron ăm′ōr-än
Amnah ăm′nä
Amnigaddah ăm-nĭ-găd′ä
Amnihu ăm-nī′hū
Amnor ăm′nōr
Amoron a-mōr′än
Amos ā′mus
Amoz ā′muz
Amulek ăm′yū-lĕk
Amulon ăm′yū-län
Amulonites ăm′ya-län′īts
Anathoth ăn′a-tōth
Angola ăn-gō′la
Ani-Anti ăn′ī—ăn′tī
Anti-Nephi-Lehi ăn′tī—nē′fī—lē′hī
Anti-Nephi-Lehies ăn′tī—nē′fī—lē′hīz
Antiomno ăn-tē-äm′nō
Antion ăn′tē-än
Antionah ăn-tē-än′a
Antionum ăn-tē-ō′num
Antiparah ăn-tĭ-pär′a
Antipas ăn′tĭ-päs
Antipus ăn′tĭ-pus
Antum ăn′tum
Archeantus är-kē-ăn′tus
Arpad är′păd
Assyria a-sĭr′ē-a

Babylon băb′ĭ-län
Bashan bā′shän
Benjamin bĕn′ja-mĭn
Bethabara bĕth-ăb′a-ra
Boaz bō′ăz
Bountiful boun′tĭ-ful

Cain kān
Calno kăl′nō
Carchemish kär-kĕm′ĭsh
Cezoram sē-zōr′um

Chaldeans kăl-dē′unz
Chaldees kăl-dēz′
Chemish kĕm′ĭsh
Cherubim chĕr′a-bĭm
Cohor kō′hōr
Com kōm
Comnor kōm′nōr
Corianton kōr-ē-ăn′tun
Coriantor kōr-ē-ăn′tōr
Coriantum kōr-ē-ăn′tum
Coriantumr kōr-ē-ăn′ta-mer
Corihor kōr′ĭ-hōr
Corom kōr′um
Cumeni kū′ma-nī
Cumenihah kū-ma-nī′hä
Cumom kū′mum
Cumorah ka-mōr′a
Curelom kū-rē′lum

Deseret dĕz-a-rĕt′
Desolation dĕs-ō-lā′shun

Edom ē′dum
Egypt ē′jĭpt
Egyptian ē-jĭp′shun
Elam ē′lum
Elijah ē-lī′ja
Emer ē′mer
Emron ĕm′rän
Enos ē′nus
Ephah ē′fä
Ephraim ē′frĕm *or* ē′frum
Esrom ĕz′rum
Ethem ē′thum
Ether ē′ther
Eve ēv
Ezias ē-zī′us
Ezrom ĕz′rum

Gad găd
Gadiandi găd-ē-ăn′dī
Gadianton găd-ē-ăn′tun
Gadiomnah găd-ē-äm′na
Gallim găl′ĭm
Gazelem ga-zā′lĭm
Geba gē′ba
Gebim gē′bĭm
Gibeah gĭb′ē-a
Gid gĭd
Giddonah gĭd-dō′nä
Giddianhi gĭd-ē-ăn′hī
Gideon gĭd′ē-un
Gidgiddonah gĭd-gĭd-dō′nä
Gidgiddoni gĭd-gĭd-dō′nī
Gilead gĭl′ē-ud
Gilgah gĭl′gä
Gilgal gĭl′gäl
Gimgimno gĭm-gĭm′nō
Gomorrah ga-mōr′a

Hagoth hā′gäth
Hamath hā′muth
Hearthom hē-är′thum
Helam hē′lum
Helaman hē′la-mun
Helem hē′lĕm
Helorum hē-lōr′um
Hem hĕm
Hermounts her′mounts
Heshlon hĕsh′län
Heth hĕth
Himni hĭm′nī
Horeb hōr′ĕb

Immanuel ĭm-măn′yū-ĕl
Irreantum ĭ-rē-ăn′tum
Isaac ī′zĭk
Isabel ĭz′a-bĕl
Isaiah ī-zā′a
Ishmael ĭsh′mul *or* ĭsh′mĕl
Ishmaelite ĭsh′mul-īt *or* ĭsh′mĕl-īt
Israel ĭz′rĕl *or* ĭz′rul
Israelite ĭz′rĕl-īt *or* ĭz′rul-īt

Jacob jā′kub
Jacobite jā′kub-īt
Jacobugath jā′ka-bū′găth
Jacom jā′kum
Jared jĕr′ud
Jaredite jĕr′a-dīt
Jarom jĕr′um
Jashon jā′shän
Jeberechiah jĕb-a-ra-kī′a
Jehovah jē-hō′va
Jeneum jĕn′ē-um
Jeremiah jĕr-a-mī′a
Jershon jĕr′shän
Jerusalem ja-rū′sa-lĕm
Jesse Jĕs′ē
Jew jū
John jän
Jonas jō′nus
Jordan jōr′dun
Joseph jō′zĕf
Josephite jō′zĕf-īt
Josh jäsh
Joshua jäsh′ū-wa
Jothan jō′thun
Judah jū′da
Judea jū-dē′a

Kib kĭb

Kim kĭm
Kimnor kĭm′nōr
Kish kĭsh
Kishkumen kĭsh-kū′mun
Korihor kō′rĭ-hōr
Kumen kū′mun
Kumenonhi kū′ma-nän′hī

Laban lā′bun
Lachoneus la-kō′nē-us
Laish lā′ĭsh
Lamah lā′mä
Laman lā′mun
Lamanite lā′mun-īt
Lamoni la-mō′nī
Lebanon lĕb′a-nän
Lehi lē′hī
Lehi-Nephi lē′hī—nē′fī
Lehonti lē-hän′tī
Lemuel lĕm′yūl
Lemuelite lĕm′yūl-īt
Levi lē′vī
Liahona lē′a-hō′na
Lib lĭb
Limhah lĭm′hä
Limher lĭm′her
Limhi lĭm′hī
Limnah lĭm′nä
Luram lūr′um

Madmenah măd-mĕn′a
Mahah mā′hä
Maher-shalal-hash-baz mā′her—shăl-ăl—hăsh′bäz
Mahonri ma-hän′rī
Malachi măl′a-kī
Manasseh ma-năs′a
Manti măn′tī
Mary mĕ′rē
Mathoni ma-thō′nī
Mathonihah măth-ō-nī′hä
Medes mēdz
Melchizedek mĕl-kĭz′a-dĭk
Melek mē′lĕk
Michmash mĭk′măsh
Middoni mĭd-dō′nī
Midian mĭd′ē-un
Migron mī′grän
Minon mī′nän
Moab mō′ăb
Mocum mō′kum
Moriancumer mōr-ē-ăn′ka-mer
Morianton mōr-ē-ăn′tun
Moriantum mōr-ē-ăn′tum
Mormon mōr′mun
Moron mōr′un

Moroni mō-rō′nī
Moronihah mō-rō-nī′hä
Moses mō′zus
Mosiah mō-sī′a *or* mō-zī′a
Mulek myū′lĕk
Muloki myū′la-kī

Nahom nā′hum
Naphtali năf′ta-lī
Nazareth năz′a-rĕth
Neas nē′äs
Nehor nē′hōr
Nephi nē′fī
Nephihah nē-fī′hä
Nephite nē′fīt
Neum nē′um
Nimrah nĭm′rä
Nimrod nĭm′räd
Noah nō′a

Ogath ō′găth
Omega ō-mā′ga
Omer ō′mer
Omner äm′ner
Omni äm′nī
Onidah ō-nī′da
Onihah ō-nī′hä
Onti än′tī
Opher ō′fer
Oreb ōr′ĕb
Orihah ō-rī′hä

Paanchi pā-ăn′kī
Pachus pā′kus
Pacumeni pā-kyū′mĕn-ī
Pagag pā′găg
Pahoran pa-hōr′un
Palestina păl-a-stī′na
Pathros pā′thrōs
Pekah pē′kä
Pharaoh fā′rō *or* fĕ′rō
Philistine fĭl′a-stēn

Rabbanah ra-băn′a
Rahab rā′hăb
Ramah rä′mä
Ramath rā′muth
Rameumptom răm-ē-ump′tum
Remaliah rĕm-a-lī′a
Rezin rē′zĭn
Riplah rĭp′lä
Riplakish rĭp-lā′kĭsh
Ripliancum rĭp-lē-ăn′kum

Salem sā′lĕm
Sam săm

Samaria sa-mĕr′ē-a
Samuel săm′yū-ĕl
Sarah sĕr′a
Sariah sa-rī′a
Saul säl
Seantum sē-ăn′tum
Sebus sē′bus
Seezoram sē-zōr′um
Senine sē′nīn
Senum sē′num
Seraphim sĕr′a-fĭm
Seth sĕth
Shared shā′rud
Shazer shā′zer
Shearjashub shĭr-jā′shub
Shelem shē′lĕm
Shem shĕm
Shemlon shĕm′län
Shemnon shĕm′nän
Sherem shĕr′um
Sherrizah shĕr-ī′za
Sheum shē′um
Shez shĕz
Shiblom shĭb′lum
Shiblon shĭb′lun
Shiblum shĭb′lum
Shiloah shī-lō′a
Shilom shī′lum
Shim shĭm
Shimnilon shĭm-nī′län
Shinar shī′när
Shiz shĭz
Shule shūl
Shum shum
Shurr sher
Sidom sī′dum
Sidon sī′dun
Sinai sī′nī
Sinim sī′nĭm
Siron sī′run
Syria sĭr′ē-a

Tarshish tär′shĭsh
Teancum tē-ăn′kum
Teomner tē-äm′ner
Thummim thum′ĭm
Timothy tĭm′a-thē
Tubaloth tū′ba-läth

Uriah yū-rī′a
Urim yūr′ĭm
Uzziah yū-zī′a

Zarahemla zĕr-a-hĕm′la
Zebulun zĕb′yū-lun
Zechariah zĕk′a-rī′a
Zedekiah zĕd′a-kī′a
Zeezrom zē-ĕz′rum
Zemnarihah zĕm-na-rī′hä
Zenephi zēn′a-fī
Zeniff zē′nĭf
Zenoch zē′nuk
Zenos zē′nus
Zerahemnah zĕr-a-hĕm′nä
Zeram zē′rum
Zerin zē′rĭn
Ziff zĭf
Zion zī′un
Zoram zōr′um
Zoramite zōr′um-īt

INDEX

AARON[1]—*brother of Moses* (*see* BD Aaron)
No references in Book of Mormon.

AARON[2]—*Jaredite king*

Ether 1: 16 descendant of Heth[2]; 10: 31 dwells in captivity.

AARON[3]—*son of Mosiah[2]* [c. 100 B.C.] (*see also* Mosiah[2], Sons of)

Mosiah 27: 8–10 an unbeliever, seeks to destroy church; 27: 32 converted by angel; 27: 34 named among sons of King Mosiah[2]; 27: 35–37 preaches gospel; 28: 1–9 is allowed to preach in land of Nephi; 29: 3 (28: 10; Alma 17: 6) refuses to become king; **Alma** 17: 1–3 (27: 16–19) meets Alma[2] with joy; 21: 1–4 goes to land of Jerusalem; 21: 4–10 Amalekites contend as he preaches about atonement; 21: 11 goes to Ani-Anti, meets Muloki and Ammah; 21: 12–14 (20: 2, 28) goes to Middoni, preaches, is imprisoned, is delivered by Ammon[2] and Lamoni; 21: 15–17 preaches in synagogues, converts many; 22: 1 is led by Spirit to land of Nephi; 22: 2–16 teaches Lamanite king; 22: 17–22 raises fallen king; 23: 1 is protected by proclamation; 23: 4 establishes churches in cities; 23: 16–17 consulted by king in naming Anti-Nephi-Lehies; 24: 5 travels with brothers in lands of Midian and Ishmael; 25: 6 people are stirred up to remember A's words; 26: 10 rebukes Ammon[2]; 31: 6–7 goes with Ammon[2] and Alma[2] to Zoramites; 35: 14 returns to Zarahemla.

AARON[4]—*king of Lamanites* [c. A.D. 330]

Morm. 2: 9 is defeated by armies of Mormon[2]; 3: 4 sends epistle to Mormon[2]; **Moro.** 9: 17 many Nephites fall to A's army.

AARON, CITY OF [possibly two different cities]

Alma 8: 13–14 was in vicinity of Ammonihah; 50: 14 near cities of Moroni and Nephihah.

ABEL—*son of Adam* (*see also* BD Abel)

Hel. 6: 27 Satan plots with Cain to murder A.

ABHOR, ABHORRENCE (*see also* Allowance; Despise; Hate)

2 Ne. 9: 49 my soul *a.* sin; **Alma** 13: 12 those sanctified cannot look upon sin save with *a.*; 27: 28 Anti-Nephi-Lehies look upon shedding of blood with *a.*; 37: 29 teach them to *a.* such wickedness.

ABIDE (*see also* Dwell; Obedience; Remain)

1 Ne. 11: 27 Holy Ghost *a.* upon the Lamb in form of dove; **Alma** 1: 1 people obliged to *a.* by laws of Mosiah[2]; **3 Ne.** 24: 2 who may *a.* day of the Lord's coming; **Morm.** 2: 26 Spirit *a.* not with Nephite army; **Ether** 12: 41 (Moro. 9: 26) grace *a.* in you forever.

ABINADI—*Nephite prophet* [c. 150 B.C.]

Mosiah 11: 20 prophesies afflictions of people of King Noah[3]; 11: 26–29 Noah[3] angry over A's words; 12: 1–8 comes in disguise, commanded to prophesy; 12: 16–18 is delivered to king, imprisoned, questioned; 12: 19–37 confounds and challenges questioners; 12: 34–36 (13: 12–24) quotes Ten Commandments; 13: 1–5 protected by Spirit; 13: 27–28 teaches salvation not by Mosaic law alone, but also by atonement; 14: 1–12 (15: 6) quotes Isaiah; 15: 1–9 prophesies that God will come among men, redeem them; 16: 1–15 preaches Christ only Redeemer, teaches resurrection and judgment; 17: 1 condemned to death; 17: 2–4 (24: 9; 26: 15; Alma 5: 11) Alma[1] believes and writes A's words; 17: 5–7 imprisoned and accused; 17: 15–19 prophesies priests' death by fire; 17: 20 is burned to death; 18: 1 Alma[1] teaches A's words; 20: 21 (25: 9; Morm. 1: 19) A's words fulfilled; 21: 30 A's death mourned; 24: 5 A's words not taught by Amulon.

ABINADOM—*Nephite historian, son of Chemish* [between 279 and 130 B.C.]

Omni 1: 10 participates in war; 1: 11 writes on plates; 1: 12 is father of Amaleki[1].

ABISH—*Lamanite woman, servant of Lamoni*

Alma 19: 16 converted to the Lord; 19: 17 calls people to king's house; 19: 28 grieves because of tumult; 19: 29 raises queen.

ABLOM—*Jaredite city*

Ether 9: 3 Omer flees to A. by seashore.

ABOMINATION, ABOMINABLE (*see also* Church, Great and Abominable; Church of the Devil; Evil; Sin; TG Abomination; BD Abomination of Desolation)

Jacob 2: 21 pride is *a.* in sight of the Lord; **Mosiah** 3: 25 the wicked are consigned to view of own *a.*; **Alma** 13: 17 Melchizedek's people waxed strong in *a.*; 39: 5 unchastity is most *a.* above all sins save murder and denying Holy Ghost; **Hel.** 4: 11 (13: 14; 3 Ne. 9: 2) slaughter of Nephites caused by *a.*; **3 Ne.** 5: 6 (Hel. 7: 25; 3 Ne. 16: 10; Ether 8: 18; 11: 22) secret and *a.* combinations; 16: 10 Gentiles to receive gospel when they are full of secret *a.*; **Ether** 11: 22 Jaredites reject prophets because of *a.*; 14: 25 Jaredites' *a.* prepared way for destruction; **Moro.** 9: 8–9 *a.* of Lamanites and Nephites during war.

ABOUND

Mosiah 5: 15 (Alma 7: 24; Ether 12: 4) always *a.* in good works; 27: 5 Nephites *a.* in grace of God.

ABRAHAM—*father of faithful* (*see also* Abrahamic Covenant; BD Abraham)

2 Ne. 8: 2 look unto A., your father; 27: 33 the Lord redeemed A.; **Jacob** 4: 5 A. obedient in offering Isaac; **Alma** 5: 24 (7: 25; Hel. 3: 30) murderers cannot sit in kingdom with A.; 13: 15 A. paid tithes to Melchizedek; **Hel.** 8: 16–17 A. and prophets testified of the Son.

ABRAHAMIC COVENANT (*see also* Israel; TG Abrahamic Covenant; BD Abraham, Covenant of)

1 Ne. 15: 18 covenant with A. to be fulfilled; 17: 40 (22: 9; 2 Ne. 29: 14; 3 Ne. 20: 25, 27; Morm. 5: 20; Ether 3: 11) God covenants with A.

ABRIDGMENT, ABRIDGE (*see also* Record)

Title Page Book of Mormon an *a.* of Nephite record and Book of Ether; **1 Ne.** 1: 17 Nephi[1] *a.* father's record; **W of M** 1: 3 Mormon *a.* record of Nephi[1]; **Morm.** 5: 9 Mormon[2] makes small *a.* of things he has seen; **Moro.** 1: 1 Moroni *a.* Jaredites' record.

ABYSS

Mosiah 27: 29 Alma[2] in darkest *a.*; **Alma** 26: 3 Lamanites in darkest *a.*

ACCEPTABLE

Moro. 7: 44 none is *a.* before God except meek and lowly.

ACCOMPLISH (*see also* Do; Fulfill; Perform)

1 Ne. 3: 7 (17: 3) the Lord prepares way to *a.* that which he commands; 9: 6 the Lord prepares way to *a.* all his works.

ACCOUNT (*see also* Accountable; History; Record)

1 Ne. 1: 16–17 (6: 3) Nephi[1] does not make full *a.* on small plates; 9: 2–4 large plates of Nephi contain *a.* of secular history; 10: 1 Nephi[1] records *a.* of his ministry on small plates.

ACCOUNTABILITY, AGE OF (*see also* Accountable)

Moro. 8: 5–26 little children need no repentance, neither baptism.

ACCOUNTABLE (*see also* Accountability, Age of; Responsibility; TG Accountability)

Moro. 8: 10 teach repentance and baptism unto those *a.*

ACCURSED (*see also* Curse; Slippery)

Hel. 12: 18 hidden treasure to be *a.* because of iniquity; **Ether** 4: 8 he who contends against word of the Lord shall be *a.*

ACCUSE (*see also* Condemn)

2 Ne. 1: 25 brothers of Nephi[1] *a.* him of seeking power; **Mosiah** 2: 15 Benjamin does not *a.* his people; 12: 19 priests question Abinadi that they might *a.* him; **Alma** 10: 31 Zeezrom foremost to *a.* Amulek and Alma[2]; 30: 31 Korihor *a.* priests of leading people away; **Hel.** 9: 19 judges question Nephi[2] that they might *a.* him to death.

ACKNOWLEDGE (*see also* Confess)

Alma 1: 1 laws of Mosiah[2] are *a.* by people; 1: 15 Nehor *a.* false teachings; 38: 14 *a.* your unworthiness before God; 39: 13 *a.* your faults; **Moro.** 10: 6 that which is good *a.* that Christ is.

ACT (*see also* Agency; Deed; Walk; Work [noun])

2 Ne. 2: 13 if no God, there could have been no creation of things, neither to *a.* nor to be *a.* upon; 2: 16 (Hel. 14: 30) God gave unto man to *a.* for himself; 2: 26 because of atonement men become free to *a.* for themselves and not to be *a.* upon; 31: 13 to receive Holy Ghost, men must *a.* no hypocrisy or deception before God; **Alma** 12: 31 through transgression man was placed in state to *a.* according to his will.

ADAM—*first man created on earth* (*see also* Eden, Garden of; Eve; Fall of Man; Man; TG Adam; BD Adam)

1 Ne. 5: 11 A. and Eve our first parents; **2 Ne.** 2: 19 driven from garden; 2: 22 if A. had not transgressed, he would not have fallen; 2: 25 A. fell that men might be; 9: 21 Holy One suffered pains of all who belong to family of A.; **Mosiah** 3: 11 Christ's blood atones for all who have fallen by transgression of A.; 3: 16 as in A., or by nature, men fall; 3: 19 natural man an enemy to God since fall of A.; 3: 26 justice could not deny A. should fall because of partaking of forbidden fruit.

ADD (*see also* Increase)

3 Ne. 13: 27 who can *a.* one cubit to his stature; 13: 33 all things shall be *a.* unto you.

ADHERE (*see also* Keep)

Alma 60: 34 *a.* to word of God.

ADMINISTRATION, ADMINISTER (*see also* Impart; Minister [verb])

Jacob 2: 19 seek riches to *a.* relief to sick and afflicted; **Mosiah** 4: 16 *a.* of your substance to those in need; 4: 26 to retain remission of sins, *a.* relief to needy; **Alma** 10: 14 lawyers hired to *a.* law at trials; 15: 18 Alma[2] *a.* to Amulek in his tribulations; 35: 9 Ammonites *a.* unto Zoramites according to their wants; **3 Ne.** 6: 28 covenant of secret combinations *a.* by devil; **4 Ne.** 1: 27 wicked churches *a.* that which was sacred unto the unworthy; **Ether** 10: 33 robbers *a.* oaths after manner of the ancients; **Moro.** 4: 1 elders and priests *a.* flesh and blood of Christ unto church; 5: 1–2 manner of *a.* sacrament wine.

ADMONISH, ADMONITION (*see also* Rebuke; Warn, Warning)

Jacob 2: 9 Jacob[2] sorrows that he is commanded to *a.* people according to crimes; **Enos** 1: 1 father of Enos[2] taught him in nurture and *a.* of the Lord; **Omni** 1: 13 people of Mosiah[2] were *a.* continually by word of God; **Mosiah** 26: 6, 39 church members who committed sin were *a.* by the church; **Alma** 1: 7 Gideon *a.* Nehor with word of God.

ADORN (*see also* Pride; Vanity)

4 Ne. 1: 41 (Morm. 8: 37) Nephites *a.* churches with precious things; **Morm.** 8: 39 why do ye *a.* yourselves with that which hath no life.

ADULTERY, ADULTERER (*see also* Chastity, Chaste; Fornication; Lust; Whore; TG Adulterer, Adultery; Sexual Immorality; BD Adultery)

Mosiah 13: 22 thou shalt not commit *a.*; **Alma** 16: 18 priests preach against *a.*; 23: 3 Lamanite king teaches people not to commit *a.*; 30: 10 those who commit *a.* are punished; 39: 3–5 *a.* is most abominable above all sins save murder and denying Holy Ghost; **Hel.** 4: 11–12 slaughter of Nephites caused by committing *a.*; 7: 5 Nephites rule that they might more easily commit *a.*; **3 Ne.** 12: 28 (Matt. 5: 28) whoso lusts after a woman has already committed *a.* in heart; 12: 32 (Matt. 5: 32) whoso puts away his wife causes her to commit *a.*

ADVANTAGE (*see also* Gain)

2 Ne. 28: 8 the wicked to say, Take *a.* of one because of words; **Ether** 12: 26 fools shall take no *a.* of your weakness.

ADVERSARY (*see also* Devil)

1 Ne. 15: 24 fiery darts of *a.* cannot overpower those who hearken to God's word; **Alma** 12: 5 Zeezrom's plan is plan of the *a.*; **3 Ne.** 12: 25 (Matt. 5: 25) agree with thine *a.* quickly.

ADVERSITY (*see* Affliction; Infirmity; Opposition; Oppression; Patience; Persecution; Sorrow; Suffering; Tempt; Trial; Tribulation; Wind)

ADVOCATE (*see* Jesus Christ—Advocate)

AFFECTION (*see also* Love)

Alma 37: 36 let *a.* of heart be placed upon the Lord forever.

AFFIXED (*see* Punish, Punishment)

AFFLICTED (*see also* Affliction)

1 Ne. 21: 13 the Lord will have mercy upon his *a.*; **Jacob** 2: 19 administer relief to the *a.*; **Mosiah** 14: 4, 7 (Isa. 53: 4) we did esteem him smitten of God, and *a.*; **Alma** 1: 27 Nephites impart substance to the *a.*; 34: 28 if ye turn away the *a.*, your prayer is vain; **3 Ne.** 17: 9 Nephites brought their *a.* for the Savior's blessing; **Morm.** 8: 39 why do ye suffer the *a.* to pass by you without notice.

AFFLICTION (*see also* Afflicted; Chasten; Needy; Oppression; Pain; Suffering; Trial; Tribulation)

1 Ne. 15: 5 Nephi[1] is overcome because of *a.*; **2 Ne.** 2: 2 God shall consecrate thine *a.* for thy gain; 4: 26 why should my strength slacken because of mine *a.*; **Jacob** 3: 1 God will console you in your *a.*; **Mosiah** 24: 13–14 the Lord visits his people in their *a.*; **Alma** 1: 23 (4: 6–7) pride a cause of great *a.* to church; 7: 11 Son of God to go forth suffering *a.*; 17: 11 (26: 27; 31: 31; 34: 41) be patient in *a.*; 32: 6 *a.* of poor Zoramites humble them; 33: 11 the Lord hears Alma[2] because of his *a.*; 61: 4 those who try to take away judgment-seat are cause of sore *a.*; 62: 41 many are softened because of their *a.*; **Hel.** 3: 34 (3 Ne. 6: 13) the proud cause the humble to wade through much *a.*; 12: 3 except the Lord chastens his people with *a.*, they will not remember him.

AGAINST

2 Ne. 10: 16 they who are not for God are *a.* him.

AGE (*see also* Accountability, Age of; Old)

Mosiah 10: 9 men placed in army ranks according to *a.*

AGENCY, AGENT (*see also* Accountable; Act; Choose; Evil; Fall of Man; Freedom; Fruit, Forbidden; Knowledge; Law; Liberty; Obedience; Opposition; Tempt; Transgression; Will; TG Agency)

2 Ne. 2: 11 opposition in all things; 2: 16 man could not act for himself save he was enticed by good and evil; 2: 27 men are free to choose; 10: 23 ye are free to act for yourselves; 26: 10 those who choose works of darkness must go down to hell; **Mosiah** 2: 21 God preserves men that they may do according to their own will; 5: 8 under Christ's head, men are made free; **Alma** 12: 31 having transgressed temporal commandments, men placed themselves in state to act according to their own wills; 13: 3 man left to choose good or evil; 30: 8 choose ye this day; 41: 7 the redeemed are their own judges, whether to do good or evil; **Hel.** 14: 30 ye are free, ye are permitted to act for yourselves; **Moro.** 7: 15 it is given unto you to judge, that ye may know good from evil.

AGOSH—*Jaredite area*

Ether 14: 15–16 Lib² pursues Coriantumr² to plains of A.

AGREE (*see also* Unite)

3 Ne. 12: 25 *a.* with thine adversary quickly.

AHA—*Nephite military officer* [c. 80 B.C.]

Alma 16: 5–6 son of Zoram², frees captive Nephites.

AHAH—*Jaredite king, son of Seth²*

Ether 1: 9 father of Ethem; 11: 10 commits iniquity while king.

AIATH [possibly Ai] (*see also* BD Ai)

2 Ne. 20: 28 (Isa. 10: 28) Assyrians have come to A.

AKISH—*Jaredite king, son of Kimnor*

Ether 8: 10 daughter of Jared³ conspires to marry A.; 8: 11–13 A. agrees to kill the king; 8: 14–18 initiates secret combination; 9: 1 overthrows kingdom of Omer; 9: 4 marries daughter of Jared³; 9: 5 causes death of Jared³ and obtains kingdom; 9: 6–7 reigns, kills own son; 9: 12 has war with other sons, kingdom destroyed.

AKISH, WILDERNESS OF

Ether 14: 3–4, 14 scene of battles of Coriantumr².

ALIKE (*see also* Equal, Equality; Respect; Respecter; Same)

2 Ne. 26: 33 all are *a.* unto God; **Mosiah** 29: 32 every man may enjoy his rights and privileges *a.*; **Moro.** 8: 17 all children are *a.* unto me.

ALIVE (*see also* Living; Quicken)

2 Ne. 25: 25 we are made *a.* in Christ; **Jacob** 5: 34 roots of wild olive-tree are *a.*; **Moro.** 8: 12, 19, 22 little children are *a.* in Christ.

ALLOT (*see also* Give)

Alma 29: 3–4 the Lord *a.* unto men according to their wills.

ALLOWANCE (*see also* Abhor)

Alma 45: 16 the Lord cannot look upon sin with least degree of *a.*

ALMA¹—*Nephite prophet, founder of the church* [c. 173-91 B.C.]

Mosiah 17: 1–2 priest of Noah³, descendant of Nephi¹; 17: 2 (24: 9) believes Abinadi; 17: 3–4 cast out by king, flees, hides, writes words of Abinadi; 18: 1 repents, teaches words of Abinadi; 18: 5 hides by waters of Mormon; 18: 7–11 people gather to hear A.; 18: 12–14 baptizes Helam; 18: 15–16 baptizes 204 souls; 18: 17 (21: 30) organizes church; 18: 18 has authority from God, ordains priests; 18: 19–26 instructs priests; 18: 27–29 commands people to share substance; 18: 34 (23: 1) is warned of approaching army, departs into wilderness; 21: 30 departure of A. is mourned; 21: 34 people want to become like A.; 23: 1 account of A. begins; 23: 6–7 declines to be king; 23: 8–25 teaches people; 23: 16 high priest, founder of church; 23: 17 consecrates priests and teachers; 23: 26 flees with brethren to city of Helam; 23: 27–29 surrenders to Lamanites; 23: 35 discovered by Amulon; 23: 36–37 is deceived by Lamanites; 24: 8 is oppressed by Amulon; 24: 12–15 pours out heart to the Lord; 24: 16–20 A. and people are delivered through faith; 24: 23 is warned to flee in haste; 24: 25 arrives in Zarahemla, meets Mosiah²; 25: 6 account of A. is read to people; 25: 14–16 preaches repentance; 25: 17–18 baptizes Limhi and people; 25: 19–24 establishes churches; 26: 7 dissenters brought before A.; 26: 8 is given authority over church; 26: 20 is promised eternal life; 26: 21–33 is instructed concerning wrong-doers and unbelievers; 26: 34–39 judges, regulates church, walks in diligence, teaches, suffers afflictions; 27: 1 people complain to A.; 27: 8 son of

A. an unbeliever; 27: 14 prays for son; 29: 42 (Alma 4: 4; 5: 3) ordains son high priest; 29: 45 dies; **Alma** 5: 11 son lauds A's beliefs.

ALMA[2]—*son of Alma*[1], *first chief judge, high priest* [c. 100-73 B.C.]

Mosiah 27: 8–10 seeks to destroy church; 27: 11 (Alma 36: 6–10) with sons of Mosiah[2] sees angel; 27: 19 becomes helpless and dumb; 27: 20 father rejoices over him; 27: 23 is revived; 27: 24–31 (Alma 36: 5–24) relates experience; 27: 32 teaches people; 28: 20 receives records and interpreters; 29: 42 (Alma 4: 4; 5: 3) is appointed chief judge and high priest; **Alma** 1: 11–15 sentences Nehor; 2: 16 leads Nephite army; 2: 30 asks the Lord for mercy to save people; 2: 31 slays Amlici; 2: 32–38 contends with Lamanites and Amlicites; 4: 4 baptizes in river Sidon; 4: 7 (6: 1; 15: 3) consecrates teachers, priests, elders; 4: 11–13 sees great wickedness in church; 4: 16–17 resigns judgment-seat to Nephihah; 4: 18 retains office of high priest; 5: 1–2 preaches in Zarahemla; 5: 3–61 preaches about his mighty change in heart; 5: 62 speaks by way of commandment; 6: 7–8 preaches in valley of Gideon; 7: 1–27 preaches about coming of Redeemer; 8: 1 leaves Gideon for Zarahemla; 8: 3–5 teaches and baptizes in Melek; 8: 6–8 preaches at Ammonihah; 8: 10 wrestles with God in mighty prayer; 8: 11–13 is reviled and cast out of Ammonihah; 8: 14 is visited by angel; 8: 16–18 returns to Ammonihah; 8: 19–21 meets Amulek; 8: 27 tarries many days; 8: 30–32 with Amulek, goes forth with power; 9: 1–7 people of Ammonihah contend with A.; 9: 8–30 boldly testifies; 10: 31 with Amulek, is accused by Zeezrom; 12: 1–18 speaks to Zeezrom; 12: 20 is questioned by Antionah; 12: 21–37 teaches of tree of life, fall, probationary state, commandments, plan of redemption; 13: 1–20 teaches of holy priesthood, responsibilities, foreknowledge, Melchizedek; 13: 21, 27–30 calls people to repent; 13: 22–26 teaches joyful news of salvation; 14: 2–4 with Amulek, bound, taken before judge; 14: 9–10 sees converts burned; 14: 11 is constrained by Spirit; 14: 13 cannot be burned till work is finished; 14: 17–24 imprisoned, mistreated; 14: 26–28 (Ether 12: 13) freed from prison; 15: 1 goes to Sidom with Amulek; 15: 10–12 heals and baptizes Zeezrom; 15: 13 establishes church in Sidom; 15: 18 takes Amulek to Zarahemla; 16: 5 sons of Zoram[2] ask for A's counsel in battles; 16: 13 preaches repentance with Amulek; 17: 1–2 (27: 16, 19) meets sons of Mosiah[2] journeying to Gideon; 27: 20 takes brethren back to Zarahemla; 27: 25 returns to wilderness with Ammon[2]; 29: 1–3 desires to be angel; 29: 8 teaches that the Lord grants in wisdom to all nations; 30: 29–30 confronts Korihor; 30: 33 labors in ministry not for pay; 30: 49–50 strikes Korihor dumb; 31: 1–2 sorrowful because of Zoramites; 31: 6–7 takes several brethren to preach to Zoramites; 31: 12–38 grieves over use of Rameumptom, prays for people; 32: 4 preaches on hill Onidah; 32: 12 preaches to the poor; 32: 13–43 teaches about faith; 33: 2–15 urges reading of scripture; 33: 17–23 encourages faith in the Son; 35: 1 goes to Jershon with brethren; 35: 14 returns to Zarahemla; 35: 15 grieves over people's iniquity; 36: 1–30 gives charge to Helaman[1]; 37: 1–18 (50: 38) gives Helaman[1] records; 37: 21 speaks of twenty-four plates; 37: 24–47 further instructs Helaman[1]; 38: 1–15 gives commandments and instructions to his son Shiblon; 39: 1 gives commandments to his son Corianton; 39: 5–6 teaches about unpardonable sin; 40: 11–15 describes state of soul between death and resurrection; 40: 16–24 (41: 1–15) teaches about restoration of body and soul; 42: 1–31 teaches of Fall, probationary state, temporal death, spiritual death, plan of mercy, plan of happiness, law, punishment, justice, and salvation; 42: 31 sends Corianton to preach; 43: 1 goes forth to preach; 43: 24 receives word of the Lord for Moroni[1]; 45: 2 instructs Helaman[1]; 45: 9–16 prophesies about wickedness and destruction of people; 45: 16–17 blesses land and church; 45: 18 departs, not heard of again; 45: 19 taken up by Spirit or buried by the Lord, as Moses; **Hel.** 4: 21 people remember A's prophecies; 5: 41 A's teachings cited by Aminadab.

ALMA, VALLEY OF—*a day's travel north of city of Helam*

Mosiah 24: 20 named after Alma[1]; 24: 21 people poured out thanks in A.

ALMIGHTY (*see* God, Power of)

ALMS (*see also* Charity; Impart; Needy; Poor; Relief; TG Almsgiving; BD Almsgiving)

3 Ne. 13: 1 ye should do *a.* unto the poor; 13: 2–4 *a.* should be in secret.

ALONE

1 Ne. 7: 1 not meet for Lehi[1] to take family into wilderness *a.*; **Jacob** 4: 13 Nephites are not witnesses *a.*; **Mosiah** 13: 28 salvation comes not by law *a.*

ALPHA (*see also* TG Omega; BD Alpha; Omega)

3 Ne. 9: 18 Christ is A. and Omega.

ALTAR (*see also* Idolatry; Offering; Sacrifice; Worship; BD Altar)

1 Ne. 2: 7 Lehi[1] builds *a.* of stones; **Alma** 15: 17 people gather in sanctuaries to worship God before *a.*; 17: 4 sons of Mosiah[2] bring many before *a.* of God.

ALTER (*see also* Change)

Alma 51: 2–5 some desire that law be *a.* to overthrow free government; **Hel.** 4: 22 Nephites had *a.* laws of Mosiah[2]; **Morm.** 9: 32–33 Nephites' written language *a.* according to speech.

AMALEKI[1]—*Nephite record keeper* [c. 130 B.C.]

Omni 1: 12 son of Abinadom; 1: 12–22 records doings of Mosiah[1]; 1: 23–24 records beginning of Benjamin's reign; 1: 25 will deliver records to Benjamin; 1: 26 calls brethren to come unto Christ; 1: 27–30 records expedition that returns to land of Nephi; **W of M** 1: 10 delivered plates to Benjamin.

AMALEKI[2]—*part of expedition that seeks Zeniff's group* [c. 121 B.C.] (*see also* Ammon[1])

Mosiah 7: 6 accompanies Ammon[1] in returning to land of Nephi.

AMALEKITES—*group of Nephite apostates*

Alma 21: 2 help build city of Jerusalem; 21: 3 more hardened than Lamanites; 21: 4 after order of Nehors; 21: 5 contend with Aaron[3]; 22: 7 say there is a God; 23: 14 only one A. is converted; 24: 1 stir up Lamanites against Anti-Nephi-Lehies; 43: 6 are appointed captains because of murderous dispositions; 43: 13 dissenters from Nephites; 43: 20 better armed than Lamanites; 43: 44 inspire Lamanites to fight.

AMALICKIAH—*Nephite traitor* [c. 70 B.C.]

Alma 46: 3 leader of revolt against Helaman[2]; 46: 4 desires to be king; 46: 4–10 leads people from church by flattery; 46: 11 angers Moroni[1]; 46: 28–33 flees with followers; 47: 1 stirs up Lamanites in land of Nephi; 47: 3 heads Lamanite army; 47: 4 seeks overthrow of Lamanite king; 47: 10–12 sends messages to Lehonti; 47: 13 conspires with Lehonti; 47: 17–19 poisons Lehonti, becomes Lamanite commander; 47: 21–24 has king slain; 47: 35 takes king's wife and kingdom; 48: 1 stirs up Lamanites against Nephites; 48: 5 appoints Zoramites as captains; 48: 7 obtains power by fraud; 49: 10–11 does not himself come to battle; 49: 27 enraged over defeat of his army; 51: 12 heads army in person; 51: 23 takes city of Moroni; 51: 26 takes other cities; 51: 29 meets Teancum; 51: 34 slain by Teancum; 52: 3 brother of A. is made king.

AMALICKIAHITES—*followers of Amalickiah*

Alma 46: 28 are dissenters; 46: 35 refuse covenant, put to death; 49: 9 astonished by Nephite preparation.

AMARON—*son of Omni, Nephite record keeper*

Omni 1: 3 receives plates; 1: 8 delivers plates to Chemish.

AMGID—*Jaredite king*

Ether 10: 32 overthrown by Com[2].

AMINADAB—*Nephite dissenter living among Lamanites* [c. 30 B.C.]

Hel. 5: 35–37 sees faces of Nephi[2] and Lehi[4] shining in prison; 5: 39–41 tells Lamanites to repent.

AMINADI—*descendant of Nephi[1], ancestor of Amulek*

Alma 10: 2–3 interprets writings on temple wall.

AMISS

2 Ne. 4: 35 God will give me, if I ask not *a.*

AMLICI—*Nephite dissenter* [c. 87 B.C.] (*see also* Amlicites)

Alma 2: 1 incites people to contention and attempts to become king by cunning ways; 2: 4 would deny privileges of church; 2: 7 voice of people comes against A.; 2: 9 is consecrated king by dissenters; 2: 11 A's followers are called Amlicites; 2: 31 slain by Alma[2].

AMLICITES—*Nephite faction desiring king*

Alma 2: 11 followers of Amlici; 2: 12–13 Nephites prepare to meet A.; 2: 24 join Lamanites; 2: 35 are defeated; 3: 3 the slain are thrown in waters of Sidon; 3: 4, 13 mark foreheads like Lamanites; 3: 18 are in open rebellion against God and are cursed.

AMMAH—*missionary companion of Aaron[3]*

Alma 20: 2 imprisoned at Middoni; 21: 11–17 preaches at Ani-Anti and Middoni.

AMMARON—*Nephite record keeper* [c. A.D. 306]

4 Ne. 1: 47 brother of Amos[2], keeps records; 1: 48 hides all records; **Morm.** 1: 2–4 tells Mormon[2] how and when to hide the plates; 2: 17 deposits records near city of Jashon.

AMMON[1]—*leader of expedition to land of Nephi* [c. 121 B.C.]

Mosiah 7: 3 strong and mighty man, descendant of Zarahemla; 7: 6 leads brethren to land of Nephi; 7: 7 is imprisoned by king Limhi; 7: 8 is brought before king; 7: 16 is honored; 8: 2 addresses people; 8: 6 reads record of Limhi; 8: 8–11 is told of ancient relics and twenty-four gold plates; 8: 13–17 tells of Mosiah², seer who can translate; 21: 23 is suspected of being a priest of Noah³; 21: 33 declines to baptize king; 22: 11 leads Limhi and people to freedom.

AMMON²—*son of Mosiah², missionary to Lamanites* [c. 100 B.C.] (*see also* Ammon², People of; Mosiah², Sons of)

Mosiah 27: 8 unbeliever; 27: 10 seeks to destroy church; 27: 11 angel appears to A.; 27: 32 begins preaching word of God; 27: 34–35 with brethren, travels throughout Zarahemla; 28: 1–8 desires mission to Lamanites; 28: 10 (29: 3) refuses to be king; **Alma** 17: 1–4 with brethren, meets Alma²; 17: 6–8 departs for land of Nephi; 17: 13 separates from brethren; 17: 18 chief among missionaries; 17: 20–21 taken bound to Lamoni; 17: 25 becomes servant; 17: 26–39 saves king's flocks; 18: 2–4 Lamoni believes A. is Great Spirit; 18: 10 prepares chariots; 18: 16 discerns king's thoughts; 18: 22–32 teaches king, recites history; 19: 2 is called before queen; 19: 14 thanks God, overpowered with joy; 19: 22–23 cannot be slain, according to the Lord's promises; 19: 33 revives, ministers to people; 20: 1 organizes church; 20: 2 is commanded to go to Middoni; 20: 8 meets Lamoni's father; 20: 14–18 is threatened, but saves Lamoni; 20: 20–21 overpowers king; 20: 22–28 frees brethren from prison; 21: 18 returns with Lamoni to land of Ishmael; 21: 23 teaches Lamoni's people; 23: 1 proclamation for A's protection; 23: 6 A's converts never fall away; 24: 5 with brethren, holds council with Lamoni and his brother; 26: 1–34 reviews success; 26: 10 is rebuked by Aaron³; 26: 35 praises God; 27: 5 proposes migration to Zarahemla; 27: 10–15 leads his people toward Zarahemla; 27: 16 (17: 1–4) with brethren, meets Alma²; 27: 17 is swallowed up in joy; 27: 25 returns with Alma²; 30: 20 is high priest over Ammonites; 30: 21 banishes Korihor; 31: 6 goes with Alma² on mission to Zoramites; 31: 32 Alma² prays for his success; 31: 37–38 is provided for through faith; 35: 1 returns to Jershon; 35: 14 returns to Zarahemla; 37: 9 needs plates for missionary work; 48: 18 a man of God; **Ether** 12: 15 A's faith wrought miracle among Lamanites.

AMMON, CHILDREN OF—*people in Palestine descended from Lot* (*see also* BD Ammon, Ammonites)

2 Ne. 21: 14 (Isa. 11: 14) to obey gathered Israel.

AMMON², PEOPLE OF—*converted Lamanites; also known as Anti-Nephi-Lehies or Ammonites* (*see also* Helaman², Sons of)

Alma 21: 23 (23: 4–5) thousands of Lamanites converted by sons of Mosiah²; 23: 6 after conversion, never fall away; 23: 16–17 (24: 1) take the name of Anti-Nephi-Lehies; 23: 18 friendly to Nephites, curse no longer follows them; 24: 1–2 unconverted Lamanites take up arms against them; 24: 6 will not take up arms; 24: 12–19 refuse to shed blood, bury weapons; 24: 20–22 do not resist Lamanite attack, and 1005 are slain; 24: 24–27 over one thousand Lamanites converted through example; 24: 28 slain mainly by Amalekites and Amulonites; 25: 13 joined by many Lamanites; 25: 15 (30: 3) observe law of Moses; 25: 16 look forward to Christ; 27: 2 Amalekites stir up Lamanites again to slay them; 27: 8 offer to become slaves to Nephites; 27: 14 depart into wilderness near Zarahemla; 27: 21–25 are given land of Jershon by Nephites; 27: 23 (28: 1; 43: 12) protected by Nephites; 27: 26 called people of Ammon²; 27: 27 numbered with church, distinguished for zeal; 35: 8 Zoramites angry with them; 35: 9 accept converted Zoramites; 35: 11 Zoramites prepare for war with them; 35: 13 remove to Melek; 43: 11 hated by Lamanites; 43: 11 will not break covenant; 43: 13 give great substance to Nephites; 47: 29 joined by Lehonti's servants; 53: 10–14 willing to break oath, dissuaded by Helaman²; 53: 16–19 their sons prepare for war, choose Helaman² as their leader; 56: 54 sons of A. defeat Lamanites; 56: 55–56 sons of A. miraculously saved from death; 62: 16–17 joined by four thousand Lamanites who enter covenant; **Hel.** 3: 12 may go to land northward.

AMMONIHAH, CITY OF—*in West, near cities of Melek, Noah, and Aaron*

Alma 8: 6–8 (9:1) Alma² preaches at A.; 8: 7 land of A. named after first possessor; 8: 9–13 Alma² cast out of A.; 8: 16–18 Alma² returns to A.; ch. 9–14 words of Alma² and Amulek to people at A.; 10: 23 destruction of people predicted; 14: 8 people at A. burn scriptures, slay believers; 14: 22 Alma² and Amulek are imprisoned; 14: 27 falling prison walls slay leaders; 14: 28 Alma² and Amulek are freed; 14: 29 people flee from prophets; 15: 1 Alma² and Amulek banished from A.; 15: 15 people remain hard-hearted; 16: 2–3, 9 (25: 2) Lamanites destroy people of A.; 16: 11 called Desolation of Nehors; 49: 3 rebuilt; 49: 10–11 Lamanites dare not attack A.

AMMONIHAH, LAND OF—*to the west of River Sidon* (*see* Ammonihah, City of)

AMMONIHAHITES (*see* Ammonihah, City of)

AMMONITES (*see* Ammon[2], People of)

AMMORON—*Nephite traitor, brother of Amalickiah, descendant of Zoram*[1] [c. 66-61 B.C.]

Alma 52: 3 appointed king of Lamanites; 52: 12 attacks Nephites; 54: 1 proposes prisoner exchange; 54: 4–14 receives epistle from Moroni[1]; 54: 16–24 A's reply; 55: 1 knows his cause is not just; 55: 2 Moroni[1] refuses prisoner exchange with A.; 56: 18 abandons attack; 57: 1 offers to deliver city of Antiparah in exchange for prisoners; 57: 17 sends new provisions; 59: 7 strengthens Lamanites; 62: 33 is with combined Lamanite armies; 62: 36 is slain by Teancum.

AMNIGADDAH—*Jaredite king*

Ether 1: 14–15 son of Aaron[2], father of Coriantum[2]; 10: 31 dwells in captivity.

AMNIHU—*hill on east of River Sidon*

Alma 2: 15 where Amlicites fight Nephites.

AMNOR[1]—*spy for Nephites* [c. 87 B.C.]

Alma 2: 22 sent to watch camp of Amlicites.

AMNOR[2]—*Nephite coin*

Alma 11: 6 *a.* of silver; 11: 11 equal to two senums.

AMORON—*a Nephite* [c. A.D. 400-421]

Moro. 9: 7 reports to Mormon.

AMOS[1]—*Nephite record keeper* [c. A.D. 110-194]

4 Ne. 1: 19–20 son of Nephi[4], keeps records; 1: 21 gives records to his son.

AMOS[2]—*Nephite record keeper* [c. A.D. 194-306]

4 Ne. 1: 21 receives records from his father, Amos[1]; 1: 47 gives records to Ammaron.

AMOZ—*father of Isaiah*[1] [c. 8th century B.C.]

2 Ne. 12: 1 (23: 1; Isa. 2: 1; 13: 1) Isaiah[1], son of A.

AMULEK—*missionary companion of Alma*[2] [c. 82-74 B.C.]

Alma 8: 20 (10: 7) visited by angel; 8: 21 receives Alma[2]; 8: 31–32 goes forth with power; 10: 1–11 preaches to people in Ammonihah; 10: 2–3 son of Giddonah, grandson of Ishmael[2], descendant of Aminadi, Nephi[1], Lehi[2], and Manasseh; 10: 4 man of reputation, friends, riches; 10: 5–6 had rebelled against God; 10: 8 obeys angel; 10: 11 family and kindred blessed by Alma[2]; 10: 12 a second witness; 10: 17 perceives questioners' thoughts; 10: 22 prophesies destruction of Ammonihahites; 10: 31 accused by Zeezrom; 11: 20 judges stir up people against A.; 11: 21–38 questioned by Zeezrom; 11: 39–40 testifies of Redeemer; 11: 41–45 teaches of resurrection, judgment, and restoration; 12: 1 words silence Zeezrom; 12: 8–18 Alma[2] explains the words of A.; 12: 24 speaks of temporal death; 14: 2 people desire his destruction; 14: 10 wants to stop martyrdom of believers; 14: 17 imprisoned with Alma[2]; 14: 18 refuses to answer judge; 14: 26 breaks bonds by faith; 14: 26–27 people flee, persecutors slain; 15: 1 with Alma[2], commanded to leave city; 15: 16 rejected by relatives and friends; 15: 18 goes with Alma[2] to Zarahemla; 16: 13 preaches repentance; 31: 6 among missionaries to Zoramites; 31: 32 Alma[2] prays for A's success; 34: 1 teaches the poor; 34: 10–16 explains great and last sacrifice, meaning of law, mercy, justice; 34: 17 teaches about prayer; 34: 32 warns against procrastination; 35: 1 goes to Jershon; **Hel.** 5: 10 quoted on redemption; **Ether** 12: 13 faith of Alma[2] and A. causes prison walls to tumble.

AMULON—*leader of priests of Noah*[3], *tributary monarch under Laman*[3] (*see also* Amulon, Children of; Amulon, Land of; Amulonites; Noah[3], Priests of)

Mosiah 23: 32 leader of priests of Noah[3]; 23: 33 pleads with Lamanites for life; 23: 35 joins Lamanites, discovers land of Helam; 23: 39 made king; 24: 1 A. and brethren made teachers over people of Alma[1]; 24: 8 exercises authority over Alma[1] and people; 24: 11 threatens believers with death.

AMULON, CHILDREN OF—*children of priests of Noah*[3] (*see also* Amulonites)

Mosiah 25: 12 children of A. and brethren want to be called Nephites.

AMULON, LAND OF—*settled by Amulon and priests, between Zarahemla and Nephi*

Mosiah 23: 31 priests of Noah[3] are found in A.; 24: 1 Amulon and brethren appointed teachers in A.

AMULONITES—*descendants and followers of Amulon and priests of Noah*[3] (*see also* Noah[3], Priests of)

Alma 21: 3 are more wicked than Lamanites; 21: 4 after order of Nehors;

23: 14 (24: 29) none converted; 24: 1 stir up Lamanites; 24: 2 rebel against king, take up arms against Ammonites; 24: 28 (25: 7) slay believers; 25: 4 slain by Nephites; 25: 5 usurp leadership and persecute Lamanites; 25: 8 hunted, slain by Lamanites; 25: 9 Abinadi's prophecy fulfilled.

ANATHOTH—*Levite city near old Jerusalem*

2 Ne. 20: 30 (Isa. 10: 30) O poor A.

ANCIENT (*see also* Old)

2 Ne. 13: 2 (Isa. 3: 2) the Lord takes the *a.* away from Jerusalem; 19: 15 the *a.*, he is the head; 29: 4–5 (Morm. 8: 15) Jews are the Lord's *a.* covenant people; **Mosiah** 8: 13 Mosiah[2] can translate all records of *a.* date; **Ether** 9: 5 (10: 33) oaths of the *a.*

ANGEL (*see also* Angels, Ministering of; Angels of the Devil; Messenger; TG Angels; BD Angels)

1 Ne. 1: 8 (Alma 36: 22) numberless concourses of *a.* praising God; 3: 29 (17: 45) *a.* reproves Laman[1] and Lemuel; 11: 14—14: 30 (15: 29; 19: 8, 10) *a.* of the Lord shows Nephi[1] vision interpreting father's dream; **2 Ne.** 10: 3 *a.* reveals Christ's name to Jacob[2]; 32: 3 *a.* speak by power of Holy Ghost; **Mosiah** 3: 2—4: 1 *a.* speaks to Benjamin; 27: 11–18, 32 (Alma 17: 2; 36: 5; 38: 7) *a.* of the Lord appears to Alma[2] and sons of Mosiah[2]; **Alma 8: 14–18 (9: 19–30) *a.* gives Alma[2] instructions; 10: 7 (11: 31) *a.* appears to Amulek; 13: 29 voice of the Lord declares repentance by mouth of *a.* unto all nations; 18: 30 heaven is place where God and *a.* dwell; 19: 34 many Lamanites see and converse with *a.*; 21: 5 an Amalekite asks why *a.* do not appear unto them; 27: 4 Anti-Nephi-Lehies treat Ammon[2] and brothers as *a.*; 29: 1 O that I were an *a.*; 32: 23 God imparts his word by *a.*; 39: 19 as easy for the Lord to send *a.* at this time as to our children; 40: 11 *a.* teaches Alma[2] about existence between death and resurrection;** **Hel.** 5: 36 faces of Nephi[2] and Lehi[4] shine as faces of *a.*; 13: 7 *a.* taught Samuel the Lamanite; 16: 14 *a.* appear unto wise men to declare glad tidings; **3 Ne.** 7: 15, 18 Nephi[3] is visited by *a.* ; 11: 8 Nephites think Christ is *a.* descending; 28: 30 three Nephites are as *a.* of God; **Moro.** 7: 22–25 *a.* sent to teach men of Christ's coming; 7: 37 it is by faith that *a.* appear and minister unto men.

ANGELS, MINISTERING OF (*see also* Angel; TG Angels, Ministering)

Jacob 7: 5 *a.* ministered to Jacob[2]; 7: 17 Sherem confesses power of Holy Ghost and ministering of *a.*; **Omni** 1: 25 Amaleki exhorts all men to believe in ministering of *a.*; **3 Ne.** 7: 18 *a.* minister unto Nephi[3] daily; 17: 24 *a.* minister to Nephite children; **Moro.** 7: 25 by ministering of *a.*, men begin to exercise faith in Christ; 7: 29 *a.* have not ceased to minister unto men; 7: 37 by faith *a.* appear and minister unto men.

ANGELS OF THE DEVIL (*see also* Demon; Devil; Devils)

2 Ne. 2: 17 (9: 8) *a.* of God fell from heaven, became devil; 9: 8–9 without resurrection, men's spirits must become *a.* to devil; 9: 9 (Alma 30: 53) Satan transformed himself into *a.* of light; 9: 16 the filthy shall be devil and his *a.*; **Jacob** 3: 11 loose yourselves from pains of hell that ye become not *a.* to devil; **Mosiah** 26: 27 everlasting fire prepared for devil and his *a.*; **Hel.** 13: 37 people will say, We are surrounded by devil's *a.*

ANGER (*see also* Fury; Indignation; Offend; Passion; Provoke; Rage; Wrath)

3 Ne. 11: 29 devil stirs men up to contend with *a.*; **Ether** 15: 22 Jaredites drunken with *a.*; **Moro.** 9: 3 Satan stirs Lamanites up continually to *a.*

ANGOLA—*Nephite City*

Morm. 2: 4 Nephites take possession of A.

ANGUISH (*see also* Misery; Pain; Remorse; Sorrow; Suffering; Torment)

1 Ne. 17: 47 (Morm. 6: 16) my soul is rent with *a.*; **Mosiah** 2: 38 awareness of guilt fills breast with *a.*; 3: 7 Christ's *a.* will cause blood to come from every pore; 25: 11 Nephites filled with *a.* for welfare of Lamanites' souls; 28: 4 sons of Mosiah[2] suffered much *a.* of soul because of their iniquities; **Alma** 38: 8 Alma[2] passed three days and nights in bitter *a.* of soul.

ANI-ANTI—*Lamanite village in land of Nephi*

Alma 21: 11 Aaron[3] finds Muloki and brethren preaching in A.

ANIMAL (*see also* Ass; Bear; Beast; Bee; Calf, Calves; Cattle; Chickens; Cow; Creature; Cummoms; Cureloms; Dog; Dove; Dragon; Elephant; Fish; Flock; Food; Fowl; Game; Goat; Hen; Horse; Insect; Lamb; Meat; Ox, Oxen; Serpent; Sheep; Swine; Vultures; BD Animals)

1 Ne. 18: 25 beasts of every kind found during journey through wilderness; **2 Ne.** 5: 11 Nephites begin to raise *a.* of every kind; **Alma** 22: 31 Bountiful filled with wild *a.* of every kind; **Ether** 9: 18 Jaredites raise many kinds of *a.* useful for food; 10: 19 land southward covered with *a.* of the forest.

ANOINTING, ANOINT (*see also* Consecrate; Ordinance; TG Anointing; BD Anoint)

2 Ne. 20: 27 (Isa. 10: 27) yoke shall be destroyed because of the *a.*; **Jacob** 1: 9 Nephi[1] is *a.* king; **3 Ne.** 13: 17 (Matt. 6: 17) when thou fastest, *a.*

ANSWER (*see also* Open; Prayer; Receive)

2 Ne. 2: 7 Christ a sacrifice to *a.* ends of law; 2: 10 punishment affixed to *a.* ends of atonement; **Mosiah** 29: 38 every man expresses willingness to *a.* for own sins; **Alma** 9: 26 Son quick to *a.* prayers of his people; **Morm.** 9: 37 may the Lord grant that their prayers be *a.* according to their faith.

ANTICHRIST (*see also* Prophets, False; TG Antichrist; BD Antichrist)

Jacob 7: 1–2 Sherem; **Alma** 1: 2–15 Nehor; 30: 6–21 Korihor.

ANTI-NEPHI-LEHI—*a brother of Lamoni, king over converted Lamanites*

Alma 24: 3 name given son of Lamanite king, receives kingdom; 24: 5 holds council with Ammon[2] and Lamoni.

ANTI-NEPHI-LEHIES (*see* Ammon[2], People of)

ANTIOMNO—*Lamanite king* [early first century B.C.]

Alma 20: 4 king in land of Middoni, friend of Lamoni.

ANTION—*Nephite coin* (*see also* Coin)

Alma 11: 19 *a.* of gold equal to three shiblons.

ANTIONAH—*a chief ruler in Ammonihah*

Alma 12: 20 questions Alma[2].

ANTIONUM—*Nephite commander* [c. A.D. 385]

Morm. 6: 14 falls with his ten thousand.

ANTIONUM, LAND OF—*east of Sidon*

Alma 31: 3 Zoramites gathered in A.; 43: 5 Lamanites arrive under Zerahemnah; 43: 22 Lamanites retire from A.

ANTIPARAH—*Nephite city*

Alma 56: 14 possessed by Lamanites; 56: 31–34 Helaman[2] decoys Lamanite forces in A.; 57: 1–4 regained by Nephites.

ANTIPAS, MOUNT

Alma 47: 7 Lamanites gather on A.; 47: 10 Amalickiah sends message to Lehonti, leader of Lamanites on A.

ANTIPUS—*Nephite commander* [c. 65 B.C.]

Alma 56: 9 appointed a leader; 56: 10 A's army reduced by Lamanites; 56: 15 fortifies city of Judea; 56: 18 strength of A's army feared; 56: 30–33 orders Helaman[2] and sons to march; 56: 37 pursues Lamanites; 56: 51 is slain; 56: 57 remainder of A's men join Ammonite striplings.

ANTUM, LAND OF

Morm. 1: 3 place of hill Shim and records.

ANXIETY, ANXIOUS, ANXIOUSLY (*see also* Fear; Trouble; Worry)

2 Ne. 1: 16 *a.* of Lehi[1] that his people observe the Lord's statutes; 6: 3 great *a.* of Jacob for welfare of his people's souls; **Jacob** 1: 5 future manifested unto Nephi[1] and Jacob[2] because of *a.* for people; **Mosiah** 29: 38 Nephites *a.* that every man have equal chance; **Alma** 13: 27 Alma[2] wishes with *a.* unto pain that people of Ammonihah hearken to his words; **3 Ne.** 3: 3 robbers wait with *a.* to destroy Nephites.

APOSTASY (*see also* Ammonihah, City of; Antichrist; Church, Great and Abominable; Church of the Devil; Darkness, Spiritual; Dissenter; Doctrine, False; Gadianton Robbers; Priestcraft; Prophets, False; Sin; Transgression; Unbelief; Zoramites[2]; TG Apostasy of Individuals)

1 Ne. 8: 23 (12: 17) those who commence path lose way in mist; 8: 28 those who partake of fruit fall into forbidden paths because of shame of world; 15: 10 (17: 45) Nephi[1] warns brothers about hardheartedness; **2 Ne.** ch. 28 prophecies of Nephi[1] regarding corrupt churches in latter days; **Jacob** ch. 2–3 Jacob[2] denounces Nephites' sins; **Mosiah** 11: 1–7 Noah[3] leads his people into *a.*; **Alma** 4: 6–12 pride, contention, wickedness grow in church, lead unbelievers astray; 24: 30 those enlightened by Spirit who fall into transgression become more hardened; ch. 31 Zoramites have fallen into great errors; 37: 27 knowledge of secret oaths to be kept from Nephites lest they fall into darkness; **Hel.** 3: 33–34 (4: 11–13; 5: 2–3) many members of church become proud, wicked, less righteous than Lamanites; 12: 2 when the Lord prospers his people, they harden hearts and forget him; 13: 38 Nephites have sought happiness in doing iniquity; **3 Ne.** 2: 1–3 Nephites forget signs, harden hearts, fall under Satan's power; 14: 24–27 (18: 13; Matt. 7: 24–27) parable of houses built on rock and on sand; 18: 15 watch and pray lest ye be tempted and led away by devil; **4 Ne.** 1: 24–34, 38–39 Nephites fall away from truth, build false churches; **Morm.** 8: 28, 31–33 Mormon[2] prophesies about corrupt churches in latter days.

APOSTLE (*see also* Disciple; TG Apostles; BD Apostle)

1 Ne. 1: 10–11 Lehi[1] sees twelve in vision; 11: 29 Nephi[1] sees twelve in vision; 11: 34–36 multitudes to fight against *a.* of the Lamb; 12: 9 twelve *a.* shall judge twelve tribes of Israel, twelve Nephite disciples; 13: 24 twelve *a.* to bear record of the Lamb; 13: 26, 39–41 record of gospel to go forth by hand of twelve *a.*; **Morm.** 9: 18 many mighty miracles wrought by *a.*; **Ether** 12: 41 prophets and *a.* have written of Jesus; **Moro.** 2: 2 Nephite disciples to give Holy Ghost, as do the Lord's *a.*

APPAREL (*see also* Clothing; Garment; Raiment; TG Apparel)

Jacob 2: 13 (Alma 1: 6, 32; 4: 6; 5: 53; 31: 28; 4 Ne. 1: 24; Morm. 8: 36) Nephites proud because of costly *a.*; **Alma** 1: 27 church members do not wear costly *a.*; 32: 2 poor Zoramites cast out of synagogues because of coarse *a.*; **Hel.** 13: 28 the wicked clothe false prophets in costly *a.*

APPEAL (*see also* Plead)

Alma 37: 16 you must *a.* unto the Lord.

APPEAR, APPEARANCE (*see also* Jesus Christ, Appearances of; Show)

2 Ne. 4: 31 wilt thou make me shake at *a.* of sin; **Mosiah** 27: 11 angel *a.* to Alma[2] and sons of Mosiah[2]; **Alma** 8: 14 angel *a.* to Alma[2] on road from Ammonihah; 10: 7 angel *a.* to Amulek; 21: 5 why do not angels *a.* unto us; 30: 53 devil *a.* to Korihor in form of angel; **Hel.** 12: 15 it *a.* to man that sun stands still; 14: 3 because of lights in heavens, night shall *a.* as day; 14: 25 (3 Ne. 25: 11) risen saints shall *a.* to many; 16: 14 angels *a.* to wise men to fulfill scriptures; **Moro.** 7: 37 it is by faith that angels *a.*

APPEASE (*see also* Satisfy)

Alma 42: 15 atonement *a.* demands of justice; **Hel.** 11: 11 may the Lord's anger be *a.* in destruction of wicked already destroyed.

APPLY

Mosiah 4: 2 *a.* the atoning blood of Christ; 12: 27 ye have not *a.* your hearts to understanding.

APPOINT (*see also* Ordain)

2 Ne. 24: 31 none shall be alone in his *a.* times; **Mosiah** 2: 4 the Lord *a.* just men to be teachers; 29: 11 let us *a.* judges; **Alma** 12: 27 (42: 6) it was *a.* unto men that they must die; 40: 4–5, 7–9 time *a.* for all to come forth from the dead; 40: 4–5, 10 God knows the time *a.* for the resurrection.

ARCHEANTUS—*Nephite military officer* [c. A.D. 385]

Moro. 9: 2 falls by sword.

ARISE (*see also* Rise)

3 Ne. 23: 11 many saints did *a.*

ARK (*see also* BD Ark)

Ether 6: 7 Jaredite vessels were tight like *a.* of Noah[1].

ARM (*see also* Armed; Arms; Might; Strength; TG Trust Not in the Arm of Flesh)

1 Ne. 22: 10 kindreds of earth cannot be blessed unless the Lord makes bare his *a.*; **2 Ne.** 1: 15 I am encircled eternally in *a.* of the Lord's love; 4: 34 I will not trust in *a.* of flesh; 8: 5 (Isa. 51: 5) the Lord's *a.* shall judge the people, and isles shall trust on his *a.*; 28: 31 cursed is he who makes flesh his *a.*; **Jacob** 6: 5 (Alma 5: 33) the Lord's *a.* of mercy is extended; **Omni** 1: 13 Nephites led by power of the Lord's *a.*; **Alma** 17: 37 Ammon[2] smites off Lamanites' *a.* with sword; 20: 20 Ammon[2] smites *a.* of Lamoni's father; 34: 16 mercy encircles the repentant in *a.* of safety; **Morm.** 5: 11 Nephites might have been clasped in *a.* of Jesus.

ARMED (*see also* Arms)

1 Ne. 14: 14 saints *a.* with righteousness.

ARMOR (*see also* Breastplate)

1 Ne. 4: 19 Nephi[1] girds on Laban's *a.*; **2 Ne.** 1: 23 put on *a.* of righteousness; **Alma** 43: 21 Lamanites fear Nephite armies because of *a.*; **3 Ne.** 4: 7 appearance of Giddianhi's army is terrible because of their *a.*

ARMS (*see also* Weapon)

Alma 51: 13 (62: 9) king-men refuse to take up *a.* against Lamanites; 53: 11 because of oath, Ammonites do not take up *a.*; 53: 16 sons of Ammonites take up *a.*

ARMY, ARMIES (*see also* Battle; Soldier; War)

1 Ne. 4: 2 (17: 27; Hel. 8: 11) *a.* of Pharaoh drowned in Red Sea.

AROUSE (*see also* Awake; Prick; Stir)

Jacob 3: 11 (Alma 32: 27) *a.* the faculties of your souls; **Morm.** 2: 24 words of Mormon[2] *a.* Nephites to vigor.

ARRAIGN

Alma 11: 44 every soul to be *a.* before bar of Godhead to be judged.

ARROW (*see also* Bow; Weapon)

1 Ne. 16: 23 Nephi[1] makes *a.* out of straight stick.

ART (*see also* Skill)

Alma 10: 15 lawyers are learned in all *a.* and cunning; **Hel.** 12: 2 the Lord prospers his people in precious things of every kind and *a.*; 16: 21 wicked Nephites fear prophets work some great mystery by *a.* of the evil one; **Morm.** 2: 10 no man could keep that which was his own, because of magic *a.* in land; **Ether** 13: 16 Coriantumr[2] studies all *a.* of war.

ASCEND (*see also* Rise)

2 Ne. 24: 13–14 Lucifer claims he will *a.* into heaven; **Jacob** 2: 35 sobbings of wives and children *a.* to God against Nephites.

ASHAMED (*see also* Shame)

1 Ne. 8: 25–28 those who partake of fruit are *a.* because of scoffers; 21: 23 (2 Ne. 6: 7; Isa. 49: 23) they shall not be *a.* who wait for the Lord; **2 Ne.** 6: 13 people of the Lord shall not be *a.*; 7: 7 (Isa. 50: 7) I know that I shall not be *a.*; **Alma** 46: 21 if Nephites become *a.* to take name of Christ, the Lord shall rend them; **3 Ne.** 22: 4 fear not, for thou shalt not be *a.*; **Morm.** 8: 38 why are ye *a.* to take upon you name of Christ.

ASHES (*see also* Sackcloth)

Mosiah 11: 25 except Noah's people repent in sackcloth and *a.*, the Lord will not hear prayers; **3 Ne.** 25: 3 wicked shall be *a.* under feet of those who fear God.

ASK (*see also* Inquire; Knock; Pray; Question; Seek; TG Prayer)

1 Ne. 15: 11 (Moro. 10: 4) if ye *a.* the Lord in faith, he will make things known; **2 Ne.** 4: 35 (3 Ne. 14: 7; 18: 20; James 1: 5) God will give liberally to him that *a.*; 4: 35 God will give if I *a.* not amiss; 32: 4 if people cannot understand words of Nephi[1], it is because they *a.* not; **Enos** 1: 15 (3 Ne. 18: 20; 27: 29; Moro. 7: 26) whatsoever ye *a.* in faith ye shall receive; **Mosiah** 4: 10 *a.* in sincerity of heart that God forgive you; 4: 21 (3 Ne. 18: 20; Moro. 7: 26) God grants whatsoever men *a.* that is right; **Hel.** 10: 5 Nephi[2] would not *a.* what is contrary to the Lord's will; **3 Ne.** 13: 8 the Father knows what men need before they *a.*; 14: 7 (18: 20) *a.*, and it shall be given; 14: 8 every one who *a.* receives; 17: 3 (18: 20; 27: 28; Morm. 9: 21; Moro. 7: 26) *a.* the Father in Christ's name; **Morm.** 9: 28 *a.* not that ye may consume it on your lusts, but *a.* with firmness unshaken that ye will yield to no temptation; **Moro.** 10: 4 *a.* God if these things are true.

ASLEEP (*see* Sleep)

ASS (*see also* Animal)

1 Ne. 18: 25 Nephites find *a.* in wilderness; **Mosiah** 5: 14 doth a man take neighbor's *a.* and keep him; 12: 5 (21: 3) people of Noah[3] shall be driven like dumb *a.*; **Ether** 9: 19 Jaredites have *a.*

ASSEMBLE (*see also* Church of God; Meet, Meeting; Worship)

Mosiah 18: 25 one day in week set apart for people to *a.* to be taught and to worship; 25: 21 Nephites *a.* in different bodies, called churches; **Alma** 6: 5 none are deprived of privilege of *a.* to hear God's word; 15: 17 Nephites in Sidom *a.* in sanctuaries to worship.

ASSYRIA—*country in western Asia* (*see also* Assyrian; BD Assyria and Babylonia)

2 Ne. 17: 17 (Isa. 7: 17) king of A. attacks Judah; 17: 18 (Isa. 7: 18) the Lord to hiss for bee in land of A.; 17: 20 (Isa. 7: 20) king of A. brings terror; 18: 4 (Isa. 8: 4) riches of Damascus and spoils of Samaria to be taken before king of A.; 18: 7 (Isa. 8: 7) king of A. and his glory shall come up over his channels; 20: 12 (Isa. 10: 12) the Lord will punish fruit of stout heart of king of A.; 21: 11, 16 (Isa. 11: 11, 16) the Lord to recover his people from A.

ASSYRIAN—*native of Assyria* (*see also* Assyria; BD Assyria)

2 Ne. 20: 5 (Isa. 10: 5) O A., rod of the Lord's anger; 20: 24 (Isa. 10: 24) people in Zion not to be afraid of A.; 24: 25 (Isa. 14: 25) the Lord will tread A. under foot.

ASTRAY (*see also* Apostasy; Err; Lose, Lost; Wander)

2 Ne. 12: 5 house of Jacob have all gone *a.*; 28: 14 false churches have all gone *a.*; **Mosiah** 14: 6 (Isa. 53: 6) all we, like sheep, have gone *a.*; 27: 10 Alma[2] seeks to lead *a.* the Lord's people; **Alma** 5: 37 unrighteous have gone *a.*, as sheep having no shepherd; 13: 17 Melchizedek's people had all gone *a.*; 30: 53 devil tells Korihor people have gone *a.* after unknown God; 41: 1 some have gone far *a.* because of wresting the scriptures.

ASTRONOMY (*see also* Moon; Star; Sun; World)

Alma 30: 44 motion of earth and planets in regular form witness Supreme Creator; **Hel.** 12: 15 earth moves, not sun; 14: 5 (3 Ne. 1: 21) new star to arise as sign of Christ's birth.

ATE (*see* Eat)

ATHIRST (*see also* Thirst)

Alma 1: 30 Nephites do not send away those who are *a.*; 4: 12 some church members turn backs on those who are *a.*

ATONE, ATONEMENT (*see* Jesus Christ, Atonement through)

AUTHOR (*see also* Founder)

Hel. 6: 30 Satan is *a.* of all sin; 8: 28 *a.* of secret band is Gadianton and the evil one; **Moro.** 6: 4 Christ is *a.* and finisher of members' faith.

AUTHORITY (*see also* Calling; Dominion; Office; Ordain; Ordinance; Power; Priesthood; Reign; Rule; Scepter; TG Authority)

1 Ne. 10: 22 Holy Ghost gives *a.* to speak; **2 Ne.** 1: 25 brothers of Nephi[1] accuse him of seeking *a.*; **Mosiah** 13: 6 Abinadi speaks with *a.* from God; 18: 13 Alma[1] baptizes, having *a.* from God; 21: 33 none in Limhi's land have *a.* to baptize; 23: 17 none receive *a.* to teach except by Alma[1] from God; 26: 8 (Alma 5: 3) Alma[2] has *a.* over church; **Alma** 9: 6 who is God that sendeth no more *a.* than one man among this people; 17: 3 sons of Mosiah[2] teach with *a.* of God; 25: 5 Amulon's followers usurp *a.* over Lamanites; 30: 23 Korihor accuses ancient priests of usurping *a.*; **Hel.** 5: 18 Nephi[2] and Lehi[4] preach to Lamanites with great *a.*; 7: 4 Gadianton robbers usurp *a.*; 11: 18 (3 Ne. 7: 17) Nephi[2] a man of God, having great *a.* from God; **3 Ne.** 6: 15 Satan tempts people to seek power and *a.*; 11: 25 (12: 1) baptism performed by *a.* of Christ; **Moro.** 8: 16 Moroni[2] preaches with boldness, having *a.* from God.

AVAIL (*see also* Profit)

Mosiah 3: 15 law of Moses *a.* nothing except through Christ's atonement; **Alma** 34: 28 without charity toward the needy, prayer *a.* nothing; **Moro.** 8: 22 baptism *a.* nothing unto him who is under no condemnation.

AVENGE (*see also* Revenge; Vengeance)

Alma 54: 16 Ammoron threatens to *a.* his brother's blood on Nephites; 61: 6 Nephites flock to army to *a.* their wrongs; **Morm.** 3: 9 Nephites swear to *a.* themselves of brethren's blood; 8: 41 God will *a.* saints' blood upon the wicked; **Ether** 8: 22 the Lord will not suffer saints' blood to cry for vengeance without *a.* them; 14: 24 Shiz swears to *a.* himself upon Coriantumr[2] of his brother's blood.

AWAKE, AWAKEN (*see also* Arouse; Consciousness; Rise)

2 Ne. 4: 28 *a.*, my soul; 9: 47 expedient that I should *a.* you to awful reality of these things; 27: 3 those who oppose Zion shall be as hungry man who *a.* from dream of eating and soul is empty; **Jacob** 3: 11 shake yourselves that ye may *a.* from slumbers of death; **Mosiah** 2: 38 divine justice *a.* the unrepentant to sense of guilt; 2: 40 *a.* to remembrance of awful situation of those fallen into transgression; 4: 5 God's goodness *a.* man to sense of his own nothingness; **Alma** 4: 3 Nephites are *a.* to remembrance of duty by afflictions; 5: 7 church members *a.* unto God; 7: 22 Alma[2] teaches that he might *a.* people to sense of duty to God; 32: 27 Alma[2] warns people to *a.*; **Morm.** 9: 13 all men shall be *a.* from endless sleep by power of God; **Ether** 8: 24 when they see secret combinations come among them, Gentiles are to *a.* to sense of awful situation.

AWKWARDNESS

Ether 12: 24 Nephites can write but little because of *a.* of hands.

AX

Enos 1: 20 (Morm. 6: 9) Lamanites have skill with *a.*; **Alma** 5: 52 *a.* is laid at root of tree.

BABBLINGS

Alma 1: 32 those who do not belong to church indulge themselves in *b.*

BABE (*see also* Child; Infant)

2 Ne. 13: 4 (Isa. 3: 4) *b.* shall rule over Judah; **3 Ne.** 26: 16 during Christ's visit *b.* utter marvelous things.

BABEL, TOWER OF (*see* Tower)

BABYLON—*capital of Babylonia, in southwest Asia* (*see also* Assyria; Church of the Devil; TG Babylon; BD Babylon)

1 Ne. 1: 13 (10: 3; 2 Ne. 25: 10; Omni 1: 15) Jerusalem to be carried captive into *B.*; 20: 14 (Isa. 48: 14) the Lord will do his pleasure on *B.*; 20: 20 (Isa. 48: 20) go ye forth of *B.*; **2 Ne.** 23: 1 (Isa. 13: 1) burden of *B.*, which Isaiah[1] saw; 23: 19 (Isa. 13: 19) *B.* shall be as when God overthrew Sodom and Gomorrah; 24: 4 (Isa. 14: 4) take up proverb against king of *B.*; 24: 22 (Isa. 14: 22) the Lord will cut off from *B.* the name; 25: 15 *B.* shall be destroyed.

BACK

Alma 4: 12 (5: 55; Hel. 6: 39) the proud turn their *b.* upon the needy.

BAD (*see also* Evil; Worse)

2 Ne. 2: 11 opposition necessary that good and *b.* may be brought to pass; **Jacob** 5: 65–77 good and *b.* branches in the vineyard; **Alma** 3: 26 the dead reap rewards according to works, whether good or *b.*

BALL (*see* Liahona)

BAND (*see also* Bind; Chain; Cord; Gadianton Robbers)

Mosiah 15: 8 (Alma 11: 41–42; Morm. 9: 13) through Christ, God breaks *b.* of temporal death; 23: 12 people of Noah[3] are bound with *b.* of iniquity; **Alma** 5: 7 the fathers were encircled by *b.* of death; 14: 24 chief judge commands Alma[2] and Amulek to deliver themselves from *b.*

BANISHED

Alma 36: 15 oh, that I could be *b.* and not be brought before God to be judged.

BANNER (*see also* Title of Liberty)

2 Ne. 23: 2 (Isa. 13: 2) lift a *b.* upon high mountain.

BAPTISM, BAPTIZE (*see also* Accountability, Age of; Born of God; Church of God; Conversion; Faith; Fire; Forgive; Grave; Holy Ghost; Holy Ghost, Baptism of; Immersion; Name of the Lord; Ordinance; Remission; Repentance; Sacrament; Salvation; Wash; Water; Witness; TG Baptism; Baptism, Essential; Baptism, Immersion; Baptism, Qualifications for; BD Baptism)

1 Ne. 10: 9–10 John the Baptist to *b.* Messiah; 20: 1 (Isa. 48: 1) house of Jacob comes forth out of waters of Judah, or out of waters of *b.*; **2 Ne.** 9: 23 God commands all men to repent and be *b.* in his name; 31: 4–12 Nephi[1] explains why Messiah must be *b.*; 31: 11 (3 Ne. 11. 37–38; 18: 16; 21: 6; 27: 20; Morm. 3: 2; 7: 8; Ether 4: 18; Moro. 7: 34) repent and be *b.* in name of the Son; 31: 12–13 (3 Ne. 26: 17) he who is *b.* shall receive Holy Ghost; **Mosiah** 18: 8–10 Alma[1] describes qualities of those to be *b.* in name of the Lord; 18: 12–16 Alma[1] *b.* Helam and others at Waters of Mormon; 18: 17 (3 Ne. 18: 16) those who are *b.* by authority of God are added to his church; 21: 35 Limhi's people desire to be *b.* as witness they are willing to serve God; **Alma** 5: 62 Alma[2] invites nonmembers to be *b.* unto repentance; 9: 27 the Son redeems those who are *b.* unto repentance through faith; 15: 6–12 Alma[2] *b.* Zeezrom; 32: 16 blessed is he who believes and is *b.* without stubbornness; **Hel.** 5: 19 (3 Ne. 9: 20; Ether 12: 14) eight thousand Lamanites are *b.* with water and fire; **3 Ne.** 7: 24–25 none are brought to repentance who are not *b.* with water; 7: 25 Nephi[3] ordains men to *b.* as witness that people have repented and received remission of sins; 9: 20 (12: 1–2; Morm. 7: 10) Christ will *b.* with fire those who come to him with broken heart; 11: 21–22 (12: 1) the Lord gives Nephite disciples power to *b.*; 11: 23–28 (Moro. 6: 1–4) conditions and mode of *b.*; 11: 33–34 (Morm. 9: 23; Ether 4: 18) only those who believe and are *b.* shall be saved; 18: 5, 11, 30 sacrament to be given to those who are *b.*; 19: 11–13 Nephi[3] and other disciples are *b.*; 21: 6 Gentiles who repent and are *b.* may be numbered among the Lord's people; 26: 17 Nephite disciples *b.* those who come unto them; 27: 16 whoso repents and is *b.* shall be filled; **Morm.** 7: 10 if ye believe and are *b.* with water and fire, it shall be well in day of judgment; 9: 29 see that ye are not *b.* unworthily; **Moro.** 8: 5, 8, 10–15, 20–22 *b.* of little children is unnecessary; 8: 25 first fruits of repentance is *b.*

BAR (*see also* Judgment; Judgment-Seat)

2 Ne. 33: 11 (Jacob 6: 13; Moro. 10: 27, 34) you and I shall stand face to face before Christ's *b.*; **Jacob** 6: 9 (Morm. 9: 13) power of redemption will bring wicked before *b.* of God; **Mosiah** 16: 10 mortal shall put on immortality and be brought before *b.* of God to be judged; **Alma** 5: 22 how will you feel to stand before the *b.* of God with stained garments; 11: 44 everything shall be restored and arraigned before *b.* of Son, Father, and Holy Spirit.

BARE

1 Ne. 22: 10–11 (Mosiah 12: 24; 15: 31; 3 Ne. 16: 20; Isa. 52: 10) the Lord makes *b.* his holy arm; **3 Ne.** 20: 35 Father hath made *b.* his holy arm.

BARGE (*see also* Dish; Ship; Vessel)

Ether 2: 6, 16–18 Jaredites build *b.*; 6: 4 Jaredites aboard *b.*

BARREN

Alma 32: 39 if you neglect tree, your ground is *b.*; **3 Ne.** 22: 1 (Isa. 54: 1) sing, O *b.*, thou that didst not bear.

BATHE (*see* Tears)

BATTLE (*see also* Army; Carnage; Fight; Slaughter; War; TG God to Fight Our Battles)

1 Ne. 12: 2 Nephi[1] sees multitudes gathered together to *b.*; **Jarom** 1: 7 Lamanites come many times against Nephites to *b.*; **Mosiah** 9: 16 Zeniff and his people go forth against Lamanites to *b.*; 10: 6 Lamanites prepare to come to *b.* against Zeniff's people; **Alma** 2: 16 Alma[2] goes at head of armies against Amlicites to *b.*; 28: 2 tremendous *b.* between Nephites and Lamanites; 43: 26 Moroni[1] gathers people to *b.* against Lamanites; 62: 19 Lamanites do not come to *b.* because of Nephites' great courage and numbers; **3 Ne.** 4: 1 armies of robbers prepare to *b.*; 4: 16 armies of robbers do not come to *b.*; **Morm.** 4: 1 Nephite armies go up to *b.* against Lamanites; 8: 2 after great *b.* at Cumorah, Nephites hunted by Lamanites; **Ether** 15: 15 Jaredites march forth one against another to *b.*; **Moro.** 9: 2 Mormon[2] has sore *b.* with Lamanites.

BEAM (*see* Mote)

BEAR [noun] (*see also* Animal)

2 Ne. 21: 7 (30: 13; Isa. 11: 7) cow and *b.* shall be fed.

BEAR, BORE, BORNE (*see also* Born; Burden; Carry; Endure; Record; Tolerable)

1 Ne. 11: 20 Nephi[1] beholds virgin *b.* child in arms; 16: 1 thou has declared hard things, more than we are able to *b.*; **2 Ne.** 17: 14 a virgin shall conceive, and shall *b.* a son; **Mosiah** 10: 9 all old and young men able to *b.* arms gather for battle; 13: 23 (Hel. 7: 21; Ex. 20: 16) thou shalt not *b.* false witness; 26: 18 blessed is this people who are willing to *b.* the Lord's name; **Alma** 4: 19 Alma[2] sees no way to reclaim people save in *b.* down in pure testimony against them; 13: 28 pray that ye be not tempted above that which ye can *b.*; 26: 27 (34: 40; 38: 4) *b.* with patience thine afflictions; **3 Ne.** 20: 41 be ye clean that *b.* the vessels of the Lord.

BEAST (*see also* Animal)

1 Ne. 7: 16 Laman[1] and Lemuel seek to leave Nephi[1] in the wilderness to be devoured by wild *b.*; 16: 31 Nephi[1] slays wild *b.* for food; 18: 25 Lehites find *b.* in forest of every kind; **Enos** 1: 3 Enos[2] hunts *b.* in forests; **Jarom** 1: 6 Lamanites drink blood of *b.*; **Alma** 34: 10 great and last sacrifice not to be sacrifice of *b.*; **3 Ne.** 4: 2 no wild *b.* in lands deserted by Nephites; 20: 16 (21: 12) house of Jacob[1] to be among Gentiles as lion among *b.* of forest; 28: 22 (4 Ne. 1: 33) disciples cast into den of wild *b.*; **Morm.** 8: 24 wild *b.* could not harm saints; **Ether** 10: 26 Jaredites make tools with which they work their *b.*; **Moro.** 9: 9–10 Nephites devour flesh of Lamanite daughters like wild *b.*

BEAT (*see also* Smite; Strike)

2 Ne. 28: 8 God will *b.* us with a few stripes; **3 Ne.** 20: 19 (Micah 4: 13) thou shalt *b.* in pieces many people.

BEATITUDES (*see also* BD Beatitudes)

3 Ne. 12: 3–12 (Matt. 5: 5–2) the Savior teaches B. to Nephites.

BEAUTY, BEAUTIFUL (*see also* Comely; Delightsome; Fair)

1 Ne. 11: 8 *b.* of tree exceeds all *b.*; 11: 15 Nephi[1] sees virgin, most *b.*; 13: 37 (Mosiah 12: 21; 15: 15–18; 3 Ne. 20: 40; Isa. 52: 7) how *b.* upon the mountain are they who publish peace; **2 Ne.** 8: 24 (3 Ne. 20: 36; Moro. 10: 31) Zion to put on *b.* garments; 14: 2 branch of the Lord shall be *b.* and glorious; **Mosiah** 14: 2 (Isa. 53: 2) when we shall see him there is no *b.* that we should desire him; 18: 30 how *b.* are the environs of Mormon to those who came to knowledge of the Redeemer.

BEE (*see also* Animal)

2 Ne. 17: 18 (Isa. 7: 18) the Lord shall hiss for *b.* in Assyria; **Ether** 2: 3 deseret is interpreted as honey *b.*; 2: 3 Jaredites carry swarms of *b.*

BEFOREHAND

1 Ne. 4: 6 Nephi[1] led by Spirit, not knowing *b.* what he should do.

BEG, BEGGAR (*see also* Plead; Poor)

Mosiah 4: 16–25 ye will not suffer the *b.* to put up his petition to you in vain; 4: 20 Nephites *b.* the Lord for forgiveness; **Alma** 30: 56 Korihor *b.* from house to house for food.

BEGINNING (*see also* Creation; End)

1 Ne. 5: 12–13 (Alma 37: 3) brass plates contain record of Jews from *b.*; 9: 6 (Acts 15: 18) the Lord knows all things from *b.*; 12: 18 Holy Ghost bears record of Lamb from *b.* of world; 20: 3, 5, 16 (Isa. 48: 3, 5, 16) the Lord has declared former things from *b.*; **2 Ne.** 9: 2 the Lord has spoken through his prophets from *b.*; 11: 4 all things given of God from *b.* typify Christ; 27: 7 sealed book shall be revelation from God, from *b.* of world to end; **Mosiah** 3: 8 (Hel. 14: 12) Christ the Creator of all things from *b.*; 7: 27 (Ether 3: 15–16) Christ to take image after which man was created in *b.*; 28: 14 Urim and Thummim were prepared from *b.*; **Alma** 11: 39 (3 Ne. 9: 18; Rev. 1: 8) Son is the *b.* and the end; 13: 7–8 (Heb. 7: 1–3) priesthood is without *b.* of days or end of years; 13: 9 Only Begotten is without *b.* of days or end of years; 18: 32 by God's hand men were all created from *b.*; 18: 34 (Ether 3: 15) man in *b.* was created after image of God; 26: 24 Lamanites' ways have been ways of transgressor from *b.*; **Hel.** 6: 29 devil has brought forth works of darkness from *b.* of man; **3 Ne.** 9: 15 (John 1: 1–2) Christ was with Father from *b.*; 11: 11 Christ has suffered will of Father in all things from *b.*; 26: 3 Christ expounds all things from *b.*; **4 Ne.** 1: 38 fathers dwindled from *b.*; 1: 39 Lamanites taught to hate Nephites from *b.*; **Ether** 8: 15 Cain a murderer from *b.*; 8: 19 the Lord has forbidden secret combinations from *b.* of man; 8: 25 devil has caused people to murder and to cast out prophets from *b.*; 13: 2 Ether tells Jaredites of all things from *b.* of man.

BEGOTTEN (*see also* Born of God; Children of God; Jesus Christ—Only Begotten Son; Son)

Mosiah 5: 7 Christ hath spiritually *b.* his people.

BEGUILE (*see also* Deceit; Lying)

2 Ne. 9: 9 (Mosiah 16: 3; Ether 8: 25) devil *b.* our first parents.

BEHOLD, BEHELD (*see also* Look; See; View)

Ether 3: 19 brother of Jared[2] could not be kept from *b.* within the veil; **Moro.** 10: 14 gift of *b.* of angels.

BEING [noun]

2 Ne. 9: 9 devil is that *b.* who beguiled first parents; **Jacob** 2: 21 one *b.* is as precious in God's sight as other; 7: 7 Sherem claims people should not worship a *b.* who is to come in hundreds of years; **Mosiah** 2: 17 when ye are in service of fellow *b.* ye are in service of God; 8: 18 God provides means that man can become great benefit to fellow *b.*; **Alma** 26: 35 God is a merciful *b.*; **Hel.** 16: 18 people claim it is not reasonable that a *b.* such as Christ should come; **Moro.** 8: 18 God is not a changeable *b.*

BELIEF, BELIEVE, BELIEVING (*see also* Believer; Doubt; Faith; Opinion; Religion; Unbelief; TG Belief)

1 Ne. 2: 13 Laman[1] and Lemuel do not *b.* Jerusalem could be destroyed; 15: 11 (Enos 1: 15; Mosiah 4: 21; Alma 22: 16; 3 Ne. 18: 20; Moro. 7: 26) if ye ask, *b.* that ye shall receive, these things shall be made known to you; **2 Ne.** 2: 9 (3 Ne. 11: 33–35) they who *b.* in Christ shall be saved; 5: 6 those who go with Nephi[1] *b.* in God's warnings; 6: 14 (25: 16; 30: 7; 3 Ne. 20: 31) day cometh when Messiah's people shall *b.* in him; 6: 14 Messiah will destroy none who *b.* in him; 9: 18 saints who have *b.* in Holy One shall inherit kingdom of God; 25: 16 Jews will be persecuted until persuaded to *b.* in Christ; 25: 28 right way is to *b.* in Christ; 28: 6 false churches teach not to *b.* in miracles; 30: 7 scattered Jews shall also begin to *b.* in Christ; 33: 10 hearken unto these words and *b.* in Christ; 33: 10 if ye *b.* in Christ, ye shall *b.* in these words; **Jacob** 4: 5 all prophets *b.* in Christ; 7: 10 *b.* thou the scriptures; **Jarom** 1: 11 priests teach people to *b.* in Messiah as though he had already come; **Mosiah** 4: 9 *b.* in God, *b.* that he is; 4: 10 *b.* that ye must repent of sins; 4: 10 if ye *b.* these things, see that ye do them; 15: 22 those who *b.* words of prophets will come forth in first resurrection; 26: 22 whosoever is baptized shall *b.* in the Lord's name; **Alma** 1: 17 false priests pretend to teach according to *b.*; 4: 8 people of church persecute those who do not *b.* according to their will; 11: 40 the Son will take upon him transgressions of those who *b.* on his name; 18: 24, 26, 28 *b.* thou that there is a God, a Great Spirit; 21: 7 *b.* thou that the Son shall come to redeem mankind from sins; 22: 11 Lamanite king *b.* that the Great Spirit created all things; 24: 19 when brought to *b.*, converted Lamanites were firm; 30: 7 no law against a man's *b.*; 30: 42 Alma[2] knows that Korihor *b.*; 31: 17 Zoramites claim traditions bind brethren down to *b.* in Christ; 32: 16 blessed is he who *b.* in word of God without being compelled to know word before he will *b.*; 32: 18 if a man knows a thing, he has no cause to *b.*; 32: 27 if ye can no more than desire to *b.*, let this desire work in you; 33: 20 few looked upon Moses' serpent because they did not *b.* it would heal them; 33: 22 cast about your eyes and begin to *b.* in the Son; 46: 15 believers called Christians because of *b.* in Christ; **Hel.** 14: 13 if ye *b.* on Christ's name ye will repent; 15: 10 the Lord will prolong days of Ammonites because of steadfastness when they *b.*; **3 Ne.** 11: 35 whoso *b.* in Christ *b.* in the Father also; 12: 1 blessed are ye if ye *b.* in me after ye have seen me; 12: 2 more blessed are those who shall *b.* in your words; 16: 6–7 blessed are Gentiles because of *b.* in Christ; 18: 20 whatsoever ye ask, *b.* that ye shall receive, it shall be given; 19: 20 Christ chooses disciples because of their *b.* in him; **4 Ne.** 1: 29 church persecuted because of *b.* in Christ; **Morm.** 3: 20–21 Mormon writes so that people will *b.* gospel; 9: 27 doubt not, but be *b.*; **Ether** 3: 11 *b.* thou the words I shall speak; 3: 15 never has man *b.* in the Lord as brother of Jared[2]; 4: 12 he who will not *b.* Christ's words will not *b.* Christ, will not *b.* the Father; 12: 18 men first *b.* in the Son before working miracles; **Moro.** 7: 16 everything which persuades to *b.* in Christ is sent by power of Christ; 7: 17 whatsoever persuades not to *b.* in Christ is of devil; 7: 45 (1 Cor. 13: 7) charity *b.* all things.

BELIEVER (*see also* Christian; Saint; Worshipper)

Alma 46: 14–15 true *b.* in Christ are

called Christians; **4 Ne.** 1: 36–37 true *b.* in Christ are called Nephites.

BELLOWS

1 Ne. 17: 11 Nephi[1] makes a *b.*

BELOVED (*see also* Jesus Christ—Son of God; John the Beloved)

BENEFIT (*see also* Blessing, Gain; Profit)

Mosiah 8: 18 God provides means that man can become great *b.* to fellow beings.

BENJAMIN—*Nephite prophet-king* [c. 120 B.C.]

Omni 1: 23 *B.*, son of Mosiah[1], begins reign; 1: 24 (W of M 1: 13–14) drives out Lamanites; 1: 25 (W of M 1: 10) given plates by Amaleki[1]; **W of M** 1: 11 hands down plates; 1: 13 uses sword of Laban against Lamanites; 1: 16–18 (Mosiah 1: 1) holy man, establishes peace; **Mosiah** 1: 2 sons of *B.* named; 1: 3 teaches concerning records; 1: 10, 15 (2: 30; 6: 3) confers kingdom on Mosiah[2]; 1: 16 gives Mosiah[2] records and artifacts; 2: 9—4: 30 addresses people from tower; 2: 12–14 serve , labors with hands; 2: 17 urges service to fellow men; 3: 7 teaches of Jesus' suffering; 3: 15–19 teaches about atonement; 3: 18–27 teaches about judgment; 4: 16–19 teaches people to help beggars, for all are beggars; 5: 5 *B*'s people covenant with the Lord; 6: 1 takes names of those who enter covenant; 6: 3 consecrates Mosiah[2], appoints priests; 6: 5 dies; 8: 2–3 *B*'s word rehearsed by Ammon[1]; 26: 1 rising generation do not understand *B*'s words; 29: 13 if people could have kings like *B.*, it would be well; **Hel.** 5: 9 Helaman[3] asks sons to remember words of *B.*

BESET

2 Ne. 4: 18 I am encompassed about because of sins which so easily *b.* me; **Alma** 7: 15 lay aside every sin which easily doth *b.* you.

BETHABARA (*see also* BD Bethabara)

1 Ne. 10: 9 John to baptize Messiah in *B.*

BETTER (*see also* Good; Well)

1 Ne. 4: 13 *b.* that one man perish than nation dwindle in unbelief; **2 Ne.** 31: 14 it would have been *b.* for you that ye had not known me; **Jacob** 2: 13 some Nephites persecute brethren because they suppose they are *b.*; **Mosiah** 29: 12 *b.* that a man be judged of God than of man; **Alma** 1: 26 preacher and teacher no *b.* than hearer and learner; 37: 45 words of Christ shall carry us into far *b.* land of promise; 43: 45 Nephites inspired by *b.* cause; **3 Ne.** 12: 30 *b.* to deny yourselves of these things than to be cast into hell; 28: 35 it would be *b.* for them if they had not been born; **Ether** 12: 4 whoso believeth in God might hope for *b.* world.

BIBLE (*see also* Book; Scriptures; BD Bible)

2 Ne. 29: 3–10 Gentiles shall say, A *B.*, we have got a *B.*

BIND, BOUND (*see also* Band; Bondage; Priesthood; Seal)

2 Ne. 1: 13 awful chains *b.* men that they are carried captive to gulf of misery; 9: 45 shake off chains of him who would *b.* you; 26: 22 devil leads men with flaxen cord until he *b.* them; **Alma** 7: 15 lay aside every sin which doth *b.* you down to destruction; 44: 5 liberty *b.* Nephites to lands and country.

BIRTH (*see* Bear, Bore, Borne; Born; Jesus Christ, First Coming of)

BIRTHRIGHT (*see* Heir; Inherit; BD Birthright)

BITTER, BITTERNESS (*see also* Taste)

2 Ne. 2: 15 tree of life, being sweet, is in opposition to forbidden fruit, being *b.*; 15: 20 (Isa. 5: 20) wo unto them that put *b.* for sweet; **Jacob** 5: 52, 57, 65 *b.* fruit of olive-trees; **Mosiah** 27: 29 (Alma 36: 18) Alma[2] redeemed from gall of *b.*; **Alma** 36: 21 nothing could be so *b.* as pains of Alma[2]; 41: 11 (Morm. 8: 31) men in carnal state are in gall of *b.*; **3 Ne.** 11: 11 Christ has drunk out of the *b.* cup; **Moro.** 7: 11 *b.* fountain cannot bring forth good water; 8: 14 he who supposes little children need baptism is in gall of *b.*

BLACK, BLACKNESS (*see also* Darkness, Physical)

2 Ne. 5: 21 skin of *b.* to come upon brethren of Nephi[1]; 7: 3 the Lord clothes heavens with *b.*; 26: 33 the Lord denies none who come unto him, *b.* and white; **3 Ne.** 12: 36 thou canst not make one hair *b.* or white.

BLAMELESS (*see also* Guiltless; Innocence; Spotless)

Mosiah 3: 21 none shall be found *b.* before God except little children; **Alma** 5: 27 have ye kept yourselves *b.* before God; 7: 3 Alma[2] hopes to find people of Gideon *b.* before God; 29: 5 he who knows not good from evil is *b.*

BLASPHEMY, BLASPHEME (*see also* TG Blaspheme; BD Blasphemy)

Jacob 7: 7 Sherem claims teachings about Christ are *b.*; **Alma** 30: 30 Korihor *b.*

BLESSING, BLESS (*see also* Benefit; Blessed [adj.]; Indebted; Obedience; Ordinance; Privilege; Reward)

1 Ne. 15: 18 (22: 9; 3 Ne. 20: 25, 27; Gen. 12: 3) in Abraham's seed shall all kindreds of earth be *b.*; 17: 2 great *b.* of the Lord upon family of Lehi[1] in wilderness; 17: 35 the Lord *b.* land unto Israelites; 19: 17 every nation, kindred, tongue, and people shall be *b.*; 22: 10 kindreds of earth cannot be *b.* unless the Lord makes bare his arm; **2 Ne.** 1: 28 Lehi[1] leaves first *b.* if sons will hearken unto Nephi[1]; 4: 3–11 Lehi[1] leaves *b.* upon children of Laman[1] and Lemuel; **Mosiah** 2: 24 if men do what the Lord commands, he immediately *b.* them; 2: 41 those who keep commandments are *b.* in all things; 13: 19 the Lord *b.* sabbath day; **Alma** 45: 16 the cursing and *b.* of God upon the land; **Hel.** 12: 1 the Lord *b.* and prospers those who put trust in him; **3 Ne.** 10: 18 great *b.* poured out upon Nephites and Lamanites; 12: 44 (Matt. 5: 44) *b.* them that curse you; 17: 21 Christ *b.* little children; 18: 3, 5 (26: 13) Christ *b.* bread, gives power to *b.* it; 20: 26 Father sent Christ to *b.* people by turning them away from iniquities; **Ether** 1: 43 the Lord will *b.* brother of Jared[2] in choice land; 10: 28 never could be a people more *b.* than Jaredites; **Moro.** 4: 3 (5: 2) prayers to *b.* and sanctify bread and wine.

BLESSED [adj.] (*see also* Bless; Happiness; BD Beatitudes)

1 Ne. 13: 37 *b.* are they who seek to bring forth Zion; **2 Ne.** 3: 23 because of covenant Joseph[1] is *b.*; **Jacob** 6: 3 *b.* are they who have labored in vineyard; **Enos** 1: 1 (Alma 26: 8; 57: 35; 3 Ne. 4: 32; 11: 17) *b.* be name of my God; **Mosiah** 3: 16 little children are *b.*; **Alma** 32: 13–16 *b.* are they who humble themselves; 38: 2 *b.* is he who endures to end; **3 Ne.** 9: 14 *b.* are those who come unto Christ; 12: 1 *b.* are they who give heed to disciples; 12: 1 *b.* are those who believe in Christ, having seen him; 12: 2 more *b.* are they who believe testimony of others; 12: 3–12 (Matt. 5: 3–12) the Beatitudes; 17: 20 *b.* are ye because of your faith; 27: 22 if ye do these things *b.* are ye.

BLINDNESS, BLIND (*see also* Darkness, Spiritual; Ignorance; BD Blindness)

1 Ne. 7: 8 Nephi[1] asks brethren why they are so *b.* in minds; 12: 17 mists of darkness, devil's temptations, *b.* eyes; 13: 27 abominable church perverts right ways of the Lord to *b.* men's eyes; 13: 32 the Lord will not allow Gentiles to remain in awful state of *b.*; 14: 7 men will be delivered to *b.* of their minds; 15: 24 adversary cannot overpower unto *b.* those who hold to iron rod; 17: 30 Israelites *b.* their minds; **2 Ne.** 9: 32 wo unto the *b.* who will not see; 27: 29 (Isa. 29: 18) the *b.* shall see out of obscurity; **Jacob** 4: 14 Jews' *b.* came from looking beyond the mark; **Jarom** 1: 3 much to be done among people because of *b.* of minds; **Mosiah** 3: 5 (3 Ne. 17: 9; 26: 15) the Lord will cause the *b.* to receive their sight; 11: 29 eyes of the people were *b.*; **Alma** 10: 25 people give Satan power to *b.* their eyes; 13: 4 men reject Spirit on account of *b.* of minds; 14: 6 Zeezrom knows concerning *b.* of minds he has caused; **4 Ne.** 1: 5 the Lord's disciples cause the *b.* to receive sight; **Ether** 4: 15 veil of unbelief causes Israelites to remain in *b.* of mind; 15: 19 Jaredites given up to *b.* of minds that they might be destroyed.

BLOCK (*see* Stumbling Block)

BLOOD (*see also* Blood, Shedding of; Blood-thirsty; Jesus Christ, Atonement through; Sacrament; Sacrifice; TG Blood; Blood, Eating of; Blood, Shedding of; Blood, Symbolism of; BD Blood)

1 Ne. 12: 10 (Ether 13: 10) garments of righteous made white in *b.* of Lamb; 22: 13 (2 Ne. 6: 18) abominable church to be drunk with own *b.*; **2 Ne.** 26: 3 (28: 10; 3 Ne. 9: 5–9, 11, 19; Morm. 8: 27; Ether 8: 22) *b.* of saints to cry up to God; **Jacob** 1: 19 (Mosiah 2: 27–28) the Lord's servants magnify offices, that people's *b.* might not come upon their garments; **Jarom** 1: 6 Lamanites drink *b.* of beasts; **Mosiah** 3: 7 Christ will suffer so greatly that *b.* will come from every pore; 3: 11 Christ's *b.* atones for sins of those who have fallen by Adam's transgression or sinned ignorantly; 4: 2 apply the atoning *b.* of Christ; 7: 27 God will take upon him flesh and *b.*; **Alma** 5: 21 garments cleansed from stain through *b.* of him who comes to redeem his people; 5: 22 how will ye feel to stand before God having garments stained with *b.*; 14: 11 *b.* of innocent shall stand as witness against people of Ammonihah; 24: 13 *b.* of Son to be shed for atonement of sins; 34: 11 no man can sacrifice own *b.* to atone for another's sins; **Hel.** 9: 31 *b.* will be found upon skirts of murderer's cloak; **3 Ne.** 9: 5, 7–9, 11, 19 (Morm. 8: 41; Ether 8: 22) the Lord avenges *b.* of saints; 18: 11 (20: 8; Moro. 5: 2) wine in remembrance of the Lord's *b.*; 18: 28–30 the unworthy are not to partake of the Lord's *b.* unless they repent; 27: 19 only those who wash garments in the Lord's *b.* enter his rest; **Ether** 3: 6, 8–9 finger of the Lord appears like unto flesh and *b.*; 13: 10 garments of those in New Jerusalem made white in *b.* of Lamb; **Moro.** 4: 1—5: 2 manner of administering flesh and *b.* of the Lord; 10: 33 men are sanctified through shedding of *b.* of Christ.

BLOOD, SHEDDING OF (*see also* Blood; Kill; Martyrdom; Murder; Sacrifice; War; TG Blood, Shedding of)

1 Ne. 4: 10 Nephi[1] has never shed *b.* of man; **2 Ne.** 1: 12 Lehi[1] predicts bloodshed and great visitations; 6: 15 they who believe not in Christ will be destroyed by bloodshed; 10: 6 because of Jews' iniquities, bloodshed shall come upon them; **Mosiah** 17: 10 (Alma 14: 11) *b.* of the innocent shall stand as witness against the wicked; **Alma** 24: 12–13, 15, 18 converted Lamanites refuse to stain swords with *b.* of brethren; 24: 13 *b.* of Son to be shed for atonement of sins; 24: 17–18 converted Lamanites bury all weapons used for shedding of *b.*; 34: 13 shedding of *b.* to stop after last and great sacrifice; 39: 3–5 shedding of innocent *b.* more abominable than whoredom; 43: 47 ye shall defend your families even unto bloodshed; 48: 11 (55: 19) Moroni[1] does not delight in bloodshed; 48: 14 Nephites taught to defend themselves against enemies, even to shedding of *b.*; 48: 23 Nephites do not delight in shedding of *b.*; 51: 9 Amalickiah has sworn to drink *b.* of Moroni[1]; 53: 11 converted Lamanites to take oath never to shed *b.*; 61: 10 Nephites will resist wickedness even unto bloodshed; **Hel.** 9: 31 *b.* will be found upon skirts of murderer's cloak; **3 Ne.** 10: 12 those who did not shed *b.* of saints are spared; 18: 11 (Moro. 5: 2) wine in remembrance of *b.* which Christ shed for men; **Moro.** 10: 33 men are sanctified through shedding of Christ's *b.*

BLOOD-THIRSTY (*see also* Blood; Blood, Shedding of)

Enos 1: 20 (Mosiah 10: 12) Lamanites a *b*-thirsty people; **Mosiah** 9: 2 ruler is austere and *b*-thirsty man; **Moro.** 9: 5 Nephites thirst after *b.* and revenge continually.

BLOT (*see also* Cast; Cut; Excommunication)

Mosiah 1: 12 (5: 11) Benjamin gives his people a name that shall never be *b.* out; 26: 36 (Alma 1: 24; 5: 57; Moro. 6: 7) names of the unrighteous are *b.* out.

BOAST, BOASTING (*see also* Pride; TG Boast, Boasting)

Mosiah 2: 15 Benjamin does not do things to *b.*; 11: 19 people of Noah[3] *b.* in own strength; **Alma** 26: 12 Ammon[2] will not *b.* of himself; 26: 36 if this is *b.*, even so will I *b.*; 38: 11 see that ye do not *b.* in your own wisdom; **Hel.** 4: 13 because of *b.*, Nephites are left to own strength; 5: 8 Helaman[3] counsels sons not to do things to *b.*; 12: 5 how quick are men to *b.*; 13: 22 Nephites' hearts swell with pride unto *b.*; **3 Ne.** 6: 10 pride and *b.* among Nephites because of riches; **Morm.** 3: 9 (4: 8) Nephites *b.* in own strength.

BOAZ, CITY OF

Morm. 4: 20–21 Nephites flee to *B.* and are slaughtered.

BODY, BODIES (*see also* Death, Physical; Flesh; Resurrection; Soul; Tabernacle; TG Body; Body, Sanctity of; Spirit Body)

1 Ne. 15: 13 Messiah shall be manifested in *b.*; 15: 31–32 torment of *b.* or final state of soul after death of temporal *b.*; **2 Ne.** 1: 22 warning against incurring God's displeasure unto eternal destruction of soul and *b.*; 4: 25 *b.* of Nephi[1] carried away on wings of Spirit; 9: 4 in *b.* we shall see God; 9: 10 God prepares way for escape from death of *b.*; 9: 13 grave must deliver up *b.* of righteous; **Mosiah** 3: 7 the Lord will suffer pain of *b.*; 4: 6 salvation comes to him who continues in faith unto end of life of mortal *b.*; 18: 13 baptism a covenant to serve God until man is dead as to mortal *b.*; **Alma** 5: 15 (11: 45) mortal *b.* to be raised in immortality; 11: 43–45 spirit and *b.* to be reunited in perfect form; 29: 16 soul of Alma[2] carried away from *b.* because of great joy; 34: 34 same spirit that possesses mortal *b.* will possess *b.* in eternal world; 36: 15 oh that I could become extinct both soul and *b.*; 40: 11–14 state of soul after it leaves mortal *b.*; 40: 18 first resurrection means reuniting of soul with *b.* of those from Adam to Christ's resurrection; 40: 21 space between death and resurrection of *b.*; 40: 23 soul shall be restored to *b.*; 41: 2 every part of *b.* to be restored; **3 Ne.** 10: 19 Christ shows *b.* unto Nephites; 13: 22 (Matt. 6: 22) light of *b.* is the eye; 18: 7 (20: 8; Moro. 4: 3) broken bread is in remembrance of Christ's *b.*; 28: 15, 37 three Nephites seem to be transfigured from *b.* of flesh into immortal state; **Morm.** 6: 21 *b.* moldering in corruption must soon become incorruptible *b.*; **Ether** 3: 16–17 brother of Jared[2] sees *b.* of the Lord's spirit; **Moro.** 10: 34 *b.* and spirit shall soon reunite.

BOLDNESS, BOLDLY

Jacob 2: 7 Jacob[2] grieved that he must use *b.* of speech; **Alma** 38: 12 use *b.*, but not overbearance; **3 Ne.** 6: 20 inspired men testify *b.* of sins; **Moro.** 8: 16 Mormon[2] speaks with *b.*, having authority from God.

BOND (*see also* Bondage; Freedom)

2 Ne. 10: 16 (26: 33; Alma 1: 30; 5: 49; 11: 44; 4 Ne. 1: 3) both *b.* and free; **Mosiah** 23: 13 people of Alma[1] delivered by power of God out of *b.*; 27: 29 (Alma 36: 27) soul of Alma[2] redeemed from *b.* of iniquity; **Alma** 38: 4 Shiblon was in *b.*

among Zoramites; 41: 11 all men that are in a carnal state are in *b.* of iniquity; **Morm.** 8: 31 those who say the Lord will uphold sinner are in *b.* of iniquity; **Moro.** 8: 14 he who supposes little children need baptism is in *b.* of iniquity.

BONDAGE (*see also* Blindness; Bond; Captive, Captivity; Liberty; Prison; Slavery; Subject; Yoke; TG Bondage, Physical; Bondage, Spiritual)

1 Ne. 17: 25 children of Israel were in *b.*; 19: 10 (Alma 29: 12; 36: 28) the Lord leads his people out of *b.* in Egypt; **Mosiah** 7: 15 Limhi's people in *b.* to Lamanites; 12: 2 (29: 18) because of iniquities, this generation shall be brought into *b.*; 21: 36 (22: 1) Limhi's people study how to deliver themselves from *b.*; 23: 12 (29: 18) people of Noah[3] had been in *b.* to him and his priests; 24: 17, 21 the Lord to deliver people of Alma[2] out of *b.*; 29: 18–20 the Lord delivers people of Noah[3] from *b.* because of humility and repentance; 29: 40 Mosiah[2] grants that his people be delivered from all manner of *b.*; **Alma** 9: 22 (36: 29) Nephites are brought out of *b.* time after time; 30: 24, 27 Korihor claims Nephites are in *b.* to foolish traditions; 36: 2 only God of Abraham could deliver the fathers from *b.*; 43: 8 Zerahemnah seeks to bring Nephites into *b.*; 48: 4 Amalickiah seeks to bring Nephites into *b.*; 48: 11 Moroni[1] finds joy in freedom of brethren from *b.*; 61: 12 Nephites would subject themselves to yoke of *b.* if requisite with justice of God; 62: 5 Nephites take up swords that they might not come into *b.*; **Ether** 2: 12 nation that possesses this land shall be free from *b.*

BONE (*see also* Body)

Omni 1: 22 (Mosiah 8: 8; 21: 26–27; Alma 22: 30) Jaredites' *b.* lie scattered in land northward; **Ether** 11: 6 prophets testify that Jaredites' *b.* will become as heaps of earth upon land.

BOOK (*see also* Bible; Book of Mormon; Read; Record; Scriptures; Write; TG Book; Book of Life; Book of Remembrance; Education; BD Book of Life; Lost Books)

1 Ne. 1: 11, 19 first angel gives Lehi[1] a *b.*; 5: 11 brass plates contain five *b.* of Moses; 10: 15 Nephi[1] does not write all prophecies of Lehi[1] in *b.*; 13: 23–29 (14: 23) Nephi[1] beholds *b.* going from Jews to Gentiles; 13: 39 other *b.* to come forth from Gentiles to seed of Nephi[1]; 19: 23 Nephi[1] reads to his people things written in *b.* of Moses; **2 Ne.** 3: 23 seed of Joseph[2] will not be destroyed, for they shall hearken to words of *b.*; 26: 17 history of Nephites to be written and sealed up in *b.*; 27: 6–22 Nephi[1] sees coming forth of sealed *b.*; 28: 2 things written in *b.* shall be of great worth to children of men; 29: 11 (3 Ne. 27: 25–26) out of *b.* will the Lord judge world; 30: 3 many shall believe words of *b.* and carry them forth to seed of Nephi[1]; **Omni** 1: 4 Amaron writes in *b.* of his father; 1: 9 Chemish writes in same *b.* with brother; **Mosiah** 1: 8 Benjamin teaches sons many things not written in *b.*; 8: 1 only a few of Limhi's words are recorded in *b.*; **Alma** 5: 58 names of righteous shall be written in *b.* of life; 9: 34 only part of Amulek's words are written in *b.*; 13: 31 many words of Alma[2] not written in *b.*; **Hel.** 2: 13–14 in end of *b.* of Nephi, Gadianton will prove the overthrow of Nephites; 3: 15 many *b.* and records kept by Nephites; **3 Ne.** 5: 8 (26: 6) not all marvelous things can be written in *b.*; 24: 16 *b.* of remembrance written for them who fear the Lord; 26: 6, 9 when Gentiles believe things written in *b.*, greater things shall be revealed.

BOOK OF MORMON (*see also* Book; Record; Scriptures; Smith, Joseph, Jr.; Translation, Translate; Witnesses, Three; TG Book of Mormon; BD Ephraim, Stick of)

Title Page abridgment of record of Nephites and Jaredites, written to testify of Christ; **1 Ne.** 13: 40 last records shall establish truth of the first; **2 Ne.** 3: 12 (Ezek. 37: 15–20) writings of descendants of Joseph[1] and of Judah shall grow together to bring knowledge of covenants; 3: 19–20 descendants of Joseph[1] shall cry from dust; 25: 18 the Lord will bring his word to Jews to convince them of true Messiah; 25: 23 we write to persuade our children and brethren to believe in Christ; 26: 14–18 (Isa. 29: 4) those who have been destroyed will whisper out of dust; 27: 6–26 (Isa. 29: 9–14) prophecy concerning coming forth of *B. of M.*; 27: 29 (Isa. 29: 18) deaf shall hear words of *b.*; 29: 8 testimony of two nations is witness that the Lord is God; 29: 12–14 the Lord will speak to Jews, Nephites, other tribes, and they shall write; 33: 10 if ye believe in Christ, ye shall believe in these words; **Enos** 1: 16 the Lord covenants to bring records to Lamanites; **Morm.** 5: 12 record to be hid up to come forth in the Lord's due time; 8: 16 (Ps. 85: 11) record to be brought out of earth to shine forth out of darkness; **Ether** 2: 11 writings to come unto Gentiles that they may know decrees of God and repent; 5: 4 (2 Ne. 27: 12–14) in mouth of three witnesses shall these things be established; **Moro.** 10: 4 ask God if these things are not true; 10: 29 God shall show unto you that that which I have written is true.

BORN (*see also* Bear, Bore, Borne; Born of God; Firstborn; Jesus Christ, First Coming of)

1 Ne. 1: 1 Nephi[1] *b.* of goodly parents; **2 Ne.** 3: 1 Joseph[2] is last-*b.* of Lehi[1]; **3 Ne.** 28: 35 better for those who do not receive Jesus not to have been *b.*

BORN OF GOD (*see also* Baptism; Begotten; Change; Children of God; Conversion; Faith; Fire; Holy Ghost, Baptism of; Remission; Spirit, Holy/Spirit of the Lord; TG Man, New, Spiritually Reborn)

Mosiah 5: 7 those who enter covenant are *b.* of Christ; 27: 25 (Alma 5: 49) all people must be *b.* again, *b.* of God; 27: 28 (Alma 36: 23) Alma[2] is *b.* of God; **Alma** 5: 14 Alma[2] asks, Have ye spiritually been *b.* of God; 22: 15 what shall I do that I may be *b.* of God; 36: 5 (38: 6) if Alma[2] had not been *b.* of God, he would not have known these things.

BORNE (*see* Bear, Bore, Borne)

BORROW

Mosiah 4: 28 he who *b.* should return it; **3 Ne.** 12: 42 (Matt. 5: 42) from him that would *b.* of thee turn thou not away; **Ether** 14: 2 Jaredites would not *b.* or lend.

BOUGHT (*see* Buy, Bought)

BOUND (*see* Bind, Bound)

BOUNTIFUL, CITY OF—*Nephite city in land of Bountiful*[2] (*see also* Bountiful, Land of[2])

Alma 52: 15, 17 Teancum is based in *B.*; 52: 27 Lamanites attack *B.*; 53: 3 ditch dug around *B.*; 53: 4 *B.* is encircled with timber wall; 55: 26 prisoners taken to *B.*; **Hel.** 1: 23 Coriantumr[3] marches toward *B.*; 5: 14 people taught, beginning at *B.*

BOUNTIFUL, LAND OF[1]—*area in southern Arabia, near sea*

1 Ne. 17: 5 Lehites come to land they called *B.* because of fruit and honey; 17: 7 voice of the Lord comes to Nephi[1] in *B.*

BOUNTIFUL, LAND OF[2]—*Nephite territory north of Zarahemla* (*see also* Bountiful, Land of[1])

Alma 22: 29 Nephites take possession of *B.*; 22: 31 *B.* lies south of land of Desolation; 22: 33 *B.* runs from east to west sea; 27: 22 *B.* is joined on southeast by Jershon; 50: 11 Nephites possess land north of *B.*; 50: 32 Moroni[1] fears people in *B.* will hearken to Morianton; 51: 28 Nephites driven to borders of *B.*; 51: 30–32 Amalickiah repulsed from *B.*; 52: 9 Moroni[1] orders *B.* fortified; 52: 15, 18 Moroni[1] marches toward *B.*; 52: 39 Lamanite prisoners taken to *B.*; 63: 5 Hagoth builds ships in *B.*; **Hel.** 1: 28 Lehi[3] sent to defend *B.*; 4: 6 Nephites driven into *B.*; **3 Ne.** 3: 23 Nephites prepare to defend *B.*; 11: 1 Christ appears to people gathered at temple in *B.*

BOUNTY

Alma 26: 15 converted Lamanites encircled with matchless *b.* of God's love.

BOW [noun] (*see also* Arrow; Weapon)

1 Ne. 16: 18 Nephi[1] breaks his *b.*; 16: 23 Nephi[1] makes *b.* out of wood, arms himself with *b.* and arrows; **Mosiah** 9: 16 Zeniff arms his people with *b.*; **Alma** 2: 12 Nephites arm themselves with *b.*; 43: 20 army of Zerahemnah armed with *b.*; **Hel.** 1: 14 Lamanite army armed with *b.*; **Morm.** 6: 9 Lamanites fall upon Nephites with sword, *b.*, arrow.

BOW, BOWED [verb] (*see also* Worship)

1 Ne. 7: 20 brethren of Nephi[1] *b.* before him; 21: 23 (Isa. 49: 23) kings and queens shall *b.* to house of Israel; **Mosiah** 13: 13 (Ex. 20: 5) thou shalt not *b.* down thyself unto graven images; 27: 31 every knee shall *b.* before Redeemer; **Alma** 22: 16 if Lamanite king *b.* before the Lord, he will receive desired hope; 31: 1 Zoram[3] leads Zoramites to *b.* to dumb idols; **3 Ne.** 17: 10 Nephites *b.* down at Savior's feet.

BOWELS (*see also* Mercy)

Mosiah 15: 9 the Son has *b.* of mercy; **Alma** 7: 12 the Son takes their infirmities that his *b.* may be filled with mercy; **3 Ne.** 17: 6–7 the Savior's *b.* filled with compassion, mercy.

BRANCH (*see also* Israel; Root; Tree; TG Branch; Jesus Christ, Davidic Descent of; Vineyard of the Lord)

1 Ne. 10: 12 Lehi[1] compares Israel to olive-tree whose *b.* are broken off; 10: 14 (15: 7, 13, 16) natural *b.* of olive-tree to be grafted in; 15: 12 (19: 24; 2 Ne. 3: 5; 9: 53; Alma 26: 36) Lehites are *b.* of house of Israel; **2 Ne.** 3: 5 (9: 53; 10: 1; Jacob 2: 25) the Lord would raise righteous *b.*, from descendants of Joseph[1], Nephites; 14: 2 (Isa. 4: 2) *b.* of the Lord shall be beautiful and glorious; 21: 1 (Isa. 11: 1) *b.* shall grow out of Jesse's roots; **Jacob** 5: 3–77 parable of natural and wild *b.* of olive-trees; 6: 4 God remembers house of Israel, both roots and *b.*; **Alma** 16: 17 word preached among Nephites that as *b.* they might be grafted into true vine; **3 Ne.** 25: 1 day of the Lord shall leave the proud neither root nor *b.*

BRASS (*see also* Plates, Brass)

1 Ne. 16: 10 Liahona made of fine *b.*; **2 Ne.** 5: 15 (Jarom 1: 8) Nephi[1] teaches people to work in *b.*; **Mosiah** 8: 7–10 people of Ammon[1] discover breastplates of *b.*; 11: 8, 10 Noah[3] ornaments buildings and temple with *b.*; **Ether** 10: 23 Jaredites make *b.*

BRAZEN SERPENT (*see* Serpent)

BREAD (*see also* Sacrament; TG Bread; Bread of Life)

2 Ne. 14: 1 (Isa. 4: 1) seven women shall say, We will eat own *b.*, only let us be called by thy name; **Alma** 5: 34 come unto me and ye shall eat *b.* of life freely; **3 Ne.** 18: 1–7 (20: 3–9; 26: 13) Christ administers *b.* and wine of sacrament to Nephites; 18: 7 (Moro. 4: 3) *b.* is in remembrance of Christ's body; **Moro.** 4: 1–3 manner of administering sacrament *b.*; 6: 6 Nephite church partakes oft of *b.* and wine of sacrament.

BREAK, BRAKE, BROKEN (*see also* Broken Heart and Contrite Spirit)

1 Ne. 12: 4 in vision Nephi[1] sees plains *b.* up; 16: 18 Nephi[1] *b.* his bow; **2 Ne.** 3: 5 righteous branch raised from loins of Joseph[1] will be *b.* off; **Jacob** 2: 35 unrighteous Nephites have *b.* wives' hearts; **Mosiah** 15: 8–9, 20, 23 (16: 7; Alma 5: 9) Christ *b.* bands of death; 20: 14 Limhi's people have not *b.* oath made to Lamanites; **Alma** 43: 11 Anti-Nephi-Lehies would not *b.* oath; **Hel.** 14: 21–22, 24 (3 Ne. 8: 13, 18) rocks and highways *b.* up at Christ's death; **3 Ne.** 6: 14 church *b.* up because of inequality; 13: 19–20 (27: 32; Matt. 6: 19) lay not up treasures on earth, where thieves *b.* through and steal; 18: 25 whosoever *b.* commandment to come unto Christ suffers himself to be led into temptation; **Ether** 6: 10 no monster of sea could *b.* Jaredite vessels.

BREAST (*see also* Breastplate; Heart)

Mosiah 2: 38 justice fills *b.* of the unrepentant with guilt; **Alma** 22: 15 what shall I do to have wicked spirit rooted out of my *b.*; 32: 28 true seed will swell within *b.*; **Morm.** 6: 7 Lamanite armies fill *b.* of wicked with fear.

BREASTPLATE (*see also* BD Breastplate)

Mosiah 8: 10 Limhi's people have found large *b.* in wilderness; **Alma** 43: 19–21, 38, 44 (44: 9) Nephite armies wear *b.*, Lamanites do not; 49: 6 (Hel. 1: 14) Lamanites wear *b.*; **Ether** 15: 15 Jaredite armies armed with *b.*

BREATH, BREATHE (*see also* TG Breath of Life)

2 Ne. 9: 26 God gave men *b.*; 21: 4 (30: 9; Isa. 11: 4) with *b.* of lips shall the Lord slay the wicked; **Mosiah** 2: 21 God preserves men from day to day by lending them *b.*; **Ether** 2: 19 Jaredites fear they cannot *b.* in vessels.

BRETHREN (*see* Brother)

BRIDE (*see also* TG Bride; BD Bride, Bridegroom)

1 Ne. 21: 18 (Isa. 49: 18) Israel shall bind her destroyers on even as a *b.*

BRIDLE

Alma 38: 12 *b.* all your passions.

BRIGHTNESS, BRIGHTER (*see also* Light)

1 Ne. 1: 10 *b.* of twelve followers exceeds stars; 15: 30 *b.* of God's justice is like *b.* of flaming fire; **2 Ne.** 9: 44 Jacob[1] to stand with *b.* before God; 31: 20 press forward, having perfect *b.* of hope; **Alma** 37: 5 (1 Ne. 5: 19) brass plates will retain *b.*

BRIMSTONE (*see* Lake; BD Brimstone)

BRING, BROUGHT

1 Ne. 13: 37 blessed are they who seek to *b.* forth Zion; **2 Ne.** 1: 7 land is consecrated unto him whom the Lord shall *b.*; 4: 5 (Prov. 22: 6) if ye are *b.* up in way ye should go, ye will not depart from it; 32: 4 because men ask not, they are not *b.* into light; **Mosiah** 4: 17 perhaps thou shalt say, The man has *b.* upon himself his misery; 12: 22 (15: 29; 3 Ne. 16: 18) they shall see eye to eye when the Lord shall *b.* again Zion; **Alma** 46: 18 God will not suffer believers to be destroyed until they *b.* it upon themselves by transgressions; **Hel.** 15: 7 faith and repentance *b.* change of heart; **3 Ne.** 15: 17, 21 (John 10: 16) other sheep I have, them also I must *b.*

BROAD (*see also* Wide)

1 Ne. 12: 17 mists of darkness are temptations of devil, which lead men away into *b.* roads; **3 Ne.** 14: 13 (Matt. 7: 13) *b.* is way which leads to destruction; 27: 33 *b.* is way which leads to death.

BROKEN HEART AND CONTRITE SPIRIT (*see also* Humble; Offering; Sacrifice; TG Contrite Heart)

2 Ne. 2: 7 Christ's sacrifice answers ends of law unto all who have *b.h.* and contrite spirit; 4: 32 may gates of hell be shut before me, because my heart is *b.* and spirit is contrite; **Jacob** 2: 10 Jacob[2] must tell people of wickedness in presence of the *b.h.*; **3 Ne.** 9: 20 offer for sacrifice unto the Lord a *b.h.* and contrite spirit; 12: 19 come unto Christ with *b.h.* and contrite spirit; **Morm.** 2: 14 Nephites do not come unto Jesus with *b.h.* and contrite spirits; **Ether** 4: 15 call upon the Father with *b.h.* and contrite spirit; **Moro.** 6: 2 only those with *b.h.* and contrite spirit are received unto baptism.

BROTHER, BRETHREN (*see also* Family; Jared[2], Brother of; Neighbor; TG Brethren; Brother; Brotherhood and Sisterhood)

1 Ne. 2: 5 elder *b.* of Nephi[1] are Laman[1], Lemuel, and Sam; 2: 22 Nephi[1] to be made ruler and teacher over *b.*; 4: 26 Zoram[1] supposes Nephi[1] speaks of *b.* of church; 22: 6 prophecies of Nephi[1] refer to *b.* who are of house of Israel; **2 Ne.** 4: 11 Sam's inheritance shall be like his *b.* Nephi[1]; 25: 23 we write to persuade our *b.* to believe in Christ; **Jacob** 2: 17 think of your *b.* like unto yourselves; **Mosiah** 9: 2 *b.* fights against *b.* among Nephite expedition; **Alma** 10: 3 Joseph[1] sold into Egypt by his *b.*; 13: 4–5 except for hardheartedness, the unfaithful might have had as great privilege as their faithful *b.*; 24: 6 converted Lamanites refuse to take up arms against *b.*; **3 Ne.** 3: 7 Giddianhi tempts Nephite leaders to become *b.* with robbers; 7: 19 (19: 4) Nephi[3] raises *b.* from dead; 12: 22 (Matt. 5: 22) he who is angry with his *b.* is in danger of judgment; 14: 3 (Matt. 7: 3) why beholdest thou the mote in thy *b*'s eye; 15: 14 Father has not commanded Christ to tell *b.* at Jerusalem about Nephites.

BRUISE (*see also* Wound)

Mosiah 14: 5 (Isa. 53: 5) the Lord *b.* for our iniquities; 14: 10 (Isa. 53: 10) it pleased the Lord to *b.* Messiah.

BUILD, BUILT (*see also* Building [noun]; Church of God; Foundation; House; Rock)

1 Ne. 18: 2 Nephi[1] does not *b.* ship after manner of men; 22: 22–23 kingdom of devil shall be *b.* up among men; **Ether** 13: 5 Jerusalem to be *b.* up again; 13: 6, 8 New Jerusalem to be *b.* upon this land; 13: 8 remnant of house of Jacob shall be *b.* upon this land.

BUILDING [noun] (*see also* Build; House; Palace; Sanctuary; Synagogue; Tabernacle; Temple; Tower)

1 Ne. 8: 26–33 (11: 35–36; 12: 18) great and spacious *b.* in dream of Lehi[1]; **2 Ne.** 5: 15 Nephi[1] teaches people to build *b.*; **Mosiah** 9: 8 Zeniff's people begin to build *b.*; 11: 8–15 Noah[3] builds many elegant *b.*; 23: 5 people of Alma begin to build *b.*; **Hel.** 3: 14 hundredth part of Nephites' *b.* of ships, temples, synagogues cannot be contained in record; **3 Ne.** 8: 14 *b.* fall to earth at Christ's death; **Ether** 10: 5–6 Riplakish builds spacious *b.*

BURDEN, BURDENSOME (*see also* Affliction; Bear; Laden; Oppression; Suffering; Task; Weigh)

Mosiah 6: 7 Mosiah[2] tills earth, that he might not become *b.* to people; 18: 8–10 those willing to bear one another's *b.* should be baptized; 21: 3 Lamanites put heavy *b.* on backs of Limhi's people; 24: 14–15, 21 the Lord eases *b.* placed on Alma[1] and his people; 29: 34 *b.* should come upon all, that every man might bear his part; **Alma** 33: 23 may God grant that your *b.* be light, through joy of the Son; **Ether** 10: 10 Morianton[1] eases *b.* of people.

BURN, BURNT, BURNING (*see also* Destruction; Devour; Fire; Hell; Oven; Stubble; BD Burnt Offering)

1 Ne. 5: 9 (7: 22; Mosiah 2: 3) Nephites offer *b.* offerings according to law of Moses; 12: 4 (3 Ne. 8: 14; 9: 3, 9–10) many cities are *b.* with fire; 22: 15 (2 Ne. 26: 4; 3 Ne. 25: 1) day comes that wicked must be *b.*; **2 Ne.** 14: 4 the Lord purges by spirit of *b.*; 19: 18 wickedness *b.* as the fire; **Jacob** 5: 7, 9 main branches of olive-tree cast into fire and *b.*; 5: 47 the Lord grieved that trees should be cut down and *b.*; 5: 77 the Lord will cause vineyard to be *b.*; 6: 3 world shall be *b.* with fire; **Mosiah** 27: 28 the Lord has seen fit to snatch Alma[2] out of everlasting *b.*; **Alma** 14: 12–13 Alma[2] and Amulek not to be *b.* because work not finished; **Hel.** 5: 23–24 Nephi[2] and Lehi[4] are encircled by fire, but not *b.*; **3 Ne.** 9: 19 the Lord will no longer accept *b.* offerings; 10: 13 more righteous part of people are not *b.*; 11: 3 voice from heaven causes hearts to *b.*; 25: 1 (Mal. 4: 10) day cometh that shall *b.* as oven; **4 Ne.** 1: 7 Nephites build cities where cities had been *b.*; **Morm.** 5: 5 Nephite cities *b.* by Lamanites; **Ether** 14: 17 Shiz *b.* cities.

BURY, BURIAL (*see also* Earth; Grave; BD Burial)

Mosiah 18: 14–15 Alma[1] and Helam *b.* in water at baptism; **Alma** 24: 19 (25: 14; 26: 32; Hel. 15: 9) converted Lamanites *b.* weapons; 45: 19 Alma[2] said to be *b.* by hand of the Lord; **3 Ne.** 8: 25 if Nephites had repented, families would not have been *b.* in great city; 9: 6, 8 the Lord causes inhabitants of cities to be *b.* in earth; 10: 13 righteous part of Nephites are not *b.* in earth; **Ether** 6: 6–7 Jaredite vessels are *b.* in depths of sea; 14: 22 no Jaredites left to *b.* the dead.

BUSHEL (*see* Candle)

BUSINESS (*see also* Gain; Merchants; Trade; Traffic)

Mosiah 29: 26 law to do *b.* by voice of people; **Alma** 10: 31 Zeezrom has much *b.* to do among the people.

BUY, BOUGHT

2 Ne. 9: 50 (26: 25; Isa. 55: 1) he who has no money, come *b.* and eat; **Hel.** 6: 8 Lamanites and Nephites have free intercourse to *b.* and sell; **Ether** 10: 22 Jaredites *b.*, sell, and traffic one with another.

BY-WORD (*see* Hiss)

CAIN—*son of Adam* (*see also* BD Cain)

Hel. 6: 27 plotted with Lucifer; **Ether** 8: 15 murderer, handed down oaths.

CALAMITY (*see also* Destruction; Tribulation; Trouble)

Morm. 2: 27 Mormon[2] sorrows because of Nephites' *c.*; 5: 11 Gentiles will sorrow for *c.* of Israel.

CALF, CALVES (*see also* Animal; BD Calves)

1 Ne. 22: 24 righteous to be led up as *c.* of stall; **2 Ne.** 21: 6 (30: 12; Isa. 11: 6) leopard shall lie down with kid and *c.*; **3 Ne.** 25: 2 (Mal. 4: 2) they who fear the Lord shall grow up as *c.* in a stall.

CALL (*see also* Calling; Name; Ordain; Prayer; TG Called of God)

2 Ne. 3: 15 name of latter-day seer shall be *c.* after Joseph[1]; 15: 20 (Isa. 5: 20) wo unto them that *c.* evil good; **Mosiah** 3: 8 (15: 21) he shall be *c.* Jesus Christ, his mother shall be *c.* Mary; 4: 11 *c.* on the name of the Lord daily; 5: 9 (3 Ne. 27: 5) the obedient shall know name by which he is *c.*, shall be *c.* by name of Christ; 5: 12 retain in your hearts name by which the Lord shall *c.* you; 16: 11–12 those delivered to devil have never *c.* upon the Lord; 18: 17 (Alma 46: 14–15; 3 Ne. 26: 21) those baptized are *c.* the church of Christ; 25: 12 children of Amulon and his brethren would no longer be *c.* by fathers' names; 25: 21 Nephites assemble in different bodies, *c.* churches; 26: 4 rising generation would not *c.* upon the Lord; **Alma** 3: 17 he that departeth from thee shall no more be *c.* thy seed; 5: 37–38, 60 good shepherd hath *c.* and is still *c.* you in his own name; 5: 49 (6: 8; 8: 4; 43: 2) Alma[2] preaches according to holy order by which he was *c.*; 9: 17 the Lord will be merciful unto all who *c.* on his name; 10: 6 Amulek was *c.* many times but would not hear; 12: 30 after angels' visits, men began to *c.* on God's name; 12: 33 God did *c.* on men, in name of the Son; 13: 3 priests were *c.* and prepared from foundations of world; 13: 27–28 *c.* upon the Lord's holy name that ye be not tempted above that which ye can bear; 18: 34 (22: 4) Ammon[2] is *c.* by Holy Spirit to teach people; 22: 16 if thou wilt *c.* upon God's name in faith, thou shalt receive hope desired; 28: 14 great *c.* of diligence to labor in the Lord's vineyards; 29: 6 why should I desire more than to perform the work to which I have been *c.*; 46: 14–15 true believers in Christ are *c.* Christians; **Hel.** 8: 18 many before days of Abraham were *c.* by order of Son of God; **3 Ne.** 4: 30 Nephites ask God to protect people so long as they *c.* on his name for protection; 11: 23–25 person being baptized should be *c.* by name during prayer; 12: 1 number of disciples who had been *c.* by Christ was twelve; 12: 9 (Matt. 5: 9) peacemakers shall be *c.* children of God; 21: 27 dispersed shall *c.* on the Father in Christ's name; 22: 5 Holy One shall be *c.* God of whole earth; 27: 7–9 church should be *c.* in the Lord's name; 27: 8 if church be *c.* in name of man, it is church of man; 27: 9 ye shall *c.* whatsoever things ye do *c.* in my name; **Ether** 2: 14–15 brother of Jared[2] chastised because he did not remember to *c.* upon name of the Lord; 4: 15 when men *c.* upon the Father, they shall know he remembers covenant; 12: 10 by faith that they of old were *c.* after holy order of God; **Moro.** 2: 2 disciples to *c.* upon the Father in Christ's name to bestow Holy Ghost; 3: 1 Nephite disciples were *c.* elders of church; 7: 29–31 office of angels' ministry is to *c.* men unto repentance; 8: 2 Christ has *c.* Moroni[2] to his ministry; 8: 8 Christ came not to *c.* righteous but sinners to repentance.

CALLING (*see also* Authority; Call; Errand; Inspire, Inspiration; Ministry; Office; TG Called of God; Calling)

Jacob 2: 3 Jacob[2] has been diligent in office of his *c.*; **Alma** 13: 3–8 priests are called with a holy *c.*; 29: 13 God has called Alma[2] with a holy *c.*; **Moro.** 3: 4 priests and teachers are ordained according to gifts and *c.* of God unto men; 7: 2 Mormon[2] permitted to speak because of gift of Christ's *c.* unto him.

CALM (*see also* Peace)

1 Ne. 18: 21 after Nephi[1] prays, great *c.* on sea.

CALNO—*possibly town near Babylon*

2 Ne. 20: 9 (Isa. 10: 9) is not C. as Carchemish.

CALVES (*see* Calf, Calves)

CAMP

2 Ne. 26: 15 the Lord shall *c.* against seed of Nephi[1] and his brethren.

CANDLE (*see also* Candlestick; Light)

3 Ne. 8: 21 because of vapor of darkness there could be no c.; 12: 15 (Matt. 5: 15) do men light a c. and put it under a bushel.

CANDLESTICK

3 Ne. 12: 15 (Matt. 5: 15) men put lighted candle on c. and it giveth light.

CANKER (*see also* Corrupt)

Mosiah 8: 11 blades of swords are c. with rust; **Morm.** 8: 38 ye hypocrites who sell yourselves for that which will c.

CAPITAL PUNISHMENT (*see also* Blood, Shedding of; Death, Physical; Executed; Hang; Kill; Murder; TG Capital Punishment)

2 Ne. 9: 35 murderer who deliberately kills shall die; **Alma** 1: 13–14 Nehor condemned to die because he shed blood of righteous man; 1: 18 (30: 10) he who murders is punished unto death; 34: 12 law requires the life of him who has murdered.

CAPTAIN (*see also* Commander)

Mosiah 20: 17 Gideon is king's c.; **Alma** 2: 13 c. appointed among Nephites; 16: 5 Zoram[2] is appointed chief c. over Nephite armies; 43: 6 Zerahemnah appoints chief c. over Lamanites; 43: 16–17 (60: 36; 61: 2) Moroni[1] is appointed chief c. over all Nephite armies; 48: 5 Amalickiah appoints Zoramites as chief c. over his armies; 49: 5 chief c. of Lamanites are astonished at wisdom of Nephites; 49: 16 Moroni[1] appoints Lehi[3] chief c. of men of city of Noah; 52: 19 chief c. of Nephites hold council of war; 57: 29 Gid is chief c. over band appointed to guard prisoners; **3 Ne.** 3: 17 Lachoneus[1] appoints chief c. over Nephite armies; 3: 18–19 Gidgiddoni is appointed chief c. and chief judge; 3: 19 Nephites appoint men of revelation as chief c.

CAPTIVATE, CAPTIVATION (*see also* Captive, Captivity; Seduce)

2 Ne. 2: 29 will of flesh gives devil power to c.; **Alma** 9: 28 those who have been evil shall reap damnation according to power and c. of devil.

CAPTIVE, CAPTIVITY (*see also* Bondage; Captivate; Destruction; Ensnare; Freedom; Prison; Sin; Slavery; TG Captivity)

1 Ne. 1: 13 (10: 3; 2 Ne. 6: 8; 25: 10; Omni 1: 15) inhabitants of Jerusalem to be carried away c. into Babylon; 13: 5 abominable church brings saints down into c.; 13: 13 Gentiles to go forth out of c., upon the many waters; 14: 4, 7 (2 Ne. 1: 18; Alma 12: 6, 17) the wicked will be brought down into c. of devil; 22: 12 the Lord will bring house of Israel again out of c.; **2 Ne.** 2: 27 men are free to choose liberty and eternal life or c. and death; 3: 4 Joseph[1] is carried c. into Egypt; 9: 12 hell must deliver up its c. spirits; 25: 10 Jews have been destroyed, except those carried c. into Babylon; **Omni** 1: 15 people of Zarahemla came from Jerusalem when Zedekiah was carried c. into Babylon; **Mosiah** 27: 16 (Alma 5: 6; 29: 11–12; 36: 2, 29) remember the c. of your fathers; **Alma** 12: 11 they who harden hearts are taken c. by devil; 16: 3 Lamanites take some Nephites c. into wilderness; **Hel.** 11: 33 robbers carry many c. into wilderness; **3 Ne.** 18: 15 pray always, lest ye be tempted and led away c. by devil; 27: 32 fourth generation led away c. by devil; **Ether** 6: 23 to have a king leads into c.; 7: 17 (8: 4; 10: 14–15, 30–31; 11: 9, 18-19) Jaredite kings in c.

CARCASS (*see also* Body)

Alma 16: 10 c. of inhabitants of Ammonihah mangled by dogs and wild beasts; **Ether** 9: 34 people devour c. of them which fell by the way.

CARE (*see also* Carefully)

Alma 32: 37 if ye nourish seed with great c., it will get root; 37: 47 Alma[2] admonishes Helaman[1] to take great c. of sacred things; 40: 12 paradise a state of rest from all c.; **Morm.** 5: 10 Mormon[2] speaks to Gentiles who have c. for house of Israel.

CAREFULLY

2 Ne. 28: 21 devil leads souls c. down to hell.

CARNAGE (*see also* Battle; Slaughter; War)

3 Ne. 2: 11 Gadianton robbers spread great c. throughout land; **Morm.** 2: 8 because people do not repent, blood and c. spread among Nephites and Lamanites; 4: 11 impossible for tongue to describe horrible scene of c.; 5: 8 Mormon[2] does not desire to harrow up souls by describing scene of c.; **Ether** 14: 21 so long had been scene of c. that whole land is covered with dead bodies.

CARNAL, CARNALLY (*see also* Devilish; Evil; Fall of Man; Flesh; Lasciviousness; Law of Moses; Lust; Nature, Natural; Sensual; Temporal; Wicked; World)

2 Ne. 9: 39 (Rom. 8: 6) to be c-minded is death; 28: 21 devil lulls men away into c. security; **Mosiah** 4: 2 Benjamin's people view themselves in c. state; 16: 3 (Alma 42: 10) the wicked are c. and devilish; 16: 3 Fall caused all mankind to become c.; 16: 5 he who persists in his c. nature remains in his fallen state;

16: 12 those delivered up to damnation have gone according to their own *c.* wills; 26: 4 many in rising generation refuse baptism and remain in *c.* state; 27: 25 those born of God are changed from c. and fallen state to state of righteousness; **Alma** 22: 13 Aaron[2] explains fall of man and *c.* state; 30: 53 Korihor teaches devil's words because they are pleasing to *c.* mind; 36: 4 knowledge of Alma[2] comes not of *c.* mind but of God; 41: 11 all men in *c.* state are in gall of bitterness; 41: 13 restoration is to bring back c. for c.

CARRY (*see also* Bear, Bore, Borne; Catch)

1 Ne. 1: 8 (14: 30) Lehi[1] is c. away in vision; 11: 29 the twelve are c. away in Spirit; 21: 22 (22: 6, 8; 2 Ne. 6: 6; Isa. 49: 22) daughters of the Lord's people shall be c. upon Gentiles' shoulders; **2 Ne.** 33: 1 when man speaks by Holy Ghost, power of Holy Ghost c. it into men's hearts; **Alma** 37: 45 words of Christ shall c. us beyond vale of sorrow; **3 Ne.** 6: 17 people delivered for long time to be c. about by temptations of devil.

CAST (*see also* Blot; Cut; Devils; Excommunication; Fire; Throw; Thrust; Toss)

1 Ne. 1: 20 Jews c. out prophets; 15: 33 those who die in wickedness must be c. off; **2 Ne.** 26: 3 (Hel. 13: 24; 3 Ne. 8: 25; 9: 10–11) wicked shall perish because they c. out prophets; 30: 2 (Hel. 14: 18) Jews who do not repent shall be c. off; **Mosiah** 16: 2 (Alma 40: 13, 26) wicked shall be c. out; 28: 4 Lamanites suffer much, fearing they should be c. off forever; **Alma** 10: 23 (Hel. 13: 14) if people c. out the righteous, the Lord will not stay his hand; 11: 2 man in debt must pay or be c. out from people; 22: 15 Lamanite king asks what he should do to avoid being c. off at last day; 32: 28 if ye do not c. out good seed by unbelief, it will swell; 32: 32 if seed does not grow, it is c. away; 32: 38 neglected tree withers, is c. out; **Hel.** 12: 25 in last days some shall be c. off from God's presence; **3 Ne.** 18: 23, 30, 32 the unworthy should not be c. out from places of worship; 24: 11 (Mal. 3: 11) neither shall your vine c. her fruit before the time; **Ether** 8: 25 devil causes men to c. out prophets; 13: 13 Jaredites c. Ether out.

CATCH, CAUGHT (*see also* Carry; Ensnare)

1 Ne. 11: 1 Nephi[1] *c.* away in Spirit into high mountain; **Alma** 10: 13 lawyers try to c. Alma[2] and Amulek in their words; 12: 1 Amulek c. Zeezrom in his lying; 12: 6 adversary had laid a snare to c. people of Ammonihah; 18: 23 Ammon[2] c. Lamoni with guile; **3 Ne.** 28: 13 disciples c. up into heaven.

CATTLE (*see also* Animal; Beast; Herd; Ox)

Enos 1: 21 Nephites raise c.; **3 Ne.** 3: 22 (4: 4) Nephites gather c. to defend themselves; 6: 1 Nephites return to land, with c.; **Ether** 9: 18 Jaredites have all manner of c.

CAUSE (*see also* Reason)

2 Ne. 8: 22 (Moro. 1: 28) God pleads the c. of his people; **Mosiah** 16: 3 serpent's beguiling of our first parents was c. of fall; 29: 5 consider the c. which ye are called to consider; **Alma** 11: 25 Zeezrom seeks c. to destroy Amulek; 19: 14 Lamanites have been c. of much mourning among Nephites; 32: 18 if a man knoweth a thing, he hath no c. to believe; 43: 45 Nephites inspired by better c.; 46:16 Moroni[1] prays that c. of Christians might be favored; 46: 35 Amalickiahites who will not support c. of freedom are put to death; 46: 40 God prepared plants and roots to remove c. of diseases; 48: 10 Nephites prepare to maintain what enemies call c. of Christians; 50: 39 chief judge appointed with oath to maintain c. of God; 51: 7, 17 king-men obliged to maintain c. of freedom; 54: 10 Nephites will maintain their religion and c. of their God; 56: 11 Nephites have died in c. of their country and their God; 58: 12 Nephites fixed with determination to maintain c. of liberty; 60: 16 if all Nephites had been true to c. of freedom, they would have dispersed their enemies; 60: 28 Moroni[1] defends c. of his country according to God's commandments; 61: 14 Pahoran rejoices in c. of his Redeemer and his God; 62: 1 Pahoran not a traitor to c. of his country; 62: 11 death inflicted upon those who are not true to c. of freedom; **Hel.** 14: 28 signs given that there should be no c. for unbelief; **Moro.** 7: 28 Christ advocates c. of children of men.

CAVITY

1 Ne. 3: 27 sons of Lehi[1] hide themselves in c. of rock; **Ether** 13: 13–14, 18, 22 Ether hides in c. of rock.

CEASE (*see also* Miracle; Refrain; Stop; Strive)

2 Ne. 23: 11 (Isa. 13: 11) the Lord will cause the arrogancy of the proud to c.; **Mosiah** 26: 39 (3 Ne. 19: 26, 30) pray without c.; **Alma** 42: 13, 22–23, 25 if justice were destroyed, God would c. to be God; **Morm.** 9: 19 if God changed he would c. to be God.

CEDARS (*see* Lebanon)

CEMENT

Hel. 3: 7, 9, 11 Nephites become expert in working c.

CENTER

1 Ne. 16: 2 truth cuts the guilty to c.; **Hel.** 12: 12 by power of the Lord's voice do foundations rock to c.; **3 Ne.** 11: 3 small voice pierces Nephites to c.

CEZORAM—*wicked chief judge of Nephites* [c. 30 B.C.]

Hel. 5: 1 receives judgment-seat; 6: 15–19 murdered, as is his son, who is appointed in his stead.

CHAFF

2 Ne. 15: 24 (Isa. 5: 24) as flame consumeth the c.; 26: 18 multitude of terrible ones shall be as c. that passes away; **Mosiah** 7: 30 if people sow filthiness, they shall reap c.; **Alma** 37: 15 Satan to sift the transgressor as c. before wind; **Morm.** 5: 16, 18 Nephites driven about as c. before wind.

CHAIN (*see also* Band; Captivate; Hell; TG Bondage, Spiritual)

2 Ne. 1: 13 (9: 45) shake off awful c. by which ye are bound; 28: 19 devil will grasp the wicked with his everlasting c.; **Alma** 5: 7, 9–10 fathers loosed from c. of hell that encircled them; 12: 6 adversary lays snares that he might encircle people with his c.; 12: 11 c. of hell means to be taken captive by devil and led by his will; 12: 17 those who die in their sins shall be c. down to everlasting destruction; 13: 30 may the Lord grant unto you repentance, that ye not be bound down by c. of hell; 36: 18 have mercy on me, who am encircled by c. of death.

CHALDEA, CHALDEAN, CHALDAIC (*see also* Language; BD Chaldea)

1 Ne. 20: 14 (Isa. 48: 14) the Lord's arm to come upon C.; 20: 20 (Isa. 48: 20) flee ye from the C.; 2 Ne. 23: 19 (Isa. 13: 19) Babylon, beauty of C's excellency, shall be as when God overthrew Sodom.

CHANCE

Mosiah 29: 38 Nephites are anxious that every man have equal c.; **3 Ne.** 6: 12 people distinguished by ranks, according to c. for learning.

CHANGE, CHANGING (*see also* Alter; Born of God; Changeable; Conversion; God, Eternal Nature of; Heart; Mend; Repentance; Transfigure, Transfiguration; Transform; Translated Beings; Unchangeable; Vary)

1 Ne. 16: 29 writing on Liahona c. from time to time; **Mosiah** 5: 7 hearts are c. through faith; 27: 25 all mankind must be c. from fallen state to state of righteousness; 5: 2 Spirit has wrought mighty c. in Benjamin's people; **Alma** 5: 12–13 mighty c. wrought in hearts of Alma[1] and his people; 5: 14–26 have ye experienced this mighty c. in your hearts; 12: 20 man to be c. from mortal to immortal state; 19: 33 Lamoni and household declare their hearts have been c.; **Hel.** 15: 7 repentance brings c. of heart; **3 Ne.** 8: 12 whole face of land is c.; 24: 6 I am the Lord, I c. not; 28: 8, 15 three Nephites c. from mortality to immortality; 28: 37–40 c. wrought upon bodies of three Nephites; **Morm.** 9: 9–10 no shadow of c. in God; 9: 19 if God c., he would cease to be God; **Ether** 12: 14 faith of Nephi[2] and Lehi[4] wrought c. upon Lamanites.

CHANGEABLE (*see also* Change)

Moro. 8: 12 if little children were not alive in Christ, God would be a c. God; 8: 18 God is not a c. being.

CHARACTERS (*see also* Language; Writing)

Morm. 9: 32 record written in c. known as reformed Egyptian.

CHARGE (*see also* Instruction)

Mosiah 1: 15–16 Benjamin gives Mosiah[2] c. concerning affairs of kingdom, records; 29: 42 Alma[1] gives Alma[2] c. concerning affairs of church; **Alma** 35: 16 Alma[2] gathers sons to give them his c.

CHARIOT (*see also* BD Chariot)

Alma 18: 9 (20: 6) Lamoni commands servants to prepare horses and c.; 18: 10, 12 Ammon[2] prepares Lamoni's c.; **3 Ne.** 3: 22 Nephites gather with horses and c.; 21: 14 (Micah 5: 10) the Father will destroy c. of Gentiles.

CHARITY, CHARITABLE (*see also* Alms; Compassion; God, Love of; Impart; Love; Needy; Neighbor; Relief; Substance; TG Charity; BD Charity)

2 Ne. 26: 30 the Lord has commanded that all men should have c.; 26: 30 c. is love; 26: 30 (Moro. 7: 44, 46) except men have c. they are nothing; 26: 30 if men have c., they will not suffer laborer in Zion to perish; 33: 7–9 Nephi[1] has c. for his people, the Jew, and the Gentiles; **Alma** 7: 24 see that ye have faith, hope, and c.; 13: 29 have faith, hope, the love of God in your hearts; 34: 29 if ye do not remember to be c., ye are as dross; **Ether** 12: 28 faith, hope, and c. bring unto the Lord; 12: 34 love that the Lord has for men is c.; 12: 34 (Moro. 10: 20–21) without c. men cannot inherit place prepared in the Father's mansions; 12: 35–37 if Gentiles have not c., the Lord will prove them; **Moro.** 7: 1 Moroni[2] writes words of Mormon[2] on faith, hope, and c.; 7: 44 if man is meek and confesses Christ, he must have c.; 7: 45 (1 Cor. 13: 4–7) qualities of c. described; 7: 46 (1 Cor. 13: 8) c. never faileth; 7: 46 cleave unto c., which is the greatest of all; 7: 47 (8: 17) c. is pure love of Christ and endures forever; 10: 20–21 except ye have c., ye can in nowise be saved in the kingdom of God.

CHASTEN, CHASTISEMENT (*see also* Affliction; Persecution; Prove; Punishment; Rebuke; Refine; Reprove; Scourge; Suffering; Trial; Tribulation; Warn; TG Chastening)

1 Ne. 16: 25 Lehi[1] c. because of murmuring against the Lord; 16: 39 voice of the Lord c. Laman[1] and Lemuel; **Mosiah** 14: 5 (Isa. 53: 5) the c. of our peace was upon Messiah; 23: 21 the Lord sees fit to c. his people; **Hel.** 12: 3 except the Lord c. his people, they will not remember him; 15: 3 the Lord has c. Nephites because he loves them; **Ether** 2: 14 brother of Jared[2] is c. because he remembered not to call upon the Lord.

CHASTITY, CHASTE (*see also* Adultery; Clean; Fornication; Lust; Purity; Virtue; TG Chastity, Chaste)

Jacob 2: 7 feelings of Nephites' wives and children are tender and c.; 2: 28 the Lord delights in c. of women; **Moro.** 9: 9 Nephites deprive Lamanites' daughters of that which is most precious, c.

CHEAT (*see also* Deceit)

2 Ne. 28: 21 devil c. men's souls.

CHECK (*see also* Restrain)

Alma 15: 17 people are c. as to pride.

CHEEK (*see* Smite)

CHEER (*see also* Cheerful; Happiness; Joy; TG Cheer)

2 Ne. 10: 23 c. up your hearts; **Alma** 17: 31 (3 Ne. 1: 13) be of good c.

CHEERFULLY (*see also* Cheer; TG Cheerful, Cheerfulness)

Mosiah 24: 15 Alma[1] and his followers submit c. to will of the Lord.

CHEMISH—*Nephite record keeper, son of Omni*

Omni 1: 8 receives plates from brother, Amaron; 1: 9 writes few things; 1: 10 father of Abinadom.

CHERUBIM (*see also* TG Cherubim; BD Cherubim)

Alma 12: 21 (42: 2–3; Gen. 3: 24) God placed c. and flaming sword east of Eden.

CHICKENS (*see also* Animal; Hen)

3 Ne. 10: 4–6 (Matt. 23: 37) the Lord would have gathered people as a hen gathers c.

CHIEF (*see also* Captain; Judge, Chief)

3 Ne. 7: 3, 14 every tribe appoints c.

CHILD, CHILDREN (*see also* Babe; Children of God; Daughter; Son; TG Child; Children; Family; Children, Duties of; Family, Children, Responsibilities toward; Honoring Father and Mother; Salvation of Little Children)

1 Ne. 5: 21 (Mosiah 1: 4) brass plates of great worth in preserving the Lord's commandments unto c.; 11: 20 Nephi[1] sees virgin bearing c. in arms; 14: 3 abominable church founded by devil and his c.; 17: 1–2 women bear c. in wilderness; 22: 6, 8 (21: 22; Isa. 49: 22) c. of Jews to be carried in Gentiles' arms; **2 Ne.** 2: 23 without fall, Adam and Eve would have had no c.; 4: 15 Nephi[1] writes scriptures for learning and profit of his c.; 13: 12 (Isa. 3: 12) c. to be oppressors of the Lord's people; 19: 6 (Isa. 9: 6) for unto us a c. is born; 21: 6 (30: 12; Isa. 11: 6) leopard, kid, calf, lion to lie down together, and little c. shall lead them; 25: 26–27 Nephites write of Christ, that c. may know source of remission of sins; **Jacob** 2: 35 (3: 10) Nephites have lost confidence of c. because of bad example; **Mosiah** 3: 16 (Moro. 8: 8–24) blood of Christ atones for sins of little c.; 3: 18 men drink damnation to souls except they become as little c.; 3: 19 c. is submissive, humble, full of love; 3: 21 none shall be found blameless except little c.; 4: 14 ye will not suffer your c. to go hungry, to transgress, to quarrel, to serve devil; 6: 2 all except little c. enter covenant; 15: 25 little c. have eternal life; **Alma** 5: 25, 38–41 the wicked are c. of devil; 30: 25 Korihor says c. not guilty because of parents; 30: 60 devil will not support his c.; 32: 23 words given to little c. which confound the wise and learned; 39: 12 command thy c. to do good; 43: 45 (48: 10; 58: 12) Nephites fight for homes, wives, c.; **Hel.** 15: 2 wo unto them which are with c., for they shall be heavy and cannot flee; **3 Ne.** 9: 22 the Lord will receive those who repent and come unto him as little c.; 11: 37–38 men must become as little c. or they cannot inherit kingdom of God; 17: 11–12, 21–23 Christ blesses c.; 17: 24–25 angels minister to Nephite c.; 18: 21 pray in your families that your wives and c. may be blessed; 22: 1 (Isa. 54: 1) more are the c. of the desolate than the c. of the married wife; 22: 13 (Isa. 54: 13) all thy c. shall be taught of the Lord, and great shall be peace of thy c.; 26: 14 Christ teaches and ministers to c. of multitude, looses their tongues; 28: 22 (4 Ne. 1: 33) Nephite disciples play with beasts as c. with lamb; **4 Ne.** 1: 38 those who reject gospel teach c. they should not believe; **Morm.** 1: 2 Mormon[2] a sober c.; 4: 12 there never had been so great wickedness among all c. of Lehi[1]; **Moro.** 8: 3 Father's Holy C., Jesus; 8: 8–24 little c. do not need repentance or baptism; 8: 12, 22 (Mosiah 3: 16) little c. are alive in Christ; 8: 15 wickedness to suppose God saves one c. because of baptism and the other must perish; 8: 17 all c. are alike unto the Lord; 8: 17 the Lord loves little c. with perfect love.

CHILDREN OF GOD (*see also* Begotten; Born of God; Heir; Inherit; Saint; Son; TG Children of Light)

1 Ne. 11: 17 God loves his c.; 17: 36 the Lord has created his c. that they should possess earth; **Alma** 36: 14 Alma[2] had led many of God's c. to destruction; **3 Ne.** 12: 9 (Matt. 5: 9) peacemakers shall be called c. of God; 12: 44–45 (Matt. 5: 44–45) love your enemies, that you may be c. of Father in heaven; **Moro.** 7: 19 lay hold upon every good thing and you will be c. of Christ.

CHOICE (*see also* Choose; Chosen [adj.]; Precious; Promised Land)

2 Ne. 1: 19 Lehi[1] wishes that sons might be a c. people of the Lord; 3: 6–7 the Lord will raise up c. seer from loins of Joseph[1]; **Jacob** 5: 43 branch planted in c. spot in vineyard; **W of M** 1: 6 Mormon[2] puts plates containing c. revelations with remainder of record.

CHOOSE, CHOSE, CHOSEN (*see also* Agency; Chosen [adj.])

1 Ne. 12: 7 the twelve were ordained of God and c.; 20: 10 (Isa. 48: 10) I have c. thee in the furnace of affliction; **2 Ne.** 2: 27–29 (10: 23; Hel. 14: 31) men are free to c. liberty and eternal life or captivity and death; 2: 30 I have c. the good part; 17: 16 (Isa. 7: 16) before child knows to c. good, land shall be forsaken of both kings; 26: 10 (Alma 40: 13) because Nephites c. works of darkness, they must go down to hell; **Mosiah** 29: 25 c. judges by voice of people; 29: 27 (Alma 10: 19) if voice of people c. iniquity, judgments will come; **Alma** 13: 3 those fore-ordained were left to c. good or evil; 13: 3, 10 having c. good and exercised faith, priests were called with holy calling; 30: 8 (Josh. 24: 15) c. ye this day whom ye will serve; **Hel.** 5: 2 they who c. evil were more numerous than they who c. good; 13: 29 how long will ye c. darkness rather than light; **3 Ne.** 12: 1 Christ c. twelve to minister unto Nephites; 19: 20 Christ c. Nephite disciples because of their belief in him.

CHOSEN [adj.] (*see also* Choice; Choose; Covenant)

Mosiah 7: 26 Abinadi a c. man of God; **Alma** 7: 10 Mary a precious and c. vessel; 10: 7 Alma[2] a c. man of God; 46: 17 (Ether 13: 2) all the land on the north and the south a c. land.

CHRIST (*see* Jesus Christ)

CHRISTIAN (*see also* Believer; Saint; Worshipper; TG Christian; BD Christians)

Alma 46: 13, 16 Moroni[1] prays for blessings of liberty as long as C. remain to possess land; 46: 14–15 true believers are called C.; 48: 10 cause of liberty is called cause of C.

CHRISTS, FALSE (*see also* Prophets, False)

2 Ne. 25: 18 not any Messiah come save false Messiah; **W of M** 1: 15–16 are punished according to crimes.

CHURCH (*see also* Church, Great and Abominable; Church of God; Church of the Devil; Churches, False; TG Church)

1 Ne. 4: 26 Zoram[1] supposes Nephi[1] speaks of brethren of c.

CHURCH, GREAT AND ABOMINABLE (*see also* Church of the Devil; Churches, False; Harlot; Whore)

1 Ne. 13: 5, 9 abominable c. slays saints; 13: 6 (14: 3, 9, 17) devil is founder of great and abominable c.; 13: 7–8 precious clothing and harlots are desires of great and abominable c.; 13: 26–28, 32, 34 great and abominable c. takes away plain and precious parts of gospel; 14: 3 (22: 14) great and abominable c. digs pit for saints; 14: 9–10, 13, 16 great and abominable c. is mother of abominations; 14: 10 those who do not belong to c. of Lamb belong to great c.; 14: 17 wrath of God to be poured out on great and abominable c.; 22: 13 blood of great and abominable c. shall turn upon their own heads; 22: 14 (2 Ne. 28: 18) great and abominable c. shall tumble to dust; **2 Ne.** 6: 12 if Gentiles do not unite themselves to great and abominable c., they shall be saved.

CHURCH OF CHRIST (*see* Church of God)

CHURCH OF GOD (*see also* Assemble; Baptism; Build; Flock; Kingdom of God; Officer; Priesthood; Religion; Saint; Stake; TG Church; Church, Name of; Church before Christ; Church Organization; BD Church)

1 Ne. 14: 10 only two c., c. of Lamb and c. of devil; 14: 12, 14 c. of Lamb are saints of God; **2 Ne.** 9: 2 Jews shall be restored to true c. of God; 25: 14 wo unto those who fight against God and people of his c.; **Mosiah** 18: 17 (25: 18; 26: 22; Alma 4: 5; 3 Ne. 26: 21; 28: 23; Moro. 6: 4) those baptized are called c. of God, or c. of Christ; 21: 30 (23: 16; 25: 18; 29: 47) Alma[1] and his people form c. of God; 25: 18–19 (29: 47; Alma 4: 7; 6: 1) Mosiah[2] grants that Alma[1] might establish c. throughout land and ordain priests and teachers over every c.; 25: 22 notwithstanding many c., they are all one c.; 26: 8 Mosiah[2] gives Alma[1] authority over c.; 26: 22 this is my c.; 27: 1–2 (Alma 1: 19) great persecutions inflicted on c.; 27: 9–10 (36: 6, 9, 11) Alma[2] seeks to destroy c. of God; 27: 13 angel asks Alma[2], Why persecutest thou c. of God; 29: 42 (Alma 4: 4; 5: 3) Alma[1] gives son, Alma[2], charge concerning all affairs of c.; **Alma** 1: 30 members of c. do not send away any, whether out of c. or in the c.; 1: 31 members of c. prosper more than those who do not belong; 2: 4 Amlici seeks to destroy c.; 4: 4–5 (5: 5) c. established more fully through many baptisms; 4: 11 wickedness in c. leads unbelievers to further iniquity; 5: 5 (8: 23) Alma[2] high priest over c.; 6: 4 (8: 1) order of c. established; 45: 22 (62: 46) Helaman[2] and brethren go forth to establish c. again; 46: 10 Amalickiah seeks to destroy c. of God; 46: 13–14 true believers who belong to c. are called Christians; **Hel.** 3: 33 pride enters hearts of those who profess to belong to c.; 4: 11 wickedness among those who profess to belong to c.; 11: 21 c. spreads throughout land; **3 Ne.** 6: 14 c. begins to be broken up; 18: 5 one to be ordained with power to give broken bread to people of c.; 18: 16 prayers in c. to follow Savior's pattern; 21: 22 if they will repent, I will establish my c. among them; 27: 3–11 those who build upon gospel should call c. in Christ's name; 27: 21 ye know the things that ye must do in my c.; 28: 18 disciples unite as many to c. as believe in their preaching; **4 Ne.** 1: 1 disciples form c. of Christ in all lands; 1: 26 Nephites begin to build up c. to get gain, and deny true c. of Christ; 1: 27–29 c. that deny Christ's gospel persecute true c.; **Morm.** 8: 38 O ye hypocrites, why have ye polluted the holy c. of God; **Moro.** 3: 1 disciples are called elders of c.; 4: 2 (5: 2; D&C 20: 76) elders and priests kneel down with c. and pray over bread and wine; 6: 5 c. meets oft to fast, pray, speak; 7: 39 if ye have not faith in Christ, ye are not fit to be numbered among people of his c.

CHURCH OF THE DEVIL (*see also* Church, Great and Abominable; Churches, False; Devil; TG Devil, Church of)

1 Ne. 13: 6 (14: 3, 9, 17) devil is founder of great and abominable c.; 14: 10 only two c., c. of Lamb and c. of devil; **Alma** 5: 39 if ye are not sheep of good shepherd, devil is your shepherd; **3 Ne.** 27: 11 those who build c. upon works of devil have joy for season, then comes the end.

CHURCH OF THE LAMB (*see* Church of God)

CHURCHES, FALSE (*see also* Church, Great and Abominable; Church of the Devil; Denominations; Doctrine, False; Priestcraft; Priests, False; Prophets, False; Tradition)

1 Ne. 22: 23 c. built up to get gain or power shall be brought low; **2 Ne.** 26: 20 Gentiles shall stumble because they build many c.; 28: 3–4 c. built by men shall contend against each other; **3 Ne.** 27: 8 if c. is called in name of man, it is c. of man; 27: 11 those who build c. upon works of men will have joy for season, then comes the end; **4 Ne.** 1: 26 c. built up to get gain deny true c.; 1: 27 many c. in land deny parts of gospel; 1: 28 false c. multiplies because of iniquity and power of Satan; 1: 29–30 c. denies Christ and persecutes true c.; **Morm.** 8: 28 c. will become defiled and leaders will rise up in pride; 8: 32 c. will forgive sins for money.

CIMETER (*see also* Sword; Weapon)

Enos 1: 20 Lamanites skilled in c.; **Mosiah** 9: 16 (10: 8; Alma 2: 12; 43: 18, 20, 37; 60: 2; Hel. 1: 14) c. used in wars between Nephites and Lamanites.

CIRCUMCISION (*see also* Uncircumcised; TG Circumcision; BD Circumcision)

Moro. 8: 8 law of c. done away in Christ.

CIRCUMSPECTLY

Mosiah 26: 37 (Hel. 15: 5; 16: 10) walk c. before God.

CITIZENSHIP (*see also* Government, Civil)

Mosiah 2: 17 when in service of fellow beings ye are in service of God; 4: 13 live peaceably, and render to every man his due; 29: 25 choose judges by voice of people; **Alma** 1: 1, 14 people are obliged to abide by laws; 43: 9, 26, 47 (55: 28) Nephites fight to defend rights, privileges, liberty; 46: 20 (48: 13; 51: 6) Nephites and converted Lamanites enter covenant to preserve rights and free government.

CITY (*see also* Jerusalem; Jerusalem, New; Town; Villages; Zarahemla, City of[1])

1 Ne. 12: 4 (3 Ne. 8: 14–16) in vision, Nephi[1] sees many *c.* destroyed; **2 Ne.** 16: 8–11 (Isa. 6: 8–11) Isaiah[1] is called to preach until *c.* be wasted without inhabitants; **Alma** 8: 7 Nephite custom to call *c.* after him who first possessed them; 50: 1 Nephite armies dig up heaps of earth round about all *c.*; 62: 32 (Hel. 4: 16; Morm. 8: 7) battles fought from *c.* to *c.*; **Hel.** 3: 9 trees allowed to grow for timber to build *c.*; 8: 6 Nephites do not believe they can be destroyed because *c.* are great; **3 Ne.** 6: 7 many *c.* are built anew and many old *c.* are repaired; 8: 8–10, 14–15 (9: 3–10) many *c.* destroyed at time of Crucifixion; 12: 14 (Matt. 5: 14) *c.* set on hill cannot be hid; 21: 15 (Micah 5: 11) I will cut off the *c.* of thy land; **4 Ne.** 1: 7–9 many *c.* are rebuilt; **Ether** 9: 23 Coriantum[1] builds many mighty *c.*; 13: 5 Jerusalem to be built up again and become holy *c.*

CIVIL (*see also* Government, Civil)

Moro. 9: 12 Nephites were a *c.* people.

CIVILIZATION

Alma 51: 22 Moroni[1] subjects his people to peace and *c.*; **Moro.** 9: 11 Nephites are without *c.*

CLAIM (*see also* Justice; Mercy; Profess)

Mosiah 29: 9 Mosiah[2] fears son might later *c.* right to kingdom; **Moro.** 7: 28 Christ *c.* all those who have faith in him.

CLAP (*see also* Hands, Laying on of)

Alma 31: 36 Alma[2] *c.* his hands upon them, and they were filled with Spirit.

CLASS (*see also* Ranks)

4 Ne. 1: 26 Nephites began to be divided into *c.*

CLAY (*see also* Tabernacle)

2 Ne. 27: 27 (Isa. 29: 16) turning of things upside down shall be esteemed as potter's *c.*

CLEAN, CLEANLINESS (*see also* Chastity; Cleanse; Holy; Purify; Virtue; White; Worthy; TG Cleanliness)

2 Ne. 25: 16 worship the Father with pure hearts and *c.* hands; **Alma** 5: 19 can ye look to God with pure heart and *c.* hands; 24: 15 God imparted his word and has made us *c.* thereby; **3 Ne.** 20: 41 (Isa. 52: 11) be ye *c.* that bear vessels of the Lord; **Ether** 4: 6 Gentiles shall not receive interpreters until they repent of sins and become *c.* before the Lord; 12: 37 thy garments shall be made *c.*

CLEANSE (*see also* Baptism; Clean; Fire; Purify; Rid; Sanctification; Spotless; Wash)

Alma 5: 21 no man can be saved except his garments are *c.* from all stain; 5: 24 garments of all holy prophets are *c.*; 5: 27 if called to die, could you say your garments have been *c.*; 7: 14 the Lamb is mighty to save and *c.* from all unrighteousness; 60: 23 inward vessel to be *c.* first, then outward vessel; 60: 24 Nephites not to contend with Lamanites until they have *c.* their inward vessel; **3 Ne.** 8: 1 no man could do miracle in Jesus' name save he were *c.* from iniquity; 28: 36 Mormon[2] did not know whether three Nephites had been *c.* from mortality to immortality; **Morm.** 9: 6 turn unto Father that ye might be *c.* by blood of Lamb; **Moro.** 6: 4 after baptism people are *c.* by Holy Ghost.

CLEAR (*see also* Plain)

2 Ne. 4: 33 wilt thou *c.* my way before me; **Jacob** 5: 65 ye shall *c.* away branches which bring forth bitter fruit.

CLEAVE, CLAVE [join] (*see also* Join; Mount; Rock)

Jacob 6: 5 *c.* unto God as he *c.* unto you; **Hel.** 4: 25 except Nephites *c.* unto the Lord, they must perish; **3 Ne.** 10: 10 earth *c.* together again; **Ether** 14: 2 every man *c.* unto that which was his; **Moro.** 7: 28 they who have faith in Christ will *c.* unto every good thing; 7: 46 *c.* unto charity.

CLIMATE

Alma 46: 40 men subject to diseases by nature of *c.*

CLOAK

3 Ne. 12: 40 (Matt. 5: 40) if any man will take away thy coat, let him have *c.* also.

CLOSET (*see also* Private; Secret)

Alma 33: 7 when I turned unto my *c.*, and prayed, the Lord did hear me; 34: 26 pour out your souls in your *c.*; **3 Ne.** 13:6 when thou prayest, enter into thy *c.*

CLOTH (*see also* Clothe; Clothing; Linen; Silk)

Mosiah 10: 5 (Hel. 6: 13) Nephite women work all manner of *c.*; **Alma** 1: 29 church becomes rich, having all manner of good homely *c.*; **Ether** 10: 24 Jaredites work all manner of *c.*

CLOTHE (*see also* Clothing)

2 Ne. 7: 3 (Isa. 50: 3) the Lord *c.*

heavens with blackness; 9: 14 the righteous shall be c. with purity; **Jacob** 2: 19 obtain riches to c. the naked; **Mosiah** 4: 26 impart of your substance to the poor, c. the naked; 10: 5 (Hel. 6: 13) women work cloth that Nephites might c. their nakedness; **Alma** 35: 9 people of Ammon[2] c. poor Zoramites; **Hel.** 13: 28 people will c. false prophet in costly apparel; **3 Ne.** 11: 8 Christ c. in white robe.

CLOTHING, CLOTHES (*see also* Apparel; Cloak; Coat; Garment; Raiment; Robe)

1 Ne. 13: 7–8 Nephi[1] sees precious c. in abominable church; **2 Ne.** 13: 6 (Isa. 3: 6) men shall say, Thou hast c., be thou our ruler; 28: 13 latter-day churches will rob the poor because of fine c.; **Alma** 14: 22 people of Ammonihah take away c. of Alma[2] and Amulek; 43: 19 Nephite army dressed with thick c.; **Hel.** 4: 12 Nephites withhold c. from the naked; **3 Ne.** 14: 15 (Matt. 7: 15) beware of false prophets, who come in sheep's c.

CLOUD (*see also* Smoke; Vapor)

2 Ne. 14: 5 (Isa. 4: 5) the Lord will create upon every dwelling-place of mount Zion a c. and smoke by day; 15: 6 (Isa. 5: 6) the Lord will command c. that they rain no rain; 24: 14 (Isa. 14: 14) the Lord will ascend above heights of c.; **Mosiah** 27: 11 angel descended as in c.; **Alma** 19: 6 light of God's glory dispels c. of darkness in Lamoni's mind; **Hel.** 5: 28 those in prison are overshadowed with c. of darkness; **3 Ne.** 18: 38 c. overshadows multitude, that they cannot see Jesus; **Ether** 2: 4–5, 14 the Lord speaks with brother of Jared[2] in c.

COAT (*see also* Clothing)

Alma 46: 12 Moroni[1] rends c. to make title of liberty; 46: 24 remnant of c. of Joseph[1] was preserved; **3 Ne.** 12: 40 (Matt. 5: 40) if any man will take away thy c., let him have thy cloak also.

COHOR[1]—*brother of Noah[2]*

Ether 7: 15 drawn away by brother.

COHOR[2]—*early Jaredite king*

Ether 7: 20 son of Noah[2], rules one of two kingdoms; 7: 21 slain by Shule in battle; 7: 22 father of Nimrod[2], who gives up kingdom.

COHOR[3]—*late Jaredite*

Ether 13: 17 sons and daughters of C. are unrepentant.

COIN (*see also* Amnor; Ezrom; Limnah; Money; Onti; Senine; Senum; Seon; Shiblon; Shiblum; Shum)

Alma 11: 1–9 Nephite c. and measures explained.

COM[1]—*early Jaredite king*

Ether 1: 26–27 (9: 25) father of Heth[1], son of Coriantum[1]; 9: 25 reigns in father's stead.

COM[2]—*late Jaredite king*

Ether 1: 12–13 (10: 31) son of Coriantum[2], father of Shiblon[1]; 10: 32 reigns over half of kingdom; 10: 33–34 fails to prevail over robbers; 11: 1 many prophets come in C's days; 11: 2–3 blessed for protecting prophets.

COMBINATION (*see* Secret Combination)

COME, CAME (*see also* Enter; Jesus Christ, First Coming of; Jesus Christ, Second Coming of)

1 Ne. 6: 4 intent of Nephi[1] to persuade men to c. unto God; 13: 40 all men must c. unto the Son, or they cannot be saved; **2 Ne.** 2: 10 because of intercession for all, all men c. unto God; 9: 45 c. unto that God who is rock of your salvation; 9: 51 (Omni 1: 26) c. unto the Holy One of Israel; 26: 33 the Lord invites all to c. to him, denies none that c.; 28: 32 the Lord will be merciful unto Gentiles if they repent and c. unto him; **Jacob** 6: 5 c. with full purpose of heart, and cleave unto God; **Alma** 5: 16 can you imagine hearing the Lord's voice say, C. unto me; 5: 34 c. unto me and ye shall partake of fruit of tree of life; 5:35 c. unto me and bring forth works of righteousness; 12: 15 we must c. forth and stand before God in his glory; **3 Ne.** 12: 3 (Matt. 5: 3) blessed are poor in spirit who c. unto the Lord; 12: 20 c. unto me and be ye saved; 12: 24 first be reconciled and c. unto me; 21: 27 work to commence among dispersed to prepare way whereby they may c. unto Christ; **Morm.** 9: 27 c. unto the Lord with all your heart; **Ether** 12: 27 if men will c. unto the Lord, he will show them their weaknesses; 13: 3 New Jerusalem to c. down out of heaven; **Moro.** 10: 32 c. unto Christ, and be perfected in him.

COMELY, COMELINESS (*see also* Beauty)

2 Ne. 14: 2 (Isa. 4: 2) fruit of earth shall be c. to them that are escaped of Israel; **Mosiah** 14: 2 (Isa. 53: 2) he hath no form nor c.; **Alma** 1: 27 Nephites do not wear costly apparel, yet they are neat and c.

COMFORT (*see also* Consolation; Holy Ghost—Comforter; Mourn; Rest)

2 Ne. 8: 12 I am he that c. you; **Mosiah** 12: 23 (15: 30; Alma 17: 10; 3 Ne. 16: 19; 20: 34; Isa. 52: 9) the Lord hath c. his people; 18: 9 those baptized should be willing to c. those in need of c.; **Alma** 31: 31 wilt thou c. my soul in Christ; **3 Ne.** 12: 4 (Matt. 5: 4) blessed are they that mourn, for they shall be c.; **Ether** 15: 3 soul of Coriantumr[2] refused to be c.

COMFORTER (*see* Holy Ghost–Comforter)

COMFORTER, SECOND (*see* TG Jesus Christ–Second Comforter)

COMING (*see* Jesus Christ, First Coming of; Jesus Christ, Second Coming of)

COMMAND (*see also* Commandments of God; Decree; Instruction; Require)

1 Ne. 17: 48 Nephi[1] c. brothers not to touch him; **Mosiah** 18: 19–24, 27, 29 Alma[1] c. priests how church should be administered; 27: 3 strict c. throughout all churches that there should be no persecution; **Alma** 11: 35–36 Zeezrom claims Amulek speaks as though he had authority to c. God; 37: 27 (Hel. 6: 25) Alma[2] c. Helaman[2] to retain secret oaths and covenants.

COMMANDER (*see also* Captain)

Alma 43: 44 Zerahemnah chief c. of Lamanites; 46: 11 Moroni[1] chief c. of Nephites; 47: 19 Amalickiah is appointed chief c. of Lamanites; **3 Ne.** 3: 18 Gidgiddoni, great c. of all Nephite armies; **Morm.** 3: 11 Mormon[2] refuses to be c. of Nephite armies.

COMMANDMENTS OF GOD (*see also* Decree; Forbid; Law; Law of Moses; Obedience; Precept; Require; Sayings; Scriptures; Statute; Ten Commandments; TG Commandments of God)

Title Page book written by way of c.; **1 Ne.** 2: 10 Lehi[1] prays that Laman[1] might be immovable as valley in keeping c.; 3: 7 I will go and do things that the Lord has c.; 3: 7 the Lord gives no c. save he prepares a way to accomplish it; 5: 21 brass plates enable people to preserve c. unto children; 15: 25 Nephi[1] exhorts brethren to remember God's c. always in all things; 17: 3 c. of God must be fulfilled; 22: 31 those who are obedient to c. shall be saved; **2 Ne.** 1: 9 (4: 4; Jarom 1: 9; Mosiah 2: 22, 31; Alma 9: 13; 50: 20) if those brought out of Jerusalem keep the Lord's c., they shall prosper; 2: 21 the Lord gives c. that all men must repent; 9: 27 wo unto him that has all c. of God and transgresses them; 25: 25 Nephites keep law of Moses because of the c.; 26: 24 the Lord c. none that they shall not partake of salvation; 26: 29 the Lord c. that there shall be no priestcrafts; 26: 32 the Lord has c. that men should not murder; 29: 11 the Lord c. all men to write words he speaks to them; 30: 1 except ye keep c. of God, ye shall perish; **Jacob** 2: 10 I must do according to strict c. of God; 2: 30 if the Lord will raise up seed, he will c. his people; 4: 6 our faith becometh unshaken insomuch that we can c. trees, mountains, waves to obey; **Mosiah** 2: 22 all that God requires of you is to keep his c.; 2: 41 consider the blessed and happy state of those who keep c. of God; 5: 5 Benjamin's people willing to be obedient in all things the Lord shall c.; 12: 33—13: 25 Abinadi reviews Ten C.; 18: 10 baptism a covenant to serve God and keep his c.; 23: 14 trust no man to be your teacher except he be a man of God, keeping his c.; **Alma** 5: 18 can ye imagine yourselves brought before God's tribunal with perfect remembrance that ye have set at defiance his c.; 5: 44 Alma[2] is c. to testify of things to come as spoken by fathers; 5: 61–62 I, Alma[2], c. you in language of him who hath c. me; 6: 6 children of God are c. to gather together oft; 12: 9 those who know mysteries are under strict c. to impart only that which God grants unto children of men; 12: 31–32 God gave c. to men, they having first transgressed the first c.; 12: 37 let us not provoke God to pull down his wrath upon us in these his second c.; 29: 9 I know that which the Lord has c. me; 37: 35 learn in thy youth to keep the c.; **Hel.** 4: 22 Nephites trample under feet that which the Lord c. Mosiah[1] to give them; 6: 31 more part of Nephites trample under feet the c. of God; 7: 7 in days of Nephi[1], the Lord's people were firm to keep c.; 14: 9–10 (3 Ne. 23: 9) the Lord c. Samuel the Lamanite to preach repentance; **3 Ne.** 15: 16, 18–19 Father c. Christ what to speak; 16: 4 (23: 13) Christ c. Nephites to write his sayings after he is gone; 16: 16 (20: 14) the Father c. Christ to give land for inheritance; 18: 3, 8, 12 the Lord gives c. to administer bread and wine to those who have repented and been baptized; 18: 27–28 the Lord gives c. not to suffer any one unknowingly to partake of bread and wine unworthily; 23: 14 Jesus c. Nephites to teach what he has expounded; 26: 2 the Father c. Christ to give Nephites scriptures they do not have; **Morm.** 5: 23 at God's great c., earth shall be rolled together as scroll; 7: 4 Lamanites should not take weapons of war save God c. them; **Ether** 4: 9 at Christ's c., inhabitants of earth shall pass away; **Moro.** 8: 25 baptism comes by faith unto fulfilling the c., which brings remission of sins.

COMMIT (*see* Adultery; Murder; Sin)

COMMON

Mosiah 29: 26 not c. that voice of

people desires anything contrary to what is right; **3 Ne.** 26: 19 (4 Ne. 1: 3, 25) Nephites have all things c. among them.

COMMUNICATION (*see also* Correspondence; Hearken; Heed; Language; Prayer; Speak; Think; Understand; Word; TG Communication)

3 Ne. 12: 37 let your c. be Yea, yea.

COMMUNION, COMMUNE (*see also* TG Sacrament; BD Communion)

Jarom 1: 4 as many as are not stiffnecked and have faith c. with Spirit.

COMNOR—*hill near Valley of Shur*

Ether 14: 28 Coriantumr[2] gathers armies near hill C.

COMPASS (*see* Liahona)

COMPASSION (*see also* Charity; God, Love of; Kindness; Love; Mercy; Pity; TG Compassion)

1 Ne. 21: 15 (Isa. 49: 15) can woman forget sucking child, that she have not c. on son of her womb; **Mosiah** 15: 9 the Son is filled with c. toward children of men; 19: 14 (20: 26) Lamanites have c. on people of Limhi; 23: 34 Lamanites have c. on Amulon and brethren; **Alma** 27: 4 Ammon[2] and brethren moved with c. by destruction among people; **3 Ne.** 17: 6 Christ's bowels are filled with c. toward Nephites; **Ether** 1: 35 the Lord had c. upon Jared[2].

COMPEL (*see also* Agency; Constrain; Dominion; Liberty)

Alma 32: 13–16 blessings of those who are humble because they are c. or are not c.; 42: 27 whosoever will not come to waters of life is not c. to come; 47: 3 Lamanite king commands Amalickiah to c. reluctant soldiers to arms; 51: 15, 20 Moroni[1] requests permission to c. dissenters to defend country; **3 Ne.** 2: 12 converted Lamanites are c. to take up arms against robbers; 12: 41 (Matt. 5: 41) whosoever shall c. thee to go a mile, go with him twain.

COMPLAIN (*see also* Murmur; Reproach)

1 Ne. 5: 2–3 Sariah c. against Lehi[1]; 17: 18 brethren c. against Nephi[1]; **Mosiah** 27: 1 church c. against leaders because of persecution; **Alma** 60: 4 were this all we had suffered we would not c.

COMPREHEND (*see also* God, Omniscience of; Know; Learn; Perceive; Understand)

Mosiah 4: 9 man doth not c. all things which the Lord can c.; **Alma** 26: 35 God c. all things; **Morm.** 9: 16 who can c. works of God.

CONCEIVE (*see also* Bear, Bore, Borne; TG Conceived in Sin)

2 Ne. 17: 14 (18: 3; Alma 7: 10; Isa. 7: 14; 8: 3) virgin shall c. and shall bear a son; **Mosiah** 15: 3 Christ is called Father because he was c. by power of God; **3 Ne.** 17: 17 hearts cannot c. marvelous things Nephites heard Jesus speak.

CONCUBINE (*see also* Adultery; Chastity; Wife; TG Concubine)

Jacob 1: 15 (2: 24) David and Solomon desired c.; 2: 27 Nephites not to have c.; 3: 5 Lamanites do not have c.; **Mosiah** 11: 2, 4, 14 Noah[3] has c.; **Ether** 10: 5 Riplakish has c.

CONDEMN, CONDEMNATION (*see also* Accuse; Judge [verb]; Spurn)

Title Page c. not the things of God; **2 Ne.** 7: 9 (Isa. 50: 9) all who c. God shall wax old as garment; 9: 25 where no punishment, there is no c.; 9: 25 where no c., mercies of Holy One have claim; 33: 14 (Alma 12: 14) words shall c. men at last day; **Mosiah** 4: 22 c. of those who withhold their substance will be just; 26: 31 he who forgives not brings himself under c.; **Alma** 3: 19 every man who is cursed brings upon himself his own c.; 41: 15 the word restoration more fully c. the sinner; 60: 2 Moroni[1] writes to civil leaders by way of c.; **Hel.** 7: 5 people c. the righteous because of their righteousness; 8: 1 wicked judges want to c. Nephi[2]; 14: 19 by knowing things and not doing them, men come under c.; 14: 29 those who do not believe bring upon themselves their own c.; **3 Ne.** 6: 22 people could be c. to death only with signature of governor; 6: 25 judges c. prophets to death; 22: 17 (Isa. 54: 17) every tongue that shall rise against thee in judgment thou shalt c.; **Morm.** 8: 12 record not to be c. because of imperfections; 9: 31 c. me not for my imperfection; **Moro.** 6: 7 three witnesses are needed to c. transgressor; 7: 19 lay hold upon every good thing and c. it not; 8: 22 he who is under no c. cannot repent; 9: 6 if we cease to labor, we will be brought under c.

CONDESCENSION (*see* Jesus Christ, Condescension of)

CONDUCT (*see* Lead)

CONFER (*see also* Give; Ordain; Ordinance)

Omni 1: 3 Omni c. plates upon Amaron; **Mosiah** 28: 20 Mosiah[2] c. records on Alma[2]; 29: 42 Alma[1] c. office of high priest upon Alma²; **Alma** 63: 11 Shiblon c. sacred things upon Helaman².

CONFESS (*see also* Acknowledge; Confession of Sins; TG Confess)

Jacob 7: 17 Sherem c. Christ; **Mosiah** 16: 1 every nation shall c. before God that his judgments are just; 26: 27 (Matt. 7: 23) the Lord will c. he never knew those who never knew him; 27: 31 every tongue shall c. before Redeemer; **Moro.** 7: 44 if man is meek and c. Christ, he must have charity.

CONFESSION OF SINS (*see also* Forgive; Humble; Repentance; TG Confession)

Mosiah 26: 29, 35 transgressor who c. his sins shall be forgiven; 26: 36 (Moro. 6: 7) those who do not c. sins are not numbered among church; **Alma** 17: 4 by power of words of sons of Mosiah² many Lamanites c. sins; **3 Ne.** 1: 25 Nephites come to knowledge of error and c. faults.

CONFIDENCE (*see also* Faith; Trust)

Jacob 2: 35 Nephites lose c. of children through bad example.

CONFIRM (*see also* Establish; Hands, Laying on of; Holy Ghost, Gift of; BD Confirmation)

Mosiah 27: 33 Alma² and sons of Mosiah² c. faith; **Morm.** 9: 25 unto whosoever believes in his name will the Lord c. his words.

CONFOUND (*see also* Rebuke)

1 Ne. 14: 2 (15: 20; Ether 13: 8; Moro. 10: 31) Israel shall no more be c.; 17: 52 Nephi¹ c. his brethren; 22: 5, 7 Israel shall be scattered and c.; 22: 22 the righteous shall not be c.; **2 Ne.** 3: 12 writing shall grow unto c. of false doctrines; 3: 14 they who seek to destroy latter-day seer shall be c.; **Jacob** 7: 8 Jacob² c. Sherem; **Omni** 1: 22 (Mosiah 28: 17; Ether 1: 33–37) the Lord c. language at time of tower; **Mosiah** 12: 19 Abinadi c. priests; **Alma** 32: 23 children given words that c. the wise; 37: 6–7 by small means the Lord c. the wise; **Hel.** 5: 17 Nephi² and Lehi⁴ c. dissenters; **Ether** 1: 34–37 the Lord does not c. language of Jared² and his family; 3: 24 the Lord c. language written by brother of Jared².

CONQUER, CONQUEROR (*see also* Overcome; Prevail; Subject; Win)

Jacob 7: 25 trusting in God, Nephites become c. of enemies; **Alma** 30: 17 Korihor claims every man c. according to his strength; 44: 8 if swords not taken, Lamanites will perish or c.; **Moro.** 9: 6 labor to c. enemy of all righteousness.

CONSCIENCE (*see also* Light; TG Conscience; BD Conscience)

Mosiah 2: 27 Benjamin teaches people so that he can answer God with clear c.; 4: 3 Benjamin's people have peace of c. because of faith in Christ; **Alma** 29: 5 to him who knows good and evil is given according to his desires, whether joy or remorse of c.; 42: 18 punishment and just law bring remorse of c.

CONSCIOUSNESS (*see also* Awake; Knowledge)

Alma 12: 1 (14: 6) Zeezrom trembles under c. of guilt; **Morm.** 9: 3–4 man cannot dwell with God under c. of guilt.

CONSECRATE (*see also* Anointing; Ordain; Sanctification)

2 Ne. 1: 7, 32 (3: 2; 10: 19) land is c. unto him whom the Lord brings to it; 2: 2 God shall c. thy afflictions for thy gain; 5: 26 (Jacob 1: 18) Nephi¹ c. Jacob² and Joseph² as priests; 32: 9 pray that the Father will c. thy performance unto thee; 33: 4 the Lord will c. prayers of Nephi¹ for gain of his people; **Mosiah** 2: 11 Benjamin c. by Mosiah¹; 6: 3 Benjamin c. Mosiah² to be ruler; 23: 17 Alma¹ c. just men as priests; **Alma** 5: 3 Alma¹ c. son, Alma², to be high priest; 15: 13 Alma² c. priests; 23: 4 Aaron³ and brethren c. priests among Lamanites.

CONSEQUENCES (*see also* Reward; Wages)

2 Ne. 9: 48 (Jacob 3: 12) because people are unholy, Jacob² must teach c. of sin.

CONSIDER (*see also* Think)

Mosiah 3: 9 his people shall c. Christ a man; **Hel.** 14: 16 by the fall, all mankind are c. dead, temporally and spiritually; **3 Ne.** 20: 45 (21: 8) that which kings had not heard shall they c.

CONSIGN (*see also* Condemn; Judgment)

Mosiah 3: 25 the evil are c. to awful view of own guilt; **Alma** 9: 11 except for God's power, man would be c. to state of endless misery; 26: 19 why did God not c. us to awful destruction; 28: 11 mourners fear that dead are c. to state of endless wo; 40: 26 wicked are c. to partake of fruits of their labors; 42: 1 Corianton supposes injustice that sinner is c. to state of misery; 42: 14 justice c. fallen mankind to be cut off; **Hel.** 12: 26 those cast off shall be c. to state of endless misery.

CONSOLATION, CONSOLE (*see also* Comfort)

Jacob 3: 1 God will c. you in your

afflictions; Mosiah 27: 33 Alma[2] and sons of Mosiah[2] impart c. to church; **Alma** 56: 11 we may c. ourselves that we have died in cause of country and God; **Hel.** 3: 35 firmer faith in Christ fills souls with joy and c.

CONSTRAIN, CONSTRAINT (*see also* Compel)

1 Ne. 4: 10 Nephi[1] is c. by Spirit to kill Laban; 7: 15 (2 Ne. 4: 14; 28: 1) Spirit c. Nephi[1] to speak; **Alma** 14: 11 Spirit c. Alma[2] not to stretch forth hand on behalf of martyrs; **4 Ne.** 1: 48 Ammaron is c. by Spirit to hide up records.

CONSUME, CONSUMING, CONSUMPTION (*see also* Devour; Eat)

1 Ne. 17: 48 Nephi[1] is filled with power of God, even unto c. of flesh; 22: 23 churches built up for gain will be c. as stubble; **2 Ne.** 4: 21 God has filled Lehi[1] with his love, even unto c. of flesh; 26: 6 the wicked shall be c.; 26: 7 loss of the slain well nigh c. Nephi[1] before presence of the Lord; 27: 31 the scorner is c.; **Alma** 5: 52 tree that bringeth not forth good fruit will be cast into fire which cannot be c.

CONTENTION, CONTEND (*see also* Devil; Disputations; Dissension; Doctrine, False; Hardheartedness; Murmur; Prophets, False; Quarrel; Rebel; Stir; Strife; TG Contention)

1 Ne. 9: 4 (19:4) account of c. of people engraven on other plates; 12: 3 (Jarom 1: 13) Nephi[1] beholds many generations pass away after manner of wars and c.; 21: 25 (2 Ne. 6: 17; Isa. 49: 25) the Lord will c. with him who c. with Israel; **2 Ne.** 26: 2 (4 Ne. 1: 24–39) several generations after Christ's visit, wars and c. arise; 26: 32 the Lord commands that men not c. one with another; 28: 4 churches shall c. one with another; **Omni** 1: 17 Mulekites had had many wars and serious c.; **W of M** 1: 12 Benjamin had somewhat of c. among his own people; **Mosiah** 2: 32 beware lest c. arise among you; 9: 13 Laman[2] stirs up Lamanites to wars and c. with people of Zeniff; 18: 21 Alma[1] commands no c. among church members; 29: 7 Mosiah[2] fears that giving kingdom to someone other than son might raise c.; **Alma** 2: 5 people have much dispute and wonderful c. regarding Amlici; 4: 9 great c. arise among people of church; 19: 28 c. regarding Ammon[2] among household of Lamanite king; 34: 38 Amulek admonishes people not to c. against Holy Ghost; 50: 25 c. among Nephites concerning land of Lehi; 51: 9 critical time for c. because Amalickiah stirs up Lamanites; **Hel.** 16: 22 Satan spreads rumors and c.; **3 Ne.** 2: 11 wars and c. throughout land because of Gadianton robbers; 11: 29 devil is father of c., stirs up men to c. with anger; **4 Ne.** 1: 2, 13, 15, 18 no c. in land because of love of God; **Ether** 4: 8 he who c. against word of the Lord will be accursed; 11: 7 wars and c. among Jaredites because of wicked combinations.

CONTINUE, CONTINUATION (*see also* Endure; Eternal Life; Faint; Increase)

2 Ne. 33: 9 c. in path until end of day of probation; **Jacob** 6: 11 c. in the way which is narrow; **Ether** 2: 11 people to know God's decrees, that they may not c. in iniquities.

CONTRARY

Mosiah 2: 36 if men go c. to what they have been taught, they withdraw themselves from Spirit; 29: 26 not common that voice of people desireth anything c. to that which is right; **Alma** 11: 22 Amulek will say nothing c. to the Spirit of the Lord; **Hel.** 8: 3 Nephi[2] speaks nothing c. to God's commandments; 10: 5 Nephi[2] will not seek that which is c. to the Lord's will; 13: 38 to seek happiness in doing iniquity is c. to nature of righteousness of God; 16: 12 people begin to do more of that which is c. to God's commandments.

CONTRITE (*see* Broken Heart and Contrite Spirit; Meek; TG Contrite Heart)

CONTROVERSY (*see* Contention; Disputations)

CONVERSION, CONVERT (*see also* Baptism; Born of God; Change; Convince; Fire; Heart; Holy Ghost; Repentance; TG Conversion, Convert; BD Conversion)

1 Ne. 2: 16 c. of Nephi[1]; **2 Ne.** 16: 10 (Isa. 6: 10) make the heart of this people fat lest they be c. and healed; **Jacob** 7: 7 Sherem claims Nephites c. law of Moses into worship of being which shall come many hundred years hence; **Enos** 1: 2–4 c. of Enos; **Mosiah** 5: 1–5 c. of King Benjamin's people; 18: 1 (Alma 5: 11) c. of Alma[1]; 18: 7–11 c. of people of Alma[1]; 25: 14–17 c. of Limhi; 27: 11–32 (Alma 36: 6–24) c. of Alma[2]; 27: 33–35 c. of sons of Mosiah[2]; **Alma** 5: 12–14, 26 c. of people of Zarahemla; 15: 5–12 c. of Zeezrom; 18: 40–41 c. of Lamoni; 19: 16–17 c. of Abish; 22: 15 c. of Lamoni's father; 22: 23 c. of Lamoni's household; 23: 14 only one Amalekite is c.; 53: 10 people of Ammon[2] are c. by word and power of God; **Hel.** 5: 49–50 (6: 3) c. of Lamanites; **3 Ne.** 1: 22 notwithstanding Satan's lyings, most Nephites are c. unto the Lord; 7: 21 those who are c. have been visited by Spirit; 7: 26 (28: 23; 4 Ne. 1: 2) c. of Nephites; 9: 13 be c. that the Lord may heal you; 15: 22 Gentiles to be *c.* through preaching of Jews.

CONVINCE, CONVINCING (*see also* Conversion; Persuade; Witness; BD Convince)

Title Page (2 Ne. 25: 18; 26: 12) Book of Mormon written to the *c.* of Jew and Gentile that Jesus is the Christ; **Alma** 21: 17 (24: 7; 26: 24; 37: 9; Hel. 5: 19) Nephite missionaries *c.* many Lamanites of wickedness of fathers' traditions; 37: 8–9 records *c.* many of error of their ways; **3 Ne.** 1: 25 those who preached to no longer observe law of Moses are *c.* of error.

COPPER (*see also* Metal; Ore)

1 Ne. 18: 25 (2 Ne. 5: 15; Jarom 1: 8; Mosiah 11: 3, 8, 10) Nephites use *c.*; **Mosiah** 8: 10 (Ether 10: 23) Jaredites use *c.*

CORD (*see also* Band)

1 Ne. 7: 16 (18: 11) brethren of Nephi[1] bind him with *c.*; **2 Ne.** 26: 22 devil leads the wicked by neck with flaxen *c.*; **Alma** 14: 4, 22–23, 26 Alma[2] and Amulek bound with *c.*; 62: 21, 23 Moroni[1] has army prepare *c.* and ladders to enter city; **3 Ne.** 22: 2 (Isa. 54: 2) lengthen thy *c.* and strengthen thy stakes.

CORIANTON—*son of Alma*[2] [c. 75 B.C.]

Alma 31: 7 goes to Zoramites; 39: 3 had forsaken ministry to go after harlot; 39: 11 because of C's conduct, Zoramites do not believe words of Alma[2]; ch. 39–42 Alma[2] instructs C. on state of soul after death, on resurrection, probation, redemption, justice, atonement, repentance, and agency; 42: 31 is called to preach again; 63: 10 sails northward.

CORIANTOR—*a late Jaredite*

Ether 1: 6–7 (11: 18, 23) son of Moron; 11: 19 lives in captivity; 11: 20 many prophets in C's days.

CORIANTUM[1]—*early Jaredite king*

Ether 1: 27–28 (9: 21–25) son of Emer, father of Com[1]; 9: 21 is anointed king; 9: 23 righteous reign, great builder; 9: 24 begets sons and daughters, lives to 142 years.

CORIANTUM[2]—*middle Jaredite*

Ether 1: 13–14 (10: 31) son of Amnigaddah, father of Com[2]; 10: 31 lives in captivity.

CORIANTUMR[1]—*early Jaredite*

Ether 8: 4 son of Omer; 8: 5–6 restores kingdom to father, spares brother.

CORIANTUMR[2]—*Jaredite king, last Jaredite survivor*

Omni 1: 21 discovered by people of Zarahemla; **Ether** 12: 1–2 king over all land in days of Ether; 13: 15 many seek to destroy C.; 13: 16 skilled in warfare; 13: 20 warned by Ether; 13: 21 to be buried by another people; 13: 23 captured by Shared; 13: 24 liberated by sons; 13: 28–31 meets Shared in battle, wounded; 14: 3–5 battles with brother of Shared; 14: 6 C's throne is taken by Gilead; 14: 12 battles with Lib[2]; 14: 14–15 is pursued to Agosh; 14: 16 slays Lib[2], battles with Shiz; 14: 17 flees from Shiz; 14: 24 not to fall by sword; 14: 30 wounded by Shiz; 15: 3 repents; 15: 4, 18 writes to Shiz; 15: 11 camps at hill Ramah; 15: 13 is watched by Ether; 15: 15 final battle; 15: 30 slays Shiz; 15: 32 falls wounded.

CORIANTUMR[3]—*apostate Nephite, commander of Lamanite forces* [c. 51 B.C.]

Hel. 1: 15 descendant of Zarahemla, Nephite dissenter; 1: 17 leads Lamanites against Zarahemla; 1: 20 takes Zarahemla; 1: 21 kills judge; 1: 23 marches toward Bountiful; 1: 30 is killed; 1: 32 C's army is captured.

CORIHOR[1]—*early Jaredite rebel*

Ether 7: 3 son of Kib; 7: 4 rebels against father; 7: 5 takes father captive; 7: 9 brother, Shule, restores kingdom to Kib; 7: 13 repents and gains favor.

CORIHOR[2]—*late Jaredite*

Ether 13: 17 sons and daughters of C. repent not.

CORIHOR, LAND AND VALLEY OF—*Jaredite area*

Ether 14: 27–28 scene of battles of Coriantumr[2] with Shiz.

COROM—*middle Jaredite king*

Ether 1: 19–20 (10: 15–16) son of Levi[2], father of Kish; 10: 16 anointed king; 10: 17 righteous ruler, succeeded by son.

CORRESPONDENCE (*see also* Communication)

Alma 23: 18 (24: 8–9) Anti-Nephi-Lehies open *c.* with Nephites; 31: 4 Nephites fear Zoramites will enter *c.* with Lamanites.

CORRUPT, CORRUPTION (*see also* Canker; Corruptness; Defile; Filthiness; Pervert; Pollute; Unclean; Wickedness)

2 Ne. 2: 11 without opposition, body must remain as dead, having neither *c.* nor incorruption; 9: 7 without infinite atonement, *c.* could not put on incorruption; 9: 51 feast upon that which cannot be *c.*; 28: 11–12 churches will become *c.*; **Jacob** 5: 39 fruit of natural branches become *c.*; 5: 42, 46–48 fruit of vineyard has become *c.*; 5: 75 vineyard is no more *c.*; **Omni** 1: 17 language of Mulekites had become *c.*; **Mosiah** 16: 10 this *c.* shall put on incorruption; 29: 40 Mosiah² does not seek lucre which *c.* soul; **Alma** 5: 15 do you view this *c.* raised in incorruption; 40: 2 this *c.* does not put on incorruption until after resurrection of Christ; 41: 4 all things shall be restored to proper order, *c.* to incorruption; **Hel.** 4: 22 laws of Nephites had become *c.*; 8: 25 (3 Ne. 13: 20) nothing *c.* treasures of heaven; **3 Ne.** 13: 19–20 (Matt. 6: 19–20) lay not up for yourselves treasures upon earth, where moth and rust *c.*; 14: 17–18 (Matt. 7: 17–18) *c.* tree brings forth evil fruit; **Morm.** 6: 21 bodies moldering in *c.* must soon become incorruptible bodies; **Ether** 9: 6 wicked and secret society *c.* hearts of Jaredites.

CORRUPTNESS (*see also* Corrupt)

Hel. 8: 3 Nephi² speaks of *c.* of laws.

COSTLY, COSTLINESS (*see* Apparel; Pride)

COUNCIL

Alma 52: 19 chief captains hold *c.* of war; **3 Ne.** 12: 22 (Matt. 5: 22) whosoever shall say unto his brother, Raca, shall be in danger of *c.*

COUNSEL (*see also* Guide; Instruction; God, Wisdom of)

1 Ne. 19: 7 men hearken not to voice of God's *c.*; **2 Ne.** 9: 28 when men are learned, they think they are wise and hearken not unto God's *c.*; 9: 29 to be learned is good, if they hearken to *c.* of God; 27: 27 (28: 9) wo unto them that seek deep to hide their *c.* from the Lord; 28: 30 blessed are those who lend ear unto the Lord's *c.*; **Jacob** 4: 10 seek not to *c.* the Lord, but to take *c.* from his hand; **Alma** 29: 8 (37: 12) the Lord *c.* in wisdom; 37: 37 *c.* with the Lord in all thy doings; 39: 10 Corianton is commanded to *c.* with elder brothers; **Hel.** 12: 5 how slow are men to give ear unto the Lord's *c.*; 12: 6 notwithstanding God's goodness and mercy, men set at naught his *c.*

COUNSELOR

2 Ne. 19: 6 (Isa. 9: 6) Messiah's name shall be called, Wonderful, C.

COUNTENANCE (*see also* Face; Visage)

2 Ne. 13: 9 (Isa. 3: 9) show of their *c.* witnesses against them; **Alma** 5: 14, 19 have ye received God's image in your *c.*; **3 Ne.** 13: 16 (Matt. 6: 16) when ye fast, be not as the hypocrites, of sad *c.*; 19: 25 light of Jesus' *c.* smiles upon disciples.

COUNTRY, COUNTRIES (*see also* Government, Civil; Land; Nation; North)

Alma 43: 26, 47 (56: 11; 58: 8; 61: 6; Hel. 4: 7; Morm. 5: 4) Nephites fight to defend *c.*; 48: 11–13 (60: 36) Moroni¹ swears oath to defend freedom of *c.*; 51: 13, 15, 20 (62: 9–10) dissenters are compelled to defend *c.*; 53: 13, 18 (56: 5) Ammonites desire to take up arms in defense of *c.*; 60: 28 according to God's commandments, Moroni¹ takes sword to defend *c.*

COURAGE (*see also* Faith; Fear; Strength; Valiant)

Alma 15: 4 Zeezrom's heart begins to take *c.*; 53: 20 (56: 45) 2,000 stripling warriors are exceedingly valiant for *c.*; 62: 19 because of Nephites' *c.*, Lamanites dare not come to battle.

COURSE (*see also* Direction; Lead; Path)

1 Ne. 10: 19 (Alma 7: 20; 37: 12) *c.* of the Lord is one eternal round; **Mosiah** 7: 4 Nephite expedition knows not *c.* to travel in wilderness; **Alma** 37: 42 Lehites do not travel direct *c.*, because of transgressions; 37: 44–45 (Hel. 3: 29) word of Christ points straight *c.* to eternal bliss.

COVENANT (*see also* Abraham; Abrahamic Covenant; Baptism; Chosen; Gospel; Inherit; Israel; Oath; Promise; Promised Land; Sacrament; TG Covenants; Priesthood, Oath and Covenant; Seed of Abraham; BD Abrahamic Covenant; Covenant)

1 Ne. 13: 23 book is record of Jews, contains *c.* of the Lord; 13: 26 abominable church takes away from gospel many *c.*; 14: 14 power of the Lamb descends upon *c.* people of the Lord; 15: 18 (3 Ne. 15: 8; 16: 5, 11–12; 20: 12, 25–27, 29; 21: 7; Morm. 5: 20; 8: 23; 9: 37; Ether 4: 15; 13: 11) *c.* made to Abraham to be fulfilled in latter days; 17: 40 the Lord *c.* with Abraham, Isaac, Jacob; 17: 40 the Lord remembered *c.* made to fathers and brought them out of Egypt; 19: 15 when Jews no more turn aside hearts from Holy One, he will remember *c.* made to fathers; 22: 9 marvelous work among Gentiles shall make known Father's *c.* unto Abraham; **2 Ne.** 1: 5 the Lord *c.* with Nephi¹ that land should be inheritance to his seed; 6: 12 if Gentiles fight not against Zion, the Lord will fulfill *c.* made unto his children; 9: 1 Jacob² reads Isaiah¹ that brethren might know the Lord's *c.* with Israel; 10: 7 Christ has *c.* with fathers that Jews will be restored to lands of inheritance when they believe in him; 10: 15 the Lord must destroy secret works of darkness so c. may be fulfilled; 11: 5 Jacob[2] delights in c. of the Lord made unto fathers; 29: 1 the Lord will do marvelous work, that he may remember c.; 29: 4 Jews are the Lord's ancient c. people; 29: 14 (3 Ne. 20: 25, 27) the Lord c. with Abraham to remember his seed forever; **Mosiah** 5: 5 Benjamin's people are willing to enter c. with God to do his will; 18: 13 baptism a testimony that man has entered c. to serve God; **Alma** 24: 18 Ammonites c. to give own lives rather than shed blood; 37: 27 Helaman[1] to hold back c. of secret combinations; 43: 11 (24: 15–18; 56: 6) Ammonites enter c. not to take up arms; 46: 20 those who will maintain title of liberty should enter c. to maintain their rights; 51: 6 freemen c. to maintain rights of religion by free government; 53: 16–18 sons of Ammonites enter c. to fight for liberty of Nephites; **Hel.** 6: 21–26 (3 Ne. 6: 28–29) robbers enter c. to protect and preserve one another; 6: 26–30 (3 Ne. 6: 28) secret oaths and c. are handed down by Satan; **3 Ne.** 5: 4–5 (6: 3) robbers who enter c. to murder no more are set at liberty; 6: 27–29 (7: 11) judges, lawyers, high priests enter c. to combine against all righteousness, destroy government; 20: 26 ye are children of c.; 21: 4 Gentiles to be established as free people in land so that c. unto Israel may be fulfilled; 22: 10 c. of peace shall not be removed; **Moro.** 7: 31–32 angels do work of c. of the Father; 10: 33 Christ's blood is in c. of the Father unto remission of sins.

COVET, COVETOUSNESS (*see also* Desire; Envy; Jealous; Lust; TG Covet, Covetousness)

Mosiah 4: 25 your condemnation is just for ye c. that which ye have not received; 13: 24 (Ex. 20: 17; Deut. 5: 21) thou shalt not c. thy neighbor's house, wife.

COW (*see also* Animal; Cattle)

1 Ne. 18: 25 Lehites find c. in wilderness; **2 Ne.** 21: 7 (30: 13; Isa. 11: 7) c. and bear shall feed; **Ether** 9: 18 Jaredites have c.

CRAFTINESS, CRAFT (*see also* Art; Cunning; Deceit; Guile; Profession; Skill; Subtlety)

Mosiah 7: 21 (9: 10; 10: 18) Zeniff deceived by c. of King Laman[2]; **Alma** 4: 19 Alma[2] seeks to pull down, by word of God, the c. among his people; 12: 3 Zeezrom taken in lying and c.; 35: 3 Amulek's words destroy c. of Zoramites; **Hel.** 2: 4 Gadianton exceedingly expert in his c. of murder and robbery.

CREATION, CREATE (*see also* Adam; Beginning; Creature; Earth; Framed [verb]; God—Creator; Heaven; Jesus Christ—Creator; Make; Man; Work [noun]; World; TG Creation, Create; Earth, Purpose of; Man, Physical Creation of; Spirit Creation)

1 Ne. 5: 11 books of Moses give account of c. of world; 17: 36 the Lord has c. earth that it should be inhabited; **2 Ne.** 1: 10 those coming from Jerusalem have received great blessings, having knowledge of c.; 2: 12–13 there would have been no purpose in end of its c.; 2: 14 (Alma 18: 28; 22: 10; Morm. 9: 11) God has c. all things; 11: 7 if there be no God, there could have been no c.; 29: 7 the Lord has c. all men; Jacob 2: 21 God has c. all flesh that they should keep his commandments and glorify him forever; 4: 9 earth c. by power of God's word; **Mosiah** 2: 20–24 God hath c. you and granted unto you your lives; 2: 25 ye were c. of dust of earth; 4: 9 believe in God, that he c. all things; 7: 27 God to take upon himself the image after which man was c. in beginning; 28: 17 (Ether 1: 3) Jaredite records give account of people back to c. of Adam; **Alma** 18: 36 Ammon[2] teaches Lamoni, beginning at c. of world; 22: 12–13 Aaron[2] begins from c. of Adam, reading scriptures to Lamanite king; **3 Ne.** 9: 15 Christ c. heavens and earth; **Morm.** 9: 12 God c. Adam; **Ether** 3: 15–16 all men were c. in beginning after the Lord's own image; **Moro.** 10: 3 remember how merciful the Lord has been, from c. of Adam to present.

CREATOR (*see* God—Creator; Jesus Christ—Creator)

CREATURE

Mosiah 28: 3 sons of Mosiah[2] desire that gospel be declared to every c.; **Alma** 42: 21–22 mercy claims repentance, otherwise justice claims the c.; **Morm.** 9: 22 (Matt. 28: 19) go ye into all the world, and preach the gospel to every c.

CRIME (*see also* Law; Law, Civil; Offense; Punishment; Sin; Transgression)

Jacob 2: 9 Jacob[2] is constrained to admonish people according to c.; 2: 22–23 Jacob must speak concerning grosser c. than pride—whoredom; **Mosiah** 26: 11 unbelievers are brought before Alma[1] to be judged according to c.; 29: 15 he who commits iniquity is punished according to c.; **Alma** 10: 13 people seek to slay or imprison Alma[2] and Amulek according to c. they could make appear against them; 30: 17 Korihor claims that whatsoever a man does is not c.; 39: 7 I would not dwell upon your c. to harrow up your soul if it were not for your good; 39: 8 ye cannot hide your c. from God; 50: 39 chief judge takes oath to bring the wicked to justice according to c.; **3 Ne.** 6: 26 judges who condemned prophets to be judged of c. according to law.

CRISIS

Alma 34: 34 ye cannot say, when ye are brought to that awful c., I will repent.

CROOKED (*see also* Straight)

Alma 7: 20 God cannot walk in c. paths.

CROP (*see also* Grain)

Alma 34: 24 cry unto God over c. of fields.

CROSS (*see also* Jesus Christ, Death of)

2 Ne. 9: 18 righteous saints who have endured c. of world shall inherit kingdom of God; **Jacob** 1: 8 we would to God that all men would believe in Christ and suffer his c.; **Mosiah** 12: 19 priests question Abinadi that they might c. him; **Alma** 10: 16 lawyers question Amulek that they might make him c. his words; 39: 9 c. yourself in all these things; **Hel.** 9: 19 judges question Alma[2] that they might c. him; **3 Ne.** 12: 30 better to deny yourselves of these things, wherein ye take up your c.

CRUCIFIXION, CRUCIFY (*see* Cross; Jesus Christ, Death of)

CRY (*see also* Lament; Mourn; Plead; Prayer; Wail; Weep)

1 Ne. 2: 16 (17: 7; 2 Ne. 5: 1; 33: 3) Nephi[1] c. unto the Lord; 10: 7–8 prophet to prepare way before Messiah, c. in wilderness; **2 Ne.** 26: 3 (28: 10; Morm. 8: 27) blood of saints shall c. to God from ground; 33: 13 I speak unto you as voice of one c. from dust; **Enos** 1: 4 Enos[2] c. unto his Maker in mighty prayer; **Mosiah** 11: 24 except they repent, the Lord will be slow to hear his people's c.; 21: 14 Limhi's people c. mightily to God to deliver them out of afflictions; **Alma** 9: 26 Son quick to hear c. of his people; 31: 27 Zoramites c. unto God, but hearts are swallowed up in pride; 34: 20–25 c. unto God over household, against enemies and devil, over crops and flocks; 34: 27 when ye do not c. unto God, let your hearts be full; 36: 18 Alma[2] c. within his heart unto Jesus; 37: 36 c. unto God for all thy support; 43: 49–50 Nephites c. unto the Lord for liberty and freedom from bondage; **Morm.** 3: 2 c. unto this people, Repent ye; **Ether** 12: 3 Ether c. from morning to sunset, exhorting people to believe in God; 15: 16 great were Jaredites' c. for loss of the slain; **Moro.** 9: 15 my heart c., Wo unto this people.

CUMENI, CITY OF—*Nephite city to southwest*

Alma 56: 13–14 captured by Lamanites; 57: 7–8, 12 recaptured by Helaman[1]; 57: 23 retained; 57: 31 Lamanites march toward; 57: 34 is preserved.

CUMENIHAH—*Nephite commander* [c. A.D. 385]

Morm. 6: 14 fell with his ten thousand.

CUMMOMS—*unidentified animals* (*see also* Animal)

Ether 9: 19 useful to man, abundant in days of Emer.

CUMORAH, LAND AND HILL OF (*see also* Ramah, Hill)

Morm. 6: 2–4 Nephites gather at C.; 6: 4 land of many waters; 6: 5 Nephites at C. by A.D. 385; 6: 6 records hidden; 6: 11 all but 24 Nephites slain at C.; 8: 2 aftermath of battle.

CUNNING (*see also* Craftiness; Deceit; Device; Lying; Subtlety; Wiles)

2 Ne. 9: 28 O that c. plan of the evil one; **Mosiah** 24: 7 Lamanites begin to be c. and wise people; **Alma** 2: 2 by c., Amlici draws away many; 10: 13, 15 lawyers try to catch Alma[2] and Amulek by c. devices; 28: 13 power of devil comes by c.; 46: 10 (51: 27) Amalickiah a man of c. device; **Hel.** 3: 29 word of God shall divide c. of devil; 16: 21 the hardhearted fear they will work some great mystery by c. of evil one; **3 Ne.** 21: 10 Father will show that his wisdom is greater than c. of devil.

CUP (*see also* Drink)

2 Ne. 8: 17 Jerusalem has drunk c. of the Lord's fury; **Mosiah** 3: 26 (5: 5) the evil will drink out of c. of God's wrath; **Alma** 40: 26 the wicked drink dregs of bitter c.; **3 Ne.** 11: 11 Christ has drunk out of bitter c. which the Father gave him; 18: 8 disciples commanded to take wine of c. and drink it; **Moro.** 5: 1 those administering sacrament should take c. and offer prayer.

CURE (*see also* Heal; Restoration, Restore)

Mosiah 3: 5 the Lord will come down among men and c. all manner of diseases; 28: 2 sons of Mosiah[2] seek to c. Lamanites of hatred; **3 Ne.** 26: 15 Christ does all manner of c. among Nephites.

CURELOMS—*unidentified animals* (*see also* Animal)

Ether 9: 19 useful to man, abundant in days of Emer.

CURIOUS (*see* Workmanship)

CURSE, CURSING (*see also* Accursed;

Cursed [adj.]; Destruction; Insect; Mark; Punishment; TG Curse)

1 Ne. 2: 23 the Lord will *c.* brothers of Nephi[1] because of rebellion; 17: 35 the Lord *c.* land against house of Israel because of iniquity; **2 Ne.** 1: 7 (Jacob 2: 29; Hel. 13: 17–19, 23, 30, 35; Morm. 1: 17–18; Ether 14: 1) land is *c.* because of people's wickedness; 4: 6 *c.* to be taken from grandchildren of Lehi[1] and answered upon parents' heads; 5: 21–24 (Jacob 3: 3, 5; Alma 3: 6) the Lord causes sore *c.* to come upon Lamanites' skin because of iniquity; 29: 5 Gentiles have *c.* Jews; **Jacob** 2: 33 the Lord will visit with sore *c.* those who lead away captive the daughters of his people; **Alma** 17: 15 *c.* had fallen upon Lamanites because of traditions of fathers; 23: 18 (3 Ne. 2: 15) *c.* of God no more follows Lamanites; 30: 50, 53–56 Korihor brought upon himself the *c.* of being stricken dumb; 45: 16 this is the *c.* and blessing of God upon the land; 49: 27 Amalickiah *c.* God; **3 Ne.** 3: 24 great *c.* upon land northward; 25: 6 (Mal. 4: 6) Elijah shall turn hearts of fathers and children to each other lest earth be smitten with *c.*; **Ether** 14: 1 great *c.* upon land because of Jaredites' iniquity; **Moro.** 8: 8 *c.* of Adam is taken from little children in Christ; 8: 24 repentance is made unto them who are under *c.* of broken law.

CURSED [adj.] (*see also* Accursed; Curse)

2 Ne. 1: 7 (Jacob 2: 29) if iniquity abound, *c.* be land for people's sake; 4: 34 (28: 31) *c.* is he who puts trust in arm of flesh; 5: 23 *c.* shall be seed of him who mixes with Lamanites' seed; **Alma** 32: 19 how much more *c.* is he who knows God's will and does it not; 37: 31 *c.* be land forever unto workers of darkness; **Hel.** 13: 19–21 *c.* are people because they set hearts upon riches.

CURTAIN (*see also* Veil)

3 Ne. 22: 2 (Isa. 54: 2) let them stretch forth the *c.* of thy habitations.

CUSTOM (*see also* Tradition)

Alma 8: 7 *c.* of Nephites to call lands, cities, villages after him who first possessed them; 17: 20 Lamanite *c.* to bind all Nephites who fall into their hands; 47: 17 *c.* among Lamanites, if chief leader killed, to appoint second leader as chief; **3 Ne.** 3: 19 *c.* among Nephites to appoint as chief captains men who have spirit of revelation.

CUT (*see also* Blot; Cast; Excommunication; God, Presence of; Hew; Prune)

1 Ne. 2: 21 (2 Ne. 5: 20) if brothers of Nephi[1] rebel, they shall be *c.* off from the Lord's presence; 16: 2 truth *c.* the guilty to center; 22: 19 all who fight against Zion shall be *c.* off; **2 Ne.** 1: 20 (4: 4; Alma 9: 13–14; 36: 30; 37: 13; 38: 1; 50: 20; Hel. 12: 21) if people do not keep commandments, they shall be *c.* off from the Lord's presence; 2: 5 by law men are *c.* off; 27: 31 all who watch for iniquity shall be *c.* off; **Alma** 42: 6 Adam and Eve *c.* off from tree of life; 42: 7 Adam and Eve *c.* off temporally and spiritually from presence of the Lord; **3 Ne.** 21: 13–17 (Micah 5: 8–13) all Israel's enemies shall be *c.* off; 21: 20 whosoever will not repent and come unto Son will the Lord *c.* off; **Ether** 2: 15 if ye will sin until fully ripe ye shall be *c.* off from the Lord's presence; **Moro.** 8: 14 man who thinks little children need baptism to be *c.* off.

DAMNATION, DAMNED (*see also* Condemn, Condemnation; Death, Spiritual; Hell; Punishment; Torment; BD Damnation)

2 Ne. 9: 24 (3 Ne. 11: 34; Morm. 9: 23; Ether 4: 18) if men will not repent, believe in Christ's name, be baptized, and endure to end, they must be *d.*; **Mosiah** 2: 33 (3: 25) if man obeys evil spirit and dies in sins, he drinketh *d.* to his soul; 3: 18 men bring *d.* to their souls except they humble themselves; 16: 11 to be delivered up to devil is *d.*; **Alma** 9: 28 if men have been evil, they shall reap *d.* of their souls; 36: 16 Alma[2] was wracked with pains of *d.* soul; **Hel.** 12: 26 they who have done evil shall have everlasting death; **3 Ne.** 18: 29 whoso eateth and drinketh Christ's flesh and blood unworthily eateth and drinketh *d.* to his soul; 26: 5 if men be evil, they are brought forth to resurrection of *d.*; **Morm.** 2: 13 Nephites' sorrowing is sorrowing of the *d.*; 8: 33 why have ye transfigured the holy word of God, that ye might bring *d.* upon your souls.

DANCE, DANCING (*see also* BD Dancing)

1 Ne. 18: 9 followers of Lehi[1] begin to make merry, *d.*, sing; **Mosiah** 20: 1 daughters of Lamanites gather themselves together to sing, *d.*; **Ether** 8: 10 daughter of Jared[2] will *d.* before Akish.

DANGER (*see also* Threaten)

3 Ne. 12: 21 (Matt. 5: 21) he who kills shall be in *d.* of judgment; 12: 22 (Matt. 5: 22) he who says, Thou fool, shall be in *d.* of hell fire; **Morm.** 8: 17 he who condemns should be aware lest he be in *d.* of hell fire; **Moro.** 8: 20–21 he who says little children need baptism is in *d.* of hell.

DARK, DARKEN (*see* Darkness, Physical; Darkness, Spiritual; Light)

DARKNESS, PHYSICAL (*see also* Black; Darkness, Spiritual; Light; Night; Skin)

1 Ne. 8: 4, 7–8 in dream, Lehi[1] travels in *d.*; 12: 4–5 (19: 11) mist of *d.* to cover land at Christ's death; 12: 23 (Alma 3: 6; Morm. 5: 15) Lamanites become *d.* and loathsome people; 19: 10 (Hel. 14: 20, 27; 3 Ne. 8: 3, 19–23; 10: 9) three days of *d.* to be sign of Christ's death; **Jacob** 3: 9 commandment not to revile against Lamanites because of *d.* of skins; **Hel.** 5: 28–43 cloud of *d.* overshadows prison of Nephi[2] and Lehi[4]; 14: 3–4 (3 Ne. 1: 15, 19) no *d.* in night before Christ's birth; **3 Ne.** 10: 12–13 more righteous part of people are not overpowered by vapor of *d.*; **Ether** 6: 3 the Lord causes stones to shine in *d.*

DARKNESS, SPIRITUAL (*see also* Apostasy; Blindness; Ignorance; Light; Mist; Night; Obscurity; Sin; Spirit World; Wicked, Wickedness; Withdraw; TG Darkness, Spiritual; Walking in Darkness; BD Darkness)

1 Ne. 8: 23–24 (12: 17) mist of *d.* in dream of Lehi[1] is temptations of devil; 21: 9 go forth to them that sit in *d.*; 22: 12 Israel shall be brought out of obscurity and *d.*; **2 Ne.** 3: 5 Messiah to be made manifest unto branch of Israel to bring them out of hidden *d.* unto light; 10: 15 the Lord will destroy secret works of *d.*; 15: 20 (Isa. 5: 20) wo unto them that put *d.* for light and light for *d.*; 26: 10 because the Lord's people choose *d.* rather than light, they must go down to hell; 26: 23 God works not in *d.*; 27: 27 (28: 9) wo unto people whose works are in *d.*; 27: 29 deaf shall hear words of book, and blind shall see out of obscurity and *d.*; 30: 6 scales of *d.* shall fall from Lamanites' eyes; 30: 17 no work of *d.* save it shall be made manifest; 32: 4 those who ask not must perish in *d.*; **Alma** 5: 7 fathers were in midst of *d.*; 19: 6 *d.* veil of unbelief is cast from Lamoni's mind; 26: 3 Lamanites in *d.* abyss before brought to light of God; 34: 33 if we do not improve our time in this life, then cometh night of *d.*; 37: 23–24 the Lord will prepare stone which shall shine forth in *d.* unto light; 37: 23, 25–26 the Lord will bring forth secret works out of *d.* unto light; 37: 27 Helaman[2] to hold back secret covenants lest people fall into *d.*; 37: 28, 30 curse upon land, judgments of God, destruction upon workers of *d.*; 40: 13–14 spirits of the wicked to be cast into outer *d.*; 41: 7 the repentant are delivered from endless night of *d.*; **Hel.** 6: 28–30 devil is the being who spreads works of *d.*; 13: 29 how long will ye choose *d.* rather than light; **3 Ne.** 13: 23 (Matt. 6: 23) if eye be evil, whole body shall be full of *d.*; **Morm.** 8: 16 record shall be brought out of *d.* unto light, shall shine forth in *d.*

DART (*see also* Spear; Weapon)

1 Ne. 15: 24 fiery *d.* of adversary cannot overpower those who hold fast to word of God; **Jarom** 1: 8 Nephites make weapons of war, arrow, *d.*

DAUGHTER (*see also* Child; Family; Woman)

1 Ne. 7: 6 two *d.* of Ishmael[1] rebel with Laman[1] and Lemuel; 16: 7 Nephi[1] and brothers take *d.* of Ishmael[1] to wife; 21: 22 (22: 6; Isa. 49: 22) Israel's *d.* shall be carried on Gentiles' shoulders; **2 Ne.** 4: 3–9 Lehi[1] calls sons and *d.* of Laman[1] together; 13: 16 (Isa. 3: 16) *d.* of Zion are haughty; 14: 4 (Isa. 4: 4) the Lord shall wash away filth of *d.* of Zion; **Jacob** 2: 31–33 the Lord has heard mourning of *d.* of his people in Jerusalem; **Mosiah** 5: 7 (Ether 3: 14) because of covenant, ye shall be called sons and *d.* of Christ; 20: 4–5 priests of Noah[3] carry off *d.* of Lamanites; **3 Ne.** 2: 16 *d.* of converted Lamanites become exceedingly fair; **Ether** 8: 8–17 *d.* of Jared[2] conspires to save his kingdom; **Moro.** 9: 9–10 Nephites murder many *d.* of Lamanites; 10: 31 put on thy beautiful garments, O *d.* of Zion.

DAVID—*king of Israel* (*see also* BD David)

2 Ne. 19: 7 (Isa. 9: 7) no end to throne of *D.*; **Jacob** 1: 15 (2: 23–24) *D*'s practice of having many wives and concubines was abominable before the Lord.

DAY (*see also* Day of the Lord; Daylight; Judgment; Light; Sabbath; Time; BD Day of Atonement)

2 Ne. 2: 21 *d.* of children of men were prolonged, that they might repent while in flesh; 2: 26 men are free to not be acted upon save by punishment at last *d.*; 3: 5 Joseph[1] truly saw our *d.*; 33: 9 men must continue in path until end of *d.* of probation; **W of M** 1: 11 people shall be judged out of records at last *d.*; **Alma** 33: 22 all shall stand before God to be judged at last *d.*; 34: 31 now is *d.* of your salvation; 34: 32 *d.* of this life is *d.* for men to perform labors; 34: 33 do not procrastinate *d.* of repentance until end; 40: 8 all is as one *d.* with God; 41: 5 those who desire to do evil all *d.* shall have reward of evil when night comes; 45: 13–14 *d.* to come when those now numbered among Nephites shall be numbered among Lamanites; **Hel.** 4: 7 from west sea to east is a *d*'s journey; 12: 14 if God say unto earth to lengthen the *d.* for many hours, it is done; 12: 25 in last *d.* some shall be cast out; 14: 4 (3 Ne. 1: 8, 19) sign of Christ's birth to be one *d.* and a night and *d.* as one *d.*; **3 Ne.** 1: 9 *d.* set apart that believers should be put to death except sign be given; 8: 24 O that we had repented before this great and dreadful *d.*; 13: 34 (Matt. 6: 34) sufficient is *d.* unto evil thereof; 16: 7 in latter *d.* shall truth come unto Gentiles; 25: 1 (Mal. 4: 1) *d.* cometh that shall burn as oven; **Ether** 13: 13 Ether hid himself in cavity of rock by *d.*

DAY OF THE LORD (*see also* Day; Jesus Christ, Second Coming of; Judgment; Last Days; Millennium; TG Day of the Lord)

2 Ne. 12: 12–13 (Isa. 2: 12–13) *d.* of the Lord shall come upon the proud and lofty; 23: 6, 9 (Isa. 13: 6) *d.* of the Lord is at hand; **3 Ne.** 24: 2 (Mal. 3: 2) who may abide *d.* of the Lord's coming; 25: 1 (Mal. 4: 1) *d.* cometh that shall burn as oven; 25: 5 (Mal. 4: 5) Elijah to be sent before coming of great and dreadful *d.* of the Lord.

DAYLIGHT (*see also* Light)

Moro. 7: 15 way to judge is as plain as *d.* is from dark night.

DEAD, DEADNESS (*see also* Death, Physical; Death, Spiritual; Jesus Christ, Resurrection of; Raise; Resurrection)

2 Ne. 18: 19 should not a people seek unto their God for the living to hear from the *d.*; 25: 25 the law hath become *d.* unto us; 25: 27 by knowing *d.* of the law, men may look forward to that life which is in Christ; 27: 13 (Morm. 8: 26; 9: 30; Moro. 10: 27) words of the faithful shall speak as if it were from the *d.*; **Mosiah** 18: 13 baptism a covenant to serve God until *d.* as to mortal body; **Alma** 5: 41–42 he that becomes a child of the devil is *d.* unto all good works; 18: 43—19: 8, 18 Lamoni lies as though *d.* for two days and nights; 30: 18 Korihor claims that when a man is *d.*, that is the end; **Hel.** 14: 16 all mankind, being cut off from presence of the Lord by fall of Adam, are considered as *d.*; **Moro.** 8: 23 it is mockery before God, putting trust in *d.* works; 10: 34 Jehovah, the Eternal Judge of both quick and *d.*

DEAF, DEAFNESS (*see also* Heal; Hear)

2 Ne. 9: 31 wo unto the *d.* that will not hear; 27: 29 the *d.* shall hear words of book; **Jarom** 1: 3 much should be done among Nephites because of *d.* of ears; **Mosiah** 3: 5 (3 Ne. 17: 7–9; 26: 15) Christ will cause the *d.* to hear; **4 Ne.** 1: 5 Christ's disciples cause the *d.* to hear.

DEARTH (*see* Famine)

DEATH, PHYSICAL (*see also* Body; Capital Punishment; Dead; Death, Spiritual; Die; Fall of Man; Grave; Immortality; Jesus Christ, Death of; Jesus Christ, Resurrection of; Kill; Life; Martyrdom; Paradise; Raise; Resurrection; Slay; Sleep; Spirit World; TG Death; Death, Power over)

1 Ne. 15: 31 doth this thing mean the final state of the soul after *d.* of temporal body; **2 Ne.** 9: 6 as *d.* has passed upon all men, there must be a power of resurrection; 9: 10, 19 God prepares way for escape from monster, *d.* and hell, *d.* of body and of spirit; 9: 11–12 temporal and spiritual *d.* shall deliver up their dead; 10: 25 may God raise you from *d.* by power of resurrection; **Mosiah** 15: 8 (16: 7) Christ breaks bands of *d.*; 16: 8–9 (Alma 22: 14; 27: 28; Morm. 7: 5) sting of *d.* is swallowed up in Christ, and there can be no more *d.*; 27: 28 Alma[2] repents nigh unto *d.*; **Alma** 1: 18 he who murders is punished unto *d.*; 7: 12 (11: 42) Christ to take upon him *d.* that he may loose the bands of temporal *d.*; 11: 45 mortal body is raised from first *d.* unto life; 12: 23–24 because Adam partook of forbidden fruit, temporal *d.* comes upon mankind; 15: 17 people pray continually that they might be delivered from Satan and *d.*; 27: 28 people of Ammon[2] never look upon *d.* with any degree of terror; 40: 11–14 state of soul between *d.* and resurrection; 42: 9 (Hel. 14: 16) fall brought upon mankind both a spiritual *d.* and a temporal *d.*; 55: 3 Moroni[1] will seek *d.* among Lamanites until they sue for peace; **Hel.** 12: 3 except the Lord visits his people with *d.*, they will not remember him; **3 Ne.** 27: 7–8, 25, 37–38 (Ether 12: 17) three Nephite disciples shall never taste of *d.*

DEATH, SPIRITUAL (*see also* Damnation; Dead; Death, Physical; Die; Fall of Man; God, Presence of; Hell; Redemption; Repentance; Sin; Sleep; Sons of Perdition; Spirit World; TG Death, Spiritual, First; Death, Spiritual, Second)

2 Ne. 2: 27 (10: 23; Alma 29: 5; Hel. 14: 31) men are free to choose eternal life or *d.*; 9: 10 God prepares way for escape from monster, *d.* and hell, *d.* of body and of spirit; 9: 11–12 temporal and spiritual *d.* shall deliver their dead; 9: 39 (Rom. 8: 6) to be carnally-minded is *d.*; **Jacob** 3: 11 shake yourselves that ye awake from slumber of *d.*; 3: 11 lake of fire and brimstone is second *d.*; **Mosiah** 15: 8–9 (Alma 7: 12) Christ breaks bands of *d.*; **Alma** 5: 7 fathers encircled by bands of *d.*, chains of hell; 12: 16 whosoever dies in sin shall suffer second *d.*, which is spiritual *d.*; 12: 32 penalty for doing evil is second *d.*, which is everlasting *d.*; 13: 30 may the Lord grant unto you repentance, that you may not suffer second *d.*; 15: 17 people pray continually that they might be delivered from Satan and *d.*; 29: 5 unto him who knows good and evil is given according to his desires, life or *d.*; 36: 18 Alma[2] was encircled by everlasting bands of *d.*; 40: 26 awful *d.* comes upon the wicked, for they die as to things of righteousness; 42: 9 (Hel. 14: 16) fall brought upon mankind a spiritual *d.* as well as temporal *d.*; **Hel.** 14: 16 (Morm. 9: 13) Christ's *d.* redeems all mankind from first *d.*, that spiritual *d.*; 14: 18 those who do not repent suffer again a spiritual *d.*, a second *d.*

DEBT (*see also* Indebted; Trespass; TG Debt)

3 Ne. 13: 11 (Matt. 6: 12) forgive us our *d.* as we forgive our debtors.

DECEIT, DECEIVE (*see also* Beguile; Cheat; Craftiness; Cunning; Deception; Device; False, Falsehood; Flatter; Fraud; Guile; Hypocrisy; Lying; Pretend; Sincerity; Wicked; Wiles)

1 Ne. 16: 38 Laman[1] claims Nephi[1] tries to *d.* their eyes; **2 Ne.** 9: 41 the Lord cannot be *d.*; 25: 18 no other Messiah to come, save false Messiah which should *d.* people; **Jacob** 7: 18 Sherem confesses he was *d.* by power of devil; **Mosiah** 7: 21 (10: 18) Zeniff is *d.* by cunning of king Laman[2]; 11: 7 people of Noah[3] are *d.* by flattering words of king and priests; 14: 9 (Isa. 53: 9) no *d.* in Messiah's mouth; 26: 6 unbelievers *d.* many with flattering words; **Alma** 12: 1 Amulek catches Zeezrom in *d.*; 16: 18 priests preach against all *d.*; 20: 13 Lamanites believe Nephites seek to *d.* them; 30: 47 Korihor shall not *d.* people any more; 30: 53 Korihor confesses that devil has *d.* him; 48: 7 Amalickiah obtains power by fraud and *d.*; **3 Ne.** 2: 1–2 Nephites imagine that signs are wrought by power of devil to *d.*; 16: 10 Gentiles shall be filled with all manner of lyings and *d.*; 21: 19 all *d.* shall be done away; 30: 2 repent of your lyings and *d.*; **Morm.** 8: 31 it shall come in a day when there is lying and *d.*

DECEPTION (*see also* Deceit)

2 Ne. 31: 13 if ye follow the Son, acting no *d.* before God, ye shall receive Holy Ghost.

DECLARE (*see also* Preach; Proclamation; Prophecy; Publish; Tell)

Mosiah 15: 10 (Isa. 53: 8) who shall *d.* Son's generation; **3 Ne.** 11: 40 whoso shall *d.* more or less than this as the Lord's doctrine comes of evil.

DECOY (*see also* Stratagem)

Alma 52: 21 Moroni[1] resolves upon plan to *d.* Lamanites out of strongholds; 58: 1 Nephites could not *d.* Lamanites from strongholds because they remembered former plan.

DECREE (*see also* Command; Commandments of God; Consume, Consumption; Law; Ordain; Proclaim; Statute)

2 Ne. 20: 1 (Isa. 10: 1) wo unto them that *d.* unrighteous *d.*; **Alma** 23: 2 Lamanite king sends *d.* not to lay hands on sons of Mosiah[2]; 29: 4 I ought not to harrow up in my desires the firm *d.* of a just God; 41: 8 *d.* of God are unalterable; **Ether** 2: 9 *d.* of God that this is a promised land; 2: 10 everlasting *d.* of God that those who possess land must serve him; 2: 11 this message comes unto Gentiles, that they may know *d.* of God.

DEED (*see also* Act; Do; Doing; Judgment; Work [noun])

Mosiah 4: 30 if ye do not watch words and *d.*, ye must perish; **Alma** 5: 15 (36: 15) men will be judged according to *d.* done in mortal body; 42: 27 in last day it shall be restored unto him according to his *d.*; **Hel.** 10: 5 the Lord will make Nephi[2] mighty in word and *d.*; 13: 26 Nephites would call a prophet false because he testified their *d.* were evil; 15: 4 the Lord has hated Lamanites because their *d.* have been evil.

DEFENCE, DEFENSE, DEFEND (*see also* Fight; Maintain; Preserve; Safe; Security)

2 Ne. 14: 5 (Isa. 4: 5) glory of Zion shall be a *d.*; **Alma** 35: 14 converted Zoramites take up arms to *d.* families and lands; 43: 47 ye shall *d.* your families even unto bloodshed; 48: 13 Moroni[1] swears oath to *d.* people, country, religion; 48: 14 Nephites taught to *d.* themselves against enemies; 48: 16 God reveals to Nephites where they should go to *d.* themselves; 51: 13 king-men would not take up arms to *d.* country; 54: 13 Nephites have only sought to *d.* themselves; 60: 28 Moroni[1] takes up sword to *d.* country according to God's commandments; 61: 6 (62: 5) Nephites take up arms in *d.* of country; **3 Ne.** 3: 2 ye do stand well, as if ye were supported by hand of a god in *d.* of your liberty; **Ether** 14: 2 every man keeps sword in right hand in *d.* of property and family.

DEFIANCE (*see also* Rebel)

Alma 5: 18 can ye imagine yourselves brought before God with remembrance that ye have set at *d.* his commandments; **3 Ne.** 6: 30 judges set at *d.* the law and rights of their country.

DEFILE (*see also* Corrupt; Filthiness; Pollute; Unclean)

Morm. 8: 28 churches shall become *d.*

DELAY (*see also* Procrastinate)

3 Ne. 29: 2 ye need not say the Lord *d.* his coming.

DELICATE (*see* Tender)

DELIGHT (*see also* Delightsome; Happiness; Joy; Pleased; Pleasure)

2 Ne. 4: 15–16 (11: 2, 4–6; 25: 5) Nephi[1] *d.* in scriptures, in things of the Lord; 9: 37 devil *d.* in those who worship idols; 9: 49 my heart *d.* in righteousness; 9: 51 let your soul *d.* in fatness; 25: 4 (31: 3) Nephi[1] *d.* in plainness; 25: 13 Nephi[1] *d.* to prophesy concerning Christ; **Jacob** 2: 28 God *d.* in chastity; **Alma** 48: 11 Moroni[1] does not *d.* in bloodshed; **Moro.** 9: 19 Nephites *d.* in everything save that which is good.

DELIGHTSOME (*see also* Beauty; Fair)

2 Ne. 5: 21 (Morm. 5: 17) Lamanites were fair and *d.* people; 30: 6–7 (W of M 1: 8) Lamanites and Jews who believe in Christ shall become *d.* people; **3 Ne.** 24: 12 ye shall be a *d.* land; **4 Ne.** 1: 10 Nephites become fair and *d.* people; **Moro.** 9: 12 few years have passed since Nephites were civil and *d.* people.

DELIVER, DELIVERANCE (*see also* Escape; Freedom; Give; Help; Loose; Ransom; Reclaim; Redemption; Salvation; Save; Snatch)

1 Ne. 1: 20 the Lord makes those he has chosen mighty unto power of *d.*; 3: 29 the Lord will *d.* Laban into brothers' hands; 4: 3 the Lord is able to *d.* us; 17: 14 the Lord *d.* Lehites from destruction in Jerusalem; **2 Ne.** 9: 11–12 temporal and spiritual deaths must *d.* up their dead; 9: 19 God *d.* his saints from awful monster of death; 11: 5 mercy of God in eternal plan of *d.* from death; 27: 9–22 book shall be *d.* unto a man; **Mosiah** 9: 17 Zeniff's people are awakened to remembrance of *d.* of their fathers; **Alma** 4: 14 resurrection of the dead according to *d.* of Christ from bands of death; 7: 13 Son blots out transgressions according to power of his *d.*; 9: 28 righteous shall reap salvation according to *d.* of Christ; 14: 26 give us strength according to our faith in Christ, even unto *d.*; 15: 2 those cast out of Ammonihah relate power of *d.*; 46: 7 Nephites' great rejoicing because of *d.* by hand of the Lord; 58: 11 the Lord causes that Nephites hope for *d.* in him; 58: 37 we trust God will *d.* us; **3 Ne.** 13: 12 (Matt. 6: 13) *d.* us from evil.

DEMANDS (*see* Justice)

DEMON (*see also* Angels of the Devil; Devils; Spirit, Evil)

Hel. 13: 37 we are surrounded by *d.*

DENY (*see also* Refuse; Reject; Resist)

2 Ne. 26: 33 the Lord *d.* none who come unto him; 28: 4 churches shall *d.* Holy Ghost; 31: 14 if men receive Holy Ghost and then *d.* Christ, better that they had not known him; **Jacob** 6: 8 will ye *d.* good word of Christ; 7: 9 *d.* thou the Christ who shall come; 7: 19 Sherem fears he has committed unpardonable sin by *d.* Christ; **Omni** 1: 17 Mulekites *d.* the being of their Creator; **Mosiah** 4: 24 they who *d.* beggar should say, If I had, I would give; 17: 20 Abinadi put to death because he would not *d.* God's commandments; **Alma** 30: 39 Alma[2] asks Korihor whether he will again *d.* God and Christ; 39: 6 to *d.* Holy Ghost when it once has had place in you is unpardonable sin; 46: 35 few *d.* covenant of freedom; **Hel.** 8: 24 ye cannot *d.* these things except ye shall lie; **3 Ne.** 12: 30 *d.* yourselves of these things; 29: 6 wo unto him that shall *d.* revelations of the Lord; **4 Ne.** 1: 27 churches profess to know Christ, but *d.* more parts of gospel; 1: 29 false church *d.* Christ; **Morm.** 9: 7–8 he who *d.* revelations and spiritual gifts knows not gospel of Christ; **Moro.** 1: 2 Lamanites put to death every Nephite who will not *d.* Christ; 10: 7 *d.* not the power of God; 10: 32 *d.* yourselves of all ungodliness.

DEPART (*see also* Die; Flight; Go; Journey; Leave)

1 Ne. 2: 2–4 (3: 18) Lehi[1] and family *d.* into wilderness; **2 Ne.** 5: 5–7 Nephi[1] and followers *d.* into wilderness; **Omni** 1: 12–14 Mosiah[1] and his people *d.* into wilderness; **3 Ne.** 20: 41 cry to go forth, *D.* ye, *d.* ye.

DEPEND, DEPENDENT (*see also* Rely; Trust)

Mosiah 4: 19, 21 do we not all *d.* upon God for substance and life; 10: 11 Lamanites *d.* upon own strength; 18: 26 priests not to *d.* upon people for support; **Hel.** 16: 15 people *d.* upon own strength.

DEPRAVITY (*see also* Wicked)

Moro. 9: 18 O the *d.* of my people.

DEPRESSED (*see also* Despair)

Alma 26: 27 when our hearts were *d.*, the Lord comforted us; 56: 16 Nephite soldiers are *d.* in body as well as in spirit.

DEPRIVE (*see also* Take)

Alma 2: 4 Amlici would *d.* people of their rights and privileges of church; 6: 5 none are *d.* of privilege of assembling to hear word of God; **Moro.** 9: 9 Nephites *d.* Lamanite daughters of chastity and virtue.

DEPTH

1 Ne. 12: 16 *d.* of fountain of filthy water are *d.* of hell; 16: 25 Lehi[1] brought down into *d.* of sorrow for murmuring; **2 Ne.** 9: 42 (Mosiah 4: 11; Alma 62: 41; Hel. 6: 5; 3 Ne. 12: 2) men must humble themselves in *d.* of humility; 17: 11 (Isa. 7: 11) ask a sign of the Lord, either in *d.* or in heights; 26: 5 *d.* of earth shall swallow up those who kill prophets and saints; **Jacob** 4: 8 how unsearchable are *d.* of mysteries of the Lord.

DESCEND (*see also* Descendant; Fall; Jesus Christ, Condescension of; Jesus Christ, Second Coming of)

1 Ne. 1: 19 (11: 7; 12: 6; 3 Ne. 11: 8) Lehi[1] and Nephi[1] see Christ *d.* out of heaven; 11: 30 (3 Ne. 17: 24) Nephi[1] sees angels *d.* out of heaven to minister to men.

DESCENDANT (*see also* Genealogy; Loins; Seed)

1 Ne. 5: 14 (6: 1–2; 2 Ne. 3: 4; Alma 10: 3) Lehi[1] a *d.* of Joseph[1]; 5: 16 Laban a *d.* of Joseph[1]; **2 Ne.** 30: 4 Nephites' seed shall know they are *d.* of Jews; **Mosiah** 7: 3, 13 Ammon[1] a *d.* of Zarahemla; 25: 2 among Nephites, fewer *d.* of Nephi[1] than people of Zarahemla; 25: 2 Zarahemla a *d.* of Mulek; 25: 13 kingdom conferred on none but *d.* of Nephi[1]; Alma 10: 3 Lehi[1] a *d.* of Manasseh; 17: 21 Lamoni a *d.* of Ishmael[1]; 24: 29 (56: 3) Lamanites who join Nephites are actual *d.* of Laman[1] and Lemuel, not of dissenters; 43: 13 Lamanite armies include *d.* of priests of Noah[3]; **Hel.** 11: 24 group of Nephite dissenters and real *d.* of Laman[1] commence war with Nephites; **3 Ne.** 10: 4 how oft has the Lord wanted to gather *d.* of Jacob[1] as hen gathereth chickens; **Morm.** 1: 5 (8: 13) Mormon[2] a *d.* of Nephi[1]; **Ether** 1: 6 Ether a *d.* of Coriantor; 10: 8 *d.* of Riplakish driven out of land; 11: 17–18 *d.* of brother of Jared[2] overthrows Moron and obtains kingdom.

DESERET

Ether 2: 3 Jaredites carry with them *d.*, by interpretation, a honey bee.

DESIRABLE (*see also* Desire)

1 Ne. 8: 15 (15: 36) fruit of the tree of life is *d.* above all other fruit; 11: 22 love of God is most *d.* above all other things; **Alma** 32: 38–39 tree withers, but not because fruit would not be *d.*

DESIRE (*see also* Covet; Desirable; Intent; List; Lust; Pleasure; Purpose; Search; Seek; Will; Willing; Wish)

Enos 1: 9 Enos feels *d.* for welfare of Nephites; **Mosiah** 18: 10–11 *d.* of Benjamin's people is to be baptized; **Alma** 29: 4 God grants unto men according to their *d.*; 32: 27 if ye can no more than *d.* to believe, let this *d.* work in you; 41: 5 man will be raised to happiness, goodness, or evil according to *d.*; **3 Ne.** 18: 18 Satan *d.* to have you.

DESOLATION, DESOLATE (*see also* Desolation, City of; Desolation, Land of; Destruction; Empty; Ruin; Waste; Wilderness)

Hel. 3: 5 Nephites spread into parts of land that have not been rendered *d.*; 14: 24 (3 Ne. 4: 1) many cities to become *d.*; **3 Ne.** 10: 7 places of Israel's dwellings shall become *d.* until fulfilling of covenant; 22: 3 (Isa. 54: 3) Israel's seed shall make *d.* cities to be inhabited.

DESOLATION, CITY OF—*Nephite city to the north*

Morm. 3: 7 Lamanites come to *D.* to battle; 4: 2 possessed by Lamanites; 4: 3 near city of Teancum; 4: 8 regained by Nephites; 4: 13 possessed again by Lamanites; 4: 19 great battle of *D.*

DESOLATION, LAND OF—*north of the land Bountiful*

Alma 22: 30–31 land far northward that had been peopled and destroyed; 22: 30 place of first landing of people of Zarahemla; 22: 32 day and a half journey from east to west sea; 46: 17 Moroni[1] names land south of *D.* a land of liberty; 50: 33–34 Nephites overtake Morianton in *D.*; 63: 5 Hagoth's ships built near *D.*; **3 Ne.** 3: 23 land appointed for gathering extends to line between Bountiful and *D.*; **Morm.** 3: 5 Mormon[2] causes people to gather in *D.*; 4: 1–2, 19 Lamanites possess *D.*; **Ether** 7: 6 near land of Moron.

DESOLATION OF NEHORS (*see* Ammonihah, City of)

DESPAIR (*see also* Depressed; Mourn; Sorrow; Suffering; Torment; Tribulation; TG Despair)

Alma 26: 19 why did God not doom us to eternal *d.*; **Moro.** 10: 22 if ye have no hope, ye must needs be in *d.*

DESPISE (*see also* Abhor; Despisers; Despitefully; Hate; Malice)

1 Ne. 19: 14 because Jews have *d.* Holy One, they shall wander; **2 Ne.** 9: 30 the rich *d.* the poor; 9: 42 the rich and proud are they whom God *d.*; 15: 24 the

Lord's anger is kindled against his people because they *d.* word of Holy One; **Jacob** 4: 8 *d.* not the revelations of God; **Mosiah** 14: 3 (Isa. 53: 3) Messiah is *d.* and rejected of men; **Alma** 46: 18 surely God shall not suffer that we, who are *d.* because we take upon us Christ's name, shall be destroyed; **3 Ne.** 13: 24 (Matt. 6: 24) man with two masters will hold to one and *d.* the other; **4 Ne.** 1: 29 false church *d.* true church because of miracles; **Morm.** 9: 26–27 who will *d.* works of the Lord.

DESPISERS (*see also* Despise)

Morm. 9: 26 *d.* of the Lord's works shall wonder and perish.

DESPITEFULLY (*see also* Despise)

3 Ne. 12: 44 (Matt. 5: 44) pray for them who *d.* use you.

DESTROY (*see* Destruction)

DESTRUCTION (*see also* Burn; Calamity; Captive, Captivity; Chasten; Earthquake; Famine; Fire; Flood; Hail; Iniquity; Judgment; Last Days; Lightning; Overthrow; Pestilence; Ruin; Scatter; Scourge; Slaughter; Slay; Smite; Sweep; Tempest; Thrash; Throw; Tribulation; Vengeance; War; Waste; Wrath)

1 Ne. 1: 4 (7: 13; 17: 43; 2 Ne. 1: 4; Hel. 8: 20–21) Jerusalem must be *d.*; 13: 8–9 abominable church *d.* saints of God; 14: 7 the hardhearted to be brought down to *d.*, both temporally and spiritually; 17: 32, 35 the Lord curses land against children of land unto their *d.*; 17: 37–38 the Lord *d.* nations of the wicked; 22: 14 all who fight against Zion shall be *d.*; 22: 16 God shall not suffer that the wicked *d.* the righteous; **2 Ne.** 1: 22 Lehi[1] exhorts sons to unity, that they not incur God's displeasure unto *d.*; 3: 3 seed of Joseph[2] shall not utterly be *d.*; 4: 9 seed of Lemuel shall not utterly be *d.*; 6: 15 they that believe not in Messiah shall be *d.*; 10: 6 (25: 9) because of iniquities, *d.* shall come upon Jews; 21: 9 (30: 15; Isa. 11: 9) they shall not hurt or *d.* in all my holy mountain; 25: 9 *d.* of Jews from generation to generation always foretold by prophets; 25: 14 after Messiah rises from dead, Jerusalem shall be *d.* again; 26: 5–6 they who kill prophets shall be visited with all manner of *d.*; 26: 8 the righteous who *d.* not the prophets shall not perish; 30: 10 the Lord will *d.* the wicked, even by fire; **Enos** 1: 23 (Ether 11: 1) prophets prophesy of *d.* among people; **Mosiah** 27: 10 (Alma 36: 6) Alma[2] and sons of Mosiah[2] seek to *d.* church; 29: 27 (Alma 10: 18–19) when voice of people chooses iniquity, God will visit them with *d.*; **Alma** 1: 12 priestcraft would prove entire *d.* of Nephites; 2: 4 Amlici's intent is to *d.* church; 10: 22 (Hel. 13: 13) if not for prayers of righteous, people would be visited now with *d.*; 10: 27 foundation of *d.* of people is laid by unrighteous lawyers and judges; 12: 17, 36 those who die in sins will be chained down to everlasting *d.*; 35: 3 the word *d.* craft of Zoramites; 36: 9 if thou wilt of thyself be *d.*, seek no more to *d.* church; 36: 14 Alma[2] had murdered many, or led them away unto *d.*; 42: 8 to reclaim man from temporal death would *d.* plan of happiness; 42: 13 work of justice could not be *d.*; 46: 10 Amalickiah seeks to *d.* church; **Hel.** 5: 2 (6: 40; 11: 37) Nephites are ripening for *d.* because laws are corrupt; 6: 28 devil dragged Jaredites down to *d.*; 13: 14 when people cast out the righteous, they are ripe for *d.*; 13: 32, 38 your *d.* is made sure; **3 Ne.** 9: 12 many great *d.* has the Lord caused to come upon Nephites because of iniquity; 10: 14 see if all these *d.* are not unto fulfilling of prophecies; 12: 17 (Matt. 5: 17) Christ came not to *d.* law or prophets, but to fulfill; 24: 11 (Mal. 3: 11) the Lord will rebuke the devourer and he shall not *d.* fruits; **Morm.** 6: 22 O that you had repented before this great *d.* came upon you; 8: 3 Moroni[2] remains alone to write tale of his people's *d.*; **Ether** 1: 5 Moroni[2] gives account of Jaredites from tower to *d.*; 7: 23 Jaredites to be *d.* if they do not repent; 8: 21 secret combinations have caused *d.* of Jaredites and Nephites; 8: 23 suffer not that murderous combinations bring work of *d.* upon you; 9: 20 those who possess land to be *d.* when ripened in iniquity; 13: 14 Ether views *d.* which came upon Jaredites; 15: 19 Jaredites given up to hardness of hearts, that they might be *d.*

DETERMINE, DETERMINATION

2 Ne. 1: 21 be *d.* in one mind, united in all things; **Moro.** 6: 3 none baptized save they have *d.* to serve Christ to end.

DEVICE (*see also* Cunning; Deceit)

Alma 11: 21 Zeezrom is expert in *d.* of devil; 30: 42 devil works *d.* that he may destroy children of God.

DEVIL (*see also* Adversary; Angels of the Devil; Church of the Devil; Contention; Devilish; Devils; Evil; Hell; Lucifer; Lying; Perdition; Rebel; Satan; Serpent; Spirit, Evil; Tempt; Wicked; TG Devil; BD Devil)

1 Ne. 12: 17 mists of darkness in vision are temptations of *d.*; 12: 19 Lamanites to contend against Nephites because of temptations of *d.*; 13: 6 (14: 3, 9, 17) *d.* is founder of abominable church; 14: 7 (2 Ne. 1: 18) the wicked are brought down to captivity of *d.*; 14: 10 only two churches—church of Lamb and church of *d.*; 15: 35 *d.* is preparator of hell; **2 Ne.** 2: 17 (9: 8) angel of God fell, became *d.*; 2: 18 (9: 9; Mosiah 16: 3; Hel. 6: 26; Ether 8: 25) *d.* beguiled our first parents; 9: 8–9 except for resurrection our spirits should become like *d.* and we should become angels to *d.*; 9: 16 they who are filthy are *d.* and his angels; 9: 37 *d.* of all devils delights in those who worship idols; 26: 22 (Hel. 6: 26, 30; 8: 28; Ether 8: 16) *d.* is founder of secret combinations; 28: 19 kingdom of *d.* must shake; 28: 20–23 *d.* will rage, pacify, flatter; **Jacob** 7: 18 Sherem confesses he had been deceived by *d.*; **Omni** 1: 25 (Alma 5: 40; Moro. 7: 12, 17) that which is evil comes from *d.*; **Mosiah** 2: 32 beware lest contentions arise and ye obey evil spirit; 4: 14 (Alma 34: 23; Hel. 6: 30; Moro. 7: 17) *d.* is master of sin, enemy to righteousness; 16: 3, 5 *d.* has power over the wicked; **Alma** 5: 39 if ye are not sheep of good shepherd, *d.* is your shepherd; 9: 28 the evil shall reap damnation according to captivation of *d.*; 30: 53 Korihor confesses that *d.* deceived him; 30: 60 *d.* will not support his children; 34: 23 cry unto God against *d.*; 34: 39 pray continually that ye may not be led away by temptations of *d.*; 40: 13 spirit of *d.* takes possession of spirits of the wicked; 48: 17 if all men were like Moroni[1], *d.* would never have power over them; **Hel.** 5: 12 build your foundation, that *d*'s mighty storm shall have no power over you; 6: 30 *d.* is author of all sin; 8: 28 *d.* seeks to destroy souls of men; **3 Ne.** 11: 29 he who has spirit of contention is of the *d.*; **Ether** 8: 25 *d.* is father of all lies; **Moro.** 7: 12 *d.* is an enemy to God; 7: 17 whatsoever persuadeth men not to believe in Christ is of *d.*

DEVILISH (*see also* Carnal; Devil)

Mosiah 16: 3 the wicked are carnal and *d.*; 16: 3 (Alma 42: 9–10) fall caused all mankind to become carnal, sensual, *d.*; **Alma** 41: 13 meaning of restoration is to bring back *d.* for *d.*; **Hel.** 12: 4 how *d.* are children of men.

DEVILS (*see also* Angels of the Devil; Demon; Devil; Spirit, Evil)

1 Ne. 11: 31 (Mosiah 3: 6) Lamb casts out *d.*; **2 Ne.** 9: 8–9 without resurrection we would have become *d.*, angels to devil; **Jacob** 3: 11 *d.* to be cast into lake of fire and brimstone; **3 Ne.** 7: 19 Nephi[3] casts out *d.* in name of Lamb; 14: 22 (Matt. 7: 22) many will say they have cast out *d.* in the Lord's name; **Morm.** 9: 24 believers shall cast out *d.* in the Lord's name.

DEVOTE, DEVOTION (*see* Consecration, Law of; Worship)

DEVOUR (*see also* Burn; Consume; Eat; Fire)

Alma 5: 59 shepherd watches flocks, that wolf does not *d.*; **Moro.** 9: 10 Nephites *d.* human flesh like wild beasts.

DIE (*see also* Death, Physical; Death, Spiritual; Depart; Jesus Christ, Death of; Lay; Perish)

2 Ne. 2: 18 partake of forbidden fruit, and ye shall not *d.*; 9: 35 murderer who deliberately kills shall *d.*; 28: 7–8 (Isa. 22: 13; 1 Cor. 15: 32) eat, drink, and be merry, for tomorrow we *d.*; **Jacob** 2: 35 because of strictness of word of God against Nephites, many hearts *d.*; **Mosiah** 15: 26 the Lord redeems none who rebel against him and *d.* in their sins; **Alma** 12: 16 (40: 26) those who *d.* in sins shall *d.* second death, *d.* as pertaining to righteousness; **Morm.** 2: 14 Nephites curse God and wish to *d.*; 8: 38 greater is value of endless happiness than misery which never *d.*; **Moro.** 10: 26 those who *d.* in sins cannot be saved in kingdom of God.

DIG (*see also* Pit)

Jacob 5: 5, 11, 27, 63–64 master *d.* about trees in vineyard.

DILIGENCE, DILIGENT, DILIGENTLY (*see also* Endure; Faithful; Neglect; Obedience; Single; Slothful; Steadfast; Valiant; Zeal)

1 Ne. 10: 19 he who *d.* seeks shall find; 16: 28–29 (Mosiah 1: 16) pointers and writing on Liahona affected by *d.* of people; **Jacob** 1: 19 priests answer sins of people on own heads if they do not teach with *d.*; **Mosiah** 1: 7 (3 Ne. 23: 1) search records *d.*, that ye may profit thereby; 1: 11 Benjamin's people have been *d.* in keeping commandments; 4: 27 man should be *d.*, that thereby he might win prize; 7: 33 if ye will serve God with all *d.* of mind, he will deliver you; **Alma** 7: 23 I would that ye should be *d.* in keeping commandments; 12: 9 men are granted portion of mysteries according to *d.* they give God; 17: 2 sons of Mosiah[2] wax strong in knowledge of truth, for they searched scriptures *d.*; 32: 42–43 because of *d.* in nourishing word, ye may pluck fruit; 38: 10 be *d.* and temperate; 40: 3 Alma[2] has inquired *d.* of God regarding mystery of resurrection; 49: 30 Nephites enjoy peace and prosperity because of *d.* they give unto word of God; **3 Ne.** 6: 14 a few of converted Lamanites still willing with *d.* to keep commandments; **Moro.** 8: 26 love endures by *d.* unto prayer.

DIMMED

1 Ne. 5: 19 brass plates should never be *d.* by time.

DIRECT [adj.] (*see* Course; Straight)

Alma 37: 42 fathers did not travel *d.* course in wilderness because of transgressions.

DIRECTION, DIRECT [verb] (*see also* Course; Guide; Lead; Liahona; Path; Way)

1 Ne. 16: 16, 30 Lehites follow *d.* on Liahona; **Alma** 37: 36 let all thoughts be *d.* unto the Lord; 37: 37 counsel with the Lord, and he will *d.* thee for good; **Ether** 2: 5–6 the Lord gives Jaredites *d.* where to travel.

DISCERN (*see also* Discernible; Enlighten; Light; Perceive; Tell; TG Discernment, Spiritual)

Alma 18: 18 Ammon[2] can *d.* king's thoughts; **3 Ne.** 24: 18 (Mal. 3: 18) ye shall *d.* between him that serveth God and him that serveth him not.

DISCERNIBLE

Alma 32: 35 whatsoever is light is good, because it is *d.*

DISCIPLE (*see also* Apostle; Follow, Follower; Servant; Three Nephite Disciples; TG Disciple; BD Disciple)

1 Ne. 12: 8 Nephi[1] sees twelve *d.* of Lamb chosen to minister to his seed; 12: 10 (Morm. 3: 19) twelve *d.* shall judge Nephites; **Alma** 45: 14 all shall be like Lamanites except *d.* of the Lord; **3 Ne.** 5: 13 Mormon[2] is *d.* of Christ; 11: 22 Christ calls *d.* and gives power to baptize; 12: 1 (15: 11) number of those called and given authority is twelve; 15: 12 ye are my *d.*, and ye are a light to this people; 18: 26–34 Christ gives *d.* instructions on sacrament; 18: 37 (Moro. 2: 1–3) *d.* bear record that Christ gave them power to give Holy Ghost; 18: 39 *d.* bear record that Christ ascended into heaven; 19: 4 names of twelve *d.*; 19: 5–6 twelve *d.* teach multitude in twelve groups; 28: 1 Christ asks *d.*, one by one, what they desire; 28: 4–10 three *d.* shall not taste of death; 28: 26 (Morm. 8: 11) three *d.* minister unto Nephi[3], Mormon[2], Moroni[2]; **4 Ne.** 1: 1 disciples of Jesus form church of Christ; 1: 5 miracles wrought by *d.* of Jesus; 1: 30 false church exercises authority over three *d.* of Jesus; 1: 31–33 people try to kill three *d.*; 1: 37 three *d.* are among true believers; **Morm.** 1: 13 the Lord takes away his beloved *d.* because of people's wickedness; 8: 10 none know true God, save *d.* of Jesus; **Ether** 12: 17 it was by faith that three *d.* obtained promise not to taste of death; **Moro.** 3: 1–4 manner in which *d.* ordained priests and teachers.

DISEASE (*see also* Infirmity; Leprous; Sick, Sickness)

1 Ne. 11: 31 (Mosiah 3: 5; 3 Ne. 17: 7) Lamb heals multitudes afflicted with *d.*; **Mosiah** 17: 16 people of Noah[3] to be afflicted with *d.* because of iniquities; **Alma** 9: 22 Nephites saved from all manner of *d.*; 46: 40 God had prepared plants and roots to remove cause of *d.*

DISGUISE

Mosiah 12: 1 Abinadi comes among people in *d.*; **Hel.** 1: 12 Kishkumen in *d.* when he murders Pahoran[2]; 2: 6 servant obtains, by *d.*, knowledge of Kishkumen's plan to murder Helaman[3].

DISH (*see also* Barge)

Ether 2: 17 (6: 7) Jaredite vessels are tight like *d.*

DISOBEDIENCE (*see also* Murmur; Obedience; Rebel; Reject; Sin; Trample; Transgression; Unfaithful; Wicked; TG Disobedience, Disobey)

Alma 42: 12 man had brought fallen state upon himself because of *d.*

DISPERSE, DISPERSION (*see also* Israel, Scattering of; Scatter; TG Israel, Scattering of; BD Dispersions)

2 Ne. 10: 8 (3 Ne. 21: 1) Jews shall be gathered from long *d.*; 21: 12 (3 Ne. 5: 26; Isa. 11: 12) the Lord shall gather *d.* of Israel; **3 Ne.** 21: 26 work of the Father to commence among *d.* tribes; **Morm.** 8: 15 records to be brought forth for welfare of long *d.* covenant people.

DISPLEASURE, DISPLEASED (*see also* Indignation; Wrath)

2 Ne. 1: 21–22 be united, that ye may not incur *d.* of God; **Mosiah** 1: 17 followers of Lehi[1] were unfaithful and incurred *d.* of God; 25: 12 children of Amulon and his brethren are *d.* with conduct of their fathers.

DISPOSITION (*see also* Nature; Will)

Mosiah 5: 2 Benjamin's people experience mighty change and have no more *d.* to do evil; 9: 5 Zeniff goes to Lamanite king to learn his *d.*; **Alma** 43: 6 Amalekites are of more wicked and murderous *d.* than Lamanites.

DISPUTATIONS, DISPUTE (*see also* Contention; Dissension)

3 Ne. 8: 4 there began to be *d.* among the people; 11: 22, 28 the Lord commands that there be no *d.* regarding baptism or other points of doctrine; 18:

34 Christ gives commandments because of *d.* among people; 27: 3 *d.* among people regarding name of church; **4 Ne.** 1: 2 no contentions or *d.* among Nephites; **Ether** 12: 6 *d.* not because ye see not; **Moro.** 8: 4–5 Mormon[2] is grieved because of *d.* regarding baptism of little children.

DISSENSION (*see also* Contention; Dissenter, Dissent; Divide; Murmur)

Mosiah 26: 5 because of *d.* among members, unbelievers become more numerous; 27: 9 Alma[2] causes much *d.* among people; **Alma** 46: 6 those who desire king are led away by Amalickiah to *d.*; 53: 8–9 intrigue amongst Nephites causes *d.*, places them in dangerous circumstances; **Hel.** 4: 1 many *d.* in church; **3 Ne.** 2: 18 because of *d.* among Nephites, Gadianton robbers gain advantages.

DISSENTER, DISSENT (*see also* Amalekites; Amalickiah; Ammonihah, City of; Amulonites; Apostasy; King-men; Prophets, False; Rebel; Revolt, Revolution; Unbelief; Zoramites[2])

Alma 1: 21–25 many in church harden hearts, withdraw from people of God; 24: 29–30 no *d.*, only Lamanites, join people of the Lord; 31: 8 Zoramites are *d.* from Nephites; 43: 13 (47: 35) Lamanite armies consist of Lamanites and those who had *d.* from Nephites; 43: 13 *d.* include Amalekites, Zoramites, and descendants of priests of Noah[3]; 48: 24 Nephites protect families from barbarous cruelties of those who had *d.* from church and joined Lamanites; 51: 15–20 *d.* compelled to defend country; 62: 6 Pachus is king of *d.*; **Hel.** 1: 15 Coriantumr[3], *d.* from among Nephites, leads Lamanite army; 5: 35–41 Aminadab, who had *d.* from church, calls Lamanites to repent; **3 Ne.** 3: 11 robbers had wronged themselves by *d.*; **Moro.** 9: 24 a few Nephite survivors *d.* over to Lamanites.

DISTINGUISH

Mosiah 1: 11 Benjamin gives his people a name to *d.* them; **Alma** 2: 11 people of Amlici are *d.* by name of Amlici; 3: 4 Amlicites *d.* themselves from Nephites with red mark on foreheads; 23: 16 Anti-Nephi-Lehies desire a name to *d.* them from their brethren; 27: 26 people of Ammon[2] *d.* by that name ever after; 27: 27 people of Ammon[2] are *d.* for their zeal toward God; **3 Ne.** 6: 12 people began to be *d.* by ranks.

DIVIDE, DIVISION (*see also* Dissension)

1 Ne. 4: 2 (17: 26) waters of Red Sea were *d.*; 12: 18 terrible gulf *d.* spacious building and tree of life; 13: 10 many waters *d.* Gentiles from seed of Lamanites; **2 Ne.** 30: 10 the Lord will cause great *d.* among the people; **Mosiah** 19: 2 *d.* among people of Noah[3]; **Alma** 11: 45 spirits will be united with bodies, never to be *d.*; 51: 6 great *d.* between freemen and king-men; **Hel.** 1: 4 sons of Pahoran[1] cause three *d.* among the people; **3 Ne.** 7: 2 (4 Ne. 1: 35) people were *d.* one against another; 7: 14 Nephites *d.* into tribes; **4 Ne.** 1: 26 people are *d.* into classes; **Ether** 2: 13 the Lord brings Jaredites to great sea which *d.* the lands.

DIVORCE, DIVORCEMENT (*see also* Marriage; BD Divorce)

2 Ne. 7: 1 (Isa. 50: 1) where is the bill of your mother's *d.*; **3 Ne.** 12: 31–32 (Matt. 5: 31–32) Savior teaches concerning *d.*

DO, DID, DONE (*see also* Accomplish; Deed; Doing, Doings; Labor; Obedience; Perform; Undertake; Walk; Work [verb]; Wrought)

1 Ne. 3: 7 I will go and *d.* the things which the Lord hath commanded; 17: 30 the Lord *d.* all things for Israel that were expedient for man to receive; 17: 50 if God had commanded me to *d.* all good things, I could *d.* them; **2 Ne.** 25: 23 by grace we are saved, after all we can *d.*; 26: 24 the Lord *d.* not anything save for benefit of world; 26: 33 God *d.* nothing save it be plain unto men; **Enos** 1: 7 Lord, how is it *d.*; **Alma** 32: 19 how much more cursed is he who knows God's will and *d.* it not; **Hel.** 14: 30 whosoever *d.* iniquity *d.* it unto himself; **3 Ne.** 14: 24 (Matt. 7: 24; Luke 6: 47–48) whoso hears sayings and *d.* them is like man who built house upon rock; 18: 6 this shall ye always observe to *d.*, even as I have *d.*; 27: 21 ye know the things ye must *d.* in my church.

DOCTRINE (*see also* Doctrine, False; Gospel; Plan; Precept; Principle)

1 Ne. 15: 14 Lamanites shall come to knowledge of Redeemer and points of his *d.*; **2 Ne.** 31: 21 (32: 6) this is the *d.* of Christ; **Jacob** 7: 2 Sherem seeks to overthrow *d.* of Christ; **Alma** 41: 9 do not risk one more offense against God upon points of *d.*; **Hel.** 11: 22–23 those who know *d.* through revelation put an end to contentions; **3 Ne.** 2: 2 Satan leads men to believe *d.* of Christ is foolish; 11: 28 there shall be no disputations concerning points of *d.*; 11: 30 it is not Christ's *d.* to stir up hearts of men with anger; 11: 32, 35, 39 this is my *d.*; 11: 40 whoso establishes more or less for Christ's *d.* comes of evil; 21: 6 Gentiles to know true points of *d.*

DOCTRINE, FALSE (*see also* Antichrist; Apostasy; Churches, False; Contention; Err, Error; Prophets, False)

2 Ne. 3: 12 writings of descendants of Joseph[1] and Judah shall confound false *d.*; 28: 9 many shall teach vain, foolish, false *d.*; 28: 12 because of false *d.*, churches will be corrupted; **Alma** 1: 16 many go forth preaching false *d.* for riches and honor.

DOG (*see also* Animal; BD Dog)

3 Ne. 7: 8 people turned from righteousness as *d.* to his vomit; 14: 6 (Matt. 7: 6) give not that which is holy unto *d.*

DOING, DOINGS (*see also* Deed; Do)

1 Ne. 10: 20 for all thy *d.* thou shalt be brought into judgment; **2 Ne.** 25: 2 *d.* of Jews were *d.* of abominations; **Alma** 37: 36 let all thy *d.* be unto the Lord; **Morm.** 8: 35 Christ hath shown you unto me, and I know your *d.*

DOMINION (*see also* Authority; Kingdom; Power; Reign; Rule; Scepter; Throne)

1 Ne. 14: 12 *d.* of church of God will be small; **Alma** 5: 50 Son cometh in his majesty, power, *d.*

DOOR (*see also* Gate)

Hel. 8: 26–27 destruction is even now at your *d.*; **3 Ne.** 13: 6 (Matt. 6: 6) when thou hast shut *d.* of closet, pray to the Father.

DORMANT (*see also* Sleep)

Alma 32: 34 your faith is *d.*

DOUBT, DOUBTINGS (*see also* Belief; Faith; Hardheartedness; Unbelief; TG Doubt, Doubtful)

Alma 56: 47 (57: 26) stripling warriors were taught God would deliver them if they did not *d.*; 56: 48 striplings do not *d.* mothers; **3 Ne.** 5: 1 none of Nephites *d.* words of prophets; 8: 4 great *d.* among people notwithstanding many signs; **Morm.** 9: 21 whoso believes in Christ, *d.* nothing, shall be granted whatsoever he asks; 9: 25 the Lord will confirm his words to those who believe in his name, *d.* nothing; 9: 27 *d.* not, but be believing; **Ether** 3: 19 brother of Jared[2] has faith no longer, for he knows, nothing *d.*

DOVE (*see also* Holy Ghost; TG Holy Ghost, Sign of; BD Dove; Dove, Sign of)

1 Ne. 11: 27 (2 Ne. 31: 8) Holy Ghost abides upon Lamb in form of *d.*

DRAGON (*see also* TG Dragon; BD Dragon)

2 Ne. 8: 9 (Isa. 51: 9) art thou not he that wounded the *d.*; 23: 22 (Isa. 13: 22) *d.* shall cry in their pleasant palaces; **Mosiah** 20: 11 (Alma 43: 44) people of Limhi fight like *d.*

DRAW, DREW, DRAWN

2 Ne. 26: 24 (3 Ne. 27: 14–15) the Lord lays down his life that he may *d.* men unto him; 27: 25 (Isa. 29: 13) this people *d.* near the Lord with mouth, but have removed hearts from him; **Alma** 34: 27 let your hearts be full, *d.* out in prayer unto the Lord; 42: 2 after God sent first parents from Eden, he *d.* out the man; **Hel.** 13: 22 hearts of Nephites not *d.* out unto the Lord.

DREADFUL (*see* Day; Day of the Lord)

DREAM (*see also* Revelation; Vision; BD Dreams)

1 Ne. 1: 16 Lehi[1] has written many things which he saw in *d.*; 2: 1–2 the Lord speaks to Lehi[1] in *d.*; 3: 2 (8: 2) I have *d.* a *d.*; 8: 36 (10: 2) Lehi[1] speaks words of *d.*; 15: 21 what means this thing our father saw in *d.*; **2 Ne.** 27: 3 (Isa. 29: 7) nations that fight against Zion shall be as *d.* of night vision; **Jacob** 7: 26 our lives passed away as a *d.*; **Alma** 30: 28 Korihor claims priests bring people to believe, by traditions and *d.*, that they should offend some unknown being; **Ether** 9: 3 the Lord warns Omer in a *d.*

DRESS (*see also* Apparel; Clothing)

1 Ne. 8: 4, 7 *d.* of those in spacious building is exceeding fine.

DRINK, DRUNK (*see also* Cup; Drunk, Drunken; Eat; Partake; Sacrament; Thirst; Wine)

2 Ne. 27: 4 they who do iniquity shall stagger, but not with strong *d.*; **Mosiah** 2: 33 (3: 18, 25) he who dies in his sins *d.* damnation to his soul; **Alma** 5: 34 come unto me and ye shall *d.* of waters of life freely; 49: 27 (51: 9) Amalickiah swears to *d.* blood of Moroni[1]; **Morm.** 9: 24 believers shall *d.* any deadly thing and it shall not hurt them.

DROSS

Alma 32: 3 the poor are esteemed by their brethren as *d.*; 34: 29 if ye do not remember to be charitable, ye are as *d.*

DROUGHT (*see* Famine)

DROWNED

1 Ne. 4: 2 (17: 27; Alma 36: 28; Hel. 8: 11) Egyptians *d.* in Red Sea; 8: 32 many *d.* in depths of fountain; **Alma** 63: 8 those who left in ships are supposed to be *d.*; **3 Ne.** 8: 9 inhabitants of Moroni are *d.* in sea.

DRUNK, DRUNKEN, DRUNKENNESS (*see also* Wine; TG Drunkenness)

1 Ne. 4: 7 Nephi[1] finds Laban *d.* with wine; 21: 26 (22: 13; Isa. 49: 26) those who oppress the Lord's people shall be *d.* with own blood; **2 Ne.** 8: 21 hear this, thou *d.*, and not with wine; 27: 1 in last days Gentiles and Jews shall be *d.* with iniquity; **Mosiah** 22: 7 Lamanites will be *d.*, so that Limhi's people can escape; **Alma** 55: 14 Nephites cause Lamanites to become *d.*; 55: 19 Nephites would not destroy Lamanites in their *d.*; 55: 30 Lamanites try to destroy Nephites with poison or *d.*; **Ether** 15: 22 Jaredites *d.* with anger, as man who is *d.* with wine.

DUMB (*see also* Heal)

Mosiah 12: 5 (21: 3) people of Noah[3] shall be driven like *d.* ass; 14: 7 (15: 6; Isa. 53: 7) as a sheep before her shearers is *d.*, so he opened not his mouth; 27: 19 astonishment of Alma[1] was so great that he became *d.*; **Alma** 30: 49–50 Korihor is struck *d.*; **Hel.** 5: 25 Lamanites stand as if struck *d.* with amazement; **3 Ne.** 17: 9 Christ heals the *d.*

DUNG

Jacob 5: 64 Lord of vineyard commands servant to *d.* trees once more; **Morm.** 2: 15 thousands hewn down and heaped up as *d.*

DUNGEON (*see also* Prison)

Mosiah 2: 13 neither have I suffered that ye should be confined in *d.*; **Alma** 8: 31 Alma[2] and Amulek could not be confined in *d.*

DUST (*see also* Ashes; Earth; Ground)

1 Ne. 21: 23 (2 Ne. 6: 7, 13; Isa. 49: 23) kings and queens shall lick up *d.* of thy feet; 22: 14 abominable church shall tumble to *d.*; **2 Ne.** 1: 14 (Moro. 10: 31) awake and arise from the *d.*; 3: 19–20 fruit of loins of Nephi[1] to cry as from *d.*; 26: 15 Nephites and Lamanites to be brought low in *d.*; 26: 16 (Isa. 29: 4) speech of those who are destroyed shall be low out of *d.*; 27: 9 words of book are words of those who have slumbered in *d.*; 33: 13 Nephi[1] speaks as voice of one crying from *d.*; **Jacob** 2: 21 all flesh is of the *d.*; **Mosiah** 2: 25 (Morm. 9: 17) men were created of *d.* of earth; **Alma** 34: 38 humble yourselves even to *d.*; **Hel.** 12: 7 (Mosiah 2: 25) children of men are less than *d.* of earth; **Morm.** 8: 23 saints who have gone before will cry, even from the *d.*; **Moro.** 10: 27 Moroni[2] declares his words like one speaking out of dust.

DUTY (*see also* Obedience; Office; Perform; Responsibility; Serve)

Mosiah 1: 17 Lehites smitten with afflictions to stir them up in remembrance of *d.*; 13: 30 law of performances and ordinances to keep Israel in remembrance of *d.* toward God; **Alma** 4: 19 (7: 22) Alma[2] preaches to stir Nephites up in remembrance of *d.*; 43: 46 Nephites were doing what they felt was *d.* they owed to God; **Hel.** 15: 5 more part of Lamanites are in path of *d.*

DWELL, DWELLING (*see also* Abide; God, Presence of; Home; Inhabit; Live; Sojourn)

1 Ne. 10: 21 no unclean thing can *d.* with God; 15: 33 if men are filthy, they cannot *d.* in kingdom of God; 22: 28 all nations shall *d.* safely in Holy One if they repent; **2 Ne.** 2: 8 no flesh can *d.* in presence of God save through grace of Messiah; 21: 6 (30: 12; Isa. 11: 6) wolf shall *d.* with lamb; **Mosiah** 2: 37 (Alma 7: 21; 34: 36; Hel. 4: 24) the Lord *d.* not in unholy temples; 2: 41 those who keep commandments *d.* with God in never-ending happiness; 3: 5 (Alma 7: 8) the Lord shall come down and *d.* in tabernacle of clay; 3: 6 the Lord shall cast out evil spirits that *d.* in men's hearts; 15: 23 prophets are raised to *d.* with God, who has redeemed them; **Alma** 18: 35 portion of Spirit *d.* in Ammon[2]; 34: 36 the Lord *d.* in hearts of the righteous; 39: 7 Alma[2] would not *d.* upon Corianton's sins if it were not for his good; **3 Ne.** 28: 9 disciples shall not have pain while they *d.* in flesh; **4 Ne.** 1: 15 love of God *d.* in Nephites' hearts; **Morm.** 7: 7 he who is found guiltless shall *d.* in presence of God; 9: 3–4 men could not *d.* with Christ with consciousness of guilt; **Ether** 13: 2 all men who *d.* upon land should serve the Lord; 13: 10 blessed are they who *d.* in New Jerusalem; **Moro.** 8: 26 all saints shall *d.* with God.

DWINDLE, DWINDLING (*see* Unbelief)

EAR (*see also* Hear)

1 Ne. 20: 8 (Isa. 48: 8) from that time thine *e.* was not opened; **2 Ne.** 7: 4–5 (Isa. 50: 4–5) the Lord waketh mine *e.* to hear; 16: 10 (Isa. 6: 10) make the *e.* of this people heavy; 28: 22 devil whispers in men's *e.* until he grasps them; **Jarom** 1: 3 much should be done among Nephites because of deafness of their *e.*; **Mosiah** 2: 9 open your *e.* that ye may hear; **3 Ne.** 11: 5 survivors open *e.* to hear voice from heaven; 17: 16 *e.* has not heard such great things as Jesus spoke unto Father; 26: 15 Christ unstopped *e.* of the deaf.

EARTH (*see also* Bury; Creation; Dust; Earthquake; Ground; Land; World; TG Earth; Earth, Cleansing of; Earth, Curse of; Earth, Destiny of; Earth, Dividing of; Earth, Purpose of; Earth, Renewal of)

1 Ne. 4: 1 the Lord is mightier than all the *e.*; 11: 6 (3 Ne. 11: 14; 22: 5) the Lord is God over all the *e.*; 13: 41 one Shepherd over all the *e.*; 17: 36 (Mosiah 4: 2; 13: 19; Morm. 9: 17) the Lord hath created the *e.*; 19: 17 all the *e.* shall see salvation of the Lord; **2 Ne.** 8: 6 (Isa. 51: 6) *e.* to wax old like a garment; 21: 4 (Isa. 11: 4) the Lord shall smite *e.* with rod of his mouth; 23: 13 (Isa. 13: 13) *e.* shall remove out of her place; **Jacob** 4: 9 by power of the Lord's word, *e.* was created and man came upon *e.*; **Alma** 5: 50 behold the glory of the King of all the *e.*; 11: 39 the Son is Eternal Father of heaven and *e.*; **Hel.** 12: 13–15 (Jacob 4: 9) if the Lord say unto *e.*, Move, it is moved; 12: 18 (13: 18; Morm. 1: 18) whoso shall hide treasure in *e.* shall find it no more; **3 Ne.** 8: 17 whole *e.* becomes deformed; 10: 9 *e.* ceases to tremble; 12: 5 (Matt. 5: 5) meek shall inherit the *e.*; 13: 10 (Matt. 6: 10) thy will be done on *e.* as it is in heaven; 26: 3 (Morm. 5: 23; 9: 2; Ether 13: 9) *e.* to be wrapt together as scroll, and heaven and *e.* to pass away; **Ether** 13: 9 a new heaven and new *e.*; **Moro.** 7: 36 will God withhold power of Holy Ghost as long as *e.* shall stand.

EARTHQUAKE (*see also* Earth; Quake; Shake; Tremble; TG Earthquake)

1 Ne. 12: 4 in dream Nephi[1] hears thunderings and *e.*; **2 Ne.** 6: 15 unbelievers will be destroyed in *e.*; 26: 6 they who kill prophets shall be visited with *e.*; 27: 2 Jews and Gentiles shall be visited with *e.*; **Morm.** 8: 30 wars and *e.* in divers places.

EASE (*see also* Comfort; Easiness)

2 Ne. 28: 24 wo unto him who is at *e.* in Zion; **Hel.** 12: 2 people harden hearts because of their *e.*

EASINESS, EASY (*see also* Light, Lightly [adj.]; Simple)

1 Ne. 14: 23 things written in book were *e.* to understand; 17: 41 because of *e.* of requirement for healing, many perished; **Alma** 7: 23 be *e.* to be entreated; 37: 44 *e.* to give heed to word of Christ; 37: 46 do not be slothful because of *e.* of way; 39: 6 not *e.* for man who has denied Holy Ghost to obtain forgiveness; **Hel.** 6: 36 the Lord pours out Spirit on Lamanites because of their *e.* to believe; 7: 7 earlier Nephites were *e.* to be entreated.

EAT, EATEN (*see also* Consume; Devour; Drink; Food; Partake; Taste)

2 Ne. 13: 10 (Isa. 3: 10) the righteous shall *e.* fruit of their doings; 14: 1 (Isa. 4: 1) we will *e.* our own bread; 19: 20 every man shall *e.* flesh of his own arm; 21: 7 (30: 12; Isa. 11: 7) lion shall *e.* straw like ox; 28: 7–8 *e.*, drink, and be merry; **Alma** 31: 37 (3 Ne. 13: 25, 31; Matt. 6: 25, 31) missionaries take no thought for what they should *e.* or drink; 42: 3 God placed cherubim and flaming sword lest man should *e.* of tree of life; **3 Ne.** 18: 29 whoso *e.* Christ's flesh unworthily *e.* damnation to his soul; 20: 8 he that *e.* this bread *e.* Christ's body to his soul; **Moro.** 4: 3 *e.* sacrament bread in remembrance of body of Son.

EDEN, GARDEN OF—*home of Adam and Eve* (*see also* Adam; Fruit, Forbidden; BD Eden, Garden of)

2 Ne. 2: 19 (Alma 42: 2) Adam and Eve are driven out of *E.*; 2: 22 if Adam had not transgressed, he would have remained in *E.*; 8: 3 (Isa. 51: 3) the Lord will make Zion's wilderness like *E.*; **Alma** 12: 21 (42: 3) God placed cherubim and flaming sword on east of *E.*

EFFECT

Mosiah 7: 30 *e.* of reaping whirlwind is poison; **Alma** 12: 26 if first parents could have partaken of tree of life, word of God would have been void, taking none *e.*; 31: 5 preaching of word has more powerful *e.* on people than sword.

EGYPT—*land of Israel's captivity* (*see also* Egyptian; BD Egypt)

1 Ne. 5: 14 (2 Ne. 3: 4; 4: 1; Alma 10: 3) Joseph[1] sold into *E.*; 5: 15 (17: 40; 19: 10; 2 Ne. 3: 10; 21: 16; 25: 20; Mosiah 7: 19; 12: 34; Alma 36: 28) God led Israel out of captivity, out of *E.*; **2 Ne.** 17: 18 (Isa. 7: 18) the Lord shall hiss for fly in uttermost part of *E.*; 20: 24, 26 (Isa. 10: 24, 26) Assyrian shall lift up staff against Zion after manner of *E.*; 21: 11 (Isa. 11: 11) the Lord shall set his hand the second time to recover remnant of his people left in *E.*; **Ether** 13: 7 Joseph[1] brought father into *E.*

EGYPTIAN (*see also* Egypt; Language)

1 Ne. 1: 2 language of Lehi[1] consists of learning of Jews and language of *E.*; 4: 3 the Lord is able to destroy Laban, even as *E.*; 17: 27 (Alma 36: 28; Hel. 8: 11) the Lord swallowed up *E.* in Red Sea; 17: 23 (Alma 29: 12) would fathers have been led out of hands of *E.* if they had not hearkened to the Lord's words; **2 Ne.** 21: 15 (Isa. 11: 15) the Lord destroys tongue of *E.* sea; **Mosiah** 1: 4 Lehi[1] could read engravings because he had been taught in language of *E.*; **Morm.** 9: 32 record written in characters called reformed *E.*

ELDER (*see also* Priesthood; TG Elder; Elder—Melchizedek Priesthood; BD Elders)

1 Ne. 4: 22, 27 Zoram[1] speaks with Nephi[1] concerning *e.* of Jews; **Alma** 4: 7 (6: 1) Alma[2] consecrates *e.* over church; 4: 16 Alma[2] gives one of *e.* power to enact laws; **Moro.** 3: 1 disciples are called *e.* of church; 4: 1 *e.* and priests administer sacrament; 6: 1 *e.*, priests, and teachers are baptized; 6: 7 those who commit iniquity are brought before *e.*

ELECT (*see also* Choose; Chosen)

Alma 31: 16–17 Zoramites believe God has *e.* them to be his holy children.

ELEMENT (*see also* Materials; Matter)

3 Ne. 26: 3 (Morm. 9: 2) *e.* shall melt with fervent heat.

ELEPHANT (*see also* Animal; BD Elephant)

Ether 9: 19 Jaredites have *e.*

ELIJAH—*prophet of Israel* [ca. 900 B.C.] (*see also* BD Elijah)

3 Ne. 25: 5 (Mal. 4: 5) I will send you *E.* the prophet.

EMER—*early Jaredite king*

Ether 1: 28–29 son of Omer, father of Coriantum[1]; 9: 14 anointed king; 9: 15–16 has peaceful, prosperous reign; 9: 21 executes judgment in righteousness.

EMPLOY

2 Ne. 9: 41 Holy One *e.* no servant at the gate; **Alma** 10: 32 (11: 20) lawyers got gain according to their *e.*

EMPTY

2 Ne. 27: 3 (Isa. 29: 8) enemies of Zion shall be as hungry man who dreams he eats, but soul is *e.*

EMRON—*Nephite soldier*

Moro. 9: 2 is slain.

END, ENDS, ENDING (*see also* Beginning; Endless; Endure; Final; Finish; Last; Last Days; Pass; Purpose; TG World, End of)

1 Ne. 14: 3 casting of soul into that hell which hath no *e.*; 14: 22 John the Beloved to write of *e.* of world; **2 Ne.** 2: 7 (Moro. 7: 28) Christ offers himself a sacrifice for sin, to answer *e.* of law; 2: 12 without opposition, no purpose in *e.* of its creation; 2: 22 except for Adam's fall, all things must have had no *e.*; 25: 25 law of Moses given for *e.* of preparing for Christ; 26: 25 (3 Ne. 9: 22) come unto me, all ye *e.* of earth; 27: 7 sealed book shall be revelation from God, from beginning of world to *e.*; 31: 21 Godhead is one God, without *e.*; 33: 9 continue in straight path until *e.* of day of probation; **Mosiah** 26: 23 the Lord grants unto him that believeth unto the *e.* a place at right hand; **Alma** 5: 13 because fathers were faithful unto *e.*, they were saved; 27: 27 Ammonites are firm in faith of Christ unto *e.*; 30: 12, 18 Korihor claims that when man is dead, that is *e.*; 41: 6 he who desires righteousness until *e.* is rewarded unto righteousness; **3 Ne.** 16: 20 (20: 35) all *e.* of earth to see salvation of God; **Morm.** 7: 7 he who is found guiltless will dwell in state of happiness which hath no *e.*; **Moro.** 6: 3 (Mosiah 18: 9) those received unto baptism must have determination to serve Christ to *e.*; 8: 26 love endures by diligence unto prayer, until *e.* come.

ENDLESS (*see also* End; Eternal; Everlasting; God, Eternal Nature of; Infinite; Misery; Torment)

Mosiah 16: 9 Christ is light and life of world, a light and life that is *e.*; 16: 11 (Alma 41: 4; Hel. 12: 26) the good are resurrected to *e.* life and happiness, the evil to *e.* damnation; **Alma** 12: 24 life a time to prepare for *e.* state after resurrection; **Hel.** 7: 16 devil seeks to hurl souls down to *e.* wo; **Morm.** 8: 38 greater is value of *e.* happiness than misery that never dies; 9: 13 resurrection brings to pass redemption from *e.* sleep.

ENDURE, ENDURANCE (*see also* Bear; Continue; Diligence; Faint; Faithful; Firmness; Obedience; Probation; Steadfast)

1 Ne. 13: 37 those who *e.* to end shall be lifted up; 22: 31 (2 Ne. 31: 15; Omni 1: 26; Alma 5: 13; 32: 13; 3 Ne. 27: 6) those who *e.* to end shall be saved; **Alma** 32: 15 (38: 2) blessed is he who *e.* to end; **3 Ne.** 15: 9 *e.* to end, and ye shall live; 27: 16 he who *e.* to end will be held guiltless; **Morm.** 9: 29 those who *e.* to end shall not be cast out; **Moro.** 3: 3 (8: 3) remission of sins, through Christ, by *e.* of faith on his name to end; 7: 45 charity *e.* all things; 8: 26 love *e.* by diligence unto prayer.

ENEMY (*see also* Adversary; Oppressor)

2 Ne. 4: 28 give place no more for *e.* of my soul; **Mosiah** 2: 31 if Nephites keep commandments, *e.* shall have no power over them; 2: 37 man who transgresses against what he has been taught becomes *e.* to righteousness; 3: 19 (16: 5) natural man is *e.* to God; 4: 14 (16: 5; Alma 34: 23; Moro. 7: 12; 9: 6) devil is *e.* to all righteousness, *e.* to God; **Alma** 26: 6 those who are gathered shall not be driven whithersoever *e.* listeth to carry them; 58: 10 Nephites pray that God will deliver them from *e.*; **Hel.** 8: 6 corrupt judges do not believe *e.* can have power over them; **3 Ne.** 12: 43–44 (Matt. 5: 43–44) love your *e.*

ENGRAVE, ENGRAVEN, ENGRAVINGS (*see also* Plates, Brass; Plates of Ether; Plates of Nephi, Large; Plates of Nephi, Small; Record; Write)

Jacob 4: 1–3 difficulty of *e.* on plates; **Omni** 1: 20 large stone with *e.* on it brought to Mosiah[2] to be translated; **Mosiah** 21: 28 Mosiah[2] has gift of God whereby he can interpret *e.*; **Alma** 5: 19 can ye look up, having image of God *e.* on countenances; 63: 12 all *e.* in possession of Helaman[1] are sent forth among people; **Morm.** 1: 3 Ammaron had deposited sacred *e.* in hill Shim.

ENJOY (*see* Enjoyment; Rights)

ENJOYMENT

2 Ne. 9: 14 the righteous shall have perfect knowledge of their *e.*

ENLARGE (*see also* Grow; Increase)

Jacob 2: 9 it burdens soul of Jacob[2] to *e.* wounds of those already wounded; **Alma** 32: 28 word must be good, for it begins to *e.* my soul; **3 Ne.** 22: 2 (Isa. 54: 2) *e.* the place of thy tent; **Moro.** 10: 31 *e.* thy borders forever.

ENLIGHTEN (*see also* Discern; Illuminate; Inspire; Light; Quick [=living]; Shine)

Alma 24: 30 people once *e.* by Spirit who have fallen into sin become more hardened; 32: 28 word must be good, for it begins to *e.* my understanding.

ENOS[1]—*grandson of Adam* (*see also* BD Enos)

No references in Book of Mormon.

ENOS[2]—*Nephite prophet, record keeper*

Jacob 7: 27 son of Jacob[2], given plates; **Enos** 1: 1, 3 is taught by father; 1: 2 wrestles before God to receive remission of sins; 1: 4 prays all day; 1: 5–8 hears voice of the Lord, sins forgiven through faith in Christ; 1: 9 concerned for welfare of Nephites; 1: 19 prophesies and testifies; **Jarom** 1: 1 gives plates to son, Jarom.

ENSIGN (*see also* Standard)

2 Ne. 15: 26 (21: 12; Isa. 5: 26; 11: 12) the Lord will lift an *e.* to the nations; 21: 10 root of Jesse shall stand for *e.*

ENSNARE (*see also* Captive; Catch; Snare)

1 Ne. 22: 14 nations which war against Israel shall fall into pit digged to *e.* people of the Lord; **Alma** 28: 13 devil devises cunning plans to *e.* hearts of men.

ENTER (*see also* Come; Gate; Rest)

1 Ne. 15: 34 (10: 21; 3 Ne. 27: 19) no unclean thing can *e.* kingdom of God; **2 Ne.** 32: 5 *e.* in by the way and Holy Ghost will show what to do; **Mosiah** 5: 5 Benjamin's people willing to *e.* covenant with God; **Alma** 40: 13 spirit of devil *e.* into spirits of wicked; **3 Ne.** 14: 21 (Matt. 7: 21) not every one that saith Lord, Lord, shall *e.* kingdom of heaven; 18: 18 pray always lest ye *e.* into temptation.

ENTICE, ENTICINGS (*see also* Agency; Invite; Tempt)

2 Ne. 2: 16 man could not act for himself save he should be *e.* by the sweet or the bitter; 5: 21 Lamanites given skin of blackness that they might not be *e.* to Nephites; 9: 39 remember the awfulness of yielding to the *e.* of cunning one; **Mosiah** 3: 19 natural man will be enemy to God until he yields to *e.* of Spirit; **Hel.** 6: 26 Satan *e.* first parents to partake of forbidden fruit; 7: 16 how could you have given way to *e.* of devil; **Moro.** 7: 12 devil *e.* to sin; 7: 13 that which is of God *e.* to do good continually.

ENTREAT (*see also* Exhort)

Alma 7: 23 be easy to be *e.*; **Hel.** 7: 7 people of Nephi were easy to be *e.*

ENTRUSTED (*see also* Give)

Alma 37: 14 Helaman[1] *e.* with sacred things; 39: 4 Corianton should have tended to ministry with which he was *e.*; 53: 20 sons of Helaman[2] are true in all they are *e.*; **Morm.** 6: 6 Mormon[2] hides records *e.* to him by the Lord.

ENVY, ENVYING (*see also* Covet; Jealous; Pride; TG Envy)

2 Ne. 21: 13 (Isa. 11: 13) *e.* of Ephraim shall depart; 26: 21 (Morm. 8: 28) false churches will cause *e.*; 26: 32 the Lord has commanded that men should not *e.*; **Alma** 1: 32 those who do not belong to church indulge in *e.*; 4: 9 *e.* among people of church; 5: 29 is there one among you who is not stripped of *e.*; 16: 18 priests preach against *e.*; **Hel.** 13: 22 hearts of Nephites swell with great pride, unto *e.*; **3 Ne.** 30: 2 Mormon[2] calls Gentiles to repent of *e.*; **4 Ne.** 1: 16 no *e.* among people after Christ's visit; **Morm.** 8: 28 in latter days teachers and leaders of churches will lift themselves up in pride, unto *e.*

EPHRAIM—*kingdom of Israel* (*see also* Israel; Joseph[1], Seed of; BD Ephraim; Israel; Israel, Kingdom of; Joseph, People of)

2 Ne. 17: 2, 5 (Isa. 7: 2, 5) Syria is confederate with *E.*; 17: 8 (Isa. 7: 8) *E.* to be broken that it be not a people; 17: 9 (Isa. 7: 9) Samaria is head of *E.*; 17: 17 (Isa. 7: 17) the Lord shall bring upon house of David days that have not come from the day that *E.* departed from Judah; 19: 8–9 (Isa. 9: 8–9) all people, even *E.*, to know the Lord's word; 19: 21 (Isa. 9: 21) Manasseh and *E.* shall be against Judah; 21: 13 (Isa. 11: 13) *E.* shall not envy Judah, and Judah shall not vex *E.*

EPHRAIM, HILL OF

Ether 7: 9 iron ore for swords obtained from hill *E.*

EPISTLE

Alma 54: 4, 15 Moroni[1] writes *e.* to Ammoron; 54: 15 (55: 1) Ammoron writes *e.* to Moroni[1]; 56: 1 Moroni[1] receives *e.* from Helaman[2]; 57: 1 Helaman[2] had received *e.* from Ammoron; 57: 2 Helaman[2] wrote *e.* to Ammoron; 59: 3 Moroni[1] writes *e.* to Pahoran[1]; 60: 1 Moroni[1] writes second *e.* to Pahoran[1]; 61: 1 (62: 1) Moroni[1] receives *e.* from Pahoran[1]; **3 Ne.** 3: 1–2, 11 Lachoneus[1] receives *e.* from leader of robbers; **Morm.** 3: 4 Lamanite king sends *e.* to Mormon[2]; 6: 2 Mormon[2] writes *e.* to Lamanite king; **Ether** 15: 4–5 Coriantumr[2] sends *e.* to Shiz; 15: 5 Shiz writes *e.* to Coriantumr[2]; 15: 18 Coriantumr[2] writes second *e.* to Shiz; **Moro.** ch. 8–9 Moroni[2] records two *e.* from Mormon[2].

EQUAL, EQUALITY (*see also* Alike; Equity; Inequality; Judgment; Respect, Respecter; Same)

Jacob 5: 66, 73 root and top of tree should be *e.* in strength; 5: 74 fruits of trees become *e.*; **Mosiah** 27: 3 commandment throughout all churches that there should be *e.* among all men; 29: 38 every man should have *e.* chance; **Alma** 1: 26 teacher and learner are all *e.*; 30: 11 all men are on *e.* grounds before law; **3 Ne.** 28: 39 change in three Nephite disciples not *e.* to change to take place at last day.

EQUITY (*see also* Equal; Justice)

2 Ne. 21: 4 (30: 9; Isa. 11: 4) the Lord will reprove with *e.* for the meek; **Alma** 9: 26 (10: 21; 13: 9) the Lord is full of grace, *e.*; **Hel.** 3: 20 Helaman[2] and Nephi[2] fill judgment-seat with *e.*; **3 Ne.** 6: 4 Nephites form laws according to *e.*

ERR, ERROR (*see also* Astray; Doctrine, False; Sin; Stumble; Transgression; Wander)

2 Ne. 13: 12 (19: 16; 28: 14; Isa. 3: 12; 9: 16) they who lead the Lord's children cause them to *e.*; 25: 20 (Alma 5: 43; 13: 23) the Lord's word is taught plainly, so that people cannot *e.*; 27: 35 they who *e.* in spirit shall come to understanding; 28: 14 people *e.* because they are taught precepts of men; **Alma** 37: 8 sacred records convince many of *e.* of their ways; **3 Ne.** 1: 25 those who preach against law of Moses are convinced of their *e.*; **Moro.** 8: 6 gross *e.* that little children need baptism.

ERRAND (*see also* Calling)

Jacob 1: 17 Jacob[2] first obtained his *e.* from the Lord.

ESCAPE (*see also* Deliver; Flight; Refuge; Salvation)

2 Ne. 9: 10 God prepares *e.* from grasp of death and hell; 14: 2 (Isa. 4: 2) fruit of earth shall be comely to them that are *e.* of Israel.

ESROM—*early Jaredite*

Ether 8: 4–6 son of Omer, helps return kingdom to father.

ESTABLISH, ESTABLISHMENT (*see also* Confirm; Prepare)

1 Ne. 13: 40 last records shall *e.* truth of the first; **2 Ne.** 12: 2 (Isa. 2: 2) mountain of the Lord's house shall be *e.* in top of mountains; **Alma** 1: 6 Nehor *e.* church; 2: 3 king must be *e.* by voice of people; 8: 1 Alma[2] *e.* order of church; **Hel.** 5: 2 laws and government *e.* by voice of people; **3 Ne.** 7: 11, 14 laws and government *e.* by chiefs and leaders of tribes; 11: 40 whoso shall declare more or less than this and *e.* it for Christ's doctrine comes of evil; 21: 1 the Lord will *e.* Zion again among house of Israel; 21: 22 the Lord will *e.* his church among house of Israel if they will hearken; **Ether** 5: 4 in mouth of three witnesses shall these things be *e.*

ESTEEM (*see also* Love; Value; Worth)

1 Ne. 17: 35 the Lord *e.* all flesh in one; 19: 7 things which some *e.* to be of great worth, others set at naught; **2 Ne.** 3: 7 choice seer will be *e.* highly among descendants of Joseph[1]; 33: 2 many things written are *e.* as things of naught by those who harden hearts; 33: 3 Nephi[1] *e.* things he has written as of great worth; **Mosiah** 14: 4 (Isa. 53: 4) we did *e.* Messiah stricken and afflicted: 23: 7 ye shall not *e.* one flesh above another; 27: 4 every man should *e.* his neighbor as himself; 29: 40 people of Mosiah[2] *e.* him more than any other man; **Alma** 1: 26 priest does not *e.* himself above hearers; **Hel.** 11: 18 people *e.* Nephi[2] as great prophet; **Ether** 13: 13 Jaredites *e.* Ether as naught.

ETERNAL, ETERNALLY (*see also* Endless; Eternal Life; Eternity; Everlasting; God, Eternal Nature of; Infinite)

1 Ne. 10: 19 (Alma 7: 20) course of the Lord is one *e.* round; **2 Ne.** 1: 13 men carried captive down to *e.* gulf of misery; **Mosiah** 2: 34 ye are *e.* indebted to the Father; **Alma** 3: 26 in one year tens of thousands of souls sent to *e.* world; 3: 26 men reap *e.* happiness, *e.* misery, according to spirit they obey; 34: 10 great and last sacrifice must be infinite and *e.* sacrifice; 37: 44 word of Christ will point straight course to *e.* bliss; 42: 16 repentance could not come except there were a punishment which also was *e.* as life of soul; **3 Ne.** 28: 40 three Nephites will dwell with God *e.*; **Ether** 3: 14 in Christ shall mankind have light *e.*; **Moro.** 7: 28 Christ dwells *e.* in the heavens.

ETERNAL FATHER, GOD THE (*see* God, Eternal Nature of; God the Father)

ETERNAL LIFE (*see also* Continue, Continuation; Immortality; Live; Redemption; Resurrection; Salvation; TG Eternal Life)

2 Ne. 2: 27–29 (10: 23) men are free to choose *e.* life or *e.* death; 9: 39 to be spiritually minded is life *e.*; 31: 18 those who repent and are baptized are in narrow path which leads to *e.* life; 33: 4 to believe in Christ and endure to end is life *e.*; **Jacob** 6: 11 continue in narrow way until ye obtain *e.* life; **Enos** 1: 3 Jacob[2] taught Enos[2] concerning *e.* life; **Mosiah** 26: 20 the Lord covenants with Alma[1] that he shall have *e.* life; **Alma** 19: 6 light of everlasting life lit up Lamoni's soul; 28: 14 great reason of rejoicing because of light of Christ unto life; **Hel.** 12: 26 (3 Ne. 26: 5) they who have done good shall have everlasting life; 14: 31 God has given unto man to choose life or death; **3 Ne.** 5: 13 Mormon[2] declares Christ's word, so that his people might have everlasting life; 15: 9 unto him who endures to end shall the Lord give *e.* life; **Ether** 3: 14 in Christ shall mankind have life; **Moro.** 7: 41 ye shall have hope, through atonement and resurrection, to be raised unto life *e.*

ETERNITY (*see also* Eternal; God, Eternal Nature of; Time)

Jacob 7: 18 Sherem speaks of *e.* and eternal punishment; **Mosiah** 3: 5 the Lord was and is from all *e.* to all *e.*; **Alma** 13: 7 high priesthood prepared from *e.* to all *e.*; 34: 33 this day of life given to prepare for *e.*; **Moro.** 8: 18 God is unchangeable from all *e.* to all *e.*

ETHEM—*later Jaredite king*

Ether 1: 8–9 son of Ahah, father of Moron; 11: 11, 14 executes judgment in wickedness; 11: 12 many prophets during *E*'s reign.

ETHER—*last great Jaredite prophet, record keeper*

Ether 1: 2, 6 record on twenty-four gold plates called Book of *E.*; 1: 6 (11: 23) son of Coriantor; 12: 1–2 prophet in days of Coriantumr[2]; 12: 5 prophesies great and marvelous things; 13: 2 is rejected; 13: 4 speaks of Christ and New Jerusalem; 13: 13–14, 18 hides in cave, views destruction of Jaredites; 13: 20–22 calls Coriantumr[2] to repentance; 13: 21, 24 *E*'s prophecies are fulfilled; 15: 1 *E*'s words remembered by Coriantumr[2]; 15: 12–13 watches, but does not join others; 15: 33 finishes and hides record; 15: 34 last words.

EVE—*mother of all living* (*see also* Adam; Eden, Garden of; Parent; Woman; BD Eve)

1 Ne. 5: 11 brass plates give account of Adam and *E.*; **2 Ne.** 2: 15–20 tempted, partakes of forbidden fruit; **Alma** 42: 2, 7 cut off temporally and spiritually from presence of God.

EVERLASTING, EVERLASTINGLY (*see also* Endless; Eternal; Eternal Life; God, Eternal Nature of)

1 Ne. 14: 7 the Lord will do a work among men which will be *e.*; **Alma** 26: 15 Lamanites were encircled with *e.* darkness, but God has brought them into *e.* light; 37: 32 teach this people an *e.* hatred against sin and iniquity; **Hel.** 13: 38 ye have procrastinated day of salvation until *e.* too late; **Ether** 2: 10 *e.* decree of God that those who inhabit land must serve him or be swept off; **Moro.** 8: 17 charity is *e.* love.

EVIDENCE (*see also* Witness)

Alma 11: 2 judges judge according to law and *e.*; 30: 40 what *e.* have ye that there is no God; **Hel.** 5: 50 Lamanites are convinced because of greatness of *e.*; 8: 24 corrupt judges have rejected truth notwithstanding many *e.* they have received.

EVIL (*see also* Abomination; Agency; Bad; Carnal; Devil; Filthiness; Iniquity; Sin; Spirit, Evil; Transgression; Unclean; Wicked; Wrong)

2 Ne. 2: 5 (Hel. 14: 31; Moro. 7: 16) men are instructed sufficiently that they know good from *e.*; 2: 17 fallen angel became devil, having sought that which was *e.*; 2: 18 (Alma 12: 31) ye shall be as God, knowing good and *e.*; 2: 26 because men are redeemed from fall, they have become free, knowing good from *e.*; 2: 29 not choose eternal death, according to will of flesh and *e.* therein; 15: 20 (Isa. 5: 20) wo unto them that call *e.* good, and good *e.*; **Jacob** 5: 37–38 trees in vineyard have brought forth *e.* fruit; 5: 59 because of the change of branches, the good may overcome the *e.*; **Omni** 1: 25 (Alma 5: 40; Moro. 7: 12, 17) that which is *e.* comes from devil; **Mosiah** 5: 2 (Alma 19: 33) the Spirit has wrought mighty change in Benjamin's people, that they have no more disposition to do *e.*; **Alma** 12: 31 through the fall, men are in position to act according to wills, whether to do *e.* or good; 29: 5 he who knows not good from *e.* is blameless; 29: 5 to him who knows good from *e.* is given according to his desires; 40: 13 spirits of wicked have no portion of Spirit, for they choose *e.* works rather than good; 41: 4–5 (Hel. 14: 31) *e.* works shall be restored unto men for *e.*; 41: 5 if man has desired *e.* all day long, he shall have reward of *e.* when night comes; 41: 7 those who repent and desire righteousness are their own judges, whether to do good or *e.*; 41: 13 word restoration means to bring back *e.* for *e.*; **Hel.** 12: 4 how *e.* and devilish are children of men; 15: 4 the Lord has hated Lamanites because their deeds have been *e.* continually; **3 Ne.** 13: 12 (Matt. 6: 13) deliver us from *e.*; **Ether** 3: 2 because of fall, men's natures have become *e.* continually; **Moro.** 7: 6 man being *e.* cannot do that which is good; 7: 8 if a man being *e.* gives a gift, he does it grudgingly; 7: 9 it is counted *e.* unto a man if he pray without real intent; 7: 17 whatsoever thing persuadeth men to do *e.* comes of devil; 7: 45 (1 Cor. 13: 5) charity thinketh no *e.*

EXALT, EXALTED (*see also* Raise; TG Exalt)

2 Ne. 12: 2 (Isa. 2: 2) mountain of the Lord's house shall be *e.* above the hills; 24: 13 (Isa. 14: 13) I will *e.* my throne above the stars.

EXAMPLE (*see also* Ensign; Follow; Light; Standard; TG Example)

1 Ne. 7: 8 Nephi[1] must set *e.* for elder brethren; **2 Ne.** 31: 9 (3 Ne. 18: 16; Morm. 7: 10) Christ's baptism sets *e.*; 31: 16 unless a man endures to end in following the *e.* of the Son, he cannot be saved; **Jacob** 2: 35 (3: 10) Nephites have lost confidence of children because of bad *e.*; **Alma** 4: 11 *e.* of church leads unbelievers into iniquity; 17: 11 the Lord admonishes sons of Mosiah[2] to show good *e.* unto Lamanites; 39: 1 Shiblon has set good example for Corianton; **3 Ne.** 18: 16 Christ has set *e.* for men.

EXCELLENT

Ether 12: 11 God prepared a more *e.* way; 12: 32 in Father's mansions, man may have more *e.* hope.

EXCOMMUNICATION (*see also* Blot; Cast; Cut)

3 Ne. 18: 31 he who repents not should not be numbered among the Lord's people.

EXCUSE

1 Ne. 19: 6 Nephi[1] does not *e.* himself because of other men, but because of own weakness; **Jacob** 2: 23 Nephites seek to *e.* themselves in committing whoredoms because of David and Solomon; **Alma** 39: 4 Isabel stole away hearts of many, but this is no *e.* for Corianton; 42: 30 do not endeavor to *e.* yourself by denying justice of God.

EXECUTED (*see also* Capital Punishment)

Alma 2: 1 (1: 15) Nehor *e.* according to law; 11: 2 judge *e.* authority; 62: 9–10 king-men and many others who deny freedom are *e.* according to law; **Hel.** 2: 10 Helaman[2] tries to take robbers, that they might be *e.*

EXERCISE (*see* Dominion; Faith; Power)

EXHORT, EXHORTATION (*see also* Entreat; Persuade; Preach; Urge; Warn)

1 Ne. 8: 37 Lehi[1] *e.* sons to hearken; 17: 15 Nephi[1] *e.* his brethren to faithfulness; **Jarom** 1: 11 prophets *e.* people to diligence; **Omni** 1: 25 Amaleki[1] *e.* all men to come unto God; **Alma** 34: 40 Amulek *e.* Zoramites to have patience; **Hel.** 6: 4 Lamanites *e.* Nephites to faith and repentance; **Moro.** 10: 2 Moroni[2] speaks by way of *e.*; 10: 3 Moroni[2] *e.* readers to remember God's mercy; 10: 4 Moroni[2] *e.* readers to ask God whether writings are true.

EXPEDIENT

1 Ne. 17: 30 the Lord did for Israelites all things *e.* for man to receive; **2 Ne.** 2: 27 all things are given unto men which are *e.*; **Moro.** 7: 33 (10: 23) if ye have faith in Christ, ye shall have power to do whatsoever is *e.* in him.

EXPERIMENT

Alma 32: 27, 33, 36 (34: 4) Alma[2] exhorts Zoramites to try *e.* to know whether seed is good.

EXPERT, EXPERTNESS (*see also* Skill)

Alma 10: 31 Zeezrom one of most *e.* lawyers in Ammonihah; 11: 21 Zeezrom *e.* in devices of devil; 18: 3 Lamoni's flocks cannot be scattered because of *e.*

of Ammon[2]; **Hel.** 2: 4 Gadianton is *e.* in many words; 3: 7 Nephites become *e.* in working of cement; **Ether** 8: 8 daughter of Jared[2] is exceedingly *e.*

EXPOUND (*see also* Preach; Teach)

Alma 18: 38 Ammon[2] *e.* all records and scriptures since time of Lehi[1]; 22: 13 Aaron[2] *e.* all scriptures from creation of Adam; **3 Ne.** 23: 14 Christ *e.* all scriptures in one; 26: 3 Christ *e.* all things from creation to his coming in glory.

EXQUISITE

Alma 36: 21 nothing so *e.* and bitter as pains of Alma[2].

EXTINCT

Alma 36: 15 oh that I could become *e.* both soul and body; 45: 11 Nephites shall become *e.*; **Hel.** 11: 10 band of Gadianton have become *e.*; **3 Ne.** 3: 8 Giddianhi threatens to slay Nephites until they become *e.*

EYE (*see also* See; Sight)

1 Ne. 22: 23 churches built up to become popular in *e.* of world; **2 Ne.** 9: 44 Nephi[1] prays that God will view him with all-searching *e.*; 15: 21 (Isa. 5: 21) wo unto the wise in their own *e.*; 16: 10 (Isa. 6: 10) shut *e.* of this people, lest they see with their *e.*; 27: 12 book shall be hid from *e.* of world; 27: 29 (Isa. 29: 18) *e.* of blind shall see out of obscurity; **Jacob** 2: 10 Jacob[2] must tell Nephites of their wickedness under glance of piercing *e.* of God; **Mosiah** 12: 22 (15: 29; 16: 1; Alma 36: 26; 3 Ne. 16: 18; 20: 32; Isa. 52: 8) they shall see *e.* to *e.*; 18: 21 Alma[1] commands that there should be no contention, but that people look forward with one *e.*; 27: 22 priests pray that Alma[2] might receive strength, that *e.* of people might be opened to goodness of God; **Alma** 5: 15 (32: 40) look forward with *e.* of faith; **3 Ne.** 2: 2 Satan blinds people's *e.*; 12: 38 (Ex. 21: 24; Lev. 24: 20; Matt. 5: 38) it is written, an *e.* for an *e.*; 13: 22 (Matt. 6: 22) light of body is the *e.*; 14: 3 (Matt. 7: 3) why beholdest thou the mote in brother's *e.*, but not beam in own *e.*; 26: 15 Christ opens *e.* of the blind; 28: 8 three Nephites to be changed in twinkling of *e.*; **Morm.** 8: 15 plates to be brought to light with *e.* single to God's glory; **Ether** 12: 19 many see with their *e.* things which they behold with *e.* of faith.

EZIAS—*a prophet*

Hel. 8: 20 testified of Christ.

EZROM—*silver coin* (*see also* Coin)

Alma 11: 6, 12 as great as four senums.

FACE (*see also* Countenance; God, Presence of; Visage)

2 Ne. 9: 38 those who die in their sins shall return to God, see his *f.*; 23: 8 (Isa. 13: 8) men's *f.* shall be as flames; 33: 11 you and I shall stand *f.* to *f.* before Christ's bar; **Mosiah** 13: 5 Abinadi's *f.* shines as Moses on mount Sinai; **Hel.** 5: 36 *f.* of Nephi[2] and Lehi[4] shine as *f.* of angels; **3 Ne.** 9: 11 the Lord destroys cities to hide their wickedness from before his *f.*; 13: 16 (Matt. 6: 16) when hypocrites fast, they disfigure their *f.*

FACULTY

1 Ne. 15: 25 Nephi[1] exhorts his brethren with all his *f.*; **Jacob** 3: 11 (Alma 32: 27) arouse the *f.* of your souls; **W of M** 1: 18 by laboring with *f.* of his whole soul, Benjamin establishes peace.

FAIL

Alma 4: 15 Spirit of the Lord does not *f.* Alma[2]; **Moro.** 7: 46 charity never *f.*

FAINT (*see also* Continue; Endure)

2 Ne. 32: 9 (Luke 18: 1) ye must pray always, and not *f.*

FAIR (*see also* Beauty; Delightsome)

1 Ne. 11: 13, 15 virgin is exceedingly *f.*; 13: 15 Gentiles who obtain land will be exceedingly *f.*; **3 Ne.** 2: 16 young men and daughters of Lamanites become exceedingly *f.*; **4 Ne.** 1: 10 Nephites become exceedingly *f.* people; **Morm.** 9: 6 cry unto Father that ye may be found *f.*

FAITH (*see also* Baptism; Belief; Born of God; Confidence; Doubt; Faithful; Forgive, Forgiveness; Gospel; Hope; Knowledge; Miracle; Obedience; Prayer; Religion; Repentance; Salvation; Sanctification; Sign; Testimony; Trial; Trust; TG Faith; BD Faith)

1 Ne. 7: 12 the Lord is able to do all things for men if they exercise *f.* in him; 10: 17 Lehi[1] received Holy Ghost by *f.* on the Son; 12: 10 because of *f.* in the Lamb, apostles' garments are made white; 16: 28 pointers in Liahona work according to *f.*; **2 Ne.** 1: 10 power given to do all things by *f.*; 9: 23 men are commanded to be baptized, having *f.* in the Holy One; 25: 25 Nephites made alive in Christ because of *f.*; 26: 13 (27: 23; Ether 12: 12; Moro. 7: 27–29, 34–38) Christ works miracles according to men's *f.*; 31: 19 ye have not come thus far save by word of Christ with unshaken *f.* in him; **Jacob** 4: 6 our *f.* becomes unshaken; **Enos** 1: 8 sins forgiven because of *f.* in Christ; **Jarom** 1: 4

as many as have *f.* have communion with Holy Spirit; 1: 4 Holy Spirit makes manifest among men according to their *f.*; **Mosiah** 3: 9, 12 (Moro. 7: 26, 38) salvation comes through *f.* on Christ's name; 5: 4 *f.* on things spoken by Benjamin brings his people to knowledge; 5: 7 hearts of Benjamin's people are changed through *f.* on the Lord's name; 21: 30 Alma[1] and his people form church through *f.* on Abinadi's words; 25: 15 (Alma 37: 33) preach repentance and *f.* on the Lord; 26: 15 Alma[1] is blessed because of *f.* in words of Abinadi; 27: 14 the Lord hears prayers of Alma[1] because of his *f.*; **Alma** 1: 24–25 withdrawal of many from church is great trial to those who stand fast in the *f.*; 2: 30 being exercised with much *f.*, Alma[2] cries unto the Lord to preserve his people; 7: 6 look forward for remission of your sins with everlasting *f.*; 14: 26 give us strength according to our *f.* in Christ; 15: 10 heal this man according to his *f.* in Christ; 18: 35 Spirit gives knowledge and power according to *f.*; 22: 16 if thou wilt call on God's name in *f.*, thou shalt receive the hope thou desirest; 26: 22 unto him who exercises *f.* is given to know mysteries; 32: 18 (Ether 3: 19) if a man knows a thing, he has no cause to have *f.*; 32: 21 *f.* is not a perfect knowledge; 32: 21 (Ether 12: 6) *f.* is hope for things which are not seen; 32: 36 (34: 4) exercise your *f.* to plant the seed; 32: 40 if ye will not nourish the word, looking forward with eye of *f.* to fruit, ye can never pluck fruit of tree of life; 33: 23 as word begins to swell, nourish it by *f.*; 44: 5 Nephites gain power over Lamanites by *f.*; 48: 13 Moroni[1] is firm in *f.* of Christ; 48: 15–16 *f.* that God will prosper Nephites if they fight only in defense; 57: 26–27 stripling warriors spared because of *f.* in what they had been taught; 61: 17 Nephites march against dissenters in strength of God, according to *f.*; **Hel.** 5: 47 peace be unto you because of *f.* in Well Beloved; 8: 15 those who look upon Son with *f.* will have life eternal; 13: 6 nothing can save Nephites from destruction save repentance and *f.* on Christ; **3 Ne.** 7: 18 so great is *f.* of Nephi[3] that angels minister unto him daily; 13: 30 (Matt. 6: 30) even so will God clothe you, if ye are not of little *f.*; 17: 8 your *f.* is sufficient that I should heal you; 19: 35 so great *f.* have I never seen among all the Jews; 26: 9 Lamanites to have record to try their *f.*; 26: 11 Nephi[3] is commanded not to write all from plates of Nephi, in order to try people's *f.*; 27: 19 none enter the Lord's rest save those who wash garments in Christ's blood because of *f.*; **Morm.** 9: 37 may the Lord grant that prayers be answered according to *f.*; **Ether** 3: 19 brother of Jared[2] has *f.* no longer, because he knows; 4: 7 when Gentiles exercise *f.* in the Lord, they may become sanctified; 12: 4 hope comes of *f.*; 12: 6 receive no witness until after trial of *f.*; 12: 7 by *f.* Christ showed himself; 12: 10 by *f.* were they of old called after holy order; 12: 11 by *f.* was law of Moses given; 12: 12 without *f.* among men, God can do no miracle among them; 12: 14–15 *f.* of missionaries caused change among Lamanites; 12: 28 *f.*, hope, charity bring men unto the Lord; 12: 30 the Lord works after men have *f.*; **Moro.** 3: 3 remission of sins comes through Christ, by endurance of *f.* on his name; 6: 4 Christ is author and finisher of *f.*; ch. 7 letter of Mormon[2] on *f.*, hope, charity; 7: 26 by *f.* men become sons of God; 7: 26 whatsoever ye ask in *f.*, believing that ye shall receive, it shall be done; 7: 33 (10: 23) if ye have *f.* in Christ, ye shall have power to do whatsoever is expedient in him; 7: 41 hope to be raised unto life eternal because of *f.* in Christ; 7: 42 without *f.* there cannot be any hope; 7: 43 man cannot have *f.* and hope save he shall be meek; 10: 4 if ye ask with *f.* in Christ, God will manifest truth unto you.

FAITHFUL, FAITHFULNESS (*see also* Diligence; Faith; Obedience; Righteousness; Steadfast; Work [noun]; Worthy; Zeal)

1 Ne. 3: 16 let us be *f.* in keeping the Lord's commandments; **2 Ne.** 6: 11 many shall not be suffered to perish, because of prayers of the *f.*; 21: 5 (30: 11; Isa. 11: 5) *f.* shall be the girdle of his reins; 26: 15 prayers of the *f.* shall be heard; **Mosiah** 2: 41 if the righteous hold out *f.* to end, they are received into heaven; 10: 13 Nephi[1] is favored of the Lord because more *f.* in keeping commandments; **Alma** 5: 13 fathers saved because they were *f.* until end; **3 Ne.** 27: 19 garments washed in Christ's blood because of *f.* unto end; **Ether** 4: 19 he who is found *f.* unto the Lord's name shall dwell in kingdom.

FALL, FELL, FALLEN (*see also* Apostasy; Descend; Fall of Man; Tumble)

1 Ne. 12: 7 Holy Ghost *f.* upon twelve apostles; 22: 13 sword of abominable church shall *f.* upon own heads; 22: 14 those who fight against Zion shall *f.* into pit digged to ensnare the Lord's people; **2 Ne.** 2: 17 (24: 12; Luke 10: 18; Isa. 14: 12) angel had *f.* from heaven; **Hel.** 13: 5 (3 Ne. 20: 20) within four hundred years sword of justice shall *f.* upon this people; **3 Ne.** 11: 12, 17 when Jesus had spoken these words, multitude *f.* to earth; 14: 24–27 (18: 13; Matt. 7: 24–27) house built upon sand *f.*; 19: 13

Holy Ghost *f.* upon Nephite disciples; **Ether** 3: 6 brother of Jared[2] *f.* down before the Lord; **Moro.** 2: 3 Holy Ghost *f.* on those on whom disciples laid hands.

FALL OF MAN (*see also* Adam; Carnal; Death, Physical; Death, Spiritual; Fruit, Forbidden; Jesus Christ, Atonement through; Nature, Natural; Resurrection; Sin; Transgression; TG Fall of Man; BD Fall of Adam)

1 Ne. 10: 6 all mankind were in a lost and fallen state; **2 Ne.** 2: 4 the way is prepared from the *f.* of man; 2: 19 after partaking of forbidden fruit, Adam and Eve were driven from Eden; 2: 25 Adam fell that men might be; 9: 6 resurrection must come unto man by reason of the *f.*; 9: 6 the *f.* came by reason of transgression; **Mosiah** 3: 11 Christ's blood atones for sins of those who have fallen by transgression of Adam; 3: 16 in Adam, or by nature, children *f.*; 3: 19 natural man has been enemy to God since *f.* of Adam; 4: 5 knowledge of God's goodness awakens men to sense of fallen state; 4: 7 atonement prepared for all mankind since *f.* of Adam; 16: 3 *f.* caused by serpent's beguiling of first parents; 16: 4 mankind would have been endlessly lost, had not God redeemed his people from lost and fallen state; **Alma** 12: 22 by Adam's *f.* all mankind become lost and fallen; 18: 36 Ammon[2] teaches Lamoni many things concerning *f.* of man; 22: 13 Aaron[3] expounds scriptures, laying *f.* of man before Lamanite king; 22: 14 since man had fallen, he could not merit anything of himself; 34: 9 all mankind are fallen and lost; 42: 6–7 first parents become fallen man, cut off temporally and spiritually; 42: 9 the *f.* brought upon mankind spiritual death as well as temporal; **Hel.** 14: 16 mankind, being cut off from presence of the Lord by *f.* of Adam, are dead as to things spiritual and temporal; **Morm.** 9: 12 by Adam came the *f.* of man; **Ether** 3: 2 because of the *f.* our natures have become evil continually.

FALLEN (*see* Fall, Fell, Fallen; Fall of Man)

FALSE, FALSEHOOD (*see also* Christs, False; Churches, False; Deceit; Doctrine, False; Incorrect; Lying; Prophets, False; Wrong)

2 Ne. 25: 18 no other Messiah shall come, save *f.* Messiah; **Mosiah** 13: 23 (Ex. 20: 16; Hel. 7: 21) thou shalt not bear *f.* witness; **3 Ne.** 24: 5 (Mal. 3: 5) the Lord will be swift witness against *f.* swearers.

FALSE CHRISTS (*see* Christs, False)

FALSE DOCTRINE (*see* Doctrine, False)

FALSE PRIESTHOODS (*see* Priestcraft; TG False Priesthoods)

FALSE PROPHETS (*see* Prophets, False)

FAMILIAR (*see also* Spirit, Evil)

2 Ne. 18: 19 (Isa. 8: 19) they shall say, Seek unto them that have *f.* spirits; 26: 16 (Isa. 29: 4) voice shall be as one that hath a *f.* spirit; **Jacob** 2: 17 be *f.* with all.

FAMILY (*see also* Brother; Child; Daughter; Father; Household; Husband; Mother; Sister; Son; Wife; TG Family, Children, Duties of; Family, Children, Responsibilities toward; Family, Eternal; Family, Love within; Family, Patriarchal; BD Family)

1 Ne. 2: 2 the Lord commands Lehi[1] to take his *f.* and depart into wilderness; 2 **Ne.** 2: 20 Adam and Eve have brought forth the *f.* of all the earth; **Alma** 43: 47 ye shall defend your *f.* even unto bloodshed; **3 Ne.** 7: 14 tribes organized according to *f.*; 18: 21 pray in your *f.*; **Morm.** 3: 20 every soul who belongs to human *f.* shall stand before judgment-seat; **Ether** 1: 41 Jared[2] and friends to gather their *f.*

FAMINE (*see also* Destruction; Hunger; Rain)

2 Ne. 1: 18 (Mosiah 1: 17) because of hardness of hearts, Nephites may be visited by *f.*; 6: 15 they who believe not on Messiah shall be destroyed by *f.*; 24: 30 (Isa. 14: 30) I will kill thy root with *f.*; **Mosiah** 9: 3 Zeniff's people smitten with *f.*; **Alma** 9: 22 the Lord has saved Israel from *f.*; 10: 22 if it were not for prayers of righteous, ye would be visited now by *f.*; 53: 7 Moroni[1] delivers women and children from *f.*; 62: 35, 39 war between Nephites and Lamanites causes much *f.*; **Hel.** 10: 6 Nephi[2] is given power to smite earth with *f.*; 11: 4 let there be *f.* in land to stir people up in remembrance of the Lord; 13: 9 four hundred years will not pass away before the Lord visits Nephites with *f.*; **Ether** 9: 28 great *f.* to destroy people if they do not repent; 9: 30 great dearth upon the land.

FAR

2 Ne. 27: 25 (Isa. 29: 13) this people draw near the Lord with lips, but remove hearts *f.* from him; **Mosiah** 5: 13 how knoweth a man the stranger who is *f.* from thoughts of heart.

FAST (*see also* Faster; Fasting; Firmness; Steadfast)

1 Ne. 8: 30 many hold *f.* to rod of iron; **Alma** 1: 24–25 withdrawal of some is great trial to those that stand *f.* in the faith.

FASTER (*see also* Swift)

Mosiah 4: 27 not requisite that man run *f.* than he has strength.

FASTING, FAST (*see also* Humble; Prayer; TG Fasting; BD Fasts)

Omni 1: 26 (4 Ne. 1: 12) continue in *f.* and prayer; **Mosiah** 27: 22 priests *f.* and pray for Alma[2]; **Alma** 5: 46 Alma[2] has *f.* and prayed many days to know things of himself; 6: 6 children of God are commanded to gather together oft and join in *f.* and prayer; 17: 3, 9 sons of Mosiah[2] had given themselves to much *f.* and prayer to obtain Spirit; 45: 1 Nephites *f.* much and pray much; **Hel.** 3: 34–35 humble part of people *f.* and pray oft; **3 Ne.** 13: 16–18 (Matt. 6: 16–18) when ye *f.*, be not as hypocrites, but appear not unto men to *f.*; 27: 1 disciples unite in mighty prayer and *f.*

FATHER (*see also* Abraham; Family; Forefathers; God the Father; Husband; Mother; Parent; Son; TG Honoring Father and Mother; Marriage, Fatherhood; Fatherhood)

1 Ne. 1: 1 Nephi[1] is taught in learning of his *f.*; 15: 18 the Lord made covenant with *f.* Abraham; 17: 55 (Mosiah 13: 20; Ex. 20: 12) honor thy *f.* and thy mother; 21: 23 (2 Ne. 6: 7; 10: 9; Isa. 49: 23) kings shall be Israel's nursing *f.*; **2 Ne.** 2: 18 (9: 9; Ether 8: 25) devil is *f.* of all lies; 8: 2 look unto Abraham, your *f.*; 24: 21 (Isa. 14: 21) prepare slaughter for the Lord's children for iniquities of their *f.*; **Enos** 1: 1 Enos knows his *f.* is just man; **Mosiah** 13: 13 (Ex. 20: 5) the Lord visits iniquities of *f.* upon children; **Alma** 28: 5 cries heard of *f.* mourning for sons, brother for *f.*; **3 Ne.** 11: 29 devil is *f.* of contention; 25: 6 (Mal. 4: 6; D&C 110: 15; JS-H 1: 39) the Lord will turn hearts of *f.* to children and hearts of children to *f.*; **Moro.** 9: 8 Lamanites kill husbands and *f.* and feed flesh to wives and children.

FATHERLESS (*see* Orphan)

FAULT (*see also* Transgression; Weak, Weakness)

Alma 39: 13 acknowledge your *f.*; **3 Ne.** 1: 25 those who had ceased practicing law of Moses confess their *f.*; **Morm.** 8: 17 if there be *f.* in record, they be *f.* of man.

FAVORED (*see also* Blessing; Please)

1 Ne. 1: 1 Nephi[1] highly *f.* of the Lord; 17: 35 he who is righteous is *f.* of God; **2 Ne.** 1: 19 O that ye might be a choice and *f.* people of the Lord; **Alma** 9: 20 Nephites have been *f.* above every other nation; **Ether** 1: 34 brother of Jared[2] a man highly *f.* of the Lord.

FEAR, FEARFUL (*see also* Anxiety; Courage; Fear of God; Quake; Shake; Terror; Tremble; Worry)

2 Ne. 8: 7 (Isa. 51: 7) *f.* not the reproach of men; **Jacob** 7: 19 Sherem *f.* he has committed unpardonable sin; **Alma** 1: 18 many durst not steal for *f.* of law; 14: 26 inhabitants of Ammonihah flee, for *f.* of destruction; **Morm.** 6: 7 awful *f.* of death fills breasts of the wicked; **Moro.** 8: 16 *f.* not what man can do; 8: 16 perfect love casteth out *f.*

FEAR OF GOD (*see also* Obedience; Worship; TG Fear of God)

2 Ne. 12: 10 (Isa. 2: 10) *f.* of the Lord shall smite the wicked; 21: 1–2 (Isa. 11: 1–2) spirit of knowledge and *f.* of the Lord shall rest upon branch from Jesse's roots; 27: 34 children of Jacob[1] shall *f.* God of Israel; **Enos** 1: 23 prophecies of war and destruction keep Nephites in *f.* of the Lord; **Mosiah** 4: 1 Benjamin's people fall to earth, for *f.* of the Lord; 29: 30 Nephites are commanded to handle judicial matters in *f.* of the Lord; **Alma** 19: 15 *f.* of the Lord comes upon Lamoni's household; 36: 7 Alma[2] and sons of Mosiah[2] fell to earth, for *f.* of the Lord came upon them; 39: 12 Alma[2] commands Corianton, in *f.* of the Lord, to refrain from iniquities; 60: 28 Moroni[2] does not *f.* civil authority but he *f.* God; **3 Ne.** 4: 10 Nephites do not *f.* robbers, but they *f.* God; 25: 2 unto those who *f.* the Lord's name will Son of Righteousness arise with healing in wings; **Morm.** 9: 27 work out your salvation with *f.* and trembling before the Lord; **Ether** 3: 6 brother of Jared is struck with *f.* when he sees the Lord's finger.

FEAST (*see also* Partake)

2 Ne. 9: 51 *f.* upon that which perisheth not; 31: 20 (32: 3) press forward, *f.* upon word of Christ; **Jacob** 2: 9 those who have been wounded have daggers to pierce their souls, instead of *f.* upon word of God; 3: 2 *f.* upon God's love.

FEED (*see also* Eat; Food; Nourish)

2 Ne. 21: 7 (30: 13: Isa. 11: 7) cow and bear shall *f.*; **Jacob** 2: 19 seek riches for intent to do good—to *f.* the hungry; **Mosiah** 4: 26 to retain remission of sins, men must impart of substance, *f.* the hungry; **Alma** 4: 13 some Nephites *f.* the hungry; **3 Ne.** 13: 26 (Matt. 6: 26) Father *f.* fowls of the air; **Moro.** 9: 8 Lamanites *f.* women upon flesh of husbands.

FEEL, FELT (*see also* Feeling; Touch)

1 Ne. 17: 45 Laman[1] and Lemuel cannot *f.* words of still small voice; **Alma** 5: 26 if ye have *f.* to sing song of redeeming love, can ye *f.* so now; 26: 16 Ammon[2] cannot say smallest part which he *f.*; 32: 28 when ye *f.* swelling motions, ye will say seed is good; **3 Ne.** 8: 20 inhabitants of land can *f.* vapor of darkness; 11: 14–15 (18: 25) multitude *f.* prints of nails in Christ's hands.

FEELING (*see also* Feel; Passion)

1 Ne. 8: 37 Lehi[1] exhorts Laman[1] and Lemuel with *f.* of tender parent; 17: 45 (Moro. 9: 20) Laman[1] and Lemuel are past *f.*, cannot feel words of still small voice; **2 Ne.** 4: 12 Lehi[1] speaks according to *f.* of heart; **Jacob** 2: 7 *f.* of wives and children are tender and chaste.

FEET (*see* Foot, Feet)

FELL (*see* Fall, Fell, Fallen)

FELLOWSHIP (*see also* TG Brotherhood and Sisterhood; Fellowship; Fellowshipping)

Hel. 6: 3 Nephites and Lamanites *f.* one with another.

FELT (*see* Feel, Felt)

FEMALE (*see also* Woman)

1 Ne. 8: 27 spacious building filled with people, both male and *f.*; **2 Ne.** 10: 16 those who fight against Zion, both male and *f.*, shall perish; 26: 33 the Lord denies none who come unto him, male and *f.*; **Alma** 1: 30 Nephites are liberal to all, both male and *f.*; 11: 44 restoration shall come to all, both male and *f.*; **Ether** 1: 41 (2: 1) Jaredites gather flocks, both male and *f.*

FEROCIOUS (*see also* Fury; Wild)

Enos 1: 20 (Mosiah 10: 12) Lamanites led by evil nature to become *f.*; **Mosiah** 17: 17 people of Noah[3] shall be driven, even as wild flock is driven by *f.* beasts; **Alma** 17: 14 sons of Mosiah[2] preach to hardened and *f.* people; 47: 36 dissenters become more wicked and *f.* than Lamanites; **Hel.** 3: 16 Nephites are no more called Nephites, becoming wicked and *f.*

FERVENT (*see* Heat)

FEVER (*see also* Disease; Sick)

Alma 15: 3, 5 Zeezrom sick with *f.*; 46: 40 God prepares plants and roots to treat *f.*

FEW (*see also* Scarce)

1 Ne. 14: 12 numbers of church of Lamb were *f.*; 17: 43 *f.* Jews not destroyed shall be led into captivity; **2 Ne.** 28: 14 latter-day churches are all gone astray, save a *f.*; **Alma** 21: 12 *f.* believe on words of missionaries; 33: 19–26 *f.* understood prophecies and types of Christ; **3 Ne.** 7: 7 *f.* righteous men among Nephites; 7: 21 *f.* are converted unto the Lord; 14: 14 (27: 33; Matt. 7: 14) narrow is the way, and *f.* that find it; **Morm.** 8: 36 none save a *f.* who do not lift themselves up in pride.

FIELD

1 Ne. 8: 9, 20 Lehi[1] beholds large *f.* in dream; **2 Ne.** 27: 28 Lebanon to be turned into fruitful *f.*; **Alma** 26: 5 *f.* was ripe and missionaries thrust in sickle; 33: 5 God was merciful when Alma[2] cried unto him in *f.*; 34: 20, 24–25 cry unto God in your *f.*

FIERCENESS (*see* Wrath)

FIERY (*see* Dart; Fire; Furnace; Serpent)

FIG (*see also* Tree; BD Fig Tree)

3 Ne. 14: 16 (Matt. 7: 16) do men gather *f.* of thistles.

FIGHT, FOUGHT (*see also* Battle; Persecution; Struggle; War)

1 Ne. 11: 34–35 (14: 13) multitudes of earth shall *f.* against apostles; 11: 36 (2 Ne. 10: 16) those who *f.* against apostles shall be destroyed; 22: 14, 19 (2 Ne. 6: 13; 10: 13–16) all who *f.* against Zion shall be destroyed; **2 Ne.** 6: 12 blessed are Gentiles if they *f.* not against Zion; 25: 14 wo unto them who *f.* against God and his church; 27: 3 (Isa. 29: 8) all who *f.* against Zion shall be as dream of night vision; 29: 14 the Lord will show unto them who *f.* against Zion that he is God; **Mosiah** 4: 14 ye will not suffer your children to *f.* one with another; 20: 11 people of Limhi *f.* for their lives; **Alma** 23: 7 Lamanites do not *f.* against God any more; 43: 45 Nephites inspired by better cause *f.* for homes and families; 51: 21 those who profess nobility are brought to *f.* for freedom; 53: 17 sons of Ammonites enter covenant to *f.* for liberty of Nephites; 56: 56 sons of Ammonites *f.* with strength of God.

FILL (*see also* Full)

1 Ne. 1: 12 as Lehi[1] reads book, he is *f.* with Spirit; 14: 3 pit shall be *f.* by those who digged it; **Mosiah** 2: 4 by keeping commandments, Nephites might be *f.* with love toward God and men; **Alma** 8: 30 Alma[2] and Amulek are *f.* with Holy Ghost; 38: 12 bridle passions, that ye may be *f.* with love; **3 Ne.** 12: 6 (Matt. 5: 6) blessed are those who hunger and thirst after righteousness, for they shall be *f.* with Holy Ghost; 18: 5, 9 when multitude has partaken of bread and wine, they are *f.*; 19: 13 those baptized are *f.* with Holy Ghost and fire; 20: 9 when multitude has partaken of bread and wine, they are *f.* with Spirit; 27: 16 whoso repents and is baptized shall be *f.*; **Moro.** 7: 47–48 pray unto Father that ye may be *f.* with pure love of Christ; 8: 26 Comforter *f.* with hope and perfect love.

FILTHINESS, FILTHY (*see also* Corrupt; Defile; Evil; Pollute; Spot; Stain; Unclean; Wicked)

1 Ne. 12: 16 (15: 27) Nephi[1] sees fountain of *f.* water in vision; 12: 23 (Enos 1: 20) Lamanites to become *f.* people; 15: 33–34 (Alma 7: 21) kingdom of God is not *f.*; **2 Ne.** 9: 16 (Morm. 9: 14) they who are *f.* shall be *f.* still; **Jacob** 3: 3 land to be cursed for sake of those who are *f.* before God; 3: 3, 5 Lamanites are not *f.* like Nephites; 3: 5 Nephites hate Lamanites because of their *f.*; **Mosiah** 7: 30 if the Lord's people sow *f.*, they shall reap chaff in whirlwind; **Alma** 5: 22 how will you feel to stand before bar of God with garments stained in *f.*; 7: 21 no *f.* can be received into kingdom of God; 32: 3 the poor are esteemed as *f.* by Zoramites; **Morm.** 5: 15 descendants of Lehites shall become *f.* people.

FINAL (*see also* End; Last)

1 Ne. 15: 35 *f.* state of men's souls is to dwell in kingdom of God or to be cast out; **Mosiah** 2: 38–39 *f.* doom of those who repent not is to endure never-ending torment; **Alma** 34: 35 *f.* state of the wicked is that devil has all power over them.

FIND, FOUND (*see also* Blameless; Spotless; Unclean)

1 Ne. 10: 19 (3 Ne. 14: 7; Matt. 7: 7) he who diligently seeks shall *f.*; **Jacob** 4: 8 impossible that man should *f.* out all the Lord's ways; **Mosiah** 5: 8–9 whosoever enters covenant with God and is obedient shall be *f.* at his right hand; **Alma** 32: 13 whosoever repents shall *f.* mercy; **3 Ne.** 14: 14 (27: 33; Matt. 7: 14) narrow is the way, and few that *f.* it; **Moro.** 6: 7 whoso is *f.* to commit iniquity is brought before elders.

FINGER

Alma 10: 2 writing on wall of temple written by *f.* of God; **Ether** 3: 6–9, 19 (12: 20–21) brother of Jared sees *f.* of the Lord.

FINISH (*see also* End; Finisher)

Alma 14: 13 work of Alma[2] and Amulek is not *f.*

FINISHER

Moro. 6: 4 Christ is author and *f.* of believers' faith.

FIRE (*see also* Born of God; Burn; Cleanse; Destruction; Flame; Furnace; Hell; Holy Ghost, Baptism of; Purify; Remission; TG Earth, Cleansing of; Fire, Baptism of; Holy Ghost, Baptism of; BD Fire)

1 Ne. 1: 6 pillar of *f.* comes down and dwells on rock before Lehi[1]; 15: 30 brightness of God's justice is like brightness of *f.*; **2 Ne.** 6: 15 they who believe not in Messiah shall be destroyed by *f.*; 9: 16 (Mosiah 26: 27) the filthy shall go away into everlasting *f.*; 9: 16, 19 (28: 23; Jacob 3: 11; 6: 10; Mosiah 3: 27; Alma 12: 17; 14: 14) lake of *f.* and brimstone; 15: 24 (Isa. 5: 24) as *f.* devoureth stubble, root of the wicked shall be rottenness; 19: 18 (Isa. 9: 18) wickedness burneth as the *f.*; 20: 17 (Isa. 10: 17) light of Israel shall be for a *f.*; 30: 10 the Lord will spare his people even if he must destroy the wicked by *f.*; 31: 13–14 (3 Ne. 9: 20; 12: 1; 19: 13; Ether 12: 14) baptism of *f.*; **Jacob** 5: 26, 37, 42, 45–47, 49, 58, 66 branches that do not bring forth good fruit are cast into *f.*; 5: 77 the Lord will cause vineyard to be burned with *f.*; 6: 3 world shall be burned with *f.*; **Mosiah** 2: 38 (Morm. 9: 5) awareness of guilt fills the breast with anguish like unquenchable *f.*; 19: 20 Noah[3] suffers death by *f.*; **Alma** 5: 35, 52 those who bring forth works of righteousness shall not be cast into *f.*; 25: 5 Amulonites cause many believing Lamanites to perish by *f.*; **Hel.** 5: 23 Nephi[2] and Lehi[4] encircled as by flaming *f.*; 13: 13 (3 Ne. 9: 11) except for the righteous in city, the Lord would destroy it by *f.*; **3 Ne.** 12: 22 (Matt. 5: 22) whosoever shall say to his brother, Thou fool, shall be in danger of hell *f.*; 24: 2 (Mal. 3: 2) he is like a refiners' *f.*; 27: 11 those who build church on works of men or devil will be cast into *f.*; 27: 17 he who endures not to end shall be cast into *f.*; **4 Ne.** 1: 32 disciples cast into furnaces of *f.*; **Morm.** 8: 17 he who condemns shall be in danger of hell *f.*; 9: 5 when ye are brought to see your nakedness before glory of God, it will kindle unquenchable *f.* in you.

FIRMNESS, FIRM, FIRMER (*see also* Endure; Fast; Fixed; Immoveable; Steadfast; Unshaken)

1 Ne. 2: 10 Lehi[1] admonishes Lemuel to be *f.* like valley; **Jacob** 3: 1 look unto God with *f.* of mind; 3: 2 if minds are *f.*, ye may feast upon God's love forever; 4: 18 Jacob[2] will unfold mysteries if not shaken from *f.* in spirit; **Alma** 24: 19 when Lamanites were brought to believe truth, they were *f.*; 27: 27 Ammonites are *f.* in faith of Christ; 34: 41 bear with afflictions with *f.* hope that ye shall one day rest from afflictions; 48: 13 Moroni[1] is *f.* in faith of Christ; 57: 27 minds of Ammonites are *f.*; **Hel.** 3: 35 more humble part of people wax *f.* and *f.* in faith of Christ; 6: 1 Lamanites' righteousness exceeds that of Nephites because of *f.*; 7: 7 earlier Nephites were *f.* to keep commandments; 15: 7–8 those who come to change of heart are *f.* in faith; 15: 10 because of Lamanites' *f.*, God will bless them; **3 Ne.** 6: 14 church broken up, except for a few Lamanites who are *f.*; **Morm.** 2: 25 Nephite army stands before Lamanite army with *f.*; 9: 28 ask with *f.* unshaken that ye will yield to no temptation; **Moro.** 7: 30 miracles and angels show themselves unto them of strong faith and *f.* mind.

FIRST (*see also* Death, Spiritual; Firstborn; Fruit; Resurrection)

1 Ne. 5: 11 (Mosiah 16: 3) Adam and Eve our *f.* parents; 13: 42 (Ether 13: 12) last shall be *f.* and *f.* shall be last; 20: 12 (Isa. 48: 12) I am the *f.* and I am the last; **2 Ne.** 1: 29 if brethren of Nephi[1] do not hearken unto him, Lehi[1] will take *f.* blessing and give it to him; **Jacob** 1: 17 Jacob[2] *f.* obtains errand from the Lord before teaching; 5: 63 (Ether 13: 12) begin at the last, that they may be *f.*, and the *f.* may be last; **Alma** 11: 38–39 Son is the *f.* and the last; 12: 36 hard-heartedness provokes the Lord to send down destruction, unto the last death as well as the *f.*; 43: 46 if not guilty of *f.* or second offense, ye shall not suffer yourselves to be slain by enemies; **3 Ne.** 13: 33 (Matt. 6: 33) seek ye *f.* the kingdom of God; 20: 26 the Father raised Christ up unto men *f.*; **Ether** 12: 18 men *f.* believe in the Son, then work miracles.

FIRSTBORN (*see also* Firstling; BD Firstborn)

2 Ne. 2: 1 Jacob[2], my *f.* in days of tribulation; 4: 3 Lehi[1] speaks to children of his *f.* Laman[1].

FIRST-FRUITS (*see* Fruit)

FISH (*see also* Animal; Whale)

3 Ne. 14: 9–10 (Matt. 7: 10) if son ask a *f.*, what man will give him a serpent; **Ether** 2: 2 Jaredites carry *f.* with them in vessel.

FIXED (*see also* Firmness)

Enos 1: 20 Lamanites' hatred is *f.*; **Alma** 47: 6 disobedient Lamanites are *f.* in their minds with a determination not to go against Nephites; 58: 12 small Nephite force is *f.* with determination to conquer enemies.

FLAME (*see also* Fire; Sword)

2 Ne. 20: 17 (Isa. 10: 17) Holy One shall be for a *f.*; 23: 8 (Isa. 13: 8) their faces shall be as *f.*; **Jacob** 6: 10 (Mosiah 3: 27) lake of fire and brimstone, whose *f.* are unquenchable; **Mosiah** 2: 38 sense of guilt fills breast with anguish, whose *f.* ascends forever; **Morm.** 9: 5 to see our nakedness before glory of God will kindle a *f.* of unquenchable fire.

FLATTER, FLATTERING, FLATTERY (*see also* Deceit; Hypocrisy; Lying)

2 Ne. 28: 22 devil *f.* men that there is no hell; **Jacob** 7: 4 Sherem uses much *f.*; **Mosiah** 11: 7 people deceived by *f.* and vain words of Noah[3] and priests; 26: 6 unbelievers deceive many with *f.* words; 27: 8 Alma[2] and sons of Mosiah[2] speak *f.* to lead people into iniquity; **Alma** 17: 31 Ammon[2] *f.* fellow-servants by his words; 30: 47 better that Korihor's soul be lost than that he bring down many to destruction by *f.* words; 46: 7 many in church believe *f.* words of Amalickiah; 61: 4 those who seek judgment-seat use much *f.* to lead away hearts; **3 Ne.** 7: 12 Jacob[4] *f.* dissenters that many would join his band.

FLEE (*see* Flight)

FLESH (*see also* Body; Carnal; Man; Mankind; Mortal; Nature, Natural; Sacrament; Sensual; Temporal; Word; TG Flesh; Flesh and Blood; Trust Not in the Arm of Flesh; BD Flesh)

1 Ne. 17: 35 the Lord esteems all *f.* in one; 22: 18 destruction comes unto men according to *f.* if they harden hearts; 22: 22 kingdom of devil established among them which are in the *f.*; 22: 23 all who seek lusts of the *f.* shall be brought low; **2 Ne.** 2: 5 by law no *f.* is justified; 2: 27 men are free according to the *f.* to choose life or death; 4: 17 my heart sorrows because of my *f.*; 4: 34 I will not put trust in arm of *f.*; 9: 4–7 *f.* must waste away and die; 9: 53 Nephites' seed shall not be utterly destroyed according to the *f.*; 10: 24 reconcile yourselves to will of God and not to will of devil and the *f.*; 28: 31 cursed is he who makes *f.* his arm; **Jacob** 2: 21 pride is abominable unto him who created all *f.*; **Mosiah** 7: 27 (Ether 3: 6, 8–9) God will take upon him *f.* and blood; 15: 2–3 because the Lord dwells in *f.*, he shall be called the Son; 15: 2 the Son shall subject the *f.* to will of Father; 23: 7 ye shall not esteem one *f.* above another; **Alma** 7: 13 Son suffers according to the *f.*; **3 Ne.** 18: 28–30 whoso eats and drinks Christ's *f.* and blood unworthily eats and drinks damnation to soul; 28: 15, 39 three Nephites are sanctified in *f.*, transfigured from body of *f.* into immortal state; **Ether** 15: 34 it matters not whether Ether is translated or suffers will of the Lord in *f.*; **Moro.** ch. 4–5 manner of administering Christ's *f.* and blood to church; 9: 8 Nephite women are fed *f.* of husbands.

FLIGHT, FLEE, FLED (*see also* Depart; Escape; Journey; Leave)

1 Ne. 4: 36 sons of Lehi[1] do not want Jews to know of *f.*; **2 Ne.** 1: 3 the Lord has been merciful in warning Lehites to *f.* Jerusalem; **Mosiah** 20: 12 speedy *f.* of Limhi's people; **Alma** 50: 33 Moroni[1] sends army to head *f.* of people of Morianton[2]; **Hel.** 1: 10 speedy was *f.* of Kishkumen; 2: 11 Gadianton's band takes *f.* out of land; 15: 2 ye shall attempt to *f.*, and there shall be no refuge; **3 Ne.** 1: 28 Nephite dissenters *f.* to robbers; 7: 12 Jacob[4] orders his band to take *f.* into northernmost part of land; 20: 42 (21: 29; Isa. 52: 12) ye shall not go out with haste nor go by *f.*; **Morm.** 5: 7 those whose *f.* was swifter than Lamanites escape.

FLOCK (*see also* Church of God; Fold; Sheep)

2 Ne. 5: 11 (Enos 1: 21) Nephites begin to raise *f.*; **Mosiah** 2: 3 Nephites take firstlings of *f.* to offer sacrifice; 8: 21 children of men are wild *f.* which fleeth from shepherd; 9: 12 Lamanites bring people of Zeniff into bondage, to feast on *f.*; 10: 2 Zeniff guards his people and *f.*; 17: 17 people of Noah[3] shall be driven as wild *f.* is driven by wild beasts; **Alma** 5: 59 if wolf enter *f.* doth not shepherd drive him out; 17: 25 Ammon[2] set to watch Lamoni's *f.*; 18: 2 faithfulness of Ammon[2] in defending *f.* astonishes Lamoni; 34: 20, 25 cry unto the Lord over all your *f.*; **3 Ne.** 4: 4 Nephites reserve *f.* and provisions for seven years' subsistence; 20: 16 (21: 12; Micah 5: 8) remnant of Jacob[1] shall be among Gentiles as young lion among *f.* of sheep; **Ether** 1: 41 Jaredites are commanded to gather *f.*; 10: 12 people of Morianton[1] become exceeding rich in *f.*

FLOOD (*see also* Destruction; Noah[1]; Sea; Water; TG Flood, Noah's)

Alma 10: 22 people would not be destroyed by *f.*, but by famine, pestilence, sword; **3 Ne.** 11: 40 (14: 26–27; 18: 13) when *f.* come, gates of hell stand open to receive those built upon sandy foundation; **Ether** 2: 24–25 Jaredites could not cross sea, save the Lord prepared them against *f.*; 3: 2 Jaredites to be encompassed about by *f.*; 13: 2 after waters receded, land became choice.

FLYING SERPENTS (*see* Serpent)

FOLD (*see also* Flock; Sheep)

1 Ne. 15: 15 will not Israel come into true *f.* of God; 22: 25 (3 Ne. 16: 3; John 10: 16) one *f.* and one shepherd; **2 Ne.** 9: 2 Jews to be restored to true church and *f.* of God; **Mosiah** 18: 8–10 those who desire to come unto *f.* of God should be baptized; **Alma** 5: 39 if ye are not sheep of good shepherd, of what *f.* are ye; 26: 4 thousands of Lamanites have been brought into *f.* of God; **3 Ne.** 15: 17–21 (John 10: 16) the Lord has other sheep not of same *f.*

FOLLOW, FOLLOWER (*see also* Disciple; Example; Obedience; Saint)

2 Ne. 28: 14 all have gone astray save a few humble *f.* of Christ; 31: 10 the Lamb says, F. me; 31: 10 can we *f.* Jesus save we keep Father's commandments; 31: 12 *f.* me, and do the things ye have seen me do; 31: 13 by *f.* Son down into water ye shall receive Holy Ghost; 31: 16 unless a man endure to end, in *f.* Christ's example, he cannot be saved; **Alma** 4: 15 Alma[2] sees afflictions of humble *f.* of God; 5: 41 if man brings forth good works, he *f.* the good shepherd; 5: 57 all who desire to *f.* good shepherd must come out from among the wicked; 37: 45 if we *f.* Christ's words, they will carry us to far better land of promise; 42: 7 first parents became subject to *f.* after own will; **Hel.** 6: 5 many brought down to depths of humility to be humble *f.* of God and the Lamb; **3 Ne.** 27: 10–12 works of churches built upon works of men or devil *f.* them; **Morm.** 9: 24 (Ether 4: 18) signs *f.* them who believe; **Moro.** 7: 3 peaceable *f.* of Christ shall enter rest of the Lord; 7: 11 servant of devil cannot *f.* Christ; 7: 48 pure love of Christ bestowed upon all true *f.* of the Son.

FOLLY (*see also* Fool; Foolish)

2 Ne. 19: 17 (Isa. 9: 17) every mouth speaketh *f.*

FOOD (*see also* Eat; Feed; Grain; Meat; Nourish)

1 Ne. 16: 31–32 Nephi[1] obtains *f.*; **Mosiah** 4: 19 do we not all depend upon God for *f.*; **Alma** 8: 20 Amulek imparts *f.* to Alma[2]; 14: 22 people of Ammonihah withhold *f.* from Alma[2] and Amulek; 30: 56 Korihor goes from house to house, begging for *f.*; 58: 7 Nephite armies about to perish for want of *f.*; **Hel.** 4: 12 Nephites withhold *f.* from the hungry; 5: 22 Nephi[2] and Lehi[4] cast into prison many days without *f.*; **3 Ne.** 4: 3 robbers could not exist for want of *f.*; **Ether** 6: 4 Jaredites prepare all manner of *f.* for journey; **Moro.** 9: 16 because of armies, widows and daughters wander whithersoever they can for *f.*

FOOL (*see also* Folly; Foolish)

1 Ne. 17: 17 brethren call Nephi[1] a *f.*; **2 Ne.** 9: 42 the Lord will not open to those puffed up in learning, save they consider themselves *f.* before him; 29: 6 *f.* shall say, We need no more Bible; **Hel.** 9: 21 ye *f.*, how long will the Lord suffer you to go on in this way of sin; **3 Ne.** 12: 22 (Matt. 5: 22) whosoever shall say, Thou *f.*, shall be in danger of hell fire; **Ether** 12: 26 *f.* mock, but they shall mourn.

FOOLISH, FOOLISHNESS (*see also* Doctrine, False; False; Folly; Fool)

1 Ne. 2: 11 elder sons believe Lehi[1] is led away by *f.* imaginations of his heart; **2 Ne.** 9: 28 O the *f.* of men; 26: 10 for reward of their *f.*, Nephites shall reap destruction; 28: 9 many shall teach *f.* doctrines; **Alma** 8: 11 (21: 8; 30: 13–14, 23, 27; 31: 17) dissenters believe church teaches *f.* traditions; 37: 6 ye suppose this is *f.* in me; **Hel.** 12: 4 how *f.* are children of men; 13: 29 how long will ye suffer yourselves to be led by *f.*; **3 Ne.** 14: 26 (Matt. 7: 26) those who hear Christ's sayings but do them not are likened to *f.* man who builds house upon sand.

FOOT, FEET (*see also* Footstool; Trample; Tread)

1 Ne. 11: 24 (3 Ne. 17: 10) many will fall down at Son's *f.* and worship; **Mosiah** 12: 21 (15: 14–18; 3 Ne. 20: 40; Isa. 52: 7) how beautiful upon mountains are *f.* of him who brings good tidings; **Alma** 36: 7 earth trembles under *f.* of Alma[2] and friends; 46: 22 God may cast us at enemies' *f.*, even as we cast garments at thy *f.*, if we transgress; **3 Ne.** 11: 14–15 multitude feels prints of nails in Christ's *f.*

FOOTSTOOL

1 Ne. 17: 39 (3 Ne. 12: 35; Isa. 66: 1; Matt. 5: 35) earth is God's *f.*

FORBID, FORBADE, FORBIDDEN (*see also* Commandments of God; Fruit, Forbidden; Hinder)

1 Ne. 8: 28 those who are ashamed fall away into *f.* paths; 14: 28 Nephi[1] is *f.* to write remainder of what he saw; **2 Ne.** 26: 28 none are *f.* to partake of God's goodness; **3 Ne.** 18: 22 ye shall not *f.* any man from coming into meeting; 18: 29 (4 Ne. 1: 27) *f.* the unworthy from partaking sacrament; 26: 11 Christ *f.* Nephi[3] to write all things from plates of Nephi; 26: 16 (27: 23; 28: 14) men are *f.* to write all of marvelous things uttered or heard; 28: 25 the Lord *f.* Nephi[3] to write names of three Nephites; **Morm.** 1: 16–17 Mormon[2] is *f.* to preach unto people; **Ether** 4: 1 things written by brother of Jared[2] were *f.* to come unto men until after Crucifixion; 5: 1 to translate sealed things is *f.*; 8: 18–19 God has *f.* that men work in secret combinations; 13: 13 Moroni[2] is *f.* to write more of Ether's prophecies.

FOREFATHERS (*see also* Father)

1 Ne. 3: 3 (5: 14; Alma 37: 3) brass plates contain genealogy of *f.*; 15: 14 Lamanites to come to knowledge of *f.*; **Alma** 7: 10 Jerusalem, the land of our *f.*

FOREHEAD

Alma 3: 4 Amlicites mark themselves with red in *f.*

FOREKNOWLEDGE (*see* God, Foreknowledge of)

FOREORDINATION (*see* Calling; Elect; God, Foreknowledge of; Premortal Existence; TG Foreordination; Jesus Christ, Foreordained; Man, Antemortal Existence of)

FORGET, FORGOT, FORGOTTEN (*see also* Forgive; Remember, Remembrance)

1 Ne. 21: 15 (Isa. 49: 15) can woman *f.* her sucking child; 21: 15 (2 Ne. 29: 5) the Lord will not *f.* Israel; **Alma** 37: 41 because miracles were worked by small means, forefathers *f.* to exercise faith; 46: 8 (Hel. 11: 36; 12: 2) how quick do men *f.* the Lord; 47: 36 dissenters entirely *f.* the Lord; **Hel.** 7: 20 (12: 2) how could you have *f.* your God in very day he has delivered you; **3 Ne.** 2: 1 people begin to *f.* signs and wonders given at Christ's birth; 22: 4 (Isa. 54: 4) thou shalt *f.* shame of thy youth.

FORGIVE, FORGIVEN, FORGIVENESS (*see also* Baptism; Confession of Sins; Forsake; Jesus Christ, Atonement through; Reconcile; Remission; Repentance; TG Forgive, Forgiven)

1 Ne. 7: 21 Nephi[1] frankly *f.* brethren; **Enos** 1: 5 sins of Enos[2] are *f.*; **Mosiah** 4: 2 apply atoning blood of Christ that we may receive *f.* of sins; 4: 10 (Moro. 6: 8) ask in sincerity of heart that God would *f.* you; 26: 22 whosoever is baptized will the Lord freely *f.*; 26: 29–30 whosoever confesses and repents should be *f.*; 26: 31 *f.* one another your trespasses; 26: 31 (3 Ne. 13: 14–15) he who *f.* not his neighbor's trespasses brings himself under condemnation; **Alma** 39: 6 not easy for those who deny Holy Ghost or murder against light of God to receive *f.*; **3 Ne.** 13: 11 (Matt. 6: 12) *f.* us our debts, as we *f.* our debtors; 13: 14–15 (Matt. 6: 14–15) if ye *f.* men their trespasses, Father will *f.* you; **Morm.** 8: 32 churches will *f.* sins for money.

FORM [noun] (*see also* Frame [noun]; Image; TG Holy Ghost, Dove, Sign of)

1 Ne. 11: 11 Spirit in *f.* of man; 11: 27 (2 Ne. 31: 8) Holy Ghost will abide upon Christ in *f.* of dove; **Mosiah** 13: 34 God shall take upon himself *f.* of man; 14: 2 (Isa. 53: 2) Messiah hath no *f.* or comeliness; **Alma** 11: 43 spirit and body shall be reunited in perfect *f.*; 30: 44 all planets which move in regular *f.* witness there is a Supreme Creator; 30: 53 devil appeared unto Korihor in *f.* of angel; **3 Ne.** 20: 44 (Isa. 52: 14) Messiah's *f.* was more marred than sons of men; **Moro.** 7: 30 angels show themselves in every *f.* of godliness.

FORMATION (*see also* Foundation; Founder)

1 Ne. 13: 4 Nephi[1] sees *f.* of great church among Gentiles.

FORMED [verb] (*see also* Creation; Formation: Framed [verb]; Make)

1 Ne. 21: 5 the Lord *f.* me from womb; **3 Ne.** 22: 17 (Isa. 54: 17) no weapon that is *f.* against thee shall prosper.

FORNICATION, FORNICATOR (*see also* Adultery; Chastity; Lust; Whore; TG Fornication; Sexual Immorality)

Jacob 3: 12 Jacob[2] warns Nephites against *f.*; **Hel.** 8: 26 Nephites are ripening for destruction because of murders and *f.*; **3 Ne.** 12: 32 (Matt. 5: 32) whosoever puts away his wife, save for *f.*, causes her to commit adultery.

FORSAKE, FORSAKEN (*see also* Forgive, Forgiveness; Leave; Repentance)

Mosiah 4: 10 (Alma 39: 9) repent of your sins and *f.* them; **Alma** 46: 21 Nephites enter covenant that they would not *f.* their Lord; **3 Ne.** 22: 7 (Isa. 54: 7) for a small moment have I *f.* thee.

FORT, FORTIFY (*see also* Defence, Defense; Protect)

2 Ne. 10: 12 the Lord will *f.* land against all other nations; 26: 15 the Lord shall raise *f.* against seed of Nephi[1] and brethren.

FOUGHT (*see* Fight, Fought)

FOUND (*see* Find, Found; Founded; Founder)

FOUNDATION (*see also* Formation; Founded; Founder; Preparator; Rock)

2 Ne. 28: 28 he who is built upon sandy *f.* trembles lest he fall; **Jacob** 4: 15–17 Jews to reject only stone upon which they might build safe *f.*; **Alma** 10: 17–27 lawyers and hypocrites are laying *f.* of devil; 13: 3 those ordained were called and prepared from *f.* of world; **Hel.** 5: 12 upon rock of Redeemer ye must build *f.*; **3 Ne.** 11: 40 whoso declares more or less than Christ's doctrine builds upon sandy *f.*; 18: 13 those who do more or less than these are built upon sandy *f.*

FOUNDED (*see also* Build; Foundation; Founder)

1 Ne. 14: 3 great and abominable church *f.* by devil; **3 Ne.** 14: 25 (Matt. 7: 25) house *f.* upon rock does not fall because of floods, winds, rain.

FOUNDER (*see also* Author; Devil; Foundation; Founded; Preparator)

1 Ne. 13: 6 (14: 9, 17) devil is *f.* of great and abominable church; **2 Ne.** 26: 22 devil is *f.* of secret combinations, works of darkness; **Mosiah** 15: 18 how beautiful upon mountains are feet of *f.* of peace; 23: 16 (29: 47) Alma[1] *f.* of church.

FOUNTAIN (*see also* River; Spring; Water)

1 Ne. 2: 9 Lehi[1] exhorts Lemuel to be like river, continually running into *f.* of righteousness; 8: 20 straight and narrow path leads by head of *f.*; 11: 25 iron rod leads to *f.* of living waters; 12: 16 *f.* of filthy waters is depths of hell; **Mosiah** 18: 5 Alma[1] hides by *f.* of pure water in Mormon; **Ether** 8: 26 Moroni[2] writes so that men may come to *f.* of all righteousness; 12: 28 the Lord is the *f.* of all righteousness; **Moro.** 7: 11 bitter *f.* cannot bring forth good water, nor good *f.* bitter water.

FOWL (*see also* Animal)

2 Ne. 2: 15 God created *f.* of air; **Ether** 2: 16 Jaredite barges are light like *f.* upon water.

FRAME [noun] (*see also* Body)

1 Ne. 17: 47 Nephi[1] is full of Spirit, so that his *f.* has no strength; **Mosiah** 2: 26 Benjamin about to yield mortal *f.* to mother earth; **Alma** 11: 43 (40: 23; 41: 4) limb and joint shall be restored to proper *f.*; 19: 6 light of everlasting life has overcome Lamoni's natural *f.*; **3 Ne.** 11: 3 no part of people's *f.* that small voice does not cause to quake.

FRAMED [verb] (*see also* Creation; Formed [verb])

2 Ne. 27: 27 shall the thing *f.* say of him that *f.* it, he had no understanding.

FRAUD (*see also* Deceit; Lying)

Alma 47: 30, 35 (48: 7) Amalickiah obtains power by *f.*; 55: 1 Ammoron has perfect knowledge of his *f.*

FREEDOM, FREE (*see also* Agency; Bondage; Captive; Deliver; Freely; Freemen; Government, Civil; King-men; Liberty; Redemption; Salvation)

2 Ne. 2: 4 salvation is *f.*; 2: 26 because men are redeemed from fall, they have become *f.* forever; 2: 27 men are *f.* to choose eternal life through great Redeemer; 3: 5 Messiah to be made manifest unto seed of Joseph[1] unto bringing them out of captivity unto *f.*; 10: 23 (Hel. 14: 30) men are *f.* to act for themselves; **Jacob** 2: 17 be *f.* with your substance; **Mosiah** 5: 8 under this head ye are made *f.*, and there is no other head whereby ye can be made *f.*; **Alma** 30: 24 Korihor claims Nephites are not a *f.* people; 43: 48 Moroni[1] inspires his men with thoughts of *f.*; 46: 35 Amalickiahites required to enter covenant to support cause of *f.*; 48: 11 Moroni[1] delights in *f.* of his country; 48: 20 because Nephites humble themselves, they are *f.* from wars and dissension; 50: 39 chief judge given oath to keep peace and *f.*; 51: 6 freemen swear to maintain privileges of religion by *f.* government; 51: 7 king-men are obliged to maintain cause of *f.*; 60: 36 Moroni[1] seeks not honor of world, but *f.* of his country; 61: 6 Nephites flock to army in defense of *f.*; 61: 15 Spirit of God is Spirit of *f.*; 62: 1 Pahoran[1] not a traitor to *f.* of his country; **3 Ne.** 2: 12 converted Lamanites take up arms against robbers to maintain *f.*; 21: 4 Gentiles set up as *f.* people by power of the Father; **Ether** 2: 12 nations that possess this land shall be *f.* from bondage; 8: 25 they who build secret combinations seek to overthrow *f.* of all lands.

FREELY

Mosiah 26: 22 whosoever is baptized unto repentance will the Lord *f.* forgive; **Alma** 5: 34 (42: 27) partake of waters of life *f.*

FREEMEN—*Nephite group vowing to defend freedom* [c. 67 B.C.]

Alma 51: 6–7 *f.* save judgment-seat for Pahoran[1]; 60: 25 *f.* serve in army of Moroni[1]; 61: 3–4 *f.* of Pahoran[1] are daunted by dissenters, that they do not come unto Moroni[1]; 62: 6 *f.* are driven out of Zarahemla.

FRIEND, FRIENDSHIP (*see also* TG Brotherhood and Sisterhood; Fellowshipping)

2 Ne. 1: 30 Zoram[1] a true *f.* to Nephi[1]; **Mosiah** 29: 22 iniquitous king has his *f.* in iniquity; **Alma** 15: 16 Amulek is rejected by those who were once his *f.*; 62: 37 Teancum a true *f.* to liberty; **Morm.** 8: 5 Moroni[2] has no *f.*; **Ether** 1: 36 Jared[1] pleads that the Lord might have compassion on *f.*

FRUIT, FRUITFUL (*see also* Food; Fruit, Forbidden; Tree; Tree of Life; Work [noun])

1 Ne. 8: 10–35 Lehi[1] beholds tree whose *f.* is desirable to make one happy; 15: 36 *f.* of tree of life is most precious and desirable above all other *f.*; **2 Ne.** 2: 9 Messiah is first-*f.* unto God; **Jacob** 4: 11 be presented as first-*f.* of Christ unto God; 5: 3–77 Zenos's parable of vineyard with good and evil *f.*; 5: 18 wild branches grafted into tame roots bring forth tame *f.*; 5: 26 branches that have not brought forth good *f.* shall be cast into fire; 5: 25–26 wild branches overcome tame branches, so that corrupted tree brings forth no good *f.*; 5: 64 if grafted branches bring forth natural *f.*, tree shall be spared; 5: 65 branches bringing forth bitter *f.* shall be cleared away; 5: 74 trees become again natural *f.*, and the Lord preserves unto himself the natural *f.*; 6: 7 after ye have been nourished by word of God, will ye bring forth evil *f.*; **Alma** 5: 36 whosoever brings not forth good *f.* shall have cause to mourn; 5: 62 be baptized unto repentance that ye may be partakers of *f.* of tree of life; 12: 15 (13: 13; 34: 30) bring forth *f.* meet for repentance; 26: 30–31 Ammon[2] and brethren can see *f.* of labors; 29: 17 may God grant that those who are *f.* of missionaries' labors may go no more out; 32: 40 if ye will not nourish the word, ye can never pluck of *f.* of tree of life; 36: 25 the Lord gives Alma[2] great joy in *f.* of labors; 40: 26 the wicked are consigned to partake of *f.* of their works; 42: 3 the Lord places cherubim and flaming sword so that Adam should not partake of *f.* of tree of life; **Hel.** 11: 13, 17 Nephi[2] prays the Lord to send rain, that earth may bring forth *f.*; **3 Ne.** 14: 16, 20 (Matt. 7: 16, 20) ye shall know them by their *f.*; 14: 17–18 (Matt. 7: 17–18) good tree brings forth good *f.*, evil tree evil *f.*; 24: 11 (Mal. 3: 11) the Lord will rebuke devourer that he shall not destroy *f.* of ground; **Moro.** 6: 1 elders, priests, teachers not baptized save they brought forth *f.* meet that they are worthy; 8: 25 first *f.* of repentance is baptism.

FRUIT, FORBIDDEN (*see also* Agency; Eden, Garden of; Fall of Man; Tree)

2 Ne. 2: 15 *f. f.* set in opposition to tree of life; 2: 18–19 (Hel. 6: 26) devil beguiled Adam and Eve into partaking of *f. f.*; **Mosiah** 3: 26 justice could not deny that Adam should fall because he took of *f. f.*; **Alma** 12: 22 Adam fell by partaking of *f. f.*

FRUSTRATED (*see also* Hinder)

Alma 12: 26 (42: 5) if first parents

could have partaken of tree of life, plan of redemption would have been *f.*; **3 Ne.** 1: 16 plan of destruction laid for believers is *f.*

FULFIL, FULFILL (*see also* Accomplish; Perform)

1 Ne. 20: 14 the Lord will *f.* his word; **2 Ne.** 9: 17 (25: 24; Alma 34: 13; 3 Ne. 1: 25) God's law must be *f.*; 10: 17 the Lord will *f.* his promises; 25: 7 (3 Ne. 16: 17; 20: 11) prophecies of Isaiah shall be *f.*; 25: 24 Nephites look forward to Christ until law shall be *f.*; 31: 5 Lamb baptized by water to *f.* all righteousness; **Alma** 34: 13 great and last sacrifice shall *f.* law of Moses; **Hel.** 16: 13–14 words of prophets, scriptures begin to be *f.*; **3 Ne.** 1: 25 law not yet *f.*; 5: 14 prayers of holy ones shall be *f.* according to their faith; 9: 17 (12: 46; 15: 5) in Christ is the law of Moses *f.*; 28: 7 three Nephite disciples to live until all things shall be *f.*; **Ether** 12: 3 by faith all things are *f.*

FULL (*see also* Fill; Fulness)

1 Ne. 1: 16 (6: 3) Nephi[1] does not make *f.* account; **Jacob** 6: 5 (3 Ne. 10: 6; 12: 24; 18: 32; Acts 11: 23) come unto the Lord with *f.* purpose of heart; **Alma** 12: 10 he who hardens not his heart shall know mysteries until he knows them in *f.*; 34: 27 let your hearts be *f.*, drawn out in prayer unto the Lord; **Morm.** 2: 18 (5: 9) Mormon[2] makes *f.* account on plates of Nephi, not upon these plates; **Ether** 3: 17 Moroni[2] does not make *f.* account; 15: 19 Satan has *f.* power over hearts.

FULLER [noun]

3 Ne. 24: 2 (Mal. 3: 2) the Lord is like refiner's fire and *f*'s soap.

FULNESS (*see also* Full; Gospel)

1 Ne. 17: 35 *f.* of God's wrath was upon those who inhabited promised land before Israel; 22: 16 time will come when *f.* of God's wrath shall be poured out; 22: 17 God will preserve the righteous if *f.* of his wrath must come; **2 Ne.** 1: 17 because of hardness of hearts, God may come out in *f.* of his wrath; 2: 3 in *f.* of time Redeemer comes to bring salvation unto men; 11: 7 Christ comes in *f.* of his own time; **3 Ne.** 27: 30 Christ's joy is great, even unto *f.*; 28: 10 disciples shall have *f.* of joy; **Ether** 2: 10 not until *f.* of iniquity are children of land swept off.

FURNACE (*see also* Fire; Oven)

1 Ne. 20: 10 (Isa. 48: 10) I have chosen thee in *f.* of affliction; **Mosiah** 12: 3 life of Noah[3] shall be valued as garment in hot *f.*; **3 Ne.** 28: 21 (4 Ne. 1: 32; Morm. 8: 24) Nephite disciples cast into fiery *f.*, without harm.

FURY (*see also* Anger; Ferocious; Passion; Wrath)

2 Ne. 8: 13 (Isa. 51: 13) thou hast feared continually every day because of *f.* of oppressor; 8: 20 (Isa. 51: 20) as wild bull in net, thy two sons are full of *f.* of the Lord; **Alma** 52: 33 Jacob[3] leads Lamanites to battle with exceeding *f.*; **3 Ne.** 21: 21 Father will execute *f.* upon those who do not come unto Son.

GAD, CITY OF

3 Ne. 9: 10 burned because inhabitants cast out prophets.

GADIANI, CITY OF

3 Ne. 9: 8 destroyed because of iniquity.

GADIANTON—*leader of robber bands* [c. 50 B.C.] (*see also* Gadianton Robbers)

Hel. 2: 4 expert in wickedness, becomes leader of robber band; 2: 11 flees with band; 2: 13 almost proves destruction of Nephites; 6: 24 gave wicked laws; 6: 26, 29 received secret oaths and covenants from devil.

GADIANTON ROBBERS (*see also* Gadianton; Kishkumen; Rob, Robbery; Secret Combination)

Hel. 2: 4 Gadianton becomes leader of band of Kishkumen; 2: 11 flee out of land by secret way, into wilderness; 3: 23 unknown to government, therefore not destroyed; 6: 18 (7: 25) include many Nephites, more numerous among wicked part of Lamanites; 6: 18 called G's robbers and murderers; 6: 24 those who reveal their wickedness unto world are tried according to laws given by G. and Kishkumen; 6: 26–29 secret oaths and covenants given to G. by devil; 6: 37 Lamanites hunt robbers, preach word of God, destroy band of G. among Lamanites; 7: 4 (8: 1, 27–28) fill judgment-seats, usurp power and authority; 11: 10 Nephites sweep away band of G.; 11: 24–26 dissenters form new band, become robbers of G.; **3 Ne.** 1: 27 robbers dwell in mountains, cannot be overpowered; 1: 29 Lamanite children are led away by Zoramites to join G. robbers; 2: 11 robbers spread death and carnage; 2: 12 converted Lamanites and Nephites unite against robbers; 2: 18 robbers gain many advantages because of people's iniquity; 3: 9 secret society of G. is of ancient date; 3: 15 unless people repent and cry unto the Lord, they will not be delivered from G. robbers; **4 Ne.** 1: 42, 46 robbers of G. spread again over the land; **Morm.** 1: 18 people try to hide treasures because G. robbers infest the land; 2: 27–28 Nephites regain some lands from robbers of G.

GADIOMNAH, CITY OF

3 Ne. 9: 8 is sunk, hills and valleys in place.

GAIN (*see also* Advantage; Benefit; Business; Profit; Riches; Wealth)

1 Ne. 22: 23 (4 Ne. 1: 26) churches built up to get g. will be consumed; **2 Ne.** 26: 29 priestcrafts are that men preach to get g.; 27: 15–16 the learned shall say, Bring book and I will read, to get g.; **Alma** 11: 3, 20 judges stir people up to wickedness to get g.; 30: 35 (Mosiah 2: 14; Alma 1: 26) missionaries receive no g.; **Hel.** 6: 8 Nephites and Lamanites have free intercourse to get g.; 7: 4–5 Gadianton robbers fill judgment-seats to get g.; 7: 21 Nephites have forgotten God to get g.; **3 Ne.** 29: 7 wo unto him who shall say to get g. that there can be no miracle; **Morm.** 8: 14 no one shall have plates to get g.; 8: 40 (Ether 8: 16, 22–23; 11: 15) secret combinations built up to get g.; **Ether** 10: 22 Jaredites traffic one with another to get g.

GALL (*see* Bitter, Bitterness; BD Gall)

GAME (*see also* Animal)

3 Ne. 4: 2 Nephites leave no g. for robbers in deserted lands; 4: 20 wild g. in wilderness becomes scarce; 29: 8 ye need not any longer make g. of Jews; **Ether** 10: 21 Jaredites preserve land southward for wilderness, to get g.

GARDEN (*see also* Eden, Garden of)

2 Ne. 8: 3 the Lord will make Zion's desert like g. of the Lord; **Hel.** 7: 10 Nephi[2] prays upon tower in g.

GARMENT (*see also* Apparel; Clothing; Raiment; Robe)

1 Ne. 4: 19 Nephi[1] puts on Laban's g.; 12: 10 g. made white in blood of Lamb; **2 Ne.** 7: 9 (Isa. 50: 9) all who condemn the Lord shall wax old as a g.; 8: 6 (Isa. 51: 6) earth shall wax old like a g.; 8: 24 (Isa. 52: 1; 3 Ne. 20: 36) put on beautiful g., O Jerusalem; **Jacob** 1: 19 Jacob[2] and Joseph[2] labor that people's blood might not come upon their g.; 2: 2 Jacob[2] under responsibility to magnify office, that he might rid g. of his people's sins; **Mosiah** 12: 3 life of Noah[3] to be valued as g. in hot furnace; **Alma** 5: 21 no man can be saved except g. are washed white; 7: 25 may the Lord bless you and keep your g. spotless; 46: 24 as remnant of g. of Joseph[1] was preserved, so shall remnant of his seed be preserved; **3 Ne.** 27: 19 only those who wash g. in Christ's blood can enter Father's rest; **Morm.** 9: 35 these things are written that we may rid g. of blood of our brethren; **Ether** 12: 37 g. of Moroni[2] shall be made clean.

GATE (*see also* Door; Way)

2 Ne. 4: 32 may g. of hell be shut continually before me; 9: 41 keeper of g. is Holy One of Israel; 27: 32 (Isa. 29: 21) they who lay snare for him that reproves in g. shall be cut off; 31: 8–9 Christ's baptism shows men narrowness of g.; 31: 17–18 baptism and repentance are g. by which men should enter; 33: 9 men cannot be reconciled unto Christ except they enter narrow g.; **Jacob** 6: 11 (3 Ne. 14: 13; 27: 33; Matt. 7: 13) enter in at the strait g.; **Hel.** 3: 28 g. of heaven is open unto all who believe on Christ; **3 Ne.** 11: 39 (Matt. 16: 18) g. of hell shall not prevail upon those built on rock of Christ; 14: 13 (27: 33; Matt. 7: 13–14) wide is g. which leads to destruction; 14: 14 (27: 33; Matt. 7: 14) strait is g. which leads to life; 18: 13 g. of hell are open to receive those not built on rock of Christ.

GATHER (*see also* Assemble; Israel, Gathering of; Recover; Remnant; Restoration; Return; Scatter; Zion)

1 Ne. 22: 25 (3 Ne. 16: 5) Holy One g. his children from four quarters of earth; **2 Ne.** 10: 8 (3 Ne. 21: 1) the Lord will g. in Israel from long dispersion; 21: 12 (Isa. 11: 12) the Lord shall g. the dispersed of Judah from four corners of earth; 23: 4 (Isa. 13: 4) tumultuous noise of kingdoms g. together; 29: 14 Israel shall be g. home unto lands of possessions, and the Lord's word shall be g. in one; **Mosiah** 18: 25 one day in week set apart for people to g. to worship; **Alma** 6: 6 children of God are commanded to g. oft in fasting and prayer; **3 Ne.** 10: 6 (Matt. 23: 37; Luke 13: 34) how oft will I g. you as a hen g. her chickens; 13: 26 (Matt. 6: 26) behold the fowls, for they do not g. into barns; 20: 18 the Lord will g. his people as a man g. his sheaves.

GAZELEM—*name given to servant of God*

Alma 37: 23 the Lord will prepare unto his servant G. a stone.

GENEALOGY (*see also* Descendant; Father; Forefather; TG Genealogy and Temple Work; BD Genealogy)

1 Ne. 3: 3, 12 (5: 14, 16; Alma 37: 3) brass plates contain g. of forefathers; **Jarom** 1: 1 (Omni 1: 1) Jarom writes, that g. may be kept; **Omni** 1: 18 Zarahemla gives g. of fathers.

GENERATION

1 Ne. 12: 11–12 (2 Ne. 26: 9; Alma 45: 12; 3 Ne. 27: 32; 4 Ne. 1: 22–24) Nephites to pass into third and fourth g.

after Christ's appearance before iniquity arises; **2 Ne.** 4: 2 Lehi[1] prophesies about future g.; 9: 53 in future g. seed of Nephites shall become righteous branch unto Israel; **Mosiah** 13: 13 (Deut. 5: 9) God visits iniquities of fathers upon children unto third and fourth g.; 14: 8 (15: 10; Isa. 53: 8) who shall declare his g.; **Alma** 9: 8 (10: 17, 25; Hel. 13: 29) O ye wicked and perverse g.; 37: 14, 18–19 the Lord will preserve records, that he might show his power unto future g.; **Hel.** 13: 10 fourth g. of enemies shall visit Nephites' destruction; **3 Ne.** 26: 2 Christ gives Nephites scriptures so that future g. will have them; **Moro.** 10: 28 God's word shall hiss forth from g. to g.

GENEROSITY (*see* TG Generosity)

GENTILE (*see also* Heathen; Nation; BD Gentile)

Title Page book written to convince Jew and G. that Jesus is the Christ; **1 Ne.** 10: 11 risen Messiah to manifest himself unto G. by Holy Ghost; 13: 3 Nephi[1] sees nations and kingdoms of G.; 13: 4, 26 formation of abominable church among G.; 13: 12 Nephi[1] beholds man among G. who goes forth upon many waters unto Lamanites; 13: 15 G. prosper in promised land; 13: 25 (Morm. 7: 8) book containing gospel goes from Jews in purity unto G.; 13: 29 after plain and precious parts are taken from gospel, it goes unto nations of G.; 13: 32 the Lord will not suffer G. to remain in blindness; 13: 35 Nephite writings shall come unto G.; 13: 42 Lamb shall manifest unto Jews and G., then unto G. and Jews; 14: 1 if G. hearken unto Lamb, he shall manifest himself; 15: 13, 17 grafting in of natural branches through fulness of G. means fulness of gospel shall come to G.; 15: 17 (2 Ne. 10: 18; 26: 15–19) Lamanites shall be scattered by G.; 22: 6 (1 Ne. 21: 22–23; 2 Ne. 6: 7; 10: 9; Isa. 49: 23) G. to nurse Israel, be set up as standard; 22: 7 the Lord will raise up mighty nation among G. upon this land; 22: 8 (3 Ne. 28: 32) the Lord will do marvelous work among G.; **2 Ne.** 10: 11 this land shall be land of liberty among G.; 10: 16 he who fights against Zion, both Jew and G., shall perish; 10: 18 G. shall be like father to Lamanites, shall be numbered among house of Israel; 26: 33 all are alike unto God, both Jew and G.; 29: 3 many G. shall say, A Bible! A Bible! we have a Bible; 30: 3 (3 Ne. 21: 5; 26: 8; Morm. 5: 15; 7: 8) G. shall carry gospel, book unto Lamanites; **3 Ne.** 15: 22 G. to be converted through preaching of Jews; 16: 10 when G. reject fulness of gospel, Father will bring gospel from among them; 21: 12 (Micah 5: 8) remnant of Jacob[1] shall be among G. as lion among beasts of forest; 28: 27 three Nephites shall be among G., and G. shall know them not; **Morm.** 3: 17 Mormon[2] writes unto G.; **Ether** 12: 23 Moroni[2] fears G. will mock these writings because of Nephites' weakness in writing; 12: 36 Moroni[2] prays the Lord will give G. grace, that they might have charity.

GENTLE (*see also* Kindness; Meek; Tender)

Alma 7: 23 be humble, submissive, g.

GHOST (*see also* Holy Ghost; Spirit)

Jacob 7: 20 Sherem gives up the g.; **Hel.** 14: 21 when Christ yields up the g., there shall be thunderings and lightnings.

GID—*Nephite military officer* [c. 63 B.C.] (*see also* Gid, City of)

Alma 57: 28–29 chief captain over band appointed to guard prisoners; 57: 30–35 reports death and escape of rebellious prisoners; 58: 16–23 takes part in strategy to capture Lamanite cities.

GID, CITY OF

Alma 51: 26 possessed by Amalickiah; 55: 7–24 Moroni[1] takes G. without bloodshed; 55: 25–26 Lamanite prisoners labor to fortify G.

GIDDIANHI—*chief Gadianton robbers* [c. A.D. 16-21]

3 Ne. 3: 9 governor of secret society; 3: 10–12 demands Nephite lands; 4: 5–6 commands armies to go to battle against Nephites; 4: 10–12 Nephites defeat G's army; 4: 14 is slain.

GIDDONAH[1]—*Amulek's father*

Alma 10: 2–3 descendant of Nephi[1].

GIDDONAH[2]—*high priest in Gideon* [c. 75 B.C.]

Alma 30: 21–29 is challenged by Korihor.

GIDEON—*Nephite patriot* [c. 145-91 B.C.]

Mosiah 19: 4 strong man, enemy to king Noah[3]; 19: 5–8 fights with king, spares king's life; 19: 18–24 sends men into wilderness to search for king and priests; 20: 17–22 counsels with Limhi regarding dealings with Lamanite king; 22: 3–9 proposes plan for escaping from Lamanites; **Alma** 1: 7–8 a teacher in the church, withstands Nehor; 1: 9 (2: 1, 20; 6: 7; 14: 16) is slain by Nehor; 2: 20 valley named after G.; 6: 7 city named after G.

GIDEON, CITY OF—*east of River Sidon*

Alma 6: 7 built in valley of G.; **Hel.** 13: 15 wo unto city of G. for wickedness.

GIDEON, LAND AND VALLEY OF—*east of River Sidon*

Alma 2: 20–26 people of Alma[2] pitch tents in valley of G.; 6: 7—8: 1 Alma[2] preaches in G., establishes church; 17: 1 Alma[2] meets sons of Mosiah[2] while journeying from G.; 30: 21 Korihor preaches in land of G. without success; 61: 5 Pahoran[1] flees to land of G.; 62: 3–6 Moroni[1] unites with Pahoran[1] in land of G.

GIDGIDDONAH—*Nephite commander* [c. A.D. 385]

Morm. 6: 13 is fallen with his ten thousand.

GIDGIDDONI—*Nephite commander* [c. A.D. 16]

3 Ne. 3: 18 great commander of armies; 3: 19 has spirit of revelation and prophecy; 3: 20–21 refuses people's petition for offensive campaign against robbers; 3: 26 causes Nephites to make weapons; 4: 13–14 defeats robbers; 4: 24–26 cuts off robbers' retreat; 6: 6 establishes great peace.

GIFT (*see also* Give; Holy Ghost, Gift of; Spirit; Tongue; TG God, Gifts of)

Title Page (1 Ne. 13: 35) book to come forth by g. and power of God; **1 Ne.** 10: 17 power of Holy Ghost is g. of God unto all who diligently seek him; 15: 36 fruit of tree of life is greatest of all the g. of God; **Omni** 1: 20 Mosiah[1] interprets engravings on stones by g. and power of God; 1: 25 Amaleki[1] exhorts all men to believe in g. of speaking with tongues; **Mosiah** 8: 16 no man can have g. greater than to be seer; **Alma** 9: 21 Nephites have had many g., g. of speaking with tongues, of preaching, of Holy Ghost, of translation; **Hel.** 5: 8 Helaman[2] admonishes his sons to do good, that they may have g. of eternal life; **3 Ne.** 29: 6 wo unto him who says the Lord no longer works by g.; **4 Ne.** 1: 3 Nephites have all things in common, so that all are partakers of heavenly g.; **Morm.** 1: 14 Nephites have no g. from the Lord, because of their wickedness; 9: 7–8 he who says there are no g. knows not the gospel of Christ; **Ether** 12: 8 Christ prepared a way that others might be partakers of heavenly g.; 12: 9 ye may be partakers of heavenly g. if ye have faith; **Moro.** 7: 8 if a man being evil gives a g., he does it grudgingly; 10: 8 deny not the g. of God; 10: 8 different ways that g. are administered, but all are given by manifestations of Spirit; 10: 18 every good g. cometh of Christ; 10: 24 if g. of God are ever done away, it shall be because of unbelief; 10: 30 lay hold upon every good g., touch not the evil g.

GILEAD—*Jaredite military commander*

Ether 14: 3–5 is defeated by Coriantumr[2]; 14: 6 places himself upon throne of Coriantumr[2]; 14: 8 army of G. is strengthened by secret combinations; 14: 8–9 is murdered by his high priest.

GILGAH—*early Jaredite*

Ether 6: 14 one of four sons of Jared[2]; 6: 24–27 refuses to be king.

GILGAL—*Nephite commander* [c. A.D. 385]

Morm. 6: 14 is slain with army.

GILGAL, CITY OF

3 Ne. 9: 6 sinks into depths of earth.

GILGAL, VALLEY OF

Ether 13: 27–30 site of battle between Shared and Coriantumr[2].

GIMGIMNO, CITY OF

3 Ne. 9: 8 sinks into depths of earth.

GIVE, GIVEN (*see also* Confer; Deliver; Gift; Grant; Impart; Mete; Provide; Render)

2 Ne. 2: 27 all things are g. men that are expedient unto man; 4: 35 God will g. liberally to him that asketh; 4: 35 my God will g. me if I ask not amiss; **Mosiah** 4: 24 those who do not g. to the beggar should be able to say, I g. not because I have not; **3 Ne.** 14: 7 (Matt. 7: 7) ask and it shall be g. unto you; 14: 11 (Matt. 7: 11) how much more shall Father in heaven g. good things to them that ask him; **Morm.** 8: 15 none can have power to bring record to light save it be g. him of God.

GLASS (*see also* BD Glass)

Ether 3: 1 brother of Jared[2] brings the Lord sixteen stones, transparent as g.

GLORIFY (*see also* Exalt; Glorious; Glory; Honor; Praise; Sanctification)

2 Ne. 6: 4 Jacob[2] speaks so that people may learn and g. name of God; **3 Ne.** 12: 16 (Matt. 5: 16) let light so shine that they see good works and g. Father; 23: 9 Father to g. his name in Christ; **Ether** 3: 21 the Lord shall g. his name in the flesh; 12: 4 hope makes men abound in good works, being led to g. God; 12: 8 because of faith of men, Christ has shown himself, g. name of Father.

GLORIOUS (*see also* Glorify; Glory)

1 Ne. 21: 5 (Isa. 49: 5) yet shall I be g. in eyes of the Lord; **2 Ne.** 9: 46 prepare for g. day when justice shall be administered; 14: 2 (Isa. 4: 2) branch of the Lord shall be g.; 21: 10 (Isa. 11: 10) his rest shall be g.

GLORY [noun] (*see also* Eternal Life;

Glorify; Glory [verb]; Glory of the World; Light; Majesty; Power; Reward; Transfigure, Transfiguration; TG Glory; God, Glory of)

1 Ne. 22: 24 Holy One of Israel to reign in great g.; **2 Ne.** 1: 15 Nephi[1] has beheld the Lord's g.; 1: 25 Nephi[1] has sought the Lord's g.; 12: 19 (Isa. 2: 19) g. of the Lord's majesty shall smite them; 16: 3 (Isa. 6: 3) whole earth is full of the Lord's g.; **Jacob** 4: 4 not only Nephites, but all holy prophets, have hope of Christ's g.; **Mosiah** 4: 12 grow in knowledge of g. of him who created you; **Alma** 5: 50 (9: 26; 13: 24; 3 Ne. 26: 3; 28: 7–8) Son to come in g.; 5: 50 g. of King of all the earth shall soon shine forth; 14: 11 the Lord receives martyrs unto himself in g.; 19: 6 Lamoni's mind is enlightened by light of g. of God; 36: 28 I know that the Lord will raise me up at last day, to dwell with him in g.; 60: 36 Moroni[1] seeks not honor of world, but g. of God; **3 Ne.** 13: 13 (Matt. 6: 13) thine is the kingdom, the power, and the g. forever; 20: 9–10 multitude gives g. to Jesus; **Morm.** 8: 15 bringing forth of record must be done with eye single to g. of God.; 9: 5 when ye are brought to see g. of God, it will kindle unquenchable fire in you; **Moro.** 9: 25 may hope of Christ's g. rest in your mind forever.

GLORY [verb]

2 Ne. 33: 6 Nephi[1] g. in plainness, in truth, in Jesus; **Mosiah** 23: 11 Alma[1] is not worthy to g. of himself; **Alma** 26: 16 who can g. too much in the Lord; 29: 9 I do not g. of myself, but I g. in that which the Lord hath commanded me; 48: 16 heart of Moroni[1] g. in his faith.

GLORY OF THE WORLD

2 Ne. 27: 15–16 the learned will offer to read book for g. of world; **Hel.** 7: 5 robbers rule in government to get g. of world; **3 Ne.** 13: 2 (Matt. 6: 2) hypocrites give alms to have g. of men; **Ether** 8: 7 Jared[3] had set heart upon kingdom and g. of world.

GNASH, GNASHING (*see also* Hell; Torment)

Mosiah 16: 2 (Alma 40: 13) the wicked shall have cause to g. teeth; **Alma** 14: 21 people of Ammonihah g. teeth upon Alma[2] and Amulek.

GO

1 Ne. 3: 7 I will g. and do the things which the Lord hath commanded; 21: 9 (Isa. 49: 9) say to prisoners, G. forth; **2 Ne.** 12: 3 (Isa. 2: 3) let us g. up to mountain of the Lord; 12: 3 (Isa. 2: 3) out of Zion shall g. forth the law; **3 Ne.** 12: 41 (Matt. 5: 41) whosoever shall compel thee to g. a mile, g. with him twain; 17: 4 (18: 27) Christ g. unto the Father; **Morm.** 9: 22 (Matt. 28: 19) g. ye into world and preach gospel to every creature; **Ether** 1: 42 the Lord will g. before Jaredites into choice land.

GOAT (*see also* Animal)

1 Ne. 18: 25 (Enos 1: 21) Nephites find g. upon land; **Alma** 14: 29 people flee Alma[2] and Amulek as g. fleeth with her young from two lions; **Ether** 9: 18 Jaredites have g.

GOD (*see also* Born of God; Children of God; Church of God; Commandments of God; Faith; Fear of God; Gift; Glory [noun]; God, Body of; God—Creator; God, Eternal Nature of; God, Foreknowledge of; God, Goodness of; God, Love of; God, Manifestations of; God, Omniscience of; God, Power of; God, Presence of; God, Wisdom of; God the Father; Godhead; Godliness; Gods; Grace; Holy Ghost; Indignation; Jesus Christ; Jesus Christ—Creator; Jesus Christ—Holy One of Israel; Jesus Christ—Jehovah; Jesus Christ—Lord; Judgment; Justice; Kingdom of God; Knowledge; Law; Mercy; Mystery; Name of the Lord; Praise; Prayer; Redemption; Spirit, Holy/Spirit of the Lord; Trust; Will; Word of God/Word of the Lord; Work [noun]; Worship; Wrath; TG God; BD God)

Title Page condemn not the things of God; **1 Ne.** 5: 9–10 (19: 7, 13; 20: 1–2; 2 Ne. 27: 34; 3 Ne. 11: 14) G. of Israel; 5: 15 (19: 10) G. preserved Israel, led them from Egypt; 6: 3–5 (2 Ne. 5: 32) Nephi[1] writes things pleasing to G. upon plates; 6: 4 (Mosiah 7: 19; 23: 23; Alma 29: 11; 36: 2; 3 Ne. 4: 30; Morm. 9: 11) G. of Abraham, Isaac, and Jacob[1]; 10: 21 no unclean thing can dwell with G.; 11: 6 (3 Ne. 11: 14; 22: 5) the Lord is G. over all the earth; 13: 41 there is one G., and one Shepherd over all the earth; 17: 14 ye shall know that I, the Lord, am G.; 17: 30 (2 Ne. 1: 10) G. is the Redeemer of Israel; 17: 30 (31: 16; Alma 5: 13; 7: 6; 11: 25–27; 43: 20; 3 Ne. 30: 1; Morm. 5: 14; 9: 28–29) the living G.; 17: 40 the Lord loves those who will have him to be their G.; 18: 16 (Jacob 3: 1) look unto G.; 19: 10 G. of our fathers; 19: 12 G. of nature suffers; 21: 5 (Isa. 49: 5) my G. shall be my strength; **2 Ne.** 2: 2 thou knowest greatness of G.; 2: 10 (2 Ne. 9: 38; Alma 40: 11; 42: 23) all men come unto G.; 2: 13 if there is no law, sin, righteousness, happiness, punishment, there is no G.; 2: 14 there is a G.; 2: 18 (Alma 42: 3) through the fall, man became as G., knowing good and evil; 2: 21 G. gave commandment that all men must repent; 4: 20 my G. hath been my support; 4: 30 (Jacob 7: 25) my G. and rock of my salvation; 4: 35 (James 1: 5) G. will give liberally to him that asketh; 6: 15 they who believe not shall know that the Lord is G.; 6: 17 Mighty G. shall deliver his covenant people; 8: 22 thy G. pleadeth the cause of his people; 9: 4 in our bodies we shall see G.; 11: 3 G. proveth all his words; 11: 4 all things given of G. from beginning are the typifying of Christ; 11: 7 if there be no Christ, there be no G.; 15: 16 (Isa. 5: 16) G. that is holy shall be sanctified in righteousness; 18: 10 (Isa. 8: 10) G. is with us; 19: 6 (Isa. 9: 6) Messiah shall be called, The Mighty G.; 26: 17 those who have dwindled in unbelief seek to destroy the things of G.; 26: 33 all are alike unto G.; 27: 23 I am G., and I am a G. of miracles; 28: 6 churches will say G. is not a G. of miracles; 29: 8 testimony of two nations is witness that I am G.; 31: 21 (Mosiah 15: 1–5; Alma 11: 44) Father, Son, and Holy Ghost are one G.; 2: 5 sin appears abominable unto G.; 4: 5 Abraham's offering up of Isaac is in similitude of G. and his Only Begotten Son; 6: 5 cleave unto G.; **Enos** 1: 6 (Ether 3: 12) G. could not lie; **Mosiah** 2: 16–19 when ye are in service of fellow beings, ye are in service of G.; 4: 22 your substance and your life belong to G.; 5: 5, 8 (6: 1; 21: 31–32; Alma 46: 22; Ether 13: 11) enter covenant with G.; 5: 15 G. is above all; 7: 27 Christ is the G., the Father of all things; 8: 18 G. has provided means for man to become great benefit to fellow beings; 11: 21, 23 (Hel. 7: 17) turn to G.; 11: 22 (13: 13) they shall know that I am the Lord their G., and am a jealous G.; 12: 21 (15: 14; 3 Ne. 20: 40) G. reigneth; 12: 24 (15: 31) all ends of earth shall see salvation of our G.; 12: 30 you ought to tremble before G.; 12: 35 (Ex. 20: 3) thou shalt have no other G. before me; 13: 28 (Alma 42: 15) G. himself shall make atonement for sins of his people; 13: 32–33 (15: 23; 16: 4) G. to redeem his people; 13: 34 (15: 1; 17: 8) prophets have prophesied that G. would come down and take form of man; 15: 8 G. breaks the bands of death; 17: 19 G. executes vengeance; 21: 35 baptism a testimony that they were willing to serve G.; 24: 5 Lamanites know not G.; 27: 15 I am sent from G.; 27: 31 all men shall confess that he is G.; **Alma** 5: 19 can ye look up to G. at day of judgment with pure heart and clean hands; 5: 28 if ye are not stripped of pride, ye are not prepared to meet G.; 5: 40 (Moro. 7: 12) good comes from G.; 9: 5 (16: 9) people of Ammonihah knew not that G. could do such marvelous works; 11: 24 thou knowest there is a G.; 11: 28–29 there is no more than one G.; 12: 24 (34: 32; 42: 4) life a probationary time to prepare to meet G.; 12: 30 G. conversed with men and made known the plan of redemption; 12: 33 G. called on men in name of the Son; 12: 37 provoke not G.; 18: 24–28 Ammon[2] teaches Lamoni about G.; 18: 30 G. dwells in the heavens; 18: 34 (22: 12) man was created after image of G.; 22: 7–11 Aaron[3] teaches Lamanite king about Great Spirit, who is G.; 22: 18 if thou art G., wilt thou make thyself known to me; 24: 12 G. has taken away our stains; 26: 37 G. is mindful of every people; 27: 4 (36: 6) angels sent from G.; 30: 37–39 Alma[2] testifies to Korihor that there is a G.; 30: 44 what evidence have you there is no G.; 30: 44 will ye tempt G.; 30: 48, 52 Korihor does not deny existence of G.; 30: 53 devil said there is no G.; 37: 12 records preserved for wise purpose known unto G.; 37: 47 (38: 2) look to G. and live; 39: 8 ye cannot hide your crimes from G.; 39: 17 souls always precious unto G.; 40: 4–5, 10, 21 G. knows time appointed for all to come forth from the dead; 40: 8 all is as one day with G.; 41: 8 G's decrees are unalterable; 41: 11 the wicked are without G. in the world and have gone contrary to nature of G.; 42: 13, 22–23, 25 if work of justice could be destroyed, G. would cease to be G.; 42: 26 G. brings about his great and eternal purposes; 44: 4 G. will support the faithful; 46: 10 foundation of liberty granted by G.; 48: 10 Moroni[1] prepares to support liberty, that Nephites might live unto G.; 58: 11 G. visited Nephites with assurances he would deliver them; 58: 40 (61: 9, 21; Hel. 14: 30) Ammonite youth stand fast in liberty wherewith G. has made them free; 60: 10 sufferings are known unto G.; **Hel.** 3: 35 sanctification comes because of yielding hearts unto G.; 7: 20 how could you have forgotten your G. in very day he has delivered you; 9: 21 how long will G. suffer us to remain in sin; 12: 2 when G. prospers his people they forget him; 13: 11 return unto G.; **3 Ne.** 11: 14 Christ is G. of whole earth; 13: 24 (Matt. 6: 24) ye cannot serve G. and Mammon; **Morm.** 3: 21 Jews to have witnesses that that Jesus whom they slew was the very G.; 5: 17 Lamanites were once led by G.; 8: 10 none know true G. save disciples of Jesus; 8: 15 none can have power to bring record to light save it be given him of G.; 9: 2 in day of visitation will ye say there is no G.; 9: 9 G. is same yesterday, today, forever; 9: 16 are not the things G. hath wrought marvelous; **Ether** 2: 8–12 whoso possesses this land should serve G.; 3: 12 thou art a G. of truth; 3: 18–21 Christ ministers unto brother of Jared[2] that he might know he is G.; 12: 11 G.

prepared a more excellent way; 12: 12 G. can do no miracle among the faithless; **Moro.** 7: 12 devil an enemy to G.; 7: 13–16 that which is of G. invites and entices to do good; 7: 14, 17 that which persuades to do evil is not of G.; 7: 23 G. declared unto prophets that Christ should come; 7: 35 (10: 4–5, 29) G. will show things that are true; 7: 44 only meek and lowly are acceptable before G.; 8: 12–18 G. is not a changeable G.

GOD, BODY OF (*see also* TG God, Body of—Corporeal Nature)

Mosiah 3: 5 (Alma 7: 8) the Lord shall dwell in tabernacle of clay; 7: 27 Christ to take upon himself image of man, flesh and blood: 7: 27 (Ether 3: 15; Gen. 1: 26–27) man created after image of G.; **3 Ne.** 11: 14–15 Nephites feel Christ's resurrected body; **Ether** 3: 15–16 Christ shows brother of Jared[2] body of his spirit, which appears as body he will have in flesh.

GOD—CREATOR (*see also* Creation; Jesus Christ—Creator; TG God, Creator)

1 Ne. 17: 36 the Lord has created earth and his children to possess it; **2 Ne.** 2: 14 (Mosiah 4: 9; Alma 18: 28; 22: 10; Morm. 9: 11) G. created all things in heaven and earth; 8: 13 (Isa. 51: 13) the Lord thy maker stretched forth the heavens, laid foundations of earth; 9: 40 I have spoken words of your Maker; 11: 7 if there were no G., there could have been no creation; 29: 7 G. has created all men; **Jacob** 2: 6 Nephites' sins make Jacob[2] shrink before his Maker; 2: 21 G. has created men to keep his commandments and glorify him; 4: 9 earth was created by power of G's word; **Enos** 1: 4 Enos[2] kneels before his Maker; **Omni** 1: 17 people of Zarahemla deny being of their Creator; **Mosiah** 2: 20–23 G. has created you and granted unto you your lives; 29: 19 except for interposition of all-wise Creator, people of Noah[3] must remain in bondage; **Alma** 30: 44 all things witness there is a Supreme Creator; **Morm.** 9: 11–12 G. of Abraham, Isaac, and Jacob created heavens and earth.

GOD, ETERNAL NATURE OF (*see also* God the Father; TG God, Eternal Nature of)

Title Page (2 Ne. 26: 12) Jesus is the Christ, the Eternal G.; **1 Ne.** 10: 19 (Alma 7: 20) the course of the Lord is one eternal round; 11: 21 (13: 40; Mosiah 15: 4; 16: 15; Alma 11: 38–39; Morm. 6: 22; Moro. 4: 3; 5: 2; 10: 4, 31) the Eternal Father; 11: 32 (15: 15; 2 Ne. 4: 35; Hel. 12: 8; Moro. 10: 28) the Everlasting G.; 12: 18 (2 Ne. 9: 8; Alma 34: 9; Ether 8: 23) the Eternal G.; **2 Ne.** 19: 6 (Isa. 9: 6) Messiah shall be called, The Everlasting Father; **Mosiah** 16: 9 Christ is the light of the world, a light that is endless; **Alma** 11: 44 Godhead is one eternal G.; 13: 9 Only Begotten is without beginning of days or end of years; **Hel.** 1: 11 everlasting Maker; 13: 38 (Alma 41: 10–11) to seek happiness in iniquity is contrary to nature of righteousness which is in our Eternal Head; **3 Ne.** 24: 6 (Moro. 8: 18) the Lord changes not; **Morm.** 9: 9 G. is same yesterday, today, forever; 9: 9–10 no variableness or shadow of changing in G.; 9: 19 G. changes not, or he would cease to be G.; **Moro.** 7: 22 G. knows all things, being from everlasting to everlasting; 10: 34 Jehovah, the Eternal Judge of both quick and dead.

GOD, FOREKNOWLEDGE OF (*see also* Elect; God, Omniscience of; TG God, Foreknowledge of)

1 Ne. 20: 5 before it came to pass I showed them thee; **2 Ne.** 27: 10 G. reveals all things from foundation of world to end; **W of M** 1: 7 the Lord knows all things which are to come; **Alma** 13: 3 priests were called and ordained from foundation of world according to foreknowledge of G.; 13: 7 high priesthood prepared from eternity to eternity according to G's foreknowledge of all things; 40: 4–5, 10, 21 G. knows time when all shall come forth from the dead; 40: 10 G. knows all the times appointed unto man.

GOD, GOODNESS OF (*see also* Kindness)

1 Ne. 1: 1 Nephi[1] has great knowledge of goodness of G.; 5: 4 except for vision, Lehi[1] would not have known goodness of G.; **2 Ne.** 9: 10 how great the goodness of G.; 33: 14 you that will not partake of goodness of G., I bid you an everlasting farewell; **Jacob** 1: 7 we labored diligently to persuade our people to partake of goodness of G.; **Mosiah** 4: 5–6 knowledge of goodness of G. awakens man to sense of nothingness; 5: 3 through goodness of G. we have great views of things to come; 25: 10 G's goodness in delivering people of Alma[1]; **Alma** 12: 32 justice could not be destroyed, according to supreme goodness of G.; 57: 25 goodness of G. preserves stripling Ammonites; **3 Ne.** 4: 33 Nephites weep because of goodness of G.; **Morm.** 2: 13 Nephites' sorrowing was not unto repentance because of goodness of G.

GOD, LOVE OF (*see also* Charity; Compassion; Love; Mercy; TG God, Love of)

1 Ne. 11: 17 G. loveth his children; 11: 22, 25 tree of life represents love of G.; 11: 25 waters are representation of love of G.; 17: 40 the Lord loveth those who will have him to be their G.; **2 Ne.** 1: 15 Lehi[1] is encircled eternally in arms of G's love; 4: 21 G. hath filled me with his love; 26: 24 the Lord loveth the world, layeth down life; **Jacob** 3: 2 feast upon G's love; **Mosiah** 4: 11–12 if ye retain in remembrance the greatness of G., ye shall be filled with his love; **Alma** 24: 14 G. has made gospel known to Lamanites because he loves them; **Hel.** 15: 3 the Lord has chastened Nephites because he loves them; **Ether** 12: 34 the Lord's love is charity; **Moro.** 7: 47 charity is pure love of Christ.

GOD, MANIFESTATIONS OF (*see also* Dream; God, Presence of; Jesus Christ, Appearances of; Jesus Christ, Second Coming of; Revelation; Vision; Voice; TG God, Manifestations of; God, Privilege of Seeing)

1 Ne. 1: 8 (5: 4; Alma 36: 22) Lehi[1] is carried away in vision and sees G. on throne; 10: 11 Messiah to rise from dead and *m.* himself to Gentiles; **2 Ne.** 2: 4 (11: 3) Jacob[2] has beheld Redeemer's glory in his youth; 9: 4 in our bodies we shall see G.; 11: 2 Isaiah[1] saw Redeemer, as did Nephi[2]; 26: 13 Christ manifests himself to all who believe in him; **Alma** 19: 6 light of glory of G. lights up Lamoni's mind and he is carried away in G.; 19: 13 Lamoni has seen his Redeemer; **3 Ne.** 11: 8 Nephites see Man descending from heaven; 12: 8 (Matt. 5: 8) the pure in heart shall see G.; 28: 37 Mormon[2] inquires of the Lord and he makes truth manifest; **Ether** 3: 13–16 Christ shows himself to brother of Jared[2]; 12: 39 Moroni[2] talked with Jesus face to face.

GOD, OMNISCIENCE OF (*see also* God, Foreknowledge of; God, Wisdom of; Knowledge; TG God, Omniscience of)

2 Ne. 2: 24 all things done in wisdom of him who knoweth all things; 9: 20 (Morm. 8: 17) G. knows all things, there is not anything except he knows it; 27: 10 G's revelation reveals all things from foundation of world to end; 27: 27 the Lord knows all works in dark; **Jacob** 2: 5 by help of Creator Jacob[2] can tell his people their thoughts; **Alma** 7: 13 Spirit knoweth all things; 18: 32 G. knows all thoughts and intents of heart; 26: 35 G. comprehends all things; 26: 37 G. is mindful of every people; 39: 8 ye cannot hide your crimes from G.; 40: 4–5, 10, 21 G. knows time when all shall come forth from the dead; 60: 10 known unto G. were all their cries and sufferings; **3 Ne.** 28: 6 Christ knows his disciples' thoughts; **Ether** 3: 25 the Lord shows brother of Jared[2] all inhabitants of earth who had been or would be; **Moro.** 7: 22 G. knows all things, being from everlasting to everlasting.

GOD, POWER OF

1 Ne. 1: 14 (17: 48; Mosiah 11: 23; 18: 13; Hel. 10: 11; 3 Ne. 4: 32) G. Almighty; 1: 14 the Lord's power is over all inhabitants of earth; 4: 1 the Lord is mightier than all the earth; 7: 12 the Lord is able to do all things; 9: 6 the Lord has all power unto fulfilling all his words; 11: 31 the afflicted are healed by power of Lamb; 13: 18–19, 30 (Mosiah 23: 13) Gentiles in promised land delivered by power of G. out of hands of all other nations; 17: 46 by power of his almighty word G. can cause earth to pass away; 17: 48 Nephi[1] filled with power of G.; 17: 51 the Lord has such great power and has wrought so many miracles; 18: 20 (Alma 30: 52) only power of G. threatening destruction could soften hearts; 21: 26 (22: 12; 2 Ne. 6: 18) the Lord is the Mighty One of Jacob; **2 Ne.** 6: 17 Mighty G. shall deliver his covenant people; 10: 25 may G. raise you by power of resurrection and by power of atonement; 19: 16 (Isa. 9: 16) Messiah's name shall be called, The Mighty God; 26: 20 false churches will put down power and miracles of G.; 27: 10 book shall be sealed by power of G.; 27: 12 (Ether 5: 3–4) three witnesses shall behold book by power of G.; 27: 20 the Lord is able to do his own work; 28: 3–5, 26 (Jacob 6: 8; Morm. 8: 28) churches shall deny power of G.; 31: 19 rely upon merits of him who is mighty to save; **Jacob** 2: 5 by help of all-powerful Creator, I can tell you your thoughts; 4: 11 power of resurrection which is in Christ; 7: 21 power of G. comes down upon multitude; **Enos** 1: 26 (Alma 37: 40; Morm. 7: 9) Enos[2] wrought upon by power of G., that he must preach and prophesy; **Mosiah** 3: 5, 17–18, 21 (5: 2, 15) the Lord Omnipotent; 4: 9 believe that G. has all power in heaven and earth; 8: 16 no man can have greater gift than to be seer, except he possess power of G.; 11: 23 none to deliver this people except the Almighty G.; 15: 3 Christ is called the Father because he was conceived by power of G.; 21: 30 Alma[1] and his people form church through power of G.; 27: 14 angel comes to convince Alma[2] of power of G.; 27: 15 can ye dispute the power of G.; 27: 18 nothing save power of G. could make earth tremble as though it would part asunder; **Alma** 5: 50 Son cometh in his might, majesty, power; 7: 8 G. has power to do all things according to his word; 9: 28 the righteous shall reap salvation according to power of Christ; 14: 10 Amulek asks Alma[2] to exercise power of G. on behalf of martyrs; 14: 24 if ye have power of G., deliver yourselves;

19: 6, 17 Lamoni is under power of G.; 23: 6 power of G. works miracles in Ammon[2] and his brethren; 26: 35 (Morm. 5: 23; Ether 3: 4) G. has all power; 30: 51–52 Korihor knows he is struck dumb by power of G.; 31: 5 preaching of word of G. has powerful effect upon minds; 34: 18 G. is mighty to save; 37: 15 if ye transgress, sacred things shall be taken away by power of G.; 37: 16 G. is powerful to fulfilling his words; 44: 5 the all-powerful G.; 56: 56 stripling Ammonites fight with strength of G.; 57: 26 stripling Ammonites are preserved by miraculous power of G.; **Hel.** 5: 11 Father gives the Lord power to redeem men from their sins; 9: 36 Nephi[2] knows nothing concerning murder of chief judge save given by power of G.; 12: 10–12 by power of G's voice, whole earth shakes; **3 Ne.** 13: 13 (Matt. 6: 13) thine is the kingdom, the power, and the glory; **Morm.** 5: 22 how can ye stand before power of G.; 7: 5 believe that Christ has risen by power of Father; 8: 16 bringing forth of record shall be by power of G.; 9: 13 all men shall be awakened from endless sleep by power of G.; **Ether** 3: 4 the Lord has all power and can do whatsoever he will for benefit of man; **Moro.** 7: 16 everything which invites to do good is sent by power of Christ; 7: 35 G. will show with power that these things are true; 10: 7, 32–33 deny not the power of G.; 10: 7 G. works by power according to men's faith.

GOD, PRESENCE OF (*see also* Death, Spiritual; Redemption; Resurrection)

1 Ne. 10: 21 no unclean thing can dwell with G.; **2 Ne.** 2: 8 no flesh can dwell in presence of G. save through mercy and grace of Messiah; 2: 10 (9: 38; Alma 40: 11; 42: 23) all men will stand in presence of G. to be judged; 9: 6 because man became fallen, they were cut off from presence of the Lord; 9: 8 angel fell from presence of Eternal G.; 9: 8–9 except for resurrection, spirits must be shut out from presence of G.; **Mosiah** 2: 38 sense of guilt causes man to shrink from presence of the Lord; 2: 41 those who keep commandments dwell with God in state of never-ending happiness; 15: 23 prophets and believers are raised to dwell with God; **Alma** 36: 14–15 thought of standing in presence of G. racks Alma[2] with horror; 36: 30 (38: 1) those who keep not commandments are cut off from G's presence; 42: 7 first parents were cut off temporally and spiritually from presence of the Lord; 42: 23 (Hel. 14: 15) resurrection brings men back into G's presence; **Hel.** 12: 25 in last day some shall be cast off from presence of the Lord; **Morm.** 9: 4–5 the miserable to dwell with G. under consciousness of filthiness; 9: 13 (Ether 3: 13) because of redemption, men are brought back into presence of the Lord.

GOD, WISDOM OF (*see also* God, Omniscience of; TG God, Wisdom of)

1 Ne. 9: 5 (W of M 1: 7) the Lord commands Nephi[1] to make plates for wise purpose; **2 Ne.** 2: 24 all things have been done in wisdom of him who knows all things; 9: 8 O the wisdom of G.; 27: 22 sealed book to be revealed when the Lord sees fit in his wisdom; **Jacob** 4: 10 (Alma 29: 8; 37: 12) the Lord counsels in wisdom; **Mosiah** 4: 9 (Alma 26: 35) believe that G. has all wisdom; 29: 19 the all-wise Creator; **Alma** 37: 2 record to be kept for a wise purpose; **3 Ne.** 28: 29 when the Lord sees fit in wisdom, three Nephites will minister to scattered tribes; 29: 1 (Morm. 5: 13) writings to come forth when the Lord sees fit in his wisdom.

GOD THE FATHER (*see also* Children of God; Jesus Christ—Creator; TG God the Father—Elohim/Eloheim; God the Father—Jehovah; Man, a Spirit Child of Heavenly Father)

1 Ne. 11: 21 (13: 40) Lamb of God is Son of Eternal Father; 14: 8 remember covenants of Father unto house of Israel; **2 Ne.** 19: 6 (Isa. 9: 6) Messiah shall be called, The Everlasting Father; 25: 16 Jews shall worship Father in Christ's name; 31: 21 (Alma 11: 44; 3 Ne. 11: 27; Morm. 7: 7) Father, Son, and Holy Ghost are one God; 32: 9 (3 Ne. 18: 19–20; 21: 27; Morm. 9: 27; Ether 4: 15; Moro. 2: 2; 7: 26; 8: 3; 10: 4) pray unto Father in name of Christ; **Jacob** 4: 5 prophets worshipped Father in Christ's name; **Mosiah** 2: 34 ye are eternally indebted to heavenly Father; 3: 8 (15: 4; 16: 15; Alma 11: 38–39; Hel. 14: 12; 16: 18; Ether 4: 7) Jesus Christ is Father of heaven and earth; 7: 27 Christ is Father of all things; 15: 2 (Morm. 9: 12; Ether 3: 14) Christ is Father and Son; 15: 3 Christ is the Father because he was conceived by power of God; **3 Ne.** 1: 14 Christ comes to do will both of Father and of Son; 9: 15 Christ was with Father from beginning; 9: 15 (11: 27) Christ is in Father, and Father in Christ; 9: 15 in Christ has Father glorified his name; 11: 25 baptism performed in name of Father, Son, and Holy Ghost; 11: 32 Father, Son, and Holy Ghost bear record of each other; 12: 48 (Matt. 5: 48) be perfect even as Christ, or Father in heaven, is perfect; 13: 6 (Matt. 6: 6) pray to thy Father who is in secret; 13: 9 (Matt. 6: 9) our Father who art in heaven; 13: 14–15 (Matt. 6: 14–15) if ye forgive men their trespasses, heavenly Father will forgive you; 13: 26 fowls sow not, yet heavenly Father feeds them; 13: 32 Heavenly Father knows ye have need of all these things; 14: 21 (Matt. 7: 21) he who does will of Father will enter kingdom of heaven; 17: 15–18 Jesus speaks marvelous things in prayer to Father; 18: 21 pray in your families unto Father; 18: 27 Christ must go to Father to fulfill other commandments; 28: 11 Father gives Holy Ghost unto men because of Christ; **Morm.** 6: 22 the Eternal Father knows your state; **Moro.** 4: 3 (5: 2) O God, the Eternal Father; 10: 4 ask God, the Eternal Father, if these things are true; 10: 31 covenants of Eternal Father to house of Israel shall be fulfilled.

GODHEAD (*see also* God; God the Father; Holy Ghost; Jesus Christ; TG Godhead)

2 Ne. 31: 21 doctrine of Christ is only true doctrine of Father, Son, Holy Ghost; 31: 21 (Mosiah 15: 2–5; Alma 11: 44; 3 Ne. 11: 27, 36; Morm. 7: 7) Father, Son, and Holy Ghost are one God; **Alma** 11: 44 all must be arraigned before bar of Christ the Son, God the Father, and Holy Ghost; **Morm.** 7: 7 sing unto Father, Son, and Holy Ghost; **Ether** 12: 41 grace of Father, Christ, Holy Ghost to abide in you forever.

GODLINESS, GODLY (*see also* TG Godliness; Mysteries of Godliness)

Moro. 7: 30 miracles are shown unto them of strong faith in every form of g.

GODS (*see also* Idolatry)

Alma 12: 31 having transgressed first commandments, first parents became as G., knowing good from evil; **Morm.** 4: 14 Lamanites offer women and children as sacrifices unto their idol g.

GOLD (*see also* Metal; Ore)

1 Ne. 13: 7 Nephi[1] sees g. and silver in abominable church; 18: 25 Nephites find g. in promised land; **2 Ne.** 23: 12 (Isa. 13: 12) I will make a man more precious than fine g.; **Jacob** 2: 12 many Nephites have begun to search for g.; **Mosiah** 2: 12 Benjamin has not sought g. of his people for his service; 19: 15 Limhi's people must give Lamanites half their g. as tribute; **Alma** 1: 29 (Hel. 6: 9) Nephites have abundance of g.; **3 Ne.** 24: 3 (Mal. 3: 3) the Lord shall purge sons of Levi[1] as g. and silver; **Ether** 10: 5–7 Riplakish causes fine g. to be refined in prison.

GOOD (*see also* Better; God, Goodness of; Tidings; Work [noun])

2 Ne. 2: 5 (Hel. 14: 31) men are instructed sufficiently that they know g. from evil; 2: 18 (Alma 12: 31) Satan tells Eve partaking of forbidden fruit will make her as God, knowing g. and evil; 2: 26 because men are redeemed from fall, they have become free forever, knowing g. and evil; 2: 30 I have chosen the g. part; 15: 20 (Isa. 5: 20) wo unto them that call evil g. and g. evil; 17: 15 (Isa. 7: 15) butter and honey shall he eat, that he may know to refuse evil and choose g.; 33: 4, 10 words of Jacob[2] persuade men to do g.; **Jacob** 2: 19 seek riches for the intent to do g.; 5: 25, 43 trees planted in g. spot of ground; **Omni** 1: 25 believe in all things which are g.; **Mosiah** 5: 2 Benjamin's people experience mighty change of heart to do g. continually; 16: 3 (Alma 12: 31) fall is cause of mankind's knowing g. from evil; **Alma** 5: 40 whatsoever is g. cometh of God; 29: 5 he that knoweth not g. from evil is blameless; 32: 35 whatsoever is light is g.; 37: 37 counsel with the Lord in all thy doings and he will direct thee for g.; 41: 13 restoration means to bring back g. for g.; 41: 14 do g. continually; **Hel.** 12: 4 children of men are slow to do g.; 14: 31 ye can do g. and be restored unto g.; **3 Ne.** 12: 44 (Matt. 5: 44) do g. to them that hate you; 14: 17 (Matt. 7: 17) every g. tree bringeth forth g. fruit; **Ether** 4: 11 Spirit persuadeth men to do g.; 4: 12 whatsoever persuadeth men to do g. is of Christ, for g. cometh of none save Christ; **Moro.** 7: 12 all things which are g. come of God; 7: 13, 16 that which is of God inviteth to do g. continually; 7: 19 search diligently in the light of Christ that ye may know g. from evil; 7: 19 if ye lay hold upon every g. thing, ye will be child of Christ; 10: 6 nothing that is g. denieth Christ, but acknowledgeth that he is.

GOOD SHEPHERD (*see* Jesus Christ—Good Shepherd)

GOODLY

1 Ne. 1: 1 Nephi[1] born of g. parents.

GOSPEL (*see also* Baptism; Covenant; Faith; Holy Ghost, Gift of; Jesus Christ; Obedience; Plan; Religion; Repentance; Salvation; Tidings; Truth; Word of God/Word of the Lord)

1 Ne. 10: 14 (15: 13) after Gentiles receive fulness of g. Israel shall come to knowledge of Messiah; 13: 24 when book proceeded from Jews, it had fulness of g.; 13: 26, 32, 34 plain and precious parts of g. kept back by abominable church; **2 Ne.** 30: 5 g. of Christ shall be declared among Lamanites; **3 Ne.** 16: 10–12 when Gentiles reject fulness of g., it shall come to Israel; 27: 10 if church is built upon Christ's g., Father will show his works in it; 27: 13–21 this is my g.; 28: 23 disciples preach g. of Christ unto all people; **4 Ne.** 1: 38 those who reject g. are called Lamanites; **Morm.** 9: 8 he that denieth these things knoweth not the g. of Christ; 9: 22 (Matt.

28: 19) go ye into world and preach g. to every creature; **Ether** 4: 18 repent all ye ends of the earth, and believe in my g.

GOSSIP (*see also* Babbling; Backbiting; Lying; Slander)

Hel. 16: 22 Satan spreads rumors and contentions.

GOVERN, GOVERNMENT (*see also* Government, Civil; Order; Regulate; Rule)

2 Ne. 19: 6 (Isa. 9: 6) unto us a child is born, and the g. shall be upon his shoulders; 19: 7 (Isa. 9: 7) of the increase of g. and peace there is no end.

GOVERNMENT, CIVIL (*see also* Country; Freedom; Govern; Governor; Law, Civil; Liberty; Nation; Right [noun]; Tax; TG Governments)

Alma 43: 17 Moroni[1] takes command and g. of wars; 46: 35 Amalickiahites who will not covenant to maintain free g. are put to death; 51: 5 king-men desire to alter law to overthrow free g.; 54: 17, 24 Ammoron claims Nephites' fathers robbed their brethren of right to g.; 58: 36 Helaman[2] fears some faction in g. does not send more men; 59: 13 Moroni[1] is angry with g.; 60: 14 Moroni[1] fears God's judgments will come because of slothfulness of g.; 60: 24 necessary to cleanse g. before contending with Lamanites; **Hel.** 1: 18 because of contention in g. Nephites do not keep sufficient guards in Zarahemla; 5: 2 laws and g. established by voice of people; 6: 39 robbers obtain sole management of g.; 7: 5 robbers held in office at head of g. to get gain; **3 Ne.** 3: 10 Giddianhi claims he desires to help his people recover g.; 7: 2, 6 people separate into tribes and destroy g. of land; 7: 11 tribes united in hatred of those who entered covenant to destroy g.; 7: 14 tribes not united as to laws and manner of g.; 9: 9 people of king Jacob[4] destroy peace and g. of land.

GOVERNOR (*see also* Government, Civil; Judge, Chief; Ruler)

Alma 2: 16 Alma[2] is g. of Nephites; 50: 39 (61: 1) Pahoran[1] is appointed g.; **3 Ne.** 1: 1 Lachoneus[1] is g.

GRACE (*see also* Jesus Christ, Atonement through; Mercy; Redemption; Salvation; Work [noun]; BD Grace)

2 Ne. 2: 6 (Alma 5: 48; 9: 26; 13: 9) Messiah is full of g. and truth; 9: 8 O the wisdom of God, his mercy and g.; 9: 53 because of g. and mercy, the Lord has promised that Nephites' seed shall not be destroyed; 10: 24 only in and through g. of God that men are saved; 11: 5 my soul delighteth in the Lord's g.; 25: 23 by g. we are saved, after all we can do; **Jacob** 4: 7 the Lord showeth us our weakness that we may know it is by his g. that we have power; **Mosiah** 18: 16 people of Alma[1] are baptized and filled with g. of God; 18: 26 (27: 5) for their labor priests were to receive g. of God; **Alma** 7: 3 continue in supplicating of the Lord's g.; **Hel.** 12: 24 men should repent that they might be restored unto g. for g.; **Morm.** 2: 15 day of g. is past with Nephites; **Ether** 12: 26–27 the Lord's g. is sufficient for the meek; 12: 36, 41 Moroni[2] prays the Lord will give the Gentiles g.; **Moro.** 7: 2 by g. of Father and Christ Mormon[2] is permitted to speak; 8: 3 continually praying that God, through infinite g., will keep you; 10: 32–33 ye may be perfect in Christ, by his g.

GRAFT

1 Ne. 10: 14 (15: 13–18; Jacob 5: 3–77; Alma 16: 17) after Gentiles receive gospel, natural branches or remnant of Israel should be g. in, or come to knowledge of Messiah.

GRAIN (*see also* Food; Wheat)

Hel. 11: 17 the Lord causes rain to fall, that earth brings forth g.

GRANT (*see also* Give)

Mosiah 26: 23 the Lord g. unto him that believeth unto end a place at his right hand; **Alma** 17: 9 sons of Mosiah[2] pray that the Lord g. them portion of Spirit; 29: 4 God g. unto men according to their desire; 42: 4 probationary time g. unto man to repent; 42: 22 law given, a punishment affixed, a repentance g.

GRAPE (*see also* Vineyard; Wine)

2 Ne. 15: 2 (Isa. 5: 2) well-beloved's vineyard brought forth wild g.; **3 Ne.** 14: 16 (Matt. 7: 16) do men gather g. of thorns.

GRAVE (*see also* Baptism; Bury; Death, Physical; Resurrection; Sepulchre)

2 Ne. 1: 14 hear words of parent, whose limbs ye must soon lay down in g.; 9: 11–13 g. must deliver up its dead; **Mosiah** 16: 7–8 (Alma 22: 14) because of resurrection, g. hath no victory; **Hel.** 14: 25 many g. shall be opened at time of Christ's resurrection; **Morm.** 7: 5 Christ hath gained victory over g.

GRAVEN (*see* Engrave; Image)

GREAT, GREATER, GREATEST (*see also* Day of the Lord; Mighty)

1 Ne. 7: 11 ye have forgotten what g. things the Lord hath done for us; 15: 36 fruit of tree of life is g. of all gifts of God; **2 Ne.** 3: 9 latter-day seer shall be g. like Moses; 12: 9 (Isa. 2: 9) g. man humbleth himself not, therefore forgive him not; **Alma** 18: 2–21 (19: 25) Lamoni mistakes Ammon[2] for G. Spirit; 18: 22–35 Ammon[2] teaches Lamoni about G. Spirit; **Morm.** 9: 13 when trump shall sound, all shall come forth, both small and g.; **Ether** 7: 27 Shule remembers g. things the Lord hath done for forefathers in bringing them across g. deep.

GRIEVE (*see also* Lament; Mourn; Remorse; Sorrow)

1 Ne. 2: 18 (15: 4) Nephi[1] g. because of hardness of brothers' hearts; **Jacob** 5: 7, 11, 32, 46–47, 51, 66 the Lord g. that he must lose trees; **3 Ne.** 7: 16 Nephi[3] g. for hardness of hearts.

GROSS, GROSSER, GROSSEST

Jacob 2: 22 Jacob[2] must speak to his people concerning g. crime; **Alma** 8: 28 people wax more g. in iniquities; 26: 24 Lamanites' days spent in g. iniquities.

GROUND (*see also* Dust; Earth; Grounds)

1 Ne. 4: 2 (17: 26; Mosiah 7: 19; Hel. 8: 11) fathers come through Red Sea on dry g.; **2 Ne.** 26: 16 those who shall be destroyed shall speak out of g.; **Jacob** 5: 22 tree planted in poor spot of g. brings forth much fruit; 5: 23 tree planted in poorer spot of g. also brings forth much fruit; 5: 25, 43 tree planted in good spot of g. brings forth tame and wild fruit; **Alma** 32: 39 if neglected tree withers, it is because g. is barren.

GROUNDS (*see also* Ground)

Alma 5: 10 what g. had fathers to hope for salvation; 30: 7, 11 law should not bring men on to unequal g.

GROW (*see also* Enlarge; Increase; Multiply; Spread; Swell; Wax)

Alma 32: 28–41 word compared to good seed which will g. if planted in heart; **3 Ne.** 25: 2 (Mal. 4: 2) ye shall g. up as calves in stall.

GRUDGINGLY

Moro. 7: 8 if a man being evil giveth a gift, he doeth it g.

GUIDE (*see also* Counsel; Direction; Enlighten; God, Wisdom of; Holy Ghost; Inspire; Reveal; TG Guidance, Divine)

Mosiah 2: 36 if ye transgress, Spirit shall have no place in you to g. you in wisdom's paths; **Hel.** 13: 29 how long will ye be led by blind g.

GUILE

Alma 18: 23 Ammon[2] catches king with g.

GUILT, GUILTY (*see also* Bondage; Repentance; Shame; Sin; Spot; Stain; Torment; Transgression)

1 Ne. 16: 2 the g. take truth to be hard; **2 Ne.** 9: 14 we shall have perfect knowledge of all our g.; 28: 8 if we are g., God will beat us with a few stripes; **Jacob** 6: 9 resurrection will bring you to stand with awful g. before God; **Enos** 1: 6 my g. was swept away; **Mosiah** 2: 38 justice awakens soul to lively sense of g.; 3: 25 those who have done evil works are consigned to awful view of own g.; **Alma** 1: 12 Nehor is g. of priestcraft; 5: 18 can ye imagine yourselves brought before God's tribunal filled with g.; 5: 23 these things will testify ye are g. of all manner of wickedness; 11: 43 we shall be brought to stand before God with bright recollection of all our g.; 12: 1 Zeezrom trembles under consciousness of g.; 14: 7 Zeezrom confesses he is g.; 24: 10 God has forgiven us and taken away g. from hearts; 30: 25 Korihor says child is not g. because of parents; 39: 7 I would to God ye had not been g. of so great a crime; 43: 46 inasmuch as ye are not g. of first or second offense, ye shall not suffer yourselves to be slain by enemies; **Hel.** 7: 5 wicked judges let the g. go unpunished; **3 Ne.** 6: 29 lawyers and judges enter covenant to deliver those g. of murder from grasp of justice; **Morm.** 9: 3 can ye dwell with God under consciousness of your g.

GUILTLESS (*see also* Blameless; Spotless)

Mosiah 4: 25–26 that ye may walk g. before God, impart of your substance to the poor; 13: 15 (Ex. 20: 7) the Lord will not hold him g. that taketh his name in vain; **3 Ne.** 27: 16 whoso repents, is baptized, and endures to end will Christ hold g. before the Father.

GULF (*see also* Hell; Misery)

1 Ne. 12: 18 (15: 28) awful g. separates the wicked from tree of life; **2 Ne.** 1: 13 (Alma 26: 20; Hel. 5: 12) chains bind men captive down to eternal g. of misery and woe; **Hel.** 3: 29 word leads man of Christ across g. of misery.

HAGOTH—*Nephite ship builder* [c. 55 B.C.]

Alma 63: 5–8 builds and launches many ships.

HAIL (*see also* Destruction; Storm)

Mosiah 12: 6 the Lord will smite people of Noah[3] with *h.*; **Hel.** 5: 12 devil shall send forth *h.*

HAIR (*see also* Head; Shave)

2 Ne. 13: 24 (Isa. 3: 24) instead of well-set *h.* there shall be baldness; **Alma** 11: 44 (40: 23) not so much as *h.* of head shall be lost in restoration; **3 Ne.** 12: 36

(Matt. 5: 36) neither shalt thou swear by head, for thou canst not make one *h.* black or white.

HALLOWED (*see also* Holy)

Mosiah 13: 19 (Ex. 20: 11) the Lord blessed sabbath day and *h.* it; **3 Ne.** 13: 9 (Matt. 6: 9) our Father who art in heaven, *h.* be thy name.

HAND (*see also* Hand of the Lord; Hands, Laying on of; Labor; Right Hand)

1 Ne. 1: 3 Nephi[1] makes record with own *h.*; 17: 54 Nephi[1] stretches *h.* unto brethren, and the Lord shakes them; **2 Ne.** 25: 16 worship Father in Christ's name with pure hearts and clean *h.*; **Alma** 5: 19 can ye look up to God with pure heart and clean *h.*; 5: 28, 50 (10: 20; Hel. 5: 32) kingdom of heaven is soon at *h.*; **3 Ne.** 11: 14–15 Christ invites Nephites to thrust *h.* into his side, feel nail prints in *h.* and feet.

HAND OF THE LORD

1 Ne. 5: 14 Joseph[1] preserved by *h.* of the Lord; 21: 22 (2 Ne. 6: 6; Isa. 49: 22) the Lord will lift up *h.* to Gentiles; **2 Ne.** 1: 5 land covenanted unto all those led out of other countries by *h.* of the Lord; 1: 6 (Omni 1: 16) none shall come into land save they who were brought by *h.* of the Lord; 1: 10 (Alma 9: 23) Nephites receive great blessings from *h.* of the Lord; 1: 24 (Mosiah 23: 10; Alma 1: 8; 2: 30; 17: 9; 26: 3; 29: 9; 35: 14) instrument in *h.* of the Lord; 5: 12 (Mosiah 1: 16) compass prepared for Lehi[1] by *h.* of the Lord; 7: 2 (Isa. 50: 2) is the Lord's *h.* shortened that it cannot redeem; 8: 17 Jerusalem has drunk at *h.* of the Lord the cup of his fury; 15: 25 (19: 12, 21; 20: 4; Isa. 5: 25; 9: 12, 21; 10: 4) the Lord's *h.* is outstretched still; 21: 11 (25: 17; 29: 1; Jacob 6: 2; Isa. 11: 11) the Lord shall set his *h.* second time to recover his people; 28: 6 churches shall deny miracle wrought by *h.* of the Lord; **Jacob** 5: 47 has the Lord slackened his *h.* that he has not nourished his vineyard; 6: 4 the Lord stretches forth his *h.* unto house of Israel all the day long; **Mosiah** 1: 2 prophecies delivered to fathers by *h.* of the Lord; 2: 11 Benjamin made ruler by *h.* of the Lord; 28: 15 (Alma 37: 4) records preserved by *h.* of the Lord; **Alma** 2: 28 Nephites strengthened by *h.* of the Lord; 9: 22 Nephites delivered out of Jerusalem by *h.* of the Lord; 26: 3, 7 converted Lamanites are in *h.* of the Lord; 45: 19 Alma[2] buried by *h.* of the Lord; 46: 7 Nephites delivered by *h.* of the Lord; **4 Ne.** 1: 16 no happier people among all created by *h.* of God; **Morm.** 5: 23 know ye not that ye are in *h.* of the Lord; 6: 6 records had been entrusted to Mormon[2] by *h.* of the Lord; 8: 8 *h.* of the Lord has brought destruction on Nephites; 8: 26 none can stay *h.* of the Lord; **Ether** 1: 1 Jaredites destroyed by *h.* of the Lord; 2: 6 Jaredites continually directed by *h.* of the Lord; 3: 6 the Lord stretches forth his *h.* and touches stones with finger; 10: 28 Jaredites blessed and prospered by *h.* of the Lord.

HANDS, LAYING ON OF (*see also* Anointing; Confirm; Heal; Holy Ghost, Gift of; Ordain; Ordinance; Priesthood; TG Hands, Laying on of; BD Laying on of Hands)

Alma 6: 1 Alma[2] ordains priests and elders by laying on his *h.*; 31: 36 Alma[2] claps his *h.* upon those with him, and they are filled with Holy Ghost; **3 Ne.** 18: 36–37 Christ gives disciples Holy Ghost by laying on of *h.*; **Morm.** 9: 24 believers shall lay *h.* on the sick, and they shall recover; **Moro.** 2: 2 disciples given power to bestow Holy Ghost by laying on of *h.*; 3: 1–2 disciples ordain priests and teachers by laying on of *h.*

HANG (*see also* Capital Punishment; Sword)

3 Ne. 4: 28 Zemnarihah is *h.* upon tree until dead.

HAPPINESS, HAPPY, HAPPIER (*see also* Blessed [adj.]; Cheer; Delight; Joy; Merry; Pleased; Pleasure)

1 Ne. 8: 10 fruit of tree of life is desirable to make one *h.*; **2 Ne.** 2: 13 if there be no righteousness, there be no *h.*; **Mosiah** 2: 41 those who keep commandments unto the end shall dwell with God in state of never-ending *h.*; 16: 11 the good are resurrected to endless life of *h.*; **Alma** 3: 26 those whose works are good reap eternal *h.*; 27: 18 none receive joy of God save penitent and humble seeker of *h.*; 28: 12 survivors of war rejoice that dead may be raised to dwell with God in state of never-ending *h.*; 40: 12–17 spirits of those who are righteous are received into state of *h.*; 41: 5 souls will be raised to *h.* according to their desires of *h.*; 41: 10 (Hel. 13: 38) ye shall not be restored from sin to *h.*; 41: 10 wickedness never was *h.*; 42: 16 punishment affixed opposite plan of *h.*; 44: 5 Nephites owe all their *h.* to sacred word of God; 46: 41 those who die in faith of Christ are *h.* in him; 50: 23 there never was *h.* time among Nephites than in days of Moroni[1]; **Hel.** 12: 2 at very time when Lord does all things for welfare and *h.* of his people they harden their hearts; 13: 38 Nephites have sought for *h.* in doing iniquity; **4 Ne.** 1: 16 could not be a *h.* people among all those created by God; **Morm.**

2: 13 the Lord would not always suffer Nephites to take *h.* in sin; 7: 7 he that is found guiltless shall dwell in state of *h.* which hath no end.

HARD (*see also* Hardheartedness; Harsh)

1 Ne. 3: 28 Laman[1] and Lemuel speak *h.* words unto younger brothers; 15: 3 Lehi[1] spoke many things that were *h.* to understand; 16: 2 the guilty take the truth to be *h.*; **2 Ne.** 9: 40 words of truth are *h.* against all uncleanness; **Hel.** 14: 10 Nephites seek to destroy Samuel the Lamanite because his words are *h.* against them.

HARDHEARTEDNESS (*see also* Contention; Doubt; Hate; Pride; Rebel; Resist; Soften; Stiffnecked; Stubbornness; Unbelief; Wicked; TG Hardheartedness)

1 Ne. 2: 18 (7: 8) Nephi[1] grieves for hardness of brothers' hearts; 12: 17 temptations of devil harden hearts of men; 13: 27–28 abominable church takes away plain parts of gospel to harden hearts of men; 14: 7 men to be delivered to hardness of their hearts; 15: 3 being hard in hearts, Laman[1] and Lemuel look not to God for understanding; 15: 11 if ye harden not hearts and ask in faith, these things shall be made known; 22: 5 (2 Ne. 6: 10; 25: 10; Mosiah 3: 15) Jews will harden hearts against Holy One; **2 Ne.** 33: 2 many harden hearts against Holy Spirit; **Jacob** 6: 4–5 those of house of Israel who harden not hearts shall be saved in kingdom of God; **Mosiah** 11: 29 people of Noah[3] harden hearts against Abinadi's words; **Alma** 12: 10 he who hardens heart receives lesser portion of word; 12: 34 whoso repenteth and hardeneth not his heart shall have claim on mercy; 12: 37 let us repent and harden not our hearts lest we provoke the Lord to wrath; 13: 4 men reject Spirit because of hardness of hearts; 21: 3 dissenters are harder than Lamanites, cause Lamanites to harden hearts; 24: 30 enlightened people who fall into sin become more hardened; 33: 21 if ye could be healed by merely casting about your eyes, would ye harden your hearts in unbelief and not cast about your eyes; 34: 31 come forth and harden not your hearts any longer; 37: 10 Nephites harden hearts in sin and iniquities; **Hel.** 6: 35 (13: 8) Spirit withdraws from Nephites because of hardness of hearts; 13: 8 because of Nephites' hardness of heart, the Lord will withdraw his word; 16: 12 people become more hardened in iniquity; **3 Ne.** 1: 22 lyings sent forth among people by Satan to harden their hearts; 20: 28 if Gentiles harden hearts against him, the Lord will return their iniquities upon their own heads; 21: 22 if Israel will repent and harden not hearts, the Lord will establish church among them; **Morm.** 3: 2 Mormon[2] prays for Nephites, but without faith because of their *h.*; **Ether** 8: 25 devil hardens men's hearts, that they murder prophets; **Moro.** 9: 4 when Mormon[2] uses no sharpness, Nephites harden hearts against God's word.

HARLOT (*see also* Adultery; Church, Great and Abominable; Fornication; Whore)

1 Ne. 13: 7–8, 34 (14: 16–17) abominable church is mother of *h.*; **Mosiah** 11: 14 (12: 29) priests of Noah[3] spend their time with *h.*; **Alma** 39: 3 Corianton goes after *h.* Isabel.

HARM (*see also* Harmless; Hurt; Mischief)

Hel. 5: 44 Nephi[2] and Lehi[4] encircled by fire, yet it *h.* them not; **3 Ne.** 28: 21 (4 Ne. 1: 32–33; Morm. 8: 24) Nephite disciples cast into furnace and den of wild beasts and receive no *h.*

HARMLESS

Alma 18: 22 Ammon[2] is wise, yet *h.*

HARROW (*see also* Terror; Torment)

2 Ne. 9: 47 would I *h.* up your souls if your minds were pure; **Alma** 15: 3 Zeezrom's sins *h.* up his mind; 39: 7 Alma[2] would not dwell upon Corianton's sins, to *h.* up his soul, if it were not for his good; **Morm.** 5: 8 Mormon[2] does not desire to *h.* up men's souls in describing carnage.

HARSH, HARSHLY, HARSHNESS (*see also* Hard)

2 Ne. 33: 5 record speaks *h.* against sin; **Enos** 1: 23 prophets preach and prophesy in *h.*; **3 Ne.** 11: 3 voice from heaven is not *h.*

HARVEST (*see also* Reap; Thrash)

Alma 17: 13 sons of Mosiah[2] trust that they shall meet at close of their *h.*; 26: 7 converts are in hands of the Lord of the *h.*

HASTE, HASTEN (*see also* Rash)

2 Ne. 15: 19 (Isa. 5: 19) wo unto them that say, Let him *h.* his work; **3 Ne.** 20: 42 (Isa. 52: 12) ye shall not go out with *h.*, for the Lord will go before you.

HATE, HATRED (*see also* Abhor; Despise; Malice; Persecution; Revile)

1 Ne. 19: 14 (2 Ne. 6: 10–11; 3 Ne. 16: 9) because Jews have despised the Holy One, they shall be *h.* among all nations; **2 Ne.** 5: 14 (Jacob 7: 24; Enos 1: 20) *h.* of Lamanites against Nephites; 29: 5 Gentiles have *h.* Jews and not sought to recover them; **Mosiah** 10: 17

(4 Ne. 1: 39) Lamanites are taught to *h.* children of God; 13: 13 (Ex. 20: 5) the Lord visits iniquities of fathers upon children unto third and fourth generation of them that *h.* him; **Alma** 24: 1–2 *h.* of Lamanites against people of Anti-Nephi-Lehi becomes sore; 37: 32 teach an everlasting *h.* against sin and iniquity; **Hel.** 5: 51 converted Lamanites lay down their *h.*; **3 Ne.** 7: 11 tribes united in *h.* of robbers; 12: 43–44 (Matt. 5: 43–44) do good to them that *h.* you; 13: 24 (Matt. 6: 24) man who serves two masters will *h.* one and love other; **Moro.** 1: 2 because of *h.*, Lamanites put to death every Nephite who will not deny Christ.

HAVOC

Hel. 11: 27 robbers make great *h.*

HEAD (*see also* Hair)

1 Ne. 22: 13 blood of abominable church shall turn upon own *h.*; **2 Ne.** 4: 6 cursing taken from you and answered upon *h.* of parents; **Jacob** 4: 17 is it possible for Jews to build upon rejected foundation that it may become *h.* of their corner; **Mosiah** 5: 8 under this *h.* ye are made free; 10: 8 (Alma 3: 5; 3 Ne. 4: 7) warriors shave their *h.*; 29: 30 sins shall be answered upon people's *h.*; **Alma** 3: 4–5 Amlicites do not shave *h.* like Lamanites; **3 Ne.** 1: 13 lift up your *h.* and be of good cheer; 12: 36 (Matt. 5: 36) thou shalt not swear by the *h.*; 20: 28 Father will return Gentiles' iniquities upon their own *h.*

HEAL, HEALING (*see also* Cure; Deaf; Dumb; Hands, Laying on of; Jesus Christ, Atonement through; Miracle; Ordinance; Raise; Recover; Save; Sick; TG Heal, Healing)

1 Ne. 11: 31 multitudes of sick and afflicted *h.* by Lamb; 17: 41 the Lord prepared way that Israelites might be *h.* of serpent bites; **2 Ne.** 16: 10 (Isa. 6: 10; Acts 28: 27) make people's heart fat, lest they understand, be converted and *h.*; 25: 20 the Lord gave Moses power to *h.* nations after being bitten by serpents; **Jacob** 2: 8 pleasing word of God *h.* wounded soul; **Mosiah** 14: 5 (Isa. 53: 5) with his stripes we are *h.*; **Alma** 15: 8 if thou believest in redemption of Christ, thou canst be *h.*; 33: 20 Israelites would not look upon serpent because they did not believe it would *h.* them; 33: 21–22 if ye could be *h.* by casting about your eyes, would ye not behold quickly; **3 Ne.** 7: 22 those who are *h.* manifest unto people that they have been wrought upon by Spirit; 9: 13 repent of your sins and be converted, that I may *h.* you; 17: 9 Christ *h.* all Nephite sick who are brought to him; 18: 32 those who repent and come unto Christ will be *h.*

HEAR, HEARD (*see also* Communication; Deaf; Ear; Hearken; Heed; Listen)

1 Ne. 10: 17 Nephi[1] desires to see, *h.* things seen by his father; 17: 45 Laman[1] and Lemuel have *h.* God's voice from time to time; 19: 24 Nephi[1] admonishes people to *h.* words of Moses; 22: 20 latter-day prophet shall ye *h.* in all things he shall say unto you; **2 Ne.** 9: 31 wo unto the deaf that will not *h.*; 16: 10 (Isa. 6: 10; Matt. 13: 13–15) make ears of this people heavy lest they *h.* and be converted; 27: 29 (Isa. 29: 18) the deaf shall *h.* words of book; **Jacob** 7: 5 Jacob[2] *h.* voice of the Lord from time to time; **Mosiah** 9: 18 God *h.* cries of Zeniff's people; 11: 23–24 (21: 15) except this people repent, the Lord will be slow to *h.* their cries; 26: 28 he who will not *h.* the Lord's voice shall not be received in his church; 27: 14 the Lord hath *h.* prayers of his people; **3 Ne.** 11: 3 voice from heaven pierces them that *h.*; 14: 24 (Matt. 7: 24) whoso *h.* Christ's sayings and doeth them is like wise man who built house upon rock; 15: 17, 21–23 (John 10: 16) other sheep not of this fold shall *h.* Christ's voice; 17: 16 ear hath not *h.* so marvelous things as Nephites *h.* Jesus speak unto Father; 17: 25 multitude did see, *h.*, bear record; 27: 9 if ye call upon Father in Christ's name, Father will *h.* you; **Ether** 1: 40 the Lord *h.* brother of Jared[2]; **Moro.** 2: 3 multitude did not *h.* Jesus give disciples authority to bestow Holy Ghost.

HEARKEN (*see also* Communication; Hear; Heed; Listen; Obedience)

1 Ne. 14: 2 if Gentiles *h.* unto Lamb, they shall be numbered among Israel; 19: 7 men *h.* not unto God's counsels; **2 Ne.** 8: 1 (Isa. 51: 1) *h.* unto me, ye that follow after righteousness; 9: 29 to be learned is good if they *h.* unto counsels of God; 26: 8 the righteous that *h.* unto words of prophets shall not perish; 28: 26, 31 wo unto him that *h.* unto precepts of men; 32: 8 if ye *h.* unto Spirit which teacheth man to pray, ye would know that ye must pray; **Alma** 5: 38 (Hel. 7: 18) if ye will not *h.* unto voice of good shepherd, ye are not his sheep; 5: 41 if a man bringeth forth good works, he *h.* unto voice of good shepherd; **3 Ne.** 28: 34 wo unto him who will not *h.* unto words of Jesus.

HEART (*see also* Breast; Broken Heart and Contrite Spirit; Change; Conversion; Hardheartedness; Humble; Intent; Lowliness; Pride; Purpose)

1 Ne. 17: 44 elder sons of Lehi[1] are

murderers in *h.*; 18: 20 only power of God threatening destruction could soften *h.* of brothers of Nephi[1]; 22: 26 Satan has no power over people's *h.* because they dwell in righteousness; **2 Ne.** 1: 21 Lehi[1] exhorts sons to be determined in one mind and one *h.*; 4: 16 *h.* of Nephi[1] ponders continually upon what he has seen and heard; 4: 26 why should my *h.* weep; 4: 28, 30 rejoice, O my *h.*; 9: 30 the *h.* of the rich are upon their treasures; 9: 49 my *h.* delighteth in righteousness; 16: 10 (Isa. 6: 10) make *h.* of this people fat lest they understand with their *h.* and be converted; 25: 16 Israel shall worship Father in Christ's name with pure *h.* and clean hands; 27: 25 (Isa. 29: 13) people draw near the Lord with mouth, but have removed *h.* far from him; 28: 20 devil shall rage in *h.* of men; 33: 1 when a man speaks by power of Holy Ghost, it carries unto *h.* of men; **Jacob** 2: 35 Nephites have broken *h.* of tender wives; **Mosiah** 2: 9 Benjamin admonishes people to open *h.* that they may understand; 4: 2 apply atoning blood of Christ that our *h.* may be purified; 5: 12 remember to retain the name written always in *h.*; 12: 27 ye have not applied your *h.* to understanding; 18: 8–12 if this be the desire of your *h.*, what have you against being baptized; 18: 21 people of church should have *h.* knit together in unity; 24: 12 Alma[1] and his people pour out *h.* to God; **Alma** 5: 7 the Lord changed fathers' *h.*; 5: 19 can ye look to God with pure *h.* and clean hands; 5: 26 if ye have experienced a change of *h.*, can ye feel so now; 13: 29 have love of God always in *h.*; 16: 16 the Lord pours out Spirit to prepare *h.* to receive word; 32: 16 blessed is he that believeth and is baptized without stubbornness of *h.*; 32: 28 plant seed in your *h.*; 34: 27 when ye do not cry unto the Lord, let your *h.* be full; 37: 37 let thy *h.* be full of thanks unto God; **Hel.** 3: 35 sanctification of *h.*, which cometh of yielding *h.* unto God; 6: 17 Nephites begin to set *h.* upon riches; 6: 30 Satan hands down works of darkness as he can get hold upon *h.* of men; 12: 4 how quick are men to set *h.* upon vain things of world; 13: 2–4 Samuel prophesies whatsoever things the Lord puts into his *h.*; **3 Ne.** 11: 3 voice from heaven causes *h.* to burn; 11: 30 not Christ's doctrine to stir up *h.* with anger; 12: 28 (Matt. 5: 28) whoso looketh upon woman to lust after her hath committed adultery in *h.*; 12: 29 suffer none of these things to enter *h.*; 19: 33 multitude understands in their *h.* the words Jesus prays; 25: 6 (Mal. 4: 6) Elijah shall turn *h.* of fathers to children and *h.* of children to fathers; **4 Ne.** 1: 28 (Ether 15: 19) Satan gets hold upon *h.* of church; **Morm.** 9: 27 come unto the Lord with all your *h.*; **Moro.** 7: 48 pray unto Father with all energy of *h.*; 10: 3 ponder these things in your *h.*

HEARTHOM—*early Jaredite king*

Ether 1: 16–17 (10: 16) father of Heth[1], son of Lib[1]; 10: 30 reigns twenty-four years, taken into captivity.

HEAT

2 Ne. 14: 6 (Isa. 4: 6) tabernacle shall be shadow in daytime from *h.*; **3 Ne.** 26: 3 (Morm. 9: 2; 2 Pet. 3: 10, 12) elements shall melt with fervent *h.*

HEATHEN (*see also* Gentile)

2 Ne. 26: 33 the Lord remembereth the *h.*; **3 Ne.** 13: 7 (Matt. 6: 7) use not vain repetitions, as the *h.*; 21: 21 the Lord will execute vengeance and fury upon the unrepentant, as upon the *h.*

HEAVEN (*see also* Astronomy; Creation; God—Creator; Heavenly; Jesus Christ—Creator; Kingdom of God; Paradise; BD Heaven)

1 Ne. 1: 8 Lehi[1] sees *h.* open; 11: 14, 27, 30 (12: 6) Nephi[1] sees *h.* open; **2 Ne.** 7: 3 (Isa. 50: 3) the Lord clothes the *h.* with blackness; 23: 13 (Isa. 13: 13) the Lord will shake the *h.*; 24: 13 (Isa. 14: 13) Lucifer says, I will ascend into *h.*; **Mosiah** 2: 41 those who keep commandments unto end are received into *h.*; **Alma** 18: 30 *h.* is a place where God dwells; **Hel.** 3: 28 gate of *h.* is open unto all; 5: 8 (3 Ne. 13: 20; Matt. 6: 20) lay up for yourselves treasures in *h.*; 5: 48 Nephi[2] and Lehi[4] behold *h.* open; 14: 3, 6 signs in *h.* at Christ's coming; **3 Ne.** 11: 3 Nephites hear voice as if it comes out of *h.*; 13: 10 (Matt. 6: 10) thy will be done on earth as it is in *h.*; 28: 7 Christ shall come in glory with powers of *h.*; 28: 13–16, 36 three Nephites caught up into *h.*; **Ether** 13: 9 (Isa. 65: 17) there shall be a new *h.* and a new earth.

HEAVENLY (*see also* Heaven)

4 Ne. 1: 3 (Ether 12: 8) all made partakers of the *h.* gift.

HEAVENLY FATHER (*see* God the Father)

HEBREW (*see also* Language; BD Hebrew)

Morm. 9: 33 Nephites have altered the *H.*; 9: 33 if Nephites could have written in *H.*, there would have been no imperfections in record.

HEDGE (*see also* Punishment)

2 Ne. 4: 33 Lord, *h.* not up my way, but the ways of mine enemy; **Mosiah** 7: 29 in day of their transgression, the Lord will *h.* up his people's ways that they prosper not.

HEED (*see also* Communication; Hear; Hearken; Listen; Notice; Obedience)

1 Ne. 15: 25 give *h.* unto word of the Lord; **Mosiah** 1: 16 Liahona would lead the people according to the *h.* they gave the Lord; 5: 11 take *h.* that ye do not transgress; **Alma** 12: 9 portion of word granted unto men according to *h.* they give the Lord; 37: 43 fathers slothful to give *h.* to compass; 37: 44 it is easy to give *h.* to word of Christ.

HEIR (*see also* Children of God; Elect; Inherit; Seed)

Mosiah 15: 11 those who hearken unto prophets and look forward to remission of sins are *h.* of kingdom of God; **4 Ne.** 1: 17 people are in one, children of Christ and *h.* of kingdom of God.

HELAM—*convert from among people of Noah*[3] [c. 147 B.C.]

Mosiah 18: 12–14 baptized by Alma[1].

HELAM, CITY OF (*see also* Helam, Land of)

Mosiah 23: 20 built by people of Alma[1] in land of Helam; 23: 25–26 people flee to *H.* when Lamanites come.

HELAM, LAND OF—*land inhabited by people of Alma*[1]

Mosiah 23: 3–4 beautiful land, eight days' journey from land of Nephi; 23: 19 given name; 23: 20 people multiply, prosper, build city of *H.*; 23: 25 Lamanites invade; 23: 29 Lamanites take possession of *H.*; 23: 35 Amulon and his brethren discover *H.* while searching for land of Nephi; 23: 37 Lamanites set guards around *H.*; 23: 38 Lamanites bring families to *H.*; 23: 39 Amulon appointed king over *H.*; 24: 18–20 people of Alma[1] flee from *H.*; 27: 16 remember the captivity of thy fathers in land of *H.*; **Alma** 24: 1 Amalekites and Amulonites stir up Lamanites in *H.* against people of Anti-Nephi-Lehi.

HELAMAN[1]—*son of King Benjamin* [c. 130 B.C.]

Mosiah 1: 2 taught in language and prophecies by father.

HELAMAN[2]—*son of Alma*[2]*, prophet, military commander* [c. 74 B.C.]

Alma 31: 7 eldest son of Alma[2], not taken to preach to Zoramites; ch. 36–37 commandments of Alma[2] to *H.*; 37: 1–2 (45: 2–3; 50: 38) is entrusted with plates, to keep record; 37: 21 is given twenty-four plates of Jaredites; 37: 21, 23–24 is commanded to preserve Urim and Thummim; ch. 45–62 *H*'s account of the Nephites; 45: 2–8 is blessed because of belief; 45: 9–14 to write prophecy of Nephite destruction; 45: 15 is blessed by father; 45: 20 (48: 19; 62: 44) preaches; 45: 22 reestablishes church; 45: 23 appoints priests; 46: 1 is opposed by unrepentant; 46: 6 a high priest over church; 46: 38 maintains order in church; 49: 30 people have peace and prosperity because they heed *H.*; 53: 14 persuades Ammonites not to break oath; 53: 19, 22 young Ammonites ask *H.* to be their leader; ch. 56–58 writes letter to Moroni[1]; 56: 9 assists Antipus; 56: 30–54 armies of *H.* and Antipus defeat Lamanites by means of decoy; 57: 1–3 receives letter from Ammoron and sends reply; 57: 7–12 surrounds city Cumeni, intercepts Lamanites' provisions, obtains city; 57: 17–27 *H.* and two thousand stripling Ammonites battle Lamanites, are preserved by faith; 58: 7 complains of rulers' indifference; 58: 13–29 takes possession of Manti by decoying Lamanites from city; 60: 3 *H.* and his men have suffered much; 62: 12 receives six thousand additional soldiers; 62: 42 returns to Zarahemla; 62: 45 causes many to repent; 62: 52 dies.

HELAMAN[3]—*son of Helaman*[2]*, record keeper, chief judge* [c. 53 B.C.]

Alma 63: 11 receives records; **Hel.** 2: 2 is appointed chief judge; 2: 3–5 Kishkumen plots to murder *H.*; 2: 6–9 is saved by servant; 2: 14 takes his account from book of Nephi; 3: 20 serves righteously; 3: 37 dies; 5: 5–13 *H*'s instructions to his sons.

HELAMAN[2], SONS OF—*children of converted Lamanites known as Ammonites* [c. 64 B.C.] (*see also* Ammon[2], People of)

Alma 53: 14–15 *H.* convinces Lamanites not to break oath, never to shed blood; 53: 16 sons had not entered covenant, assemble, call themselves Nephites; 53: 17–18 two thousand enter covenant to protect liberty; 53: 19 ask *H.* to be their leader; 53: 20–21 (56: 46–47) are courageous, obedient to commandments; 53: 22 (56: 57) march to support of people in borders; 56: 3 *H.* tells Moroni[1] about sons of Ammonites; 56: 10 *H.* calls them his sons; 56: 45 have greatest courage among Nephites; 56: 47–48 were taught not to doubt by their mothers; 56: 52–54 defeat Lamanites; 56: 55–56 none slain; 57: 6 sixty additional sons of Ammonites join *H.*; 57: 19–21 fight valiantly; 57: 22 are selected to convey prisoners; 57: 24 (58: 39) two hundred wounded, none perish; 57: 26

are preserved by faith; 58: 39 in city of Manti with *H*.

HELEM—*brother of Ammon*[1]

Mosiah 7: 6 accompanies Ammon[1] on expedition to land of Nephi.

HELL (*see also* Captive, Captivity; Damnation; Darkness, Spiritual; Death, Spiritual; Devil; Jesus Christ, Atonement through; Lake; Redemption; Resurrection; Torment; Wicked; TG Hell; BD Hell)

1 Ne. 12: 16 (15: 26–29) depths of fountain of filthy water are depths of *h.*; 14: 3 abominable church founded by devil, that he might lead souls down to *h.*; 15: 35 devil is preparator of *h.*; **2 Ne.** 1: 13 O that ye would awake from deep sleep of *h.*; 2: 29 will of flesh giveth devil power to bring men down to *h.*; 9: 10 God prepareth a way for escape from death and *h.*; 9: 12 spiritual death is *h.*; 9: 12 death and *h.* must deliver up dead; 9: 26 atonement delivereth those who have not law from death and *h.*; 9: 34 liar shall be thrust down to *h.*; 28: 15 those who are proud, preach false doctrines, commit whoredoms, pervert right way of the Lord shall be thrust down to *h.*; 28: 21 devil lulls some into carnal security and leads them away carefully down to *h.*; 28: 22 devil tells men there is no *h.*; 33: 6 I glory in my Jesus, for he hath redeemed my soul from *h.*; **Jacob** 3: 11 loose yourselves from pains of *h.*; **Alma** 5: 7 chains of *h.* awaited fathers; 12: 11 chains of *h.* means to be taken captive by devil; 13: 30 the Lord grant unto you repentance, that you may not be bound down by chains of *h.*; 26: 13 how many thousands of our brethren has God loosed from pains of *h.*; 30: 60 devil will not support his children, but speedily drags them down to *h.*; 48: 17 if all men would be like unto Moroni[1], powers of *h.* would be shaken forever; 54: 7 awful *h.* awaits murderers; **Hel.** 6: 28 devil dragged Jaredites down to destruction, to everlasting *h.*; **3 Ne.** 11: 39 (Matt. 16: 18) gates of *h.* shall not prevail against those who build on Christ's doctrine; 11: 40 gates of *h.* stand open to receive those who declare more or less than Christ's doctrine; 12: 22 (Matt. 5: 22) he who says to brother, Thou fool, is in danger of *h.* fire; **Morm.** 8: 17 he who condemns shall be in danger of *h.* fire; 9: 4 more miserable to dwell with God under consciousness of filthiness than to dwell with damned in *h.*; **Moro.** 8: 20–21 he that saith little children need baptism is in danger of *h.*

HELORUM—*son of Benjamin* [c. 130 B.C.]

Mosiah 1: 2–3 taught in language of fathers, that he might become man of understanding and know prophecies.

HELP (*see also* Deliver; Relief; Serve; Succor; Support; BD Help)

Jacob 2: 5 by *h.* of Creator I can tell you your thoughts; **W of M** 1: 18 with *h.* of holy men, Benjamin establishes peace; **Mosiah** 1: 4 Lehi[1] could not have taught all these things without *h.* of brass plates; **Ether** 8: 16 oaths of secret combinations administered to *h.* those who sought power to gain power.

HEM—*brother of Ammon*[1]

Mosiah 7: 6 accompanies Ammon[1] on expedition to land of Nephi.

HEN (*see also* Animal; Chickens)

3 Ne. 10: 4–6 (Matt. 23: 37; Luke 13: 34) the Lord would gather Israel as *h.* gathers her chickens.

HERD (*see also* Animal; Cattle; Flock)

2 Ne. 5: 11 (Enos 1: 21; Hel. 6: 12) Nephites begin to raise *h.*; **Mosiah** 7: 22 Limhi's people give one half their *h.* as tribute to Lamanites; **Alma** 1: 29 because of steadiness of church, Nephites have abundance of *h.*; 62: 29 prisoners of Lamanites join Ammonites in raising *h.*; **3 Ne.** 3: 13 Nephites gather *h.* in one place; **Ether** 6: 4 Jaredites prepare food for *h.* during journey; 10: 12 Jaredites become exceeding rich in raising *h.*

HERITAGE (*see also* Inherit)

1 Ne. 21: 8 (Isa. 49: 8) isles of sea to inherit desolate *h.*; **3 Ne.** 22: 17 *h.* of the Lord's servants is to be preserved from weapons, tongues.

HERMOUNTS—*wilderness on west and north*

Alma 2: 37 Lamanites driven until they reach wilderness called *H*.

HESHLON, PLAINS OF

Ether 13: 28 Coriantumr[2] pursues Shared until he comes to plains of *H*.

HETH[1]—*early Jaredite*

Ether 1: 16 ancestor of Aaron[2], son of Hearthom; 10: 31 lives in captivity.

HETH[2]—*middle Jaredite*

Ether 1: 25–26 son of Com[1], father of Shez; 9: 26 embraces secret plots; 9: 29 commands persecution of prophets; 10: 1 perishes by famine.

HEW, HEWN (*see also* Cut)

Jacob 5: 42 all trees of vineyard good for nothing save to be *h.* down; 5: 66 bad trees shall be *h.* down; **Alma** 5: 35 bring forth works of righteousness and ye shall not be *h.* down; 5: 52 (3 Ne. 14: 19; Matt. 7: 19) every tree that bringeth not forth good fruit shall be *h.* down; 5: 56 they who persist in wickedness shall be *h.* down; **Hel.** 14: 18 whoso repents shall not be *h.* down; **3 Ne.** 27: 11–12 churches built upon works of men or devil shall be *h.* down; 27: 17 he who endures not to end shall be *h.* down.

HIDE, HID, HIDDEN (*see also* Secret)

2 Ne. 9: 43 things of the wise and prudent shall be *h.*; 27: 12 book shall be *h.* from world; 27: 22 after book has been read, it should be sealed and *h.* up unto the Lord; 27: 26 (Isa. 29: 14) understanding of their prudent shall be *h.*; 27: 27 (28: 9; Isa. 29: 15) wo unto them that seek deep to *h.* counsel from the Lord; **Jacob** 5: 14, 20 the Lord of vineyard *h.* natural branches of tame olive-tree; **Mosiah** 8: 17 *h.* things shall come to light; 14: 3 (Isa. 53: 3) we *h.* our faces from him; **Alma** 39: 8 ye cannot *h.* your crimes from God; **Hel.** 13: 18–20 (Morm. 1: 18) if men *h.* treasures in earth, they shall find them no more; 13: 19 men should *h.* up their treasures unto the Lord; **3 Ne.** 9: 5 the Lord has covered city of Moronihah with earth to *h.* iniquities from his face; 12: 14 (Matt. 5: 14) city set on hill cannot be *h.*; 28: 25 names of those who should never taste death are *h.* from world; **Morm.** 5: 8 all things which are *h.* must be revealed upon housetops; **Ether** 4: 3 Moroni[2] is commanded to *h.* writings again in earth; **Moro.** 9: 15 come out in judgment, O God, and *h.* this people's sins from before thy face.

HIGH, HIGHER, HIGHEST (*see also* High Priest; Highway; Pride)

1 Ne. 11: 6 the Lord, the most *h.* God; **2 Ne.** 24: 14 (Isa. 14: 14) I will be like unto the Most *H.*; **Alma** 51: 8 those who are in favor of kings are those of *h.* birth; **3 Ne.** 11: 17 blessed be the name of the Most *H.* God.

HIGH PRIEST (*see also* Priesthood; TG High Priest—Melchizedek Priesthood; BD High Priest)

Mosiah 23: 16 (26: 7) Alma[1] the *h.p.* over the people; **Alma** 4: 4 Alma[2] consecrated *h.p.* by father; 4: 18 Alma[2] retains office of *h.p.*; 13: 1–11 *h.p.* ordained unto high priesthood after order of Son; 30: 20 Ammon[2] a *h.p.* over Ammonites; 46: 6 Helaman[2] and his brethren are *h.p.* over church; **3 Ne.** 6: 20–21 they who had been *h.p.* are angry with men who preach against sins of people.

HIGH PRIESTHOOD (*see* Priesthood)

HIGHWAY (*see also* Path; Road; Street; Way)

2 Ne. 21: 16 (Isa. 11: 16) there shall be a *h.* for remnant of the Lord's people; **Hel.** 14: 24 (3 Ne. 6: 8; 8: 13) many *h.* to be broken up in destruction at Christ's death.

HILL (*see also* Cumorah, Land and Hill of; Ephraim, Hill of; Mount, Mountain; Ramah, Hill; Riplah, Hill; Shim, Hill)

2 Ne. 20: 32 (Isa. 10: 32) he shall shake his hand against the mount of daughter of Zion, the *h.* of Jerusalem; **3 Ne.** 12: 14 (Matt. 5: 14) city set on *h.* cannot be hid.

HIMNI—*son of Mosiah*[2] [c. 100-74 B.C.] (*see also* Mosiah[2], Sons of)

Mosiah 27: 8 an unbeliever; 27: 10 seeks to destroy church; 27: 32 is converted by angel; 27: 34–35 travels through Zarahemla with brothers to repair injuries they had done to church; 28: 1–9 Mosiah[2] allows sons to preach to Lamanites; 28: 10 (29: 3; Alma 17: 6) refuses to be king; **Alma** 23: 1–7 *H*'s successful missionary efforts among Lamanites; 25: 17 rejoices with brethren for success among Lamanites; 27: 16–19 *H*'s great joy at reunion with Alma[2]; 31: 6 is left in charge of church when Alma[2] and companions begin missionary journey.

HINDER (*see also* Forbid; Frustrated; Restrain; Stay; Stop; Withhold)

3 Ne. 6: 5 nothing to *h.* people from prospering except transgression.

HISS (*see also* Whisper)

1 Ne. 19: 14 (3 Ne. 16: 9) because Jews despise the Holy One, they shall become *h.* and by-word; **2 Ne.** 15: 26 (Isa. 5: 26) the Lord will *h.* unto Israel from end of earth; 17: 18 (Isa. 7: 18) the Lord shall *h.* for fly that is in uttermost part of Egypt; 29: 2 the Lord's words shall *h.* forth unto ends of earth; **3 Ne.** 29: 8 ye need not any longer *h.* nor spurn Jews; **Moro.** 10: 28 God's word shall *h.* forth generation to generation.

HISTORY (*see also* Account; Record)

1 Ne. 9: 2 (2 Ne. 4: 14; 5: 33; Jacob 1: 3) account of *h.* of Nephites recorded on large plates of Nephi; **Jacob** 1: 2 small plates touch but lightly on *h.* of Nephites.

HOLD (*see also* Keep; Power; Retain; Withhold)

1 Ne. 15: 24 whoso would *h.* fast to word of God would not perish; **Alma** 8: 9 (27: 12) Satan has great *h.* upon hearts; 30: 12 law could have no *h.* upon Korihor; **Hel.** 3: 29 whosoever will may lay *h.* upon word of God; 13: 31 riches to become slippery, that men cannot *h.* them; **4 Ne.**

1: 28 false church multiplies because Satan gets *h.* upon hearts; **Moro.** 7: 19 lay *h.* upon every good thing; 10: 30 lay *h.* upon every good gift.

HOLE

2 Ne. 8: 1 (Isa. 51: 1) look unto the *h.* of the pit whence ye are digged; **Ether** 2: 20 Jaredites to make *h.* in tops and bottoms of vessels for air.

HOLINESS (*see also* Holy; Purity; Righteousness; Sacred; Sanctification)

2 Ne. 2: 10 men to be judged according to truth and *h.* which is in God; 9: 20 how great the *h.* of our God; **Mosiah** 18: 12 pour out thy Spirit upon thy servant, that he may do work with *h.* of heart; **3 Ne.** 26: 5 men resurrected to everlasting life or damnation, according to mercy, justice, and *h.* of Christ; **Morm.** 9: 5 when ye are brought to see your nakedness and the *h.* of Christ, it will kindle unquenchable fire.

HOLY (*see also* Holiness; Holy Ghost; Order; Spirit, Holy)

1 Ne. 20: 2 (Isa. 48: 2) house of Jacob call themselves of the *h.* city; **2 Ne.** 31: 5 Lamb of God, being *h.*, had need to be baptized; **Jarom** 1: 5 Nephites keep sabbath *h.* unto the Lord; **W of M** 1: 17 Benjamin a *h.* man; 1: 17 many *h.* men among Nephites speak word of God with sharpness; **Mosiah** 13: 16 (Ex. 20: 8) remember the sabbath day, to keep it *h.*; **Alma** 10: 9 Alma[2] is a *h.* man; 12: 30 plan of redemption made known unto men according to faith, repentance, and *h.* works; 13: 1–11 high priests called with *h.* calling, ordained with *h.* ordinance unto high priesthood; 13: 26 news of Christ's coming to be made known unto *h.* men by angels; **3 Ne.** 28: 39 three Nephites sanctified in the flesh, that they are *h.*; **Ether** 13: 5 Jerusalem to be built again, a *h.* city; **Moro.** 8: 3 continually pray unto Father in name of his *H.* Child, Jesus.

HOLY GHOST (*see also* Holy Ghost, Baptism of; Holy Ghost—Comforter; Holy Ghost, Gift of; Spirit, Gifts of; Spirit, Holy/Spirit of the Lord; TG God, Spirit of; Holy Ghost; Holy Ghost, Dove, Sign of; Holy Ghost, Gifts of; Holy Ghost, Loss of; Holy Ghost, Mission of; Holy Ghost, Source of Testimony; Holy Ghost, Unpardonable Sin against; Holy Spirit; Lord, Spirit of; Spirit; BD Holy Ghost)

1 Ne. 10: 11 Messiah shall manifest himself to Gentiles by *H.G.*; 10: 17 *H.G.* is gift of God unto all who diligently seek him; 10: 19 mysteries of God shall be unfolded by power of *H.G.*; 10: 22 *H.G.* gives Nephi[1] authority to speak these things; 11: 27 (2 Ne. 31: 8) after baptism of Christ, *H.G.* comes down from heaven and abides upon him in form of dove; 12: 7 *H.G.* falls upon the twelve ordained of God; 12: 18 *H.G.* beareth record of Messiah; 13: 37 those who seek to bring forth Zion shall have gift and power of *H.G.*; 2 Ne. 26: 13 Christ manifests himself unto believers by power of *H.G.*; 28: 4 priests shall deny *H.G.*, which gives utterance; 28: 26 wo unto him that denieth the gift of the *H.G.*; 28: 31 cursed is he who hearkens to precepts of men, save given by power of *H.G.*; 31: 18 (3 Ne. 11: 32, 36; 16: 6; 28: 11) *H.G.* bears record of Father and Son; 31: 21 (Mosiah 15: 2–5; Alma 11: 44; 3 Ne. 11: 27, 36; Morm. 7: 7) Father, Son, and *H.G.* are one God; 32: 2 speaking with tongues of angels comes by *H.G.*; 32: 3 angels speak by power of *H.G.*; 33: 1 when man speaks by power of *H.G.*, power of *H.G.* carries it unto hearts of man; **Jacob** 6: 8 will ye reject the gift of the *H.G.* and quench the *H.* Spirit; 7: 12 Jacob[2] testifies of Christ by power of *H.G.*; 7: 13 Sherem asks for sign by power of *H.G.*; 7: 17 Sherem confesses Christ and power of *H.G.*; **Alma** 7: 10 Mary shall conceive by power of *H.G.*; 8: 30–31 Alma[2] and Amulek are filled with *H.G.* and given power; 34: 38 contend no more against *H.G.*: 39: 6 to deny *H.G.* when it has had place in you is unpardonable sin; **3 Ne.** 11: 25 I baptize you in name of the Father, Son, and *H.G.*; 15: 23 Christ does not manifest himself unto Gentiles, save by *H.G.*; 20: 27 in Abraham's seed shall all kindreds of earth be blessed, unto pouring out of *H.G.* through Christ upon Gentiles; 21: 2 things which Jesus declared are by power of *H.G.*; 29: 6 wo unto him who says the Lord no longer works by power of *H.G.*; **4 Ne.** 1: 48 Ammaron is constrained by *H.G.* to hide up sacred records; **Morm.** 1: 14 *H.G.* does not come upon any of Nephites because of their wickedness and unbelief; **Ether** 12: 23 Nephites could speak much because of *H.G.*; **Moro.** 3: 4 disciples ordain priests and teachers by power of *H.G.*; 6: 9 meetings conducted by power of *H.G.*; 7: 32 God prepares way that men may have faith, that *H.G.* may have place in their hearts; 7: 36 has God withheld power of *H.G.* from men; 7: 44 if a man confesses by power of *H.G.* that Jesus is the Christ, he must have charity; 8: 7 word of the Lord comes unto Mormon[2] by power of *H.G.*; 8: 9 *H.G.* manifests word of God; 8: 26 because of meekness and lowliness of heart cometh visitation of *H.G.*; 8: 28 Spirit ceaseth to strive with Nephites because they are denying *H.G.*; 10: 4–5 by power of *H.G.*

ye may know the truth of all things; 10: 7 ye may know that Christ is by power of *H.G.*

HOLY GHOST, BAPTISM OF (*see also* Born of God; Conversion; Fire; Holy Ghost, Gift of; Remission; Sanctification; TG Holy Ghost, Baptism of)

2 Ne. 31: 13–14 (3 Ne. 12: 1–2; 19: 13; 26: 17; 28: 18; 4 Ne. 1: 1; Morm. 7: 10) after baptism of water comes baptism of fire and *H.G.*; 31: 17 after repentance and baptism by water cometh remission of sins by fire and *H.G.*; **Mosiah** 4: 3 Spirit comes upon Nephites, and they are filled with joy, having received remission of sins; **Alma** 13: 12 after being sanctified by *H.G.*, high priests could not look upon sin without abhorrence; 36: 24 Alma[2] labors that men might be born of God and filled with *H.G.*; **3 Ne.** 9: 20 whoso comes unto Christ will be baptized with fire and *H.G.*; 11: 35 whoso believes in Christ will Father visit with fire and *H.G.*; 19: 9–13, 20–22 after Nephite disciples are baptized, *H.G.* falls upon them and they are filled with *H.G.* and fire; 27: 20 repent and be baptized, that ye may be sanctified by reception of *H.G.*; **Ether** 12: 14 after mighty change wrought upon Lamanites, they are baptized with fire and *H.G.*; **Moro.** 6: 4 after baptism, the people are cleansed by power of *H.G.*

HOLY GHOST—COMFORTER (*see also* Holy Ghost; TG Holy Ghost, Comforter; BD Comforter)

Moro. 8: 26 *H.G.*, Comforter which fills with hope and perfect love.

HOLY GHOST, GIFT OF (*see also* Confirm; Gift; Gospel; Hands, Laying on of; Holy Ghost; Holy Ghost, Baptism of; Ordinance; Spirit, Gifts of; TG Holy Ghost, Gift of)

2 Ne. 31: 12 to him who is baptized will Father give *H.G.*; **Alma** 9: 21 Nephites have been visited by Spirit with many gifts, including gift of *H.G.*; **3 Ne.** 18: 36–37 (Moro. 2: 1–3) Christ gives disciples power to bestow *H.G.*

HOLY ONE (*see* Jesus Christ—Holy One of Israel)

HOME (*see also* Dwell, Dwelling)

2 Ne. 9: 2 (29: 14; 3 Ne. 21: 28) Jews shall be gathered *h.* to lands of inheritance; **Alma** 40: 11 when spirits depart mortal body, they are taken *h.* to God.

HONEST (*see also* Uprightness; TG Honesty)

Alma 27: 27 Ammonites are perfectly *h.*

HONEY (*see also* Bee)

1 Ne. 17: 5 land called Bountiful because of much fruit and wild *h.*; 18: 6 Lehites prepare *h.* in abundance for voyage; **2 Ne.** 17: 15, 22 (Isa. 7: 15) butter and *h.* shall Messiah eat, that he may know to refuse evil and choose good; 26: 25 buy milk and *h.* without money and without price.

HONOR (*see also* Esteem; Glorify; Glory; Honorable; Praise; Respect)

1 Ne. 17: 55 (Mosiah 13: 20; Ex. 20: 12) *h.* thy father and thy mother; **Alma** 1: 16 men preach false doctrines for sake of riches and *h.*; 60: 36 Moroni[1] seeks not for *h.* of world.

HOPE (*see also* Faith; Trust)

2 Ne. 31: 20 press forward, having perfect brightness of *h.*; **Jacob** 2: 19 after ye have obtained *h.* in Christ, ye shall obtain riches; 4: 4 Nephites have *h.* of Christ's glory many hundred years before his coming; **Alma** 7: 24 see that ye have faith, *h.*, and charity; 30: 13 Korihor claims Nephites are bound down under foolish and vain *h.*; 32: 21 (Ether 12: 6; Heb. 11: 11) faith is to *h.* for things not seen which are true; **Ether** 12: 4 whoso believeth in God might with surety *h.* for better world; 12: 4 *h.* cometh of faith; 12: 28 faith, *h.* and charity bringeth unto the Lord; 12: 32 house prepared in Father's mansions in which man might have more excellent *h.*; 12: 32 without *h.* man cannot receive inheritance in place prepared; **Moro.** ch. 7 teaching of Mormon[2] on faith, *h.*, and charity; 7: 40 how can ye attain unto faith save ye shall have *h.*; 7: 41 ye shall have *h.*, through atonement and resurrection of Christ, to be raised unto life eternal; 7: 42 without faith there cannot be any *h.*; 7: 45 charity *h.* all things; 8: 14 he who supposeth little children need baptism hath neither faith, *h.*, nor charity; 8: 26 the Comforter filleth with *h.*; 10: 20 if there must be faith there must be *h.*, if there must be *h.* there must be charity.

HORROR (*see also* Fear of God; Terror; Torment)

Alma 36: 14 thought of coming into presence of God racked soul of Alma[2] with inexpressible *h.*

HORSE (*see also* Animal)

1 Ne. 18: 25 Lehites find *h.* in wilderness; **2 Ne.** 12: 7 (Isa. 2: 7) their land is full of *h.*; **Enos** 1: 21 Nephites raise many *h.*; **Alma** 18: 9–12 Ammon[2] prepares Lamoni's *h.* and chariots; **3 Ne.** 3: 22

Nephites gather with *h.* and other possessions in one place; 21: 14 (Micah 5: 10) I will cut off thy *h.* out of midst of thee; **Ether** 9: 19 Jaredites have *h.*

HOSANNA (*see also* BD Hosanna)

1 Ne. 11: 6 (3 Ne. 4: 32; 11: 17) *h.* to the Lord, the most high God.

HOUR (*see also* Time; BD Hour)

Alma 5: 29 *h.* is close at hand.

HOUSE (*see also* Household; Housetop; Israel; Jacob, House of; Temple; BD House)

2 Ne. 12: 2 (Isa. 2: 2) mountain of the Lord's *h.* shall be established in top of mountains; 12: 3 (Isa. 2: 3) let us go up to *h.* of the God of Jacob; **Mosiah** 13: 24 (Ex. 20: 17) thou shalt not covet thy neighbor's *h.*; **Alma** 30: 56 Korihor goes from *h.* to *h.* begging; **3 Ne.** 14: 24–27 (Matt. 7: 24–27) parable of those who build *h.* upon rock and sand.

HOUSEHOLD (*see also* Family)

Alma 22: 23 whole *h.* of Lamanite king is converted unto the Lord; 34: 21 cry unto the Lord over all your *h.*

HOUSETOP

2 Ne. 27: 11 words of sealed book to be read on *h.*; **Morm.** 5: 8 all hidden things must be revealed on *h.*

HUMAN (*see also* Man; Mankind)

Mosiah 28: 3 sons of Mosiah[2] cannot bear that any *h.* soul should perish; **Alma** 34: 10 great and last sacrifice shall not be *h.* sacrifice; **Morm.** 3: 20 every soul who belongs to whole *h.* family of Adam must stand before judgment-seat of Christ.

HUMBLE, HUMILITY (*see also* Boast; Broken Heart and Contrite Spirit; Fasting; Low, Lowliness; Poor; Submissive; Weak; TG Humility, Humble)

1 Ne. 13: 16 Gentiles *h.* themselves before the Lord; 15: 20 (16: 5, 32; 18: 4) brethren of Nephi[1] *h.* themselves before the Lord; **2 Ne.** 9: 42 save they come down in depths of *h.*, the Lord will not open to the proud: 12: 11 (Isa. 2: 11) lofty looks of man shall be *h.*; 15: 15 (Isa. 5: 15) the mighty man shall be *h.*; 20: 33 the haughty shall be *h.*; 28: 14 all have gone astray, save a few *h.* followers of Christ; 31: 7 by baptism, Christ *h.* himself before the Father; **Mosiah** 3: 19 natural man is enemy to God unless he becometh as child, *h.*; 4: 11 *h.* yourselves, even in depths of *h.*; **Alma** 5: 27 could ye say that ye have been sufficiently *h.*; 32: 13 blessed is he who is compelled to be *h.*; 32: 14–15 more blessed is he that *h.* himself without being compelled; 37: 33 Helaman[2] is admonished to teach people to *h.* themselves; 48: 20 people *h.* themselves because of words of Helaman[2] and brethren; **Hel.** 3: 34 more *h.* part of people suffer great persecutions; 3: 35 (6: 39) *h.* part of people fast and pray oft, and wax stronger in *h.*; 6: 5 powerful preachers bring many down into depths of *h.*, to be *h.* followers of Christ; **3 Ne.** 6: 13 some Nephites lifted up in pride, others exceedingly *h.*; 12: 2 blessed are they who shall believe in your words and come down into depths of *h.*; **4 Ne.** 1: 29 false church persecutes true church because of their *h.*; **Ether** 6: 12 when Jaredites land in promised land, they *h.* themselves before the Lord; 9: 35 when Jaredites have sufficiently *h.* themselves, the Lord sends rain; 12: 27 the Lord gives men weakness that they may be *h.*; 12: 39 Jesus told Moroni[2] these things in plain *h.*; **Moro.** 8: 10 parents must *h.* themselves as their little children.

HUNGER, HUNGRY (*see also* Charity; Famine)

2 Ne. 27: 3 (Isa. 29: 8) nations that fight against Zion shall be like *h.* man who dreams he eats, but soul is empty; **Jacob** 2: 19 seek riches to feed the *h.*; **Enos** 1: 4 soul of Enos[2] is *h.*; **Mosiah** 3: 7 Christ shall suffer *h.*; 4: 26 impart our substance to the poor, such as feeding the *h.*; **Alma** 4: 12 some lift themselves up in pride, turning their backs upon the *h.*; 8: 26 (10: 7) Alma[2] was an *h.* when Amulek took him in; 32: 42 feast upon word until ye are filled, that ye *h.* not; **3 Ne.** 4: 20 robbers about to perish with *h.*; 12: 6 (Matt. 5: 6) blessed are they who *h.* and thirst after righteousness; 20: 8 soul of him who partakes of Christ's flesh and blood shall never *h.*; **Morm.** 8: 39 why do ye adorn yourselves with that which hath no life, yet suffer the *h.* to pass by you.

HUSBAND (*see also* Family; Marriage; Wife; TG Husband; Marriage, Husband)

Jacob 2: 31 daughters of the Lord's people mourn because of wickedness of *h.*; 3: 7 Lamanite *h.* love wives, and wives love *h.*; Moro. 9: 8 Lamanites feed Nephite women upon flesh of *h.*

HYPOCRISY, HYPOCRITE (*see also* Deceit; Guile; Lying; Sincerity; Wicked; BD Hypocrite)

2 Ne. 31: 13 if ye follow Son, acting no *h.*, ye shall receive Holy Ghost; **Alma** 10: 17 lawyers and *h.* are laying foundation of devil; 34: 28 if saints turn away the needy, they are as *h.* who deny the faith; **3 Ne.** 13: 2 (Matt. 6: 2) when ye do your alms, do not sound trumpet as *h.* do; 13: 5 (Matt. 6: 5) when thou prayest, thou shalt not do as *h.*; 16: 10 when Gentiles are full of *h.*, the Lord will bring gospel from among them; **Morm.** 8: 38 *h.* sell themselves for that which will canker, pollute church of God.

IDLENESS, IDLE, IDLER (*see also* Industry; Labor; Laziness; Procrastinate; Sleep; Slothful)

1 Ne. 12: 23 (2 Ne. 5: 24) Lamanites become an *i.* people; **Alma** 1: 32 those who do not belong to church indulge in *i.*; 22: 28 more *i.* part of Lamanites live in wilderness in tents; 24: 18 converted Lamanites covenant that they will labor rather than spend days in *i.*; 38: 12 refrain from *i.*

IDOLATRY, IDOLATROUS, IDOL (*see also* Altar; Gods; Image; Priests, False; Sacrifice; BD Idol)

2 Ne. 9: 37 wo unto those who worship *i.*; 12: 8 (Isa. 2: 8) land is full of *i.*; **Enos** 1: 20 (Mosiah 9: 12; Alma 17: 15) Lamanites are full of *i.*; **Mosiah** 11: 6 priests of Noah[3] are supported in *i.* by taxes; 11: 7 people of Noah[3] become *i.* because of flattery of king and priests; 12: 35 (Ex. 20: 3) thou shalt have no other God before me; 13: 12–13 (Ex. 20: 4–5) thou shalt not make unto thee any graven image; 27: 8 Alma[2] became a wicked and *i.* man; **Alma** 1: 32 those who do not belong to church indulge in *i.*; 31: 1 Zoram[3] leads his people to bow down to dumb *i.*; 50: 21 *i.* brings wars and destructions upon Nephites; **Hel.** 6: 31 Nephites build *i.* of gold and silver; **Morm.** 4: 14, 21 Lamanites offer Nephite women and children as sacrifices to *i.*; 5: 15 Nephites to become loathsome people because of *i.*; **Ether** 7: 23 prophets testify that *i.* will bring curse upon land.

IGNORANCE, IGNORANT, IGNORANTLY (*see also* Accountable; Blindness; Darkness, Spiritual; Knowledge)

Mosiah 1: 3 except for records, Nephites must have suffered in *i.*; 3: 11 Christ's blood atoneth for those who have *i.* sinned; 15: 24 those who died in *i.* before Christ came shall come forth in first resurrection; 19: 17 Limhi not *i.* of father's iniquities; **Alma** 34: 2 impossible that Zoramites are *i.* of prophecies of Christ's coming; **3 Ne.** 6: 12 some are *i.* because of poverty; 6: 18 people do not sin *i.*, for they know will of God.

ILLUMINATE (*see also* Enlighten)

Alma 5: 7 fathers' souls were *i.* by light of everlasting word.

IMAGE (*see also* Creation; Form [noun]; Idolatry; Likeness)

Mosiah 7: 27 Christ to take upon himself the *i.* of man; 7: 27 (Alma 18: 34; 22: 12; Ether 3: 15) man created in *i.* of God; 12: 36 (13: 12–13) thou shalt not make unto thee any graven *i.*; **Alma** 5: 14, 19 have ye received God's *i.* in your countenances; **3 Ne.** 21: 17 (Micah 5: 13) thy graven *i.* I will cut off.

IMAGINATION, IMAGINE (*see also* Think; Thoughts)

1 Ne. 2: 11 (17: 20) elder sons murmur that Lehi[1] follows foolish *i.* of heart; 12: 18 spacious building is vain *i.* of men; **Alma** 5: 16–18 can you *i.* you hear the Lord's voice calling you; **Hel.** 16: 22 (3 Ne. 2: 2) Nephites *i.* up foolish and vain things in hearts; **3 Ne.** 29: 3 ye need not *i.* that words spoken are vain; **Morm.** 9: 10, 15 if ye have *i.* a changing God, he is not a God of miracles.

IMMANUEL (*see* Jesus Christ—Immanuel)

IMMERSION, IMMERSE (*see also* Baptism; Water; TG Baptism, Immersion)

Mosiah 18: 14 Alma[1] and Helam are buried in water in baptism; 18: 14–16 Alma[1] baptizes by burying in water; **3 Ne.** 11: 26 during baptism, disciples should *i.* person in water; 19: 11–13 Nephi[3] goes down into water to baptize.

IMMORTALITY, IMMORTAL (*see also* Body; Death, Physical; Eternal Life; Incorruptible; Jesus Christ, Resurrection of; Life; Live; Mortal; Redemption; Resurrection; TG Immortality)

2 Ne. 9: 13 all men shall become *i.*; 9: 15 when men have become *i.*, they must appear before judgment-seat; **Enos** 1: 27 (Mosiah 16: 10; Alma 5: 15; 12: 12; 41: 4; Morm. 6: 21) mortal must put on *i.*; **Alma** 11: 45 mortal body to be raised to *i.* body; 40: 2 mortal does not put on *i.* until after Christ's coming; **3 Ne.** 28: 8, 17 three Nephites shall be changed in twinkling of eye from mortality to *i.*

IMMOVABLE (*see also* Firmness; Steadfast)

1 Ne. 2: 10 Lehi[1] exhorts Lemuel to be *i.* in keeping commandments; **Mosiah** 5: 15 I would that ye should be steadfast and *i.*; **Alma** 1: 25 those who stand fast in the faith are *i.* in keeping commandments; **3 Ne.** 6: 14 church broken up, save few Lamanites who are *i.*

IMPART (*see also* Alms; Charity; Give; Poor)

Mosiah 4: 21, 26 (18: 27–28; 21: 17; Alma 1: 27; 34: 28) saints commanded to *i.* of substance for support of needy; 28: 1 sons of Mosiah[2] desire to *i.* word of God to Lamanites; **Alma** 12: 9 men commanded to *i.* only that portion of word which God grants unto men; 16: 14 Alma[2] and Amulek *i.* word of God without any respect of persons; 32: 23 God *i.* his word by angels unto men.

IMPOSSIBLE

Jacob 4: 8 *i.* that man should find out all God's ways; **Alma** 11: 34 *i.* for God to deny his word; **Hel.** 8: 5–6 Nephite judges believe destruction is *i.*; **Morm.** 4: 11 *i.* to write perfect description of carnage.

IMPROVE (*see also* Increase)

Alma 34: 33 if we do not *i.* our time while in this life, then cometh night of darkness.

INCORRECT (*see also* False)

Alma 3: 8 (9: 17; 26: 24; 37: 9) *i.* traditions of Lamanites.

INCORRUPTIBLE (*see also* Immortality)

2 Ne. 9: 13 all men shall become *i.*; **Morm.** 6: 21 bodies moldering in corruption must become *i.*

INCORRUPTION (*see* Corrupt, Corruption)

INCREASE (*see also* Add; Continue, Continuation; Enlarge; Grow; Improve; Lengthen; Multiply; Prolong; Reward; Seed; Spread; Swell; Wax)

2 Ne. 19: 3 (Isa. 9: 3) thou hast *i.* in the joy; 19: 7 (Isa. 9: 7) of *i.* of government and peace there is no end; 27: 30 the meek also shall *i.*; **Alma** 32: 28–29 would not the swelling of the seed *i.* your faith.

INDEBTED (*see also* Blessing; Debt; Owe)

Mosiah 2: 23 ye are *i.* unto God for creating you; 2: 24 ye will forever be *i.* unto God because of his blessings; 2: 34 ye are eternally *i.* to heavenly Father to render to him all that you have and are.

INDIGNATION (*see also* Anger; Displeasure; Judgment; Provoke; Punishment; Wrath)

2 Ne. 20: 25 (Isa. 10: 25) *i.* shall cease; **Alma** 40: 14 souls of wicked look for fiery *i.* of wrath of God upon them.

INDUSTRY, INDUSTRIOUS (*see also* Idleness; Labor; Work [verb]; TG Industry; Work, Value of)

2 Ne. 5: 17 Nephi[1] causes his people to be *i.*; **Mosiah** 23: 5 people of Alma[1] are *i.*; Alma 4: 6 people of church prosper by their *i.*; 10: 4 Amulek has acquired much riches by his *i.*; 23: 18 Anti-Nephi-Lehies become very *i.* people; **Ether** 10: 22 Jaredites are exceedingly *i.*

INEQUALITY (*see also* Equal; Pride; Ranks)

Mosiah 29: 32 *i.* should be no more in land; **Alma** 4: 12, 15 great *i.* among Nephites; 16: 16 no *i.* among Nephites; 28: 13 how great the *i.* of man is because of sin; **3 Ne.** 6: 14 great *i.* in all the land.

INFANT (*see also* Accountability, Age of; Babe; Child)

Mosiah 3: 18 the *i.* perisheth not that dieth in infancy.

INFINITE (*see also* Endless; Eternal; God, Eternal Nature of)

2 Ne. 1: 10 (Mosiah 5: 3; Hel. 12: 1; Moro. 8: 3) *i.* goodness of God; 9: 7 (25: 16; Alma 34: 10–14) atonement must be *i.*; **Mosiah** 28: 4 the Lord in *i.* mercy spares sons of Mosiah[2].

INFIRMITY (*see also* Disease; Suffering; Weak)

Mosiah 2: 11 like all men, Benjamin is subject to *i.* in body and mind; **Alma** 7: 12 Son will take upon him the *i.* of his people; 31: 30 O Lord, wilt thou give me strength, that I may bear my *i.*; **3 Ne.** 7: 22 those healed of *i.* manifest that they had been wrought upon by Spirit.

INFLICT

2 Ne. 2: 10 (Alma 42: 22) law given unto *i.* of punishment; **Mosiah** 3: 19 man must be willing to submit to all which the Lord seeth fit to *i.* upon him.

INHABIT, INHABITANT (*see also* Dwell; Possess)

1 Ne. 17: 36 the Lord created earth that it should be *i.*; 21: 19 (Isa. 49: 19) desolate places shall be too narrow by reason of *i.*; **2 Ne.** 20: 46 (Zech. 12: 6) Jerusalem shall be *i.* again; 22: 3 (Isa. 54: 3) desolate cities to be *i.*

INHERIT, INHERITANCE (*see also* Children of God; Covenant; Heir; Heritage; Kingdom of God; Possess; Promised Land; BD Inheritance)

1 Ne. 21: 8 (Isa. 49: 8) I will give thee my servant for covenant of the people, to cause to *i.* desolate heritages; 22: 12 (2 Ne. 25: 11) Israel shall be gathered into lands of *i.*; **2 Ne.** 1: 5 the Lord covenants with Lehi[1] to give his seed land of *i.*; 1: 9 if those coming out of Jerusalem keep commandments, none shall take away land of *i.*; 3: 2 may the Lord consecrate this land unto thee for thine *i.*; 9: 18 righteous saints shall *i.* kingdom of God; 10: 7 Jews to be restored to lands of *i.* when they believe in Christ; **Jacob** 3: 4 unless Nephites repent, Lamanites will possess land of *i.*; **Omni**

1: 27 (Mosiah 9: 1, 3) Zeniff and others desire to possess land of first *i.*; **Mosiah** 27: 26 unless they become new creatures, mankind cannot *i.* kingdom of God; **Alma** 5: 51 (9: 12; 39: 9; 3 Ne. 11: 38) except ye repent, ye cannot *i.* kingdom of heaven; 5: 58 unto the righteous will the Lord grant *i.* at right hand; 40: 26 no unclean thing can *i.* kingdom of God; 41: 4 those raised to endless happiness *i.* kingdom of God, those raised to endless misery *i.* kingdom of devil; **3 Ne.** 11: 33 whoso believeth in Christ and is baptized shall *i.* kingdom of God; 12: 5 (Matt. 5: 5) blessed are the meek, for they shall *i.* earth; 16: 16 (20: 14) Nephites to be given this land for *i.*; 22: 3 (Isa. 54: 3) thy seed shall *i.* the Gentiles; **Ether** 2: 15 Jaredites to be given this land for *i.*; 7: 16 Noah[2] obtains land of first *i.*; 12: 34 except men have charity, they cannot *i.* place prepared in Father's mansions.

INIQUITY, INIQUITOUS (*see also* Destruction; Evil; Judgment; Rebel; Sin; Transgression; Trespass; Ungodliness; Unrighteous; Wicked; TG Iniquity)

1 Ne. 17: 35 Canaanites driven out because they were ripe in *i.*; 17: 41 the Lord straitened Israel in wilderness because of *i.*; 17: 45 (Mosiah 13: 29; Alma 46: 8; Hel. 12: 4) ye are swift to do *i.*, but slow to remember the Lord; **2 Ne.** 1: 7 if *i.* abound, land to be cursed; 1: 31 nothing save *i.* shall disturb prosperity; 7: 1 (Isa. 50: 1) for your *i.* have ye sold yourselves; 25: 9 Jews have been destroyed from generation to generation according to *i.*; 27: 31 (Isa. 29: 20) all who watch for *i.* shall be cut off; 28: 16 when inhabitants of earth are fully ripe in *i.*, they shall perish; **Mosiah** 11: 22 the Lord visits the *i.* of his people; 13: 11 priests of Noah[3] have studied and taught *i.*; 14: 5 (Isa. 53: 5) Messiah was bruised for our *i.*; 14: 6 (Isa. 53: 6) the Lord hath laid on Messiah the *i.* of us all; 14: 11 (Isa. 53: 11) Messiah shall bear their *i.*; 21: 15 the Lord is slow to hear cries of Limhi's people because of *i.*; 27: 29 soul of Alma[2] has been redeemed from bonds of *i.*; 29: 17 how much *i.* doth one wicked king cause; 29: 21 ye cannot dethrone *i.* king save through contention and bloodshed; **Alma** 26: 24 Lamanites' days have been spent in grossest *i.*; 41: 11 all men in state of nature, or carnal state, are in bonds of *i.*; **Hel.** 7: 7 early Nephites were slow to be led to do *i.*; 13: 38 ye have sought happiness in doing *i.*; **3 Ne.** 9: 5 the Lord has covered city with earth to hide *i.*; 14: 23 (Matt. 7: 23) depart from me, ye that work *i.*; 20: 28 if Gentiles harden hearts against the Lord, he will return their *i.* upon their own heads; **Ether** 2: 9 (9: 20) God's wrath shall come upon inhabitants of land when they are ripened in *i.*; **Moro.** 6: 7 church members strict to observe that there should be no *i.* among them; 7: 45 (1 Cor. 13: 6) charity rejoiceth not in *i.*; 10: 22 despair cometh because of *i.*

INJUSTICE (*see* Justice; Malice; Persecution; Unjust; Unlawful)

INNOCENCE, INNOCENT (*see also* Blameless; Blood, Shedding of; Guiltless; Purity; Righteousness; Spotless)

2 Ne. 2: 23 Adam and Eve would have remained in state of *i.*

INQUIRE (*see also* Ask; Prayer; Question; Seek)

1 Ne. 15: 3 words hard to understand save a man *i.* of God; 15: 8 have ye *i.* of the Lord; 16: 23–24 Lehi[1] *i.* of the Lord where Nephi[1] should hunt; **Jacob** 2: 11 as Jacob[2] *i.* of the Lord, his word came; **Mosiah** 28: 6 Mosiah[2] *i.* of the Lord whether sons should preach to Lamanites; **Alma** 27: 7 Ammon[2] *i.* of the Lord whether Ammonites should go to Nephites; 40: 3, 9 Alma[2] has *i.* diligently of the Lord to know concerning resurrection; 43: 23 Moroni[1] asks Alma[2] to *i.* of the Lord whether Nephites should defend themselves against Lamanites; **3 Ne.** 28: 37 Mormon[2] *i.* of the Lord regarding three Nephites; **Ether** 1: 38 Jared[2] asks brother to *i.* of the Lord whether he will drive them out of land; **Moro.** 8: 7 Mormon[2] *i.* of the Lord regarding baptism of little children.

INSECT (*see also* Curse; Judgment)

Mosiah 12: 6 *i.* shall pester land of people of Noah[3].

INSPIRE, INSPIRATION (*see also* Calling; Enlighten; Holy Ghost; Revelation; Spirit, Holy/Spirit of the Lord; TG Inspiration)

Alma 43: 45 Nephites are *i.* by better cause; **3 Ne.** 6: 20 men *i.* from heaven are sent forth to preach; **Moro.** 7: 13 everything which inviteth to do good, love God, and serve him is *i.* of God.

INSTRUCTION, INSTRUCT (*see also* Charge; Command; Counsel; Revelation; Teach)

1 Ne. 17: 18 Nephi[1] *i.* of the Lord to build ship; 19: 3 things written on plates should be kept for *i.* of people; **2 Ne.** 2: 5 men are sufficiently *i.* that they know good from evil; 18: 11 (Isa. 8: 11) the Lord *i.* me that I should not walk in way of this people; **Alma** 47: 36 dissenters, who have been *i.* in knowledge of the Lord, become more hardened than Lamanites; 49: 8 Nephites prepared to battle after manner of *i.* of Moroni[1]; **3 Ne.** 3: 26 Gidgiddoni causes Nephites to make armor after manner of his *i.*; **Ether** 2: 16 Jaredites build barges according to *i.* of the Lord.

INSTRUMENT, INSTRUMENTALITY

2 Ne. 1: 24 (3: 24; Mosiah 23: 10; 27: 36; Alma 1: 8; 2: 30; 17: 9, 11; 26: 3, 15; 29: 9; 35: 14; 3 Ne. 22: 16) *i.* in hands of God.

INTENT (*see also* Desire; Purpose; Sincerity; Thoughts; Will)

1 Ne. 6: 4 fulness of mine *i.* is to persuade men to come unto God; **2 Ne.** 31: 13 if ye follow Son with real *i.*, ye shall receive Holy Ghost; **Jacob** 2: 19 seek riches for *i.* to do good; 4: 5 Nephites keep law of Moses for *i.* of pointing souls to Christ; **Mosiah** 5: 13 how knoweth a man the master who is far from *i.* of his heart; **Alma** 18: 32 God knows thoughts and *i.* of heart; 34: 15 *i.* of last sacrifice is to bring about bowels of mercy; **Moro.** 6: 8 as oft as they repented with real *i.*, they were forgiven; 7: 6 except a man offereth a gift with real *i.*, it profiteth him nothing; 7: 9 if a man prays without real *i.*, it profiteth him nothing; 10: 4 if ye ask God with real *i.*, he will manifest the truth unto you.

INTERCESSION (*see* Jesus Christ—Mediator)

INTEREST

Mosiah 4: 18 unrepentant have no *i.* in kingdom of God.

INTERPRETATION, INTERPRET (*see also* Interpreters; Language; Spirit, Gifts of; Tongue; Translation)

1 Ne. 11: 10–11 Nephi[1] desires to know *i.* of father's dream; 17: 5 Irreantum, being *i.*, is many waters; **Omni** 1: 20 Mosiah[1] *i.* engravings by gift and power of God; 1: 25 Amaleki[1] exhorts all men to believe in gift of *i.* of languages; **Mosiah** 8: 11 no one among Limhi's people can *i.* language on plates; 28: 13–14 two stones prepared for purpose of *i.* languages; **Alma** 10: 2 Aminadi *i.* writing upon temple wall; 18: 13 Rabbanah, being *i.*, is powerful or great king; 31: 21 Rameumptom, being *i.*, is holy stand; 37: 38 Liahona, being *i.*, is a compass; **Morm.** 9: 7 who can say there are no speaking with tongues and *i.* of tongues; **Ether** 2: 3 deseret, by *i.*, is honey bee; 3: 22 brother of Jared[2] shall seal record of experience, and no one can *i.* it; 4: 5 the Lord has commanded Moroni[2] to seal up *i.* of what brother of Jared[2] saw; 15: 8 Ripliancum, by *i.*, is large, or to exceed all; **Moro.** 10: 16 (1 Cor. 12: 10) to another is given the *i.* of languages.

INTERPRETERS (*see also* Interpretation; Seer; Translation; BD Urim and Thummim)

Mosiah 8: 13 *i.* a gift of God to seer for translating all ancient records; 8: 19 (Alma 37: 24–25) *i.* prepared for unfolding mysteries; 28: 20 Mosiah[2] confers *i.* upon Alma[2]; **Alma** 37: 21 Alma[2] admonishes Helaman[2] to preserve *i.*; **Ether** 4: 5 Moroni[2] commanded to seal up *i.*

INVENT

Mosiah 9: 16 Zeniff arms his people with all manner of weapons they can *i.*

INVITE (*see also* Entice; Lead)

2 Ne. 26: 33 God *i.* all to come unto him; **Moro.** 7: 12 devil *i.* to sin; 7: 13 that which is of God *i.* to do good; 7: 13, 16 every thing which *i.* to do good is of God.

INWARD, INWARDLY (*see* Prophets, False; Vessel)

IRON (*see also* Metal; Ore; Rod; Steel; Yoke)

2 Ne. 5: 15 Nephi[1] teaches his people to work in all manner of *i.*; 20: 34 (Isa. 10: 34) he shall cut down thickets of forests with *i.*; **Jarom** 1: 8 Nephites become rich in workmanship in *i.*; **Mosiah** 11: 8 Noah[3] ornaments buildings with all manner of *i.*; **Ether** 10: 23 Jaredites work in all manner of *i.*

IRREANTUM—*probably an arm of Indian Ocean off southeastern Arabia*

1 Ne. 17: 5 Lehites behold sea, which they call *I.*

ISAAC—*son of Abraham* (*see also* BD Isaac)

1 Ne. 6: 4 (19: 10; Mosiah 7: 19; 23: 23; Alma 29: 11; 36: 2; 3 Ne. 4: 30; Morm. 9: 11) God of Abraham, *I.*, and Jacob; 17: 40 God covenanted with Abraham, *I.*, and Jacob; **Jacob** 4: 5 Abraham's offering of *I.* is similitude of God and Son; **Alma** 5: 24 (7: 25; Hel. 3: 30) righteous shall sit down in kingdom of God with Abraham, *I.*, and Jacob.

ISABEL—*harlot in land of Siron* [c. 73 B.C.]

Alma 39: 3 Corianton forsakes ministry and goes after harlot *I.*

ISAIAH[1]—*Hebrew prophet* [c. eighth century B.C.] (*see also* BD Isaiah)

1 Ne. 15: 20 Nephi[1] rehearses to his brethren the words of *I.*; 19: 23 Nephi[1] reads prophecies of *I.* to persuade his people to believe in Redeemer; **2 Ne.** 6: 4 Jacob[2] speaks of things to come by reading words of *I.*; 6: 5 *I.* spake concerning all house of Israel; 11: 2 *I.* saw Redeemer; 11: 8 Jacob[2] writes words of *I.* to lift hearts; 25: 1 *I.* spake things hard to understand; 25: 4 *I*'s words plain to those with spirit of prophecy; 25: 5 my soul delighteth in words of *I.*; 25: 6 judgments spoken of by *I.* have come to pass; 25: 7 men shall know when prophecies of *I.* are fulfilled; **Mosiah** 15: 6 Messiah shall be led as sheep before shearer, as *I.* said; **Hel.** 8: 18–20 *I.* testified of redemption; **3 Ne.** 16: 17–20 words of *I.* shall be fulfilled; 20: 11–12 when words of *I.* should be fulfilled, then is fulfilling of the Father's covenant with Israel; 23: 1 (Morm. 8: 23) search these things diligently, for great are words of *I.* *Compare also* 1 Ne. 20/Isa. 48; 1 Ne. 21/Isa. 49; 2 Ne. 7/Isa. 50; 2 Ne. 8/Isa. 51; 2 Ne. 12/Isa. 2; 2 Ne. 13/Isa. 3; 2 Ne. 14/Isa. 4; 2 Ne. 15/Isa. 5; 2 Ne. 16/Isa. 6; 2 Ne. 17/Isa. 7; 2 Ne. 18/Isa. 8; 2 Ne. 19/Isa. 9; 2 Ne. 20/Isa. 10; 2 Ne. 21/Isa. 11; 2 Ne. 22/Isa. 12; 2 Ne. 23/Isa. 13; 2 Ne. 24/Isa. 14; 2 Ne. 27/Isa. 29; Mosiah 14/ Isa. 53; Mosiah 15/parts of Isa. 52; 3 Ne. 22/Isa. 54.

ISAIAH[2]—*one of the twelve Nephite disciples* [c. A.D. 34]

3 Ne. 19: 4 chosen by Christ to minister to Nephites.

ISHMAEL[1]—*an Ephraimite from Jerusalem* [c. 600 B.C.] (*see also* Ishmael[1], Sons of; Ishmaelite)

1 Ne. 7: 2 sons of Lehi[1] return to Jerusalem to bring *I.* and family into wilderness; 7: 4–5 the Lord softens heart of *I.*; 7: 19 part of *I*'s family pleads with rebellious brethren; 7: 22 house of *I.* joins Lehites in thanking God and offering sacrifice; 16: 7 Zoram[1] and sons of Lehi[1] marry *I*'s daughters; 16: 34 dies.

ISHMAEL[2]—*grandfather of Amulek*

Alma 10: 2 father of Giddonah, descendant of Aminadi.

ISHMAEL, LAND OF—*portion of land of Nephi*

Alma 17: 19 Ammon[2] goes to land of *I.*; 17: 21 (20: 14–15) Lamoni king over land of *I.*; 21: 20–21 synagogues built and word preached in land of *I.*; 22: 4 Ammon[2] and Lamoni return to land of *I.*; 22: 4 Ammon[2] called by Spirit to teach people in land of *I.*; 23: 7–9 converted Lamanites in land of *I.* lay down arms; 24: 5 council held in land of *I.* to plan defense against Lamanites; 25: 13 other Lamanites join people of Anti-Nephi-Lehi in land of *I.*

ISHMAEL[1], SONS OF (*see also* Ishmaelite)

1 Ne. 7: 6 (18: 17) two sons of *I.* join Laman[1] and Lemuel in rebelling; 16: 20 murmuring by Laman[1], Lemuel, and sons of *I.*; 16: 37 encouraged to slay Lehi[1] and Nephi[1]; 18: 9 begin to make merry; **2 Ne.** 1: 28 admonished to hearken unto Nephi[1]; 4: 13 angry with Nephi[1]; **Alma** 3: 7 the Lord set mark upon sons of *I.*; 17: 19 became Lamanites; 43: 13 (47: 35) Lamanites consist of Laman[1], Lemuel, sons of *I.*, and dissenters.

ISHMAELITE, ISHMAELITISH—*descendants of Ishmael[1]*

Alma 3: 7 mark of Lamanites also placed upon *I.* women; 47: 35 (43: 13; Morm. 1: 8–9) Lamanites composed of Lamanites, Lemuelites, Ishmaelites, and dissenters; **4 Ne.** 1: 38 willfully reject gospel.

ISLAND, ISLE

1 Ne. 19: 10 three days of darkness a sign of Christ's death to those on *i.* of sea; 22: 4 more part of all tribes have been scattered upon *i.* of sea; **2 Ne.** 10: 8 Jews shall be gathered in from long dispersion, from *i.* of sea; 10: 20 we are upon an *i.* of sea; 21: 11 (Isa. 11: 11) the Lord shall set his hand the second time to recover his people from *i.* of sea; 29: 7 the Lord remembers those upon *i.* of sea; 29: 11 the Lord commands all men, in *i.* of sea.

ISRAEL—*name of Jacob[1] and, by extension, of all his descendants* (*see also* Abrahamic Covenant; Branch; Covenant; Ephraim; Israel, Gathering of; Israel, Scattering of; Israel, Ten Lost Tribes of; Israelites; Jacob[1]; Jew; Joseph[1]; Joseph[1], Seed of; Judah; Remnant; TG Israel; Israel, Blessings of; Israel, Bondage of, in Other Lands; Israel, Deliverance of; Israel, Joseph, People of; Israel, Judah, People of; Israel, Land of; Israel, Mission of; Israel, Origins of; Israel, Remnant of; Israel, Twelve Tribes of; BD Israel; Israel, Kingdom of)

Title Page (1 Ne. 12: 9; 15: 12; 2 Ne. 6: 5; 3 Ne. 20: 10; Morm. 7: 2) Nephites and Lamanites are remnant of house of *I.*; **1 Ne.** 10: 12 (15: 12; Jacob 5: 3—6: 1) house of *I.* compared to olive-tree; 10: 14 (15: 12–18) house of *I.* to come to knowledge of true Messiah; 12: 9 (Morm. 3: 18) twelve tribes of *I.* to be judged by twelve apostles; 13: 23 (14: 5, 8, 17; 22: 6, 9, 11; 2 Ne. 9: 1; 3 Ne. 16: 5, 11–12; 20: 12, 27; 21: 4, 7; 29: 3, 8; Morm. 5: 20; 9: 37; Ether 4: 15; Moro. 10: 31) covenants with house of *I.*; 13: 33–34 (19: 11) the Lamb will visit remnant of house of *I.*; 14: 2 (2 Ne. 10: 18; 3 Ne. 16: 13–15; 21: 6; 30: 2) if Gentiles harden not hearts, they shall be numbered among house of *I.*; 14: 26 sealed writings shall come forth unto house of *I.*; 15: 14 (2 Ne. 28: 2; 3 Ne. 20: 10; Morm. 7: 1) remnant of Lehites' seed shall know they are of house of *I.*; 15: 17 the Lord shall be rejected of Jews, or of house of *I.*; 17: 23 children of *I.* were led out of Egypt because they hearkened to the Lord; 17: 25 children of *I.* were in bondage; 17: 29 Moses smote rock, that children of *I.* might quench thirst; 19: 10 sign of Christ's death to be given house of *I.*; 20: 1 (Isa. 48: 1) house of Jacob are called by name of *I.*; 20: 12 hearken, O Jacob, and *I.* my called; 21: 3 (Isa. 49: 3) thou art my servant, O *I.*; 21: 7 (Isa. 49: 7) the Lord, the Redeemer of *I.*; 22: 12 those who are of house of *I.* shall know that the Lord is their Savior, the Mighty One of *I.*; 22: 14 nations that war against house of *I.* shall be turned one against another; **2 Ne.** 3: 9 Moses raised up to deliver house of *I.*; 6: 5 (3 Ne. 23: 2) Isaiah[1] spake concerning all house of *I.*; 9: 53 our seed shall become righteous branch unto house of *I.*; 14: 2 (Isa. 4: 2) fruit of earth shall be comely to them that are escaped of *I.*; 15: 7 (Isa. 5: 7) vineyard of the Lord is house of *I.*; 18: 14 (Isa. 8: 14) he shall be for a rock of offense to both the houses of *I.*; 19: 8 (Isa. 9: 8) the Lord sent his word unto Jacob and it hath lighted upon *I.*; 19: 12 (Isa. 9: 12) Syrians and Philistines shall devour *I.*; 19: 14 (Isa. 9: 14) the Lord will cut off from *I.* head and tail; 20: 17 (Isa. 10: 17) the light of *I.* shall be for a fire; 21: 16 (Isa. 11: 16) highway shall be left, as when *I.* came up out of Egypt; 24: 1 (Isa. 14: 1) the Lord will have mercy on Jacob and will yet choose *I.*; 25: 20 the Lord brought *I.* up out of Egypt; 29: 2 the Lord's words shall hiss forth as standard unto house of *I.*; **Jacob** 1: 7 provocation in days of temptation while children of *I.* were in wilderness; **Mosiah** 7: 19 trust in that God who brought children of *I.* out of Egypt; 13: 29 expedient that law should be given to children of *I.*; **3 Ne.** 15: 5 Christ is the one who covenanted with his people *I.*; 16: 7 because of unbelief of house of *I.*, truth shall come unto Gentiles; 17: 14 Jesus troubled because of wickedness of house of *I.*; 21: 20 unrepentant to be cut off from house of *I.*; 25: 4 (Mal. 4: 4) the Lord commanded law of Moses for all *I.*; 29: 1 covenant which Father made with children of *I.* shall be fulfilled; 29: 2 ye need not say the Lord delays his coming to children of *I.*; **Morm.** 5: 10–11 Gentiles who have care for house of *I.* will have sorrow for calamity of house of *I.*; 8: 21 he who breathes out wrath against house of *I.* is in danger to be hewn down.

ISRAEL, GATHERING OF (*see also* Israel, Scattering of; TG Israel, Gathering of; Israel, Restoration of)

1 Ne. 10: 14 (15: 12–18; 3 Ne. 16: 4, 11–12) *I.* to be gathered again, to come to knowledge of Messiah; 10: 14 (Jacob 5: 52–74) natural branches of olive-tree, remnants of *I.*, to be grafted in; 15: 18–20 (2 Ne. 3: 21; 3 Ne. 10: 7; 16: 5, 11–12; 20: 12–13, 29; 21: 4, 7; 29: 1, 3, 8–9) God to remember covenant to restore *I.*; 19: 16 (3 Ne. 5: 24) all people who are of house of *I.* will the Lord gather in; 21: 5–6 (Isa. 49: 5–6) Isaiah[1] to be servant to raise up tribes of Jacob and restore preserved of *I.*; 21: 22 (Isa. 49: 22) Gentiles shall bring *I*'s sons and daughters; **2 Ne.** 3: 11–13 latter-day seer to be raised up when work commences unto restoring house of *I.*; 3: 24 mighty one to rise up as instrument of the Lord in bringing to pass much restoration unto house of *I.*; 6: 14 (21: 11; 25: 17; 29: 1; Jacob 6: 2; Isa. 11: 11) Messiah will set hand second time to recover covenant people of *I.*; 9: 2 the Lord speaks to *I.* by prophets until time when they are restored to true church and gathered to lands of inheritance; 10: 2 (30: 5; Hel. 15: 11; 3 Ne. 5: 23) descendants of Nephites and Lamanites to be restored to knowledge of Christ; 20: 21–22 (Isa. 10: 21–22) remnant of Jacob shall return; 20: 22 (Isa. 10: 22) though I be as sand of sea, yet a remnant shall return; 21: 12 (Isa. 11: 12) the Lord shall assemble outcasts of *I.*; 24: 2 (Isa. 14: 2) house of *I.* to return to lands of promise; 30: 7–8 (3 Ne. 20: 31–33; Morm. 5: 14) Jews shall begin to believe in Christ, and God will commence work of restoration; **3 Ne.** 10: 4–6 (Matt. 23: 37) the Lord would gather *I.* as hen gathers chickens; 16: 4 through fulness of Gentiles, remnant of *I.* shall be brought to knowledge of Redeemer; 20: 21 the Lord will establish his people, O house of *I.*; 20: 29 the Lord will remember covenant to gather his people and give them Jerusalem as land of inheritance; 21: 22–24 Gentiles shall assist remnant of Jacob in gathering unto New Jerusalem; 21: 27 work to commence among the dispersed to prepare way, that they call upon Father in Christ's name; 29: 1 when scriptures come to Gentiles, Father's covenant to restore *I.* to lands of inheritance will be fulfilled; **Morm.** 3: 17 when work commences, *I.* shall be about to prepare to return to land of inheritance; 5: 14 writings to convince Jews, that Father restore house of *I.* to land of inheritance; **Ether** 4: 14 come unto me, ye house of *I.*; 13: 10 seed of Joseph[1], who are of house of *I.*, shall dwell in New Jerusalem.

ISRAEL, SCATTERING OF (*see also* Destruction; Israel, Gathering of; Israel, Ten Lost Tribes of; Remnant; TG Israel, Scattering of)

1 Ne. 10: 3 Jerusalem to be carried captive into Babylon; 10: 12 (Jacob 5: 7–8, 13–14) house of *I.* compared to olive-tree whose branches should be broken off and scattered; 10: 13 Lehites to be scattered upon the land; 10: 14 (15: 16–17; 2 Ne. 6: 11; 10: 67; 3 Ne. 20: 13) after *I.* is scattered, they will be gathered; 13: 14 (22: 7; 3 Ne. 16: 8; Morm. 5: 9) seed of Lamanites to be scattered by Gentiles; 15: 20 after being gathered, *I.* will be scattered no more; 21: 1 house of *I.* are broken off and driven out because of wickedness of pastors; 22: 3, 7 (2 Ne. 25: 15) house of *I.* to be scattered among all nations; 22: 4 many are already lost from knowledge of those at Jerusalem; **2 Ne.** 3: 5 from loins of Joseph[1] would come righteous branch to be broken off; 10: 22 God has led away from time to time from house of *I.*; **Omni** 1: 15 (Hel. 8: 21) people of Zarahemla come from Jerusalem when Zedekiah was taken captive into Babylon; **3 Ne.** 10: 7 place of I's dwellings shall be desolate until fulfilling of covenant; 20: 27 Gentiles to be made mighty unto scattering of Israel; 28: 29 three Nephites to minister to scattered tribes of Israel; **Ether** 13: 7 the Lord brought remnant of seed of Joseph[1] out of Jerusalem.

ISRAEL, TEN LOST TRIBES OF (*see also* Israel, Gathering of; Israel, Scattering of; TG Israel, Ten Lost Tribes of)

1 Ne. 22: 4 many are already lost from knowledge of those at Jerusalem; **2 Ne.** 29: 12 the Lord will speak to Jews, Nephites, other tribes, and they shall write; 29: 13 Jews, Nephites, and lost tribes shall have each others' writings; **3 Ne.** 15: 15 Father has not commanded Christ to tell Jews about other tribes whom Father led away; 15: 20 Father separated other tribes from Jews because of iniquity; 17: 4 Christ will show himself to lost tribes; 21: 26 gospel to be preached to lost tribes; 28: 29 three Nephites shall minister unto all scattered tribes; **Ether** 13: 11 they who were scattered and gathered from north countries are partakers of fulfilling of covenant.

ISRAELITES (*see also* Israel)

Hel. 8: 11 *I.*, who were our fathers, came through Red Sea.

-ITES

4 Ne. 1: 17 no manner of *i.* among the people.

JACOB[1]—*father of twelve tribes, name changed to Israel* [c. 1800 B.C.] (*see also* Israel; Jacob, House of; BD Israel; Jacob)

1 Ne. 5: 14 Lehi[1] a descendant of Joseph[1], who was son of *J.*; 6: 4 (19: 10; Mosiah 7: 19; 23: 23; Alma 29: 11; 36: 2; 3 Ne. 4: 30; Morm. 9: 11) God of Abraham, Isaac, and *J.*; 17: 40 the Lord covenanted with Abraham, Isaac, and *J.*; 20: 20 (Isa. 48: 20) the Lord hath redeemed his servant *J.*; **2 Ne.** 12: 3 (Isa. 2: 3) let us go up to the house of the God of *J.*; 19: 8 the Lord sent his word unto *J.*, and it hath lighted upon Israel; **Alma** 5: 24 (7: 25; Hel. 3: 30) the righteous shall sit down in kingdom of God with Abraham, Isaac, and *J.*; 46: 24–26 remember the words of *J.* before his death; **3 Ne.** 10: 17 father *J.* testified concerning remnant of the seed of Joseph[1]; 20: 22 this people will Christ establish in this land unto fulfilling of covenant made with father *J.*

JACOB[2]—*son of Lehi[1]* [c. 599 B.C.] (*see also* Jacobites)

1 Ne. 18: 7 (2 Ne. 2: 2) elder son of Lehi[1] born in wilderness; 18: 19 is grieved by afflictions of mother; **2 Ne.** 2: 1 suffered afflictions and sorrow in childhood because of brothers' rudeness; 5: 6 goes with Nephi[1] into wilderness; 5: 26 (6: 2; Jacob 1: 18) is consecrated as priest and teacher; 6: 1—11: 1 (31: 1) exhorts people, citing prophecies of Isaiah; 6: 2 called of God and ordained after his holy order; 6: 8 the Lord has shown *J.* that Jerusalem has been destroyed; 10: 1 speaks concerning righteous branch of Israel; 11: 3 has seen Redeemer; **Jacob** 1: 1–2, 8 (W of M 1: 3) given small plates and commanded to write precious things; 1: 14 distinguished between Lamanites and Nephites according to righteousness; 1: 17 teaches in temple, having first obtained errand from the Lord; 1: 19 (2: 2–3) magnifies office, taking responsibility for sins of people if he does not teach them; 2: 1—3: 14 record of *J's* words to people after death of Nephi[1]; 2: 11 is commanded by the Lord to declare word in temple; 3: 1 admonishes people to look unto God; 3: 12 warns against every kind of sin; 3: 14 writes on plates of *J.*, made by Nephi[1]; 4: 1 ministers much unto his people; 4: 15 is led by Spirit to prophesy; 7: 3–15 confronts and confounds Sherem; 7: 27 gives plates to son Enos[2]; **Alma** 3: 6 Lamanites cursed because of rebellion against *J.* and his brothers.

JACOB[3] —*Nephite apostate of Zoramite sect* [c. 64 B.C.]

Alma 52: 20 leader of Lamanite army, refuses to fight; 52: 21–31 victim of decoy strategy by Moroni[1]; 52: 33–

34 having unconquerable spirit, leads Lamanites against Moroni[1]; 52: 35 is killed.

JACOB[4]—*apostate Nephite chosen king by secret combination* [c. 29-30 B.C.] (*see also* Jacobugath, City of)

3 Ne. 7: 9 placed at head of secret combination; 7: 12–14 king of band, commands his people to flee and establish kingdom in north; 9: 9 the Lord has burned city inhabited by people of king *J.*

JACOB, CITY OF

3 Ne. 9: 8 the Lord causes city of *J.* to sink into earth.

JACOB, HOUSE OF (*see also* Israel; Jacob[1]; Remnant)

1 Ne. 20: 1, 12 hear this, O house of *J.*, who are called by name of Israel; 20: 20 the Lord hath redeemed his servant *J.*; 21: 5 Isaiah[1] to be the Lord's servant to bring tribes of *J.* again to him; **2 Ne.** 12: 5 (Isa. 2: 5) O house of *J.*, let us walk in light of the Lord; 12: 6 (Isa. 2: 6) O Lord, thou hast forsaken thy people, the house of *J.*; 18: 17 (Isa. 8: 17) the Lord hideth his face from house of *J.*; 19: 8 the Lord sent his word unto *J.*, and it hath lighted upon Israel; 20: 20 such as are escaped of house of *J.* shall no more stay upon him that smote them; 20: 21 remnant of *J.* shall return unto the mighty God; 24: 1 the Lord will have mercy on *J.* and strangers shall cleave to house of *J.*; 46: 23 (3 Ne. 20: 16; 21: 2; Morm. 7: 10) Nephites are remnant of seed of *J.*; **3 Ne.** 5: 24 the Lord to gather all remnant of seed of *J.*; 5: 25 the Lord hath covenanted with all the house of *J.*; 10: 4 how oft would the Lord have gathered descendants of *J.*; 20: 16 (21: 12; Morm. 5: 24) remnant of house of *J.* shall go forth among Gentiles; 21: 22 if Gentiles repent, they will be numbered among this remnant of *J.*; 21: 23 Gentiles to assist remnant of *J.* in building New Jerusalem; 24: 6 (Mal. 3: 6) ye sons of *J.* are not consumed; **4 Ne.** 1: 49 (Morm. 5: 12) sacred records to come again unto remnant of house of *J.*

JACOBITES—*descendants of Jacob[2]*

Jacob 1: 13 (4 Ne. 1: 36; Morm. 1: 8) included among Nephites; **4 Ne.** 1: 37 true believers in Christ.

JACOBUGATH—*city of followers of Jacob[4]*

3 Ne. 9: 9 the Lord causes to be burned by fire.

JACOM

Ether 6: 14 one of four sons of Jared[2]; 6: 27 refuses to be king.

JARED[1]—*father of Enoch[2]*

No references in Book of Mormon.

JARED[2]—*founder of Jaredites* (*see also* Jared[2], Brother of; Jaredites)

Ether 1: 32 father of Orihah; 1: 33—2: 1 comes from Tower of Babel with brother and friends; 1: 34–35 asks brother to pray that the Lord will not confound their language; 1: 36–37 language not confounded; 1: 38–43 asks brother to inquire of the Lord where they should go; 2: 1 journeys to valley of Nimrod with family and friends; 2: 13 dwells in tent at Moriancumer, by seashore, for four years; 6: 4–12 sails for promised land; 6: 14, 20 has four sons, eight daughters; 6: 19–21 gathers and counts his people; 6: 24 argues that people should have king; 6: 29 dies.

JARED[3]—*early Jaredite king*

Ether 8: 1 son of Omer; 8: 2 seizes kingdom from father; 8: 5–7 battles against brothers' army, loses kingdom; 8: 8–18 accepts daughter's plan to regain kingdom through secret combination with Akish; 9: 1, 4 overthrows kingdom of Omer, anointed king; 9: 5 killed by Akish's band.

JARED[2], BROTHER OF—*first Jaredite prophet*

Ether 1: 34 a large and mighty man, highly favored of the Lord; 1: 34–37 asks the Lord not to confound language; 1: 38–42 (2: 7) is promised a choice land; 1: 43 posterity to be great nation; 2: 4–5 is visited and led by the Lord; 2: 14–15 is chastened by the Lord, repents, and is forgiven; 2: 16 is instructed to build barges; 3: 1 melts stones for light in barges; 3: 6, 19 (12: 20) sees finger of the Lord; 3: 13—4: 1 sees, converses with Christ because of great faith; 3: 20, 26 (12: 21) the Lord could not withhold anything from brother of *J.* because of faith; 3: 22, 27–28 told to write, then seal up record; 3: 23, 28 is given Urim and Thummim; 3: 25 is shown all inhabitants of earth, past, present, and future; 4: 1 writings not to come forth before Christ's resurrection; 6: 2 puts stones in vessels for light; 6: 9 sings praises to the Lord; 6: 15, 20 begets twenty-two sons and daughters; 6: 23 warns against having kings; 6: 25–26 sons refuse to be king; 6: 29 dies; 7: 5 warnings of captivity are fulfilled; 12: 24 mighty in writing; 12: 30 caused mountain Zerin to be removed.

JAREDITES—*descendants of Jared[2], his brother, and his friends*

Ether 1: 33–37 language not confounded at Babel; 2: 1 travel to valley of Nimrod; 2: 13 dwell in tents at Moriancumer, by great sea, for four years; 2: 16–17 build barges according to the Lord's instructions; 6: 4 gather food, flocks, and herds and set forth in barges; 6: 9 sing praises unto the Lord; 6: 11–12 land on shores of promised land after 344 days; 6: 13, 18 multiply upon land; 6: 17 are taught to walk humbly before Lord; 6: 22–27 desire king; 6: 28 become exceedingly rich; 7: 20 are divided into two kingdoms; 7: 23–25 prophets warn of wickedness and idolatry and are mocked, but supported by king; 7: 26–27 repent, regain prosperity and peace; 8: 13–26 secret combination founded among *J.*; 9: 12 wars destroy all save thirty souls; 9: 15–25 period of peace and prosperity; 9: 26 secret combinations arise again; 9: 30–33 are plagued by dearth of rain, poisonous serpents; 9: 31–32 some flee to land southward; 9: 34–35 repent, and the Lord relieves dearth; 10: 28 never could be people more blessed; 11: 1–6 prophets prophesy destruction, are rejected; 11: 7 wars and contentions; 11: 8 people repent; 11: 12–13, 20–22 prophets again warn of destruction, are rejected; ch. 13–15 final wars.

JAROM—*Nephite prophet* [c. 420 B.C.]

Jarom 1: 1 son of Enos[2], writes that genealogy may be kept; 1: 2, 14 writes little because plates are small; **Omni** 1: 1 commands son, Omni, to write.

JASHON, CITY AND LAND OF

Morm. 2: 16 Lamanites pursue Nephites to land of; 2: 17 is near land where Ammaron deposits records.

JAVELIN (*see also* Weapon)

Jarom 1: 8 Nephites make *j.*; **Alma** 51: 34 Teancum puts *j.* through Amalickiah's heart; 62: 36 Teancum kills Ammoron with *j.*

JEALOUS, JEALOUSY (*see also* Covet; Envy)

Mosiah 11: 22 (13: 13; Ex. 20: 5) the Lord is a *j.* God; **Ether** 9: 7 Akish *j.* of his son.

JEHOVAH (*see* Jesus Christ—Jehovah)

JENEAM—*Nephite commander* [c. A.D. 385]

Morm. 6: 14 had fallen with his ten thousand.

JEREMIAH[1]—*Hebrew prophet, contemporary of Lehi[1]* [c. end of seventh century B.C.] (*see also* BD Jeremiah)

1 Ne. 5: 13 brass plates contain prophecies of *J.*; 7: 14 Jews have cast *J.* into prison; **Hel.** 8: 20 testified of Jerusalem's destruction.

JEREMIAH[2]—*one of twelve Nephite disciples* [c. A.D. 34]

3 Ne. 19: 4 is chosen by Jesus to minister to Nephites.

JERSHON, LAND OF—*land on east by sea, south of land Bountiful* (*see also* Ammon[2], People of)

Alma 27: 22, 26 Nephites give *J.* to people of Ammon; 27: 23–24 (28: 1) is protected by Nephites; 28: 1 church established in *J.*; 28: 1–3 (30: 1) is attacked by Lamanites; 30: 19–21 Korihor teaches in *J.*; 35: 6, 14 outcast Zoramites come into *J.*; 35: 13 (43: 3, 15) Ammonites leave land so that Nephite armies can gather to fight Lamanites; 43: 18 Nephites battle Lamanites in borders of *J.*; 43: 25 Moroni[2] leaves part of army in *J.*

JERUSALEM[1]—*chief city of Jews and surrounding area* (*see also* Jerusalem, New; Jew; BD Jerusalem; Judea)

1 Ne. 1: 4, 7 Lehi[1] dwells at *J.*; 1: 4, 13, 18 (2: 13; 3: 17; 7: 13; 10: 3; **2 Ne.** 25: 14; **Alma** 9: 9; **Hel.** 8: 20–21; **Ether** 13: 5) destruction of *J.*; 2: 4 (17: 20; Alma 10: 3; Hel. 5: 6) Lehi[1] and family leave *J.*; 2: 11 (2 Ne. 1: 1, 3; Jacob 2: 25, 32; Omni 1: 6; Mosiah 2: 4; 7: 20; Alma 9: 22; 22: 9; 36: 29; 3 Ne. 5: 20; Ether 13: 7) the Lord leads Lehites out of land of *J.*; 3: 2—4: 38 (5: 6; 7: 2) sons of Lehi[1] return to *J.* for records; 5: 4 (19: 20) family of Lehi[1] would have perished if they had remained at *J.*; 7: 3–5 sons of Lehi[1] return to *J.* to get family of Ishmael[1]; 7: 7, 15 (16: 35–36; 17: 20) the rebellious desire to return to land of *J.*; 10: 4 (19: 8) Messiah to come six hundred years after Lehi[1] left *J.*; 11: 13 Nephi[1] sees *J.* in vision; 18: 24 Lehites bring seeds from land of *J.*; 19: 13 (4 Ne. 1: 31) those at *J.* shall crucify God of Israel; 22: 4 many already lost from knowledge of those at *J.*; **2 Ne.** 1: 4 (6: 8) Lehi[1] sees in vision that *J.* is destroyed; 8: 17 (Isa. 51: 17) *J.* has drunk cup of the Lord's fury; 8: 24 (Isa. 52: 1) put on thy beautiful garments, O *J.*, the holy city; 8: 25 (Isa. 52: 2) arise, sit down, O *J.*; 9: 5 God shall show himself to those at *J.*; 10: 5 those at *J.* shall stiffen their necks; 12: 1 (Isa. 2: 1) word Isaiah[1] saw concerning Judah and *J.*; 13: 1 (Isa. 3: 1) the Lord takes away from *J.* the stay and the staff; 13: 8 (Isa. 3: 8) *J.* is ruined; 14: 3 (Isa. 4: 3) they who remain in *J.* shall be called holy; 17: 1 (Isa. 7: 1) kings of Syria and Israel went up toward *J.* to war against it; 18: 14 (Isa. 8: 14) the Lord shall be for gin and snare to inhabitants of *J.*; 20: 32 (Isa. 10: 32) the Lord shall shake hand against mount of daughter of Zion, the hill of *J.*; 25: 6 Nephi[1] has dwelt at *J.*; 25: 11 Jews will return and possess land of *J.*; 30: 4 remnant of Nephites' seed shall know they came from *J.*: **Jacob** 2: 31 the Lord has heard mourning of his people in land of *J.*; 7: 26 Nephites a lonesome people, cast out from *J.*; **Omni** 1: 15 people of Zarahemla came from *J.* when Zedekiah was carried captive into Babylon; **Mosiah** 1: 6 records contain sayings of fathers from time they came from *J.*; 10: 12 (Hel. 8: 21) Lamanites believe they were driven from land of *J.* because of fathers' iniquities; 12: 23 (15: 30; 3 Ne. 16: 19) the Lord has redeemed *J.*; **Alma** 3: 11 (10: 17) brass plates brought out of land of *J.*; 7: 10 Son shall be born at *J.*; **3 Ne.** 4: 11 greatest slaughter among people of Lehi[1] since he left *J.*; 10: 5 how oft would the Lord have gathered his people that dwell at *J.*; 15: 14 Christ not commanded to tell those at *J.* about Nephites; 16: 1 the Lord has other sheep not of this land or land of *J.*; 16: 4 if those at *J.* do not ask Father, they must learn of other tribes from writings; 17: 8 Nephites desire that Christ show what he has done unto brethren at *J.*; 20: 29 land of *J.* is Israel's promised land forever; 20: 46 *J.* shall be inhabited again; 21: 26 work shall commence among tribes which Father led out of *J.*; **Morm.** 3: 18 twelve tribes of Israel shall be judged by twelve disciples in land of *J.*; **Ether** 13: 8 remnant of house of Joseph[1] shall build holy city, like *J.* of old; 13: 11 then cometh the *J.* of old; **Moro.** 10: 31 awake and arise from dust, O *J.*

JERUSALEM[2]—*Lamanite city and land in land of Nephi*

Alma 21: 1–2 Aaron[3] journeys toward land called by Lamanites *J.*; 21: 2 Lamanites and dissenters had built great city, called *J.*; 21: 4 Aaron[3] comes to city of *J.*; 24: 1 dissenters stir up Lamanites in land of *J.* against people of Anti-Nephi-Lehi; **3 Ne.** 9: 7 the Lord causes water to come upon city of *J.*

JERUSALEM, NEW (*see also* Zion; TG Jerusalem, New)

3 Ne. 20: 22 the Lord will establish this people in this land, and it shall be a *N.J.*; 21: 23 Gentiles shall assist remnant of Israel in building *N.J.*; 21: 24 those scattered shall be gathered unto *N.J.*; **Ether** 13: 2–6 *N.J.* shall come down out of heaven unto this land; 13: 5 rebuilt Jerusalem could not be a new *J.*; 13: 10 blessed are they who dwell in *N.J.*

JESSE—*father of David* [c. 1100 B.C.] (*see also* BD Jesse)

2 Ne. 21: 1 (Isa. 11: 1) there shall come forth a rod out of stem of *J.*; 21: 10 (Isa. 11: 10) there shall be a root of *J.*, which shall stand for an ensign.

JESUS CHRIST (*see also* Baptism; Belief, Believe; Blood; Charity; Church of God; Day of the Lord; Faith; Fall of Man; Firstborn; Glory [noun]; God; God, Body of; God, Eternal Nature of; God, Foreknowledge of; God, Goodness of; God, Love of; God, Manifestations of; God, Omniscience of; God, Power of; God, Presence of; God, Wisdom of; God the Father; Godhead; Gospel; Grace; Hand of the Lord; Jesus Christ—Advocate; Jesus Christ, Appearances of; Jesus Christ, Atonement through; Jesus Christ, Condescension of; Jesus Christ—Creator; Jesus Christ, Death of; Jesus Christ, First Coming of; Jesus Christ—Good Shepherd; Jesus Christ—Holy One of Israel; Jesus Christ—Immanuel; Jesus Christ—Jehovah; Jesus Christ—Lamb of God; Jesus Christ—Lord; Jesus Christ—Lord of Hosts; Jesus Christ – Mediator; Jesus Christ—Messiah; Jesus Christ—Only Begotten Son; Jesus Christ—Redeemer; Jesus Christ, Resurrection of; Jesus Christ—Savior; Jesus Christ, Second Coming of; Jesus Christ—Son of God; Jesus Christ, Types of; Judgment; King; Light; Love; Mercy; Name of the Lord; Rest; Rock; Spirit, Holy/Spirit of the Lord; Word of God/Word of the Lord; TG Jesus Christ; Jesus Christ, Antemortal Existence of; Jesus Christ, Ascension of; Jesus Christ, Authority of; Jesus Christ, Baptism of; Jesus Christ, Betrayal of; Jesus Christ, Davidic Descent of; Jesus Christ, Exemplar; Jesus Christ, Family of; Jesus Christ, Firstborn; Jesus Christ, Foreordained; Jesus Christ, Glory of; Jesus Christ, Head of the Church; Jesus Christ, Judge; Jesus Christ, King; Jesus Christ, Light of the World; Jesus Christ, Messenger of the Covenant; Jesus Christ, Millennial Reign of; Jesus Christ, Mission of; Jesus Christ, Power of; Jesus Christ, Prophecies about; Jesus Christ, Relationship with the Father; Jesus Christ, Rock; Jesus Christ, Second Comforter; Jesus Christ, Spirit of; Jesus Christ, Taking Name of; Jesus Christ, Teaching Mode of; Jesus Christ, Temptation of; Jesus Christ, Trials of; BD Jesus)

Title Page (2 Ne. 26: 12) convince Jews and Gentiles that Jesus is the Christ; **1 Ne.** 10: 9 Messiah to be baptized by John in Bethabara; **2 Ne.** 10: 3 (25: 19; Mosiah 3: 8) Messiah's name to be Jesus Christ; 25: 24 (26: 8; 31: 20) look forward with steadfastness unto Christ; 25: 26 we talk of Christ, we rejoice in Christ, we preach of Christ, we prophesy of Christ; 31: 2, 21 (32: 6; Jacob 7: 6; 3 Ne. 2: 2) doctrine of Christ; 31: 10 can we follow Jesus save we are willing to keep Father's commandments; 32: 3 feast upon words of Christ, for they tell you all ye should do; 33: 4 writings persuade people to believe in Jesus; 33: 6 I glory in my Jesus; 33: 10 if ye believe in Christ, ye will believe these words; **Jacob** 1: 6 through revelations and prophecies the Nephites know of Christ; 4: 4 Nephites' writings show they know of Christ; 4: 15 Jews reject stone upon which they might build safe foundation; 7: 11, 19 (3 Ne. 6: 23; 7: 10) scriptures and prophets testify of Christ; 7: 19 Sherem has lied to God in denying Christ; **Mosiah** 3: 7 (15: 5; Alma 7: 11) Christ to suffer temptation; 16: 9 (Alma 38: 9; 3 Ne. 9: 18; 11: 11; Ether 4: 12) Christ is light and life of world; **Alma** 5: 44 holy order of God which is in Christ Jesus; 6: 8 Alma[2] teaches according to testimony of Jesus Christ; 28: 14 (Moro. 7: 18–19) reason for joy because of light of Christ unto life; 31: 31–32 comfort my soul in Christ; 31: 34 Lamanites to be brought again unto Christ; 31: 38 sons of Mosiah[2] are swallowed up in Christ; **Hel.** 3: 29 word of God leads man of Christ across gulf of misery; 5: 12 rock of our Redeemer is Christ; **3 Ne.** 9: 15 (11: 10; Ether 3: 14) I am Jesus Christ; 28: 33 scriptures give account of marvelous works of Christ; 29: 5 wo unto him who denies Christ; **4 Ne.** 1: 27 many churches profess to know Christ, but deny his gospel; **Morm.** 3: 21 Jews to have other witnesses that Jesus, whom they slew, was the very Christ; 5: 11 if Nephites had repented, they might have been clasped in arms of Jesus; 6: 17 how could ye have rejected that Jesus, who stood with open arms to receive you; 9: 5 holiness of Jesus Christ will kindle unquenchable fire in the guilty; **Ether** 2: 12 God of this land is Jesus Christ; 3: 14 Christ was prepared from foundation of world; 4: 12 (Moro. 7: 16–17) whatsoever persuades men to do good is of Christ; 12: 41 seek this Jesus of whom the prophets have written; **Moro.** 7: 11 servant of devil cannot follow Christ, follower of Christ cannot be servant of devil; 7: 16, 18–19 light of Christ is given to every man, that he may know good from evil; 7: 44 if a man confesses by Holy Ghost that Jesus is the Christ, he must have charity; 7: 47 charity is pure love of Christ; 10: 17–18 every good gift cometh of Christ.

JESUS CHRIST—ADVOCATE (*see also* Jesus Christ, Atonement through; Jesus Christ—Mediator)

2 Ne. 2: 9 Messiah shall make intercession for all men; 8: 22 (Isa. 51: 22) the Lord pleads the cause of his people; 13: 13 (Isa. 3: 13) the Lord standeth to plead and judge the people; **Jacob** 3: 1 God will plead your cause; **Mosiah** 14: 12 (Isa. 53: 12) Messiah made intercession for transgressors; 15: 8 God gives Son power to make intercession for men; **Moro.** 7: 28 Christ advocates the cause of men.

JESUS CHRIST, APPEARANCES OF (*see also* God, Manifestations of; Vision; TG God, Manifestations of; God, Privilege of Seeing; Jesus Christ, Appearances, Antemortal; Jesus Christ, Appearances, Postmortal)

1 Ne. 13: 42 Lamb shall manifest himself in body unto all nations; **2 Ne.** 2: 4 Jacob[2] has beheld Redeemer; 11: 2 (16: 1, 5; Isa. 6: 1, 5) Isaiah[1] has seen Redeemer; 11: 2 Nephi[1] has seen Redeemer; 25: 14 Messiah shall rise from dead and manifest himself to his people; **Enos** 1: 8 Christ shall manifest himself in flesh; **Alma** 19: 13 Lamoni has seen Redeemer; **3 Ne.** 10: 18–19 (11: 2) Christ will show his body to those who are spared; ch. 11–28 Christ's appearances among Nephites; 11: 8 Nephites see Man descending from heaven; 16: 2 Christ has not yet manifest himself to other sheep; 17: 4 Christ will show himself to the lost tribes; 19: 15 Jesus comes again and stands in Nephites' midst; 27: 2 Jesus again shows himself to disciples; **Morm.** 1: 15 Mormon[2] is visited of the Lord; **Ether** ch. 3 Christ's appearance to brother of Jared[2]; 3: 13 the Lord has never shown himself before to man; 3: 16 as Christ appears to brother of Jared[2], so will he appear in flesh; 9: 22 Emer sees Son; 12: 7 it was by faith that Christ showed himself to fathers; 12: 39 Moroni[2] has seen Jesus and talked with him face to face; **Moro.** 7: 48 (1 Jn. 3: 2) when Christ appears, we shall be like him.

JESUS CHRIST, ATONEMENT THROUGH (*see also* Fall of Man; Firstborn; Firstborn; Forgive; Grace; Jesus Christ—Advocate; Jesus Christ, Death of; Jesus Christ, First Coming of; Jesus Christ—Lamb of God; Jesus Christ—Mediator; Jesus Christ—Messiah; Jesus Christ—Only Begotten Son; Jesus Christ—Redeemer; Jesus Christ, Resurrection of; Jesus Christ—Savior; Jesus Christ, Types of; Mercy; Merit; Offering; Plan; Reconcile; Remission; Sacrifice; Salvation; Sanctification; Transgression; TG Jesus Christ, Atonement through; BD Atonement)

1 Ne. 11: 33 Son to be lifted up upon cross and slain for sins of world; **2 Ne.** 2: 7 Messiah offers himself a sacrifice for sin, to answer ends of law; 2: 10 punishment affixed to law to answer ends of atonement; 9: 7 (25: 16) atonement must be infinite; 9: 26 atonement satisfies demands of justice; 10: 25 God raises man from everlasting death by power of atonement; 11: 5 justice, power, and mercy in great and eternal plan of deliverance from death; 11: 6 save Christ should come, all must perish; **Jacob** 4: 11 be reconciled unto God through atonement of Christ; 7: 12 (Alma 34: 9; 42: 15) if no atonement, all mankind must be lost; **Mosiah** 3: 11 Christ's blood atones for sins of those fallen by Adam's transgression; 3: 15 (13: 28) law of Moses avails nothing except through atonement of Christ's blood; 4: 6–7 (Alma 13: 5) atonement prepared from foundation of world; 13: 28 (Alma 34: 9) except for atonement, all must perish, notwithstanding law of Moses; 14: 5 (Isa. 53: 5) he was wounded for our transgressions; 14: 10 (Isa. 53: 10) thou shalt make his soul an offering for sin; **Alma** 7: 11 Son will take upon him pains and sicknesses of his people; 22: 14 sufferings and death of Christ atone for men's sins; 24: 13 Christ's blood shed for atonement of sins; 30: 17 Korihor teaches there could be no atonement; 34: 8 Christ shall take upon him the transgressions of his people and atone for sins of world; 34: 11 no man can sacrifice own blood which will atone for sins of another; 42: 15 plan of mercy could not be brought about without an atonement; 42: 23 mercy comes because of atonement; 42: 23 atonement brings to pass the resurrection; **Hel.** 5: 9 only means whereby man can be saved is through atoning blood of Jesus Christ; **3 Ne.** 11: 14 Christ has been slain for sins of world; **Moro.** 7: 41 ye shall have hope through atonement of Christ; 8: 20 he who says children need baptism sets at naught Christ's atonement; 10: 33 ye are sanctified in Christ, by grace of God, through shedding of blood of Christ.

JESUS CHRIST, CONDESCENSION OF (*see also* TG Jesus Christ, Condescension of)

1 Ne. 11: 16 knowest thou the condescension of God; 11: 26 behold the condescension of God; 19: 10 God yieldeth himself into hands of wicked men; **2 Ne.** 4: 26 the Lord in condescension has visited men; 9: 53 how great the Lord's condescension unto men; **Jacob** 4: 7 by the Lord's great condescension men have power to do these things; **Alma** 7: 13 Son suffers according to flesh; 19: 13 Redeemer shall be born of woman; **Ether** 3: 9 Christ shall take upon him flesh and blood.

JESUS CHRIST—CREATOR (*see also* Creation; God—Creator; God the Father; Jesus Christ—Jehovah)

2 Ne. 9: 5 Creator to die for all men; **Mosiah** 3: 8 Jesus Christ, the Creator of all things: 5: 15 man to have eternal life through mercy of him who created all things; 26: 23 I take upon me sins of world, for I have created them; **Alma** 5: 15 exercise faith in redemption of him who created you; **3 Ne.** 22: 5 thy maker, thy Redeemer; **Ether** 3: 16 Christ has created man after body of his spirit.

JESUS CHRIST, DEATH OF (*see also* Death, Physical; Jesus Christ, Resurrection of; TG Jesus Christ, Crucifixion of; Jesus Christ, Death of)

1 Ne. 10: 11 after Messiah has been slain by Jews, he shall rise from dead; 11: 33 (Alma 30: 26; 3 Ne. 11: 14) Son to be lifted up upon cross and slain for sins of world; 19: 10 God to yield himself to wicked men to be crucified; 19: 10 (Hel. 14: 14, 20, 27; 3 Ne. 8: 3, 19–23; 10: 9) three days of darkness to be sign of Christ's death; 19: 13 (2 Ne. 10: 3, 5; 25: 13; Morm. 3: 21) Jews to crucify God; **2 Ne.** 2: 8 Messiah lays down life according to flesh; 6: 9 (Mosiah 3: 9) Jews will scourge and crucify Holy One, Jesus Christ; 9: 5 great Creator suffers himself to die for all men; 10: 3 no other nation would crucify their God; 26: 3 signs to be given of Messiah's birth, death, resurrection; 26: 24 (3 Ne. 27: 14) God lays down his life that he might draw men unto him; **Mosiah** 14: 5 (Isa. 53: 5) he was wounded for our transgressions, bruised for our iniquities; 14: 9 (Isa. 53: 9) he made his grave with the wicked and with the rich in his death; 14: 12 (Isa. 53: 12) he has poured out his soul unto death, was numbered with transgressors, bore sins of many; 15: 7 Son shall be led, crucified, and slain; 18: 2 (Hel. 14: 16; Morm. 9: 13) resurrection and redemption brought to pass through power, sufferings, death of Christ; **Alma** 7: 12 (11: 42) Son will take upon him death, that he may loose bands of death; 16: 19 priests hold forth coming, sufferings, death of Son; 21: 9 no redemption save through death and sufferings of Christ; 22: 14 sufferings and death of Christ atone for sins; **Hel.** 8: 14 as Moses lifted up brazen serpent, so shall Son be lifted up; 14: 15 Son must die that salvation may come; **3 Ne.** 6: 20 prophets testify boldly of Christ's death and sufferings; 9: 22 for the repentant Christ has laid down his life; 27: 14 Father sent Christ that he might be lifted up upon cross; 28: 6 before Christ was lifted up by Jews, John desired to tarry; **Morm.** 9: 13 all men are redeemed because death of Christ brings to pass resurrection; **Ether** 4: 1 writings of brother of Jared[2] not to come forth until after the Lord is lifted up upon cross; 12: 33 the Lord has loved the world, even unto laying down life for world; **Moro.** 9: 25 may Christ's sufferings and death rest in your mind forever.

JESUS CHRIST, FIRST COMING OF (*see also* Jesus Christ, Second Coming of; TG Jesus Christ, Birth of)

1 Ne. 10: 4 (19: 8; 2 Ne. 25: 19) Messiah to come six hundred years after Lehi[1] left Jerusalem; 11: 13–14, 18–20 Nephi[1] sees virgin carried away in Spirit, mother of Son of God; **2 Ne.** 10: 3 Christ to come among Jews, more wicked part of world; 11: 6 save Christ should come, all men must perish; 17: 14 (Isa. 7: 14) virgin shall conceive and bear son, Immanuel; 19: 6 (Isa. 9: 6) unto us a child is born, unto us a son is given; **Mosiah** 3: 5 (4: 2; 7: 27; 13: 34; 15: 1; 17: 8) God shall come down from heaven among men; 3: 13 whoso should believe that Christ should come might receive remission of sins; 16: 6 if Christ did not come, there could be no redemption; **Alma** 7: 10 Son to be born of Mary at Jerusalem; **Hel.** 8: 22 Lehi[1], Nephi[1], almost all fathers have testified of coming of Christ; 14: 2 in five years comes the Son; 14: 3–6 (3 Ne. 1: 15–21) signs to be given of Christ's coming; **3 Ne.** 1: 13–14 on the morrow come I into the world; 9: 16 I came unto my own, and my own received me not; 9: 16 scriptures concerning Christ's coming are fulfilled; 12: 17 (Matt. 5: 17) Christ is come not to destroy, but to fulfill.

JESUS CHRIST—GOOD SHEPHERD

1 Ne. 13: 41 one God and one Shepherd over all; 22: 25 (3 Ne. 18: 31) Holy One numbers his sheep, and they know him; **Mosiah** 26: 21 he who will hear my voice will be my sheep; **Alma** 5: 38–39 good shepherd calls you in his own name; 5: 57 he who desires to follow good shepherd should come out from the wicked; **Hel.** 7: 18 Nephites will not hearken to voice of good shepherd; 15: 13 Lamanites to be brought to knowledge of Redeemer, great and true shepherd; **3 Ne.** 15: 21 (16: 3) one fold and one s.; **Morm.** 5: 17 Nephites once had Christ for their shepherd.

JESUS CHRIST—HOLY ONE OF ISRAEL (*see also* BD Holy One of Israel)

1 Ne. 19: 14 (22: 5; 2 Ne. 6: 10) because Jews have despised Holy One, they shall wander in flesh; 19: 15 when Jews no more turn hearts against Holy One, God will remember covenants; 20: 17 (21: 7) the Lord, thy Redeemer, the Holy One; 22: 18 (2 Ne. 1: 10; 6: 10, 15; 15: 24) wrath to be poured out on those who harden hearts against Holy One; 22: 21 prophet of whom Moses spoke was Holy One; 22: 24, 26 Holy One to reign in power and glory; 22: 28 all who repent will dwell safely in Holy One; **2 Ne.** 2: 10 ends of law which Holy One hath given: 3: 2 land to be consecrated unto those who keep commandments of Holy One; 6: 9 Holy One to manifest himself to Jews in flesh; 9: 11–12 temporal death to deliver its dead through power of resurrection of Holy One; 9: 15 (Morm. 9: 13–14) those resurrected must appear before judgment-seat of Holy One; 9: 18 those who have believed in Holy One shall inherit kingdom of God; 9: 19 Holy One delivers his saints from death and hell; 9: 23 men must be baptized having faith in Holy One; 9: 25 mercies of Holy One have claim because of atonement; 9: 26 all to be restored to the God who gave them breath, Holy One; 9: 41 keeper of gate is Holy One; 25: 29 (30: 2; Omni 1: 26) Christ is Holy One of Israel; 27: 34 children of Jacob[1] shall sanctify Holy One; **Hel.** 12: 2 when he prospers his people, they trample under feet the Holy One; **3 Ne.** 22: 5 (Isa. 54: 5) thy maker, thy Redeemer, the Holy One.

JESUS CHRIST—IMMANUEL (*see also* BD Immanuel)

2 Ne. 17: 14 (Isa. 7: 14) virgin shall conceive, bear son, call his name Immanuel.

JESUS CHRIST—JEHOVAH (*see also* Jesus Christ—Creator; BD Jehovah)

2 Ne. 22: 2 (Isa. 12: 2) the Lord Jehovah is my strength; **Moro.** 10: 34 meet before pleasing bar of the great Jehovah, the Eternal Judge.

JESUS CHRIST—LAMB OF GOD (*see also* TG Jesus Christ, Lamb of God)

1 Ne. 11: 34–36 (12: 9; 13: 26, 40–41; 14: 20, 24, 27) twelve apostles of Lamb; 12: 8, 10 twelve disciples of Lamb among Nephites; 12: 11 (Alma 13: 11; 34: 36; Morm. 9: 6; Ether 13: 10–11) garments made white in blood of Lamb; 13: 26, 29, 32, 34 truths taken away from gospel of Lamb; 13: 35 records will come to Gentiles by gift and power of Lamb; 13: 37 saved in everlasting kingdom of Lamb; 13: 39 books which came forth by power of Lamb; 13: 40 Lamb is Son of Father and Savior of world; 13: 41 words of Lamb to be made known by records; 14: 12, 14 church of Lamb; 14: 26 records will come forth according to truth which is in Lamb; **Hel.** 6: 5 preachers bring many to be humble followers of God and Lamb.

JESUS CHRIST—LORD (*see also* Day of the Lord; God; Jesus Christ—Lord of Hosts; Name of the Lord; Spirit, Holy/Spirit of the Lord; Word of God/Word of the Lord; TG Jesus Christ, Lord; Lord; BD Lord)

1 Ne. 3: 7 the Lord giveth no commandment save he shall prepare way that they may accomplish it; 4: 13 slays the wicked to bring forth righteous purposes: 7: 11 ye have forgotten what great things the Lord hath done; 10: 7–8 (Alma 7: 9; Hel. 14: 9; 3 Ne. 24: 1) prepare way of the Lord; 15: 18 the Lord made covenant with Abraham; 16: 29 (Alma 37: 7) by small means the Lord brings to pass great things; 17: 14 (2 Ne. 6: 7) ye shall know that I, the Lord, am God; 17: 30 (19: 23; 2 Ne. 28: 15; Alma 28: 8) the Lord their God, their Redeemer; 17: 35 the Lord esteems all flesh in one; 17: 45 ye are slow to remember the Lord; 22: 20 the Lord will prepare way for his people; **2 Ne.** 1: 15 the Lord has redeemed my soul from hell; 2: 16 the Lord gives unto man to act for himself; 4: 16 my soul delights in things of the Lord; 6: 12 the Lord God will fulfill his covenants; 9: 16 word of the Lord God cannot pass away; 9: 41 come unto the Lord, the Holy One; 9: 41 he cannot be deceived, for the Lord God is his name; 10: 7 (Mosiah 5: 15) Christ is the Lord God; 10: 9, 21 (Alma 3: 17; 9: 24; 17: 15; 28: 11; 4 Ne. 1: 49) promises of the Lord; 31: 13 follow your Lord and Savior down into water; **Jacob** 1: 17 Jacob[2] first obtains his errand from the Lord; 4: 10 seek not to counsel the Lord; **Omni** 1: 25 nothing good save it comes from the Lord; **Mosiah** 3: 5, 17–18, 21 (5: 15) Christ the Lord Omnipotent reigns; 3: 12 salvation through faith on the Lord Jesus Christ; **Alma** 24: 27 the Lord works in many ways to save people; 26: 16 we will glory in the Lord; 34: 36 the Lord dwells not in unholy temples; 37: 36 let all thy doings be unto the Lord; **3 Ne.** 1: 12–14 voice of the Lord comes to Nephi[3], saying, On the morrow come I into the world; 14: 21–22 (Matt. 7: 21–22) not everyone who says Lord, Lord, shall enter kingdom of heaven; 19: 18 multitude pray unto Jesus, calling him their Lord; **Ether** 3: 6–18 brother of Jared[2] sees the Lord, who is Jesus Christ.

JESUS CHRIST—LORD OF HOSTS (*see also* Jesus Christ—Lord; TG Lord of Hosts; BD Lord of Hosts)

1 Ne. 20: 2 (Isa. 48: 2) God of Israel is the Lord of Hosts; **2 Ne.** 8: 15 (Isa. 51: 15) Lord of Hosts is my name; 12: 12 (Isa. 2: 12) day of the Lord of Hosts is soon to come; 15: 7 (Isa. 5: 7) vineyard of the Lord of Hosts is the house of Israel; 15: 16 (Isa. 5: 16) the Lord of Hosts shall be exalted; 19: 13 (Isa. 9: 13) people do not seek the Lord of Hosts; 24: 22 (Isa. 14: 22) the Lord of Hosts will rise up against them; 27: 2 all nations shall be visited of the Lord of Hosts; **Jacob** 2: 30 if the Lord of Hosts will raise up seed, he will command his people; **3 Ne.** 22: 5 (Isa. 54: 5) the Lord of Hosts is name of thy husband; 24: 7 (Mal. 3: 7) return unto me and I will return unto you, saith the Lord of Hosts; 24: 10 (Mal. 3: 10) prove me now herewith, saith the Lord of Hosts.

JESUS CHRIST—MEDIATOR (*see also* Jesus Christ, Atonement through; Jesus Christ—Advocate; TG Jesus Christ, Mediator)

2 Ne. 2: 27 men are free to choose eternal life through great Mediator of all men; 2: 28 look to the great Mediator.

JESUS CHRIST—MESSIAH (*see also* TG Jesus Christ—Messiah; BD Messiah)

1 Ne. 1: 19 things which Lehi[1] saw manifest plainly coming of Messiah; 10: 4 Messiah shall come six hundred years after Lehi[1] left Jerusalem; 10: 4 God to raise up Messiah, or in other words, a Savior; 10: 5 (Jarom 1: 11; Mosiah 13: 33; Hel. 8: 13) prophets spoke of Messiah, or Redeemer; 10: 7–10 prophet will come to prepare way of Messiah; 10: 11 Jews to slay Messiah; 10: 14 Israel to come to knowledge of true Messiah, their Redeemer; 10: 17 Son of God, the Messiah who should come; 12: 18 Messiah the Lamb of God; 15: 13 fulness of Messiah's gospel will come to Gentiles after he manifests body unto men; **2 Ne.** 1: 10 judgments to come upon people if they reject Holy One, the true Messiah, their Redeemer and God; 2: 6–8 redemption comes in and through Holy Messiah; 2: 26 Messiah comes in fulness of time; 3: 5 (25: 14) the Lord's covenant that Messiah shall appear to righteous branch of Israel; 6: 13 people of the Lord are they who wait for Messiah; 6: 14 Messiah will set himself the second time to recover his people; 25: 14 Messiah shall rise from dead; 25: 16 Israel shall believe in Christ and not look forward to another Messiah; 25: 18 Christ's words shall be given to Israel to convince them of true Messiah; 25: 18 there should not any other come, save false Messiah; 26: 3 signs to be given of Messiah's birth; **Jarom** 1: 11 prophets and teachers persuade people to look forward to Messiah; **Mosiah** 13: 33 (Hel. 8: 13) Moses spoke of coming of Messiah.

JESUS CHRIST—ONLY BEGOTTEN SON (*see also* Jesus Christ—Son of God; TG Jesus Christ, Only Begotten Son)

2 Ne. 25: 12 (Alma 5: 48; 9: 26) Only Begotten of the Father shall manifest himself in flesh; **Jacob** 4: 5 Abraham's offering up of Isaac is similitude of God and Only Begotten Son; 4: 11 (Alma 13: 5) be reconciled unto God through atonement of Christ, his Only Begotten Son; **Alma** 5: 48 Christ, Only Begotten, shall come to take away sins of world; 9: 26 Son's glory shall be glory of Only Begotten; 12: 33–34 mercy comes through Only Begotten Son; 13: 9 high priests after order of Son, the Only Begotten.

JESUS CHRIST—REDEEMER (*see also* Jesus Christ, Atonement through; Jesus Christ—Savior; Redemption; TG Jesus Christ, Redeemer)

1 Ne. 10: 5 prophets have spoken of Redeemer; 10: 6 all mankind lost unless they rely on Redeemer; 11: 27 Redeemer seen by Nephi[1] in vision; 15: 14 (2 Ne. 6: 11; 10: 2; Mosiah 18: 30; 26: 26; 27: 36; Alma 37: 10; Hel. 15: 13; 3 Ne. 16: 4) seed of Nephites shall come to knowledge of Redeemer; 17: 30 Redeemer led Israel by day and gave light by night; 19: 18, 23 Nephi[1] persuades his people to believe in Redeemer; 21: 26 (2 Ne. 6: 18; Isa. 49: 26) all flesh shall know the Lord is their Redeemer; **2 Ne.** 1: 10 if those in promised land reject Redeemer, judgment shall rest upon them; 1: 15 the Lord has redeemed my soul from hell; 2: 3 Jacob[2] is redeemed because of righteousness of Redeemer; 2: 6 redemption comes in and through Holy Messiah; 11: 2 Isaiah[1] saw Redeemer, as did Nephi[1]; 28: 5 many will say Redeemer has done his work; 31: 17 do the things the Redeemer has done; **Enos** 1: 27 my rest is with my Redeemer; **Mosiah** 15: 10 Son's soul to be made an offering for sin; 15: 24 those who die in ignorance are redeemed by the Lord; 16: 15 redemption comes through Christ, who is Eternal Father; 18: 2 redemption to be brought to pass through power, sufferings, death of Christ; 18: 30 how beautiful are waters of Mormon to those who there came to knowledge of Redeemer; 26: 25–26 they who never knew the Lord shall know he is their Redeemer; 27: 30 Alma[2] had rejected his Redeemer; 27: 32, 36 Alma[2] and companions are instruments in bringing many to knowledge of Redeemer; **Alma** 5: 27 Christ will come to redeem his people from their sins; 7: 13 (11: 40) Son of God suffers to take upon him sins of his people; 9: 27 Son comes to redeem those who will be baptized; 61: 14 Nephites resist evil, that they may rejoice in cause of Redeemer; **Hel.** 5: 9 Christ comes to redeem the world; 5: 11–12 we must build upon rock of Redeemer; 14: 16 Christ's death redeems all mankind from first spiritual death; 14: 17 resurrection of Christ redeems all mankind; **3 Ne.** 9: 17 (Morm. 9: 12) by Christ redemption comes; 10: 10 lamentations of Nephites are turned into praise of Christ, their Redeemer; 11: 11 Christ has taken upon himself the sins of the world; 22: 5 (Isa. 54: 5) thy Redeemer, the God of the whole earth, shall he be called; **Ether** 3: 14 Christ was prepared from foundation of world to redeem his people; **Moro.** 8: 8 listen to the words of Christ, your Redeemer.

JESUS CHRIST, RESURRECTION OF (*see also* Death, Physical; Immortality; Jesus Christ, Atonement through; Jesus Christ, Death of; Jesus Christ—Redeemer; Resurrection; TG Jesus Christ, Resurrection of)

1 Ne. 10: 11 Messiah shall rise from the dead; **2 Ne.** 2: 8 (Mosiah 13: 35; 15: 20; Alma 33: 22; 40: 3; Hel. 14: 15) Christ lays down life, takes it up again, to bring to pass resurrection of dead; 9: 11–12 (Alma 40: 21, 23; Moro. 10: 34) bodies and spirits of men shall be restored to one another by power of resurrection of Holy One; 26: 1 after Christ rises from dead, he will show himself to Nephites; **Jacob** 4: 11 be reconciled to God through atonement of Christ, and ye may obtain resurrection according to power of resurrection in Christ; 6: 9 power of redemption and resurrection in Christ will bring you to stand before God; **Mosiah** 15: 20 Son has power over the dead and brings to pass resurrection; 15: 21–26 (Alma 40: 15–18) those who died before Christ's resurrection will have part in first resurrection; 16: 7 if Christ had not risen from the dead, there could have been no resurrection; 16: 8 (Morm. 7: 5) sting of death is swallowed in Christ; **Alma** 11: 42 death of Christ shall loose bands of temporal death; 33: 22 (Hel. 14: 20) Son shall rise from dead to bring to pass the resurrection; **Hel.** 14: 17 resurrection of Christ redeems mankind; 14: 25 (3 Ne. 23: 9, 11) at time of Christ's resurrection many saints shall be resurrected; **3 Ne.** 6: 20 prophets testify of redemption which the Lord would make for his people, the resurrection of Christ; **Morm.** 7: 5 by power of Father, Christ has risen again; 9: 13 death of Christ brings to pass the resurrection; **Ether** 12: 7 by faith Christ showed himself to Nephites after he had risen; **Moro.** 7: 41 ye shall have hope through Christ's atonement and resurrection.

JESUS CHRIST—SAVIOR (*see also* Jesus Christ, Atonement through; Jesus Christ—Redeemer; Salvation; Save; TG Jesus Christ—Savior)

1 Ne. 10: 4 God will raise up Messiah, or in other words, Savior of world; 13: 40 Lamb is Savior; 21: 26 (22: 12; 2 Ne. 6: 18) all flesh shall know that the Lord is Savior; **2 Ne.** 6: 17 Mighty God shall deliver his covenant people; 31: 13 (Morm. 7: 10) are you willing to follow Savior into water; **Mosiah** 3: 20 knowledge of Savior will spread to every nation; **Hel.** 14: 15 Christ must die that salvation may come; **3 Ne.** 5: 20 Mormon[2] has reason to bless his Savior Jesus Christ; **Morm.** 3: 14 our Lord and Savior Jesus Christ; **Moro.** 8: 29 words of Savior will be fulfilled.

JESUS CHRIST, SECOND COMING OF (*see also* Day of the Lord; Last Days; Millennium; TG Jesus Christ, Second Coming of)

3 Ne. 24: 1 (Mal. 3: 1) the Lord shall suddenly come to temple; 24: 2 (Mal. 3: 2) who may abide day of the Lord's coming; 25: 5 (Mal. 4: 5) Elijah to be sent before coming of day of the Lord; 27: 16 he who endures to end will be held guiltless when Christ stands to judge world; 29: 2 ye need not say the Lord delays his coming unto Israel; **Morm.** 8: 26–32 signs of the Lord's coming in latter days.

JESUS CHRIST–SON OF GOD (*see also* God the Father; Jesus Christ–Creator; Jesus Christ–Jehovah; Jesus Christ–Lamb of God; Jesus Christ–Messiah; Jesus Christ–Only Begotten Son; TG Jesus Christ, Divine Sonship; BD Son of God)

1 Ne. 10: 17 Son of God is Messiah who should come; 11: 7 Nephi[1] to see, bear record of Son of God; 11: 18 virgin is mother of Son of God; 11: 21 (13: 40) Lamb of God is Son of the Eternal Father; 11: 24 Son of God to go forth among men; **2 Ne.** 17: 14 (Isa. 7: 14) virgin shall conceive and bear a son, Immanuel; 19: 6 (Isa. 9: 6) unto us a child is born, unto us a son is given; 25: 16, 19 (Mosiah 3: 8; 4: 2; Alma 6: 8; 36: 17–18; Hel. 3: 28; 5: 12; 14: 12; 3 Ne. 5: 13, 26; 9: 15; 20: 31; Morm. 5: 14; 7: 5; Ether 4: 7) name of Son of God shall be Jesus Christ; 26: 9 (Alma 16: 20) Son of righteousness shall appear unto Nephites; 31: 11–12 be baptized in name of Son; 31: 21 (Mosiah 15: 4–5; Alma 11: 44; 3 Ne. 11: 27, 36; 28: 10; Morm. 7: 7) Father, Son, and Holy Ghost are one God; **Jacob** 4: 5 Abraham's offering up Isaac is similitude of God and Son; 4: 5, 11 (Alma 5: 48; 9: 26; 12: 33–34; 13: 5–9) Christ is the Father's Only Begotten Son; **Mosiah** 3: 8 (Alma 7: 9–10) mother of Son of God to be Mary; 15: 2–3 because he dwells in flesh, he shall be called Son of God; 15: 3 he shall be Father and Son; 15: 7 will of Son swallowed up in will of Father; 15: 8 God gives Son power to make intercession for men; **Alma** 5: 50 (9: 26) Son of God will come in his glory; 6: 8 (7: 13; 11: 40; Hel. 14: 2) Jesus Christ, the Son of God who should come to redeem his people from sins; 7: 11–13 ministry of Son foretold; 11: 32 (34: 5) who shall come, is it Son of God; 11: 38–39 (Mosiah 15: 1–5; Hel. 16: 18) Son is the Eternal Father; 12: 33 God calls on men in name of his Son; 12: 33 (36: 18) God will have mercy upon men through Son; 13: 1–9 (Hel. 8: 18) high priesthood after order of Son; 13: 16 ordinances given that people might look forward on Son; 24: 13 blood of Son to be shed for atonement of sins; 33: 14–19 (34: 7–8; Hel. 8: 13–22) prophets have spoken of Son; 34: 2 Nephites teach that Christ is to be Son of God; 34: 10–14 great and last sacrifice will be Son of God; 36: 18 Jesus, thou Son of God, have mercy; **Hel.** 14: 2 Son of God to come in five years; 14: 8 whosoever believes on Son shall have everlasting life; **3 Ne.** 1: 14 Christ to do will both of Father and Son; 1: 17 Son must shortly appear; 11: 7 behold my Beloved Son, in whom I am well pleased; 25: 2 (Mal. 4: 2) unto them who fear the Lord's name will Son of Righteousness arise; **Morm.** 5: 14 Jesus is the Christ, the Son of the living God; 7: 5 believe in Jesus Christ, that he is the Son of God; **Ether** 12: 18 miracles are not wrought until after men believe in Son of God.

JESUS CHRIST, TYPES OF (*see also* Type, Typify; TG Jesus Christ, Types of, in Anticipation; Jesus Christ, Types of, in Memory)

2 Ne. 11: 4 (Jacob 4: 5; Mosiah 13: 30–31; 16: 14; Alma 25: 15; 34: 14; Gal. 3: 24; Heb. 10: 1) law of Moses given as type pointing to Christ; 11: 4 all things given of God from beginning typify Christ; **Jacob** 4: 5 Abraham's offering up of Isaac is similitude of God and Son; **Mosiah** 3: 15 the Lord showed his people many types of his coming; **Alma** 33: 19–21 (1 Ne. 17: 41; 2 Ne. 25: 20; Hel. 8: 14–15; Num. 21: 8–9) serpent raised in wilderness a type of Christ; 37: 38–46 working of Liahona a type of word of Christ; **3 Ne.** 18: 7, 11 bread and wine of sacrament to be taken in remembrance of body and blood of Christ.

JEW, JEWISH—*descendant of Judah, or inhabitant of kingdom of Judah* (*see also* Israel; Israel, Gathering of; Israel, Scattering of; Israelites; Jacob, House of; Jerusalem[1]; Judah; Israel; TG Israel, Judah, People of; Jew, Jewish; BD Jew)

Title Page (2 Ne. 26: 12) book written to convincing of J. and Gentile that Jesus is the Christ; **1 Ne.** 1: 2 language of Lehi[1] consists of learning of J. and language of Egyptians; 1: 19–20 J. mock Lehi[1]; 2: 13 (17: 44) J. seek to kill Lehi[1]; 3: 3 (5: 6) Laban has record of J.; 4: 22–37 Zoram[1] speaks to Nephi[1] concerning elders of J.; 4: 36 Lehites do not want J. to know of flight; 5: 12 (Omni

1: 14; Ether 1: 3) brass plates contain record of J. down to Zedekiah; 10: 2–4 Lehi[1] speaks to family about J.; 10: 4 the Lord will raise up Messiah among J.; 10: 11 J. to hear gospel, dwindle in unbelief; 13: 23–24, 38 (14: 23; 2 Ne. 29: 4–13) book containing record of J., covenants of the Lord to come from J.; 13: 25–26 (Morm. 7: 8) gospel goes forth in purity from J. to Gentiles; 13: 39 (2 Ne. 25: 15; 30: 7) J. to be scattered; 13: 42 Lamb shall be manifest to J., then Gentiles, to Gentiles, then J.; 15: 17 (2 Ne. 25: 18) the Lord will be rejected of J.; 15: 19–20 Nephi[1] rehearses words of Isaiah[1] concerning restoration of J.; **2 Ne.** 9: 2 the Lord has spoken unto J. by mouth of prophets; 10: 3 (4 Ne. 1: 31; Morm. 7: 5) Christ to come among J., for no other nation would crucify their God; 10: 16 he who fights against Zion, both J. and Gentile, will perish; 25: 1, 5–6 difficulty of understanding manner of prophesying among J.; 25: 2 Nephi[1] has not taught many things concerning manner of J., for their works were works of darkness; 25: 9 J. have been destroyed from generation to generation according to iniquities; 26: 33 all are alike unto God, both Gentile and J.; 27: 1 in last days all nations of Gentiles and J. shall be drunken with iniquity; 29: 5 O Gentiles, have ye remembered the J.; 30: 2 J. who will not repent shall be cast off; 30: 4 remnant of Nephites' seed shall know they are descendants of J.; 33: 8 Nephi[1] has charity for J., whence he came; 33: 10 Nephi[1] admonishes J. to believe in Christ; 33: 14 words of J. will condemn those who do not accept them; **Jacob** 4: 14 J. a stiffnecked people; 4: 15–17 by stumbling of J., they will reject stone upon which they might build safe foundation; **Alma** 11: 4 Nephites do not reckon after manner of J.; 16: 13 synagogues built after manner of J.; **3 Ne.** 19: 35 so great faith have I never seen among all the J.; 28: 28 three Nephites will be among J.; 29: 8 Gentiles need no longer spurn or make game of J.; **Morm.** 3: 21 J. shall have other witnesses that Jesus, whom they slew, is the Christ; 5: 12, 14 writings shall go unto unbelieving of J.

JEWEL

2 Ne. 13: 21 (Isa. 3: 21) the Lord will take away nose j. of daughters of Zion; **3 Ne.** 24: 16–17 they who fear the Lord shall be his when he makes up his j.

JOHN THE BELOVED—*also known as the Revelator* [c. first century A.D.] (*see also* BD John)

1 Ne. 14: 19–27 Nephi[1] beholds J. in vision; **3 Ne.** 28: 4–6 three Nephite disciples desire to tarry, as did J. the beloved; **Ether** 4: 16 revelation written by J. to be unfolded in eyes of all people.

JOIN (*see also* Cleave; Unite)

2 Ne. 15: 8 (Isa. 5: 8) wo unto them who j. house to house; 23: 15 every one who is j. to the wicked shall fall by sword; **Mosiah** 25: 23 (Alma 4: 4; Hel. 3: 24) those who desire to take upon themselves name of Christ are baptized and j. churches of God.

JOINT

1 Ne. 19: 20 workings in spirit weary Nephi[1], that j. are weak; **Alma** 11: 43 (40: 23) both limb and j. shall be restored in resurrection.

JONAS[1]—*son of Nephi[3], one of twelve disciples* [c. A.D. 34]

3 Ne. 19: 4 chosen by Jesus to minister to Nephites.

JONAS[2]—*one of twelve disciples* [c. A.D. 34]

3 Ne. 19: 4 chosen by Jesus to minister to Nephites.

JORDAN—*river in Palestine* (*see also* BD Jordan River)

1 Ne. 10: 9 prophet shall baptize in Bethabara, beyond J.; 17: 32 after crossing river J., Israelites drove out children of land; **2 Ne.** 19: 1 (Isa. 9: 1) the Lord did afflict by way of Red Sea beyond J. in Galilee.

JORDAN, CITY OF

Morm. 5: 3 Nephites flee to the city of J.

JOSEPH[1]—*son of Jacob[1]* [c. 1700 B.C.] (*see also* Ephraim; Israel; Joseph[1], Seed of; Manasseh; Smith, Joseph, Jr.; BD Joseph; Joseph, Stick of)

1 Ne. 5: 14 (6: 2; 2 Ne. 3: 4) Lehi[1] a descendant of J.; 5: 16 Laban a descendant of J.; **2 Ne.** 3: 4 great were the covenants made unto J.; 3: 5 J. truly saw our day; 3: 6–21 J. testifies of latter-day seer named J.; 4: 1 J. is carried into Egypt; **Alma** 10: 3 Aminadi a descendant of J.; 46: 24 part of remnant of J. shall be preserved, as remnant of coat of J.; **Ether** 13: 7 J. brought his father down into Egypt.

JOSEPH[2]—*son of Lehi[1]* [c. 595 B.C.] (*see also* Josephites)

1 Ne. 18: 7 younger son of Lehi[1] born in wilderness; 18: 19 is grieved because of mother's afflictions; **2 Ne.** ch. 3 words of Lehi[1] to J.; 3: 1 thou wast born in wilderness of mine affliction; 3: 3, 23 may the Lord bless thee forever, for thy seed shall not be destroyed; 3: 25 is admonished to hearken unto words of Nephi[1]; 5: 5–6 follows Nephi[1] from land; 5: 26 (Jacob 1: 18) is consecrated a priest; **Alma** 3: 6 is a just and holy man.

JOSEPH[1], SEED OF—*descendants of Joseph*[1] (*see also* Israel; Joseph[1])

2 Ne. 3: 16 (25: 21) the Lord promised *J.* to preserve his seed forever; **Jacob** 2: 25 Nephites to be righteous branch from loins of *J.*; **Alma** 46: 23 (Ether 13: 7) Nephites are remnant of seed of *J.*; 46: 24–27 (3 Ne. 10: 17) part of remnant of *J.* shall be preserved, as remnant of coat of *J.*, remainder shall perish; **3 Ne.** 5: 21 the Lord has been merciful unto seed of *J.*; 5: 23 the Lord will bring remnant of seed of *J.* to knowledge of the Lord; 15: 12 Nephites a remnant of house of *J.*; **Ether** 13: 6–10 New Jerusalem to be built unto remnant of seed of *J.*

JOSEPHITES—*descendants of Joseph*[2] (*see also* Joseph[2])

Jacob 1: 13 (4 Ne. 1: 36–37; Morm. 1: 8) included among Nephites.

JOSH—*Nephite commander* [c. A.D. 385]

Morm. 6: 14 had fallen with his ten thousand.

JOSH, CITY OF

3 Ne. 9: 10 is burned.

JOSHUA, LAND OF—*land in borders west, by seashore*

Morm. 2: 6 Nephites march to land of *J.*

JOT

Alma 34: 13 law shall be fulfilled, every *j.* and tittle; **3 Ne.** 1: 25 (12: 18; Matt. 5: 18) not one *j.* or tittle should pass away until whole law of Moses was fulfilled.

JOURNEY (*see also* Depart; Flight; Sail; Sojourn; Travel; Wander)

1 Ne. 2: 2–4 (3: 18) Lehi[1] and family depart into wilderness; 3: 9 Nephi[1] and brothers *j.* back to Jerusalem for records; 16: 33 Lehites *j.* in nearly same course as in beginning; **2 Ne.** 5: 7 Nephi[1] and followers *j.* many days in wilderness; **Omni** 1: 12 Mosiah[1] and his people depart into wilderness, discover people of Zarahemla; 1: 29 considerable number of Nephites *j.* into wilderness; **Mosiah** 1: 17 (1 Ne. 16: 28–29; Alma 37: 39–41) when Lehites were unfaithful, no progress in *j.*; 23: 3 people of Alma[1] flee eight days' *j.* into wilderness; **Alma** 8: 6 Alma[2] travels three days' *j.* to Ammonihah; 22: 32 distance of day and a half's *j.* from east to west sea; **Hel.** 3: 3–5 many Nephites depart from Zarahemla and travel to land northward; 4: 7 from west sea to east is a day's *j.* for a Nephite.

JOY, JOYOUS (*see also* Cheer; Delight; Happiness; Pleasure; Rejoice)

1 Ne. 8: 12 (11: 21–23) fruit of tree of life fills soul with *j.*; 13: 37 how beautiful upon mountains shall be they who publish tidings of *j.*; **2 Ne.** 2: 23 if Adam had not transgressed, he would have had no *j.*, knowing no misery; 2: 25 men are that they might have *j.*; 9: 18 *j.* of righteous saints shall be full forever; 27: 30 *j.* of the meek shall be in the Lord; **Mosiah** 3: 3 angel declares unto Benjamin glad tidings of *j.*; 4: 20 the Lord has poured out Spirit and caused hearts to be filled with *j.*; **Alma** 4: 14 people filled with *j.* because of resurrection; 19: 6 light of God's glory infuses *j.* into Lamoni's soul; 19: 14 Ammon[2] overpowered with *j.*; 22: 15 what shall I do to be born of God, receive Spirit, be filled with *j.*; 26: 11 heart of Ammon[2] is brim with *j.*; 26: 35 *j.* of Ammon[2] is carried away, unto boasting in God; 28: 8 account of incomprehensible *j.* of Ammon[2] and his brothers; 28: 14 great reason of *j.* because of light of Christ unto life; 29: 9 my *j.*, that I may be instrument in hands of God to bring some soul to repentance; 29: 13–14 I do not *j.* in my own success, but my *j.* is more full because of success of brethren; 30: 34 have rejoicings in *j.* of our brethren; 33: 23 may God grant that your burdens be light, through *j.* of Son; 36: 20 soul of Alma[2] filled with *j.* as exceeding as his pain; 36: 24 Alma[2] labors to bring other souls to taste exceeding *j.* which he tasted; **3 Ne.** 17: 18 so great is *j.* of multitude that they are overcome; 17: 20 Christ's *j.* is full; 27: 11 if church is built upon works of men or devil, they have *j.* for season; **Morm.** 2: 13 *j.* of Mormon[2] is vain, for Nephites' sorrowing is not unto repentance; **Ether** 6: 12 when Jaredites land in promised land, they shed tears of *j.*

JUDAH—*southern kingdom of Israelites* (*see also* Hebrew; Israel; Jacob[1]; Jacob, House of; Jerusalem[1]; Jew; TG Israel, Judah, People of; BD Judah, Kingdom of)

1 Ne. 1: 4 (5: 12; Omni 1: 15) Zedekiah, king of *J.*; 20: 1 (Isa. 48: 1) house of Jacob are come forth out of waters of *J.*, or waters of baptism; **2 Ne.** 3: 12 fruit of loins of *J.* shall write; 12: 1 (Isa. 2: 1) word that Isaiah[1] saw concerning *J.* and Jerusalem; 13: 8 (Isa. 3: 8) *J.* is fallen; 17: 6 (Isa. 7: 6) let us go up against *J.* and vex it; 17: 17 (Isa. 7: 17) the day that Ephraim departed from *J.*; 21: 13 (Isa. 11: 13) Ephraim shall not envy *J.*, and *J.* shall not vex Ephraim.

JUDEA, CITY OF—*Nephite city*

Alma 56: 9 Helaman[1] marches with two thousand stripling warriors to *J.*; 56: 15 Antipus and his men fortify city of *J.*; 56: 18 when Lamanites see Nephite reinforcements, they do not come against *J.*; 56: 57 Helaman[1] and stripling warriors march back to *J.*; 57: 11 Nephites send provisions to *J.*

JUDGE [noun] (*see also* Judge [verb]; Judge, Chief; Judgment; Lawyers)

Mosiah 29: 11, 25 let us appoint *j.* to judge according to law; 29: 25, 39 *j.* chosen by voice of people; 29: 29 lower *j.* shall judge higher *j.* according to voice of people; 29: 44 commencement of reign of *j.* throughout land of Zarahemla; **Alma** 10: 27 foundation of destruction of Ammonihah being laid by lawyers and *j.*; 11: 1–3 compensation of *j.*; 14: 18–27 *j.* of Ammonihah torment of Alma[2] and Amulek; 41: 7 those who repent and desire righteousness are own *j.*; **3 Ne.** 6: 23–24 *j.* secretly put prophets to death; 6: 25–26 *j.* who condemned prophets to death are brought before governor; 6: 27–30 *j.*, lawyers, and friends form secret combination; 27: 27 (1 Ne. 11: 32; Morm. 3: 19) Nephite disciples shall be *j.* of Nephites; **Moro.** 10: 34 great Jehovah, the Eternal *J.* of both quick and dead.

JUDGE [verb] (*see also* Condemn; Judge [noun]; Judgment; Justice)

1 Ne. 11: 32 Son was *j.* of world; 12: 9 (Morm. 3: 18–19) twelve apostles shall *j.* twelve tribes of Israel, twelve Nephite disciples; 12: 10 (3 Ne. 27: 27; Morm. 3: 19) twelve Nephite disciples shall *j.* Nephites; 15: 32–33 (2 Ne. 9: 15; 28: 23; Mosiah 16: 10; Alma 5: 15; 11: 41; 12: 12; 41: 3; 3 Ne. 26: 4; Morm. 3: 20) men must be *j.* before God according to their works; **2 Ne.** 8: 5 (Isa. 51: 5) the Lord's arm shall *j.* the people; 25: 18 the Lord shall bring forth his word, which shall *j.* the Jews; 30: 9 with righteousness shall the Lord God *j.* the poor; **Mosiah** 4: 22 if ye *j.* and condemn the beggar, how much more just will be your condemnation; 26: 29 whosoever transgresseth against the Lord shall ye *j.* according to sins; 29: 11, 25 let us appoint judges to *j.* this people according to law; 29: 12 better to be *j.* of God than of man; 29: 29 lower judges shall *j.* higher judges according to voice of people; **Alma** 41: 14 deal justly, *j.* righteously; **3 Ne.** 14: 1 (Matt. 7: 1) *j.* not, that ye be not *j.*; 27: 16 Christ shall stand to *j.* the world; 27: 25–26 out of books shall world be *j.*; **Morm.** 8: 19 he who *j.* rashly shall be *j.* rashly; **Moro.** 7: 15 given unto you to *j.*, that ye may know good from evil; 7: 15–18 way to *j.* is shown; 7: 18 *j.* by light of Christ; 7: 18 with that same judgment which ye *j.* ye shall be *j.*

JUDGE, CHIEF (*see also* Governor; Judge [noun])

Mosiah 29: 42–43 (Alma 2: 16) Alma[2] appointed to be first chief *j.*; **Alma** 4: 16–17 (50: 37) Nephihah appointed chief *j.*; 14: 14–27 chief *j.* of land of Ammonihah, who is after order of Nehor, mocks Alma[2] and Amulek; 27: 21 chief *j.* asks for voice of people concerning people of Anti-Nephi-Lehi; 50: 39 Pahoran[1] succeeds father as chief *j.*; **Hel.** 1: 5 Pahoran[2] appointed by voice of people to be chief *j.*; 1: 13, 21 Pacumeni appointed by voice of people to be chief *j.*; 2: 2 Helaman[2] appointed to fill judgment-seat; 3: 37 Nephi[2] fills judgment seat; 5: 1 (6: 15, 19) Nephi[2] delivers judgment seat to Cezoram; 6: 15 Cezoram's son appointed in his stead and is also murdered; 8: 27 (9: 2–17, 23) Seezoram, chief *j.*, murdered; **3 Ne.** 1: 1 Lachoneus[1] the chief *j.*; 3: 18–19 Gidgiddoni appointed chief captain and chief *j.*; 6: 19 Lachoneus[2] fills seat of his father; 7: 1 secret combination murders chief *j.*

JUDGMENT (*see also* Anger; Bar; Condemn, Condemnation; Day of the Lord; Destruction; Equal; Iniquity; Jesus Christ; Judge [verb]; Judgment-seat; Just; Justice; Last Days; Reward; Scourge; Thrash; Transgression; Visitation; Wicked; Wrath; TG God, Justice of; Judgment; Judgment, the Last)

1 Ne. 10: 20 for all thy doings thou shalt be brought into *j.*; 12: 5 Nephi[1] beholds multitudes who had not fallen because of great and terrible *j.* of the Lord; 22: 21 Holy One shall execute *j.* in righteousness; **2 Ne.** 1: 10 if Nephites reject Holy One, the *j.* of him who is just shall rest upon them; 9: 7 without atonement, first *j.* which came upon man must have remained to endless duration; 9: 15 when all men pass from first death unto life, then comes *j.*; 9: 46 prepare your souls for day of *j.*; 18: 15 brothers of Nephi[1] see that *j.* of God are upon them; 25: 3 Nephi[1] writes so that people may know *j.* of God; **Mosiah** 3: 18 (29: 12; Alma 12: 15) the Lord judgeth, and his *j.* is just; 16: 1 every people shall confess before God that his *j.* are just; 17: 11 Noah[3] fears *j.* of God would be upon him; 29: 12 *j.* of God are always just, *j.* of men not always just; 29: 27 when voice of people chooses iniquity, *j.* of God will come; 29: 43 Alma[2] judges righteous *j.*; **Alma** 12: 27 after death, men must come to *j.*; 14: 11 (60: 13) the Lord suffers martyrs to die, that his *j.* may be just;

37: 30 *j.* of God come upon workers of secret combinations; 58: 9 (60: 14) Nephites filled with fear lest *j.* of God come upon land to destruction; **Hel.** 4: 23 because of iniquity, *j.* of God stare Nephites in face; 14: 11 *j.* of God await the wicked; **3 Ne.** 12: 21 (Matt. 5: 21) whosoever shall kill shall be in danger of *j.* of God; **Ether** 11: 20 prophets warn Jaredites that God will execute *j.* to their utter destruction; **Moro.** 7: 18 with same *j.* which ye judge ye shall also be judged; 9: 14 how can we expect God will stay his hand in *j.* against us; 9: 15 come out in *j.*, O God.

JUDGMENT-SEAT (*see also* Bar; Judge, Chief; Judgment; Throne; Tribunal)

Title Page condemn not the things of God that ye may be found spotless at *j-s.* of Christ; **1 Ne.** 10: 21 if ye have sought to do wickedly, ye are found unclean before *j-s.* of God; **2 Ne.** 9: 15 (3 Ne. 28: 31; Morm 3: 20; 6: 21; 7: 6) all men must appear before *j-s.* of Christ; 33: 7 Nephi[1] has faith he will meet many souls spotless at Christ's *j-s.*; 33: 15 what I seal on earth shall be brought against you at the *j.* bar; **Alma** 1: 2 (4: 17–18; 50: 39; Hel. 1: 2–9; 2:2; 3: 37; 5: 1; 6: 15; 8: 27; 3 Ne. 6: 19; 7: 1) chief judge among Nephites sits upon *j-s.*; **Morm.** 3: 22 all should repent and prepare to stand before *j-s.* of Christ; **Ether** 12: 38 Moroni[2] bids farewell until we meet before *j-s.* of Christ; **Moro.** 8: 20–21 listen unto them and give heed, or they stand against you at *j-s.* of Christ.

JUST, JUSTLY (*see also* Justice; Perfect; Righteousness; Uprightness)

2 Ne. 1: 10 if Nephites reject Holy One, judgments of him who is *j.* shall rest upon them; 1: 22 do not incur displeasure of a *j.* God; 26: 7 I must cry unto my God, Thy ways are *j.*; 27: 32 (28: 16) they who turn aside the *j.* for thing of naught shall be cut off; **Enos** 1: 1 Enos knows his father is *j.* man; **Omni** 1: 22 (Mosiah 3: 18; 16: 1; 29: 12) God's judgment is *j.*; **Mosiah** 2: 4 God appointed *j.* men to be Nephites' teachers; 4: 22, 25 if ye condemn the beggar, how much more *j.* will be your condemnation; 19: 17 Limhi is a *j.* man; 23: 8 (29: 13) if it were possible always to have *j.* men as kings, it would be well to have kings; 27: 31 (Alma 12: 15) men shall confess that judgment of everlasting punishment is *j.* upon them; 29: 12 God's judgments are always *j.*, judgments of man not always *j.*; **Alma** 3: 6 Nephi[1] and followers were *j.* and holy men; 12: 8 all shall rise from dead, both *j.* and unjust; 13: 25–26 time of Christ's coming shall be made known unto *j.* and holy men; 29: 4 I ought not to harrow up in my desires the firm decree of a *j.* God; 41: 13 restoration means to bring back *j.* for that which is *j.*; 41: 14 deal *j.*; 42: 15 God atoneth for sins of world so that he might be a *j.* and merciful God; **3 Ne.** 26: 19 (4 Ne. 1: 2) every man deals *j.* one with another; 27: 27 ye shall be judges of this people according to *j.* judgment I shall give you; **Morm.** 9: 4 ye would be miserable to dwell with holy and *j.* God under consciousness of filthiness; **Moro.** 10: 6 whatsoever thing is good is *j.* and true.

JUSTICE (*see also* Equity; Judge [verb]; Judgment; Just; Mercy; Punishment; Sacrifice; Vengeance; TG God, Justice of)

1 Ne. 14: 4 *j.* of God will fall upon those who work wickedness; 15: 30 *j.* of God divides wicked from righteous; **2 Ne.** 2: 11–12 absence of opposition would destroy *j.* of God; 9: 17 O the greatness and *j.* of our God; 9: 26 (Alma 42: 15) atonement satisfies demands of *j.*; 19: 7 (Isa. 9: 7) kingdom to be established with judgment and *j.*; **Jacob** 4: 10 God counsels in *j.* and great mercy; 6: 10 *j.* cannot be denied; **Mosiah** 2: 38 demands of divine *j.* awaken soul of unrepentant to sense of guilt; 5: 15 salvation through *j.* and mercy of Creator; **Alma** 12: 32 works of *j.* could not be destroyed; 41: 2–3 (61: 12) requisite with *j.* of God that men should be judged according to works; 42: 14 all mankind fallen and in grasp of *j.* of God; 42: 25 do ye suppose mercy can rob *j.*; 42: 30 do not excuse yourself by denying God's *j.*, but let his *j.* and mercy have full sway in your heart; 54: 6 *j.* of God hangs over you unless you repent; 60: 13 the Lord suffereth the righteous to be slain that his *j.* may come upon the wicked; **3 Ne.** 26: 5 the good to be resurrected to everlasting life, the evil to damnation, according to Christ's *j.*; 29: 4 sword of *j.* is in the Lord's right hand.

JUSTIFY (*see also* Jesus Christ, Atonement through; Sanctification; TG Justification)

1 Ne. 16: 2 the righteous have I *j.*; **2 Ne.** 2: 5 by law no flesh is *j.*; 7: 8 the Lord is near, and he *j.* me; 15: 22–23 (Isa. 5: 23) wo unto the mighty who *j.* the wicked for reward; 28: 8 many shall say, God will *j.* you in committing a little sin; **Mosiah** 14: 11 (Isa. 53: 11) by his knowledge shall my righteous servant *j.* many; **Alma** 41: 15 the word restoration *j.* the sinner not at all.

KEEP, KEPT (*see also* Keeper; Maintain; Obedience; Observe; Preserve; Restrain; Retain; Withhold)

1 Ne. 19: 5 more sacred things to be

k. for knowledge of Nephites; **2 Ne.** 1: 9 (Mosiah 1: 7; 2: 22; Alma 36: 1, 30; 38: 1) if those brought out of Jerusalem *k.* commandments, they shall prosper and be *k.* from all nations; 25: 24 (Jacob 4: 5; Mosiah 13: 27–35; Alma 25: 15–16) Nephites *k.* law of Moses to look forward to Christ; **Mosiah** 2: 4 *k.* God's commandments, to be filled with love toward God and all men; 13: 16 (18: 23; Ex. 20: 8) remember the Sabbath day, to *k.* it holy; **Alma** 37: 35 learn in thy youth to *k.* commandments; 42: 2 cherubim and flaming sword placed to *k.* tree of life; **Hel.** 15: 5 more part of Lamanites *k.* commandments, according to law of Moses; **3 Ne.** 16: 4 writings shall be *k.* and manifested unto Gentiles; **Ether** 3: 19–20 (12: 21) brother of Jared[2] could not be *k.* from within veil; **Moro.** 6: 4 those baptized should be nourished by word, to *k.* them in right way; 8: 3 Mormon[2] prays that God will *k.* Moroni[2] through endurance of faith.

KEEPER

2 Ne. 9: 41 *k.* of gate is Holy One.

KIB—*early Jaredite king*

Ether 1: 31–32 (7: 3, 7) son of Orihah, father of Shule and Corihor; 7: 5, 7 taken captive by Corihor, dwells in captivity; 7: 8–9 restored to throne by Shule.

KID (*see also* Animal)

2 Ne. 21: 6 (30: 12; Isa. 11: 6) leopard shall lie down with *k.*

KILL (*see also* Blood, Shedding of; Capital Punishment; Death, Physical; Martyrdom; Murder; Slaughter; Slay; Smite)

1 Ne. 4: 10 Nephi[1] constrained by Spirit to *k.* Laban; **2 Ne.** 9: 35 murderer who deliberately *k.* shall die; 26: 5 (3 Ne. 8: 25) earth to swallow up those who *k.* prophets and saints; **Jacob** 4: 14 Jews *k.* the prophets; **Mosiah** 13: 21 (3 Ne. 12: 21; Ex. 20: 13) thou shalt not *k.*; **Hel.** 7: 5 robbers fill judgment-seat, that they might more easily *k.*; 13: 32–33 (3 Ne. 8: 25) Nephites to lament that they *k.* prophets; **4 Ne.** 1: 30–31 people seek to *k.* disciples of Jesus.

KIM—*Jaredite king*

Ether 1: 21–22 (10: 13–14) son of Morianton[1], father of Levi[2]; 10: 13 does not reign righteously; 10: 14 brought into captivity by brother.

KIMNOR—*early Jaredite*

Ether 8: 10 the father of Akish, who founded secret combination.

KINDLE (*see* Anger)

KINDNESS, KIND (*see also* Charity; Compassion; Gentle; Love)

1 Ne. 19: 9 Christ to suffer mockery because of his loving *k.*; **3 Ne.** 22: 8 (Isa. 54: 8) with everlasting *k.* will I have mercy on thee; **Moro.** 7: 45 (1 Cor. 13: 4) charity suffereth long and is *k.*

KING (*see also* Jesus Christ; Kingdom; King-men; Prince)

1 Ne. 16: 38 brothers think Nephi[1] wants to make himself *k.*; 21: 23 (2 Ne. 6: 7; 10: 9; Isa. 49: 23) *k.* of Gentiles shall be Israel's nursing fathers; **2 Ne.** 5: 18 people want Nephi[1] to be *k.*, but he desires they have no *k.*; 6: 2 Nephites look unto Nephi[1] as *k.* or protector; 10: 11 land shall be land of liberty unto Gentiles, with no *k.*; 10: 14 the Lord is *k.* of heaven; **Jacob** 1: 11 those who reign in stead of Nephi[1] are called second Nephi, third Nephi, according to reigns of *k.*; **Omni** 1: 12 Mosiah[1] made *k.* over Zarahemla; **Mosiah** 2: 19 if earthly *k.* merits any thanks, how you ought to thank heavenly *K.*; 2: 26 Benjamin, whom ye call your *k.*, is no better than ye yourselves are; 2: 30 Benjamin declares Mosiah[2] is *k.* over Nephites; 7: 9 Zeniff made *k.* by voice of people; 23: 6–7 (29: 16) Nephites ask Alma[1] to be *k.*, but he advises against *k.*; 23: 8 (29: 13, 16) if possible always to have just men as *k.*, it would be well to have *k.*; 29: 1–3 sons of Mosiah[2] not willing to become *k.*; 29: 21 ye cannot dethrone iniquitous *k.*, save through contention; 29: 22–23 unrighteous *k.* perverts ways of righteousness; 29: 31 sins of many people have been caused by iniquities of *k.*; 29: 35–36 Mosiah[2] unfolds disadvantages of having unrighteous *k.*; **Alma** 5: 50 *K.* of heaven shall soon shine forth among all men; 13: 17–18 Melchizedek was *k.* over land of Salem; 46: 4 Amalickiah desires to be *k.*; **3 Ne.** 6: 30 judges and lawyers covenant to destroy governor and establish *k.*; 7: 9–10 secret combination calls Jacob[4] *k.*; 20: 45 (21: 8; Isa. 52: 15) *k.* shall shut their mouths at the Lord's servant; **Ether** 6: 22–28 Jaredites desire a son of Jared[1] or his brother be anointed *k.*

KINGDOM (*see also* Church of the Devil; Dominion; Government, Civil; King; Kingdom of God; Nation)

1 Ne. 13: 1 Nephi[1] beholds many nations and *k.* in vision; 22: 22 *k.* of devil shall be built up among men; 22: 23 those who belong to *k.* of devil should fear and tremble; **2 Ne.** 20: 10 (Isa. 10: 10) my hand hath founded the *k.* of idols; 23: 4 (Isa. 13: 4) tumultuous noise of *k.* of nations gathered together; 24: 16 (Isa. 14: 16) is this the man that did shake *k.*;

28: 19 *k.* of devil must shake; **Mosiah** 29: 6 he to whom *k.* rightly belongs has declined; 29: 6–9 Mosiah[2] fears son might later claim right to *k.*; **Alma** 41: 4 those whose works are evil shall inherit *k.* of devil.

KINGDOM OF GOD (*see also* Church of God; Heaven; Millennium; TG Kingdom of God, in Heaven; Kingdom of God, on Earth; BD Kingdom of Heaven, or Kingdom of God)

1 Ne. 13: 37 those who seek to bring forth Zion shall be lifted up in everlasting *k.* of Lamb; 15: 34 *k.* of God is not filthy; 15: 35 righteous souls to dwell in *k.* of God; **2 Ne.** 9: 18 they who have endured crosses of world shall inherit *k.* of God, prepared from foundation of world; 9: 23 (31: 11–21; Alma 9: 12; 3 Ne. 11: 38; Moro. 10: 26) only those who repent, are baptized, and have faith can be saved in *k.* of God; 10: 25 may God raise up by power of resurrection and atonement to receive eternal *k.* of God; 25: 13 (Mosiah 15: 11; 3 Ne. 11: 33) believers shall be saved in *k.* of God; 33: 12 I pray that many of us, if not all, may be saved in God's *k.*; **Jacob** 2: 18 before ye seek riches, seek *k.* of God; 6: 4 those who do not harden hearts shall be saved in *k.* of God; **Mosiah** 4: 16–18 he who succors not the beggar has no interest in *k.* of God; 18: 18 priests ordained to teach things pertaining to *k.* of God; 27: 26 (Alma 7: 14) unless men become new creatures, they cannot inherit *k.* of God; **Alma** 5: 23–24 murderers cannot have place to sit down in *k.* of God; 5: 50 (9: 25; 10: 20; Hel. 5: 32) *k.* of heaven is at hand; 7: 14 if ye are not born again, ye cannot inherit *k.* of heaven; 7: 19 path of righteousness leads to *k.* of God; 7: 21 (11: 37; 40: 26) no unclean thing can be received into *k.* of God; 29: 17 may God grant that my brethren may sit down in *k.* of God; 39: 9 the unrepentant and lustful cannot inherit *k.* of God; 40: 25 the righteous shall shine forth in *k.* of God; 41: 4 all shall be raised to endless happiness to inherit *k.* of God or endless misery in *k.* of devil; **3 Ne.** 9: 22 (11: 38; Ether 5: 5) those who repent and come as little child will be received in *k.* of God; 12: 3 (Matt. 5: 3) blessed are poor in spirit who come unto Christ, for theirs is *k.* of heaven; 12: 10 (Matt. 5: 10) blessed are they who are persecuted, for theirs is *k.* of heaven; 13: 33 (Matt. 6: 33) seek ye first *k.* of God, and all these things shall be added; 14: 21 (Matt. 7: 21) not every one who says, Lord, shall enter *k.* of heaven; **4 Ne.** 1: 17 people are all in one, children of Christ and heirs of *k.* of God; **Ether** 15: 34 whether Ether is translated or dies matters not if he is saved in *k.* of God; **Moro.** 9: 6 conquer enemy of all righteousness and rest souls in *k.* of God; 10: 21 except ye have charity, ye cannot be saved in *k.* of God.

KING-MEN (*see also* Dissenter; Freedom)

Alma 51: 5 those who desire to alter law to establish king over land are called *k.*; 51: 13 refuse to defend country; 51: 17–19 (60: 16) are slain by army of Moroni[1] or cast into prison; 51: 20–21 are compelled to defend country; 60: 16 prevent Nephites from dispersing enemies; 62: 9 receive trial and are executed.

KISH—*Jaredite king*

Ether 1: 18–19 (10: 17–18) son of Corom, father of Lib[1].

KISHKUMEN—*leader of robbers* (*see also* Gadianton Robbers)

Hel. 1: 9–10 (2: 3) murders Pahoran[2]; 1: 11–12 (2: 3) not found because of covenant of secret combination; 2: 3–9 plans to murder Helaman[3]; 2: 9 killed by servant of Helaman[3]; 6: 18, 24 cofounder of Gadianton robbers.

KISS (*see also* Worship)

3 Ne. 11: 19 Nephi[3] bows himself before the Lord and *k.* his feet; 17: 10 many of the multitude *k.* Christ's feet.

KNEE (*see also* Kneel)

Mosiah 27: 31 (Isa. 45: 23) every *k.* shall bow and every tongue confess before Redeemer; **Alma** 19: 14 Ammon[2] falls upon *k.* and pours out soul to God in thanksgiving; 22: 17 Lamanite king bows down before the Lord upon *k.* and prays.

KNEEL (*see also* Knee)

Enos 1: 4 Enos[2] *k.* before Maker; **3 Ne.** 17: 13 (19: 16) Jesus commands multitude to *k.*; **Moro.** 4: 1–2 elders and priests *k.* with church to offer sacrament prayer.

KNOCK (*see also* Ask)

2 Ne. 9: 42 (3 Ne. 14: 7; 27: 29; Matt. 7: 7) *k.*, and it shall be opened unto you; 32: 4 if ye cannot understand, it is because ye ask not, neither do ye *k.*

KNOW, KNEW, KNOWN (*see also* Comprehend; God, Omniscience of; Knowingly; Knowledge; Learn; Perceive; Revelation, Reveal; Testimony; Understand)

1 Ne. 4: 6 Nephi[1] is led by Spirit, not *k.* beforehand what he should do; 9: 6 (2 Ne. 2: 24; 9: 20; W of M 1: 7; Alma 18: 18; 40: 5; Hel. 8: 8) the Lord *k.* all things from beginning; 15: 9 Laman[1] and Lemuel claim the Lord does not make things *k.* unto them; 17: 13 ye shall *k.* that it is by me that ye are led; 21: 26 (22: 12) all flesh shall *k.* that the Lord is Savior and Redeemer; 22: 2 by Spirit all things are made *k.* unto prophets; **2 Ne.** 2: 18 (Alma 12: 31; 42: 3) by partaking of forbidden fruit, Adam and Eve become as God, *k.* good and evil; 4: 19 I *k.* in whom I have trusted; 9: 20 there is not anything save God *k.* it; 9: 28 the learned set aside God's counsel, thinking they *k.* of themselves; 27: 27 the Lord will show unto those who hide their counsels that he *k.* all their works; 31: 14 if ye deny Christ after receiving Holy Ghost, it would have been better not to have *k.* him; **Jacob** 1: 6 because of revelations, Nephites *k.* of Christ and his kingdom; 4: 4 Nephites write so that those to come will *k.* that they *k.* of Christ; 4: 8 no man *k.* of God's ways save it be revealed unto him; **Mosiah** 4: 11 if ye have *k.* of God's goodness, remember always his greatness; 5: 13 how *k.* a man the master whom he has not served or who is far from his thoughts; 8: 17 seer can *k.* of things past and future, makes *k.* things that could not otherwise be *k.*; 11: 22 people of Noah[3] shall *k.* that I am the Lord their God; 16: 3 all mankind became carnal, *k.* evil from good; 26: 24 if they *k.* me, they shall have place eternally at my right hand; **Alma** 5: 45–46 these things are made *k.* by Spirit; 7: 13 Spirit *k.* all things; 12: 3 (18: 32) God *k.* all thy thoughts, and they are made *k.* by his Spirit; 12: 9 given unto many to *k.* the mysteries of God; 12: 11 to those who harden hearts is given lesser portion of word until they *k.* nothing of mysteries; 26: 21 what natural man *k.* these things; 26: 21 none *k.* these things save the penitent; 26: 22 unto those who repent, exercise faith, bring forth good works, and pray continually, it is given to *k.* mysteries of God; 29: 5 he who *k.* not good from evil is blameless; 32: 18 (Ether 3: 19) if a man *k.* a thing, he hath no cause to believe, for he *k.* it; 32: 19 more cursed is he who *k.* will of God and doeth it not; 36: 4 I would not that ye think I *k.* of myself, but of God; 40: 10 God *k.* all the times appointed unto man; **Hel.** 9: 41 some believe Nephi[2] is a god, otherwise he could not *k.* of all things; 14: 31 God has given unto you to *k.* good from evil; **3 Ne.** 6: 18 Nephites do not sin ignorantly, for they *k.* will of God; 9: 20 converted Lamanites were baptized with fire and Holy Ghost and *k.* it not; 11: 14 multitude feels prints of nail, to *k.* Christ is God of Israel; 13: 3 (Matt. 6: 3) let not left hand *k.* what right hand doest; 13: 8 (Matt. 6: 8) Father *k.* what ye have need before ye ask him; 14: 23 (Matt. 7: 23) the Lord will profess unto many, I never *k.* you; 18: 31 the Lord *k.* his sheep; 20: 39 Christ's people shall *k.* his name; 21: 6 Gentiles to *k.* true points of Christ's doctrine; 28: 27 three Nephites will be among Gentiles, but Gentiles shall *k.* them not; **Morm.** 6: 22 ye are gone and the Father *k.* your state; **Ether** 3: 19 brother of Jared has faith no longer, for he *k.*; 4: 11 he who believeth these things shall be visited with Spirit, shall *k.* and bear record; 5: 3 three witnesses shall *k.* these things are true; **Moro.** 7: 15 given unto you to judge, that ye may *k.* good from evil; 7: 16 Spirit of Christ is given to every man, to *k.* good from evil; 7: 18 ye *k.* the light by which ye may judge; 7: 19 search diligently in light of Christ that ye may *k.* good from evil; 10: 5 by power of Holy Ghost ye may *k.* the truth of all things; 10: 7 by power of Holy Ghost ye may *k.* that Christ is.

KNOWINGLY

3 Ne. 18: 28 ye shall not suffer anyone *k.* to partake of sacrament unworthily.

KNOWLEDGE (*see also* Agency; Faith; God, Omniscience of; Holy Ghost; Ignorance; Know; Learn; Mystery; Scriptures; Study; Testimony; Truth; Understand; Wisdom; TG Knowledge; BD Knowledge)

1 Ne. 22: 4 many are already lost from *k.* of Jews; **2 Ne.** 4: 23 God hath given Nephi[1] *k.* by visions in nighttime; 6: 11 Jews shall come to *k.* of Redeemer; 9: 13 after the resurrection our *k.* shall be perfect; 9: 14 we shall have a perfect *k.* of guilt; 15: 13 (Isa. 5: 13) my people are gone into captivity because they have no *k.*; 21: 2 (Isa. 11: 2) spirit of *k.* shall rest upon him; 21: 9 (30: 15; Isa. 11: 9) earth shall be full of *k.* of the Lord; 32: 7 men will not search *k.*, nor understand great *k.*; **Jacob** 4: 12 why not speak of atonement and attain perfect *k.* of Christ; **W of M** 1: 8 Mormon[2] prays his brethren may come to *k.* of God; **Mosiah** 3: 20 *k.* of Savior shall spread throughout every nation; 4: 12 ye shall grow in *k.* of glory of him who created you; 4: 11 (Isa. 53: 11) by his *k.* shall my righteous servant justify many; 18: 26 priests to wax strong in Spirit, having *k.* of God; 28: 1–2 (Alma 23: 5; 37: 9) sons of Mosiah[2] to bring Lamanites to *k.* of the Lord; 28: 17–18 account of Jaredites gives Nephites much *k.* in which they rejoice; **Alma** 9: 19 Lamanites to destroy Nephites if they fall into sin after receiving so much *k.* from God; 18: 35 portion of Spirit dwelleth in me, which giveth me *k.*; 32: 34 your *k.* is perfect in that thing, and your faith is dormant; 37: 8–9 sacred records bring Lamanites to *k.* of the Lord; 47: 36 dissenters, who were instructed in same *k.* of the Lord, became more hardened; **Hel.** 6: 34 Lamanites grow in *k.* of God; 14: 30 God hath given you *k.* and hath made you free; 15: 13 Lamanites to be brought to *k.* of Redeemer; **3 Ne.** 5: 20 Christ has given much *k.* unto salvation; 5: 23 Christ to bring remnant of seed of Joseph[1] to *k.* of their Lord; 16: 4 if Jews do not ask for *k.* of Nephites, they shall receive it from writings; 20: 13 scattered remnant of Israel shall be brought to *k.* of Redeemer; **Ether** 3: 19–20 because of perfect *k.* brother of Jared[2] could not be kept from beholding within veil; 4: 13 the Lord will show unto Gentiles greater things, *k.* of which is hidden because of unbelief; **Moro.** 7: 15–17 way to judge is plain, that ye may know with perfect *k.*; 10: 10 to another is given to teach word of *k.* by same Spirit.

KORIHOR—*an antichrist* [c. 74 B.C.]

Alma 30: 6, 12–17 preaches against Christ; 30: 18 leads many into wickedness; 30: 19–21 tries to preach to people of Ammon[2], but is rejected; 30: 21 preaches in land of Gideon, but is bound and carried before high priest; 30: 22–29 confrontation with Giddonah, the high priest; 30: 30–55 confrontation with Alma[2]; 30: 43–48 asks for sign; 30: 49–50 is struck dumb; 30: 52–53 confesses he has been deceived by devil; 30: 54–55 Alma[2] refused to remove curse; 30: 56, 58 begs from house to house; 30: 59 is killed by Zoramites.

KUMEN—*one of twelve Nephite disciples* [c. A.D. 34]

3 Ne. 19: 4 is chosen by Jesus to minister to Nephites.

KUMENONHI—*one of twelve Nephite disciples* [c. A.D. 34]

3 Ne. 19: 4 is chosen by Jesus to minister to Nephites.

LABAN—*custodian of brass plates* [c. 600 B.C.] (*see also* Plates, Brass)

1 Ne. 3: 3 has record of Jews; 3: 4–11 sons of Lehi[1] sent to get records from; 3: 12–14 refuses to give up record; 3: 25–26 takes sons' property without giving plates of brass; 3: 29—4: 3 to be delivered into sons' hands; 4: 7–18 is slain by Nephi[1]; 4: 9, 18–19, 21 (2 Ne. 5: 14; Jacob 1: 10; W of M 1: 13; Mosiah 1: 16) sword of; 5: 16 descendant of Joseph[1].

LABOR (*see also* Do; Idleness; Industry; Laborer; Task; Travail; Wages; Work [verb])

1 Ne. 17: 41 *l.* which Israelites had to perform to be healed was to look; **2 Ne.** 5: 17 Nephi[1] causes his people to *l.* with hands; 9: 51 do not *l.* for that which cannot satisfy; 29: 4 do Gentiles remember the *l.* of the Jews; **Jacob** 1: 19 by *l.* with our might their blood should not come upon our garments; 5: 15, 29, 61–62, 71 servants called to *l.* in vineyard; **Mosiah** 2: 14 Benjamin has *l.* with his hands to serve his people; 13: 17 (Ex. 20: 9) six days shalt thou *l.* and do all thy work; 18: 24 (27: 5; Alma 1: 26) priests should *l.* with own hands for their support; 27: 4 every man should *l.* with own hands for his support; **Alma** 1: 3, 12 Nehor claims priests ought not *l.* with hands; 8: 10 Alma[2] *l.* much in spirit, wrestling with God in mighty prayer; 24: 18 converted Lamanites covenant to *l.* abundantly with hands rather than spend days in idleness; 29: 15 missionaries have *l.* exceedingly and brought forth much fruit; 30: 31 Korihor accuses priests of glutting on people's *l.*; 30: 32 Alma[2] has *l.* with own hands for support; 30: 34 if we receive nothing for *l.* in church, what doth it profit us to *l.* in church save to declare truth; 34: 32 this life is day for men to perform *l.*; 36: 24 Alma[2] has *l.*, without ceasing, to bring souls unto repentance; 36: 25 the Lord gives joy in fruit of *l.*; **Moro.** 9: 6 if we cease to *l.*, we should be brought under condemnation.

LABORER (*see also* Labor)

2 Ne. 26: 30 if men have charity, they would not suffer *l.* in Zion to perish; 26: 31 *l.* in Zion shall labor for Zion.

LACHONEUS[1]—*Nephite chief judge* [c. A.D. 1]

3 Ne. 1: 1 chief judge and governor over the land; 3: 1–10 receives epistle from robber leader; 3: 11–13, 22–25 gathers all the people and provisions in one place; 3: 14, 25 causes fortifications to be built; 3: 15 calls people to repentance; 3: 16 marvelous words and prophecies of *L.* cause people to fear; 3: 17 appoints chief captains over armies; 6: 6 helps establish peace; 6: 19 succeeded by son.

LACHONEUS[2]—*son of Lachoneus[1]* [c. A.D. 29-30]

3 Ne. 6: 19 follows father as chief judge.

LADEN (*see also* Burden)

1 Ne. 17: 25 children of Israel were *l.* with grievous tasks in bondage; **Mosiah** 2: 14 Benjamin labors so people will not be *l.* with taxes.

LAID (*see* Lay, Laid)

LAKE (*see also* Hell; Torment)

2 Ne. 9: 16 (28: 23; Jacob 3: 11; 6: 10; Mosiah 3: 27; Alma 12: 17; 14: 14) torment of the unrighteous is as *l.* of fire and brimstone; 9: 19, 26 God delivers saints and those without law from *l.* of fire and brimstone.

LAMAH—*Nephite commander* [c. A.D. 385]

Morm. 6: 14 and his ten thousand have fallen.

LAMAN[1]—*eldest son of Lehi[1]* [c. 600 B.C.] (*see also* Laman, River; Lamanite)

1 Ne. 2: 5 travels into wilderness with family; 2: 9 is admonished to be like river, continually running into fountain of all righteousness; 2: 11–12 (3: 28; 16: 36) murmurs against father; 2: 18 does not hearken unto Nephi[1]; 3: 11–14 tries unsuccessfully to obtain brass plates from Laban; 3: 28 smites Nephi[1] and Sam with rod; 7: 6 rebels; 8: 35–36 does not partake of fruit of tree of life; 16: 7 takes daughter of Ishmael[1] to wife; 16: 20 murmurs because of afflictions in wilderness; 16: 37–38 stirs up Lemuel and sons of Ishmael[1] to kill Nephi[1]; 17: 17–18 murmurs against desire of Nephi[1] to build ship; 18: 11–19 binds Nephi[1] in cords; **2 Ne.** 1: 24–29 Lehi[1] exhorts *L.* to hearken unto Nephi[1]; 4: 3–7 Lehi[1] counsels *L.* and his family; 5: 21 (Alma 3: 7) cursing comes upon followers of *L.*; **Alma** 18: 38 Ammon[2] rehearses unto Lamanites concerning rebellion of *L.* and Lemuel.

LAMAN[2]—*Lamanite king* [c. 200 B.C.]

Mosiah 7: 21 (9: 10; 10: 18) deceives Zeniff; 9: 11–13 stirs up his people against people of Zeniff; 10: 6 dies.

LAMAN[3]—*son of Laman[2]* [c. 178 B.C.]

Mosiah 10: 6 replaces father as king; 24: 3 is called after his father, king over numerous people; 24: 9 Amulon is subject to *L.*

LAMAN[4]—*Nephite soldier*

Alma 55: 4 sought out by Moroni[1], who desires a descendant of Laman[1]; 55: 5 (47: 29) formerly servant of Lamanite king; 55: 6–15 entices Lamanite guards into becoming drunk.

LAMAN, CITY OF

3 Ne. 9: 10 is burned at time of crucifixion.

LAMAN, RIVER—*river emptying into Red Sea* (*see also* Laman[1])

1 Ne. 2: 6–9 named by Lehi[1]; 16: 12 Lehites cross river.

LAMANITE—*descendant of Laman[1], later any person who rejects the gospel* (*see also* Ammon[2], People of; Lamanitish)

1 Ne. 12: 20 will overcome seed of Nephi[1]; 12: 23 (2 Ne. 5: 21–24; Jacob 3: 3–5; Alma 3: 6, 15–16, 19; Morm. 5: 15) cursed; **2 Ne.** 5: 14 a threat to Nephites; 5: 25 to be a scourge to Nephites; 30: 6 to be pure and delightsome people; **Jacob** 1: 13–14 seek to destroy Nephites; 2: 35 treat families better than Nephites; 3: 3 not filthy like Nephites; 7: 24 many means devised to restore *L.* to truth are vain; **Enos** 1: 11–13 Enos[2] prays for preservation of *L.*; 1: 16 records to be brought to *L.*; 1: 20 (Jarom 1: 6; Mosiah 9: 12; 10: 12) are bloodthirsty and idolatrous; 1: 24 (Jarom 1: 7; Omni 1: 10, 24; Alma 25: 3; 28: 3–10; 35: 13; 43: 3; 48: 21–22; Morm. 2: 1) wars between Nephites and *L.*; **Jarom** 1: 2 records written for *L.*; **W of M** 1: 13–14 are driven back by Nephites; **Mosiah** 1: 5 (10: 12–17; Alma 9: 16) traditions of fathers cause unbelief of *L.*; 7: 15, 22 Limhi's people in bondage to *L.*; 9: 14–15 slay Zeniff's flocks, but are driven out; 10: 8 (Alma 3: 4, 6, 15–16, 18) appearance of *L.*; 19: 10–22 defeat people of Noah[3] and make them pay tribute; 20: 3–6 daughters of *L.* taken by priests of Noah[3]; 21: 15 the Lord softens *L*'s hearts; 22: 10–11 Limhi's people escape from *L.*; 23: 29 possess land of Helam; 23: 35 priests of Noah[3] join *L.*; 24: 4 are taught by priests of Noah[3]; 24: 7 prosper; 28: 1–9 (Alma ch. 17–28) sons of Mosiah[2] preach gospel among *L.*; **Alma** 2: 24 joined by Amlicites; 3: 10 dissenters marked like *L.*; 9: 16 the Lord extends merciful promises to *L.*; 16: 2–3 (25: 2) destroy city of Ammonihah; 17: 4 (19: 31–36; 23: 3–13) many *L.* converted; 17: 16–19 Ammon[2] begins ministry among *L.*; 19: 35–36 (23: 4–5) many *L.* are converted and baptized; 21: 23 converted *L.* are zealous for keeping commandments; 22: 27 division of land between Nephites and *L.*; 23: 6 after conversion, *L.* stand steadfast in truth; 23: 7 (24: 6) *L.* lay down weapons; 23: 17 (24: 3) *L.* converts take new name, Anti-Nephi-Lehies; 24: 1–2, 20–26 slaughter converts, more are converted; 25: 1 swear vengeance on Nephites; 25: 3 are driven and slain in battles with Nephites; 25: 4–5 many converts perish by fire; 27: 26 converted *L.* are called people of Ammon[2]; 28: 1–2 follow and slaughter converts; 28: 2–3 are slain and driven out; 43: 19, 37–38 are not as well equipped for war as Nephites; 43: 43 fight with great courage; 44: 15 make covenant of peace; 45: 14 in end, surviving Nephites will be numbered among *L.*; 47: 4–35

Amalickiah becomes king of *L.*; 49: 4 are astonished at Nephite fortifications; 49: 25 are defeated; 50: 7 are driven by army of Moroni[1]; 52: 2 retreat to captured cities; 52: 8 kept prisoner for ransom by Nephites; 54: 3 take women and children as prisoners; 55: 33 fortify Morianton; 56: 12 slay all prisoners except captains; 56: 24 fear the Nephites; 57: 22 are driven to city of Manti; 58: 28 lose city of Manti; 59: 7–11 take city of Nephihah; 62: 14–15 many *L.* captured by Moroni[1]; 62: 24–25 flee to land of Moroni; 63: 15 are driven back to own lands; **Hel.** 1: 22, 27, 33 capture and lose Zarahemla; 4: 5 recapture Zarahemla; 5: 17–19, 50 many *L.* are converted by sons of Helaman[3]; 5: 50–52 yield up lands; 6: 1, 36 (13: 1) many *L.* become more righteous than Nephites; 6: 4 many *L.* preach to Nephites; 6: 6–8 peace between Nephites and *L.*; 6: 9 *L.* and Nephites become exceedingly rich; 6: 37 hunt Gadianton robbers and preach gospel to them; **3 Ne.** 2: 12–14 unite with and are called Nephites; 2: 15 curse taken from *L.* when converted; 2: 16 children become fair like Nephites; 6: 14 church broken up except among a few *L.*; 9: 20 baptized by fire and Holy Ghost because of faith; 10: 18 *L.* and Nephites receive great blessings; **4 Ne.** 1: 2–3 Nephites and *L.* all converted, all things held common; 1: 17 name abolished; 1: 20 name revived; 1: 38 unbelievers called *L.*; 1: 39 are taught to hate; **Morm.** 4: 1–2 drive Nephites to land of Desolation; 4: 11 *L.* and Nephites delight in shedding blood; 4: 13–14 take cities Desolation and Teancum, sacrifice women and children; 4: 18 sweep Nephites before them from this time on; 6: 7–15 slay all Nephites, except twenty-four; 7: 1–10 *L.* are of Israel; 8: 8 (Moro. 1: 2) dissension among *L.*; 8: 9 with robbers, *L.* possess land; **Ether** 4: 3 reject gospel of Christ; 8: 20 secret combinations among *L.*; **Moro.** 1: 1–2 *L.* put to death believers in Christ

LAMANITISH

Alma 17: 26 Ammon[2] tends flocks with *L.* servants; 19: 16 Abish a *L.* woman who had been converted to the Lord.

LAMB (*see also* Animal; Jesus Christ—Lamb of God; Sheep)

2 Ne. 21: 6 (30: 12; Isa. 11: 6) wolf shall dwell with *l.*; **Mosiah** 14: 7 (Isa. 53: 7) he is brought as *l.* to slaughter; **3 Ne.** 28: 22 (4 Ne. 1: 33) disciples play with wild beasts as child with *l.*

LAME (*see also* Heal)

Mosiah 3: 5 (3 Ne. 17: 7–9; 26: 15) the Lord shall cause the *l.* to walk; **4 Ne.** 1: 5 disciples of Jesus cause the *l.* to walk.

LAMENT, LAMENTATION (*see also* Cry; Grieve; Mourn; Sorrow; Wail; Weep)

2 Ne. 13: 26 (Isa. 3: 26) her gates shall *l.*; **Mosiah** 21: 9 great *l.* among people of Limhi; **Alma** 28: 4 time of great *l.* among Nephites; **Hel.** 6: 33 Nephites grow in iniquity, to great *l.* of the righteous; 7: 15 because of *l.* of Nephi[2] the people gather around him; 13: 32–33 in days of destruction, Nephites will *l.* that they did not repent; **3 Ne.** 10: 2 survivors of destruction cease to *l.* for loss of kindred; 10: 10 *l.* is turned into praise and thanksgiving unto Christ; **Morm.** 2: 11 *l.* in land because of robbers; **Ether** 15: 16 Jaredite survivors take up *l.* for loss of the slain.

LAMONI—*Lamanite king converted by Ammon*[2]

Alma 17: 21 descendant of Ishmael[2]; 17: 21–23 Ammon[2] carried before *L.*; 17: 24 offers to give Ammon[2] one of his daughters to wife; 17: 25–39 sets Ammon[2] to watch flocks; 18: 1–5, 8–12 is astonished at power of Ammon[2], believes him to be Great Spirit; 18: 11–15 fears Ammon[2]; 18: 18–21 asks Ammon[2] about Great Spirit; 18: 22–39 is taught by Ammon[2]; 18: 40–41 believes and cries unto the Lord; 18: 42–43 (19: 6) falls to earth, overcome by Spirit; 19: 12–13 arises, testifies of Redeemer, and sinks again with joy; 20: 1 asks Ammon[2] to go with him to land of Nephi to teach his father; 20: 2–7 journeys with Ammon[2] toward Middoni to free brethren from prison; 20: 8–16 meets father, who threatens to kill him for befriending a Nephite; 20: 17–25 is defended by Ammon[2]; 20: 28 proceeds to land of Middoni and frees brethren of Ammon[2] from prison; 21: 18 returns to land of Ishmael with Ammon[2]; 21: 20–22 builds synagogues and teaches his people; 22: 1–27 Aaron[2] teaches *L.*'s father; 24: 5–17 Ammon[2] and his brethren hold council with *L.* and his brother concerning defense of Anti-Nephi-Lehies.

LAND (*see also* Country; Earth; Ground; Inherit; Law, Civil; Nation; Promised Land)

1 Ne. 2: 20 (4: 14; 14: 1–2; 2 Ne. 1: 9, 20; Jarom 1: 9; Omni 1: 6; Ether 2: 8–11) if people keep commandments, they will prosper in the *l.*; 2: 20 (2 Ne. 1: 5; 3: 2; 10: 19; Ether 1: 38, 42; 2: 7, 10, 15; 9: 20; 10: 28; 13: 2) this *l.* is choice above all other lands; 17: 38 the Lord leadeth away the righteous into precious *l.*; **2 Ne.** 1: 7 (10: 11; Mosiah 29: 32; Ether 2: 12) this *l.* is to be a *l.* of liberty; 1: 7 if iniquity abound, *l.* to be cursed; 23: 14 (Isa. 13: 14) every man shall flee into his own *l.*; **Alma** 22: 32 small neck of *l.*

between *l.* northward and *l.* southward; 35: 14 (43: 47; 48: 10) Nephites fight to defend their *l.*; **3 Ne.** 8: 18 broken rocks found upon all the face of the *l.*; 20: 22 (21: 22–23; Ether 13: 4, 8) New Jerusalem to be built upon this *l.*

LANGUAGE (*see also* Chaldea, Chaldaic; Characters; Communication; Egyptian; Hebrew; Interpretation; Speak; Speech; Tongue; Translation; Word; Write; Writing; TG Language)

1 Ne. 1: 2 (Mosiah 1: 4) Nephi[1] writes in *l.* of father, which consists of learning of Jews and *l.* of Egyptians; **2 Ne.** 31: 3 the Lord speaks unto men according to their *l.*; **Omni** 1: 17 *l.* of people of Zarahemla has become corrupted; 1: 22 (Mosiah 28: 17; Ether 1: 33–37) the Lord confounded *l.* at time of tower; 1: 25 (Moro. 10: 16) believe in gift of interpreting *l.*; **Mosiah** 1: 2 Benjamin teaches his sons in all *l.* of his fathers; 1: 4 Lehi[1] could read brass plates because he had been taught in *l.* of Egyptians; 8: 11–12 Limhi desires to have twenty-four gold plates translated into his *l.*; 24: 4 *l.* of Nephi[1] is taught among Lamanites; 28: 13–14 (Morm. 9: 34–35; Ether 3: 22–23) Urim and Thummim prepared for purpose of interpreting *l.*; **Alma** 5: 61 Alma[2] commands in *l.* of him who hath commanded him; **3 Ne.** 5: 18 many things which Nephites, according to their *l.*, cannot write; **Morm.** 9: 34–35 because no other people know Nephites' *l.*, the Lord has prepared means for interpretation.

LASCIVIOUSNESS (*see also* Carnal; Lust)

Jacob 3: 12 Jacob[2] warns against *l.*; **Alma** 16: 18 priests preach against all manner of *l.*; 45: 11–12 Nephites to become extinct because of *l.*; 47: 36 dissenters give way to all manner of *l.*; **4 Ne.** 1: 16 no *l.* among people after Christ's visit.

LAST (*see also* End; Final; First; Last Days)

Alma 12: 36 the Lord sends down wrath according to his word in *l.* provocation, unto *l.* death as well as first; 34: 10–15 Son will be great and *l.* sacrifice.

LAST DAYS (*see also* Day of the Lord; Destruction; Israel, Gathering of; Jesus Christ, Second Coming of; Judgment; Lift; Millennium; Restoration; TG Last Days)

2 Ne. 25: 8 prophecies of Isaiah[1] to be of great worth in *l.* days; 26: 14 I prophesy unto you concerning *l.* days, when the Lord shall bring these things forth; 27: 1 in *l.* days, or days of Gentiles, all nations shall be drunken with iniquity; **Mosiah** 26: 28 he who will not hear my voice I will not receive at *l.* day; **3 Ne.** 15: 1 (27: 22) whoso does Christ's sayings shall be lifted up at *l.* day; 16: 7 in latter day, truth shall come unto Gentiles.

LATCHET

1 Ne. 10: 8 (Mark 1: 7) John the Baptist to feel unworthy to unloose *l.* of Christ's shoe; **2 Ne.** 15: 27 (Isa. 5: 27) *l.* of their shoes shall not be broken.

LATTER DAY (*see* Last Days)

LAUGH, LAUGHTER (*see also* Scorn; TG Laughter, Laugh)

Alma 26: 23 Nephites *l.* at sons of Mosiah[2] for preaching to Lamanites; **3 Ne.** 9: 2 the devil *l.* because of the slain.

LAW (*see also* Agency; Commandments of God; Crime; Decree; Law, Civil; Law of Moses; Lawful; Obedience; Ordinance; Punishment; Statute; Transgression; TG Law)

2 Ne. 2: 5 by *l.* is not flesh justified; 2: 5 by temporal *l.* were men cut off, and by spiritual *l.* they perish from the good; 2: 26 men are free not to be acted upon, save by punishment of *l.* at last day; 8: 4 (Isa. 51: 4) *l.* shall proceed from me; 8: 7 (Isa. 51: 7) hearken unto me, ye in whose heart I have written my *l.*; 9: 25 where no *l.* is given, there is no punishment; 12: 3 (Isa. 2: 3) out of Zion shall go forth the *l.*; **Mosiah** 29: 13 if you could have just men as kings, who would establish *l.* of God, it would be expedient to have kings; **Alma** 42: 17 how could he sin if there was no *l.*; 42: 17 how could there be a *l.* save there was a punishment; 42: 21 if there was no *l.*, what could justice or mercy do; 42: 22 there is a *l.* given, and a punishment fixed; 42: 23 men will be judged according to their works, according to *l.* and justice; **Moro.** 8: 22 all they who are without *l.* are alive in Christ; 8: 22 power of redemption cometh on all them who have no *l.*

LAW, CIVIL (*see also* Crime; Government, Civil)

Mosiah 29: 15 he who commits iniquity is punished according to *l.* given by fathers; 29: 25 choose ye judges that ye may be judged according to *l.* given by fathers; **Alma** 1: 1 Mosiah[2] had established *l.* acknowledged by people; 1: 32–33 *l.* is put in force upon all who transgress it; 30: 7, 11 no *l.* among Nephites against a man's belief; 34: 12 *l.* requires life of him who has murdered; **Hel.** 4: 22 Nephites have trampled under feet the *l.* of Mosiah[2]; 5: 2 *l.* and governments established by voice of people; **3 Ne.** 6: 4 Nephites have formed their *l.* according to equity and justice; 6: 24 contrary to *l.* of land for anyone to be put to death except power is given by governor; 6: 30 judges and lawyers set at defiance the *l.* and rights of country.

LAW OF MOSES (*see also* Carnal; Commandments of God; Jesus Christ, Types of; Law; Offering; Sacrifice)

1 Ne. 4: 16 *l.* was engraven upon brass plates; 17: 22 people of Jerusalem were righteous, kept commandments according to *l.* of Moses; **2 Ne.** 5: 10 (25: 24; Jarom 1: 5; Alma 30: 3) Nephites kept commandments according to *l.* of Moses; 11: 4 (25: 24–30; Jacob 4: 5–6; Alma 25: 15; 34: 14) *l.* of Moses has been given to point the people toward Christ; 25: 25 *l.* is dead unto us, and we are alive in Christ; 25: 25 we keep the *l.* because of the commandments; **Mosiah** 3: 14 because his people were stiffnecked, the Lord gave them *l.* of Moses; 12: 28–29 if ye teach *l.* of Moses, why do ye not keep it; 13: 30–32 *l.* of performances and ordinances given to keep people in remembrance of God; **Hel.** 13: 1 Lamanites observe commandments, according to *l.* of Moses; **3 Ne.** 1: 24–25 some teach that Nephites should not observe *l.* of Moses because Christ has been born; 9: 17 (12: 17–18; 15: 4–5; Matt. 5: 17–18) in Christ is *l.* of Moses fulfilled; 12: 17 (Matt. 5: 17) think not that I am come to destroy the *l.*; 12: 18 (Matt. 5: 18) not one jot nor one tittle hath passed away from the *l.*; 14: 12 (Matt. 7: 12) all things ye would that men should do to you, do ye to them, for this is the *l.* and the prophets; 15: 5 Christ is he that gave the *l.*; 25: 4 (Mal. 4: 4) remember ye *l.* of Moses; **4 Ne.** 1: 12 Nephites do not walk any more after performances and ordinances of *l.* of Moses; **Ether** 12: 11 by faith was *l.* of Moses given.

LAWFUL (*see also* Right [adj.])

3 Ne. 26: 18 not *l.* to write unspeakable things seen by those filled with Holy Ghost.

LAWYERS (*see also* Judge [noun])

Alma 10: 15 *l.* are learned in arts and cunning; 10: 27 foundation of destruction is being laid by unrighteousness of *l.* and judges; **3 Ne.** 6: 11 many merchants and *l.* in land; 6: 21 chief judges, *l.*, and high priests are angry with prophets; 6: 27–30 *l.* and high priests enter into secret combination.

LAY, LAID (*see also* Die; Foundation; Hands, Laying on of; Hold; Jesus Christ, Death of; Life)

2 Ne. 3: 12 writings shall *l.* down contentions; **Jacob** 5: 13, 18–20, 23, 27, 29, 71, 76 Lord of vineyard will *l.* up fruit; **Alma** 7: 15 *l.* aside every sin.

LAZINESS, LAZY (*see also* Idleness; Labor; Slothful)

Mosiah 9: 12 Lamanites are *l.* and idolatrous; 11: 6 priests of Noah[3] are supported in *l.* by taxes.

LEAD, LED (*see also* Course; Direction; Guide; Inspire; Invite; Preside)

1 Ne. 4: 6 Nephi[1] is *l.* by Spirit; 14: 3 abominable church founded by devil to *l.* souls down to hell; 16: 16 directions of Liahona *l.* Lehites in more fertile parts of wilderness; 17: 24 the Lord commanded Moses to *l.* Israelites out of bondage; 17: 38 the Lord *l.* the righteous into precious lands; **2 Ne.** 10: 22 the Lord has *l.* away from time to time from house of Israel; 13: 12 (Isa. 3: 12) they who *l.* thee cause thee to err; 21: 6 (30: 12; Isa. 11: 6) little child shall *l.* them; 28: 14 they are *l.* that they do err because they are taught precepts of men; 28: 21 by lulling them into carnal security, devil *l.* men carefully down to hell; **Mosiah** 27: 8–10 Alma[2] and sons of Mosiah[2] *l.* astray people of the Lord; **Alma** 1: 7 Nehor tries to *l.* away people of church; 4: 11 because of wickedness, example of church *l.* unbelievers into iniquity; 13: 28 be *l.* by Holy Spirit; 21: 16 missionaries go forth whithersoever they are *l.* by Spirit; 34: 39 pray continually that ye be not *l.* away by temptations of devil; 36: 28 the Lord *l.* Israelites by his power into promised land; 39: 12 command thy children to do good, lest they *l.* away hearts of many; **Hel.** 3: 29 word of God *l.* man of Christ across everlasting gulf of misery; 15: 7 holy scriptures *l.* Lamanites to faith and repentance; **3 Ne.** 13: 12 (Matt. 6: 13) *l.* us not into temptation; **Morm.** 5: 17 Nephites were once *l.* by God; **Ether** 4: 12 I am the same that *l.* men to all good; **Moro.** 6: 9 Holy Ghost *l.* church whether to preach, exhort, pray, or sing.

LEADER (*see also* Lead; Ruler; TG Leadership)

2 Ne. 19: 16 (Isa. 9: 16) *l.* of this people cause them to err; **Jarom** 1: 7 Nephite *l.* were mighty men in faith of the Lord; **Omni** 1: 28 their *l.*, Zeniff, was a strong, mighty, stiffnecked man; **3 Ne.** 7: 11 *l.* of tribes establish laws; **Morm.** 2: 1 Nephites appoint Mormon[2] their *l.*; 8: 28 *l.* of churches shall rise in pride.

LEARN (*see also* Comprehend; Know; Learned [adj.]; Learning; Study; Teach; Understand)

2 Ne. 12: 4 (Isa. 2: 4) neither shall

they *l.* war any more; 27: 35 (Isa. 29: 24) they that murmured shall *l.* doctrine; **Alma** 32: 12 it is well that ye are cast out of synagogues, that ye may *l.* wisdom; 37: 35 *l.* wisdom in thy youth; 38: 9 I have told you this that ye may *l.* wisdom; **Morm.** 9: 31 God hath manifested unto you our imperfections, that ye may *l.* to be more wise than we have been.

LEARNED [adj.] (*see also* Learn; Learning; Wisdom)

2 Ne. 9: 29 to be *l.* is good if they hearken to counsels of God; 9: 42 the Lord despises the *l.* who are puffed up; 27: 15–20 prophecy concerning *l.* man who will not read sealed book; **Jacob** 7: 4 Sherem is *l.* with perfect knowledge of language; **Alma** 10: 15 lawyers are *l.* in arts and cunning.

LEARNER (*see* Teacher)

LEARNING (*see also* Knowledge; Learn; Learned [adj.]; Scriptures; Truth; Wisdom)

1 Ne. 1: 1 Nephi[1] is taught in *l.* of father; 19: 23 Nephi[1] likens scriptures unto Nephites, to be for their *l.*; **2 Ne.** 2: 14 I speak unto you these things for your *l.*; 4: 15 Nephi[1] writes scriptures for *l.* of his children; 26: 20 Gentiles will preach up unto themselves their own *l.*; **3 Ne.** 6: 12 people distinguished by ranks, according to chances for *l.*, which depend upon riches.

LEAST (*see also* Less)

Alma 42: 30 do not endeavor to excuse yourself in the *l.* point; 45: 16 the Lord cannot look upon sin with *l.* degree of allowance.

LEAVE, LEFT (*see also* Depart; Left [adj.])

1 Ne. 3: 26 sons of Lehi[1] are obliged to *l.* behind property with Laban; **2 Ne.** 14: 3 (Isa. 4: 3) they that are *l.* in Zion shall be called holy; **Alma** 1: 26 priests *l.* labors to preach, and people *l.* labors to hear; 13: 3 those called according to God's foreknowledge are *l.* to choose good or evil; **3 Ne.** 25: 1 (Mal. 4: 1) day of the Lord will *l.* the wicked neither root nor branch; **Morm.** 2: 26 Nephites are *l.* to themselves, that Spirit does not abide in them.

LEBANON (*see also* BD Lebanon)

2 Ne. 12: 13 (Isa. 2: 13) day of the Lord shall come upon cedars of *L.*; 20: 34 (Isa. 10: 34) *L.* shall fall by a mighty one; 24: 8 (Isa. 14: 8) cedars of *L.* rejoice at thee; 27: 28 *L.* shall be turned into fruitful field.

LED (*see* Lead, Led)

LEFT [adj.] (*see also* Leave, Left; Right Hand)

Mosiah 5: 10 whosoever shall not take upon himself the name of Christ shall find himself on *l.* hand of God.

LEHI[1]—*Hebrew prophet who led his followers to promised land in western hemisphere* [c. 600 B.C.] (*see also* Lehi, Book of)

1 Ne. 1: 5 prays to the Lord on behalf of his people; 1: 6–15 sees visions; 1: 16 writes many things he has seen in visions and dreams; 1: 18–20 (Hel. 8: 22) prophesies among Jews, is rejected; 2: 1–4 (Alma 9: 9; 10: 3; Hel. 8: 22; Ether 13: 5) flees Jerusalem with family; 2: 9–14 admonishes elder sons; 2: 15 dwells in tent; 3: 2–4 sends sons to obtain brass plates; 5: 6 comforts Sariah; 5: 10–15 (Mosiah 1: 4) reads brass plates; 5: 14 (2 Ne. 3: 4; Alma 10: 3) a descendant of Joseph[1]; 5: 17–19 prophesies concerning his seed and brass plates; 7: 1–2 sends sons to bring family of Ishmael[1] into wilderness; 8: 2–28 explains dream of tree of life; 10: 2–16 prophesies Babylonian captivity, coming of Christ, future of Jews; 16: 9, 11–12 voice of the Lord commands *L.* to take journey into wilderness; 16: 10 finds Liahona; 16: 20 begins to murmur against the Lord because of afflictions; 16: 23–31 asks the Lord where Nephi[1] should hunt for food; 16: 25 is chastened because of murmuring against the Lord; 18: 7 begets two sons in wilderness; 18: 8–23 sails to promised land; **2 Ne.** 1: 1–3 speaks unto family concerning great things the Lord has done for them; 1: 4 sees in vision that Jerusalem has been destroyed; 1: 6–12 prophesies concerning promised land; 1: 13–23 admonishes sons to keep commandments; 1: 24–29 admonishes sons to hearken unto Nephi[1]; 1: 30–32 blesses Zoram[1]; 2: 1–30 teachings to Jacob[2] concerning Christ, opposition, the Fall, and redemption; 3: 1–4, 25 blesses Joseph[2]; 3: 5–24 teaches concerning prophecy of Joseph[1]; 4: 3–11 blesses grandchildren; 4: 12 dies; **Jacob** 2: 34 commandments were given to *L.*; **Alma** 10: 3 descendant of Manasseh; **Hel.** 6: 10 the Lord brought *L.* into land south.

LEHI[2]—*son of Zoram[2], possibly same as Lehi[3]* [c. 81 B.C.]

Alma 16: 5–8 goes with father and brother to rescue captured brethren.

LEHI[3]—*Nephite military commander* [c. 74 B.C.]

Alma 43: 35 encircles Lamanites with his army; 43: 36–53 pursues Lamanite army; 49: 16–17 is appointed chief captain over city of Noah; 52: 27–36 (62: 32–34) assists Moroni[1] in defeating

Lamanites; 53: 2 is given command of city of Mulek; 61: 15–21 (62: 3, 13) is left in charge of men and provisions; 62: 37 laments Teancum's death; **Hel.** 1: 28 assists Moronihah.

LEHI[4]—*son of Helaman[2], great missionary* [c. 45 B.C.]

Hel. 3: 21 younger son of Helaman[2]; 4: 14 preaches and prophesies many things; 5: 4 with brother, Nephi[2], preaches all his days; 5: 18–19 converts eight thousand Lamanites; 5: 20–21 goes to land of Nephi, cast into prison with Nephi[2]; 5: 22–25 is miraculously freed from prison; 5: 26–37 preaches to Lamanites, face shines in darkness; 5: 44 is encircled with fire, has unspeakable joy; 6: 6 goes with Nephi[2] to preach in land northward; 11: 19 not a whit behind Nephi[2] in righteousness; 11: 23 preaches, putting end to much strife; **Ether** 12: 14 by faith of Nephi[2] and *L.* was change wrought upon Lamanites.

LEHI, BOOK OF

1 Ne. 19: 1 Nephi[1] engraves record of *L.* on plates.

LEHI, CITY OF AND LAND OF[1]—*land adjoining land of Morianton and containing city of Lehi*

Alma 50: 15 city of *L.* built in north by seashore; 50: 25–26 border dispute between lands of *L.* and Morianton; 50: 26 people of Morianton take up arms against people of *L.*; 50: 27–28 people of *L.* flee to Moroni[1]; 50: 36 peace and union between people of *L.* and people of Morianton; 51: 24 people of *L.* gather, prepare for battle; 51: 26 city of *L.* is captured by Amalickiah; 62: 30 Moroni[1] goes to land of *L.* to battle Lamanites.

LEHI, LAND OF[2]—*apparently the entire land south*

Hel. 6: 10 the land south was called *L.*

LEHI-NEPHI, CITY OF AND LAND OF—*also called land of Nephi, of which it is a part* (*see also* Nephi, Land of)

Mosiah 7: 1–4 Mosiah[2] sends expedition to find those who had returned to land of *L-N.*; 9: 1, 6 Zeniff is allowed to possess land; 9: 8 Zeniff repairs walls of city of *L-N.*

LEHONTI—*Lamanite officer* [c. 72 B.C.]

Alma 47: 8–19 is lured into trap by Amalickiah and poisoned.

LEMUEL—*second son of Lehi[1]* [c. 600 B.C.] (*see also* Lemuel, Valley of; Lemuelites)

1 Ne. 2: 5 one of four sons of Lehi[1], travels in wilderness with family; 2: 10 Lehi[1] admonishes *L.* to be steadfast, like valley; 2: 11–13 murmurs against father; 2: 14 is confounded by father; 2: 18 does not hearken unto Nephi[1]; 2: 21, 23 is threatened with curse; 3: 4–10 is sent with brothers for brass plates; 3: 28 (2 Ne. 4: 13) angry with Nephi[1], hearkens unto Laman[1]; 3: 29–31 smites younger brothers with rod, is stopped by angel; 7: 6 rebels against Nephi[1] and Lehi[1]; 8: 4, 17–18, 35–36 Lehi[1] fears for *L.* because of dream; 16: 7 takes a daughter of Ishmael[1] to wife; 16: 20 murmurs because of afflictions; 16: 37 plots with Laman[1] against lives of father and brother; 16: 39 is chastened by voice of the Lord; 18: 11 with Laman[1], binds Nephi[1]; **2 Ne.** 1: 28 Lehi[1] admonishes *L.* to hearken unto Nephi[1]; 4: 8–9 Lehi[1] blesses *L*'s family; 5: 21 (Alma 3: 7) is cursed because of iniquity; **Alma** 18: 38 Ammon[2] speaks about rebellion of *L.*

LEMUEL, CITY OF—*Lamanite city*

Alma 23: 12–13 inhabitants are converted to the Lord.

LEMUEL, VALLEY OF—*near borders of Red Sea*

1 Ne. 2: 10 Lehi[1] admonishes *L.* to be steadfast like valley; 2: 14 Lehi[1] speaks to Laman and Lemuel in valley of *L.*; 9: 1 (10: 16; 16: 6) family of Lehi[1] dwells in valley of *L.*; 16: 12 Lehites depart.

LEMUELITES—*descendants of Lemuel*

Jacob 1: 13 people called Lamanites, *L.*, Ishmaelites; **Alma** 24: 29 those who join people of the Lord are actual descendants of Laman[1] and Lemuel; 43: 13 Lamanites are compound of Laman and Lemuel and Nephite dissenters; 47: 35 (Morm. 1: 8–9) Lamanites composed of Lamanites, *L.*, Ishmaelites, Nephite dissenters; **4 Ne.** 1: 38 those who reject gospel are called Lamanites, *L.*, Ishmaelites.

LEND (*see also* Borrow; Give)

2 Ne. 28: 30 blessed are they who *l.* ear to the Lord's counsel; **Mosiah** 2: 21 God preserves you from day to day, *l.* you breath; **Ether** 14: 2 people would not borrow or *l.*

LENGTHEN (*see also* Increase; Prolong; Stretch)

2 Ne. 2: 21 men's time was *l.*. that they might repent in flesh; 28: 32 the Lord will *l.* his arm unto Gentiles; **Hel.** 7: 24 the Lord will *l.* Lamanites' days because they have not sinned against greater knowledge; 12: 14 if the Lord says to earth, Go back, that it *l.* the day, it is done; **3 Ne.** 22: 2 (Isa. 54: 2) *l.* thy cords and strengthen thy stakes.

LEOPARD

2 Ne. 21: 6 (30: 12; Isa. 11: 6) *l.* shall lie down with kid.

LEPROUS (*see also* Disease; Heal; BD Leper; Leprosy)

3 Ne. 17: 7 Nephites to bring the *l.* to Christ to be healed.

LESS, LESSER (*see also* Dust; Least)

Alma 12: 10–11 he who hardens heart receives *l.* portion of word; **3 Ne.** 2: 1 people become *l.* and *l.* astonished at sign or wonder from heaven; 11: 40 (18: 13) whoso declares more or *l.* than Christ's doctrine is not built upon rock.

LEVI[1]—*son of Jacob[1]* (*see also* BD Levi)

3 Ne. 24: 3 (Mal. 3: 3) the Lord shall purify sons of *L.*

LEVI[2]—*middle Jaredite king*

Ether 1: 20–21 (10: 14, 16) son of Kim, father of Corom; 10: 15 serves in captivity forty-two years after father's death; 10: 15 obtains kingdom by war; 10: 16 rules righteously.

LIAHONA—*compass given to Lehi[1]*

1 Ne. 16: 10 Lehi[1] finds brass ball of curious workmanship, with two spindles; 16: 10 (Alma 37: 38–39) points way Lehites should go into wilderness; 16: 16 leads Lehites to more fertile parts of wilderness; 16: 26–27, 29 writing on *L.* gives understanding of the Lord's ways; 16: 28–29 (Mosiah 1: 16; Alma 37: 40) works according to faith and diligence; 18: 12–14 after brothers bind Nephi[1], compass ceases to work; 18: 21 when Nephi[1] is unbound, compass works; **2 Ne.** 5: 12 Nephi[1] takes compass with him; **Mosiah** 1: 16 Benjamin gives ball to Mosiah[2]; **Alma** 37: 38 called *L.*, being interpreted, a compass; 37: 41–42 when Lehites were slothful, compass ceased to work and they did not progress in journey; 37: 43–45 *L.* a shadow or type of word of Christ.

LIB[1]—*middle Jaredite king*

Ether 1: 17–18 son of Kish, father of Hearthom; 10: 18 becomes king; 10: 19 good king, great hunter, serpents destroyed during *L*'s reign; 10: 20–29 lives long, and people prosper.

LIB[2]—*late Jaredite king*

Ether 14: 10 man of great stature, obtains kingdom through secret combination and murder; 14: 11–15 battles with Coriantumr[2]; 14: 16 is killed.

LIBERAL, LIBERALLY

2 Ne. 4: 35 (James 1: 5) God giveth *l.* to him that asketh; **Alma** 1: 30 Nephites are *l.* to all in need; 6: 5 word of God is *l.* unto all.

LIBERTY (*see also* Agency; Bondage; Freedom; Freemen; Government, Civil; Promised Land; Right [noun]; TG Liberty)

2 Ne. 1: 7 (10: 11; Mosiah 29: 32; Alma 46: 17) promised land shall be land of *l.*; 2: 27 men are free to choose *l.* or captivity; **Mosiah** 23: 13 (Alma 58: 40; 61: 9) stand fast in *l.* wherewith ye have been made free; 29: 39 Nephites rejoice in *l.*; **Alma** 8: 17 people of Ammonihah study to destroy *l.*; 21: 22 Lamanites have *l.* of worshipping the Lord according to their desires; 43: 9 Nephites to preserve *l.* of worshipping God according to their desire; 43: 26, 30, 45, 48–49 (58: 12) Nephites fight to preserve their lands and *l.*; 44: 5 God strengthens Nephites, by *l.* which binds them to lands; 46: 10 Amalickiah seeks to destroy foundation of *l.*; 46: 13, 36 (51: 20; 62: 4) Moroni[1] raises title of *l.*; 46: 24 let us preserve our *l.* as a remnant of Joseph[1]; 46: 28 Moroni[1] gathers all those who desire to maintain *l.*, to stand against Amalickiah; 48: 10–11 Moroni[1] prepares to support *l.*; 50: 32 Moroni[1] fears that Morianton[2] could cause overthrow of *l.*; 51: 7 people of *l.* rejoice in victory of freemen; 51: 13 king-men are wroth with people of *l.*; 51: 17, 20 king-men are compelled to support cause of *l.* of Nephites; 56: 47 Ammonite youth think more upon *l.* of fathers than upon their lives; 62: 37 Teancum a true friend to *l.*; **Hel.** 1: 7–8 Paanchi condemned to death for seeking to destroy *l.*; **3 Ne.** 2: 12 converted Lamanites join Nephites against robbers to maintain *l.*; 3: 2 Nephites are firm in maintaining *l.*; 5: 4 robbers who covenant to murder no more were set at *l.*

LICK (*see* Dust)

LIE, LAY, LAIN (*see also* Lying, Lie, Liar)

2 Ne. 21: 6 (30: 12; Isa. 11: 6) leopard shall *l.* down with kid; 24: 30 (Isa. 14: 30) the needy shall *l.* down in safety; **Alma** 37: 37 when thou *l.* down at night, *l.* down unto the Lord.

LIFE, LIVES (*see also* Death, Physical; Eternal Life; Immortality; Jesus Christ, Death of; Live; Mortal; Resurrection; Tree of Life; TG Breath of Life; Life; Life, Sanctity of; Life after Death; Mortality)

1 Ne. 1: 20 (2: 1) Jews seek *l.* of Lehi[1]; **Jacob** 7: 26 our *l.* passed away like a dream; **Mosiah** 4: 6 continue in faith unto end of *l.* of mortal body; 7: 22 Lamanite king exacts tribute from Zeniff's people, or their *l.*; 13: 11 ye have studied and taught iniquity the most part of your *l.*; 16: 9 (Alma 38: 9; 3 Ne. 9: 18; 11: 11; Ether 4: 12) Christ is light and *l.* of world; **Alma** 5: 34 ye shall eat and drink of the bread and waters of *l.*; 5: 58 names of the righteous shall be written in book of *l.*; 11: 45 mortal body is raised from first death unto *l.*; 12: 24 (34: 32–33; 42: 4) this *l.* became probationary state; 26: 32 converted Lamanites would rather sacrifice their *l.* than take *l.* of enemy; 26: 36 this is my *l.* and my light; 28: 14 great reason of rejoicing because of light of Christ unto *l.*; 34: 12 law requireth the *l.* of him who hath murdered; 34: 33 after day of this *l.* cometh night of darkness; 40: 11 spirits of all men are taken home to God, who gave them *l.*; 41: 3 if men's works were good in this *l.*, they shall be restored unto that which is good; 42: 16 repentance could not come except there were punishment as eternal as *l.* of soul; 48: 14 Nephites are taught never to raise sword except to preserve *l.*; 48: 24 Nephites could not suffer to lay down *l.*, that wives and children be massacred; 53: 17 Ammonite youths covenant to protect land unto laying down of *l.*; 54: 12 it shall be blood for blood, *l.* for *l.*; **3 Ne.** 13: 25 (Matt. 6: 25) take no thought for your *l.*; **Ether** 3: 14 in Christ shall all mankind have *l.*

LIFT (*see also* Exalt; Jesus Christ, Death of; Magnify; Pride; Raise)

1 Ne. 13: 37 they who seek to bring forth Zion shall be *l.* up at last day; 16: 2 the righteous shall be *l.* up at last day; 18: 9 Laman[1], Lemuel, and sons of Ishmael[1] are *l.* up unto exceeding rudeness; **2 Ne.** 12: 4 (Isa. 2: 4) nation shall not *l.* up sword against nation; **Mosiah** 23: 22 (Alma 36: 3; 38: 5) whosoever puts trust in the Lord shall be *l.* up at last day; **Alma** 13: 29 have love of God always in heart, that you may be *l.* up at last day; 31: 25 Alma[2] sees that people's hearts are *l.* up unto great boasting; 37: 37 counsel with the Lord in all your doings, and you shall be *l.* up at last day; **Hel.** 6: 17 Nephites seek to get gain that they might be *l.* up one above another; 8: 14 as Moses *l.* up brazen serpent, so shall Son be *l.* up; **Moro.** 9: 25 may Christ *l.* thee up.

LIGHT [adj. = little] (*see also* Ease; Easiness; Light; Little; Simple; Small)

1 Ne. 21: 6 (Isa. 49: 6) *l.* thing that thou shouldst be my servant to raise up tribes of Jacob.

LIGHT (*see also* Brightness; Candle; Darkness, Physical; Darkness, Spiritual; Enlighten; Example; Glory [noun]; Holy Ghost; Illuminate; Jesus Christ; Knowledge; Lamp; Shine; Spirit, Holy; Truth; TG Light; Light of Christ; BD Light of Christ)

1 Ne. 17: 13 the Lord will be your *l.* in wilderness; **2 Ne.** 10: 14 the Lord will be *l.* unto them that hear his words; 12: 5 (Isa. 2: 5) let us walk in *l.* of the Lord; 15: 20 (Isa. 5: 20) wo unto them that put darkness for *l.* and *l.* for darkness; 18: 20 (Isa. 8: 20) if they speak not according to this word, it is because there is no *l.* in them; 19: 2 (Isa. 9: 2) people who walked in darkness have seen a great *l.*; 23: 10 (Isa. 13: 10) stars of heaven shall not give *l.*; 26: 10 Nephites shall reap destruction because they choose works of darkness rather than *l.*; 26: 29 priestcrafts are that men set themselves up for *l.* unto world to get gain and praise; 31: 3 the Lord giveth *l.* unto the understanding; **Mosiah** 16: 9 (Alma 38: 9; 3 Ne. 9: 18; 11: 11; Ether 4: 12) Christ is the *l.* and life of world; **Alma** 9: 23 if Nephites transgress against *l.*, it would be more tolerable for Lamanites than for them; 19: 6 *l.* which *l.* up Lamoni's mind is *l.* of God's glory, marvelous *l.* of his goodness; 28: 14 great cause of rejoicing because of *l.* of Christ unto life; 32: 35 whatsoever is *l.* is good; 32: 35–36 after tasting this *l.* your knowledge is not perfect; 36: 20 what marvelous *l.* did Alma[2] behold; 37: 23 stone shall shine forth in darkness unto *l.*; **Hel.** 13: 29 how long will ye choose darkness rather than *l.*; 14: 3 great *l.* in heaven shall be sign of Christ's coming; **3 Ne.** 1: 19 at going down of sun there is *l.* as at mid-day; 8: 21 no *l.* because of thick darkness; 12: 16 (Matt. 5: 16) let your *l.* so shine that they see your good works; 15: 12 twelve disciples are *l.* unto Nephites; 18: 16 Christ is the *l.*, has set example; **Ether** 3: 4 (6: 2) brother of Jared[2] asks the Lord to touch stones, that Jaredites might have *l.*; **Moro.** 7: 18 *l.* by which ye should judge is *l.* of Christ; 7: 19 search diligently in *l.* of Christ that ye may know good from evil.

LIGHTNING (*see also* Destruction; Thunder)

1 Ne. 12: 4 (Hel. 14: 21; 3 Ne. 8: 7, 17, 19) at time of Christ's death, there shall be great *l.*; 19: 11 the Lord will visit house of Israel with *l.* of his power; **2 Ne.** 26: 6 they who kill prophets shall be visited with *l.*

LIKEN (*see also* Likeness; Parable; Teach)

1 Ne. 19: 23 Nephi[1] *l.* all scriptures unto his people; 22: 8 the Lord's marvelous work is *l.* unto Israel's being nourished by Gentiles; **2 Ne.** 6: 5 (11: 2, 8) words of Isaiah[1] concerning house of Israel may be *l.* unto Nephites; **Jacob** 5: 3 (6: 1)

Israel is *l.* unto tame olive-tree; **3 Ne.** 14: 24 they who do Christ's sayings are *l.* unto man who built house upon rock.

LIKENESS (*see also* Image; Similitude)

Mosiah 12: 36 (13: 12; Ex. 20: 4) thou shalt not make any graven image or any *l.* of any thing in heaven or earth; **Alma** 32: 31 every seed bringeth forth unto its own *l.*; **Ether** 3: 17 Jesus shows himself to brother of Jared[2] in *l.* of same body he showed unto Nephites.

LILIES

3 Ne. 13: 28 (Matt. 6: 28) consider *l.* of field.

LIMHAH—*Nephite commander* [c. A.D. 385]

Morm. 6: 14 has fallen with his ten thousand.

LIMHER—*Nephite soldier* [c. 87 B.C.]

Alma 2: 22 sent out to watch camp of Amlicites; 2: 23–25 reports that Amlicites have joined large Lamanite army.

LIMHI—*king of Nephites in land of Nephi* [c. 121 B.C.] (*see also* Ammon[1]; Nephi, Land of)

Mosiah 7: 7–8 (21: 22–23) commits Ammon[1] and brethren to prison; 7: 9 son of Noah[3]; 7: 9–11 questions Ammon[1]; 7: 14 (21: 24) rejoices over news from Zarahemla; 7: 15, 21–23 is in bondage to Lamanites; 7: 17–18 gathers people to hear his words; 7: 19–20 exhorts people to put trust in God; 7: 24–33 laments over his people's transgressions; 8: 1 tells of brethren from Zarahemla; 8: 2–3 causes Ammon[1] to speak to people; 8: 5–14 (21: 25–28) brings forth twenty-four gold plates found by his people; 8: 15–18 is taught about seers by Ammon[1]; 19: 17 is a just man; 19: 26 is made king by people, makes oath with Lamanite king to pay tribute; 19: 27–29 establishes peace among his people; 20: 8 discovers Lamanites and lays ambush; 20: 9–11 drives Lamanites from lands; 20: 12–16 counsels with Lamanite king; 20: 23–26 pacifies Lamanites by telling of father's priests; 21: 2–6 *L*'s people complain to him of Lamanites' persecution; 21: 7–8, 11–12 is defeated by Lamanites three times; 21: 17 commands that every man impart to support of widows and children; 21: 19 always takes guards with him; 21: 32 enters into covenant to serve God; 21: 36—22: 2 studies how to deliver people from bondage; 22: 9–12 follows Gideon's plan to escape into wilderness; 22: 13 joins people of Mosiah[2]; 25: 16–18 is taught and baptized by Alma[1]; 28: 11 delivers twenty-four gold plates to Mosiah[2].

LIMNAH (*see also* Coin)

Alma 11: 5, 10 *l.* of gold is value of all the coins.

LINE

2 Ne. 28: 30 (Isa. 28: 10) the Lord gives unto men *l.* upon *l.*

LINEN (*see also* Cloth; Clothing)

1 Ne. 13: 7–8 silks and fine-twined *l.* in abominable church; **Mosiah** 10: 5 Zeniff causes women to work all manner of fine *l.*; **Alma** 1: 29 (Hel. 6: 13) Nephites have abundance of silk and fine-twined *l.*; 4: 6 church begins to wax proud because of silks and fine-twined *l.*; **Ether** 10: 24 Jaredites have silks and fine-twined *l.*

LION (*see also* Animal; Beast)

2 Ne. 21: 7 (30: 13; Isa. 11: 7) *l.* shall eat straw like ox; **Mosiah** 20: 10 they fought like *l.* for their prey; **3 Ne.** 20: 16 (21: 12; Morm. 5: 24; Micah 5: 8) house of Jacob shall be among Gentiles as *l.* among beasts of forest.

LIPS (*see also* Mouth; Speak; Tongue; Word)

2 Ne. 16: 6 (Isa. 6: 5) I am a man of unclean *l.*; 27: 25 (Isa. 29: 13) with their *l.* this people honor the Lord; 30: 9 with breath of his *l.* the Lord shall slay the wicked.

LIST (*see also* Desire)

Mosiah 2: 32 beware lest contentions arise and ye *l.* to obey evil spirit; 2: 33, 37 whoso *l.* to obey evil spirit drinks damnation to his soul; **Alma** 3: 27 every man receiveth wages of him whom he *l.* to obey.

LISTEN (*see also* Communication; Hear; Hearken; Heed)

Jacob 2: 16 O that ye would *l.* to word of God's commands; **Mosiah** 22: 4 Gideon asks Limhi to *l.* to his words; **Moro.** 8: 8 *l.* to the words of Christ.

LITTLE (*see also* Child; Light [adj.]; Season; Small)

2 Ne. 28: 8 many shall say God justifieth in committing a *l.* sin; 28: 30 (Isa. 28: 10) the Lord gives unto men here a *l.*, there a *l.*; **Mosiah** 18: 27 of him that has but *l.*, but *l.* should be required; **3 Ne.** 13: 30 (Matt. 6: 30) so will God clothe you if ye are not of *l.* faith.

LIVE [verb] (*see also* Alive; Dwell; Eternal Life; Immortality; Inhabit; Life; Living)

Mosiah 4: 13 ye will not have a mind to injure one another, but to *l.* peaceably; 27: 31 they who *l.* without God in world shall confess that his judgment is just;

Alma 33: 19 (37: 46–47; Hel. 8: 15) type was raised in wilderness that whosoever would look upon it might *l.*; 37: 47 look to God and *l.*; 42: 3 if Adam had partaken of tree of life, he would have *l.* forever; **3 Ne.** 15: 9 look unto Christ and endure to end, and ye shall *l.*; 28: 2 disciples desire to come speedily into Christ's kingdom after they have *l.* unto age of man.

LIVING (*see also* Alive; Live; TG Living; Living Water)

1 Ne. 11: 25 iron rod leads to fountain of *l.* waters; 17: 30 (2 Ne. 31: 16; Alma 5: 13; 7: 6; 3 Ne. 30: 1; Morm. 5: 14; 9: 28) the true and *l.* God; **2 Ne.** 9: 13 in resurrection all men will be *l.* souls.

LOATHSOME (*see also* Hate; Wicked)

1 Ne. 12: 23 (2 Ne. 5: 22) Lamanites become *l.* people; **Morm.** 5: 15 Nephites shall become *l.* people.

LOINS (*see also* Descendant; Seed)

2 Ne. 3: 4–22 prophecy of Joseph[1] concerning fruit of his *l.*; **Jacob** 2: 25 the Lord has led Nephites from Jerusalem to raise up righteous branch from *l.* of Joseph[1].

LONG-SUFFERING (*see also* Patience)

1 Ne. 19: 9 Christ to suffer mockery because of his *l-s.* toward men; **Mosiah** 4: 6 come to knowledge of God and his *l-s.*; 27: 33 Alma[2] and sons of Mosiah[2] exhort people with *l-s.*; **Alma** 7: 23 be full of patience and *l-s.*; 9: 26 Son's glory shall be full of *l-s.*; 13: 28 be led by Spirit, become patient, full of all *l-s.*; 17: 11 be patient in *l-s.*; 26: 16 who can say too much of the Lord's *l-s.*; 32: 43 ye shall reap reward of your *l-s.*; 38: 3 Alma[2] has great joy in Shiblon's *l-s.* among Zoramites; 42: 30 let justice of God and his *l-s.* have full sway in your heart; **Morm.** 2: 12 Mormon[2] knows *l-s.* of God; **Moro.** 7: 45 (1 Cor. 13: 4) charity suffereth *l.*; 9: 25 may Christ's *l-s.* rest in your mind forever.

LOOK (*see also* Behold; See)

1 Ne. 17: 40–41 (Alma 33: 19–20; Hel. 8: 14–15) labor which Israelites had to perform to be healed was to *l.* upon serpent; **2 Ne.** 2: 28 *l.* to the great Mediator; 8: 1 (Isa. 51: 1) *l.* unto rock from whence ye are hewn; 24: 16 (Isa. 14: 16) they that see thee shall narrowly *l.* upon thee; 25: 24 (26: 8) *l.* forward unto Christ; 25: 26 Nephites write of Christ, that children may know to what source they may *l.* for remission of sins; 25: 27 by knowing deadness of law, they may *l.* forward unto that life which is in Christ; **Jacob** 4: 14 Jews' blindness came by *l.* beyond mark; **Jarom** 1: 11 prophets persuade men to *l.* forward unto Messiah; **Mosiah** 8: 13 Mosiah[2] has wherewith that he can *l.* and translate records; **Alma** 5: 15 *l.* forward with eye of faith and view mortal body raised in immortality; 13: 12 high priests could not *l.* upon sins save with abhorrence; 37: 47 *l.* to God and live; 45: 16 the Lord cannot *l.* upon sin with least degree of allowance; **Hel.** 8: 15 as many as *l.* upon Son might live; **3 Ne.** 12: 28 (Matt. 5: 28) whosoever *l.* on woman to lust hath committed adultery in heart.

LOOSE (*see also* Bind; Deliver)

2 Ne. 3: 17 the Lord will not *l.* Moses' tongue; 15: 27 (Isa. 5: 27) girdle of loins shall not be *l.*; **Jacob** 3: 11 *l.* yourselves from pains of hell; **Alma** 7: 12 (11: 42) Son to take upon him death, that he might *l.* bands of death; **Hel.** 10: 7 (Matt. 16: 19) whatsoever he *l.* on earth shall be *l.* in heaven; **3 Ne.** 20: 37 *l.* thyself from bands of neck, daughter of Zion; 26: 14 Christ *l.* children's tongues; **Morm.** 9: 13 all shall be redeemed and *l.* from eternal band of death.

LORD (*see* Jesus Christ—Lord)

LORD OF HOSTS (*see* Jesus Christ—Lord of Hosts)

LORD'S DAY (*see* Day of the Lord; Sabbath)

LORD'S HOUSE (*see* House; Temple)

LORD'S PRAYER (*see also* Prayer; BD Lord's Prayer)

3 Ne. 13: 9–13 (Matt. 6: 9–13) the Lord's Prayer given to the Nephites.

LOSE, LOST (*see also* Astray; Israel, Ten Lost Tribes of)

1 Ne. 8: 23 those on path *l.* their way in mist of darkness; 10: 6 (Mosiah 16: 4; Alma 34: 9) all mankind were in *l.* and fallen state; **2 Ne.** 25: 17 the Lord will restore his people from *l.* and fallen state; **Jacob** 2: 35 Nephites have *l.* confidence of children because of bad example; **Mosiah** 20: 22 better that we should be in bondage than *l.* our lives; **Alma** 9: 30 people of Ammonihah are *l.* and fallen people; 16: 8 not one Nephite taken captive by Lamanites is *l.*; 30: 47 better that thy soul should be *l.* than that thou shouldst bring many down to destruction; 42: 6 man became *l.* forever; 60: 13 ye need not suppose that the righteous are *l.* because they are slain; **Hel.** 13: 33 if ye had remembered God, your riches would not have become slippery that ye *l.* them; **3 Ne.** 12: 13 (Matt. 5: 13) if salt *l.* its savor, wherewith shall earth be salted; 16: 15 Gentiles shall be as salt that has *l.* its savor; **Moro.** 9: 5 Nephites have *l.* their love one toward another.

LOST TRIBES (*see* Israel, Ten Lost Tribes of)

LOT (*see also* BD Lots, Casting of)

1 Ne. 3: 11 *l.* falls upon Laman[1] to visit Laban.

LOVE (*see also* Charity; Compassion; Esteem; God, Love of; TG Love)

2 Ne. 9: 40 the righteous *l.* the truth and are not shaken; 26: 30 (Moro. 8: 17) charity is everlasting *l.*; 31: 20 (Mosiah 2: 4) press forward with steadfastness in Christ, having *l.* of God and all men; **Jacob** 3: 7 Lamanite husbands and wives *l.* each other and their children; **Mosiah** 3: 19 natural man must become a child, patient, full of *l.*; 4: 15 teach children to *l.* and serve one another; 23: 15 (Lev. 19: 18) every man should *l.* his neighbor as himself; **Alma** 5: 26 if ye have felt to sing song of redeeming *l.*, can ye feel so now; 11: 24 thou *l.* lucre more than God; 13: 28 be led by Holy Ghost, becoming patient, full of *l.*; 38: 12 bridle your passions, that ye may be filled with *l.*; **4 Ne.** 1: 15 no contention in land because of *l.* of God in hearts of people; **Morm.** 8: 37 ye *l.* your money and substance more than ye *l.* the poor and needy; **Moro.** 7: 13 every thing which inviteth to *l.* God is inspired of God; 7: 47 charity is pure *l.* of Christ; 7: 48 pray that ye may be filled with this *l.*; 8: 16 perfect *l.* casteth out fear; 8: 26 Comforter filleth with hope and perfect *l.*; 10: 32 if ye *l.* God with all your might, his grace is sufficient.

LOVING KINDNESS (*see* Kindness)

LOW, LOWER (*see also* Humble; Lowliness)

1 Ne. 22: 23 those who belong to kingdom of devil must be brought *l.* in dust; **2 Ne.** 12: 12 (Isa. 2: 12) the proud and lofty to be brought *l.*; 12: 17 haughtiness of men shall be made *l.*; 26: 15 after Lehites' seed have been brought *l.* in dust, they shall not be forgotten; 26: 16 speech of those destroyed shall be *l.* out of dust; **Alma** 28: 11 bodies of many thousands are laid *l.* in earth; **Hel.** 14: 23 many mountains shall be laid *l.*

LOWLINESS, LOWLY (*see also* Humble; Low; Meek; Poor)

1 Ne. 2: 19 Nephi[1] is blessed because he has sought the Lord with *l.* of heart; **Alma** 32: 8 blessed are ye if ye are *l.* in heart; 32: 12 because the poor are cast out, they are brought to *l.* of heart; 37: 33–34 teach people to be meek and *l.* in heart; **Moro.** 7: 43 man cannot have faith and hope save he be *l.* of heart; 7: 44 none is acceptable before God save the *l.* in heart; 8: 26 remission of sins brings *l.* of heart, which brings Comforter.

LUCIFER (*see also* Devil; BD Lucifer)

2 Ne. 24: 12 (Isa. 14: 12) how art thou fallen from heaven, *L.*, son of morning.

LUCRE (*see also* Money; Riches)

Mosiah 29: 40 *l.* corrupts soul; **Alma** 11: 24 Zeezrom loves *l.* more than God.

LURAM—*Nephite officer* [c. A.D. 385]

Moro. 9: 2 has fallen by sword.

LUST (*see also* Adultery; Carnal; Chastity; Covet; Desire; Fornication; Lasciviousness; TG Lust; Sexual Immorality)

1 Ne. 3: 25 Laban *l.* after property brought by sons of Lehi[1]; 22: 23 those who seek *l.* of flesh should fear and tremble; **Alma** 39: 9 go no more after *l.* of your eyes; **3 Ne.** 12: 28 (Matt. 5: 28) whoso looketh on woman to *l.* hath committed adultery in heart; **Morm.** 9: 28 ask not, that ye may consume it on your *l.*

LYING, LIE, LIAR (*see also* Beguile; Cunning; Deceit; Devil; False; Flatter; Fraud; Guile; Honest; Hypocrisy)

2 Ne. 2: 18 (9: 9) devil is father of *l.*; 9: 34 *l.* shall be thrust down to hell; 28: 8 many shall say, *L.* a little; **Jacob** 7: 19 Sherem fears he has committed unpardonable sin by *l.* unto God; **Enos** 1: 6 (Ether 3: 12) God cannot *l.*; **Mosiah** 10: 18 Laman[3], by *l.* craftiness, deceives Zeniff; **Alma** 1: 17 *l.* are punished according to law; 5: 17 do ye imagine ye can *l.* to the Lord; 5: 25 except ye make Creator a *l.*, wicked cannot have place in heaven; 12: 1 Amulek has caught Zeezrom in his *l.*; 12: 3 thou hast not *l.* unto men only, but thou hast *l.* unto God; 12: 23 if Adam had partaken of tree of life, there would have been no death, making God a *l.*; 16: 18 priests preach against all *l.*; 30: 42 Korihor is possessed with *l.* spirit; 30: 47 better that Korihor's soul be lost than that he bring many souls to destruction by his *l.*; **Hel.** 4: 12 destruction of Nephites caused by their *l.*; 8: 24 ye cannot deny these things except ye *l.*; **3 Ne.** 1: 22 *l.* sent forth among people by Satan to harden hearts; 16: 10 when Gentiles are filled with all manner of *l.*, Father will bring gospel from among them; 21: 19 all *l.* shall be done away; 30: 2 Gentiles called to repent of *l.*; **4 Ne.** 1: 16 no *l.* among the people;

Morm. 8: 31 day of the Lord to come in day when much *l.* upon earth.

MADE

2 Ne. 27: 27 (Isa. 17: 27) shall the work say to him who *m.* it, he *m.* me not.

MAGIC (*see also* Sorceries, Sorcerer; Witchcraft)

Morm. 1: 19 (2: 10) *m.* art and witchcraft in the land.

MAGNIFY (*see also* Enlarge; Exalt; Lift; TG Priesthood, Magnifying Callings within)

2 Ne. 20: 15 (Isa. 10: 15) shall the saw *m.* itself against him that shaketh it; 25: 13 heart of Nephi[1] *m.* Only Begotten's holy name; **Jacob** 1: 19 (2: 2) Jacob[2] *m.* his office.

MAHAH

Ether 6: 14 one of four sons of Jared[2].

MAHER-SHALAL-HASH-BAZ—*son of Isaiah*[1] [c. eighth century B.C.]

2 Ne. 18: 1 (Isa. 8: 1) Isaiah is commanded to write concerning M.; 18: 3 (Isa. 8: 3) prophetess bears son, called M.

MAIMED (*see also* Heal)

3 Ne. 17: 7 Christ asks that the *m.* be brought to him.

MAINTAIN, MAINTENANCE (*see also* Defence; Keep; Preserve; Provide; Retain; Support)

Alma 44: 5 Nephites gain power over Lamanites by the *m.* of sacred word of God; 46: 20 whosoever will *m.* title of liberty should come forth; 46: 28 those desirous of *m.* liberty are gathered; 46: 35 dissenters who do not covenant to *m.* free government are put to death; 48: 10 Moroni[1] prepares people to *m.* cause of Christians; 50: 39 chief judge takes oath to *m.* cause of God; 51: 6 freemen swear to *m.* rights of religion by free government; 51: 7 king-men are obliged to *m.* cause of freedom.

MAJESTY (*see also* Glory [noun])

2 Ne. 12: 10, 19, 21 (Isa. 2: 10, 19, 21) glory of the Lord's *m.* shall smite wicked ones; **Alma** 5: 50 Son cometh in *m.*; 12: 15 men must stand before God in his *m.*

MAKE (*see* Made)

MAKER (*see* God—Creator; Jesus Christ—Creator)

MALACHI—*Jewish prophet* [c. late fifth century B.C.] (*see also* BD Malachi)

3 Ne. 24 compare Malachi 3; **3 Ne.** 25 compare Malachi 4.

MALE (*see also* Man)

1 Ne. 8: 27 spacious building filled with people, both *m.* and female; **2 Ne.** 10: 16 he who fights against Zion, both *m.* and female, shall perish; 26: 33 the Lord denies none who come to him, *m.* and female; **Alma** 1: 30 Nephites are liberal to all, both *m.* and female; 11: 44 restoration shall come to all, both *m.* and female; **Ether** 1: 41 gather thy flocks, both *m.* and female.

MALICE (*see also* Despise; Hate; Love; Mischief; Mock; Oppression; Persecution; Revile; Rudeness; Scorn)

2 Ne. 26: 21 churches shall cause *m.*; 26: 32 the Lord has commanded that men should not have *m.*; **Alma** 4: 9 (Hel. 13: 22; Morm. 8: 36) *m.* among the Nephites; 16: 18 priests preach against *m.*

MAMMON (*see also* Riches; BD Mammon)

3 Ne. 13: 24 (Matt. 6: 24) ye cannot serve God and *m.*

MAN, MEN (*see also* Adam; Agency; Body; Fall of Man; Flesh; Human; Male; Mankind; Nature, Natural; Soul; World; TG Man; Man, a Spirit Child of Heavenly Father; Man, Antemortal Existence of; Man, Natural, Not Spiritually Reborn; Man, New, Spiritually Reborn; Man, Physical Creation of; Man, Potential to Become like Heavenly Father; Man of God)

1 Ne. 8: 5 (14: 19) Lehi[1] sees *m.* in white robe in vision; 11: 7 (12: 6; 3 Ne. 11: 8) Nephi[1] to behold *m.* descending out of heaven; 11: 11 Nephi[1] speaks to Spirit of the Lord as a man speaks; 13: 12 Nephi[1] beholds *m.* among Gentiles who goes forth upon waters; **2 Ne.** 1: 21 arise, my sons, and be *m.*; 2: 25 Adam fell that *m.* might be; 4: 17 O wretched *m.* that I am; 4: 34 (28: 31) cursed is he that puts trust in *m.*; 8: 7 (Isa. 51: 7) fear not the reproach of *m.*; 9: 5 Creator to become subject unto *m.* in flesh; 14: 1 (Isa. 4: 1) seven women shall take hold of one *m.*; 23: 12 (Isa. 13: 12) the Lord will make a *m.* more precious than fine gold; 26: 11 Spirit of the Lord will not always strive with *m.*; 27: 9 book to be delivered to a *m.* who will deliver it to another; 27: 25 their fear toward God is taught by precepts of *m.*; 28: 14 they err because they are taught by precepts of *m.*; 28: 26, 31 wo unto him who hearkens to precepts of *m.*; 29: 7 (Alma 1: 4) the Lord has created all *m.*; **Jacob** 2: 27 no *m.* among *m.* shall have more than one wife; 4: 8 no *m.* knows God's ways, save through revelation; 4: 9 God spoke, and *m.* was created; **Mosiah** 3: 19 natural *m.* is enemy to God; 7: 27 Christ to take upon him image of *m.*; 7: 27 (Alma 18: 34; 22: 12; Ether 3: 15–16) *m.* was created after image of God; 8: 16 *m.* may have great power given him from God; **Alma** 2: 30 Alma[2] a *m.* of God; 26: 21 what natural *m.* knows these things; 30: 11 law that all *m.* should be on equal grounds; 32: 23 God imparts his words not only to *m.*, but to women also; 40: 8 time is measured only unto *m.*; 41: 11 all *m.* in natural, carnal state, are in gall of bitterness; **Hel.** 11: 8, 18 Nephi[2] is esteemed a *m.* of God; **3 Ne.** 14: 12 (Matt. 7: 12) whatsoever ye would that *m.* should do to you, do to them; 27: 8 church called in name of *m.* is church of *m.*; 27: 27 what manner of *m.* ought ye to be; **Morm.** 9: 17 *m.* was created of dust; **Ether** 3: 15 never before has the Lord shown himself unto *m.*; 3: 16 the Lord has created *m.* after body of his spirit; 12: 39 Moroni[2] has talked with Jesus as *m.* talks with another; **Moro.** 8: 16 fear not what *m.* can do.

MANASSEH—*son of Joseph*[1], *father of a tribe of Israel* [c. seventeenth century B.C.]

2 Ne. 19: 21 (Isa. 9: 21) M. and Ephraim will be against Judah; **Alma** 10: 3 Lehi a descendant of M.

MANIFEST, MANIFESTATION (*see also* God, Manifestations of; Jesus Christ, Appearances of; Revelation; Show; Testify; Unfold)

1 Ne. 1: 19 vision of Lehi[1] *m.* coming of Messiah; **Mosiah** 8: 17 (Alma 37: 21) secret things shall be made *m.*; **Alma** 5: 46 the Lord *m.* these things to Alma[2] by Holy Spirit; 5: 47 spirit of prophecy is by *m.* of Spirit of God; **3 Ne.** 7: 22 those who are healed *m.* that Spirit has wrought upon them; 26: 9 if they believe, greater things shall be made *m.* unto them; **Ether** 2: 12 Christ has been *m.* by the things we have written; **Moro.** 10: 4 Father will *m.* truth of book by power of Holy Ghost; 10: 8 spiritual gifts are given by *m.* of Spirit.

MANKIND (*see also* Flesh; Human; Man)

1 Ne. 10: 6 (Alma 12: 22; 42: 14) all *m.* were in lost and fallen state; **2 Ne.** 2: 18 devil sought misery of all *m.*; **Mosiah** 16: 3 fall was cause of *m.* becoming carnal; **Alma** 19: 13 Redeemer shall redeem all *m.* who believe on his name; 34: 9 except for atonement, all *m.* must unavoidably perish; **Hel.** 14: 16 all *m.* redeemed from first death; 14: 17 Christ's resurrection redeems all *m.*; **Ether** 3: 14 in Christ shall all *m.* have light eternally.

MANNA (*see also* BD Manna)

1 Ne. 17: 28 (Mosiah 7: 19) children of Israel were fed with *m.* in wilderness.

MANNER

2 Ne. 25: 2 Nephi[1] has not taught his people much concerning *m.* of Jews; **Alma** 11: 4 Nephites do not reckon after *m.* of Jews; **3 Ne.** 13: 9 (Matt. 6: 9) after this *m.* pray ye; 27: 27 what *m.* of men ought ye to be.

MANSION (*see also* House)

Enos 1: 27 place is prepared for you in *m.* of Father; **Ether** 12: 32, 34, 37 the Lord has prepared house for man among Father's *m.*

MANTI—*Nephite soldier* [c. 87 B.C.]

Alma 2: 22 sent out to watch Amlicites.

MANTI, CITY OF—*chief city in land of Manti* (*see also* Manti, Land of)

Alma 56: 13–14 possessed by Lamanites; 57: 22 Lamanites driven back to M.; 58: 1 Helaman[2] desires to take M.; 58: 13 Nephites go forth against Lamanites in M.; 58: 39 Ammonite youth are with Helaman[2] in M.

MANTI, HILL OF—*near city of Zarahemla*

Alma 1: 15 Nehor put to death on M.

MANTI, LAND OF—*most southerly land of Nephites* (*see also* Manti, City of)

Alma 16: 6–7 Zoram[2] and sons march beyond borders of M.; 17: 1 Alma[2] meets sons of Mosiah[2] while on way to M.; 22: 27 proclamation sent to people of M.; 43: 22 head of river Sidon near M.; 43: 24–25 Nephite and Lamanite armies converge on M.; 43: 26 Moroni[1] gathers people in land to battle Lamanites; 43: 27–54 Nephites defeat Lamanites near borders of M.; 56: 13–14 Lamanites possess M.; 58: 26–30 (59: 6) Nephites march toward M. by night.

MARK (*see also* Curse; Skin)

Jacob 4: 14 Jews' blindness came by looking beyond the *m.*; **Alma** 3: 4, 13, 18 Amlicites *m.* themselves with red in forehead; 3: 6 Lamanites' skins were dark, according to *m.* set upon fathers; 3: 7, 14 the Lord set *m.* upon Laman[1], Lemuel, sons of Ishmael[1]; 3: 10, 15–16, 18 those who are led away by Lamanites receive *m.*

MARRIAGE, MARRY (*see also* Divorce; Father; Husband; Mother; Wife; TG Marriage; Marriage, Celestial; Marriage, Continuing Courtship in; Marriage, Fatherhood; Marriage, Husbands; Marriage, Interfaith; Marriage, Motherhood;

Marriage, Plural; Marriage, Temporal; Marriage, Wives; BD Marriage)

1 Ne. 16: 7 Zoram[1] and sons of Lehi[1] take daughters of Ishmael[1] to wife; **Jacob** ch. 2 Jacob[2] denounces plurality of wives and concubines among Nephites; **3 Ne.** 12: 32 (Matt. 5: 32) whoso *m.* her who is divorced committeth adultery; 22: 1 (Isa. 54: 1) more are the children of the desolate than the children of the *m.* wife; **4 Ne.** 1: 11 Nephites are *m.* and given in *m.*

MARTYRDOM, MARTYR (*see also* Blood, Shedding of; Death, Physical; Kill; Murder; Persecution; TG Martyrdom; Prophets, Rejection of; BD Martyr)

Mosiah 7: 26 people of Limhi have slain a prophet; 17: 13–20 Abinadi is put to death by fire; **Alma** 14: 8–11 converted Ammonihahites are cast into fire; 24: 12–26 converted Lamanites refuse to fight, are killed, more converted; 25: 5–7 converted Lamanites put to death by children of Amulon; 25: 8 *m.* stirs up other Lamanites to hunt seed of Amulon; **3 Ne.** 6: 25 judges condemn prophets to death, not according to law; **Ether** 8: 25 devil has caused men to murder prophets.

MARVEL (*see also* Marvelous; Wonder)

Alma 22: 23 queen and others *m.* that Aaron[2] raises Lamanite king; **Hel.** 5: 49 converted Lamanites bidden not to *m.* at manifestation of Spirit; **3 Ne.** 15: 2 some *m.* at Jesus' words; 15: 3 *m.* not that I said old things have passed away.

MARVELOUS (*see also* Marvel; Wonderful)

1 Ne. 14: 7 (22: 8; 2 Ne. 25: 17; 27: 26; 29: 1; 3 Ne. 21: 9; 28: 31–32; Isa. 29: 14) the Lord to bring forth great and *m.* work among men; **Alma** 19: 6 light of God's glory, which is *m.* light of his goodness, enlightens Lamoni's mind; **4 Ne.** 1: 5 Jesus' disciples do great and *m.* works; **Ether** 4: 15 when Israel rends veil of unbelief, great and *m.* things shall come forth; 12: 5 (13: 13) Ether prophesies great and *m.* things.

MARY—*mother of Jesus* (*see also* Virgin; BD Mary)

Mosiah 3: 8 Christ's mother shall be called M.; **Alma** 7: 10 Son of God shall be born of M.

MASTER (*see also* Lord; Mahan)

1 Ne. 4: 21 Zoram[1] supposes Nephi[1] to be his *m.*; **Jacob** 5: 4 *m.* of vineyard goes forth; **Mosiah** 4: 14 devil is the *m.* of sin; 5: 13 how knoweth a man the *m.* he has not served; 24: 9 Amulon puts task-*m.* over people of Alma[1]; **3 Ne.** 13: 24 (Matt. 6: 24) no man can serve two *m.*

MATHONI—*one of twelve Nephite disciples* [c. A.D. 34]

3 Ne. 19: 4 called by Jesus to minister to Nephites.

MATHONIHAH—*one of twelve Nephite disciples* [c. A.D. 34]

3 Ne. 19: 4 called by Jesus to minister to Nephites.

MEANING, MEAN, MEANT (*see also* Interpretation; Knowledge; Means)

1 Ne. 11: 17 Nephi[1] does not know *m.* of all things; 11: 21 (15: 21) knowest thou *m.* of tree; 13: 21 knowest thou *m.* of book; 15: 23 what *m.* rod of iron; 15: 26 what *m.* river of water; 22: 1 what *m.* these things ye have read; **Mosiah** 12: 20 what *m.* words which are written; **Alma** 12: 11 this is what is *m.* by chains of hell; 34: 14 whole *m.* of law is to point toward Christ; 40: 18 first resurrection *m.* reuniting of soul with body of those from Adam to Christ; 41: 12–13 *m.* of word restoration is to bring back evil for evil, good for good.

MEANS (*see also* Meaning)

1 Ne. 16: 29 (Alma 37: 6–7) by small *m.* the Lord can bring about great things; **Mosiah** 28: 13 Mosiah[2] translates records by *m.* of two stones; **Alma** 30: 47 better that thy soul be lost than that thou shouldst be *m.* of bringing others to destruction; 38: 9 (Hel. 5: 9) no other *m.* whereby man can be saved, only in and through Christ; **3 Ne.** 18: 32 ye shall be *m.* of bringing salvation unto the unworthy; **Morm.** 9: 34 the Lord has prepared *m.* for interpretation of writings.

MEASURE (*see also* Mete)

Alma 11: 4 Nephites do not *m.* after manner of Jews; 40: 8 time is *m.* only unto men; **3 Ne.** 14: 2 (Matt. 7: 2) with what *m.* ye mete, it shall be *m.* unto you.

MEAT (*see also* Flesh; Food)

1 Ne. 17: 2 Lehites live on raw *m.* in wilderness; 18: 6 Lehites prepare *m.* for voyage; **Enos** 1: 20 many Lamanites eat nothing but raw *m.*; **Alma** 8: 21 Amulek sets bread and *m.* before Alma[2]; **3 Ne.** 4: 19 robbers have nothing save *m.* for their subsistence; 13: 25 (Matt. 6: 25) is not life more than *m.*; 24: 10 (Mal. 3: 10) bring tithes into storehouse, that there may be *m.* in the Lord's house.

MEDIATION, MEDIATOR (*see* Jesus Christ—Mediator)

MEEK, MEEKNESS (*see also* Contrite; Gentle; Humble; Lowliness; Poor)

2 Ne. 9: 30 (28: 13) wo unto the rich,

for they persecute the *m.*; 21: 4 (30: 9; Isa. 11: 4) the Lord will reprove with equity for the *m.*; 27: 30 the *m.* also shall increase; **Mosiah** 3: 19 natural man is enemy to God, unless he becomes *m.*; **Alma** 13: 28 be led by Holy Spirit, becoming *m.*; **Hel.** 6: 39 Nephites turn backs upon the poor and *m.*; **3 Ne.** 12: 5 (Matt. 5: 5; Ps. 37: 11) blessed are the *m.*, for they shall inherit earth; **Ether** 12: 26 my grace is sufficient for the *m.*; **Moro.** 7: 39 ye have faith in Christ because of your *m.*; 7: 44 none is acceptable before God, save the *m.*; 8: 26 remission of sins brings *m.*

MEET, MET, MEETING (*see also* Assemble; Church; Conference; Congregation; Meet [adj.]; Mete; Worship)

2 Ne. 33: 7 Nephi[1] has great faith in Christ that he will *m.* many souls spotless at judgment; **Alma** 5: 28 if ye are not stripped of pride, ye are not prepared to *m.* God; 12: 24 (34: 32) this life a time to prepare to *m.* God; 48: 23 Nephites sorry to send Lamanites into eternal world unprepared to *m.* God; **4 Ne.** 1: 12 Nephites *m.* together oft to pray and hear word of God; **Ether** 12: 38 (Moro. 10: 34) I bid farewell until we *m.* before judgment-seat; **Moro.** 6: 5–6 church *m.* together oft to fast, pray, discuss, partake of sacrament; 6: 9 *m.* are conducted after workings of Spirit.

MELCHIZEDEK—*king of Salem* (*see also* Priesthood; BD Melchizedek)

Alma 13: 14 a priest after order of Son of God; 13: 15 received Abraham's tithes; 13: 17–18 persuaded his people to repent.

MELCHIZEDEK PRIESTHOOD (*see* Priesthood, Melchizedek)

MELEK—*Nephite land west of Sidon*

Alma 8: 3–4 Alma[2] journeys into M. to teach; 35: 13 Ammonites come to M.; 45: 18 Alma[2] leaves Zarahemla as if to go to M.

MELT (*see also* Molten)

2 Ne. 23: 7 (Isa. 13: 7) every man's heart shall *m.*; **3 Ne.** 26: 3 (Morm. 9: 2; 2 Pet. 3: 10) elements to *m.* with fervent heat.

MEMORY (*see also* Remember, Remembrance)

Alma 36: 17, 19 Alma[2] is harrowed by *m.* of many sins; 46: 12 Moroni[1] writes on coat, In *m.* of our God.

MEN (*see* Man)

MEND (*see also* Change; Repair; Repentance)

Hel. 11: 36 Nephites do not *m.* their ways.

MENTION

1 Ne. 20: 1 (Isa. 48: 1) Israel makes *m.* of God, yet they swear not in truth; 21: 1 (Isa. 49: 1) from bowels of my mother hath the Lord made *m.* of my name; **2 Ne.** 22: 4 (Isa. 12: 4) make *m.* that the Lord's name is exalted; **Alma** 13: 19 of Melchizedek they have more particularly made *m.*

MERCHANTS (*see also* Business; Trade; Traffic)

3 Ne. 6: 11 many *m.* in the land.

MERCY, MERCIFUL (*see also* Compassion; God, Love of; Grace; Jesus Christ, Atonement through; Justice; Love; Merit; Pity; Repentance; TG Mercy, Merciful)

1 Ne. 1: 20 tender *m.* of the Lord are over all whom he has chosen; 8: 8 Lehi[1] prays the Lord will have *m.* on him; 13: 33 the Lord will be *m.* unto Gentiles; **2 Ne.** 1: 3 how *m.* the Lord was in warning Lehites to flee Jerusalem; 4: 26 the Lord has visited men in so much *m.*; 9: 25 where there is no condemnation, *m.* of Holy One have claim; 9: 53 because of his *m.*, the Lord has promised Nephites' seed will not be utterly destroyed; 19: 17 (Isa. 9: 17) the Lord shall have no *m.* on Israel's fatherless and widows; **Jacob** 6: 5 while the Lord's arm of *m.* is extended, harden not your hearts; **Mosiah** 2: 38–39 *m.* hath no claim on the unrepentant; 15: 8–9 God breaks bands of death, having bowels of *m.*; **Alma** 2: 30 Lord, have *m.* and spare my life; 5: 33 the Lord's arms of *m.* are extended to all men; 7: 12 the Lord will take upon him their infirmities, that his bowels may be filled with *m.*; 9: 11 if it had not been for the Lord's *m.* we should unavoidably have been cut off; 12: 33–34 whoso repents and hardens not his heart has claim on *m.* through Son; 15: 10 Lord, have *m.* on this man; 26: 37 the Lord's bowels of *m.* are over all the earth; 29: 10 then do I remember his *m.* arm; 32: 13 (Ether 11: 8) whoso repents shall find *m.*; 32: 22 God is *m.* unto all who believe; 34: 15 intent of last sacrifice is to bring about the bowels of *m.*, which overpowers justice; 34: 16 (42: 15) *m.* can satisfy demands of justice; 41: 14 if ye do all these things, ye shall have *m.* restored to you; 42: 15 plan of *m.* could not be brought about except an atonement be made; 42: 22 which repentance *m.* claimeth; 42: 25 do ye suppose that *m.* can rob justice; **3 Ne.** 12: 7 (Matt. 5: 7) blessed are the *m.*, for they shall obtain *m.*; 17: 7

Christ's bowels are filled with *m.*; 29: 7 no *m.* for son of perdition; **Moro.** 8: 19 awful wickedness to deny pure *m.* of God unto little children, for they are alive in him because of *m.*; 8: 20 he that saith little children need baptism denieth *m.* of Christ.

MERIT (*see also* Grace; Jesus Christ, Atonement through; Mercy; Virtue; Worth)

2 Ne. 2: 8 no flesh can dwell in God's presence, save through *m.* of Messiah; 31: 19 rely wholly upon *m.* of him who is mighty to save; **Alma** 22: 14 since man had fallen, he could not *m.* anything of himself; 24: 10 God has taken away guilt from hearts through *m.* of his Son; **Hel.** 14: 13 have remission of sins through Christ's *m.*; **Moro.** 6: 4 rely alone upon *m.* of Christ.

MERRY (*see also* Glad; Happiness; Lightmindedness)

1 Ne. 18: 9 wives begin to make themselves *m.*; **2 Ne.** 28: 7–8 many shall say, Eat, drink, and be *m.*; **Mosiah** 20: 1 Lamanite daughters gather to make themselves *m.*; **Alma** 55: 14 Lamanite soldiers drink and are *m.*

MESSENGER (*see also* Angel; Servant)

3 Ne. 24: 1 (Mal. 3: 1) behold, I will send my *m.*

MESSIAH (*see* Jesus Christ—Messiah)

METAL (*see also* Gold; Iron; Ore; Silver; Steel)

Hel. 6: 9 Nephites and Lamanites have all manner of precious *m.*; **Ether** 10: 23 Jaredites make all manner of *m.*

METE (*see also* Give; Measure)

3 Ne. 14: 2 (Matt. 7: 2) with what measure ye *m.* it shall be measured to you.

MIDDONI—*Lamanite land*

Alma 20: 2–3 the Lord tells Ammon[2] to go to M., where brethren are in prison; 20: 4–7 Lamoni offers to go with Ammon[2] to M. to release brethren; 20: 14–15 Lamoni refuses his father's order not to go to M.; 20: 28–30 (21: 12–13) brethren of Ammon[2] had been cast into prison in M., released by Ammon[2] and Lamoni; 21: 18 Ammon[2] and Lamoni return from M.; 23: 8–10 Lamanites in M. are converted unto the Lord.

MIDIAN, LAND OF—*Lamanite land east of Lehi-Nephi*

Alma 24: 5 Ammon[2] meets his brethren in M.

MIDST

3 Ne. 11: 8 (17: 12–13; 27: 2) Christ stands in *m.* of Nephites.

MIGHT (*see also* Arm; God, Power of; Mighty; Power; Strength)

2 Ne. 25: 29 worship Christ with all your *m.*; **Jacob** 1: 19 by laboring with their *m.*, the Lord's servants would not have people's blood on their garments; 5: 61, 71 call servants, that we may labor diligently with our *m.* in vineyard; 7: 25 Nephites fortify against Lamanites with all their *m.*, trusting in God; **Mosiah** 2: 11 Benjamin has served his people with all *m.*; **Alma** 5: 50 Son comes in his *m.*; **3 Ne.** 3: 16 Nephites exert themselves in their *m.* to do according to words of Lachoneus; **Moro.** 10: 32 love God with all *m.*, mind, and strength.

MIGHTY, MIGHTIER (*see also* God, Power of; Strong)

1 Ne. 17: 32 the Lord makes Israelites *m.* unto driving out children of land; 22: 7 God will raise up a *m.* nation among Gentiles; **2 Ne.** 3: 24 one *m.* shall rise up to do much good in restoring Israel; 6: 17 (Isa. 49: 25) captives of the *m.* shall be taken away; 15: 15 (Isa. 5: 15) the *m.* shall be humbled; 31: 19 rely wholly upon merits of him who is *m.* to save; **Mosiah** 5: 2 the Lord has wrought *m.* change in Benjamin's people; **Alma** 5: 14 have ye experienced this *m.* change; 34: 18 cry unto God for mercy, for he is *m.* to save; **Hel.** 10: 5 the Lord will make Nephi[2] *m.* in word and deed; **Morm.** 9: 18 Christ and apostles did many *m.* miracles; **Ether** 2: 1 valley of Nimrod named after *m.* hunter.

MILDNESS

Hel. 5: 29–33 still voice of perfect *m.* calls Lamanites to repent.

MILE

3 Ne. 12: 41 (Matt. 5: 41) whosoever shall compel thee to go a *m.*, go with him twain.

MILK

2 Ne. 9: 50 (26: 25) come buy wine and *m.* without money.

MILLENNIUM (*see also* Day of the Lord; Jesus Christ, Second Coming of; Kingdom of God; Zion; TG Millennium; Millennium, Preparing a People for)

1 Ne. 22: 26 (2 Ne. 30: 18) because of people's righteousness, Satan bound, cannot be loosed for many years.

MIND, MINDED (*see also* Heart; Knowledge; Mindful; Spirit)

2 **Ne.** 1: 21 my sons, to be determined in one *m.*; 9: 39 to be carnally *m.* is death, to be spiritually *m.* is life eternal; 25: 29 worship Christ with all your *m.*; **Jacob** 2: 9 instead of feasting on pleasing word of God, daggers are placed to wound their delicate *m.*; 3: 2 ye may feast upon God's love if your *m.* are firm; **Enos** 1: 10 voice of the Lord came into *m.* of Enos[2]; **Mosiah** 2: 9 open your *m.*, that mysteries of God may be unfolded; 4: 13 ye will not have a *m.* to injure one another; **Alma** 15: 3 Zeezrom's fever is caused by great tribulations of *m.* on account of his wickedness; 17: 5 sons of Mosiah[2] suffer much, both in body and *m.*; 19: 6 glory of God lights up Lamoni's *m.*; 30: 53 Korihor teaches devil's words because they are pleasing to carnal *m.*; 31: 5 word has more powerful effect upon *m.* of people than sword; 32: 34 when word swells in soul, *m.* begins to expand; 36: 4 Alma[2] obtains knowledge not of carnal *m.*, but of God; 36: 18 as *m.* of Alma[2] caught hold on Christ, he cried for mercy; 39: 13 turn to the Lord with all your *m.*; 40: 1 (41: 1) Corianton's *m.* is worried concerning resurrection; 57: 27 *m.* of Ammonite youths are firm; **Ether** 4: 15 veil of unbelief causes men to remain in blindness of *m.*; **Moro.** 7: 30 angels show themselves unto them of firm *m.* in every form of godliness; 9: 25 may Christ's mercy, long-suffering rest in your *m.* forever; 10: 32 (Matt. 22: 37) love God with all your might, *m.*

MINDFUL

Alma 26: 37 God is *m.* of every people; **Moro.** 8: 2 Christ hath been *m.* of you.

MINGLE (*see also* Mix)

Alma 3: 9 he who *m.* seed with Lamanites brings same curse on his seed; 5: 57 names of the wicked not to be *m.* with names of the Lord's people; 50: 22 wicked Nephites dwindle in unbelief and *m.* with Lamanites; **Hel.** 1: 12 robbers *m.* with people.

MINISTER [noun] (*see also* Disciple; Minister [verb], Ministration; Ministry; Officer; Preacher; Servant)

1 Ne. 12: 9–10 twelve *m.* shall judge Nephites; **Mosiah** 23: 14 trust no man to be your *m.* except he be a man of God.

MINISTER [verb], **MINISTRATION** (*see also* Administration; Angels, Ministering of; Ministry; Serve)

3 Ne. 7: 17 Nephi[3] *m.* with power and great authority; 10: 19 Christ *m.* unto Nephites; 13: 25 Christ chooses twelve disciples to *m.* unto Nephites; 26: 19 disciples *m.* one to another; 28: 29 three Nephites shall administer unto scattered tribes of Israel; **Moro.** 4: 1 elders and priests *m.* bread.

MINISTRY (*see also* Calling; Minister [noun]; Minister [verb]; Office; Preach; Serve, Service; TG Ministry; BD Ministry)

1 Ne. 9: 3 Nephi[1] to engrave on plates an account of *m.* of his people; **Alma** 39: 3 Corianton did forsake the *m.*; **3 Ne.** 7: 15 Nephi[3] given power to know concerning *m.* of Christ; **Moro.** 7: 31 office of the *m.* is to call men unto repentance; 8: 2 Christ has called Moroni[2] to his *m.*

MINON—*Nephite land on west bank of river Sidon*

Alma 2: 24 Nephite scouts see many Lamanites in M.

MIRACLE, MIRACULOUS (*see also* Faith; God, Manifestations of; God, Power of; Marvel; Raise; Sign; Wonder; TG Miracle; BD Miracle)

1 Ne. 17: 51 the Lord has wrought many *m.* among men; **2 Ne.** 10: 4 should mighty *m.* be wrought among other nations, they would repent; 26: 13 Christ works *m.* among men according to their faith; 27: 23 (Morm. 9: 11) I am a God of *m.*; 28: 6 (Morm. 8: 26) churches shall deny that God is God of *m.*; **Mosiah** 3: 5 (15: 6) God shall come down among men and work mighty *m.*; 8: 18 God has provided a means that man, through faith, might work mighty *m.*; **Alma** 23: 6 many Lamanites brought to knowledge of truth by power of God working *m.* in missionaries; 57: 26 preservation of Ammonite striplings ascribed to *m.* power of God; **Hel.** 4: 25 the Lord ceases to preserve Nephites by *m.* power; 16: 4 Nephi[2] works *m.* that people might know Christ must shortly come; **3 Ne.** 1: 4 greater *m.* wrought among the people in preparation for Christ's coming; 8: 1 no man could do *m.* in Jesus' name save he were cleansed from iniquity; 19: 35 Christ could not show so great *m.* to Jews because of their unbelief; 29: 7 wo unto him who says, to get gain, that no *m.* can be wrought by Christ; **4 Ne.** 1: 5 Jesus' disciples work all manner of *m.* in his name; **Morm.** 1: 3 *m.* cease because of iniquity; 9: 15–19 God has not ceased to be a God of *m.*; 9: 17 creation of earth and of men were *m.*; 9: 17 by power of God's word have *m.* been wrought; 9: 18 many mighty *m.* wrought by apostles; 9: 20 (Ether 12: 12) if God ceases to do *m.*, it is because of unbelief of men; **Ether** 12: 16 (Moro. 7: 37) all who work *m.* work them by faith; **Moro.** 7: 27, 29, 35–36 *m.* have not ceased because Christ ascended into heaven; 7: 37–38 if *m.* cease, it is because faith has ceased; 10: 12 to another is given gift of working mighty *m*.

MIRE

2 Ne. 20: 6 (Isa. 10: 6) I will give him charge to tread them down like *m*. of streets; **3 Ne.** 7: 8 people have turned from righteousness like sow to her wallowing in *m*.

MISCHIEF (*see also* Harm; Malice; Wicked)

2 Ne. 5: 24 Lamanites become idle, full of *m*.; **3 Ne.** 16: 10 when Gentiles are filled with *m*., Father will bring gospel from them.

MISERY, MISERABLE (*see also* Anguish; Hell; Sorrow; Suffering; Torment; Tribulation; Unhappy; Wretched)

2 Ne. 1: 13 those bound by chains of hell are carried away to eternal gulf of *m*.; 2: 18 because devil became *m*. forever, he sought *m*. of all mankind; 2: 23 Adam and Eve could have had no joy, for they knew no *m*.; 2: 27 devil seeks that all men might be *m*. like himself; **Mosiah** 3: 25 view of own guilt causes wicked to shrink from the Lord into state of *m*.; 4: 17 perhaps thou shalt say, The man has brought upon himself his *m*.; **Alma** 3: 26 men will reap eternal happiness or *m*. according to works; 9: 11 except for the Lord's mercy, we might have been consigned to state of endless *m*.; 40: 15 consignation of soul to happiness or *m*. might be termed first resurrection; 42: 1 Corianton supposes it is unjust to consign sinner to *m*.; **Hel.** 3: 29 word of God leads man of Christ across everlasting gulf of *m*. prepared for the wicked; 5: 12 devil will have no power to drag those built in Christ's foundation down to gulf of endless *m*.; 12: 25–26 they who have done evil will be consigned to state of endless *m*.; **Morm.** 8: 38 greater is value of endless happiness than *m*. that never dies; 9: 4 men would be more *m*. to dwell with God under consciousness of filthiness than with damned souls.

MIST (*see also* Cloud; Darkness, Physical; Darkness, Spiritual; Smoke; Vapor)

1 Ne. 8: 23 *m*. of darkness arises in dream of Lehi[1]; 12: 4 (3 Ne. 8: 22) Nephi[1] sees *m*. of darkness in promised land; 12: 17 *m*. of darkness are temptations of devil.

MISUNDERSTAND

2 Ne. 25: 28 Nephi[1] has spoken plainly, that his people cannot *m*.

MIX, MIXTURE

1 Ne. 13: 30 the Lord will not suffer Gentiles to destroy *m*. of seed of Nephi[1] among his brethren; **2 Ne.** 5: 23 cursed shall be the seed of him who *m*. with Lamanites; **Alma** 3: 7–8 Lamanites are marked so that Nephites might not *m*. with them; 35: 10 Zoramites *m*. with Lamanites; **Hel.** 3: 16 Nephites *m*. with Lamanites until they are no longer called Nephites.

MOCK, MOCKERY (*see also* Malice; Persecution; Revile; Scorn)

1 Ne. 1: 19 Jews *m*. Lehi[1]; 8: 27 people in spacious building are in attitude of *m*.; **Jacob** 6: 8 will ye deny good word of Christ and make *m*. of plan of redemption; **Mosiah** 15: 5 Son suffereth himself to be *m*.; **Alma** 5: 30–31 he who makes *m*. of brother cannot be saved unless he repents; **Hel.** 4: 12 slaughter of Nephites is caused because they make *m*. of that which is sacred; **Ether** 7: 24 Jaredites revile against prophets and *m*. them; 12: 25 Moroni[2] fears Gentiles will *m*. his words; 12: 26 fools *m*., but they shall mourn; **Moro.** 8: 9, 23 solemn *m*. before God to baptize little children.

MOCUM, CITY OF

3 Ne. 9: 7 covered with water.

MOLTEN (*see also* Melt)

1 Ne. 17: 16 Nephi[1] makes tools with ore which he did *m*. out of rock; **Ether** 3: 1 brother of Jared[2] did *m*. out of rock sixteen small stones; 7: 9 Shule did *m*. out of hill and made swords.

MOMENT

3 Ne. 22: 7–8 (Isa. 54: 7–8) for small *m*. have I forsaken thee.

MONEY (*see also* Coin; Debt; Lucre; Mammon; Price; Riches; Tithing; Treasure; Wealth)

2 Ne. 9: 50 (Isa. 55: 1) he that hath no *m*., come buy and eat; 26: 25 buy milk and honey without *m*.; 26: 31 if laborers in Zion labor for *m*., they shall perish; **Alma** 1: 20 saints are persecuted because they impart word of God without *m*.; 11: 4–19 Nephite *m*. system; 11: 20 judges stir up people to disturbances, that they might get *m*.; **Hel.** 7: 5 the wicked go unpunished because of their *m*.; 9: 20 Nephi[2] is offered *m*. to reveal murderer; **3 Ne.** 20: 38 ye shall be redeemed without *m*.; **Morm.** 8: 32 churches shall say, For your *m*. you shall be forgiven of sins; 8: 37 ye love *m*. more than the poor.

MOON

2 Ne. 23: 10 (Isa. 13: 10) *m*. shall not cause her light to shine; **Hel.** 14: 20 (3 Ne. 8: 22) as sign of Christ's death, *m*. shall not give light.

MORE

3 Ne. 11: 40 whoso shall declare *m.* or less than Christ's doctrine is not built upon his rock; 18: 13 whoso shall do *m.* or less than these is not built upon Christ's rock.

MORIANCUMER, LAND OF

Ether 2: 13 Jaredites camp in M.

MORIANTON[1]—*Jaredite king*

Ether 1: 22–23 (10: 9, 13) descendant of Riplakish, father of Kim; 10: 9–13 gathers army of outcasts, establishes himself as king; 10: 10–11 eases people's burden, rules justly; 10: 12 builds many cities; 10: 13 lives to great age.

MORIANTON[2]—*founder of Nephite city* [c. 68 B.C.] (*see also* Morianton, City of and Land of; Morianton, People of)

Alma 50: 28 leader of people of Morianton; 50: 29 plans to lead his people to land northward; 50: 30–31 beats maid servant, who flees and tells Moroni[1] about plans; 50: 32 Moroni[1] fears consequences of his flight to north; 50: 35 is slain by Teancum.

MORIANTON, CITY OF AND LAND OF—*area settled by* Morianton[2] (*see also* Morianton[2]; Morianton, People of)

Alma 50: 25 land of M. next to land of Lehi, near seashore; 50: 36 people restored to land of M.; 51: 26 is possessed by Amalickiah; 55: 33 is fortified by Lamanites; 55: 33 (59: 4) Moroni[1] prepares attack; 59: 5 people flee to Nephihah, are attacked by Lamanites.

MORIANTON, PEOPLE OF—*followers of Morianton*[2] (*see also* Morianton, City of and Land of)

Alma 50: 26 claim part of land of Lehi, take up arms; 50: 28 fear Moroni[1] will destroy them; 50: 29–32 plan to flee to land northward; 50: 33–36 are stopped and brought back by Moroni[1]; 51: 1 peace is established between people of Lehi and people of M.

MORIANTUM—*Nephite area*

Moro. 9: 9–10 people in M. take Lamanite daughters prisoner, rape and murder them.

MORMON[1] [c. A.D. 322]

Morm. 1: 5 father of Mormon[2].

MORMON[2]—*Nephite prophet, general, record keeper, abridger* [c. A.D. 333]

W of M 1: 1 is about to deliver record to Moroni[2]; 1: 3 after abridging large plates of Nephi, finds small plates; 1: 6 puts small plates with others; 1: 9 makes record according to understanding God has given him; 1: 11 prays plates will be preserved; **3 Ne.** 5: 12 is called after land of Mormon; 5: 20 (Morm. 1: 5) a pure descendant of Nephi[1]; **Morm.** 1: 1 calls his record the Book of M.; 1: 2 when ten years old, is visited by Ammaron; 1: 3–4 is instructed to take record from hill when twenty-four; 1: 5 son of Mormon[1]; 1: 6 is taken by father to Zarahemla; 1: 15 visited by the Lord; 1: 16–17 is forbidden to preach because of hardness of Nephites' hearts; 2: 12 hopes people will become righteous; 2: 17 takes large plates and makes record according to instructions; 3: 11 refuses to be leader because of people's wickedness; 3: 17 writes for future generations; 4: 23 takes all records hidden by Ammaron; 6: 2 writes epistle to Lamanite king; 6: 4–5 gathers Nephites to Cumorah; 6: 6 makes record out of plates of Nephi and places record in hill; 8: 1 record is finished by son, Moroni[2]; 8: 3 is killed by Lamanites; **Ether** 15: 11 hid records in hill Ramah; **Moro.** ch. 7 teachings on faith, hope, and charity; ch. 8 letter concerning baptism of little children; ch. 9 second epistle to Moroni[2].

MORMON, FOREST OF—*near waters of Mormon* (*see also* Mormon, Place of; Mormon, Waters of)

Mosiah 18: 30 beautiful to eyes of those who there came to knowledge of Redeemer.

MORMON, PLACE OF—*region near city of Lehi-Nephi* (*see also* Mormon, Forest of; Mormon, Waters of)

Mosiah 18: 4–7 those who believe Alma[1] go to M., where he is hiding, to hear him; 18: 5 fountain of pure water in M.; 18: 30 Alma[1] establishes order of church; 18: 31–33 people in M. are discovered by king; 18: 34–35 people depart into wilderness.

MORMON, WATERS OF—*fountain in land of Mormon*

Mosiah 18: 5 in M. a fountain of pure water; 18: 8–16, 30 (25: 18; 26: 15; Alma 5: 3) converts are baptized in waters of M.; 18: 30 beautiful to eyes of those who there came to knowledge of Redeemer.

MORNING

2 Ne. 24: 12 (Isa. 14: 12) Lucifer, son of *m.*; **Alma** 34: 21 cry unto the Lord *m.*, mid-day, and evening; 37: 37 when thou risest in *m.*, let heart be full of thanks unto God.

MORON—*late Jaredite king*

Ether 1: 7–8 (11: 14) son of Ethem, father of Coriantor; 11: 14 reigns wickedly; 11: 15–17 battles for kingdom; 11: 18 is overthrown, dwells in captivity.

MORON, LAND OF—*north of the great land of Desolation*

Ether 7: 5–6 is invaded by Corihor[1], king taken captive; 7: 6 is near Desolation; 7: 17 Shule is carried captive into M.; 14: 6 brother of Shared places himself on throne of Coriantumr[2] in M.; 14: 11 Coriantumr[2] battles Lib[2] in M.

MORONI[1]—*righteous Nephite military commander* [c. 100 B.C.]

Alma 43: 16–17 chief captain of all Nephite armies; 43: 19–21 equips army, prepares armor for soldiers; 43: 22–23 sends spies into wilderness; 43: 24–25 marches into Manti; 43: 27–42 prepares stratagem to surround Lamanite army; 43: 47–50 inspires soldiers to fight for freedom; 43: 51–54 defeats Lamanites; 44: 1–6 demands surrender of Zerahemnah; 44: 8–12 Zerahemnah fails in attempt on M's life; 44: 16–18 commands soldiers to slay Zerahemnah's soldiers; 44: 19–20 Zerahemnah surrenders to M.; 46: 11 angered by Amalickiah's dissension; 46: 12–13 makes title of liberty; 46: 21–28 gathers army; 46: 30–33 cuts off armies of Amalickiah, who flees; 46: 34 is appointed by chief judges and voice of people; 46: 35 puts to death those who deny covenant of freedom; 46: 36 hoists title of liberty from every tower; 48: 7–10 strengthens his armies; 48: 11–18 character of M.; 49: 2–8 fortifies army with trenches; 50: 1–6 builds more fortifications; 50: 7–12 drives out Lamanites; 50: 31–36 sends army to stop flight of Morianton[2] and his people; 51: 13–21 has conflict with king-men; 52: 5–11 sends orders and reinforcements to Teancum; 52: 18–19 enters Bountiful, joins Teancum; 52: 21–26 takes city of Mulek by stratagem; 52: 35 is wounded; 52: 34–40 subdues remaining Lamanites near city of Mulek; 53: 1–5 fortifies Bountiful; 54: 4–14 epistle to Ammoron; 55: 6–15 sends Laman[4] with wine to Lamanites; 55: 16–24 arms prisoners in Gid and takes city; ch. 56–58 receives epistle from Helaman[2]; 59: 3 writes to Pahoran[1]; 59: 13 is angry with government because of indifference; ch. 60 writes second epistle to Pahoran[1]; 62: 1 is filled with joy over faithfulness of Pahoran[1]; 62: 4 raises standard of liberty wherever he goes; 62: 6, 14 joins Pahoran[1]; 62: 18–26 takes city of Nephihah; 62: 42–43 after fortifying land, yields command of army to son; 63: 3 dies.

MORONI[2]—*son of Mormon[2], last of Nephites* [c. A.D. 421]

W of M 1: 1 Mormon[2] plans to deliver record to M.; **Morm.** 6: 6 Mormon[2] stores records except few plates given to M.; 6: 11–12 one of only twenty-four remaining Nephites; 8: 1 is finishing record of his father; 8: 10–11 testifies of three Nephite disciples; 8: 12 would make all things known if possible; 8: 14 (Moro. 10: 2) seals up plates; ch. 9 address to unbelievers; **Ether** 1: 1 gives account of Jaredites; 3: 17 does not make full account of Jesus' appearance to brother of Jared[2]; 4: 5 is commanded to seal records with the interpreters; 5: 1–6 instructs future translator; 6: 1 (9: 1) continues history of Jaredites; 8: 20 does not give secret oaths; 12: 6–12 discourse on faith; 12: 23–28 not mighty in writing, fears Gentiles will mock; 12: 29 is comforted by Ether's words; 12: 38–41 bids farewell to Gentiles; 13: 1 tells of Jaredites' destruction; **Moro.** 1: 1 adds to his record; ch. 2–6 records ordinances and church discipline; ch. 7 records father's teachings on faith, hope, and charity; ch. 8 father's epistle concerning baptism of little children; ch. 9 father's second epistle; 10: 1–2 writes few more words to Lamanites before sealing records; 10: 34 to meet readers before judgment-bar of God.

MORONI, CITY OF AND LAND OF—*in southeast of Nephite lands*

Alma 50: 13 is built by Nephites near east sea, by possessions of Lamanites; 51: 22 Lamanites come into land of M.; 51: 23–24 (59: 5) Nephites are driven from city of M. to Nephihah; 62: 25 Lamanites again flee to land of M.; 62: 32–34 Lamanites encircled in land of M.; **3 Ne.** 8: 9 (9: 4) city of M. sinks into sea.

MORONIHAH[1]—*righteous Nephite general, son of Moroni[1]* [c. 60 B.C.]

Alma 62: 43 Moroni[1] turns armies over to son, M.; 63: 15 drives back Lamanites; **Hel.** 1: 25–27 is surprised by Lamanite invasion; 1: 28–30 defeats and captures enemy; 1: 33 retakes city of Zarahemla; 2: 1 establishes peace, but contention arises; 4: 6 is driven into land Bountiful; 4: 9–10 regains half of Nephites' possessions; 4: 14–20 brings Lamanites to repentance, regains control over land.

MORONIHAH[2]—*Nephite general* [c. A.D. 385]

Morm. 6: 14 fallen with his ten thousand.

MORONIHAH, CITY OF—*iniquitous Nephite city*

3 Ne. 8: 10, 25 (9: 5) is buried under earth.

MORROW (*see also* Tomorrow)

3 Ne. 1: 13 on the *m.* come I into the world.

MORTAL, MORTALITY (*see also* Body; Flesh; Immortality; Life; Man; Probation; Temporal; World; TG Mortality)

Enos 1: 27 (Mosiah 16: 10; Morm. 6: 21) *m.* shall put on immortality; **Mosiah** 4: 6 continue in faith even unto end of life of *m.* body; **Alma** 5: 15 do you view this *m.* body raised in immortality; 11: 45 (12: 12, 20; 41: 4) *m.* body is raised to immortal body; 40: 2 this *m.* does not put on immortality until after coming of Christ; **3 Ne.** 28: 8, 17, 36 when Christ comes, three Nephites will be changed in twinkling of eye from *m.* to immortality.

MOSES—*great Hebrew prophet* [c. fifteenth century B.C.] (*see also* Law of Moses; Moses, Books of; BD Moses)

1 Ne. 4: 2 let us be strong like unto M.; 17: 24–26 (2 Ne. 3: 10) M. is commanded to lead Israel out of bondage; 17: 24 M. smote rock and water came forth; 17: 30, 42 Israelites reviled against M.; 22: 20–21 (3 Ne. 20: 23; 21: 11; Deut. 18: 15) Christ is prophet like unto M. that the Lord would raise; **2 Ne.** 3: 9–17 latter-day prophet like unto M. to be named Joseph; 25: 20 (Hel. 8: 11–13) M. was given power by God; **Mosiah** 12: 33 the Lord delivered commandments to M. in mount of Sinai; 13: 5 Abinadi's face shines even as M.; 13: 33 M. prophesied about Messiah; **Alma** 45: 19 Alma[2] is buried by hand of the Lord even as M.; **3 Ne.** 27: 8 if church is called by M. name, it is M. church.

MOSES, BOOKS OF

1 Ne. 5: 11 brass plates contain books of M.; 19: 23 Nephi[1] reads many things written in books of M.

MOSIAH[1]—*Nephite prophet, king in Zarahemla, father of Benjamin*

Omni 1: 12 is warned to flee out of land of Nephi; 1: 14–15 discovers people of Zarahemla; 1: 18 causes people of Zarahemla to be taught in his language; 1: 19 is appointed king of united peoples; 1: 23 son, Benjamin, reigns after his death; **Mosiah** 2: 32 spoke of evil spirit.

MOSIAH[2]—*Nephite king, son of Benjamin* [c. 154-91 B.C.] (*see also* Mosiah[2], Sons of)

Mosiah 1: 2 son of Benjamin, taught in language of his fathers; 1: 10 (2: 30; 6: 3) is proclaimed king; 1: 18 is told to gather the people; 6: 4–7 walks in ways of his father; 7: 1–2 sends expedition to Lehi-Nephi; 21: 28 has gift of interpretation; 22: 14 (24: 25) receives people from Lehi-Nephi with joy; 25: 1–7 reads records of Alma[1] and Zeniff; 25: 14–19 (26: 12) allows Alma[1] to establish churches; 27: 1–3 forbids unbelievers to persecute believers; 28: 11–19 translates records; 28: 20 confers records and sacred articles on Alma[2]; 29: 11, 25, 39 recommends that people select judges; 29: 30–36 discourses on kings; 29: 46 dies; 29: 47 last of Nephite kings; **Alma** 1: 1 accomplishments of M.; 10: 19 had warned of destruction through transgression; 11: 4 established permanent system of measures; 17: 35 (19: 23) was promised that his sons would be saved; **Hel.** 4: 21–22 words of M. were being trampled; **Ether** 4: 1 was instructed not to make experience of brother of Jared[2] known to people.

MOSIAH[2], SONS OF—*great Nephite missionaries* (*see also* Aaron[2]; Ammon[2]; Himni; Omner)

Mosiah 27: 8–10 (Alma 36: 6) among unbelievers trying to destroy church; 27: 11–12, 18–20 are rebuked by angel; 27: 32–35 preach throughout Zarahemla; 27: 34 (Alma 22: 35; 23: 1; 25: 17; 31: 6) names are Ammon[2], Aaron[3], Omner, and Himni; 28: 1–7 obtain permission to go to preach to Lamanites; 28: 10 (29: 3; Alma 17: 6) unwilling to be king; **Alma** ch. 17–26 record of ministry among Lamanites; 17: 1 meet Alma[2] again; 23: 4 establish churches; 31: 6 accompany Alma[2] to Zoramites; 48: 18 all men of God.

MOTE

3 Ne. 14: 3 (Matt. 7: 3) why beholdest thou the *m.* in thy brother's eye.

MOTH

3 Ne. 13: 19–20 (27: 32; Matt. 6: 19–20) lay not up for yourselves treasures upon earth, where *m.* and rust corrupt.

MOTHER (*see also* Child; Family; Father; Marriage; Parent; Wife; TG Marriage, Motherhood; Mother)

1 Ne. 2: 5 (5: 1; 8: 14) Sariah, *m.* of Nephi[1]; 11: 18 the virgin whom thou seest is *m.* of Son of God; 13: 17 *m.* Gentiles gather against Gentiles in promised land; 13: 34 abominable church is *m.* of harlots; 14: 9 abominable church is *m.* of abominations; 17: 55 (Mosiah 13: 20; Ex. 20: 12) honor father and *m.*; 18: 19 Jacob[2] and Joseph[2] are grieved because of afflictions of their *m.*; 21: 23 (2 Ne. 6: 7; 10: 9; Isa. 49: 23) queens shall be Israel's nursing *m.*; **2 Ne.** 3: 1 in days of greatest sorrow did *m.* bear Joseph[2]; 7: 1 (Isa. 50: 1) where is bill of *m*'s divorcement, for your transgressions is *m.* put away; 9: 7 flesh must have crumbled to *m.* earth; **Jacob** 5: 54 branches of *m.* tree grafted into roots of natural branches; 5: 56, 60 branches of natural trees grafted into roots of *m.* tree; **Mosiah** 2: 26 Benjamin about to yield mortal frame to *m.* earth; 3: 8 Christ's *m.* shall be called Mary; **Alma** 56: 47 (57: 21) Ammonite youths taught by *m.* that if they did not doubt, God would deliver them; **3 Ne.** 8: 25 if we had repented, our *m.* and daughters would have been spared; **Morm.** 6: 15 Nephites' bodies left to crumble and return to *m.* earth; 6: 19 O ye fathers and *m.*, how is it ye could have fallen.

MOUNT, MOUNTAIN (*see also* Antipas, Mount; Hill; Sinai, Mount; Zerin, Mount; Zion, Mount)

1 Ne. 11: 1 Nephi[1] is caught away in Spirit into high *m.*; 12: 4 Nephi[2] beholds *m.* tumbling into pieces; 13: 37 (Mosiah 12: 21; 15: 15–18; 3 Ne. 20: 40; Isa. 52: 7) how beautiful upon *m.* are feet of them that publish peace and tidings of great joy; 16: 30 Nephi[1] goes into top of *m.* to hunt; 17: 7 Nephi[1] is commanded to get into *m.* to speak with the Lord; 18: 3 Nephi[1] goes into *m.* oft to pray; **2 Ne.** 12: 2–3 (Isa. 2: 2–3) *m.* of the Lord's house shall be established in top of *m.*; 21: 9 (30: 15; Isa. 11: 9) they shall not hurt nor destroy in all the Lord's holy *m.*; 24: 25 (Isa. 14: 25) upon my *m.* shall I tread the Assyrian under foot; 26: 5 *m.* shall cover those who kill prophets; **Jacob** 4: 6 (Morm. 8: 24; Ether 12: 30) we can command in Jesus' name and *m.* obey; **Alma** 12: 14 we would be glad if we could command *m.* to fall upon us to hide us from the Lord's presence; **Hel.** 12: 9 at the Lord's voice *m.* tremble; 12: 17 if the Lord commands *m.* to fall on city, it is done; 14: 23 *m.* to be made low and valleys to become *m.* at Christ's death; **3 Ne.** 8: 10 in place of Moronihah there became a great *m.*; 22: 10 (Isa. 54: 10) *m.* shall depart and hills be removed; **Ether** 3: 1—4: 1 brother of Jared[2] speaks with the Lord upon *m.*; 12: 30 brother of Jared[2] tells *m.* to remove.

MOURN, MOURNING (*see also* Comfort; Cry; Grieve; Lament; Sorrow; Suffering; Wail; Weep)

2 Ne. 8: 11 (Isa. 51: 11) sorrow and *m.* shall flee away; 32: 7 Nephi[1] is left to *m.* because of wickedness of men; **Jacob** 7: 26 Nephites *m.* out their days; **Mosiah** 7: 23 how great reason Limhi's people have to *m.*; 18: 9–10 those willing to *m.* with those that *m.* should be baptized; 21: 9 (Alma 28: 4; 30: 2) great *m.* because of war; **Hel.** 7: 6–11 Nephi[2] *m.* for wickedness of his people; 9: 10 people assemble to *m.* death of chief judge; **3 Ne.** 8: 23 great *m.* because of destruction; 10: 10 *m.* turns into joy; 12: 4 (Matt. 5: 4) blessed are all who *m.*, for they shall be comforted; **Morm.** 2: 11–13 Nephites *m.* because God will not always suffer them to take happiness in sin; 6: 18 ye are fallen, and I *m.* your loss; 8: 40 why do ye cause widows and orphans to *m.* before the Lord; **Ether** 11: 13 prophets *m.* and withdraw from the people; 12: 26 fools mock, but they shall *m.*; 15: 3 Coriantumr[2] *m.* and refuses to be comforted.

MOUTH (*see also* Lips; Speak; Tongue; Word)

1 Ne. 21: 2 (Isa. 49: 2) he hath made my *m.* like a sharp sword; **2 Ne.** 27: 14 (Ether 5: 4) in *m.* of witnesses will the Lord establish his word; 27: 25 (Isa. 29: 13) this people draw near the Lord with mouth, but remove hearts from him; **Mosiah** 14: 7 (Isa. 53: 7) he was oppressed and afflicted, yet he opened not his *m.*; **Alma** 13: 22 voice of the Lord, by *m.* of angels, declares repentance to all nations; **3 Ne.** 20: 45 (21: 8) kings shall shut their *m.*; 26: 16 even babes open *m.* and utter marvelous things; **Ether** 5: 2–4 in *m.* of three witnesses shall these things be established; **Moro.** 7: 23 God declared to prophets, by own *m.*, that Christ should come; 7: 25 by every word that proceeded out of *m.* of God, men began to exercise faith in Christ; 10: 28 these things shall proceed out of *m.* of everlasting God.

MOVE (*see also* Remove)

Mosiah 2: 21 God lends men breath, that they may live and *m.*; **Hel.** 12: 13 if the Lord says unto earth, M., it is *m.*; 12: 15 it is the earth that *m.*, and not the sun; **Ether** 12: 30 if brother of Jared[2] had not had faith, mountain would not have *m.*

MULEK—*son of Jewish king Zedekiah* [c. 589 B.C.]

Mosiah 25: 2 Zarahemla a descendant of M.; **Hel.** 6: 10 son of Zedekiah was brought into land north; 8: 21 all Zedekiah's sons slain except M.

MULEK, CITY OF—*Nephite city south of Bountiful*

Alma 51: 25–26 on east borders by seashore, possessed by Amalickiah; 52: 2 Lamanite army retreats to M.; 52: 16–26 (53: 2, 6) Moroni[1] retakes M.

MULEK, LAND OF (*see also* Desolation, Land of)

Hel. 6: 10 land north is called M.

MULOKI—*missionary companion of Aaron*[3]

Alma 20: 2 imprisoned in land of Middoni; 21: 11 preaches in Ani-Anti; 21: 12 travels to Middoni with Aaron[3].

MULTIPLY (*see also* Enlarge; Grow; Increase)

2 Ne. 5: 13 (4 Ne. 1: 10) Nephites *m.* in land; **3 Ne.** 19: 24 Jesus' disciples pray without *m.* words; **Ether** 6: 18 Jaredites *m.*

MULTITUDE (*see also* Nation)

1 Ne. 11: 34–35 *m.* of earth gathered together to fight apostles; 12: 13–15 Nephi[1] sees *m.* of his seed battling against seed of brethren; 13: 14 Nephi[1] beholds *m.* of Gentiles upon promised land; **2 Ne.** 23: 4 (Isa. 13: 4) noise of *m.* in mountains like a great people; **Mosiah** 2: 7 *m.* of his people so great that Benjamin must speak from tower; **3 Ne.** 11: 12 *m.* of Nephites falls to earth; 17: 18 so great is joy of *m.* that they are overcome; 18: 37 (Moro. 2: 3) *m.* does not hear Christ give disciples authority to bestow Holy Ghost.

MURDER, MURDERER, MURDEROUS (*see also* Blood, Shedding of; Capital Punishment; Kill; Martyrdom; Secret Combination; Slay; BD Murder)

1 Ne. 17: 44 elder sons of Lehi[1] are *m.* in hearts; **2 Ne.** 9: 9 (Hel. 6: 29; Ether 8: 16) devil is source of secret combinations of *m.*; 9: 35 wo unto *m.* who deliberately kills; 10: 15 the Lord will destroy secret works of *m.*; 26: 32 (Mosiah 2: 13) the Lord commands that men should not *m.*; **Alma** 1: 18 those who practice priestcraft dare not *m.* for fear of law; 17: 14 Lamanites delight in *m.* Nephites; 30: 10 (34: 12) if a man *m.*, he was punished unto death; 36: 14 Alma[2] had *m.* many, or led them unto destruction; 37: 30 secret workers of darkness *m.* the prophets; 39: 6 not easy for him who *m.* against light to gain forgiveness; 42: 19 if no law was given, would a man fear he would die if he *m.*; 54: 7 hell awaits *m.* except they withdraw *m.* purposes; **Hel.** 2: 4 Gadianton expert in craft of secret work of *m.*; 6: 17 Nephites begin to commit secret *m.*; 6: 21 robbers covenant they should not suffer for *m.*; 8: 26 Nephites are ripening for destruction because of *m.*; **3 Ne.** 5: 4 robbers who covenant not to *m.* are set at liberty; 7: 6 government destroyed by secret combination of friends and kindred of those who *m.* prophets; 9: 9 people of Jacob[4] are burned because of secret *m.* and combinations; 16: 10 when Gentiles are filled with *m.*, Father will bring gospel from among them; 30: 2 Mormon[2] calls Gentiles to repent of *m.*; **Morm.** 8: 8 whole face of land is one continual round of *m.*; **Ether** 8: 15 Cain was a *m.* from beginning; 8: 23 suffer not that *m.* combinations shall get above you; 8: 25 devil caused man to commit *m.* from beginning; **Moro.** 9: 10 Nephites *m.* Lamanite daughters in most cruel manner.

MURMUR, MURMURING (*see also* Complain; Contention; Disobedience; Disputations; Dissension; Hardheartedness; Rebel)

1 Ne. 2: 11 (3: 31; 16: 20; 2 Ne. 1: 26; 5: 4) Laman[1] and Lemuel *m.* in many things; 3: 6 Nephi[1] is favored of the Lord because he has not *m.*; 16: 20 Lehi[1] begins to *m.* against the Lord; 17: 2 Lehites begin to bear journeyings without *m.*; 17: 49 Nephi[1] admonishes brethren to *m.* no more; **2 Ne.** 27: 35 they who *m.* shall learn doctrine; **Alma** 22: 24 great *m.* among Lamanites because of Aaron[2] and his companions.

MUSIC (*see* Dance; Sing)

MYSTERY (*see also* Godliness; Hide, Hidden; Knowledge; Secret; TG Mysteries of Godliness; BD Mystery)

1 Ne. 2: 16 Nephi[1] has great desires to know *m.* of God; 10: 19 *m.* of God shall be unfolded unto them that seek diligently, by power of Holy Ghost; **Jacob** 4: 8 how unsearchable are the depths of *m.* of God; 4: 18 (Alma 40: 3) I will unfold this *m.* unto you; **Mosiah** 1: 5 records are preserved that people might read and understand *m.* of God; 2: 9 open your minds that *m.* of God may be unfolded to your view; 8: 19 interpreters prepared for purpose of unfolding *m.* to men; **Alma** 10: 5 Amulek had never known much of the Lord's *m.* and marvelous power; 12: 9 given unto many to know *m.* of God; 26: 22 conditions for knowing God; 30: 28 Korihor claims priests yoke people with pretended *m.*; 37: 4 plates to go forth to every people, that they shall know *m.* contained thereon; 37: 11 these *m.* are not yet fully made known unto me, therefore I shall forbear; 37: 21 twenty-four plates to be kept, that *m.* and works of darkness may be made manifest; 40: 3 many *m.* that are kept that no one knoweth save God himself; **Hel.** 16: 21 people fear that prophets will work some great *m.* which they cannot understand.

NAHOM—*place in Arabian desert*

1 Ne. 16: 34 Ishmael[1] is buried at *N.*

NAIL

3 Ne. 11: 14–15 multitude feels prints of *n.* in Christ's hands and feet.

NAKED, NAKEDNESS (*see also* Charity; Clothing; Judgment; Needy; Poor)

2 Ne. 9: 14 we shall have perfect knowledge of our guilt and *n.*; **Jacob** 2: 19 seek riches to do good, to clothe the *n.*; **Mosiah** 4: 26 to retain remission of sin, impart substance, clothing the *n.*; 10: 5 (Hel. 6: 13) women work cloth, that Nephites might clothe their *n.*; 18: 28 Nephites are commanded to impart of substance to every needy, *n.* soul; **Alma** 1: 30 Nephites do not send away any who are *n.*; 3: 5 (43: 20) Lamanites are *n.* save loincloth; 14: 22 Ammonihahites take clothes from Alma[2] and Amulek, that they are *n.*; 20: 28–29 Ammon[2] finds brothers *n.* in prison; 34: 28 if ye turn away the *n.*, your prayer is vain; **Hel.** 4: 11–12 slaughter of Nephites caused by pride, withholding clothing from *n.*; **Morm.** 8: 39 why do ye suffer the *n.* to pass by you and notice them not; 9: 5 to see your *n.* before glory of God will kindle unquenchable fire; **Ether** 10: 24 Jaredites work cloth to clothe themselves from *n.*

NAME (*see also* Call; Name of the Lord)

1 Ne. 14: 27 *n.* of apostle of Lamb is John; 20: 1 (Isa. 48: 1) hearken, O house of Jacob, who are called by *n.* of Israel; **2 Ne.** 3: 15 *n.* of latter-day seer shall be called after Joseph[1], and after *n.* of his father; **Mosiah** 1: 11–12 (5: 9–12) Benjamin gives his people a *n.* to distinguish them, never to be blotted out; 25: 12 children of Amulon and brethren are no longer called after *n.* of fathers, take *n.* of Nephi; 26: 36 (Alma 1: 24; 5: 57; Moro. 6: 7) *n.* of unrepentant transgressors are blotted out; **Alma** 5: 57 *n.* of wicked shall not be numbered among *n.* of righteous; 23: 17 converted Lamanites call their *n.* Anti-Nephi-Lehies; **Hel.** 5: 6 I have given you *n.* of first parents who came out of Jerusalem; **3 Ne.** 27: 8 if church is called in *n.* of man, it is church of man; 28: 25 the Lord forbids that *n.* of three Nephites be written.

NAME OF THE LORD (*see also* Jesus Christ; Prayer; TG Name of the Lord; BD Christ, Names of)

1 Ne. 17: 48 in *n.* of Almighty God I command you not to touch me; 20: 1 (Isa. 48: 1) Israel swears by *n.* of the Lord, but not in truth; 20: 11 (Isa. 48: 11) I will not suffer my *n.* to be polluted; **2 Ne.** 9: 23–24 (31: 11–12; Mosiah 18: 10; 3 Ne. 11: 23–27, 37–38; 18: 5, 11, 16, 30; 21: 6; 26: 17, 21; 27: 1, 16, 20; 30: 2; 4 Ne. 1: 1; Morm. 7: 8; Ether 4: 18; Moro. 7: 34) be baptized in *n.* of Christ; 9: 24 (25: 13–14; Mosiah 3: 9, 21; 5: 7; 26: 22; Alma 5: 48; 9: 27; 11: 40; 12: 15; 19: 13, 36; 22: 13; 26: 35; 32: 22; 34: 15; Hel. 3: 28; 14: 2, 12–13; 3 Ne. 9: 17; 18: 5; Morm. 9: 25, 37; Ether 3: 14; 4: 18; Moro. 7: 26, 38; 8: 3) believe and have faith in Christ's *n.*; 9: 41 the Lord God is his *n.*; 10: 3 angel tells Jacob[2] that the Lord's *n.* will be Christ; 17: 14 (Isa. 7: 14) virgin shall bear a son and call his *n.* Immanuel; 19: 6 (Isa. 9: 6) Messiah's *n.* shall be called, Wonderful, Counselor, The Mighty God, The Everlasting Father, The Prince of Peace; 25: 16 (Jacob 4: 5) worship Father in Christ's *n.*; 25: 19 according to prophets and word of angel, Messiah's *n.* shall be Jesus Christ; 25: 20 (31: 21; Mosiah 3: 17; 5: 8) none other *n.* given, save Jesus Christ, whereby man can be saved; 26: 32 (Mosiah 13: 15; Ex. 20: 7) not take *n.* of the Lord thy God in vain; 27: 34 (Isa. 29: 23) they shall sanctify my *n.*; 31: 13 (Mosiah 5: 8; 6: 2; Alma 34: 38; 46: 18, 21; 3 Ne. 27: 5–6; Moro. 6: 3) men must take upon themselves *n.* of Christ; 32: 9 (33: 12; 3 Ne. 16: 4; 17: 3; 18: 19–23, 30; 19: 6–8; 20: 31; 27: 2, 7, 28; 28: 30; Morm. 9: 6, 21, 27; Ether 4: 15; Moro. 2: 2; 3: 2; 4: 2–3; 5: 2; 7: 26; 8: 3; 10: 4) pray unto Father in *n.* of Christ; **Jacob** 4: 6 (Morm. 8: 24) the Lord's servants can command trees or mountains in *n.* of Jesus; **Mosiah** 1: 11–12 (5: 9–12) Benjamin gives his people a *n.* to distinguish them; 4: 11 (Alma 19: 16; 24: 21; Ether 2: 15) call on *n.* of the Lord; 5: 9 whosoever enters covenant shall know *n.* by which he is called, *n.* of Christ; 5: 12 retain *n.* written always in your hearts, that ye may know *n.* by which ye shall be called; 26: 18 blessed is this people who are willing to bear the Lord's *n.*, for in his *n.* shall they be called; **Alma** 5: 38 good shepherd calls in his own *n.*, *n.* of Christ; **3 Ne.** 8: 1 no man could do miracle in *n.* of Jesus save he were cleansed from iniquity; 11: 17 blessed be *n.* of Most High God; 13: 9 (Matt. 6: 9) our Father who art in heaven, hallowed be thy *n.*; 14: 22 (Matt. 7: 22) in the Lord's *n.* many will cast out devils; 27: 5 men must take upon themselves the *n.* of Christ, for by that *n.* shall they be called; 27: 6 whoso taketh upon himself *n.* of Christ shall be saved; 27: 7 whatsoever ye do, do it in Christ's *n.*; 27: 7 church to be called in Christ's *n.*; **Ether** 2: 14 the Lord chastens brother of Jared[2] because he remembers not to call upon *n.* of the Lord; 3: 21 time cometh when the Lord will glorify his *n.* in the flesh; 4: 19 blessed is he who is found faithful unto the Lord's *n.* at last day; **Moro.** 4: 3 in sacrament, saints covenant to take upon themselves *n.* of Christ; 7: 26 men saved by faith in Christ's *n.*; 8: 3 the Lord will keep you through endurance of faith on his *n.*

NARROW (*see also* Strait)

1 Ne. 8: 20 Lehi[1] beholds straight

and *n.* path in vision; **2 Ne.** 9: 41 way for man is *n.*; 31: 18–19 (3 Ne. 14: 14; 27: 33; Matt. 7: 14) straight and *n.* path leads to eternal life; 33: 9 enter into the *n.* gate; **Jacob** 6: 11 continue in the way which is *n.*; **Alma** 50: 34 (52: 9; 63: 5; Morm. 2: 29; 3: 5; Ether 10: 20) *n.* pass leads by sea into land northward; **Hel.** 3: 29 word of God leads man of Christ in straight and *n.* course across gulf of misery.

NATION (*see also* Country; Gentile; Government, Civil; Heathen; Land; Multitude; People)

1 Ne. 5: 18 brass plates to go to every *n.*; 13: 2 Nephi[1] beholds many *n.* in vision; 13: 42 Lamb shall manifest himself unto all *n.*; 17: 37 the Lord raises up righteous *n.* and destroys *n.* of wicked; 19: 17 every *n.* shall be blessed; 22: 5 (2 Ne. 25: 15) Israel shall be scattered among all *n.*; 22: 14 every *n.* which wars against Israel shall be turned one against another; **2 Ne.** 1: 8 this land to be kept from knowledge of other *n.*; 12: 2 (Isa. 2: 2) all *n.* shall flow unto mountain of the Lord's house; 12: 12 day of the Lord soon cometh upon all *n.*; 15: 26 (Isa. 5: 26) the Lord will lift ensign to the *n.*; 25: 16 the Lord will scourge Jews by other *n.*; 27: 3 all *n.* that fight against Zion shall be as dream of night vision; 29: 7 the Lord brings his word unto all *n.*; 29: 8 testimony of two *n.* is witness that the Lord is God; 30: 8 the Lord will commence his work among all *n.*; **Mosiah** 3: 13 the Lord has sent prophets to declare these things to every *n.*; 15: 28 salvation of the Lord shall be declared to every *n.*; 16: 1 every *n.* shall confess before God that his judgments are just; **Alma** 9: 20 Nephites are favored above every other *n.*; 13: 21–22 voice of the Lord declares unto all *n.* that now is time to repent; 29: 8 the Lord grants unto all *n.*, of their own *n.* and tongue, to teach his word; 37: 4 records to go forth unto every *n.*; 45: 16 land cursed unto every *n.* that does wickedly; **3 Ne.** 28: 29 three Nephites shall minister unto all *n.*; **Ether** 2: 9 whatsoever *n.* possesses promised land should serve God or be swept off; 2: 12 whatsoever *n.* shall possess this land shall be free from all other *n.* if they serve God; 8: 22 whatsoever *n.* upholds secret combinations until they spread over the *n.* shall be destroyed; 8: 25 whoso builds secret combination seeks to overthrow freedom of all *n.*

NATURE, NATURAL (*see also* Carnal; Earth; Fall of Man; Flesh; Mortal; Temporal; World; TG Natural; Nature, Earth; Nature, Human)

1 Ne. 10: 14 (15: 7) *n.* branches of olive-tree are remnant of house of Israel; 19: 12 the God of *n.* suffers; **Jacob** 5: 3–77 parable of olive-tree, with *n.* branches and fruit; **Mosiah** 3: 16 in Adam, or by *n.*, men fall; 3: 19 *n.* man is enemy to God; 16: 5 he who persists in carnal *n.* remains in fallen state; **Alma** 19: 6 light of everlasting life overcomes Lamoni's *n.* frame; 26: 21 what *n.* man knows these things; 41: 4 every thing shall be restored to its *n.* frame; 41: 11 all men who are in state of *n.* have gone contrary to *n.* of God; 41: 12 restoration does not mean to take a thing of *n.* state and place it in unnatural state; 42: 10 men become carnal, sensual, and devilish, by *n.*; **Hel.** 13: 38 ye have sought for happiness in doing iniquity, which is contrary to *n.* of God's righteousness; **Ether** 3: 2 because of the fall our *n.* have become evil continually.

NAUGHT (*see also* Nothing; Vain)

1 Ne. 17: 48 whoso lays hands upon Nephi[1] shall be as *n.* before power of God; 19: 7–9 because of iniquity, world will judge Lord a thing of *n.*; **2 Ne.** 2: 11–12 without opposition, it must have been created for thing of *n.*; 27: 31 terrible one to be brought to *n.*; 27: 32 (28: 16) they who turn aside the just for a thing of *n.* shall be cut off; 33: 2 because they harden hearts, many cast away writings as things of *n.*; **Hel.** 4: 21 Nephites see they had set at *n.* God's commandments; 12: 6 men set at *n.* God's counsels; **3 Ne.** 20: 38 ye have sold yourselves for *n.*; **Morm.** 5: 9 this people to be counted as *n.* among Gentiles; **Ether** 13: 13 Jaredites esteem Ether as *n.*; **Moro.** 8: 20 he who says little children need baptism sets at *n.* the atonement.

NAZARETH—*city of Christ's childhood* (*see also* BD Nazareth)

1 Ne. 11: 13 Nephi[1] beholds virgin in N.

NEAR (*see also* Nigh)

2 Ne. 27: 25 (Isa. 29: 13) this people draw *n.* the Lord with mouth, but hearts are far from him.

NEAS—*unidentified plant* (*see also* Grain)

Mosiah 9: 9 people of Zeniff grow *n.*

NECK (*see also* Captive; Pride; Stiffnecked)

1 Ne. 20: 4 (Isa. 48: 4) thy *n.* is an iron sinew; **2 Ne.** 26: 22 devil leads men by *n.* with flaxen cord; **Alma** 22: 32 (50: 34; 52: 9; 63: 5; Morm. 2: 29; 3: 5; Ether 10: 20) small *n.* of land between land northward and land southward.

NEED (*see also* Needy; Want)

2 Ne. 28: 29 wo unto him that shall

say, we *n.* no more of word of God; **Mosiah** 4: 16 succor those that stand in *n.* of your succor; 18: 9 be willing to comfort those that stand in *n.* of comfort; **Alma** 1: 29 Nephites have abundance of all things they *n.*; 7: 23 (Morm. 9: 27) ask for whatsoever things ye *n.*, spiritual and temporal; 34: 28 if ye do not impart of substance to those in *n.*, your prayer is vain.

NEEDY (*see also* Afflicted; Alms; Charity; Hunger; Naked; Needs; Orphan; Poor; Relief; Widow)

2 Ne. 20: 2 (Isa. 10: 2) wo unto them that turn away the *n.* from judgment; 24: 30 (Isa. 14: 30) the *n.* shall lie down in safety; **Mosiah** 18: 28 (Alma 1: 27) Nephites should impart of substance to every *n.*, naked soul; **Alma** 4: 12–13 (5: 55) the proud turn backs on *n.*, the humble impart their substance to *n.*; 34: 28 if ye turn away the *n.*, your prayer is vain; **Morm.** 8: 37 ye love your substance more than ye love the *n.*; 8: 39 why do ye adorn yourselves, yet suffer the *n.* to pass by.

NEGLECT (*see also* Diligence; Slothful)

Alma 32: 38 if ye *n.* the tree, it will not get any root.

NEHOR[1]—*brother of Abraham* (*see* BD Nahor)

No references in Book of Mormon.

NEHOR[2]—*Nephite apostate* [c. 91 B.C.] (*see also* Nehors, Order of)

Alma 1: 2–3 proclaims against church; 1: 7 is withstood by Gideon; 1: 9 (2: 20) slays Gideon; 1: 14–15 is condemned by Alma[2] and executed.

NEHOR, CITY OF—*Jaredite city*

Ether 7: 9 Shule battles Corihor[1] in city of *N.*

NEHORS, ORDER OF—*wicked combination of those who follow Nehor*

Alma 14: 16–18 judge in Ammonihah is after order of *N.*; 15: 15 stiffnecked people of Ammonihah are of order of *N.*; 16: 11 many are slain on order of *N.*; 21: 4 Amalekites and Amulonites build synagogues after order of *N.*; 24: 28–29 more wicked part of Lamanites, who do not join church, are of order of *N.*

NEIGHBOR (*see also* Brother; Charity; Love)

2 Ne. 28: 8 many shall say, dig a pit for thy *n.*; **Mosiah** 4: 28 he who borrows from *n.* should return what he borrows; 5: 14 doth a man take an ass that belongs to his *n.* and keep it; 13: 23 (Ex. 20: 16) thou shalt not bear false witness against thy *n.*; 13: 24 (Ex. 20: 17) thou shalt not covet anything that is thy *n*'s; 23: 15 (3 Ne. 12: 43; Matt. 22: 39) every man should love his *n.* as himself; 26: 31 he who forgives not his *n*'s trespasses brings himself under condemnation; 27: 4 every man should esteem his *n.* as himself.

NEPHI[1]—*son of Lehi[1], great prophet, founder of Nephites* [c. 600 B.C.] (*see also* Nephites; Plates of Nephi, Large; Plates of Nephi, Small)

1 Ne. 1: 1 born of goodly parents; 1: 2 makes record; 1: 16–17 (8: 29) abridges father's record, will add his own account; 2: 16 character of *N.*; 2: 19–24 the Lord speaks to *N.*; 2: 19 is blessed because of faith; 2: 20 to be led to land of promise; 2: 22 chosen to be a ruler; 3: 7 will go and do things the Lord hath commanded; 3: 9 returns to Jerusalem with brothers to obtain brass plates; 3: 24 asks Laban for brass plates; 3: 27 hides in cave with brothers; 3: 28–29 is smitten by elder brothers, protected by an angel; 4: 18 slays Laban; 4: 24 obtains plates; 4: 31 is large in stature; 4: 32–35 convinces Zoram[1] to join his family; 6: 2 is a descendant of Joseph[1]; 7: 2–6 returns to Jerusalem for Ishmael[1] and family; 7: 16 (18: 11) is bound by brothers; 8: 3 Lehi[1] rejoices because of *N.*; 8: 14–16 is seen by Lehi[1] in dream; 9: 1 concludes father's account; 9: 1–5 (19: 1–2) makes two sets of plates; 9: 2–3 (19: 3) records ministry and prophecies on small plates; 9: 2, 4 (19: 4) records wars, contentions, and destructions on large plates; 10: 1 gives account of his reign and ministry; 10: 17 wants to know about father's vision; ch. 11–14 beholds father's dream and vision of future of promised land; 11: 6 is blessed for belief in Son; 11: 32–33 in vision sees Christ crucified; 14: 28 is forbidden to write all he sees; 15: 12 explains olive-tree as symbol of house of Israel; 15: 19–20 speaks concerning restoration of Jews and words of Isaiah[1]; 16: 7 marries; 16: 18, 23 breaks bow, makes another; 16: 22 speaks much to brothers; 16: 37 Laman[1] stirs the rebellious up to slay Lehi[1] and *N.*; 17: 8–11, 16 (18: 1–4) is commanded to build ship; 17: 15 keeps the commandments; 17: 17 is mocked by brothers; 17: 52–53 is filled with power of God; 18: 3 goes oft to mount to pray, sees great things; 18: 6–23 crosses ocean with Lehites; 18: 22 guides the ship; 19: 22 teaches from brass plates; 19: 23 reads Isaiah[1] to persuade brethren of Christ; 20: 1—21: 26 quotes Isaiah[1]; 22: 1–26 expounds writings of Isaiah[1]; 22: 20–21 (2 Ne. 1: 10; 25: 23; 26: 1) preaches about Christ; **2 Ne.** 1: 24 Lehi[1] exhorts sons not to rebel against *N.*; 5: 1 cries unto Lord because of brothers; 5: 6–7 flees from Laman[1] and Lemuel, with many followers; 5: 9 followers call themselves the people of N.; 5: 12, 14 brings plates, sword of Laban; 5: 15–16 teaches people to work, builds temple; 5: 18 people desire that N. be king; 5: 18 he recommends no king; 11: 2 writes more words of Isaiah[1]; ch. 12–24 quotes Isaiah 2–14; 25: 1–6 comments on prophecies of Isaiah[1]; 25: 7—31: 21 gives his own prophecies; 26: 1 teaches of Christ's resurrection; 27: 6–22 foretells coming forth of Book of Mormon; 29: 14 prophesies all records to be gathered as one; 30: 2 prophesies Gentiles to be numbered with covenant people; 31: 4–9 explains why Christ will be baptized; 32: 5 explains office of Holy Ghost; 33: 1–15 parting testimony; **Jacob** 1: 1 gives Jacob[2] commandment concerning small plates; 1: 12 dies; 1: 18 had consecrated Jacob[2] and Joseph[2] as priests; 3: 14 plates of Jacob made by N.; **Mosiah** 10: 13 the Lord heard and answered prayers of N.; **Hel.** 8: 22 had testified God was with Israel.

NEPHI[2]—*son of Helaman[3], great Nephite missionary* [c. 45 B.C.]

Hel. 3: 21 elder son of Helaman[3], brother of Lehi[4]; 3: 37 is appointed chief judge; 4: 14 (5: 14; 7: 2) preaches and prophesies with Lehi[4]; 5: 1 resigns position as chief judge; 5: 4 is weary over people's iniquity; 5: 18–19 preaches to Lamanites, converts eight thousand; 5: 20 goes to land of Nephi; 5: 21 is imprisoned with Lehi[4]; 5: 22–25, 43–44 is encircled with fire, protected from those who would slay them; 5: 27–31 prison is shaken, overshadowed with a cloud; 5: 36–39 converses with angels; 5: 50 converts more part of Lamanites; 6: 6 goes to land northward with Lehi[4]; 7: 1 returns to Zarahemla; 7: 4–6 sorrows over rise of Gadianton band; 7: 7 laments that he did not live in days of Lehi[1]; 7: 10 prays on garden tower; 7: 12 teaches multitude from tower; 7: 19 predicts calamity unless people repent; 8: 5 arouses opposition; 8: 27 reveals secret murder of chief judge; 9: 16 is accused of the murder; 9: 26–36 identifies murderer; 9: 37–38 innocence is established; 10: 3–5 is praised by voice from heaven; 10: 6–7 is given great power; 10: 16 is conveyed away from persecutors by Spirit; 11: 4 invokes famine in land; 11: 10–16 prays for rain; 11: 17 the Lord answers N's prayer; 11: 18 is esteemed as great prophet; 11: 23 receives revelations, preaches, puts end to strife; 16: 1 Samuel's converts ask that N. baptize them; 16: 3–4 continues baptizing, prophesying, preaching repentance, working miracles; **3 Ne.** 1: 2 (2: 9) disappears.

NEPHI[3]—*son of Nephi[2], one of the twelve Nephite disciples* [c. A.D. 1] (*see also* Disciple; Nephi[4])

3 Ne. 1: 2 eldest son of Nephi[2], given charge of plates; 1: 10 sorrows for wickedness of people; 1: 11–12 cries unto the Lord in behalf of his people, 1: 12–13 hears voice of the Lord, sign of Christ's birth to be given; 1: 23 performs baptisms; 5: 9–10 makes record on plates of Nephi[1]; 7: 15, 18 was visited by angels and voice of the Lord; 7: 17 ministers with great power; 7: 19 (19: 4) casts out devils, raises brother from dead; 7: 20 arouses people's anger because of many miracles; 11: 18–20 Jesus calls N. forward; 11: 21–22 (12: 1) is given power to baptize; 19: 4 is called by Jesus to minister as one of twelve disciples; 19: 11–12 is baptized, baptizes other eleven disciples; 23: 7–8 is told to bring forth the records; 23: 9–13 is commanded to write missing parts of record.

NEPHI[4]—son of *Nephi[3]* [c. A.D. 34]

4 Ne. 1: heading—son of Nephi; 1: 19 keeps last record, dies.

NEPHI, CITY OF—*chief city in land of Nephi* (*see also* Lehi-Nephi, City of and Land of; Nephi, Land of)

Mosiah 9: 15 persecuted Nephites flee to N. for Zeniff's protection; 20: 3 priests of Noah[3] are ashamed to return to N.; 21: 1, 12 Limhi and his people return to N. after battles; **Alma** 23: 8, 11 Lamanites in N. are converted; 47: 20 chief city in land of Nephi; 47: 31 Amalickiah takes possession of N.

NEPHI, LAND OF—*land of Lehites' first inheritance, also a smaller part of that land, sometimes called land of Lehi-Nephi* (*see also* Lehi-Nephi, City of and Land of[1]; Limhi; Nephi, City of; Noah[3]; Zeniff)

2 Ne. 5: 8 named after Nephi[1]; Omni 1: 12 Mosiah[1] flees from N. as directed; 1: 27–30 large number of Nephites return to N.; **W of M** 1: 13 Lamanite armies come from N. to battle Nephites; **Mosiah** 7: 6 Ammon[2] and brethren go to N.; 7: 7–8 Ammon[2] and brethren imprisoned in N.; 7: 9 (19: 26) Limhi, king of N.; ch. 9–22 record of Zeniff's people in land of N.; 9: 1 Zeniff has knowledge of land of N.; 9: 6 Zeniff obtains possession of land of N.; 9: 14 Lamanites invade, steal flocks; 10: 1 peace established in N.; 11: 1 Noah[3] succeeds father as king in N.; 11: 20 Abinadi preaches in N.; 18: 4–5 Alma[1] teaches in Mormon, in borders of land of N.; 19: 15 Lamanites carry away Nephites' wives and children in N.; 19: 24 husbands return to N.; 20: 7 Lamanites go to destroy Nephites in N.; 20: 11 Lamanites repulsed; 21: 1–4 Limhi's people in bondage in N.; 21: 11 Limhi's people escape from N.; 21: 21 wicked priests come into land of N. to steal; 28: 1–9 (Alma 17: 6–8) sons of Mosiah[2] are permitted to go on mission to N.; 29: 3 (Alma 22: 1) Aaron[3] goes to N.; Alma 2: 24 Amlicites join Lamanites in N.; ch. 17–26 account of mission of sons of Mosiah to Lamanites in N.; 18: 9 Lamoni's father is king over land of N.; 20: 1 Lamoni desires Ammon[2] to accompany him to N.; 20: 2 the Lord tells Ammon[2] not to go to N.; 22: 28 idle Lamanites inhabit borders of N.; 22: 32 land of N. nearly surrounded by water; 22: 34 Nephites kept Lamanites to south in N.; 24: 20–23 Lamanites invade and slaughter many converted Lamanites in N.; 25: 13 many Lamanites join converts in N.; 27: 1 Lamanites return to N.; 27: 20 (28: 8) sons of Mosiah[2] tell of mission in N.; 27: 26 Ammonites leave N.; 47: 1, 20 Amalickiahites go to N.; 50: 8 land of N. runs in straight course from east sea to west; 53: 6 Moroni[1] captures city of Mulek in N.; 58: 38 Lamanites flee to N.; **Hel.** 4: 12 Nephite dissenters join Lamanites in N.; 5: 20 Nephi[2] and Lehi[2] go to N.

NEPHI, PEOPLE OF (*see* Nephites)

NEPHI, PLATES OF (*see* Plates of Nephi, Large; Plates of Nephi, Small)

NEPHIHAH—*second chief judge of Nephites* [c. 83 B.C.]

Alma 4: 17–18 (8: 12) Alma[2] delivers judgment-seat to N.; 50: 37–39 dies, son is appointed in his stead.

NEPHIHAH, CITY OF—*possibly two cities by this name*

Alma 50: 14 is built between cities of Aaron and Moroni; 51: 24 those who flee out of Moroni come to N.; 51: 26 captured by Amalickiah; 59: 5–11 is attacked by Lamanites; 62: 18–26 is retaken by Moroni[1].

NEPHIHAH, LAND OF (*see also* Nephihah, City of)

Alma 50: 14 Nephites call name of city, or the land, N.; 62: 14, 18 Moroni[1] goes to N.; 62: 30 Moroni[1] leaves N.

NEPHIHAH, PEOPLE OF—*residents of city or land of Nephihah*

Alma 59: 5 include people from other cities; 59: 7–8 are slaughtered and scattered.

NEPHIHAH, PLAINS OF—*near the city of Nephihah*

Alma 62: 18 Nephites pitch their tents in plains of N.

NEPHITES—*descendants of Nephi[1] and his followers, later any person who accepts gospel*

1 Ne. 12: 20 (Hel. 15: 17) to be overcome by Lamanites; **2 Ne.** 5: 25 to be scourged by Lamanites; 29: 12 the Lord will speak unto N. and they shall write; 29: 13 to have Jews' words, Jews to have words of N.; **Jacob** 1: 13 all who are not Lamanites are N.; 2: 35 treat families worse than Lamanites; 3: 3 more filthy than Lamanites; **Enos** 1: 13–16 Enos prays for preservation of N. records; 1: 20 seek to restore Lamanites to faith in God; 1: 21 till earth; 1: 22 a stiffnecked people; 1: 24 (Jarom 1: 7; Omni 1: 10, 24; Alma 25: 3; 28: 3–10; 35: 13; 43: 3; 48: 21–22; Morm. 2: 1) N's wars with Lamanites; **Jarom** 1: 5 wax strong, observe the law; **Omni** 1: 2 Omni fights to preserve N.; 1: 5 more wicked part destroyed; **W of M** 1: 1 Mormon[2] witnesses destruction of most of N.; 1: 13–14 drive back Lamanites; **Mosiah** 19: 28 Lamanite guards supported by tribute from N.; 21: 2–5 afflicted by Lamanites; 25: 12 children of Amulonites desire to be called N.; 25: 13 people of Zarahemla all called N.; 29: 44 reign of judges commences among N.; **Alma** 2: 11–38 contention with Amlicites; 3: 4 dissenters marked; 3: 11 believe in records; 8: 7 call cities and land after first possessor; 22: 27 land divided between Lamanites and N.; 25: 1 Lamanites swear vengeance on N.; 28: 1–3 defend Ammonites, great slaughter among Lamanites and N.; 30: 20 Ammonites wiser than N.; 43: 4 armies assemble in Jershon; 43: 7–9 N. fight for liberties; 43: 19, 37–38 better equipped for war; 43: 45 inspired by better cause; 45: 10–12 destruction of N. foretold; 47: 36 dissenters become more hardened; 48: 14 are taught to defend themselves; 49: 4 fortify Ammonihah; 49: 13 fortify city of Noah; 49: 21 are attacked at city of Noah; 49: 25 Amalickiah, by birth a N.; 50: 23 N. never happier than at time of Moroni[1]; 52: 8 keep prisoners for ransom; 53: 8 dissension among N. gives enemy the advantage; 53: 16 sons of Ammonites call themselves N.; 55: 5–22 strategy secures release of captured N.; 56: 24 are feared by Lamanites; 58: 28 take city of Manti by stratagem; 59: 7–11 lose city of Nephihah; 62: 15 capture many prisoners; 62: 25 drive Lamanites to land of Moroni; 62: 40 are spared because of prayers of the righteous; 62: 41 many are hardened because of war, others softened from afflictions; 63: 6 many sail north; 63: 14 dissenters are stirred up against

N.; 63: 15 drive Lamanites back to own lands; **Hel.** 1: 22, 27, 33 lose and retake Zarahemla; 3: 15 many records kept by N.; 4: 11–13 slaughtered because of wickedness; 6: 2, 31 (13: 1) less righteous than Lamanites; 6: 4–5 are converted by Lamanites; 6: 6–8 peace between *N.* and Lamanites; 6: 9 *N.* and Lamanites become exceedingly rich; 6: 18–21, 38 many take Gadianton oaths and covenants; 6: 34 dwindle in unbelief; 16: 1 some repent, join church; **3 Ne.** 2: 1 become hardened after sign of Christ's birth given; 2: 8 reckon time from time of sign; 2: 12 unite with converted Lamanites; 3: 13–14, 22–25 gather in one place, fortify against robbers; 3: 19 appoint chief captains who have spirit of revelation; 4: 7–28 defeat robbers; 5: 1 believe words of prophets; 6: 1 return to own families and lands; 6: 3 have peace after subduing Gadianton band; 7: 2 have dissension and form tribes; 10: 18 N. and Lamanites receive great blessings; ch. 11–26 ministry of Jesus among *N.*; **4 Ne.** 1: 2–3 all are converted unto the Lord, have all things in common; 1: 7–23 prosper during reign of righteousness; 1: 24 begin to be proud; 1: 36 factions arise among *N.*; 1: 43 become proud and vain; **Morm.** 2: 1 appoint Mormon[2] leader of armies; 3: 1 prepare for battle; 3: 9–11 increase in wickedness, Mormon[2] refuses to lead *N.*; 4: 1–2 are driven to land of Desolation; 4: 11 *N.* and Lamanites delight to shed blood; 4: 18 gain no power over Lamanites from this time; 5: 1 Mormon[2] assumes command of *N.*; 6: 7–15 all are slain, save twenty-four; 8: 2 *N.* who escape are hunted, destroyed; **Moro.** 1: 2 are put to death unless they deny Christ; 9: 9 become depraved, lustful, and barbarous; 9: 11 are without civilization.

NEUM—*a Hebrew prophet quoted by Nephi*[1]

1 Ne. 19: 10 God to yield himself to be crucified, according to words of N.

NEW (*see also* Jerusalem, New; Renew)

2 Ne. 31: 14 if man who can speak with *n.* tongue, tongue of angels, denies the Lord, it would have been better not to have known him; **Mosiah** 27: 26 those born of the Spirit become *n.* creatures; **Hel.** 14: 5 (3 Ne. 1: 21) *n.* star to appear at Christ's birth; **3 Ne.** 12: 47 (15: 2; 2 Cor. 5: 17) all things have become *n.*; **Morm.** 9: 24 (Mark 16: 17) they who believe shall speak with *n.* tongues; **Ether** 13: 9 there shall be a *n.* heaven and a *n.* earth.

NIGH (*see also* Near)

2 Ne. 15: 19 (Isa. 5: 19) let counsel of Holy One draw *n.*; **Jacob** 5: 47, 62, 64, 71 end draweth *n.*; **Mosiah** 27: 28 after repenting *n.* unto death, Alma[2] is snatched out of everlasting burning; **Alma** 9: 25 kingdom of heaven is *n.* at hand; 13: 21 day of salvation draweth *n.*

NIGHT (*see also* Darkness, Physical; Darkness, Spiritual)

1 Ne. 16: 9 the Lord speaks unto Lehi[1] by *n.*; **2 Ne.** 4: 23 the Lord has given Nephi[1] knowledge by visions in *n.*; 27: 3 (Isa. 29: 7) all nations that fight against Zion shall be as dream of *n.* vision; **Alma** 34: 33 after day of this life comes *n.* of darkness; 41: 5 he who has desired evil all day long shall have reward of evil when *n.* comes; 41: 7 the redeemed shall be delivered from endless *n.* of darkness; **Hel.** 14: 4 (3 Ne. 1: 8, 15–19) at Christ's birth one day and *n.* and day shall be as one day; **3 Ne.** 27: 33 many travel broad way to death until *n.* cometh; **Moro.** 7: 15 way to judge is as plain as daylight is from dark *n.*

NIMRAH—*Jaredite, son of Akish*

Ether 9: 8–9 angry with father, flees with small group of men to Omer.

NIMROD[1]—*grandson of Ham* (*see also* Nimrod, Valley of; BD Nimrod)

Ether 2: 1 valley named after N., mighty hunter.

NIMROD[2]—*Jaredite, son of Cohor*[1]

Ether 7: 22 gives up kingdom to Shule, gains favors.

NIMROD, VALLEY OF—*in Mesopotamia*

Ether 2: 1 Jaredites travel north to valley of *N.*; 2: 4 the Lord talks to brother of Jared[2] in *N.*

NOAH[1]—*patriarch at time of flood* (*see also* BD Noah)

Alma 10: 22 the Lord would not destroy people by flood as in days of *N.*: **3 Ne.** 22: 9 (Isa. 54: 9) waters of *N.* no more to go over earth; **Ether** 6: 7 Jaredite vessels are tight like ark of *N.*

NOAH[2]—*early Jaredite king, son of Corihor*[1]

Ether 7: 14–15 rebels against his father and the king; 7: 16–17 becomes king through battle; 7: 18 is slain by sons of Shule.

NOAH[3]—*son of Zeniff, king over Nephites in land of Nephi* [c. 160 B.C.] (*see also* Nephi, Land of; Noah[3], Priests of)

Mosiah 7: 9 father of Limhi; 11: 1 Zeniff confers kingdom on *N.*; 11: 2–15 commits many iniquities; 11: 16–19 *N's* armies drive back the Lamanites; 11: 27 angry with words of Abinadi; 12: 17 imprisons Abinadi; 13: 1 (17: 1) orders Abinadi slain; 18: 33 accuses Alma[1] of sedition; 19: 8 life spared by Gideon; 19: 9 flees before Lamanites; 19: 11 commands men to desert wives and children; 19: 20 is burned to death; 23: 9 (29: 18) Alma[1] reminds of *N*'s iniquities; 23: 12–13 (Alma 5: 4) people freed from bonds of *N*.

NOAH, CITY AND LAND OF—*in land of Zarahemla, near Ammonihah*

Alma 49: 12–13 Amalickiah marches toward *N*.; 49: 14–15 is strengthened by Moroni[1].

NOAH[3], PRIESTS OF—*wicked priests appointed by Noah*[3] (*see also* Amulon; Amulon, Children of; Amulonites)

Mosiah 11: 5 *N*. puts down priests of his father and appoints new priests; 11: 11 priests' seats are ornamented with gold; 11: 19 people lifted up in pride because of priests; 12: 17 hold council to determine Abinadi's fate; 12: 19 question Abinadi; 12: 25–37 are challenged by Abinadi; 13: 2 are withstood by Abinadi; 13: 5—16: 15 Abinadi preaches to *N*. and priests; 17: 1 are commanded by king to slay Abinadi; 17: 2–4 Alma[1], one of priests, is converted, flees; 17: 5–20 priests burn Abinadi to death; 17: 15–19 (Alma 25: 7–12) Abinadi prophesies future afflictions of priests' seed; 19: 21 priests flee from angry people; 20: 3 are ashamed to return to wives; 20: 4–5, 18, 23 take daughters of Lamanites for wives; 21: 20–21 Limhi desires to punish priests; 23: 9, 12 Alma[1] reminds of priests' iniquities; 23: 30–31 Lamanite army finds priests; 23: 32–35 priests join Lamanites; 24: 1, 4–6 are appointed teachers over Lamanites; **Alma** 25: 3–5 most of priests are slain in battles with Nephites.

NOBILITY (*see also* Pride; Rich)

Alma 51: 8 those of high birth are favored of kings, seek to be kings; 51: 17–18 Moroni[1] commands army to pull down pride and *n*. of king-men; 51: 21 Moroni[1] puts end to stubbornness and pride of those who profess *n*. of blood.

NOISE (*see also* Roar; Sound [noun and verb]; Tumult)

2 Ne. 23: 4 (Isa. 13: 4) *n*. of multitude in mountain like a great people; 27: 2 nations shall be visited of the Lord with great *n*.; **Alma** 14: 29 having heard great *n*., people see Alma[2] and Amulek walk out of fallen prison; **Hel.** 5: 30 voice calling to repentance is not voice of great tumultuous *n*.; **3 Ne.** 10: 9 tumultuous *n*. passes away.

NOON-DAY (*see also* Light)

1 Ne. 1: 9 Lehi[1] sees one descending from heaven whose luster is above sun at *n*.

NORTH, NORTHERN (*see also* Israel, Ten Lost Tribes of)

2 Ne. 29: 11 the Lord commands all men in east, west, *n*., south; **3 Ne.** 20: 13 scattered remnant shall be gathered from east, west, south, *n*.; **Ether** 1: 1 Jaredites are destroyed upon face of *n*. country; 9: 35 rain brings fruit in *n*. countries; 13: 11 Israel to be gathered from four quarters, from *n*. countries.

NOTHING, NOTHINGNESS (*see also* Avail; Humble; Naught; Profit)

1 Ne. 2: 4 Lehi[1] takes *n*. into wilderness save family, provisions, tents; **2 Ne.** 26: 30 (1 Cor. 13: 2) except men have charity they are *n*.; **Mosiah** 4: 5 knowledge of God's goodness awakens men to sense of their *n*.; 4: 11 always retain in remembrance the greatness of God and your own *n*.; **Alma** 26: 12 I know that I am *n*.; **Hel.** 12: 7 how great is *n*. of men; **3 Ne.** 12: 13 (16: 15; Matt. 5: 13) salt that has lost savor is good for *n*. but to be trampled under foot; **Morm.** 9: 21 believe in Christ, doubting *n*.; **Moro.** 10: 6 *n*. that is good denieth Christ.

NOTICE (*see also* Heed)

Morm. 8: 39 why do ye suffer the needy to pass by you and *n*. them not.

NOURISH, NOURISHMENT (*see also* Feed; Food; Nurse; Strength; Strengthen)

1 Ne. 15: 15 remnant of Nephites' seed will receive *n*. from true vine; 17: 3 if men keep God's commandments, he *n*. them; 22: 8 (21: 22–23; 22: 6; 2 Ne. 6: 6) remnant of Nephites' seed to be *n*. by Gentiles; **Jacob** 5: 71 last time the Lord will *n*. his vineyard; **Alma** 32: 37 if you *n*. tree with much care, it will get root; 32: 42 because of your diligence in *n*. the word, ye shall pluck fruit; 33: 23 plant this word in your hearts and *n*. it by faith; **Moro.** 6: 4 those baptized to be *n*. by good word of God.

NUMBER

1 Ne. 14: 12 *n*. of church of Lamb are few; 22: 25 (3 Ne. 18: 31) the Lord *n*. his sheep; **Mosiah** 14: 12 (Isa. 53: 12) Messiah was *n*. with transgressors; **Alma** 5: 57 (6: 3; 3 Ne. 18: 31; Moro. 6: 7) names of wicked shall not be *n*. among names of righteous; **3 Ne.** 16: 3 other sheep to whom Christ will go shall be *n*. among his sheep.

NURSE, NURSING (*see also* Care; Nourish)

1 Ne. 21: 23 (22: 6; 2 Ne. 6: 7; 10: 9;

Isa. 49: 23) kings and queens shall be Israel's *n.* fathers and mothers.

OATH (*see also* Covenant; Promise; Secret Combination; Swear)

1 Ne. 4: 35–37 Zoram[1] makes *o.* to tarry with Lehites; **Alma** 37: 27, 29 (Hel. 6: 25) Alma[2] commands Helaman[1] not to reveal *o.* of secret combinations; 44: 8 Zerahemnah refuses to take *o.* not to wage further wars; 49: 27 Amalickiah swears *o.* to drink blood of Moroni[1]; 50: 39 chief judge swears *o.* to keep peace and freedom; 53: 11, 14 (24: 17–19; 56: 8) Ammonites swear *o.* not to take up arms; **Hel.** 6: 21 Nephites enter *o.* of secret combinations; 6: 30 devil hands down *o.* of secret combinations; **3 Ne.** 12: 33 (Matt. 5: 33) perform unto the Lord thine *o.*; **4 Ne.** 1: 42 wicked part of people again build up secret *o.* of Gadianton; **Morm.** 5: 1 Mormon[2] repents of *o.* not to assist Nephites; **Ether** 8: 15 (9: 5) Akish administers secret *o.* handed down from Cain; 8: 20 secret *o.* and combinations have been had among all people; 10: 33 robbers administer *o.* after manner of ancients.

OBEDIENCE, OBEDIENT, OBEY (*see also* Abide; Agency; Baptism; Blessing; Commandments of God; Diligence; Disobedience; Do; Duty; Endure; Faith; Faithful; Fear of God; Follow; Gospel; Hearken; Heed; Humble; Keep; Law; Observe; Steadfast; Submissive; TG Obedience, Obedient, Obey)

1 Ne. 4: 18 Nephi[1] *o.* voice of Spirit; 22: 31 if ye are *o.* to commandments, ye shall be saved; **2 Ne.** 31: 7 Lamb witnesses that he would be *o.* in keeping commandments; 33: 15 thus hath the Lord commanded me, and I must *o.*; **Jacob** 7: 27 Enos[2] promises *o.* unto commands; **Mosiah** 2: 32–33, 37 he who listeth to *o.* evil spirit receiveth for wages everlasting punishment; 5: 8 all who have entered covenant to be *o.* take upon themselves name of Christ; 29: 23 he who does not *o.* iniquitous king is destroyed; **Alma** 3: 26–27 men reap their reward according to spirit they list to *o.*; 57: 20 Ammonite youth *o.* every command with exactness.

OBSCURITY (*see also* Darkness, Spiritual)

1 Ne. 22: 12 Israel shall be brought out of *o.*; **2 Ne.** 1: 23 Lehi[1] admonishes sons to come forth out of *o.*; 27: 29 (Isa. 29: 18) eyes of blind shall see out of *o.*

OBSERVE (*see also* Obedience; Perform)

2 Ne. 32: 6 when Christ manifests himself in flesh, ye shall *o.* to do the things he shall say; **Jacob** 3: 5–6 because Nephites *o.* commandment to have only one wife, the Lord will not destroy them; **Mosiah** 13: 30 Israelites given law of performances to *o.*; 18: 23 Alma[1] commands his people to *o.* Sabbath day; **Alma** 5: 61 Alma[2] commands people to *o.* words he has spoken; 62: 10 Nephites *o.* law of putting to death king-men who do not take up arms in defence of country; **3 Ne.** 18: 6 Christ commands disciples to *o.* sacrament.

OBTAIN (*see also* Receive)

2 Ne. 3: 14 promise which Joseph[1] has *o.* of the Lord shall be fulfilled; 9: 46 the devil hath *o.* me; **Jacob** 1: 17 Jacob[2] *o.* his errand from the Lord; 2: 19 after ye have *o.* hope in Christ ye shall *o.* riches; **Hel.** 6: 39 secret combinations *o.* sole management of government; 13: 38 ye have sought all the days of your lives for that which ye could not *o.*; **Ether** 12: 20 brother of Jared[2] *o.* word by faith; **Moro.** 7: 3 peaceable followers of Christ have *o.* sufficient hope to enter his rest.

OFFEND, OFFENDER (*see also* Anger; Offense)

Alma 35: 15 people are *o.* by strictness of word of Alma[2]; **3 Ne.** 28: 35 do ye suppose ye can get rid of justice of an *o.* God.

OFFENSE (*see also* Crime; Offend; Transgression; Trespass)

2 Ne. 18: 14 (Isa. 8: 14) he shall be for rock of *o.* to both houses of Israel; **Alma** 41: 9 do not risk one more *o.* against God; 43: 46 if people are not guilty of first or second *o.*, they should not suffer themselves to be slain; 48: 14 Nephites are taught never to give *o.*

OFFERING, OFFER (*see also* Altar; Broken Heart and Contrite Spirit; Gift; Give; Jesus Christ, Atonement through; Law of Moses; Sacrifice)

1 Ne. 2: 7 Lehi[1] builds altar and makes *o.* unto the Lord; 5: 9 (7: 22) Lehites *o.* sacrifice and burnt *o.* unto the Lord; **2 Ne.** 2: 7 Messiah *o.* himself a sacrifice for sin; **Jacob** 4: 5 Abraham was obedient to God's commands in *o.* up Isaac; **Omni** 1: 26 *o.* your whole souls as *o.* unto Christ; **Mosiah** 2: 3 Nephites take firstlings of flock to *o.* sacrifice according to law of Moses; 14: 10 (Isa. 53: 10) thou shalt make his soul an *o.* for sin; **Alma** 31: 23 Zoramites *o.* up thanks upon Rameumptom; **3 Ne.** 9: 19 ye shall *o.* up unto the Lord no more the shedding of blood; 24: 3 (Mal. 3: 3) sons of Levi[1] to *o.* unto the Lord an *o.* in righteousness; **Morm.** 4: 14 Lamanites *o.* women and children as sacrifices to idols.

OFFICE (*see also* Authority; Calling; Duty;

Ministry; Officer; Ordain; Priesthood, Melchizedek)

Jacob 1: 19 (2: 2–3) Jacob[2] magnifies *o.*, that blood might not come upon his garments; **Mosiah** 29: 42 Alma[1] confers *o.* of high priest upon Alma[2]; **Alma** 4: 18 Alma[2] retains *o.* of high priest; 13: 18 Melchizedek received *o.* of high priesthood according to holy order of God; **Hel.** 7: 5 robbers held in *o.* at head of government; **Moro.** 7: 31 *o.* of angels' ministry is to call men to repentance.

OFFICER (*see also* Church of God; Government, Civil; Leader; Minister [noun]; Office)

Alma 11: 2 judge sends forth *o.* to bring man before him; 14: 17 judge delivers Alma[2] and Amulek to *o.* to be cast into prison; 30: 29 Korihor delivered into hands of *o.* and sent to Alma[2]; **3 Ne.** 6: 11 many merchants, lawyers, *o.* in land.

OGATH—*place near hill Ramah*

Ether 15: 10 Jaredites pitch tents in O.

OLD (*see also* Age; Ancient)

1 Ne. 1: 20 Jews angry with Lehi[1], as with prophets of *o.*; 8: 27 spacious building filled with people, both *o.* and young; **2 Ne.** 4: 12 Lehi[1] waxes *o.* and dies; **Mosiah** 1: 9 Benjamin waxes *o.*; 2: 40 all ye *o.* men, and young, awake to remembrance of awful situation of transgressors; 10: 10 Zeniff goes up to battle against Lamanites in *o.* age; 10: 22 being *o.*, Zeniff confers kingdom upon son; **Alma** 1: 30 Nephites are liberal to all, both *o.* and young; 5: 49 Alma[2] preaches unto all, both *o.* and young; 11: 44 restoration shall come to all, both *o.* and young; 46: 41 many die of *o.* age; **3 Ne.** 15: 2–3, 7 *o.* things have passed away; **Ether** 10: 16 Levi[2] lives to good *o.* age; 13: 8 remnant of Joseph[1] shall build holy city like Jerusalem of *o.*; **Moro.** 9: 19 Nephites spare none, neither *o.* nor young.

OLIVE (*see also* Tree; BD Olive Tree)

1 Ne. 10: 12 (15: 12) house of Israel compared to *o.* tree; 10: 14 (15: 7, 12–13) natural branches of *o.* tree, remnants of Israel, to be grafted in; **Jacob** 5: 3 (6: 1) the Lord likens house of Israel to tame *o.* tree.

OMEGA (*see* Alpha)

OMER—*early Jaredite king*

Ether 1: 29–30 (8: 1; 9: 14) son of Shule, father of Emer; 8: 1 reigns in father's stead, begets Jared[3]; 8: 2 Jared[3] rebels against O., gains half of kingdom; 8: 3–4 battles with Jared[3], in captivity half his days; 8: 4 begets Esrom and Coriantumr[1] in captivity; 8: 5–6 sons regain kingdom for O.; 8: 7–12 Jared[3] and daughter plot with Akish to murder O.; 9: 1 secret combination of Akish overthrows kingdom of O.; 9: 2–3 escapes with family because of the Lord's warning; 9: 9 Nimrah flees to O.; 9: 12–13 is restored to land of his inheritance; 8: 14 anoints Emer king to reign in his stead.

OMNER—*son of Mosiah[2]* [c. 100 B.C.] (*see also* Mosiah[2], Sons of)

Mosiah 27: 8 an unbeliever; 27: 10 seeks to destroy church; 27: 32 is converted by angel; 27: 34 is named among sons of Mosiah[2]; 27: 35–37 preaches gospel; 28: 1–9 is allowed to preach in land of Nephi; 28: 10 (29: 3; Alma 17: 6) refuses to become king; **Alma** 17: 1–3 (27: 16–19) meets Alma with joy; 23: 1 is protected by proclamation of king; 24: 5 travels with brothers to Midian; 25: 17 rejoices with brethren over their success; 31: 6–7 goes with Ammon[2] to Zoramites; 35: 14 returns to Zarahemla.

OMNER, CITY OF—*Nephite city by seashore on east borders*

Alma 51: 26 possessed by Amalickiah.

OMNI—*Nephite record keeper* [c. 361 B.C.]

Jarom 1: 15 (Omni 1: 1) son of Jarom, is given plates; **Omni** 1: 2 fights with Lamanites, has not fully kept commandments; 1: 3 confers plates upon his son Amaron.

OMNIPOTENT (*see* God, Power of)

ONE (*see also* Unite, Unity)

1 Ne. 13: 41 records of Nephites' seed and of twelve apostles shall be established in *o.*; 13: 41 there is *o.* God over all the earth; 17: 35 the Lord esteemeth all flesh in *o.*; 22: 25 (3 Ne. 15: 17; 16: 3; John 10: 16) *o.* fold and *o.* shepherd; **2 Ne.** 25: 18 *o.* Messiah spoken of by prophets; 31: 21 (Mosiah 15: 2–5; Alma 11: 44; 3 Ne. 11: 27, 36; Morm. 7: 7) Father, Son, and Holy Ghost are *o.* God; **Jacob** 2: 21 the *o.* being is as precious in God's sight as the other; **Mosiah** 15: 4 (3 Ne. 11: 27; 19: 23, 29; 20: 35; 28: 10; John 10: 30; 17: 11, 21–22) Christ and the Father are *o.*; 18: 21 (Eph. 4: 4–6) Nephites should look forward with *o.* eye, having *o.* faith and *o.* baptism; 23: 7 ye shall not esteem *o.* flesh above another; **Alma** 11: 28–29, 35 (14: 5; Deut. 6: 4; Gal. 3: 20; Eph. 4: 5–6) there is only *o.* God; **3 Ne.** 23: 14 Jesus expounds all the scriptures in *o.*; **4 Ne.** 1: 17 Nephites are in *o.*, children of Christ; **Moro.** 7: 17 devil persuades no man to do good, no, not *o.*

ONIDAH—*gathering place for dissatisfied Lamanites*

Alma 47: 5 Amalickiah goes to place of O.

ONIDAH, HILL—*in land of Antionum*

Alma 32: 4 Alma[2] speaks to multitude from hill O.

ONIHAH, CITY OF

3 Ne. 9: 7 destroyed at time of crucifixion.

ONLY BEGOTTEN (*see* Jesus Christ—Only Begotten Son)

ONTI—*silver coin* (*see also* Coin)

Alma 11: 6, 13 silver coin whose value is as great as them all; 11: 22 Zeezrom offers Amulek six *o.* to deny God.

OPEN (*see also* Answer; Openly)

1 Ne. 1: 8 Lehi[1] sees heavens *o.*; 11: 14 (12: 6) Nephi[1] sees heavens *o.*; **2 Ne**: 7: 5 (Isa. 50: 5) the Lord hath *o.* mine ear; 9: 42 (3 Ne. 14: 7–8; 27: 29; Matt. 7: 7–8) whoso knocketh, to him will the Lord *o.*; **Mosiah** 2: 9 *o.* your ears that ye may hear; 14: 7 (15: 6; Isa. 53: 7) he was afflicted, yet he *o.* not his mouth; 27: 22 priests fast and pray that the Lord might *o.* mouth of Alma[2] and *o.* eyes of people to see goodness and glory of God.

OPENLY (*see also* Open)

3 Ne. 13: 4, 6 (Matt. 7: 4, 6) give alms and pray in secret, that Father reward thee *o.*

OPINION (*see also* Belief)

Alma 40: 20 Alma[2] gives *o.* that souls and bodies are reunited at resurrection of Christ.

OPPOSITION, OPPOSITE (*see also* Agency; Probation; Sweet; Trial, Try; TG Opposition)

2 Ne. 2: 10 punishment that is affixed is in *o.* to happiness which is affixed; 2: 11, 15 *o.* in all things; 2: 15 forbidden fruit set in *o.* to tree of life; **Alma** 41: 12–13 restoration does not mean to place a thing in state *o.* to its nature; 42: 16 eternal punishment affixed *o.* plan of eternal happiness.

OPPRESSION, OPPRESS (*see also* Affliction; Malice; Oppressor; Persecution; Suffering; Trial, Try; Tribulation)

1 Ne. 21: 26 (Isa. 49: 26) I will feed them that *o.* thee with their own flesh; **2 Ne.** 13: 5 (Isa. 3: 5) the people shall be *o.*, every one by another; 15: 7 (Isa. 5: 7) he looked for judgment, and behold, *o.*; **Mosiah** 13: 35 (14: 7; Isa. 53: 7) he himself should be *o.* and afflicted; 23: 12 people of Alma[1] have been *o.* by king Noah[3]; **Hel.** 4: 11–12 great slaughter among Nephites caused by their *o.* to the poor; **3 Ne.** 22: 14 (Isa. 54: 14) thou shalt be far from *o.*; 24: 5 (Mal. 3: 5) I will be swift witness against those that *o.* hireling in his wages.

OPPRESSOR (*see also* Oppression)

2 Ne. 8: 13 (Isa. 51: 13) thou hast feared continually every day because of fury of the *o.*; 13: 12 (Isa. 3: 12) children are *o.* of the Lord's people; 19: 4 (Isa. 9: 4) thou hast broken the rod of his *o.*; 24: 2 (Isa. 14: 2) they shall rule over their *o.*

ORDAIN, ORDINATION (*see also* Appoint; Authority; Confer; Decree; Hands, Laying on of; Office; Ordinance; Priesthood; TG Priesthood, Ordination)

1 Ne. 12: 7 Twelve were *o.* and chosen; 14: 25 the Lord hath *o.* apostle of Lamb to write these things; **2 Ne.** 6: 2 Jacob[2] is *o.* after manner of God's holy order; **Mosiah** 18: 18 having authority from God, Alma[1] *o.* priests; 25: 19 Mosiah[2] gives Alma[1] power to *o.* priests and teachers over every church; **Alma** 6: 1 Alma[2] *o.* priests and teachers by laying on of hands; 13: 1–3 (49: 30) the Lord *o.* priests after his holy order to teach people; 13: 6–8 men are *o.* unto high priesthood with holy ordinances; **3 Ne.** 7: 25 Nephi[3] *o.* men to baptize; 18: 5 one to be *o.* to administer sacrament to people; **4 Ne.** 1: 14 other disciples are *o.* instead of original disciples; **Moro.** ch. 3 manner of *o.* priests and teachers.

ORDER (*see also* Authority; Govern; Head; Law; Priesthood; Regulate; Unite; TG Order)

2 Ne. 6: 2 (Alma 5: 44; 6: 8; 13: 1–3, 6–11; 43: 2; Hel. 8: 18; Ether 12: 10) teachers are ordained after manner of God's holy *o.*; 19: 7 (Isa. 9: 7) of increase of government and peace there is no end upon his kingdom to *o.* it; **Mosiah** 4: 27 all things must be done in *o.*; **Alma** 4: 20 (13: 1, 6–11) high priesthood of holy *o.* of God; 6: 4 (8: 1) Alma[2] establishes *o.* of church; 13: 2, 6–9 (Hel. 8: 18) high priesthood after *o.* of the Son; 14: 16 (21: 4; 24: 28) apostates are after *o.* of Nehors; 41: 2 all things should be restored to proper *o.*; **3 Ne.** 6: 4 great *o.* in the land; **Moro.** 9: 18 Nephites are without *o.* and mercy.

ORDINANCE (*see also* Anointing; Authority; Baptism; Blessing; Confer; Confirm; Covenant; Hands, Laying on of; Heal; Holy Ghost, Gift of; Law; Ordain; Priesthood; Sacrament; Sacrifice; Statute; Temple; TG Ordinance)

2 Ne. 25: 30 keep performances and *o.* until law is fulfilled; **Mosiah** 13: 30 children of Israel given law of performances and *o.* to keep them in remembrance of God; **Alma** 13: 8 high priests ordained with holy *o.*; 13: 16 *o.* given that people might look forward on Son; 30: 3 Nephites are strict in observing *o.* according to law of Moses; 50: 39 chief judge appointed with sacred *o.* to judge righteously; **3 Ne.** 24: 7 (Mal. 3: 7) ye are gone away from mine *o.*, 24: 14 (Mal. 3: 14) what doth it profit that we have kept God's *o.*; **4 Ne.** 1: 12 Nephites no longer walk after *o.* of law of Moses.

ORE (*see also* Copper; Gold; Iron; Metal; Silver; Stone [noun])

1 Ne. 17: 9 Nephi[1] asks the Lord where he can find *o.* for tools; 18: 25 Lehites find all manner of *o.* in wilderness; 19: 1 Nephi[1] makes plates of *o.*; **2 Ne.** 5: 15 Nephi[1] teaches people to work in precious *o.*; **Jacob** 2: 12 Nephites search for precious *o.*; **Mosiah** 21: 27 record of Jaredites engraven on plates of *o.*; **Hel.** 6: 11 precious *o.* of every kind in promised land; **Ether** 10: 23 Jaredites work in all manner of *o.*

ORIHAH—*first Jaredite king*

Ether 1: 32 (6: 27; 7: 3) son of Jared[2], father of Kib; 6: 27 is anointed king; 6: 28—7: 1 reigns righteously; 7: 2 begets twenty-three sons, eight daughters; 7: 3 is succeeded by son Kib.

ORPHAN (*see also* Needy)

Morm. 8: 40 why do ye cause *o.* to mourn before the Lord.

OUTER (*see* Darkness, Spiritual; Outward; Vessel)

OUTWARD (*see also* Temporal)

Alma 25: 15 Nephites keep *o.* performances until time when Christ shall be revealed; **3 Ne.** 4: 16 robbers plan to make Nephites yield by cutting them off from *o.* privileges.

OVEN (*see also* Furnace)

3 Ne. 13: 30 (Matt. 6: 30) grass of field tomorrow is cast into *o.*; 25: 1 (Mal. 4: 1) day cometh that shall burn as *o.*

OVERBEARANCE (*see also* Compel)

Alma 38: 12 use boldness, but not *o.*

OVERCOME (*see also* Conquer; Overpower; Prevail)

1 Ne. 1: 7 Lehi[1] casts himself upon bed, *o.* with Spirit; 12: 20 Lamanites to *o.* Nephites; **Jacob** 5: 59, 66 good branches may *o.* evil; **Alma** 19: 6 light of everlasting light had *o.* Lamoni's natural frame; **3 Ne.** 17: 18 so great is joy of multitude that they are *o.*

OVERPOWER (*see also* Overcome)

1 Ne. 15: 24 fiery darts of adversary cannot *o.* those who hearken to word of God; **Alma** 19: 13–14 Lamanite king and queen *o.* by Spirit; 34: 15 bowels of mercy *o.* justice; 34: 39 be watchful unto prayer continually, that devil may not *o.* you; 53: 14 Ammonites *o.* by persuasions of Helaman[2] not to break oath; **3 Ne.** 10: 13 righteous are not *o.* by vapor of smoke and darkness; **Ether** 12: 24 things written by brother of Jared[2] were mighty unto *o.* of man to read them.

OVERSHADOW

Alma 7: 10 Mary shall be *o.* and conceive by power of Holy Ghost; **Hel.** 5: 28, 34 Lamanites are *o.* with cloud of darkness; **3 Ne.** 18: 38–39 cloud *o.* multitude, that they cannot see Jesus.

OVERTAKE, OVERTOOK, OVERTAKEN

3 Ne. 29: 4 if ye spurn at the Lord's doings, sword of his justice will *o.* you; **Morm.** 4: 5 judgments of God will *o.* the wicked.

OVERTHROW, OVERTHREW (*see also* Conquer; Destruction; Overcome)

2 Ne. 23: 19 (Isa. 13: 19) Babylon shall be as when God *o.* Sodom and Gomorrah; **Jacob** 7: 2 Sherem flatters people that he might *o.* doctrine of Christ; **Mosiah** 27: 13 nothing shall *o.* God's church save transgression; **Alma** 50: 32 flight of people of Morianton[2] to north may lead to *o.* of liberty; 51: 5 king-men desire to alter law to *o.* free government; **Hel.** 2: 13 Gadianton proves *o.* of Nephites; **Ether** 8: 25 he who builds secret combinations seeks to *o.* freedom of all lands.

OWE (*see also* Debt; Duty; Indebted)

Alma 11: 2 if a man would not pay what he *o.* to another, he was complained of to judge; 44: 5 Nephites *o.* sacred support to wives and children; 44: 5 Nephites *o.* all happiness to sacred word of God; 57: 22 Nephites *o.* victory to Ammonite youths.

OX, OXEN (*see also* Animal; Cattle)

1 Ne. 18: 25 Lehites find *o.* in wilderness in promised land; **2 Ne.** 21: 7 (Isa. 11: 7) lion shall eat straw like *o.*; **Ether** 9: 18 Jaredites have *o.*

PAANCHI—*son of Pahoran*[1] [c. 52 B.C.] (*see also* Pacumeni; Pahoran[2])

Hel. 1: 3 contends for judgment-seat;

1: 7 plans to flatter people into rebellion; 1: 8 is tried and condemned to death.

PACHUS—*king of Nephite dissenters* [c. 61 B.C.]

Alma 62: 6 king of dissenters who had driven freemen from Zarahemla; 62: 7 battles with Moroni[1] and Pahoran[1]; 62: 8 is slain.

PACIFY (*see also* Peace)

1 Ne. 15: 20 through words of Nephi[1] his brothers are *p.* and humbled; **2 Ne.** 28: 21 devil will *p.* men and lull them into carnal security; **Mosiah** 20: 20 except Limhi *p.* Lamanites, his people perish.

PACUMENI—*son of Pahoran*[1] [c. 52 B.C.] (*see also* Paanchi; Pahoran[2])

Hel. 1: 3 contends for judgment-seat; 1: 6 submits to voice of people; 1: 13 is appointed chief judge and governor; 1: 21 is slain by Coriantumr[3].

PAGAG—*son of brother of Jared*[2]

Ether 6: 25 refuses to be king.

PAHORAN[1]—*third Nephite chief judge* [c. 68 B.C.]

Alma 50: 39–40 fills judgment-seat of his father, Nephihah; 51: 2–5 contends with king-men; 51: 6 *P*'s supporters are called freemen; 51: 7 retains judgment-seat by voice of people; 51: 15–16 grants Moroni[1] power to compel dissenters to defend country; 59: 3 Moroni[1] writes to *P.* requesting reinforcements; ch. 60 Moroni[1] writes second epistle, complaining of neglect; ch. 61 *P*'s reply to epistle; 61: 5, 8 is driven from Zarahemla by king-men; 61: 9 seeks not power, but to preserve rights and liberty of people; 62: 6 is joined by Moroni[1]; 62: 7–8 returns to Zarahemla, is restored to judgment-seat; 62: 11 helps in restoring peace; 62: 14 marches to Nephihah; 62: 26 takes city of Nephihah without losses; 62: 44 returns to judgment-seat; **Hel.** 1: 2 dies.

PAHORAN[2]—*son of Pahoran*[1], *fourth Nephite chief judge* [c. 52 B.C.] (*see also* Paanchi; Pacumeni)

Hel. 1: 3 contends for judgment-seat; 1: 5 is appointed chief judge by voice of people; 1: 9 is murdered by Kishkumen.

PAID (*see* Pay, Paid)

PAIN (*see also* Affliction; Anguish; Grieve; Sorrow; Suffering; Torment)

1 Ne. 17: 47 heart of Nephi[1] is *p.* because of brothers; **2 Ne.** 9: 21 God suffereth *p.* of all men; 26: 7 Nephi[1] feels *p.* for the slain of his people; **Jacob** 3: 11 loose yourselves from *p.* of hell; **Mosiah** 2: 38 demands of justice fill breast of wicked with *p.* like unquenchable fire; 3: 7 the Lord shall suffer *p.* of body; 25: 11 Nephites filled with *p.* for welfare of Lamanites' souls; 27: 29 Alma[2] is snatched, and his soul is *p.* no more; **Alma** 7: 11 Son will take upon him the *p.* of his people; 13: 27 Alma[2] wishes with anxiety unto *p.* that people would hearken; 14: 6 Zeezrom is encircled by *p.* of hell; 26: 13 how many thousands of Lamanites has God loosed from *p.* of hell; 31: 30 wickedness among Zoramites *p.* soul of Alma[2]; 36: 13, 16 (38: 8) Alma[2] remembered all his sins and was tormented by *p.* of hell; 36: 19–20 Alma[2] was filled with joy as exceeding as was his *p.*; **3 Ne.** 28: 8–9, 38 three Nephites will not have *p.* in flesh or endure *p.* of death.

PALACE (*see also* Building)

2 Ne. 23: 22 (Isa. 13: 22) dragons shall cry in their pleasant *p.*; **Mosiah** 11: 9 Noah[3] builds spacious *p.*; **Alma** 22: 2 Aaron[3] goes to Lamanite king in his *p.*

PARABLE (*see also* Liken; BD Parables)

Jacob ch. 5 allegory of tame and wild olive-trees.

PARADISE (*see also* Death, Physical; Eden, Garden of; Heaven; Prison; Rest; Resurrection; Spirit World; TG Paradise, Paradisiacal; BD Paradise)

2 Ne. 9: 13 *p.* of God must deliver up its dead; **Alma** 40: 12, 14 spirits of righteous remain in state of happiness, called *p.*, until resurrection; **4 Ne.** 1: 14 Jesus' disciples are gone to *p.* of God; **Moro.** 10: 34 Moroni[2] will soon go to rest in *p.* of God.

PARENT (*see also* Child; Family; Father; Mother; TG Family, Children, Responsibilities toward; Honoring Father and Mother; Marriage, Fatherhood; Marriage, Motherhood)

1 Ne. 1: 1 Nephi[1] born of goodly *p.*; 5: 11 Adam and Eve, our first *p.*; 8: 37 Lehi[1] exhorts elder sons with all the feeling of tender *p.*; **2 Ne.** 1: 14 hear the words of trembling *p.*; 4: 6 Lehi[1] takes cursing from grandchildren, to be answered upon heads of *p.*; **Jacob** 4: 3 Nephites labor, that children may learn with joy concerning first *p.*; **Omni** 1: 22 first *p.* of Coriantumr[2] came out from tower; **Alma** 30: 25 child is not guilty because of *p.*; **Hel.** 5: 5–6 Helaman[2] reminds sons of names of first *p.* who came out of Jerusalem; **Moro.** 8: 10 teach *p.* that they must repent, be baptized, and humble themselves as their little children.

PART (*see also* Partake; Portion)

2 Ne. 2: 30 Lehi[1] has chosen the good *p.*; **Mosiah** 15: 24 (Rev. 20: 6) those who died before Christ came shall have *p.* in first resurrection; 29: 34 every man should bear his *p.*; **Alma** 40: 13 spirits of wicked have no *p.* or portion of Spirit of the Lord.

PARTAKE, PARTAKEN, PARTAKER (*see also* Drink; Eat; Inherit; Receive; Taste)

1 Ne. 8: 11–12 Lehi[1] *p.* of fruit of tree of life; 8: 15–16 Sariah, Sam, and Nephi[1] *p.* of fruit; 8: 17–18 Laman[1] and Lemuel do not *p.* of fruit; 8: 24 those who cling to iron rod *p.* of fruit; **2 Ne.** 2: 18 (Hel. 6: 26) devil tempts Eve to *p.* of forbidden fruit; 26: 24 the Lord commands none that they shall not *p.* of salvation; **Jacob** 1: 7 come unto Christ and *p.* of goodness of God; **Omni** 1: 26 come unto Christ and *p.* of his salvation; **Alma** 5: 34 come unto the Lord and you shall *p.* of fruit of tree of life; 5: 62 those who are baptized may be *p.* of fruit of tree of life; 12: 23, 26 (42: 5) if Adam had *p.* of tree of life, there would have been no death; 42: 27 whosoever will may come and *p.* of waters of life; **3 Ne.** 18: 28 (Morm. 9: 29) ye shall not suffer any one knowingly to *p.* of sacrament unworthily; **4 Ne.** 1: 3 Nephites are all made free, and *p.* of the heavenly gift; **Ether** 12: 8 Christ has prepared way by which others may be *p.* of heavenly gift; **Moro.** 4: 3 bread is blessed to souls of those who *p.*; 6: 6 saints meet together oft to *p.* of bread and wine; 8: 17 all children are alike and *p.* of salvation.

PASS (*see also* Cease; End; Judgment; Past; Vanish)

1 Ne. 17: 46 (Alma 9: 2; 3 Ne. 26: 3; Ether 13: 8; Matt. 24: 35) earth shall *p.* away; **3 Ne.** 1: 25 (Matt. 5: 18) not one jot or tittle should *p.* away until all should be fulfilled.

PASSION (*see also* Anger; Feeling; Fury; Rage)

Alma 38: 12 bridle all your *p.*; 50: 30 Morianton[2] a man of much *p.*

PAST (*see also* Pass; Present)

1 Ne. 17: 45 brothers of Nephi[1] are *p.* feeling; **Mosiah** 8: 17 a seer can know of things that are *p.*; **Hel.** 13: 38 your days of probation are *p.*; **3 Ne.** 1: 5–6 some say time is *p.* when signs of Christ's birth should be given; **Moro.** 9: 20 Nephites are without principle, and *p.* feeling.

PASTOR (*see also* Shepherd; TG Pastor)

1 Ne. 21: 1 Israel is broken off because of wickedness of *p.*

PASTURE (*see* Sheep)

PATH (*see also* Course; Direction; Highway; Road; Street; Walk; Way)

1 Ne. 8: 20–23 Lehi[1] beholds strait and narrow *p.* leading to tree of life; 8: 28 those who have tasted fruit but become ashamed fall into forbidden *p.*; 10: 8 (Alma 7: 19) John shall cry, Prepare way of the Lord, make his *p.* strait; 16: 5 Nephi[1] hopes brothers will walk in *p.* of righteousness; **2 Ne.** 4: 32–33 wilt thou make my *p.* straight before me; 12: 3 (Isa. 2: 3) God will teach us his ways, and we will walk in his *p.*; 13: 12 (Isa. 3: 12) they who lead the Lord's people cause them to destroy the way of their *p.*; 31: 9 Christ's baptism shows men the straitness of the *p.*; 31: 19 after ye have gotten into strait and narrow *p.*, is all done; 33: 9 only those who walk in strait *p.* which leads to life have hope; **Mosiah** 2: 36 if men withdraw themselves from Spirit, it has no place to guide them in wisdom's *p.*; **Alma** 7: 9 repent, prepare way of the Lord, walk in his *p.*; 7: 19 I perceive ye are in *p.* of righteousness, *p.* which leads to kingdom of God; 7: 20 God cannot walk in crooked *p.*; 37: 12 God's *p.* are straight; **Hel.** 15: 5 more part of Lamanites are in *p.* of their duty.

PATIENCE, PATIENT, PATIENTLY (*see also* Affliction; Humble; Long-suffering)

Mosiah 3: 19 natural man is enemy to God unless he becomes as child, *p.*; 23: 21 the Lord tries his people's *p.*; 24: 15 Alma[1] and his people submit with *p.* to the Lord's will; **Alma** 1: 25 the faithful bear persecution with *p.*; 7: 23 be humble, full of *p.*; 9: 26 Son of God shall be full of *p.*; 13: 28 be led by Holy Spirit, becoming *p.*; 17: 11 sons of Mosiah[2] are commanded to be *p.* among Lamanites; 20: 29 brothers of Ammon[2] had been *p.* in sufferings; 26: 27 bear with *p.* thine afflictions; 32: 41 if ye nourish tree with *p.*, it shall spring forth unto everlasting life; 32: 43 ye shall reap rewards of your *p.*; 34: 3 Alma[2] exhorted poor Zoramites unto faith and *p.*; 34: 40 Amulek exhorts poor Zoramites to have *p.*, bear afflictions; 38: 4 Shiblon bore persecutions with *p.* because the Lord was with him.

PAY, PAID (*see also* Debt; Repay; Reward; Tax; Tithing; Tribute; Wages)

Mosiah 2: 24 the Lord will bless the obedient, therefore he hath *p.* them; **Alma** 11: 2 if a man did not *p.* another what he owed, he was taken before judge; **3 Ne.** 12: 26 (Matt. 5: 26) thou shalt not come from prison until thou hast *p.* the uttermost senine.

PEACE (*see also* Calm; Pacify; Peaceable,

Peaceably; Peacemaker; Rest; War; TG Peace of God)

1 Ne. 13: 37 (Mosiah 12: 21; 15: 15–18; 3 Ne. 20: 40; Isa. 52: 7) how beautiful upon mountains are feet of him who publishes *p.*; 14: 7 the Lord will convince men unto *p.* or deliver them to hardness of heart; 20: 18 (Isa. 48: 18) if thou hadst hearkened unto my commandment, then had thy *p.* been as a river; 20: 22 (Isa. 48: 22) there is no *p.* unto the wicked; **2 Ne.** 3: 12 writings of Nephites and Jews shall grow together unto establishing *p.*; 4: 27 why should I yield to temptation, that evil one have place in my heart to destroy my *p.*; 19: 6 (Isa. 9: 6) Messiah shall be called, The Prince of *P.*; 19: 7 (Isa. 9: 7) of increase of government and *p.* there is no end; 26: 9 (4 Ne. 1: 4) Son shall appear, and Nephites shall have *p.* until three generations have passed; **Jacob** 7: 23 (W of M 1: 18; Alma 3: 24) *p.* restored again among Nephites; **Mosiah** 4: 3 Benjamin's people receive remission of sins and have *p.* of conscience; 19: 27 Limhi establishes *p.* among his people; 27: 37 sons of Mosiah² publish *p.*; 29: 14, 40 Mosiah² has labored to establish *p.* throughout the land; **Alma** 7: 27 may *p.* of God rest upon you; 13: 18 Melchizedek established *p.*, was called prince of *p.*; 24: 19 converted Lamanites bury weapons of war for *p.*; 38: 8 after three days and nights of anguish Alma² cried unto the Lord and found *p.*; 40: 12 spirits of righteous are received into paradise, a state of *p.*; 44: 14 Nephites will slay Lamanites unless they depart with covenant of *p.*; 58: 11 the Lord speaks *p.* to our souls; **Hel.** 5: 47 *p.* be unto you because of your faith; **3 Ne.** 22: 10 covenant of *p.* shall not be removed; **4 Ne.** 1: 4 *p.* in land following Christ's visit.

PEACEABLE, PEACEABLY (*see also* Peace)

Mosiah 4: 13 ye will not have mind to injure one another, but to live *p.*; **Moro.** 7: 3–4 Mormon² speaks to *p.* followers of Christ, whom he recognizes because of their *p.* walk with men.

PEACEMAKER

3 Ne. 12: 9 (Matt. 5: 9) blessed are *p.*, for they shall be called children of God.

PEARL (*see also* Precious)

3 Ne. 14: 6 (Matt. 7: 6) cast not your *p.* before swine; **4 Ne.** 1: 24 Nephites begin to be proud, wearing fine *p.*

PENALTY (*see also* Punishment)

Alma 12: 32 *p.* of doing evil is second death.

PENETRATE (*see also* Pierce)

Alma 26: 6 storm shall not *p.* to converts.

PENITENT (*see also* Humble; Repentance)

Alma 26: 21 none knoweth these things save the *p.*; 27: 18 none receive joy of God save truly *p.* seeker of happiness; 29: 10 when I see many of my brethren truly *p.*, my soul is filled with joy; 32: 7 Alma² says no more to multitude, but cries unto *p.*; 42: 23 mercy claimeth the *p.*; 42: 24 none but truly *p.* are saved; **3 Ne.** 6: 13 some are lifted up in pride, others are humble and *p.*

PEOPLE (*see also* Nation)

1 Ne. 5: 18 brass plates to go to every *p.*; 11: 36 thus shall be destruction of all *p.* that fight against apostles; 13: 40 records shall make known to all *p.* that Lamb is Son of Father; 14: 11 whore of all the earth has dominion among all *p.*; 17: 35 this *p.* had rejected every word of God; 19: 17 (Mosiah 16: 1) every *p.* shall see salvation of the Lord; 22: 28 all *p.* shall dwell safely in Holy One if they repent; **2 Ne.** 5: 9 those who are with Nephi¹ call themselves the *p.* of Nephi; 8: 16 (Isa. 51: 16) Zion, thou art my *p.*; 23: 14 (Isa. 13: 14) every man shall turn to own *p.*; 26: 13 Christ will manifest himself unto every *p.* that believe; 29: 4–5 Jews, the Lord's ancient covenant *p.*; 29: 14 the Lord's *p.*, who are of house of Israel, shall be gathered; **Omni** 1: 14 Nephites discover a *p.* called the *p.* of Zarahemla; **Mosiah** 1: 11 Benjamin will give his *p.* a name; 3: 20 knowledge of Savior shall spread through every *p.*; 15: 28 salvation of the Lord shall be declared to every *p.*; 18: 8, 10 as ye desire to be called God's *p.*, what have ye against being baptized; 27: 25 all *p.* must be born again; **Alma** 4: 12 great inequality among the *p.*; 26: 37 God is mindful of every *p.*; **3 Ne.** 20: 39 my *p.* shall know my name; 28: 29 three Nephites shall minister unto all *p.*; **4 Ne.** 1: 16 there could not be happier *p.* among all *p.* created by God.

PERCEIVE (*see also* Comprehend; Discern; Know; See; Understand)

2 Ne. 16: 9 (Isa. 6: 9) see ye indeed, but they *p.* not; 32: 8 I *p.* that ye ponder still; **Jacob** 4: 15 Jacob² *p.* by workings of Spirit; **Mosiah** 13: 7 I *p.* that my message cuts you to your hearts; 13: 11 I *p.* that commandments are not written in your hearts; **Alma** 7: 19 I *p.* that ye are in paths of righteousness; 10: 17 Amulek *p.* lawyers' thoughts; 18: 16 Ammon², filled with Spirit, *p.* king's thoughts; 40: 1 (41: 1; 42: 1) I *p.* that thy mind is worried; 43: 48 Moroni¹ *p.* intent of his men to shrink from Lamanites; **3 Ne.**

15: 2 Jesus *p.* that some wonder concerning law of Moses; 17: 2 I *p.* that ye are weak, that ye cannot understand all my words; **Morm.** 1: 2 I *p.* that thou art a sober child.

PERFECT, PERFECTED, PERFECTION (*see also* Godliness; Just; Perfectness; Righteousness; Uprightness; TG Perfection)

2 Ne. 9: 13 in resurrection our knowledge shall be *p.*; 9: 14 we shall have *p.* knowledge of our guilt; 9: 23 be baptized, having *p.* faith in Holy One; 31: 20 press forward with steadfastness in Christ, having *p.* brightness of hope; **Jacob** 4: 12 attain unto *p.* knowledge of Christ; 7: 4 Sherem has *p.* knowledge of language; **Alma** 5: 18 can ye imagine yourselves brought before God with *p.* remembrance of guilt; 11: 43–44 (40: 23) spirit and body shall be reunited in *p.* form; 32: 21, 26 faith is not to have *p.* knowledge; 32: 26 ye cannot know of their surety at first unto *p.*; 32: 34 your knowledge is *p.* in that thing and your faith is dormant; 42: 15 atonement made that God might be *p.*, just, and merciful God; 48: 11 Moroni[1] a man of *p.* understanding; 50: 37 Nephihah filled judgment-seat with *p.* uprightness before God; 55: 1 Ammoron has *p.* knowledge of his fraud; **Hel.** 5: 30 those in prison hear still small voice of *p.* mildness; **3 Ne.** 12: 48 (Matt. 5: 48) I would that ye should be *p.*, even as I, or your Father is *p.*; **Ether** 3: 7, 20 having *p.* knowledge of God, brother of Jared could not be kept within veil; **Moro.** 7: 15–17 way to judge is plain, that ye may know with *p.* knowledge; 8: 16 (1 John 4: 18) *p.* love casteth out fear; 10: 32 come unto Christ and be *p.* in him; 10: 32 by God's grace ye may be *p.* in Christ.

PERFECTNESS (*see also* Perfect)

2 Ne. 9: 46 prepare your souls that ye may not remember your awful guilt in *p.*

PERFORM, PERFORMANCE (*see also* Accomplish; Do; Duty; Fulfil; Observe; Undertake)

1 Ne. 17: 41 labor which Israelites had to *p.* was to look; **2 Ne.** 25: 30 ye must keep *p.* and ordinances of God until law is fulfilled; 32: 9 ye must not *p.* any thing unto the Lord without first praying that Father consecrate thy *p.*; **Mosiah** 13: 30 Israelites given law of *p.* and ordinances to keep them in remembrance of God; **Alma** 25: 15 Nephites keep outward *p.* until Christ shall be revealed; 31: 10 Zoramites would not observe *p.* of church; 34: 32 this life is day for men to *p.* labors; 34: 33 after this life cometh night of darkness, wherein no labor can be *p.*; 57: 21 Ammonite youth *p.* every command with exactness; **4 Ne.** 1: 12 Nephites do not walk any more after *p.* and ordinances of law of Moses; **Moro.** 9: 6 we have labor to *p.* while in tabernacle of clay.

PERISH (*see also* Destruction; Die)

1 Ne. 4: 13 better that one man should *p.* than nation dwindle in unbelief; 5: 19 brass plates should never *p.*; 15: 10 how is it ye will *p.* because of hardness of heart; 17: 41 (Alma 33: 20) because of simpleness of means of healing, many *p.*; 22: 19 the righteous shall not *p.*; **2 Ne.** 1: 4 if Lehites had stayed in Jerusalem, they would have *p.*; 6: 11 many Jews shall be afflicted in flesh and not suffered to *p.* because of prayers of righteous; 9: 30 treasure of the rich shall *p.* with them; 9: 51 feast upon that which *p.* not; 10: 13 they who fight against Zion shall *p.*; 25: 21 Joseph[1] received promise that his seed should never *p.*; 26: 30 if men have charity, they would not suffer laborer in Zion to *p.*; 26: 31 if laborers in Zion labor for money, they shall *p.*; 27: 26 (Isa. 29: 14) wisdom of wise and learned shall *p.*; 28: 16 when men are fully ripe in iniquity, they shall *p.*; 30: 1 except ye keep commandments of God, ye shall *p.*; **Jacob** 5: 4 master to nourish tree that it *p.* not; 5: 11 master will preserve roots, that they *p.* not; **Mosiah** 3: 18 the infant *p.* not who dies in infancy; 4: 22–23 wo unto him who withholds his substance, for it shall *p.* with him; 4: 30 O man, remember and *p.* not; 13: 28 (Alma 34: 9) except for atonement, men must unavoidably *p.*; 28: 3 sons of Mosiah[2] cannot bear that any soul should *p.*; **Alma** 53: 11 according to oath not to take up arms, Ammonites would have *p.*; **Hel.** 4: 25 except Nephites cleave unto the Lord, they must unavoidably *p.*; 14: 30 whosoever *p.*, *p.* unto himself; **Ether** 2: 19 without air in vessels, Jaredites would *p.*; **Moro.** 8: 16 they who pervert ways of the Lord shall *p.*

PERMIT (*see also* Suffer)

Mosiah 7: 8 Ammon[1] and brethren are *p.* to answer king's questions; **Hel.** 14: 30 men are *p.* to act for themselves; **Moro.** 7: 2 because of gift of his calling from the Lord, Mormon[2] is *p.* to speak to people.

PERSECUTION, PERSECUTE (*see also* Affliction; Chasten; Hate; Malice; Martyrdom; Mock; Oppression; Revile; Scourge; Smite; Spurn; Stone [verb]; Tread; Tribulation; Trial)

2 Ne. 9: 30 because they are rich, they *p.* the meek; 26: 8 the righteous who look forward to Christ, notwithstanding *p.*, shall not perish; **Jacob** 2: 13 because some have obtained more abundantly, they *p.* their brethren; **Mosiah** 26: 38 Alma[1] and fellow laborers are *p.* by those not of church; 27: 1 *p.* inflicted on church by unbelievers become so great the church murmurs; 27: 2 Mosiah[2] sends proclamation that no unbeliever should *p.* church member; 27: 13 why *p.* thou the church of God; 27: 32 Alma[2] and companions are *p.* by unbelievers; **Alma** 1: 21 strict law in church that no member should *p.* one who does not belong; 1: 25 those who stand steadfast in faith bear the *p.* with patience; 5: 54 will ye persist in *p.* your brethren; **Hel.** 3: 34 many who profess to belong to church are lifted up in pride unto *p.* their brethren; 13: 22 your hearts swell with great pride, unto *p.*; **3 Ne.** 6: 13 some receive *p.* and do not turn and revile again; 12: 10–11 (Matt. 5: 10–11) blessed are all who are *p.* for their Lord's sake, for theirs is kingdom; 12: 12 so *p.* they the prophets before you; 12: 44 (Matt. 5: 44) pray for them that *p.* you; **4 Ne.** 1: 29 other church *p.* true church of Christ; **Morm.** 8: 36 only a few do not lift themselves in pride, unto *p.*

PERSIST (*see also* Remain)

Jacob 2: 14 if ye *p.* in these things, God's judgments must speedily come upon you; **Mosiah** 16: 5 he who *p.* in carnal nature remains in fallen state; **Alma** 5: 54 will ye *p.* in persecuting brethren; 5: 55 will you *p.* in turning backs upon the needy; 5: 56 (9: 18) all who *p.* in their wickedness shall be hewn down and cast into fire; **Morm.** 4: 10 Nephites repent not and *p.* in wickedness.

PERSON (*see* Respect, Respecter)

PERSUADE, PERSUASION (*see also* Convince; Doctrine, False; Exhort; Plead; Urge)

1 Ne. 3: 21 Nephi[1] *p.* brethren to be faithful in keeping commandments; 6: 4 intent of Nephi[1] is to *p.* men to come unto God; 19: 23 (2 Ne. 25: 23; 33: 4; Morm. 5: 14) writings to *p.* people to believe in Redeemer; **2 Ne.** 26: 27 the Lord has commanded his people to *p.* all men to repentance; 33: 4 (Ether 8: 26) writings *p.* men to do good; **Jacob** 1: 8 Jacob[2] would *p.* all men not to rebel against God; **Jarom** 1: 11 law of Moses *p.* men to look forward to Messiah; **Morm.** 3: 22 Mormon[2] would *p.* all ends of earth to repent; **Ether** 4: 11 Spirit *p.* men to do good; 4: 12 whatsoever *p.* to do good is of the Lord; **Moro.** 7: 16 that which *p.* men to believe in Christ is of God; 7: 17 that which *p.* men to do evil is of devil.

PERVERT, PERVERSE, PERVERSION (*see also* Corrupt; Wrest)

1 Ne. 13: 27 (22: 14) abominable church *p.* right ways of the Lord; **2 Ne.** 28: 15 all who *p.* right way of the Lord shall be thrust down to hell; **Jacob** 7: 7 Sherem leads away people, that they *p.* right way of God; **Mosiah** 12: 26 priests of Noah[3] have *p.* ways of the Lord; 29: 23 unrighteous king *p.* the ways of righteousness; **Alma** 9: 8 (10: 17, 25; Hel. 13: 29) ye wicked and *p.* generation; 10: 18 lawyers lay plans to *p.* ways of righteous; 30: 22, 60 Korihor *p.* ways of the Lord; 31: 1, 11 Zoramites *p.* ways of the Lord; 31: 24 Zoramites a wicked and *p.* people; **Morm.** 8: 33 ye wicked, *p.*, stiffnecked people; **Moro.** 8: 15–16 they who say little children need baptism *p.* ways of the Lord; 9: 19 Nephites have become strong in *p.*

PESTILENCE (*see also* Destruction)

2 Ne. 6: 15 they who believe not in Messiah shall be destroyed by *p.*; 10: 6 because of iniquities, *p.* shall come upon Jews; **Mosiah** 12: 4, 7 the Lord will smite people of Noah[3] with *p.* because of iniquities; **Alma** 10: 22–23 except for prayers of the righteous, the Lord would smite people of Ammonihah with *p.*; 45: 10–11 when Nephites dwindle in unbelief, they shall see *p.*; **Hel.** 10: 6 Nephi[2] is given power to smite earth with *p.*; 12: 3 except the Lord chastens his people with *p.*, they will not remember him; **Ether** 11: 7 because Jaredites hearken not to the Lord, *p.* come.

PETITION (*see also* Beg; Plead)

Mosiah 4: 16 ye will not suffer beggar to put up his *p.* in vain; 4: 22 if ye condemn the man who puts his *p.* to you, how much more just will your condemnation be; **Alma** 51: 15 Moroni[1] sends *p.* to governor requesting power to compel dissenters to fight.

PHARAOH—*ruler of ancient Egypt* (*see also* BD Pharaoh)

1 Ne. 4: 2 (17: 27; Ex. 14: 26–30) armies of *P.* drowned in Red sea.

PHYSICIAN

Moro. 8: 8 (Matt. 9: 12) the whole need no *p.*

PIERCE, PIERCING (*see also* Penetrate)

Jacob 2: 9 those who have not been wounded must have daggers placed to *p.* their souls; 2: 10 Jacob[2] tells Nephites of wickedness under glance of *p.* eye of God; **Hel.** 5: 30 still voice in prison *p.* to very soul; **3 Ne.** 11: 3 survivors hear small voice that *p.* to very center.

PILLAR

1 Ne. 1: 6 *p.* of fire comes down before Lehi[1]; **Hel.** 5: 24, 43–44 Nephi[2] and Lehi[4] are encircled in *p.* of fire.

PILLOW

2 Ne. 33: 3 eyes of Nephi[1] water his *p.* by night because of his people.

PIT (*see also* Persecution; Snare)

1 Ne. 14: 3 great *p.* digged by abominable church for destruction of men; 22: 14 they shall fall into *p.* which they digged to ensnare people of the Lord; **2 Ne.** 8: 1 (Isa. 51: 1) look to hole of *p.* from whence ye are digged; 24: 15 (Isa. 14: 15) thou shalt be brought down to hell, to sides of *p.*; 28: 8 many shall say, Dig *p.* for thy neighbor; **3 Ne.** 28: 20 wicked could not dig *p.* sufficient to hold disciples; **Ether** 9: 29 Jaredites cast prophets into *p.* to perish.

PITY (*see also* Compassion; Mercy)

2 Ne. 23: 18 (Isa. 13: 18) they shall have no *p.* on fruit of womb; **Alma** 53: 11 Ammonites would allow themselves to fall into brethren's hands except for *p.* of Ammon[2] and brethren; **Ether** 3: 3 Lord, look upon me in *p.*

PLACE

1 Ne. 17: 46 (3 Ne. 8: 13) by power of his word the Lord can cause rough *p.* to be made smooth; 21: 20 (Isa. 49: 20) the *p.* is too strait for me, give *p.* to me that I may dwell; **2 Ne.** 4: 27 why should I yield to temptation, that evil one have *p.* in my heart; 23: 13 (Isa. 13: 13) earth shall remove out of her *p.*; 28: 23 after judgment, wicked must go to *p.* prepared for them; 33: 2 many harden hearts against Spirit, that it have no *p.* in them; **Enos** 1: 27 *p.* prepared for you in mansions of Father; **Mosiah** 2: 36 if ye transgress what has been spoken, ye withdraw yourselves from Spirit, that it has no *p.* in you; 2: 37 the Lord has no *p.* in those who obey evil spirit; 12: 23 (15: 30; 3 Ne. 16: 19; 20: 34; Isa. 52: 9) ye waste *p.* of Jerusalem; 26: 24 if they know me, they shall have *p.* at my right hand; **Alma** 5: 25 ye cannot suppose the wicked have *p.* in kingdom of heaven; 20: 30 brethren of Ammon[2] are driven from *p.* to *p.*; 32: 27 give *p.* for portion of my words; 34: 26 pour out your souls in secret *p.*; 34: 35 if ye have procrastinated day of repentance, Spirit has withdrawn that it has no *p.* in you; 39: 6 to deny Holy Ghost when it once has had *p.* in you is unpardonable sin; **Hel.** 14: 23 many *p.* that are now valleys shall become mountains; **Morm.** 8: 30 earthquakes in divers *p.*; **Moro.** 7: 32 the Lord prepares way that men may have faith in Christ, that Holy Ghost may have *p.* in hearts.

PLAIN, PLAINLY, PLAINNESS (*see also* Clear; Simple)

1 Ne. 13: 26–29, 32, 34 great and abominable church takes many *p.* and precious things from book; 13: 29 because things are taken from book which were *p.* to men's understanding, according to *p.* which is in Lamb, many stumble; 13: 34–40 the Lord will reveal many *p.* and precious parts of gospel that have been taken away; 14: 23 when book proceeded from Jews, it was *p.* and true; **2 Ne.** 1: 26 brothers murmur because Nephi[1] has been *p.* unto them; 4: 32 may I be strict in the *p.* road; 9: 47 would I be *p.* unto you according to *p.* of truth if ye were freed from sin; 25: 4 words of Isaiah[1] are *p.* unto all who are filled with spirit of prophecy; 25: 4 (33: 6) my soul delighteth in *p.*; 25: 20 I have spoken *p.*, that ye cannot err; 26: 33 the Lord doeth nothing save it be *p.* unto men; 32: 7 men will not understand great knowledge when given them in *p.*; 33: 5 writings of Nephi[1] speak harshly against sin, according to *p.* of word of God; **Jacob** 4: 13 these things are manifested unto us *p.*, for salvation of souls; 4: 14 Jews despised words of *p.*; **Enos** 1: 23 prophets speak with great *p.* of speech; **Mosiah** 2: 40 Benjamin speaks *p.*, that his people might understand; **Alma** 13: 23 glad tidings are made known in *p.* terms; 14: 2 people are angry with Alma[2] because of *p.* of his words; **Moro.** 7: 15 way to judge is as *p.* as daylight is from dark night.

PLAINS (*see also* Agosh; Hershlon, Plains of; Nephihah, Plains of)

1 Ne. 12: 4 Nephi[1] beholds *p.* of earth broken up in vision; **Alma** 52: 20 Nephites desire to meet Jacob[3] on *p.* between cities.

PLAN (*see also* Gospel; Plot; Redemption; Salvation; Secret Combination; TG Salvation, Plan of)

2 Ne. ch. 2, 9 (Alma ch. 12, 42) summary of *p.* of redemption; 9: 6 (Alma 12: 25) to fulfill merciful *p.* of Creator, there must be resurrection; 9: 13 how great the *p.* of our God; 9: 28 (Alma 28: 13) cunning *p.* of evil one; **Jacob** 6: 8 will ye make a mock of great *p.* of redemption; **Jarom** 1: 2 fathers have revealed *p.* of salvation on plates; **Alma** 12: 4 Zeezrom's *p.* was very subtle *p.*; 12: 25, 30 *p.* of redemption laid from foundation of world; 12: 30–32 God made *p.* of redemption known unto man; 12: 33 God called on men in name of Son, this being *p.* of redemption; 34: 9 according to great *p.* of God, atonement must be made; 34: 16 only unto him who has faith is brought about *p.* of redemption; 37: 29, 32 trust not those secret *p.* of murder unto this people; 41: 2 *p.* of restoration is requisite with justice of God; 42: 5 if Adam had partaken of tree of life, *p.* of salvation would have been frustrated; 42: 8 to reclaim man from temporal death would destroy great *p.* of happiness; 42: 11 except for *p.* of redemption, men would be cut off from presence of the Lord; 42: 15 *p.* of mercy could not be brought about except atonement should be made; **Hel.** 2: 6 servant obtains knowledge of *p.* to destroy Helaman[2]; 11: 10 secret *p.* of Gadianton robbers are concealed in earth; 11: 26 great band of robbers search out secret *p.* of Gadianton; **3 Ne.** 1: 16 *p.* of destruction laid for believers has been frustrated; **Ether** 8: 8 daughter of Jared[3] devises *p.* to redeem kingdom unto father.

PLANT (*see also* Grain; Seed; Sow [verb]; Till)

1 Ne. 18: 24 Lehites begin to *p.* seeds; **2 Ne.** 8: 16 (Isa. 51: 16) I have covered thee in shadow of mine hand that I may *p.* heavens; 15: 2 (Isa. 5: 2) well-beloved *p.* vineyard with choicest vine; **Jacob** 5: 21 how comest thou hither to *p.* this tree; **Mosiah** 14: 2 (Isa. 53: 2) he shall grow up before him as tender *p.*; **Alma** 32: 28, 33 (33: 23) give place, that seed may be *p.* in your heart; 32: 36 (34: 4) ye have exercised faith to *p.* seed to know if it is good; 33: 1 people ask how to *p.* seed, or word.

PLATES (*see* Book; Book of Mormon; Characters; Engrave; Plates, Brass; Plates of Ether; Plates of Jacob; Plates of Mormon; Plates of Nephi, Large; Plates of Nephi, Small; Plates of Zeniff; Record; Scriptures)

PLATES, BRASS (*see also* Laban)

1 Ne. 3: 3, 12 (19: 2) Laban has record of Jews and genealogy of fathers engraven on *b.p.*; 3: 9—4: 38 sons of Lehi[1] obtain *b.p.*; 4: 16 law is engraven upon *b.p.*; 4: 24 Nephi[1] to carry engravings on *b.p.* to brothers; 5: 10–16 (19: 23; Omni 1: 14; Alma 37: 3) *b.p.* contain five books of Moses, history of Jews to reign of Zedekiah, genealogy; 5: 18 *b.p.* to go to every people of seed of Lehi[1]; 5: 19 *b.p.* should never perish; 7: 11 ye have forgotten what great things the Lord hath done that we should obtain record; 13: 23 Bible is like engravings on *b.p.*; 19: 1–2 Nephi[1] reads many scriptures engraven on *b.p.*; 19: 22—22: 1 Nephi[1] reads writings of Isaiah[1] from *b.p.*; 22: 30 writings on *b.p.* testify man must be obedient; **2 Ne.** 4: 2 prophecies of Joseph[1] are written on *b.p.*; 4: 14–15 Nephi[1] engraves scriptures from *b.p.* on his *p.*; 5: 12 (Mosiah 10: 16) Nephi[1] takes records engraven on *b.p.* with him; **Omni** 1: 14 Zarahemla rejoices because of *b.p.*; **Mosiah** 1: 3–4 Lehi[1] could not have taught his children all these things without *b.p.*; 1: 4 engravings on *b.p.* are in Egyptian; 1: 16 Benjamin gives *b.p.* to Mosiah[2]; 28: 11, 20 Mosiah[2] gives Alma[2] records engraven on *b.p.*; **Alma** 37: 1–3 Alma[2] gives *b.p.* to Helaman[2]; 37: 3 engravings on *b.p.* are records of holy scriptures; **3 Ne.** 1: 2 Nephi[2] gives *b.p.* to son Nephi[3]; 10: 17 prophecy of Jacob[1] concerning seed of Joseph[1] is on *b.p.*

PLATES OF ETHER (*see also* Ether; Jaredites)

Mosiah 8: 9 expedition from Limhi discovers twenty-four *p.* of gold filled with engravings; 21: 27 people of Limhi find Jaredite record of engraven plates of ore; 22: 14 Limhi gives record to Mosiah[2]; 28: 11 Mosiah[2] translates record on *p.* of gold found by Limhi; **Alma** 37: 21–32 twenty-four *p.* contain record of secret works of darkness of people who were destroyed; **Hel.** 6: 26 secret oaths did not come to Gadianton from record, but from devil; **Ether** 1: 2 Moroni[2] takes account of Jaredites from twenty-four gold *p.* found by Limhi, called Book of Ether; 3: 22 (4: 1) brother of Jared[2] is commanded to write what he has seen and heard, seal it; 15: 33 Ether finishes record and hides it.

PLATES OF JACOB (*see also* Jacob[2]; Plates of Nephi, Small)

Jacob 3: 14 Jacob[2] writes upon *p.* called *p.* of Jacob, made by Nephi[1].

PLATES OF MORMON (*see also* Mormon[2]; Moroni[2])

W of M 1: 3 (Morm. 6: 6) Mormon[2] makes abridgment from *p.* of Nephi; 1: 6 Mormon[2] puts small *p.* with remainder of his record; 1: 9 Mormon[2] proceeds to finish his record; **3 Ne.** 5: 10–11 Mormon[2] makes record on *p.* he has made with own hands; **Morm.** 2: 18 upon these *p.* Mormon[2] does not make full account of wickedness; 6: 6 Mormon[2] gives Moroni[2] few plates; 8: 1 Moroni[2] finishes father's record; **Moro.** 10: 2 Moroni[2] seals up record.

PLATES OF NEPHI, LARGE—*secular history abridged by Mormon[2], whose abridgment constitutes books of Mosiah, Alma, Helaman, 3 Nephi, and 4 Nephi* (*see also* Lehi, Book of; Mormon[2]; Plates of Mormon; Plates of Nephi, Small)

1 Ne. 9: 2, 4 (19: 4; 2 Ne. 4: 14; 5: 29, 33; Jacob 1: 3; 3: 13; 7: 26; Mosiah 1: 6) Nephi[1] makes account of history, kings, wars on other *p.*, also called *p.* of Nephi; **2 Ne.** 4: 14 many sayings of Lehi[1] and Nephi[1] are recorded on other *p.*; **Jacob** 1: 3 (Jarom 1: 14; Omni 1: 11) secular history to be engraven on larger *p.*; **W of M** 1: 3 after abridging larger *p.* down to reign of Benjamin, Mormon[2] finds small *p.*; **Mosiah** 1: 3 Benjamin teaches of records engraven on larger *p.*; 1: 6 Benjamin testifies *p.* of Nephi are true; **Alma** 37: 2 Alma[2] commands Helaman[2] to keep sacred record upon *p.* of Nephi; **3 Ne.** 5: 8–10 (26: 6–7) Mormon[2] gives only small part of record engraven on *p.* of Nephi; 26: 6–7 *p.* of Nephi contain more part of things Jesus taught the people; 26: 8–11 Mormon[2] is commanded not to record all Christ's sayings engraven on *p.* of Nephi; **Morm.** 1: 4 Mormon[2] is instructed to engrave on *p.* of Nephi all he observes among Nephites; 2: 18 upon *p.* of Nephi Mormon[2] makes full account of Nephites' wickedness; 6: 6 Mormon[2] makes record out of *p.* of Nephi.

PLATES OF NEPHI, SMALL—*spiritual history of Nephites, which constitutes the books of 1 Nephi, 2 Nephi, Jacob, Enos, Jarom, Omni* (*see also* Nephi[1])

1 Ne. 1: 17 (19: 1) Nephi[1] abridges record of father upon *p.* he has made; 6: 1 Nephi[1] does not include genealogy in this part of his record; 6: 3 Nephi[1] does not make full account of history on these *p.* so he can write of things of God; 9: 2–4 (10: 1; 19: 3; Jacob 1: 1–2) these *p.* do not contain full account of people, but rather an account of the ministry; 19: 1 on *p.* of ore Nephi[1] engraves father's record, journey in wilderness, father's prophecies, own prophecies; **2 Ne.** 4: 15 upon these *p.* Nephi[1] writes things of his soul and scriptures engraven on brass *p.*; 5: 30–32 Nephi[1] is commanded by the Lord to make and engrave many things for profit of his people; **Jacob** 1: 1–2, 4 Nephi[1] instructs Jacob[2] to engrave most precious, sacred things on small *p.*; 3: 13 hundredth part of Nephites' proceedings cannot be written upon these *p.*; 3: 14 *p.* of Jacob included among small *p.*; 7: 27 Jacob[2] confers *p.* upon Enos[2]; **Jarom** 1: 2, 14 Jarom writes little because *p.* are small; **Omni** 1: 1 Jarom instructs Omni to write upon *p.*; 1: 8–9 Omni delivers *p.* to Chemish; 1: 10 Abinadom writes upon *p.*; 1: 12–30 Amaleki writes upon *p.*; 1: 25 Amaleki delivers *p.* to king Benjamin; 1: 30 *p.* are full; **W of M** 1: 3 after abridging large *p.* to reign of Benjamin, Mormon[2] discovers these *p.*, which contain small account of prophets; 1: 4 small *p.* contain prophecies of coming of Christ; 1: 6 Mormon[2] puts small *p.* with remainder of his record.

PLATES OF ZENIFF (*see also* Limhi; Nephi, Land of; Noah[3]; Zeniff)

Mosiah 8: 5 Limhi brings Ammon[1] *p.* containing record of his people; 22: 14 Mosiah[2] receives with joy records of Limhi's people.

PLAY

2 Ne. 21: 8 (30: 14; Isa. 11: 8) sucking child shall *p.* on hole of asp; **3 Ne.** 28: 22 (4 Ne. 1: 33) disciples cast into den of beasts, *p.* with them.

PLEAD (*see also* Appeal; Cry; Exhort; Jesus Christ—Advocate; Persuade; Petition)

2 Ne. 8: 22 (Isa. 51: 22) the Lord *p.* cause of his people; 13: 13 (Isa. 3: 13) the Lord standeth up to *p.* and judge the people; **Jacob** 3: 1 God will *p.* your cause; **Alma** 1: 15 Nehor stands before Alma[2] and *p.* for himself with much boldness.

PLEASANT (*see also* Pleased, Pleasing)

Mosiah 23: 4, 19 people of Alma[1] come to *p.* land; **Alma** 55: 13 wine was *p.* to Lamanites' taste; **Hel.** 5: 46–47 *p.* voice whispers peace to Nephi[2] and Lehi[4]; **3 Ne.** 24: 4 (Mal. 3: 4) offering of Judah and Jerusalem shall be *p.* unto the Lord.

PLEASED, PLEASING (*see also* Delight; Favored; Happiness; Pleasant; Pleasure)

1 Ne. 6: 5 (2 Ne. 5: 32) Nephi[1] writes things *p.* unto God, not *p.* unto world; **2 Ne.** 5: 32 if Nephites are *p.* with things of God, they will be *p.* with engravings of Nephi[1]; **Jacob** 2: 7 tenderness and chasteness of feelings are *p.* unto God; 2: 8 Jacob[2] supposes people come to hear *p.* word of God; 6: 13 (Moro. 10: 34) meet before *p.* bar of God; **Mosiah** 14: 10 (Isa. 53: 10) it *p.* the Lord to bruise him; **Alma** 30: 53 Korihor taught devil's words because they were *p.* to carnal mind; **3 Ne.** 11: 7 (Matt. 3: 17) behold my Beloved Son, in whom I am well *p.*

PLEASURE (*see also* Delight; Desire; Happiness; Joy; Will)

1 Ne. 16: 38 brothers accuse Nephi[1] of desiring to be ruler, that he might do according to his *p.*; **2 Ne.** 25: 22 these things shall go according to *p.* of God; **Jacob** 4: 9 God commands earth according to his *p.*; **Enos** 1: 27 Enos[2] will see Redeemer's face with *p.*; **Mosiah** 7: 33 the Lord will deliver you out of bondage, according to *p.*; **Alma** 4: 8 people of church persecute those who do not believe according to their *p.*

PLOT (*see also* Plan)

Alma 2: 21 Alma[2] sends spies to know *p.* of Amlicites; **Hel.** 6: 30 devil, who *p.* with Cain, hands down secret *p.* for workers of darkness.

PLOW (*see also* Till)

2 Ne. 12: 4 (Isa. 2: 4) they shall beat their swords into *p*-shares; **Ether** 10: 25 Jaredites make tools to *p.* and sow.

PLUCK (*see also* Destruction; Prune; Reap)

Jacob 5: 7, 26, 52, 57–58 branches *p.* off olive-tree; **Alma** 32: 38 if tree is not nourished, it withers and ye *p.* it up; 32: 40 if ye will not nourish word, ye can never *p.* fruit of tree of life.

PLUNDER (*see* Rob)

POINT (*see also* Direction, Direct; Doctrine)

1 Ne. 8: 33 those in building *p.* finger of scorn at partakers of fruit; **Jacob** 4: 5 (Alma 34: 14) law of Moses *p.* souls to Christ; **Alma** 34: 40 faith causes spindles to *p.* direction Lehites should go; 37: 44 word of Christ will *p.* straight course to eternal bliss; 51: 5 king-men desire that a few *p.* of law be altered.

POINTERS (*see* Liahona)

POISON, POISONOUS (*see also* Serpent)

Mosiah 7: 30 effect of whirlwind is *p.*; **Alma** 47: 18 Amalickiah causes servant to administer *p.* by degrees to Lehonti; 55: 30 Lamanites attempt to destroy Nephites with *p.*

POLLUTE, POLLUTION (*see also* Corrupt; Defile; Filthiness; Sin)

1 Ne. 20: 11 (Isa. 48: 11) the Lord will not suffer his name to be *p.*; **Mosiah** 25: 11 when Nephites think of Lamanites' *p.* state, they are filled with anguish; **Alma** 26: 17 who could have supposed God would have snatched us from *p.* state; **Morm.** 8: 31 the Lord's promises will be fulfilled in day when great *p.* are upon land; 8: 38 why have ye *p.* church of God.

POLYGAMY (*see* Marriage; Wife)

PONDER (*see also* Consider; Reasoning; Study; Think)

1 Ne. 11: 1 as Nephi[1] sits *p.*, he is caught away in Spirit; **2 Ne.** 4: 15–16 my heart *p.* the scriptures; 32: 1 brothers of Nephi[1] *p.* what to do after entering the way; **Hel.** 10: 2–3 Nephi[2] *p.* upon things the Lord has shown him; **3 Ne.** 17: 3 Christ tells people to *p.* upon what he has said; **Moro.** 10: 3 when ye read these things, *p.* them in your hearts.

POOL (*see* Water)

POOR, POORER, POOREST (*see also* Alms; Charity; Humble; Lowliness; Meek; Naked; Needy; Poverty; Relief)

2 Ne. 9: 30 because they are rich, they despise the *p.*; 13: 15 (Isa. 3: 15) ye grind the faces of the *p.*; 21: 4 (30: 9; Isa. 11: 4) with righteousness shall the Lord judge the *p.*; 26: 20 Gentiles grind upon face of the *p.*; 27: 30 the *p.* shall rejoice in Holy One; 28: 13 false churches rob the *p.* because of fine sanctuaries; **Jacob** 5: 21 branch of tree planted in *p.* spot in all vineyard; 5: 22 the Lord knew it was *p.* spot of ground; 5: 23 the Lord has planted another branch in spot of ground *p.* than first; **Mosiah** 4: 26 impart of substance to the *p.*; **Alma** 5: 55 will you persist in turning your backs upon the *p.*; 32: 2–3 Alma[2] and missionaries have success among *p.* class of people; 32: 4 those who seek out Alma[2] are *p.* in heart because of poverty as to things of world; **Hel.** 4: 12 slaughter of Nephites is caused by their oppression of *p.*; 6: 39 robbers obtain government, turn backs upon the *p.*; **3 Ne.** 12: 3 (Matt. 5: 3) blessed are the *p.* in spirit who come unto Christ; **4 Ne.** 1: 3 Nephites have all things in common, there were not rich and *p.*; **Morm.** 8: 37 ye love money more than ye love the *p.*

POPULAR

1 Ne. 22: 23 churches built up to become *p.* in eyes of world shall be brought low; **Alma** 1: 15 Nehor declares that every priest should become *p.*; 35: 3 more *p.* part of Zoramites are angry because of word.

PORE

Mosiah 3: 7 (Luke 22: 44) blood shall come from every *p.* of Messiah.

PORTION (*see also* Part)

Mosiah 14: 12 (Isa. 53: 12) I will divide him a *p.* with the great; **Alma** 12: 10–11 he who hardens heart receives lesser *p.* of word; 17: 9 sons of Mosiah[2] pray that the Lord will grant them a *p.* of Spirit; 18: 35 *p.* of Spirit gives knowledge and power; 24: 8 Lamoni thanks God he has given converted Lamanites *p.* of Spirit; 27: 24 Nephites will defend Ammonites if they will give *p.* of substance to assist armies; 32: 27 let this desire work in you until you can give place for *p.* of my words; 40: 13 spirits of wicked have no *p.* of Spirit.

POSSESS (*see also* Inhabit)

Alma 30: 42 Korihor is *p.* with lying spirit; 34: 34 same spirit that *p.* body at death will *p.* body in eternal world; **Morm.** 5: 19 the Lord hath reserved Nephites' blessings for Gentiles who shall *p.* land; **Ether** 2: 8–10 he who *p.* land shall serve God or be swept off; **Moro.** 7: 47 whoso is found *p.* of charity, it shall be well with him.

POTTER

2 Ne. 27: 27 your turning of things upside down shall be esteemed as *p*'s clay.

POUR

1 Ne. 14: 15 wrath of God to be *p.* out upon abominable church; **2 Ne.** 27: 5 the Lord has *p.* out upon the wicked the spirit of deep sleep; **Jacob** 7: 8 the Lord *p.* his Spirit into soul of Jacob[2]; **Enos** 1: 9 Enos[2] *p.* out whole soul unto God for Nephites; **Mosiah** 4: 20 the Lord has *p.* out his Spirit upon Benjamin's people; 14: 12 (Isa. 53: 12) he hath *p.* out his soul unto death; 18: 10 the Lord will *p.* out Spirit upon those who are baptized; 25: 24 the Lord *p.* out Spirit upon people of God; **Alma** 19: 14 Spirit is *p.* out upon Lamanites; 34: 26 *p.* out your souls in your closets; **Hel.** 3: 25 (3 Ne. 10: 18) many blessings are *p.* out upon church; **3 Ne.** 20: 27 in Abraham's seed shall all kindreds be blessed, unto *p.* out of Holy Ghost; 24: 10 (Mal. 3: 10) the Lord will open windows of heaven and *p.* out blessing; **Morm.** 3: 12 soul of Mormon[2] is *p.* out in prayer for Nephites; **Ether** 9: 20 the Lord *p.* out blessings upon choice land.

POVERTY (*see also* Poor)

Alma 32: 4 great multitude are poor in heart because of *p.* as to things of world; 34: 40 do not revile against those who cast you out because of your *p.*; **Hel.** 13: 31 in days of your *p.* ye cannot retain your riches; **3 Ne.** 6: 12 some have no chance for learning, because of *p.*

POWER, POWERFUL (*see also* Authority; Dominion; Glory [noun]; God, Power of; Might; Priesthood; Strength; TG God, Power of; Jesus Christ, Power of; Power; Priesthood, Power of)

1 Ne. 2: 14 (10: 17) Lehi[1] speaks with *p.*; 10: 17 Lehi[1] received *p.* by faith on Son; 10: 17 *p.* of Holy Ghost is gift of God unto all who diligently seek him; 17: 52 Spirit is so *p.*, brothers fear they should wither; 22: 15 Satan shall have no more *p.* over hearts of men; 22: 23 churches built up to get *p.* over flesh shall be brought low; 22: 26 because of righteousness of people, Satan has no *p.*; **2 Ne.** 1: 25 elder brothers accuse Nephi[1] of seeking *p.* and authority over them; 10: 25 may God raise you from death by *p.* of resurrection and from everlasting death by *p.* of atonement; 32: 3 angels speak by *p.* of Holy Ghost; 33: 1 when a man speaks by *p.* of Holy Ghost, *p.* of Holy Ghost carries it unto hearts; **Jacob** 4: 11 ye may obtain a resurrection according to *p.* of resurrection which is in Christ; 7: 4 Sherem's knowledge of language enables him to use much *p.* of speech; 7: 18 Sherem confesses he was deceived by *p.* of devil; **W of M** 1: 17 many holy men in land speak word of God with *p.* and authority; **Mosiah** 8: 16 man may have great *p.* given him of God; 13: 6 Abinadi speaks with *p.* and authority from God; 16: 3 (Alma 34: 35) devil has *p.* over the wicked; 23: 39 Amulon given no *p.* to do anything contrary to will of Lamanite king; 25: 19 Mosiah[2] gives Alma[1] *p.* to ordain priests and teachers; **Alma** 1: 17 law could have no *p.* over any man for his belief; 9: 28 the evil shall reap damnation according to *p.* of devil; 12: 5 adversary exercises *p.* in Zeezrom; 17: 3 sons of Mosiah[2] teach with *p.* and authority; 19: 4 Ammon[2] has *p.* to do many mighty works in God's name; 30: 42 devil has *p.* over Korihor; 3: 15 preaching of word has more *p.* effect than sword; 34: 34 same spirit that possesses body at death shall have *p.* to possess it in eternal world; 46: 4 lower judges seek for *p.* by declaring king; 48: 7 Amalickiah obtains *p.* by fraud and deceit; 48: 17 if all men were like Moroni,[1] *p.* of hell would be broken and devil would have no *p.*; 60: 36 Moroni[1] seeks not for *p.*, but to pull it down; **Hel.** 3: 29 word is quick and *p.*; 6: 5 many preach with great *p.* and authority; 7: 4 Gadianton robbers usurp *p.* and authority of land; **3 Ne.** 2: 2 people imagine signs are wrought by men and *p.* of devil; 6: 15 (7: 5) cause of iniquity is that Satan has great *p.*; 7: 17 Nephi[3] ministers with *p.* and great authority; 11: 21–22 Jesus gives disciples *p.* to baptize; 16: 12 Gentiles shall not have *p.* over Israel; 18: 37 (Moro. 2: 1–3) Jesus gives disciples *p.* to bestow Holy Ghost; 28: 39 three Nephites are changed, that Satan should have no *p.* over them and *p.* of earth could not hold them; 29: 6 wo unto him who says the Lord no longer works by *p.* of Holy Ghost; **Ether** 8: 16 secret combinations were kept up by *p.* of devil; 8: 22 nation that upholds secret combinations to get *p.* shall be destroyed; 8: 23 (11: 15) combinations built up to get *p.* and gain; 8: 26 Moroni[2] writes, that Satan may have no *p.* over men; 12: 25 God has made prophets' words *p.*; 15: 19 Satan has full *p.* over hearts of people; **Moro.** 7: 44 if a man confesses by *p.* of Holy Ghost that Jesus is the Christ, he must have charity; 8: 8 curse of Adam has no *p.* over little children; 10: 4–5 by *p.* of Holy Ghost ye may know the truth of all things.

PRAISE (*see also* Glorify; Honor; Rejoice; Shout; Thank; Vain; Worship)

1 Ne. 13: 9 for *p.* of world abominable church destroys saints; 18: 16 Nephi[1] *p.* God all day long; **2 Ne.** 9: 49 Jacob[2] will *p.* holy name of God; 22: 4 *p.* the Lord, call upon his name; 26: 29 priestcraft is to preach to get *p.* of world; **Mosiah** 2: 20–21 if you surrender all *p.* to God, yet would ye be unprofitable servants; **Alma** 24: 23 converted Lamanites *p.* God in very act of perishing under sword; 26: 8 let us sing to God's *p.*; 38: 13 Zoramites pray to be *p.* of men; **Morm.** 8: 38 why are you ashamed to take upon you name of Christ, to get *p.* of world; **Ether** 6: 9 brother of Jared[2] did sing *p.* to the Lord.

PRAYER, PRAY (*see also* Answer; Ask; Call; Communication; Cry; Faith; Fasting; Name of the Lord; Supplicate; TG Prayer; BD Prayer)

1 Ne. 18: 3 Nephi[1] *p.* oft unto the Lord; **2 Ne.** 4: 24 Lehi[1] has waxed bold in mighty *p.* unto God; 26: 15 *p.* of the faithful shall be heard; 32: 8 if ye would hearken unto Spirit which teaches man to *p.*, ye would know ye must *p.*; 32: 8 evil spirit teaches man that he must not *p.*; 32: 9 *p.* always; 33: 12 Nephi[1] *p.* that many may be saved in God's kingdom; **Jacob** 7: 22 Father has answered *p.* of Jacob[2]; **Enos** 1: 4 Enos[2] cries unto his Maker in mighty *p.*; **Omni** 1: 26 continue in fasting and *p.*; **Mosiah** 27: 14 Alma[1] has *p.* much concerning Alma[2]; 27: 22–23 Alma[1] has priests *p.* that the Lord will open mouth of Alma[2]; **Alma** 5: 46 Alma[2] has fasted and *p.* many days to know these things; 8: 10 Alma[2] wrestles with God in mighty *p.* that he might pour out his Spirit; 10: 22–23 people of Ammonihah are spared because of *p.* of the righteous; 17: 3 sons of Mosiah[2] teach with power because they have given themselves to much fasting and *p.*; 26: 22 to know mysteries of God, men must *p.* without ceasing; 28: 6 following tremendous slaughter is time of much fasting and *p.*; 31: 12, 22 every Zoramite offers selfsame *p.*; 34: 19 continue in *p.* unto God; 34: 27 when ye do not cry unto the Lord, let your hearts be drawn out in *p.* unto him continually; 38: 13 Zoramites *p.* to be heard of men; 45: 1 Nephites fast and *p.* much to give God thanks; 62: 51 Nephites *p.* unto the Lord continually; **Hel.** 3: 35 members of church fast and *p.* oft; **3 Ne.** 12: 44 (Matt. 5: 44) *p.* for them that despitefully use you; 13: 5 (Matt. 6: 5) when thou *p.*, do not as the hypocrites; 13: 9 (Matt. 6: 9) after this manner therefore *p.* ye; 17: 15 Jesus *p.* unto Father; 18: 15 watch and *p.* always; 18: 16 as Jesus has *p.* among them, so should saints *p.* in church; 18: 21 *p.* in your families; 19: 6 twelve disciples cause multitude to kneel and *p.* to Father; 19: 17–18, 22, 24 disciples *p.* unto Jesus because he is with them; 19: 24 disciples *p.* without multiplying words; 20: 1 Jesus commands multitude to cease to *p.*, but not to cease to *p.* in hearts; 27: 1 disciples are united in mighty *p.* and fasting when Jesus appears again; **Moro.** 6: 4 those baptized are numbered among people of church, to keep them watchful unto *p.*; 6: 5 church meets together oft to fast and *p.*; 7: 6, 9 if man *p.* without real intent, it profits him nothing; 7: 48 *p.* unto Father with all energy of heart; 8: 26 perfect love endures by diligence unto *p.*

PREACH, PREACHING (*see also* Declare; Exhort; Gospel; Ministry; Preacher; Prophecy; Publish; Teach; Testify; Warn; TG Preaching)

2 Ne. 25: 26 Nephites *p.* of Christ; 26: 29 priestcrafts are that men *p.* for gain and praise; **Enos** 1: 23 prophets among Nephites *p.* of wars; **Mosiah** 18: 20 priests should *p.* nothing save repentance and faith; 23: 17 none receive authority to *p.* save by Alma[1] from God; **Alma** 1: 16 many go forth *p.* false doctrines; 9: 21 Nephites have been visited with gift of *p.*; 29: 13 God hath called me by a holy calling to *p.* word unto this people; 31: 5 *p.* of word has great tendency to lead people to do that which is just; 37: 33 Alma[2] calls Helaman[2] to *p.* repentance; 43: 2 Alma[2] and sons *p.* word according to spirit of prophecy, after holy order of God; **Hel.** 5: 17 Nephi[2] and Lehi[4] *p.* with great power; **3 Ne.** 5: 4 word of God is *p.* to robbers in prison; 6: 20 men sent from heaven *p.* against sins of people; 20: 30 fulness of gospel shall be *p.* to the Lord's people; **Morm.** 1: 16 Mormon[2] endeavors to *p.*, but is forbidden; **Moro.** 6: 9 Holy Ghost leads church whether to *p.*, pray, sing.

PREACHER (*see also* Elder; Minister [noun]; Preach)

W of M 1: 16 false *p.* are punished according to their crimes; **Alma** 1: 26 *p.* is no better than hearer.

PRECEPT (*see also* Commandments of God; Doctrine; Doctrine, False; Law; Persuade, Persuasion; Principle)

2 Ne. 27: 25 (Isa. 29: 13) fear of this people toward the Lord is taught by *p.* of men; 28: 14 false churches err in many instances because they are taught by *p.* of men; 28: 26, 31 wo unto him who hearkens unto *p.* of men; 28: 30 (Isa. 28: 10) the Lord gives line upon line, *p.* upon *p.*; 28: 30 blessed are they who hearken unto the Lord's *p.*

PRECIOUS (*see also* Choice; Pearl; Value; Worth)

1 Ne. 11: 9 (15: 36; Alma 32: 42) in vision, Nephi[1] sees tree *p.* above all; 13: 7–8 abominable church has all manner of *p.* clothing; 13: 26–29, 32, 34 abominable church takes away many plain and *p.* parts of gospel; 13: 34 Gentiles to stumble because plain and *p.* parts of gospel are taken away; 13: 34–35, 40 the Lord will make known plain and *p.* truths that have been taken away; 14: 23 when writings proceed from Jew, they are most *p.*; **2 Ne.** 1: 10 Nephites brought into *p.* land of promise by goodness of God; 5: 16 Nephites' temple constructed after manner of Solomon's, without so many *p.* things; **Jacob** 1: 2 Jacob[2] is commanded to write on plates those things he considers most *p.*; 5: 61, 74 natural fruit is most *p.* above all other fruit; **Alma** 7: 10 Mary a *p.* and chosen vessel; 31: 35 souls of Zoramites are *p.*; 39: 17 is not a soul at this time as *p.* unto God as a soul at the time of his coming; **Hel.** 5: 8 Helaman[3] desires that his sons have *p.* gift of eternal life; **Moro.** 9: 9 Nephites have deprived Lamanites' daughters of that which is most *p.*, chastity and virtue.

PREMORTAL EXISTENCE

Alma 13: 3 priests were called and prepared from foundation of world.

PREPARE, PREPARATION, PREPARATORY (*see also* Establish; Make; Preparator; Probation; Read)

1 Ne. 2: 20 the Lord has *p.* land for Lehites; 3: 7 (9: 6) the Lord gives not commandments save he *p.* way to accomplish them; 10: 7–8 (3 Ne. 24: 1; Mal. 3: 1) prophet shall come to *p.* way of the Lord; 10: 8 (Alma 7: 9; Hel. 14: 9) *p.* ye the way of the Lord; 10: 18 (Ether 3: 14) way is *p.* for all men from foundation of world; 15: 29 river of filthy water represents hell *p.* for the wicked; 15: 34 place of filthiness is *p.* for that which is filthy; 22: 20 the Lord will surely *p.* way for all people; **2 Ne.** 9: 10 God *p.* way for escape from death and hell; 9: 43 happiness *p.* for saints shall be hid from the wise and prudent; 9: 46 *p.* your souls for day when justice shall be administered; **Jacob** 5: 61 call servants to labor diligently in vineyard, that we may *p.* way; **Mosiah** 4: 6–7 atonement *p.* from foundation of world; **Alma** 5: 28 if ye are not stripped of pride, ye are not *p.* to meet God and must *p.* quickly; 12: 24 (34: 32; 42: 10, 13) this life became probationary state, a *p.* state, time to *p.* to meet God; 12: 26 if first parents had partaken of tree of life, they would have had no *p.* state; 13: 3 priests are called with holy calling which was *p.* with a *p.* redemption; 13: 5 holy calling *p.* in and through atonement of Only Begotten Son, who was *p.*; 16: 16 the Lord pours out Spirit to *p.* men's minds and hearts to receive word; 32: 6 afflictions humble poor Zoramites in *p.* to hear word; 34: 3 Alma[2] has spoken to *p.* Zoramites' minds; 37: 24–25 interpreters were *p.* that word of God might be fulfilled; 48: 15 Nephites have faith God will warn them to flee or *p.* for war; **3 Ne.** 17: 3 Jesus tells Nephites to *p.* minds for morrow; 21: 27 work to commence in *p.* way whereby Father's people may come unto Christ; **Ether** 3: 14 Christ was *p.* from foundation of world; 9: 28 prophets cry repentance, to *p.* way of the Lord; 12: 11 God *p.* a more excellent way; **Moro.** 7: 31 office of angel's ministry is to *p.* way among men by declaring word unto chosen vessels; 7: 32 the Lord *p.* way that men may have faith in Christ.

PREPARATOR (*see also* Founder)

1 Ne. 15: 35 devil is *p.* of hell.

PRESENCE (*see* God, Presence of)

PRESENT [adj.]

Morm. 8: 35 Moroni[2] speaks unto readers as though they were *p.*

PRESERVE (*see also* Defence; Keep; Maintain; Protect; Safe; Spare; Support; Uphold)

1 Ne. 3: 19–20 sons of Lehi[1] should obtain brass plates to *p.* language and words of prophets; 5: 21 brass plates of great value in *p.* commandments; 22: 17 the Lord will *p.* the righteous; **2 Ne.** 3: 16 the Lord covenants to *p.* seed of Joseph[1] forever; 27: 22 latter-day seer to seal up book that unread words may be *p.*; **Enos** 1: 15 the Lord is able to *p.* Nephites' records; **Mosiah** 2: 20–21 God has kept and *p.* you from day to day; **Alma** 37: 12–14 records are *p.* for wise purpose known unto God; 37: 21 Alma[2] commands Helaman[2] to *p.* interpreters; 46: 24 remnant of seed of Joseph[1] to be *p.* as remnant of his garment was *p.*; 57: 26 Ammonite youths believe that those who do not doubt will be *p.* by God's marvelous power; 61: 9 Pahoran[1] seeks only to *p.* rights and liberty of his people; **Hel.** 4: 24 Spirit no longer *p.* Nephites; **Ether** 2: 7 the Lord had *p.* land of promise for righteous people.

PRESIDE (*see also* Lead; Watch)

Alma 6: 1 Alma[2] ordains priests and teachers to *p.* over church.

PRESS (*see also* Wine-press)

1 Ne. 8: 24 Lehi[1] beholds others *p.*

forward through mist; **2 Ne.** 31: 20 *p.* forward with steadfastness in Christ.

PRETEND (*see also* Deceit; False; Lying)

Mosiah 12: 12 priests say Abinadi *p.* the Lord hath spoken; **Alma** 1: 17 those practicing priestcraft *p.* to preach according to belief; 30: 28 Korihor claims priests yoke people with *p.* mysteries; 47: 27 Amalickiah *p.* to be wroth concerning murder of king.

PREVAIL (*see also* Conquer; Overcome; Overpower; Overthrow; Prey)

3 Ne. 11: 39 (Matt. 16: 18) gates of hell shall not *p.* against those who build upon Christ's doctrine.

PREY (*see also* Captive, Captivity; Prevail; Subject)

2 Ne. 9: 46 those whom devil obtains are *p.* to his awful misery; 20: 1–2 (Isa. 10: 1–2) wo unto those who decree unrighteous decrees that widows may be their *p.*; **Alma** 49: 3 because Lamanites had destroyed city of Ammonihah once, they suppose it will be easy *p.*; **Ether** 14: 22 Jaredites leave bodies of slain upon land to become *p.* to worms of flesh.

PRICE (*see also* Money)

2 Ne. 9: 50 (26: 25; Isa. 55: 1) come buy wine and milk without *p.*; **Alma** 1: 20 nonbelievers persecute saints because they impart word without *p.*

PRICK (*see also* Arouse; Stir)

Jarom 1: 12 prophets and priests *p.* people's hearts with word.

PRIDE, PROUD (*see also* Adorn; Boast; Envy; Hardheartedness; High; Inequality; Puffed; Rich; Stiffnecked; Stubbornness; Vanity)

1 Ne. 11: 36 (12: 18) spacious building is *p.* of world; 22: 15 (3 Ne. 25: 1; Mal. 4: 1) the *p.* shall be as stubble; **2 Ne.** 12: 12 (Isa. 2: 12) the *p.* and lofty shall be brought low; 26: 20 Gentiles are lifted up in *p.* of eyes; 28: 12 because of *p.* latter-day churches are puffed up; 28: 15 the wise, learned, and rich who are puffed up in *p.* of hearts shall be thrust down to hell; **Jacob** 1: 16 Nephites search much gold and silver, begin to be lifted up in *p.*; 2: 13 because some obtain more abundantly, they are lifted up in *p.* of heart; **Alma** 1: 6 Nehor is lifted up in *p.* of heart; 1: 20 unbelievers persecute saints because they are not *p.*; 4: 6 people of church wax *p.*; 4: 12 great inequality among people, some lifting themselves up with *p.*; 5: 23 he who is not stripped of *p.* is not prepared to meet God; 38: 11 see that ye are not lifted up unto *p.*; **Hel.** 3: 33 *p.* enters hearts of those who profess to belong to church; 12: 5 how quick to be lifted up in *p.* are children of men; 13: 27 people would receive man who said, Walk after *p.* of your own hearts; **3 Ne.** 6: 10 (4 Ne. 1: 24) some of people are lifted up unto *p.* and boastings; **Morm.** 8: 28 churches shall be lifted up in *p.* of hearts; 8: 36 only a few do not lift themselves up in *p.* of hearts; **Moro.** 8: 27 *p.* of Nephites has proven their destruction.

PRIEST (*see also* High Priest; Noah[3], Priests of; Priestcraft; Priesthood; Priests, False; TG Priest, Aaronic Priesthood; Priest, False; Priest, Melchizedek Priesthood; BD Priests)

2 Ne. 5: 26 (Jacob 1: 18) Nephi[1] consecrates Jacob[2] and Joseph[2] as *p.*; **Jarom** 1: 1 *p.* labor diligently exhorting people to diligence, teaching law of Moses; **Mosiah** 6: 3 Benjamin appoints *p.* to teach people; 11: 5 Noah[3] puts down *p.* consecrated by father and appoints new ones; 18: 18 (23: 17) Alma[1], having authority from God, ordains *p.*; 18: 24, 26 (27: 5; Alma 1: 26) Alma[1] commands *p.* to labor with own hands for support; 18: 28 people impart of substance to *p.* that stand in need; 23: 17 only just men are ordained *p.*; 25: 21 every church has *p.* and teachers; 25: 21 *p.* preach word as delivered by Alma[1]; 26: 7 unbelievers are delivered unto *p.* by teachers; **Alma** 1: 26 *p.* leave labors to impart word, then return to labors; 1: 26 *p.* does not esteem himself above his hearers; 4: 7 *p.* are sorely grieved by wickedness among people; 6: 1 Alma[2] ordains *p.* and elders by laying on of hands; 13: 1–12 the Lord ordained *p.* after his holy order, order of Son; 13: 3, 5 *p.* were called and prepared from foundation of world; 13: 4 *p.* are called on account of their faith; 15: 13 Alma[2] consecrates *p.* and teachers to baptize; 23: 4 Aaron[3] and brethren establish churches, consecrate *p.* among Lamanites; 45: 22 Helaman[2] and brethren appoint *p.* throughout land over all churches; **Moro.** ch. 3 manner in which disciples ordain *p.* and teachers; **Moro.** ch. 4–5 manner in which elders and *p.* administer sacrament; 6: 1 elders, *p.*, teachers were baptized if fruits showed they were worthy.

PRIESTCRAFT (*see also* Churches, False; Nehors, Order of; Priests, False; Prophets, False; TG Priestcraft)

2 Ne. 10: 5 because of *p.*, Jews will crucify Christ; 26: 29 *p.* are that men preach to get gain and praise of world; **Alma** 1: 12 Nehor is first to introduce *p.* among Nephites; 1: 12 if *p.* were enforced among Nephites, it would prove their destruction; 1: 16 death of Nehor does not end *p.*, for many preach false doctrines for riches and honor; **3 Ne.** 16: 10 when Gentiles are filled with *p.*, Father will bring gospel from among them; 21: 19 all *p.* shall be done away; 30: 2 Mormon[2] calls Gentiles to turn from *p.*

PRIESTHOOD (*see also* Apostle; Authority; Calling; Elder; High Priest; Minister [verb]; Ministry; Office; Officer; Ordain; Order; Ordinance; Power; Preside; Priest; Teacher; TG Priesthood; Priesthood, Aaronic; Priesthood, Authority; Priesthood, History of; Priesthood, Keys of; Priesthood, Magnifying Callings within; Priesthood, Melchizedek; Priesthood, Oath and Covenant; Priesthood, Power of; Priesthood, Qualifying for)

Alma 4: 20 Alma[2] confines himself wholly to high *p.* of holy order of God; 13: 1–12 men are ordained unto high *p.* of holy order of God, after order of Son; 13: 7–9 high *p.* after order of Son was from foundation of world, without beginning of days or end of years; 13: 14, 18 Melchizedek took upon himself the high *p.* forever.

PRIESTS, FALSE (*see also* Idolatry; Nehors, Order of; Noah[3], Priests of; Priestcraft)

2 Ne. 28: 4 *p.* of latter-day churches shall contend with one another; Mosiah 11: 5 Noah[3] appoints new *p.*; **Alma** 14: 18, 27 *p.* after order of Nehor question Alma[2] and Amulek in prison; **4 Ne.** 1: 34 people are led by many *p.* and false prophets to build up many churches.

PRINCE (*see also* King)

2 Ne. 13: 4 (Isa. 3: 4) I will give children unto them to be their *p.*; 19: 6 (Isa. 9: 6) Messiah shall be called, The *P.* of Peace; **Alma** 13: 18 Melchizedek called the *p.* of peace.

PRINCIPLE

Moro. 9: 20 Nephites are without *p.*

PRINTS (*see* Nail)

PRISON (*see also* Bondage; Captive; Dungeons; Hell; Prisoner)

1 Ne. 7: 14 Jews have cast Jeremiah[1] into *p.*; **Mosiah** 7: 7 Ammon[1] and brethren are cast into *p.*; 12: 17 Abinadi is cast into *p.*; 14: 8 (Isa. 53: 8) Messiah was taken from *p.* and from judgment; **Alma** 14: 17 Alma[2] and Amulek are cast into *p.*; 14: 27 (Ether 12: 13) walls of *p.* are rent in twain; 20: 2–7, 22–30 (21: 13–15) brethren of Ammon[2] are in *p.* in Middoni; 62: 50 Nephites had been delivered from *p.*; **Hel.** 5: 21 Nephi[2] and Lehi[4] are cast into same *p.* in which Ammon[1] and brethren were cast; 5: 27, 31 walls of *p.* shake and tremble; 9: 39 some who believe Nephi[2] were converted in *p.*; **3 Ne.** 12: 25 (Matt. 5: 25) agree with thine adversary quickly lest thou shalt be cast into *p.*; 28: 19 (4 Ne. 1: 30) *p.* could not hold three Nephites; **Morm.** 8: 24 by power of the Lord's word saints cause *p.* to tumble; **Ether** 10: 5–6 Riplakish builds many *p.*

PRISONER (*see also* Captive; Prison)

1 Ne. 21: 9 (Isa. 49: 9) thou mayest say to *p.*, Go forth; **Alma** 52: 8 Moroni[1] orders Teancum to retain all *p.*; 53: 1 *p.* of Lamanites are compelled to bury dead; 54: 1 Ammoron desires to exchange *p.* with Moroni[1]; 54: 11 Moroni[1] sets conditions for exchanging *p.*; 55: 25 Nephites cause Lamanite *p.* to fortify city; 57: 11–18 Lamanite *p.* are sent to Zarahemla, are killed during rebellion; 62: 27–29 Lamanite *p.* join Ammonites; 62: 30 Nephites take many Lamanite *p.* and regain Nephite *p.*; **3 Ne.** 5: 4 all robbers taken *p.* and cast into prison; **Morm.** 4: 2 Lamanites take many Nephite *p.*; 4: 14 Lamanites offer women and children *p.* as sacrifices to idols; **Moro.** 9: 7–8 Lamanites take *p.*, feed wives flesh of husbands.

PRIVATE, PRIVATELY (*see also* Closet; Privily; Secret)

Mosiah 18: 1 Alma[1] teaches Abinadi's words *p.*

PRIVILEGE, PRIVILEGED (*see also* Blessing; Right [noun])

2 Ne. 26: 28 all men are *p.* to partake of God's goodness; **Mosiah** 29: 32 every man should enjoy his *p.* alike; **Alma** 2: 4 if Amlici could gain voice of people, he would deprive them of *p.* of church; 6: 5 none are denied *p.* of assembling to hear word of God; 13: 4 except for blindness of minds, those who reject Spirit might have had as great *p.* as brethren; 30: 9 if man desires to serve God, it is his *p.*; 30: 27 Korihor accuses priests of leading people away, that they durst not enjoy *p.*; 43: 9 design of Nephites is to preserve rights and *p.*; 51: 6 freemen swear to maintain *p.* of religion by free government; **3 Ne.** 2: 12 converted Lamanites and Nephites take up arms against robbers to maintain *p.* of worship; 4: 16 robbers believe they can make Nephites yield by cutting off outward *p.*

PRIVILY (*see also* Private; Secret)

Alma 14: 3 people desire to put away Alma[2] and Amulek *p.*; 35: 5 rulers of Zoramites find out *p.* the minds of the people.

PRIZE (*see also* Reward)

Mosiah 4: 27 man should be diligent, that thereby he might win the *p.*

PROBATION, PROBATIONARY (*see also* Endure; Mortal, Mortality; Opposition; Prepare, Preparatory; Prove; Tempt; Trial)

1 Ne. 10: 21 if men have sought to do wickedly during days of *p.*, they are found unclean before judgment; 15: 32 men must be judged of works done in days of *p.*; **2 Ne.** 2: 21 men's state became state of *p.*; 9: 27 wo unto him who wasteth days of *p.*; 33: 9 continue in straight and narrow path until end of day of *p.*; **Alma** 12: 24 this life became *p.* state; 42: 4 *p.* time granted to man to repent; 42: 10 *p.* state became state for men to prepare; 42: 13 plan of redemption can be brought about only on condition of repentance in this *p.* state; **Hel.** 13: 38 your days of *p.* are past; **Morm.** 9: 28 be wise in days of *p.*

PROCLAMATION (*see also* Declare; Decree)

Mosiah 7: 17 Limhi sends *p.* among people to gather; 22: 6 *p.* to be sent to gather flocks and drive them into wilderness by night; 27: 2 Mosiah[2] sends *p.* that unbelievers should not persecute believers; **Alma** 22: 27 (23: 1) Lamanite king sends *p.* throughout land not to harm Aaron[3] and brethren; 30: 57 *p.* calls followers of Korihor to repent; **Hel.** 9: 9 *p.* announces murder of chief judge and capture of murderers; **3 Ne.** 3: 13, 22 Lachoneus sends *p.* that all people should gather in one place.

PROCRASTINATE (*see also* Delay; Idleness; Slothful)

Alma 13: 27 (34: 33–34) do not *p.* day of repentance; 34: 35 if ye have *p.* day of repentance, ye have become subjected to spirit of devil; **Hel.** 13: 38 ye have *p.* day of salvation until it is everlastingly too late.

PROFESS (*see also* Claim; Profession)

Alma 5: 37 ye that have *p.* to know ways of righteousness have gone astray; 51: 21 Moroni[1] puts end to pride of those who *p.* blood of nobility; **Hel.** 3: 33 pride enters hearts of those who *p.* to belong to church; 4: 11 slaughter of Nephites caused by wickedness of those who *p.* to belong to church; **4 Ne.** 1: 27 many churches *p.* to know Christ, but deny his gospel.

PROFESSION (*see also* Craftiness, Craft)

Alma 10: 15 lawyers are learned in arts and cunning that they might be skillful in their *p.*; 14: 18 (15: 15; 16: 11) priests of Ammonihah are of *p.* of Nehor.

PROFIT (*see also* Advantage; Avail; Benefit; Gain; Prosper; Reward)

1 Ne. 19: 23 Nephi[1] likens scriptures to Nephites, that they might be for their *p.*; 20: 17 (Isa. 48: 17) the Lord teacheth thee to *p.*; **2 Ne.** 2: 14 Lehi[1] speaks to sons for their *p.*; 4: 15 Nephi[1] writes scriptures for learning and *p.* of his children; 9: 28 the wisdom of the learned *p.* them not; **Jacob** 5: 32, 35, 42 tree *p.* master of vineyard nothing; **W of M** 1: 2 writings may some day *p.* Nephites; **Alma** 30: 34 what doth it *p.* us to labor in church save to declare truth; **3 Ne.** 24: 14 (Mal. 3: 14) what doth it *p.* that we have kept his ordinances; **Moro.** 7: 6 if evil man offers gift without real intent, it *p.* him nothing; 7: 6, 9 if a man prays without real intent it *p.* him nothing; 10: 8 gifts of Spirit are given unto men to *p.* them.

PROGRESS

Mosiah 1: 17 (Alma 37: 14) when Lehites were unfaithful, they did not *p.* on journey; **Alma** 4: 10 church fails to *p.* because of wickedness; 60: 30 Moroni[1] will strike those who impede *p.* of Nephites in cause of freedom.

PROLONG (*see also* Increase; Lengthen)

2 Ne. 2: 21 men's days were *p.*, that they might repent while in flesh; **Mosiah** 14: 10 (Isa. 53: 10) he shall *p.* his days; **Alma** 9: 16 (Hel. 15: 4, 11) the Lord will *p.* Lamanites' existence in land; 9: 18 if Nephites persist in wickedness, their days will not be *p.*

PROMISE (*see also* Covenant; Oath; Promised Land; Swear)

2 Ne. 3: 5, 14 Joseph[1] obtained *p.* that righteous branch of Israel would rise out of fruit of his loins; 10: 2 *p.* which Nephites have obtained are *p.* according to flesh; 10: 17 (Alma 37: 17) the Lord will fulfill his *p.* to men; 25: 21 the Lord *p.* that records will be preserved; 25: 21 the Lord *p.* Joseph[1] his seed should never perish; **Alma** 9: 16, 24 many *p.* are extended to Lamanites; 9: 24 the Lord's *p.* are not extended to Nephites if they transgress; 50: 21 the Lord's *p.* have been verified to Nephites; **4 Ne.** 1: 11 Nephites are blessed according to the multitude of *p.* which the Lord had made to them; **Morm.** 8: 22 eternal purposes of the Lord to roll on until all his *p.* are fulfilled; 9: 21 *p.* that Father will answer prayers is unto all; **Ether** 8: 17 Akish leads friends and kindred away by fair *p.*; 12: 17 by faith, three Nephites obtained *p.* not to taste death; **Moro.** 7:

41 men will be raised unto life eternal because of faith in Christ, according to the *p.*

PROMISED LAND (*see also* Covenant; Inherit; Land; Liberty; Zion; TG Promised Land)

1 Ne. 2: 20 (4: 14; 7: 13; 14: 1–2; 2 Ne. 1: 9, 20; Jarom 1: 9; Omni 1: 6; Ether 2: 8–11) if people keep commandments, they will prosper in land of *p.*; 2: 20 (5: 5; 7: 13; 2 Ne. 1: 5) Lehites are given land of *p.*; 2: 20 (2 Ne. 1: 5; 3: 2; 10: 19; Ether 1: 38, 42; 2: 7, 10, 15; 9: 20; 10: 28; 13: 2) *p.l.* is choice above all other lands; 5: 5 Lehi[1] has obtained a land of *p.*; 10: 13 Lehites must be led into land of *p.* unto fulfilling of the Lord's word that Israel should be scattered; ch. 12–14 Nephi[1] beholds vision of future of land of *p.*; 17: 38 the Lord leads away the righteous into precious lands; 18: 23 Lehites arrive at *p.l.*; 22: 12 (2 Ne. 6: 11; 9: 2; 10: 7; 25: 11; 3 Ne. 20: 33; 29: 1) Israel to be gathered to land of inheritance; **2 Ne.** 9: 2 Jews shall be established in all their lands of *p.*; 24: 2 (Isa. 14: 2) Israel shall return to lands of *p.*; **Jacob** 2: 12 land of *p.* abounds in precious metals; Enos 1: 10 I have given thy brethren this holy land; **Mosiah** 10: 15 brethren were wroth with Nephi[1] when they had arrived in *p.l.*; **3 Ne.** 20: 29 Father will remember covenant to give his people again the land of Jerusalem, which is *p.l.* unto them forever; 21: 22 the Lord has given land to remnant of Jacob for their inheritance; **Ether** 2: 7–15 (1: 42–43) the Lord leads Jaredites to land of *p.*; 6: 12 Jaredites land upon shore of land of *p.*

PROPERTY

1 Ne. 3: 25–26 (4: 11) Laban takes *p.* of sons of Lehi[1].

PROPHECY, PROPHESY (*see also* Declare; Holy Ghost; Inspire; Preach; Prophet; Revelation; TG Prophecy)

2 Ne. 25: 1 words of Isaiah[1] are hard for Nephites to understand because they know not Jew's manner of *p.*; 25: 4 Nephi[1] will *p.* with plainness; 25: 4 words of Isaiah[1] are plain to all who are filled with spirit of *p.*; 25: 7 Nephi[1] proceeds with his own *p.*; 25: 26 Nephites *p.* of Christ; **Jacob** 4: 6 Nephites have many revelations and spirit of *p.*; 4: 13 let him who *p.* *p.* to understanding of men; **W of M** 1: 4 *p.* of Christ's coming are pleasing to Mormon[2]; **Mosiah** 5: 3 were it expedient, Nephites could *p.* of all things; 12: 29 (13: 26) the Lord has sent Abinadi to *p.* great evil against people of Noah[3]; **Alma** 4: 20 Alma[2] confines himself wholly to testimony of the word, according to spirit of *p.*; 9: 4 Ammonihahites will not believe his words if Alma[2] *p.* destruction; 17: 3 sons of Mosiah[2] have spirit of *p.*; 25: 16 Nephites retain hope through faith, unto eternal salvation, relying upon spirit of *p.*; 30: 12 Korihor preaches against *p.* of Christ's coming; 45: 9 that which Alma[2] *p.* to Helaman[2] shall not be made known until *p.* has been fulfilled; **Hel.** 4: 23 Nephites deny spirit of *p.*; 14: 1 (3 Ne. 23: 9–13) Samuel *p.* many things that are not written; **3 Ne.** 1: 4 *p.* of prophets begin to be fulfilled more fully; 29: 6 wo unto him who says the Lord no longer works by *p.*; **Morm.** 8: 23 search the *p.* of Isaiah[1]; **Ether** 12: 5 Ether *p.* many great things, which people do not believe; **Moro.** 10: 13 to another is given that he may *p.* concerning all things; 10: 28 I declare these things unto the fulfilling of *p.*

PROPHET (*see also* Apostle; Martyrdom; Preach; Prophecy; Prophetess; Prophets, False; Revelation; Revelator; Seer; Servant; TG Prophets, Mission of; Prophets, Rejection of; BD Prophet)

1 Ne. 3: 18 (7: 14; 2 Ne. 27: 5) Jews have rejected words of *p.*; 10: 4 six hundred years after Lehi[1] left Jerusalem, the Lord would raise up a *p.*, a Messiah; 11: 27 *p.* should prepare way before Redeemer; 19: 20 had not the Lord shown Nephi[1] concerning Jews, as he had *p.* of old, he should have perished; 22: 2 by Spirit are all things made known unto *p.*; 22: 20–21 (3 Ne. 20: 23) the Lord will raise up *p.* like unto Moses, the Holy One; **2 Ne.** 25: 5 Jews understand words of *p.*; 25: 18 only one Messiah spoken of by *p.*; 26: 3 (Jacob 4: 14) Jews shall perish because they killed *p.*; 26: 5 depths of earth shall swallow up those who kill *p.*; **Jacob** 4: 6 we search the *p.*; 6: 8 will ye reject words of *p.*; **Enos** 1: 22–23 many *p.* among Nephites, preaching destruction; **Jarom** 1: 11 *p.* exhort people to diligence, teach law of Moses; **Mosiah** 7: 26 Limhi's people have slain *p.*; 8: 15 seer is greater than *p.*; 8: 16 seer is revelator and *p.*; **Alma** 20: 15 Lamoni knows Ammon[2] and brethren are holy *p.*; 37: 30 (Ether 9: 29; 11: 2) Jaredites were destroyed because they murdered *p.*; **Hel.** 9: 2 people do not believe Nephi[2] is *p.*; 13: 24 Nephites cast out *p.*; 13: 25–28 Nephites reject true *p.* and accept false *p.*; 13: 32–33 (3 Ne. 8: 25) Nephites will lament that they killed *p.*; **3 Ne.** 1: 13 on morrow Christ comes into world to fulfill that spoken by *p.*; 6: 23–25 (7: 6, 10) judges put *p.* to death secretly; 7: 14 Nephites stone the *p.*; 10: 12 more righteous people are saved, for they had received *p.*; 10: 14 destruction fulfills prophecies of many of the holy *p.*; 11: 10 I am Jesus Christ, whom the *p.* testified shall come; 12: 11–12 (Matt. 5: 11–12) blessed are you when men persecute you, for so persecuted they the *p.*; 23: 5 search the *p.*, for many testify of these things; **Ether** 7: 24 Jaredites revile against *p.* and mock them; 9: 28 *p.* come into land crying repentance; 9: 29 (11: 22) Jaredites believe not the *p.*; **Moro.** 7: 23 God declared unto *p.* that Christ should come.

PROPHETESS

2 Ne. 18: 3 (Isa. 8: 3) I went unto the *p.*, and she conceived and bare a son.

PROPHETS, FALSE (*see also* Antichrist; Apostasy; Christs, False; Dissenter; Doctrine, False; Priestcraft)

W of M 1: 15–16 false *p.* among the people; **Hel.** 13: 25–28 Nephites reject true *p.* and accept false *p.*; **3 Ne.** 14: 15 (Matt. 7: 15) beware of false *p.* who come in sheep's clothing; **4 Ne.** 1: 34 Nephites are led by false *p.* to build many churches.

PROSPER, PROSPERITY (*see also* Blessing; Gain; Profit; Reward; Rich; Riches; Righteousness)

1 Ne. 2: 20 (2 Ne. 1: 9, 20, 31; Jarom 1: 9; Mosiah 1: 7; Alma 37: 13; 49: 30; 50: 20) if ye keep commandments, ye shall *p.*; **2 Ne.** 5: 11 Nephites *p.* exceedingly; 28: 21 devil will lull some, that they say, Zion *p.*, all is well; **Jarom** 1: 9 because Nephites are prepared, Lamanites do not *p.* against them; **Mosiah** 7: 29 in day of transgression the Lord will hedge up people's ways that they *p.* not; 21: 16 people of Limhi begin to *p.* by degrees; 27: 9 Alma[2] becomes great hindrance to *p.* of church; **Hel.** 3: 25 so great is *p.* of church that high priests are astonished; 3: 26 work of the Lord *p.*; 12: 1 the Lord *p.* those who put trust in him; 12: 2 when the Lord *p.* his people, they harden hearts and forget him; **3 Ne.** 22: 17 (Isa. 54: 17) no weapon that is formed against thee shall *p.*; **4 Ne.** 1: 23 Nephites become rich because of *p.* in Christ.

PROTECT, PROTECTION (*see also* Preserve; Refuge; Safe; Security; Spare)

1 Ne. 5: 8 the Lord has *p.* sons of Sariah; **Mosiah** 9: 15 people call upon Zeniff for *p.*; **3 Ne.** 4: 10, 30 Nephites supplicate God for *p.*

PROUD (*see* Pride, Proud)

PROVE, PROVEN (*see also* Evidence; Probation; Reprove; Tempt; Testify; Trial, Try; Witness)

2 Ne. 11: 3 God sends witnesses to *p.* all his words; **Alma** 34: 6–7 Alma[2] has appealed to Moses to *p.* prophecies of Christ are true; **Hel.** 9: 38 brother of chief judge is brought to *p.* he is murderer; **3 Ne.** 1: 24 some try to *p.* by scriptures that Nephites no longer need to observe law of Moses; 24: 10 (Mal. 3: 10) bring tithes into storehouse and *p.* the Lord; **Ether** 12: 35 if Gentiles have not charity because of Nephites' weakness, the Lord will *p.* them.

PROVIDE (*see also* Give; Maintain; Prepare)

1 Ne. 17: 3 if men keep commandments, God *p.* means to accomplish what is commanded; **Mosiah** 8: 18 God has *p.* a means that man might work mighty miracles.

PROVISION (*see also* Substance)

3 Ne. 4: 4, 18–19 Nephites gather all *p.* in one place to deny food for robbers.

PROVOKE, PROVOCATION (*see also* Anger; Indignation; Stir)

2 Ne. 13: 8 (Isa. 3: 8) doings of Judah have *p.* eyes of the Lord's glory; **Jacob** 1: 7 teachers labor diligently lest the Lord swear Nephites not enter his rest, as in *p.* in days of temptation; 1: 8 (Alma 12: 37) teachers persuade men not to *p.* God to anger; **Alma** 12: 36 your iniquity *p.* the Lord to send down wrath as in first *p.*; **Hel.** 7: 18 Nephites have *p.* the Lord to anger; **Moro.** 7: 45 (1 Cor. 13: 5) charity is not easily *p.*

PRUDENCE, PRUDENT, PRUDENTLY (*see also* Wisdom; Wise)

2 Ne. 9: 43 things of the wise and *p.* shall be hid from them; 13: 1–2 (Isa. 3: 1–2) the Lord doth take away from Judah the *p.*; 15: 21 (Isa. 5: 21) wo unto the *p.* in their own sight; 20: 13 (Isa. 10: 13) the Lord is *p.*; 27: 26 (Isa. 29: 14) the understanding of their *p.* shall be hid; **3 Ne.** 20: 43 my servant shall deal *p.*

PRUNE, PRUNING (*see also* Cut; Pluck)

2 Ne. 12: 4 (Isa. 2: 4) nations shall beat their spears into *p*-hooks; 15: 6 (Isa. 5: 6) vineyard shall not be *p.* nor digged; **Jacob** 5: 4, 27, 62, 69 the Lord *p.* vineyard; 6: 2 the Lord's servants to go forth last time to *p.* vineyard.

PUBLISH (*see also* Declare; Preach)

1 Ne. 13: 37 (Mosiah 12: 21; 15: 14–15; 27: 37; 3 Ne. 20: 40; Isa. 52: 7) how beautiful upon mountains are feet of those who *p.* peace; **Mosiah** 27: 32 Alma[2] and companions *p.* unto people things they have heard and seen; **Alma** 30: 57 knowledge of what happened to Korihor is *p.* throughout land.

PUFFED, PUFFING (*see also* Pride; Vanity)

2 Ne. 9: 42 the Lord despises those who are *p.* up because of learning, wisdom, riches; 28: 9, 12–15 many shall be *p.* up in hearts and seek deep to hide counsels from the Lord; **Alma** 5: 37 those who are *p.* up in vain things of world have gone astray; 31: 27 men cry unto God with mouths while they are *p.* up with vain things of world; **3 Ne.** 6: 15 Satan *p.* people up in pride; **Moro.** 7: 45 (1 Cor. 13: 4) charity is not *p.* up.

PULL (*see also* Destruction)

Alma 4: 19 Alma[2] seeks to *p.* down, by preaching word, the pride and contention among his people; 12: 37 let us repent, that we provoke not the Lord to *p.* down his wrath; 51: 17–18 Moroni[1] *p.* down pride of king-men; 54: 9 Ammoron will *p.* down wrath of God to his utter destruction; 60: 36 Moroni[1] seeks not for power, but to *p.* it down; **3 Ne.** 14: 4 (Matt. 7: 4) wilt thou say to brother, Let me *p.* mote from thine eye.

PUNISHMENT, PUNISH (*see also* Chasten; Crime; Curse; Damnation; Hedge; Hell; Indignation; Justice; Law; Penalty; Sin; Transgression; Vengeance; Wrath; TG Punish, Punishment)

2 Ne. 2: 10 law given unto inflicting of *p.*; 2: 10 (Alma 42: 16) punishment affixed to law is in opposition to happiness affixed; 2: 13 if there be no righteousness nor happiness, there be no *p.* nor misery; 2: 26 men are free not to be acted upon, save by *p.* of law; 9: 25 where no law is given, no *p.*, where no *p.* no condemnation; 23: 11 the Lord will *p.* world for evil; **Jacob** 7: 18 Sherem confesses and speaks of eternal *p.*; **W of M** 1: 15 false Christs are *p.* according to crimes; **Mosiah** 2: 33 he who listeth to obey evil spirit receiveth for his wages everlasting *p.*; 29: 15 those who commit iniquity are *p.* according to law; **Alma** 1: 17 liars are *p.*; 30: 9 no law to *p.* unbelievers; 30: 10 those who murder, steal, commit adultery are *p.*; 30: 11 man is *p.* only for his crimes; 42: 1 Corianton is concerned over justice of God in *p.* of sinner; 42: 16 repentance could not come unto men except there were a *p.*; 42: 17–18 how could there be a law save there was a *p.*; 42: 18, 22 a law given and a *p.* affixed; 42: 22 the law inflicteth the *p.*; **3 Ne.** 5: 5 those who continue in secret murders and threatenings are *p.* according to law; **Morm.** 4: 5 the wicked are *p.* by the wicked.

PURGE (*see also* Purify; Refine)

3 Ne. 24: 3 (Mal. 3: 3) the Lord shall *p.* sons of Levi[1] as gold and silver.

PURIFIER

3 Ne. 24: 3 (Mal. 3: 3) he shall sit as refiner and *p.* of silver.

PURIFY (*see also* Cleanse; Fire; Purge; Purifier; Purity; Refine; Sanctification; Wash)

Mosiah 4: 2 apply atoning blood of Christ, that hearts may be *p.*; **Alma** 5: 21 no man can be saved except his garments are *p.*; **Hel.** 3: 35 saints fast and pray oft, even unto *p.* of their hearts; **3 Ne.** 19: 28–29 disciples have been *p.* and those who believe their words shall be *p.*; **Moro.** 7: 48 pray unto Father that we may be *p.* even as he is pure.

PURITY, PURE (*see also* Blameless, Chastity; Clean; Guiltless; Holiness; Innocence; Righteousness; Purify; Sanctification; Spotless; Virtue; White)

1 Ne. 13: 25 gospel goes forth in *p.* from Jews to Gentiles; 14: 26 sealed writings shall come forth in *p.*; **2 Ne.** 9: 14 the righteous shall have perfect knowledge of their righteousness, being clothed in *p.*; 9: 47 would I harrow up your souls if your minds were *p.*; 25: 16 when Jews worship Father with *p.* hearts and clean hands, they will believe in Christ; 30: 6 Lamanites to be *p.* and delightsome; **Jacob** 3: 2 ye who are *p.* in heart, receive word of God; **Alma** 4: 19 Alma[2] sees no way to reclaim his people save in bearing down in *p.* testimony against them; 5: 19 can ye look up to God with *p.* heart and clean hands; 13: 12 priests, being *p.* and spotless before God, could not look upon sin without abhorrence; 16: 21 word of God is preached in *p.* in all the land; 32: 42 fruit of word is *p.* above all that is *p.*; **3 Ne.** 12: 8 (Matt. 5: 8) blessed are *p.* in heart, for they shall see God; **Morm.** 9: 6 cry unto Father that ye may be found *p.*; **Moro.** 7: 47 charity is *p.* love of Christ; 7: 48 pray unto Father that we may be purified even as he is *p.*

PURPOSE (*see also* Desire; End, Ends; Intent; Reason; Will)

1 Ne. 9: 3, 5 (19: 3; W of M 1: 7; Alma 37: 2, 12, 14, 18) plates made for special *p.*; **2 Ne.** 2: 11–12 without opposition there would have been no *p.* in end of its creation; 2: 15 (Alma 37: 7; 42: 26; Morm. 8: 22) the Lord brings about his eternal *p.*; 31: 13 follow Son with full *p.* of heart; **Mosiah** 7: 33 turn to the Lord with full *p.* of heart; **Alma** 11: 20 judges stir up people for sole *p.* to get gain; **3 Ne.** 10: 6 (12: 24; 18: 32; Acts 11: 23) come unto Christ with full *p.* of heart; **Morm.** 5: 14 Father brings about eternal *p.* through Son.

PUT (*see also* Trust)

Mosiah 3: 19 natural man is enemy to God unless he *p.* off natural man; **Alma** 30: 42 ye have *p.* off Spirit, that it has no place in you; **3 Ne.** 12: 31–32 (Matt. 5: 31–32) whosoever *p.* away his wife, save for fornication, causes her to commit adultery; 13: 25 (Matt. 6: 25) take no thought for your body, what ye shall *p.* on.

QUAKE, QUAKING (*see also* Earthquake; Fear; Fear of God; Shake; Tremble)

1 Ne. 1: 6 because of what he sees, Lehi[1] *q.* and trembles; 12: 4 many cities to tumble to earth because of *q.*; 22: 23 all who belong to kingdom of devil need *q.*; **2 Ne.** 4: 22 the Lord has confounded mine enemies, causing them to *q.*; **Mosiah** 28: 3 thought that any soul should endure endless torment causes sons of Mosiah[2] to *q.*; **Hel.** 12: 9 at the Lord's voice hills and mountains *q.*; **3 Ne.** 8: 12 whole face of land is changed because of great *q.* of whole earth; 11: 3 small voice pierces to center, that no part of frame does not *q.*

QUARREL (*see also* Contention; Disputations)

Mosiah 4: 14 ye will not suffer your children to *q.* with each other.

QUEEN (*see also* King; Ruler)

1 Ne. 21: 23 (2 Ne. 6: 7; 10: 9; Isa. 49: 23) *q.* of Gentiles shall be Israel's nursing mothers; **Alma** 19: 2–11 Lamoni's *q.* has faith in Ammon; 19: 12–18 *q.* overcome by Spirit; 19: 29–30 *q.* is raised, praises Jesus, raises Lamoni; 47: 32–34 Amalickiah reports death of Lamanite king to *q.*; 47: 35 Amalickiah takes Lamanite *q.* to wife.

QUENCH (*see also* Fire; Satisfy)

1 Ne. 17: 29 Moses brings water from rock to *q.* Israelites' thirst; **Jacob** 6: 8 will ye reject gift of Holy Ghost and *q.* Holy Spirit.

QUESTION (*see also* Ask; Inquire)

Mosiah 12: 18–19 priests of Noah[3] begin to *q.* Abinadi; **Alma** 10: 13–14 lawyers of Ammonihah think to *q.* Alma[2] and Amulek; 34: 5 great *q.* in Zoramites' minds is whether there will be a Christ; **Hel.** 9: 19 multitude begins to *q.* Nephi[2] to cross him.

QUICK, QUICKLY [=fast] (*see also* Faster; Haste; Quick [=living]; Rash; Slow; Swift)

Mosiah 13: 29 children of Israel *q.* to do iniquity; **Alma** 5: 28 ye must prepare *q.*, for kingdom is at hand; 9: 26 Son is *q.* to hear cries of his people; 33: 21 if ye could be healed by casting eyes, would ye not behold *q.*; 46: 8 how *q.* men forget the Lord; **Hel.** 3: 29 word of God is *q.* and powerful; 12: 5 how *q.* are men to be lifted up in pride; **3 Ne.** 7: 15 Nephites *q.* return from righteousness to wickedness; 12: 25 (Matt. 5: 25) agree with thine adversary *q.*

QUICK [=living] (*see also* Alive; Living)

Moro. 10: 34 Jehovah, the Eternal Judge of both the *q.* and dead.

QUIVER

1 Ne. 21: 2 (Isa. 49: 2) in his *q.* hath the Lord hid me.

RABBANAH

Alma 18: 13 *R.*, meaning powerful or great king.

RACA—*word suggesting contempt in Aramaic and Greek*

3 Ne. 12: 22 (Matt. 5: 22) whosoever says to brother, *R.*, shall be in danger of council.

RACK

Mosiah 27: 29 (Alma 36: 12, 14) soul of Alma[2] is *r.* with eternal torment; **Alma** 26: 9 if Ammon[2] and brethren had not come from Zarahemla, Lamanites would still be *r.* with hatred.

RAGE (*see also* Fury)

2 Ne. 28: 20 devil shall *r.* in men's hearts.

RAILING (*see also* Revile)

3 Ne. 6: 13 some return *r.* for *r.*, others receive *r.* humbly.

RAIMENT (*see also* Apparel; Clothing; Garment)

Mosiah 4: 19 do we not all depend upon God for food and *r.*; **3 Ne.** 13: 25 (Matt. 6: 25) is not the body more than *r.*; 13: 28 (Matt. 6: 28) why take ye thought for *r.*

RAIN (*see also* Destruction; Famine; Flood; BD Rain)

2 Ne. 15: 6 (Isa. 5: 6) the Lord will command clouds that they *r.* no *r.*; **Hel.** 11: 13, 17 Nephi[2] prays for *r.*; **Ether** 2: 24 *r.* and floods has the Lord sent forth; 9: 30 Jaredites begin to be destroyed because of no *r.*; 9: 35 when Jaredites have humbled themselves, the Lord sends *r.*

RAISE (*see also* Death, Physical; Exalt; Heal; Jesus Christ, Resurrection of; Miracle; Resurrection; Rise)

1 Ne. 7: 1 sons of Lehi[1] take wives, that they might *r.* up seed; 10: 4 the Lord will *r.* Messiah among Jews; 17: 37 the Lord *r.* up a righteous nation and destroys wicked nations; 22: 7 the Lord will *r.* up mighty nation among Gentiles; **2 Ne.** 3: 5 from descendants of Joseph[1] the Lord would *r.* righteous branch of Israel; 3: 7 the Lord will *r.* choice seer from descendants of Joseph[1]; 3: 10 the Lord will *r.* Moses to deliver Israel; 10: 25 may God *r.* you from death by power of resurrection; **Jacob** 2: 30 if the Lord will *r.* seed unto himself, he will command his people; **Mosiah** 3: 5 (3 Ne. 26: 15) Messiah shall *r.* the dead; **Alma** 5: 15 (11: 45) this mortal body to be *r.* in immortality; 11: 42 because of Christ's death, all shall be *r.* from temporal death; 33: 19 (Hel. 8: 14; Num. 21: 9; John 3: 14) type of Christ *r.* up in wilderness; 41: 4 all things shall be *r.* to endless happiness or endless misery; **Hel.** 12: 17 if the Lord says to mountain, Be *r.* up, it is done; **3 Ne.** 7: 19 (19: 4) Nephi[3] *r.* brother from dead; 15: 1 the Lord will *r.* him who remembers these sayings; 20: 26 Father *r.* Christ first unto Israel; **4 Ne.** 1: 5 Jesus' disciples *r.* the dead; **Moro.** 7: 41 ye shall have hope through Christ's atonement and resurrection to be *r.* unto life eternal.

RAMAH, HILL—*Jaredite name for Hill Cumorah* (*see also* Cumorah, Land and Hill of)

Ether 15: 11 army of Coriantumr[2] pitch tents by hill *R.*, where Mormon[2] hid records.

RAMEUMPTOM—*elevated place in synagogues of Zoramites*[2]

Alma 31: 13–14 those who worship must stand upon top and recite prayer; 31: 21 *R.*, being interpreted, is the holy stand.

RANKS (*see also* Inequality)

Mosiah 10: 9 men in Zeniff's army placed in *r.* according to age; **3 Ne.** 6: 12 people distinguished by *r.* according to riches and chances for learning.

RANSOM (*see also* Deliver; Redemption)

2 Ne. 8: 10 (Isa. 51: 10) art thou not he who hath made depths of sea a way for the *r.* to pass over; **Alma** 52: 8 Moroni[1] retains Lamanite prisoners as *r.* for those taken by Lamanites.

RASH, RASHLY (*see also* Foolish; Haste; Quick, Quickly)

Alma 51: 10 Amalickiah's promise is *r.*; **Morm.** 8: 19 he who judgeth *r.* shall be judged *r.*

RAVENING, RAVENOUS (*see* Wolf)

RAW (*see* Meat)

READ (*see also* Book; Language; Rehearse; Scriptures; Search; Study; Word; Writing)

1 Ne. 16: 29 new writing upon Liahona is plain to be *r.*; 19: 22–23 (ch. 20–21) Nephi[1] *r.* many things engraven upon brass plates; **2 Ne.** 6: 4–7, 16–18 (ch. 7–8) Jacob[2] *r.* the words of Isaiah to Nephites; **Jacob** 5: 1–77 do ye not remember having *r.* the words of Zenos comparing Israel to tame olive-tree; **Mosiah** 1: 5 records preserved that people might *r.* and understand God's mysteries; 25: 5–6 Mosiah[2] *r.* to his people records of Zeniff and Alma[1]; **Alma** 22: 12–14 Aaron[3] *r.* scriptures to Lamanite king; 33: 14 if ye have *r.* the scriptures, how can ye disbelieve on Son of God; **3 Ne.** 10: 14 whoso *r.*, let him understand; 27: 4–5 why do the people dispute, have they not *r.* scriptures; **Morm.** 9: 8 he who denies God's revelations has not *r.* the scriptures; **Ether** 3: 22 brother of Jared[2] to record experience in language that cannot be *r.*; 12: 24 things written by brother of Jared[2] are mighty unto overpowering of man to *r.* them; **Moro.** 10: 3 when ye have *r.* these things, remember how merciful God has been to men.

READY (*see also* Prepare)

3 Ne. 18: 13 gates of hell are *r.* to receive those who build on sandy foundation.

REALITY, REAL, REALLY (*see also* Intent; True)

2 Ne. 9: 47 Jacob[2] must awaken brethren to awful *r.* of judgment; **Jacob** 4: 13 Spirit speaks of things as they *r.* are and *r.* will be; **Alma** 32: 35 is not this *r.*

REAP (*see also* Harvest; Pluck; Receive; Reward; Sow [verb]; Thrash)

Mosiah 7: 30–31 if people sow filthiness, they shall *r.* chaff in whirlwind; **Alma** 26: 5 ye did thrust in your sickle and *r.* with your might; **3 Ne.** 13: 26 (Matt. 6: 26) fowls of air neither sow nor *r.*; **Ether** 10: 25 Jaredites make tools to *r.*

REASON, REASONS [noun] (*see also* Cause; Reasoning)

2 Ne. 9: 6 resurrection must come unto man by *r.* of fall; **Mosiah** 7: 24 great are *r.* which ye have to mourn; **Alma** 24: 26 because the slain were righteous, we have no *r.* to doubt they are saved; 26: 1 how great *r.* have we to rejoice; 28: 11 thousands mourn loss of kindred because they have *r.* to fear they are consigned to endless wo; 33: 20 the *r.* Israelites would not look upon type is that they did not believe it would heal them; **3 Ne.** 5: 20 Mormon[2] has *r.* to bless his God; **Morm.** 9: 20 *r.* why God ceases to do miracles is unbelief.

REASONING, REASON, REASONABLE (*see also* Consider; Ponder; Teach; Think)

Hel. 16: 17 Nephites *r.* and contend among themselves; 16: 18 Nephites say it is not *r.* that such a being as Christ should come.

REBEL, REBELLION, REBELLIOUS (*see also* Apostasy; Contention; Defiance; Devil; Disobedience; Disputations; Dissenter; Excommunication; Hardheartedness; Iniquity; Murmur; Reject; Resist; Stiffnecked; Trample; Transgression; Unbelief; TG Rebellion)

1 Ne. 2: 21, 23–24 (7: 6) if brothers of Nephi[1] *r.*, they will be cut off; **2 Ne.** 1: 2 Lehi[1] speaks to sons concerning their *r.*; **Jacob** 1: 8 we would persuade all men not to *r.* against God; **Mosiah** 2: 36–37 man who transgresses against his knowledge comes out in open *r.* against God; 15: 26 the Lord redeems none who *r.* against him; 15: 26 those who willfully *r.* against God have no part in first resurrection; 27: 11 (Alma 36: 13) Alma[2] and sons of Mosiah[2] *r.* against God; **Alma** 3: 18 Amlicites are cursed because they come out in open *r.* against God; 23: 7 converted Lamanites lay down weapons of *r.*; 57: 32 Lamanite prisoners rise in *r.*; 62: 2 Moroni[1] mourns because of those who *r.* against country and God; **Hel.** 4: 2 the *r.* are slain and driven out of land; 8: 25 Nephites have rejected truth and *r.* against God; **3 Ne.** 6: 18 Nephites know will of God, but *r.* willfully against him; **4 Ne.** 1: 38 those who willfully *r.* against God are called Lamanites; **Morm.** 1: 16 Mormon[2] is forbidden to preach to people, because they willfully *r.* against God; 2: 15 thousands of Nephites are hewn down in open *r.* against God.

REBUKE (*see also* Admonish; Chasten; Confound; Reproach; Reprove; Warn)

2 Ne. 7: 2 (Isa. 50: 2) at his *r.*, the Lord dries up sea; 8: 20 (Isa. 51: 20) two sons are full of *r.* of God; 12: 4 (Isa. 2: 4) the Lord will judge among nations and *r.* many; **Alma** 19: 20 other Lamanites *r.* those who murmur against Ammon[2]; **3 Ne.** 24: 11 (Mal. 3: 11) the Lord will *r.* the devourer for your sakes.

RECEIVE (*see also* Answer; Obtain; Partake; Reap)

1 Ne. 17: 30 the Lord did all things for Israelites which were expedient for man to *r.*; **2 Ne.** 25: 3 Nephi[1] writes unto those who will hereafter *r.* what he writes; 28: 27 wo unto him who says, We have *r.*, and we need no more; 28: 28 he that is built upon rock *r.* it with gladness; **Jacob** 3: 2 *r.* the pleasing word of God; **Enos** 1: 15 (Mosiah 4: 21; Alma 22: 16; 3 Ne. 18: 20; Moro. 7: 26) ask, believing ye shall *r.*, and ye shall *r.* it; **Mosiah** 4: 6–7 this is the man who *r.* salvation; 22: 14 Mosiah[2] *r.* Limhi's people with joy; 26: 21 he who hears the Lord's voice shall be *r.* into church and *r.* by the Lord; 26: 37 church *r.* many, baptizes many; **Alma** 5: 14 have ye *r.* God's image in your countenances; 12: 10 he who hardens heart *r.* lesser portion of words; 16: 16 the Lord pours out Spirit to prepare men to *r.* the word; 35: 9 people of Ammon[2] *r.* all the poor of the Zoramites; **3 Ne.** 9: 16 Christ came unto his own and they *r.* him not; 9: 22 whoso comes unto the Lord as little child will he *r.*; 14: 8 (Matt. 7: 8) every one who asketh *r.*; 27: 29 (Matt. 7: 7–8) ask and ye shall *r.*; **Moro.** 10: 4 when ye *r.* these things, ask God if they are true.

RECKON, RECKONING (*see also* Measure; Record; Time)

Alma 11: 4 Nephites do not *r.* after manner of Jews; 11: 5–19 system of *r.* among Nephites; **3 Ne.** 2: 8 Nephites *r.* time from period when sign of Christ's birth was given.

RECLAIM (*see also* Deliver; Recover; Restoration; Save)

Jacob 7: 24 many means were devised to *r.* Lamanites to knowledge of truth; **Alma** 4: 19 Alma[2] sees no way to *r.* his people save by bearing down in pure testimony against them; 42: 8 not expedient that man should be *r.* from temporal death; 42: 9 expedient that man should be *r.* from spiritual death; 42: 12 no means to *r.* man from fallen state; 55: 28 Nephites *r.* their rights and privileges.

RECONCILE, RECONCILIATION (*see also* Forgive; Jesus Christ, Atonement through; Satisfy; Subject; Submissive)

2 Ne. 10: 24 *r.* yourselves to will of God; 25: 23 we labor diligently to persuade men to be *r.* to God; 33: 9 for none can I hope except they shall be *r.* unto Christ; **Jacob** 4: 11 be *r.* unto God through atonement of Christ; **3 Ne.** 12: 24 (Matt. 5: 24) first be *r.* to thy brother.

RECORD (*see also* Account; Book; Book of Mormon; Engrave, Engravings; History; Plates, Brass; Plates of Ether; Plates of Mormon; Plates of Nephi, Large; Plates of Nephi, Small; Scriptures; Testify; Witness; Write)

1 Ne. 1: 1 Nephi[1] makes *r.* of his proceedings; 1: 17 Nephi[1] abridges *r.* of father; 3: 3 Laban has *r.* of Jews; 3: 19 Lehites should obtain *r.* to preserve language of fathers; 5: 12 brass plates contain *r.* of Jews from beginning to reign of Zedekiah; 5: 16 Laban and fathers had kept *r.* because they were descendants of Joseph[1]; 6: 1 *r.* of Lehi[1] gives genealogy: 10: 10 John the Baptist will bear *r.* that he baptized Lamb; 11: 7 Nephi[1] to bear *r.* of Son; 12: 18 Holy Ghost bears *r.* of Messiah; 13: 23 Nephi[1] beholds book that is *r.* of Jews; 13: 24 twelve apostles bear *r.* according to truth which is in Lamb; 13: 41 words of Lamb shall be made known in *r.* of Nephites and *r.* of apostles; 14: 27 Nephi[1] bears *r.* that name of apostle was John; 19: 1 Nephi[1] is commanded to make plates that he might engrave *r.* of his people; **2 Ne.** 5: 29 Nephi[1] kept *r.* upon plates; **Enos** 1: 13–15 Enos[2] desires that the Lord preserve *r.* of Nephites; **Omni** 1: 9 Nephites keep *r.* according to commandments of fathers; 1: 17 language of people of Zarahemla is corrupted because they brought no *r.* with them; **W of M** 1: 1 Mormon[2] to deliver *r.* to Moroni[2]; **Mosiah** 1: 16 Benjamin gives Mosiah[2] charge concerning *r.*; 8: 12–13 (21: 27) Limhi desires that *r.* on twenty-four gold plates be translated; 22: 14 Mosiah[2] receives *r.* of Limhi's people and *r.* on gold plates; 25: 5 Mosiah[2] reads *r.* of Zeniff's people to his people; 28: 20 Mosiah[2] confers all *r.* upon Alma[2]; **Alma** 18: 36 Ammon[2] lays before Lamoni *r.* of scriptures; 37: 2 Alma[2] commands Helaman[2] to keep *r.* of Nephites; 37: 3 brass plates contain *r.* of scriptures; **Hel.** 3: 13, 15 (3 Ne. 5: 9) many *r.* kept of proceedings of Nephites; 6: 26 secret covenants did not come to Gadianton from *r.*, but from devil; **3 Ne.** 5: 11 Mormon[2] makes *r.* on plates he has made; 5: 18 Mormon[2] testifies his *r.* is true; 8: 1 *r.* of Nephi[3] is true; 11: 32, 35–36 Father, Son, and Holy Ghost bear *r.* of each other; 17: 25 multitude knows *r.* is true for they saw and heard; 21: 5 *r.* shall come forth from Gentiles to descendants of Nephites; 23: 7–8 Nephi[3] brings *r.* before Jesus; 23: 9–13 Jesus instructs that missing part of *r.* be written; **4 Ne.** 1: 19 Nephi[4] kept *r.*; **Morm.** 1: 1 Mormon[2] makes *r.* of what he has seen and heard; 6: 6 Mormon[2] is commanded not to suffer *r.* to fall into hands of Lamanites; 8: 1 Moroni[2] finishes *r.* of Mormon[2]; 8: 14 (Moro. 10: 2) Moroni[2] hides *r.*; **Ether** 1: 6 *r.* of Jaredites written by Ether; 5: 4 Father, Son, and Holy Ghost bear *r.* of word; 13: 1 Moroni[2] finishes *r.* of destruction of Jaredites.

RECOVER (*see also* Gather; Heal; Reclaim; Restoration)

2 Ne. 6: 14 (21: 11; 29: 1; Jacob 6: 2; Isa. 11: 11) Messiah shall set himself the second time to *r.* his people; **3 Ne.** 3: 10 Giddianhi claims his people should *r.* rights and government; **Morm.** 9: 24 (Mark 16: 18) believers shall lay hands on the sick and they shall *r.*

RED SEA (*see also* BD Red Sea)

1 Ne. 2: 5 (16: 14) Lehites camp near shores of *R.S.*; 2: 8–9 river Laman empties into *R.S.*; 4: 2 (17: 26–27; Mosiah 7: 19; Alma 36: 28; Hel. 8: 11) Moses divided waters of *R.S.*; **2 Ne.** 19: 1 (Isa. 9: 1) he did more grievously afflict by way of *R.S.* beyond Jordan.

REDEEMER (*see* Jesus Christ—Redeemer)

REDEMPTION, REDEEM (*see also* Death, Spiritual; Deliver; Eternal Life; Freedom; Immortality; Jesus Christ—Redeemer; Plan; Ransom; Resurrection; Salvation; Save; TG Redeem, Redemption; BD Redemption)

1 Ne. 20: 20 (Isa. 48: 20) the Lord has *r.* his servant Jacob[1]; **2 Ne.** 1: 15 the Lord has *r.* my soul from hell; 2: 6 *r.* comes in and through Messiah; 2: 26 Messiah will *r.* men from fall; 7: 2 (Isa. 50: 2) is the Lord's hand shortened that it cannot *r.*; 27: 33 the Lord *r.* Abraham; **Jacob** 6: 8 will ye make a mock of great plan of *r.*; **W of M** 1: 8 Mormon[2] prays his brethren will come again to knowledge of *r.* of Christ; **Mosiah** 12: 23 (15: 30; 3 Ne. 16: 19; 20: 34) the Lord has *r.* Jerusalem; 15: 22–23 prophets and those who believe them are raised to dwell with God who has *r.* them; 15: 25–26 the Lord *r.* none who rebel against him; 16: 6 (Alma 21: 9) if Christ had not come, there could have been no *r.*; 18: 2 *r.* of people brought to pass by power, sufferings, death of Christ; 26: 26 those who never knew the Lord will know he is their Redeemer, but they would not be *r.*; 27: 24, 29 Alma[2] is *r.* of the Lord; Alma 5: 9 fathers did sing *r.* love; 5: 21 Messiah shall come to *r.* his people from sins; 5: 26 if ye have felt to sing song of *r.* love, can ye feel so now; 9: 27 Son comes to *r.* those who will be baptized; 11: 41 the wicked remain as though there had been no *r.*; 12: 18 whosoever dies in his sins cannot be *r.* according to God's justice; 12: 25 without plan of *r.*, there could have been no resurrection; 13: 2 priests are ordained in manner that people might know in what manner to look forward to Son for *r.*; 13: 3 holy calling was prepared with, and according to, a preparatory *r.*; 17: 16 sons of Mosiah[2] to bring Lamanites to knowledge of plan of *r.*; 18: 39 Ammon[2] expounds plan of *r.* to Lamanite king; 26: 13 Lamanites are brought to sing *r.* love because of power of word; 29: 2 I would declare unto every soul with voice of thunder the plan of *r.*; 34: 16 only unto him who has faith unto repentance is brought about the great plan of *r.*; 42: 13 according to justice, plan of *r.* could be brought about only on conditions of repentance; **Hel.** 5: 9 Christ comes to *r.* the world; 5: 9–10 (Alma 11: 34–37) the Lord shall not *r.* his people in their sins, but from their sins; 14: 16–17 (Morm. 9: 13) Christ's death and resurrection *r.* all men from temporal death; **3 Ne.** 6: 20 prophets testify of *r.* which Christ would make; 9: 17 by Christ *r.* comes; 9: 21 Christ has come into world to bring *r.*; 20: 38 (Isa. 52: 3) ye shall *r.* without money; **Morm.** 7: 7 Christ has brought to pass the *r.* of the world; 9: 12 because of Jesus Christ came the *r.* of man; **Ether** 3: 13 brother of Jared[2] is *r.* from fall; **Moro.** 7: 38 men without faith are as though there had been no *r.*; 8: 22 power of *r.* comes on all who have no law.

REFINE, REFINER (*see also* Chasten; Purge; Purify)

1 Ne. 20: 10 (Isa. 48: 10) I have *r.* thee; **Alma** 34: 29 if ye are not charitable, ye are as dross which *r.* cast out; **Hel.** 6: 11 Nephites *r.* ore; **3 Ne.** 24: 2 (Mal. 3: 2) the Lord is like *r*'s fire; **Ether** 10: 7 Riplakish causes fine gold to be *r.* in prison.

REFORMED EGYPTIAN (*see* Egyptian)

REFRAIN (*see also* Cease)

Alma 38: 12 see that ye *r.* from idleness; 39: 12 Alma[1] commands Corianton to *r.* from iniquities.

REFUGE (*see also* Escape; Protect; Safe, Safety)

2 Ne. 14: 6 (Isa. 4: 6) there shall be a tabernacle for a place of *r.*; **Hel.** 15: 2 ye shall attempt to flee and there shall be no place for *r.*

REFUSE (*see also* Deny; Reject)

2 Ne. 17: 15 (Isa. 7: 15) butter and honey shall he eat, that he may know to *r.* evil and choose good; **Mosiah** 29: 1–3 (Alma 17: 6) sons of Mosiah[2] *r.* to be king; **Alma** 27: 3 (51: 13) people of Anti-Nephi-Lehi *r.* to take up arms; **Hel.** 14: 20 sun shall *r.* to give light; **Morm.** 3: 11 Mormon[2] *r.* to be commander of Nephites; **Ether** 10: 6 Riplakish puts to death those who *r.* to labor; 15: 3 Coriantumr[2] *r.* to be comforted.

REGULATE, REGULATION (*see also* Govern; Government, Civil; Order)

Mosiah 26: 37 Alma[1] *r.* all affairs of church; **Alma** 45: 21 (62: 44) *r.* made throughout church; **3 Ne.** 7: 6 *r.* of government are destroyed.

REHEARSE (*see also* Read)

1 Ne. 15: 20 Nephi[1] *r.* words of Isaiah[1]; **Mosiah** 8: 3 Ammon[1] *r.* words of Benjamin.

REIGN (*see also* Authority; Dominion; King; Millennium; Power; Rule)

1 Ne. 22: 26 Holy One of Israel *r.*; **2 Ne.** 2: 29 devil will *r.* over the wicked in his kingdom; **Mosiah** 3: 5 Lord God Omnipotent who *r.* shall come down among men; 6: 4 Mosiah[2] begins to *r.* in father's stead; 11: 1 Noah[3] begins to *r.* in father's stead; 12: 21 (15: 14; Isa. 52: 7) how beautiful upon mountains are feet of him that saith unto Zion, Thy God *r.*

REJECT (*see also* Apostasy; Deny; Disobedience; Rebel; Refuse; Resist; Unbelief; Withstand; TG Prophets, Rejection of)

1 Ne. 3: 18 Jews have *r.* words of prophets; 15: 17 the Lord will show his power unto Gentiles because Jews will *r.* him; 19: 13 Jews shall be scourged because they *r.* signs and power of God; **2 Ne.** 1: 10 when those upon promised land *r.* Holy One, judgments shall rest upon them; 25: 12 Jews will *r.* Christ because of iniquities; 25: 18 word given to Israel to convince them of true Messiah, whom they *r.*; 27: 14 wo unto him who *r.* word of God; **Jacob** 4: 15–17 by stumbling of Jews they will *r.* stone upon which they might build safe foundation; **Mosiah** 14: 3 (Isa. 53: 3) he is despised and *r.* of men; 27: 30 Alma[2] *r.* his Redeemer; **Alma** 6: 3 church members who do not repent are *r.*; 13: 4 men *r.* Spirit because of hardness of heart and blindness of mind; **Hel.** 6: 2 many Nephites *r.* word of God; **3 Ne.** 16: 10 when Gentiles *r.* fulness of gospel, Father will bring it from them; **4 Ne.** 1: 38 those who *r.* gospel are called Lamanites; **Morm.** 6: 17 how could ye have *r.* Jesus; **Ether** 4: 3 Lamanites have *r.* gospel of Jesus Christ; 11: 22 Jaredites *r.* words of prophets because of secret society; **Moro.** 8: 29 after *r.* so great knowledge Nephites must soon perish.

REJOICE, REJOICING (*see also* Delight; Glorify; Joy; Praise; Shout; Sing; Thank)

1 Ne. 8: 3 Lehi[1] has reason to *r.* in the Lord because of Nephi[1] and Sam; **2 Ne.** 9: 52 let your hearts *r.*; 25: 26 we *r.* in Christ; 27: 30 (Isa. 29: 19) poor among men shall *r.* in Holy One; **Mosiah** 2: 4 Benjamin teaches his people to keep commandments that they might *r.*; 5: 4 because of great knowledge, people *r.*; 18: 14 Alma[1] and Helam come forth out of water *r.*; **Alma** 46: 38 peace and *r.* in church for four years; 61: 9 Pahoran[1] *r.* in greatness of heart of Moroni[1]; **Hel.** 8: 22 fathers have *r.* in Christ's day; **3 Ne.** 9: 2 devil laughs and his angels *r.* because of the slain.

RELIEF (*see also* Alms; Charity; Help; Needy; Poor; Serve; Succor)

Jacob 2: 19 obtain riches to administer *r.* to the needy; **Mosiah** 4: 26 to retain remission of sins, administer *r.* to needy, both spiritually and temporally.

RELIGION, RELIGIOUS (*see also* Belief; Church of God; Faith; Gospel; Worship)

Alma 43: 47 Nephites contend with Lamanites to defend their *r.*; 44: 2 Lamanites are angry with Nephites because of *r.*; 44: 5 God strengthens Nephites to gain power over Lamanites, by their faith, *r.*; 46: 20 those who will maintain title of liberty should covenant to maintain their rights, *r.*; 48: 13 Moroni[1] has sworn oath to defend his *r.*; 51: 6 freemen covenant to maintain privileges of *r.* by free government.

RELY (*see also* Depend; Trust)

1 Ne. 10: 6 all mankind would be lost save they *r.* on Redeemer; **2 Ne.** 31: 19 *r.* wholly upon merits of him who is mighty to save; **Alma** 24: 25 Lamanites who throw down weapons *r.* upon mercies of those whose arms are lifted to slay them; 25: 16 converted Lamanites *r.* upon spirits of prophecy; 26: 28 sons of Mosiah[2] travel from house to house, *r.* upon mercies of world; 27: 9 people of Anti-Nephi-Lehi *r.* upon mercies of Nephites; **Moro.** 6: 4 those baptized *r.* alone upon merits of Christ.

REMAIN (*see also* Abide; Persist; Sojourn; Tarry)

1 Ne. 13: 32 the Lord will not suffer Gentiles to *r.* in blindness; **2 Ne.** 2: 11 if it should be one body, it must *r.* as dead; 2: 22–23 if Adam had not transgressed, he would have *r.* in garden; 9: 7 without infinite atonement, first judgment must have *r.* endlessly; 9: 8–9 without resurrection, our spirits would have *r.* with devil; **Mosiah** 2: 38 if willful transgressor *r.* enemy to God, justice fills breast with guilt; 7: 18 Limhi trusts an effectual struggle *r.* to be made; 16: 5 he who persists in carnal nature *r.* in fallen state; **Alma** 7: 21 he who is filthy shall *r.* in filthiness; 9: 15 more tolerable for Lamanites if Nephites *r.* in sins; 15: 15 people of Ammonihah *r.* hardhearted; 40: 14 the wicked *r.* in darkness and righteous in paradise until resurrection; **3 Ne.** 28: 40 three Nephites to *r.* in sanctified state until judgment day.

REMEMBER, REMEMBRANCE (*see also* Book; Forget; Forgive; Memory; Type)

1 Ne. 2: 24 (2 Ne. 5: 25) Lamanites to scourge Nephites to stir them up in *r.*; 14: 8 *r.* Father's covenants with Israel; 15: 25 Nephi[1] exhorts brothers to *r.* to keep commandments; 17: 45 (Mosiah 9: 3; Alma 62: 49; Hel. 12: 5) men are slow to *r.* the Lord; **2 Ne.** 3: 25 *r.* the words of thy dying father; 9: 39 *r.* awfulness in transgressing against God; 9: 40 *r.* greatness of Holy One; 9: 46 prepare your souls that ye may not *r.* your awful guilt; 29: 5 have Gentiles *r.* Jews; **Jacob** 1: 11 people desire to obtain name of Nephi[1] in *r.*; 3: 9 *r.* your own filthiness; **Mosiah** 1: 7 *r.* to search records diligently; 1: 17 Lehites smitten with afflictions to stir them up in *r.* of duty; 2: 40 awake to *r.* of awful situation of transgressors; 4: 30 *r.*, and perish not; 27: 30 the Lord has *r.* every creature of his creating; **Alma** 4: 19 Alma[2] preaches to stir up people in *r.* of duty; 5: 6 (36: 29) have you sufficiently retained in *r.* the captivity of fathers; 5: 18 souls brought before God filled with remorse, having *r.* of guilt; 36: 13 Alma[2] *r.* all his sins; **Hel.** 12: 3 except the Lord chastens his people, they will not *r.* him; 13: 33 O that we had *r.* the Lord; 16: 5 Nephi[2] prophesies concerning Christ's coming, that people might *r.* that they had known signs beforehand; **3 Ne.** 16: 10–11 (3 Ne. 20: 29) when Gentiles reject gospel, the Lord will *r.* Israel; 18: 7, 11 (Moro. 4: 3; 5: 2; 6: 6) partake of sacrament in *r.* of Christ's flesh and blood; 24: 16 (Mal. 3: 16) book of *r.* written for those who fear the Lord; **Morm.** 5: 21 the Lord will *r.* prayers of the righteous; 8: 21 he who says the Lord *r.* not his covenant shall be hewn down; **Moro.** 10: 27 I exhort you to *r.* these things.

REMISSION, REMIT (*see also* Baptism; Born of God; Faith; Fire; Forgive; Holy Ghost, Baptism of; Jesus Christ, Atonement through; Mercy; Pardon; Repentance)

2 Ne. 25: 26 Nephites preach of Christ, that children may know source of *r.* of sins; 31: 17 (3 Ne. 12: 2; 30: 2) after baptism comes *r.* of sins by fire and Holy Ghost; **Enos** 1: 2 Enos[2] wrestles before God before receiving *r.* of sins; **Mosiah** 3: 13 those who believe Christ should come can receive *r.* of sins; 4: 3 Spirit comes upon Benjamin's people and they are filled with joy, having received *r.* of sins; 4: 11–12 always remember God's goodness in order to retain *r.* of sins; 4: 26 for sake of retaining *r.* of sins, impart substance to the poor; 15: 11 (Alma 4: 14) those who look forward to Christ's coming for *r.* of sins are his seed; **Alma** 7: 6 (30: 16) look forward for *r.* of sins with everlasting faith; 12: 34 he who repents has claim on mercy through Son, unto *r.* of sins; 38: 8 never until he cried out to Christ for mercy did Alma[2] receive *r.* of sins; **3 Ne.** 1: 23 baptism unto repentance, in which there is great *r.* of sins; 7: 16 Nephi[3] testifies boldly, *r.* of sins through faith on the

Lord; 7: 52 baptism a witness that they had repented and received *r.* of sins; 30: 2 be baptized, that ye may receive *r.* of sins and be filled with Holy Ghost; **Moro.** 3: 3 priests and teachers are ordained to preach repentance and *r.* of sins through Christ; 8: 11 baptism is unto repentance to fulfilling commandments unto *r.* of sins; 8: 26 *r.* of sins bringeth meekness; 10: 33 sanctification by grace through shedding of blood is Father's covenant unto *r.* of sins.

REMNANT (*see also* Gather; Israel; Israel, Gathering of; Israel, Scattering of; Jacob, House of; Residue)

1 Ne. 10: 14 (15: 12–13) natural branches of olive-tree, or *r.* of Israel, shall be grafted in; 13: 34 the Lord will visit *r.* of Israel, seed of Lehi[1]; **2 Ne.** 20: 21 (Isa. 10: 21) *r.* of Jacob shall return unto God; 28: 2 (Alma 46: 23; 3 Ne. 20: 16; Morm. 7: 10) Nephites' seed is *r.* of house of Israel, or Jacob[1]; 30: 3 Gentiles shall carry words of book to *r.* of Nephites' seed; **Alma** 46: 23 (3 Ne. 10: 17; 15: 12) Nephites are *r.* of seed of Joseph[1]; **3 Ne.** 5: 23 the Lord will again bring *r.* of seed of Joseph[1] to knowledge of the Lord; 5: 24 the Lord will gather all *r.* of seed of Jacob[1]; 21: 12 the Lord's people who are *r.* of Jacob[1], shall be among Gentiles; 21: 22 Gentiles can be numbered among this *r.* of Jacob[1], to whom the Lord has given this land; **Morm.** 5: 24 Gentiles called to repent, lest *r.* of Jacob[1] go among them as a lion; **Ether** 13: 7 the Lord brought *r.* of seed of Joseph[1] out of Jerusalem; 13: 10 those who dwell in New Jerusalem are numbered among *r.* of seed of Joseph[1].

REMORSE (*see also* Anguish; Grieve; Sackcloth; Sorrow; Torment)

Alma 5: 18 souls brought before God are filled with *r.*, having remembrance of guilt; 29: 5 to him who knoweth good and evil is given according to his desire, joy or *r.*; 42: 18 just law brings *r.*

REMOVE (*see also* Move)

2 Ne. 16: 12 (Isa. 6: 12) the Lord will *r.* men far away; 23: 13 (Isa. 13: 13) earth shall *r.* out of her place; 27: 25 (Isa. 29: 13–14) men draw near the Lord with mouths, but have *r.* hearts far from him; **Alma** 46: 40 God has prepared plants and roots to *r.* cause of disease; **Hel.** 5: 40–41 cloud of darkness to be *r.* by faith; **3 Ne.** 22: 10 (Isa. 54: 10) hills shall be *r.*; **Morm.** 8: 24 in the Lord's name saints could *r.* mountains; **Ether** 12: 30 brother of Jared[2] said to mountain, *R.*, and it was *r.*

REND, RENT

1 Ne. 12: 4 (19: 12; Hel. 14: 22; 3 Ne. 8: 18; 10: 9) earth and rocks shall be *r.*; 17: 47 soul of Nephi[1] is *r.* with anguish because of brothers; **Alma** 46: 12–13 Moroni[1] *r.* coat for title of liberty; 46: 21 Nephites *r.* garments as covenant not to forsake the Lord; 46: 23 let us keep commandments or our garments shall be *r.* by brethren; **Hel.** 6: 39 robbers obtain government, that they smite, *r.*; 10: 8 if Nephi[3] says to temple it should be *r.* in twain, it shall be done; **3 Ne.** 14: 6 (Matt. 7: 6) cast not your pearls before swine lest they turn again and *r.* you; **Morm.** 6: 16 soul of Mormon[2] is *r.* with anguish because of the slain; **Ether** 4: 15 when Israel *r.* veil of unbelief, they shall know Father remembers covenants.

RENDER (*see also* Give)

Mosiah 2: 20–21 if you *r.* all thanks to God, ye would be unprofitable servants; 2: 34 men are eternally indebted to Father, to *r.* unto him all that they have and are; 4: 13 *r.* to every man according to his due.

RENEW (*see also* New; Repair; TG Earth, Renewal of)

4 Ne. 1: 9 sunken cities could not be *r.*

RENT (*see* Rend, Rent)

REPAIR (*see also* Mend; Renew)

Mosiah 9: 8 Nephites *r.* walls of cities; 27: 35 sons of Mosiah[2] strive to *r.* all injuries they had done to church; **Alma** 27: 8 people of Anti-Nephi-Lehi are willing to be Nephites' slaves until they have *r.* their many murders and sins; **Hel.** 5: 17 converted dissenters endeavor to *r.* wrongs they had done; **3 Ne.** 6: 7 many old cities *r.*

REPAY (*see also* Pay)

Morm. 3: 15 (8: 20; Rom. 12: 19) vengeance is the Lord's, and he will *r.*

REPENTANCE, REPENT (*see also* Baptism; Change; Confession of Sins; Death, Spiritual; Excommunication; Faith; Forgive; Forsake; Gospel; Guilt; Mend; Mercy; Penitent; Redemption; Remission; Salvation; Work [noun]; Work [verb]; TG Repent, Repentance; BD Repentance)

1 Ne. 1: 4 many prophets prophesy that Jews must *r.* or be destroyed; 10: 18 way is prepared for all men if they *r.* and come unto the Lord; 14: 5 if Gentiles *r.*, it shall be well with them; 18: 20 when they see they will be swallowed in sea, brothers of Nephi[1] *r.*; 22: 28 all nations shall dwell safely in Holy One if they will *r.*; **2 Ne.** 2: 21 days of men were prolonged, that they might *r.*; 2: 21 (31: 11; Alma 9: 12; 3 Ne. 11: 32) God commands that all men must *r.*; 6: 12 if Gentiles *r.*, they shall be saved; 9: 23 God commands that all must *r.* and be baptized; 26: 27 the Lord commands his people to persuade all men to *r.*; 28: 19 they who belong to devil's kingdom must be stirred up unto *r.*; 30: 2 (3 Ne. 16: 13) Gentiles who *r.* are covenant people of the Lord; 30: 2 Jews who will not *r.* shall be cast off; 30: 2 the Lord covenants with none save those who *r.*; 31: 13 those who follow Son, *r.* of sins, shall receive Holy Ghost; 31: 17 gate by which men should enter is *r.* and baptism; **Jacob** 3: 3 except ye *r.*, the land is cursed; **Mosiah** 2: 38 if willful transgressor *r.* not, he shall be filled with sense of guilt; 3: 12 salvation cometh to none who knowingly rebel, except through *r.* and faith; 3: 21 men can be found blameless before God only through *r.* and faith; 4: 10 believe that ye must *r.* of your sins; 4: 18 he who turns away beggar has great cause to *r.*; 18: 20 preach nothing save *r.* and faith; 26: 29 if transgressor confesses and *r.*, ye shall forgive him; 26: 35–36 (3 Ne. 18: 29–32; Moro. 6: 7) only those who *r.* and confess sins are numbered among people of church; 27: 28 after *r.* nigh unto death, Alma[2] is snatched from everlasting burning, born of God; **Alma** 5: 31 he who persecutes his brother must *r.* or he cannot be saved; 5: 49 (7: 9) Alma[2] is called to cry unto people that they must *r.* and be born again; 5: 54 those sanctified by Spirit bring forth works meet for *r.*; 6: 2 all who *r.* are baptized unto *r.*; 7: 9 (Hel. 14: 9) *r.* ye, and prepare way of the Lord; 9: 12 except men *r.*, they cannot inherit kingdom of God; 9: 25 (10: 20; Hel. 5: 32) *r.* ye, for kingdom of heaven is at hand; 12: 24 (42: 4) man was granted time in which he might *r.*; 13: 10 many are ordained high priests because they choose to *r.* and work righteousness rather than perish; 13: 18 Melchizedek preached *r.* unto his people, and they *r.*; 14: 1 many people begin to *r.* and search scriptures; 26: 22 to know mysteries of God, men must *r.*; 29: 1 O that I were an angel and could cry *r.* unto every people; 32: 13 if a man is compelled to be humble, he sometimes seeks *r.*; 32: 13 all who *r.* shall find mercy; 34: 33 do not procrastinate day of *r.*; 34: 34 when brought to night of darkness, men cannot say they will *r.*; 37: 31 cursed be land unto secret combinations except they *r.*; 42: 16 *r.* could not come unto men except there were a punishment; 42: 22 there is punishment affixed and *r.* granted, which *r.* mercy claimeth; 42: 29 only let your sins trouble you, with that trouble which shall bring you down unto *r.*; **Hel.** 5: 11 the Lord is given power from Father to redeem his people because of *r.*; 5: 11 the Lord has sent his angels to declare tidings of conditions of *r.*; 5: 29 *r.* ye, and seek no more to destroy my servants; 5: 40–41 to remove cloud of darkness, Lamanites must *r.* and have faith; 12: 22 *r.* has been declared that men might be saved; 12: 23 (3 Ne. 23: 5) those who *r.* shall be saved; 13: 33, 36 (3 Ne. 8: 24–25) O that I had *r.* and not killed prophets; 15: 1 except ye *r.*, your houses will be left to you desolate; 15: 7 prophecies of holy prophets lead men to faith and *r.*, which bring change of heart; **3 Ne.** 7: 24 all who are brought unto *r.* are baptized; 9: 2 wo unto inhabitants of earth, except they *r.*; 9: 22 the Lord will receive all who *r.* and come unto him as little child; 16: 13 if Gentiles *r.*, they shall be numbered among the Lord's people; 18: 32 if a man *r.*, ye shall not cast him out; 27: 16 whoso *r.* and is baptized shall be filled; 30: 2 Mormon[2] calls Gentiles to *r.* of evil doings; **Ether** 2: 11 this message cometh unto Gentiles that they may *r.*; 11: 1 many prophets prophesy destruction of Jaredites unless they *r.*; **Moro.** 6: 2 only those who witness unto church that they have *r.* are received unto baptism; 6: 8 as oft as men *r.* and seek forgiveness, they are forgiven; 7: 31 office of angels' ministry is to call men to *r.*; 8: 8 Christ came into world to call not the righteous but sinners to *r.*; 8: 11, 19 little children need no *r.*; 8: 22 he that is under no condemnation cannot *r.*; 8: 24 *r.* is unto them that are under condemnation and under curse of broken law; 8: 25 first fruits of *r.* is baptism; 9: 3 Mormon[2] fears Lamanites will destroy Nephites, for they do not *r.*

REPETITION

3 Ne. 13: 7 when ye pray, use not vain *r.*

REPORT (*see also* Rumor)

Mosiah 14: 1 (Isa. 53: 1) who hath believed our *r.*

REPRESENTATION (*see also* Shadow; Type)

1 Ne. 11: 25 living waters and tree of life are *r.* of love of God; 15: 21–22 tree in dream of Lehi[1] was *r.* of tree of life; 15: 28–29 gulf separating wicked from tree of life is *r.* of hell; 15: 32 *r.* of things both temporal and spiritual.

REPROACH, REPROACHFULLY (*see also* Rebuke; Reprove; Scorn; Shame)

2 Ne. 8: 7 (Isa. 51: 7) fear not the *r.* of men; 14: 1 (Isa. 4: 1) seven women will want to be called by one man's name to take away *r.*; **3 Ne.** 22: 4 (Isa. 54: 4) not remember the *r.* of thy youth.

REPROVE (*see also* Prove; Punishment; Rebuke; Reproach; Warn)

2 Ne. 21: 3 (Isa. 11: 3) he shall not *r.*

after the hearing of his ears; 21: 4 (30: 9; Isa. 11: 4) he shall *r.* with equity for the meek; 27: 32 they who lay a snare for him that *r.* at the gate shall be cut off.

REPUGNANT (*see also* Loathsome; Opposition)

Mosiah 29: 36 iniquities and abominations of unrighteous king are expressly *r.* to commandments of God.

REQUIRE (*see also* Command; Commandments of God; Requisite)

1 Ne. 3: 5 brothers murmur that it is hard thing Lehi[1] *r.* of them; **Mosiah** 2: 22–24 all that God *r.* of men is to keep his commandments; 18: 27 of him who has but little, little is *r.*; **Alma** 34: 12 law *r.* the life of him who murders.

REQUISITE

Mosiah 4: 27 not *r.* that man should run faster than he has strength; **Alma** 41: 2 plan of restoration is *r.* with justice of God; 41: 2 *r.* that all things be restored to proper order; 41: 3 *r.* with justice of God that men be judged according to works.

RESIDUE (*see also* Remnant)

Moro. 7: 32 the Lord prepared way that *r.* of men may have faith in Christ.

RESIST (*see also* Deny; Hardheartedness; Rebel; Refuse; Reject; Withstand)

Alma 30: 46 Korihor *r.* Spirit of truth; 32: 28 if ye do not cast out seed by unbelief, that ye *r.* Spirit, it will swell; 48: 16 Moroni[1] glories in *r.* iniquity; 61: 14 whatsoever evil we cannot *r.* with words, let us *r.* with swords; **3 Ne.** 12: 39 (Matt. 5: 39) ye shall not *r.* evil, but turn other cheek to him who smites right cheek.

RESPECT, RESPECTER (*see also* Alike; Equal; Esteem; Honor; Regard; Worth)

2 Ne. 33: 14 Nephi[1] bids farewell to those who will not *r.* words of God; **Alma** 1: 30 Nephites are liberal to all, having no *r.* to persons as to those in need; 16: 14 Alma[2] and Amulek impart word of God without any *r.* of persons. **Moro.** 8: 12 if little children need baptism, God would be *r.* of persons.

RESPONSIBILITY (*see also* Accountable; Duty)

Jacob 1: 19 priests and teachers take upon themselves *r.* for sins of people if they do not teach word of God; 2: 2 Jacob[2] is under *r.* to magnify office.

REST (*see also* Abide; Comfort; Paradise; Peace; Sabbath)

2 Ne. 21: 2 (Isa. 11: 2) Spirit of the Lord shall *r.* upon rod out of stem of Jesse; 21: 10 (Isa. 11: 10) *r.* of root of Jesse shall be glorious; **Jacob** 1: 7 we persuade our people to come unto Christ, that they might enter into his *r.*; **Enos** 1: 27 Enos[2] soon goes to place of his *r.*; **Alma** 7: 27 may peace of God *r.* upon you; 10: 11 the Lord's blessing has *r.* upon Amulek and household; 12: 34–37 only those who repent and harden not hearts shall enter the Lord's *r.*; 13: 6 priests are ordained to teach men, that they might enter into God's *r.*; 13: 12 many are made pure and enter *r.* of the Lord; 13: 13 humble yourselves, bring forth fruit meet for repentance, enter *r.* of the Lord; 13: 16 look forward to Son for remission of sins, that they may enter *r.* of the Lord; 13: 29 have love of God always in your hearts, that ye may enter into his *r.*; 16: 17 receive word with joy that they may enter *r.* of the Lord; 37: 34 the meek and lowly in heart shall find *r.* to their souls; 40: 12 righteous will be received into paradise, a state of *r.* and peace, where they *r.* from troubles; 60: 13 the righteous enter *r.* of the Lord; **3 Ne.** 27: 19 only those who have washed garments in Christ's blood enter into Father's *r.*; 28: 3 disciples shall find *r.* with Christ in his kingdom; **Moro.** 7: 3 obtain sufficient hope by which ye can enter into *r.* of the Lord; 9: 6 we have labor to perform, that we may conquer enemy and *r.* our souls in kingdom of God; 9: 25 may Christ's mercy and long-suffering *r.* in your mind forever; 10: 34 Moroni[2] soon goes to *r.* in paradise of God.

RESTITUTION (*see* Repair)

RESTORATION, RESTORE (*see also* Church of God; Gather; Gospel; Israel, Gathering of; Judgment; Last Days; Reclaim; Recover; Resurrection; Return; TG Israel, Restoration of; Restoration of the Gospel; BD Restitution; Restoration)

1 Ne. 15: 19 Nephi[1] speaks concerning *r.* of Jews in latter days; 21: 6 (Isa. 49: 6) it is a light thing that thou shouldst be servant to *r.* the preserved of Israel; **2 Ne.** 3: 24 mighty one shall rise up to do much good unto bringing to pass *r.* unto Israel; 9: 2 the Lord has spoken unto Jews by prophets, from beginning until they are *r.* to true church; 9: 12 (Alma 40: 23) bodies and spirits of men shall be *r.* to one another; 10: 2 (30: 5; Hel. 15: 11) Nephites' and Lamanites' children shall be *r.* to knowledge of Christ; 25: 17 the Lord will set his hand second time to *r.* his people; 30: 8 the Lord will commence work among all nations to bring about *r.* of his people; **Jacob** 7: 23 peace and love of God is *r.* again among Nephites; **Enos** 1: 14 Nephites' struggles are vain in *r.*

Lamanites to true faith; **Alma** 11: 44 this *r.* shall come to all; 11: 44 (40: 23; 41: 4) every thing shall be *r.* to its perfect frame; 40: 21–22 resurrection brings about *r.* of those things spoken by prophets; 41: 2 plan of *r.* is requisite with justice of God; 41: 4 all things shall be *r.* to proper order; 41: 10 do not suppose ye shall be *r.* from sin to happiness; 41: 12–13 meaning of *r.* is to bring back evil for evil, good for good; 41: 14 be merciful, deal justly, judge righteously, and do good, and you shall have mercy, justice, righteous judgment, and good *r.* to you; 42: 23 because of resurrection, men are *r.* to God's presence; 42: 27–28 if man has desired evil, evil shall be done unto him, according to *r.* of God; **Hel.** 12: 24 may men be brought to repentance and good works, that they might be *r.* unto grace for grace; 14: 31 ye can do good and be *r.* unto that which is good, or evil and be *r.* unto that which is evil; **3 Ne.** 29: 1 when gospel comes to Gentiles, *r.* of Israel is beginning to be fulfilled; **Morm.** 9: 36 *r.* of Lamanites to knowledge of Christ is according to prayers of all saints.

RESTRAIN (*see also* Hinder; Keep; Stay; Stop; Withhold)

2 Ne. 1: 26 Nephi[1] could not *r.* the truth; **Ether** 12: 2 Ether could not be *r.* from prophesying because of Spirit.

RESURRECTION (*see also* Body; Death, Physical; Eternal Life; Fall of Man; Grave; Immortality; Jesus Christ, Resurrection of; Life; Paradise; Quick [=living]; Raise; Redemption; Restoration; Reunite; Rise; Spirit World; TG Resurrection; BD Resurrection)

2 Ne. 2: 8 (Mosiah 13: 35; 15: 20; Alma 33: 22; 40: 3; Hel. 14: 15) Christ lays down life, takes it up again, to bring to pass *r.* of the dead; 9: 6 *r.* must come unto man by reason of the fall; 9: 11–12 (Alma 40: 21, 23; Moro. 10: 34) bodies and spirits of men shall be restored to one another by power of *r.* of Holy One; 9: 22 *r.* will pass upon all men; 10: 25 may God raise you from death by power of the *r.*; **Jacob** 4: 11 be reconciled to God through atonement of Christ, and ye may obtain *r.* according to power of *r.* which is in Christ; 6: 9 power of redemption and *r.*, which is in Christ, will bring you to stand before God; **Mosiah** 13: 34–35 God himself shall come down and bring to pass the *r.*; 15: 20 Son hath power over the dead and bringeth to pass *r.*; 15: 21–26 (Alma 40: 15–18) those who died before Christ's *r.* will have part in first *r.*; 15: 22 all prophets and those who believe in them shall come forth in first *r.*; 15: 26 those who rebel against God shall have no part in first *r.*; 16: 7 if Christ had not risen from dead, there could have been no *r.*; 16: 8 (Morm. 7: 5) grave has no victory, sting of death is swallowed in Christ; 18: 9–10 those who would be numbered among first *r.* must be baptized; **Alma** 11: 41 the wicked remain as though there had been no redemption, except for loosing of bands of death; 11: 42 (12: 8; 40: 4–5, 9) all shall rise from the dead; 11: 45 mortal body is raised to an immortal body; 12: 24 man given a time to prepare for endless state which is after *r.*; 21: 9 Aaron[3] opens to Lamanites scriptures concerning *r.*; 33: 22 (Hel. 14: 20) Son shall rise from dead to bring to pass *r.*; 40: 4–10 time appointed that all shall come from the dead; 40: 6, 11–14 state of souls between death and *r.*; 40: 15–17 state between death and *r.* is not first *r.*; 40: 16 first *r.* includes those who died before Christ's *r.*; 40: 21 space between death and *r.*; 40: 23 soul shall be restored to body and body to soul; **Hel.** 14: 25 (3 Ne. 23: 9–13) at time of Christ's *r.* many saints shall be resurrected; **3 Ne.** 26: 4–5 men will be judged of their works, if they be good, to *r.* of everlasting life, if evil, to *r.* of damnation; **Morm.** 9: 13 death of Christ bringeth to pass the *r.*; **Moro.** 7: 41 ye shall have hope through Christ's atonement and *r.* to be raised unto life eternal; 10: 34 I soon go to rest in paradise of God until my spirit and body shall again reunite.

RETAIN (*see also* Hold; Keep; Maintain)

Jacob 1: 11 Nephites desire to *r.* in remembrance the name of Nephi[1]; **Mosiah** 4: 11–12 always *r.* in remembrance God's goodness and ye will always *r.* remission of your sins; 4: 26 to *r.* remission of sins, impart of substance to the poor; 5: 12 *r.* name of Christ written always in your heart; **Alma** 4: 14 Nephites look forward to Christ's coming, thus *r.* remission of sins; 5: 6 have you sufficiently *r.* in remembrance the captivity of your fathers; 25: 16 converted Lamanites *r.* hope through faith unto eternal salvation; 37: 5 brass plates must *r.* their brightness; **Hel.** 13: 31 (Morm. 1: 18) in days of your poverty ye cannot *r.* your riches; **Moro.** 7: 8 if man gives gift grudgingly, it is counted to him the same as if he had *r.* it.

RETURN (*see also* Gather; Israel, Gathering of; Recover; Restoration)

1 Ne. 10: 3 (2 Ne. 6: 9; 25: 11) Jews shall *r.* out of captivity; **2 Ne.** 1: 14 Lehi[1] soon to lie in grave, from which no traveler can *r.*; 8: 11 (Isa. 51: 11) the redeemed of the Lord shall *r.*; 16: 13 (Isa. 6: 13) they shall *r.* and be eaten; 20: 21 (Isa. 10: 21) remnant of Jacob[1] shall *r.*; **Mosiah** 4: 28 whosoever borrows of his neighbor should *r.* what he borrows; **Alma** 7: 23 always *r.* thanks unto God for whatsoever ye receive; 34: 34 when brought to awful crisis of night of darkness, ye cannot say I will *r.* to my God; **Hel.** 13: 11 if ye repent and *r.* to the Lord, he will turn away his anger; **3 Ne.** 6: 13 some *r.* railing for railing; 10: 6 Israel should repent and *r.* unto the Lord with full purpose of heart; 16: 13 if Gentiles will repent and *r.* unto Father, they shall be numbered among house of Israel; 20: 28 Father shall *r.* Gentiles' iniquities upon own heads; 24: 7 (Mal. 3: 7) *r.* unto the Lord and he will *r.* unto you; 27: 11 those built upon devil's works shall be cast into fire from which there is no *r.*; **Morm.** 6: 15 bodies of slain left to *r.* to mother earth; **Moro.** 9: 22 Mormon[2] prays the Lord will spare life of Moroni[2] to witness *r.* of his people.

REUNITE (*see also* Resurrection)

Alma 11: 43 (40: 18–21; Moro. 10: 34) spirit and body shall be *r.* in perfect form.

REVELATION, REVEAL (*see also* Dream; God, Manifestations of; Guide; Holy Ghost; Inspire; Instruction; Knowledge; Manifest; Prophecy; Prophet; Revelator; Scriptures; Spirit, Holy/Spirit of the Lord; Testimony; Vision; Visitation; Voice; TG Revelation; BD Revelation)

2 Ne. 5: 6 those who go with Nephi[1] are those who believe *r.* of God; 27: 7 in sealed book shall be *r.* from beginning of world to end; 27: 10 *r.* sealed in book *r.* all things from foundation of world unto end; 27: 11 (30: 18) all things shall be *r.* which ever have been or ever will be; 30: 17 nothing is secret save it shall be *r.*; **Jacob** 1: 6 (Alma 9: 21) Nephites have many *r.* and spirit of prophecy; 4: 8 no man knows God's ways save they are *r.* to him; 4: 8 despise not the *r.* of God; **Omni** 1: 11 Abinadom knows of no *r.* save those that have been written; **Mosiah** 14: 1 (Isa. 53: 1) to whom is the arm of the Lord *r.*; **Alma** 4: 20 (8: 24) Alma[2] confines himself to testimony of word, according to spirit of *r.*; 5: 46 the Lord has made manifest many things by Holy Spirit, which is spirit of *r.*; 17: 3 sons of Mosiah teach with spirit of prophecy and *r.*; 25: 15 outward ordinances must be kept until Christ is *r.*; 26: 22 things never *r.* shall be *r.* to those who repent, exercise faith, bring forth good works, and pray without ceasing; 43: 2 Alma[2] and sons preach according to spirit of prophecy and *r.*; **Hel.** 4: 12, 23 Nephites deny spirit of prophecy and *r.*; 11: 23 Nephi[2] and Lehi[4] have many *r.* daily; **3 Ne.** 3: 19 Nephites appoint as chief captains those who have spirit of *r.*; 26: 14 children speak greater things than Jesus had *r.* to people; 29: 6 wo unto him who denies *r.* of the Lord and says the Lord no longer works by *r.*; **Morm.** 5: 8 things which are hid must be *r.*; 8: 33 look unto *r.* of God; 9: 7–8 those who deny *r.* know not the gospel of Christ.

REVELATOR (*see also* Prophet; Revelation; Seer)

Mosiah 8: 16 a seer is a *r.*

REVENGE (*see also* Avenge; Vengeance)

Mosiah 19: 19 those who fled with Noah[3] swear to return and seek *r.*; **Alma** 27: 2 Amalekites see they cannot seek *r.*; **Moro.** 9: 5, 23 Nephites thirst after blood and *r.* continually.

REVILE (*see also* Backbiting; Hate; Malice; Mock; Persecution; Railing; Scorn; Spit)

1 Ne. 17: 42 Israelites *r.* against Moses; **2 Ne.** 9: 40 if ye say I have spoken hard things against you, ye *r.* against truth; 28: 16 those who *r.* against that which is good; **Jacob** 3: 9 *r.* no more against Lamanites because of darkness of skin; **Alma** 8: 9, 13 people of Ammonihah *r.* against Alma[2]; 14: 2 people of Ammonihah claim Amulek has *r.* against their law; 16: 18 priests preach against all *r.*; 34: 40 Amulek admonishes poor Zoramites not to *r.* against those who cast them out; **Hel.** 10: 15 Nephites *r.* against Nephi[2]; **3 Ne.** 6: 13 some receive railing and do not turn and *r.* again; 12: 11 (Matt. 5: 11) blessed are ye when men shall *r.* you; 22: 17 the Lord's servants to condemn every tongue that *r.* against them; **Ether** 7: 24 Jaredites *r.* against prophets.

REVIVE

Ether 9: 35 Jaredites begin to *r.* after drought.

REVOLT, REVOLUTION (*see also* Dissenter; War)

4 Ne. 1: 20 small group *r.* from church and took name of Lamanites; **Morm.** 2: 8 one complete *r.* throughout all the land.

REWARD (*see also* Blessing; Increase; Judgment; Pay; Prize; Profit; Prosper; Reap; Wages; Work [noun])

2 Ne. 13: 9 (Isa. 3: 9) they have *r.* evil unto themselves; 15: 22–23 (Isa. 5: 23) wo unto those who justify the wicked for *r.*; 26: 10 for *r.* of their pride, Nephites will reap destruction; **Alma** 3: 26 in one year tens of thousands were sent into eternal world to reap *r.* according to works; 9: 28 all men shall reap *r.* of works; 11: 25 for evil of bribery Zeezrom will have his *r.*; 29: 15 how great shall be *r.* of sons of Mosiah[2]; 32: 43 reap *r.* of faith and diligence; 34: 39 devil *r.* men no good thing; 41: 6 if man has repented and desired righteousness, he shall be *r.* unto righteousness; 41: 14 if you do good continually, you shall receive your *r.*; **3 Ne.** 12: 11–12 (Matt. 5: 11–12) great shall be *r.* in heaven of those who are persecuted for Christ's sake; 13: 5 (Matt. 6: 5) hypocrites, who pray to be seen of men, have their *r.*

RICH (*see also* Nobility; Pride; Prosper, Prosperity; Riches; Wealth)

2 Ne. 9: 30 wo unto *r.* who are *r.* as to things of world, for they despise the poor; 9: 42 the *r.* who are puffed up in riches are they whom the Lord despises; 28: 15 the *r.* who are puffed up in pride shall be thrust down to hell; **Mosiah** 4: 23 their substance shall perish with those who are *r.* in things of this world; 14: 9 (Isa. 53: 9) he made his grave with the *r.* in his death; **Alma** 1: 29 because of steadiness of church, they began to be exceedingly *r.*; **4 Ne.** 1: 3 Nephites have all things in common, so there are no *r.* or poor; 1: 23 Nephites become exceedingly *r.* because of prosperity in Christ.

RICHES (*see also* Gain; Lucre; Mammon; Money; Prosper, Prosperity; Rich; Treasure; Wealth)

Jacob 2: 18 before ye seek *r.*, seek kingdom of God; 2: 19 after ye have obtained hope in Christ, ye shall obtain *r.* if ye seek them; 2: 19 seek *r.* for intent to do good; **Mosiah** 2: 12 Benjamin has not sought *r.* of his people; 12: 29 (Alma 5: 53; Hel. 7: 21; 13: 20) do ye set hearts upon *r.*; 29: 40 Mosiah[2] does not exact *r.* of his people; **Alma** 1: 30 Nephites do not set hearts upon *r.*; 4: 6 (45: 24; Hel. 3: 36; 4: 12; 6: 17) people of church begin to wax proud because of *r.*; 7: 6 I trust ye have not set your hearts upon *r.*; 39: 14 seek not after *r.*; 62: 49 in spite of *r.* Nephites are not lifted up in pride; **Hel.** 13: 20–21 Nephites are cursed because of *r.*; 13: 22 ye always remember your *r.*, not to thank the Lord for them; 13: 31–33 (Morm. 1: 18) the Lord will curse *r.* that they become slippery; **3 Ne.** 6: 12 people are distinguished by ranks, according to *r.*; 6: 12 some receive great learning because of their *r.*; 6: 15 Satan tempts people to seek for *r.*; **Ether** 10: 3 Shez smitten by robber because of *r.*

RID (*see also* Cleanse)

2 Ne. 9: 44 Jacob[2] is *r.* of brethren's blood; **Jacob** 2: 2 Jacob[2] magnifies office to *r.* his garments of people's sins; 2: 16 O that God would *r.* you from this iniquity; **Mosiah** 2: 28 Benjamin teaches people to *r.* himself of their blood; **3 Ne.** 28: 35 do ye suppose ye can get *r.* of justice of an offended God; **Morm.** 9: 35 these things are written that we may *r.* our garments of blood of brethren.

RIGHT [adj.=correct], **RIGHTLY** (*see also* Right Hand; Right [noun]; True)

1 Ne. 13: 27 (22: 14) abominable church takes away parts of gospel to pervert *r.* ways of the Lord; **2 Ne.** 25: 28 words of Nephi[1] are sufficient to teach any man the *r.* way to believe in Christ; **Jacob** 7: 7 Sherem claims Jacob[2] has led away many, that they pervert *r.* way of God; 7: 7 Sherem claims law of Moses is *r.* way; **Mosiah** 29: 6 he to whom kingdom *r.* belongs has refused it; **Moro.** 6: 4 those baptized are nourished by good word of God, to keep them in *r.* way.

RIGHT [noun] (*see also* Government, Civil; Liberty; Privilege; Right [adj.]; Right Hand)

Mosiah 29: 32 this land should be land of liberty, that every man may enjoy *r.* alike; **Alma** 2: 4 Amlici would deprive people of *r.* and privileges of church; 30: 27 Korihor claims priests do not allow Nephites to enjoy *r.*; 43: 9, 26, 47 design of Nephites is to preserve *r.*; 48: 13 Moroni[1] had sworn oath to defend his people, his *r.*; 51: 6 freemen covenant to maintain their *r.* by free government; 61: 9 Pahoran seeks to retain judgment-seat to preserve *r.* of his people; **3 Ne.** 3: 10 Giddianhi claims Lamanites desire to recover their *r.* and government; 6: 30 secret combination sets at defiance the law and *r.* of country; **Moro.** 7: 27 Christ claims of Father his *r.* of mercy.

RIGHT HAND (*see also* Left; Right [adj.]; Right [noun])

1 Ne. 20: 13 (Isa. 48: 13) my *r.* hand hath spanned the heavens; **Mosiah** 5: 9 those who enter covenant will be found at *r.* hand of God; 26: 23 the Lord grants unto them who believe place at his *r.* hand; 26: 24 if men know the Lord, they shall have place at *r.* hand; **Alma** 5: 58 unto the righteous will the Lord grant inheritance at *r.* hand; 7: 20 God hath no shadow of turning from *r.* to left; 24: 23 converted Lamanites would not flee from sword nor turn aside to *r.* hand or to left; 56: 37, 40 Lamanites dare not turn to *r.* or left, lest they be surrounded; **3 Ne.** 12: 39 (Matt. 5: 39) whosoever shall smite thee on *r.* cheek, turn to him the other; 13: 3 (Matt. 6: 3) let not thy left hand know what thy *r.* hand doeth; 22: 3 (Isa. 54: 3) thou shalt break forth on *r.* hand and on left; **Moro.** 9: 26 Christ sits on *r.* hand of Father's power.

RIGHTEOUSNESS, RIGHTEOUS, RIGHTEOUSLY (*see also* Faithful; Godliness; Holiness; Honest; Innocence; Just; Obedience; Perfect; Prosper, Prosperity; Purity; Uprightness)

1 Ne. 2: 9 Lehi[1] admonishes Laman[1] to be like river, continually running into fountain of *r.*; 14: 14 saints are armed with *r.*; 15: 36 the wicked are rejected from the *r.*; 16: 3 if ye were *r.*, ye would not murmur; 17: 35 he who is *r.* is favored of God; 19: 11 the Lord will visit house of Israel because of *r.*; 22: 16 God will not suffer that the wicked shall destroy the *r.*; 22: 17, 22 the *r.* need not fear; 22: 26 because of *r.* of the Lord's people, Satan has no power; **2 Ne.** 1: 19 the Lord's ways are *r.* forever; 1: 23 put on armor of *r.*; 2: 3 Jacob[2] is redeemed, because of *r.* of Redeemer; 2: 13 if no sin, then no *r.*, if no *r.*, then no happiness; 4: 33 encircle me in robe of thy *r.*; 9: 14 the *r.* shall have perfect knowledge of their *r.*, being clothed with robe of *r.*; 9: 16 (Morm. 9: 14) they who are *r.* shall be *r.* still; 9: 18 the *r.*, the saints of God, shall inherit kingdom of God; 9: 40 the *r.* fear not words of truth; 9: 49 my heart delights in *r.*; 21: 4 (30: 9; Isa. 11: 4) with *r.* shall the Lord judge the poor; 26: 8 the *r.* who look forward unto Christ shall not perish; 26: 9 the Son of *r.* shall appear unto the *r.*; 31: 5–6 the Lamb is baptized to fulfill all *r.*; **Jacob** 2: 25 the Lord has led Nephites from Jerusalem to raise up *r.* branch from fruit of loins of Joseph[1]; 4: 5 law of Moses is sanctified unto Nephites for *r.*; **Mosiah** 2: 37 man who listeth to obey evil spirit becometh enemy to all *r.*; 3: 10 Christ to be resurrected that *r.* judgment might come upon men; 4: 14 (Alma 34: 23) devil is enemy to all *r.*; 23: 18 priests nourish people with things pertaining to *r.*; 27: 25 all mankind must be born of God, changed from carnal state to state of *r.*; **Alma** 5: 42 whoso hearkens to devil receives wages of death as to things pertaining to *r.*; 5: 58 names of the *r.* shall be written in book of life; 7: 19 people of Gideon are in paths of *r.*; 12: 16 whosoever dies in sins shall die spiritual death, as to things pertaining to *r.*; 13: 10 many are ordained high priests on account of *r.*; 26: 8 the Lord works *r.* forever; 34: 36 in hearts of the *r.* doth the Lord dwell; 34: 36 the *r.* shall sit down in the Lord's kingdom; 38: 9 Christ is the word of truth and *r.*; 40: 12, 14 spirits of those who are *r.* are received into state of happiness; 41: 14 judge *r.* and you shall have *r.* judgment; 45: 15 Alma[2] blesses earth for the *r*'s sake; 50: 39 chief judge appointed with oath to judge *r.*; 60: 13 the Lord suffers the *r.* to be slain, that justice might come upon the wicked; 62: 40 Nephites spared because of prayers of the *r.*; **Hel.** 6: 1 Lamanites' *r.* exceeds that of Nephites; 7: 5 robbers condemn the *r.* because of their *r.*; 13: 13 were it not for the *r.*, the Lord would destroy Zarahemla; 13: 38 ye have sought happiness in doing iniquity, which is contrary to nature of God's *r.*; 14: 29 signs given that *r.* judgment may come upon nonbelievers; **3 Ne.** 4: 29 may the Lord preserve his people in *r.*; 22: 14 (Isa. 54: 14) in *r.* shalt thou be established; 24: 3 (Mal. 3: 3) sons of Levi[1] to offer unto the Lord an offering in *r.*; 24: 18 (Mal. 3: 18) then shall ye return and discern between the *r.* and the wicked; 25: 2 (Mal. 4: 2) unto you that fear my name shall Son of *R.* arise; **4 Ne.** 1: 46 there are none who are *r.* save disciples of Jesus; **Morm.** 2: 12 Mormon[2] supposes the Lord will be merciful unto Nephites that they would again become *r.* people; **Ether** 2: 7 promised land preserved for *r.* people; 8: 26 writings to persuade people to come unto fountain of all *r.*; **Moro.** 7: 6–7 if man prays without real intent, it is not counted unto him for *r.*; 8: 8 Christ came into world to call not the *r.*, but sinners to repentance; 9: 6 we have labor to perform to conquer enemy of all *r.*

RIOTINGS, RIOTOUS (*see also* Uproar; TG Rioting and Reveling)

Mosiah 11: 14 Noah[3] spends his time in *r.* living; **Alma** 11: 20 judges stir people up to *r.*

RIPE, RIPEN

1 Ne. 17: 35 Jews were *r.* in iniquity; **2 Ne.** 28: 16 when inhabitants of earth are fully *r.* in iniquity, they shall perish; **Jacob** 5: 58 we will pluck from trees branches which are *r.*; **Mosiah** 12: 12 when blossoms of thistle are *r.*, they are driven by wind; **Alma** 10: 19 (Hel. 5: 2) if voice of people should choose iniquity, they are *r.* for destruction; 26: 5 field was *r.* and missionaries thrust in their sickles; 37: 31 (45: 16) land to be cursed unto workers of darkness unless they repent before fully *r.*; **Hel.** 6: 40 (8: 26; 11: 37) Nephites are *r.* for everlasting destruction; 13: 14 when Nephites cast the righteous out, they will be *r.* for destruction; **Ether** 2: 9 (9: 20) fulness of God's wrath will come upon inhabitants of promised land when they are *r.* in iniquity; 2: 15 if ye sin until ye are fully *r.*, ye shall be cut off from presence of the Lord.

RIPLAH, HILL—*east of river Sidon, near land of Manti*

Alma 43: 31, 35 armies of Lehi[3] attack Lamanites from hill *R.*

RIPLAKISH—*Jaredite king*

Ether 1: 23–24 (10: 4) ancestor of Morianton[1], son of Shez; 10: 4 reigns in father's stead; 10: 5–7 reigns unrighteously, afflicts people with abominations; 10: 8 is killed in rebellion.

RIPLIANCUM, WATERS OF

Ether 15: 8 both Coriantumr[2] and Shiz and his people pitch tents by waters of *R.*, which by interpretation is large, or to exceed all.

RISE, RISEN, RISING (*see also* Arise; Ascend; Awake; Jesus Christ, Resurrection of; Raise; Resurrection)

1 Ne. 10: 11 (2 Ne. 25: 13–14; 26: 1; Mosiah 3: 10; Morm. 7: 5; Ether 12: 7) Messiah to *r.* from dead; **2 Ne.** 2: 8 Messiah brings to pass the resurrection, being first to *r.* from dead; 3: 5 the Lord will *r.* up righteous branch from loins of Joseph[1]; 9: 8 if flesh should *r.* no more, men must become subject to devil; 9: 8 angel fell from God's presence, became devil, to *r.* no more; **Mosiah** 3: 10 Christ will *r.* the third day from the dead; 16: 7 if Christ had not *r.* from dead, there could have been no resurrection; 26: 1 many in *r.* generation do not understand Benjamin's words; **Alma** 5: 49 Alma[2] is called to preach to the aged, middle aged, and *r.* generation; 11: 41 (12: 8) all shall *r.* from the dead; 37: 37 when thou *r.* in morning, let heart be full of thanks unto God; 40: 4–10 time appointed to all men to *r.* from the dead; **Hel.** 14: 4 people shall know of *r.* of sun after night without darkness at birth of Christ; **3 Ne.** 1: 30 Lamanites also decrease in righteousness because of wickedness of *r.* generation; 12: 45 (Matt. 5: 45) Father maketh his sun to *r.* on the evil and the good; **Morm.** 7: 5 by power of Father, Christ hath *r.* again; 8: 28 leaders of churches shall *r.* in pride of hearts.

RITES (*see* Worship)

RIVER (*see also* Fountain; Jordan; Sidon, River; Water)

1 Ne. 2: 6–9 (16: 12) Lehi[1] names *r.* Laman; 8: 13, 17, 19, 26 Lehi[1] beholds *r.* of water near tree in vision; 12: 16 (15: 26–29) Nephi[1] beholds same *r.*, representing depths of hell; **Hel.** 3: 4 those traveling in north come to large bodies of water and many *r.*

ROAD (*see also* Highway; Path; Street; Way)

1 Ne. 8: 32 many are lost from view wandering in strange *r.*; 12: 17 mists of darkness, devil's temptations, lead men away into broad *r.*; **2 Ne.** 4: 32 shut gates of thy righteousness before me, that I may be strict in plain *r.*; **3 Ne.** 6: 8 many *r.* are made, leading from city to city; 8: 13 many level *r.* are spoiled in destruction.

ROAR (*see also* Noise; Tumult)

2 Ne. 8: 15 (Isa. 51: 15) I am the Lord thy God, whose waves *r.*; 15: 29 (Isa. 5: 29) they shall *r.* like young lions; 15: 30 (Isa. 5: 30) they shall *r.* against them like *r.* of sea.

ROB, ROBBERY, ROBBING (*see also* Robber; Steal; Thief)

2 Ne. 28: 13 false churches *r.* the poor because of fine sanctuaries; **Mosiah** 10: 17 Lamanites have taught children they should *r.* Nephites; **Alma** 1: 18 those practicing priestcraft dare not *r.* for fear of law; 16: 18 priests preach against *r.*; 20: 13 Lamanites believe Nephi[1] *r.* their fathers and that Nephites will *r.* them of property; 37: 21 *r.* of secret combinations among Jaredites should be manifest to Nephites; 42: 25 do you suppose mercy can *r.* justice; **Hel.** 2: 4 Gadianton robbers are expert in secret craft of *r.* and murder; 2: 8 (3 Ne. 4: 5) object of those in Kishkumen's band is to murder, *r.*, and gain power; 3: 14 hundredth part of Nephites' proceedings, including *r.*, cannot be contained in record; **3 Ne.** 24: 8 (Mal. 3: 8) will a man *r.* God; **Morm.** 8: 31 record shall come in day when there shall be *r.*

ROBBER (*see also* Gadianton Robbers)

Alma 11: 2 man is compelled to pay what he owed or be cast out as thief and *r.*; **4 Ne.** 1: 17 no *r.* or murderers in land.

ROBE (*see also* Apparel; Garment)

1 Ne. 8: 5 man in white *r.* stands before Lehi[1]; 14: 19–20 Nephi[1] beholds one of twelve apostles, dressed in white *r.*; **2 Ne.** 4: 33 encircle me in *r.* of thy righteousness; 9: 14 the righteous shall be clothed in *r.* of righteousness; **3 Ne.** 11: 8 Christ descends from heaven clothed in white *r.*

ROCK (*see also* Stone [noun]; TG Jesus Christ, Rock)

1 Ne. 12: 4 (19: 12; Hel. 14: 21; 3 Ne. 8: 18; 10: 9) Nephi[1] beholds *r.* rending; 13: 36 in Nephites' records shall be written the Lamb's gospel, his *r.* and salvation; 15: 15 will they not give praise to their God, their *r.* and salvation; 17: 16 Nephi[1] makes tools of ore out of *r.*; 17: 29 (2 Ne. 25: 20) Moses smote *r.* and water came forth; 20: 21 (Isa. 48: 21) the Lord clave *r.* and waters gushed forth;

2 Ne. 4: 30 my soul will rejoice in thee, my God, and *r.* of my salvation; 4: 35 God, *r.* of my righteousness; 9: 45 come unto that God who is *r.* of your salvation; 18: 14 (Isa. 8: 14) he shall be for *r.* of offense to both houses of Israel; 28: 28 he who is built upon *r.* receives truth with gladness; **Alma** 12: 14 the guilty would be glad if *r.* hid them from God's presence; **Hel.** 5: 12 upon *r.* of Redeemer ye must build foundation; **3 Ne.** 11: 39–40 whoso builds upon Christ's doctrine builds upon his *r.*; 14: 24–27 (18: 12–13; Matt. 7: 24–28) he who does Christ's sayings is compared to wise man who built house upon *r.*; **Ether** 3: 1 brother of Jared[2] makes sixteen small stones out of *r.*

ROD

1 Ne. 3: 28 Laman[1] and Lemuel smite younger brothers with *r.*; 8: 19–20, 24, 30 Lehi[1] beholds iron *r.*; 11: 25 (15: 23–24) iron *r.* is word of God; 17: 41 the Lord straitened Israel in wilderness with his *r.*; **2 Ne.** 3: 17 the Lord will give Moses power in a *r.*; 21: 1 (Isa. 11: 1) *r.* shall come forth out of stem of Jesse; 21: 4 (30: 9; Isa. 11: 4) the Lord shall smite earth with *r.* of his mouth.

ROLL (*see also* Scroll)

2 Ne. 18: 1 (Isa. 8: 1) take *r.* and write in it with pen; **Morm.** 5: 23 (9: 2) earth shall be *r.* together as scroll; 8: 22 purposes of the Lord shall *r.* on.

ROOT (*see also* Branch; Israel; Tree)

2 Ne. 15: 24 (Isa. 5: 24) their *r.* shall be rottenness; 21: 1 (Isa. 11: 1) branch shall grow out of Jesse's *r.*; 21: 10 (Isa. 11: 10) *r.* of Jesse shall stand for ensign; **Jacob** 5: 8 *r.* of this tree shall perish; 5: 18 because of strength of *r.*, wild branches bring forth tame fruit; 5: 66, 73 *r.* and top of tree to be equal; **Mosiah** 14: 2 (Isa. 53: 2) he shall grow up before him as *r.* out of dry ground; **Alma** 5: 52 the ax is laid at *r.* of tree; 22: 15 what shall I do to be born of God, having wicked spirit *r.* out of breast; 32: 37–38, 41 if ye nourish tree, it will get *r.*; 32: 42 because of diligence, faith, and patience with the word, that it may take *r.* in you, ye shall pluck its fruit; 46: 40 God prepared plants and *r.* to remove cause of disease; **3 Ne.** 25: 1 (Mal. 4: 1) day that cometh will leave the proud neither *r.* nor branch.

ROUGH (*see* Smooth)

ROUND (*see also* God, Eternal Nature of; Unchangeable)

1 Ne. 10: 19 (Alma 7: 20; 37: 12) course of the Lord is one eternal *r.*; **Morm.** 8: 8 whole face of land is one continual *r.* of murder.

RUDENESS (*see also* Malice; Revile)

1 Ne. 18: 9 elder sons of Lehi[1] and Ishmael speak with *r.*; **2 Ne.** 2: 1 Jacob[2] has suffered afflictions because of *r.* of brethren.

RUIN (*see also* Desolation; Destruction; Waste)

2 Ne. 13: 6 (Isa. 3: 6) let not this *r.* come under thy hand; 13: 8 (Isa. 3: 8) Jerusalem is *r.*; **Mosiah** 8: 8 Limhi's people discover land covered with *r.* of buildings.

RULE (*see also* Authority; Dominion; Govern; Government, Civil; Kingdom; Kingdom of God; Millennium; Regulate; Reign; Ruler)

1 Ne. 17: 39 the Lord *r.* high in heavens; **2 Ne.** 5: 3 elder brothers claim Nephi[1] thinks to *r.* over them; 13: 4, 12 (Isa. 3: 4, 12) babes and women shall *r.* over Judah; 24: 2 (Isa. 14: 2) Israel shall *r.* over oppressors; **Mosiah** 29: 13 if kings were always just men, Nephites should have kings *r.* over them; 29: 41 Nephites appoint judges to *r.* over them; **Hel.** 7: 5 robbers *r.* to get gain and glory; 12: 6 men do not desire that the Lord should *r.* over them.

RULER (*see also* Government, Civil; King; Leader; Rule; Tyrant)

1 Ne. 2: 22 (3: 29; 2 Ne. 5: 19) Nephi[1] to be made *r.* over brothers; 16: 37–38 (18: 10; 2 Ne. 5: 3) elder brothers do not want Nephi[1] to be *r.* over them; **2 Ne.** 27: 5 your *r.* and seers hath the Lord covered because of your iniquity; **Mosiah** 1: 10 (2: 30) Benjamin to proclaim Mosiah[2] *r.* over Nephites; **Alma** 2: 14 Amlici appoints *r.* over his people; 12: 20 Antionah a chief *r.* among people of Ammonihah; 35: 8 chief *r.* of Zoramites a very wicked man; 46: 5 people would establish Amalickiah as king that he might make them *r.*

RUMOR (*see also* Backbiting; Report)

1 Ne. 12: 2, 21 (14: 15–16; 2 Ne. 25: 12; Morm. 8: 30) wars and *r.* of wars; **Hel.** 16: 22 Satan spreads *r.* and contentions upon land.

RUN

2 Ne. 29: 8 when two nations *r.* together, their testimonies shall *r.* together; **Mosiah** 4: 27 not requisite that man *r.* faster than he has strength; 12: 11 thou shalt be as dry stalk which is *r.* over by beasts.

RUST

Mosiah 8: 11 Limhi's people have found sword blades cankered with *r.*;

3 Ne. 13: 19–20 (Matt. 6: 19–20) lay not up treasures upon earth, where r. corrupts.

SABBATH (*see also* BD Sabbath)

Jarom 1: 5 Nephites keep s. day holy unto the Lord; **Mosiah** 13: 16–19 (Ex. 20: 8–11) remember the s. day, to keep it holy; 18: 23 Alma[1] commands priests to keep s. day holy.

SACKCLOTH (*see also* Darkness, Physical; Grieve; Humble; Remorse; Sorrow)

2 Ne. 7: 3 (Isa. 50: 3) I make s. the covering of the heavens; **Mosiah** 11: 25 people must repent in s. and ashes; **Hel.** 11: 9 Nephites repent and humble themselves in s.

SACRAMENT (*see also* Baptism; Blood; Bread; Flesh; Jesus Christ, Types of; Ordinance; Remember, Remembrance; Wine; TG Sacrament)

3 Ne. 18: 1–4, 8–9 (20: 3–7; 26: 13) Jesus administers s. to Nephites; 18: 5 one shall be ordained with power to administer s.; 18: 6–7 (20: 8) bread in remembrance of Christ's body; 18: 10 partaking of s. witnesses that partaker will keep commandments; 18: 11 those baptized shall receive s.; 18: 11 (20: 8) wine in remembrance of Christ's blood; 18: 28–29 the unworthy not to be allowed to partake of s.; **Moro.** 4: 3 prayer for s. bread; 5: 2 prayer for s. wine; 6: 6 Nephites meet oft to partake of bread and wine in remembrance of Jesus.

SACRED (*see also* Godliness, Godly; Holiness; Holy)

1 Ne. 19: 5–6 (Jacob 1: 4) Nephi[1] records s. things on plates; **Alma** 37: 2, 14–16, 47 (50: 38; 63: 1; 3 Ne. 1: 2; 4 Ne. 1: 48; Morm. 6: 6; Ether 15: 11; Moro. 9: 24) plates are s., to be kept s.; 44: 5 s. support owed to wives and children; 50: 39 chief judge appointed with s. ordinance to judge righteously, to grant s. privilege to worship; **Hel.** 4: 12 Nephites make mock of that which is s.; **4 Ne.** 1: 27 false churches administer that which is s. unto the unworthy.

SACRIFICE (*see also* Altar; Blood; Blood, Shedding of; Broken Heart and Contrite Spirit; Idolatry; Jesus Christ, Atonement through; Jesus Christ, Types of; Justice; Law of Moses; Mercy; Offering; Ordinance; TG Sacrifice; BD Sacrifices)

1 Ne. 5: 9 Lehites offer s. and burnt offerings; **2 Ne.** 2: 7 Messiah offers himself a s. for sin; **Mosiah** 2: 3 Nephites take firstlings and offer s. according to law of Moses; **Alma** 34: 10–15 must be great and last s., infinite and eternal; 34: 11 no man can s. own blood to atone for another's sins; 34: 13 shedding of blood to stop after great and last s.; 34: 14 law points to great and last s. of Son; 34: 15 last s. brings about mercy, which overpowers justice; **3 Ne.** 9: 20 offer for s. to Christ a broken heart and contrite spirit; **Morm.** 4: 14–15, 21 Lamanites offer Nephite women and children as s. to idols.

SAD (*see also* Sorrow)

3 Ne. 13: 16 fast not as hypocrites, of s. countenance; **Morm.** 8: 3 Moroni[2] alone left to write s. tale of Nephites' destruction.

SAFE, SAFELY, SAFETY (*see also* Defence; Preserve; Protect; Refuge; Security)

1 Ne. 22: 28 all nations shall dwell s. in Holy One if they repent; **2 Ne.** 1: 9 those who keep commandments shall dwell s. in promised land; 6: 2 Nephites depend upon Nephi[1] for s.; 24: 30 (Isa. 14: 30) the needy shall lie down in s.; **Jacob** 4: 15 Jews will reject stone upon which they might build s. foundation; **Alma** 34: 16 mercy encircles the repentant in arms of s.; 48: 12 Moroni[1] labors for s. of his people; 62: 10 law strictly observed for s. of country; **3 Ne.** 2: 12 converted Lamanites and Nephites take up arms for s.; **Moro.** 1: 3 Moroni[2] wanders for s. of his life.

SAIL (*see also* Journey; Ship)

1 Ne. 18: 22–23 Lehites s. to promised land; **Alma** 63: 6, 8 many Nephites s. northward; **Morm.** 5: 18 Nephites are led by Satan as vessel tossed without s. or anchor.

SAINT, SAINTS (*see also* Believer; Children of God; Christian; Church of God; Flock; Sheep; TG Saints; BD Saints)

1 Ne. 13: 5, 9 abominable church slays s.; 14: 12 church of Lamb are s.; 14: 14 power of Lamb descends upon s.; 15: 28 awful gulf separates wicked from tree of life and s.; **2 Ne.** 9: 18 (Moro. 8: 26) s. shall inherit kingdom of God; 9: 19 God delivers s. from death and hell; 26: 3 (28: 10; Morm. 8: 27, 41) cry of blood of s. ascends to God against wicked; **Enos** 1: 3 words concerning joy of s. sink into heart of Enos[2]; **Mosiah** 3: 19 natural man is enemy to God unless he becomes s. through atonement; **Hel.** 14: 25 (3 Ne. 23: 9–13) many graves shall open, and s. shall appear; **Morm.** 8: 23 s. who have possessed land shall cry from dust; 8: 41 (Ether 8: 22) the Lord will avenge blood of s.; **Moro.** 8: 26 all s. shall dwell with God.

SALEM—*earlier name for Jerusalem in Palestine* (*see also* BD Salem)

Alma 13: 17–18 Melchizedek, king of S.

SALT (*see also* Example)

3 Ne. 12: 13 (Matt. 5: 13) you are s. of earth; 16: 15 Gentiles shall be as s. that has lost savor.

SALVATION (*see also* Baptism; Deliver; Escape; Eternal Life; Faith; Gospel; Grace; Jesus Christ, Atonement through; Jesus Christ—Savior; Obedience; Plan; Redemption; Repentance; Sanctification; Save; TG Salvation; Salvation, Plan of)

2 Ne. 2: 4 s. is free; 26: 24, 27 the Lord commands none not to partake of s.; **Enos** 1: 13 Enos prays Lamanites might be brought unto s.; **Mosiah** 3: 9 Christ comes unto his own that s. might come unto men; 3: 18 s. comes through atoning blood of Christ; 4: 6–8 atonement prepared that s. might come to those who trust in the Lord; 5: 8 no other name given whereby s. comes, except Christ; 12: 21 (15: 14; 3 Ne. 20: 40; Isa. 52: 7) how beautiful upon mountains are feet of him who publishes s.; 13: 28 s. comes not by law alone; 15: 26–27 s. comes to none who rebel against God; 15: 28 s. shall be declared to all; 15: 31 (16: 1; 3 Ne. 16: 20; 20: 35) all shall see s. of God; **Alma** 9: 28 the righteous shall reap s.; 11: 40 s. comes only to believers; 13: 21 day of s. draws nigh; 34: 31 now is the day of your s.; 34: 37 (Morm. 9: 27) work out your s. with fear before God; **Hel.** 13: 38 ye have procrastinated the day of your s.; **3 Ne.** 18: 32 ye may be means of bringing s. to repentant; **Moro.** 8: 17 little children are alike and partakers of s.

SAM—*third son of Lehi*[1] [c. 600 B.C.]

1 Ne. 2: 5 third son of Lehi[1], older brother of Nephi[1]; 2: 17 is told of the Lord's manifestations by Nephi[1]; 7: 6 (Alma 3: 6) elder brothers rebel against Nephi[1] and *S.*; 8: 3 Lehi[1] rejoices because of *S.*; **2 Ne.** 1: 28 is admonished to hearken unto Nephi[1]; 4: 11 is blessed by Lehi[1]; 5: 6 goes with Nephi[1].

SAME (*see also* Alike; Equal; Unchangeable)

1 Ne. 10: 18 (2 Ne. 27: 23; 29: 9; Alma 31: 17; Moro. 10: 7, 19) the Lord is s. yesterday, today, forever; **2 Ne.** 2: 4 Spirit is s. yesterday, today, forever; 2: 22 without the fall, Adam would have stayed in s. state; **Alma** 34: 34 s. spirit shall possess body after death.

SAMUEL[1]—*Hebrew prophet* [c. 1100 B.C.] (*see also* BD Samuel)

3 Ne. 20: 24 *S.* and all prophets have testified of Christ.

SAMUEL[2]—*Lamanite prophet* [c. 6 B.C.]

Hel. ch. 13–15 prophecy of *S.* the Lamanite to the Nephites; 13: 2 comes into Zarahemla; 13: 5 (3 Ne. 23: 9–10) speaks words of the Lord; 14: 2–6 foretells signs of Christ's birth; 14: 14, 20–28 foretells signs of Christ's death; 14: 15–19 teaches concerning resurrection and redemption; 16: 1, 3 those who believe *S.* desire baptism; 16: 2, 6 many are angry with *S.* and try to kill him; 16: 7 flees.

SANCTIFICATION, SANCTIFY (*see also* Born of God; Cleanse; Consecrate; Faith; Glorify; Grace; Holiness; Holy; Holy Ghost, Baptism of; Jesus Christ, Atonement through; Justify; Purify; Righteousness; Salvation; TG Sanctification, Sanctify)

2 Ne. 15: 16 (Isa. 5: 16) God shall be s. in righteousness; 18: 13 (Isa. 8: 13) s. the Lord himself; 27: 34 (Isa. 29: 23) they shall s. the Lord's name; **Jacob** 4: 5 law of Moses is s. unto Nephites for righteousness; **Alma** 5: 54 those brought into church have been s. by Holy Ghost; 13: 11–12 high priests are s. by Holy Ghost; **Hel.** 3: 35 s. comes from yielding heart to God; **3 Ne.** 27: 20 be baptized that ye may be s. by reception of Holy Ghost; 28: 39 three Nephites are s. in flesh; **Ether** 4: 7 Gentiles shall exercise faith, that they may become s. in the Lord; **Moro.** 4: 3 bless and s. this bread; 5: 2 bless and s. this wine; 10: 33 if ye by grace are perfect in Christ, ye are s. in Christ by grace of God.

SANCTUARY (*see also* Building [noun]; Refuge; Synagogue)

2 Ne. 28: 13 false churches rob poor because of fine s.; **Alma** 15: 17 people assemble in s. to worship; 21: 6 Amalekites in Jerusalem have built s.; **Hel.** 3: 9 people in land northward use timber to build s.; **Ether** 13: 3 New Jerusalem the holy s. of the Lord.

SAND, SANDY (*see also* Innumerable; Rock)

1 Ne. 12: 1 multitude in promised land as many as s. of sea; 20: 19 (Isa. 48: 19) thy seed also had been as the s.; **2 Ne.** 20: 22 (Isa. 10: 22) though Israel be as s. of sea, yet remnant shall return; 28: 28 (3 Ne. 11: 40; 14: 26; 18: 13) house built upon s. foundation; **Alma** 2: 27 Lamanites and Amlicites almost as numerous as s. of sea; **Morm.** 1: 7 Nephites numerous as s. of sea.

SARAH, SARAI—*wife of Abraham* [c. twentieth century B.C.] (*see also* BD Sarah)

2 Ne. 8: 2 (Isa. 51: 2) look unto *S.*, who bare you.

SARIAH—*wife of Lehi*[1] [c. 600 B.C.]

1 Ne. 2: 5 accompanies Lehi[1] from Jerusalem; 5: 1, 7 rejoices over sons' return from Jerusalem; 5: 2–3 murmurs against Lehi[1]; 5: 4–6 is comforted by Lehi[1]; 8: 14–16 is seen by Lehi[1] in vision of tree of life; 18: 19 Jacob[1] and Joseph[1] are grieved because of mother's afflictions.

SATAN (*see also* Adversary; Devil; Evil; Lucifer; TG Satan; BD Satan)

1 Ne. 13: 29 because scriptures are missing, *S.* has power over men; 22: 15, 26 (2 Ne. 30: 18; Ether 8: 26) *S.* shall have no more power over men because of righteousness; **Alma** 8: 9 (10: 25; 27: 12; Hel. 16: 23; 3 Ne. 2: 2–3; 6: 15–16; 4 Ne. 1: 28) *S.* has gotten hold of people's hearts; 12: 17 *S.* will subject the wicked according to his will; 15: 17 people pray to be delivered from *S.*; 37: 15 transgressors will be delivered up unto *S.*; **Hel.** 6: 21 (16: 22; Moro. 9: 3) *S.* stirs up hearts of Nephites; **3 Ne.** 1: 22 *S.* sends lyings among people; 7: 5 iniquity comes because people yield themselves to *S.*; 18: 18 *S.* desires to have you, that he may sift you as wheat; 28: 39 *S.* could have no power over three Nephites; **Morm.** 5: 18 Nephites are led by *S.* as chaff is driven before wind; **Ether** 15: 19 *S.* has full power over hearts of Jaredites.

SATISFY (*see also* Appease; Jesus Christ, Atonement through; Quench; Reconcile)

2 Ne. 9: 26 atonement *s.* demands of justice; 9: 51 do not spend your labor for that which cannot *s.*; **Mosiah** 14: 11 (Isa. 53: 11) he shall see the travail of his soul and be *s.*; 15: 8–9 Son *s.* demands of justice; **Alma** 34: 16 mercy can *s.* demands of justice.

SAVE (*see also* Deliver; Reclaim; Redemption; Salvation)

1 Ne. 6: 4 come unto God and be *s.*; 13: 40 all men must come unto Son or they cannot be *s.*; **2 Ne.** 2: 9 they who believe in Messiah shall be *s.*; 9: 21 (3 Ne. 9: 21) God comes into world to *s.* all men if they hearken; 9: 23 those without repentance, baptism, faith cannot be *s.*; 25: 20 (Acts 4: 12) no name other than Jesus Christ whereby man can be *s.*; 25: 23 *s.* by grace after all we can do; 28: 8 false churches claim sinner will be beaten with few stripes, then *s.*; 31: 15 (Alma 32: 13) he who endures to end shall be *s.*; 31: 19 (Alma 7: 14; 34: 18) rely upon merits of him who is mighty to *s.*; **Mosiah** 4: 8 no other conditions whereby man can be *s.*; **Alma** 2: 30 Alma[2] asks to be instrument in the Lord's hand to *s.* this people; 5: 21 no man can be *s.* except his garments are washed white; 11: 34–37 God will not *s.* his people in their sins; 12: 15 God has all power to *s.* every man who believes; 14: 10 Amulek would *s.* martyrs from flames; 26: 30 sons of Mosiah[2] suffered afflictions that they might be instruments of *s.* some soul; 27: 4 sons of Mosiah[2] are treated as angels sent to *s.* people; **Hel.** 13: 6 nothing can *s.* this people except repentance and faith; 13: 12 Zarahemla is *s.* because of the righteous; **3 Ne.** 9: 21 Christ is come into world to *s.* it from sin; 11: 33 (23: 5; Morm. 9: 23; Ether 4: 18) whoso believes and is baptized shall be *s.*; **Morm.** 2: 21 Mormon[2] gathers people to *s.* them from destruction; 7: 3 ye must come unto repentance or ye cannot be *s.*; **Moro.** 7: 26 men are *s.* by faith in Christ; 8: 15 awful wickedness to suppose God *s.* one child because of baptism, while another perishes.

SAVIOR (*see* Jesus Christ—Savior)

SAVOR

3 Ne. 12: 13 (16: 15; Matt. 5: 13) if salt loses *s.*, wherewith will earth be salted.

SAW (*see* See, Saw, Seen)

SAY (*see also* Sayings; Speak)

1 Ne. 21: 21 (Isa. 49: 21) then shalt thou *s.* in thine heart, Who hath begotten me these; **Mosiah** 2: 25 ye cannot *s.* ye are even as much as dust of earth.

SAYINGS (*see also* Commandments of God; Say; Teach; Word)

2 Ne. 4: 14 many *s.* of Nephi[1] and Lehi[1] are written on other plates; 30: 18 Nephi[1] makes end of his *s.*; **Mosiah** 1: 6 remember that these *s.* are true; **3 Ne.** 15: 1 whoso remembers and does Christ's *s.* shall be raised up; 16: 4 Christ's *s.* to be written; 18: 33 keep these *s.* which I have commanded you; 27: 33 Jesus ends his *s.*; **Morm.** 9: 26 who can deny the Lord's *s.*

SCALES

2 Ne. 30: 6 *s.* of darkness shall begin to fall from eyes.

SCARCE (*see also* Few)

Hel. 3: 10 timber exceedingly *s.* in land northward; **3 Ne.** 4: 20 wild game becomes *s.* in wilderness.

SCARLET

1 Ne. 13: 7–8 Nephi[1] beholds *s.* in abominable church.

SCATTER, SCATTERING (*see also* Destruction; Disperse; Gather; Israel, Scattering of; Israel, Ten Lost Tribes of; Remnant)

1 Ne. 17: 32 the Lord made Israel mighty, unto s. children of land to destruction.

SCENT

Alma 16: 11 great s. of dead bodies in Ammonihah; **Ether** 14: 23 s. of dead bodies troubles Jaredites.

SCEPTER (*see also* Authority; Dominion; Rule)

2 Ne. 24: 5 (Isa. 14: 5) the Lord has broken s. of the rulers.

SCOFF (*see also* Mock; Scorn)

1 Ne. 8: 26–28 those in spacious building s. at those partaking of fruit.

SCORN, SCORNFUL (*see also* Laugh; Malice; Mock; Reproach; Revile; Scoff)

1 Ne. 8: 33 those in spacious building point finger of s. at those partaking of fruit; **Alma** 4: 8 people of church are s. toward each other; 26: 23 Nephites laughed sons of Mosiah[2] to s. over preaching to Lamanites.

SCOURGE (*see also* Chasten; Destruction; Judgment; Persecution)

1 Ne. 2: 24 (2 Ne. 5: 25; Jacob 3: 3) Lamanites to be s. unto Nephites; 19: 9 (2 Ne. 6: 9; Mosiah 3: 9) world shall s. God when he comes; 19: 13 (2 Ne. 25: 16) Jews to be s. by all people for crucifying God; **Mosiah** 15: 5 Son will suffer himself to be s.; 17: 13 wicked priests s. Abinadi; **3 Ne.** 20: 28 Gentiles to be a s. to descendants of Nephites.

SCRIPTURES (*see also* Bible; Book; Book of Mormon; Commandments of God; Knowledge; Learn; Prophecy; Read; Record; Revelation; Truth; Word of God; Write; Writing; TG Scriptures; Scriptures, Lost; Scriptures, Preservation of; Scriptures, Study of; Scriptures, Value of; Scriptures, Writing of; Scriptures to Come Forth; BD Scriptures)

1 Ne. 19: 23 Nephi[1] likens s. unto Nephites; **2 Ne.** 4: 15 Nephi[1] writes on his plates many s. from brass plates; 4: 15 my soul delighteth in s.; **Jacob** 2: 23 Nephites understand not the s.; 7: 23 Nephites search s., hearken not to Sherem's words; **Alma** 12: 1 Alma[2] unfolds s. beyond what Amulek has done; 13: 20 (41: 1) if men wrest s., it will be to own destruction; 14: 1 repentant people of Ammonihah search s.; 18: 38 Ammon[2] expounds to Lamanites all s. since Lehi[1] left Jerusalem; 30: 44 s. are laid before thee and all things denote there is a God; 33: 2 (3 Ne. 10: 14) ye ought to search the s.; 37: 3 brass plates have records of holy s. on them; **Hel.** 16: 14 s. begin to be fulfilled; **3 Ne.** 1: 24 those who use s. to preach against law of Moses have not understood s.; 9: 16 s. concerning Christ's coming are fulfilled; 10: 14 he who has s. should search them; 23: 6 Jesus expounds s. to Nephites; 23: 6 Nephites to write other s. that they have not; 23: 14 Jesus expounds all s. in one which Nephites have written; 27: 5 have they not read the s.

SCROLL (*see also* Roll)

3 Ne. 26: 3 (Morm. 5: 23; 9: 2) earth to be wrapt together as s.

SEA (*see also* Flood; Island, Isle; Red Sea; Water; Waves)

2 Ne. 7: 2 (Isa. 50: 2) at his rebuke, the Lord dries up s.; 10: 20 the Lord has made s. our path; 21: 9 (Isa. 11: 9) earth to be full of knowledge of the Lord, as waters cover s.; **Mosiah** 13: 19 in six days the Lord made heaven, earth, and s.; **Ether** 2: 13 the Lord brings Jared[2] and brethren to great s.

SEAL, SEALING (*see also* Bind; Elect; Hide; Marriage; Temple)

Title Page (Moro. 10: 2) Book of Mormon is s. by hand of Moroni[2]; **1 Ne.** 14: 26 records of visions are s. to come forth in purity; **2 Ne.** 18: 16 (Isa. 8: 16) s. the law among my disciples; 27: 7 book shall be s.; 27: 22 thou shalt s. book again and hide it unto me; 33: 15 what I s. on earth shall be brought against you at judgment bar; **Mosiah** 5: 15 abound in good works, that Christ may s. you his; 17: 20 Abinadi s. truth of his words by death; **Alma** 34: 35 if ye have procrastinated day of repentance, devil s. you his; **Hel.** 10: 7 Nephi[2] given power that what he s. on earth shall be s. in heaven; **Ether** 3: 22 brother of Jared[2] to write, s. up things seen and heard.

SEANTUM—*Nephite belonging to Gadianton band* [c. 23 B.C.]

Hel. 9: 6 murders brother, chief judge; 9: 26–36 Nephi[2] sends men to house of S.; 9: 37 confesses.

SEARCH, SOUGHT (*see also* Desire; Inquire; Read; Seek; Study)

1 Ne. 2: 19 Nephi[1] has s. the Lord diligently; 5: 10 Lehi[1] s. brass plates; 10: 21 if men have s. to do wickedly, they are found unclean; **2 Ne.** 1: 25 Nephi[1] has not s. for power and authority, but for glory of God; 2: 17 fallen angel became devil, having s. evil; 9: 4 many Nephites have s. much to know things to come; 9:

44 I pray God that he view me with his all-*s.* eye; 32: 7 men will not *s.* knowledge; **Jacob** 4: 6 (3 Ne. 23: 5) *s.* the prophets; 4: 14 Jews *s.* for things they could not understand; 7: 23 Nephites *s.* the scriptures; **W of M** 1: 3 Mormon[2] *s.* among records and finds small plates; **Mosiah** 1: 7 *s.* records diligently; 27: 31 those who live without God will shrink beneath glance of his all-*s.* eye; **Alma** 14: 1 repentant people of Ammonihah *s.* scriptures; 17: 2 sons of Mosiah[2] *s.* scriptures diligently to know word of God; 33: 2 (3 Ne. 10: 14; 23: 1) ye ought to *s.* the scriptures; **Hel.** 11: 26 robbers *s.* out secret plans of Gadianton; **Morm.** 8: 23 *s.* the prophecies of Isaiah; **Ether** 8: 17 daughter of Jared[3] puts it into Akish's heart to *s.* out secret oaths; **Moro.** 6: 8 as oft as men *s.* forgiveness, they were forgiven; 7: 19 *s.* diligently in light of Christ to know good from evil.

SEASON (*see also* Time)

2 Ne. 7: 4 (Isa. 50: 4) the Lord has given me tongue of the learned that I know how to speak word in *s.*

SEAT (*see* Judgment-seat)

SEBUS, WATERS OF—*watering place in land of Ishmael*

Alma 17: 26 Ammon[2] goes where flocks are watered, called *S.*; 17: 34 Ammon[2] contends with Lamanites who stand by waters of *S.*; 18: 7 practice among Lamanites of scattering flocks at waters of *S.*; 19: 20 king slew servants whose flocks were scattered at *S.*

SECOND (*see also* Death, Spiritual; Jesus Christ, Second Coming of)

2 Ne. 6: 14 (21: 11; 25: 17; 29: 1; Jacob 6: 2) Messiah will set himself *s.* time to recover his people; **Mosiah** 26: 25 when *s.* trump sounds, they who never knew the Lord shall stand before him; **Alma** 43: 46 if ye are not guilty of first or *s.* offense, ye shall not suffer yourselves to be slain; **Morm.** 4: 20 Lamanites do not beat Nephites in Boaz until *s.* attack.

SECRET (*see also* Closet; Hide; Private; Privily; Secret Combination)

1 Ne. 20: 16 (Isa. 48: 16) I have not spoken in *s.*; **2 Ne.** 30: 17 (Mosiah 8: 17) all things *s.* shall be revealed; **Alma** 34: 26 pour out your souls to the Lord in *s.* places; 58: 20 Gid and Teomner rise from *s.* places and cut off Lamanite spies; **3 Ne.** 13: 6 (Matt. 6: 6) pray to thy Father who is in *s.*

SECRET COMBINATION (*see also* Gadianton Robbers; Murder; Oath; Plan)

2 Ne. 9: 9 (26: 22; Hel. 6: 26–30; 3 Ne. 6: 28–29; Ether 8: 15, 25; 10: 33) devil is founder of all *s.c.* of murder; 10: 15 Lord must destroy *s.* works of darkness and murder; 26: 20, 22 *s.c.* to be among Gentiles, as in times of old; **Alma** 37: 21 *s.* works of Jaredites to be made manifest; 37: 27–29 (Ether 8: 20) record of *s.* covenants of Jaredites not to be made manifest to Nephites; 37: 22, 25–26 the Lord destroyed Jaredites because they did not repent of *s.* works; 37: 23–25 the Lord will bring *s.* works out of darkness into light; 37: 28, 31 curse on land against *s.c.*; 37: 29–30 *s.c.* murdered prophets; 37: 30 God's judgments come upon workers of darkness and *s.c.*; **Hel.** 2: 8 Kishkumen's *s.c.* plans to murder, rob, get power; 2: 13 (Ether 8: 21) *s.c.* cause destruction of Nephites and Jaredites; 6: 15, 18–19 (Ether 14: 8–10) *s.c.* murder to get kingdom; 6: 22 robber bands have *s.* signs and words; 6: 22 those who enter covenant swear brother shall not be injured because of wickedness; 6: 26 *s.* covenants came to Gadianton not from records, but from devil; 6: 37–38 Lamanites hunt, Nephites support *s.c.*; 7: 25 Nephites have united themselves to *s.* band established by Gadianton; **3 Ne.** 3: 9 Giddianhi, governor of *s.* society of Gadianton; 5: 5–6 punishment puts end to *s.c.*; 6: 27–30 friends of wicked judges enter covenant to combine against righteousness; 7: 6, 9 government is destroyed by *s.c.*; **4 Ne.** 1: 42 wicked part of Nephites again build up *s.c.* of Gadianton; **Morm.** 8: 27 blood of saints will cry unto the Lord because of *s.c.*; 8: 40 why do ye build up your *s.* abominations to get gain; **Ether** 8: 13–18 Akish and followers form *s.c.*; 8: 19 the Lord works not in *s.c.*; 8: 20 *s.c.* are had among all people; 8: 22–23 nations that uphold *s.c.* shall be destroyed; 8: 24 Gentiles to awake to awful situation because of *s.c.*; 9: 26 Heth[1] embraces *s.* plans of old; 10: 33 robbers administer oaths after manner of ancients; 11: 15 rebellion arises because of *s.c.*; 11: 22 Jaredites reject words of prophets because of *s.* society; 13: 18 many are slain by sword of *s.c.*

SECURITY (*see also* Defence; Protect; Refuge; Safe, Safety)

2 Ne. 1: 32 the Lord has consecrated this land for *s.* of seed of Nephi[1] and Zoram[1]; 28: 21 devil lulls men away into carnal *s.*; **Alma** 49: 13 Moroni[1] builds forts of *s.*; 49: 21 Lamanites contend with Nephites to get into their place of *s.*; 50: 4 places of *s.* built upon towers; 60: 19 have ye neglected us because ye are surrounded by *s.*; **3 Ne.** 4: 15 Nephite armies return again to places of *s.*

SEDUCE (*see also* Captivate; Tempt)

Hel. 6: 38 robbers s. more part of the righteous Nephites.

SEE, SAW, SEEN (*see also* Behold; Eye; Look; Observe; Perceive; Sight; View; Vision; Watch)

1 Ne. 1: 8 Lehi[1] s. God sitting on throne; **2 Ne.** 3: 5 Joseph[1] truly s. our day; 9: 4 in our bodies we shall s. God; 9: 32 the blind that will not s. shall perish; 11: 2–3 Isaiah[1], Nephi[1], and Jacob[2] s. the Lord; 16: 5 (Isa. 6: 5) mine eyes have s. the King; 16: 9 (Isa. 6: 9) he said, s. ye, but they perceived not; 16: 10 (Isa. 6: 10) shut this people's eyes lest they s. and be converted; 27: 29 (Isa. 29: 18) eyes of the blind shall s. out of obscurity; **Mosiah** 15: 29 (3 Ne. 20: 32) the Lord's watchmen s. eye to eye when he brings Zion; **Alma** 19: 13 Lamoni has s. Redeemer; 30: 15 Korihor claims man cannot know of things he cannot s.; 36: 26 because of the word, many have s. eye to eye; **Hel.** 8: 17 Abraham s. of Son's coming; **3 Ne.** 11: 8 multitude s. Christ descending from heaven; 13: 6 (Matt. 6: 6) Father, who s. in secret, shall reward you openly; 17: 16–17 eye hath never s. so great and marvelous things; 17: 25 multitude bear record because each man s. for himself; 26: 18 many of those baptized s. unspeakable things; **Ether** 3: 20 brother of Jared[2] s. Jesus; 9: 22 Emer s. Son of Righteousness; 12: 6 faith is things hoped for and not s.; 12: 6 dispute not because ye s. not; 12: 39 Moroni[2] has s. Jesus.

SEED (*see also* Children of God; Descendant; Heir; Loins; Plant; BD Seed of Abraham)

1 Ne. 5: 19 (7: 1) Lehi[1] prophesies many things concerning his s.; 8: 1 (16: 11; 18: 6) Lehites gather s. of every kind; 12: 9–10 twelve ministers from s. of Nephi[1] will judge his s.; 13: 11 wrath of God to be upon s. of Lamanites; 13: 34 the Lord will manifest himself to s. of Nephi[1]; 15: 13–14 remnant of s. of Nephites to receive gospel from Gentiles; 15: 18 (22: 9; 3 Ne. 20: 25) the Lord covenants with Abraham, In thy s. shall all earth be blessed; 18: 24 (2 Ne. 5: 11; Mosiah 9: 9) Lehites plant s.; 20: 19 (Isa. 48: 19) thy s. also had been as sand; **2 Ne.** 3: 3 s. of Joseph[2] shall not utterly be destroyed; 10: 19 the Lord to consecrate this land to s. of Lehi[1]; 24: 20 (Isa. 14: 20) s. of evil-doers shall never be renowned; 29: 14 the Lord covenanted to remember Abraham's s. forever; **Jacob** 2: 30 if the Lord will raise up s., he will command his people; **Mosiah** 14: 10 (15: 10–12; Isa. 53: 10) when thou shalt make his soul an offering for sin, he shall see his s.; 15: 11–12 those who hearken to prophets are Son's s.; **Alma** 3: 9 whoever mingles his s. with Lamanites brings same curse upon his s.; 32: 28–39 word compared to s.; 46: 23 (Morm. 7: 10) Nephites are remnant of s. of Jacob[1], of Joseph[1]; **Hel.** 8: 21 s. of Zedekiah are with Nephites; **3 Ne.** 5: 23 the Lord will bring remnant of s. of Joseph[1] to knowledge of God; 5: 24 the Lord will gather remnant of s. of Jacob[1]; 22: 3 (Isa. 54: 3) thy s. shall inherit the Gentiles; **Ether** 1: 41 (2: 3) Jaredites gather s. of every kind; 13: 6, 10 New Jerusalem to be built unto remnant of s. of Joseph[1]; 13: 7 the Lord brought remnant of s. of Joseph[1] out of Jerusalem.

SEEK, SOUGHT (*see also* Ask; Desire; Inquire; Look; Pray; Search; Watch)

1 Ne. 2: 19 Nephi[1] has s. the Lord diligently; 10: 17 power of Holy Ghost is gift of God unto all who diligently s. him; 10: 19 (3 Ne. 14: 7–8; Matt. 7: 7–8) he who diligently s. shall find; 10: 21 those who have s. to do wickedly shall be found unclean; 13: 37 blessed are they who s. to bring forth Zion; **2 Ne.** 1: 25 Nephi[1] has not s. power and authority, but glory of God; 2: 17 fallen angel became devil, having s. evil; 2: 27 devil s. that all men might be miserable; 21: 10 (Isa. 11: 10) Gentiles shall s. to ensign; 26: 29 those practicing priestcraft do not s. welfare of Zion; 27: 27 (28: 9) wo unto them that s. deep to hide counsel from the Lord; **Jacob** 2: 18 (3 Ne. 13: 33) before ye s. riches, s. kingdom of God; 2: 19 after obtaining hope in Christ, ye shall obtain riches if ye s. them; 2: 19 s. riches to do good; 4: 10 s. not to counsel the Lord, but to take counsel; 4: 14 Jews s. for things they could not understand; **Mosiah** 27: 10 (Alma 36: 6) Alma[2] and sons of Mosiah[2] s. to destroy church; **Alma** 32: 13 sometimes if man is compelled to be humble, he s. repentance; 39: 14 s. not after riches or vain things of world; 46: 10 Amalickiah leads many to s. to destroy church; 60: 36 Moroni[1] s. not for power or honor, but glory of God; **3 Ne.** 13: 33 (Matt. 6: 33) s. ye first the kingdom of God; **Ether** 8: 25 those who build up secret combinations s. to overthrow freedom of all lands; 12: 41 s. this Jesus of whom prophets have written; **Moro.** 6: 8 as oft as men s. repentance with real intent, they were forgiven; 7: 45 charity s. not her own; 8: 28 Nephites s. to put down all power and authority from God.

SEEN (*see* See, Saw, Seen)

SEER (*see also* Prophet; Revelator; Translation; BD Seer)

2 Ne. 3: 6–8, 11–15 the Lord to raise choice latter-day s. from fruit of loins of Joseph[1]; 27: 5 the Lord has covered s. because of people's iniquity; **Mosiah** 8: 13 (28: 16) whoever is commanded to look in interpreters is called s.; 8: 15–16 s. is revelator and prophet, no greater gift; 8: 17 s. can know past, future, reveal all things.

SEEZORAM—*member of Gadianton band, elected chief judge* [c. 26 B.C.]

Hel. 8: 27–28 member of Gadianton band; 9: 23 Nephi[2] is accused of murdering *S.*; 9: 26–37 Nephi[2] reveals *S.* was murdered by brother.

SELL, SOLD

1 Ne. 5: 14 (Alma 10: 3) Joseph[1] was s. into Egypt; **2 Ne.** 7: 1 (Isa. 50: 1) for your iniquities you have s. yourselves; 26: 10 (3 Ne. 20: 38) Nephites s. themselves for naught; **Alma** 46: 23 let us keep commandments, or we be cast into prison or s. or slain; **Hel.** 6: 8 Nephites and Lamanites have free intercourse to buy and s.; **3 Ne.** 27: 32 fourth generation will s. the Lord for silver and gold; **Morm.** 8: 38 Nephites s. themselves for that which will canker; **Ether** 10: 22 Jaredites buy and s. to get gain.

SEND, SENT

2 Ne. 16: 8 (Isa. 6: 8) here am I, s. me; **Mosiah** 3: 13 the Lord has s. his holy prophets among men; **3 Ne.** 20: 26 Father s. Son; 24: 1 (Mal. 3: 1) the Lord will s. messenger to prepare way; 25: 5 (Mal. 4: 5) the Lord will s. Elijah the prophet; 27: 13 Christ came into world to do Father's will because Father s. him; 28: 34 wo unto those who will not hearken to words of those whom Jesus has s. among them; **Ether** 4: 12 he who will not believe Christ will not believe Father who s. him; **Moro.** 7: 16 every thing which persuades to believe in Christ is s. by power and gift of Christ.

SENINE—*Nephite coin* (*see also* Coin)

Alma 11: 3 judges receive s. of gold for a day; 11: 3, 7 senum of silver is equal to s. of gold; 11: 5, 8 s. is half value of seon; 30: 33 Alma[2] has never received so much as one s. for labor in church; **3 Ne.** 12: 26 thou shalt not come out of prison until thou hast paid the uttermost s.

SENSE

2 Ne. 2: 11 without opposition, it must have neither s. nor insensibility; **Mosiah** 2: 38 justice awakens the unrepentant to lively s. of guilt; 4: 5 knowledge of God's goodness awakens s. of own nothingness; **Alma** 7: 22 Alma[2] speaks to awaken people to s. of duty toward God; **Ether** 8: 24 Jaredites will awake to s. of awful situation.

SENSUAL (*see also* Carnal; Flesh; Lust; Nature, Natural)

Mosiah 16: 3 (Alma 42: 10) because of fall, mankind became carnal, s., devilish.

SENT (*see* Send, Sent)

SENUM—*Nephite coin* (*see also* Coin)

Alma 11: 3 judges receive s. of silver each day; 11: 3, 7 s. of silver is equal to senine of gold; 11: 11 two s. equal one amnor; 11: 12 four s. equal one ezrom; 11: 15 shiblon is half of a s.

SEON—*Nephite coin* (*see also* Coin)

Alma 11: 5, 8 twice the value of senine; 11: 9 shum of gold equals two s.

SEPARATION, SEPARATE, SEPARATELY (*see also* TG Separation)

1 Ne. 13: 12 man among Gentiles is s. from Lamanites by many waters; **Mosiah** 26: 4 unbelievers in rising generations are s. people as to faith; **Alma** 3: 14 the Lord sets mark on Lamanites that they may be s. from Nephites; 5: 57 come ye out from the wicked and be s.; 29: 16 my soul is carried away, even unto s. from body, because of joy; 31: 2 Alma[2] sorrows because of s. of Zoramites from Nephites; 35: 16 Alma[2] will give charge to sons s.; **3 Ne.** 15: 19 Nephites were s. from Jews because of Jews' iniquity.

SEPULCHRE (*see also* Grave)

1 Ne. 19: 10 (2 Ne. 25: 13) Christ to be buried in s.; **Alma** 19: 1, 5 king Lamoni to be laid in s.

SERAPHIM (*see also* BD Seraphim)

2 Ne. 16: 2 (Isa. 6: 2) s. stand above God's throne; 16: 6–7 (Isa. 6: 6–7) s. touches lips of Isaiah[1] with coal.

SERMON ON THE MOUNT

3 Ne. ch. 12–14 (Matt. ch. 5–7) Christ teaches Nephites as he taught the Jews.

SERPENT (*see also* Devil; Jesus Christ, Types of; BD Fiery Serpents; Serpent, Brazen)

1 Ne. 17: 41 (2 Ne. 25: 20) the Lord sent fiery flying s. among Israelites and prepared way for healing; **2 Ne.** 2: 18 (Mosiah 16: 3) old s., the devil, tempted Eve; **2 Ne.** 24: 29 (Isa. 14: 29) out of s's root shall come cockatrice, and his fruit shall be fiery flying s.; 25: 20 the Lord gave Moses power to heal nations bitten by poisonous s.; 25: 20 if Israelites would cast eyes unto s. raised by Moses in wilderness, they would be healed; **Hel.** 8: 14–15 (Alma 33: 19–22) brazen s. lifted up by Moses in wilderness is type of Christ; **3 Ne.** 14: 10 (Matt. 7: 10) if son asks for fish, will father give him s.; **Morm.** 8: 24 poisonous s. could not harm saints; 9: 24 those that believe shall take up s.; **Ether** 9: 31–33 poisonous s. come upon land; 10: 19 poisonous s. are destroyed.

SERVANT (*see also* Angel; Angels of the Devil; Disciple; Follow, Follower; Messenger; Minister [noun]; Prophet; Serve, Service)

1 Ne. 20: 20 (Isa. 48: 20) the Lord hath redeemed his s. Jacob[1]; 21: 3 (Isa. 49: 3) thou art my s., O Israel; **2 Ne.** 9: 41 Holy One employs no s. at gate; **Jacob** ch. 5 s. aids lord in caring for vineyard; **Mosiah** 2: 21 if ye serve God with whole souls, yet ye would be unprofitable s.; 14: 11 (Isa. 53: 11) the Lord's righteous s. shall justify many; 21: 33 Ammon[1] declines to baptize, considering himself unworthy s.; 22: 4 if thou hast not found me to be unprofitable s., listen to my words; **Alma** 17: 25 Ammon[2] desires to be Lamoni's s.; 17: 27–39 Ammon[2] helps king's s. tend flocks; **Hel.** 5: 29, 32 seek no more to destroy my s.; **3 Ne.** 20: 43 the Lord's s. shall deal prudently; 21: 10 life of the Lord's s. shall be in his hand; 22: 17 (Isa. 54: 17) this is the heritage of s. of the Lord; **Moro.** 7: 11 s. of devil cannot follow Christ, follower of Christ cannot be s. of devil.

SERVE, SERVICE (*see also* Duty; Help; Minister [verb]; Ministry; Obedience; Relief; Servant; Work [noun]; Worship)

2 Ne. 1: 7 if people s. the Lord according to his commandments, land shall have liberty; **Mosiah** 2: 12 as I have been suffered to spend my days in your s., I have not sought riches of you; 2: 17 when ye are in s. of fellow beings, ye are in s. of God; 2: 18 if king labors to s. you, ought not ye to labor to s. one another; 2: 21 if ye s. Creator with whole souls, yet are ye unprofitable servants; 4: 14 ye will not suffer children to s. devil; 5: 13 how knoweth a man the master whom he has not s.; 7: 33 if ye s. God with full diligence of mind, he will deliver you from bondage; **3 Ne.** 13: 24 (Matt. 6: 24) no man can s. two masters; **Morm.** 9: 28 ask that ye will s. the true and living God; **Ether** 2: 8 those who possess land of promise must s. God or be swept off; **Moro.** 7: 13 every thing which invites to s. God is inspired of God.

SET (*see* Defiance; Heart; Naught; Order)

SETH[1]—*son of Adam* (*see* BD Seth)

No references in Book of Mormon.

SETH[2]—*Jaredite*

Ether 1: 10–11 (11: 10) son of Shiblon, father of Ahah; 11: 9 brought into captivity all his days.

SEVEN, SEVENTH (*see also* Sabbath)

2 Ne. 14: 1 (Isa. 4: 1) s. women will take hold of one man; **Mosiah** 13: 18 the s. day, the sabbath, thou shalt not do any work.

SHADOW (*see also* Jesus Christ, Types of; Type)

1 Ne. 21: 2 (2 Ne. 8: 16; Isa. 49: 2; 51: 16) in s. of his hand he hath hid me; **2 Ne.** 14: 6 (Isa. 4: 6) tabernacle shall be for s. in daytime from heat; **Mosiah** 3: 15 the Lord shows many types and s. to his people; 13: 10 what Noah[3] will do with Abinadi shall be type and s. of things to come; 16: 14 law of Moses is s. of things to come; **Alma** 7: 20 God has no s. of turning from right to left; 37: 43 workings of Liahona are not without a s.; **Morm.** 9: 10 no s. of changing in God.

SHAFT

1 Ne. 21: 2 (Isa. 49: 2) the Lord has made me a polished s.; **Hel.** 5: 12 devil will send s. in whirlwind.

SHAKE, SHOOK, SHAKEN (*see also* Earthquake; Fear; Fear of God; Quake; Tremble)

1 Ne. 2: 14 Lehi[1] speaks to Laman[1] and Lemuel until their frames s.; 17: 45 (Mosiah 27: 15; Hel. 12: 11) God's voice causes earth to s.; **2 Ne.** 1: 13, 23 s. off awful chains that bind you; 4: 31 wilt thou make me s. at appearance of sin; 9: 40 the righteous love the truth and are not s. by it; 9: 44 Jacob[2] s. brethren's iniquities from his soul; 12: 19 (Isa. 2: 19) he ariseth to s. terribly the earth; 23: 13 (Isa. 13: 13) the Lord will s. the heavens; 24: 16 (Isa. 14: 16) is this the man that did s. kingdoms; 28: 19 kingdom of devil must s.; **Jacob** 7: 5 Sherem hopes to s. Jacob[2] from faith, but he cannot be s.; **Mosiah** 27: 18 (Alma 38: 7) voice of angel s. earth; **Alma** 14: 27 earth s., prison walls rent in twain; 29: 1 O that I might speak with a voice to s. the earth; 48: 17 if all men were like Moroni[1], power of hell would have been s.; **Hel.** 5: 27, 42 the Lord causes earth and prison walls to s.; **3 Ne.** 8: 6 thunder causes whole earth to s. at Christ's death; 20: 37 s. thyself from the dust, O Jerusalem;

Morm. 8: 24 in the Lord's name saints could cause earth to s.; **Ether** 4: 9 at the Lord's word, earth shall s.

SHAME (*see also* Ashamed; Guilt; Humble; Reproach)

2 Ne. 7: 6 (Isa. 50: 6) I hid not my face from s. and spitting; 9: 18 saints who have endured crosses of world and despised s. of it shall inherit kingdom; **Jacob** 1: 8 all men should suffer Christ's cross and bear s. of world; 2: 6 to testify of Nephites' wickedness causes Jacob[2] to shrink with s. before presence of Maker; 6: 9 power of resurrection will bring men to stand with s. before God; **Alma** 12: 15 men will acknowledge to their s. that God's judgments are just; **3 Ne.** 22: 4 be not confounded, for thou shalt not be put to s., shalt forget s. of youth.

SHARED—*Jaredite military leader*

Ether 13: 23–24, 27–29 gives battle to Coriantumr[2] and sons; 13: 30 is slain.

SHARED, BROTHER OF (*see* Gilead)

SHARP, SHARPNESS (*see also* Cut)

1 Ne. 21: 2 (Isa. 49: 2) he hath made my mouth like a s. sword; **2 Ne.** 1: 26 s. of words of Nephi[1] is s. of power of word of God; **3 Ne.** 8: 7 exceeding s. lightnings at Christ's death; **Moro.** 9: 4 when Mormon[2] speaks word of God with s., Nephites tremble.

SHAVE, SHAVEN (*see also* Shorn)

2 Ne. 17: 20 (Isa. 7: 20) the Lord shall s. with razor that is hired; **Enos** 1: 20 (Mosiah 10: 8) Lamanites wander about with heads s.

SHAZER—*campsite in Arabian desert*

1 Ne. 16: 13–14 Lehites camp at *S.*

SHEAR (*see* Shorn)

SHEARERS

Mosiah 14: 7 (15: 6; Isa. 53: 7) as sheep before s. is dumb, so Son opened not his mouth.

SHEAVES

Alma 26: 5 all the day long did ye labor, and behold the number of your s.; **3 Ne.** 20: 18 the Lord will gather his people as man gathers s. into floor.

SHED (*see also* Blood, Shedding of)

1 Ne. 11: 22 tree represents love of God, which s. itself abroad in hearts; **Mosiah** 25: 9 when Nephites think of brethren slain by Lamanites, they s. many tears of sorrow.

SHEEP (*see also* Animal; Flock; Fold; Jesus Christ—Good Shepherd; Lamb; Saint; Shepherd; BD Sheep)

1 Ne. 22: 25 the Lord numbers, feeds his s.; **Mosiah** 14: 6 (Isa. 53: 6) all we, like s., have gone astray; 14: 7 (15: 6; Isa. 53: 7) as s. before shearers is dumb, so he opened not his mouth; 26: 20 Alma[1] is called to gather the Lord's s.; 26: 21 (Alma 5: 60) he who hears the Lord's voice is his s.; **Alma** 5: 37 the wicked have gone astray, as s. having no shepherd; 5: 38–39 those who do not hearken to voice of good shepherd are not his s.; 25: 12 priests of Noah[3] to be scattered and slain as s. without shepherd; **Hel.** 15: 13 Lamanites to come to knowledge of true shepherd and be numbered among his s.; **3 Ne.** 14: 15 (Matt. 7: 15) beware of false prophets who come in s's clothing; 15: 17 (John 10: 16) other s. I have which are not of this fold; 15: 21 Nephites are the other s.; 15: 24 Nephites are numbered among the Lord's s.; 16: 1–3 the Lord has yet other s. not of this fold; 18: 31 the Lord knows his s.; 20: 16 (21: 12; Micah 5: 8) Israel shall be among Gentiles as lion among flocks of s.; **Ether** 9: 18 Jaredites have s.

SHELEM, MOUNT—*mountain in Old World named by Jaredites*

Ether 3: 1 brother of Jared[2] obtains stones in *S.*

SHEM[1]—*son of Noah[1]*

No references in Book of Mormon.

SHEM[2]—*Nephite commander* [C. A.D. 385]

Morm. 6: 14 has fallen with his ten thousand.

SHEM, CITY OF AND LAND OF—*Nephite land north of Antum and Jashon*

Morm. 2: 20 Nephites driven northward to land of *S.*; 2: 21 Nephites gather to *S.* and fortify it.

SHEMLON, LAND OF—*region bordering on land of Lehi-Nephi*

Mosiah 10: 7 Zeniff sends spies round about *S.*; 11: 12 is possessed by Lamanites; 19: 6 Lamanites come from *S.* to attack people of Noah[3]; 20: 1–5 Lamanites' daughters gather in *S.*, are carried captive by priests of Noah[3]; 24: 1 Amulon and brethren are appointed teachers in *S.*; **Alma** 23: 8, 12 Lamanites in *S.* are converted to the Lord.

SHEMNON—*one of twelve Nephite disciples* [C. A.D. 34]

3 Ne. 19: 4 is called by Jesus to minister to Nephites.

SHEPHERD (*see also* Jesus Christ—Good Shepherd; Pastor; Sheep)

1 Ne. 13: 41 one *S.* over all earth; 22: 25 (3 Ne. 15: 17; 16: 3; John 10: 16) there shall be one fold and one s.; **Mosiah** 8: 21 men are as wild flock that fleeth from s.; **Alma** 5: 37 the wicked have gone astray, as sheep having no s.; 5: 39 if men are not sheep of good s., devil is their s.; 25: 12 priests of Noah³ to be scattered and slain as sheep without s.; 15: 13 Lamanites to be brought to knowledge of true s.; **Morm.** 5: 17 Nephites once had Christ for their s.

SHEREM—*antichrist* [c. fifth century B.C.]

Jacob 7: 1–2 denies Christ; 7: 7 challenges Jacob²; 7: 13 demands a sign; 7: 15–20 is stricken and dies.

SHERRIZAH

Moro. 9: 7 Lamanites take prisoners from tower of *S.*; 9: 16–17 many women survivors in *S.*

SHEUM—*unidentified crop cultivated by Nephites*

Mosiah 9: 9 people of Zeniff till ground with seed of s.

SHEZ¹—*middle Jaredite king*

Ether 1: 24–25 son of Heth, father of Riplakish; 10: 1–2 attempts to build up broken nation; 10: 4 builds cities, lives to old age.

SHEZ²—*son of Shez¹*

Ether 10: 3 rebels against father, but is slain by robber.

SHIBLOM¹ [or Shiblon]—*late Jaredite king*

Ether 1: 11–12 son of Com², father of Seth²; 11: 4 is anointed king; 11: 5–7 great wickedness and destruction in days of *S.*; 11: 9 is slain.

SHIBLOM²—*Nephite commander* [c. A.D. 385]

Morm. 6: 14 falls with his ten thousand.

SHIBLON—*son of Alma²* [c. 74 B.C.] (*see also* Shiblom¹)

Alma 31: 7 (38: 1) second son of Alma², goes on mission to Zoramites; ch. 38 commandments of Alma² to *S.*; 49: 30 is successful in ministry; 63: 1 takes charge of sacred things; 63: 10–11 confers sacred things on Helaman³, dies.

SHIBLON—*Nephite coin* (*see also* Coin)

Alma 11: 15 s. is half a senum, a s. for half a measure of barley; 11: 16 a shiblum is half a s.; 11: 19 antion of gold equals three s.

SHIBLUM—*Nephite coin* (*see also* Coin)

Alma 11: 16 s. is half a shiblon; 11: 17 leah is half a s.

SHILOAH, WATERS OF—*pool near Jerusalem¹*

2 Ne. 18: 6 (Isa. 8: 6) people refuse waters of *S.*

SHILOM, CITY OF AND LAND OF—*small region next to land of Lehi-Nephi*

Mosiah 7: 7 Ammon¹ meets Lamanite king in *S.*; 7: 21 city of *S.* is given to Zeniff by Lamanite king; 9: 6 *S.* is possessed by Zeniff; 9: 8 walls of city of *S.* are repaired; 9: 14 Lamanites steal flocks in *S.*; 10: 8 Lamanites come upon *S.*; 10: 19–20 Lamanite army attacks, is repulsed; 11: 12–13 tower and buildings are built in *S.*; 22: 8–11 Limhi's people travel around *S.* during escape; 24: 1 Amulon and brethren are made teachers over people in *S.*; **Alma** 23: 8, 12 Lamanites in *S.* are converted.

SHIM, HILL—*in land Antum*

Morm. 1: 3 Ammaron deposited records in hill called *S.*; 4: 23 Mormon² takes records from hill *S.*; **Ether** 9: 3 Omer and family travel near hill of *S.* and place where Nephites were destroyed.

SHIMNILOM—*city in land of Nephi*

Alma 23: 8, 12 Lamanites in *S.* are converted to the Lord.

SHINE, SHINING, SHONE (*see also* Enlighten; Illuminate; Light)

2 Ne. 14: 5 (Isa. 4: 5) the Lord will create upon every dwelling-place of mount Zion the s. of flaming fire by night; 19: 2 (Isa. 9: 2) light has s. upon them that dwell in land of shadow of death; 23: 10 (Isa. 13: 10) moon shall not cause her light to s.; **Mosiah** 13: 5 Abinadi's face s. with exceeding luster; **Alma** 5: 50 glory of King shall soon s. forth among men; 37: 23 the Lord will prepare stone which will s. forth in darkness unto light; 40: 25 the righteous shall s. forth in kingdom of God; **Hel.** 5: 36 faces of Nephi² and Lehi⁴ s. as faces of angels; **3 Ne.** 12: 16 (Matt. 5: 16) let your light so s. before this people; 18: 24 hold up your light that it may s. unto the world; 19: 25 light of Jesus' countenance s. upon disciples; **Morm.** 8: 16 record shall s. forth out of darkness; **Ether** 3: 1, 4 (6: 3) brother of Jared asks the Lord to make stones s.

SHIP (*see also* Barge; Sail; Vessel)

1 Ne. 17: 8, 49–51 Nephi[1] is commanded to build s.; 17: 17 elder brothers murmur at building of s.; 18: 1–3 the Lord shows Nephi[1] how to build s.; 18: 4 Nephi[1] finishes building s.; 18: 6–8 Lehites enter s. and sail to promised land; **Alma** 63: 5 Hagoth builds large s. for voyages northward; 63: 7 other s. are built; 63: 8 s. are never heard of again; **Hel.** 3: 10 much timber sent to land northward by s.; 3: 14 record does not include full account of shipping and building of s.

SHIZ—*Jaredite military leader*

Ether 14: 17 brother of Lib, pursues Coriantumr[2]; 14: 18 fear of *S.* goes throughout land; 14: 19–20 people are divided between Coriantumr[2] and *S.*; 14: 24 swears to avenge himself upon Coriantumr[2] of brother's blood; 14: 26–31 (15: 6–28) *S*'s army battles with army of Coriantumr[2]; 15: 5 exchanges letters with Coriantumr[2]; 15: 29–31 is slain by Coriantumr[2].

SHOE (*see* Latchet)

SHORN (*see also* Shave)

Alma 3: 4–5 heads of Lamanites are s.; **3 Ne.** 4: 7 heads of robbers are s.

SHORTEN

2 Ne. 7: 2 (Isa. 50: 2) is the Lord's hand s., that he cannot redeem.

SHOULDER

1 Ne. 21: 22 (22: 6; 2 Ne. 6: 6; Isa. 49: 22) Israel's daughters shall be carried upon Gentiles' s.; **2 Ne.** 19: 6 (Isa. 9: 6) government shall be upon Messiah's s.; **Mosiah** 24: 14 the Lord will ease burdens put upon s. of people of Alma[1].

SHOUT (*see also* Praise; Rejoice)

2 Ne. 31: 13 those who receive Holy Ghost shall s. praises to Holy One.

SHOW, SHOWN (*see also* Appeal; God, Manifestations of; Jesus Christ, Appearances of; Manifest; Revelation; Sign; Unfold)

2 Ne. 32: 5 the Lord will s. all who receive Holy Ghost what they should do; 33: 11 Christ will s. that these words are his words; **Jacob** 4: 7 the Lord s. unto men their weakness; **Hel.** 7: 23 the Lord will not s. unto the wicked of his strength; **3 Ne.** 19: 35 the Lord will not s. unto Jews so great miracles because of unbelief; 28: 30 three Nephites can s. themselves to whomever it seemeth them good; **Morm.** 8: 35 Christ has s. Moroni[2] great and marvelous things to come to pass; **Ether** 3: 25 the Lord s. brother of Jared[2] all inhabitants of earth; 4: 8 unto those who deny these things, the Lord will s. no greater things; 12: 7 Christ s. himself not to the world.

SHRINK (*see also* Withdraw)

2 Ne. 9: 46 prepare yourselves for judgment, that ye may not s. with fear; **Jacob** 2: 6 to testify of wickedness causes Jacob[2] to s. from presence of maker; **Mosiah** 2: 38 (3: 25) sense of guilt causes unrepentant to s. from presence of the Lord; 27: 31 men will s. beneath glance of God's all-piercing eye; **Alma** 43: 48 men of Moroni[1] are about to s. from Lamanites.

SHULE—*early Jaredite king*

Ether 1: 30–31 (7: 7; 8: 1) son of Kib, father of Omer; 7: 7 is born in captivity; 7: 8–9 restores kingdom to father; 7: 11, 26–27 rules righteously; 7: 12 begets many children; 7: 13 gives Corihor power in kingdom; 7: 15–16 Noah[2] rebels against *S.*; 7: 15–17 Noah[2] takes *S.* captive; 7: 18–22 sons help *S.* regain kingdom; 7: 23–25 *S.* protects the prophets.

SHUM—Nephite coin (*see also* Coin)

Alma 11: 5, 9 *s.* of gold is twice the value of a seon.

SHURR, VALLEY OF

Ether 14: 28 Coriantumr[2] and army pitch tents in *S.*

SHUT

2 Ne. 4: 32 may gates of hell be s. continually before me; 4: 32 wilt thou not s. gates of righteousness before me; 9: 9 except for resurrection, our spirits must have been s. out of God's presence; 16: 10 (Isa. 6: 10) s. their eyes lest they see and be converted; **3 Ne.** 13: 6 (Matt. 6: 6) when thou has s. thy door, pray to Father who is in secret; **Ether** 4: 9 at the Lord's command, heavens are opened and are s.

SICK, SICKNESS (*see also* Disease; Fever; Heal; Infirmity; Needy)

1 Ne. 11: 31 (Mosiah 3: 5) multitudes of people who are s. are healed by Lamb; **Jacob** 2: 19 seek riches to administer relief to the s.; **Alma** 1: 30 Nephites do not send away any who are s.; 7: 11 Son will take upon himself the s. of his people; 9: 22 Nephites have been saved from s. by the Lord; 15: 3 Zeezrom lies s. at Sidom; **3 Ne.** 7: 22 those healed of s. have been wrought upon by Spirit; 17: 7–9 (26: 15) Jesus heals the s. among the Nephites; **4 Ne.** 1: 5 Jesus' disciples heal the s.; **Morm.** 8: 37 ye love your money more than ye love the s.; 8: 39 why do ye suffer the s. to pass by you without notice; 9: 24 believers shall lay hands upon the s., and they shall recover; **Moro.** 8: 8 the whole need no physician, but they who are s.

SICKLE (*see also* Reap)

Alma 26: 5 missionaries thrust in their s. and reaped.

SIDE

3 Ne. 11: 14–15 multitude thrust hands into Jesus' s.

SIDOM, LAND OF

Alma 15: 1 Alma[2] and Amulek find converts from Ammonihah in *S.*; 15: 3 Zeezrom lies sick in *S.*; 15: 10–11 Zeezrom is healed; 15: 13 Alma[2] establishes church in *S.*; 15: 14–17 people repent and are baptized.

SIDON, RIVER—*most prominent river in Nephite territory, runs north to sea* (*see also* River)

Alma 2: 15 hill Amnihu is on east of *S.*; 2: 34 Lamanites camp on west of *S.*; 4: 4 many are baptized in waters of *S.*; 22: 29 wilderness at *S.*

SIEGE

2 Ne. 26: 15 the Lord will lay s. with a mount against seed of Nephites and Lamanites; **3 Ne.** 4: 16 robbers lay s. around Nephites; **Ether** 14: 5 Coriantumr[2] lays s. to wilderness.

SIFT

Alma 37: 15 transgressors will be delivered to Satan, that he may s. them as chaff before wind; **3 Ne.** 18: 18 Satan desires to have you, that he may s. you as wheat.

SIGHT (*see also* Eye; See)

2 Ne. 15: 21 (Isa. 5: 21) wo unto the prudent in their own s.; 21: 3 (Isa. 11: 3) rod out of stem of Jesse shall not judge after s. of his eyes; **Mosiah** 3: 5 the Lord will cause the blind to receive their s.; **3 Ne.** 7: 20 Nephi[3] does many miracles in s. of people; **4 Ne.** 1: 5 Jesus' disciples cause the blind to receive s.; **Ether** 3: 25 (12: 20–21) the Lord withholds nothing from s. of brother of Jared[2].

SIGN (*see also* Faith; Jesus Christ, Second Coming of; Miracle; Prophecy; Token; Wonder; TG Sign Seekers; Signs)

1 Ne. 11: 7 Nephi[1] given s. of man descending out of heaven as s.; 19: 10 three days of darkness to be s. of Christ's death; **2 Ne.** 17: 14 (Isa. 7: 14) the Lord will give s., virgin shall conceive and bear son; 18: 18 (Isa. 8: 18) I and the children the Lord hath given me are for s. in Israel; 26: 3 s. to be given of Christ's birth, death, resurrection; **Jacob** 7: 13 Sherem asks Jacob[2] to show him a s.; 7: 14 if God shall smite thee, let that be a s.; **Mosiah** 3: 15 the Lord shows his people many s. and types of his coming; **Alma** 30: 43–50 Korihor asks for a s., is struck dumb; 30: 44 will ye say, Show me a s., when ye have testimonies of prophets; 32: 17 many will ask for s. before they will believe; 37: 27 s. and wonders of secret combinations to be kept from people; **Hel.** 2: 7 servant of Helaman[3] gives Kishkumen a s.; 6: 22 secret combinations have secret s. and words; 14: 3 Samuel the Lamanite prophesies s. of Christ's birth, night without darkness; 14: 14, 20–25 Samuel the Lamanite prophesies s. of Christ's death; **3 Ne.** 1: 13, 16 on this night will s. be given, and on the morrow come I into world; 1: 22 Satan hardens hearts, they believe not s. they have seen; 2: 1 people begin to forget s. and wonders they have seen; 8: 3 people begin to look for s. of Christ's death; 21: 1 gathering of Israel a s. that prophecies are about to be fulfilled; **Morm.** 9: 24–25 (Ether 4: 18; Mark 16: 17) these s. shall follow them that believe.

SILENCE, SILENT

2 Ne. 1: 14 Lehi[1] to lie down in cold and s. grave; **Alma** 51: 7 people of liberty put king-men to s.; 55: 17 preparations for war done in profound s.; **3 Ne.** 10: 1–2 s. in the land for many hours.

SILK (*see also* Cloth)

1 Ne. 13: 7 Nephi[1] sees s. in abominable church; **Alma** 1: 29 (4: 6) people have abundance of s.; **Ether** 9: 17 (10: 24) Jaredites have all manner of s.

SILLY (*see also* Foolish)

Alma 30: 31 Korihor accuses priests of leading people after s. traditions.

SILVER (*see also* Metal; Ore)

1 Ne. 2: 4 Lehi[1] leaves s. and precious things behind; 13: 7 gold and s. in abominable church; 18: 25 gold and s. found in promised land; **2 Ne.** 5: 15 Nephi[1] teaches people to work in s.; **Jarom** 1: 8 (Alma 1: 29; 4: 6; Hel. 6: 9) Nephites become rich in gold and s.; **Ether** 9: 17 Jaredites have all manner of s. and precious things.

SIMILITUDE (*see also* Jesus Christ, Types of; Likeness; Shadow; Type)

Jacob 4: 5 Abraham's offering Isaac is s. of God and his Son.

SIMPLE, SIMPLENESS (*see also* Ease; Easiness; Light [adj.]; Plain)

1 Ne. 17: 41 Israelites would not be

healed because of s. of the way; **2 Ne.** 3: 20 descendants of Lehi[1] will cry from dust in s.; **Alma** 37: 6 by s. things are great things brought to pass.

SIN, SINFUL (*see also* Abomination; Apostasy; Captive, Captivity; Confession of Sins; Darkness, Spiritual; Death, Spiritual; Devil; Disobedience; Err; Evil; Fall of Man; Forgive; Guilt; Iniquity; Jesus Christ, Atonement through; Jesus Christ—Savior; Justice; Offense; Pollute; Punishment; Remission; Repentance; Sinner; Transgression; Trespass; Wicked; TG Sin)

2 Ne. 2: 13 if no s., then no righteousness; 2: 23 Adam could have done no good, for he knew no s.; 4: 19 heart of Nephi[1] groans because of his s.; 4: 31 wilt thou make me shake at appearance of s.; 9: 38 those who die in s. will remain in s.; 9: 45 turn away from s.; 9: 48 Jacob[2] teaches consequences of s.; 28: 8 false churches claim God will justify in committing little s.; 33: 5 sacred record speaks harshly against s.; **Jacob** 1: 19 teachers answer s. of people upon own heads if they do not teach diligently; 2: 5 Nephites begin to labor in s. which is abominable to God; 7: 19 Sherem fears he has committed unpardonable s.; **Mosiah** 2: 33 he who remains and dies in s. receives wages of everlasting punishment; 4: 14 devil is master of s.; 4: 29 I cannot tell you all the things whereby you may commit s.; 25: 11 s. and polluted state of Lamanites; **Alma** 11: 37 God cannot save men in their s.; 13: 12 those sanctified by Holy Ghost cannot look upon s. without abhorrence; 26: 17 God has snatched us from s., polluted state; 36: 17–19 Alma[2] harrowed up by memory of s.; 39: 6 to deny Holy Ghost is unpardonable s.; 41: 9–10 do not suppose ye will be restored from s. to happiness; 42: 17 how could man s. without law; 42: 20 if no law was given against s., men would not be afraid to s.; 42: 21 if no law, what could justice or mercy do for men who s.; 42: 29 only let your s. trouble you; 45: 12 fourth generation after Christ's visit will s. against great light; 45: 16 the Lord cannot look upon s. with least degree of allowance; **Hel.** 6: 30 devil is author of all s.; 7: 24 Nephites have s. against greater knowledge than Lamanites; **3 Ne.** 6: 18 wicked Nephites do not s. ignorantly; 16: 10 when Gentiles s. against gospel, Father will take it from them; 28: 38 three Nephites are changed, that they suffer no sorrow, save for s. of world; **Morm.** 8: 32 false churches will forgive s. for money; **Ether** 2: 15 I forgive thee and thy brethren their s., but thou shalt not s. any more; 2: 15 if men s. until fully ripe, they are cut off from the Lord's presence; **Moro.** 7: 12 devil inviteth and enticeth to s.; 8: 8, 10 little children not capable of committing s.

SINAI, MOUNT (*see also* Mount, Mountain)

Mosiah 12: 33 keep commandments the Lord gave me on S.; 13: 5 Abinadi's face shines as did Moses' on S.

SINCERITY, SINCERE (*see also* Deceit; Honest; Hypocrisy; Intent)

Mosiah 4: 10 ask in s. of heart that God will forgive you; 26: 29 he who repents in s. of heart shall be forgiven; 29: 19 except for interposition of Creator and their s. repentance, people of Noah[3] must remain in bondage; **Alma** 26: 31 s. of converts is witnessed in love toward brethren; 33: 11 thou didst hear me because of my s.; **Hel.** 3: 27 the Lord is merciful to all who call upon him in s.; **Moro.** 10: 4 if ye ask with s. heart, God will manifest truth.

SING, SINGING (*see also* Praise; Rejoice)

1 Ne. 1: 8 (Alma 36: 22) God's throne surrounded by angels s. and praising God; 18: 9 the rebellious begin to dance and s.; 21: 13 (Isa. 49: 13) s., O heavens, break forth into s., O mountains; **2 Ne.** 8: 11 (Isa. 51: 11) the redeemed shall come with s. unto Zion; 15: 1 (Isa. 5: 1) then will I s. to my well-beloved a song touching his vineyard; 24: 7 (Isa. 14: 7) they break forth into s.; **Mosiah** 2: 28 Benjamin's spirit to join choirs above in s. praises of God; 12: 22 (3 Ne. 16: 18) with voice together shall watchmen s.; 20: 1 Lamanites' daughters gather in Shemlon to s. and dance; **Alma** 5: 26 if ye have felt to s. song of redeeming love, can ye feel so now; 26: 8 let us s. God's praise; 26: 13 converts are brought to s. redeeming love; **3 Ne.** 4: 31 people break forth, all as one, in s. and praising God; 22: 1 (Isa. 54: 1) s., O barren, and break forth into s.; **Morm.** 7: 7 the guiltless shall s. ceaseless praises with choirs above; **Ether** 6: 9 Jaredites s. praises unto the Lord; **Moro.** 6: 9 saints preach, pray, s. in meetings as led by Holy Ghost.

SINGLE, SINGLENESS (*see also* Diligence)

3 Ne. 13: 22 (Matt. 6: 22) if thine eye be s., thy whole body shall be full of light; **Morm.** 8: 15 record to be brought forth with eye s. to glory of God.

SINIM, LAND OF—*possibly land of China* (*see also* BD Sinim)

1 Ne. 21: 12 (Isa. 49: 12) Israel to gather from land of S.

SINK (*see* Sunk)

SINNER (*see also* Sin)

Mosiah 28: 4 sons of Mosiah[2] had been vilest of s.; **Alma** 34: 40 do not revile against those who cast you out, lest you become s. like them; 41: 15 the word restoration more fully condemns the s.; 42: 1 God's justice in condemning s. to punishment; **Hel.** 13: 26 Nephites call prophets s. because they testify of evil; **Moro.** 8: 8 Christ calls not the righteous, but s. to repentance.

SIRON, LAND OF—*land by borders of Lamanites*

Alma 39: 3 Corianton goes into land of S. after harlot.

SISTERS (*see also* Family)

2 Ne. 5: 6 s. of Nephi[1] go with him.

SITUATION (*see also* Crisis)

Mosiah 2: 40 awake to remembrance of awful s. of transgressors; **Ether** 8: 24 when secret combinations come among Gentiles, they should awake to sense of awful s.

SKILL, SKILLFUL (*see also* Art; Expert)

Enos 1: 20 Lamanites' s. was in bow; **Alma** 10: 15 lawyers are learned in cunning, that they might be s. in profession; 51: 31 every man of Teancum exceeds Lamanites in s. of war.

SKIN

1 Ne. 17: 11 Nephi[1] makes bellows of s. of beasts; **2 Ne.** 5: 21 (Alma 3: 6) the Lord causes s. of blackness to come upon Lamanites; **Jacob** 3: 8 Lamanites' s. will be whiter than Nephites' unless they repent; 3: 9 revile no more against Lamanites because of s.; **Enos** 1: 20 (Alma 3: 5; 43: 20; 3 Ne. 4: 7) Lamanites wear short s. girdle about loins; **Mosiah** 17: 13 priests scourge Abinadi's s. with faggots; **Alma** 20: 29 missionaries' s. is worn because of strong cords; 44: 18 Lamanites' naked s. exposed to Nephites' swords; 49: 6 Lamanites prepare thick garments of s.; **3 Ne.** 2: 15 Lamanites' s. becomes white.

SLACKEN (*see also* Shorten; Weak)

2 Ne. 4: 26 why should my strength s. because of my afflictions; **Jacob** 5: 47 has the Lord of vineyard s. his hand.

SLAIN (*see* Slay, Slew, Slain)

SLAUGHTER (*see also* Battle; Carnage; Kill; Slay; War)

1 Ne. 12: 2 Nephi[1] beholds great s. among his people; **Mosiah** 14: 7 (Isa. 53: 7) he is brought as lamb to s.; **Alma** 2: 18 Nephites slay Amlicites with great s.; 28: 2–3 great s. among both Lamanites and Nephites; 49: 21 (62: 38) Lamanites slain with great s.; **Hel.** 1: 27 Lamanites slay Nephites in center of land with great s.; **3 Ne.** 4: 11 great and terrible s. in battle between Nephites and robbers; **Morm.** 4: 21 Nephites driven and s.

SLAVERY, SLAVES (*see also* Bondage; Freedom)

Mosiah 2: 13 Benjamin has not suffered people to make s. of one another; 7: 15 Limhi's people willing to be s. of Nephites; **Alma** 27: 8 people of Anti-Nephi-Lehi willing to be Nephites' s. until they repair murders; 27: 9 against Nephites' law to have s.; 48: 11 Moroni[1] finds joy in brethren's freedom from s.; **3 Ne.** 3: 7 Giddianhi entices Nephites to become robbers' brethren, not s.

SLAY, SLEW, SLAIN (*see also* Death, Physical; Destruction; Jesus Christ, Death of; Jesus Christ—Lamb of God; Kill; Murder; Slaughter; Smite)

1 Ne. 1: 20 Jews had s. prophets of old; 4: 12 Spirit tells Nephi[1] to s. Laban; 4: 13 the Lord s. the wicked to bring forth righteous purposes; 13: 5 abominable church s. saints; **2 Ne.** 20: 4 (Isa. 10: 4) they shall fall under the s.; 21: 4 (30: 9) with breath of his lips shall the Lord s. the wicked; **Mosiah** 7: 26 Limhi's people have s. prophet Abinadi; **Alma** 18: 3 Lamoni's servants believe Ammon[2] cannot be s.; 19: 22–24 man who lifts sword to s. Ammon[2] falls dead; 44: 1 Nephites do not desire to s. Lamanites; 60: 13 the Lord suffers the righteous to be s. that justice might come upon the wicked; **Hel.** 1: 20 army of Coriantumr[3] s. all who oppose them; 4: 2 the rebellious are s. and driven from land; 8: 21 will ye say sons of Zedekiah were not s.; 13: 25 Nephites claim they would not have s. prophets of old; **3 Ne.** 10: 15 many have been s. for testifying of Christ's coming; 16: 9 the Lord will cause house of Israel to be s. and cast out; **Ether** 9: 27 Heth[1] s. father with sword.

SLEEP (*see also* Captive, Captivity; Death, Physical; Death, Spiritual; Dormant; Idleness; Slumber)

2 Ne. 1: 13 O that ye would awake from s. of hell; 27: 5 (Isa. 29: 10) the Lord pours out deep s. upon those that do iniquity; **Mosiah** 24: 19 the Lord causes deep s. to come upon Lamanites; **Alma** 5: 7 the Lord awakened fathers out of deep s.; 19: 8 Lamoni is not dead, but s. in God; 37: 37 lie down unto the Lord, that he may watch over you in your s.; 55: 15 Lamanite guards are drunken and in deep s.; **Morm.** 9: 13 resurrection brings to pass redemption from endless s.

SLING (*see also* Weapon)

1 Ne. 16: 23 Nephi[1] arms himself with s.; **Mosiah** 9: 16 Zeniff arms people with s.; 10: 8 (Alma 3: 5; 43: 20) Lamanites armed with s.; **Alma** 2: 12 (49: 20) Nephites armed with s.; 17: 7 sons of Mosiah[2] take s. to provide food; 17: 36–38 Ammon[2] casts stones at Lamanites with s.

SLIPPERY (*see also* Accursed)

Hel. 13: 31, 33, 36 (Morm. 1: 18) the Lord will curse riches, that they become s.

SLOTHFUL, SLOTHFULNESS (*see also* Diligence; Idleness; Industry; Laziness; Neglect; Procrastinate)

Alma 33: 21 would ye be s. and not cast eyes upon the type; 37: 41 Lehites were s. and forgot to exercise faith; 60: 14 judgments of God to come upon this people because of s.

SLOW (*see also* Quick, Quickly)

1 Ne. 17: 45 (Mosiah 9: 3; 13: 29; Hel. 12: 5) ye are s. to remember the Lord; **Mosiah** 11: 24 (21: 15) the Lord will be s. to hear cries of unrepentant; **Alma** 55: 31 (62: 49) Nephites are not s. to remember the Lord; **Hel.** 7: 7 people of Nephi[1] were s. to be led to do iniquity; 12: 4 how s. are men to do good; 12: 5 how s. are men to walk in wisdom's paths.

SLUMBER (*see also* Sleep)

2 Ne. 27: 6, 9 the Lord shall bring forth words of them which have s.; **Jacob** 3: 11 awake from s. of death.

SMALL, SMALLEST (*see also* Light [adj.]; Little; Plates of Nephi, Small; Voice)

1 Ne. 14: 12 dominions of saints are s. because of wickedness of abominable church; 16: 29 by s. means the Lord can bring about great things; **2 Ne.** 17: 13 (Isa. 7: 13) s. thing to weary men, but will ye weary God; **Alma** 10: 4 Amulek a man of no s. reputation; 26: 16 Ammon[2] cannot say s. part which he feels; 37: 7 by s. means the Lord brings about salvation of many; 37: 41 because miracles were worked by s. means, Lehites forgot to exercise faith.

SMILE

Jacob 2: 13 hand of providence has s. upon Nephites; **3 Ne.** 19: 25, 30 Jesus' countenance s. upon disciples.

SMITE, SMOTE, SMITTEN (*see also* Beat; Destruction; Kill; Persecution; Slay; Strike)

1 Ne. 17: 29 Moses s. rock, and water came forth; 21: 13 Israel shall be s. no more; **2 Ne.** 7: 8 I will s. mine adversary with strength of my mouth; 9: 33 knowledge of iniquities shall s. the uncircumcised; 12: 10 fear of the Lord shall s. the wicked; 21: 4 (30: 9; Isa. 11: 4) the Lord shall s. earth with rod of his mouth; 26: 15 seed of Nephites and Lamanites to be s. by Gentiles; **Mosiah** 1: 17 as Lehites were unfaithful, they were s. with afflictions; 12: 2 because of iniquities, this generation will be s. on cheek; 12: 31 priests of Noah[3] shall be s. for iniquities; 14: 4 (Isa. 53: 4) we did esteem him s. of God; 21: 3 Lamanites s. Limhi's people on cheeks; **Alma** 14: 14 (26: 29) chief judge s. Alma[2] and Amulek; **Hel.** 4: 12 Nephites s. the poor upon cheek; 10: 6 Nephi[2] given power to s. earth with famine; **3 Ne.** 12: 39 (Matt. 5: 39) whosoever s. thee on right cheek, turn the other; 28: 20 disciples cast into pits s. earth with word of God and are delivered; **4 Ne.** 1: 34 people s. upon people of Jesus, who do not s. again; **Morm.** 8: 19 he who s. shall be s. of the Lord; 8: 20 scripture says, Man shall not s.

SMITH, JOSEPH, JR. (*see also* Book of Mormon; Joseph[1])

2 Ne. 3: 7–19 prophecy of Joseph[1] concerning latter-day seer; 3: 15 his name shall be called after Joseph[1] and after name of his father.

SMOKE (*see also* Cloud; Mist; Vapor)

1 Ne. 19: 11 the Lord will visit some of house of Israel by s.; 22: 18 vapor of s. must come upon earth; **2 Ne.** 8: 6 (Isa. 51: 6) heavens shall vanish away like s.; 14: 5 (Isa. 4: 5) the Lord will create upon Zion's assemblies a cloud and s.; 24: 31 (Isa. 14: 31) there shall come from the north a s.; **Jacob** 6: 10 (Mosiah 3: 27) s. ascends forever from lake of fire and brimstone; **3 Ne.** 10: 13 righteous are not overpowered by vapor of s.; 10: 14 deaths and destructions by s. fulfill prophecies; **Morm.** 8: 29 there shall be heard of vapors of s. in foreign lands.

SMOOTH

1 Ne. 17: 46 (3 Ne. 8: 13) rough places to be made s., s. place to be broken up; **Hel.** 10: 9 (12: 10) Nephi[2] given power to make mountain s.

SNARE (*see also* Ensnare; Guile; Pit; Trap)

2 Ne. 27: 31–32 they who lay a s. for him who reproves shall be cut off;

Mosiah 23: 9 Alma[2] was caught in *s.*; **Alma** 10: 17 lawyers of Ammonihah lay *s.* to catch holy ones of God; 12: 6 Zeezrom's plan was *s.* of the adversary; 56: 43 Helaman[2] warns of *s.* set by Lamanites; **Hel.** 3: 29 word of God divides asunder all *s.* of devil; **Ether** 2: 2 Jaredites lay *s.* to catch fowls.

SNATCH (*see also* Deliver; Redemption; Redeem)

Mosiah 27: 28 the Lord has *s.* Alma[2] out of everlasting burning; **Alma** 26: 17 God is merciful in *s.* men from sinful state.

SNOW

1 Ne. 11: 8 whiteness of tree exceeds whiteness of driven *s.*

SOAP

3 Ne. 24: 2 (Mal. 3: 2) the Lord is like fuller's *s.*

SOBERNESS, SOBER (*see also* Solemn)

1 Ne. 18: 10 Nephi[1] speaks with much *s.*; **Jacob** 2: 2 Jacob[2] is under responsibility to magnify office with *s.*; **Mosiah** 4: 15 teach children to walk in ways of *s.*; **Alma** 37: 47 (38: 15; 42: 31) declare the word, and be *s.*; 53: 21 two thousand Ammonite youths are men of *s.*; **Morm.** 1: 2, 15 Mormon[2] is *s.* child.

SOCIETY (*see* Secret Combination)

SOFTEN (*see also* Hardheartedness)

1 Ne. 2: 16 the Lord visits Nephi[1] and *s.* his heart; 18: 20 only power of God threatening destruction could *s.* hearts of Laman[1] and Lemuel; **2 Ne.** 10: 18 the Lord will *s.* Gentiles' hearts to be like father to Lamanites' seed; **Mosiah** 21: 15 the Lord *s.* Lamanites' hearts for Limhi's people; **Alma** 24: 8 the Lord gives portion of Spirit to *s.* hearts; 62: 41 many are *s.* because of afflictions and humble themselves; **Hel.** 12: 2 when the Lord *s.* hearts of enemies, his people harden their hearts.

SOJOURN (*see also* Dwell; Journey)

1 Ne. 17: 3 the Lord provides means for Lehites during *s.* in wilderness; 17: 4 Lehites *s.* in wilderness eight years.

SOLD (*see* Sell)

SOLDIER (*see also* Army; War)

Alma 51: 9 Amalickiah gathers *s.* for war with Nephites; 53: 22 Helaman[2] marches at head of two thousand stripling *s.*

SOLEMN, SOLEMNITY (*see also* Soberness)

Jacob 7: 26 Nephites a lonesome and *s.* people; **Hel.** 5: 28 *s.* fear comes upon dissenters in prison because of overshadowing cloud; **Moro.** 8: 9 *s.* mockery before God to baptize little children.

SOLOMON—*king of Israel, son of David* [c. 1000 B.C.] (*see also* BD Solomon)

2 Ne. 5: 16 Nephi[1] builds temple after manner of temple of *S.*; **Jacob** 1: 15 *S.* had many wives and concubines; 2: 23 Nephites excuse whoredoms because of David and *S.*; 2: 24 practice of David and *S.* was abominable before the Lord; **3 Ne.** 13: 29 (Matt. 6: 29) *S.* in all his glory was not arrayed like lilies of field.

SON (*see also* Child; Children of God; Father; Jesus Christ—Only Begotten Son; Jesus Christ—Son of God; Mosiah[2], Sons of; Sons of Perdition)

1 Ne. 21: 22 (22: 6; 2 Ne. 6: 6; Isa. 49: 22) Gentiles will bring Israel's *s.* in their arms; **Jacob** 4: 5 Abraham's offering up his *s.*, Isaac, was similitude of God and his *S.*; **Mosiah** 2: 30 Benjamin declares his *s.*, Mosiah[2], king; 5: 7 those who enter covenant are called *s.* and daughters of Christ; 27: 25 those born again of God become his *s.* and daughters; **Alma** 20: 13 Lamanites believe Nephites are *s.* of a liar; 56: 5 two thousand *s.* of Ammonites have taken up weapons of war; **Hel.** 6: 10 land north called Mulek after *s.* of Zedekiah; 8: 21 *s.* of Zedekiah were slain, except Mulek; **3 Ne.** 14: 9 (Matt. 7: 9) what man, if *s.* ask bread, will given him stone; **Ether** 3: 14 those who believe on Christ's name become his *s.* and daughters.

SON OF GOD (*see* Children of God; Jesus Christ—Only Begotten Son; Jesus Christ—Son of God)

SONS OF MOSIAH (*see* Mosiah[2], Sons of)

SONS OF PERDITION (*see also* Death, Spiritual; Perdition; Unpardonable; TG Death, Spiritual, Second; Holy Ghost, Unpardonable Sin against; Sons of Perdition)

2 Ne. 2: 17 angel of God had fallen from heaven; **Mosiah** 2: 38–39 final doom of those who remain enemy to God is to endure never-ending torment; 16: 5 (Alma 11: 41) they who persist in carnal nature and go on in rebellion against God remain in fallen state as though no redemption had been made; **3 Ne.** 27: 32 many in fourth generation will be led captive as was *s.* of perdition; 29: 7 he who says Christ can work no miracle shall become like *s.* of perdition, for whom there was no mercy.

SOOTHSAYER (*see also* Prophets, False; Sorceries, Sorcerer)

2 Ne. 12: 6 (Isa. 2: 6) the Lord's people hearken unto s. like Philistines; **3 Ne.** 21: 16 (Micah 5: 12) thou shalt have no more s.

SORCERIES, SORCERER (*see also* Magic; Soothsayer)

Alma 1: 32 those who do not belong to church indulge in s.; **Morm.** 1: 19 there are s. in land.

SORE (*see also* Curse; Repentance)

Alma 15: 5 Zeezrom's mind exceedingly s. because of iniquities; **Hel.** 11: 5 work of destruction becomes s. by famine.

SORROW, SORROWFUL, SORROWING (*see also* Anguish; Despair; Grieve; Lament; Misery; Mourn; Pain; Remorse; Sad; Suffering; Torment; Tribulation; Trouble; Weep)

1 Ne. 16: 25 Lehi[1] brought down into depths of s. because of murmuring; **2 Ne.** 4: 17 heart of Nephi[1] s. because of his flesh; 4: 26 why should my soul linger in valley of s.; **Mosiah** 14: 3 (Isa. 53: 3) Messiah is man of s.; **Alma** 8: 14 Alma[2] weighed down with s. because of Nephites' wickedness; 29: 2 men should repent, that there might be no more s.; 37: 45 words of Christ can carry men beyond vale of s. to better land of promise; 40: 12 paradise a state of rest from all care and s.; **3 Ne.** 28: 5 three Nephites s. because they dare not speak their desire; 28: 38 three Nephites not to suffer s., save for sins of world; **Morm.** 2: 13 Nephites' s. was not unto repentance.

SOUGHT (*see* Seek, Sought)

SOUL (*see also* Body; Heart; Man; Mind; Spirit; TG Soul)

1 Ne. 15: 35 final state of s. is to dwell with God or be cast out; **2 Ne.** 4: 15–16 my s. delighteth in scriptures, in things of the Lord; 9: 49 my s. abhorreth sin; 11: 2 my s. delighteth in words of Isaiah[1]; 25: 4 (31: 3) my s. delighteth in plainness; 25: 29 worship Christ with whole s.; 28: 21 devil lulls men into carnal security and cheats their s.; 32: 9 ask Father to consecrate thy performance for welfare of thy s.; **Jacob** 2: 8 pleasing word of God healeth wounded s.; **Enos** 1: 4 s. of Enos[2] hungers; 1: 9 Enos[2] pours out whole s. unto God; **Omni** 1: 76 offer your whole s. as offering unto Christ; **W of M** 1: 18 Benjamin establishes peace by laboring with faculty of whole s.; **Mosiah** 14: 10 (Isa. 53: 10) thou shalt make his s. an offering for sin; 14: 12 (Isa. 53: 12) he hath poured out his s. unto death; 26: 14 Alma[1] pours out whole s. to God; 27: 29 (36: 16) s. of Alma[1] racked with eternal torment; 29: 40 Mosiah[2] seeks not lucre which corrupts s.; **Alma** 32: 28 good seed, or word, will begin to enlarge s.; 34: 26 pour out your s. unto God in your closets; 36: 15 O that I could become extinct both s. and body; 36: 20 s. of Alma[2] is filled with joy as exceeding as his pain; 40: 7, 11–14 state of s. between death and resurrection; 40: 18 first resurrection is reuniting of s. with body of those down to resurrection of Christ; 40: 21 dead shall be reunited, body and s., to be judged; 40: 23 s. shall be restored to body and body to s.; 42: 16 repentance could not come unto men except there were punishment as eternal as life of s.; **3 Ne.** 11: 3 small voice from heaven pierces to s.; 18: 29 he who partakes of sacrament unworthily eats and drinks damnation to s.; 20: 8 he who partakes of sacrament takes Christ's body and blood to s., and s. shall never hunger nor thirst, but shall be filled; **Ether** 12: 4 hope maketh an anchor to s. of men; **Moro.** 4: 3 (5: 2) bread and wine of sacrament sanctified to s. of those who partake.

SOUND [adj.]

Alma 17: 2 sons of Mosiah[2] are men of s. understanding, having searched the scriptures.

SOUND [noun and verb] (*see also* Noise; Voice)

Mosiah 26: 25 when second trump s., they who never knew the Lord shall come before him; **3 Ne.** 11: 5 eyes of multitude are toward s. from heaven; **Morm.** 9: 13 all men shall be awakened from endless sleep when trump s.

SOUTH (*see* North)

SOW [noun] (*see also* Swine)

3 Ne. 7: 8 Nephites turn from righteousness like s. to her wallowing.

SOW [verb] (*see also* Plant; Reap)

2 Ne. 5: 11 Nephites s. seed; **Mosiah** 7: 30–31 if people s. filthiness, they shall reap chaff; **3 Ne.** 13: 26 (Matt. 6: 26) fowls of air do not s.; **Ether** 10: 25 Jaredites make tools to s.

SPACE (*see also* Time)

1 Ne. 11: 19 virgin carried away in Spirit for the s. of a time; **Alma** 40: 21 s. between death and resurrection; 42: 5 if Adam had partaken of tree of life, he would have lived forever, having no s. for repentance; **3 Ne.** 8: 3, 23 darkness for s. of three days as sign of Christ's death; 8: 19 tempest and earthquakes last for s. of three hours.

SPACIOUS (*see* Building)

SPAKE (*see* Speak)

SPARE (*see also* Preserve; Protect; Salvation; Save; Withhold)

Jacob 5: 50 servant asks the Lord to s. vineyard a little longer; **Omni** 1: 7 the Lord s. the righteous; **Mosiah** 28: 4 the Lord, in infinite mercy, s. sons of Mosiah[2]; **Alma** 10: 20, 23 (62: 40; Hel. 13: 14) by prayers of the righteous are the wicked s.; **3 Ne.** 8: 24 O that we had repented, then would our brethren have been s.; 10: 6 the Lord has s. house of Israel; 22: 2 (Isa. 54: 2) s. not, lengthen thy cords; **Morm.** 3: 2 repent, be baptized, build up church, and ye shall be s.; **Moro.** 9: 19 Nephites have become brutal, s. none; 9: 22 Mormon[2] prays the Lord will s. Moroni[2].

SPEAK, SPAKE, SPOKEN (*see also* Communication; Language; Lips; Mouth; Say; Speech; Talk; Tongue; Utter; Voice; Whisper)

1 Ne. 11: 11 Nephi[1] s. with Spirit as man s.; **2 Ne.** 25: 8 unto them who suppose records are not of worth will the Lord s. particularly; 26: 16 those who shall be destroyed will s. out of ground; 27: 13 (Moro. 10: 27) words of the faithful shall s. as if from dead; 29: 12 the Lord will s. unto Jews, Nephites, other tribes, and they shall write it; 32: 3 angels s. words of Christ by power of Holy Ghost; 33: 1 when a man s. by power of Holy Ghost, that power carries it into hearts; **Jacob** 4: 9 God being able to s. created world and man; 4: 13 Spirit s. truth and lies not; 4: 13 Spirit s. of things as they are and will be; **Mosiah** 13: 33 all prophets have s. concerning coming of Messiah; **Alma** 29: 1 O that I were an angel and could s. with trump of God; 30: 52 Korihor is dumb, cannot s.; 58: 11 the Lord s. peace to our souls; **Hel.** 5: 18 what they should s. is given to Nephi[2] and Lehi[4]; 5: 45 Spirit enters hearts of Nephi[2] and Lehi[4], and they can s. marvelous words; **3 Ne.** 17: 17 (19: 32) no tongue can s. marvelous things Nephites heard Jesus s.; **Ether** 3: 12 brother of Jared[2] knows the Lord s. truth; 12: 31 after disciples s. the Lord's name, he showed himself to them in power.

SPEAR (*see also* Dart; Javelin; Weapon)

2 Ne. 12: 4 (Isa. 2: 4) nations shall beat s. into pruning-hooks; **Alma** 17: 7 sons of Mosiah[2] take s. to provide food.

SPEECH (*see also* Communication; Language; Speak; Tongue; Voice)

2 Ne. 26: 16 (Isa. 29: 4) s. of those who are destroyed shall be low out of dust; **Jacob** 2: 7 Jacob[2] grieved that he must use much boldness of s.; 7: 4 Sherem has much power of s.; **Enos** 1: 23 prophets preach with plainness of s.; **Morm.** 9: 32 reformed Egyptian characters are altered according to Nephites' manner of s.

SPIN

Mosiah 10: 5 Zeniff causes women to s. and toil; **Hel.** 6: 13 Nephite women toil and s.; **3 Ne.** 13: 28 (Matt. 6: 28) lilies of field toil not, neither do they s.

SPINDLES (*see* Liahona)

SPIRIT (*see also* Broken Heart and Contrite Spirit; Ghost; Mind; Soul; Spirit, Evil; Spirit, Holy/Spirit of the Lord; Spirit World; Spiritual; TG Spirit Body; Spirit Creation; Spirits, Disembodied; BD Spirit)

2 Ne. 9: 12 bodies and s. of men will be restored to each other; 25: 11 Nephi[1] speaks because of s. that is in him; **Mosiah** 2: 28 immortal s. to join choirs above in singing praises of God; **Alma** 3: 26 men reap eternal happiness or misery according to s. they obey; 11: 43 s. and body to be reunited in perfect form; 11: 45 s. to be united with bodies, never to be divided; 34: 34 same s. that possesses body at death will possess it in eternal world; 40: 11 after death, s. of all men are taken home to God; **3 Ne.** 12: 3 (Matt. 5: 3) blessed are poor in s. who come unto the Lord; **Ether** 3: 16 brother of Jared[2] sees body of Christ's s.; 3: 16 man is created after body of Christ's s.; **Moro.** 10: 14 to another is given the beholding of angels and ministering s.; 10: 34 Moroni[2] goes to rest in paradise until s. and body are reunited.

SPIRIT, EVIL (*see also* Angels of the Devil; Demon; Devil; Devils; Familiar; TG Spirits, Evil or Unclean)

1 Ne. 11: 31 (Mosiah 3: 6) Lamb casts out devils and unclean s.; **2 Ne.** 32: 8 evil s. teaches man not to pray; 33: 5 no man shall be angry with truth save he shall be of s. of devil; **Mosiah** 2: 32 beware lest contentions arise and ye list to obey evil s.; 2: 33 he who listeth to obey evil s. shall receive everlasting punishment; 2: 36–37 they who knowingly transgress obey evil s. and become enemies to all righteousness; 4: 14 ye will not suffer children to serve devil, who is evil s. spoken of by fathers; **Alma** 3: 26 men reap eternal happiness or misery according to s. they obey, whether good or evil; 22: 15 what shall I do to be born of God, having wicked s. rooted from breast and receive his S.; 40: 13 s. of devil takes possession of the wicked after death; **3 Ne.** 7: 19 Nephi[3] casts out devils and unclean s.; 11: 29 he who hath s. of contention is not of Christ.

SPIRIT, GIFTS OF (*see also* Holy Ghost; Holy Ghost, Baptism of; Holy Ghost, Gift of; Interpretation; Sign; Spirit, Holy/Spirit of the Lord; Tongue; Translation; TG God, Gifts of; Holy Ghost, Gifts of)

1 Ne. 10: 17 Holy Ghost is gift of God unto all who diligently seek him; 13: 37 they who seek to bring forth Zion shall have gift and power of Holy Ghost; **Jacob** 6: 8 will ye deny power of God and gift of Holy Ghost and quench Holy *S.*; **Omni** 1: 20 (Mosiah 8: 13; 21: 28) Mosiah[1] interprets engravings by gift and power of God; **Alma** 9: 21 Nephites have received spirit of prophecy and of revelation, many gifts, gifts of speaking with tongues, preaching, gift of Holy Ghost, gift of translation; **3 Ne.** 29: 6 wo to him who says the Lord no longer works by gifts or by power of Holy Ghost: **Moro.** 10: 8 gifts are given by manifestation of *S.* unto men to profit them.

SPIRIT, HOLY/SPIRIT OF THE LORD (*see also* Born of God; Holy Ghost; Holy Ghost, Baptism of; Inspire; Light; Revelation; Spirit, Gifts of; Spiritual; Truth; TG God, Spirit of; Holy Ghost; Jesus Christ, Spirit of; Lord, Spirit of; BD Spirit, the Holy)

1 Ne. 1: 7–8 Lehi[1] is overcome with *S.*; 2: 17 Nephi[1] tells Sam of things manifested to him by *H.S.*; 3: 20 words delivered to prophets by *S.* of the Lord; 4: 6 Nephi[1] led by *S.*, not knowing beforehand what he should do; 7: 14 *S.* of the Lord ceaseth soon to strive with Jews; 11: 1 Nephi[1] is caught away in *S.* into high mountain; 11: 11 Nephi[1] speaks with *S.* of the Lord in form of man; 13: 12–13 Gentiles wrought upon by *S.* of the Lord to cross many waters; 17: 49 Nephi[1] is full of *S.* of God, that his frame has no strength; 17: 52 *S.* of God is so powerful, brothers of Nephi[1] fear to touch him; 19: 12 many kings shall be wrought upon by *S.* of God; 20: 16 (Isa. 48: 16) the Lord God, and his *S.*, hath sent me; 22: 2 by *S.* are all things made known unto prophets; **2 Ne.** 2: 4 *S.* is same yesterday, today, forever; 2: 28 choose eternal life according to will of *H.S.*; 26: 11 (Ether 2: 15) *S.* of the Lord will not always strive with man; 32: 8 if ye would hearken unto *S.* that teaches man to pray, ye would know ye must pray; 33: 2 many harden hearts against *H.S.*, that it has no place in them; **Jacob** 4: 13 *S.* speaks the truth; 6: 8 will ye deny gift of Holy Ghost and quench *H.S.*; 7: 8 the Lord pours his *S.* into soul of Jacob[2]; **Jarom** 1: 4 those who are not stiffnecked and have faith have communion with *H.S.*; 1: 4 *H.S.* makes manifest unto men according to faith; **Mosiah** 3: 19 natural man will remain enemy to God unless he yields to enticings of *H.S.*; 4: 20 God has poured out *S.* upon people of Benjamin; 5: 2 *S.* of the Lord has wrought mighty change in people of Benjamin; 18: 10 be baptized, that the Lord may pour out his *S.* upon you more abundantly; 27: 24 Alma[2] has been born of the *S.*; **Alma** 5: 46 teachings are made known unto Alma[2] by *H.S.* of God; 5: 46 *H.S.* is *s.* of revelation; 5: 47 prophecy is by manifestation of *S.* of God; 5: 54 converts have been sanctified by *H.S.*; 7: 5 I trust, according to *S.* of God which is in me, that I shall have joy over you; 8: 10 Alma[2] wrestles with God that he would pour out his *S.* upon people of Ammonihah; 9: 21 Nephites have been visited by *S.* of God; 11: 22 Amulek will say nothing contrary to *S.* of the Lord; 11: 44 (2 Ne. 31: 21; 3 Ne. 11: 27, 36; 28: 10; Morm. 7: 7) Father, Son, and *H.S.* are one God; 13: 4 men reject *S.* of God because of hardness of hearts; 13: 28 pray continually and thus be led by *H.S.*; 18: 16 Ammon[2], being filled with *S.* of God, perceives king's thoughts; 18: 34 Ammon[2] has been called by *H.S.* to teach these things; 19: 36 the Lord pours out his *S.* upon Lamanites; 24: 30 if people once enlightened by *S.* fall away, they become more hardened; 30: 42 Korihor has put off *S.* of God; 30: 46 Korihor resists *s.* of the truth; 31: 36 Alma[2] clasps hands upon fellow laborers, and they are filled with *H.S.*; 34: 35 if you have procrastinated day of your repentance, *S.* of the Lord has withdrawn from you; 38: 6 *S.* of God makes things known to Alma[2]; 40: 13 spirits of the wicked have no portion of *S.* of the Lord; 45: 19 Alma[2] is taken up by *S.*; 61: 15 commanders are given power to conduct war according to *S.* of God, which is *S.* of freedom; **Hel.** 4: 24 *S.* of the Lord no more preserves Nephites; 4: 24 *S.* of the Lord dwells not in unholy temples; 5: 45 *H.S.* enters Nephi[2] and Lehi[4], that they speak marvelous words; 13: 8 because of hardness of Nephites' hearts, the Lord will withdraw his *S.* from them; **3 Ne.** 7: 21 converts signify they have been visited by *S.* of God; 18: 7, 11 (Moro. 4: 3; 5: 2) if men always remember Christ, they shall have his *S.*; **Moro.** 4: 3 (5: 2) those who partake of sacrament and always remember Christ will have his *S.*; 8: 28 (9: 4) Mormon[2] fears *S.* has ceased striving with Nephites; 10: 8, 17 gifts of God are given by manifestations of *S.* of God.

SPIRIT WORLD (*see also* Darkness, Spiritual; Death, Physical; Death, Spiritual; Hell; Paradise; Premortal Existence; Prison; Resurrection; Spirit)

Alma 40: 11 *s.* of all men are taken

home to God after death; 40: 12 s. of righteous are received in state of happiness, paradise; 40: 13–14 s. of the wicked are cast into outer darkness.

SPIRITUAL, SPIRITUALLY (*see also* Darkness, Spiritual; Death, Spiritual; Holy Ghost; Spirit; Spirit, Holy/Spirit of the Lord)

1 Ne. 14: 7 the hardhearted to be delivered unto destruction, both temporally and *s.*; 15: 26–32 river of filthy water is representation of things both temporal and *s.*; 22: 3 prophecies of Isaiah[1] pertain to things both temporal and *s.*; **2 Ne.** 2: 5 by *s.* law, men perish from that which is good; 9: 39 to be *s*-minded is life eternal; **Mosiah** 2: 41 those who keep commandments are blessed in all things, both temporal and *s.*; 4: 26 administer to relief of the poor, both *s.* and temporally; 5: 7 Christ has *s.* begotten those who enter covenant; 18: 29 Nephites impart to one another both temporally and *s.*; **Alma** 5: 14 have ye *s.* been born of God; 7: 23 ask for whatsoever things ye stand in need, both temporal and *s.*; 11: 45 through resurrection, body and spirit become *s.* and immortal; 36: 4 Alma[2] knows these things, not of the temporal but of the *s.*; 37: 43 as fathers were slothful they did not prosper, so it is with *s.* things; **Morm.** 2: 15 day of grace is past with Nephites, both temporally and *s.*; **Moro.** 10: 19 *s.* gifts will never be done away.

SPIT, SPITTING (*see also* Mock; Revile; Scorn)

1 Ne. 19: 9 world shall *s.* upon God of Israel; **2 Ne.** 7: 6 (Isa. 50: 6) I hid not my face from shame and *s.*; **Alma** 8: 13 people of Ammonihah *s.* upon Alma[2]; 14: 7 people *s.* upon Zeezrom; 26: 29 sons of Mosiah[2] have been *s.* upon.

SPOKESMAN (*see also* Speak)

2 Ne. 3: 17–18 the Lord will make a *s.* for Moses.

SPOT, SPOTTED (*see also* Filthiness; Guilt; Sin; Spot of Land; Spotless; Stain)

Ether 12: 38 garments of Moroni[1] not *s.* with Gentiles' blood; **Moro.** 10: 33 become holy, without *s.*

SPOT OF LAND

Jacob 5: 21–22 poorest *s.* of ground in vineyard; 5: 23 *s.* of ground poorer than first; 5: 25, 43–44 good *s.* of ground in vineyard.

SPOTLESS (*see also* Blameless; Cleanse; Guiltless; Innocence; Purity; Spot, Spotted)

2 Ne. 33: 7 Nephi[1] to meet many souls *s.* at judgment-seat; **Jacob** 1: 19 slothful teachers would not be found *s.* at last day; **Alma** 5: 24 (7: 25) garments of prophets are *s.*; 12: 14 our words will condemn us, and we shall not be found *s.*; 13: 12 after being sanctified by Holy Ghost, high priests are pure and *s.*; 14: 7 Zeezrom confesses Alma[2] and Amulek are *s.*; **3 Ne.** 27: 20 be sanctified by Holy Ghost, that ye may stand *s.* before the Lord; **Morm.** 9: 6 be found *s.*, having been cleansed by blood of Lamb.

SPREAD, SPREADING (*see also* Enlarge; Grow; Increase; Shed)

Mosiah 3: 20 knowledge of Savior shall *s.* throughout every nation; **Alma** 1: 15–16 death of Nehor does not end *s.* of priestcraft; **Hel.** 6: 28 devil *s.* works of darkness over land; 16: 22 Satan *s.* rumors and contentions; **3 Ne.** 4: 6 robbers dare not *s.* themselves in land lest Nephites attack; **4 Ne.** 1: 46 robbers *s.* over land; **Morm.** 2: 8 blood and carnage *s.* throughout land; **Ether** 9: 6 so great has been *s.* of secret society that hearts of all are corrupted; 9: 26 (10: 4) people have *s.* again over the land.

SPRING, SPRINGING (*see also* Fountain; Grow; Water)

1 Ne. 16: 21 bows have lost their *s.*; 21: 10 (Isa. 49: 10) he who has mercy on them shall lead them by *s.* of water; **Alma** 32: 41 (33: 23) nourish tree by faith and diligence, and it will *s.* up unto everlasting life.

SPRINKLE

3 Ne. 20: 45 (Isa. 52: 15) so shall he *s.* many nations.

SPURN (*see also* Persecution; Scorn)

3 Ne. 29: 4–5 warning not to *s.* doings of the Lord; 29: 8 ye need not any longer *s.* the Jews.

SPY

Mosiah 9: 1 Zeniff sent as *s.* among Lamanites; 10: 7 Zeniff sends *s.* around land of Shemlon; **Alma** 2: 21 Alma[2] sends *s.* to follow Amlicites; 43: 23, 28, 30 (56: 22) Moroni[1] sends *s.* to watch Lamanites; 58: 14 Lamanites send out *s.* to discover Nephites' strength.

STAFF

2 Ne. 13: 1 (Isa. 3: 1) the Lord takes from Judah whole *s.* of bread; 24: 5 (Isa. 14: 5) the Lord has broken *s.* of the wicked.

STAIN (*see also* Filthiness; Guilt; Sin; Spot, Spotted; Unclean)

Alma 5: 21 garments must be purified until cleansed from all s.; 5: 22 how will you feel to stand before God with garments s. with filthiness; 24: 11–13 since God has taken away our s., let us s. our swords no more.

STAKE

3 Ne. 22: 2 (Moro. 10: 31; Isa. 54: 2) strengthen thy s.

STAND, STOOD (*see also* Fast; Need; Rameumpton; Standing; Steadfast; Testimony; Witness)

1 Ne. 15: 33 (2 Ne. 28: 23; Alma 11: 43; Ether 5: 6) men must be brought to s. before God to be judged; **2 Ne.** 13: 13 the Lord s. up to plead and to judge; 25: 21–22 seed of Joseph[1] shall never perish as long as earth shall s.; **Mosiah** 18: 9 s. as witness of God; **Alma** 5: 44 Alma[2] is commanded to s. and testify of things to come; 31: 21 Rameumpton, being interpreted, is holy s.; **Hel.** 12: 15 it appears to man that sun s. still; **3 Ne.** 17: 12 (19: 15; 27: 2) Jesus s. in midst of Nephites; 27: 16 Jesus to s. to judge world; 27: 20 those sanctified by Holy Ghost may s. before Christ at last day; **Moro.** 7: 36–37 the Lord will not withhold power of Holy Ghost as long as earth shall s.; 10: 19 spiritual gifts shall not be done away as long as world shall s.

STANDARD (*see also* Ensign; Example; Title of Liberty; TG God, the Standard of Righteousness)

1 Ne. 21: 22 (2 Ne. 6: 6; Isa. 49: 22) the Lord will set up his s. to the people; 22: 6 the Lord will set Gentiles up for s.; **2 Ne.** 20: 18 (Isa. 10: 18) they shall be as when a s-bearer fainteth; 29: 2 the Lord's words shall hiss forth for s. unto Israel; **Alma** 46: 36 (51: 20; 62: 4–5) Moroni[1] plants s. of liberty among Nephites.

STANDING (*see also* Equal)

Alma 13: 5 those called to be high priests are on same s. with brethren.

STAR (*see also* Astronomy)

1 Ne. 1: 10 Lehi[1] beholds twelve whose brightness exceeds that of s.; **2 Ne.** 24: 13 (Isa. 14: 13) Lucifer desires to exalt his throne above s. of God; **Hel.** 14: 5 (3 Ne. 1: 21) new s. shall arise as sign of Christ's birth; 14: 20 (3 Ne. 8: 22) s. shall be darkened as sign of Christ's death.

STATE

1 Ne. 10: 6 all mankind in lost and fallen s.; 15: 31, 35 final s. of souls is to dwell with God or be cast out; **2 Ne.** 2: 21 (Alma 12: 24; 42: 10, 13) this life became s. of probation; 25: 17 the Lord will set his hand second time to restore his people from lost and fallen s.; **Mosiah** 4: 2 Benjamin's people view themselves in carnal s.; 16: 4 God redeems his people from lost and fallen s.; 27: 25 all mankind must be changed from carnal and fallen s. to s. of righteousness; **Alma** 12: 31 through first transgression men placed themselves in s. to act according to their wills; 40: 11–14 s. of soul between death and resurrection; 41: 11 men in s. of nature, or carnal s., have gone contrary to nature of God, contrary to nature of happiness; 42: 10 probationary s. became s. for men to prepare; **3 Ne.** 28: 15 three Nephites seem to be transformed from body of flesh to immortal s.

STATURE

1 Ne. 2: 16 (4: 31) Nephi[1] is large in s.; **3 Ne.** 13: 27 (Matt. 6: 27) which of you by taking thought can add one cubit unto his s.; **Morm.** 2: 1 Mormon[2] is large in s.

STATUTE (*see also* Commandments of God; Decree; Law; Ordinance)

2 Ne. 1: 16 (5: 10; Mosiah 6: 6; Alma 25: 14; 58: 40; Hel. 3: 20; 6: 34; 15: 5; 3 Ne. 25: 4) observe the s. and judgments of the Lord.

STAY (*see also* Cease; Hinder; Restrain; Stop; Withhold)

2 Ne. 13: 1 (Isa. 3: 1) the Lord takes away from Judah whole s. of water; 20: 20 (Isa. 10: 20) remnant of Israel shall no longer s. upon him that smote them, but upon the Lord; 27: 4 all ye that do iniquity, s. yourselves and wonder; **Morm.** 8: 26 records shall come by hand of the Lord, and none can s. it.

STEADFAST, STEADFASTLY, STEADFASTNESS (*see also* Diligence; Endure; Faithful; Firmness; Immovable; Obedience; Steadiness; Unshaken)

1 Ne. 2: 10 Lehi[1] exhorts Lemuel to be s. like valley; **2 Ne.** 25: 24 Nephites look forward with s. unto Christ; 26: 8 the righteous who look forward unto Christ with s. shall not perish; 31: 20 press forward with s. in Christ; **Mosiah** 4: 11 stand s. in faith of that which is to come; 5: 15 be s. and immovable; **Alma** 1: 25 the faithful stand s. in keeping commandments; 5: 48 Christ shall take away sins of those who s. believe on his name; **Hel.** 15: 8 converted Lamanites are s. in faith; 15: 10 because of their s., the Lord will prolong Lamanites' days; **3 Ne.** 1: 8 believers watch s. for sign of Christ's birth; 6: 14 church broken up except for few Lamanites who are s.; **Ether** 12: 4 hope for better world makes men sure and s.

STEADINESS (*see also* Steadfast)

Alma 38: 2 (39: 1) Alma[2] to have

great joy in Shiblon's s.; **Hel.** 6: 1 Lamanites' righteousness exceeds that of Nephites because of their s.

STEAL, STEALING, STOLEN (*see also* Fraud; Rob; Thief)

2 Ne. 26: 32 the Lord has commanded that men should not s.; **Mosiah** 2: 13 Benjamin has not suffered his people to s.; 13: 22 (Ex. 20: 15) thou shalt not s.; **Alma** 1: 18 those practicing priestcraft dare not s. for fear of law; 16: 18 priests preach against s.; 23: 3 king would convince Lamanites they ought not to s.; 39: 4 harlot Isabel s. away hearts of many; **Hel.** 4: 12 slaughter of Nephites caused by iniquities, s.; 6: 21, 23 robbers covenant they should not suffer for s.; 7: 4–5 robbers obtain management of government that they might more easily s.; **3 Ne.** 13: 19–20 (Matt. 6: 19–20) lay not up for yourselves treasures upon earth, where thieves s.; 27: 32 fourth generation will sell the Lord for that which thieves can s.

STEEL (*see also* Metal)

1 Ne. 4: 9 Laban's sword is of most precious s.; 16: 18 Nephi[1] breaks his bow, made of fine s.; **2 Ne.** 5: 15 (Jarom 1: 8) Nephi[1] teaches his people to work in s.; **Ether** 7: 9 Shule makes swords of s.

STEM OF JESSE

2 Ne. 21: 1 (Isa. 11: 1) rod shall come forth out of s. of Jesse.

STIFFNECKED, STIFFNECKEDNESS (*see also* Hardheartedness; Pride; Rebel; Stubbornness; Unbelief)

1 Ne. 2: 11 Lehi[1] speaks because of s. of elder sons; **2 Ne.** 6: 10 (10: 5; 25: 12) Jews shall stiffen necks against Holy One; 25: 28 (Enos 1: 22; Hel. 5: 3; 9: 21; 13: 29) Nephites are s. people; 28: 14 false churches wear stiff necks and high heads; 32: 7 (3 Ne. 15: 18) Spirit stops utterance because of s. of men; **Jacob** 2: 13 rich among Nephites wear stiff necks because of costly apparel; 4: 14 (6: 4; 3 Ne. 15: 18) Jews were s. people; **Jarom** 1: 4 many among Nephites have revelations, for not all are s.; **Omni** 1: 28 Zeniff a s. man; **W of M** 1: 17 holy men speak with sharpness because of s. of people; **Mosiah** 3: 14 (13: 29) the Lord saw his people were s. and appointed unto them law of Moses; **Alma** 9: 5, 31 (15: 15) people of Ammonihah are s. people; 20: 30 Lamanites in Middoni are more s. people; 26: 24 Nephites believe Lamanites are s. people; 37: 10 records may bring thousands of s. Nephites to knowledge of Redeemer; **Hel.** 4: 21 Nephites see they have been s.; **Morm.** 8: 33 s. people will build churches to get gain.

STILL (*see also* Voice)

Hel. 12: 15 it appears to man that sun stands s.

STING

Mosiah 16: 7–8 (Morm. 7: 5) s. of death is swallowed up in Christ; **Alma** 22: 14 s. of death to be swallowed up in hopes of glory.

STINK

2 Ne. 7: 2 (Isa. 50: 2) the Lord makes fish to s. because waters are dried up; 13: 24 (Isa. 3: 24) instead of sweet smell there shall be s.; **Alma** 19: 5 some say Lamoni s.

STIR (*see also* Anger; Contention; Provoke; Rebel)

Enos 1: 23 prophets s. Nephites up continually to keep them in fear of the Lord; **Mosiah** 11: 28 Abinadi s. up people; 18: 33 Noah[3] says Alma[1] is s. people up to rebellion; **Alma** 11: 20 judges s. people up to riotings to get gain; **Hel.** 6: 21 Satan s. up hearts of Nephites to unite with robbers; 16: 22 Satan s. up people to do iniquity; **Morm.** 4: 5 the wicked s. up hearts of men to bloodshed.

STONE [noun] (*see also* Foundation; Ore; Rock; Stone [verb])

1 Ne. 2: 7 Lehi[1] builds altar of s. and makes offering to the Lord; 16: 15 Lehites slay food with s. and slings; 17: 11 Nephi[1] smites two s. together to make fire; **2 Ne.** 18: 14 (Isa. 8: 14) he shall be for s. of stumbling; 19: 10 (Isa. 9: 10) we will build with hewn s.; 26: 3 Jews s. the prophets; **Jacob** 4: 15 Jews will reject s. upon which they might build safe foundation; **Omni** 1: 20 large s. with engravings brought to Mosiah[1]; **Mosiah** 10: 8 (Alma 3: 5; 43: 20) Lamanites are armed with s. and slings; 28: 11, 13–16 Mosiah[2] translates records by means of two s.; **Alma** 2: 12 (49: 20) Nephites armed with s. and slings; 17: 14 Lamanites' hearts are set upon precious s.; 37: 23 the Lord will prepare s. which will shine forth in darkness unto light; **Hel.** 16: 2 Nephites cast s. at Samuel upon the wall; **Ether** 3: 1–6 (6: 3) brother of Jared[2] makes sixteen small s. for light in vessels; 3: 23–24, 28 the Lord gives brother of Jared[2] two s. to be sealed with writings.

STONE [verb] (*see also* Martyrdom; Persecution; Reject; Stone [noun])

Alma 26: 29 sons of Mosiah[2] have been s.; 33: 17 second prophet of old was s. for testifying of Son; 38: 4 Shiblon was

s. for word's sake; **Hel.** 13: 33 (3 Ne. 8: 25) O that I had repented and not s. the prophets; **3 Ne.** 7: 14 people s. the prophets and cast them out; 10: 12 more righteous part of people receive prophets and s. them not; **Ether** 8: 25 devil causes men to s. prophets.

STOOD (*see* Stand, Stood)

STOP (*see also* Hinder; Restrain; Stay)

2 Ne. 32: 7 Spirit s. utterance of Nephi[1]; **Mosiah** 4: 20 the Lord has caused mouths to be s. that they cannot find utterance because of joy; **Alma** 36: 6 God sent angel to s. Alma[2] and companions by the way.

STORE (*see also* Storehouse)

3 Ne. 4: 18 Nephites have laid up much provision in s.; **4 Ne.** 1: 46 robbers lay up gold and silver in s.

STOREHOUSE

3 Ne. 24: 10 (Mal. 3: 10) bring ye all the tithes into the s.

STORM (*see also* Destruction; Tempest; Whirlwind; Wind)

1 Ne. 18: 13–21 great s. arises during voyage to promised land; **2 Ne.** 14: 6 (Isa. 4: 6) tabernacle shall be covert from s.; 27: 2 in day of iniquity Gentiles shall be visited with s.; **Alma** 26: 6 sheaves, or converts, shall not be beaten down by s.; **Hel.** 5: 12 those built upon foundation of Redeemer shall withstand s. of devil; **3 Ne.** 8: 5–19 great s. arises at death of Christ.

STRAIGHT, STRAIGHTNESS

1 Ne. 10: 8 (Alma 7: 19) make s. paths of the Lord; **2 Ne.** 9: 41 way for man is narrow, but lies in s. course; 31: 9 Christ's example shows men s. of path; **Alma** 7: 9 walk in the Lord's paths, which are s.; 37: 44 word of Christ will point s. course to eternal bliss.

STRAIT (*see also* Narrow; Straight; Straiten)

1 Ne. 8: 20 Lehi[1] sees s. and narrow path leading to tree; 21: 20 (Isa. 49: 20) children shall say, The place is too s. for me; **2 Ne.** 31: 18–19 s. and narrow path leads to eternal life; 33: 9 walk in the s. path; **Jacob** 6: 11 (3 Ne. 14: 13–14; 27: 33; Matt. 7: 13–14) enter in at s. gate; **Hel.** 3: 29 word of God leads in s. and narrow course across gulf of misery.

STRAITEN (*see also* Chasten)

1 Ne. 17: 41 the Lord s. Israel in wilderness.

STRANGE (*see also* Stranger; Unknown)

1 Ne. 8: 32 many in vision of Lehi[1] are lost from view, wandering in s. paths; 8: 33 great multitude enter s. building; **Alma** 13: 23 (26: 36) Nephites are wanderers in s. land; 26: 36 Nephites a branch of tree of Israel lost from body in s. land.

STRANGER (*see also* BD Stranger)

Mosiah 5: 13 how knoweth a man the master who is s. unto him; 13: 18 (Ex. 20: 10) on seventh day thou shalt not do any work, nor s. within thy gates; **Alma** 26: 9 except for sons of Mosiah[2], converted Lamanites would still be s. to God; **3 Ne.** 24: 5 (Mal. 3: 5) the Lord will be swift witness against those who turn aside the s.

STRATAGEM (*see also* Decoy)

Alma 43: 30 Moroni[1] thinks it is no sin to defend people by s.; 52: 10 Moroni[1] encourages Teancum to take cities by s.; 54: 3 Moroni[1] resolves upon s. to obtain Nephite prisoners from Lamanites; 56: 30 Nephites desire to bring s. into effect upon Lamanites; 58: 6 Lamanites resolve by s. to destroy Nephites; 58: 28 by s. Nephites take city of Manti without bloodshed.

STRAW

2 Ne. 21: 7 (30: 13; Isa. 11: 7) lion shall eat s. like ox.

STREET (*see also* Highway; Path; Road; Way)

2 Ne. 8: 20 (Isa. 51: 20) two sons lie at head of all s.; **Alma** 26: 29 (32: 1) missionaries teach in s.; **3 Ne.** 13: 2 (Matt. 6: 2) when ye do alms, do not sound trumpet as hypocrites do in s.

STRENGTH (*see also* Arm; Courage; Might; Power; Strengthen; Strong; Virtue)

1 Ne. 4: 31 Nephi[1] receives much s. of the Lord; 21: 5 (Isa. 49: 5) my God shall be my s.; **2 Ne.** 8: 24 (3 Ne. 20: 36; Isa. 52: 1) put on thy s., O Zion; 22: 2 (Isa. 12: 2) the Lord Jehovah is my s.; **Jacob** 5: 48 branches have grown faster than s. of roots; 5: 66 root and top to be equal in s.; **Mosiah** 2: 11 Benjamin serves his people with all his s.; 4: 27 not requisite that man should run faster than he has s.; 9: 17 in s. of the Lord, Zeniff's people go to battle against Lamanites; 11: 19 people of Noah[4] boast in own s.; **Alma** 20: 4 (26: 12) in s. of the Lord, Ammon[2] can do all things; 26: 12 Ammon[2] knows that as to his own s. he is weak; 39: 13 turn to the Lord with all your s.; 56: 56 Ammonite youths fight as if with s. of God; **Hel.** 4: 13 (Morm. 3: 9; 4: 8) slaughter of Nephites caused by their boasting in own s.; **3 Ne.** 3: 12

Nephites cry unto the Lord for s. against robbers; **Moro.** 9: 18 Mormon[2] has but s. of man; 10: 32 love God with all your s.

STRENGTHEN (*see also* Nourish; Strength; Strong)

1 Ne. 17: 3 if men keep commandments, God s. them; **Mosiah** 24: 15 the Lord s. people of Alma[1] to bear burdens; **Alma** 2: 28 Nephites are s. by hand of the Lord; 25: 16 law of Moses s. faith in Christ; **3 Ne.** 22: 2 (Moro. 10: 31; Isa. 54: 2) s. thy stakes.

STRETCH

1 Ne. 17: 54 Nephi[1] s. forth hand and the Lord shakes brothers; **2 Ne.** 15: 25 (19: 12, 17, 21; 20: 4; 24: 17; Jacob 6: 4; Isa. 5: 25) the Lord's hand is s. out.

STRIFE (*see also* Contention; Dissension)

2 Ne. 26: 21 many churches to be built up which cause s.; **Alma** 1: 32 those who do not belong to church indulge in envyings and s.; 4: 9 (Hel. 11: 23; 13: 22; Morm. 8: 36) s. among Nephites; 16: 18 priests preach against s.; **3 Ne.** 21: 19 all s. shall be done away; 30: 2 turn, ye Gentiles, from all your s.; **4 Ne.** 1: 16 no s. among Nephites; **Morm.** 8: 21 he who breathes out s. against work of the Lord shall be hewn down.

STRIKE, STRUCK (*see also* Beat; Smite)

Jacob 6: 13 bar of God s. wicked with fear; **Mosiah** 25: 7 Nephites are s. with wonder over records of Zeniff and Alma[1]; **Alma** 22: 18 Lamanite king is s. as if dead; 30: 50 Korihor is s. dumb; **Hel.** 5: 25 Lamanites are s. dumb with amazement over fire encircling Nephi[2] and Lehi[4].

STRIP

Alma 5: 28–29 those who are not s. of pride and envy are not prepared to meet God; 11: 2 man compelled to pay what he owes or be s.; **Morm.** 9: 28 s. yourselves of all uncleanness.

STRIPES

2 Ne. 28: 8 false churches claim sinners will be beaten with few s., then saved; **Mosiah** 14: 5 (Isa. 53: 5) with his s. are we healed.

STRIPLING (*see* Helaman[2], Sons of)

STRIVE, STRIVING (*see also* Work [verb])

1 Ne. 7: 14 Spirit ceases soon to s. with Jews; 17: 15 Nephi[1] s. to keep commandments; **2 Ne.** 26: 11 (Ether 2: 15) Spirit will not always s. with man, then comes destruction; **Mosiah** 27: 35 sons of Mosiah[2] s. to repair injuries done to church; **Hel.** 15: 6 converted Lamanites s. to bring remainder to knowledge of truth; **Morm.** 5: 16 (Moro. 8: 28; 9: 4) Spirit hath already ceased to s. with Nephites; **Ether** 15: 19 Spirit ceases to s. with Jaredites.

STRONG, STRONGER (*see also* Mighty; Power; Strength; Strengthen)

1 Ne. 4: 2 let us be s. like unto Moses; 17: 2 women among Lehites are s. like unto men; **2 Ne.** 3: 13 out of weakness, latter-day seer shall be made s.; 15: 11 (Isa. 5: 11) wo unto those who rise early that they may follow s. drink; 27: 4 (Isa. 29: 9) ye who do iniquity shall stagger, but not with s. drink; **Mosiah** 18: 26 for their labor, priests receive grace of God, that they might wax s. in Spirit; **Alma** 17: 2 sons of Mosiah[2] have waxed s. in knowledge of truth; 48: 11 Moroni[1] a s. and mighty man; 50: 18 Nephites wax s. in land; 58: 40 faith of Ammonite youths is s. in that which is to come; **Hel.** 3: 35 humble part of Nephites wax s. and s. in humility; 11: 37 Nephites wax s. and s. in pride and wickedness; **Ether** 12: 27 the Lord makes weak things become s.; 12: 37 because thou hast seen thy weakness, thou shalt be made s.; **Moro.** 7: 30 angels show themselves unto them of s. faith.

STRONGHOLD (*see also* Fort, Fortify)

Alma 50: 6 Moroni[1] prepares s.; 52: 21 Moroni[1] plans to decoy Lamanites out of s.; 58: 2 Nephites dare not attack Lamanite s.; **Hel.** 1: 27 Lamanites capture many Nephite s.

STRUGGLE (*see also* Fight; Wrestle)

Enos 1: 10 while Enos[2] s. in spirit, the Lord's voice comes; **Mosiah** 7: 18 an effectual s. remaineth to be made.

STUBBLE

1 Ne. 22: 15, 23 (2 Ne. 26: 6; 3 Ne. 25: 1; Mal. 4: 1) they who do wickedly shall be as s., to be burned; **2 Ne.** 15: 24 (Isa. 5: 24) as fire devours s., the root of the wicked shall be rottenness.

STUBBORNNESS (*see also* Hardheartedness; Pride; Stiffnecked)

Alma 32: 16 blessed is he who is baptized without s.; 51: 14 Moroni[1] is wroth because of s. of those he has labored to preserve.

STUDY (*see also* Knowledge; Learn; Ponder; Search)

Mosiah 13: 11 priests of Noah[3] have s. and taught iniquity.

STUMBLE (*see also* Err; Stumbling Block)

1 Ne. 13: 29, 34 many s. because parts of gospel are taken away; **2 Ne.** 26: 20 Gentiles have s. because of greatness of stumbling block, that they have built up many churches; **Jacob** 4: 14 God has given Jews things they could not understand, that they may *s.*; 4: 15 by *s.* of Jews, they will reject stone upon which they might build safe foundation; **Ether** 12: 25 Nephite writers s. because of placing of words.

STUMBLING BLOCK (*see also* Stumble)

1 Ne. 14: 1 Lamb will manifest himself to Gentiles to take away their *s.b.*; **2 Ne.** 4: 33 wilt thou not place *s.b.* in my way; 18: 14 (Isa. 8: 14) he shall be for a stone of s. to both houses of Israel; 26: 20 Gentiles have stumbled because of greatness of *s.b.*; **Mosiah** 7: 29 doings of the Lord's people shall be as *s.b.*; **Alma** 4: 10 wickedness of church is *s-b.* to those who do not belong to church.

STUPOR

Alma 60: 7 can you sit upon thrones in thoughtless *s.*

SUBJECT, SUBJECTION (*see also* Bondage; Captive, Captivity; Conquer; Obedience; Prey; Reconcile; Submissive; Yield; Yoke)

2 Ne. 9: 5 Creator will suffer himself to become *s.* to man, that men might become *s.* to him; **Mosiah** 7: 18 Limhi's people will not be in *s.* to enemies; 15: 2 he shall be called Son, having *s.* flesh to Father's will; 15: 5 flesh to become *s.* to Spirit; 16: 11 (Alma 12: 17; 34: 35) spirits of the wicked delivered to devil, who hath *s.* them; **Alma** 5: 20 can ye think of being saved when ye have yielded yourselves to be *s.* to devil; 12: 6 adversary lays snare to bring people into *s.*; 34: 39 pray not to be led away as *s.* of devil; 42: 7 first parents became *s.* to follow after their own will; 43: 6–7 Zerahemnah appoints Nephite dissenters as captains over Lamanites, to bring them into *s.*; **Moro.** 7: 17 neither devil nor those who *s.* themselves to him persuade men to do good; 9: 26 Christ sits on right hand of power until all things become *s.* to him.

SUBMISSIVE, SUBMIT (*see also* Humble; Obedience; Patience; Reconcile; Subject; Yield)

Mosiah 3: 19 natural man is enemy to God unless he becomes as child, *s.*, willing to *s.* to all things; **Alma** 7: 23 be *s.* and gentle; 13: 28 be led by Holy Spirit, becoming *s.*

SUBSTANCE (*see also* Charity; Property)

Jacob 2: 17 be free with your *s.*; **Mosiah** 4: 16–29 (18: 26–27; Alma 1: 27; 4: 13; 34: 28) administer of your *s.* unto those in need; **Hel.** 13: 28 Nephites would give *s.* to false prophet; **4 Ne.** 1: 25 Nephites no longer have *s.* in common; **Morm.** 8: 37 ye love your *s.* more than ye love the poor.

SUBTLETY, SUBTLE (*see also* Craftiness; Cunning; Guile; Wiles)

2 Ne. 5: 24 Lamanites an idle people, full of mischief and *s.*; **Alma** 12: 4 Zeezrom's plan was *s.*, as to *s.* of the devil; 47: 4 Amalickiah a *s.* man to do evil.

SUCCOR (*see also* Help; Relief; Strengthen)

Mosiah 4: 16 (Alma 4: 13) *s.* those who stand in need; 7: 29 the Lord will not *s.* his people in day of transgression; **Alma** 7: 12 Son to know according to flesh how to *s.* his people.

SUCK, SUCKING (*see also* Suckling)

1 Ne. 17: 2 women give plenty of *s.* for children; 21: 15 (Isa. 49: 15) can a woman forget her *s.* child; **2 Ne.** 21: 8 (30: 14; Isa. 11: 8) *s.* child shall play on hole of asp; **Hel.** 15: 2 women shall have great cause to mourn in day that they give *s.*

SUCKLING (*see also* Suck)

3 Ne. 28: 22 disciples play with wild beasts as child with *s.* lamb.

SUFFER [=allow] (*see also* Long-suffering; Suffering, Suffer)

1 Ne. 19: 9 (Mosiah 15: 5) world shall smite Messiah, and he shall *s.* it; 20: 11 (Isa. 11: 11) the Lord will not *s.* his name to be polluted; **2 Ne.** 26: 30 those who have charity would not *s.* laborer in Zion to perish; **Mosiah** 4: 14 ye will not *s.* your children to go hungry, to transgress; 4: 16 ye will not *s.* beggar to put up petition in vain; **Alma** 14: 10–11 the Lord *s.* the wicked to kill the righteous, that judgment might be just; **3 Ne.** 11: 11 Christ has *s.* will of Father in all things.

SUFFERING, SUFFER (*see also* Affliction; Anguish; Chasten; Despair; Infirmity; Misery; Mourn; Oppression; Pain; Sorrow; Tribulation; Trouble)

1 Ne. 18: 17 parents have *s.* much grief because of children; 19: 12 the God of nature *s.*; **2 Ne.** 9: 21–22 God *s.* pains of every living creature that resurrection might pass upon men; **Jacob** 1: 8 all men should *s.* Christ's cross; **Mosiah** 3: 7 (15: 5) the Lord shall *s.* temptations and pains even more than men can *s.*; 18: 1–2 Alma[1] teaches Abinadi's words concerning *s.* and death of Christ; **Alma** 7: 13 Son *s.* in flesh that he might take upon him his people's sins; 20: 29 brethren of Ammon[2] were patient in *s.*; 21: 9 no redemption for mankind, save through death and s. of Christ; 26: 30 sons of Mosiah[2] have s. all manner of affliction that they might be means of saving one soul; 31:38 the Lord has given his servants strength that they should s. no afflictions; **Hel.** 14: 20 on day that Christ s. death, sun shall be darkened; **3 Ne.** 6: 20 many prophets testify of Christ's death and s.; 28: 26, 38 change wrought in three Nephites that they might not s. pain or sorrow; **Moro.** 9: 25 may Christ's s. and death rest in your mind forever.

SUFFICIENT, SUFFICIENTLY

2 Ne. 2: 5 men are instructed s. that they know good from evil; 25: 28 words of Nephi[1] are s. to teach any man the right way; **Mosiah** 4: 24 those who have not and yet have s. should say, if I had I would give; **Alma** 5: 27 could ye say ye have been s. humble; 24: 11 it was all converted Lamanites could do to repent s.; **3 Ne.** 13: 34 (Matt. 6: 34) s. is the day unto the evil thereof; 17: 8 Nephites' faith is s. that Jesus should heal them; **Ether** 9: 35 when Jaredites humble themselves s., the Lord sends rain; 12: 26 the Lord's grace is s. for the meek; 12: 27 the Lord's grace is s. for all men who humble themselves; **Moro.** 10: 32 Christ's grace is s. for you to be perfect in him.

SUN (*see also* Astronomy)

1 Ne. 1: 9 Lehi[1] beholds one descending from heaven whose luster is above s. at noon-day; **2 Ne.** 23: 10 (Isa. 13: 10) s. shall be darkened; **Hel.** 12: 15 s. appears to stand still; 14: 4 (3 Ne. 1: 15–19) no darkness at setting of s. when Christ comes; 14: 20 (3 Ne. 8: 22) s. shall be darkened at Christ's death; **3 Ne.** 12: 45 (Matt. 5: 45) Father maketh his s. rise on the evil and the good.

SUNK

1 Ne. 12: 4 (3 Ne. 8: 14; 9: 4, 6, 8; 4 Ne. 1: 9) many cities to be s.; **3 Ne.** 10: 12–13 the righteous are spared and are not s.

SUPPLICATE, SUPPLICATION (*see also* Prayer)

Enos 1: 4 Enos[2] cries unto Maker in s. for his soul; **Alma** 7: 3 people of Gideon continue in s. of God's grace; 31: 10 Zoramites do not continue in s. to God daily; **3 Ne.** 4: 10 Nephites s. God for protection; **Moro.** 6: 9 saints preach, pray, s. in church meetings as led by Holy Ghost.

SUPPLY (*see* Provision)

SUPPORT (*see also* Help; Maintain; Preserve; Uphold)

2 Ne. 4: 20 my God hath been my s.; **Mosiah** 2: 21 God s. you from one moment to another; 2: 30 the Lord doth s. me; 11: 3–4 Noah[3] taxes people for his s.; 11: 6 priests are s. in laziness by king's taxes; 18: 24 (27: 5) priests should labor with own hands for s.; 21: 17 Limhi commands that every man impart to s. of widows; **Alma** 30: 60 devil will not s. his children; 36: 3 whosoever puts trust in God shall be s. in trials; 46: 35 those who do not covenant to s. freedom are put to death; 48: 10 Moroni[1] prepares to s. liberty; 50: 39 chief judge appointed with oath to s. cause of God; 51: 17 pride of king-men to be pulled down, or they should s. cause of liberty; **Hel.** 6: 38 Nephites s. robbers; **Ether** 10: 6 Riplakish causes people to labor continually for their s.

SUPREME

Alma 11: 22 Zeezrom offers Amulek money to deny existence of S. Being; 12: 32 works of justice could not be destroyed according to s. goodness of God; 30: 44 earth and the planets witness there is a S. Creator.

SURE, SURETY

1 Ne. 5: 8 Sariah knows of s. that the Lord commanded Lehi[1] to flee; **2 Ne.** 25: 7 men shall know of s. when prophecies of Isaiah[1] come to pass; **Jacob** 4: 15–17 (Hel. 5: 12) stone rejected by Jews shall be only s. foundation; **Mosiah** 1: 6 we can know of s. of plates because we have seen them; 24: 14 people of Alma[1] to know of s. that the Lord visits his people in their afflictions; **Alma** 23: 6 as s. as the Lord liveth, converted Lamanites never fell away; 32: 17 many say they will know of s. if shown sign; 32: 26 ye cannot know of s. of words at first any more than faith is perfect knowledge; 32: 31 are you s. this is a good seed; **Hel.** 5: 12 rock of Redeemer is s. foundation; 13: 32, 38 your destruction is made s.; 14: 4 ye shall know of s. that there are two days and a night without darkness; **3 Ne.** 11: 15 after feeling Christ's wounds, multitude know of s. and bear record; **Ether** 12: 4 whoso believeth in God might with s. hope for better world; **Moro.** 7: 26 as s. as Christ liveth, he spoke these words to our fathers.

SWALLOW

1 Ne. 15: 27 mind of Lehi[1] so s. up in other things, he did not notice filthiness of river; **2 Ne.** 26: 5 earth shall s. those who kill prophets; **Mosiah** 15: 7 will of Son is s. up in will of Father; 16: 8 (Alma 22: 14; Morm. 7: 5) sting of death is s. in Christ; **Alma** 31: 27 men's hearts are s. up in pride; 31: 38 missionaries are s. up in joy of Christ; 36: 28 (Hel. 8: 11) the

Lord has s. up Egyptians in Red Sea; **Ether** 2: 25 Jaredites need light when s. in depths of sea.

SWEAR, SWARE, SWORN, SWEARING (*see also* Oath; Promise; Swearer)

1 Ne. 20: 1 (Isa. 48: 1) Israel s. by name of the Lord but not in truth or righteousness; **Jacob** 1: 7 men should partake of goodness of God, lest he s. in wrath they should not enter in; **Mosiah** 19: 19 followers of Noah[3] have s. they will return to land of Nephi; 20: 24 Lamanite king s. oath his people will not destroy Limhi's people; **Alma** 49: 27 Amalickiah s. oath to drink blood of Moroni[1]; **Hel.** 1: 11 (Ether 8: 14) secret combination s. not to reveal murderer; **3 Ne.** 3: 8 Giddianhi s. not to destroy Nephites if they join robbers; 12: 33–37 (Matt. 5: 33–37) s. not at all; **Morm.** 3: 10, 14 Nephites s. by heavens they would go to battle against enemies; **Ether** 9: 5 secret combination s. by oath of ancients.

SWEARER

3 Ne. 24: 5 (Mal. 3: 5) the Lord will be swift witness against false s.

SWEEP, SWEPT (*see also* Destruction)

Jacob 5: 66 the Lord will s. away bad out of vineyard; **Enos** 1: 6 guilt of Enos[1] is s. away; **Jarom** 1: 3 God is merciful unto Nephites and has not s. them from land; **Ether** 2: 8 those in promised land who do not serve God shall be s. off; 14: 18 Shiz s. earth before him.

SWEET (*see also* Opposition)

1 Ne. 8: 10–11 (Alma 32: 42) fruit of tree is most s.; 17: 12 the Lord will make Lehites' food s., that they cook it not; **2 Ne.** 2: 15 forbidden fruit set in opposition to tree of life, one being s. and the other bitter; 15: 20 wo unto those who put bitter for s. and s. for bitter; **Alma** 36: 21 nothing could be so s. as joy of Alma[2] at being redeemed.

SWELL, SWELLING (*see also* Grow; Increase)

Alma 30: 31 Korihor rises up in great s. words before Alma[2]; 32: 30, 33 (33: 23) if seed s., ye must know it is good; 48: 12 heart of Moroni[1] s. with thanksgiving to God; **Hel.** 13: 22 your hearts s. with great pride.

SWIFT (*see also* Quick, Quickly)

1 Ne. 17: 45 elder brothers of Nephi[1] are s. to do iniquity; **Ether** 14: 22 so s. is war that none was left to bury dead.

SWINE (*see also* Sow [noun])

3 Ne. 14: 6 (Matt. 7: 6) do not cast your pearls before s.; **Ether** 9: 18 Jaredites have s.

SWORD (*see also* War; Weapon)

1 Ne. 1: 13 many inhabitants of Jerusalem shall perish by s.; 4: 9, 18–19 Nephi[1] cuts off Laban's head with his own s.; 21: 2 (Isa. 49: 2) the Lord hath made my mouth like sharp s.; **2 Ne.** 5: 14 (Jacob 1: 10; W of M 1: 13; Mosiah 1: 16) Nephites keep s. of Laban; 12: 4 (Isa. 2: 4) they shall beat s. into plow-shares; **Mosiah** 8: 11 Limhi's people find rusted s. in land northward; **Alma** 1: 12 Nehor has endeavored to enforce priestcraft by s.; 10: 22 Nephites would be destroyed by s. except for the righteous; 17: 37–38 Ammon[2] smites off Lamanites' arms with s.; 24: 12 since God has taken away stains and s. have become bright, let us stain s. no more; 24: 17 people of Anti-Nephi-Lehi bury s.; 26: 19 why did God not let s. of justice fall upon us; 42: 2–3 God placed cherubim and flaming s. to keep tree of life; 48: 14 Nephites are taught never to raise s. except against enemy; 60: 29 s. of justice hangs over you; 62: 5 thousands take up s. in defence of freedom; **Hel.** 11: 5 work of destruction ceases by s. and becomes sore by famine; 13: 5 s. of justice hangs over Nephites, to fall in four hundred years; **3 Ne.** 2: 19 s. of destruction hangs over Nephites; 20: 20 (Ether 8: 23) s. of the Lord's justice will fall upon Gentiles unless they repent; 29: 4 s. of the Lord's justice will overtake those who spurn his doings; **Morm.** 8: 41 s. of vengeance hangs over Nephites; **Ether** 7: 9 Shule makes s. of steel; 14: 4 many thousands fall by s.

SYNAGOGUE (*see also* Building; Sanctuary)

2 Ne. 26: 26 the Lord has not commanded any to depart out of s.; **Alma** 16: 13 Nephites build s. after manner of Jews; 21: 4, 6 Amalekites build s. after manner of Nehors; 26: 29 sons of Mosiah[2] have entered s. and taught Lamanites; 31: 12 Zoramites have built s.; 32: 2 Zoramites cast poor out of s.; **Hel.** 3: 9 people in land northward use timber to build s.; **3 Ne.** 13: 5 (Matt. 6: 5) hypocrites pray in s. to be seen of men; 18: 32 do not cast transgressor out of s.; **Moro.** 7: 1 Mormon[2] taught people in s.

TABERNACLE (*see also* Body; Building; BD Tabernacle)

2 Ne. 14: 6 (Isa. 4: 6) there shall be *t.* for shadow from heat and place of refuge; **Mosiah** 3: 5 (Alma 7: 8) God shall dwell in *t.* of clay; **Moro.** 9: 6 we have labor to perform while in *t.* of clay.

TAKE, TAKEN (*see also* Deprive)

1 Ne. 10: 10 Lamb should *t.* away sins of world; 13: 26–29, 40 plain and precious parts of gospel are *t.* away; **2 Ne.** 26: 32 (Mosiah 13: 15; Ex. 20: 7) the Lord commands that men should not *t.* his name in vain; 31: 13 (Mosiah 5: 8, 10; Alma 34: 38; 46: 18, 21; 3 Ne. 27: 6; Morm. 8: 38; Moro. 4: 3) *t.* upon you name of Christ; **Mosiah** 7: 27 (Ether 3: 9, 16) Christ to *t.* upon himself image of man, *t.* upon himself flesh and blood; **Alma** 11: 40 (34: 8) Son shall *t.* upon himself transgressions of those who believe.

TALENT (*see also* TG Talents)

Ether 12: 35 if Gentiles have not charity, the Lord will take away their *t.*

TALK (*see also* Communication; Speak)

1 Ne. 16: 38 Nephi[1] says the Lord has *t.* with him; **2 Ne.** 25: 26 Nephites *t.* of Christ; **Hel.** 5: 36 Nephi[2] and Lehi[4] are in attitude of *t.* to some being; **Ether** 2: 14 the Lord *t.* to brother of Jared[2] from cloud; 12: 39 Moroni[2] has *t.* with Jesus face to face.

TAME

Jacob 5: 3—6: 1 Israel likened to *t.* olive-tree.

TARRY (*see also* Abide; Remain; Wait)

1 Ne. 4: 35 Zoram[1] makes oath to *t.* with Lehites; 8: 2 Lehi[1] *t.* in wilderness; **Mosiah** 20: 4 priests of Noah[3] *t.* in wilderness; **3 Ne.** 17: 5 multitude ask Jesus to *t.* a little longer; 28: 4–12 (4 Ne. 1: 14, 30, 37; Morm. 8: 10; 9: 22) three Nephites allowed to *t.* until Christ's coming.

TASK (*see also* Burden; Labor)

1 Ne. 17: 25 children of Israel were laden with *t.* grievous to bear; **Jacob** 2: 10 notwithstanding greatness of *t.*, I must do according to strict commands of God; **Mosiah** 24: 9 Amulon puts *t*-masters over people of Alma[1].

TASTE (*see also* Bitter; Eat; Partake; Sweet)

1 Ne. 8: 11 (11: 7) fruit of tree is sweet above all that Lehi[1] has *t.*; 8: 28 those who *t.* of fruit become ashamed; **Jacob** 5: 31 the Lord of vineyard *t.* of fruit; **Mosiah** 4: 11 if ye have *t.* of God's love, humble yourselves; **Alma** 36: 26 because of the word, many have *t.* as I have *t.*; **3 Ne.** 28: 7, 25, 31–40 (Ether 12: 17) three Nephites shall never *t.* of death; **Morm.** 1: 15 Mormon[2] has *t.* of Jesus' goodness.

TAUGHT (*see* Teach, Taught)

TAX (*see also* Government, Civil; Support; Tribute)

Mosiah 2: 14 Benjamin labors with own hands, that people might not be laden with *t.*; **Mosiah** 7: 15 (11: 3) Limhi's people are *t.* with grievous *t.* of one-fifth of possessions; **Ether** 10: 5 Riplakish *t.* his people with heavy *t.*; 10: 6 those who would not be subject to *t.* are cast into prison.

TEACH, TAUGHT (*see also* Doctrine; Expound; Instruction, Instruct; Learn; Liken; Preach; Reasoning; Sayings; Teacher; TG Jesus Christ, Teaching Mode of; Teachable; Teaching, Teach; Teaching with the Spirit)

1 Ne. 1: 1 Nephi[1] was *t.* in learning of father; 20: 17 (Isa. 48: 17) the Lord *t.* thee to profit; **2 Ne.** 25: 28 words of Nephi[1] are sufficient to *t.* any man right way; 28: 14 men err because they are *t.* precepts of men; 32: 8 hearken unto Spirit which *t.* men to pray; 32: 8 evil spirit *t.* that man must not pray; 33: 1 Nephi[1] cannot write all things *t.* among Nephites; 33: 10 these words *t.* that all men should do good; **Jacob** 1: 19 priests answer sins of people upon own heads if they do not *t.* diligently; **Enos** 1: 1 Jacob[2] *t.* Enos[2] in his language, nurture and admonition of the Lord; **Omni** 1: 18 people of Zarahemla are *t.* language of Mosiah[1]; **Mosiah** 1: 2 Benjamin *t.* sons in language of fathers; 4: 15 *t.* children to walk in ways of soberness, to love and serve one another; 9: 1 Zeniff has been *t.* in language of Nephites; 13: 11 priests of Noah[3] have studied and *t.* iniquity; 18: 26 priests to have knowledge of God, that they might *t.* with power and authority; **Alma** 17: 3 sons of Mosiah[2] *t.* with power and authority; 29: 8 God grants unto all nations, of their own tongue, to *t.* his word; 37: 34 *t.* them never to be weary of good works, but to be meek; 48: 14 Nephites are *t.* to defend themselves, *t.* never to give offense; 53: 21 Ammonite youths had been *t.* to keep commandments; 56: 47 (57: 21) Ammonite youths had been *t.* by mothers that God would deliver them; **3 Ne.** 22: 13 (Isa. 54: 13) thy children shall be *t.* of the Lord; 26: 6 only small part of what Jesus *t.* can be recorded; **4 Ne.** 1: 38 those who rebel against gospel *t.* children not to believe; 1: 39 Lamanites are *t.* to hate children of God; **Ether** 6: 17 Jaredites are *t.* from on high to walk humbly before the Lord; **Moro.** 10: 9 to one is given to *t.* word of wisdom; 10: 10 to another is given to *t.* word of knowledge.

TEACHER (*see also* Priesthood; Teach; TG Teacher)

1 Ne. 2: 22 (16: 37; 2 Ne. 5: 19) Nephi[1] to be made *t.* over brethren; **2 Ne.** 5: 26 (Jacob 1: 18) Nephi[1] consecrates Jacob[2] and Joseph[2] as priests and *t.*; 9:

48 Nephites look to Jacob[2] as *t.*; 28: 12 churches to become corrupted because of false *t.*; **Jarom** 1: 11 *t.* labor diligently, exhorting people to diligence; **Mosiah** 2: 29 Benjamin can no longer be Nephites' *t.* and king; 23: 14 trust no man to be *t.* except he be man of God; 23: 17 (Alma 4: 7; 15: 13) Alma[1] consecrates just men as *t.*; 25: 19 Mosiah[2] gives Alma[1] power to ordain *t.* over every church; **Alma** 1: 15 Nehor declares every *t.* ought to become popular; 1: 26 *t.* is not esteemed any better than learner; 23: 4 Aaron[2] and brethren appoint *t.* over all churches in land of Lamanites; **Morm.** 8: 28 *t.* in churches shall rise in pride; **Moro.** ch. 3 manner in which elders ordained *t.*; 6: 1 *t.* are baptized.

TEANCUM—*great Nephite military leader* [c. 67 B.C.]

Alma 50: 35 slays Morianton[2]; 51: 29–32 defeats army of Amalickiah; 51: 33–34 slays Amalickiah; 52: 1–6 prepares to battle Lamanites; 52: 17–20 is ordered to attack city of Mulek; 52: 22–28 decoys Lamanites and scatters them; 53: 3 sets prisoners to work; 61: 18 (62: 13) food sought for *T*'s army; 62: 3 *T.* and Lehi[3] are given command over remainder of army of Moroni[1]; 62: 35–36 slays Ammoron and is slain.

TEANCUM, CITY OF—*by seashore near City of Desolation*

Morm. 4: 3 Nephites flee to *T.*; 4: 6–8 Lamanites attack *T.*, are repulsed; 4: 14 is taken by Lamanites, and women and children are sacrificed to idols.

TEARS (*see also* Joy; Sorrow; Weep)

1 Ne. 18: 19 wife and children of Nephi[1] and children do not soften brothers' hearts with *t.*; **Mosiah** 25: 9 Nephites shed *t.* of sorrow over brethren slain by Lamanites; **Alma** 19: 28 Abish sorrows unto *t.* over contention among Lamanites; **3 Ne.** 4: 33 Nephites' hearts are swollen with joy, unto gushing out of *t.*; 17: 5 multitude are in *t.*; 17: 10 Nephites bathe Christ's feet with *t.*; **Ether** 6: 12 Jaredites shed *t.* of joy because of the Lord's tender mercies.

TEETH (*see* Tooth, Teeth)

TELL, TOLD (*see also* Declare; Discern; Rehearse; Revelation, Reveal; Teach)

2 Ne. 28: 22 devil *t.* men there is no hell; 31: 17 do things I have *t.* you I have seen the Lord do; 32: 3 words of Christ will *t.* you all things ye should do; **Jacob** 2: 5 by help of Creator I can *t.* your thoughts; **Alma** 37: 15 Alma[2] *t.* Helaman[2] by spirit of prophecy that sacred things will be taken if he transgresses; **Hel.** 9: 41 Nephi[2] *t.* Nephites thoughts of hearts; **3 Ne.** 20: 45 (21: 8) that which kings had not been *t.* them shall they see; 28: 15 whether three Nephites were in or out of body the multitude cannot *t.*; **Ether** 13: 2 Ether *t.* Jaredites of all things from beginning; **Moro.** 7: 21 I *t.* you the way whereby ye may lay hold on every good thing; 9: 19 tongue cannot *t.* of Nephites' perversion.

TEMPERATE (*see also* TG Temperance)

Alma 7: 23 (38: 10) be *t.* in all things.

TEMPEST (*see also* Destruction; Storm; Whirlwind; Wind)

1 Ne. 18: 13–21 great *t.* arises during journey to promised land; 19: 11 the Lord will visit house of Israel by *t.*; **2 Ne.** 6: 15 they who believe not in Messiah shall be destroyed by *t.*; 27: 12 all nations of Gentiles and Jews to be visited with *t.*; **Hel.** 14: 23 (3 Ne. 8: 6) great *t.* at Christ's death; **Morm.** 8: 29 there shall be heard of *t.* in foreign lands; **Ether** 6: 6 Jaredite vessels buried in depths of sea because of great *t.*

TEMPLE (*see also* Body; Building; House; Sanctuary; Tabernacle; TG Temple; Temple, House of the Lord; BD Temple)

2 Ne. 5: 16 Nephi[1] builds *t.* after manner of Solomon; 12: 2 (Isa. 2: 2) mountain of the Lord's house shall be established in top of mountains; 16: 1 (Isa. 6: 1) the Lord's train filled the *t.*; **Jacob** 1: 17 Jacob[2] teaches in *t.*; 2: 2, 11 the Lord commands Jacob[2] to declare word in *t.*; **Mosiah** 1: 18 Benjamin gathers his people at *t.*; 2: 37 (Alma 7: 21; 34: 36) the Lord dwells not in unholy *t.*; **Alma** 10: 2 Aminadi interpreted writing upon wall of *t.*, written by finger of the Lord; 16: 13 Alma[2] and Amulek preach in *t.*; 23: 2 (26: 29) sons of Mosiah[2] are given free access to Lamanites' *t.*; 34: 36 (Hel. 4: 24) the Lord's Spirit dwells not in unholy *t.*; **Hel.** 10: 8 Nephi[2] is given power to rend *t.* in twain; **3 Ne.** 11: 1 multitude is gathered around *t.* when Christ appears; 24: 1 (Mal. 3: 1) the Lord shall suddenly come to his *t.*

TEMPORAL, TEMPORALLY (*see also* Death, Physical; Flesh; Mortal; Nature, Natural; Outward; Spiritual, Spiritually; World)

1 Ne. 14: 7 the hardhearted shall be led down to destruction, *t.* and spiritually; 15: 26–32 river of filthy water is representation of things both *t.* and spiritual; 22: 6 these things of which are spoken are *t.*; **2 Ne.** 2: 5 by *t.* law men were cut off; **Mosiah** 2: 41 those who keep commandments are blessed in all things, both *t.* and spiritual; 4: 26 administer to relief of poor, both spiritually and *t.*; 18: 29

Nephites impart to each other both *t.* and spiritually; **Alma** 7: 23 ask for whatsoever things ye stand in need, both *t.* and spiritual; 12: 31 men first transgressed first commandments as to things which were *t.* and became as Gods, knowing good and evil; 36: 4 Alma[2] knows these things, not of the *t.* but of the spiritual; 42: 7 first parents were cut off both *t.* and spiritually; 42: 9 fall brought upon mankind spiritual death as well as *t.* death; **Hel.** 14: 16 being cut off from presence of God by fall, all mankind were dead both as to things *t.* and spiritual; **Morm.** 2: 15 day of grace is past with Nephites, both *t.* and spiritually.

TEMPT, TEMPTATION (*see also* Agency; Devil; Entice; Probation; Prove; Seduce; TG Tempt, Temptation; BD Tempt)

1 Ne. 12: 17 mists of darkness are *t.* of devil; 12: 19 because of *t.* of devil, Lamanites' seed overpower Nephites' seed; 15: 24 *t.* of adversary cannot overpower those who hearken unto word of God; **2 Ne.** 4: 27 why should I give way to *t.*, that evil one have place in my heart; 17: 12 (Isa. 7: 12) neither will I *t.* the Lord; **Jacob** 7: 14 what am I that I should *t.* God; **Mosiah** 3: 7 (15: 5; Alma 7: 11) the Lord shall suffer *t.*, but shall not yield; **Alma** 11: 23 why *t.* ye me, the righteous yield to no such *t.*; 13: 28 pray that ye be not *t.* above what ye can bear; 30: 44 will ye *t.* your God; 31: 10 Zoramites do not pray that they might not enter into *t.*; 34: 39 (3 Ne. 13: 12; 18: 18; Morm. 9: 28) pray that ye may not be led away by *t.* of devil; 37: 33 teach them to withstand every *t.* of devil with faith in Christ; **3 Ne.** 2: 3 Satan leads away hearts of people, *t.* them; 6: 15 Satan causes iniquity by *t.* people to seek for power and riches; 6: 17 people had been delivered up to be carried about by *t.* of devil; 13: 12 (Matt. 6: 13) lead us not into *t.*; 18: 25 whosoever breaks this commandment suffers himself to be led into *t.*; 28: 39 change wrought in three Nephites, that Satan could not *t.* them.

TEN (*see also* Israel, Ten Lost Tribes of; Ten Commandments; Tithes)

Morm. 1: 2 Mormon[2] is *t.* years old when Ammaron comes to him.

TEN COMMANDMENTS (*see also* Commandments of God; TG Ten Commandments; BD Commandments, the Ten)

Mosiah 12: 33–36; 13: 12–24 Abinadi teaches T.C.

TENDER (*see also* Gentle; Mercy)

1 Ne. 8: 37 Lehi[1] exhorts sons with all feeling of *t.* parent; **Jacob** 2: 7, 9 Jacob[2] is grieved to speak with boldness before wives and children, whose feelings are *t.* and delicate; **Mosiah** 14: 2 (Isa. 53: 2) he shall grow up before him as *t.* plant.

TENT

1 Ne. 2: 15 Lehi[1] dwells in *t.*; 16: 12 Lehites take *t.* and depart; 18: 23 Lehites pitch *t.* in promised land; **2 Ne.** 5: 7 Nephi[1] and followers take *t.* and depart into wilderness; **Enos** 1: 20 Lamanites dwell in *t.*; **Mosiah** 2: 5–6 Benjamin's people pitch *t.* around temple; 18: 34 Alma[1] and people take *t.* and flee into wilderness; **Alma** 2: 20 Nephite army pitch *t.* in valley of Gideon; 46: 31 Nephite army marches with *t.* into wilderness; **Ether** 2: 13 Jaredites pitch *t.* by sea; 9: 3 Omer and household pitch *t.* in Ablom by seashore; 15: 11 army of Coriantumr[2] pitch *t.* by hill Ramah.

TENTH (*see* Tithes)

TEOMNER—*Nephite military officer* [c. 63 B.C.]

Alma 58: 16–23 takes part in successful ambush of Lamanites.

TERROR, TERRIBLE (*see also* Fear, Fearful; Harrow; Horror)

1 Ne. 12: 5 multitudes fall because of *t.* judgments of the Lord; 12: 18 *t.* gulf divides building and tree; **2 Ne.** 20: 33 (Isa. 10: 33) the Lord shall lop bough with *t.*; **3 Ne.** 4: 7 *t.* battle between Nephites and armies of Giddianhi; 8: 6 tempest at death of Christ; 8: 24–25 O that we had repented before great and *t.* day; 22: 14 (Isa. 54: 14) *t.* for oppressions shall not come near thee; **Morm.** 6: 8 every soul filled with *t.* because of greatness of Lamanites' numbers; **Ether** 6: 6 Jaredite vessels buried in sea because of *t.* tempests.

TESTIFY (*see also* Manifest; Preach; Prove; Record; Testimony; Verified; Witness)

1 Ne. 10: 5 (Jacob 7: 11; 3 Ne. 7: 10; 20: 24) great number of prophets have *t.* of Messiah; **2 Ne.** 3: 6–21 Joseph[1] *t.* concerning latter-day seer; 27: 12 three witnesses will *t.* to truth of book; **Jacob** 7: 11 (Alma 34: 30) scriptures *t.* of Christ; **Alma** 5: 45–46 Alma[2] *t.* to truth of what he has said; 7: 26 Alma[2] has spoken according to Spirit which *t.* in him; 14: 3 Alma[2] and Amulek have *t.* plainly against lawyers' wickedness; 34: 8 Amulek *t.* that words of prophets concerning Christ are true; **Hel.** 8: 9 if Nephi[2] were not a prophet, he could not *t.* concerning these things; 13: 26 Nephites would reject prophet who *t.* of their sins; **3 Ne.** 6: 20 inspired men *t.* boldly of Nephites' sins and redemption of Christ.

TESTIMONY (*see also* Faith; Holy Ghost; Know, Knowledge; Revelation; Testify; Witness; TG Testimony)

2 Ne. 18: 16 (Isa. 8: 16) bind up the *t.*; 25: 28 words of Nephi[1] to stand as *t.* against his people; 27: 13 few others will view book to bear *t.*; 29: 8 *t.* of two nations that the Lord is God will run together; **Alma** 4: 19 Alma[2] reclaims people by bearing down in pure *t.* against them; 4: 20 Alma[2] confines himself wholly to *t.* of word; 6: 8 Alma[2] declares word of God according to *t.* of Jesus Christ; 7: 13 Alma[2] bears *t.* of atonement through Son; 7: 16 whosoever keeps commandments shall have eternal life, according to *t.* of Holy Spirit; 30: 40–41 all things are *t.* that Christ's coming is true; **Ether** 5: 4 *t.* of three and this work shall stand as *t.* against world; **Moro.** 7: 31 angels declare word of Christ to chosen vessels that they may bear *t.* of him.

THANK, THANKS (*see also* Blessing; Indebted; Praise; Rejoice; Thankful; Thanksgiving)

1 Ne. 2: 7 (5: 9–10; 7: 22) Lehi[1] builds altar and gives *t.* to the Lord; **2 Ne.** 9: 52 give *t.* unto God's holy name by night; 29: 4 what *t.* the Gentiles the Jews for the Bible; **Mosiah** 2: 19 you ought to *t.* your heavenly King; 2: 20–21 if you should render all *t.* to God, yet would you be unprofitable servants; 8: 19 Limhi rejoices and gives *t.* to God; 24: 21 people of Alma[1] pour out *t.* unto God because he has been merciful to them; 26: 39 teachers are commanded to give *t.* in all things; **Alma** 7: 23 always return *t.* to God for whatsoever things you receive; 24: 7 Lamanite king *t.* God that he has sent Nephites to preach to them; 26: 8 let us give *t.* to God's holy name; 37: 37 when thou risest in morning, let thy heart be full of *t.* unto God; 49: 28 Nephites *t.* God because of his matchless power in delivering them; **Morm.** 9: 31 give *t.* unto God that he hath made manifest unto you your imperfections; **Ether** 6: 9 brother of Jared[2] *t.* the Lord all day long.

THANKFUL (*see also* Thank, Thanks; Thanksgiving)

Jacob 4: 3 teachers hope brethren and children will receive writings with *t.* hearts; **Mosiah** 7: 12 Ammon[1] is *t.* before God that he is permitted to speak.

THANKSGIVING (*see also* Thank, Thanks; Thankful)

2 Ne. 8: 3 (Isa. 51: 3) *t.* shall be found in Zion; **Alma** 19: 14 Ammon[2] pours out soul in *t.* to God; 34: 38 live in *t.* daily; 48: 12 heart of Moroni[1] swells with *t.* to God; **3 Ne.** 10: 10 Nephites' lamentations are turned in *t.* unto Christ.

THIEF, THIEVES, THIEVING (*see also* Rob; Robber; Steal)

Alma 1: 32 those who do not belong to church indulge in *t.*; 11: 2 those who do not pay what they owe are cast out as *t.*; **3 Ne.** 13: 19–20 (27: 32; Matt. 6: 19–20) lay not up treasures upon earth, where *t.* break through and steal; **Morm.** 2: 10 no man can keep what is his own because of *t.*

THINK, THOUGHT (*see also* Consider; Imagination; Intent; Ponder; Reasoning; Thoughts)

2 Ne. 9: 28 when men are learned, they *t.* they are wise; **Jacob** 2: 17 *t.* of your brethren like unto yourselves; **Mosiah** 23: 7 one man shall not *t.* himself above another; **Moro.** 7: 45 (1 Cor. 13: 5) charity *t.* no evil.

THIRD (*see also* Three)

Mosiah 3: 10 Christ shall rise from the dead the *t.* day; 13: 13 (Ex. 20: 5) the Lord visits iniquities of fathers upon children unto *t.* and fourth generation; **Hel.** 5: 33 voice comes *t.* time; **3 Ne.** 11: 5–6 multitude understand voice the *t.* time they hear it.

THIRST (*see also* Athirst; Blood-thirsty; Drink; Water)

1 Ne. 16: 35 (Alma 37: 42) Lehites have suffered *t.* in wilderness; 17: 29 Moses brings water from rock to quench Israel's *t.*; 20: 21 (Isa. 48: 21) they *t.* not; 21: 10 (Isa. 49: 10) they shall not hunger nor *t.*; **2 Ne.** 7: 2 (Isa. 50: 2) the Lord makes rivers a wilderness and they die of *t.*; 9: 50 every one that *t.*, come to waters; **Alma** 32: 42 those who feast upon fruit of tree shall not *t.*; **3 Ne.** 12: 6 (Matt. 5: 6) blessed are they who hunger and *t.* after righteousness; 20: 8 he who partakes of sacrament shall never hunger nor *t.*; **Moro.** 9: 5 Lamanites *t.* after blood and revenge continually.

THISTLE

Mosiah 12: 12 thou shalt be as blossoms of *t.*; **3 Ne.** 14: 16 (Matt. 7: 16) do men gather figs of *t.*

THORN

2 Ne. 15: 6 (Isa. 5: 6) I shall lay it waste and briers and *t.* shall come up; 17: 23 (Isa. 7: 23) every place shall be for briers and *t.*; 19: 18 (Isa. 9: 18) wickedness burns as fire, shall devour briers and *t.*; 20: 17 (Isa. 10: 17) light of Israel shall burn his *t.* and briers; **3 Ne.** 14: 16 (Matt. 7: 16) do men gather grapes of *t.*

THOUGHTS (*see also* Imagination; Think, Thought)

Jacob 2: 5 by help of Creator, Jacob[2]

can tell people's *t.*; **Mosiah** 4: 30 if ye do not watch your *t.*, ye must perish; 24: 12 the Lord knows *t.* of hearts of Alma[1] and his people; **Alma** 10: 17 Amulek perceives lawyers' *t.*; 12: 3 God knows Zeezrom's *t.* and makes them known through Spirit; 12: 14 our *t.* will condemn us; 18: 18 Ammon[2] discerns Lamoni's *t.*; 18: 32 God knows all *t.* and intents of our hearts; 31: 37 missionaries take no *t.* for themselves; 32: 38 if ye take no *t.* for nourishment of tree, it will take no root; 36: 14 *t.* of coming into God's presence racked Alma[2] with horror; 37: 36 let thy *t.* be directed unto the Lord; **Hel.** 9: 41 people believe Nephi[2] is a god because he tells their *t.*; **3 Ne.** 28: 6 Christ knows *t.* of three Nephites; **Moro.** 8: 14 he who is cut off in *t.* of baptism for little children must go down to hell.

THOUSAND (*see also* Millennium)

Hel. 8: 18 coming of redemption shown to people many *t.* years before Christ's coming; **3 Ne.** 3: 24 many *t.* Nephites gather in one place against robbers.

THRASH (*see also* Harvest; Reap)

Ether 10: 25 Jaredites make tools to *t.*

THREATEN, THREATENINGS (*see also* Danger; Warn)

1 Ne. 18: 20 nothing save power of God, which *t.* destruction, could soften hearts; **Jarom** 1: 10 prophets *t.* Nephites with destruction; **Alma** 26: 18 sons of Mosiah[2] went forth with mighty *t.* to destroy church; **3 Ne.** 2: 13 Nephites are *t.* with utter destruction because of war; 4: 12 notwithstanding Giddianhi's *t.*, Nephites beat robbers.

THREE (*see also* Third; Three Nephite Disciples; Thrice; Witnesses, Three)

1 Ne. 2: 6 Lehites travel *t.* days from Jerusalem; 12: 11 (2 Ne. 26: 9) *t.* generations to pass away in righteousness after Christ's visit; 19: 10 (Hel. 14: 20, 27; 3 Ne. 8: 3, 23; 10: 9) *t.* days of darkness a sign of Christ's death; **2 Ne.** 11: 3 (27: 12; Ether 5: 3–4) by words of *t.* will the Lord establish his word; 25: 13 (Mosiah 3: 10) Christ to rise from dead after *t.* days; **Alma** 36: 10, 16 (38: 8) Alma[2] was racked with torment for *t.* days and nights; **Hel.** 1: 4 *t.* sons of Pahoran[1] contend for judgment-seat, cause *t.* divisions among people; **3 Ne.** 8: 19 tempest for *t.* hours at Christ's death; 26: 13 Christ teaches Nephites for *t.* days; **Ether** 13: 28 Shared fights Coriantumr[2] for *t.* days; **Moro.** 6: 7 if *t.* witnesses condemn unrepentant transgressor, he should not be numbered among people of Christ.

THREE NEPHITE DISCIPLES

3 Ne. 28: 1–6 Christ grants *t.* disciples' desire to tarry until his coming; 28: 7–9 shall never taste of death, sorrow; 28: 10 shall have fulness of joy; 28: 13–17 are caught up into heaven; 28: 18, 23 minister unto people; 28: 19–22 endure persecution; 28: 25 names not given; 28: 26 (Morm. 8: 11) have ministered unto Mormon[2]; 28: 27–29 to minister to Gentiles, Jews, scattered tribes, all nations; 28: 30 can show themselves to whomever it seems to them good; 28: 32 (4 Ne. 1: 5) to do marvelous works; 28: 36–40 change wrought upon their bodies; 28: 39 are sanctified in flesh, Satan has no power over them; **4 Ne.** 1: 14 only disciples of original twelve who still tarry; **Morm.** 8: 10 are taken from people because of wickedness; 8: 11 have ministered unto Moroni[2].

THRICE (*see also* Three)

3 Ne. 28: 21 disciples *t.* cast into furnace without harm; **Morm.** 3: 13 *t.* has Mormon[2] delivered Nephites from enemies.

THRONE (*see also* Dominion; Judgment-seat; Kingdom of God)

1 Ne. 1: 8 Lehi[1] sees God sitting upon *t.*; 17: 39 (3 Ne. 12: 34; Matt. 5: 34) the heavens are God's *t.*; **2 Ne.** 16: 1 (Isa. 6: 1) Isaiah[1] sees God sitting upon *t.*; 24: 13 (Isa. 14: 13) Lucifer would exalt his *t.* above stars of God; 28: 23 spirits of the wicked must stand before *t.* of God to be judged; **Jacob** 3: 8 Lamanites' skins may be whiter than Nephites' when brought before *t.* of God; **Morm.** 3: 10 Nephites swear by *t.* of God they will defeat enemies; **Moro.** 9: 26 God's *t.* is high in the heavens.

THROW, THROWN (*see also* Cast; Destruction)

1 Ne. 17: 48 brothers desire to *t.* Nephi[1] into sea; **3 Ne.** 21: 15 (Micah 3: 15) I will *t.* down all thy strongholds.

THRUST (*see also* Cast)

2 Ne. 9: 34, 36 (28: 15) liars and those who commit whoredoms shall be *t.* down to hell; 23: 15 (Isa. 13: 15) the proud shall be *t.* through; 28: 15 those who are proud, preach false doctrine, pervert right way of the Lord shall be *t.* down to hell; **Alma** 26: 5 missionaries *t.* in sickle and reap; **3 Ne.** 11: 14–15 multitude *t.* hands into Christ's side.

THUNDER, THUNDERINGS (*see also* Lightning; Warn, Warning)

1 Ne. 12: 4 Nephi[1] beholds *t.* in promised land; 17: 45 the Lord has spoken to Laman[1] and Lemuel with voice of *t.*;

19: 11 (2 Ne. 26: 6) the Lord will visit Israel with *t.* of his power; **2 Ne.** 27: 2 Gentiles to be visited with *t.*; **Mosiah** 27: 11 (Alma 36: 7; 38: 7) angel speaks to Alma[2] and companions with voice of *t.*; **Hel.** 5: 30 voice of dissenters in prison was not voice of *t.*; 14: 21, 26–27 (3 Ne. 8: 6) *t.* at death of Christ.

TIDINGS (*see also* Gospel; Message)

1 Ne. 13: 37 (Mosiah 12: 21; 15: 18; 3 Ne. 20: 40; Isa. 52: 7) how beautiful upon mountains are feet of him who brings good *t.*; **Mosiah** 3: 3 angel comes to declare *t.* of great joy to Benjamin; 27: 37 sons of Mosiah[2] publish good *t.* of good; **Alma** 13: 22 the Lord declares day of salvation to all nations, that they might have glad *t.* of great joy; 39: 15 Christ comes to declare glad *t.* of salvation; **Hel.** 5: 29 seek no more to destroy my servant whom I have sent to declare good *t.*; 16: 14 angels appear and declare glad *t.* of great joy; **3 Ne.** 1: 26 appearance of signs brings glad *t.*

TIGHT

Ether 2: 17 (6: 7) Jaredite vessels are *t.* like dish.

TILL (*see also* Plant; Plow; Sow [verb])

1 Ne. 18: 24 Lehites begin to *t.* earth in promised land; **2 Ne.** 2: 19 (Alma 42: 2) Adam and Eve driven out of garden of Eden, to *t.* earth; **Enos** 1: 21 (Mosiah 6: 7) Nephites *t.* the land; **Jarom** 1: 8 Nephites make tools to *t.*; **Mosiah** 6: 7 Mosiah[2] *t.* earth to avoid burdening his people; 9: 9 (10: 4) Zeniff's people begin to *t.* ground; **Ether** 6: 13 Jaredites begin to *t.* earth in promised land; 10: 25 Jaredites make tools to *t.* earth.

TIMBER (*see also* Wood)

1 Ne. 18: 1 Nephi[1] works *t.* of ship after manner shown by the Lord; **Alma** 50: 2 (53: 4) *t.* used in fortification; **Hel.** 3: 5 Nephites spread into parts of land northward not rendered desolate and without *t.*; 3: 6–7, 9–10 *t.* scarce in land northward.

TIME (*see also* Day; Eternity; Full; Fulness; Generation; Hour; Reckon; Season; Space; Today; Tomorrow; Week; TG Time)

1 Ne. 10: 3 Jerusalem to be destroyed according to the Lord's due *t.*; 14: 26 (Morm. 5: 12) records to come forth in the Lord's due *t.*; **2 Ne.** 2: 3 in fulness of *t.* Redeemer shall come; 2: 21 (Alma 42: 4) men's *t.* was lengthened, that they might repent; 6: 14 (21: 11; 25: 17; Isa. 11: 11) Messiah will set himself the second *t.* to restore his people; 27: 10, 21 sealed revelation to be kept in book until the Lord's due *t.*; 30: 18 Satan shall have no power for long *t.*; **Jacob** 5: 15, 29 the Lord of vineyard leaves vineyard alone for long *t.*; 5: 31 this long *t.* we have nourished this tree; 5: 76 the Lord of vineyard will lay up fruit for long *t.*; 5: 76 the Lord has nourished vineyard for last *t.*; **Alma** 12: 24 (34: 32; 42: 4) this life became *t.* to prepare to meet God; 34: 33 if we do not improve *t.* in this life, then cometh night of darkness; 40: 5–10 *t.* appointed unto all men to arise from dead; **3 Ne.** 2: 8 Nephites reckon *t.* from birth of Christ; 20: 29 the Lord will gather his people in own due *t.*; 24: 11 (Mal. 3: 11) vine shall not cast fruit before *t.* in fields.

TIMOTHY—*brother of Nephi*[3] [C. A.D. 34]

3 Ne. 19: 4 had been raised from dead by Nephi[3], called by Jesus as one of twelve disciples.

TITHES (*see also* BD Tithe)

Alma 13: 15 Abraham paid *t.* to Melchizedek; **3 Ne.** 24: 8 (Mal. 3: 8) men have robbed God in *t.* and offerings; 24: 10 (Mal. 3: 10) bring *t.* into storehouse.

TITLE OF LIBERTY (*see also* Banner; Standard)

Alma 46: 12–13 Moroni[1] makes *t. of l.* on his rent coat; 46: 20 those who would maintain *t.* should enter covenant; 46: 36 Moroni[1] causes *t.* to be hoisted upon every tower; 51: 20 dissenters compelled to hoist *t.* upon their towers.

TITTLE (*see* Jot)

TODAY (*see also* Time)

1 Ne. 10: 18 (2 Ne. 27: 23; 29: 9; Alma 31: 17; Morm. 9: 9; Moro. 10: 19) God is same, yesterday, *t.*, and forever; **2 Ne.** 2: 4 Spirit is same, yesterday, *t.*, and forever; **Moro.** 10: 7 God works by power according to men's faith, same *t.*, tomorrow, forever.

TOIL (*see* Spin)

TOKEN (*see also* Sign; Type)

Alma 46: 21 people rend garments as *t.* they will not forsake the Lord; 47: 23 Lamanite king puts forth hand to raise Amalickiah's servants as *t.* of peace; **Moro.** 9: 10 Nephites devour flesh as *t.* of bravery.

TOLD (*see* Tell, Told)

TOLERABLE (*see also* Bear, Bore, Borne)

Alma 9: 15 more *t.* for Lamanites at judgment unless Nephites repent.

TOMORROW (*see also* Morrow; Time; Today)

2 **Ne.** 28: 7–8 eat, drink, and be merry, for *t.* we die.

TONGUE (*see also* Gift; Holy Ghost; Interpretation; Language; Mouth; Nation; Speak; Speech; Spirit; Gifts of; Word; TG Tongue)

1 **Ne.** 5: 18 (Alma 37: 4) records to go forth to every *t.*; 11: 36 all *t.* that fight against apostles shall be destroyed; 14: 11 abominable church has dominion among all *t.*; 19: 17 (Mosiah 16: 1) every *t.* shall see salvation of the Lord; 22: 28 all *t.* to dwell safely in Holy One if they repent; 2 **Ne.** 13: 8 (Isa. 3: 8) Judah is fallen because their *t.* have been against the Lord; 26: 13 Christ manifests himself to all who believe, every *t.*; 30: 8 the Lord shall commence his work among all *t.*; 31: 13–14 (32: 2) after receiving Holy Ghost, ye can speak with *t.* of angels; **Omni** 1: 25 believe in gift of speaking with *t.*; **Mosiah** 3: 13 the Lord has sent angels to declare word to every *t.*; 15: 28 salvation of the Lord to be declared to every *t.*; 27: 25 all *t.* must be born again; **Alma** 9: 20 Nephites have been favored above every other *t.*; 9: 21 Nephites have had gift of speaking with *t.*; 29: 8 the Lord grants unto all nations, of their own *t.*, to teach his word; 45: 16 land to be cursed to every *t.* which does wickedly; 3 **Ne.** 17: 17 (19: 32) no *t.* can speak marvelous things Jesus spoke; 22: 17 (Isa. 54: 17) every *t.* that rises against thee thou shalt condemn; 26: 14 Jesus looses *t.* of children, that they speak marvelous things; **Morm.** 4: 11 impossible for *t.* to describe scene of carnage; 9: 7–8 he who denies speaking with *t.* knows not gospel; 9: 24 those who believe shall speak with new *t.*; **Moro.** 9: 7 who can say there is no speaking with *t.*; 9: 19 *t.* cannot tell suffering of women and children; 10: 15 to another is given all kinds of *t.*; 10: 16 to another is given interpretation of languages and divers kinds of *t.*

TOOK (*see* Take, Taken)

TOOL

1 **Ne.** 17: 9–10, 16 Nephi[1] makes *t.* of ore to construct ship; **Jarom** 1: 8 Nephites make all manner of *t.*; **Hel.** 13: 34 (Ether 14: 1) we lay *t.* here and on morrow it is gone; **Ether** 10: 25–26 Jaredites make all manner of *t.*

TOOTH, TEETH

Mosiah 16: 2 (Alma 40: 13) the wicked shall be cast out, to weep, wail, gnash *t.*; **Alma** 14: 21 lawyers and judges gnash *t.* upon Alma[2] and Amulek; 3 **Ne.** 12: 38 (Matt. 5: 38) a *t.* for a *t.*

TOP (*see also* Housetop)

1 **Ne.** 16: 30 Nephi[1] goes forth into *t.* of mountain; 2 **Ne.** 12: 2 (Isa. 2: 2) mountain of the Lord's house to be established in *t.* of mountains; **Jacob** 5: 66, 73 root and *t.* of tree to be equal; **Ether** 2: 17 *t.* of Jaredite vessels tight like dish; 2: 19–20 hole in *t.* and bottom of Jaredite vessels for air; 3: 1 brother of Jared[2] carries sixteen small stones upon *t.* of mount.

TORMENT (*see also* Anguish; Damnation; Despair; Gnash; Guilt; Harrow; Hell; Lake; Misery; Pain; Remorse; Sorrow)

2 **Ne.** 9: 16, 19, 26 (28: 23; Jacob 6: 10; Mosiah 3: 27; Alma 12: 17) endless *t.* of the wicked is like lake of fire and brimstone; **Mosiah** 2: 39 (3: 25) final doom of the unrepentant is to endure endless *t.*; 27: 29 (Alma 36: 12–13) soul of Alma[2] was racked with eternal *t.*; 28: 3 thought that any soul should suffer endless *t.* causes sons of Mosiah[2] to quake; **Moro.** 8: 20–21 he who says little children need baptism is in danger of endless *t.*

TOSS (*see also* Cast; Throw)

3 **Ne.** 22: 11 (Isa. 54: 11) O thou afflicted, *t.* with tempest and not comforted; **Morm.** 5: 18 Nephites are led about by Satan as vessel is *t.* upon waves; **Ether** 6: 5 Jaredite vessels are *t.* upon waves.

TOUCH (*see also* Feel; Hand)

1 **Ne.** 17: 48–49 Nephi[1] commands brothers not to *t.* him; 2 **Ne.** 27: 21 *t.* not the things which are sealed; **Mosiah** 13: 3 Abinadi commands priests not to *t.* him; **Alma** 5: 57 (3 Ne. 20: 41; Moro. 10: 30) *t.* not unclean things of the wicked; 3 **Ne.** 18: 36 Jesus *t.* each of his disciples with his hand; **Ether** 3: 6 brother of Jared[2] asks the Lord to *t.* stones.

TOWER (*see also* Building)

Omni 1: 22 (Hel. 6: 28; Ether 1: 33) first parents of Coriantumr[2] came from *t.*; **Mosiah** 2: 7 Benjamin has *t.* erected; 11: 12–13 Noah[3] builds high *t.* to watch Lamanites; 20: 8 from *t.* Limhi discovers Lamanites' preparations for war; 28: 17 (Ether 1: 3) plates of gold give account of Jaredites back to building of *t.*; **Alma** 50: 4 Moroni[1] builds *t.* as part of fortifications; **Hel.** 6: 28 devil put it into men's hearts to build *t.* high enough to reach heaven; 7: 10–11 Nephi[2] prays upon *t.*

TOWN (*see also* City; Village)

Morm. 4: 22 Nephites flee, taking all inhabitants with them, in *t.* and villages; 5: 5 *t.* and villages burned by Lamanites.

TRADE (*see also* Business; Merchants; Traffic)

Mosiah 24: 7 Lamanites begin to *t.* one with another.

TRADITION (*see also* Custom; Doctrine, False)

Enos 1: 14 Lamanites swear to destroy Nephites' records and *t.*; **Mosiah** 1: 5 (10: 12) Lamanites do not believe truth because of incorrect *t.* of fathers; 26: 1 many in rising generations of Nephites do not believe *t.* of fathers; **Alma** 3: 8 Nephites should not mix with Lamanites and believe incorrect *t.*; 3: 11 those who do not believe Lamanites' *t.*, but records and *t.* of fathers, are called Nephites; 9: 16 *t.* of fathers cause Lamanites to remain in ignorance; 9: 17 Lamanites will be brought to know incorrectness of *t.*; 17: 9 sons of Mosiah[2] desire to bring Lamanites to knowledge of baseness of *t.*; 24: 7 Lamanite king is thankful Nephites have convinced them of *t.* of wicked fathers; 60: 32 hatred of Lamanites caused by *t.* of fathers; **Hel.** 5: 51 (15: 7) converted Lamanites lay down hatred and *t.* of fathers; 15: 4 the Lord has hated Lamanites because of evil deeds and iniquity of *t.* of fathers.

TRAFFIC (*see also* Business; Merchants; Trade)

4 Ne. 1: 46 robbers *t.* in all manner of *t.*; **Ether** 10: 22 Jaredites *t.* one with another to get gain.

TRAITOR (*see also* Apostasy)

Alma 60: 18 Moroni[1] wonders whether leaders of government are *t.*; 62: 1 Moroni[1] learns that Pahoran[1] is not *t.*

TRAMPLE (*see also* Disobedience; Rebel; Tread)

1 Ne. 19: 7 men *t.* God under feet; **Mosiah** 29: 21–22 iniquitous king *t.* under feet God's commandments; **Alma** 5: 53 can ye lay aside these things and *t.* Holy One under feet; 60: 33 (Hel. 4: 21–22; 6: 31) Nephites *t.* laws of God under their feet; **Hel.** 12: 2 when the Lord prospers his people, they forget him and *t.* him under their feet; **3 Ne.** 14: 6 (Matt. 7: 6) cast not your pearls before swine, lest they *t.* them under feet; 28: 35 do ye suppose ye can get rid of justice of offended God, who hath been *t.* under feet of men.

TRANSFIGURE, TRANSFIGURED (*see also* Change; Transform; Translated Beings; TG Transfiguration, Transfigured; Translated Beings; BD Transfiguration, Mount of)

3 Ne. 28: 15, 17, 36–39 three Nephite disciples are *t.* from body of flesh to sanctified state; **Morm.** 8: 33 why have ye *t.* word of God, that ye might bring damnation upon souls.

TRANSFORM (*see also* Change; Transfigure; Translated Beings)

2 Ne. 9: 9 devil *t.* himself nigh unto angel of light.

TRANSGRESSION, TRANSGRESS (*see also* Agency; Crime; Death, Spiritual; Disobedience; Err; Evil; Fall of Man; Fault; Guilt; Iniquity; Jesus Christ, Atonement through; Judgment; Knowledge; Law; Offense; Punishment; Rebel; Sin; Transgressor; Trespass; Wicked; TG Transgress)

2 Ne. 2: 22 if Adam had not *t.*, he would not have fallen; 9: 6 fall came by reason of *t.*; 9: 27 wo unto him that has the commandments and *t.* them; 9: 39 remember awfulness of *t.* against God; 9: 46 men will confess they have *t.* law and say, my *t.* are mine; **Enos** 1: 10 Lamanites' *t.* will the Lord bring down upon own heads; **Mosiah** 1: 12 (5: 11) new name shall never be blotted out except through *t.*; 1: 13 if Nephites fall into *t.*, the Lord will deliver them up; 2: 36–37 man who *t.* contrary to what he has been taught is in open rebellion to God; 3: 11 Christ's blood atones for sins of those who have fallen by *t.* of Adam; 4: 14 ye will not suffer your children to *t.* God's laws; 14: 5 (Isa. 53: 5) he was wounded for our *t.*; 14: 8 (Isa. 53: 8) for *t.* of my people was he stricken; 15: 9 (Alma 34: 8) Christ takes upon himself his people's *t.*; 27: 13 nothing shall overthrow church except *t.* of the Lord's people; **Alma** 7: 13 Son suffers that he might blot out his people's *t.*; 9: 19 the Lord would rather suffer that Lamanites destroy Nephites if they would fall into *t.*; 9: 23 far more tolerable for Lamanites if Nephites fall into *t.*; 10: 19 if Nephites fall into *t.*, they will be ripe for destruction; 11: 40 Christ will take upon himself *t.* of those who believe on him; 12: 31 by *t.* first commandments, men became as Gods, knowing good from evil; 24: 30 when enlightened people fall into *t.*, they become more hardened; 28: 13 how great inequality of man because of *t.*; 32: 19 how much more cursed is he who knows God's will and does it not than he who only believes and falls into *t.*; 46: 18 God will not suffer Nephites to be destroyed until they bring it upon themselves by *t.*; **Hel.** 4: 26 Nephites become weak because of *t.*

TRANSGRESSOR (*see also* Transgression, Transgress)

1 Ne. 20: 8 (Isa. 48: 8) thou wast called a *t.* from womb; **Mosiah** 14: 12 (Isa. 53: 12) he was numbered with *t.*;

Alma 26: 24 ways of Lamanites have been ways of *t.*

TRANSLATION, TRANSLATE (*see also* Book of Mormon; Gift; Holy Ghost; Interpretation; Language; Seer; Tongue; Translated Beings)

Mosiah 8: 13 Ammon[1] tells Limhi of man who can *t.* records; 8: 13–14 (28: 13) Mosiah[2] has interpreters, with which he can *t.*; 28: 11, 13 Mosiah[2] *t.* plates of gold by means of interpreters; **Alma** 9: 21 Nephites have had gift of *t.*; **Ether** 5: 1 sealed records not to be *t.*; 15: 34 whether Ether will be *t.* matters not.

TRANSLATED BEINGS (*see also* Change; John the Beloved; Three Nephite Disciples; Transfigure; Zion)

Alma 45: 19 Alma[2] is said to be taken up by Spirit or buried by hand of God, as was Moses; **3 Ne.** 28: 1–9, 36–40 three Nephite disciples who desire to tarry are sanctified, never to taste death.

TRAP (*see also* Pit; Snare)

Alma 10: 17 lawyers are laying *t.* to catch holy ones of God.

TRAVAIL (*see also* Labor)

2 Ne. 29: 4 do Gentiles remember the *t.*, labors of the Jews; **Mosiah** 14: 11 (Isa. 53: 11) he shall see *t.* of his soul; 27: 33 sons of Mosiah[2] exhort people with much *t.* to keep commandments; 29: 33 Mosiah[2] unfolds all *t.* of soul for people; **Alma** 18: 37 Ammon[2] rehearses *t.* of fathers in wilderness; **3 Ne.** 22: 1 (Isa. 54: 1) sing, O thou that didst not *t.* with child.

TRAVEL (*see also* Depart; Flight; Journey)

1 Ne. 2: 5 (7: 21; 16: 15; 17: 1) Lehites *t.* in wilderness; **Mosiah** 8: 7–8 group of Limhi's people *t.* in land of many waters; 27: 35 sons of Mosiah[2] *t.* throughout Zarahemla striving to repair injuries; **Alma** 8: 6 Alma[2] *t.* to Ammonihah; 26: 28 missionaries *t.* from house to house, relying upon mercies of world; 30: 32 Alma[2] has labored for own support, notwithstanding many *t.*

TREAD, TRODDEN (*see also* Oppression; Persecution; Trample)

Alma 30: 59 Korihor is *t.* down by Zoramites; 34: 29 if ye are not charitable, ye are as dross which is *t.* under foot; **3 Ne.** 12: 13 (Matt. 5: 13) salt that has lost savor is good for nothing but to be *t.* under foot; 16: 8 Israel has been *t.* under foot by Gentiles; 16: 15 (20: 16; 21: 12) the Lord will suffer Israel to go through Gentiles and *t.* them down; 25: 3 (Mal. 4: 3) ye shall *t.* down the wicked; **Morm.** 5: 6 Lamanites *t.* Nephites under feet.

TREASURE (*see also* Money; Riches; Treasury; Value)

2 Ne. 9: 30 hearts of the rich are upon their *t.*, which is their god; 9: 30 their *t.* shall perish with them; 12: 7 (Isa. 2: 7) neither is there any end of their *t.*; **Hel.** 5: 8 lay up for yourselves *t.* in heaven; 8: 25 Nephites have rebelled against God instead of laying up *t.* in heaven; 13: 18, 20, 35 (Morm. 1: 18) he who hides *t.* shall not find it again; 13: 19 the righteous hide up their *t.* unto the Lord; **Ether** 3: 21 brother of Jared[2] to *t.* up things he has seen and show them to no man.

TREASURY

1 Ne. 4: 20 Nephi[1] commands Zoram[1] to go to *t.* with him.

TREATY (*see also* Covenant; Oath; Promise)

Mosiah 7: 21 (9: 2) Laman[2] enters *t.* with Zeniff; **Morm.** 2: 28 Nephites make *t.* with Lamanites.

TREE (*see also* Branch; Fig; Fruit; Forbidden; Olive; Root; Tree of Life)

Jacob 4: 6 saints can command in Jesus' name and very *t.* obey; **Alma** 5: 52 ax is laid at root of *t.*; 5: 52 every *t.* that brings not good fruit shall be hewn down; 26: 36 Nephites are branch of *t.* of Israel; 32: 37 if ye nourish *t.*, it will get root, bring forth fruit; 32: 38–40 if ye do not nourish *t.*, ye can never pluck fruit; **3 Ne.** 4: 28 Zemnarihah is hanged upon *t.*; 14: 17 (Matt. 7: 17) every good *t.* brings forth good fruit, corrupt *t.* brings forth evil fruit; **Ether** 2: 17 length of Jaredites' vessels is length of *t.*

TREE OF LIFE (*see also* Eden; Tree; Vision)

1 Ne. 8: 10–35 Lehi[1] beholds *t. of l.*; 11: 8–9 Nephi[1] sees *t.* seen by father; 11: 21–22, 25 *t.* represents love of God; 11: 25 (15: 22) iron rod leads to *t. of l.*; 15: 22 *t.* in vision represents *t. of l.*; 15: 28, 36 awful gulf separates the wicked from *t. of l.*; **2 Ne.** 2: 15 forbidden fruit set in opposition to *t. of l.*; **Alma** 5: 34, 62 come unto the Lord and you shall partake of fruit of *t. of l.*; 12: 21 (42: 2–6) God placed cherubim and flaming sword lest first parents partake of fruit of *t. of l.*; 12: 23 (42: 3, 5) if Adam could have partaken of fruit of *t. of l.*, there would have been no death; 12: 26 if first parents had partaken of *t. of l.*, they would have been miserable forever; 32: 40 if ye will not nourish the word, ye can never pluck fruit of *t. of l.*; 42: 6 as men were cut off from *t. of l.*, they should be cut off from face of earth.

TREMBLE, TREMBLING (*see also* Earthquake; Fear; Fear of God; Quake; Shake)

1 Ne. 1: 6 Lehi[1] *t.* because of what he has seen; **2 Ne.** 1: 14 hear the words of *t.* parent; 24: 16 (Isa. 14: 16) is this the man who made earth to *t.*; 28: 28 he who is built upon sandy foundation *t.* lest he fall; **Alma** 36: 7 earth *t.* beneath feet of Alma[2]; **Hel.** 5: 31 walls of prison *t.*; 12: 9 at the Lord's voice, mountains *t.*; 14: 21 (3 Ne. 10: 9) earth shall *t.* at Christ's death.

TRESPASS (*see also* Offense; Sin; Transgression)

Mosiah 26: 30 as often as his people repent, the Lord will forgive their *t.* against him; 26: 31 forgive one another your *t.*; **3 Ne.** 7: 14 strict laws established that one tribe should not *t.* against another; 13: 14 (Matt. 6: 14) if ye forgive men their *t.*, Father will forgive you.

TRIAL, TRY (*see also* Chasten; Faith; Opposition; Oppression; Persecution; Probation; Prove; Trial, Judicial; Tribulation; TG Test, Try, Prove)

Mosiah 23: 21 (3 Ne. 26: 11) the Lord *t.* his people's patience and faith; 29: 33 Mosiah[2] unfolds *t.* of righteous king; **Alma** 1: 22–23 contention is cause of much *t.* with church; 27: 15 Ammon[2] and brethren will *t.* Nephites' hearts, whether converted Lamanites should enter land; 31: 5 Alma[2] to *t.* virtue of word of God; 32: 36 (34: 4) *t.* experiment by planting the seed; 36: 3 (38: 5) whosoever puts trust in God will be supported in *t.*; **3 Ne.** 26: 9 Lamanites to receive account of Savior's teachings to *t.* their faith; **Ether** 12: 6 ye receive no witness until after *t.* of faith.

TRIAL, JUDICIAL (*see also* Government, Civil; Judge [noun]; Law; Law, Civil; Transgression; Transgressor; Trial, Try)

Alma 10: 14 lawyers are hired to administer laws at times of *t.*; 51: 19 dissenters thrown into prison because no time for *t.*; **Hel.** 1: 7–8 Paanchi is *t.* by voice of people and condemned to death; 6: 24 robbers who reveal wickedness to world are *t.* by laws of Gadianton; **3 Ne.** 6: 25–27 judges who condemned prophets to death are to be *t.* according to law.

TRIBE (*see also* Israel; Israel, Ten Lost Tribes of; Jacob, House of; Judah)

3 Ne. 7: 2–4, 14 people separate into *t.*; 7: 3 each *t.* appoints leaders; 7: 11, 14 each *t.* establishes own laws; 7: 11 *t.* are united against robbers.

TRIBULATION (*see also* Affliction; Anguish; Calamity; Chasten; Despair; Destruction; Grieve; Misery; Oppression; Persecution; Sorrow; Suffering; Trial; Trouble)

2 Ne. 2: 1 Jacob[2] is firstborn in days of father's *t.*; **Jacob** 7: 26 Nephites are wanderers, born in *t.* in wilderness; **Mosiah** 23: 10 after much *t.* the Lord hears cries of Alma[1]; 27: 28 after wading through much *t.*, Alma[2] is snatched from everlasting burning; 27: 32 Alma[2] and companions preach word in much *t.*; **Alma** 8: 14 Alma[2] wades through much *t.* because of wickedness of Ammonihah; 15: 3 Zeezrom's fever caused by much *t.* of his mind; 53: 13 Ammonites see many *t.* Nephites bear for them; 60: 25–26 Nephite armies are strengthened by power of God because of patience in *t.*

TRIBUNAL (*see also* Bar; Judgment-seat)

Alma 5: 18 can ye imagine yourselves brought before God's *t.* filled with guilt.

TRIBUTE (*see also* Bondage; Tax)

Mosiah 7: 15, 22 (19: 15, 22, 26, 28) Limhi's people pay *t.* to Lamanites; 22: 7, 10 Gideon will pay last *t.* of wine to Lamanites.

TRIFLE

Mosiah 2: 9 Benjamin does not gather his people to *t.* with words.

TRODDEN (*see* Tread, Trodden)

TROUBLE (*see also* Anxiety; Calamity; Care; Sorrow; Suffering; Tribulation; Vex; Worry)

Mosiah 26: 10 Alma[2] *t.* in spirit because of false teachings; 29: 33 Mosiah[2] unfolds *t.* of righteous king; **Alma** 22: 3 Lamanite king is *t.* by generosity of Ammon[2]; 36: 3 (38: 5) those who put trust in God will be supported in *t.*; 40: 12 spirits in paradise shall rest from *t.*; 42: 29 only let your sins *t.* you with that *t.* which brings repentance; **3 Ne.** 17: 14 Jesus is *t.* because of Israel's wickedness.

TRUE (*see also* Reality; Real; Right [adj.]; Truth)

1 Ne. 10: 14 Israel to come to knowledge of *t.* Messiah; 13: 39 other books to testify that records of prophets and twelve apostles are *t.*; 15: 15 seed of Lehi[1] to receive nourishment from *t.* vine; 15: 16 seed of Lehi[1] to be grafted into *t.* olive-tree; **2 Ne.** 1: 10 if seed of Lehi[1] reject *t.* Messiah, his judgments will rest upon them; 9: 2 Jews to be restored to *t.* church and fold of God; 25: 18 words will convince Jews of *t.* Messiah; 31: 15 words of my Beloved are *t.*; 31: 21 this is doctrine of Christ, only and *t.* doctrine of Father; **Enos** 1: 20 Nephites seek diligently to restore Lamanites to *t.* faith; **Alma** 5: 13 word was preached to fathers and they put trust in *t.* and living God; 5: 48 whatsoever I say concerning what is to come is *t.*; 16: 17 those who receive word will be grafted into *t.* vine; 32: 28 *t.* seed will swell in breast; 53: 20 Ammonite youths are *t.* in whatsoever they are entrusted; **Hel.** 11: 23 those who know *t.* points of doctrine preach to people; 15: 13 Lamanites come to *t.* knowledge of great and *t.* shepherd; **3 Ne.** 8: 1 we know our record to be *t.*; 21: 6 Gentiles may know *t.* points of Christ's doctrine; **4 Ne.** 1: 29 false church persecutes *t.* church of Christ; **Morm.** 8: 10 none know *t.* God except Jesus' disciples; 9: 28 serve the *t.* and living God; **Ether** 2: 8 those in promised land must serve *t.* and only God or be swept off; **Moro.** 10: 4 ask God if these things are not *t.*; 10: 6 whatsoever thing is good is just and *t.*; 10: 29 God will show you that what I have written is *t.*

TRUMP, TRUMPET

Mosiah 26: 25 when second *t.* sounds, those who never knew the Lord will stand before him; **Alma** 29: 1 O that I were angel and could speak with *t.* of God; **3 Ne.** 13: 2 (Matt. 6: 2) when you give alms, do not sound *t.*; **Morm.** 9: 13 all men shall be awakened from endless sleep when *t.* sounds; **Ether** 14: 28 Coriantumr[2] sounds *t.* to invite armies of Shiz to battle.

TRUST (*see also* Confidence; Faith; Hope; Rely; TG Trust; Trust in God; Trust Not in Arm of Flesh; Trustworthiness)

2 Ne. 4: 19 I know in whom I have *t.*; 4: 34 O Lord, I have *t.* in thee; 4: 34 I will not put *t.* in arm of flesh; 4: 34 (28: 31) cursed is he who puts *t.* in man; 8: 5 (Isa. 51: 5) on mine arm shall isles *t.*; 22: 2 (Isa. 12: 2) I will *t.* and not be afraid; 24: 32 (Isa. 14: 32) poor of the Lord's people shall *t.* in Zion; **Jacob** 7: 25 Nephites fortify against Lamanites, putting *t.* in God; **Mosiah** 4: 6 salvation to come to him who puts *t.* in the Lord; 7: 19 rejoice and put *t.* in God; 7: 33 (Alma 61: 13) if ye will put *t.* in the Lord, he will deliver you; 23: 13 *t.* no man to be king; 23: 14 *t.* no man to be teacher except he be man of God; 29: 20 the Lord extends arms of mercy to those who put *t.* in him; **Alma** 5: 13 fathers humbled themselves and put *t.* in God; 17: 13 sons of Mosiah[2] separate, *t.* in the Lord that they should meet again; 19: 23 Mosiah[2] *t.* his son unto the Lord; 36: 3 (38: 5) whoever puts *t.* in God will be supported in trials; 37: 32 *t.* not those secret plans unto this people; 57: 27 Ammonite youths put *t.* in God continually; 58: 33 we *t.* in our God, who has given us victory; **Hel.** 12: 1 the Lord prospers those who put *t.* in him; **Morm.** 9: 20 God ceases to do miracles because men know not the God in whom they should *t.*; **Moro.** 8: 22–23 to suppose little children need baptism is putting *t.* in dead works.

TRUTH (*see also* Gospel; Knowledge; Learning; Light; Mystery; Scriptures; Spirit, Holy/Spirit of the Lord; True)

1 Ne. 13: 40 last records shall establish *t.* of first; 16: 2 the guilty take the *t.* to be hard; **2 Ne.** 9: 40 words of *t.* are hard against all uncleanness; 9: 40 the righteous love the *t.*; 27: 12 three witnesses shall testify to *t.* of book; 28: 28 wo unto all who are angry because of *t.* of God; **Jacob** 4: 13 Spirit speaketh *t.*; **Alma** 9: 26 (13: 9) Only Begotten, full of grace and *t.*; 30: 41–43 Korihor resists spirit of the *t.*; 34: 38 (John 4: 24) worship God, wherever you may be, in spirit and *t.*; 38: 9 Christ is the word of *t.* and righteousness; 43: 10 whosoever worships God in spirit and *t.*, the Lamanites would destroy; **Hel.** 6: 34 Lamanites walk in *t.* and uprightness before the Lord; **3 Ne.** 16: 7 *t.* shall come unto Gentiles; **Ether** 3: 12 thou speakest the *t.*, for thou art a God of *t.*; 4: 12 (John 14: 6) Christ is light, life, and *t.* of world; **Moro.** 7: 45 (1 Cor. 13: 4, 6) charity rejoiceth in *t.*; Moro. 10: 4 Father will manifest *t.* of book by power of Holy Ghost; 10: 5 by power of Holy Ghost ye may know *t.* of all things.

TRY (*see* Trial, Try; Trial, Judicial)

TUBALOTH—*Lamanite king* [c. 51 B.C.]

Hel. 1: 16–17 son of Ammoron, appoints Coriantumr[3] commander of armies.

TUMBLE (*see also* Fall)

1 Ne. 12: 4 Nephi[1] sees mountains *t.* into pieces and cities *t.* to earth; 22: 14 (2 Ne. 28: 18) abominable church must *t.* to earth; **Hel.** 5: 27, 31 prison walls about to *t.* to earth; **Morm.** 8: 24 by power of the Lord's word, saints cause prisons to *t.*; **Ether** 12: 13 (Alma 14: 27) faith causes prison to *t.* to earth.

TUMULT, TUMULTUOUS (*see also* Noise, Roar; Sound [noun and verb]; Uproar)

1 Ne. 12: 4 (3 Ne. 10: 9) Nephi[1] hears all manner of *t.* noises; **Hel.** 5: 30 voice to dissenters in prison is not voice of *t.* noise; **4 Ne.** 1: 16 no *t.* among Nephites.

TURN

1 Ne. 16: 39 after being chastened

by the Lord, the rebellious *t.* away anger; 19: 13 Jews shall be scourged because they *t.* hearts aside; 19: 15 when Jews no longer *t.* hearts against Holy One, he will remember covenants; 22: 13 blood of abominable church shall *t.* upon own heads; 22: 14 nations that war against Israel shall be *t.* against one another; **2 Ne.** 27: 32 (28: 16) they who *t.* aside the just for thing of naught shall be cut off; **Mosiah** 4: 16 ye will not *t.* beggar out to perish; 7: 33 (Alma 39: 13; Morm. 9: 6) *t.* to the Lord with full purpose of heart; **Alma** 4: 12 (5: 55) some *t.* their backs upon needy; 34: 28 if ye *t.* away the needy, your prayer is vain; 42: 2 the Lord placed flaming sword which *t.* every way, to keep tree of life; 56: 37 Lamanite army pursued by Antipus *t.* not to right or left; **3 Ne.** 6: 13 the humble receive persecution and do not *t.* and revile; 20: 26 Father sends Christ to *t.* people from iniquities; 24: 5 (Mal. 3: 5) I will be swift witness against those who *t.* aside stranger; **Ether** 1: 36 brother of Jared[2] to ask the Lord to *t.* away his anger.

TWAIN (*see also* Two)

Alma 14: 27 (3 Ne. 28: 19; 4 Ne. 1: 30) prison walls are rent in *t.*; **Hel.** 10: 6–8 Nephi[2] is given power to rend temple in *t.*; 14: 21–22 (3 Ne. 8: 18) rocks to be rent in *t.* at Christ's death; **3 Ne.** 12: 41 (Matt. 5: 41) whosoever shall compel thee to go a mile, go with him *t.*

TWINKLING

3 Ne. 28: 8 three Nephites to be changed in *t.* of eye from mortality to immortality.

TWO (*see also* Twain)

1 Ne. 14: 10 there are only *t.* churches; 16: 10 *t.* spindles within Liahona; **2 Ne.** 29: 8 testimony of *t.* nations is witness that the Lord is God; **Mosiah** 28: 10–13 Mosiah[2] translates record by means of *t.* stones; **Hel.** 14: 4 *t.* days and nights without darkness at Christ's birth; **3 Ne.** 13: 24 (Matt. 6: 24) no man can serve *t.* masters; **Ether** 3: 23, 28 the Lord gives brother of Jared[2] *t.* stones to seal up with record.

TYPE, TYPIFY (*see also* Remember, Remembrance; Representation; Shadow; Similitude; Token; TG Jesus Christ, Types of, in Anticipation; Jesus Christ, Types of, in Memory)

1 Ne. 17: 41 (2 Ne. 25: 20; Alma 33: 19–21; Hel. 8: 14–15; Num. 21: 8–9) serpent raised in wilderness a *t.* of Christ; **2 Ne.** 11: 4 all things given of God from beginning *t.* Christ; **Mosiah** 3: 15 the Lord showed his people many *t.* of his coming; 13: 10 (Alma 25: 10) Abinadi's death a *t.* of things to come; 13: 30–31 (16: 14; Alma 25: 15; 34: 14; Gal. 3: 24; Heb. 10: 1) law of Moses a *t.* of Christ's coming; **Alma** 13: 16 ordinances given as *t.* of Son's order; 37: 38–46 working of Liahona a *t.* of word of Christ; **Ether** 13: 6 there has been a *t.* for building of New Jerusalem.

TYRANT (*see also* King; Rule; Ruler; TG Tyranny)

Mosiah 29: 40 Nephites do not look upon Mosiah[2] as *t.*

UNALTERABLE (*see also* Unchangeable)

Alma 41: 8 decrees of God are *u.*

UNAVOIDABLY

1 Ne. 15: 4 prophecies must *u.* come to pass because of wickedness; **Mosiah** 13: 28 except for atonement, men must *u.* perish; 29: 19 except for Creator's interposition, people of Noah[3] must *u.* remain in bondage; **Alma** 9: 11 except for God's matchless power and mercy, we should *u.* have been cut off; **Hel.** 4: 25 except they cleave to the Lord, Nephites must *u.* perish in battle with Lamanites.

UNAWARES

Mosiah 10: 2 Zeniff sets guards lest Lamanites come upon them *u.*

UNBELIEF, UNBELIEVER (*see also* Apostasy; Belief; Believer; Dissenter; Doubt; Hardheartedness; Rebel; Reject; TG Unbelief, Unbelievers)

1 Ne. 4: 13 better for one man to perish than for nation to dwindle in *u.*; 10: 11 Jews to dwindle in *u.*; 12: 22–23 (2 Ne. 26: 15; Morm. 9: 35) Lamanites to dwindle in *u.*; 13: 35 (2 Ne. 26: 15; Alma 45: 10; 50: 22; Hel. 6: 34; 3 Ne. 21: 5; 4 Ne. 1: 34; Ether 4: 3) Nephites dwindle in *u.*; 17: 18 brethren will not work because they do not believe Nephi[1] can build ship; **2 Ne.** 1: 10 when Nephites dwindle in *u.*, God's judgments shall rest upon them; 10: 2 many Nephites perish in flesh because of *u.*; 26: 15 all who have dwindled in *u.* shall not be forgotten; 26: 17 those who have dwindled in *u.* shall not have book; 26: 19 those who have dwindled in *u.* shall be smitten by Gentiles; 32: 7 Nephi[1] mourns because of Nephites' *u.*; **Jacob** 3: 7 Lamanites' *u.* is caused by iniquity of fathers; **Mosiah** 26: 1–3 (3 Ne. 15: 18) because of *u.*, rising generation cannot understand word of God; 27: 2 proclamation that no *u.* should persecute church; 27: 8 Alma[2] and sons of Mosiah[2] are numbered among *u.*; 27: 32 Alma[2] and sons of Mosiah[2] are persecuted by *u.*; **Alma** 4: 11 example of church leads *u.* to iniquity; 7: 6 I trust ye are not in state of so much *u.* as your brethren; 19: 6 dark veil of *u.* being cast from Lamoni's mind; 32: 28 do not cast out seed by *u.*; 33: 21 if ye could be healed by casting eyes about, would ye harden hearts in *u.*; **Hel.** 4: 25 the Lord ceases to preserve Nephites because of *u.*; **3 Ne.** 1: 18 Nephites begin to fear because of *u.*; 1: 19 *u.* set aside day for signs of Christ's birth to be given; 16: 4 Jews to be scattered because of *u.*; 16: 8 wo unto *u.* among Gentiles; 19: 35 Jesus could not show Jews so great miracles because of *u.*; **4 Ne.** 1: 38 Lamanites do not dwindle in *u.*, but wilfully rebel against gospel; **Morm.** 1: 14 (Moro. 10: 24) gifts and Holy Ghost do not come upon any because of *u.*; 5: 14 writings to go forth among Jews; 9: 20 (Moro. 7: 37) God ceases to do miracles because of *u.*; **Ether** 4: 13 knowledge hid up because of *u.*; 4: 15 when Israel rends veil of *u.*, they shall know Father remembers covenants.

UNCHANGEABLE (*see also* Change; God, Eternal Nature of; Immutable; Round; Same; Unalterable)

Morm. 9: 19 (Moro. 8: 18) God is *u.*

UNCIRCUMCISED (*see also* Circumcision)

2 Ne. 8: 24 (3 Ne. 20: 36; Isa. 52: 1) the *u.* shall come no more to Jerusalem; 9: 33 (Hel. 9: 21) wo unto the *u.* of heart.

UNCLEAN, UNCLEANNESS (*see also* Corrupt; Defile; Evil; Filthiness; Spirit, Evil; Spot; Stain; Unholy; Wicked; TG Uncleanness, Unclean)

1 Ne. 10: 21 those who seek to do wickedly are found *u.*; 10: 21 (15: 34; Alma 7: 21; 11: 37; 40: 26; Hel. 8: 25; 3 Ne. 27: 19) no *u.* thing can dwell with God in his kingdom; **2 Ne.** 8: 24 (3 Ne. 20: 36; Isa. 52: 1) *u.* shall come no more to Jerusalem; 9: 14 we shall have perfect knowledge of our *u.*; 9: 40 truth is hard against all *u.*; **3 Ne.** 7: 17, 19 in Jesus' name Nephi[2] casts out *u.* spirits; 20: 41 (Moro. 10: 30) touch not that which is *u.*; **Morm.** 9: 28 strip yourselves of all *u.*

UNCONQUERABLE

Alma 52: 33 Jacob[3] has *u.* spirit; **3 Ne.** 3: 1, 4 robbers have *u.* spirit.

UNDERSTAND, UNDERSTOOD, UNDERSTANDING (*see also* Communication; Comprehend; Know; Knowledge; Learn; Perceive; Wisdom; TG Understand; Understanding)

1 Ne. 13: 29 (14: 23) precious things taken from book were plain to *u.*; 15: 7 Laman[1] and Lemuel cannot *u.* words of Lehi[1] concerning olive-tree; 16: 29 writing on Liahona gives *u.* concerning ways of the Lord; **2 Ne.** 21: 1–2 (Isa. 11: 1–2) spirit of *u.* shall rest upon rod from stem of Jesse; 25: 5 Jews *u.* things of prophets; 25: 8 in last days men will *u.* words of prophets; 27: 26 (Isa. 29: 14) *u.* of prudent shall be hid; 31: 3 the Lord gives light unto the *u.*; 32: 4 (3 Ne. 17: 3) if ye cannot *u.* words, it is because ye ask not; **Jacob** 2: 23–24 Nephites do not *u.* scriptures concerning wives and concubines; 4: 13 he who prophesies should prophesy to men's *u.*; 4: 14 Jews sought for things they could not *u.*; 7: 11 Sherem does not *u.* scriptures regarding Christ; **Omni** 1: 17 Mosiah[1] cannot *u.* people of Zarahemla because of corruptness of language; **W of M** 1: 9 Mormon[2] makes record according to *u.* given by God; **Mosiah** 1: 2 Mosiah[2] teaches sons language of fathers, that they might be men of *u.*; 1: 2–5 records preserved by God that men might read and *u.* prophecies, commandments, mysteries; 3: 15 Israel *u.* not that law of Moses avails nothing except for atonement; 12: 25 priests of Noah[3] pretend to *u.* spirit of prophesying; 12: 27 ye have not applied hearts to *u.*; 26: 3 (3 Ne. 15: 18) because of unbelief men cannot *u.* word of God; **Alma** 17: 2 sons of Mosiah[2] are men of sound *u.*; 26: 35 God has all *u.*; 32: 28, 34 good seed enlightens *u.*; 48: 11 Moroni[1] is man of perfect *u.*; **3 Ne.** 1: 24 those who preach against law of Moses do not *u.* scriptures; 10: 14 whoso readeth, let him *u.*; 11: 3–4 Nephites do not *u.* voice from heaven; 11: 6–8 third time, Nephites *u.* voice; 17: 2 Nephites are weak that they cannot *u.* all of Jesus' words; 17: 3 ask Father that ye may *u.*; 19: 33 multitude *u.* in hearts words Jesus prays; **Morm.** 9: 8 he who denies revelation does not *u.* scriptures; **Ether** 1: 34 brother of Jared[2] asks the Lord not to confound Jaredites that they *u.* not one another; 3: 5 the Lord is able to show forth great power, which looks small to *u.* of men.

UNDERTAKE, UNDERTAKEN (*see also* Do; Observe; Perform)

Alma 17: 13 great is work *u.* by sons of Mosiah[2]; 46: 29 Amalickiahites doubt justice of cause they have *u.*

UNEQUAL (*see also* Inequality)

Alma 30: 7 contrary to commandments that any law should bring men on *u.* grounds.

UNFAITHFUL (*see also* Disobedience)

Mosiah 1: 17 as Lehites were *u.*, they did not progress on journey.

UNFOLD (*see also* Manifest; Revelation; Show)

1 Ne. 10: 19 mysteries to be *u.* to

those who diligently seek; **Jacob** 4: 18 Jacob[2] will *u.* mystery; **Mosiah** 2: 9 open your hearts and minds that mysteries may be *u.* to your view; 8: 19 interpreters prepared to *u.* mysteries; 29: 33, 35 Mosiah[2] *u.* troubles of righteous king and disadvantages of unrighteous king; **Alma** 12: 1 Alma[2] *u.* scriptures to Zeezrom; **Ether** 4: 7 when Gentiles exercise faith, Christ will *u.* his revelations to them; 4: 16 revelation of John to be *u.* in eyes of all people.

UNGODLINESS (*see also* Iniquity; Wicked)

Moro. 10: 32 deny yourselves of all *u.*

UNHAPPY (*see also* Happiness; Misery)

Morm. 9: 14 he who is *u.* shall be *u.* still.

UNHOLY (*see also* Unclean; Unworthiness)

2 Ne. 31: 5 how much more need have we, being *u.*, to be baptized; **Mosiah** 2: 37 (Alma 7: 21; 34: 36) the Lord dwells not in *u.* temples; **Hel.** 4: 24 Spirit dwells not in *u.* temples.

UNION (*see also* Unite, Unity)

Alma 50: 36 *u.* between people of Morianton and people of Lehi.

UNITE, UNITY (*see also* Agree; Join; One; Order; Union)

2 Ne. 1: 21 be determined in one mind and one heart, *u.* in all things; **Mosiah** 18: 21 people should have hearts knit in *u.* and love; **Alma** 4: 5 three thousand five hundred souls *u.* themselves to church in baptism; 11: 45 spirits will be *u.* with bodies, never more to be divided; **Hel.** 1: 6 when he sees he cannot obtain judgment-seat, Pacumeni *u.* with voice of people; 3: 26 work of the Lord prospers unto baptizing and *u.* with church tens of thousands; **3 Ne.** 6: 27–28 lawyers and high priests *u.* with kindred of judges to form secret combinations; 7: 11 tribes are *u.* in hatred of robbers; 7: 14 tribes not *u.* in laws; 27: 1 disciples *u.* in prayer and fasting; 28: 18, 23 three disciples *u.* as many to church as believe.

UNJUST (*see* Just)

Alma 12: 8 all shall rise from dead, the just and the *u.*

UNKNOWN (*see also* Strange)

Alma 30: 28, 53 Korihor calls God an *u.* being.

UNNATURAL (*see* Nature, Natural)

UNPARDONABLE (*see also* Sons of Perdition; TG Holy Ghost, Unpardonable Sin against)

Jacob 7: 19 Sherem fears he has committed *u.* sin; **Alma** 39: 6 to deny Holy Ghost once it has had place in you is *u.* sin.

UNPREPARED (*see also* Prepare)

Alma 48: 23 Nephites sorry to send brethren into eternal world *u.* to meet God.

UNPROFITABLE

Mosiah 2: 20–21 if ye should serve God with whole souls, ye would be *u.* servants; 22: 4 if thou hast not found me to be *u.* servant, listen to my words.

UNPUNISHED

Hel. 7: 5 robbers let wicked go *u.* because of money.

UNQUENCHABLE (*see* Fire; Flame)

UNRIGHTEOUS, UNRIGHTEOUSNESS (*see also* Iniquity; Unjust; Unworthiness; Wicked; Unrighteous Dominion)

Mosiah 29: 33, 35 Mosiah[2] warns of dangers of *u.* king; **Alma** 7: 14 Lamb is mighty to cleanse from all *u.*; 10: 27 foundation of destruction laid by *u.* of lawyers and judges.

UNSEARCHABLE

Jacob 4: 8 how *u.* are depths of the Lord's mysteries.

UNSHAKEN (*see also* Steadfast)

2 Ne. 31: 19 ye have not gotten into straight path save by word of Christ with *u.* faith in him; **Jacob** 4: 6 by searching scriptures our faith becomes *u.*; **Enos** 1: 11 faith of Enos[1] begins to be *u.* in the Lord.

UNSPEAKABLE

Hel. 5: 44 Nephi[2] and Lehi[4] are filled with *u.* joy; **3 Ne.** 26: 18 many see and hear *u.* things; 28: 13 three Nephites are caught up into heaven, see and hear *u.* things.

UNSTEADINESS

Hel. 12: 1 we can behold the *u.* of hearts of men.

UNWEARIED, UNWEARYINGNESS (*see also* Diligence)

Hel. 10: 4–5 Nephi[2] declares word with *u.*; 15: 6 righteous Lamanites strive with *u.* diligence to bring brethren to knowledge of truth.

UNWISE (*see also* Foolish; Wisdom, Wise)

Alma 57: 2 by delivering up prisoners for city of Antiparah, we should suppose ourselves *u.*

UNWORTHINESS, UNWORTHY, UNWORTHILY (*see also* Iniquity; Unholy; Unrighteous; Wicked)

Mosiah 21: 33 Ammon[1] considers himself an *u.* servant; 23: 11 Alma[1] feels *u.* to glory of himself; **Alma** 38: 14 (Ether 3: 2) acknowledge your *u.* before God at all times; **3 Ne.** 18: 28–29 he who partakes of sacrament *u.* brings damnation to his soul; 18: 28–29 (Morm. 9: 29) the *u.* should be forbidden to partake of sacrament; **4 Ne.** 1: 27 false churches administer that which is sacred to the *u.*; **Morm.** 9: 29 see that ye are not baptized *u.*

UPHOLD, UPHELD (*see also* Maintain; Preserve; Support)

Hel. 2: 3 Kishkumen is *u.* by his band; **Morm.** 8: 31 many will claim the Lord will *u.* sinners; **Ether** 8: 22 nations that *u.* secret combinations shall be destroyed.

UPRIGHTNESS, UPRIGHT, UPRIGHTLY (*see also* Just; Righteousness)

1 Ne. 16: 3 (Mosiah 18: 29; Alma 1: 1; 45: 24; 53: 21; 63: 2; Hel. 6: 34) walk *u.* before God; **Alma** 27: 27 Ammonites are *u.* in all things; 50: 37 Nephihah[2] fills judgment-seat with perfect *u.* before God.

UPROAR (*see also* Noise; Riotings; Tumult)

3 Ne. 1: 7 great *u.* throughout land.

URGE (*see also* Exhort; Persuade)

Morm. 2: 23 Mormon[2] *u.* Nephites to stand boldly before Lamanites.

USE

3 Ne. 12: 44 (Matt. 5: 44) pray for those who despitefully *u.* you.

USURP (*see also* Overthrow)

Alma 25: 5 priests of Noah[3] *u.* power over Lamanites; 43: 8 Zerahemnah desires to *u.* power over Lamanites; 60: 27 Moroni[1] will destroy those who desire to *u.* power and authority; **Hel.** 7: 4 robbers *u.* power and authority of government.

UTTER, UTTERANCE (*see also* Speak; Word)

2 Ne. 28: 4 false churches shall deny Holy Ghost, which gives *u.*; 32: 7 Spirit stops *u.* of Nephi[1]; **Mosiah** 4: 20 people of Benjamin cannot find *u.* because of great joy; **Alma** 30: 49–50 Korihor is struck dumb, that he cannot have *u.*; **Hel.** 5: 33 voice speaks marvelous things, which cannot be *u.* by man; **3 Ne.** 19: 34 words of Jesus' prayer cannot be *u.* by man; 26: 14, 16 Jesus looses children's tongues that they can *u.* marvelous things.

VAIN, VAINNESS (*see also* Naught; Vanity)

1 Ne. 12: 18 spacious building is *v.* imaginations of men; **2 Ne.** 9: 28 O the *v.* of men; 26: 32 (Mosiah 13: 15; Ex. 20: 7) thou shalt not take name of the Lord in *v.*; 28: 9 many shall teach false and *v.* doctrines; **Mosiah** 4: 16 ye will not suffer beggar to put up petition in *v.*; **Alma** 1: 16 (4: 8; 5: 53; Hel. 7: 21) many love, set hearts upon *v.* things of the world; 31: 27 men cry unto God while they are puffed up with *v.* things of world; 34: 28 unless you impart of substance to needy, your prayer is *v.*; 39: 14 seek not after *v.* things of world, for you cannot carry them with you; **3 Ne.** 2: 2 men imagine up some *v.* thing in hearts regarding signs; 2: 2 devil leads men to believe doctrine of Christ is *v.*; 6: 15 Satan tempts men to seek *v.* things of world; 13: 7 (Matt. 6: 7) when ye pray, use not *v.* repetitions; 24: 14 (Mal. 3: 14) ye have said, It is *v.* to serve God.

VALE (*see also* Valley; Veil)

Alma 37: 45 words of Christ carry us beyond this *v.* of sorrow into far better land of promise.

VALIANT, VALIANTLY (*see also* Courage; Diligence; Uprightness)

2 Ne. 20: 13 (Isa. 10: 13) I have put down inhabitants like a *v.* man; **Alma** 51: 21 king-men are brought down to fight *v.* for freedom; 53: 20 Ammonite youths are exceedingly *v.* for courage; 56: 13 cities obtained by shedding blood of *v.* men; 56: 16 Nephites fight *v.* by day and toil by night to maintain cities; 62: 37 Teancum fought *v.* for his country.

VALLEY (*see also* Vale)

1 Ne. 2: 10 Lehi[1] admonishes Lemuel to be steadfast like *v.*; **2 Ne.** 4: 26 why should my soul linger in *v.* of sorrow; **Hel.** 14: 23 mountains to be laid low like *v.*, *v.* to become mountains; **3 Ne.** 9: 8 *v.* made where cities stood.

VALUE (*see also* Esteem; Precious; Treasure; Worth)

Alma 11: 4–19 *v.* of Nephite coins; **Morm.** 8: 38 greater is *v.* of endless happiness than misery.

VANISH (*see also* Pass)

2 Ne. 2: 13 if there is no God, all things must have *v.* away; 8: 6 (Isa. 51: 6) heavens shall *v.* away like smoke; **Jacob** 4: 2 whatever is written upon anything other than plates will *v.*

VANITY (*see also* Pride; Vain, Vainness)

2 Ne. 15: 18 (Isa. 5: 18) wo unto those who draw iniquity with cords of *v.*

VAPOR (*see also* Cloud; Mist; Smoke)

1 Ne. 12: 4–5 (3 Ne. 8: 20) Nephi[1] beholds *v.* of darkness upon promised land; 19: 11 the Lord will visit house of Israel, some by *v.* of darkness; 22: 18 *v.* of smoke to come if men harden hearts; **Morm.** 8: 29 there shall be heard of *v.* of smoke in foreign lands.

VARY, VARIABLENESS (*see also* Change; God, Eternal Nature of)

Mosiah 2: 22 (Alma 7: 20) the Lord never *v.* from what he has said; **3 Ne.** 19: 8 disciples minister same words as Jesus spoke, nothing *v.*; **Morm.** 9: 9 in God there is no *v.*; 9: 10 a god who *v.* would not be a God of miracles; **Ether** 8: 14–15 combinations swear that whoso *v.* from what Akish desires should lose head.

VEIL (*see also* Curtain; Vale; BD Veil)

Alma 19: 6 dark *v.* of unbelief being cast from Lamoni's mind; **Ether** 3: 19–20 (12: 21) brother of Jared[2] could not be kept from beholding within *v.*; 4: 15 when Israel rends *v.* of unbelief, they shall know Father remembers covenants; 12: 19 many before Christ's coming had such strong faith that they could not be kept from within *v.*

VENGEANCE (*see also* Avenge; Destruction; Judgment; Justice; Punishment; Revenge)

Mosiah 17: 19 God executes *v.* upon those who destroy his people; **Alma** 1: 13 if Nehor were spared, Gideon's blood would come upon judges for *v.*; 37: 30 blood of murdered prophets cries to the Lord for *v.*; **3 Ne.** 21: 21 the Lord will execute *v.* and fury upon the unrepentant; **Morm.** 3: 15 (8: 20; Rom. 12: 19) *v.* is mine, and I will repay; 8: 41 sword of *v.* hangeth over you; **Ether** 8: 22 the Lord will not suffer blood of saints to cry for *v.* and he avenge them not.

VERIFIED (*see also* Testify; Witness)

Jarom 1: 9 (Alma 9: 14) word of the Lord is *v.*

VESSEL (*see also* Barge; Ship)

Alma 7: 10 Mary a precious and chosen *v.*; 60: 23–24 inward *v.* shall be cleansed first, then outer *v.*; **3 Ne.** 20: 41 be ye clean that bear *v.* of the Lord; **Morm.** 5: 18 Nephites are led by Satan as *v.* is tossed without anchor; **Ether** 2: 2 Jaredites prepare *v.* in which to carry fish; **Moro.** 7: 31 angels bear testimony to chosen *v.*, that they may bear testimony.

VEX (*see also* Trouble)

2 Ne. 17: 6 (Isa. 7: 6) let us go up against Judah and *v.* it; 21: 13 (Isa. 11: 13) Judah shall not *v.* Ephraim.

VICTORY

Mosiah 15: 8 God gains *v.* over death; 16: 7–8 (Alma 22: 14) grave has no *v.*; **Alma** 16: 21 church established throughout land, having got *v.* over devil; 27: 28 death swallowed up in *v.* of Christ; 58: 33 God has given us *v.* over those lands.

VIEW (*see also* Behold; See; Sight)

2 Ne. 1: 24 rebel no more against your brother, whose *v.* have been glorious; 9: 44 Jacob[2] prays God to *v.* him with all-searching eye; 27: 13 none others shall *v.* book except few to bear testimony; **Mosiah** 3: 25 the wicked are consigned to awful *v.* of own guilt; 4: 2 Benjamin's people had *v.* themselves in own carnal state; **Alma** 5: 15 do you *v.* mortal body raised in immortality; 27: 28 converted Lamanites could never look upon death with any degree of terror for *v.* of Christ and his resurrection; **Ether** 13: 13–14 Ether went forth by night to *v.* destruction of his people.

VILEST (*see also* Wicked)

Mosiah 28: 4 sons of Mosiah[2] had been *v.* of sinners.

VILLAGES (*see also* City; Town)

Mosiah 27: 6 Nephites build large cities and *v.*; **Alma** 8: 7 *v.* called after him who first possessed them; **Morm.** 4: 22 Nephites flee, taking all inhabitants, both in towns and *v.*; 5: 5 towns and *v.* burned by Lamanites.

VINE (*see also* Grape; Vineyard; Wine; BD Vine)

1 Ne. 15: 15 seed of Nephites to receive nourishment from true *v.*; **2 Ne.** 15: 1–2 (Isa. 5: 1–2) well-beloved planted vineyard with choicest *v.*; **Alma** 16: 17 those who receive word are as branch grafted into true *v.*; **3 Ne.** 24: 11 (Mal. 3: 11) *v.* shall not cast her fruit before the time.

VINEYARD (*see also* Grape; Olive; Spot of Land; Vine; TG Vineyard of the Lord)

2 Ne. 15: 1–4 (Isa. 5: 1–4) well-beloved's *v.* brings forth wild grapes; 15: 7 (Isa. 5: 7) *v.* of the Lord is the house of Israel; **Jacob** ch. 5 parable of tame olive-tree in *v.*; ch. 6 Jacob[2] expounds parable of olive-tree in *v.*; **Mosiah** 11: 15 Noah[3] plants *v.* in land; **Alma** 13: 23 glad tidings declared in all parts of *v.*

VIRGIN (*see also* Jesus Christ, First Coming of; Mary)

1 Ne. 11: 13–20 Nephi[1] beholds *v.* in Nazareth, mother of Son; **2 Ne.** 17: 14 (Isa. 7: 14) *v.* shall conceive and bear son, Immanuel; **Alma** 7: 10 Christ to be born of Mary, a *v.*

VIRTUE (*see also* Chastity; Clean; Holiness; Merit; Purity; Strength; TG Virtue, Virtuous)

Alma 31: 5 Alma[2] to try *v.* of word of God; **Moro.** 9: 9 Nephites deprive Lamanite daughters of their chastity and *v.*

VISAGE (*see also* Countenance; Face)

3 Ne. 20: 44 his *v.* was so marred.

VISION, VISIONARY (*see also* Dream; God, Manifestations of; Revelation; See)

1 Ne. 1: 8 Lehi[1] carried away in *v.*; 2: 11 (5: 2, 4) Lehi[1] a *v.* man; 5: 4 if Lehi[1] had not seen things of God in *v.*, he would not have known goodness of God; ch. 8 (10: 17) Lehi[1] explains what he has seen in *v.*; **2 Ne.** 1: 1, 4 Lehi[1] has seen *v.* of destruction of Jerusalem; 4: 23 the Lord has given Nephi[1] knowledge by *v.*; 27: 3 nations that fight against Zion shall be as dream of night *v.*; **Alma** 8: 20–21 in *v.* angel tells Amulek to receive Alma[2]; 19: 16 Abish is converted because of remarkable *v.* of father.

VISIT (*see also* God, Manifestations of; Judgment; Visitation)

1 Ne. 2: 16 the Lord *v.* Nephi[1]; 13: 34 the Lord to *v.* remnant of Nephites in judgment; 19: 11 the Lord God surely will *v.* all house of Israel at that day; **2 Ne.** 4: 26 the Lord in condescension hath *v.* men in mercy; **Mosiah** 4: 26 to retain remission of sin, *v.* the sick and administer to their relief; 11: 20 (Alma 9: 12) except they repent, the Lord will *v.* this people in anger; 11: 22 the Lord is jealous God, *v.* iniquities of his people; 13: 13 (Ex. 20: 5) the Lord *v.* iniquities of fathers upon children; 27: 7 the Lord *v.* Nephites and prospers them; **Alma** 9: 21 Nephites have been *v.* by Spirit; 17: 10 the Lord *v.* sons of Mosiah[2] with Spirit; 33: 10 thou didst *v.* mine enemies in thine anger; 34: 28 if ye *v.* not the sick and afflicted, your prayer is vain; **3 Ne.** 7: 15 Nephi[3] is *v.* by angels and voice of the Lord; 7: 21 converts signify they have been *v.* by power and Spirit of God; 27: 32 in fourth generation the Lord will *v.* Nephites in turning their works upon own heads; **Morm.** 1: 15 Mormon[2] is *v.* of the Lord; **Ether** 4: 11 the Lord will *v.* believers with manifestations of Spirit.

VISITATION (*see also* Judgment; Revelation; Visit)

2 Ne. 20: 3 (Isa. 10: 3) what will ye do in day of *v.*; **Morm.** 9: 2 will ye believe in day of your *v.*; **Moro.** 8: 26 because of meekness cometh *v.* of Holy Ghost.

VOICE (*see also* God, Manifestations of; Prayer; Preach; Revelation; Sound [noun and verb]; Speech; Warn)

1 Ne. 4: 18 Nephi[1] obeys *v.* of Spirit in killing Laban; 16: 9, 25–26 (18: 5) *v.* of the Lord comes to Lehi[1]; 16: 39 *v.* of the Lord chastens rebellious brothers; 17: 45 the Lord has spoken to Laman[1] and Lemuel by *v.* of angel, still small *v.*, *v.* of thunder; 22: 2 prophecies were manifested upon Isaiah[1] by *v.* of Spirit; **2 Ne.** 4: 35 I will lift up my *v.* to thee, my God; 16: 8 (Isa. 6: 8) *v.* of the Lord says, Whom shall I send; 31: 12, 14 *v.* of Son comes to Nephi[1]; 33: 13 (Isa. 40: 3) I speak to you as *v.* of one crying from dust; **Jacob** 7: 5 *v.* of the Lord speaks to Jacob[2] from time to time; **Enos** 1: 5, 10 *v.* of the Lord comes into mind of Enos[2]; **Omni** 1: 12–13 those who hearken to *v.* of the Lord depart with Mosiah[1]; **Mosiah** 16: 2 (Ether 11: 7) the wicked hearken not to *v.* of the Lord; 24: 13, 16 *v.* of the Lord comes to people of Alma[1]; 26: 14 after Alma[1] pours out soul to God, *v.* of the Lord comes to him; 26: 21 (John 10: 16) he who will hear the Lord's *v.* shall be his sheep; 27: 11, 18 (Alma 36: 7–8; 38: 7) angel speaks to Alma[2] with *v.* of thunder; 29: 25 choose judges by *v.* of people; 29: 26 not common for *v.* of people to choose that which is not right, therefore, do business by *v.* of people; **Alma** 2: 7 *v.* of people comes against Amlici; 5: 16 can ye imagine ye hear *v.* of the Lord saying, Come unto me; 5: 38–39 they who will not hearken to *v.* of good shepherd are of devil's fold; 5: 41 if a man brings forth good works, he hearkens to *v.* of good shepherd; 5: 57 those desiring to follow *v.* of the good shepherd must come out from the wicked; 9: 21 Nephites have been spoken to by *v.* of the Lord; 10: 20 the Lord cries unto this people by *v.* of angels; 13: 22 *v.* of the Lord by mouth of angels declares repentance to all nations; 20: 2 *v.* of the Lord comes to Ammon[2]; 29: 2 I would declare repentance unto every soul with *v.* of thunder; **Hel.** 5: 29–31 still *v.* of perfect mildness speaks to dissenters in prison; 7: 18 ye will not hearken unto *v.* of good shepherd; 10: 3–11 *v.* of God comes to Nephi[1]; 12: 9–12 by power of the Lord's *v.* whole earth shakes; 12: 23 they who hearken to *v.* of the Lord shall be saved; 13: 3 *v.* of the Lord tells Samuel the Lamanite to return; **3 Ne.** 1: 12–14 (7: 15) *v.* of the Lord comes to

Nephi[3]; ch. 9 (10: 3–7) *v.* comes to inhabitants of land; 11: 3–7 three times, small piercing *v.* comes to multitude, announcing Christ; 15: 21, 24 (John 10: 16) other sheep shall hear Christ's *v.*; **Morm.** 3: 14–15 *v.* of the Lord comes to Mormon[2] prophesying destruction.

VOID (*see also* Empty)

Alma 12: 23, 26 (42: 5) if Adam had partaken of tree of life, there would have been no death, word would have been *v.*

VOMIT

3 Ne. 7: 8 people turn from righteousness like dog to *v.*

VULTURES (*see also* Animal)

Mosiah 12: 2 *v.* shall devour flesh of this generation because of iniquity; **Alma** 2: 38 many soldiers die in wilderness and are devoured by *v.*

WADE (*see* Affliction; Anguish)

WAGES (*see also* Labor; Pay; Reward)

Mosiah 2: 33 he who obeys evil spirit receives for *w.* eternal punishment; **Alma** 3: 27 every man receives *w.* of him whom he obeys; 5: 41–42 whoso hearkens to devil's voice must receive *w.* of devil; 11: 1 judges receive *w.* according to time that they labored to judge; **3 Ne.** 24: 5 (Mal. 3: 5) the Lord will be swift witness against those who oppress hireling in his *w.*; **Morm.** 8: 19 according to works shall *w.* be.

WAIL (*see also* Cry; Lament; Mourn; Weep)

Mosiah 16: 2 the wicked shall have cause to weep and *w.*; **Alma** 5: 36 those who do not works of righteousness shall have cause to *w.* and mourn; 40: 13 weeping, *w.*, gnashing of teeth in outer darkness; **3 Ne.** 10: 10 *w.* of people who are spared ceases.

WAIT (*see also* Watch)

1 Ne. 21: 23 (2 Ne. 6: 7; Isa. 49: 23) they shall not be ashamed who *w.* for the Lord; **2 Ne.** 6: 13 people of the Lord are they who *w.* for him; 8: 5 (Isa. 51: 5) isles shall *w.* upon the Lord; **Mosiah** 21: 34 Limhi's people do not form church, *w.* upon Spirit.

WALK (*see also* Act; Do; Live [verb]; Path; Way; TG Walking in Darkness; Walking with God)

1 Ne. 16: 3 (Mosiah 18: 29; Alma 1: 1; 45: 24; 53: 21; 63: 2) *w.* uprightly before God; 16: 5 *w.* in paths of righteousness; **2 Ne.** 4: 32 wilt thou not shut gates of thy righteousness, that I may *w.* in path of low valley; 13: 16 (Isa. 3: 16) daughters of Zion *w.* with stretched-forth necks; 19: 2 (Isa. 9: 2) people that *w.* in darkness have seen great light; 33: 9 for none can I hope unless they *w.* in strait path; **Mosiah** 2: 27 Benjamin *w.* with clear conscience before God; 3: 5 the Lord will cause the lame to *w.*; 4: 15 teach children to *w.* in ways of truth and soberness; 4: 26 that ye may *w.* guiltless before God, impart substance to the poor; 6: 6 Mosiah[2] *w.* in ways of the Lord; 7: 19 the Lord caused Israelites to *w.* through Red Sea; 11: 1 Noah[3] does not *w.* in father's ways; 11: 2 Noah[3] *w.* after desires of own heart; 23: 14 trust no man to be your teacher except he *w.* in God's ways; 26: 37 (Hel. 15: 5) *w.* circumspectly before God; 26: 38 Alma[1] and fellow laborers *w.* in all diligence; 29: 43 Alma[2] *w.* in ways of the Lord; **Alma** 5: 27 (7: 22) have ye *w.*, keeping yourselves blameless before God; 5: 54 (7: 22) *w.* after holy order of God; 7: 9 prepare way of the Lord, *w.* in his paths; 7: 20 God cannot *w.* in crooked paths; 15: 10–11 after being blessed by Alma[2], Zeezrom *w.*; 25: 14 converted Lamanites *w.* in ways of the Lord; 41: 8 whosoever will may *w.* in God's ways and be saved; **Hel.** 3: 20 Helaman[3] *w.* in father's ways; 13: 27 false prophets teach people to *w.* in pride of hearts; **Ether** 6: 17, 30 Jaredites are taught to *w.* humbly before the Lord; 10: 2 Shez *w.* in ways of the Lord; **Moro.** 7: 4 Mormon[2] judges people of church by peaceable *w.* with men.

WALL

1 Ne. 4: 4 sons of Lehi[1] journey to *w.* of Jerusalem; **Alma** 48: 8 (52: 6) Moroni[1] builds *w.* of stone to encircle cities; 53: 4 *w.* of timbers and earth built around Bountiful; **Hel.** 13: 4 (14: 11) Samuel preaches upon *w.*

WALLOWING (*see* Sow [noun])

WANDER, WANDERERS (*see also* Astray; Err; Flight; Journey)

1 Ne. 8: 23 those on path *w.* off and are lost in mist of darkness; 16: 35 (17: 20) the rebellious murmur because they have *w.* in wilderness many years; 19: 14 Jews to *w.* in flesh; **Jacob** 7: 26 (Alma 13: 23; 26: 36) Nephites are *w.* in strange land; **Enos** 1: 20 Lamanites *w.* about in wilderness; **Mosiah** 7: 4 expedition to Lehi-Nephi *w.* in wilderness forty days; 27: 28 Alma[2] is snatched from everlasting burning; **Moro.** 1: 3 Moroni[2] *w.* for safety of his life.

WANT (*see also* Need)

1 Ne. 16: 19 Lehites suffer much for *w.* of food; **Mosiah** 4: 26 (18: 29) administer to relief of sick, both spiritually and temporally, according to their *w.*;

27: 5 priests labor for own support, save in cases of much *w.*; **Alma** 35: 9 Ammonites administer to outcast Zoramites according to *w.*; 58: 7 Nephite army about to perish for *w.* of food; **3 Ne.** 4: 3 robbers cannot exist save in wilderness, for *w.* of food; 4: 24 robbers become weak for *w.* of food.

WAR (*see also* Army; Battle; Blood, Shedding of; Destruction; Fight; Government, Civil; Peace; Revolt; Slaughter; Sword; Warfare; TG War; BD War in Heaven)

1 Ne. 12: 2, 21 (14: 16; 2 Ne. 25: 12; Morm. 8: 30; Matt. 24: 6) there shall be *w.* and rumors of *w.*; 22: 13 abominable church shall *w.* among themselves; **2 Ne.** 12: 4 (Isa. 2: 4) nations shall not learn *w.* any more; 13: 1–2 (Isa. 3: 1–2) the Lord will take away from Judah the man of *w.*; 26: 2 there shall be great *w.* and contentions among Nephites; **Enos** 1: 24 (Omni 1: 10, 24; Alma 24: 20; 27: 1; 51: 9; Morm. 1: 8) *w.* between Nephites and Lamanites; **Omni** 1: 3 Nephites have many seasons of *w.*; **Alma** 50: 21 Nephites' iniquity brings *w.* upon them; 61: 15 Lehi[3] and Teancum given power to conduct *w.* according to Spirit; 62: 41 many become hardened because of great length of *w.*; **Hel.** 3: 22 *w.* and contentions begin to cease; 11: 1 contentions increase, causing *w.*; 11: 24 Nephite dissenters begin *w.* with brethren; **Morm.** 8: 8 Lamanites are at *w.* one with another; **Ether** 13: 15 great *w.* begins during reign of Coriantumr[2].

WARFARE (*see also* War)

Alma 1: 1 Mosiah[2] has warred a good *w.*; 56: 2 Helaman[2] and Moroni[1] brothers in the Lord as in *w.*

WARN, WARNING (*see also* Admonish; Chasten; Exhort; Preach; Rebuke; Reprove; Threaten; Thunder; Voice; Watchmen)

2 Ne. 1: 3 the Lord is merciful in *w.* Lehites to flee Jerusalem; 5: 5 the Lord *w.* Nephi[1] to depart from brethren; 5: 6 those who go with Nephi[1] believe *w.* of God; **Jacob** 3: 12 Jacob[2] *w.* people against fornication and lasciviousness; **Omni** 1: 12 Mosiah[1] is *w.* to flee out of land of Nephi; **Mosiah** 16: 12 the wicked are *w.* of iniquities, but depart not from them; 23: 1 Alma[1] is *w.* by the Lord concerning armies of Noah[3]; **Alma** 48: 15 if they keep commandments, the Lord would *w.* Nephites to flee; **Ether** 9: 3 the Lord *w.* Omer in dream.

WASH (*see also* Baptism; Cleanse; Jesus Christ, Atonement through; Purify; Sanctification)

2 Ne. 14: 4 (Isa. 4: 4) the Lord shall *w.* away filth of daughters of Zion; **Alma** 5: 21 (3 Ne. 27: 19) no man can be saved except his garments are *w.* white; 7: 14 be baptized, that ye may be *w.* from sins; 13: 11 garments of high priests have been *w.* white through blood of Lamb; 24: 13 if we should stain swords again, perhaps they can no more be *w.* bright through blood of Son; **3 Ne.** 13: 17 (Matt. 6: 17) when thou fastest, anoint thy head and *w.* thy face; **Ether** 13: 11 inhabitants of Jerusalem shall be *w.* in blood of Lamb.

WASTE (*see also* Desolation; Destruction; Empty; Ruin; TG Waste)

1 Ne. 8: 7 Lehi[1] dreams of dark and dreary *w.*; 21: 19 (Isa. 49: 19) *w.* places shall be too narrow because of inhabitants; **2 Ne.** 9: 27 awful is state of him who *w.* days of probation; 16: 11 (Isa. 6: 11) cities to be *w.* without inhabitants; **Mosiah** 12: 23 (15: 30; 3 Ne. 16: 19; 20: 34; Isa. 52: 9) sing together, ye *w.* places of Jerusalem; **Hel.** 11: 20 Nephites begin to build up *w.* places.

WATCH, WATCHFUL (*see also* Look; Preside; See; Seek; Wait; Watchmen)

2 Ne. 27: 31 all who *w.* for iniquity shall be cut off; **Mosiah** 4: 30 *w.* your thoughts and deeds; **Alma** 6: 1 priests and elders ordained to *w.* over church; 13: 28 (15: 17; 3 Ne. 18: 15, 18) *w.* and pray continually; 34: 39 (Moro. 6: 4) be *w.* unto prayer continually; **3 Ne.** 1: 8 the faithful *w.* steadfastly for sign of Christ's birth.

WATCHMEN (*see also* Warn)

Mosiah 12: 22 (15: 29; 3 Ne. 16: 18; 20: 32; Isa. 52: 8) thy *w.* shall lift up voice.

WATER (*see also* Baptism; Flood; Fountain; Immersion; Lake; Mormon, Waters of; Sea; Sebus, Waters of; Spring; Thirst; Wave)

1 Ne. 10: 9–10 John to baptize Messiah with *w.*; 13: 10, 12–13, 17, 29 Nephi[1] beholds many *w.* separating his seed from Gentiles; 14: 11–12 abominable church sits upon many *w.*; 17: 5 Lehites call sea Irreantum, meaning many *w.*; 17: 26 (Hel. 8: 11) by Moses' word, *w.* of Red Sea were divided; 17: 29 (2 Ne. 25: 20) Moses smote rock and *w.* came forth; 20: 1 (Isa. 48: 1) come forth out of *w.* of Judah, or *w.* of baptism; **2 Ne.** 9: 50 every one that thirsteth, come to *w.*; 22: 3 (Isa. 12: 3) with joy shall ye draw *w.* out of wells of salvation; 33: 3 eyes of Nephi[1] *w.* his pillow by night because of his people; **Mosiah** 18: 14 Alma[1] and Helam are buried in *w.* in baptism; **Alma** 3: 3

slain Lamanites and Amlicites are cast into *w.* of Sidon; 5: 34 (42: 27) come unto the Lord and ye shall drink *w.* of life freely; 17: 26, 34 Ammon[2] tends flocks by *w.* of Sebus; 22: 32 lands of Nephi and Zarahemla nearly surrounded by *w.*; 50: 29 (Hel. 3: 4; Morm. 6: 4) land northward covered with large bodies of *w.*; **Hel.** 12: 16 if the Lord says to *w.* of deep, Be dried up, it is done; **3 Ne.** 9: 7 the Lord causes *w.* to come up in places of cities; **Morm.** 6: 4 Cumorah a land of many *w.*; **Ether** 6: 11 Jaredites driven upon *w.* three hundred forty and four days; 13: 2 after *w.* receded, this land became choice above all others; **Moro.** 7: 11 bitter fountain cannot bring forth good *w.*, nor good fountain bitter *w.*

WAVES (*see also* Sea)

1 Ne. 20: 18 (Isa. 48: 18) thy righteousness would have been as *w.* of sea; **Jacob** 4: 6 saints can command in Jesus' name and *w.* obey; **Morm.** 5: 18 Nephites are led by Satan as vessel is tossed upon *w.* without anchor; **Ether** 2: 24 (6: 5–6) mountain *w.* shall dash upon Jaredite vessels.

WAX (*see also* Grow; Increase)

2 Ne. 4: 24 by day have I *w.* bold in mighty prayer; 7: 9 (Isa. 50: 9) those who condemn me shall *w.* old as garment; 8: 6 earth shall *w.* old like garment; **Mosiah** 18: 26 priests to receive grace of God, that they might *w.* strong in Spirit; **Alma** 4: 6 people of church begin to *w.* proud; 17: 2 sons of Mosiah[2] have *w.* strong in knowledge of truth; 50: 18 Nephites *w.* strong in land; **Hel.** 3: 35 the humble *w.* stronger and stronger in humility.

WAY (*see also* Direction; Example; Gate; Highway; Means; Path; Road; Street; Walk)

1 Ne. 3: 7 (9: 6) the Lord giveth no commandment save he shall prepare a *w.* to accomplish it; 10: 7 (3 Ne. 24: 1; Mal. 3: 1) John the Baptist to prepare *w.* of the Lord; 10: 8 (Alma 7: 9; 9: 28; Hel. 14: 9; Ether 9: 28; Isa. 40: 3) prepare ye *w.* of the Lord; 10: 18 *w.* is prepared for all men if they repent; 13: 27 (22: 14; 2 Ne. 28: 15; Jacob 7: 7; Mosiah 12: 26; 29: 7; Alma 30: 60; 31: 1, 11; Moro. 8: 16) the wicked pervert right *w.* of the Lord; 16: 10 (Alma 37: 40) one spindle in Liahona points *w.* to go in wilderness; 17: 13 the Lord will prepare *w.* in wilderness; 17: 41 the Lord prepared way that Israelites might be healed of serpents' bites; 17: 41 (Alma 37: 46) because of simpleness of *w.*, many perish; 22: 20 the Lord will prepare *w.* unto fulfilling words of Moses; **2 Ne.** 2: 4 (Alma 37: 46) *w.* is prepared from fall of man, and salvation is free; 4: 5 (Prov. 22: 6) if children are brought up in *w.* they should go, they will not depart from it; 4: 27 why should I give *w.* to temptations; 4: 33 Lord, wilt thou make a *w.* for mine escape from mine enemies; 9: 10 the Lord prepares *w.* for escape from death and hell; 9: 41 (3 Ne. 14: 14) *w.* for man is narrow; 9: 41 none other *w.* save by gate; 10: 23 men are free to choose *w.* of everlasting death or *w.* of eternal life; 12: 3 (Isa. 2: 3) the Lord will teach us his *w.*; 25: 28–29 right *w.* is to believe in Christ; 28: 11 they have all gone out of the *w.*; 31: 21 (Mosiah 3: 17; Alma 38: 9; Hel. 5: 9) none other *w.* whereby man can be saved; 32: 1 Nephites ponder what to do after entering *w.*; **Jacob** 4: 8 no man knows God's *w.* save they are revealed to him; 6: 11 continue in *w.* which is narrow; **Mosiah** 1: 9 Benjamin is soon to go *w.* of all earth; 14: 6 (Isa. 53: 6) we have turned every one to his own *w.*; 29: 23 unrighteous king perverts *w.* of righteousness; **Alma** 1: 1 Mosiah[2] has gone *w.* of all earth; 4: 19 Alma[2] sees not *w.* to reclaim Nephites save in bearing down in pure testimony; 37: 46 do not let us be slothful because of easiness of *w.*; 42: 2 flaming sword turned every *w.*, to keep tree of life; 62: 37 Teancum has gone *w.* of all earth; **Hel.** 9: 21 how long will the Lord suffer you to go in your *w.* of sin; **3 Ne.** 14: 13 (27: 33; Matt. 7: 13) broad is *w.* that leads to destruction; 14: 14 (27: 33; Matt. 7: 14) narrow is *w.* that leads to life; 21: 27 work to commence among the dispersed to prepare *w.* for them to come to Christ; **Ether** 12: 11 in his Son, God has prepared more excellent *w.*; **Moro.** 6: 4 names of converts taken to keep them in right *w.*; 7: 15 *w.* to judge is plain; 7: 21 the *w.* whereby ye may lay hold upon every good thing; 7: 32 the Lord prepared *w.* for men to have faith in Christ.

WEAK, WEAKNESS (*see also* Fault; Humble; Infirmity; Slacken; Strengthen)

1 Ne. 19: 6 Nephi[1] excuses himself because of own *w.*, not other men's; 19: 20 workings in spirit weary Nephi[1], that all his joints are *w.*; **2 Ne.** 3: 21 *w.* of their words will the Lord make strong in faith; 24: 10 (Isa. 14: 10) art thou also become *w.* as we; 33: 4 words which Nephi[1] has written in *w.* will be made strong to his people; **Jacob** 4: 7 the Lord shows Nephites *w.* that they may know power to do these things comes by his grace; **Mosiah** 1: 13 (Morm. 2: 26) if Nephites fall into transgression, they will become *w.* like brethren; 27: 19 Alma[2] becomes *w.* because of great astonishment; **Alma** 58: 37 Nephites trust God will deliver them, notwithstanding *w.* of armies; **3 Ne.** 17: 2 Nephites are *w.*, that they understand not Jesus' words; **Ether** 12: 25 Nephites behold own *w.* in writing; 12: 27 the Lord gives men *w.* that they may be humble; 12: 28 the Lord will show Gentiles their *w.*; 12: 35 Gentiles must have charity because of Nephites' *w.*; 12: 37 because thou hast seen thy *w.*, thou shalt be made strong.

WEALTH, WEALTHY (*see also* Gain; Money; Rich; Riches; TG Wealth)

Mosiah 27: 7 Nephites become large and *w.* people; **Alma** 1: 31 members of church become far more *w.* than nonmembers.

WEAPON (*see also* Arms; Arrow; Bow [noun]; Cimeter; Dart; Javelin; Sling; Spear; Sword)

Jarom 1: 8 Nephites make *w.* of war; **Mosiah** 9: 16 Zeniff arms his people with *w.*; **Alma** 2: 12 (43: 18; 60: 2) Nephites arm themselves with *w.* of war; 23: 7 (Hel. 5: 51) converted Lamanites lay down *w.* of rebellion; 24: 17–19 (26: 32; 53: 11–16; 56: 6–7; Hel. 15: 9) people of Anti-Nephi-Lehi bury *w.*; 24: 25–26 (25: 14) other Lamanites throw down *w.* and are converted; 44: 14–15 soldiers of Zerahemnah throw down *w.*; 51: 18–19 dissenters who lift *w.* against Nephite army are hewn down; 52: 25, 32 Nephites fall upon Lamanites who do not give up their *w.*; 53: 16–19 sons of Ammonites take up *w.* to support Nephites; 62: 16 Lamanite prisoners enter covenant not to take up *w.* against Nephites; **3 Ne.** 22: 17 (Isa. 54: 17) no *w.* that is formed against thee shall prosper; **Morm.** 6: 7–9 Lamanites fall upon Nephites with all manner of *w.*; 7: 4 people must lay down *w.* and delight no more in bloodshed; **Ether** 10: 27 Jaredites make all manner of *w.* of war.

WEARY

1 Ne. 19: 20 workings in spirit *w.* Nephi[1]; **2 Ne.** 7: 4 (Isa. 50: 4) when ye are *w.*, he waketh morning by morning; **Alma** 37: 34 teach people never to be *w.* of good works; **Hel.** 5: 4 Nephi[2] becomes *w.* because of Nephites' iniquity.

WEEK (*see also* Time)

Mosiah 18: 25 one day in every *w.* set apart for worship; **Alma** 31: 12 Zoramites set aside one day of *w.*, called day of the Lord, for worship; 32: 11 do ye suppose ye must worship God only once in *w.*

WEEP, WEPT, WEEPING (*see also* Cry; Lament; Mourn; Sorrow; Wail)

2 Ne. 4: 26 if I have seen so great things, why should my heart *w.*; **Jacob** 5: 41 the Lord of vineyard *w.*; **Mosiah** 16: 2 the wicked shall have cause to *w.*; **Alma** 17: 28 servants of Lamoni *w.* over scattering of flocks; 40: 13 in outer darkness there shall be *w.*, wailing; **Hel.** 13: 32 (3 Ne. 8: 23; 10: 8–10) in day of destruction ye shall *w.* and howl; **3 Ne.** 17: 21–22 Jesus *w.*

WEIGH (*see also* Burden; Oppression)

2 Ne. 1: 17 heart of Lehi[1] hath been *w.* down with sorrow because of sons; **Jacob** 2: 3 Jacob[2] is *w.* down with anxiety for welfare of Nephites' souls; **Alma** 8: 14 Alma[2] is *w.* down with sorrow because of iniquity of Ammonihah; **Moro.** 9: 25 may not the things I have written *w.* thee down to death.

WELFARE (*see also* Charity; Help)

2 Ne. 1: 25 Nephi[1] seeks brothers' eternal *w.*; 2: 30 only object of Lehi[1] is everlasting *w.* of sons' souls; 6: 3 Jacob[2] is desirous for *w.* of his people's souls; 26: 29 those practicing priestcrafts seek not *w.* of Zion; 32: 9 ask Father to consecrate thy performance for *w.* of thy soul; **Jacob** 1: 10 Nephi[1] labored all his days for his people's *w.*; 2: 3 Jacob[2] is weighed down with anxiety for *w.* of Nephites' souls; **Enos** 1: 9 Enos[2] feels desire for *w.* of Nephites; **Mosiah** 25: 11 Nephites are filled with anguish for *w.* of Lamanites' souls; **Alma** 6: 6 Nephites pray for *w.* of souls of those who know not God; 34: 27 let hearts be drawn out in prayer to God continually for *w.*; 48: 11–12 Moroni[1] labors for *w.* and safety of his people; **Hel.** 12: 2 when the Lord does all things for his people's *w.*, they harden hearts; **Morm.** 8: 15 records to come forth for *w.* of covenant people; **Moro.** 6: 5 church meets oft to speak one with another concerning *w.* of souls.

WELL [adj.] (*see also* Pleased)

2 Ne. 13: 10 (Isa. 3: 10) say unto the righteous it is *w.* with them; 28: 21 Satan lulls men into carnal security, saying, All is *w.* in Zion; 28: 25 wo unto him that crieth, All is *w.*; **Hel.** 13: 27–28 people accept false prophets because they say all is *w.*; **Morm.** 7: 10 it shall be *w.* with those who are baptized with water and with fire; **Moro.** 7: 47 whoso is found possessed of charity at last day, it shall be *w.* with him.

WHALE (*see also* Animal; BD Whale)

Ether 2: 24 Jaredite vessels shall be as *w.* in midst of sea; 6: 10 *w.* could not mar Jaredite vessels.

WHEAT (*see also* Grain)

Mosiah 9: 9 Nephites till ground with seeds of *w.*; **3 Ne.** 18: 18 Satan desires to sift you as *w.*

WHIRLWIND (*see also* Destruction; Storm; Tempest; Wind)

2 Ne. 26: 5 *w.* shall carry away those who kill prophets; **Mosiah** 7: 30 if people sow filthiness, they reap chaff in *w.*; **Alma** 26: 6 converts shall not be harrowed up by *w.*; **Hel.** 5: 12 those built upon rock of Redeemer will withstand devil's shafts in *w.*; **3 Ne.** 8: 12 whole face of land changed because of *w.*; 8: 16 some are carried away in *w.*; 10: 12–13 the righteous are not carried away in *w.*

WHISPER (*see also* Speak)

2 Ne. 26: 16 their speech shall *w.* out of dust; 28: 22 devil *w.* in men's ears until he grasps them in chains; **Hel.** 5: 30, 46 voice from heaven is perfectly mild, as a *w.*

WHITE, WHITER, WHITENESS (*see also* Brightness; Clean; Purity)

1 Ne. 8: 5 man dressed in *w.* robe stands before Lehi[1]; 8: 11 (Alma 32: 42) fruit of tree is *w.* to exceed all *w.*; 11: 13 virgin is exceedingly fair and *w.*; 12: 10–11 because of faith, garments of twelve disciples are made *w.* in Lamb's blood; 13: 15 Gentiles are *w.*; 14: 19, 27 Nephi[1] sees John the apostle dressed in *w.* robe; **2 Ne.** 5: 21 Lamanites no longer *w.*, given skin of blackness; 26: 33 the Lord denies none who come unto him, black and *w.*; **Jacob** 3: 8 Lamanites' skins will be *w.* than Nephites' unless Nephites repent; **Alma** 5: 21, 24 no man can be saved unless his garments are washed *w.*; 5: 27 (Morm. 9: 6) garments must be cleansed and made *w.* through blood of Christ; **3 Ne.** 2: 15 Lamanites' skin becomes *w.* like Nephites'; 11: 8 Christ descends from heaven clothed in *w.* robe; 12: 36 (Matt. 5: 36) thou canst not make one hair black or *w.*; 19: 25 multitude are *w.* as countenance and garments of Jesus; **Ether** 3: 1 brother of Jared[2] brings sixteen small *w.* stones to the Lord; 13: 10 New Jerusalem to be inhabited by those whose garments are *w.* through Lamb's blood.

WHOLE (*see also* Soul)

Enos 1: 8 go to, thy faith hath made thee *w.*; **Alma** 11: 45 through reuniting of spirit and body the *w.* becomes spiritual and immortal; **3 Ne.** 17: 10 both those healed and those who were *w.* worship Christ; **Moro.** 8: 8 the *w.* need no physician; 8: 8 little children are *w.*

WHORE, WHOREDOM (*see also* Adultery; Fornication; Harlot; Lust; TG Sexual Immorality; Whore; Whoredom)

1 Ne. 14: 10–12 (22: 13–14; 2 Ne. 10: 16; 28: 18) abominable church is *w.* of all earth; **2 Ne.** 9: 36 (28: 15) those who commit *w.* shall be thrust down to hell; 26: 32 (Jacob 3: 5) the Lord commands that men should not commit *w.*; 28: 14 because of *w.*, false churches have all gone astray; **Jacob** 2: 23 Nephites excuse themselves in committing *w.* because of David and Solomon; 2: 28 *w.* are abomination before the Lord; **Mosiah** 11: 6 priests of Noah[3] are supported in *w.* by taxes; **Alma** 1: 32 those who do not belong to church indulge in *w.*; 30: 18 Korihor leads many to commit *w.*; **Hel.** 6: 22–23 (Ether 8: 16) robbers enter covenant, that they might commit *w.*; **3 Ne.** 5: 3 Nephites forsake their *w.*; 16: 10 when Gentiles are filled with *w.*, Father will take gospel from them; 21: 19 all *w.* shall be done away; 30: 2 Gentiles are called to repent of *w.*; **4 Ne.** 1: 16 no *w.* among Nephites; **Ether** 10: 7 Riplakish afflicts his people with *w.*; 10: 11 Morianton[1] is cut off because of *w.*

WICKED, WICKEDLY, WICKEDNESS (*see also* Apostasy; Babylon; Carnal; Crooked; Deceit; Destruction; Devil; Disobedience; Evil; Filthiness; Hell; Hypocrisy; Iniquity; Judgment; Loathsome; Lust; Lying; Rebel; Sin; Transgression; Unclean; Ungodliness; Unholy; Unrighteous; Unworthiness; Vilest; World; TG Wickedness, Wicked)

1 Ne. 4: 13 the Lord slays the *w.* to bring forth righteous purposes; 10: 21 those who have sought to do *w.* are found unclean before God; 14: 12 numbers of church of Lamb are small because of *w.* of abominable church; 15: 36 the *w.* are rejected from the righteous; 16: 2 Nephi[1] has spoken hard things against the *w.*; 17: 37 the Lord destroys nations of the *w.*; 19: 10 God to yield himself into hands of *w.* men; 20: 22 (Isa. 48: 22) no peace unto the *w.*; 22: 16 the Lord will not suffer the *w.* to destroy the righteous; **2 Ne.** 12: 5 ye have all gone astray, every one to his *w.* ways; 15: 22–23 (Isa. 5: 22–23) wo unto those who justify the *w.* for reward; 23: 11 (Isa. 13: 11) I will punish the *w.* for their iniquity; 24: 5 (Isa. 14: 5) the Lord hath broken the staff of the *w.*; 28: 14 because of *w.*, false churches have gone astray; 30: 10 the Lord will cause division among people and will destroy the *w.*; **Jacob** 6: 13 bar of God strikes the *w.* with fear; **Mosiah** 14: 9 (Isa. 53: 9) he made his grave with the *w.*; **Alma** 1: 32–33 because of law, those who do not belong to church dare not commit *w.*; 4: 3 afflictions are judgments of God because of *w.*; 5: 57 come ye out from the *w.*; 5:

57 names of the *w.* not to be numbered among the righteous; 34: 35 (40: 13) final state of the *w.* is for devil to have all power over them; 37: 29 *w.* of Jaredites to be made known, but not secret oaths; 40: 13–14 spirits of the *w.* are cast into outer darkness until resurrection; 40: 26 an awful death cometh upon the *w.*; 41: 10 *w.* never was happiness; **Hel.** 5: 19 many Lamanites are convinced of *w.* of traditions of fathers; 6: 2 many Nephites become grossly *w.*; 6: 24 members of robber band who reveal *w.* are tried according to laws of Gadianton; 7: 5 robbers in government let *w.* go unpunished because of money; **3 Ne.** 6: 17 Nephites are in state of awful *w.*; 9: 7, 9 the Lord destroys cities to hide *w.*; 17: 14 Jesus is troubled because of *w.* of Israel; 24: 15 (Mal. 3: 15) they who work *w.* are set up; 24: 18 (Mal. 3: 18) ye shall return and discern between the righteous and the *w.*; 25: 1 all who do *w.* shall be stubble; **Morm.** 4: 5 judgments of God will overtake the *w.*; 4: 5 by the *w.* are the *w.* punished; 4: 5 the *w.* stir up hearts of men unto bloodshed; 4: 12 never so great *w.* among house of Israel; **Ether** 4: 15 Israel to rend veil of unbelief which causes them to remain in state of *w.*; **Moro.** 8: 19 awful *w.* to deny pure mercies of God unto little children.

WIDE (*see also* Broad)

3 Ne. 14: 13 (27: 33; Matt. 7: 13) *w.* is gate that leads to destruction.

WIDOW, WIDOWHOOD (*see also* Needy; Orphan)

2 Ne. 19: 17 (Isa. 9: 17) the Lord shall not have mercy upon their *w.*; 20: 1–2 (Isa. 10: 2) wo unto those who make *w.* their prey; **Mosiah** 21: 10 (Alma 28: 5; Moro. 9: 16) many *w.* in land because of war; **3 Ne.** 22: 4 (Isa. 54: 4) thou shalt not remember reproach of thy *w.*; 24: 5 (Mal. 3: 5) the Lord will be swift witness against those who oppress the *w.*; **Morm.** 8: 40 secret combinations cause *w.* to mourn before the Lord.

WIFE, WIVES (*see also* Family; Husband; Marriage; Mother; Woman; TG Marriage, Wives)

1 Ne. 7: 1 sons of Lehi[1] should take *w.* to raise up seed; 16: 7 Zoram[1] and sons of Lehi[1] take daughters of Ishmael[1] to *w.*; 18: 19 *w.* of Nephi[1] cannot soften brothers' hearts; **Jacob** 1: 15 Nephites desire many *w.* and concubines; 2: 24 taking of many *w.* by David and Solomon was abominable; 2: 27 (3: 5) no man shall have more than one *w.*; 2: 35 Nephites have broken hearts of tender *w.*; 3: 7 Lamanite husbands and *w.* love each other and their children; **Mosiah** 11: 2 Noah[3] has many *w.*; 13: 24 (Ex. 20: 17) thou shalt not covet thy neighbor's *w.*; 19: 11 Noah[3] commands all men to leave *w.* and flee from Lamanites; 19: 19–24 men return to *w.*; **Alma** 35: 14 outcast Zoramites take up arms to defend selves and *w.*; 43: 45 (46: 12; 48: 10) Nephites inspired by better cause, fighting for *w.* and children; 44: 5 sacred support owed to *w.* and children; **3 Ne.** 12: 32 (Matt. 5: 32) whosoever shall put away *w.*, save for fornication, causes her to commit adultery; 18: 21 pray in your families that *w.* and children may be blessed; **Morm.** 2: 23 Mormon[2] urges Nephites to stand boldly and fight for *w.*, children, homes.

WILD (*see also* Beast; Ferocious; Game; Wilderness)

1 Ne. 17: 5 land is called Bountiful because of fruit and *w.* honey; **2 Ne.** 15: 4 (Isa. 5: 4) what could have been done for vineyard when it brought forth *w.* grapes; **Jacob** ch. 5 parable of *w.* branches grafted into tame olive-tree; **Enos** 1: 20 (Mosiah 10: 12) Lamanites become *w.* and ferocious people; **Alma** 47: 36 Nephite dissenters become more *w.* than Lamanites; **Hel.** 3: 16 Nephites become wicked, *w.*, ferocious.

WILDERNESS (*see also* Desolate)

1 Ne. 2: 4 Lehi[1] and family depart into *w.*; 2: 5–6 Lehites travel three days in *w.* by Red Sea; 8: 4 Lehi[1] dreams of dark and dreary *w.*; 17: 4 Lehites sojourn eight years in *w.*; 18: 7 Lehi[1] begets two sons in *w.*; **2 Ne.** 2: 2 Jacob[2], firstborn in *w.*; 3: 1 Joseph[2] was born in *w.* of afflictions; 5: 5–7 the Lord warns Nephi[1] and followers to flee into *w.*; 8: 3 (Isa. 51: 3) the Lord will make Zion's *w.* like Eden; **Jacob** 1: 7 provocation in days of temptation while children of Israel were in *w.*; 4: 5 Abraham offered up Isaac in *w.*; **Mosiah** 7: 4 Ammon[1] and brethren wander forty days in *w.* looking for land of Lehi-Nephi; 21: 25 Limhi's men, searching for Zarahemla, are lost in *w.*; 23: 1, 3 Alma[1] and followers flee eight days into *w.*; **Alma** 2: 37 Lamanites flee to *w.* called Hermounts; 33: 19 (Hel. 8: 14) a type of Christ was raised in *w.*; 34: 26 pour out your souls in your secret places and *w.*; 37: 39 Liahona prepared to show way in *w.*; **Ether** 2: 5–7 Jaredites travel through *w.* to sea.

WILES (*see also* Cunning; Deceit; Subtlety)

Hel. 3: 29 word of God divides asunder all *w.* of devil.

WILFULLY (*see* Rebel)

WILL (*see also* Agency; Desire; Intent; Pleasure; Purpose; Willing; TG Will)

2 Ne. 2: 21 days of men were prolonged according to *w.* of God; 2: 28 choose eternal life according to *w.* of Holy Spirit; 2: 29 do not choose eternal death according to *w.* of flesh; 10: 24 reconcile yourselves to *w.* of God, not to *w.* of devil and flesh; 27: 13 none others shall view plates, save a few, according to *w.* of God; **Jacob** 7: 14 not my *w.* be done, if God will smite thee for a sign; 7: 14 thy *w.*, O Lord, be done, and not mine; **W of M** 1: 7 the Lord works in Mormon[2] to do according to his *w.*; **Mosiah** 2: 21 God lends you breath, that you may do according to your own *w.*; 3: 11 Christ's blood atones for sins of those who have died not knowing *w.* of God; 15: 2 Son subjects flesh to *w.* of Father; 15: 7 *w.* of Son is swallowed up in *w.* of Father; 16: 11–12 the evil to receive eternal damnation, having gone according to own carnal *w.*; 18: 28 men should impart of their substance of own free *w.*; 24: 15 people of Alma[1] submit cheerfully to *w.* of the Lord; **Alma** 12: 31 because of transgression, men are placed in state to act according to their *w.*; 29: 4 the Lord grants unto men according to their *w.*; 32: 19 how much more cursed is he who knoweth *w.* of God and doeth it not; 40: 13 spirits of the wicked are led captive by *w.* of devil; 42: 7 first parents became subjects to follow after own *w.*; **Hel.** 7: 5 robbers obtain government that they might steal and kill and do according to own *w.*; 10: 4 Nephi[2] has not sought own life, but the Lord's *w.*; 10: 5 Nephi[2] would not ask that which is contrary to the Lord's *w.*; **3 Ne.** 1: 14 Christ comes to do *w.* both of Father and of Son; 6: 18 people do not sin ignorantly, for they know *w.* of God; 11: 11 Christ has suffered *w.* of Father in all things; 13: 10 (Matt. 6: 10) thy *w.* be done on earth as it is in heaven; 27: 13 Christ came into world to do *w.* of Father; 28: 7 three Nephites to live until all things are fulfilled according to *w.* of Father; **Morm.** 8: 14–15 God *w.* that records be brought forth with eye single to his glory; **Ether** 3: 4 God has all power and can do whatsoever he *w.* for benefit of man.

WILLING, WILLINGNESS (*see also* Desire; Will)

2 Ne. 31: 13 witness unto Father you are *w.* to take name of Christ by baptism; **Mosiah** 3: 19 natural man must become as child, *w.* to submit to all things; 18: 8–9 those *w.* to bear one another's burdens should be baptized; 21: 35 baptism a testimony that men are *w.* to serve God; 26: 18 blessed is this people who are *w.* to bear the Lord's name; 29: 3 sons of Mosiah[2] not *w.* to become king; 29: 38 every man expresses *w.* to answer for his own sins; **Alma** 7: 15 show God you are *w.* to enter covenant by going into waters of baptism; **Hel.** 6: 36 the Lord pours out Spirit upon Lamanites because of their *w.* to believe his words; **3 Ne.** 6: 14 Lamanites are *w.* with all diligence to keep commandments; 18: 10 (Moro. 4: 3) partaking of sacrament witnesses to Father that men are *w.* to do what they have been commanded; **Moro.** 4: 3 (5: 2) partaking of sacrament witnesses that men are *w.* to take upon themselves Christ's name and always remember him.

WIN (*see also* Conquer; Gain)

Mosiah 4: 27 men should be diligent, that they might *w.* prize; **Alma** 17: 29 Ammon[2] shows power in restoring flocks that he might *w.* hearts of fellow-servants; **Ether** 9: 10 sons of Akish *w.* hearts of people.

WIND (*see also* Storm; Tempest; Whirlwind)

1 Ne. 18: 8 Lehites driven before *w.* toward promised land; **Alma** 26: 6 converts shall not be driven with fierce *w.* whithersoever enemy listeth to carry them; 37: 15 (Morm. 5: 18) Satan to sift transgressor as chaff before *w.*; **Hel.** 5: 12 (3 Ne. 14: 24–25; Matt. 7: 24–25) devil's *w.* have no power over those built upon rock of Redeemer; **3 Ne.** 11: 40 (14: 26–27; 18: 13; Matt. 7: 26–27) gates of hell stand open to receive those built on sandy foundation when *w.* beat upon them; 14: 25 those built on rock do not fall when *w.* blow; **Morm.** 5: 16, 18 Nephites are driven as chaff before *w.*; **Ether** 2: 24 *w.* have gone forth out of the Lord's mouth; 6: 5–8 furious *w.* blows Jaredite vessels toward promised land.

WINDOWS

3 Ne. 24: 10 (Mal. 3: 10) the Lord will open *w.* of heaven; **Ether** 2: 23 no *w.* in Jaredite barges.

WINE (*see also* Drink; Drunk, Drunken; Grape; Sacrament; Vine; Wine-press)

1 Ne. 4: 7 Laban drunken with *w.*; 21: 26 (Isa. 49: 26) they who oppress thee shall be drunken with own blood as with sweet *w.*; **2 Ne.** 8: 21 (Isa. 51: 21) hear now this, thou drunken, and not with *w.*; 9: 50 (Isa. 55: 1) come buy *w.* and milk without money; 15: 11 (Isa. 5: 11) wo unto them that follow strong drink from early in morning until night, and *w.* inflame them; 27: 4 those who do iniquity shall be drunken, but not with *w.*; **Mosiah** 11: 15 Noah[3] builds *w*-presses and makes *w.* in abundance; 22: 7–10 Limhi sends tribute of *w.* to Lamanites to make guards drunken; **Alma** 55: 8–14 Laman[4] takes *w.* to Lamanite guards to make them drunken; **3 Ne.** 18: 1–3, 8–9 (20: 5–9) Christ administers *w.* in sacrament to Nephites; 20: 8 (Moro. 5: 2) *w.* of sacrament in remembrance of Christ's blood; **Ether** 15: 22 Jaredites drunken with anger, as man who is drunken with *w.*; **Moro.** ch. 5. mode of administering sacramental *w.*; 6: 6 church meets oft to partake of bread and *w.* in remembrance of Jesus.

WINE-PRESS (*see also* Wine)

Mosiah 18: 15 Noah[3] builds *w-p.*

WING

2 Ne. 4: 25 body of Nephi[1] is carried upon *w.* of Spirit to high mountain; 16: 1–2 (Isa. 6: 1–2) seraphim with six *w.* above God's throne; 25: 13 Christ to rise from dead with healing in *w.*; **3 Ne.** 10: 4–6 (Matt. 23: 37; Luke 13: 34) the Lord would gather Israel as hen gathers chickens under *w.*; 25: 2 Son of Righteousness to arise with healing in his *w.*

WISDOM, WISE (*see also* God, Wisdom of; Knowledge; Learned [adj.]; Learning; Prudence; Understand)

1 Ne. 9: 5 (W of M 1: 6–7) the Lord commands Nephi[1] to make plates for *w.* purpose; **2 Ne.** 9: 28 when men are learned, they think they are *w.*; 9: 28 *w.* of the learned is foolishness; 9: 42 the Lord despises those who are puffed up because of *w.*; 15: 21 (Isa. 5: 21) wo unto the *w.* in their own eyes; 21: 2 (Isa. 11: 2) spirit of *w.* and understanding shall rest upon him; 27: 26 (Isa. 29: 14) *w.* of their wise and learned shall perish; 28: 30 those who hearken to the Lord's counsel shall learn *w.*; **Jacob** 6: 12 be *w.*, what can I say more; **Mosiah** 2: 17 Benjamin tells his people these things that they might learn *w.*; 2: 36 transgressors withdraw themselves from Spirit, that it has no place to guide them in *w*'s paths; 4: 27 see that all these things are done in *w.* and order; 29: 11 appoint *w.* men to be judges; **Alma** 29: 8 the Lord grants unto all nations to teach his word in *w.*; 32: 12 necessary that you should learn *w.*; 32: 23 little children are given words that confound the *w.*; 37: 2 sacred things are kept for *w.* purpose; 37: 35 learn *w.* in thy youth; 38: 9 Alma[2] speaks to son, that he may learn *w.*; 38: 11 do not boast in your own *w.*; **Hel.** 12: 5 how slow are men to walk in *w*'s paths; 16: 14 angels appear unto *w.* men; 16: 15 people depend upon own *w.*; **3 Ne.** 14: 24–25 (Matt. 7: 24–25) those who do Jesus' sayings are compared to *w.* man who builds house on rock; **Morm.** 9: 28 be *w.* in days of probation; **Moro.** 10: 9 to one is given by Spirit to teach word of *w.*

WISH (*see also* Desire; Will)

Alma 13: 27 Alma[2] *w.* that people would hearken to his words; 29: 1 O that I were an angel and could have *w.* of my heart; 29: 3 I am a man and do sin in my *w.*; **3 Ne.** 4: 16 if robbers can cut Nephites off from outward privileges, Nephites would yield themselves up according to robbers' *w.*

WITCHCRAFT (*see also* Magic; Sorceries)

3 Ne. 21: 16 (Micah 5: 12) the Lord will cut off *w.* out of land; **Morm.** 1: 19 (2: 10) *w.* in land.

WITHDRAW (*see also* Darkness, Spiritual; Excommunication; Shrink; Spirit, Holy/Spirit of the Lord)

Mosiah 2: 36 those who transgress against knowledge *w.* themselves from Spirit; **Alma** 1: 24 many *w.* themselves from church; 34: 35 Spirit *w.* from those who become subject to spirit of devil; **Hel.** 4: 24 Spirit *w.* from Nephites; 13: 8 because of hardness of hearts, the Lord will *w.* Spirit from Nephites.

WITHER, WITHERED

Jacob 5: 40 wild branch overcomes tree, that good branch *w.*; **Alma** 32: 38 if ye do not nourish tree, it will *w.* in heat; **3 Ne.** 17: 7 bring the *w.* that the Lord may heal them.

WITHHOLD, WITHHELD (*see also* Hinder; Hold; Keep; Restrain; Retain; Stay; Stop)

1 Ne. 17: 49 brothers commanded not to *w.* labor from Nephi[1]; **Mosiah** 4: 22 (Alma 5: 55) how much more just will be your condemnation for *w.* your substance; **Alma** 14: 22–23 people of Ammonihah *w.* food from Alma[2] and Amulek; **Hel.** 4: 11–12 slaughter of Nephites caused by *w.* food from hungry and clothing from the naked; **3 Ne.** 26: 10 if men do not believe these things, greater things shall be *w.*; **Ether** 3: 25–26 (12: 21) the Lord *w.* nothing from sight of brother of Jared[2]; **Moro.** 7: 36 has the Lord *w.* power of Holy Ghost.

WITHSTAND (*see also* Overcome; Reject; Resist)

Mosiah 12: 19 Abinadi *w.* priests' questions; **Alma** 5: 53 can ye *w.* these sayings; 30: 53 Korihor *w.* truth because he was deceived by devil; 37: 33 teach them to *w.* every temptation.

WITNESS (*see also* Apostle; Baptism; Convince; Evidence; Prove; Record; Revelation; See; Testify; Verified; Witnesses, Three; TG Witness; Witness of the Father)

1 Ne. 11: 7 Nephi[1] to *w.* man descending out of heaven; **2 Ne.** 11: 3 (27: 13–14) God sends more than three *w.*; 13: 9 (Isa. 3: 9) show of their countenances *w.* against them; 18: 2 (Isa. 8: 2) Isaiah[1] takes faithful *w.* to record; 27: 14 in mouth of as many *w.* as seems good the Lord will establish his word; 27: 22 book to be sealed again after *w.* have been obtained; 29: 8 testimony of two nations is *w.* that I am God; 31: 6–7 by baptism, Christ *w.* to Father that he would be obedient; 31: 13–14 (Mosiah 18: 10; 3 Ne. 18: 10; Moro. 4: 3) baptism is *w.* to Father that you are willing to take name of Christ and keep commandments; 31: 18 (3 Ne. 16: 6) Holy Ghost *w.* of Father and Son; **Jacob** 4: 6 having *w.* of prophets and revelations, we obtain a hope; 4: 13 Nephites are not *w.* alone of these things; **Mosiah** 13: 23 (Ex. 20: 16) thou shalt not bear false *w.*; 18: 9–10 those willing to stand as *w.* of God should be baptized; 18: 10 baptism a *w.* that men have entered covenant with God; 21: 35 baptism a *w.* of willingness to serve God; 24: 14 people of Alma[1] to stand as a *w.* of God; 26: 9 many *w.* against unbelievers; **Alma** 14: 11 blood of the innocent shall stand as *w.* against the wicked; 30: 45 will ye deny all these *w.*; 34: 30 after ye have received *w.*, bring fruit unto repentance; 47: 33 Lamanite queen asks Amalickiah to bring *w.* of king's death; **Hel.** 16: 20 people do not believe what they cannot *w.* with own eyes; **3 Ne.** 7: 15 Nephi[3] an eye-*w.*; 18: 11 (Moro. 4: 3; 5: 2) partake of sacrament that Christ may *w.* to Father that ye always remember him; 24: 5 (Mal. 3: 5) the Lord will be swift *w.* against the wicked; **Ether** 12: 6 ye receive no *w.* until after trial of faith; **Moro.** 6: 7 transgressor condemned by three *w.* is not numbered among church.

WITNESSES, THREE

2 Ne. 27: 12 (Ether 5: 2–4) *t.w.* to see book by power of God and testify to its truth.

WIVES (*see* Wife)

WOLF, WOLVES (*see also* Animal; Prophets, False)

2 Ne. 21: 6 (30: 12; Isa. 11: 6) *w.* shall dwell with lamb; **Alma** 5: 59 shepherd watches that no *w.* enter and devour flock; 5: 60 suffer no ravenous *w.* to enter among you; **3 Ne.** 14: 15 (Matt. 7: 15) beware of false prophets in sheep's clothing, inwardly they are ravening *w.*

WOMAN, WOMEN (*see also* Creation; Daughter; Eve; Female; Mother; Wife; TG Woman)

1 Ne. 17: 1–2, 20 Lehite *w.* bear children, are strong like unto men; 21: 15 (Isa. 49: 15) can *w.* forget her sucking child; **2 Ne.** 9: 21 Christ to suffer pains of all men, *w.*, children; 13: 12 (Isa. 3: 12) *w.* shall rule over the Lord's people; 14: 1 (Isa. 4: 1) seven *w.* shall ask to be called by one man's name to take away reproach; **Jacob** 2: 28 the Lord delights in chastity of *w.*; **Mosiah** 10: 5 (Hel. 6: 13) *w.* spin and toil; **Alma** 19: 16–17 Lamanitish *w.* named Abish makes known what has happened to Lamoni; 19: 28–29 *w.* servant takes queen by hand to raise her; 30: 18 Korihor leads away many *w.* and men to commit whoredoms; 32: 23 the Lord imparts his word by angels to men, *w.*, children; 54: 3 Lamanites take *w.* and children as prisoners; **3 Ne.** 12: 28 (Matt. 5: 28) whoso looks upon a *w.* to lust after her has committed adultery in heart; 22: 6 (Isa. 54: 6) the Lord has called thee as a *w.* forsaken; **Morm.** 4: 14, 21 Lamanites offer *w.* and children as sacrifices to idols; **Moro.** 9: 8 Lamanites feed *w.* flesh of husbands; 9: 16 many old *w.* die from hunger.

WOMB

1 Ne. 20: 8 (Isa. 48: 8) thou wast called a transgressor from *w.*; 21: 1, 5 (Isa. 49: 1, 5) the Lord has called me from *w.*; 21: 15 (Isa. 49: 15) can woman not have compassion on son of her *w.*

WONDER, WONDERFUL (*see also* Marvel; Miracle; Sign)

1 Ne. 19: 13 Jews will reject signs and *w.*; **2 Ne.** 3: 24 one shall rise up to work mighty *w.* in restoring Israel; 19: 6 (Isa. 9: 6) Messiah shall be called *W.*; 25: 17 (27: 26; Isa. 29: 14) the Lord will do marvelous work and *w.* among men; 26: 13 the Lord works *w.* among men according to their faith; **Mosiah** 3: 15 the Lord showed many signs and *w.* to Israel; **Hel.** 14: 6 (3 Ne. 1: 22; 2: 1) many signs and *w.* in heavens at Christ's birth; 16: 4 Nephi[2] shows people signs and *w.*

WOOD (*see also* Timber; Waste)

1 Ne. 16: 23 Nephi[1] makes bow out of *w.*; **2 Ne.** 5: 15 (Jarom 1: 8) Nephites work in all manner of *w.*; **Mosiah** 11: 8 Noah[3] ornaments buildings with fine *w.*; **Hel.** 3: 10–11 Nephites ship timber to land northward to build cities of *w.* and cement; **3 Ne.** 8: 21 because of darkness, no fire can be kindled with fine and dry *w.*

WORD (*see also* Communication; Language; Lips; Mouth; Read; Sayings;

Tongue; Utter, Utterance; Voice; Word of God/Word of the Lord; TG Word)

1 Ne. 3: 18 Jews have rejected *w.* of prophets; 17: 26 by Moses' *w.*, waters of Red Sea were divided; **2 Ne.** 3: 19–20 fruit of loins of Joseph[1] shall cry from dust according to simpleness of their *w.*; 3: 21 weakness of their *w.* will the Lord make strong in their faith; 9: 40 give ear to my *w.*; 9: 40 *w.* of truth are hard against all uncleanness; 25: 19 according to *w.* of prophets the Messiah comes in six hundred years after Lehi[1] left Jerusalem; 27: 6, 14 the Lord will bring forth *w.* of book, which shall be *w.* of those who have slumbered; 27: 31–32 they who make a man an offender for a *w.* shall be cut off; 28: 8 many shall say, take advantage of one because of his *w.*; 29: 2 *w.* of seed of Nephi[1] shall proceed out of the Lord's mouth; 33: 10 if ye believe in Christ, ye will believe in these *w.*; **Enos** 1: 3 *w.* Enos[2] had heard father speak concerning eternal life sink deep into his heart; **Mosiah** 4: 30 if ye do not watch thoughts and *w.*, ye must perish; 15: 11 those who have hearkened to *w.* of prophets concerning Christ are heirs of kingdom of God; **Alma** 12: 14 our *w.* will condemn us; 30: 43 Korihor has no evidence that there is no God except his own *w.*; 32: 27 try experiment upon *w.* of Alma[2]; 41: 12–15 meaning of *w.* restoration is to bring back evil for evil, good for good; 61: 14 whatsoever evil we cannot resist with our *w.*, let us resist with swords; **Hel.** 10: 5 the Lord will make Nephi[2] mighty in *w.* and deed; 12: 4 how quick are men to hearken to *w.* of evil one; **3 Ne.** 19: 24 disciples do not multiply many *w.* in prayer; **Ether** 12: 23 the Lord has made Nephites mighty in *w.* by faith, but not in writing; **Moro.** 10: 9 to one is given by Spirit to teach *w.* of wisdom; 10: 10 to another is given to teach *w.* of knowledge.

WORD OF GOD/WORD OF THE LORD (*see also* Gospel; Revelation; Word; TG Word of God; Word of the Lord)

1 Ne. 2: 3 Lehi[1] is obedient to *w.* of the Lord; 4: 14 Nephi[1] remembers *w.* of the Lord spoken in wilderness; 7: 4 sons of Lehi[1] speak *w.* of the Lord to Ishmael[1]; 7: 9 how is it ye have not hearkened to *w.* of the Lord; 7: 13 (10: 13; 2 Ne. 5: 19–20; Mosiah 21: 4; 3 Ne. 29: 2) *w.* of the Lord to be fulfilled; 11: 25 (15: 24) iron rod is *w.* of God; 15: 25 Nephi[1] exhorts brothers to give heed to *w.* of God; 17: 23 would Israel have been led out of Egypt if they had not hearkened to *w.* of the Lord; 17: 31 according to his *w.*, God did all things for Israelites; 17: 31 nothing done save it were by God's *w.*; 17: 35 children of land had rejected every *w.* of God; 17: 45 ye were past feeling that ye could not feel his *w.*; **2 Ne.** 1: 26 sharpness of Nephi[1] is sharpness of power of *w.* of God; 3: 11 the Lord will give power to latter-day seer to bring forth his *w.* and convince people of his *w.*; 9: 16 God's eternal *w.* cannot pass away; 9: 40 Nephi[1] has spoken *w.* of your maker; 12: 3 (Isa. 2: 3) *w.* of the Lord shall go out from Jerusalem; 27: 14 wo unto him who rejects *w.* of God; 28: 29 wo unto him who shall say, We have received *w.* of God and need no more; 29: 2–3 (Moro. 10: 28) the Lord's *w.* shall hiss forth to ends of earth; 29: 9 the Lord speaks forth his *w.* according to his own pleasure; 29: 9 because the Lord has spoken one *w.*, ye need not suppose he cannot speak another; 29: 14 the Lord's *w.* shall be gathered in one; 31: 15 voice from the Father says, W. of my Beloved are true; 31: 20 (32: 3) press forward, feasting upon *w.* of Christ; 32: 3 angels speak *w.* of Christ; 32: 3 *w.* of Christ will tell you all things you should do; **Jacob** 1: 19 teachers take responsibility for people's sins if they do not teach *w.* of God; 2: 4 (Morm. 7: 7) as yet, Nephites have been obedient to *w.* of the Lord; 2: 8 pleasing *w.* of God heals wounded soul; 2: 27 (Morm. 9: 27) hearken to *w.* of the Lord; 2: 35 because of strictness of *w.* of God which comes down against wicked, many hearts die pierced with deep wounds; 4: 9 by God's *w.* man came upon face of earth; 6: 7 after ye have been nourished by good *w.* of God, will ye bring forth evil fruit; **Jarom** 1: 9 (Alma 9: 14; 25: 17; 50: 19, 21) *w.* of the Lord is verified; **Omni** 1: 13 (Mosiah 26: 39) Nephites are admonished by *w.* of God; **W of M** 1: 11 people are judged out of records, according to *w.* of God; **Mosiah** 11: 29 Noah[3] hardens heart against *w.* of the Lord; 18: 32 people of Alma[1] assemble to hear *w.* of the Lord; 20: 21 Abinadi's prophecies are fulfilled because people would not hearken to *w.* of the Lord; 26: 3 because of unbelief, people could not understand *w.* of God; 26: 38 teachers teach *w.* of God in all things; 28: 1 (Alma 17: 4) sons of Mosiah[2] to impart *w.* of God to Lamanites; **Alma** 1: 15 Nehor acknowledges he has taught contrary to *w.* of God; 1: 20 members of church impart *w.* of God without money or price; 1: 26 priests leave labor to impart *w.* of God; 3: 14 *w.* of God is fulfilled; 3: 18 Amlicites fulfill *w.* of God by marking themselves in foreheads; 4: 18–19 Alma[2] gives up judgment-seat to preach *w.* of God; 4: 19 Alma[2] pulls down pride and contentions by *w.* of God; 5: 7 souls of fathers were illuminated by light of everlasting *w.*; 5: 58 *w.* of God must be fulfilled; 6: 5 *w.* of God is liberal unto all; 8: 24 Alma[2] is called to preach *w.* of God; 9: 30 Nephites' hearts have been hardened against *w.* of God; 12: 10 he who hardens heart receives lesser portion of *w.*; 12: 10 he who hardens not heart receives greater portion of *w.*; 12: 26–27 *w.* of God would have been void if first parents had lived forever; 16: 14 Alma[2] and Amulek impart *w.* of God without respect of persons; 17: 2 sons of Mosiah[2] search scriptures to know *w.* of God; 26: 13 Lamanites loosed from pains of hell by power of God's *w.*; 31: 5 preaching of *w.* has tendency to lead people to do that which is just; 31: 5 Alma[2] to try virtue of *w.* of God; 32: 23 God imparts his *w.* by angels unto men; 32: 28 if seed swells, *w.* is good; 32: 40 if ye will not nourish the *w.*, ye can never pluck fruit of tree of life; 34: 5 question in Zoramites' minds whether *w.* be in Son of God; 36: 26 because of *w.* which God has imparted to Alma[2], many have been born of God; 37: 44 easy to give heed to *w.* of Christ, which points straight course to eternal bliss; 43: 24 *w.* of the Lord comes to Alma[2], who informs Moroni[1] concerning enemies; 44: 5 Nephites owe all happiness to *w.* of God; **Hel.** 3: 29 whosoever will may lay hold upon *w.* of God; 3: 29 *w.* of God leads man of Christ in narrow course across gulf of misery; 6: 2 Nephites reject *w.* of God; 6: 37 Lamanites preach *w.* of God to robbers; 10: 12, 14 Nephi[2] declares *w.* of the Lord; 10: 13 Nephites do not hearken to *w.* of the Lord; 10: 15, 17 Nephi[2] declares or sends *w.* of God to all the people; 13: 5 Samuel the Lamanite speaks *w.* of the Lord, which he put in heart; 13: 36 O that we had repented in day when *w.* of the Lord came to us; **3 Ne.** 17: 2 Jesus perceives that Nephites are weak and cannot understand all his *w.*; 28: 20 disciples smite earth with *w.* of God and are delivered from depths; **4 Ne.** 1: 12 Nephites meet oft to hear *w.* of the Lord; **Morm.** 8: 33 why have ye transfigured holy *w.* of God; 9: 17 by power of God's *w.* heaven, earth, and man were created; 9: 17 by power of God's *w.* miracles are wrought; **Ether** 4: 8 he who contends against *w.* of the Lord shall be accursed; 4: 9 at Christ's *w.*, earth shall shake; 13: 20 (14: 24) *w.* of the Lord comes to Ether; **Moro.** 6: 4 those baptized should be nourished by good *w.* of God; 8: 7 *w.* of the Lord comes to Mormon[2]; 8: 9 Holy Ghost manifests *w.* of God to Mormon[2]; 9: 4 Mormon[2] speaks *w.* of God with sharpness.

WORK, WORKS [noun] (*see also* Act; Creation; Deed; Faithful; Fruit; Grace; Judgment; Repentance; Serve; Working; Workings; Workmanship)

1 Ne. 1: 14 (Jacob 4: 8) great and marvelous are thy *w.*, O Lord; 9: 6 the Lord prepares a way to accomplish all his *w.*; 14: 7 (22: 8; 2 Ne. 25: 17; 27: 26; 29: 1; 3 Ne. 21: 9; Isa. 29: 14) the Lord will work great and marvelous *w.*; 15: 32 (2 Ne. 9: 44; Mosiah 3: 24; Alma 41: 3) men must be judged of their *w.*; **2 Ne.** 4: 17 goodness of God in showing me great and marvelous *w.*; 27: 27 their *w.* are in dark; 27: 27 the Lord knows all their *w.*; 29: 9 the Lord's *w.* are not yet finished; 30: 8 the Lord will commence his *w.* among all nations to bring about restoration of his people; **Mosiah** 13: 17–18 (Ex. 20: 9–10) six days shalt thou do all thy *w.*, but on sabbath thou shalt not do any *w.*; **Alma** 5: 16 can you imagine the Lord saying, your *w.* have been *w.* of righteousness; 5: 41 if a man brings forth good *w.*, he hearkens to voice of good shepherd; 5: 41–42 he who brings forth evil *w.* is child of devil and is dead unto all good *w.*; 7: 24 (Ether 12: 4) see that ye have faith, hope, and charity, then ye will abound in good *w.*; 9: 28 men shall reap reward of their *w.*; 26: 15 sons of Mosiah[2] have been instruments in God's hand in doing great and marvelous *w.*; 37: 12 God counsels in wisdom over all his *w.*; 37: 34 never be weary of good *w.*; 40: 13 spirits of the wicked chose evil *w.* rather than good; 41: 3 if a man's *w.* were good in this life, he will be restored to good; 41: 4 if man's *w.* were evil, they shall be restored to him for evil; **Hel.** 15: 15 if mighty *w.* had been shown to those who dwindled in unbelief, they would not have dwindled; **3 Ne.** 12: 16 (Matt. 5: 16) let your light so shine that people will see your good *w.*; 21: 17 (Micah 5: 13) thou shalt no more worship the *w.* of thy hands; 21: 26 *w.* of Father will commence when gospel is preached to remnant of Nephites; 22: 16 (Isa. 54: 16) I have created the smith that bringeth forth an instrument for his *w.*; 27: 10 if church is built upon gospel, Father will show his *w.* in it; 27: 11 if church is built upon *w.* of men or devil, they have joy in their *w.* until cast into fire; **Morm.** 9: 16 who can comprehend the marvelous *w.* of God; **Moro.** 7: 5 by their *w.* ye shall know them; 8: 22–23 to suppose little children need baptism is putting trust in dead *w.*

WORK [verb] (*see also* Industry; Labor; Perform; Strive; Work [noun]; Working, Workings; Workmanship; Wrought; TG Work, Value of)

1 Ne. 16: 28 pointers in Liahona *w.* according to faith and diligence; **2 Ne.** 5: 15 Nephites *w.* all manner of woods and metals; 26: 13 Christ *w.* mighty miracles according to men's faith; 26: 23 the Lord *w.* not in darkness; 31: 3 the Lord *w.*

among men in plainness; **Mosiah** 3: 5 (15: 6) the Lord will go forth among men, *w.* mighty miracles; 10: 5 Zeniff causes women to *w.*; **Alma** 23: 6 power of God *w.* miracles in those who believe; 30: 42–43 devil *w.* devices in Korihor to destroy children of God; 32: 27 if ye can no more than desire to believe, let this desire *w.* in you; 34: 37 (Morm. 9: 27) *w.* out your salvation with fear before God; 37: 38, 41 because miracles were *w.* by small means, Liahona showed Lehites marvelous works; **Hel.** 6: 11 curious workmen *w.* all kinds of ore; 16: 4 Nephi[2] *w.* miracles among the people; **3 Ne.** 27: 33 many travel broad way until night comes wherein no man can *w.*; 29: 6 wo unto him that shall say the Lord no longer *w.* by revelation; **Ether** 8: 19 the Lord *w.* not in secret combinations; 10: 23 Jaredites *w.* all manner of ore, metals, fine work; 12: 30 the Lord *w.* after men have faith; **Moro.** 10: 7 God *w.* by power, according to men's faith; 10: 8 the same God *w.* different gifts; 10: 25 if there be one among you who does good, he shall *w.* by power and gifts of God.

WORKING, WORKINGS (*see also* Work [noun]; Work [verb])

1 Ne. 19: 20 Nephi[1] has *w.* in spirit which weary him; **2 Ne.** 1: 6 Lehi[1] prophesies according to *w.* of Spirit; **Jacob** 4: 15 Jacob[2] perceives by *w.* of Spirit that Jews will stumble; **W of M** 1: 17 I do this for wise purpose, for thus it whispereth me according to *w.* of Spirit; **Hel.** 3: 7 people in land northward become expert in *w.* of cement; **Moro.** 6: 9 church meetings conducted after manner of *w.* of Spirit.

WORKMANSHIP, WORKMAN

1 Ne. 4: 9 *w.* of Laban's sword exceedingly fine; 16: 10 (Alma 37: 38–39) Liahona a ball of curious *w.*; 18: 1, 4 Nephi[1] and brothers work timbers of curious *w.* for ship; **Jarom** 1: 8 Nephites become rich in fine *w.* of wood; **Hel.** 6: 11 curious *w.* work and refine all ore; **Ether** 10: 27 Jaredites work all manner of work of curious *w.*

WORLD (*see also* Babylon; Creation; Earth; Flesh; Man; Mortal; Nature, Natural; Spirit World; Temporal; Wicked, Wickedness; TG World; World, End of; Worldliness)

1 Ne. 6: 5 Nephi[1] writes things pleasing to God, not to *w.*; 8: 20 iron rod leads into spacious field, as if it were a *w.*; 11: 32 Son to be judged of the *w.*; 11: 35–36 great and spacious building is pride of *w.*; 13: 9 for praise of *w.*, abominable church destroys saints; 14: 19–22, 27 John the apostle to write concerning end of *w.*; 19: 9 *w.* will judge Christ to be thing of naught; 22: 23 church built up to become popular in eyes of *w.* shall be brought low; 22: 23 those who seek things of *w.* should fear and tremble; **2 Ne.** 9: 18 saints have endured crosses of *w.*; 9: 18 kingdom of God prepared for saints from foundation of *w.*; 9: 30 wo unto those who are rich as to things of *w.*; 23: 11 (Isa. 13: 11) the Lord will punish the *w.* for evil; 26: 24 the Lord does not anything save for benefit of *w.*, for he loves *w.*; 26: 29 priestcrafts are that men set themselves up for light unto *w.* to get praise of *w.*; 27: 10 sealed revelations reveal all things from foundation of *w.* to end; 27: 23 Lord will show *w.* he is same yesterday, today, forever; **Jacob** 6: 3 *w.* shall be burned with fire; **Mosiah** 16: 9 (Alma 38: 9; 3 Ne. 9: 18; 11: 11; Ether 4: 12) Christ is light and life of *w.*; 27: 31 those who live without God in *w.* shall confess his judgment is just; **Alma** 1: 16 many who love vain things of *w.*; 5: 37 (31: 27) those who are puffed up in vain things of *w.* have gone astray; 11: 40 Christ shall come into *w.*; 32: 3 outcast Zoramites are poor as to things of *w.*; 60: 32 Nephites' iniquity is caused by love of vain things of *w.*; **Hel.** 5: 9 (Morm. 7: 7) Christ to come to redeem *w.*; 7: 5 robbers obtain government to get glory of *w.*; **3 Ne.** 19: 20 Christ has chosen disciples out of *w.*; 19: 29 Jesus prays not for *w.*, but for those the Father has given him out of *w.*; 27: 16 Christ will stand to judge *w.*; 28: 25 names of three Nephites are hid from *w.*; **Morm.** 8: 38 men do not value endless happiness greater than undying misery because of praise of *w.*; 9: 22 go ye into all *w.* and preach gospel to every creature; **Ether** 4: 14 Father has laid up great things for Israel from foundation of *w.*; 5: 4 sacred record and witnesses shall stand as testimony against *w.*; 12: 4 those who believe in God might with surety hope for better *w.*; **Moro.** 10: 19 spiritual gifts shall not be done away as long as *w.* stands.

WORM (*see also* Corrupt, Corruption)

2 Ne. 8: 8 (Isa. 51: 8) *w.* shall eat men like wool; 24: 11 (Isa. 14: 11) *w.* is spread under thee and *w.* cover thee; **Ether** 14: 22 bodies of slain left to become prey to *w.*

WORRY (*see also* Anxiety, Anxious; Fear; Trouble)

Alma 40: 1 (41: 1) Corianton is *w.* concerning resurrection; 42: 1 Corianton is *w.* concerning God's justice in punishing sinner; 61: 19 Pahoran[1] *w.* what loyal Nephites should do.

WORSE (*see also* Bad)

Alma 24: 30 state of enlightened

people who fall into sin is *w.* than if they had never known; **Hel.** 13: 26 this people is *w.* than fathers of old.

WORSHIP (*see also* Assemble; Bow [verb]; Fear of God; Idolatry; Meet, Meeting; Praise; Religion; Serve; Worshipper; TG Worship)

1 Ne. 17: 55 elder brothers are about to *w.* Nephi[1], but he commands them to *w.* the Lord; 21: 7 (Isa. 49: 7) princes shall *w.* because of the Lord that is faithful; **2 Ne.** 12: 8 (Isa. 2: 8) they *w.* work of own hands; 25: 16 Jews to *w.* Father in Christ's name; 25: 29 *w.* Christ with all your might, mind, strength; **Jacob** 4: 5 prophets *w.* Father in Christ's name; **Alma** 15: 17 Nephites assemble in sanctuaries to *w.* God; 21: 22 Lamoni declares liberty of *w.* the Lord according to desires; 31: 12 Zoramites *w.* God in manner Alma[2] has never beheld; 32: 5 (33: 2) outcast Zoramites have no place to *w.* God; 34: 38 *w.* God in whatsoever place ye may be; 43: 10 Lamanites would destroy whoever *w.* God in spirit and truth; 50: 39 chief judge appointed with oath to grant sacred privileges to *w.* the Lord; **3 Ne.** 11: 17 (17: 10) Nephites fall at Jesus' feet and *w.* him; 21: 17 thou shalt no more *w.* works of thy hands; **Moro.** 7: 1 Mormon[2] teaches people in synagogue built for place of *w.*

WORSHIPPER (*see also* Believer; Worship)

4 Ne. 1: 37 true *w.* of Christ are called Nephites, Jacobites, Josephites, and Zoramites.

WORTH (*see also* Esteem; Merit; Precious; Respect; Value; Worthless; Worthy; TG Worth of Souls)

1 Ne. 5: 21 brass plates are of great *w.* in preserving commandments; 13: 23 covenants recorded in Bible are of great *w.* to Gentiles; 19: 7 things that some esteem of great *w.*, others set at naught; 22: 8–9 marvelous work of the Lord to be of great *w.* to Gentiles and to all Israel; **2 Ne.** 9: 51 do not spend money for that which is of no *w.*; 25: 7–8 prophecies of Isaiah[1] are of great *w.*; 33: 3 Nephi[1] esteems what he has written to be of great *w.*; **Jacob** 5: 46 trees the Lord had hoped to preserve are of no *w.*; **Alma** 34: 29 if ye are not charitable, ye are as dross which refiners cast out, being of no *w.*; **Morm.** 8: 14 plates are of no *w.*, but record is of great *w.*; **Moro.** 1: 4 Moroni[2] writes few more things that they may be of *w.* to Lamanites.

WORTHLESS

Mosiah 4: 5 knowledge of God's goodness should awaken men to sense of *w.* and fallen state.

WORTHY, WORTHINESS (*see also* Clean; Faithful; Righteousness; Uprightness)

1 Ne. 10: 8 prophet crying in wilderness feels he is not *w.* to unloose Christ's shoe latchet; **Mosiah** 17: 7 priests find Abinadi *w.* of death; **Alma** 36: 5 God has made things known to Alma[2], not of any *w.* of his; 56: 10 two thousand Ammonite youths are *w.* to be called sons; **Morm.** 9: 29 see that ye do all things in *w.*; **Moro.** 6: 1 men not baptized save they bring forth fruit meet that that they are *w.* of it.

WOUND, WOUNDED (*see also* Bruise; Stripes)

Jacob 2: 8 pleasing word of God heals the *w.* soul; 2: 9, 35 delicate minds of wives and children have been *w.*; **Mosiah** 14: 5 (Isa. 53: 5) he was *w.* for our transgressions.

WRAPT

3 Ne. 26: 3 earth to be *w.* together as scroll.

WRATH (*see also* Anger; Destruction; Displeasure; Fury; Judgment; Punishment; Rage)

1 Ne. 13: 11 *w.* of God is upon seed of Lamanites; 14: 15–17 *w.* of God poured out upon abominable church; 17: 35 fulness of *w.* of God was upon children of land; 22: 16 fulness of *w.* of God to be poured out upon all men; **2 Ne.** 1: 17 Lehi[1] fears the Lord will come out in fulness of *w.* upon sons; **Alma** 12: 36 iniquity of Ammonihah provokes God to send down *w.*; **Morm.** 8: 21 he who breathes out *w.* against work of the Lord shall be hewn down; **Ether** 2: 9 (9: 20: 14: 25) those in promised land who do not serve God will be swept off when his *w.* comes; 2: 9 fulness of the Lord's *w.* comes when people are ripened in iniquity.

WREST (*see also* Pervert)

Alma 13: 20 if ye *w.* scriptures, it will be to your destruction; 41: 1 some have *w.* scriptures and have gone far astray.

WRESTLE (*see also* Struggle)

Enos 1: 2 Enos[2] *w.* before God before receiving remission of sins; **Alma** 8: 10 Alma[2] *w.* with God in mighty prayer to pour out Spirit.

WRETCHED (*see also* Misery, Miserable)

2 Ne. 4: 17 O *w.* man that I am.

WRIT (*see also* Scriptures)

Alma 37: 5 all plates which contain holy *w.* shall retain brightness.

WRITE, WROTE, WRITTEN (*see also*

Book; Engrave; Language; Record; Scriptures; Writing)

1 Ne. 14: 25 Nephi[1] is not to *w.* what he sees, for John the apostle will *w.*; 14: 28, 30 Nephi[1] has *w.* but small part of things he saw; 14: 30 the things which Nephi[1] has *w.* are true; 19: 6 Nephi[1] *w.* only sacred things on plates; **2 Ne.** 3: 12 that which is *w.* by descendants of Joseph[1] and Judah shall grow together; 3: 17 the Lord will *w.* unto Moses his law; 4: 14 history is *w.* upon other plates; 4: 15 things of soul and scriptures *w.* upon these plates; 6: 3 Jacob[2] has spoken concerning all things *w.*, from creation of world; 25: 23 we labor diligently to *w.* to persuade our children to believe in Christ; 29: 11 the Lord commands all men to *w.* words he speaks to them; 29: 12 Jews, Nephites, scattered tribes, all nations shall *w.* what the Lord speaks to them; 33: 1 Nephi[1] cannot *w.* all things taught among his people; 33: 2 many cast away things that are *w.*; 33: 3 I, Nephi[1], have *w.* what I have *w.*; **Jacob** 1: 2 Nephi[1] commands Jacob[2] to *w.* upon plates; **Jarom** 1: 1 Jarom *w.* few words according to commandment of father; 1: 2 things *w.* on small plates are for benefit of Lamanites; **Omni** 1: 1 Omni is commanded by father to *w.* upon plates; 1: 9 Chemish *w.* in same book with brother; **W of M** 1: 2 Mormon[2] prays Moroni[2] might survive to *w.* concerning Lamanites; **Mosiah** 5: 12 retain the name *w.* always in your heart; 13: 11 Abinadi reads commandments, for they are not *w.* in priests' hearts; 24: 6 Lamanites taught to keep record, that they might *w.* one to another; **Alma** 5: 58 names of righteous shall be *w.* in book of life; 30: 52 Korihor *w.* that he is dumb; **Hel.** 8: 3 Nephi[2] speaks many things that cannot be *w.*; **3 Ne.** 16: 4 (23: 4) Jesus commands Nephites to *w.* his sayings after he is gone; 16: 4 (23: 4) sayings which Nephites *w.* to be manifested to Gentiles and Israel; 23: 9–13 Jesus asks why Samuel's prophecy of saints' resurrection is not *w.*; 23: 14 Jesus expounds all scriptures in one which they had *w.*; 26: 12 Mormon[2] *w.* things commanded of the Lord; 26: 18 many see and hear unspeakable things which are not lawful to be *w.*; 27: 23–24 Jesus commands disciples to *w.* what they have seen and heard; 27: 26 all things are *w.* by Father; 27: 26 out of books which shall be *w.* will world be judged; **Morm.** 5: 9 Mormon[2] *w.* small abridgment; 5: 12 these things are *w.* to remnant of house of Jacob; 5: 12 record *w.* upon plates to be hid and brought forth; 8: 4 Moroni[2] will *w.* and hide up records in earth; 9: 33 if plates were larger, Nephites would *w.* in Hebrew; 9: 33 if record were *w.* in Hebrew, no imperfections; **Ether** 3: 22 (4: 1) brother of Jared[2] to *w.* what he has seen and heard in language that cannot be read; 4: 16 revelations *w.* by John shall be unfolded to all; 12: 24 Nephites can *w.* but little because of awkwardness of hands; 12: 24 things which brother of Jared[2] *w.* were mighty; 12: 41 seek Jesus of whom prophets and apostles have *w.*; 15: 33 Moroni[2] has not *w.* hundredth part of Ether's record.

WRITING, WRITINGS (*see also* Write)

1 Ne. 13: 35–36 in hidden *w.* shall gospel be written; 16: 29 a new *w.* written upon Liahona; **2 Ne.** 3: 17 the Lord will give judgment to Moses in *w.*; 33: 1 Nephi[1] is not mighty in *w.* like unto speaking; **Jarom** 1: 14 on other plates are records of war, according to *w.* of kings; **Alma** 10: 2 Aminadi interpreted *w.* on temple wall, written by finger of God; **Ether** 12: 23–26, 40 the Lord has not made Nephites mighty in *w.*

WRONG, WRONGED, WRONGFULLY (*see also* Evil)

Mosiah 10: 12–13 (Alma 54: 17) Lamanites believe their fathers were *w.* in wilderness by brethren; 26: 13 Alma[1] fears he should do *w.* in sight of God; **Alma** 7: 20 the Lord has no shadow of turning from right to *w.*; **3 Ne.** 3: 10–11 robbers threaten to avenge *w.* of those who had received no *w.*; **Moro.** 7: 18 see that ye do not judge *w.*

WROUGHT (*see also* Do; Work [verb])

1 Ne. 13: 12 Spirit came down and *w.* upon Gentile across many waters; 17: 51 if the Lord has *w.* so many miracles, why cannot he instruct Nephi[1] to build ship; 19: 12 kings of isles of sea shall be *w.* upon by Spirit; **2 Ne.** 10: 4 if mighty miracles were *w.* among other nations, they would repent; **Mosiah** 5: 2 Spirit has *w.* mighty change in Benjamin's people; **Alma** 5: 12 mighty change was *w.* in heart of Alma[1]; **3 Ne.** 7: 22 those who are healed manifest that Spirit has *w.* upon them; 28: 31 great and marvelous works shall be *w.* by three Nephites; 28: 37–38 change *w.* upon bodies of three Nephites; 29: 7 he who says no miracle can be *w.* by Christ shall be like sons of perdition; **4 Ne.** 1: 13 many mighty miracles *w.* by Jesus' disciples; **Ether** 12: 16 (Moro. 7: 37) all who *w.* miracles *w.* them by faith.

YIELD (*see also* Subject; Submissive, Submit)

1 Ne. 19: 10 God to *y.* himself into hands of wicked men to be lifted up;

2 Ne. 4: 27 why should I *y.* to sin; 9: 39 remember awfulness of *y.* to enticings of cunning one; 26: 10 Nephites to reap destruction because they *y.* unto devil; **Mosiah** 3: 19 natural man is enemy to God unless he *y.* to enticings of Holy Spirit; 15: 5 the flesh becoming subject to Spirit *y.* not to temptation; **Alma** 5: 20 can ye think of being saved when ye have *y.* yourselves to become subjects to devil; 11: 23 the righteous *y.* to no such temptations; 51: 20 dissenters *y.* to standard of liberty; **Hel.** 3: 35 sanctification comes because men *y.* hearts unto God.

YOKE (*see also* Bondage; Subject)

1 Ne. 13: 5 abominable church *y.* saints with *y.* of iron; **2 Ne.** 19: 4 (Isa. 9: 4) thou hast broken *y.* of his burden; 20: 27 (Isa. 10: 27) his *y.* shall be taken from off thy neck, and the *y.* shall be destroyed because of the anointing; 24: 25 (Isa. 14: 25) *y.* of Assyrian shall depart from the Lord's people; **Alma** 44: 2 Nephites do not desire to bring anyone to *y.* of bondage; 49: 7 Lamanites suppose they will easily subject brethren to *y.* of bondage; 61: 12 we would subject ourselves to *y.* of bondage if requisite with God's justice.

YOUNG, YOUNGER (*see also* Youth)

1 Ne. 2: 16 Nephi[1] is exceedingly *y.* and large in stature; 7: 8 why do elder brothers harden hearts, that *y.* brother must speak to them; **Mosiah** 17: 2 Alma[1] a *y.* man; **Alma** 1: 30 Nephites are liberal to all, both old and *y.*; 5: 49 Alma[2] is called to preach unto all, both old and *y.*; 11: 44 restoration shall come to all, both old and *y.*; 53: 18 (56: 46) two thousand *y.* Ammonite men take up weapons to defend country; **Morm.** 2: 1 Mormon[2] is *y.* and large in stature; **Moro.** 9: 19 Nephites are brutal, sparing none, neither old nor *y.*

YOUTH (*see also* Young)

2 Ne. 2: 4 Jacob[2] has beheld God's glory in his *y.*; **Alma** 37: 35 learn wisdom in thy *y.*; 37: 35 learn in thy *y.* to keep God's commandments; **3 Ne.** 22: 4 thou shalt forget shame of thy *y.*

ZARAHEMLA—*leader of Mulek's colony* (*see also* Zarahemla, People of)

Omni 1: 14 rejoices that the Lord has sent Nephites; 1: 18 gives genealogy of fathers; **Mosiah** 7: 3, 13 Ammon[1] is a descendant of Z.; 25: 2 Z. is a descendant of Mulek; **Hel.** 1: 15 Coriantumr[3] is a descendant of Z.

ZARAHEMLA, CITY OF—*major capital of Nephites from about 200* B.C. *to* A.D. *300* (*see also* Zarahemla, Land of)

Alma 2: 26 Nephite soldiers return to city of Z.; 5: 2 (6: 1–7) church established in Z.; 7: 3–5 Alma[2] laments for condition of people in Z.; 8: 1 Alma[2] returns to Z.; 31: 6 Alma[2] leaves Himni in church in Z.; 56: 25 Lamanites dare not march against Z.; 60: 1 Moroni[1] writes to Pahoran[1] in Z.; **Hel.** 1: 18–27 Coriantumr[3] captures Z.; 1: 27–33 Z. is captured by Lamanites, retaken by Moronihah; 7: 1–6 Nephi[2] returns to Z. and sees wickedness; 13: 12 only the righteous save the wicked in Z.; **3 Ne.** 8: 8 (9: 3) Z. is burned at Christ's death; 8: 24 Z. would not have been burned if people had repented; **4 Ne.** 1: 8 Z. is rebuilt.

ZARAHEMLA, LAND OF—*region around city of Zarahemla; also area from southern wilderness to land Bountiful on north*

Omni 1: 12–13 Mosiah[1] made king over land of Z.; 1: 24 Benjamin drives Lamanites from Z.; 1: 28 (2: 4) expedition seeking land of Nephi returns to Z.; **Mosiah** 1: 1 (2: 4) no more contention in Z.; 1: 18 people are gathered in land of Z. to hear Benjamin; 7: 9 Zeniff came out of land of Z.; 7: 13–14 Ammon[1] comes from Z. to inquire after people of Zeniff; 21: 24–26 Limhi's expedition failed to find Z.; 22: 11–13 Limhi's people arrive in Z.; 24: 25 Alma[1] and his people arrive in Z.; 25: 19–23 Alma[1] is permitted to establish churches throughout Z.; 27: 34–35 sons of Mosiah[2] preach throughout Z. to repair injuries; 29: 44 reign of judges commences in Z.; **Alma** 2: 15–25 Lamanites and Nephites battle in Z.; 4: 1 no contentions in Z.; 5: 1 Alma[2] begins his mission in Z.; 15: 18 Alma[2] returns to Z. with Amulek; 16: 1 peace continues in Z.; 22: 32 lands of Nephi and Z. nearly surrounded by water; 27: 5–20 people of Anti-Nephi-Lehi come to Z.; 30: 12 Korihor comes into Z.; 35: 14 Alma[2] and sons of Mosiah[2] return to Z.; 59: 4 Moroni[1] sends epistle to Z.; 60: 30 Moroni[1] threatens to come to Z. and smite leaders with sword; 62: 6–8 Moroni[1] restores Pahoran to judgment-seat in Z.; **Hel.** 3: 31 continual rejoicing in Z.; 4: 5 Lamanites capture Z.; 5: 16–19 Nephi[2] and Lehi[4] convert eight thousand Lamanites in Z.; 6: 4 many converted Lamanites gather to Z.; 7: 1 Nephi[1] returns to Z.; 13: 2 Samuel the Lamanite preaches in Z.; **3 Ne.** 3: 22–23 Z. is appointed as place of gathering in defense against enemies; **Morm.** 1: 6 Mormon[2] is taken by his father to Z.

ZARAHEMLA, PEOPLE OF—*descendants of Mulek's colony*

Omni 1: 14 discovered by Nephites; 1: 15 had come from Jerusalem when Zedekiah was carried captive to Babylon; 1: 19 united with Nephites; 1: 21 discovered Coriantumr[2]; **Mosiah** 1: 10 Benjamin causes people of *Z.* and of Mosiah to gather; 25: 2–3 more numerous than Nephites, less than Lamanites; 25: 13 numbered with Nephites; **Alma** 22: 30 land of Desolation found by people of *Z.*

ZEAL, ZEALOUS, ZEALOUSLY (*see also* Diligence; Faithful)

Mosiah 7: 21 (9: 3) Zeniff is over-*z.* to inherit land of fathers; 27: 35 sons of Mosiah[2] strive *z.* to repair injuries they have done church; **Alma** 21: 23 people of Lamoni are *z.* in keeping commandments; 27: 27 Ammonites are distinguished for *z.* toward God.

ZEDEKIAH[1]—*last king of Judah* [c. 600 B.C.] (*see also* BD Zedekiah)

1 Ne. 1: 4 Lehi[1] and others prophesy in first year of *Z's* reign; 5: 10–13 brass plates contain record of Jews to beginning of *Z's* reign; **Omni** 1: 15 people of Zarahemla came from Jerusalem at time *Z.* was taken captive to Babylon; **Hel.** 6: 10 Mulek was son of *Z.*; 8: 21 all *Z's* sons slain except Mulek.

ZEDEKIAH[2]—*one of twelve Nephite disciples* [c. A.D. 34]

3 Ne. 19: 4 is called by Jesus to minister to Nephites.

ZEEZROM—*lawyer in Ammonihah* [c. 82 B.C.]

Alma 10: 31 accuses Alma[2] and Amulek; 11: 21–38 questions Amulek; 11: 22 tries to bribe Amulek to deny God; 11: 46 trembles at words of Amulek; 12: 1–6 is caught in his lying; 12: 7 is convinced of power of God; 12: 8 inquires diligently of Alma[2] and Amulek to learn concerning kingdom of God; 14: 2–6 is astonished by plain words; 15: 3 is sick with fever; 15: 4–11 is healed by Alma[2]; 15: 12 is baptized; 31: 5–6 with Amulek in Melek, leaves on missionary journey with Alma[2] and others; 31: 32 Alma[2] prays for *Z.* and other companions; **Hel.** 5: 41 people are reminded of *Z's* teachings concerning Christ.

ZEEZROM, CITY OF—*Nephite city on southwest frontier*

Alma 56: 13–14 is captured by Lamanites.

ZEMNARIHAH—*captain of Gadianton robbers* [c. A.D. 21]

3 Ne. 4: 16–17 lays siege to Nephites; 4: 22–23 commands forces to withdraw; 4: 28 is hanged.

ZENEPHI—*Nephite commander* [c. A.D. 400]

Moro. 9: 16 army of *Z.* carries off provisions of widows.

ZENIFF—*first king of group of Nephites who return to land of Lehi-Nephi* [c. 200 B.C.] (*see also* Lehi-Nephi, City of and Land of)

Mosiah 7: 9 father of Noah[3], grandfather of Limhi; 7: 13 Ammon[1] comes to inquire after brethren whom *Z.* brought from Zarahemla; 7: 21 (9: 3) overzealous to inherit land of fathers; 7: 21 is made king; 7: 21 (9: 6–13; 10: 18) is deceived by king Laman[2]; ch. 9–22 record of *Z.*; 9: 1 is sent as spy among Lamanites; 9: 2–3 becomes leader of group; 9: 6–7 covenants with King Laman[2] to possess land of Lehi-Nephi; 9: 13–19 (10: 19–20) drives out Lamanite invaders; 11: 1 confers kingdom on son, Noah[3].

ZENOCK—*prophet of Israel*

1 Ne. 19: 10 predicted that Christ would be lifted up by wicked men; **Alma** 33: 15–16 (34: 7) *Z's* testimony of Son of God; **Hel.** 8: 19–20 testified with other prophets concerning Christ; **3 Ne.** 10: 16 predicted destruction at Christ's death.

ZENOS—*prophet of Israel*

1 Ne. 19: 10, 12 prophesied of Christ's burial, three days of darkness; 19: 16 predicted gathering of Israel; **Jacob** 5: 1–77 Jacob[2] quotes *Z's* parable of olive-tree; 6: 1–10 Jacob[2] expounds *Z's* allegory; **Alma** 33: 3–11 *Z's* words on worship and prayer; 33: 13 *Z.* said, Thou hast turned away judgments because of thy Son; 34: 7 taught that redemption comes through Son; **Hel.** 8: 19 slain for bold testimony; 15: 11 spoke of restoration of Lamanites; **3 Ne.** 10: 15–16 testified of destruction at Christ's death.

ZERAHEMNAH—*Lamanite commander* [c. 74 B.C.]

Alma 43: 5, 44 chief captain of Lamanite army; 43: 44 inspires soldiers to fight; 43: 53 is struck with terror when surrounded; 44: 1–6 is commanded by Moroni[1] to surrender; 44: 12 attempts to kill Moroni[1], is scalped; 44: 19 begs for mercy.

ZERAM—*Nephite military officer* [c. 87 B.C.]

Alma 2: 22 is sent to watch camp of Amlicites.

ZERIN, MOUNT

Ether 12: 30 brother of Jared[2] said to mountain *Z.*, Remove, and it was removed.

ZIFF—*probably a metal used by Nephites*

Mosiah 11: 3 Noah[3] lays tax of fifth part of people's *z.*; 11: 8 Noah[3] ornaments buildings with *z.*

ZION—(*see also* Gather; Inherit, Inheritance; Jerusalem, New; Kingdom of God; Millennium; Promised Land; Zion, Mount; TG Zion, Sion; BD Zion)

1 Ne. 13: 37 blessed are they who shall seek to bring forth *Z.*; 21: 14 (Isa. 49: 14) *Z.* hath said, The Lord hath forsaken me; 22: 14, 19 (2 Ne. 6: 12–13; 10: 13, 16; 27: 3) all who fight against *Z.* shall be destroyed; **2 Ne.** 8: 3 (Isa. 51: 3) the Lord shall comfort *Z.*; 8: 11 (Isa. 51: 11) the redeemed shall come with singing unto *Z.*; 8: 16 (Isa. 51: 16) the Lord to say unto *Z.*, Thou art my people; 8: 24 (3 Ne. 20: 36; Moro. 10: 31; Isa. 52: 1) put on thy strength and beautiful garments, O *Z.*; 8: 25 (3 Ne. 20: 37; Isa. 52: 2) loose thyself from bands of thy neck, O captive daughter of *Z.*; 12: 3 (Isa. 2: 3) out of *Z.* shall go forth law; 13: 16–17 (Isa. 3: 16–17) the Lord will smite haughty daughters of *Z.*; 14: 3–4 (Isa. 4: 3–4) those left in *Z.* shall be called holy, have filth washed away; 14: 5 (Isa. 4: 5) upon glory of *Z.* shall be a defence; 24: 32 (Isa. 14: 32) the Lord has founded *Z.*, and the poor of his people shall trust in it; 26: 29 those practicing priestcrafts seek not welfare of *Z.*; 26: 30–31 laborer in *Z.* shall labor for *Z.*; 28: 21–25 devil lulls men into saying, All is well in *Z.*; **Mosiah** 12: 21 (15: 14; 3 Ne. 20: 40; Isa. 52: 7) how beautiful upon mountains are feet of him that saith unto *Z.*, Thy God reigneth; 12: 22 (15: 29; 3 Ne. 16: 18; Isa. 52: 8) the Lord shall bring again *Z.*; **3 Ne.** 21: 1 the Lord to gather Israel and establish *Z.* among them again.

ZION, MOUNT (*see also* Zion)

2 Ne. 20: 12 (Isa. 10: 12) the Lord to perform his whole work upon *M.Z.*

ZORAM[1]—*servant of Laban* [c. 600 B.C. (*see also* Zoramites[1])

1 Ne. 4: 20 has keys of treasury; 4: 21–27 thinks Nephi[1] is Laban; 4: 30 is frightened by sight of brothers of Nephi[1]; 4: 31–37 is seized, promises to accompany Lehites; 16: 7 takes eldest daughter of Ishmael[1] to wife; **2 Ne.** 1: 30–32 is blessed by Lehi[1]; 1: 30 is true friend to Nephi[1]; 5: 6 becomes follower of Nephi[1]; **Alma** 54: 23 Ammoron is a descendant of *Z.*

ZORAM[2]—*Nephite chief captain* [c. 81 B.C.]

Alma 16: 5 is appointed chief captain, seeks counsel of Alma[2]; 16: 7 crosses river Sidon and defeats Lamanites.

ZORAM[3]—*Nephite apostate* [c. 74 B.C.] (*see also* Zoramites[2])

Alma 30: 59 leads people who have separated themselves from Nephites; 31: 1 leads hearts of people to bow down to idols.

ZORAMITES[1]—*descendants of Zoram[1]*

Jacob 1: 13 (4 Ne. 1: 36; Morm. 1: 8) a group among the Nephites; **4 Ne.** 1: 37 are true believers in Christ.

ZORAMITES[2]—*apostate sect of Nephites, followers of Zoram[3]*

Alma 30: 59 (31: 8) dissenters, separate themselves from Nephites; 30: 58–59 trample Korihor to death; 31: 1, 9–11 pervert ways of the Lord, bow down to idols; 31: 3 gather in land of Antionum; 31: 4 Nephites fear *Z.* will enter into correspondence with Lamanites; 31: 5–7 Alma[2] and others undertake mission to *Z.*; 31: 9–11 *Z.* do not follow law of Moses or performances of church; 31: 12–23 perverted manner of worship, pray once a week from holy stand; 31: 26—34: 41 teachings of Alma[2] to the *Z.*; 35: 3–6 converts are expelled by *Z.*; 35: 8–11 *Z.* prepare for attack against Ammonites; 35: 14 Alma[2] and companions bring many *Z.* to repentance; 38: 13 do not pray to be heard of men, like the *Z.*; 39: 11 Corianton's bad example leads *Z.* not to believe Alma[2]; 43: 4, 6, 13 become Lamanites; 43: 43–44 inspire Lamanites to fight courageously; 48: 5 *Z.* are appointed chief captains among Lamanites because of knowledge of Nephites' strengths; **3 Ne.** 1: 29 children of converted Lamanites are led astray by lyings and flattery of *Z.*

ENGLISH
4 02309 23000 1
30923 000